Characteristics of Selected Elements

Element	Symbol	Atomic Number	Atomic Weight (amu)	Density of Solid, 20°C (g/cm^3)	Crystal Structure, 20°C	A R… (nm)	(nm)	Valence	(°C)
Aluminum	Al	13	26.98	2.71	FCC	0.143	0.053	3+	660.4
Argon	Ar	18	39.95	—	—	—	—	Inert	−189.2
Barium	Ba	56	137.33	3.5	BCC	0.217	0.136	2+	725
Beryllium	Be	4	9.012	1.85	HCP	0.114	0.035	2+	1278
Boron	B	5	10.81	2.34	Rhomb.	—	0.023	3+	2300
Bromine	Br	35	79.90	—	—	—	0.196	1−	−7.2
Cadmium	Cd	48	112.41	8.65	HCP	0.149	0.095	2+	321
Calcium	Ca	20	40.08	1.55	FCC	0.197	0.100	2+	839
Carbon	C	6	12.011	2.25	Hex.	0.071	~0.016	4+	(sublimes at 3367)
Cesium	Cs	55	132.91	1.87	BCC	0.265	0.170	1+	28.4
Chlorine	Cl	17	35.45	—	—	—	0.181	1−	−101
Chromium	Cr	24	52.00	7.19	BCC	0.125	0.063	3+	1875
Cobalt	Co	27	58.93	8.9	HCP	0.125	0.072	2+	1495
Copper	Cu	29	63.55	8.94	FCC	0.128	0.096	1+	1085
Fluorine	F	9	19.00	—	—	—	0.133	1−	−220
Gallium	Ga	31	69.72	5.90	Ortho.	0.122	0.062	3+	29.8
Germanium	Ge	32	72.64	5.32	Dia. cubic	0.122	0.053	4+	937
Gold	Au	79	196.97	19.32	FCC	0.144	0.137	1+	1064
Helium	He	2	4.003	—	—	—	—	Inert	−272 (at 26 atm)
Hydrogen	H	1	1.008	—	—	—	0.154	1+	−259
Iodine	I	53	126.91	4.93	Ortho.	0.136	0.220	1−	114
Iron	Fe	26	55.85	7.87	BCC	0.124	0.077	2+	1538
Lead	Pb	82	207.2	11.35	FCC	0.175	0.120	2+	327
Lithium	Li	3	6.94	0.534	BCC	0.152	0.068	1+	181
Magnesium	Mg	12	24.31	1.74	HCP	0.160	0.072	2+	649
Manganese	Mn	25	54.94	7.44	Cubic	0.112	0.067	2+	1244
Mercury	Hg	80	200.59	—	—	—	0.110	2+	−38.8
Molybdenum	Mo	42	95.94	10.22	BCC	0.136	0.070	4+	2617
Neon	Ne	10	20.18	—	—	—	—	Inert	−248.7
Nickel	Ni	28	58.69	8.90	FCC	0.125	0.069	2+	1455
Niobium	Nb	41	92.91	8.57	BCC	0.143	0.069	5+	2468
Nitrogen	N	7	14.007	—	—	—	0.01–0.02	5+	−209.9
Oxygen	O	8	16.00	—	—	—	0.140	2−	−218.4
Phosphorus	P	15	30.97	1.82	Ortho.	0.109	0.035	5+	44.1
Platinum	Pt	78	195.08	21.45	FCC	0.139	0.080	2+	1772
Potassium	K	19	39.10	0.862	BCC	0.231	0.138	1+	63
Silicon	Si	14	28.09	2.33	Dia. cubic	0.118	0.040	4+	1410
Silver	Ag	47	107.87	10.49	FCC	0.144	0.126	1+	962
Sodium	Na	11	22.99	0.971	BCC	0.186	0.102	1+	98
Sulfur	S	16	32.06	2.07	Ortho.	0.106	0.184	2−	113
Tin	Sn	50	118.71	7.27	Tetra.	0.151	0.071	4+	232
Titanium	Ti	22	47.87	4.51	HCP	0.145	0.068	4+	1668
Tungsten	W	74	183.84	19.3	BCC	0.137	0.070	4+	3410
Vanadium	V	23	50.94	6.1	BCC	0.132	0.059	5+	1890
Zinc	Zn	30	65.41	7.13	HCP	0.133	0.074	2+	420
Zirconium	Zr	40	91.22	6.51	HCP	0.159	0.079	4+	1852

Values of Selected Physical Constants

Quantity	*Symbol*	*SI Units*	*cgs Units*
Avogadro's number	N_A	6.023×10^{23} molecules/mol	6.023×10^{23} molecules/mol
Boltzmann's constant	k	1.38×10^{-23} J/atom-K	1.38×10^{-16} erg/atom-K 8.62×10^{-5} eV/atom-K
Bohr magneton	μ_B	9.27×10^{-24} A-m^2	9.27×10^{-21} erg/gauss[a]
Electron charge	e	1.602×10^{-19} C	4.8×10^{-10} statcoul[b]
Electron mass	—	9.11×10^{-31} kg	9.11×10^{-28} g
Gas constant	R	8.31 J/mol-K	1.987 cal/mol-K
Permeability of a vacuum	μ_0	1.257×10^{-6} henry/m	unity[a]
Permittivity of a vacuum	ϵ_0	8.85×10^{-12} farad/m	unity[b]
Planck's constant	h	6.63×10^{-34} J-s	6.63×10^{-27} erg-s 4.13×10^{-15} eV-s
Velocity of light in a vacuum	c	3×10^8 m/s	3×10^{10} cm/s

[a] In cgs-emu units.
[b] In cgs-esu units.

Unit Abbreviations

A = ampere	in. = inch	N = newton
Å = angstrom	J = joule	nm = nanometer
Btu = British thermal unit	K = degrees Kelvin	P = poise
C = Coulomb	kg = kilogram	Pa = Pascal
°C = degrees Celsius	lb_f = pound force	s = second
cal = calorie (gram)	lb_m = pound mass	T = temperature
cm = centimeter	m = meter	μm = micrometer (micron)
eV = electron volt	Mg = megagram	
°F = degrees Fahrenheit	mm = millimeter	W = watt
ft = foot	mol = mole	psi = pounds per square inch
g = gram	MPa = megapascal	

SI Multiple and Submultiple Prefixes

Factor by Which Multiplied	*Prefix*	*Symbol*
10^9	giga	G
10^6	mega	M
10^3	kilo	k
10^{-2}	centi[a]	c
10^{-3}	milli	m
10^{-6}	micro	μ
10^{-9}	nano	n
10^{-12}	pico	p

[a] Avoided when possible.

Callister's
Materials Science and Engineering

Callister's Materials Science and Engineering

William D. Callister, Jr.
Department of Metallurgical Engineering
The University of Utah

with special contributions by
David G. Rethwisch
The University of Iowa

Adapted by
R. Balasubramaniam
Department of Materials and Metallurgical Engineering
Indian Institute of Technology, Kanpur

WILEY

Callister's Materials Science and Engineering

Other Wiley Editorial Offices:

John Wiley & Sons, Inc. 111 River Street, Hoboken, NJ 07030, USA

Wiley-VCH Verlag GmbH, Pappellaee 3, D-69469 Weinheim, Germany

John Wiley & Sons Australia Ltd, 42 McDougall Street, Milton, Queensland 4064, Australia

John Wiley & Sons (Asia) Pte Ltd, 2 Clementi Loop #02-01, Jin Xing Distripark, Singapore 129809

John Wiley & Sons Canada Ltd, 22 Worcester Road, Etobicoke, Ontario, Canada, M9W 1L1

Reprint: 2013

ISBN: 978-81-265-2143-2

www.wileyindia.com

Printed at : ***Choudhary Press, New Delhi***

Preface for This Edition

Several changes have been incorporated in this revised version since the first edition of the Adapted Version was published. The most important change has been the adoption of SI units throughout the book. Some material relevant to the Indian subcontinent has been incorporated in Chapter 1. CD-ROM packaged with the book contains the latest version of *Virtual Materials Science and Engineering* (VMSE) software program, which consists of interactive simulations and animations that enhance learning of key concepts. It is anticipated that, with improved and more interactive learning modules, this revised version of the book provides a better visualization of the concepts.

Some minor mistakes in the earlier version have been corrected and the author is grateful to all the teachers and students for pointing them out.

R. Balasubramaniam
04 November 2009

Preface

In this Adapted Version of the Seventh Edition I have retained the major objectives and approaches of Professor Callister for teaching Materials Science and Engineering, namely present the basic fundamentals in sufficient detail and in logical order for university/college students with basic background in mathematics, chemistry and physics, utilizing features that enhance the learning process.

The aim of the adaptation is to synchronize the contents with the sequence of topics as taught in materials science courses in most universities in South Asia, while retaining the subject material of the Seventh Edition.

Features of The Adapted Version

New/Revised Content

The new sections and discussions that have been added and the earlier sections that have been revised and amplified in the Seventh Edition have been retained, including the "Materials of Importance" feature and "Concept Check" questions.

Modifications in Adapted Version

Several modifications have been made in this Adapted Version. The major modifications are as follows:

- Materials from Chapter 2 and part of material fromChapters 12 and 14 of the Seventh Edition have been utilized to create Chapter 3 – *Fundamentals of Structure of Crystalline Solids* – and Chapter 4 – *Structures of Crystalline Solids* – of the Adapted Version.
- Discussions on imperfections in ceramic and polymeric materials appear in Chapter 5 – *Imperfections in Solids*.
- Sections on diffusion in ceramic materials and polymers are included in Chapter 6 – *Diffusion*. An alternate method to solve Fick's Second Law of Diffusion has been introduced.
- Chapter 7 – *Phase Diagrams* – and Chapter 8 – Phase *Transformations* – precede the chapters on mechanical properties in the Adapted Version. Important mechanical properties are defined at the begining of sections 7.10 (Mechanical Properties of Isomorphous Alloys) and 8.7 (Mechanical Behavior of Iron-Carbon Alloys).
- Chapter 11 of the Seventh Edition dealing with applications and processing of metal alloys has been removed in the Adapted Version. However, sections dealing with different types of metallic alloys and annealing processes have been

introduced in Chapter 9 – *Mechanical Properties of Metals* – while the discussions related to fabrication of metals and heat treatment of steels have been moved to a new chapter devoted to fabrication of materials, Chapter 23 – *Processing of Engineering Materials*. The section on precipitation hardening now appears in Chapter 10 – *Dislocations and Strengthening Mechanisms.*

- All material, apart from ceramic structures, imperfections in ceramics and diffusion in ionic materials, from Chapters 12 and 13 of the Seventh Edition have been combined in Chapter 12 – *Applications and Processing of Ceramics.*
- Sections dealing with processing of polymers have been shifted from Chapter 15 of Seventh Edition to the last chapter of the Adapted Version devoted to processing of engineering materials. This change is also reflected in the new title of Chapter 15 – *Characteristics and Applications of Polymers*.
- Chapter 18 – *Magnetic Properties* – appears in the in-print text in the Adapted Version whereas this chapter was available on the web in the Seventh Edition.
- Discussions related to processing of metals, ceramics, polymers and composites appear in a new Chapter 23 – *Processing of Engineering Materials*. This chapter is available on CD-ROM.
- The last five chapters of the book, namely Chapter 19 – *Thermal Properties,* Chapter 20 – *Optical Properties*, Chapter 21 – *Materials Selection and Design Considerations,* Chapter 22 – *Economic, Environmental, and Societal Issues in Materials Science and Engineering*, and Chapter 23 – *Processing of Engineering Materials* are available on CD-ROM. These chapters are in Adobe Acrobat® PDF format.
- "Why Study..." section that appeared on the opening pages and "Important Terms and Concepts" section that appeared towards the end of each chapter in the Seventh Edition have been removed in the Adapted Version.
- Highlighted features in the margins of the Seventh Edition (defining key terms and description of key equations) do not appear in the Adapted Version. However, the key terms are emphasized in boldface type and they are defined in the Glossary section at the end of the book.

Student Learning Resources

A unique feature of the Adapted Version is the provision of a CD-ROM packaged with the in-print text. Besides the last five chapters, the CD-ROM contains *Virtual Materials Science and Engineering* (VMSE) software program which consists of simulations and animations to assist in learning important concepts.

The CD-ROM also contains all the answers to Concept Check questions and solutions to selected problems.

Instructor's Resources

An Instructor's resource CD-ROM is available on request (contact csupport@wiley.com). Detailed solutions of all the end-of-chapter questions, in Adobe Acrobat® PDF formats, are provided. In addition, the CD-ROM contains a set of PowerPoint® illustration slides containing photographs, illustrations and tables that appear in the book to assist the instructor in preparing handouts or presentations. A set of PowerPoint® lecture slides, originally developed by Peter M. Anderson (The Ohio State University) and Davind G. Rethwisch (The University of Iowa), is available. The original lecture slides of the Seventh Edition have been re-arranged to match the flow of topics in the text of the Abridged Version. The slides may be edited by the Instructors to suit their teaching needs.

Feedback

I solicit your comments, suggestions and criticisms on this Adapted Version via email at the following address: bala@iitk.ac.in with a copy to Professor Callister at the following address: billcallister@comcast.net.

Acknowledgments

I thank the dedicated faculty and students of IIT Kanpur for their valuable feedback regarding course contents of the introductory course in materials science and engineering. In particular, I acknowledge the valuable suggestions and ideas received from Dr. M.N. Mungole and Professors K.P. Gupta, A.K. Jena, G.S. Murty, R.K. Ray, Jitendra Kumar, Prashant Kumar, K. Shahi, R.C. Sharma, (late) V.S.R. Murthy, Sanjeev Bhargava, Sandeep Sangal, Deepak Gupta, Monica Katiyar, An-ish Upadhyaya, Bikramjit Basu, Ashish Garg and Gauthama.

I thank the following colleagues in other universities/institutions/colleges for their feedback, which was helpful in the finalization of the contents of the Adapted Version: Rajesh Prasad and Anandh Subramaniam of Indian Institute of Technology, Delhi; Uday Chatterjee of Indian Institute of Technology, Kharagpur; V.S. Raja of Indian Institute of Technology, Bombay; B.S. Murty and B.V. Phani Kumar of Indian Institute of Technology, Madras; B.S. Sundar Daniel of Indian Institute of Technology, Roorkee; Saravana Kumar of Indian Institute of Technology, Guwahati; S.N. Ojha of Institute of Technology, Benaras Hindu University, Varanasi; Rambabu Kodali of Birla Institute of Technology and Science, Pilani; M.K. Mohan of National Institute of Technology, Warangal; T. Srinivasa Rao of National Institute of Technology, Tiruchirapalli; Awanikumar Patil of Vishveswaraya National Institute of Technology, Nagpur; Rakesh Chandra of National Institute of Technology, Jamshedpur; Dipankar Chakdar of National Institute of Technology, Silchar; Viplava Kumar of Jawaharlal Nehru Technical University, Hyderabad, Geetha Manivasagam of Vellore Institute of Technology, Vellore and K.A. Padmanabhan of University of Madras, Chennai.

I am also indebted to V. Subramaniam, Rita Koul and Meenakshi Sehrawat, at Wiley India, New Delhi, for their valuable feedback, kind assistance and prompt guidance while preparing this Adapted Version.

The constant support and continued encouragement of my family and friends is highly appreciated.

R. Balasubramaniam
IIT Kanpur
March 2007

Preface of the Seventh Edition

In this Seventh Edition I have retained the objectives and approaches for teaching materials science and engineering that were presented in previous editions. **The first, and primary, objective** is to present the basic fundamentals on a level appropriate for university/college students who have completed their freshmen calculus, chemistry, and physics courses. In order to achieve this goal, I have endeavored to use terminology that is familiar to the student who is encountering the discipline of materials science and engineering for the first time, and also to define and explain all unfamiliar terms.

The second objective is to present the subject matter in a logical order, from the simple to the more complex. Each chapter builds on the content of previous ones.

The third objective, or philosophy, that I strive to maintain throughout the text is that if a topic or concept is worth treating, then it is worth treating in sufficient detail and to the extent that students have the opportunity to fully understand it without having to consult other sources; also, in most cases, some practical relevance is provided. Discussions are intended to be clear and concise and to begin at appropriate levels of understanding.

The fourth objective is to include features in the book that will expedite the learning process. These learning aids include:

- Numerous illustrations, now presented in full color, and photographs to help visualize what is being presented;
- Learning objectives;
- "Why Study . . ." and "Materials of Importance" items that provide relevance to topic discussions;
- Key terms and descriptions of key equations highlighted in the margins for quick reference;
- End-of-chapter questions and problems;
- Answers to selected problems;
- A glossary, list of symbols, and references to facilitate understanding the subject matter.

The fifth objective is to enhance the teaching and learning process by using the newer technologies that are available to most instructors and students of engineering today.

Features That Are New to This Edition

New/Revised Content

Several important changes have been made with this Seventh Edition. One of the most significant is the incorporation of a number of new sections, as well as revisions/amplifications of other sections. New sections/discussions are as follows (section numbers and chapters are with reference to Adapted Version):

- One-component (or unary) phase diagrams (Section 7.6)
- Compacted graphite iron (in Section 9.2, "Ferrous Alloys")
- Lost foam casting (in Section 23.3, "Casting")
- Temperature dependence of Frenkel and Schottky defects (in Section 5.5, "Imperfections in Ceramics")
- Fractography of ceramics (in Section 12.10, "Brittle Fracture of Ceramics")
- Crystallization of glass-ceramics, in terms of isothermal transformation and continuous cooling transformation diagrams (in Section 12.3, "Glass-Ceramics")
- Permeability in polymers (in Section 6.8, "Diffusion in Polymeric Materials")
- Magnetic anisotropy (Section 18.8)
- A new case study on chemical protective clothing (Sections 21.13 and 21.14).

Those sections that have been revised/amplified, include the following:

- Treatments in Chapter 1 ("Introduction") on the several material types have been enlarged to include comparisons of various property values (as bar charts).
- Expanded discussions on crystallographic directions and planes in hexagonal crystals (Sections 3.6 and 3.7); also some new related homework problems.
- Comparisons of (1) dimensional size ranges for various structural elements. and (2) resolution ranges for the several microscopic examination techniques (in Section 5.12, "Microscopic Techniques").
- Updates on hardness testing techniques (Section 9.8).
- Revised discussion on the Burgers vector (Section 11.4).
- New discussion on why recrystallization temperature depends on the puri of a metal (Section 10.12).
- Eliminated some detailed discussion on fracture mechanics—i.e., used "Concise Version" from sixth edition (Section 11.5).
- Expanded discussion on nondestructive testing (Section 11.5).
- Used Concise Version (from sixth edition) of discussion on crack initiatio and propagation (for fatigue, Section 11.9), and eliminated section on crack propagation rate.
- Refined terminology and representations of polymer structures (Sections 13.3 through 13.8).
- Eliminated discussion on fringed-micelle model (found in Section 14.12 of the sixth edition).
- Enhanced discussion on defects in polymers (Section 5.10).
- Revised the following sections in Chapter 14 ("Characteristics and Applications, of Polymers"): fracture of polymers (Section 14.5), deformation of semicrystalline polymers (Section 14.7), adhesives (in Section 14.18), polymerization (Section 14.20), and fabrication of fibers and films (Section 23.12).
- Revised treatment of polymer degradation (Section 16.12).

Materials of Importance

One new feature that has been incorporated in this edition is "Materials of Importance" pieces; in these we discuss familiar and interesting materials/applications of materials. These pieces lend some relevance to topical coverage, are found in most chapters in the book, and include the following:

- Carbonated Beverage Containers
- Water (Its Volume Expansion Upon Freezing)
- Tin (Its Allotropic Transformation)
- Catalysts (and Surface Defects)
- Aluminum for Integrated Circuit Interconnects
- Lead-Free Solders
- Shape-Memory Alloys
- Metal Alloys Used for Euro Coins
- Carbon Nanotubes
- Piezoelectric Ceramics
- Shrink-Wrap Polymer Films
- Phenolic Billiard Balls
- Nanocomposites in Tennis Balls
- Aluminum Electrical Wires
- Invar and Other Low-Expansion Alloys
- An Iron-Silicon Alloy That is Used in Transformer Cores
- Light-Emitting Diodes

Concept Check

Another new feature included in this seventh edition is what we call a "Concept Check," a question that tests whether or not a student understands the subject matter on a conceptual level. Concept check questions are found within most chapters; many of them appeared in the end-of-chapter Questions and Problems sections of the previous edition. Answers to these questions are on the book's Web site, *www.wiley.com/college/callister* (Student Companion Site).

And, finally, for each chapter, both the Summary and the Questions and Problems are organized by section; section titles precede their summaries and questions/problems.

Format Changes

There are several other major changes from the format of the sixth edition. First of all, no CD-ROM is packaged with the in-print text; all electronic components are found on the book's Web site (*www.wiley.com/college/callister*). This includes the last five chapters in the book—viz. Chapter 19, "Thermal Properties;" Chapter 20, "Magnetic Properties;" Chapter 21, "Optical Properties;" Chapter 22, "Materials Selection and Design Considerations;" and Chapter 23, "Economic, Environmental, and Societal Issues in Materials Science and Engineering." These chapters are in Adobe Acrobat® pdf format and may be downloaded.

Furthermore, only complete chapters appear on the Web site (rather than selected sections for some chapters per the sixth edition). And, in addition, for all sections of the book there is only one version—for the two-version sections of the sixth edition, in most instances, the detailed ones have been retained.

Six case studies have been relegated to Chapter 22, "Materials Selection and Design Considerations," which are as follows:

- Materials Selection for a Torsionally Stressed Cylindrical Shaft
- Automobile Valve Spring
- Failure of an Automobile Rear Axle
- Artificial Total Hip Replacement
- Chemical Protective Clothing
- Materials for Integrated Circuit Packages

References to these case studies are made in the left-page margins at appropriate locations in the other chapters. All but "Chemical Protective Clothing" appeared in the sixth edition; it replaces the "Thermal Protection System on the Space Shuttle Orbiter" case study.

STUDENT LEARNING RESOURCES (*WWW.WILEY.COM/COLLEGE/CALLISTER*)

Also found on the book's Web site (under "Student Companion Site") are several important instructional elements for the student that complement the text; these include the following:

1. *VMSE: Virtual Materials Science and Engineering*. This is essentially the same software program that accompanied the previous edition, but now browser-based for easier use on a wider variety of computer platforms. It consists of interactive simulations and animations that enhance the learning of key concepts in materials science and engineering, and, in addition, a materials properties/cost database. Students can access *VMSE* via the registration code included with all new copies.

Throughout the book, whenever there is some text or a problem that is supplemented by *VMSE,* a small "icon" that denotes the associated module is included in one of the margins. These modules and their corresponding icons are as follows:

Metallic Crystal Structures and Crystallography	Phase Diagrams
Ceramic Crystal Structures	Diffusion
Repeat Unit and Polymer Structures	Tensile Tests
Dislocations	Solid-Solution Strengthening

2. Answers to the Concept Check questions.

3. Direct access to online self-assessment exercises. This is a Web-based assessment program that contains questions and problems similar to those found in the text; these problems/questions are organized and labeled according to textbook sections. An answer/solution that is entered by the user in response to a question/problem is graded immediately, and comments are offered for incorrect responses. The student may use this electronic resource to review course material, and to assess his/her mastery and understanding of topics covered in the text.

4. Additional Web resources, which include the following:

- *Index of Learning Styles.* Upon answering a 44-item questionnaire, a user's learning style preference (i.e., the manner in which information is assimilated and processed) is assessed.
- *Extended Learning Objectives.* A more extensive list of learning objectives than is provided at the beginning of each chapter.
- *Links to Other Web Resources.* These links are categorized according to general Internet, software, teaching, specific course content/activities, and materials databases.

Instructors' Resources

The "Instructor Companion Site" (*www.wiley.com/college/callister*) is available for instructors who have adopted this text. Resources that are available include the following:

1. Detailed solutions of all end-of-chapter questions and problems (in both Microsoft Word® and Adobe Acrobat® PDF formats).
2. Photographs, illustrations, and tables that appear in the book (in PDF and JPEG formats); an instructor can print them for handouts or prepare transparencies in his/her desired format.
3. A set of PowerPoint® lecture slides developed by Peter M. Anderson (The Ohio State University) and David G. Rethwisch (The University of Iowa). These slides follow the flow of topics in the text, and include materials from the text and other sources as well as illustrations and animations. Instructors may use the slides as is or edit them to fit their teaching needs.
4. A list of classroom demonstrations and laboratory experiments that portray phenomena and/or illustrate principles that are discussed in the book; references are also provided that give more detailed accounts of these demonstrations.
5. Suggested course syllabi for the various engineering disciplines.

WileyPLUS

WileyPLUS gives you, the instructor, the technology to create an environment where students reach their full potential and experience academic success that will last a lifetime! With *WileyPLUS,* students will come to class better prepared for your lectures, get immediate feedback and context-sensitive help on assignments and quizzes, and have access to a full range of interactive learning resources including a complete online version of their text. *WileyPLUS* gives you a wealth of presentation and preparation tools, easy-to-navigate assessment tools including an online gradebook, and a complete system to administer and manage your course exactly as you wish. Contact your local Wiley representative for details on how to set up your *WileyPLUS* course, or visit the website at *www.wiley.com/college/wileyplus.*

Feedback

I have a sincere interest in meeting the needs of educators and students in the materials science and engineering community, and therefore would like to solicit feedback on this seventh edition. Comments, suggestions, and criticisms may be submitted to me via e-mail at the following address: *billcallister@comcast.net.*

Acknowledgments

Appreciation is expressed to those who have made contributions to this edition. I am especially indebted to David G. Rethwisch, who, as a special contributor, provided invaluable assistance in updating and upgrading important material in a number of chapters. In addition, I sincerely appreciate Grant E. Head's expert programming skills, which he used in developing the *Virtual Materials Science and Engineering* software. Important input was also furnished by Carl Wood of Utah State University and W. Roger Cannon of Rutgers University, to whom I also give thanks.

In addition, helpful ideas and suggestions have been provided by the following:

Tarek Abdelsalam, East Carolina University
Keyvan Ahdut, University of the District of Columbia
Mark Aindow, University of Connecticut (Storrs)
Pranesh Aswath, University of Texas at Arlington
Mir Atiqullah, St. Louis University
Sayavur Bakhtiyarov, Auburn University
Kristen Constant, Iowa State University
Raymond Cutler, University of Utah
Janet Degrazia, University of Colorado
Mark DeGuire, Case Western Reserve University
Timothy Dewhurst, Cedarville University
Amelito Enriquez, Canada College
Jeffrey Fergus, Auburn University
Victor Forsnes, Brigham Young University (Idaho)
Paul Funkenbusch, University of Rochester
Randall German, Pennsylvania State University
Scott Giese, University of Northern Iowa
Brian P. Grady, University of Oklahoma
Theodore Greene, Wentworth Institute of Technology
Todd Gross, University of New Hampshire
Jamie Grunlan, Texas A & M University
Masanori Hara, Rutgers University
Russell Herlache, Saginaw Valley State University
Susan Holl, California State University (Sacramento)
Zhong Hu, South Dakota State University
Duane Jardine, University of New Orleans
Jun Jin, Texas A & M University at Galveston
Paul Johnson, Grand Valley State University
Robert Johnson, University of Texas at Arlington
Robert Jones, University of Texas (Pan American)
Maureen Julian, Virginia Tech
James Kawamoto, Mission College
Edward Kolesar, Texas Christian University
Stephen Krause, Arizona State University (Tempe)
Robert McCoy, Youngstown State University
Scott Miller, University of Missouri (Rolla)
Devesh Misra, University of Louisiana at Lafayette
Angela L. Moran, U.S. Naval Academy
James Newell, Rowan University
Toby Padilla, Colorado School of Mines
Timothy Raymond, Bucknell University
Alessandro Rengan, Central State University
Bengt Selling, Royal Institute of Technology (Stockholm, Sweden)
Ismat Shah, University of Delaware
Patricia Shamamy, Lawrence Technological University
Adel Sharif, California State University at Los Angeles
Susan Sinnott, University of Florida
Andrey Soukhojak, Lehigh University
Erik Spjut, Harvey Mudd College
David Stienstra, Rose-Hulman Institute of Technology
Alexey Sverdlin, Bradley University
Dugan Um, Texas State University
Raj Vaidyanatha, University of Central Florida
Kant Vajpayee, University of Southern Mississipp
Kumar Virwani, University of Arkansas (Fayetteville)
Mark Weaver, University of Alabama (Tuscaloosa)
Jason Weiss, Purdue University (West Lafayette)

I am also indebted to Joseph P. Hayton, Sponsoring Editor, and to Kenneth Santor, Senior Production Editor at Wiley for their assistance and guidance on this revision.

Since I undertook the task of writing my first text on this subject in the early-80's, instructors and students too numerous to mention have shared their input and contributions on how to make this work more effective as a teaching and learning tool. To all those who have helped, I express my sincere "Thanks!"

Last, but certainly not least, the continual encouragement and support of my family and friends is deeply and sincerely appreciated.

William D. Callister, Jr.
Salt Lake City, Utah
January 2006

Contents

List of Symbols

The number of the section in which a symbol is introduced or explained is given in parentheses.

A = area
Å = angstrom unit
A_i = atomic weight of element i (2.2)
APF = atomic packing factor (4.2)
a = lattice parameter: unit cell x-axial length (4.2)
a = crack length of a surface crack (11.5)
at% = atom percent (5.4)
B = magnetic flux density (induction) (18.2)
B_r = magnetic remanence (18.7)
BCC = body-centered cubic crystal structure (4.3)
b = lattice parameter: unit cell y-axial length (4.2)
b = Burgers vector (5.6)
C = capacitance (17.18)
C_i = concentration (composition) of component i in wt% (5.4)
C'_i = concentration (composition) of component i in at% (5.4)
C_v, C_p = heat capacity at constant volume, pressure (19.2)
CPR = corrosion penetration rate (16.3)
CVN = Charpy V-notch (11.6)
%CW = percent cold work (10.10)
c = lattice parameter: unit cell z-axial length (4.2)
c = velocity of electromagnetic radiation in a vacuum (20.2)
D = diffusion coefficient (6.3)
D = dielectric displacement (17.19)
DP = degree of polymerization (13.5)
d = diameter
d = average grain diameter (10.8)
d_{hkl} = interplanar spacing for planes of Miller indices h, k, and l (4.20)
E = energy (2.5)
E = modulus of elasticity or Young's modulus (9.6)
$\mathscr{E}$ = electric field intensity (17.3)
E_f = Fermi energy (17.5)
E_g = band gap energy (16.6)
$E_r(t)$ = relaxation modulus (14.4)
%EL = ductility, in percent elongation (9.7)
e = electric charge per electron (17.7)
e^- = electron (17.2)
erf = Gaussian error function (6.4)
exp = e, the base for natural logarithms
F = force, interatomic or mechanical (2.5, 9.6)
$\mathscr{F}$ = Faraday constant (16.2)
FCC = face-centered cubic crystal structure (4.2)
G = shear modulus (9.6)
H = magnetic field strength (18.2)
H_c = magnetic coercivity (18.7)
HB = Brinell hardness (9.8)
HCP = hexagonal close-packed crystal structure (4.4)
HK = Knoop hardness (9.8)
HRB, HRF = Rockwell hardness: B and F scales (9.8)

HR15N, HR45W = superficial Rockwell hardness: 15N and 45W scales (9.8)

HV = Vickers hardness (9.8)

h = Planck's constant (20.2)

(hkl) = Miller indices for a crystallographic plane (3.7)

I = electric current (17.2)

I = intensity of electromagnetic radiation (20.3)

i = current density (16.3)

i_C = corrosion current density (16.4)

J = diffusion flux (6.3)

J = electric current density (17.3)

K_c = fracture toughness (11.5)

K_{Ic} = plane strain fracture toughness for mode I crack surface displacement (11.5)

k = Boltzmann's constant (5.2)

k = thermal conductivity (19.4)

l = length

l_c = critical fiber length (15.4)

ln = natural logarithm

log = logarithm taken to base 10

M = magnetization (18.2)

$\overline{M}_n$ = polymer number-average molecular weight (13.5)

$\overline{M}_w$ = polymer weight-average molecular weight (13.5)

mol% = mole percent

N = number of fatigue cycles (11.8)

N_A = Avogadro's number (4.5)

N_f = fatigue life (11.8)

n = principal quantum number (2.3)

n = number of atoms per unit cell (4.5)

n = strain-hardening exponent (9.7)

n = number of electrons in an electrochemical reaction (16.2)

n = number of conducting electrons per cubic meter (17.7)

n = index of refraction (20.5)

n' = for ceramics, the number of formula units per unit cell (4.15)

n_i = intrinsic carrier (electron and hole) concentration (17.10)

P = dielectric polarization (17.19)

P–B ratio = Pilling–Bedworth ratio (16.10)

p = number of holes per cubic meter (17.10)

Q = activation energy

Q = magnitude of charge stored (17.18)

R = atomic radius (4.2)

R = gas constant

%RA = ductility, in percent reduction in area (9.7)

r = interatomic distance (2.5)

r = reaction rate (16.3)

r_A, r_C = anion and cation ionic radii (4.10)

S = fatigue stress amplitude (11.8)

SEM = scanning electron microscopy or microscope

T = temperature

T_c = Curie temperature (18.6)

T_C = superconducting critical temperature (18.12)

T_g = glass transition temperature (12.14, 14.12)

T_m = melting temperature

TEM = transmission electron microscopy or microscope

TS = tensile strength (9.7)

t = time

t_r = rupture lifetime (11.12)

U_r = modulus of resilience (9.7)

$[uvw]$ = indices for a crystallographic direction (3.6)

V = electrical potential difference (voltage) (16.2, 17.2)

V_C = unit cell volume (4.2)
V_C = corrosion potential (16.4)
V_H = Hall voltage (17.14)
V_i = volume fraction of phase i (7.8)
v = velocity
vol% = volume percent
W_i = mass fraction of phase i (7.8)
wt% = weight percent (5.4)
x = length
x = space coordinate
Y = dimensionless parameter or function in fracture toughness expression (11.5)
y = space coordinate
z = space coordinate
α = lattice parameter: unit cell y–z interaxial angle (3.4)
α, β, γ = phase designations
α_l = linear coefficient of thermal expansion (19.3)
β = lattice parameter: unit cell x–z interaxial angle (3.4)
γ = lattice parameter: unit cell x–y interaxial angle (3.4)
γ = shear strain (9.5)
Δ = precedes the symbol of a parameter to denote finite change
ϵ = engineering strain (9.5)
ϵ = dielectric permittivity (17.18)
ϵ_r = dielectric constant or relative permittivity (17.18)
$\dot{\epsilon}_s$ = steady-state creep rate (11.12)
ϵ_T = true strain (9.7)
η = viscosity (12.12)
η = overvoltage (16.4)
θ = Bragg diffraction angle (4.20)
θ_D = Debye temperature (19.2)
λ = wavelength of electromagnetic radiation (4.20)
μ = magnetic permeability (18.2)
μ_B = Bohr magneton (18.2)
μ_r = relative magnetic permeability (18.2)
μ_e = electron mobility (17.7)
μ_h = hole mobility (17.10)
ν = Poisson's ratio (9.5)
ν = frequency of electromagnetic radiation (20.2)
ρ = density (4.5)
ρ = electrical resistivity (17.2)
ρ_t = radius of curvature at the tip of a crack (11.5)
σ = engineering stress, tensile or compressive (9.5)
σ = electrical conductivity (17.3)
σ^{*}_{cl} = longitudinal strength (composite) (15.5)
σ_c = critical stress for crack propagation (11.5)
σ_{fs} = flexural strength (12.11)
σ_m = maximum stress (11.5)
σ_m = mean stress (11.7)
σ'_m = stress in matrix at composite failure (15.5)
σ_T = true stress (9.7)
σ_w = safe or working stress (9.10)
σ_y = yield strength (9.7)
τ = shear stress (9.5)
τ_c = fiber–matrix bond strength/matrix shear yield strength (15.4)
τ_{crss} = critical resolved shear stress (10.5)
χ_m = magnetic susceptibility (18.2)

SUBSCRIPTS

c = composite
cd = discontinuous fibrous composite
cl = longitudinal direction (aligned fibrous composite)
ct = transverse direction (aligned fibrous composite)
f = final
f = at fracture
f = fiber
i = instantaneous
m = matrix
m, max = maximum
min = minimum
0 = original
0 = at equilibrium
0 = in a vacuum

Chapter 1 Introduction

A familiar item that is fabricated from three different material types is the beverage container. Beverages are marketed in aluminum (metal) cans (top), glass (ceramic) bottles (center), and plastic (polymer) bottles (bottom). (Permission to use these photographs was granted by the Coca-Cola Company. Coca-Cola, Coca-Cola Classic, the Contour Bottle design and the Dynamic Ribbon are registered trademarks of The Coca-Cola Company and used with its express permission.)

Learning Objectives

After careful study of this chapter you should be able to do the following:

1. List six different property classifications of materials that determine their applicability.
2. Cite the four components that are involved in the design, production, and utilization of materials, and briefly describe the interrelationships between these components.
3. Cite three criteria that are important in the materials selection process.
4. (a) List the three primary classifications of solid materials, and then cite the distinctive chemical feature of each.
   (b) Note the two types of advanced materials and, for each, its distinctive feature(s).
5. (a) Briefly define "smart material/system."
   (b) Briefly explain the concept of "nanotechnology" as it applies to materials.

1.1 HISTORICAL PERSPECTIVE

Materials are probably more deep-seated in our culture than most of us realize. Transportation, housing, clothing, communication, recreation, and food production—virtually every segment of our everyday lives is influenced to one degree or another by materials. Historically, the development and advancement of societies have been intimately tied to the members' ability to produce and manipulate materials to fill their needs. In fact, early civilizations have been designated by the level of their materials development (Stone Age, Bronze Age, Iron Age).[1] A historical note on the metallurgical wonder of the world, the Delhi Iron Pillar, is given on page 13.

The earliest humans had access to only a very limited number of materials, those that occur naturally: stone, wood, clay, skins, and so on. With time they discovered techniques for producing materials that had properties superior to those of the natural ones; these new materials included pottery and various metals. Furthermore, it was discovered that the properties of a material could be altered by heat treatments and by the addition of other substances. At this point, materials utilization was totally a selection process that involved deciding from a given, rather limited set of materials the one best suited for an application by virtue of its characteristics. It was not until relatively recent times that scientists came to understand the relationships between the structural elements of materials and their properties. This knowledge, acquired over approximately the past 100 years, has empowered them to fashion, to a large degree, the characteristics of materials. Thus, tens of thousands of different materials have evolved with rather specialized characteristics that meet the needs of our modern and complex society; these include metals, plastics, glasses, and fibers.

The development of many technologies that make our existence so comfortable has been intimately associated with the accessibility of suitable materials. An advancement in the understanding of a material type is often the forerunner to the stepwise progression of a technology. For example, automobiles would not have been possible without the availability of inexpensive steel or some other comparable substitute. In our contemporary era, sophisticated electronic devices rely on components that are made from what are called semiconducting materials.

[1] The approximate dates for the beginnings of Stone, Bronze, and Iron Ages were 2.5 million BC, 3500 BC and 1500 BC, respectively.

1.2 MATERIALS SCIENCE AND ENGINEERING

Sometimes it is useful to subdivide the discipline of materials science and engineering into *materials science* and *materials engineering* subdisciplines. Strictly speaking, "materials science" involves investigating the relationships that exist between the structures and properties of materials. In contrast, "materials engineering" is, on the basis of these structure–property correlations, designing or engineering the structure of a material to produce a predetermined set of properties.[2] From a functional perspective, the role of a materials scientist is to develop or synthesize new materials, whereas a materials engineer is called upon to create new products or systems using existing materials, and/or to develop techniques for processing materials. Most graduates in materials programs are trained to be both materials scientists and materials engineers.

"Structure" is at this point a nebulous term that deserves some explanation. In brief, the structure of a material usually relates to the arrangement of its internal components. Subatomic structure involves electrons within the individual atoms and interactions with their nuclei. On an atomic level, structure encompasses the organization of atoms or molecules relative to one another. The next larger structural realm, which contains large groups of atoms that are normally agglomerated together, is termed "microscopic," meaning that which is subject to direct observation using some type of microscope. Finally, structural elements that may be viewed with the naked eye are termed "macroscopic."

The notion of "property" deserves elaboration. While in service use, all materials are exposed to external stimuli that evoke some type of response. For example, a specimen subjected to forces will experience deformation, or a polished metal surface will reflect light. A property is a material trait in terms of the kind and magnitude of response to a specific imposed stimulus. Generally, definitions of properties are made independent of material shape and size.

Virtually all important properties of solid materials may be grouped into six different categories: mechanical, electrical, thermal, magnetic, optical, and deteriorative. For each there is a characteristic type of stimulus capable of provoking different responses. Mechanical properties relate deformation to an applied load or force; examples include elastic modulus and strength. For electrical properties, such as electrical conductivity and dielectric constant, the stimulus is an electric field. The thermal behavior of solids can be represented in terms of heat capacity and thermal conductivity. Magnetic properties demonstrate the response of a material to the application of a magnetic field. For optical properties, the stimulus is electromagnetic or light radiation; index of refraction and reflectivity are representative optical properties. Finally, deteriorative characteristics relate to the chemical reactivity of materials. The chapters that follow discuss properties that fall within each of these six classifications.

In addition to structure and properties, two other important components are involved in the science and engineering of materials—namely, "processing" and "performance." With regard to the relationships of these four components, the structure of a material will depend on how it is processed. Furthermore, a material's performance will be a function of its properties. Thus, the interrelationship between processing, structure, properties, and performance is as depicted in the schematic illustration shown in Figure 1.1. Throughout this text we draw attention to the

---

[2] Throughout this text we draw attention to the relationships between material properties and structural elements.

Figure 1.1 The four components of the discipline of materials science and engineering and their interrelationship.

relationships among these four components in terms of the design, production, and utilization of materials.

We now present an example of these processing-structure-properties-performance principles with Figure 1.2, a photograph showing three thin disk specimens placed over some printed matter. It is obvious that the optical properties (i.e., the light transmittance) of each of the three materials are different; the one on the left is transparent (i.e., virtually all of the reflected light passes through it), whereas the disks in the center and on the right are, respectively, translucent and opaque. All of these specimens are of the same material, aluminum oxide, but the leftmost one is what we call a single crystal—that is, it is highly perfect—which gives rise to its transparency. The center one is composed of numerous and very small single crystals that are all connected; the boundaries between these small crystals scatter a portion of the light reflected from the printed page, which makes this material optically translucent. Finally, the specimen on the right is composed not only of many small, interconnected crystals, but also of a large number of very small pores or void spaces. These pores also effectively scatter the reflected light and render this material opaque.

Thus, the structures of these three specimens are different in terms of crystal boundaries and pores, which affect the optical transmittance properties. Furthermore, each material was produced using a different processing technique. And, of course, if optical transmittance is an important parameter relative to the ultimate in-service application, the performance of each material will be different.

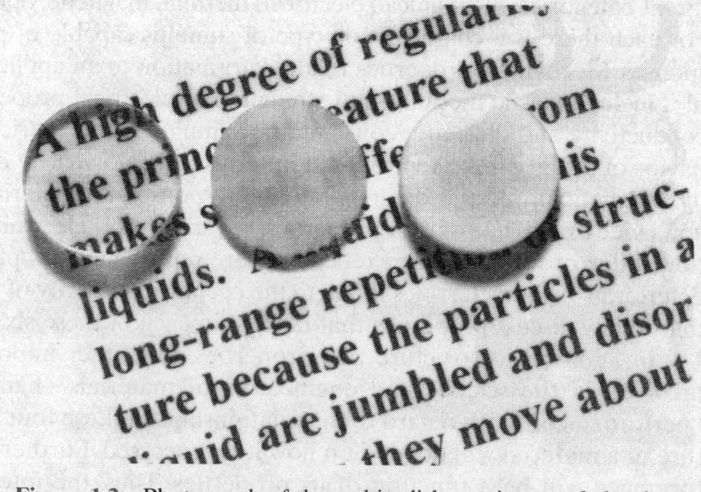

Figure 1.2 Photograph of three thin disk specimens of aluminum oxide, which have been placed over a printed page in order to demonstrate their differences in light-transmittance characteristics. The disk on the left is transparent (that is, virtually all light that is reflected from the page passes through it), whereas the one in the center is translucent (meaning that some of this reflected light is transmitted through the disk). And, the disk on the right is opaque—i.e., none of the light passes through it. These differences in optical properties are a consequence of differences in structure of these materials, which have resulted from the way the materials were processed. (Specimen preparation, P. A. Lessing; photography by S. Tanner.)

1.3 WHY STUDY MATERIALS SCIENCE AND ENGINEERING?

Why do we study materials? Many an applied scientist or engineer, whether mechanical, civil, chemical, or electrical, will at one time or another be exposed to a design problem involving materials. Examples might include a transmission gear, the superstructure for a building, an oil refinery component, or an integrated circuit chip. Of course, materials scientists and engineers are specialists who are totally involved in the investigation and design of materials.

Many times, a materials problem is one of selecting the right material from the many thousands that are available. There are several criteria on which the final decision is normally based. First of all, the in-service conditions must be characterized, for these will dictate the properties required of the material. On only rare occasions does a material possess the maximum or ideal combination of properties. Thus, it may be necessary to trade off one characteristic for another. The classic example involves strength and ductility; normally, a material having a high strength will have only a limited ductility. In such cases a reasonable compromise between two or more properties may be necessary.

A second selection consideration is any deterioration of material properties that may occur during service operation. For example, significant reductions in mechanical strength may result from exposure to elevated temperatures or corrosive environments.

Finally, probably the overriding consideration is that of economics: What will the finished product cost? A material may be found that has the ideal set of properties but is prohibitively expensive. Here again, some compromise is inevitable. The cost of a finished piece also includes any expense incurred during fabrication to produce the desired shape.

The more familiar an engineer or scientist is with the various characteristics and structure–property relationships, as well as processing techniques of materials, the more proficient and confident he or she will be to make judicious materials choices based on these criteria.

1.4 CLASSIFICATION OF MATERIALS

Solid materials have been conveniently grouped into three basic classifications: metals, ceramics, and polymers. This scheme is based primarily on chemical makeup and atomic structure, and most materials fall into one distinct grouping or another, although there are some intermediates. In addition, there are the composites, combinations of two or more of the above three basic material classes. A brief explanation of these material types and representative characteristics is offered next. Another classification is advanced materials—those used in high-technology applications—viz. semiconductors, biomaterials, smart materials, and nanoengineered materials: these are discussed in Section 1.5.

Metals

Materials in this group are composed of one or more metallic elements (such as iron, aluminum, copper, titanium, gold, and nickel), and often also nonmetallic elements (for example, carbon, nitrogen, and oxygen) in relatively small amounts.[3] Atoms in metals and their alloys are arranged in a very orderly manner (as discussed in Chapter 4), and in comparison to the ceramics and polymers, are relatively dense (Figure 1.3). With regard to mechanical characteristics, these materials are relatively stiff (Figure 1.4)

[3] The term *metal alloy* is used in reference to a metallic substance that is composed of two or more elements.

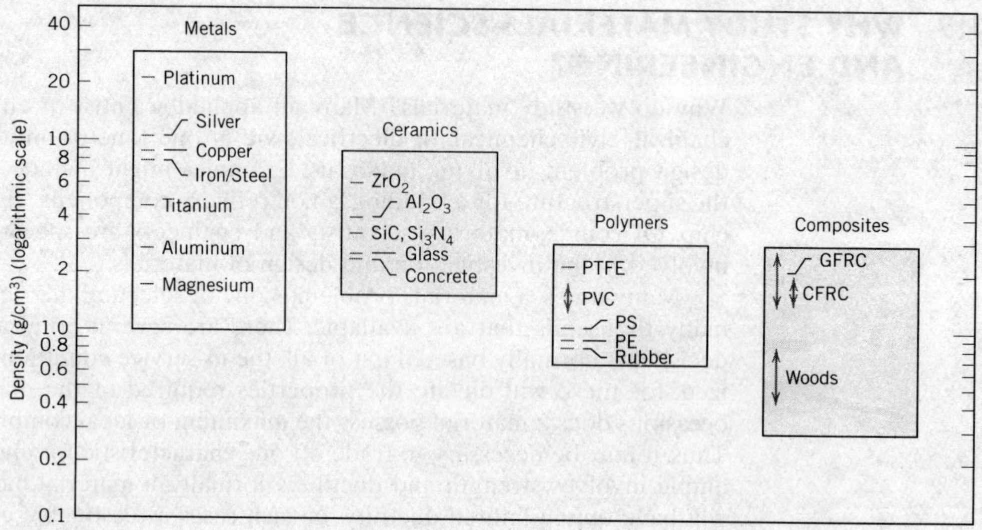

Figure 1.3 Bar-chart of room-temperature density values for various metals, ceramics, polymers, and composite materials.

and strong (Figure 1.5), yet are ductile (i.e., capable of large amounts of deformation without fracture), and are resistant to fracture (Figure 1.6), which accounts for their widespread use in structural applications. Metallic materials have large numbers of nonlocalized electrons; that is, these electrons are not bound to particular atoms. Many properties of metals are directly attributable to these electrons. For example, metals are extremely good conductors of electricity (Figure 1.7) and heat, and are not transparent to visible light; a polished metal surface has a lustrous appearance. In addition, some of the metals (viz., Fe, Co, and Ni) have desirable magnetic properties.

Figure 1.8 is a photograph that shows several common and familiar objects that are made of metallic materials. Furthermore, the types and applications of metals and their alloys are discussed in Chapter 9.

Ceramics

Ceramics are compounds between metallic and nonmetallic elements; they are most frequently oxides, nitrides, and carbides. For example, some of the common ceramic materials include aluminum oxide (or alumina, Al_2O_3), silicon dioxide (or *silica,* SiO_2), silicon carbide (SiC), silicon nitride (Si_3N_4), and, in addition, what some refer to as

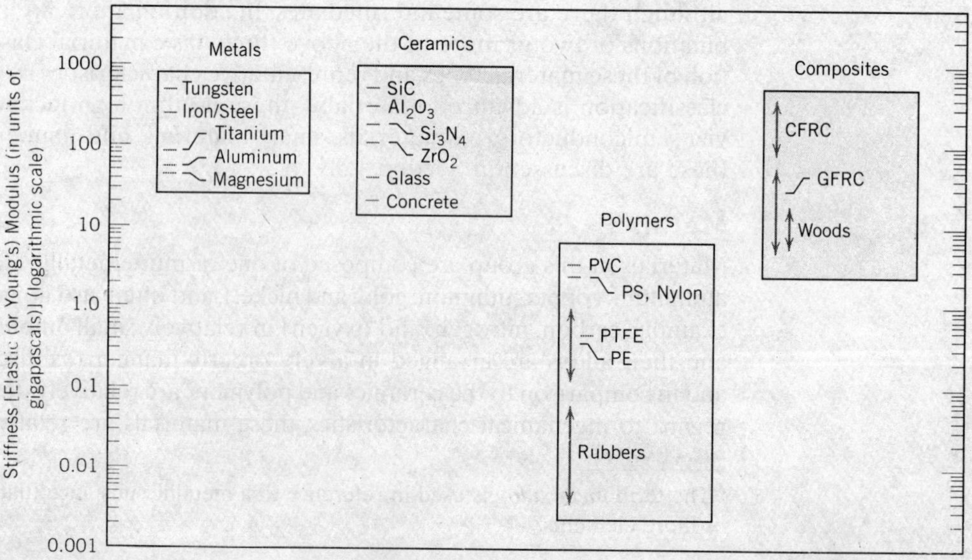

Figure 1.4 Bar-chart of room-temperature stiffness (i.e., elastic modulus) values for various metals, ceramics, polymers, and composite materials.

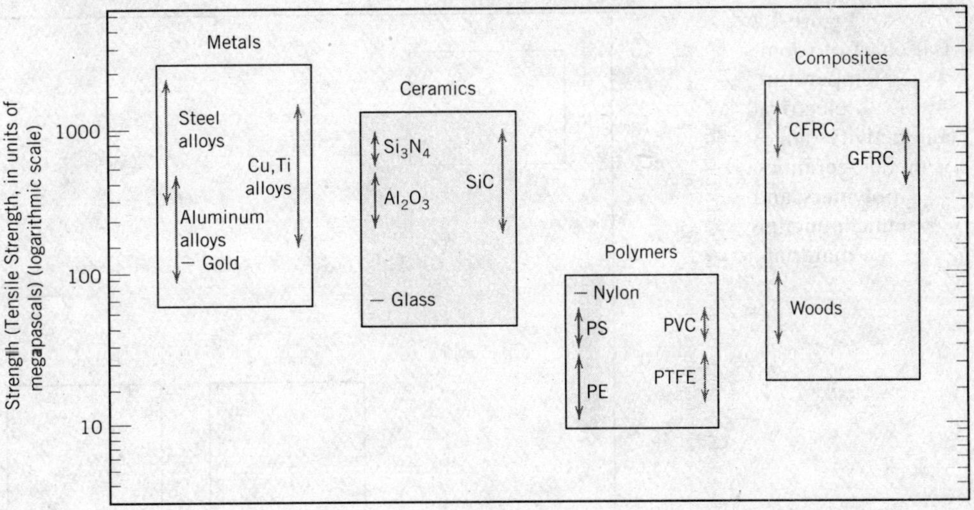

Figure 1.5 Bar-chart of room-temperature strength (i.e., tensile strength) values for various metals, ceramics, polymers, and composite materials.

the *traditional ceramics*—those composed of clay minerals (i.e., porcelain), as well as cement, and glass. With regard to mechanical behavior, ceramic materials are relatively stiff and strong—stiffnesses and strengths are comparable to those of the metals (Figures 1.4 and 1.5). In addition, ceramics are typically very hard. On the other hand, they are extremely brittle (lack ductility), and are highly susceptible to fracture (Figure 1.6). These materials are typically insulative to the passage of heat and electricity (i.e., have low electrical conductivities, Figure 1.7), and are more resistant to high temperatures and harsh environments than metals and polymers. With regard to optical characteristics, ceramics may be transparent, translucent, or opaque (Figure 1.2), and some of the oxide ceramics (e.g., Fe_3O_4) exhibit magnetic behavior.

Several common ceramic objects are shown in the photograph of Figure 1.9. The characteristics, types, and applications of this class of materials are discussed in Chapter 12.

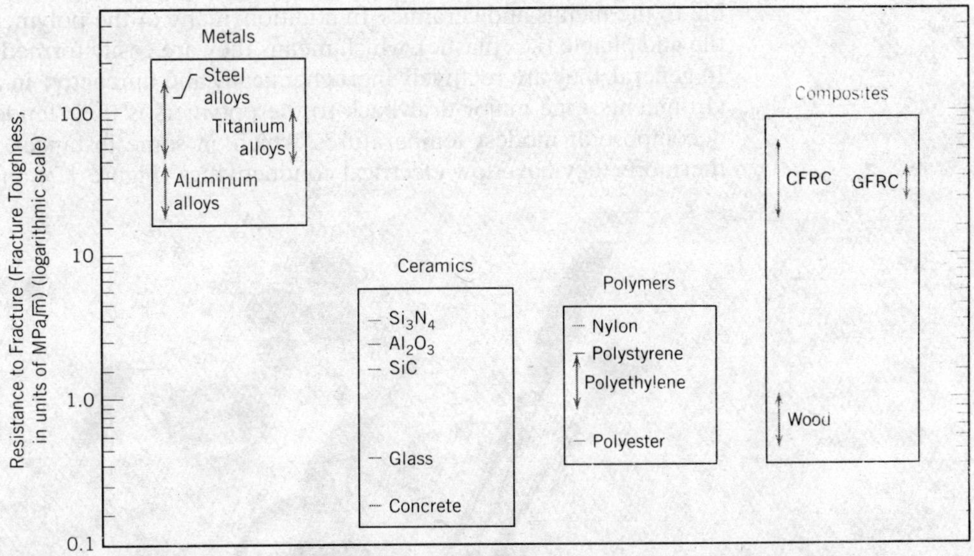

Figure 1.6 Bar-chart of room-temperature resistance to fracture (i.e., fracture toughness) for various metals, ceramics, polymers, and composite materials. (Reprinted from *Engineering Materials 1: An Introduction to Properties, Applications and Design,* third edition, M. F. Ashby and D. R. H. Jones, pages 177 and 178, Copyright 2005, with permission from Elsevier.)

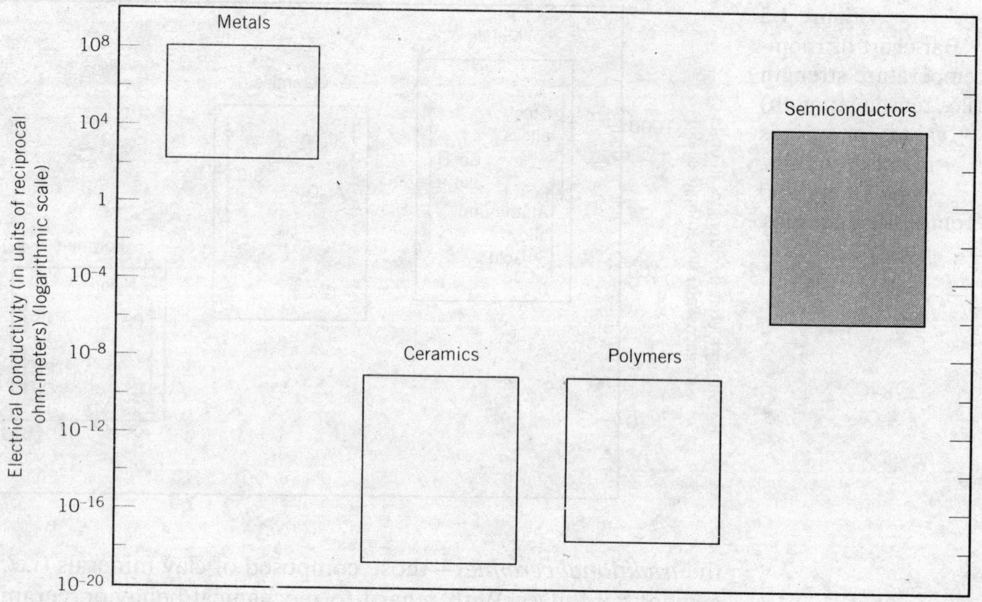

Figure 1.7 Bar-chart of room-temperature electrical conductivity ranges for metals, ceramics, polymers, and semiconducting materials.

Polymers

Polymers include the familiar plastic and rubber materials. Many of them are organic compounds that are chemically based on carbon, hydrogen, and other nonmetallic elements (viz. O, N, and Si). Furthermore, they have very large molecular structures, often chain-like in nature that have a backbone of carbon atoms. Some of the common and familiar polymers are polyethylene (PE), nylon, poly(vinyl chloride) (PVC), polycarbonate (PC), polystyrene (PS), and silicone rubber. These materials typically have low densities (Figure 1.3), whereas their mechanical characteristics are generally dissimilar to the metallic and ceramic materials—they are not as stiff nor as strong as these other material types (Figures 1.4 and 1.5). However, on the basis of their low densities, many times their stiffnesses and strengths on a per mass basis are comparable to the metals and ceramics. In addition, many of the polymers are extremely ductile and pliable (i.e., plastic), which means they are easily formed into complex shapes. In general, they are relatively inert chemically and unreactive in a large number of environments. One major drawback to the polymers is their tendency to soften and/or decompose at modest temperatures, which, in some instances, limits their use. Furthermore, they have low electrical conductivities (Figure 1.7) and are nonmagnetic.

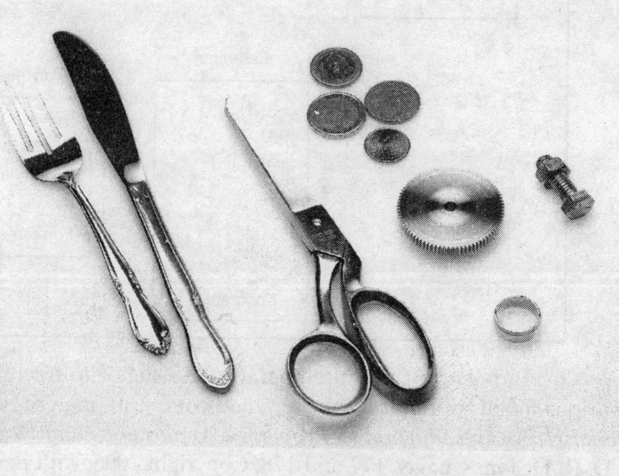

Figure 1.8 Familiar objects that are made of metals and metal alloys: (from left to right) silverware (fork and knife), scissors, coins, a gear, a wedding ring, and a nut and bolt. (Photograpy by S. Tanner.)

Figure 1.9 Common objects that are made of ceramic materials: scissors, a china tea cup, a building brick, a floor tile, and a glass vase. (Photography by S. Tanner.)

The photograph in Figure 1.10 shows several articles made of polymers that are familiar to the reader. Chapters 13 and 14 are devoted to discussions of the structures, properties, applications, and processing of polymeric materials.

Composites

A composite is composed of two (or more) individual materials, which come from the categories discussed above—viz., metals, ceramics, and polymers. The design goal of a composite is to achieve a combination of properties that is not displayed by any single material, and also to incorporate the best characteristics of each of the component materials. A large number of composite types exist that are represented by different combinations of metals, ceramics, and polymers. Furthermore, some naturally-occurring materials are also considered to be composites—for example, wood and bone. However, most of those we consider in our discussions are synthetic (or man-made) composites.

Figure 1.10 Several common objects that are made of polymeric materials: plastic tableware (spoon, fork, and knife), billiard balls, a bicycle helmet, two dice, a lawnmower wheel (plastic hub and rubber tire), and a plastic milk carton. (Photography by S. Tanner.)

MATERIALS OF IMPORTANCE

Carbonated Beverage Containers

One common item that presents some interesting material property requirements is the container for carbonated beverages. The material used for this application must satisfy the following constraints: (1) provide a barrier to the passage of carbon dioxide, which is under pressure in the container; (2) be nontoxic, unreactive with the beverage, and, preferably be recyclable; (3) be relatively strong, and capable of surviving a drop from a height of several feet when containing the beverage; (4) be inexpensive and the cost to fabricate the final shape should be relatively low; (5) if optically transparent, retain its optical clarity; and (6) capable of being produced having different colors and/or able to be adorned with decorative labels.

All three of the basic material types—metal (aluminum), ceramic (glass), and polymer (polyester plastic)—are used for carbonated beverage containers (per the chapter-opening photographs for this chapter). All of these materials are nontoxic and unreactive with beverages. In addition, each material has its pros and cons. For example, the aluminum alloy is relatively strong (but easily dented), is a very good barrier to the diffusion of carbon dioxide, is easily recycled, beverages are cooled rapidly, and labels may be painted onto its surface. On the other hand, the cans are optically opaque, and relatively expensive to produce. Glass is impervious to the passage of carbon dioxide, is a relatively inexpensive material, may be recycled, but it cracks and fractures easily, and glass bottles are relatively heavy. Whereas the plastic is relatively strong, may be made optically transparent, is inexpensive and lightweight, and is recyclable, it is not as impervious to the passage of carbon dioxide as the aluminum and glass. For example, you may have noticed that beverages in aluminum and glass containers retain their carbonization (i.e., "fizz") for several years, whereas those in two-liter plastic bottles "go flat" within a few months.

One of the most common and familiar composites is fiberglass, in which small glass fibers are embedded within a polymeric material (normally an epoxy or polyester).[4] The glass fibers are relatively strong and stiff (but also brittle), whereas the polymer is ductile (but also weak and flexible). Thus, the resulting fiberglass is relatively stiff, strong, (Figures 1.4 and 1.5) flexible, and ductile. In addition, it has a low density (Figure 1.3).

Another of these technologically important materials is the "carbon fiber-reinforced polymer" (or "CFRP") composite—carbon fibers that are embedded within a polymer. These materials are stiffer and stronger than the glass fiber-reinforced materials (Figures 1.4 and 1.5), yet they are more expensive. The CFRP composites are used in some aircraft and aerospace applications, as well as high-tech sporting equipment (e.g., bicycles, golf clubs, tennis rackets, and skis/snowboards). Chapter 16 is devoted to a discussion of these interesting materials.

1.5 ADVANCED MATERIALS

Materials that are utilized in high-technology (or high-tech) applications are sometimes termed *advanced materials.* By high technology we mean a device or product that operates or functions using relatively intricate and sophisticated principles; examples include electronic equipment (camcorders, CD/DVD players, etc.), computers, fiber-optic systems, spacecraft, aircraft, and military rocketry. These advanced materials are typically traditional materials whose properties have been enhanced, and, also newly developed, high-performance materials. Furthermore, they may be of all material types (e.g., metals, ceramics, polymers), and are normally expensive. Advanced materials include semiconductors, biomaterials, and what we may term "materials of the future"

[4] Fiberglass is sometimes also termed a "glass fiber-reinforced polymer" composite, abbreviated "GFRP."

(that is, smart materials and nanoengineered materials), which we discuss below. The properties and applications of a number of these advanced materials—for example, materials that are used for lasers, integrated circuits, magnetic information storage, liquid crystal displays (LCDs), and fiber optics—are also discussed in subsequent chapters.

Semiconductors

Semiconductors have electrical properties that are intermediate between the electrical conductors (viz. metals and metal alloys) and insulators (viz. ceramics and polymers)—Figure 1.7. Furthermore, the electrical characteristics of these materials are extremely sensitive to the presence of minute concentrations of impurity atoms, for which the concentrations may be controlled over very small spatial regions. Semiconductors have made possible the advent of integrated circuitry that has totally revolutionized the electronics and computer industries (not to mention our lives) over the past three decades.

Biomaterials

Biomaterials are employed in components implanted into the human body for replacement of diseased or damaged body parts. These materials must not produce toxic substances and must be compatible with body tissues (i.e., must not cause adverse biological reactions). All of the above materials—metals, ceramics, polymers, composites, and semiconductors—may be used as biomaterials. For example, some of the biomaterials that are utilized in artificial hip replacements are discussed in Section 21.12.

Materials of the Future

Smart Materials

Smart (or *intelligent*) *materials* are a group of new and state-of-the-art materials now being developed that will have a significant influence on many of our technologies. The adjective "smart" implies that these materials are able to sense changes in their environments and then respond to these changes in predetermined manners—traits that are also found in living organisms. In addition, this "smart" concept is being extended to rather sophisticated systems that consist of both smart and traditional materials.

Components of a smart material (or system) include some type of sensor (that detects an input signal), and an actuator (that performs a responsive and adaptive function). Actuators may be called upon to change shape, position, natural frequency, or mechanical characteristics in response to changes in temperature, electric fields, and/or magnetic fields.

Four types of materials are commonly used for actuators: shape memory alloys, piezoelectric ceramics, magnetostrictive materials, and electrorheological/magnetorheological fluids. Shape memory alloys are metals that, after having been deformed, revert back to their original shapes when temperature is changed (see the Materials of Importance piece following Section 8.9). Piezoelectric ceramics expand and contract in response to an applied electric field (or voltage); conversely, they also generate an electric field when their dimensions are altered (see Section 17.25). The behavior of magnetostrictive materials is analogous to that of the piezoelectrics, except that they are responsive to magnetic fields. Also, electrorheological and magnetorheological fluids are liquids that experience dramatic changes in viscosity upon the application of electric and magnetic fields, respectively.

Materials/devices employed as sensors include optical fibers (Section 20.14), piezoelectric materials (including some polymers), and microelectromechanical devices (MEMS, Section 12.8).

For example, one type of smart system is used in helicopters to reduce aerodynamic cockpit noise that is created by the rotating rotor blades. Piezoelectric sensors inserted into the blades monitor blade stresses and deformations; feedback signals from these sensors are fed into a computer-controlled adaptive device, which generates noise-canceling antinoise.

Nanoengineered Materials

Until very recent times the general procedure utilized by scientists to understand the chemistry and physics of materials has been to begin by studying large and complex structures, and then to investigate the fundamental building blocks of these structures that are smaller and simpler. This approach is sometimes termed "top-down" science. However, with the advent of scanning probe microscopes (Section 5.12), which permit observation of individual atoms and molecules, it has become possible to manipulate and move atoms and molecules to form new structures and, thus, design new materials that are built from simple atomic-level constituents (i.e., "materials by design"). This ability to carefully arrange atoms provides opportunities to develop mechanical, electrical, magnetic, and other properties that are not otherwise possible. We call this the "bottom-up" approach, and the study of the properties of these materials is termed "nanotechnology"; the "nano" prefix denotes that the dimensions of these structural entities are on the order of a nanometer (10^{-9} m)—as a rule, less than 100 nanometers (equivalent to approximately 500 atom diameters).[5] One example of a material of this type is the carbon nanotube, discussed in Section 4.17. In the future we will undoubtedly find that increasingly more of our technological advances will utilize these *nanoengineered materials*.

1.6 MODERN MATERIALS' NEEDS

In spite of the tremendous progress that has been made in the discipline of materials science and engineering within the past few years, there still remain technological challenges, including the development of even more sophisticated and specialized materials, as well as consideration of the environmental impact of materials production. Some comment is appropriate relative to these issues so as to round out this perspective.

Nuclear energy holds some promise, but the solutions to the many problems that remain will necessarily involve materials, from fuels to containment structures to facilities for the disposal of radioactive waste.

Significant quantities of energy are involved in transportation. Reducing the weight of transportation vehicles (automobiles, aircraft, trains, etc.), as well as increasing engine operating temperatures, will enhance fuel efficiency. New high-strength, low-density structural materials remain to be developed, as well as materials that have higher-temperature capabilities, for use in engine components.

Furthermore, there is a recognized need to find new, economical sources of energy and to use present resources more efficiently. Materials will undoubtedly play a significant role in these developments. For example, the direct conversion of solar into electrical energy has been demonstrated. Solar cells employ some rather complex and expensive materials. To ensure a viable technology, materials that are highly efficient in this conversion process yet less costly must be developed.

The hydrogen fuel cell is another very attractive and feasible energy-conversion technology that has the advantage of being non-polluting. It is just beginning to be implemented in batteries for electronic devices, and holds promise as the power plant for automobiles. New materials still need to be developed for more efficient fuel cells, and also for better catalysts to be used in the production of hydrogen.

Furthermore, environmental quality depends on our ability to control air and water pollution. Pollution control techniques employ various materials. In addition, materials

[5] One legendary and prophetic suggestion as to the possibility of nanoengineering materials was offered by Richard Feynman in his 1960 American Physical Society lecture that was entitled "There is Plenty of Room at the Bottom."

processing and refinement methods need to be improved so that they produce less environmental degradation—that is, less pollution and less despoilage of the landscape from the mining of raw materials. Also, in some materials manufacturing processes, toxic substances are produced, and the ecological impact of their disposal must be considered.

Many materials that we use are derived from resources that are nonrenewable—that is, not capable of being regenerated. These include polymers, for which the prime raw material is oil, and some metals. These nonrenewable resources are gradually becoming depleted, which necessitates: (1) the discovery of additional reserves, (2) the development of new materials having comparable properties with less adverse environmental impact, and/or (3) increased recycling efforts and the development of new recycling technologies. As a consequence of the economics of not only production but also environmental impact and ecological factors, it is becoming increasingly important to consider the "cradle-to-grave" life cycle of materials relative to the overall manufacturing process.

The roles that materials scientists and engineers play relative to these, as well as other environmental and societal issues, are discussed in more detail in Chapter 22.

MATERIALS OF IMPORTANCE

Delhi Iron Pillar

The famous Iron Pillar of Delhi[6] was erected in 402 AD originally at *Vishnupadagiri*, (now known as Udayagiri near Sanchi, about 50 km from Bhopal). The Iron Pillar was forged during the reign of the famous Gupta dynasty (320-600 AD), by Chandragupta II Vikramaditya (375-414 AD), referred to as *Chandra* in the oldest Gupta-Brahmi inscription

seen on the Pillar. The Pillar served as an astronomical gnomon at *Vishnupadagiri*, which is located on the Tropic of Cancer. The Pillar was moved to Delhi in 1233 AD by Iltutmish and erected in the Quwwat-ul-Islam mosque in the Qutub Minar Complex in New Delhi, which is its current location.

The Pillar is about 7.4 m high. The artistically meritorious decorative bell capital was originally topped with a *chakra* (circular discus), which has been removed sometime in history. The design of the capital is reminiscent of Ashokan capitals and the Pillar is wrongly referred to as Ashoka Iron Pillar. The estimated weight of the Pillar is 6511 kilograms. The construction of the massive Pillar is a marvelous engineering achievement, offering visual proof of India's metallurgical brilliance. Iron lumps of about 30 kilograms in weight were hammered together in the hot state by a process known as forge welding, with the Pillar in the horizontal position. The iron of the Pillar was extracted by the traditional direct reduction method and has been deliberately kept high in phosphorus (0.25 weight percent) and low in carbon, sulfur and manganese. The average composition of the iron of the Pillar, based on four available analyses, is (in weight percent) 0.25 phosphorus, 0.15 carbon, 0.05 manganese, 0.05 nickel, 0.03 copper, 0.02 nitrogen, 0.005 sulfur and balance iron. The Pillar is resistant to corrosion due to the formation of a thin protective passive film, aided by the relatively high phosphorus content.

[6] Balasubramaniam, R., *Story of the Delhi Iron Pillar*, Cambridge University Press, New Delhi, 2005.

REFERENCES

Ashby, M. F. and D. R. H. Jones, *Engineering Materials 1, An Introduction to Their Properties and Applications,* 3rd edition, Butterworth-Heinemann, Woburn, UK, 2005.

Ashby, M. F. and D. R. H. Jones, *Engineering Materials 2, An Introduction to Microstructures, Processing and Design,* 3rd edition, Butterworth-Heinemann, Woburn, UK, 2005.

Askeland, D. R. and P. P. Phulé, *The Science and Engineering of Materials,* 5th edition, Nelson (a division of Thomson Canada), Toronto, 2006.

Baillie, C. and L. Vanasupa, *Navigating the Materials World,* Academic Press, San Diego, CA, 2003.

Flinn, R. A. and P. K. Trojan, *Engineering Materials and Their Applications,* 4th edition, John Wiley & Sons, New York, 1994.

Jacobs, J. A. and T. F. Kilduff, *Engineering Materials Technology,* 5th edition, Prentice Hall PTR, Paramus, NJ, 2005.

Mangonon, P. L., *The Principles of Materials Selection for Engineering Design,* Prentice Hall PTR, Paramus, NJ, 1999.

McMahon, C. J., Jr., *Structural Materials,* Merion Books, Philadelphia, 2004.

Murray, G. T., *Introduction to Engineering Materials—Behavior, Properties, and Selection,* Marcel Dekker, Inc., New York, 1993.

Murthy, V. S. R., A. K. Jena, K. P. Gupta, and G. S. Murty, *Structure and Properties of Engineering Materials,* Tata McGraw Hill, New Delhi, 2003.

Raghavan, V., *Introduction to Material Science and Engineering* 5th edition, Prentice-Hall India, New Delhi, 2005.

Ralls, K. M., T. H. Courtney, and J. Wulff, *Introduction to Materials Science and Engineering,* John Wiley & Sons, New York, 1976.

Schaffer, J. P., A. Saxena, S. D. Antolovich, T. H. Sanders, Jr., and S. B. Warner, *The Science and Design of Engineering Materials,* 2nd edition, WCB/McGraw-Hill, New York, 1999.

Shackelford, J. F., *Introduction to Materials Science for Engineers,* 6th edition, Prentice Hall PTR, Paramus, NJ, 2005.

Smith, W. F. and J. Hashemi, *Principles of Materials Science and Engineering,* 4th edition, McGraw-Hill Book Company, New York, 2006.

Van Vlack, L. H., *Elements of Materials Science and Engineering,* 6th edition, Addison-Wesley Longman, Boston, MA, 1989.

White, M. A., *Properties of Materials,* Oxford University Press, New York, 1999.

Chapter 2 Atomic Structure and Interatomic Bonding

This photograph shows the underside of a gecko.

Geckos, harmless tropical lizards, are extremely fascinating and extraordinary animals. They have very sticky feet that cling to virtually any surface. This characteristic makes it possible for them to rapidly run up vertical walls and along the undersides of horizontal surfaces. In fact, a gecko can support its body mass with a single toe! The secret to this remarkable ability is the presence of an extremely large number of microscopically small hairs on each of their toe pads. When these hairs come in contact with a surface, weak forces of attraction (i.e., van der Waals forces) are established between hair molecules and molecules on the surface. The fact that these hairs are so small and so numerous explains why the gecko grips surfaces so tightly. To release its grip, the gecko simply curls up its toes, and peels the hairs away from the surface.

Another interesting feature of these toe pads is that they are self-cleaning—that is, dirt particles don't stick to them. Scientists are just beginning to understand the mechanism of adhesion for these tiny hairs, which may lead to the development of synthetic self-cleaning adhesives. Can you image duct tape that never looses its stickiness, or bandages that never leave a sticky residue?

(Photograph courtesy of Professor Kellar Autumn, Lewis & Clark College, Portland, Oregon.)

Learning Objectives

After careful study of this chapter you should be able to do the following:

1. Name the two atomic models cited, and note the differences between them.
2. Describe the important quantum-mechanical principle that relates to electron energies.
3. (a) Schematically plot attractive, repulsive, and net energies versus interatomic separation for two atoms or ions.
   (b) Note on this plot the equilibrium separation and the bonding energy.
4. (a) Briefly describe ionic, covalent, metallic, hydrogen, and van der Waals bonds.
   (b) Note which materials exhibit each of these bonding types.

2.1 INTRODUCTION

Some of the important properties of solid materials depend on geometrical atomic arrangements, and also the interactions that exist among constituent atoms or molecules. This chapter, by way of preparation for subsequent discussions, considers several fundamental and important concepts—namely, atomic structure, electron configurations in atoms and the periodic table, and the various types of primary and secondary interatomic bonds that hold together the atoms comprising a solid. These topics are reviewed briefly, under the assumption that some of the material is familiar to the reader.

Atomic Structure

2.2 FUNDAMENTAL CONCEPTS

Each atom consists of a very small nucleus composed of protons and neutrons, which is encircled by moving electrons. Both electrons and protons are electrically charged, the charge magnitude being 1.60×10^{-19} C, which is negative in sign for electrons and positive for protons; neutrons are electrically neutral. Masses for these subatomic particles are infinitesimally small; protons and neutrons have approximately the same mass, 1.67×10^{-27} kg, which is significantly larger than that of an electron, 9.11×10^{-31} kg.

Each chemical element is characterized by the number of protons in the nucleus, or the **atomic number** (Z).[1] For an electrically neutral or complete atom, the atomic number also equals the number of electrons. This atomic number ranges in integral units from 1 for hydrogen to 92 for uranium, the highest of the naturally occurring elements.

The *atomic mass* (A) of a specific atom may be expressed as the sum of the masses of protons and neutrons within the nucleus. Although the number of protons is the same for all atoms of a given element, the number of neutrons (N) may be variable. Thus atoms of some elements have two or more different atomic masses, which are called **isotopes.** The **atomic weight** of an element corresponds to the weighted average of the atomic masses of the atom's naturally occurring isotopes.[2] The **atomic mass unit (amu)** may be used for computations of atomic weight. A

---

[1] Terms appearing in boldface type are defined in the Glossary, which follows Appendix E.

[2] The term "atomic mass" is really more accurate than "atomic weight" inasmuch as, in this context, we are dealing with masses and not weights. However, atomic weight is, by convention, the preferred terminology and will be used throughout this book. The reader should note that it is *not* necessary to divide molecular weight by the gravitational constant.

scale has been established whereby 1 amu is defined as $\frac{1}{12}$ of the atomic mass of the most common isotope of carbon, carbon 12 (^{12}C) ($A = 12.00000$). Within this scheme, the masses of protons and neutrons are slightly greater than unity, and

$$A \cong Z + N \tag{2.1}$$

The atomic weight of an element or the molecular weight of a compound may be specified on the basis of amu per atom (molecule) or mass per mole of material. In one **mole** of a substance there are 6.023×10^{23} (Avogadro's number) atoms or molecules. These two atomic weight schemes are related through the following equation:

$$1 \text{ amu/atom (or molecule)} = 1 \text{ g/mol}$$

For example, the atomic weight of iron is 55.85 amu/atom, or 55.85 g/mol. Sometimes use of amu per atom or molecule is convenient; on other occasions g (or kg)/mol is preferred. The latter is used in this book.

Concept Check 2.1

Why are the atomic weights of the elements generally not integers? Cite two reasons.

[*The answer may be found in enclosed CD.*]

2.3 ELECTRONS IN ATOMS

Atomic Models

During the latter part of the nineteenth century it was realized that many phenomena involving electrons in solids could not be explained in terms of classical mechanics. What followed was the establishment of a set of principles and laws that govern systems of atomic and subatomic entities that came to be known as **quantum mechanics.** An understanding of the behavior of electrons in atoms and crystalline solids necessarily involves the discussion of quantum-mechanical concepts. However, a detailed exploration of these principles is beyond the scope of this book, and only a very superficial and simplified treatment is given.

One early outgrowth of quantum mechanics was the simplified **Bohr atomic model,** in which electrons are assumed to revolve around the atomic nucleus in discrete orbitals, and the position of any particular electron is more or less well defined in terms of its orbital. This model of the atom is represented in Figure 2.1.

Another important quantum-mechanical principle stipulates that the energies of electrons are quantized; that is, electrons are permitted to have only specific values of energy. An electron may change energy, but in doing so it must make a quantum jump either to an allowed higher energy (with absorption of energy) or to a lower energy (with emission of energy). Often, it is convenient to think of these allowed electron energies as being associated with *energy levels* or *states*. These states do not vary continuously with energy; that is, adjacent states are separated by finite energies. For example, allowed states for the Bohr hydrogen atom are represented in Figure 2.2*a*. These energies are taken to be negative, whereas the zero reference is the unbound or free electron. Of course, the single electron associated with the hydrogen atom will fill only one of these states.

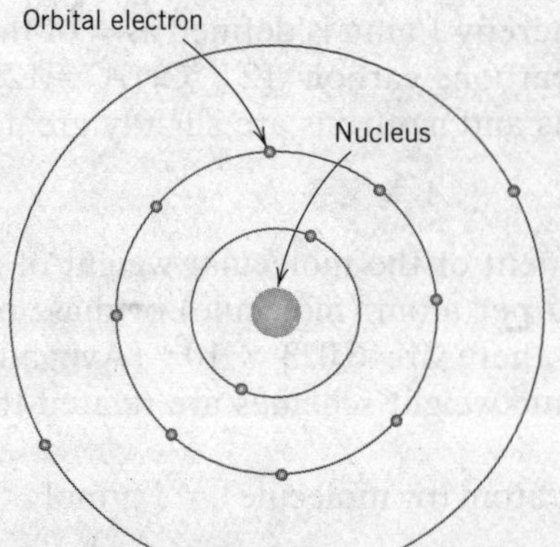

Figure 2.1 Schematic representation of the Bohr atom.

Thus, the Bohr model represents an early attempt to describe electrons in atoms, in terms of both position (electron orbitals) and energy (quantized energy levels).

This Bohr model was eventually found to have some significant limitations because of its inability to explain several phenomena involving electrons. A resolution was reached with a **wave-mechanical model,** in which the electron is considered to exhibit both wave-like and particle-like characteristics. With this model, an electron is no longer treated as a particle moving in a discrete orbital; rather, position is considered to be the probability of an electron's being at various locations around the nucleus. In other words, position is described by a probability distribution or electron cloud. Figure 2.3 compares Bohr and wave-mechanical models for the hydrogen atom. Both these models are used throughout the course of this book; the choice depends on which model allows the more simple explanation.

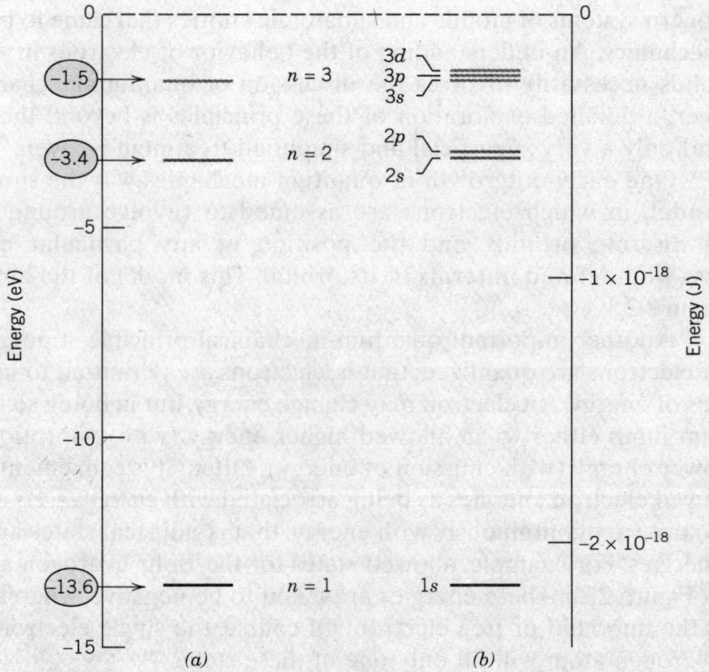

Figure 2.2 (*a*) The first three electron energy states for the Bohr hydrogen atom. (*b*) Electron energy states for the first three shells of the wave-mechanical hydrogen atom. (Adapted from W. G. Moffatt, G. W. Pearsall, and J. Wulff, *The Structure and Properties of Materials,* Vol. I, *Structure,* p. 10. Copyright © 1964 by John Wiley & Sons, New York. Reprinted by permission of John Wiley & Sons, Inc.)

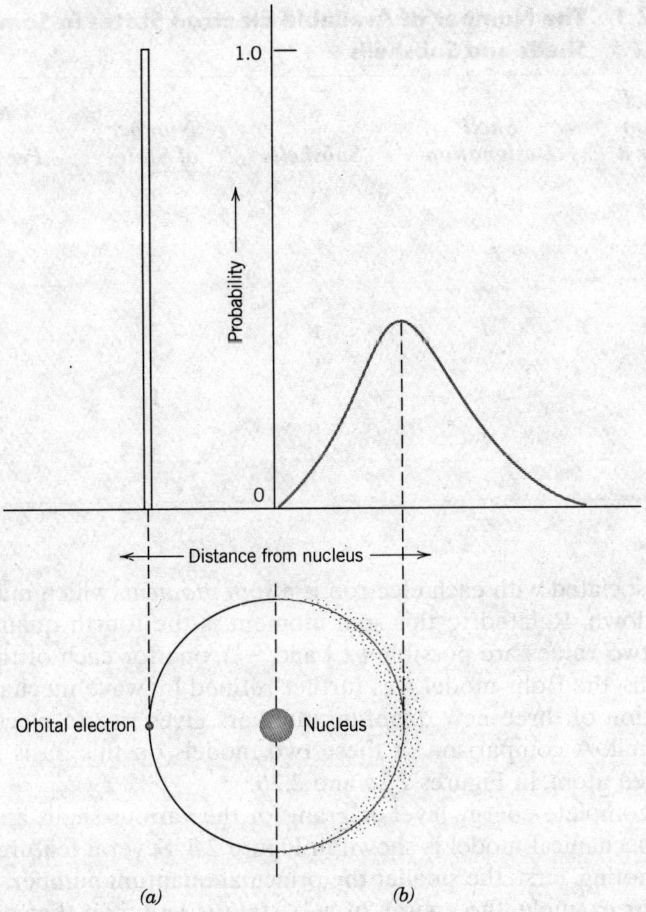

Figure 2.3 Comparison of the (*a*) Bohr and (*b*) wave-mechanical atom models in terms of electron distribution. (Adapted from Z. D. Jastrzebski, *The Nature and Properties of Engineering Materials,* 3rd edition, p. 4. Copyright © 1987 by John Wiley & Sons, New York. Reprinted by permission of John Wiley & Sons, Inc.)

Quantum Numbers

Using wave mechanics, every electron in an atom is characterized by four parameters called **quantum numbers.** The size, shape, and spatial orientation of an electron's probability density are specified by three of these quantum numbers. Furthermore, Bohr energy levels separate into electron subshells, and quantum numbers dictate the number of states within each subshell. Shells are specified by a *principal quantum number n*, which may take on integral values beginning with unity; sometimes these shells are designated by the letters *K*, *L*, *M*, *N*, *O*, and so on, which correspond, respectively, to $n = 1, 2, 3, 4, 5, \ldots$, as indicated in Table 2.1. Note also that this quantum number, and it only, is also associated with the Bohr model. This quantum number is related to the distance of an electron from the nucleus, or its position.

The second quantum number, *l*, signifies the subshell, which is denoted by a lowercase letter—an *s*, *p*, *d*, or *f*; it is related to the shape of the electron subshell. In addition, the number of these subshells is restricted by the magnitude of *n*. Allowable subshells for the several *n* values are also presented in Table 2.1. The number of energy states for each subshell is determined by the third quantum number, m_l. For an *s* subshell, there is a single energy state, whereas for *p*, *d*, and *f* subshells, three, five, and seven states exist, respectively (Table 2.1). In the absence of an external magnetic field, the states within each subshell are identical. However, when a magnetic field is applied these subshell states split, each state assuming a slightly different energy.

Table 2.1 The Number of Available Electron States in Some of the Electron Shells and Subshells

Principal Quantum Number n	*Shell Designation*	*Subshells*	*Number of States*	*Number of Electrons*	
				Per Subshell	*Per Shell*
1	*K*	*s*	1	2	2
2	*L*	*s*	1	2	8
		p	3	6	
3	*M*	*s*	1	2	18
		p	3	6	
		d	5	10	
4	*N*	*s*	1	2	32
		p	3	6	
		d	5	10	
		f	7	14	

Associated with each electron is a *spin moment,* which must be oriented either up or down. Related to this spin moment is the fourth quantum number, m_s, for which two values are possible ($+\frac{1}{2}$ and $-\frac{1}{2}$), one for each of the spin orientations.

Thus, the Bohr model was further refined by wave mechanics, in which the introduction of three new quantum numbers gives rise to electron subshells within each shell. A comparison of these two models on this basis is illustrated, for the hydrogen atom, in Figures 2.2*a* and 2.2*b*.

A complete energy level diagram for the various shells and subshells using the wave-mechanical model is shown in Figure 2.4. Several features of the diagram are worth noting. First, the smaller the principal quantum number, the lower the energy level; for example, the energy of a 1*s* state is less than that of a 2*s* state, which in turn is lower than the 3*s*. Second, within each shell, the energy of a subshell level increases with the value of the *l* quantum number. For example, the energy of a 3*d* state is greater than a 3*p*, which is larger than 3*s*. Finally, there may be overlap in

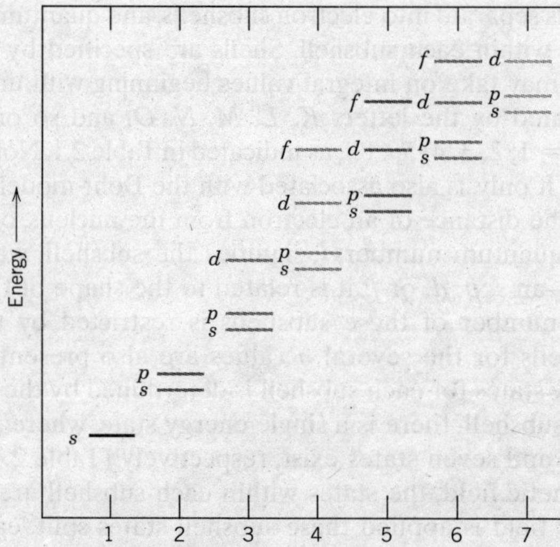

Figure 2.4 Schematic representation of the relative energies of the electrons for the various shells and subshells. (From K. M. Ralls, T. H. Courtney, and J. Wulff, *Introduction to Materials Science and Engineering,* p. 22. Copyright © 1976 by John Wiley & Sons, New York. Reprinted by permission of John Wiley & Sons, Inc.)

energy of a state in one shell with states in an adjacent shell, which is especially true of *d* and *f* states; for example, the energy of a 3*d* state is greater than that for a 4*s*.

Electron Configurations

The preceding discussion has dealt primarily with **electron states**—values of energy that are permitted for electrons. To determine the manner in which these states are filled with electrons, we use the **Pauli exclusion principle,** another quantum-mechanical concept. This principle stipulates that each electron state can hold no more than two electrons, which must have opposite spins. Thus, *s*, *p*, *d*, and *f* subshells may each accommodate, respectively, a total of 2, 6, 10, and 14 electrons; Table 2.1 summarizes the maximum number of electrons that may occupy each of the first four shells.

Of course, not all possible states in an atom are filled with electrons. For most atoms, the electrons fill up the lowest possible energy states in the electron shells and subshells, two electrons (having opposite spins) per state. The energy structure for a sodium atom is represented schematically in Figure 2.5. When all the electrons occupy the lowest possible energies in accord with the foregoing restrictions, an atom is said to be in its **ground state.** However, electron transitions to higher energy states are possible, as discussed in Chapters 17 and 20. The **electron configuration** or structure of an atom represents the manner in which these states are occupied. In the conventional notation the number of electrons in each subshell is indicated by a superscript after the shell–subshell designation. For example, the electron configurations for hydrogen, helium, and sodium are, respectively, $1s^1$, $1s^2$, and $1s^22s^22p^63s^1$. Electron configurations for some of the more common elements are listed in Table 2.2.

At this point, comments regarding these electron configurations are necessary. First, the **valence electrons** are those that occupy the outermost shell. These electrons are extremely important; as will be seen, they participate in the bonding between atoms to form atomic and molecular aggregates. Furthermore, many of the physical and chemical properties of solids are based on these valence electrons.

In addition, some atoms have what are termed "stable electron configurations"; that is, the states within the outermost or valence electron shell are completely filled. Normally this corresponds to the occupation of just the *s* and *p* states for the outermost shell by a total of eight electrons, as in neon, argon, and krypton; one exception is helium, which contains only two 1*s* electrons. These elements (Ne, Ar, Kr, and He) are the inert, or noble, gases, which are virtually unreactive chemically. Some atoms of the elements that have unfilled valence shells assume stable electron configurations by gaining or losing electrons to form charged ions,

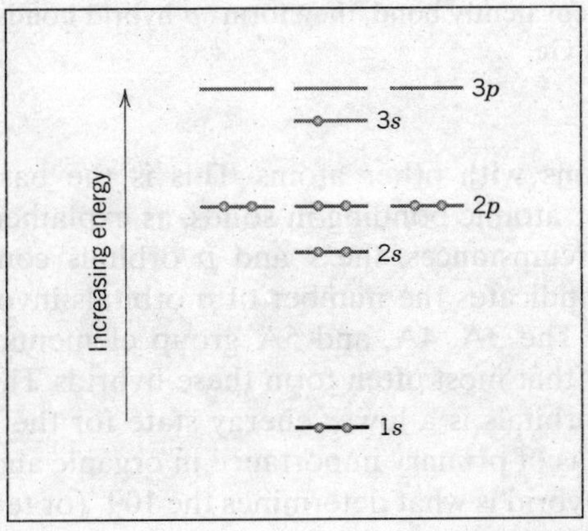

Figure 2.5 Schematic representation of the filled and lowest unfilled energy states for a sodium atom.

Table 2.2 A Listing of the Expected Electron Configurations for Some of the Common Elements[a]

Element	*Symbol*	*Atomic Number*	*Electron Configuration*
Hydrogen	H	1	$1s^1$
Helium	He	2	$1s^2$
Lithium	Li	3	$1s^2 2s^1$
Beryllium	Be	4	$1s^2 2s^2$
Boron	B	5	$1s^2 2s^2 2p^1$
Carbon	C	6	$1s^2 2s^2 2p^2$
Nitrogen	N	7	$1s^2 2s^2 2p^3$
Oxygen	O	8	$1s^2 2s^2 2p^4$
Fluorine	F	9	$1s^2 2s^2 2p^5$
Neon	Ne	10	$1s^2 2s^2 2p^6$
Sodium	Na	11	$1s^2 2s^2 2p^6 3s^1$
Magnesium	Mg	12	$1s^2 2s^2 2p^6 3s^2$
Aluminum	Al	13	$1s^2 2s^2 2p^6 3s^2 3p^1$
Silicon	Si	14	$1s^2 2s^2 2p^6 3s^2 3p^2$
Phosphorus	P	15	$1s^2 2s^2 2p^6 3s^2 3p^3$
Sulfur	S	16	$1s^2 2s^2 2p^6 3s^2 3p^4$
Chlorine	Cl	17	$1s^2 2s^2 2p^6 3s^2 3p^5$
Argon	Ar	18	$1s^2 2s^2 2p^6 3s^2 3p^6$
Potassium	K	19	$1s^2 2s^2 2p^6 3s^2 3p^6 4s^1$
Calcium	Ca	20	$1s^2 2s^2 2p^6 3s^2 3p^6 4s^2$
Scandium	Sc	21	$1s^2 2s^2 2p^6 3s^2 3p^6 3d^1 4s^2$
Titanium	Ti	22	$1s^2 2s^2 2p^6 3s^2 3p^6 3d^2 4s^2$
Vanadium	V	23	$1s^2 2s^2 2p^6 3s^2 3p^6 3d^3 4s^2$
Chromium	Cr	24	$1s^2 2s^2 2p^6 3s^2 3p^6 3d^5 4s^1$
Manganese	Mn	25	$1s^2 2s^2 2p^6 3s^2 3p^6 3d^5 4s^2$
Iron	Fe	26	$1s^2 2s^2 2p^6 3s^2 3p^6 3d^6 4s^2$
Cobalt	Co	27	$1s^2 2s^2 2p^6 3s^2 3p^6 3d^7 4s^2$
Nickel	Ni	28	$1s^2 2s^2 2p^6 3s^2 3p^6 3d^8 4s^2$
Copper	Cu	29	$1s^2 2s^2 2p^6 3s^2 3p^6 3d^{10} 4s^1$
Zinc	Zn	30	$1s^2 2s^2 2p^6 3s^2 3p^6 3d^{10} 4s^2$
Gallium	Ga	31	$1s^2 2s^2 2p^6 3s^2 3p^6 3d^{10} 4s^2 4p^1$
Germanium	Ge	32	$1s^2 2s^2 2p^6 3s^2 3p^6 3d^{10} 4s^2 4p^2$
Arsenic	As	33	$1s^2 2s^2 2p^6 3s^2 3p^6 3d^{10} 4s^2 4p^3$
Selenium	Se	34	$1s^2 2s^2 2p^6 3s^2 3p^6 3d^{10} 4s^2 4p^4$
Bromine	Br	35	$1s^2 2s^2 2p^6 3s^2 3p^6 3d^{10} 4s^2 4p^5$
Krypton	Kr	36	$1s^2 2s^2 2p^6 3s^2 3p^6 3d^{10} 4s^2 4p^6$

[a] When some elements covalently bond, they form *sp* hybrid bonds. This is especially true for C, Si, and Ge.

or by sharing electrons with other atoms. This is the basis for some chemical reactions, and also for atomic bonding in solids, as explained in Section 2.6.

Under special circumstances, the *s* and *p* orbitals combine to form hybrid sp^n orbitals, where *n* indicates the number of *p* orbitals involved, which may have a value of 1, 2, or 3. The 3A, 4A, and 5A group elements of the periodic table (Figure 2.6) are those that most often form these hybrids. The driving force for the formation of hybrid orbitals is a lower energy state for the valence electrons. For carbon the sp^3 hybrid is of primary importance in organic and polymer chemistries. The shape of the sp^3 hybrid is what determines the 109° (or tetrahedral) angle found in polymer chains (Chapter 13).

> ***Concept Check 2.2***
>
> Give electron configurations for the Fe^{3+} and S^{2-} ions.
>
> [*The answer may be found in enclosed CD.*]

2.4 THE PERIODIC TABLE

All the elements have been classified according to electron configuration in the **periodic table** (Figure 2.6). Here, the elements are situated, with increasing atomic number, in seven horizontal rows called periods. The arrangement is such that all elements arrayed in a given column or group have similar valence electron structures, as well as chemical and physical properties. These properties change gradually, moving horizontally across each period and vertically down each column.

The elements positioned in Group 0, the rightmost group, are the inert gases, which have filled electron shells and stable electron configurations. Group VIIA and VIA elements are one and two electrons deficient, respectively, from having stable structures. The Group VIIA elements (F, Cl, Br, I, and At) are sometimes termed the halogens. The alkali and the alkaline earth metals (Li, Na, K, Be, Mg, Ca, etc.) are labeled as Groups IA and IIA, having, respectively, one and two electrons in excess of stable structures. The elements in the three long periods, Groups IIIB through IIB, are termed the transition metals, which have partially filled *d* electron states and in some cases one or two electrons in the next higher energy shell. Groups IIIA, IVA, and VA (B, Si, Ge, As, etc.) display characteristics that are intermediate between the metals and nonmetals by virtue of their valence electron structures.

Key: 29 — Atomic number; Cu — Symbol; 63.54 — Atomic weight

Metal | Nonmetal | Intermediate

IA	IIA	IIIB	IVB	VB	VIB	VIIB	VIII	VIII	VIII	IB	IIB	IIIA	IVA	VA	VIA	VIIA	0
1 H 1.0080																	2 He 4.0026
3 Li 6.941	4 Be 9.0122											5 B 10.811	6 C 12.011	7 N 14.007	8 O 15.999	9 F 18.998	10 Ne 20.180
11 Na 22.990	12 Mg 24.305											13 Al 26.982	14 Si 28.086	15 P 30.974	16 S 32.064	17 Cl 35.453	18 Ar 39.948
19 K 39.098	20 Ca 40.08	21 Sc 44.956	22 Ti 47.87	23 V 50.942	24 Cr 51.996	25 Mn 54.938	26 Fe 55.845	27 Co 58.933	28 Ni 58.69	29 Cu 63.54	30 Zn 65.41	31 Ga 69.72	32 Ge 72.64	33 As 74.922	34 Se 78.96	35 Br 79.904	36 Kr 83.80
37 Rb 85.47	38 Sr 87.62	39 Y 88.91	40 Zr 91.22	41 Nb 92.91	42 Mo 95.94	43 Tc (98)	44 Ru 101.07	45 Rh 102.91	46 Pd 106.4	47 Ag 107.87	48 Cd 112.41	49 In 114.82	50 Sn 118.71	51 Sb 121.76	52 Te 127.60	53 I 126.90	54 Xe 131.30
55 Cs 132.91	56 Ba 137.34	Rare earth series	72 Hf 178.49	73 Ta 180.95	74 W 183.84	75 Re 186.2	76 Os 190.23	77 Ir 192.2	78 Pt 195.08	79 Au 196.97	80 Hg 200.59	81 Tl 204.38	82 Pb 207.19	83 Bi 208.98	84 Po (209)	85 At (210)	86 Rn (222)
87 Fr (223)	88 Ra (226)	Acti-nide series	104 Rf (261)	105 Db (262)	106 Sg (266)	107 Bh (264)	108 Hs (277)	109 Mt (268)	110 Ds (281)								

Rare earth series	57 La 138.91	58 Ce 140.12	59 Pr 140.91	60 Nd 144.24	61 Pm (145)	62 Sm 150.35	63 Eu 151.96	64 Gd 157.25	65 Tb 158.92	66 Dy 162.50	67 Ho 164.93	68 Er 167.26	69 Tm 168.93	70 Yb 173.04	71 Lu 174.97
Actinide series	89 Ac (227)	90 Th 232.04	91 Pa 231.04	92 U 238.03	93 Np (237)	94 Pu (244)	95 Am (243)	96 Cm (247)	97 Bk (247)	98 Cf (251)	99 Es (252)	100 Fm (257)	101 Md (258)	102 No (259)	103 Lr (262)

Figure 2.6 The periodic table of the elements. The numbers in parentheses are the atomic weights of the most stable or common isotopes.

IA	IIA	IIIB	IVB	VB	VIB	VIIB	VIII	VIII	VIII	IB	IIB	IIIA	IVA	VA	VIA	VIIA	0
1 H 2.1																	2 He –
3 Li 1.0	4 Be 1.5											5 B 2.0	6 C 2.5	7 N 3.0	8 O 3.5	9 F 4.0	10 Ne –
11 Na 0.9	12 Mg 1.2											13 Al 1.5	14 Si 1.8	15 P 2.1	16 S 2.5	17 Cl 3.0	18 Ar –
19 K 0.8	20 Ca 1.0	21 Sc 1.3	22 Ti 1.5	23 V 1.6	24 Cr 1.6	25 Mn 1.5	26 Fe 1.8	27 Co 1.8	28 Ni 1.8	29 Cu 1.9	30 Zn 1.6	31 Ga 1.6	32 Ge 1.8	33 As 2.0	34 Se 2.4	35 Br 2.8	36 Kr –
37 Rb 0.8	38 Sr 1.0	39 Y 1.2	40 Zr 1.4	41 Nb 1.6	42 Mo 1.8	43 Tc 1.9	44 Ru 2.2	45 Rh 2.2	46 Pd 2.2	47 Ag 1.9	48 Cd 1.7	49 In 1.7	50 Sn 1.8	51 Sb 1.9	52 Te 2.1	53 I 2.5	54 Xe –
55 Cs 0.7	56 Ba 0.9	57–71 La–Lu 1.1–1.2	72 Hf 1.3	73 Ta 1.5	74 W 1.7	75 Re 1.9	76 Os 2.2	77 Ir 2.2	78 Pt 2.2	79 Au 2.4	80 Hg 1.9	81 Tl 1.8	82 Pb 1.8	83 Bi 1.9	84 Po 2.0	85 At 2.2	86 Rn –
87 Fr 0.7	88 Ra 0.9	89–102 Ac–No 1.1–1.7															

Figure 2.7 The electronegativity values for the elements. (Adapted from Linus Pauling, *The Nature of the Chemical Bond,* 3rd edition. Copyright 1939 and 1940, 3rd edition copyright © 1960, by Cornell University. Used by permission of the publisher, Cornell University Press.)

As may be noted from the periodic table, most of the elements really come under the metal classification. These are sometimes termed **electropositive** elements, indicating that they are capable of giving up their few valence electrons to become positively charged ions. Furthermore, the elements situated on the right-hand side of the table are **electronegative;** that is, they readily accept electrons to form negatively charged ions, or sometimes they share electrons with other atoms. Figure 2.7 displays electronegativity values that have been assigned to the various elements arranged in the periodic table. As a general rule, electronegativity increases in moving from left to right and from bottom to top. Atoms are more likely to accept electrons if their outer shells are almost full, and if they are less "shielded" from (i.e., closer to) the nucleus.

Atomic Bonding in Solids

2.5 BONDING FORCES AND ENERGIES

An understanding of many of the physical properties of materials is predicated on a knowledge of the interatomic forces that bind the atoms together. Perhaps the principles of atomic bonding are best illustrated by considering the interaction between two isolated atoms as they are brought into close proximity from an infinite separation. At large distances, the interactions are negligible, but as the atoms approach, each exerts forces on the other. These forces are of two types, attractive and repulsive, and the magnitude of each is a function of the separation or interatomic distance. The origin of an attractive force F_A depends on the particular type of bonding that exists between the two atoms. The magnitude of the attractive force varies with the distance, as represented schematically in Figure 2.8*a*. Ultimately, the outer electron shells of the two atoms begin to overlap, and a strong repulsive force F_R comes into play. The net force F_N between the two atoms is just the sum of both attractive and repulsive components; that is,

$$F_N = F_A + F_R \tag{2.2}$$

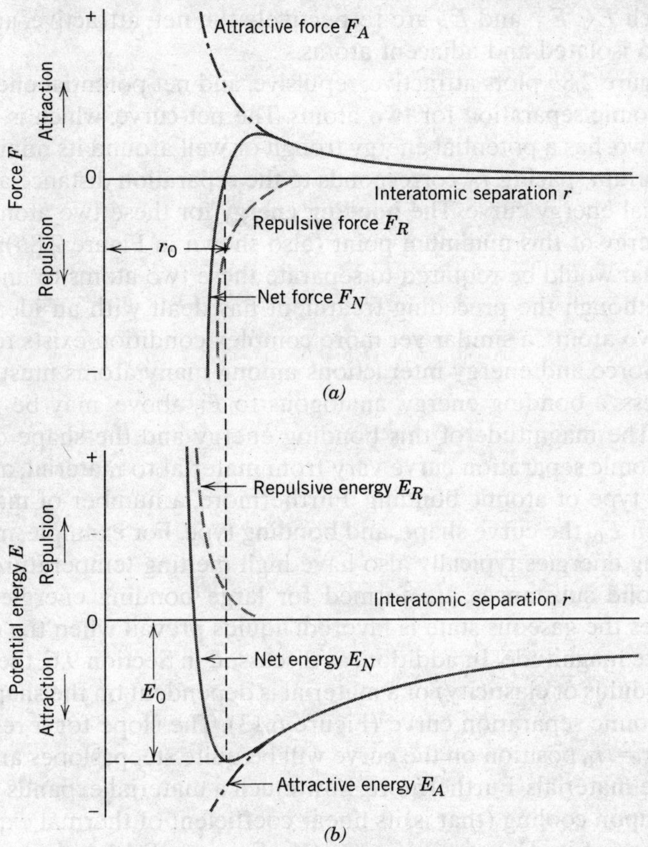

Figure 2.8 (*a*) The dependence of repulsive, attractive, and net forces on interatomic separation for two isolated atoms. (*b*) The dependence of repulsive, attractive, and net potential energies on interatomic separation for two isolated atoms.

which is also a function of the interatomic separation, as also plotted in Figure 2.8*a*. When F_A and F_R balance, or become equal, there is no net force; that is,

$$F_A + F_R = 0 \tag{2.3}$$

Then a state of equilibrium exists. The centers of the two atoms will remain separated by the equilibrium spacing r_0, as indicated in Figure 2.8*a*. For many atoms, r_0 is approximately 0.3 nm. Once in this position, the two atoms will counteract any attempt to separate them by an attractive force, or to push them together by a repulsive action.

Sometimes it is more convenient to work with the potential energies between two atoms instead of forces. Mathematically, energy (E) and force (F) are related as

$$E = \int F\,dr \tag{2.4}$$

or, for atomic systems,

$$E_N = \int_\infty^r F_N\,dr \tag{2.5}$$

$$= \int_\infty^r F_A\,dr + \int_\infty^r F_R\,dr \tag{2.6}$$

$$= E_A + E_R \tag{2.7}$$

in which E_N, E_A, and E_R are respectively the net, attractive, and repulsive energies for two isolated and adjacent atoms.

Figure 2.8*b* plots attractive, repulsive, and net potential energies as a function of interatomic separation for two atoms. The net curve, which is again the sum of the other two, has a potential energy trough or well around its minimum. Here, the same equilibrium spacing, r_0, corresponds to the separation distance at the minimum of the potential energy curve. The **bonding energy** for these two atoms, E_0, corresponds to the energy at this minimum point (also shown in Figure 2.8*b*); it represents the energy that would be required to separate these two atoms to an infinite separation.

Although the preceding treatment has dealt with an ideal situation involving only two atoms, a similar yet more complex condition exists for solid materials because force and energy interactions among many atoms must be considered. Nevertheless, a bonding energy, analogous to E_0 above, may be associated with each atom. The magnitude of this bonding energy and the shape of the energy-versus-interatomic separation curve vary from material to material, and they both depend on the type of atomic bonding. Furthermore, a number of material properties depend on E_0, the curve shape, and bonding type. For example, materials having large bonding energies typically also have high melting temperatures; at room temperature, solid substances are formed for large bonding energies, whereas for small energies the gaseous state is favored; liquids prevail when the energies are of intermediate magnitude. In addition, as discussed in Section 9.6, the mechanical stiffness (or modulus of elasticity) of a material is dependent on the shape of its force-versus-interatomic separation curve (Figure 6.13). The slope for a relatively stiff material at the $r = r_0$ position on the curve will be quite steep; slopes are shallower for more flexible materials. Furthermore, how much a material expands upon heating or contracts upon cooling (that is, its linear coefficient of thermal expansion) is related to the shape of its E_0-versus-r_0 curve (see Section 19.3). A deep and narrow "trough," which typically occurs for materials having large bonding energies, normally correlates with a low coefficient of thermal expansion and relatively small dimensional alterations for changes in temperature.

Three different types of **primary** or chemical **bond** are found in solids—ionic, covalent, and metallic. For each type, the bonding necessarily involves the valence electrons; furthermore, the nature of the bond depends on the electron structures of the constituent atoms. In general, each of these three types of bonding arises from the tendency of the atoms to assume stable electron structures, like those of the inert gases, by completely filling the outermost electron shell.

Secondary or physical forces and energies are also found in many solid materials; they are weaker than the primary ones, but nonetheless influence the physical properties of some materials. The sections that follow explain the several kinds of primary and secondary interatomic bonds.

2.6 PRIMARY INTERATOMIC BONDS

Ionic Bonding

Ionic bonding is perhaps the easiest to describe and visualize. It is always found in compounds that are composed of both metallic and nonmetallic elements, elements that are situated at the horizontal extremities of the periodic table. Atoms of a metallic element easily give up their valence electrons to the nonmetallic atoms. In the process all the atoms acquire stable or inert gas configurations and, in addition, an electrical charge; that is, they become ions. Sodium chloride (NaCl) is the classic ionic material. A sodium atom can assume the electron structure of neon (and a net single

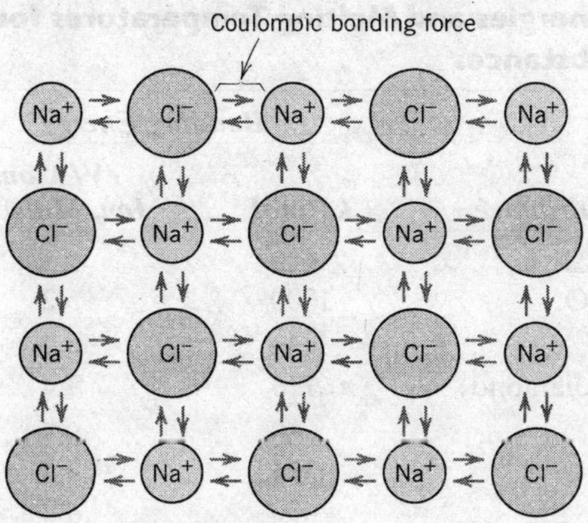

Figure 2.9 Schematic representation of ionic bonding in sodium chloride (NaCl).

positive charge) by a transfer of its one valence 3*s* electron to a chlorine atom. After such a transfer, the chlorine ion has a net negative charge and an electron configuration identical to that of argon. In sodium chloride, all the sodium and chlorine exist as ions. This type of bonding is illustrated schematically in Figure 2.9.

The attractive bonding forces are **coulombic;** that is, positive and negative ions, by virtue of their net electrical charge, attract one another. For two isolated ions, the attractive energy E_A is a function of the interatomic distance according to[3]

$$E_A = -\frac{A}{r} \tag{2.8}$$

An analogous equation for the repulsive energy is

$$E_R = \frac{B}{r^n} \tag{2.9}$$

In these expressions, *A*, *B*, and *n* are constants whose values depend on the particular ionic system. The value of *n* is approximately 8.

Ionic bonding is termed nondirectional; that is, the magnitude of the bond is equal in all directions around an ion. It follows that for ionic materials to be stable, all positive ions must have as nearest neighbors negatively charged ions in a three-dimensional scheme, and vice versa. The predominant bonding in ceramic materials is ionic. Some of the ion arrangements for these materials are discussed in Chapter 4.

Bonding energies, which generally range between 600 and 1500 kJ/mol (3 and 8 eV/atom), are relatively large, as reflected in high melting temperatures.[4] Table 2.3 contains bonding energies and melting temperatures for several ionic materials.

---

[3] The constant *A* in Equation 2.8 is equal to

$$\frac{1}{4\pi\epsilon_0}(Z_1 e)(Z_2 e)$$

where ϵ_0 is the permittivity of a vacuum (8.85×10^{-12} F/m), Z_1 and Z_2 are the valences of the two ion types, and *e* is the electronic charge (1.602×10^{-19} C).

[4] Sometimes bonding energies are expressed per atom or per ion. Under these circumstances the electron volt (eV) is a conveniently small unit of energy. It is, by definition, the energy imparted to an electron as it falls through an electric potential of one volt. The joule equivalent of the electron volt is as follows: 1.602×10^{-19} J = 1 eV.

Table 2.3 Bonding Energies and Melting Temperatures for Various Substances

		Bonding Energy		Melting
Bonding Type	*Substance*	*kJ/mol*	*eV/Atom, Ion, Molecule*	*Temperature (°C)*
Ionic	NaCl	640	3.3	801
	MgO	1000	5.2	2800
Covalent	Si	450	4.7	1410
	C (diamond)	713	7.4	>3550
Metallic	Hg	68	0.7	−39
	Al	324	3.4	660
	Fe	406	4.2	1538
	W	849	8.8	3410
van der Waals	Ar	7.7	0.08	−189
	Cl_2	31	0.32	−101
Hydrogen	NH_3	35	0.36	−78
	H_2O	51	0.52	0

Ionic materials are characteristically hard and brittle and, furthermore, electrically and thermally insulative. As discussed in subsequent chapters, these properties are a direct consequence of electron configurations and/or the nature of the ionic bond.

Covalent Bonding

In **covalent bonding,** stable electron configurations are assumed by the sharing of electrons between adjacent atoms. Two atoms that are covalently bonded will each contribute at least one electron to the bond, and the shared electrons may be considered to belong to both atoms. Covalent bonding is schematically illustrated in Figure 2.10 for a molecule of methane (CH_4). The carbon atom has four valence electrons, whereas each of the four hydrogen atoms has a single valence electron. Each hydrogen atom can acquire a helium electron configuration (two 1*s* valence electrons) when the carbon atom shares with it one electron. The carbon now has four additional shared electrons, one from each hydrogen, for a total of eight valence electrons, and the electron structure of neon. The covalent bond is directional; that is, it is between specific atoms and may exist only in the direction between one atom and another that participates in the electron sharing.

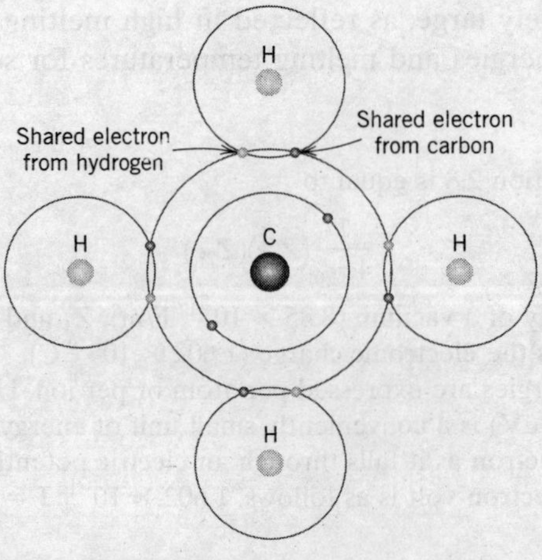

Figure 2.10 Schematic representation of covalent bonding in a molecule of methane (CH_4).

Many nonmetallic elemental molecules (H_2, Cl_2, F_2, etc.) as well as molecules containing dissimilar atoms, such as CH_4, H_2O, HNO_3, and HF, are covalently bonded. Furthermore, this type of bonding is found in elemental solids such as diamond (carbon), silicon, and germanium and other solid compounds composed of elements that are located on the right-hand side of the periodic table, such as gallium arsenide (GaAs), indium antimonide (InSb), and silicon carbide (SiC).

The number of covalent bonds that is possible for a particular atom is determined by the number of valence electrons. For N' valence electrons, an atom can covalently bond with at most $8 - N'$ other atoms. For example, $N' = 7$ for chlorine, and $8 - N' = 1$, which means that one Cl atom can bond to only one other atom, as in Cl_2. Similarly, for carbon, $N' = 4$, and each carbon atom has $8 - 4$, or four, electrons to share. Diamond is simply the three-dimensional interconnecting structure wherein each carbon atom covalently bonds with four other carbon atoms. This arrangement is represented in Figure 4.24.

Covalent bonds may be very strong, as in diamond, which is very hard and has a very high melting temperature, >3550°C (6400°F), or they may be very weak, as with bismuth, which melts at about 270°C (518°F). Bonding energies and melting temperatures for a few covalently bonded materials are presented in Table 2.3. Polymeric materials typify this bond, the basic molecular structure being a long chain of carbon atoms that are covalently bonded together with two of their available four bonds per atom. The remaining two bonds normally are shared with other atoms, which also covalently bond. Polymeric molecular structures are discussed in detail in Chapter 13.

It is possible to have interatomic bonds that are partially ionic and partially covalent, and, in fact, very few compounds exhibit pure ionic or covalent bonding. For a compound, the degree of either bond type depends on the relative positions of the constituent atoms in the periodic table (Figure 2.6) or the difference in their electronegativities (Figure 2.7). The wider the separation (both horizontally—relative to Group IVA—and vertically) from the lower left to the upper-right-hand corner (i.e., the greater the difference in electronegativity), the more ionic the bond. Conversely, the closer the atoms are together (i.e., the smaller the difference in electronegativity), the greater the degree of covalency. The percentage ionic character of a bond between elements A and B (A being the most electronegative) may be approximated by the expression

$$\% \text{ ionic character} = \{1 - \exp[-(0.25)(X_A - X_B)^2]\} \times 100 \tag{2.10}$$

where X_A and X_B are the electronegativities for the respective elements.

Metallic Bonding

Metallic bonding, the final primary bonding type, is found in metals and their alloys. A relatively simple model has been proposed that very nearly approximates the bonding scheme. Metallic materials have one, two, or at most, three valence electrons. With this model, these valence electrons are not bound to any particular atom in the solid and are more or less free to drift throughout the entire metal. They may be thought of as belonging to the metal as a whole, or forming a "sea of electrons" or an "electron cloud." The remaining nonvalence electrons and atomic nuclei form what are called *ion cores,* which possess a net positive charge equal in magnitude to the total valence electron charge per atom. Figure 2.11 is a schematic illustration of metallic bonding. The free electrons shield the positively charged ion cores from mutually repulsive electrostatic forces, which they would otherwise exert upon one another; consequently the metallic bond is nondirectional in character. In addition, these free electrons act as a "glue" to hold the ion cores together. Bonding energies

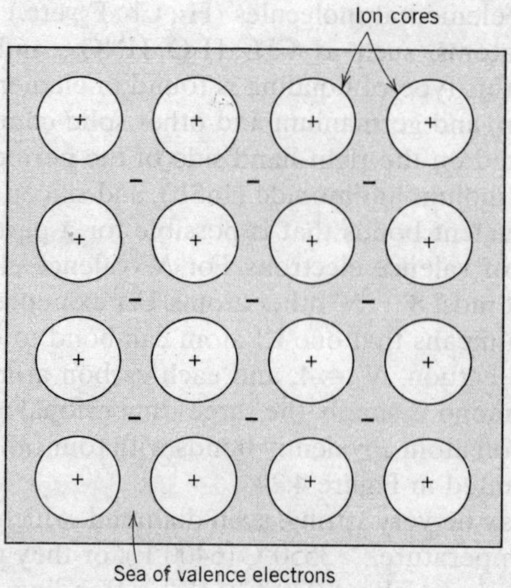

Figure 2.11 Schematic illustration of metallic bonding.

and melting temperatures for several metals are listed in Table 2.3. Bonding may be weak or strong; energies range from 68 kJ/mol (0.7 eV/atom) for mercury to 850 kJ/mol (8.8 eV/atom) for tungsten. Their respective melting temperatures are −39 and 3410°C (−38 and 6170°F).

Metallic bonding is found in the periodic table for Group IA and IIA elements and, in fact, for all elemental metals.

Some general behaviors of the various material types (i.e., metals, ceramics, polymers) may be explained by bonding type. For example, metals are good conductors of both electricity and heat, as a consequence of their free electrons (see Sections 17.5, 17.6 and 19.4). By way of contrast, ionically and covalently bonded materials are typically electrical and thermal insulators, due to the absence of large numbers of free electrons.

Furthermore, in Section 10.4 we note that at room temperature, most metals and their alloys fail in a ductile manner; that is, fracture occurs after the materials have experienced significant degrees of permanent deformation. This behavior is explained in terms of deformation mechanism (Section 10.2), which is implicitly related to the characteristics of the metallic bond. Conversely, at room temperature ionically bonded materials are intrinsically brittle as a consequence of the electrically charged nature of their component ions (see Section 12.12).

Concept Check 2.3

Offer an explanation as to why covalently bonded materials are generally less dense than ionically or metallically bonded ones.

[*The answer may be found in enclosed CD.*]

2.7 SECONDARY BONDING OR VAN DER WAALS BONDING

Secondary, van der Waals, or physical **bonds** are weak in comparison to the primary or chemical ones; bonding energies are typically on the order of only 10 kJ/mol (0.1 eV/atom). Secondary bonding exists between virtually all atoms or molecules,

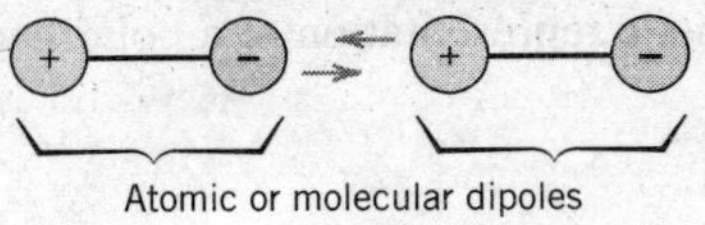

Figure 2.12 Schematic illustration of van der Waals bonding between two dipoles.

but its presence may be obscured if any of the three primary bonding types is present. Secondary bonding is evidenced for the inert gases, which have stable electron structures, and, in addition, between molecules in molecular structures that are covalently bonded.

Secondary bonding forces arise from atomic or molecular **dipoles.** In essence, an electric dipole exists whenever there is some separation of positive and negative portions of an atom or molecule. The bonding results from the coulombic attraction between the positive end of one dipole and the negative region of an adjacent one, as indicated in Figure 2.12. Dipole interactions occur between induced dipoles, between induced dipoles and polar molecules (which have permanent dipoles), and between polar molecules. **Hydrogen bonding,** a special type of secondary bonding, is found to exist between some molecules that have hydrogen as one of the constituents. These bonding mechanisms are now discussed briefly.

Fluctuating Induced Dipole Bonds

A dipole may be created or induced in an atom or molecule that is normally electrically symmetric; that is, the overall spatial distribution of the electrons is symmetric with respect to the positively charged nucleus, as shown in Figure 2.13*a*. All atoms are experiencing constant vibrational motion that can cause instantaneous and short-lived distortions of this electrical symmetry for some of the atoms or molecules, and the creation of small electric dipoles, as represented in Figure 2.13*b*. One of these dipoles can in turn produce a displacement of the electron distribution of an adjacent molecule or atom, which induces the second one also to become a dipole that is then weakly attracted or bonded to the first; this is one type of van der Waals bonding. These attractive forces may exist between large numbers of atoms or molecules, which forces are temporary and fluctuate with time.

The liquefaction and, in some cases, the solidification of the inert gases and other electrically neutral and symmetric molecules such as H_2 and Cl_2 are realized because of this type of bonding. Melting and boiling temperatures are extremely low in materials for which induced dipole bonding predominates; of all possible intermolecular bonds, these are the weakest. Bonding energies and melting temperatures for argon and chlorine are also tabulated in Table 2.3.

Polar Molecule-Induced Dipole Bonds

Permanent dipole moments exist in some molecules by virtue of an asymmetrical arrangement of positively and negatively charged regions; such molecules are

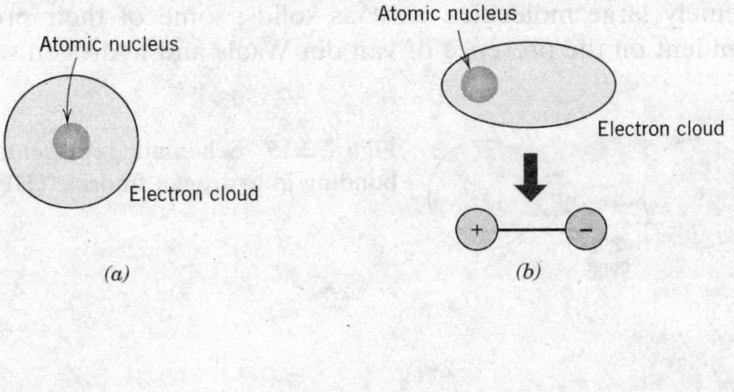

Figure 2.13 Schematic representations of (*a*) an electrically symmetric atom and (*b*) an induced atomic dipole.

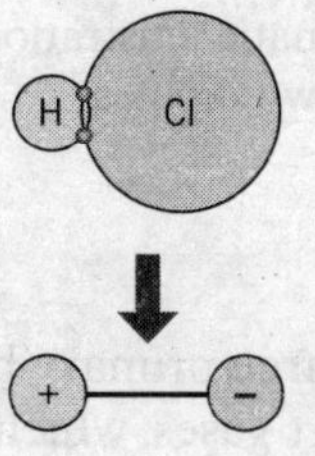

Figure 2.14 Schematic representation of a polar hydrogen chloride (HCl) molecule.

termed **polar molecules.** Figure 2.14 is a schematic representation of a hydrogen chloride molecule; a permanent dipole moment arises from net positive and negative charges that are respectively associated with the hydrogen and chlorine ends of the HCl molecule.

Polar molecules can also induce dipoles in adjacent nonpolar molecules, and a bond will form as a result of attractive forces between the two molecules. Furthermore, the magnitude of this bond will be greater than for fluctuating induced dipoles.

Permanent Dipole Bonds

Van der Waals forces will also exist between adjacent polar molecules. The associated bonding energies are significantly greater than for bonds involving induced dipoles.

The strongest secondary bonding type, the hydrogen bond, is a special case of polar molecule bonding. It occurs between molecules in which hydrogen is covalently bonded to fluorine (as in HF), oxygen (as in H_2O), and nitrogen (as in NH_3). For each H—F, H—O, or H—N bond, the single hydrogen electron is shared with the other atom. Thus, the hydrogen end of the bond is essentially a positively charged bare proton that is unscreened by any electrons. This highly positively charged end of the molecule is capable of a strong attractive force with the negative end of an adjacent molecule, as demonstrated in Figure 2.15 for HF. In essence, this single proton forms a bridge between two negatively charged atoms. The magnitude of the hydrogen bond is generally greater than that of the other types of secondary bonds and may be as high as 51 kJ/mol (0.52 eV/molecule), as shown in Table 2.3. Melting and boiling temperatures for hydrogen fluoride and water are abnormally high in light of their low molecular weights, as a consequence of hydrogen bonding.

2.8 MOLECULES

Many of the common molecules are composed of groups of atoms that are bound together by strong covalent bonds; these include elemental diatomic molecules (F_2, O_2, H_2, etc.) as well as a host of compounds (H_2O, CO_2, HNO_3, C_6H_6, CH_4, etc.). In the condensed liquid and solid states, bonds between molecules are weak secondary ones. Consequently, molecular materials have relatively low melting and boiling temperatures. Most of those that have small molecules composed of a few atoms are gases at ordinary, or ambient, temperatures and pressures. On the other hand, many of the modern polymers, being molecular materials composed of extremely large molecules, exist as solids; some of their properties are strongly dependent on the presence of van der Waals and hydrogen secondary bonds.

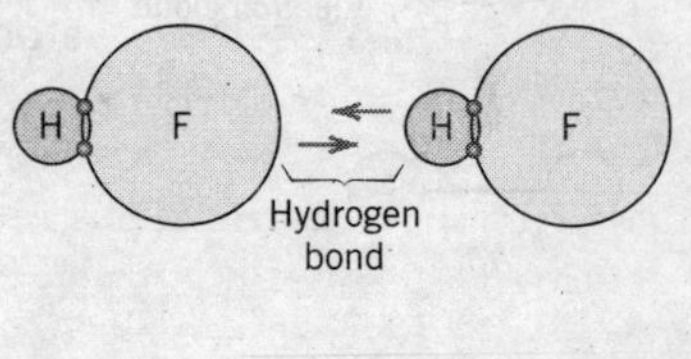

Figure 2.15 Schematic representation of hydrogen bonding in hydrogen fluoride (HF).

MATERIAL OF IMPORTANCE

Water (Its Volume Expansion Upon Freezing)

Upon freezing (i.e., transforming from a liquid to a solid upon cooling), most substances experience an increase in density (or, correspondingly, a decrease in volume). One exception is water, which exhibits the anomalous and familiar expansion upon freezing—approximately 9 volume percent expansion. This behavior may be explained on the basis of hydrogen bonding. Each H_2O molecule has two hydrogen atoms that can bond to oxygen atoms; in addition, its single O atom can bond to two hydrogen atoms of other H_2O molecules. Thus, for solid ice, each water molecule participates in four hydrogen bonds as shown in the three-dimensional schematic of Figure 2.16*a*; here hydrogen bonds are denoted by dashed lines, and each water molecule has 4 nearest-neighbor molecules. This is a relatively open structure—i.e., the molecules are not closely packed together—and, as a result, the density is comparatively low. Upon melting, this structure is partially destroyed, such that the water molecules become more closely packed together (Figure 2.16*b*)—at room temperature the average number of nearest-neighbor water molecules has increased to approximately 4.5; this leads to an increase in density.

Consequences of this anomalous freezing phenomenon are familiar. This phenomenon explains why icebergs float, why, in cold climates, it is necessary to add antifreeze to an automobile's cooling system (to keep the engine block from cracking), and why freeze-thaw cycles break up the pavement in streets and cause potholes to form.

A watering can that ruptured along a side panel-bottom panel seam. Water that was left in the can during a cold late-autumn night expanded as it froze and caused the rupture. (Photography by S. Tanner.)

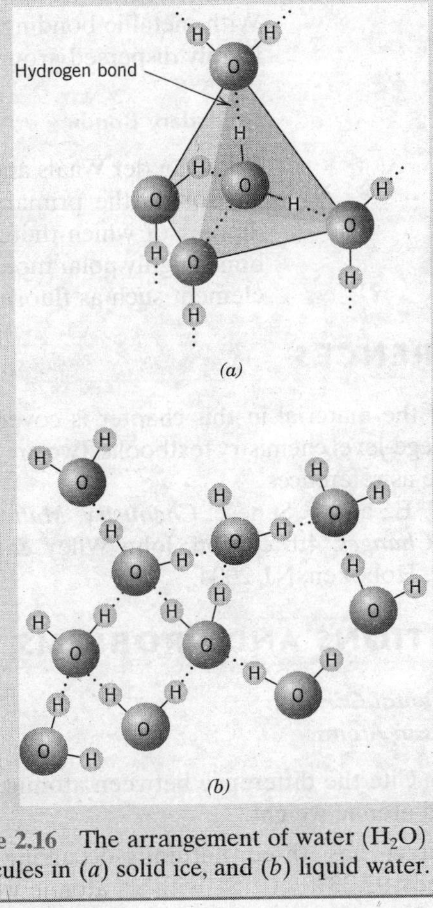

Figure 2.16 The arrangement of water (H_2O) molecules in (*a*) solid ice, and (*b*) liquid water.

SUMMARY

Electrons in Atoms
The Periodic Table

This chapter began with a survey of the fundamentals of atomic structure, presenting the Bohr and wave-mechanical models of electrons in atoms. Whereas the Bohr model assumes electrons to be particles orbiting the nucleus in discrete paths, in wave mechanics we consider them to be wave-like and treat electron position in terms of a probability distribution.

Electron energy states are specified in terms of quantum numbers that give rise to electron shells and subshells. The electron configuration of an atom corresponds to the manner in which these shells and subshells are filled with electrons in compliance with the Pauli exclusion principle. The periodic table of the elements is generated by arrangement of the various elements according to valence electron configuration.

Bonding Forces and Energies
Primary Interatomic Bonds

Atomic bonding in solids may be considered in terms of attractive and repulsive forces and energies. The three types of primary bond in solids are ionic, covalent, and metallic. For ionic bonds, electrically charged ions are formed by the transference of valence electrons from one atom type to another; forces are coulombic. There is a sharing of valence electrons between adjacent atoms when bonding is covalent. With metallic bonding, the valence electrons form a "sea of electrons" that is uniformly dispersed around the metal ion cores and acts as a form of glue for them.

Secondary Bonding or van der Waals Bonding

Both van der Waals and hydrogen bonds are termed secondary, being weak in comparison to the primary ones. They result from attractive forces between electric dipoles, of which there are two types—induced and permanent. For the hydrogen bond, highly polar molecules form when hydrogen covalently bonds to a nonmetallic element such as fluorine.

REFERENCES

Most of the material in this chapter is covered in college-level chemistry textbooks. Two are listed here as references.

Brady, J. E., and F. Senese, *Chemistry: Matter and Its Changes,* 4th edition, John Wiley & Sons, Inc., Hoboken, NJ, 2004.

Ebbing, D. D., S. D. Gammon, and R. O. Ragsdale, *Essentials of General Chemistry,* 2nd edition, Houghton Mifflin Company, Boston, 2006.

QUESTIONS AND PROBLEMS

Fundamental Concepts
Electrons in Atoms

2.1 (a) Cite the difference between atomic mass and atomic weight.

2.2 Silicon has three naturally-occurring isotopes: 92.23% of ^{28}Si, with an atomic weight of 27.9769 amu, 4.68% of ^{29}Si, with an atomic weight of 28.9765 amu, and 3.09% of ^{30}Si, with an atomic weight of 29.9738 amu. On the basis of these data, confirm that the average atomic weight of Si is 28.0854 amu.

2.3 (a) How many grams are there in one amu of a material?

(b) Mole, in the context of this book, is taken in units of gram-mole. On this basis, how many atoms are there in a pound-mole of a substance?

2.4 (a) Cite two important quantum-mechanical concepts associated with the Bohr model of the atom.

(b) Cite two important additional refinements that resulted from the wave-mechanical atomic model.

2.5 Relative to electrons and electron states, what does each of the four quantum numbers specify?

2.6 Allowed values for the quantum numbers of electrons are as follows:

$$n = 1, 2, 3, \ldots$$
$$l = 0, 1, 2, 3, \ldots, n - 1$$
$$m_l = 0, \pm 1, \pm 2, \pm 3, \ldots, \pm l$$
$$m_s = \pm \tfrac{1}{2}$$

The relationships between n and the shell designations are noted in Table 2.1. Relative to the subshells,

$l = 0$ corresponds to an s subshell
$l = 1$ corresponds to a p subshell
$l = 2$ corresponds to a d subshell
$l = 3$ corresponds to an f subshell

For the K shell, the four quantum numbers for each of the two electrons in the 1s state, in the order of nlm_lm_s, are $100(\frac{1}{2})$ and $100(-\frac{1}{2})$. Write the four quantum numbers for all of the electrons in the L and M shells, and note which correspond to the s, p, and d subshells.

2.7 Give the electron configurations for the following ions: P^{5+}, P^{3-}, Sn^{4+}, Se^{2-}, I^-, and Ni^{2+}.

2.8 Potassium iodide (KI) exhibits predominantly ionic bonding. The K^+ and I^- ions have electron structures that are identical to which two inert gases?

The Periodic Table

2.9 With regard to electron configuration, what do all the elements in Group IIA of the periodic table have in common?

2.10 To what group in the periodic table would an element with atomic number 112 belong?

2.11 Without consulting Figure 2.6 or Table 2.2, determine whether each of the electron configurations given below is an inert gas, a halogen, an alkali metal, an alkaline earth metal, or a transition metal. Justify your choices.

(a) $1s^22s^22p^63s^23p^5$
(b) $1s^22s^22p^63s^23p^63d^74s^2$
(c) $1s^22s^22p^63s^23p^63d^{10}4s^24p^6$
(d) $1s^22s^22p^63s^23p^64s^1$
(e) $1s^22s^22p^63s^23p^63d^{10}4s^24p^64d^55s^2$
(f) $1s^22s^22p^63s^2$

2.12 (a) What electron subshell is being filled for the rare earth series of elements on the periodic table?

(b) What electron subshell is being filled for the actinide series?

Bonding Forces and Energies

2.13 Calculate the force of attraction between a Ca^{2+} and an O^{2-} ion the centers of which are separated by a distance of 1.25 nm.

2.14 The net potential energy between two adjacent ions, E_N, may be represented by the sum of Equations 2.8 and 2.9; that is,

$$E_N = -\frac{A}{r} + \frac{B}{r^n} \tag{2.11}$$

Calculate the bonding energy E_0 in terms of the parameters A, B, and n using the following procedure:

1. Differentiate E_N with respect to r, and then set the resulting expression equal to zero, since the curve of E_N versus r is a minimum at E_0.

2. Solve for r in terms of A, B, and n, which yields r_0, the equilibrium interionic spacing.

3. Determine the expression for E_0 by substitution of r_0 into Equation 2.11.

2.15 For an Na^+-Cl^- ion pair, attractive and repulsive energies E_A and E_R, respectively, depend on the distance between the ions r, according to

$$E_A = -\frac{1.436}{r}$$

$$E_R = \frac{7.32 \times 10^{-6}}{r^8}$$

For these expressions, energies are expressed in electron volts per Na^+-Cl^- pair, and r is the distance in nanometers. The net energy E_N is just the sum of the two expressions above.

(a) Superimpose on a single plot E_N, E_R, and E_A versus r up to 1.0 nm.

(b) On the basis of this plot, determine (i) the equilibrium spacing r_0 between the Na^+ and Cl^- ions, and (ii) the magnitude of the bonding energy E_0 between the two ions.

(c) Mathematically determine the r_0 and E_0 values using the solutions to Problem 2.14 and compare these with the graphical results from part (b).

2.16 Consider a hypothetical X^+-Y^- ion pair for which the equilibrium interionic spacing and bonding energy values are 0.38 nm and −5.37 eV, respectively. If it is known that n in Equation 2.11 has a value of 8, using the results of Problem 2.14, determine explicit expressions for attractive and repulsive energies E_A and E_R of Equations 2.8 and 2.9.

2.17 The net potential energy E_N between two adjacent ions is sometimes represented by the expression

$$E_N = -\frac{C}{r} + D \exp\left(-\frac{r}{\rho}\right) \qquad (2.12)$$

in which r is the interionic separation and C, D, and ρ are constants whose values depend on the specific material.

(a) Derive an expression for the bonding energy E_0 in terms of the equilibrium interionic separation r_0 and the constants D and ρ using the following procedure:

1. Differentiate E_N with respect to r and set the resulting expression equal to zero.
2. Solve for C in terms of D, ρ, and r_0.
3. Determine the expression for E_0 by substitution for C in Equation 2.12.

(b) Derive another expression for E_0 in terms of r_0, C, and ρ using a procedure analogous to the one outlined in part (a).

Primary Interatomic Bonds

2.18 (a) Briefly cite the main differences between ionic, covalent, and metallic bonding.

(b) State the Pauli exclusion principle.

2.19 Compute the percentage ionic character of the interatomic bond for each of the following compounds: MgO, GaP, CsF, CdS, and FeO.

2.20 Make a plot of bonding energy versus melting temperature for the metals listed in Table 2.3. Using this plot, approximate the bonding energy for molybdenum, which has a melting temperature of 2617°C.

2.21 Using Table 2.2, determine the number of covalent bonds that are possible for atoms of the following elements: silicon, bromine, nitrogen, sulfur, and neon.

2.22 What type(s) of bonding would be expected for each of the following materials: solid xenon, calcium fluoride (CaF_2), bronze, cadmium telluride (CdTe), rubber, and tungsten?

Secondary Bonding or van der Waals Bonding

2.23 Explain why hydrogen fluoride (HF) has a higher boiling temperature than hydrogen chloride (HCl) (19.4 vs. −85°C), even though HF has a lower molecular weight.

Chapter 3 Fundamentals of Structure of Crystalline Solids

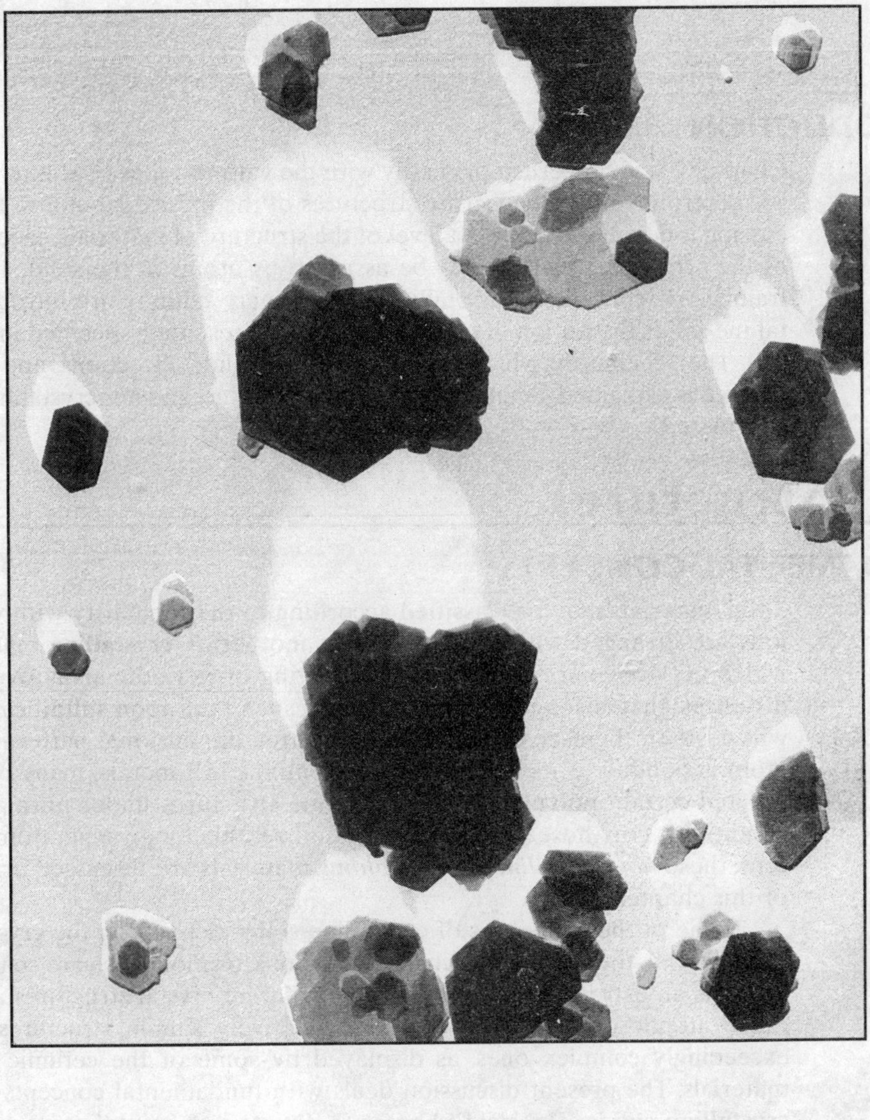

Electron micrograph of kaolinite crystals. They are in the form of hexagonal plates, some of which are stacked on top of one another. 21,000×. (Photograph courtesy of Georgia Kaolin Co., Inc.)

Learning Objectives

After studying this chapter you should be able to do the following:

1. Describe the difference in atomic/molecular structure between crystalline and noncrystalline materials.
2. Describe lattice parameters for seven crystal systems.
3. Given three direction index integers, sketch the direction corresponding to these indices within a unit cell.
4. Specify the Miller indices for a plane that has been drawn within a unit cell.
5. Distinguish between single crystals and polycrystalline materials.
6. Define *isotropy* and *anisotropy* with respect to material properties.

3.1 INTRODUCTION

Chapter 2 was concerned primarily with the various types of atomic bonding, which are determined by the electron structures of the individual atoms. The present discussion is devoted to the next level of the structure of materials, specifically, to some of the arrangements that may be assumed by atoms in the solid state. Within this framework, concepts of crystallinity and noncrystallinity are introduced. For crystalline solids the notion of crystal structure is presented, specified in terms of a unit cell. The scheme by which crystallographic points, directions, and planes are expressed is explained. Single crystals, polycrystalline, and noncrystalline materials are considered.

Crystal Structures

3.2 FUNDAMENTAL CONCEPTS

Solid materials may be classified according to the regularity with which atoms or ions are arranged with respect to one another. A **crystalline** material is one in which the atoms are situated in a repeating or periodic array over large atomic distances; that is, long-range order exists, such that upon solidification, the atoms will position themselves in a repetitive three-dimensional pattern, in which each atom is bonded to its nearest-neighbor atoms. All metals, many ceramic materials, and certain polymers form crystalline structures under normal solidification conditions. For those that do not crystallize, this long-range atomic order is absent; these *noncrystalline* or *amorphous* materials are discussed briefly at the end of this chapter.

Some of the properties of crystalline solids depend on the **crystal structure** of the material, the manner in which atoms, ions, or molecules are spatially arranged. There is an extremely large number of different crystal structures all having long-range atomic order; these vary from relatively simple structures for metals to exceedingly complex ones, as displayed by some of the ceramic and polymeric materials. The present discussion deals with fundamental concepts of structure of crystalline solids. The next chapter is devoted to crystal structures for metals, ceramics, and polymers.

When describing crystalline structures, atoms (or ions) are thought of as being solid spheres having well-defined diameters. This is termed the *atomic hard sphere model* in which spheres representing nearest-neighbor atoms touch one another. An example of the hard sphere model for the atomic arrangement found in some of the common elemental metals is displayed in Figure 3.1*c*. In this particular case all the atoms are identical. Sometimes the term **lattice** is used in the context of crystal structures; in this sense "lattice" means a three-dimensional array of points. Each lattice point has identical surroundings (i.e. motif). In the most simple case, lattice points coincide with atom positions (or sphere centers).

3.3 UNIT CELLS

The atomic order in crystalline solids indicates that small groups of atoms form a repetitive pattern. Thus, in describing crystal structures, it is often convenient to subdivide the structure into small repeat entities called **unit cells.** Unit cells for most crystal structures are parallelepipeds or prisms having three sets of parallel faces; one is drawn within the aggregate of spheres (Figure 3.1*c*), which in this case happens to be a cube. A unit cell is chosen to represent the symmetry of the crystal structure, wherein all the atom positions in the crystal may be generated by translations of the unit cell integral distances along each of its edges. Thus, the unit cell is the basic structural unit or building block of the crystal structure and defines the crystal structure by virtue of its geometry and the atom positions within.

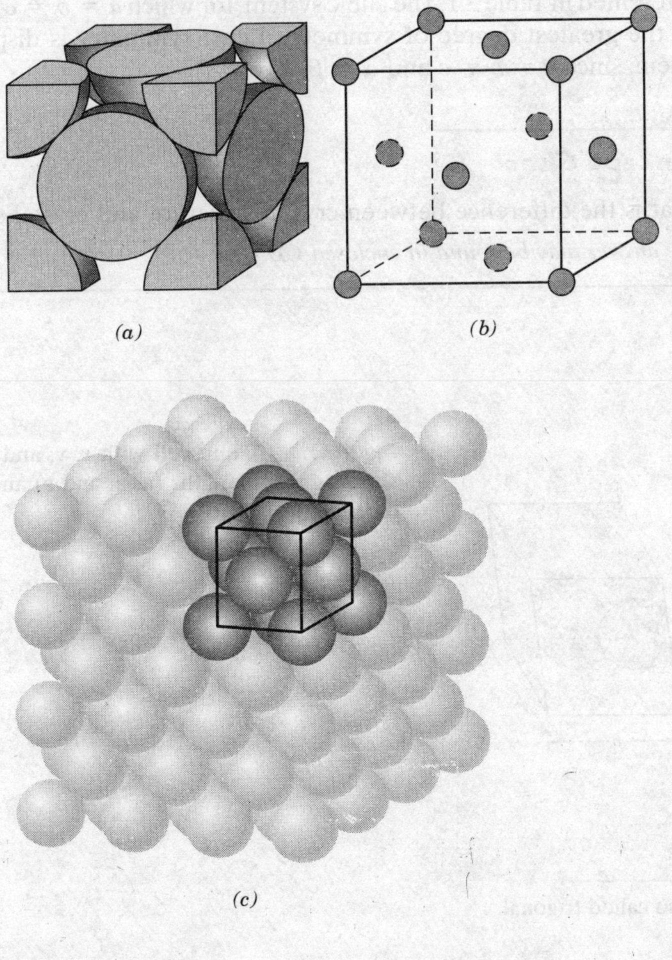

Figure 3.1 For the face-centered cubic crystal structure, (*a*) a hard sphere unit cell representation, (*b*) a reduced-sphere unit cell, and (*c*) an aggregate of many atoms. [Figure (*c*) adapted from W. G. Moffatt, G. W. Pearsall, and J. Wulff, *The Structure and Properties of Materials,* Vol. I, *Structure,* p. 51. Copyright © 1964 by John Wiley & Sons, New York. Reprinted by permission of John Wiley & Sons, Inc.]

Convenience usually dictates that parallelepiped corners coincide with centers of the hard sphere atoms. Furthermore, more than a single unit cell may be chosen for a particular crystal structure; however, we generally use the unit cell having the highest level of geometrical symmetry.

3.4 CRYSTAL SYSTEMS

Since there are many different possible crystal structures, it is sometimes convenient to divide them into groups according to unit cell configurations and/or atomic arrangements. One such scheme is based on the unit cell geometry, that is, the shape of the appropriate unit cell parallelepiped without regard to the atomic positions in the cell. Within this framework, an x, y, z coordinate system is established with its origin at one of the unit cell corners; each of the x, y, and z axes coincides with one of the three parallelepiped edges that extend from this corner, as illustrated in Figure 3.2. The unit cell geometry is completely defined in terms of six parameters: the three edge lengths a, b, and c, and the three interaxial angles α, β, and γ. These are indicated in Figure 3.2, and are sometimes termed the **lattice parameters** of a crystal structure.

On this basis there are seven different possible combinations of a, b, and c, and α, β, and γ, each of which represents a distinct **crystal system.** These seven crystal systems are cubic, tetragonal, hexagonal, orthorhombic, rhombohedral,[1] monoclinic, and triclinic. The lattice parameter relationships and unit cell sketches for each are represented in Table 3.1. The cubic system, for which $a = b = c$ and $\alpha = \beta = \gamma = 90°$, has the greatest degree of symmetry. Least symmetry is displayed by the triclinic system, since $a \neq b \neq c$ and $\alpha \neq \beta \neq \gamma$.

Concept Check 3.1

What is the difference between crystal structure and crystal system?

[*The answer may be found in enclosed CD.*]

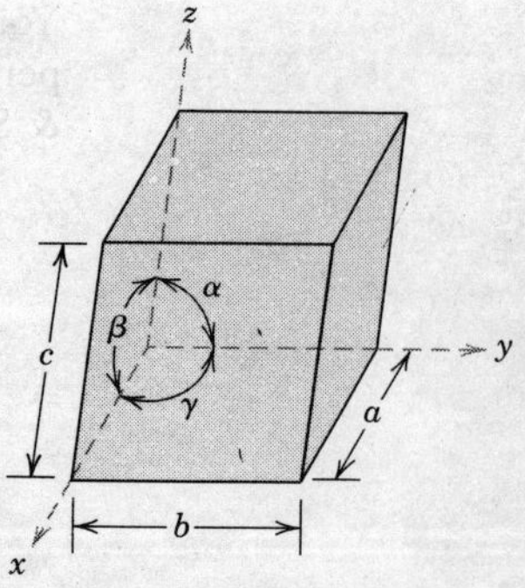

Figure 3.2 A unit cell with x, y, and z coordinate axes, showing axial lengths (a, b, and c) and interaxial angles (α, β, and γ).

[1] Also called trigonal.

Table 3.1 Lattice Parameter Relationships and Figures Showing Unit Cell Geometries for the Seven Crystal Systems

Crystal System	*Axial Relationships*	*Interaxial Angles*	*Unit Cell Geometry*
Cubic	$a = b = c$	$\alpha = \beta = \gamma = 90°$	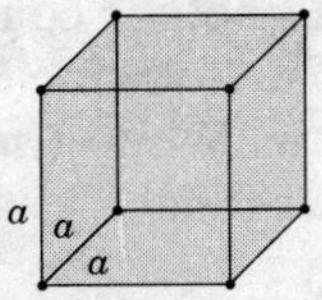
Hexagonal	$a = b \neq c$	$\alpha - \beta = 90°, \gamma = 120°$	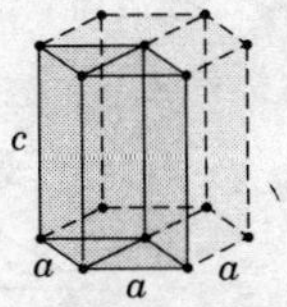
Tetragonal	$a = b \neq c$	$\alpha = \beta = \gamma = 90°$	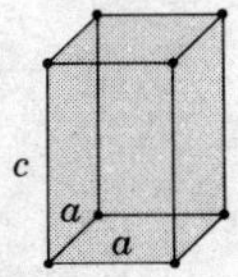
Rhombohedral (Trigonal)	$a = b = c$	$\alpha = \beta = \gamma \neq 90°$	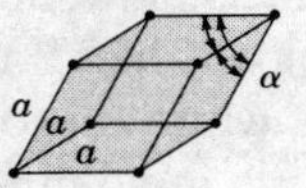
Orthorhombic	$a \neq b \neq c$	$\alpha = \beta = \gamma = 90°$	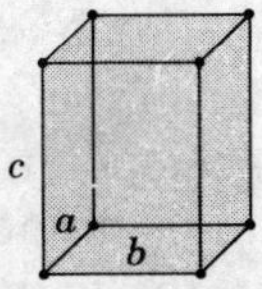
Monoclinic	$a \neq b \neq c$	$\alpha = \gamma = 90° \neq \beta$	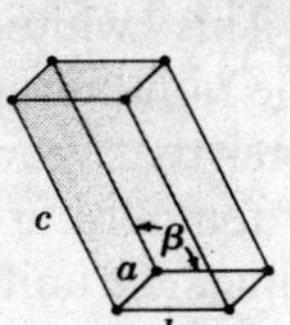
Triclinic	$a \neq b \neq c$	$\alpha \neq \beta \neq \gamma \neq 90°$	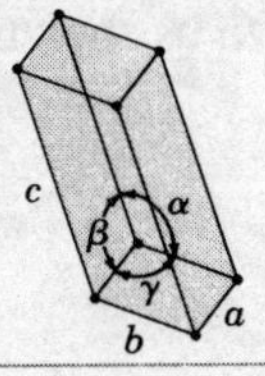

MATERIAL OF IMPORTANCE

Tin (Its Allotropic Transformation)

Another common metal that experiences an allotropic change (i.e. change in structure) is tin. White (or β) tin, having a body-centered tetragonal crystal structure at room temperature, transforms, at 13.2°C (55.8°F), to gray (or α) tin, which has a crystal structure similar to diamond (i.e., the diamond cubic crystal structure); this transformation is represented schematically as follows:

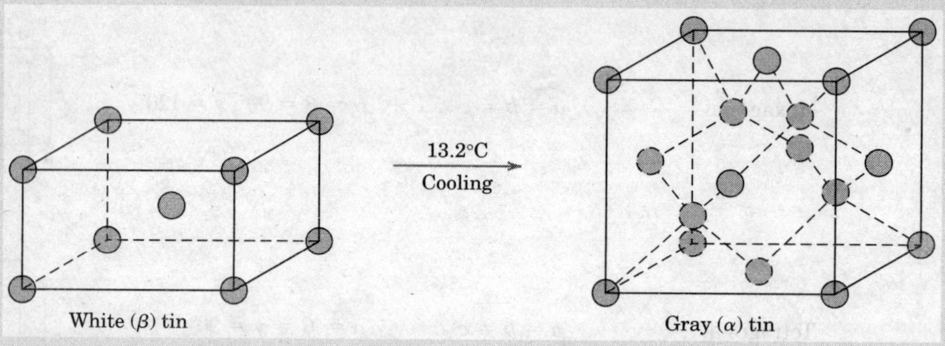

The rate at which this change takes place is extremely slow; however, the lower the temperature (below 13.2°C) the faster the rate. Accompanying this white tin-to-gray tin transformation is an increase in volume (27 percent), and, accordingly, a decrease in density (from 7.30 g/cm^3 to 5.77 g/cm^3). Consequently, this volume expansion results in the disintegration of the white tin metal into a coarse powder of the gray allotrope. For normal subambient temperatures, there is no need to worry about this disintegration process for tin products, due to the very slow rate at which the transformation occurs.

This white-to-gray-tin transition produced some rather dramatic results in 1850 in Russia. The winter that year was particularly cold, and record low temperatures persisted for extended periods of time. The uniforms of some Russian soldiers had tin buttons, many of which crumbled due to these extreme cold conditions, as did also many of the tin church organ pipes. This problem came to be known as the "tin disease."

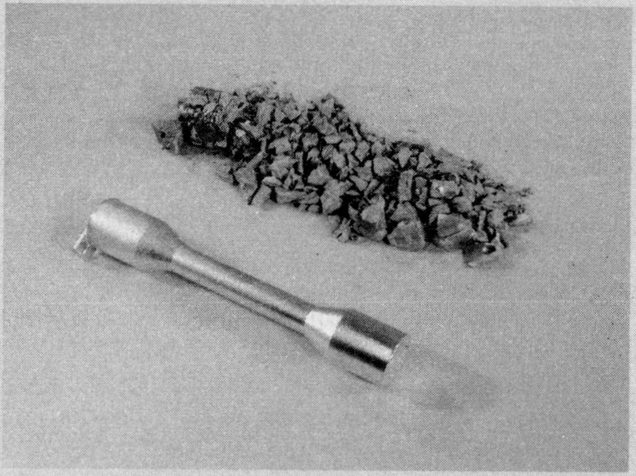

Specimen of white tin (left). Another specimen disintegrated upon transforming to gray tin (right) after it was cooled to and held at a temperature below 13.2°C for an extended period of time. (Photograph courtesy of Professor Bill Plumbridge, Department of Materials Engineering, The Open University, Milton Keynes, England.)

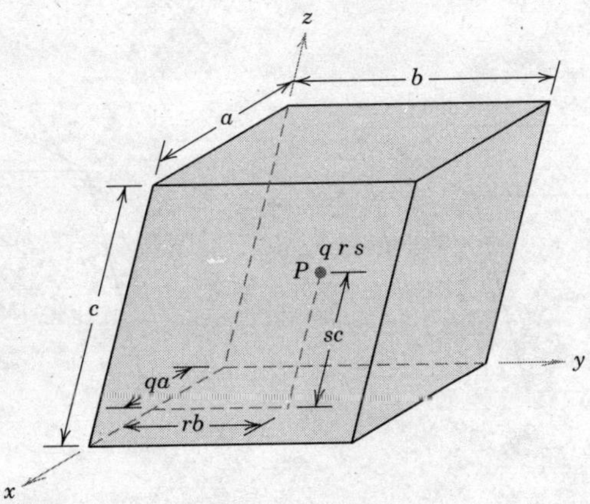

Figure 3.3 The manner in which the q, r, and s coordinates at point P within the unit cell are determined. The q coordinate (which is a fraction) corresponds to the distance qa along the x axis, where a is the unit cell edge length. The respective r and s coordinates for the y and z axes are determined similarly.

Crystallographic Points, Directions, and Planes

When dealing with crystalline materials, it often becomes necessary to specify a particular point within a unit cell, a crystallographic direction, or some crystallographic plane of atoms. Labeling conventions have been established in which three numbers or indices are used to designate point locations, directions, and planes. The basis for determining index values is the unit cell, with a right-handed coordinate system consisting of three (x, y, and z) axes situated at one of the corners and coinciding with the unit cell edges, as shown in Figure 3.2. For some crystal systems—namely, hexagonal, rhombohedral, monoclinic, and triclinic—the three axes are *not* mutually perpendicular, as in the familiar Cartesian coordinate scheme.

3.5 POINT COORDINATES

The position of any point located within a unit cell may be specified in terms of its coordinates as fractional multiples of the unit cell edge lengths (i.e., in terms of a, b, and c). To illustrate, consider the unit cell and the point P situated therein as shown in Figure 3.3. We specify the position of P in terms of the generalized coordinates q, r, and s where q is some fractional length of a along the x axis, r is some fractional length of b along the y axis, and similarly for s. Thus, the position of P is designated using coordinates $q\ r\ s$ with values that are less than or equal to unity. Furthermore, we have chosen not to separate these coordinates by commas or any other punctuation marks (which is the normal convention).

EXAMPLE PROBLEM 3.1

Location of Point Having Specified Coordinates

For the unit cell shown in the accompanying sketch (a), locate the point having coordinates $\frac{1}{4}\ 1\ \frac{1}{2}$.

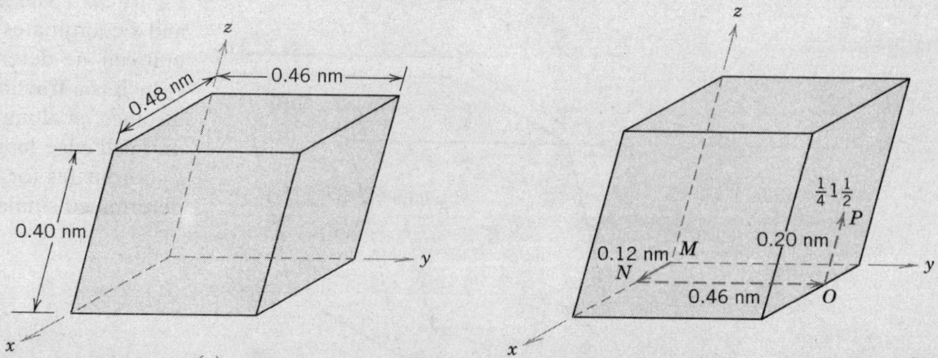

(a) (b)

Solution

From sketch (*a*), edge lengths for this unit cell are as follows: $a = 0.48$ nm, $b = 0.46$ nm, and $c = 0.40$ nm. Furthermore, in light of the above discussion, fractional lengths are $q = \frac{1}{4}$, $r = 1$, and $s = \frac{1}{2}$. Therefore, first we move from the origin of the unit cell (point *M*) $qa = \frac{1}{4}(0.48 \text{ nm}) = 0.12$ nm units along the *x* axis (to point *N*), as shown in the (*b*) sketch. Similarly, we proceed $rb = (1)(0.46 \text{ nm}) = 0.46$ nm parallel to the *y* axis, from point *N* to point *O*. Finally, we move from this position, $sc = \frac{1}{2}(0.40 \text{ nm}) = 0.20$ nm units parallel to the *z* axis to point *P* as noted again in sketch (*b*). This point *P* then corresponds to the $\frac{1}{4}\,1\,\frac{1}{2}$ point coordinates.

EXAMPLE PROBLEM 3.2

Specification of Point Coordinates

Specify point coordinates for all atom positions for a cubic unit cell with atoms at cube corners and cube center (i.e. a BCC or body centered cubic unit cell).

Solution

For the BCC unit cell of Figure 4.2, atom position coordinates correspond to the locations of the centers of all atoms in the unit cell—that is, the eight corner atoms and single center atom. These positions are noted (and also numbered) in the following figure.

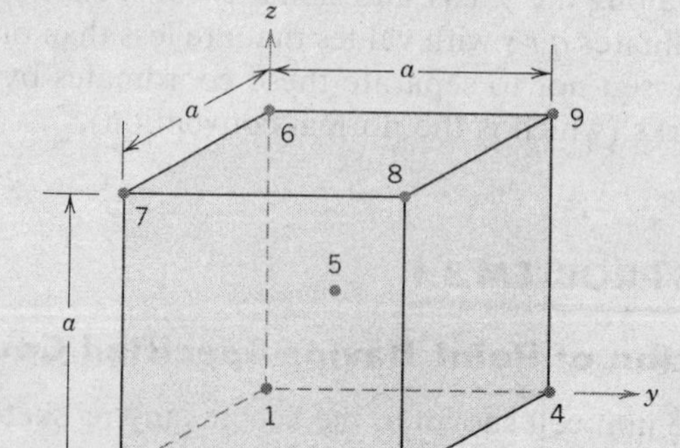

Point coordinates for position number 1 are 0 0 0; this position is located at the origin of the coordinate system, and, as such, the fractional unit cell thermore, for position number 2, since it lies one unit cell edge length along the x axis, its fractional edge lengths are a, $0a$, and $0a$, respectively, which yield point coordinates of 1 0 0. The following table presents fractional unit cell lengths along the x, y, and z axes, and their corresponding point coordinates for each of the nine points in the above figure.

Point Number	Fractional Lengths *x axis*	*y axis*	*z axis*	Point Coordinates
1	0	0	0	0 0 0
2	1	0	0	1 0 0
3	1	1	0	1 1 0
4	0	1	0	0 1 0
5	$\frac{1}{2}$	$\frac{1}{2}$	$\frac{1}{2}$	$\frac{1}{2}\frac{1}{2}\frac{1}{2}$
6	0	0	1	0 0 1
7	1	0	1	1 0 1
8	1	1	1	1 1 1
9	0	1	1	0 1 1

3.6 CRYSTALLOGRAPHIC DIRECTIONS

A crystallographic direction is defined as a line between two points, or a vector. The following steps are utilized in the determination of the three directional indices:

1. A vector of convenient length is positioned such that it passes through the origin of the coordinate system. Any vector may be translated throughout the crystal lattice without alteration, if parallelism is maintained.
2. The length of the vector projection on each of the three axes is determined; *these are measured in terms of the unit cell dimensions a, b, and c.*
3. These three numbers are multiplied or divided by a common factor to reduce them to the smallest integer values.
4. The three indices, not separated by commas, are enclosed in square brackets, thus: $[uvw]$. The u, v, and w integers correspond to the reduced projections along the x, y, and z axes, respectively.

For each of the three axes, there will exist both positive and negative coordinates. Thus negative indices are also possible, which are represented by a bar over the appropriate index. For example, the $[1\bar{1}1]$ direction would have a component in the $-y$ direction. Also, changing the signs of all indices produces an antiparallel direction; that is, $[\bar{1}1\bar{1}]$ is directly opposite to $[1\bar{1}1]$. If more than one direction (or plane) is to be specified for a particular crystal structure, it is imperative for the maintaining of consistency that a positive–negative convention, once established, not be changed.

The [100], [110], and [111] directions are common ones; they are drawn in the unit cell shown in Figure 3.4.

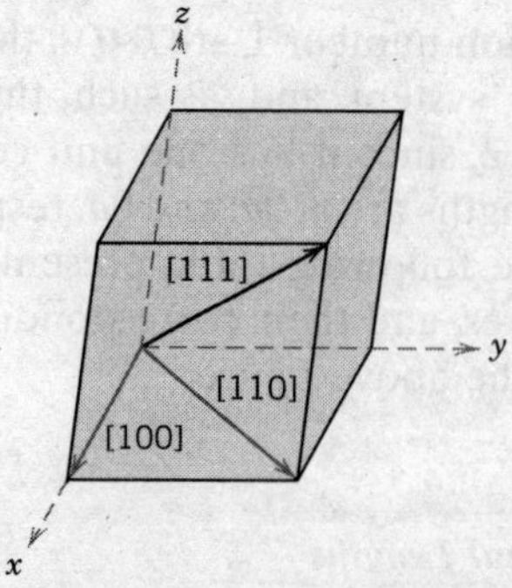

Figure 3.4 The [100], [110], and [111] directions within a unit cell.

EXAMPLE PROBLEM 3.3

Determination of Directional Indices

Determine the indices for the direction shown in the accompanying figure.

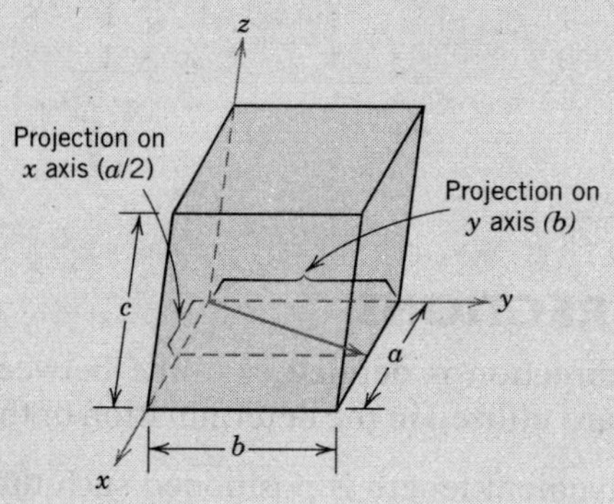

Solution

The vector, as drawn, passes through the origin of the coordinate system, and therefore no translation is necessary. Projections of this vector onto the x, y, and z axes are, respectively, $a/2$, b, and $0c$, which become $\frac{1}{2}$, 1, and 0 in terms of the unit cell parameters (i.e., when the a, b, and c are dropped). Reduction of these numbers to the lowest set of integers is accompanied by multiplication of each by the factor 2. This yields the integers 1, 2, and 0, which are then enclosed in brackets as [120].

This procedure may be summarized as follows:

	x	y	z
Projections	$a/2$	b	$0c$
Projections (in terms of a, b, and c)	$\frac{1}{2}$	1	0
Reduction	1	2	0
Enclosure		[120]	

EXAMPLE PROBLEM 3.4

Construction of Specified Crystallographic Direction

Draw a [$1\bar{1}0$] direction within a cubic unit cell.

Solution

First construct an appropriate unit cell and coordinate axes system. In the accompanying figure the unit cell is cubic, and the origin of the coordinate system, point O, is located at one of the cube corners.

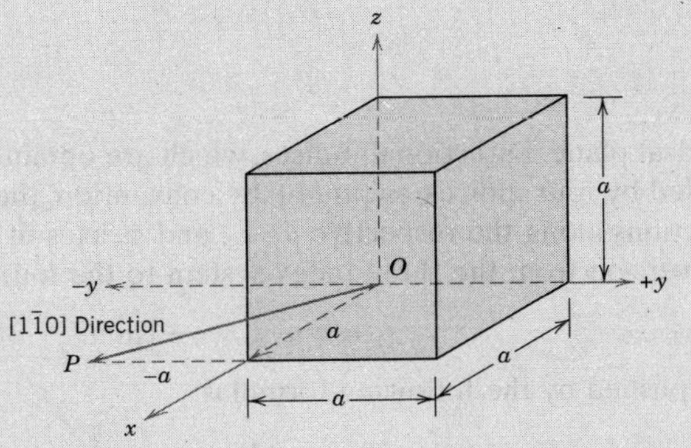

This problem is solved by reversing the procedure of the preceding example. For this [$1\bar{1}0$] direction, the projections along the x, y, and z axes are a, $-a$, and $0a$, respectively. This direction is defined by a vector passing from the origin to point P, which is located by first moving along the x axis a units, and from this position, parallel to the y axis $-a$ units, as indicated in the figure. There is no z component to the vector, since the z projection is zero.

For some crystal structures, several nonparallel directions with different indices are actually equivalent; this means that the spacing of atoms along each direction is the same. For example, in cubic crystals, all the directions represented by the following indices are equivalent: [100], [$\bar{1}00$], [010], [$0\bar{1}0$], [001], and [$00\bar{1}$]. As a convenience, equivalent directions are grouped together into a *family,* which are enclosed in angle brackets, thus: ⟨100⟩. Furthermore, directions in cubic crystals having the same indices without regard to order or sign, for example, [123] and [$\bar{2}1\bar{3}$], are equivalent. This is, in general, not true for other crystal systems. For example, for crystals of tetragonal symmetry, [100] and [010] directions are equivalent, whereas [100] and [001] are not.

Hexagonal Crystals

A problem arises for crystals having hexagonal symmetry in that some crystallographic equivalent directions will not have the same set of indices. This is circumvented by utilizing a four-axis, or *Miller–Bravais,* coordinate system as shown in Figure 3.5. The three a_1, a_2, and a_3 axes are all contained within a single plane (called the basal plane) and are at 120° angles to one another. The z axis is perpendicular

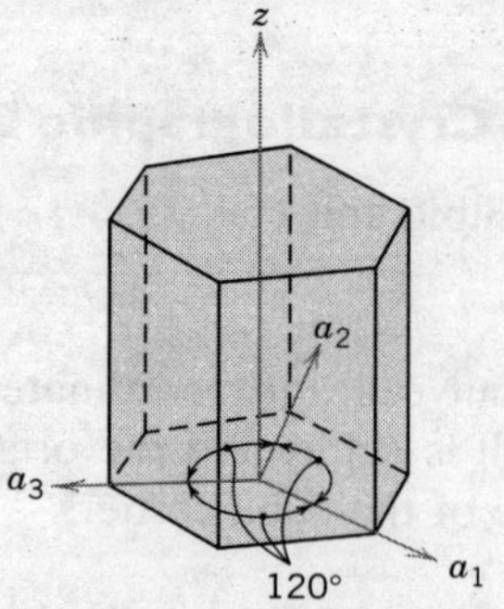

Figure 3.5 Coordinate axis system for a hexagonal unit cell (Miller–Bravais scheme).

to this basal plane. Directional indices, which are obtained as described above, will be denoted by four indices, as [*uvtw*]; by convention, the first three indices pertain to projections along the respective a_1, a_2, and a_3 axes in the basal plane.

Conversion from the three-index system to the four-index system,

$$[u'v'w'] \longrightarrow [uvtw]$$

is accomplished by the following formulas:

$$u = \frac{1}{3}(2u' - v') \tag{3.1a}$$

$$v = \frac{1}{3}(2v' - u') \tag{3.1b}$$

$$t = -(u + v) \tag{3.1c}$$

$$w = w' \tag{3.1d}$$

where primed indices are associated with the three-index scheme and unprimed with the new Miller–Bravais four-index system. (Of course, reduction to the lowest set of integers may be necessary, as discussed above.) For example, the [010] direction becomes $[\bar{1}2\bar{1}0]$. Several different directions are indicated in the hexagonal unit cell (Figure 3.6*a*).

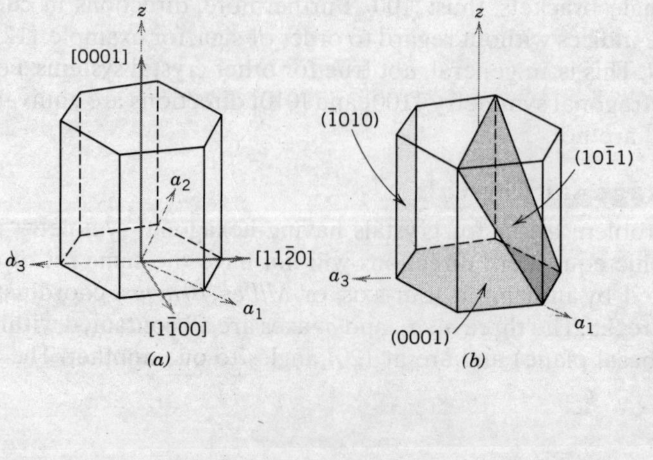

Figure 3.6 For the hexagonal crystal system, (*a*) [0001], $[1\bar{1}00]$, and $[11\bar{2}0]$ directions, and (*b*) the (0001), $(10\bar{1}1)$, and $(\bar{1}010)$ planes.

EXAMPLE PROBLEM 3.5

Determination of Directional Indices for a Hexagonal Unit Cell

Determine the indices for the direction shown in the hexagonal unit cell of sketch (*a*) below.

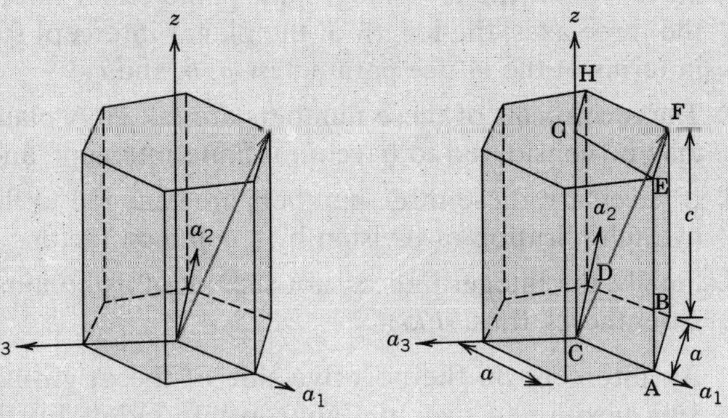

(*a*) (*b*)

Solution

In sketch (*b*), one of the three parallelepipeds comprising the hexagonal cell is delineated—its corners are labeled with letters A through H, with the origin of the a_1-a_2-a_3-z axes coordinate system located at the corner labeled C. We use this unit cell as a reference for specifying the directional indices. It now becomes necessary to determine projections of the direction vector on the a_1, a_2, and z axes. These respective projections are a (a_1 axis), a (a_2 axis) and c (z axis), which become 1, 1, and 1 in terms of the unit cell parameters. Thus,

$$u' = 1 \qquad v' = 1 \qquad w' = 1$$

Also, from Equations 3.1a, 3.1b, 3.1c, and 3.1d

$$u = \frac{1}{3}(2u' - v') = \frac{1}{3}[(2)(1) - 1] = \frac{1}{3}$$

$$v = \frac{1}{3}(2v' - u') = \frac{1}{3}[(2)(1) - 1] = \frac{1}{3}$$

$$t = -(u + v) = -\left(\frac{1}{3} + \frac{1}{3}\right) = -\frac{2}{3}$$

$$w = w' = 1$$

Multiplication of the above indices by 3 reduces them to the lowest set, which yields values for u, v, t, and w of 1, 1, −2 and 3, respectively. Hence, the direction shown in the figure is $[11\bar{2}3]$.

3.7 CRYSTALLOGRAPHIC PLANES

The orientations of planes for a crystal structure are represented in a similar manner. Again, the unit cell is the basis, with the three-axis coordinate system as represented in Figure 3.2. In all but the hexagonal crystal system, crystallographic planes are specified by three **Miller indices** as (*hkl*). Any two planes parallel to each other are equivalent and have identical indices. The procedure employed in determination of the *h*, *k*, and *l* index numbers is as follows:

1. If the plane passes through the selected origin, either another parallel plane must be constructed within the unit cell by an appropriate translation, or a new origin must be established at the corner of another unit cell.
2. At this point the crystallographic plane either intersects or parallels each of the three axes; the length of the planar intercept for each axis is determined in terms of the lattice parameters *a*, *b*, and *c*.
3. The reciprocals of these numbers are taken. A plane that parallels an axis may be considered to have an infinite intercept, and, therefore, a zero index.
4. If necessary, these three numbers are changed to the set of smallest integers by multiplication or division by a common factor.[2]
5. Finally, the integer indices, not separated by commas, are enclosed within parentheses, thus: (*hkl*).

An intercept on the negative side of the origin is indicated by a bar or minus sign positioned over the appropriate index. Furthermore, reversing the directions of all indices specifies another plane parallel to, on the opposite side of and equidistant from, the origin. Several low-index planes are represented in Figure 3.7.

One interesting and unique characteristic of cubic crystals is that planes and directions having the same indices are perpendicular to one another; however, for other crystal systems there are no simple geometrical relationships between planes and directions having the same indices.

EXAMPLE PROBLEM 3.6

Determination of Planar (Miller) Indices

Determine the Miller indices for the plane shown in the accompanying sketch (*a*).

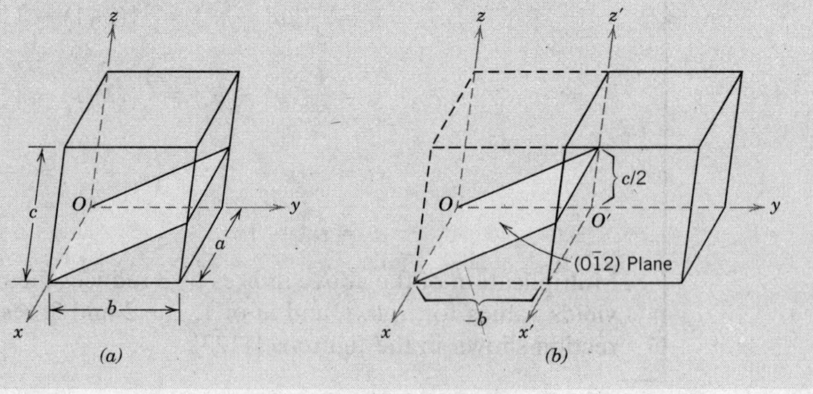

[2] On occasion, index reduction is not carried out (e.g., for x-ray diffraction studies that are described in Section 4.20); for example, (002) is not reduced to (001). In addition, for ceramic materials, the ionic arrangement for a reduced-index plane may be different from that for a nonreduced one.

Solution

Since the plane passes through the selected origin O, a new origin must be chosen at the corner of an adjacent unit cell, taken as O' and shown in sketch (b). This plane is parallel to the x axis, and the intercept may be taken as ∞a. The y and z axes intersections, referenced to the new origin O', are $-b$ and $c/2$, respectively. Thus, in terms of the lattice parameters a, b, and c, these intersections are ∞, -1, and $\frac{1}{2}$. The reciprocals of these numbers are 0, -1, and 2; and since all are integers, no further reduction is necessary. Finally, enclosure in parentheses yields $(0\bar{1}2)$.

These steps are briefly summarized below:

	x	y	z
Intercepts	∞a	$-b$	$c/2$
Intercepts (in terms of lattice parameters)	∞	-1	$\frac{1}{2}$
Reciprocals	0	-1	2
Reductions (unnecessary)			
Enclosure		$(0\bar{1}2)$	

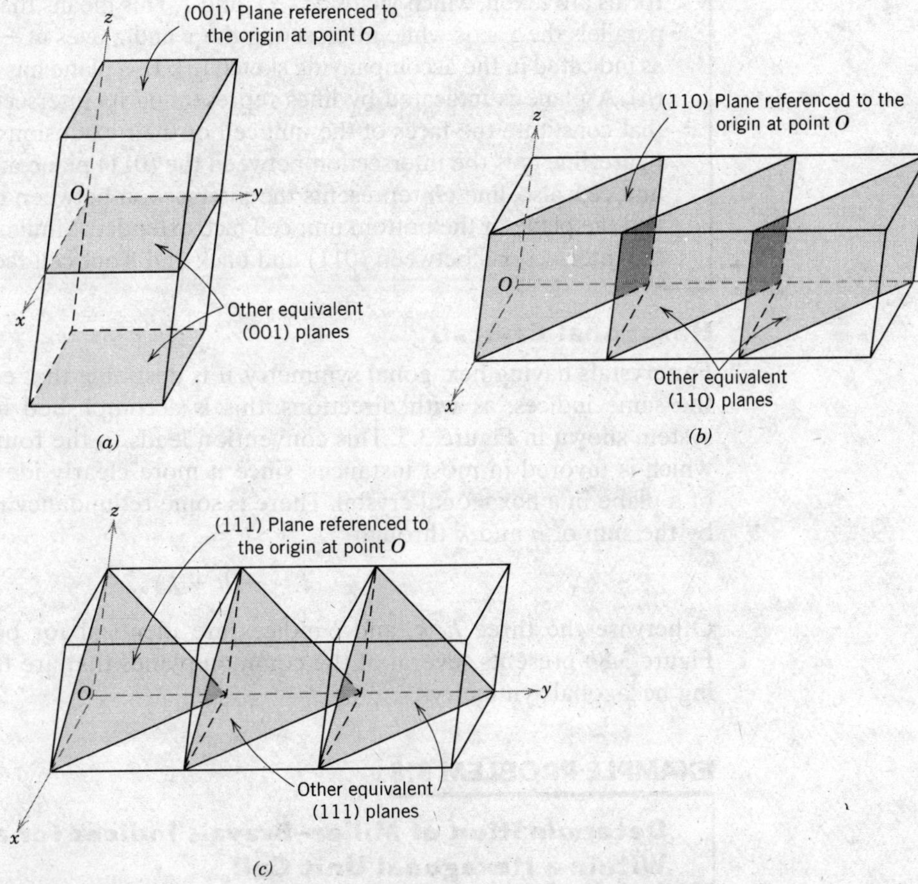

Figure 3.7 Representations of a series each of (a) (001), (b) (110), and (c) (111) crystallographic planes.

EXAMPLE PROBLEM 3.7

Construction of Specified Crystallographic Plane

Construct a $(0\bar{1}1)$ plane within a cubic unit cell.

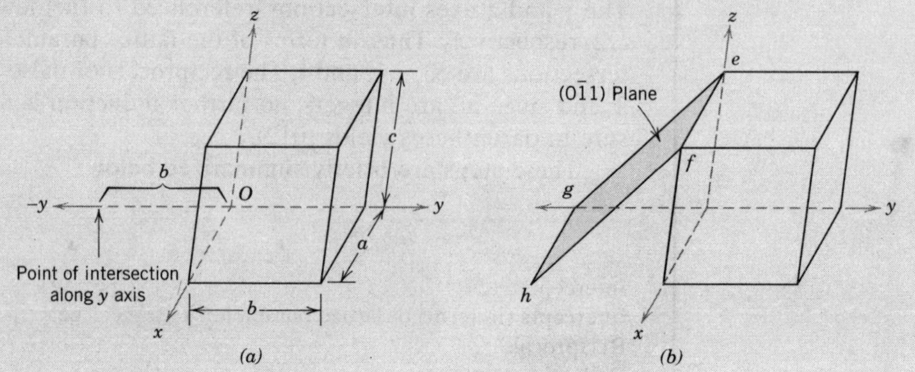

Solution

To solve this problem, carry out the procedure used in the preceding example in reverse order. To begin, the indices are removed from the parentheses, and reciprocals are taken, which yields ∞, -1, and 1. This means that the particular plane parallels the x axis while intersecting the y and z axes at $-b$ and c, respectively, as indicated in the accompanying sketch (*a*). This plane has been drawn in sketch (*b*). A plane is indicated by lines representing its intersections with the planes that constitute the faces of the unit cell or their extensions. For example, in this figure, line *ef* is the intersection between the $(0\bar{1}1)$ plane and the top face of the unit cell; also, line *gh* represents the intersection between this same $(0\bar{1}1)$ plane and the plane of the bottom unit cell face extended. Similarly, lines *eg* and *fh* are the intersections between $(0\bar{1}1)$ and back and front cell faces, respectively.

Hexagonal Crystals

For crystals having hexagonal symmetry, it is desirable that equivalent planes have the same indices; as with directions, this is accomplished by the Miller–Bravais system shown in Figure 3.5. This convention leads to the four-index (*hkil*) scheme, which is favored in most instances, since it more clearly identifies the orientation of a plane in a hexagonal crystal. There is some redundancy in that i is determined by the sum of h and k through

$$i = -(h + k) \tag{3.2}$$

Otherwise the three h, k, and l indices are identical for both indexing systems. Figure 3.8*b* presents several of the common planes that are found for crystals having hexagonal symmetry.

EXAMPLE PROBLEM 3.8

Determination of Miller–Bravais Indices for a Plane Within a Hexagonal Unit Cell

Determine the Miller–Bravais indices for the plane shown in the hexagonal unit cell.

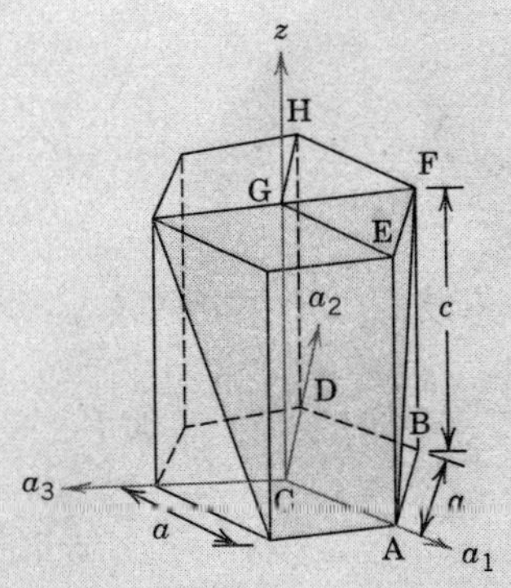

Solution

To determine these Miller–Bravais indices, consider the plane in the figure referenced to the parallelepiped labeled with the letters A through H at its corners. This plane intersects the a_1 axis at a distance a from the origin of the a_1-a_2-a_3-z coordinate axes system (point C). Furthermore, its intersections with the a_2 and z axes are $-a$ and c, respectively. Therefore, in terms of the lattice parameters, these intersections are 1, −1, and 1. Furthermore, the reciprocals of these numbers are also 1, −1, and 1. Hence

$$h = 1$$
$$k = -1$$
$$l = 1$$

and, from Equation 3.2

$$\begin{aligned} i &= -(h + k) \\ &= -(1 - 1) = 0 \end{aligned}$$

Therefore the ($hkil$) indices are ($1\bar{1}01$).

Notice that the third index is zero (i.e., its reciprocal = ∞), which means that this plane parallels the a_3 axis. Upon inspection of the above figure, it may be noted that this is indeed the case.

Crystalline and Noncrystalline Materials

3.8 SINGLE CRYSTALS

For a crystalline solid, when the periodic and repeated arrangement of atoms is perfect or extends throughout the entirety of the specimen without interruption, the result is a **single crystal.** All unit cells interlock in the same way and have the same orientation. Single crystals exist in nature, but they may also be produced artificially. They are ordinarily difficult to grow, because the environment must be carefully controlled.

If the extremities of a single crystal are permitted to grow without any external constraint, the crystal will assume a regular geometric shape having flat faces, as with some of the gem stones; the shape is indicative of the crystal structure. A photograph of a garnet single crystal is shown in Figure 3.8. Within the past few

Figure 3.8 Photograph of a garnet single crystal that was found in Tongbei, Fujian Province, China. (Photograph courtesy of Irocks.com, Megan Foreman photo.)

years, single crystals have become extremely important in many of our modern technologies, in particular electronic microcircuits, which employ single crystals of silicon and other semiconductors.

3.9 POLYCRYSTALLINE MATERIALS

Most crystalline solids are composed of a collection of many small crystals or **grains;** such materials are termed **polycrystalline.** Various stages in the solidification of a polycrystalline specimen are represented schematically in Figure 3.9. Initially, small crystals or nuclei form at various positions. These have random crystallographic orientations, as indicated by the square grids. The small grains grow by the successive addition from the surrounding liquid of atoms to the structure of each. The extremities of adjacent grains impinge on one another as the solidification process approaches completion. As indicated in Figure 3.9, the crystallographic orientation varies from grain to grain. Also, there exists some atomic mismatch within the region where two grains meet; this area, called a **grain boundary.**

3.10 ANISOTROPY

The physical properties of single crystals of some substances depend on the crystallographic direction in which measurements are taken. For example, the elastic modulus, the electrical conductivity, and the index of refraction may have different values in the [100] and [111] directions. This directionality of properties is termed **anisotropy,** and it is associated with the variance of atomic or ionic spacing with crystallographic direction. Substances in which measured properties are independent of the direction of measurement are **isotropic.** The extent and magnitude of anisotropic effects in crystalline materials are functions of the symmetry of the crystal structure; the degree of anisotropy increases with decreasing structural symmetry—triclinic structures normally are highly anisotropic. The modulus of elasticity values at [100], [110], and [111] orientations for several materials are presented in Table 3.2.

For many polycrystalline materials, the crystallographic orientations of the individual grains are totally random. Under these circumstances, even though each grain

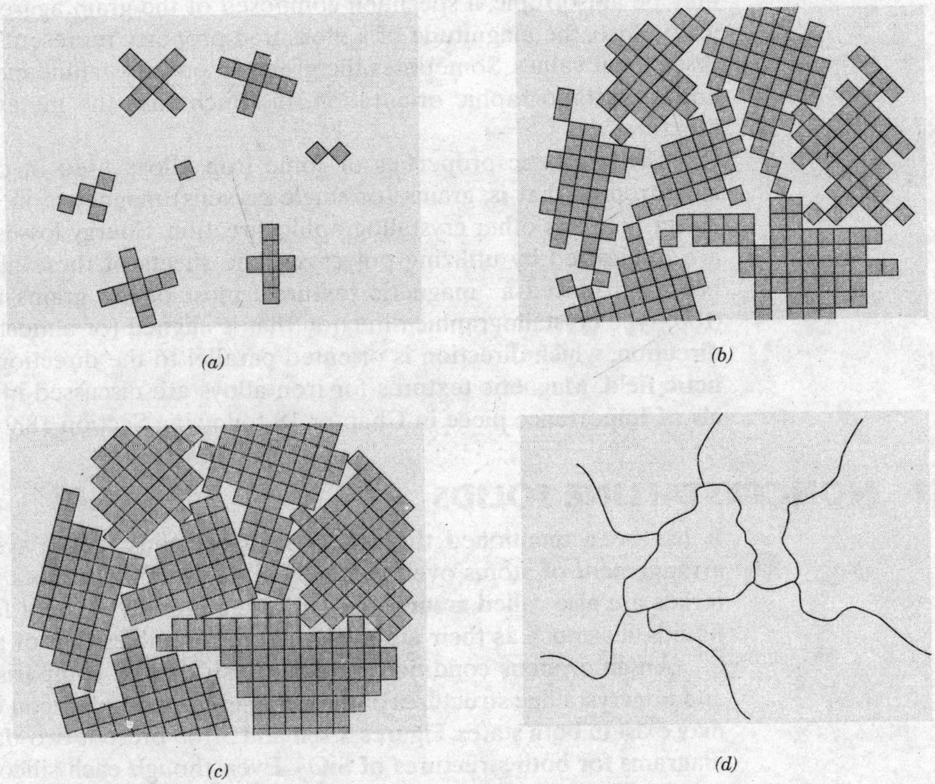

Figure 3.9 Schematic diagrams of the various stages in the solidification of a polycrystalline material; the square grids depict unit cells. (*a*) Small crystallite nuclei. (*b*) Growth of the crystallites; the obstruction of some grains that are adjacent to one another is also shown. (*c*) Upon completion of solidification, grains having irregular shapes have formed. (*d*) The grain structure as it would appear under the microscope; dark lines are the grain boundaries. (Adapted from W. Rosenhain, *An Introduction to the Study of Physical Metallurgy,* 2nd edition, Constable & Company Ltd., London, 1915.)

Table 3.2 Modulus of Elasticity Values for Several Metals at Various Crystallographic Orientations

	Modulus of Elasticity (GPa)		
Metal	*[100]*	*[110]*	*[111]*
Aluminum	63.7	72.6	76.1
Copper	66.7	130.3	191.1
Iron	125.0	210.5	272.7
Tungsten	384.6	384.6	384.6

Source: R. W. Hertzberg, *Deformation and Fracture Mechanics of Engineering Materials,* 3rd edition. Copyright © 1989 by John Wiley & Sons, New York. Reprinted by permission of John Wiley & Sons, Inc.

may be anisotropic, a specimen composed of the grain aggregate behaves isotropically. Also, the magnitude of a measured property represents some average of the directional values. Sometimes the grains in polycrystalline materials have a preferential crystallographic orientation, in which case the material is said to have a "texture."

The magnetic properties of some iron alloys used in transformer cores are anisotropic—that is, grains (or single crystals) magnetize in a ⟨100⟩-type direction easier than any other crystallographic direction. Energy losses in transformer cores are minimized by utilizing polycrystalline sheets of these alloys into which have been introduced a "magnetic texture": most of the grains in each sheet have a ⟨100⟩-type crystallographic direction that is aligned (or almost aligned) in the same direction, which direction is oriented parallel to the direction of the applied magnetic field. Magnetic textures for iron alloys are discussed in detail in the Materials of Importance piece in Chapter 18 following Section 18.9.

3.11 NONCRYSTALLINE SOLIDS

It has been mentioned that **noncrystalline** solids lack a systematic and regular arrangement of atoms over relatively large atomic distances. Sometimes such materials are also called **amorphous** (meaning literally without form), or supercooled liquids, inasmuch as their atomic structure resembles that of a liquid.

An amorphous condition may be illustrated by comparison of the crystalline and noncrystalline structures of the ceramic compound silicon dioxide (SiO_2), which may exist in both states. Figures 3.10*a* and 3.10*b* present two-dimensional schematic diagrams for both structures of SiO_2. Even though each silicon ion bonds to three oxygen ions for both states, beyond this, the structure is much more disordered and irregular for the noncrystalline structure.

Whether a crystalline or amorphous solid forms depends on the ease with which a random atomic structure in the liquid can transform to an ordered state during

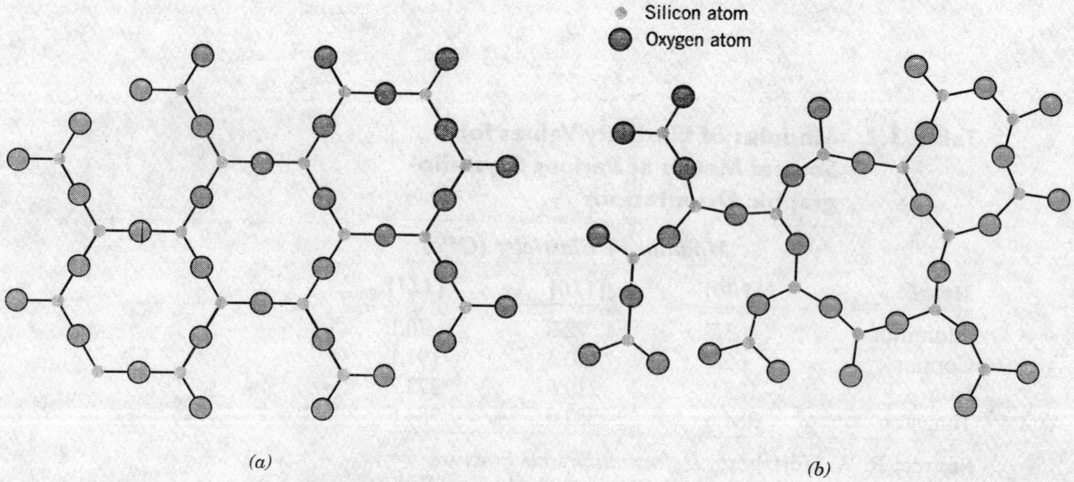

Figure 3.10 Two-dimensional schemes of the structure of (*a*) crystalline silicon dioxide and (*b*) noncrystalline silicon dioxide.

solidification. Amorphous materials, therefore, are characterized by atomic or molecular structures that are relatively complex and become ordered only with some difficulty. Furthermore, rapidly cooling through the freezing temperature favors the formation of a noncrystalline solid, since little time is allowed for the ordering process.

Metals normally form crystalline solids, but some ceramic materials are crystalline, whereas others, the inorganic glasses, are amorphous. Polymers may be completely noncrystalline and semicrystalline consisting of varying degrees of crystallinity. More about the structure and properties of amorphous ceramics and polymers is contained in Chapters 12 and 14.

Concept Check 3.2

Do noncrystalline materials display the phenomenon of allotropy (or polymorphism)? Why or why not?

[*The answer may be found in enclosed CD.*]

SUMMARY

Fundamental Concepts
Unit Cells

Atoms in crystalline solids are positioned in orderly and repeated patterns that are in contrast to the random and disordered atomic distribution found in noncrystalline or amorphous materials. Atoms may be represented as solid spheres, and, for crystalline solids, crystal structure is just the spatial arrangement of these spheres. The various crystal structures are specified in terms of parallelepiped unit cells, which are characterized by geometry and atom positions within.

Point Coordinates
Crystallographic Directions
Crystallographic Planes

Crystallographic points, directions, and planes are specified in terms of indexing schemes. The basis for the determination of each index is a coordinate axis system defined by the unit cell for the particular crystal structure. The location of a point within a unit cell is specified using coordinates that are fractional multiples of the cell edge lengths. Directional indices are computed in terms of the vector projection on each of the coordinate axes, whereas planar indices are determined from the reciprocals of axial intercepts. For hexagonal unit cells, a four-index scheme for both directions and planes is found to be more convenient.

Single Crystals
Polycrystalline Materials

Single crystals are materials in which the atomic order extends uninterrupted over the entirety of the specimen; under some circumstances, they may have flat faces and regular geometric shapes. The vast majority of crystalline solids, however, are polycrystalline, being composed of many small crystals or grains having different crystallographic orientations.

Crystal Systems
Anisotropy

Other concepts introduced in this chapter were: crystal system (a classification scheme for crystal structures on the basis of unit cell geometry), and anisotropy (the directionality dependence of properties).

REFERENCES

Azaroff, L. F., *Elements of X-Ray Crystallography,* McGraw-Hill, New York, 1968. Reprinted by TechBooks, Marietta, OH, 1990.

Buerger, M. J., *Elementary Crystallography,* Wiley, New York, 1956.

Cullity, B. D., and S. R. Stock, *Elements of X-Ray Diffraction,* 3rd edition, Prentice Hall, Upper Saddle River, NJ, 2001.

QUESTIONS AND PROBLEMS

Fundamental Concepts

3.1 What is the difference between atomic structure and crystal structure?

Unit Cells
Crystal Systems

3.2 Below is a unit cell for a hypothetical metal.

(a) To which crystal system does this unit cell belong?

(b) What would this crystal structure be called?

(c) Calculate the density of the material, given that its atomic weight is 141 g/mol.

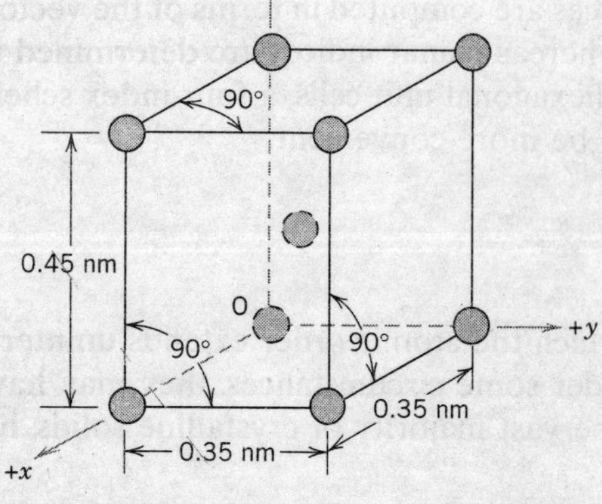

3.3 Sketch a unit cell for the face-centered orthorhombic crystal structure.

Point Coordinates

3.4 List the point coordinates for all atoms that are associated with the FCC unit cell (Figure 3.1).

3.5 List the point coordinates of both the sodium and chlorine ions for a unit cell of the sodium chloride crystal structure (Figure 4.11).

3.6 List the point coordinates of both the zinc and sulfur atoms for a unit cell of the zinc blende crystal structure (Figure 4.13).

3.7 Sketch a tetragonal unit cell, and within that cell indicate locations of the $1\,1\,\frac{1}{2}$ and $\frac{1}{2}\,\frac{1}{4}\,\frac{1}{2}$ point coordinates.

3.8 Using the Molecule Definition Utility found in the CD enclosed with the book, generate (and print out) a three-dimensional unit cell for β tin given the following: (1) the unit cell is tetragonal with $a = 0.583$ nm and $c = 0.318$ nm, and (2) Sn atoms are located at the following point coordinates:

0 0 0	0 1 1
1 0 0	$\frac{1}{2}\,0\,\frac{3}{4}$
1 1 0	$\frac{1}{2}\,1\,\frac{3}{4}$

0 1 0	$1\ \frac{1}{2}\ \frac{1}{4}$
0 0 1	$0\ \frac{1}{2}\ \frac{1}{4}$
1 0 1	$\frac{1}{2}\ \frac{1}{2}\ \frac{1}{2}$
1 1 1	

Crystallographic Directions

3.9 Draw an orthorhombic unit cell, and within that cell a [2$\bar{1}$1] direction.

3.10 Sketch a monoclinic unit cell, and within that cell a [$\bar{1}$01] direction.

3.11 What are the indices for the directions indicated by the two vectors in the sketch below?

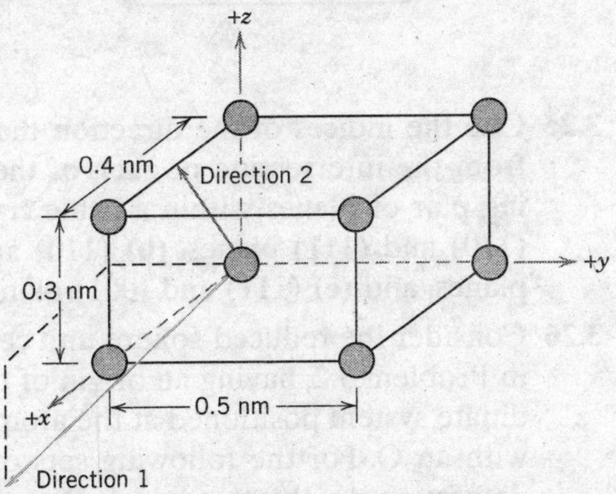

3.12 Within a cubic unit cell, sketch the following directions:

(a) [101], **(e)** [$\bar{1}\bar{1}$1],
(b) [211], **(f)** [$\bar{2}$12],
(c) [10$\bar{2}$], **(g)** [3$\bar{1}$2],
(d) [$\bar{3}\bar{1}$3], **(h)** [301].

3.13 Determine the indices for the directions shown in the following cubic unit cell:

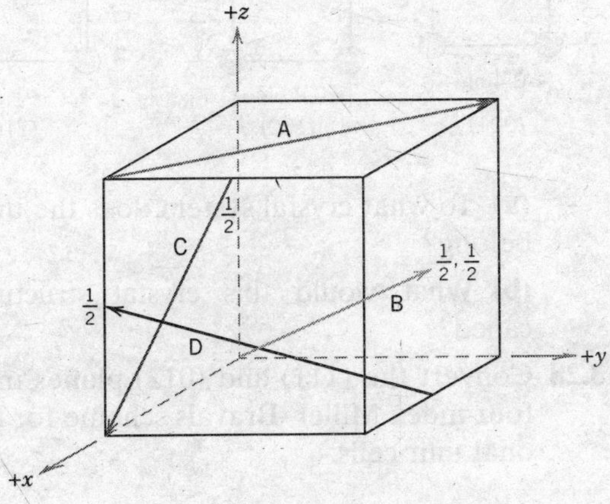

3.14 Determine the indices for the directions shown in the following cubic unit cell:

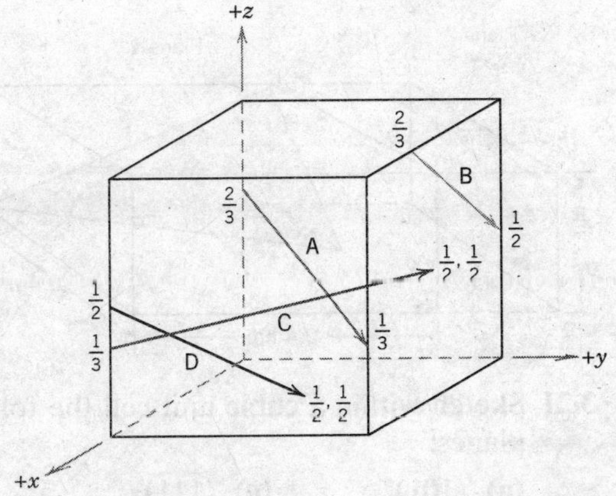

3.15 For tetragonal crystals, cite the indices of directions that are equivalent to each of the following directions:

(a) [011]

(b) [100]

3.16 Convert the [110] and [00$\bar{1}$] directions into the four-index Miller–Bravais scheme for hexagonal unit cells.

3.17 Determine the indices for the directions shown in the following hexagonal unit cell:

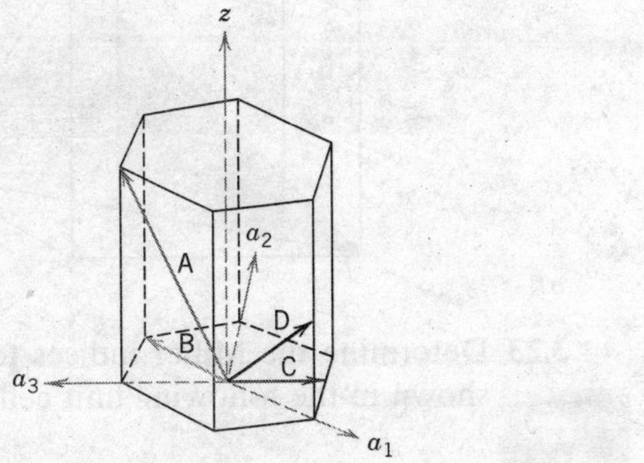

3.18 Using Equations 3.1a, 3.1b, 3.1c, and 3.1d, derive expressions for each of the three primed indices set (u', v', and w') in terms of the four unprimed indices (u, v, t, and w).

Crystallographic Planes

3.19 **(a)** Draw an orthorhombic unit cell, and within that cell a (02$\bar{1}$) plane.

(b) Draw a monoclinic unit cell, and within that cell a (200) plane.

3.20 What are the indices for the two planes drawn in the sketch below?

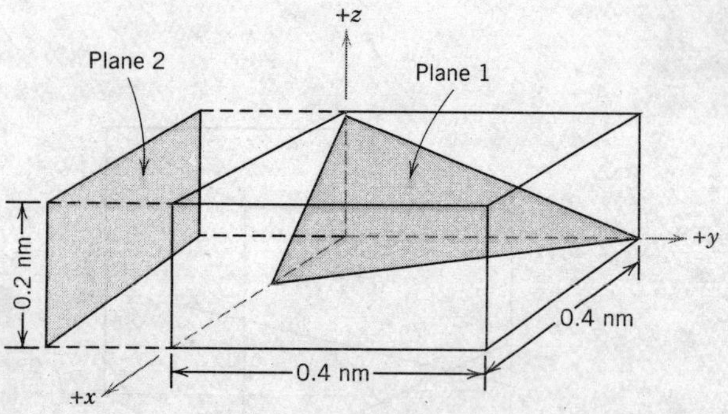

3.21 Sketch within a cubic unit cell the following planes:

(a) $(10\bar{1})$, **(e)** $(\bar{1}1\bar{1})$,
(b) $(2\bar{1}1)$, **(f)** $(\bar{2}12)$,
(c) (012), **(g)** $(3\bar{1}2)$,
(d) $(3\bar{1}3)$, **(h)** (301).

3.22 Determine the Miller indices for the planes shown in the following unit cell:

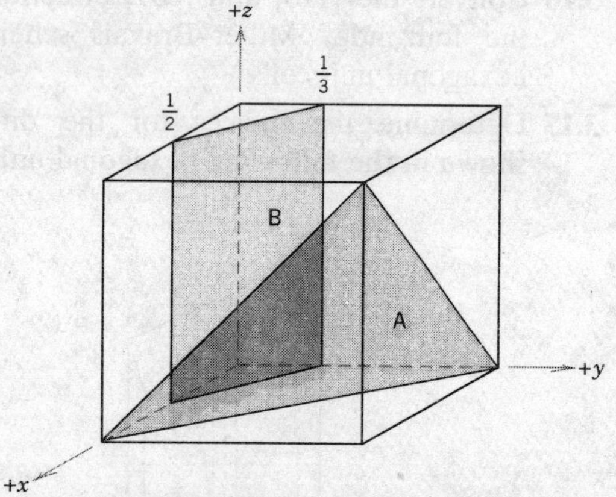

3.23 Determine the Miller indices for the planes shown in the following unit cell:

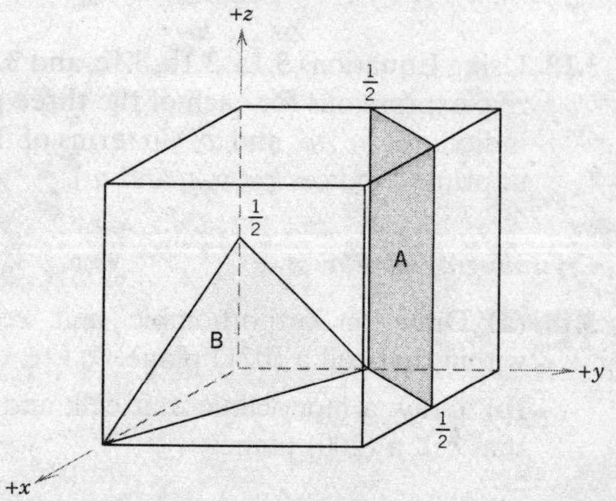

3.24 Determine the Miller indices for the planes shown in the following unit cell:

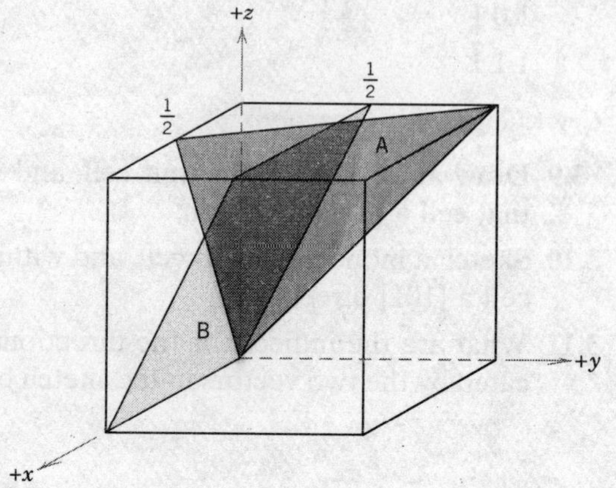

3.25 Cite the indices of the direction that results from the intersection of each of the following pair of planes within a cubic crystal: **(a)** (110) and (111) planes, **(b)** (110) and $(1\bar{1}0)$ planes, and **(c)** $(11\bar{1})$ and (001) planes.

3.26 Consider the reduced-sphere unit cell shown in Problem 3.2, having an origin of the coordinate system positioned at the atom labeled with an O. For the following sets of planes, determine which are equivalent:

(a) (100), $(0\bar{1}0)$, and (001)
(b) (110), (101), (011), and $(\bar{1}01)$
(c) (111), $(1\bar{1}1)$, $(11\bar{1})$, and $(\bar{1}1\bar{1})$

3.27 Here are three different crystallographic planes for a unit cell of a hypothetical metal. The circles represent atoms:

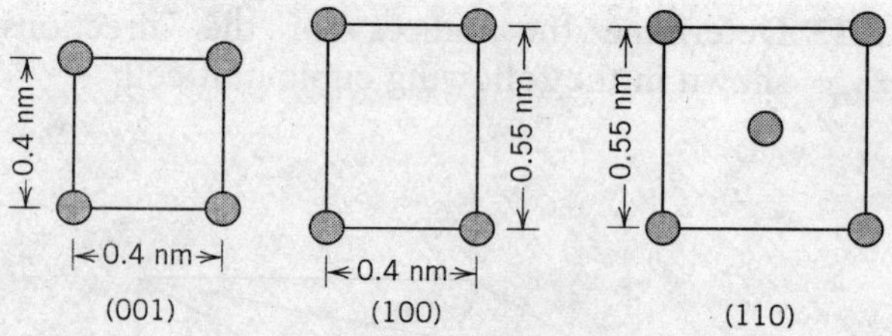

(a) To what crystal system does the unit cell belong?

(b) What would this crystal structure be called?

3.28 Convert the (111) and $(0\bar{1}2)$ planes into the four-index Miller–Bravais scheme for hexagonal unit cells.

3.29 Determine the indices for the planes shown in the hexagonal unit cells below:

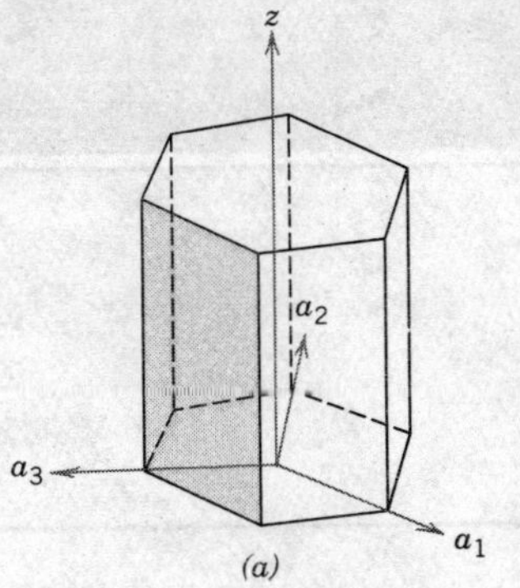

(a)

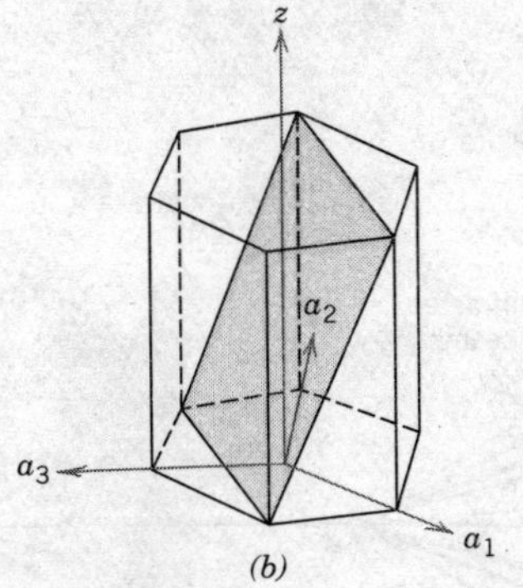

(b)

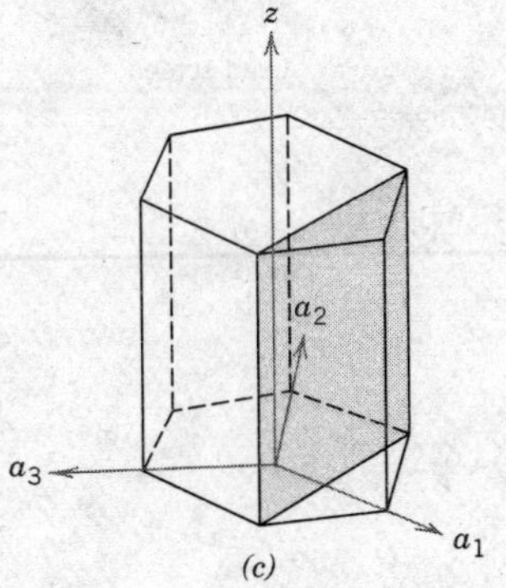

(c)

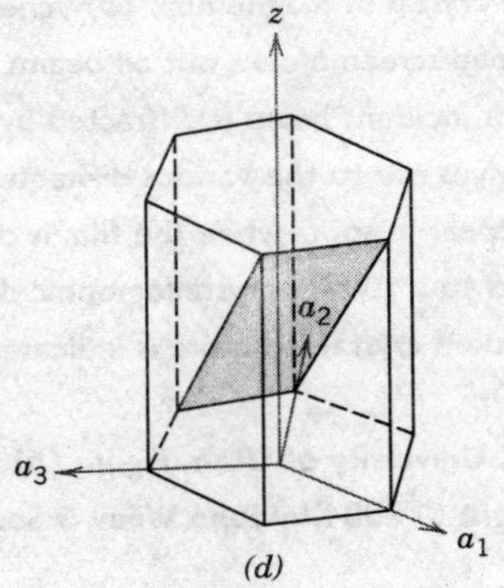

(d)

3.30 Sketch the $(01\bar{1}1)$ and $(2\bar{1}\bar{1}0)$ planes in a hexagonal unit cell.

Polycrystalline Materials

3.31 Explain why the properties of polycrystalline materials are most often isotropic.

Noncrystalline Solids

3.32 Would you expect a material in which the atomic bonding is predominantly ionic in nature to be more or less likely to form a noncrystalline solid upon solidification than a covalent material? Why?

Chapter 4 Structures of Crystalline Solids

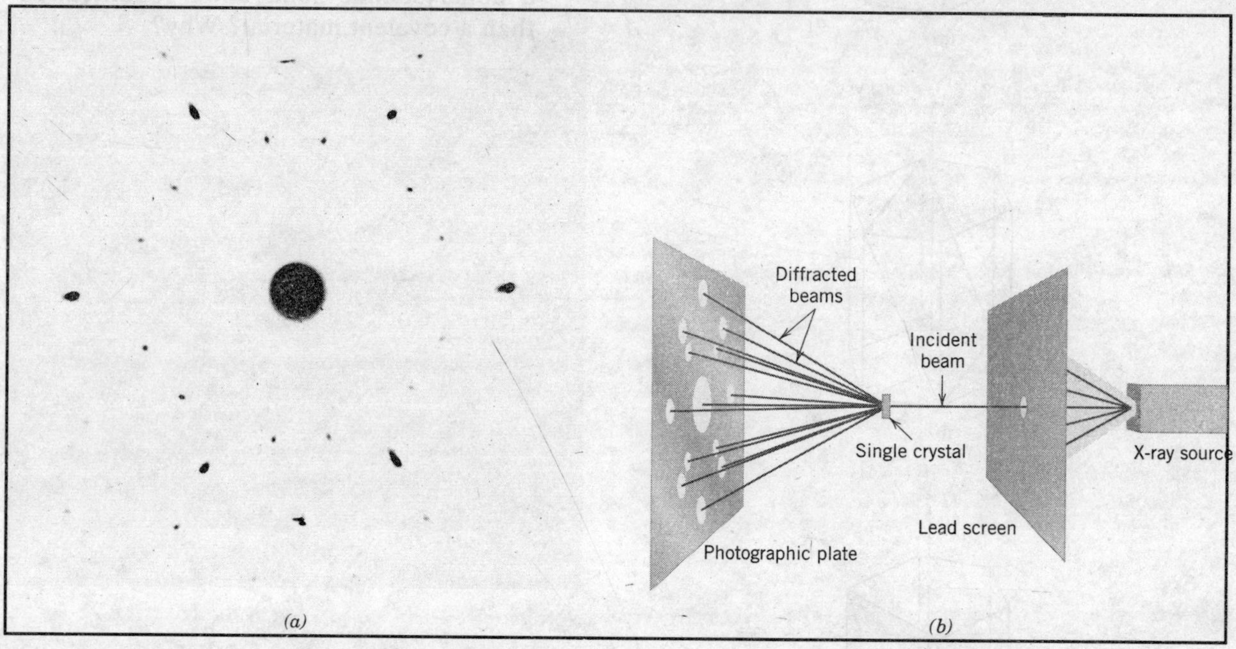

(*a*) X-ray diffraction photograph [or Laue photograph (Section 4.20)] for a single crystal of magnesium. (*b*) Schematic diagram illustrating how the spots (i.e., the diffraction pattern) in (*a*) are produced. The lead screen blocks out all beams generated from the x-ray source, except for a narrow beam traveling in a single direction. This incident beam is diffracted by individual crystallographic planes in the single crystal (having different orientations), which gives rise to the various diffracted beams that impinge on the photographic plate. Intersections of these beams with the plate appear as spots when the film is developed.

The large spot in the center of (*a*) is from the incident beam, which is parallel to a [0001] crystallographic direction. It should be noted that the hexagonal symmetry of magnesium's hexagonal close-packed crystal structure is indicated by the diffraction spot pattern that was generated.

[Figure (*a*) courtesy of J. G. Byrne, Department of Metallurgical Engineering, University of Utah. Figure (*b*) from J. E. Brady and F. Senese, *Chemistry: Matter and Its Changes,* 4th edition. Copyright © 2004 by John Wiley & Sons, Hoboken, NJ. Reprinted by permission of John Wiley & Sons, Inc.]

Learning Objectives

After studying this chapter you should be able to do the following:

1. **Draw unit cells for face-centered cubic, body-centered cubic, and hexagonal close-packed crystal structures.**
2. **Derive the relationships between unit cell edge length and atomic radius for face-centered cubic and body-centered cubic crystal structures.**
3. **Compute the densities for metals having face-centered cubic and body-centered cubic crystal structures given their unit cell dimensions.**
4. **Describe how face-centered cubic and hexagonal close-packed crystal structures may be generated by the stacking of close-packed planes of atoms.**
5. **Sketch/describe unit cells for sodium chloride, cesium, chloride, zinc blende, diamond cubic, fluorite, and perovskite crystal structures. Do likewise for the atomic structures of graphite and a silica glass.**
6. **Given the chemical formula for a ceramic compound and the ionic radii of its component ions, predict the crystal structure.**
7. **Briefly describe the crystalline state in polymeric materials.**
8. **Briefly describe/diagram the spherulitic structure for a semicrystalline polymer.**
9. **Determine crystal structure and interplanar spacing using X-ray diffractometry.**

4.1 INTRODUCTION

Concepts of crystal structure, unit cells, crystallographic points, directions and planes were explained in Chapter 3. The three common crystal structures found in metals are detailed. The types of ceramic crystal structures are discussed. Most ceramics are compounds between metallic and non-metallic elements for which the interatomic bonds are either totally ionic, or predominantly ionic but having some covalent character. Ceramic materials are discussed in greater detail in Chapter 12. Most polymeric. materials are composed of very large molecular chains with side groups of various atoms (O, Cl, etc) or organic groups such as methyl, ethyl or phenyl groups. When the molecular chains are packed in an ordered atomic arrangement, the condition of crystallinity is said to exist. Crystalline polymers are briefly discussed in this chapter. Characteristics and details of polymeric chain structures are discussed in Chapter 13. The final section of this chapter briefly describes how crystal structures are determined experimentally using X-ray diffraction techniques.

Metallic Crystal Structures

The atomic bonding in this group of materials is metallic and thus nondirectional in nature. Consequently, there are minimal restrictions as to the number and position of nearest-neighbor atoms; this leads to relatively large numbers of nearest neighbors and dense atomic packings for most metallic crystal structures. Also, for metals, using the hard sphere model for the crystal structure, each sphere represents an ion core. Table 4.1 presents the atomic radii for a number of metals. Three relatively simple crystal structures are found for most of the common metals: face-centered cubic, body-centered cubic, and hexagonal close-packed.

4.2 THE FACE-CENTERED CUBIC CRYSTAL STRUCTURE

The crystal structure found for many metals has a unit cell of cubic geometry, with atoms located at each of the corners and the centers of all the cube faces. It is aptly called the **face-centered cubic (FCC)** crystal structure. Some of the familiar

Table 4.1 Atomic Radii and Crystal Structures for 16 Metals

Metal	*Crystal Structure*[a]	*Atomic Radius*[b] *(nm)*	*Metal*	*Crystal Structure*	*Atomic Radius (nm)*
Aluminum	FCC	0.1431	Molybdenum	BCC	0.1363
Cadmium	HCP	0.1490	Nickel	FCC	0.1246
Chromium	BCC	0.1249	Platinum	FCC	0.1387
Cobalt	HCP	0.1253	Silver	FCC	0.1445
Copper	FCC	0.1278	Tantalum	BCC	0.1430
Gold	FCC	0.1442	Titanium (α)	HCP	0.1445
Iron (α)	BCC	0.1241	Tungsten	BCC	0.1371
Lead	FCC	0.1750	Zinc	HCP	0.1332

[a] FCC = face-centered cubic; HCP = hexagonal close-packed; BCC = body-centered cubic.
[b] A nanometer (nm) equals 10^{-9} m; to convert from nanometers to angstrom units (Å), multiply the nanometer value by 10.

metals having this crystal structure are copper, aluminum, silver, and gold (see also Table 4.1). Figure 4.1*a* shows a hard sphere model for the FCC unit cell, whereas in Figure 4.1*b* the atom centers are represented by small circles to provide a better perspective of atom positions. The aggregate of atoms in Figure 4.1*c* represents a section of crystal consisting of many FCC unit cells. These spheres or ion cores touch one another across a face diagonal; the cube edge length *a* and the atomic radius *R* are related through

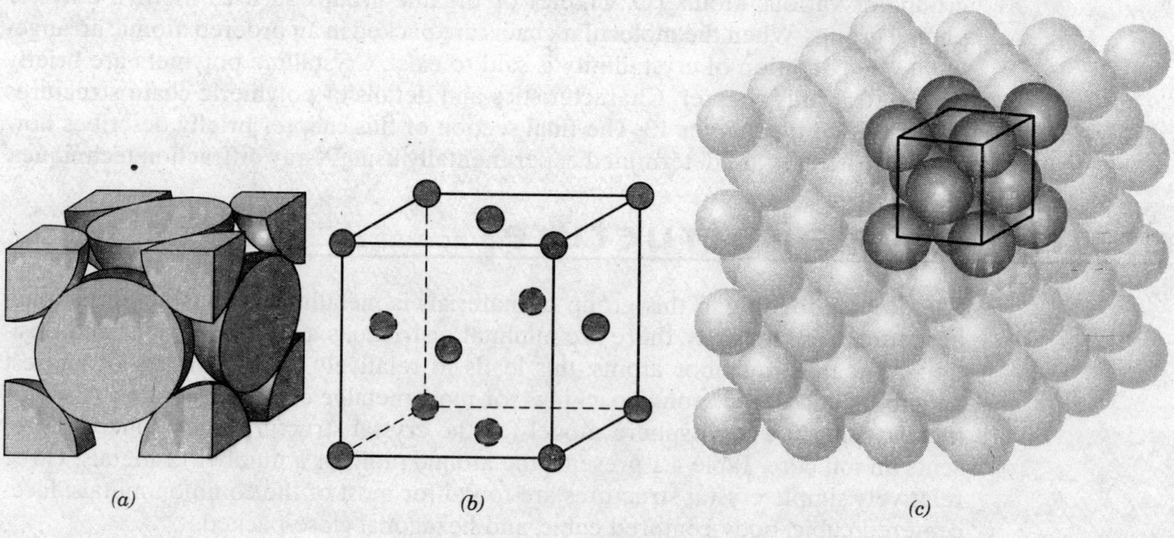

Figure 4.1 For the face-centered cubic crystal structure, (*a*) a hard sphere unit cell representation, (*b*) a reduced-sphere unit cell, and (*c*) an aggregate of many atoms. [Figure (*c*) adapted from W. G. Moffatt, G. W. Pearsall, and J. Wulff, *The Structure and Properties of Materials,* Vol. I, *Structure,* p. 51. Copyright © 1964 by John Wiley & Sons, New York. Reprinted by permission of John Wiley & Sons, Inc.]

$$a = 2R\sqrt{2} \tag{4.1}$$

This result is obtained in Example Problem 4.1.

For the FCC crystal structure, each corner atom is shared among eight unit cells, whereas a face-centered atom belongs to only two. Therefore, one-eighth of each of the eight corner atoms and one-half of each of the six face atoms, or a total of four whole atoms, may be assigned to a given unit cell. This is depicted in Figure 4.1*a*, where only sphere portions are represented within the confines of the cube. The cell comprises the volume of the cube, which is generated from the centers of the corner atoms as shown in the figure.

Corner and face positions are really equivalent; that is, translation of the cube corner from an original corner atom to the center of a face atom will not alter the cell structure.

Two other important characteristics of a crystal structure are the **coordination number** and the **atomic packing factor (APF).** For metals, each atom has the same number of nearest-neighbor or touching atoms, which is the coordination number. For face-centered cubics, the coordination number is 12. This may be confirmed by examination of Figure 4.1*a*; the front face atom has four corner nearest-neighbor atoms surrounding it, four face atoms that are in contact from behind, and four other equivalent face atoms residing in the next unit cell to the front, which is not shown.

The APF is the sum of the sphere volumes of all atoms within a unit cell (assuming the atomic hard sphere model) divided by the unit cell volume—that is For the FCC structure, the atomic packing factor is 0.74, which is the maximum

$$\text{APF} = \frac{\text{volume of atoms in a unit cell}}{\text{total unit cell volume}} \tag{4.2}$$

packing possible for spheres all having the same diameter. Computation of this APF is also included as an example problem. Metals typically have relatively large atomic packing factors to maximize the shielding provided by the free electron cloud.

4.3 THE BODY-CENTERED CUBIC CRYSTAL STRUCTURE

Another common metallic crystal structure also has a cubic unit cell with atoms located at all eight corners and a single atom at the cube center. This is called a **body-centered cubic (BCC)** crystal structure. A collection of spheres depicting this crystal structure is shown in Figure 4.2*c*, whereas Figures 4.2*a* and 4.2*b* are diagrams of BCC unit cells with the atoms represented by hard sphere and reduced-sphere models, respectively. Center and corner atoms touch one another along cube diagonals, and unit cell length a and atomic radius R are related through

$$a = \frac{4R}{\sqrt{3}} \tag{4.3}$$

Chromium, iron, tungsten, as well as several other metals listed in Table 4.1 exhibit a BCC structure.

Two atoms are associated with each BCC unit cell: the equivalent of one atom from the eight corners, each of which is shared among eight unit cells, and the single center atom, which is wholly contained within its cell. In addition, corner and

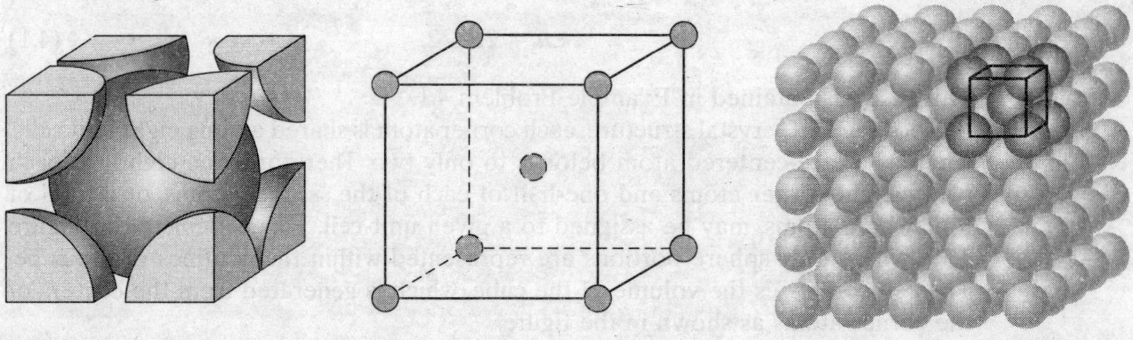

(a) (b) (c)

Figure 4.2 For the body-centered cubic crystal structure, (*a*) a hard sphere unit cell representation, (*b*) a reduced-sphere unit cell, and (*c*) an aggregate of many atoms. [Figure (*c*) from W. G. Moffatt, G. W. Pearsall, and J. Wulff, *The Structure and Properties of Materials,* Vol. I, *Structure,* p. 51. Copyright © 1964 by John Wiley & Sons, New York. Reprinted by permission of John Wiley & Sons, Inc.]

center atom positions are equivalent. The coordination number for the BCC crystal structure is 8; each center atom has as nearest neighbors its eight corner atoms.Since the coordination number is less for BCC than FCC, so also is the atomic packing factor for BCC lower—0.68 versus 0.74.

4.4 THE HEXAGONAL CLOSE-PACKED CRYSTAL STRUCTURE

Not all metals have unit cells with cubic symmetry; the final common metallic crystal structure to be discussed has a unit cell that is hexagonal. Figure 4.3*a* shows a reduced-sphere unit cell for this structure, which is termed **hexagonal close-packed**

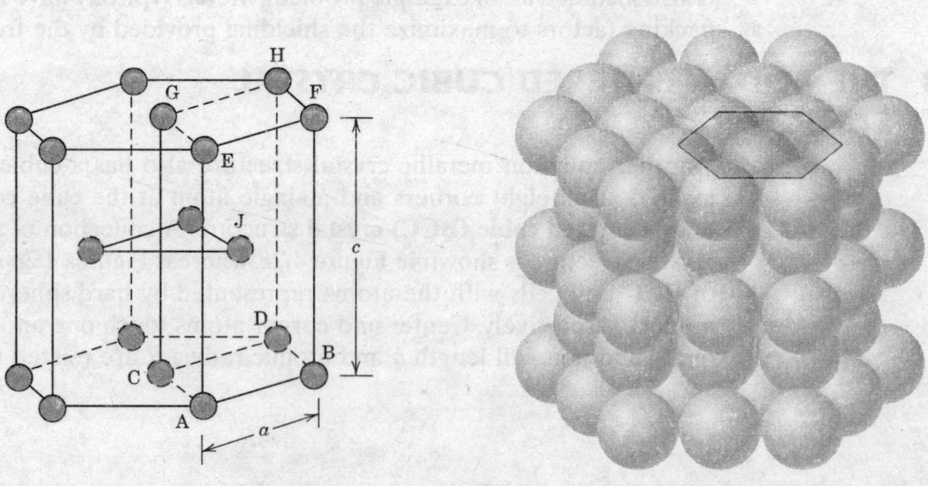

(a) (b)

Figure 4.3 For the hexagonal close-packed crystal structure, (*a*) a reduced-sphere unit cell (*a* and *c* represent the short and long edge lengths, respectively), and (*b*) an aggregate of many atoms. [Figure (*b*) from W. G. Moffatt, G. W. Pearsall, and J. Wulff, *The Structure and Properties of Materials,* Vol. I, *Structure,* p. 51. Copyright © 1964 by John Wiley & Sons, New York. Reprinted by permission of John Wiley & Sons, Inc.]

(HCP); an assemblage of several HCP unit cells is presented in Figure 4.3*b*.[1] The top and bottom faces of the unit cell consist of six atoms that form regular hexagons and surround a single atom in the center. Another plane that provides three additional atoms to the unit cell is situated between the top and bottom planes. The atoms in this midplane have as nearest neighbors atoms in both of the adjacent two planes. The equivalent of six atoms is contained in each unit cell; one-sixth of each of the 12 top and bottom face corner atoms, one-half of each of the 2 center face atoms, and all 3 midplane interior atoms. If a and c represent, respectively, the short and long unit cell dimensions of Figure 4.3*a*, the c/a ratio should be 1.633; however, for some HCP metals this ratio deviates from the ideal value.

The coordination number and the atomic packing factor for the HCP crystal structure are the same as for FCC: 12 and 0.74, respectively. The HCP metals include cadmium, magnesium, titanium, and zinc; some of these are listed in Table 4.1.

EXAMPLE PROBLEM 4.1

Determination of FCC Unit Cell Volume

Calculate the volume of an FCC unit cell in terms of the atomic radius R.

Solution

In the FCC unit cell illustrated,

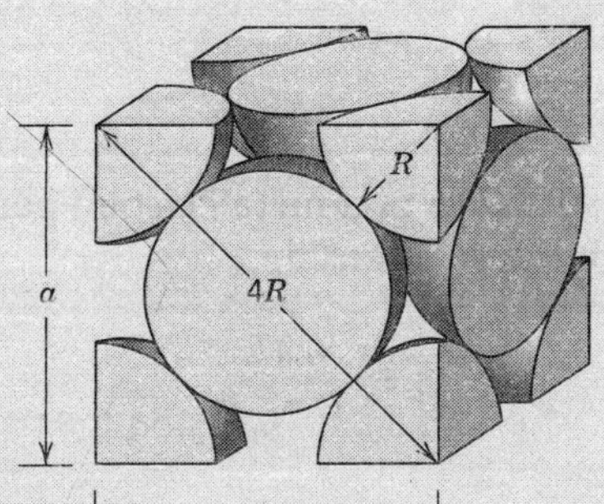

the atoms touch one another across a face-diagonal the length of which is $4R$. Since the unit cell is a cube, its volume is a^3, where a is the cell edge length. From the right triangle on the face,

$$a^2 + a^2 = (4R)^2$$

or, solving for a,

$$a = 2R\sqrt{2} \tag{4.1}$$

The FCC unit cell volume V_C may be computed from

$$V_C = a^3 = (2R\sqrt{2})^3 = 16R^3\sqrt{2} \tag{4.4}$$

[1] Alternatively, the unit cell for HCP may be specified in terms of the parallelepiped defined by atoms labeled A through H in Figure 4.3*a*. As such, the atom denoted J lies within the unit cell interior.

EXAMPLE PROBLEM 4.2

Computation of the Atomic Packing Factor for FCC

Show that the atomic packing factor for the FCC crystal structure is 0.74.

Solution

The APF is defined as the fraction of solid sphere volume in a unit cell, or

$$\text{APF} = \frac{\text{volume of atoms in a unit cell}}{\text{total unit cell volume}} = \frac{V_S}{V_C}$$

Both the total atom and unit cell volumes may be calculated in terms of the atomic radius R. The volume for a sphere is $\frac{4}{3}\pi R^3$, and since there are four atoms per FCC unit cell, the total FCC atom (or sphere) volume is

$$V_S = (4)\tfrac{4}{3}\pi R^3 = \tfrac{16}{3}\pi R^3$$

From Example Problem 4.1, the total unit cell volume is

$$V_C = 16R^3\sqrt{2}$$

Therefore, the atomic packing factor is

$$\text{APF} = \frac{V_S}{V_C} = \frac{\left(\frac{16}{3}\right)\pi R^3}{16R^3\sqrt{2}} = 0.74$$

4.5 DENSITY COMPUTATIONS

A knowledge of the crystal structure of a metallic solid permits computation of its theoretical density ρ through the relationship

$$\rho = \frac{nA}{V_C N_A} \tag{4.5}$$

where

n = number of atoms associated with each unit cell
A = atomic weight
V_C = volume of the unit cell
N_A = Avogadro's number (6.023×10^{23} atoms/mol)

EXAMPLE PROBLEM 4.3

Theoretical Density Computation for Copper

Copper has an atomic radius of 0.128 nm, an FCC crystal structure, and an atomic weight of 63.5 g/mol. Compute its theoretical density and compare the answer with its measured density.

Solution

Equation 4.5 is employed in the solution of this problem. Since the crystal structure is FCC, n, the number of atoms per unit cell, is 4. Furthermore, the atomic weight A_{Cu} is given as 63.5 g/mol. The unit cell volume V_C for FCC was determined in Example Problem 4.1 as $16R^3\sqrt{2}$, where R, the atomic radius, is 0.128 nm.

Substitution for the various parameters into Equation 4.5 yields

$$\rho = \frac{nA_{Cu}}{V_C N_A} = \frac{nA_{Cu}}{(16R^3\sqrt{2})N_A}$$

$$= \frac{(4 \text{ atoms/unit cell})(63.5 \text{ g/mol})}{[16\sqrt{2}(1.28 \times 10^{-8} \text{ cm})^3/\text{unit cell}](6.023 \times 10^{23} \text{ atoms/mol})}$$

$$= 8.89 \text{ g/cm}^3$$

The literature value for the density of copper is 8.94 g/cm^3, which is in very close agreement with the foregoing result.

4.6 ATOMIC ARRANGEMENTS

The atomic arrangement for a crystallographic plane, which is often of interest, depends on the crystal structure. The (110) atomic planes for FCC and BCC crystal structures are represented in Figures 4.4 and 4.5; reduced-sphere unit cells are also included. Note that the atomic packing is different for each case. The circles represent atoms lying in the crystallographic planes as would be obtained from a slice taken through the centers of the full-sized hard spheres.

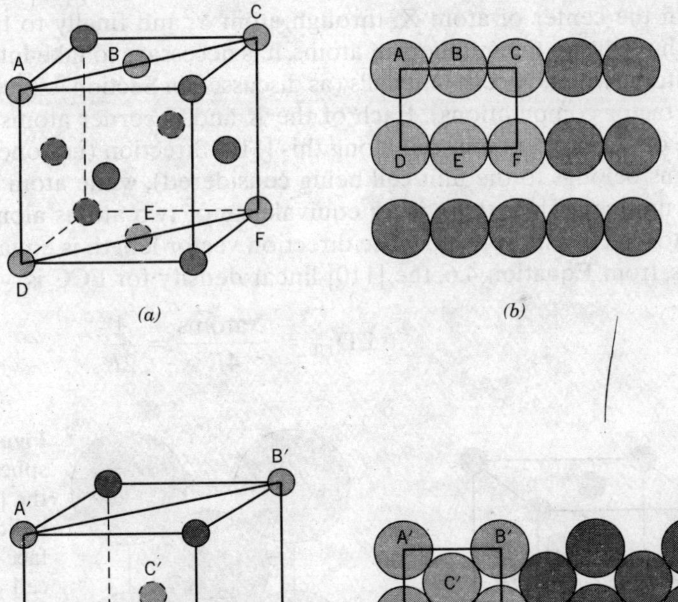

Figure 4.4 (*a*) Reduced-sphere FCC unit cell with (110) plane. (*b*) Atomic packing of an FCC (110) plane. Corresponding atom positions from (*a*) are indicated.

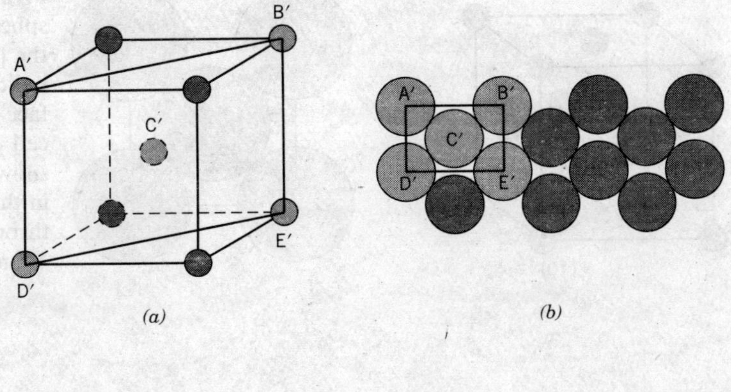

Figure 4.5 (*a*) Reduced-sphere BCC unit cell with (110) plane. (*b*) Atomic packing of a BCC (110) plane. Corresponding atom positions from (*a*) are indicated.

A "family" of planes contains all those planes that are crystallographically equivalent—that is, having the same atomic packing; and a family is designated by indices that are enclosed in braces—such as {100}. For example, in cubic crystals the (111), $(\bar{1}\bar{1}\bar{1})$, $(\bar{1}11)$, $(1\bar{1}\bar{1})$, $(11\bar{1})$, $(\bar{1}\bar{1}1)$, $(\bar{1}1\bar{1})$, and $(1\bar{1}1)$ planes all belong to the {111} family. On the other hand, for tetragonal crystal structures, the {100} family would contain only the (100), $(\bar{1}00)$, (010), and $(0\bar{1}0)$ since the (001) and $(00\bar{1})$ planes are not crystallographically equivalent. Also, in the cubic system only, planes having the same indices, irrespective of order and sign, are equivalent. For example, both $(1\bar{2}3)$ and $(3\bar{1}2)$ belong to the {123} family.

4.7 LINEAR AND PLANAR DENSITIES

The two previous sections discussed the equivalency of nonparallel crystallographic directions and planes. Directional equivalency is related to *linear density* in the sense that, for a particular material, equivalent directions have identical linear densities. The corresponding parameter for crystallographic planes is *planar density,* and planes having the same planar density values are also equivalent.

Linear density (LD) is defined as the number of atoms per unit length whose centers lie on the direction vector for a specific crystallographic direction; that is,

$$\text{LD} = \frac{\text{number of atoms centered on direction vector}}{\text{length of direction vector}} \tag{4.6}$$

Of course, the units of linear density are reciprocal length (e.g., nm^{-1}, m^{-1}).

For example, let us determine the linear density of the [110] direction for the FCC crystal structure. An FCC unit cell (reduced sphere) and the [110] direction therein are shown in Figure 4.6*a*. Represented in Figure 4.6*b* are those five atoms that lie on the bottom face of this unit cell; here the [110] direction vector passes from the center of atom X, through atom Y, and finally to the center of atom Z. With regard to the numbers of atoms, it is necessary to take into account the sharing of atoms with adjacent unit cells (as discussed in Section 4.2 relative to atomic packing factor computations). Each of the X and Z corner atoms are also shared with one other adjacent unit cell along this [110] direction (i.e., one-half of each of these atoms belongs to the unit cell being considered), while atom Y lies entirely within the unit cell. Thus, there is an equivalence of two atoms along the [110] direction vector in the unit cell. Now, the direction vector length is equal to $4R$ (Figure 4.6*b*); thus, from Equation 4.6, the [110] linear density for FCC is

$$\text{LD}_{110} = \frac{2 \text{ atoms}}{4R} = \frac{1}{2R} \tag{4.7}$$

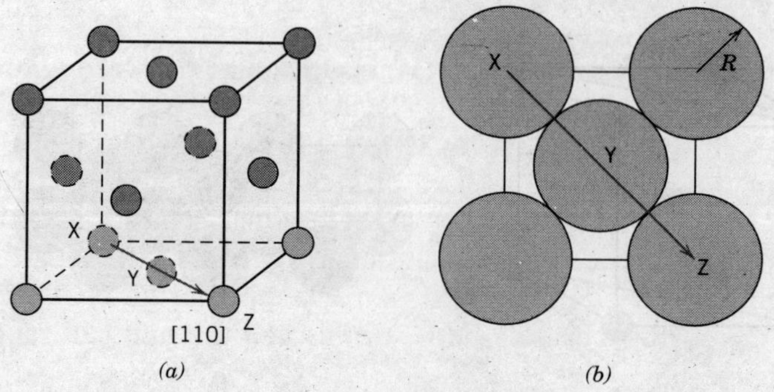

Figure 4.6 (*a*) Reduced-sphere FCC unit cell with the [110] direction indicated. (*b*) The bottom face-plane of the FCC unit cell in (*a*) on which is shown the atomic spacing in the [110] direction, through atoms labeled X, Y, and Z.

In an analogous manner, planar density (PD) is taken as the number of atoms per unit area that are centered on a particular crystallographic plane, or

$$PD = \frac{\text{number of atoms centered on a plane}}{\text{area of plane}} \tag{4.8}$$

The units for planar density are reciprocal area (e.g., nm^{-2}, m^{-2}).

For example, consider the section of a (110) plane within an FCC unit cell as represented in Figures 4.4*a* and 4.4*b*. Although six atoms have centers that lie on this plane (Figure 4.4*b*), only one-quarter of each of atoms A, C, D, and F, and one-half of atoms B and E, for a total equivalence of just 2 atoms are on that plane. Furthermore, the area of this rectangular section is equal to the product of its length and width. From Figure 4.4*b*, the length (horizontal dimension) is equal to $4R$, whereas the width (vertical dimension) is equal to $2R\sqrt{2}$, since it corresponds to the FCC unit cell edge length (Equation 4.1). Thus, the area of this planar region is $(4R)(2R\sqrt{2}) = 8R^2\sqrt{2}$, and the planar density is determined as follows:

$$PD_{110} = \frac{2 \text{ atoms}}{8R^2\sqrt{2}} = \frac{1}{4R^2\sqrt{2}} \tag{4.9}$$

Linear and planar densities are important considerations relative to the process of slip—that is, the mechanism by which metals plastically deform (Section 10.4). Slip occurs on the most densely packed crystallographic planes and, in those planes, along directions having the greatest atomic packing.

4.8 CLOSE-PACKED CRYSTAL STRUCTURES

You may remember from the discussion on metallic crystal structures that both face-centered cubic and hexagonal close-packed crystal structures have atomic packing factors of 0.74, which is the most efficient packing of equal-sized spheres or atoms. In addition to unit cell representations, these two crystal structures may be described in terms of close-packed planes of atoms (i.e., planes having a maximum atom or sphere-packing density); a portion of one such plane is illustrated in Figure 4.7*a*. Both crystal structures may be generated by the stacking of these close-packed planes on top of one another; the difference between the two structures lies in the stacking sequence.

Let the centers of all the atoms in one close-packed plane be labeled *A*. Associated with this plane are two sets of equivalent triangular depressions formed by three adjacent atoms, into which the next close-packed plane of atoms may rest. Those having the triangle vertex pointing up are arbitrarily designated as *B* positions, while the remaining depressions are those with the down vertices, which are marked *C* in Figure 4.7*a*.

A second close-packed plane may be positioned with the centers of its atoms over either *B* or *C* sites; at this point both are equivalent. Suppose that the *B* positions are arbitrarily chosen; the stacking sequence is termed *AB*, which is illustrated in Figure 4.7*b*. The real distinction between FCC and HCP lies in where the third close-packed layer is positioned. For HCP, the centers of this layer are aligned directly above the original *A* positions. This stacking sequence, *ABABAB*. is repeated over and over. Of course, the *ACACAC* . . . arrangement would be equivalent. These close-packed planes for HCP are (0001)-type planes, and the correspondence between this and the unit cell representation is shown in Figure 4.8.

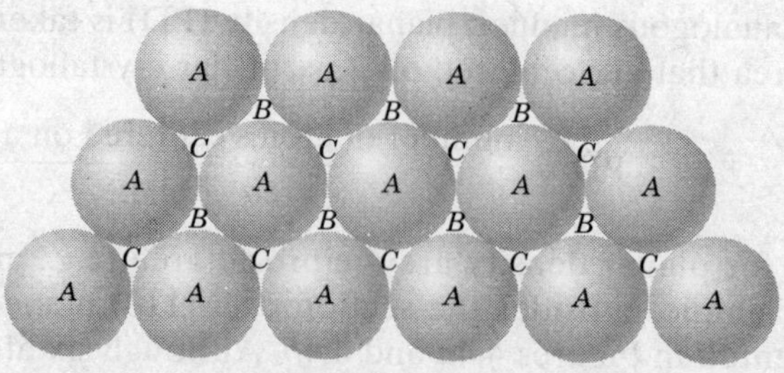

(a)

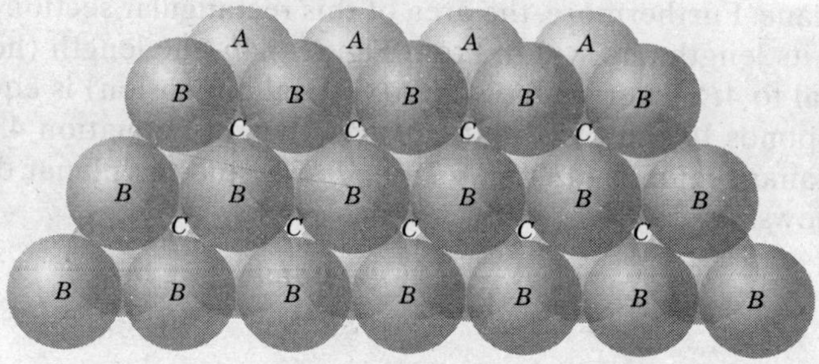

(b)

Figure 4.7 (*a*) A portion of a close-packed plane of atoms; *A*, *B*, and *C* positions are indicated. (*b*) The *AB* stacking sequence for close-packed atomic planes. (Adapted from W. G. Moffatt, G. W. Pearsall, and J. Wulff, *The Structure and Properties of Materials,* Vol. I, *Structure,* p. 50. Copyright © 1964 by John Wiley & Sons, New York. Reprinted by permission of John Wiley & Sons, Inc.)

For the face-centered crystal structure, the centers of the third plane are situated over the *C* sites of the first plane (Figure 4.9*a*). This yields an *ABCABCABC* . . . stacking sequence; that is, the atomic alignment repeats every third plane. It is more difficult to correlate the stacking of close-packed planes to the FCC unit cell. However, this relationship is demonstrated in Figure 4.9*b*. These planes are of the (111) type; an FCC unit cell is outlined on the upper left-hand front face of Figure 4.9*b*, in order to provide a perspective. The significance of these FCC and HCP close-packed planes will become apparent in Chapter 10.

4.9 POLYMORPHISM AND ALLOTROPY

Some metals, as well as nonmetals, may have more than one crystal structure, a phenomenon known as **polymorphism.** When found in elemental solids, the condition is often termed **allotropy.** The prevailing crystal structure depends on both

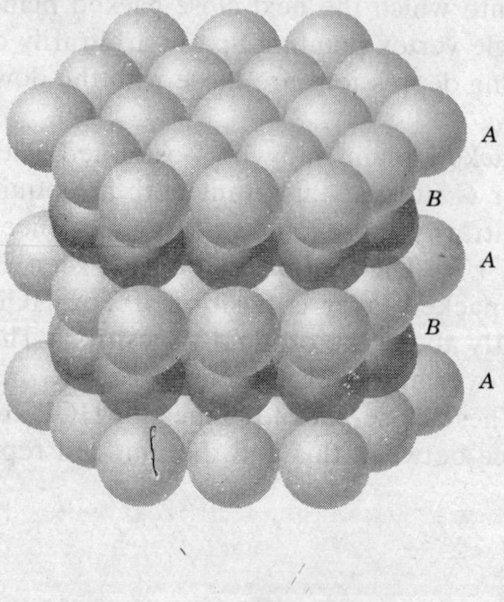

Figure 4.8 Close-packed plane stacking sequence for hexagonal close-packed. (Adapted from W. G. Moffatt, G. W. Pearsall, and J. Wulff, *The Structure and Properties of Materials,* Vol. I, *Structure,* p. 51. Copyright © 1964 by John Wiley & Sons, New York. Reprinted by permission of John Wiley & Sons, Inc.)

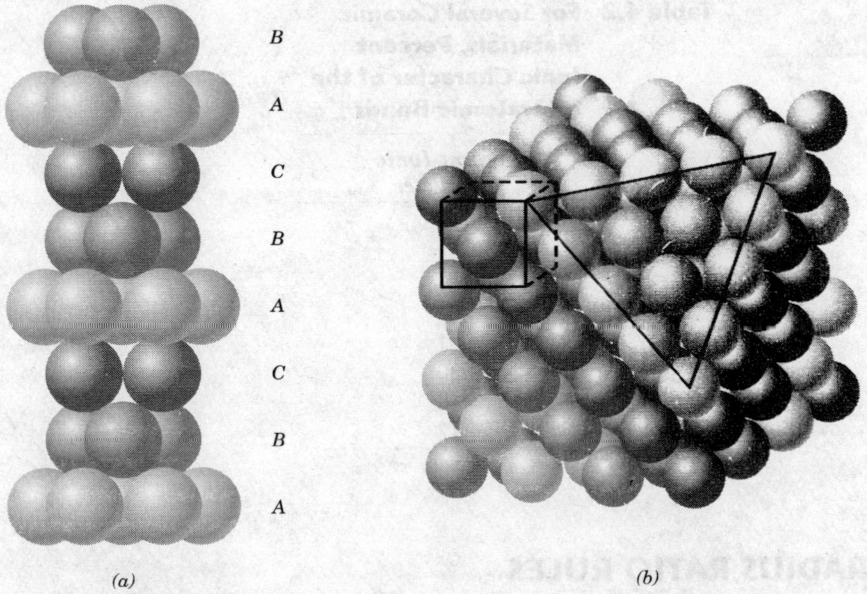

Figure 4.9 (*a*) Close-packed stacking sequence for face-centered cubic. (*b*) A corner has been removed to show the relation between the stacking of close-packed planes of atoms and the FCC crystal structure; the heavy triangle outlines a (111) plane. [Figure (*b*) from W. G. Moffatt, G. W. Pearsall, and J. Wulff, *The Structure and Properties of Materials,* Vol. I, *Structure,* p. 51. Copyright © 1964 by John Wiley & Sons, New York. Reprinted by permission of John Wiley & Sons, Inc.]

the temperature and the external pressure. One familiar example is found in carbon: graphite is the stable polymorph at ambient conditions, whereas diamond is formed at extremely high pressures. Also, pure iron has a BCC crystal structure at room temperature, which changes to FCC iron at 912°C (1674°F). Most often a modification of the density and other physical properties accompanies a polymorphic transformation.

Ceramic Crystal Structures

Ceramic materials were discussed briefly in Chapter 1, which noted that they are inorganic and nonmetallic materials. Most ceramics are compounds between metallic and nonmetallic elements for which the interatomic bonds are either totally ionic, or predominantly ionic but having some covalent character. The term "ceramic" comes from the Greek word *keramikos,* which means "burnt stuff," indicating that desirable properties of these materials are normally achieved through a high-temperature heat treatment process called firing.

Because ceramics are composed of at least two elements, and often more, their crystal structures are generally more complex than those for metals. The atomic bonding in these materials ranges from purely ionic to totally covalent; many ceramics exhibit a combination of these two bonding types, the degree of ionic character being dependent on the electronegativities of the atoms. Table 4.2 presents the percent ionic character for several common ceramic materials; these values were determined using Equation 2.10 and the electronegativities in Figure 2.7.

Table 4.2 For Several Ceramic Materials, Percent Ionic Character of the Interatomic Bonds

Material	*Percent Ionic Character*
CaF_2	89
MgO	73
NaCl	67
Al_2O_3	63
SiO_2	51
Si_3N_4	30
ZnS	18
SiC	12

4.10 RADIUS RATIO RULES

For those ceramic materials for which the atomic bonding is predominantly ionic, the crystal structures may be thought of as being composed of electrically charged ions instead of atoms. The metallic ions, or **cations,** are positively charged, because they have given up their valence electrons to the nonmetallic ions, or **anions,** which are negatively charged. Two characteristics of the component ions in crystalline ceramic materials influence the crystal structure: the magnitude of the electrical charge on each of the component ions, and the relative sizes of the cations and anions. With regard to the first characteristic, the crystal must be electrically neutral; that is, all the cation positive charges must be balanced by an equal number of anion negative charges. The chemical formula of a compound indicates the ratio of cations to anions, or the composition that achieves this charge balance. For example, in calcium fluoride, each calcium ion has a +2 charge (Ca^{2+}), and associated with each fluorine ion is a single negative charge (F^-). Thus, there must be twice as many F^- as Ca^{2+} ions, which is reflected in the chemical formula CaF_2.

The second criterion involves the sizes or ionic radii of the cations and anions, r_C and r_A, respectively. Because the metallic elements give up electrons when ionized, cations are ordinarily smaller than anions, and, consequently, the ratio r_C/r_A is less than unity. Each cation prefers to have as many nearest-neighbor anions as possible. The anions also desire a maximum number of cation nearest neighbors.

Stable ceramic crystal structures form when those anions surrounding a cation are all in contact with that cation, as illustrated in Figure 4.10. The coordination

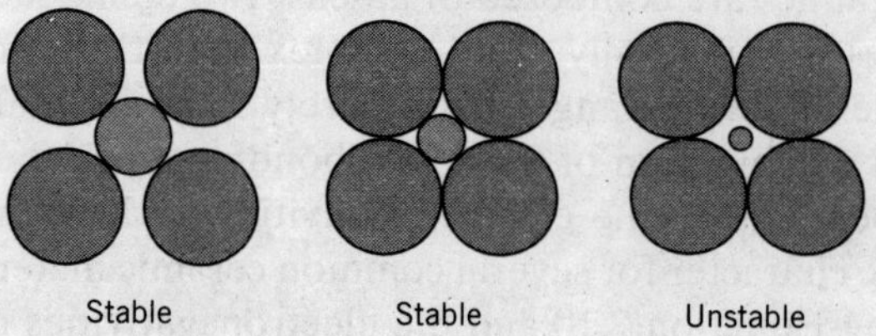

Figure 4.10 Stable and unstable anion–cation coordination configurations. Red circles represent anions; blue circles denote cations.

Table 4.3 Coordination Numbers and Geometries for Various Cation–Anion Radius Ratios (r_C/r_A)

Coordination Number	*Cation–Anion Radius Ratio*	*Coordination Geometry*
2	<0.155	
3	0.155–0.225	
4	0.225–0.414	
6	0.414–0.732	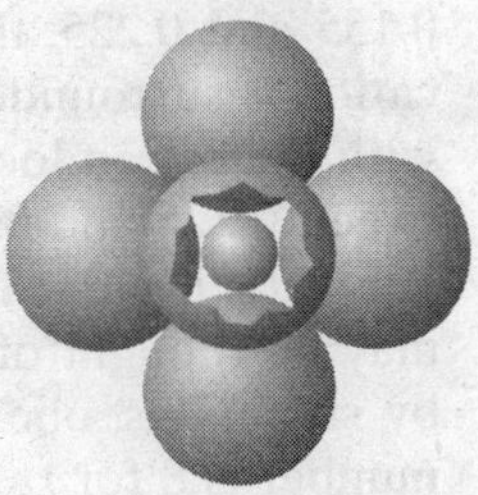
8	0.732–1.0	

Source: W. D. Kingery, H. K. Bowen, and D. R. Uhlmann, *Introduction to Ceramics,* 2nd edition. Copyright © 1976 by John Wiley & Sons, New York. Reprinted by permission of John Wiley & Sons, Inc.

number (i.e., number of anion nearest neighbors for a cation) is related to the cation–anion radius ratio. For a specific coordination number, there is a critical or minimum r_C/r_A ratio for which this cation–anion contact is established (Figure 4.10); this ratio may be determined from pure geometrical considerations (see Example Problem 4.4).

The coordination numbers and nearest-neighbor geometries for various r_C/r_A ratios are presented in Table 4.3. For r_C/r_A ratios less than 0.155, the very small

Table 4.4 Ionic Radii for Several Cations and Anions (for a Coordination Number of 6)

Cation	*Ionic Radius (nm)*	*Anion*	*Ionic Radius (nm)*
Al^{3+}	0.053	Br^-	0.196
Ba^{2+}	0.136	Cl^-	0.181
Ca^{2+}	0.100	F^-	0.133
Cs^+	0.170	I^-	0.220
Fe^{2+}	0.077	O^{2-}	0.140
Fe^{3+}	0.069	S^{2-}	0.184
K^+	0.138		
Mg^{2+}	0.072		
Mn^{2+}	0.067		
Na^+	0.102		
Ni^{2+}	0.069		
Si^{4+}	0.040		
Ti^{4+}	0.061		

cation is bonded to two anions in a linear manner. If r_C/r_A has a value between 0.155 and 0.225, the coordination number for the cation is 3. This means each cation is surrounded by three anions in the form of a planar equilateral triangle, with the cation located in the center. The coordination number is 4 for r_C/r_A between 0.225 and 0.414; the cation is located at the center of a tetrahedron, with anions at each of the four corners. For r_C/r_A between 0.414 and 0.732, the cation may be thought of as being situated at the center of an octahedron surrounded by six anions, one at each corner, as also shown in the table. The coordination number is 8 for r_C/r_A between 0.732 and 1.0, with anions at all corners of a cube and a cation positioned at the center. For a radius ratio greater than unity, the coordination number is 12. The most common coordination numbers for ceramic materials are 4, 6, and 8. Table 4.4 gives the ionic radii for several anions and cations that are common in ceramic materials.

It should be noted that the relationships between coordination number and cation–anion radii ratios (as noted in Table 4.3) are based on geometrical considerations and assuming "hard sphere" ions; therefore, these relationships are only approximate, and there are exceptions. For example, some ceramic compounds with r_C/r_A ratios greater than 0.414 in which the bonding is highly covalent (and directional), have a coordination number of 4 (instead of 6).

The size of an ion will depend on several factors. One of these is coordination number: ionic radius tends to increase as the number of nearest-neighbor ions of opposite charge increases. Ionic radii given in Table 4.4 are for a coordination number of 6. Therefore, the radius will be greater for a coordination number of 8 and less when the coordination number is 4.

In addition, the charge on an ion will influence its radius. For example, from Table 4.4, the radii for Fe^{2+} and Fe^{3+} are 0.077 and 0.069 nm, respectively, which values may be contrasted to the radius of an iron atom—viz. 0.124 nm. When an electron is removed from an atom or ion, the remaining valence electrons become more tightly bound to the nucleus, which results in a decrease in ionic radius. Conversely, ionic size increases when electrons are added to an atom or ion.

EXAMPLE PROBLEM 4.4

Computation of Minimum Cation-to-Anion Radius Ratio for a Coordination Number of 3

Show that the minimum cation-to-anion radius ratio for the coordination number 3 is 0.155.

Solution

For this coordination, the small cation is surrounded by three anions to form an equilateral triangle as shown here, triangle ABC; the centers of all four ions are coplanar.

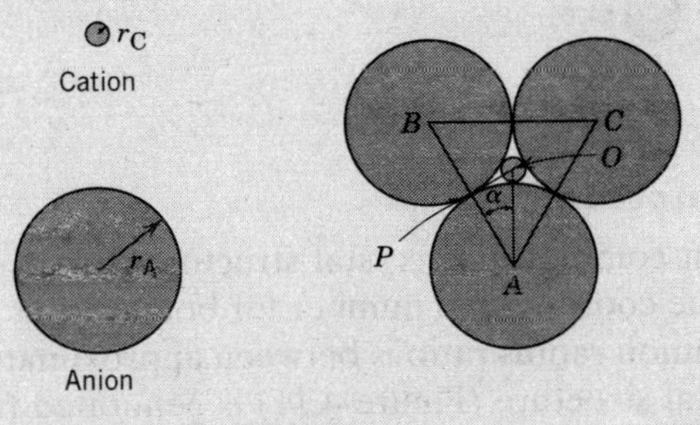

This boils down to a relatively simple plane trigonometry problem. Consideration of the right triangle APO makes it clear that the side lengths are related to the anion and cation radii r_A and r_C as

$$\overline{AP} = r_A$$

and

$$\overline{AO} = r_A + r_C$$

Furthermore, the side length ratio $\overline{AP}/\overline{AO}$ is a function of the angle α as

$$\frac{\overline{AP}}{\overline{AO}} = \cos \alpha$$

The magnitude of α is 30°, since line $\overline{AO}$ bisects the 60° angle BAC. Thus,

$$\frac{\overline{AP}}{\overline{AO}} = \frac{r_A}{r_A + r_C} = \cos 30° = \frac{\sqrt{3}}{2}$$

Solving for the cation–anion radius ratio,

$$\frac{r_C}{r_A} = \frac{1 - \sqrt{3}/2}{\sqrt{3}/2} = 0.155$$

4.11 AX-TYPE CRYSTAL STRUCTURES

Some of the common ceramic materials are those in which there are equal numbers of cations and anions. These are often referred to as AX compounds, where A denotes the cation and X the anion. There are several different crystal structures for AX compounds; each is normally named after a common material that assumes the particular structure.

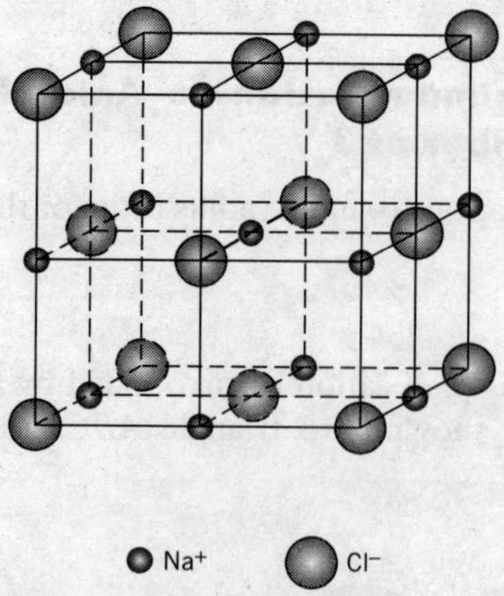

Figure 4.11 A unit cell for the rock salt, or sodium chloride (NaCl), crystal structure.

Rock Salt Structure

Perhaps the most common AX crystal structure is the *sodium chloride* (NaCl), or *rock salt,* type. The coordination number for both cations and anions is 6, and therefore the cation–anion radius ratio is between approximately 0.414 and 0.732. A unit cell for this crystal structure (Figure 4.11) is generated from an FCC arrangement of anions with one cation situated at the cube center and one at the center of each of the 12 cube edges. An equivalent crystal structure results from a face-centered arrangement of cations. Thus, the rock salt crystal structure may be thought of as two interpenetrating FCC lattices, one composed of the cations, the other of anions. Some of the common ceramic materials that form with this crystal structure are NaCl, MgO, MnS, LiF, and FeO.

Cesium Chloride Structure

Figure 4.12 shows a unit cell for the *cesium chloride* (CsCl) crystal structure; the coordination number is 8 for both ion types. The anions are located at each of the corners of a cube, whereas the cube center is a single cation. Interchange of anions with cations, and vice versa, produces the same crystal structure. This is *not* a BCC crystal structure because ions of two different kinds are involved.

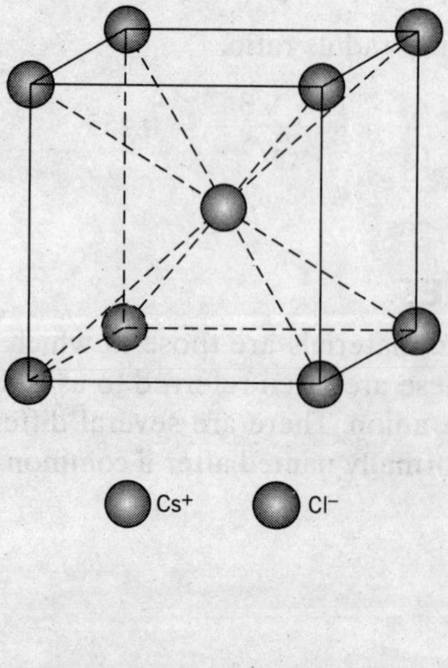

Figure 4.12 A unit cell for the cesium chloride (CsCl) crystal structure.

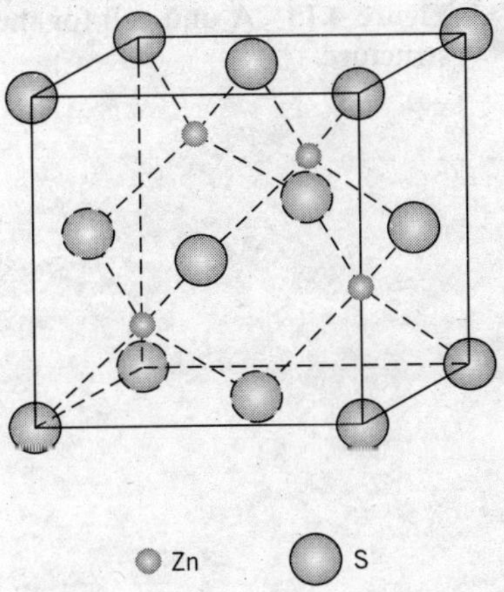

Figure 4.13 A unit cell for the zinc blende (ZnS) crystal structure.

Zinc Blende Structure

A third AX structure is one in which the coordination number is 4; that is, all ions are tetrahedrally coordinated. This is called the *zinc blende,* or *sphalerite,* structure, after the mineralogical term for zinc sulfide (ZnS). A unit cell is presented in Figure 4.13; all corner and face positions of the cubic cell are occupied by S atoms, while the Zn atoms fill interior tetrahedral positions. An equivalent structure results if Zn and S atom positions are reversed. Thus, each Zn atom is bonded to four S atoms, and vice versa. Most often the atomic bonding is highly covalent in compounds exhibiting this crystal structure (Table 4.2), which include ZnS, ZnTe, and SiC.

4.12 A_MX_P-TYPE CRYSTAL STRUCTURES

If the charges on the cations and anions are not the same, a compound can exist with the chemical formula A_mX_p, where m and/or $p \neq 1$. An example would be AX_2, for which a common crystal structure is found in *fluorite* (CaF_2). The ionic radii ratio r_C/r_A for CaF_2 is about 0.8 which, according to Table 4.3, gives a coordination number of 8. Calcium ions are positioned at the centers of cubes, with fluorine ions at the corners. The chemical formula shows that there are only half as many Ca^{2+} ions as F^- ions, and therefore the crystal structure would be similar to CsCl (Figure 4.12), except that only half the center cube positions are occupied by Ca^{2+} ions. One unit cell consists of eight cubes, as indicated in Figure 4.14. Other compounds that have this crystal structure include ZrO_2 (cubic), UO_2, PuO_2, and ThO_2.

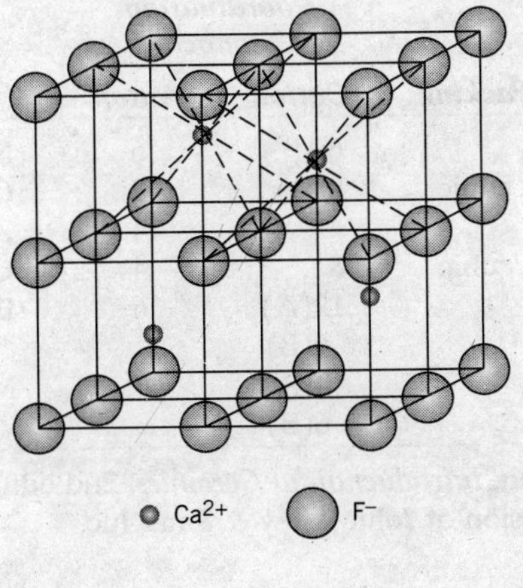

Figure 4.14 A unit cell for the fluorite (CaF_2) crystal structure.

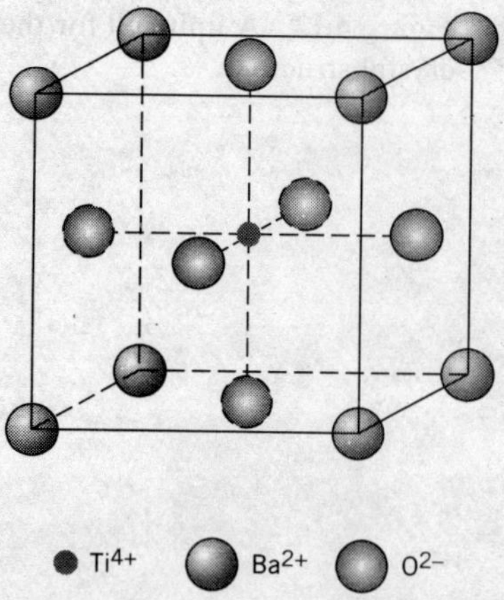

Figure 4.15 A unit cell for the perovskite crystal structure.

4.13 $A_MB_NX_P$-TYPE CRYSTAL STRUCTURES

It is also possible for ceramic compounds to have more than one type of cation; for two types of cations (represented by A and B), their chemical formula may be designated as $A_mB_nX_p$. Barium titanate ($BaTiO_3$), having both Ba^{2+} and Ti^{4+} cations, falls into this classification. This material has a *perovskite crystal structure* and rather interesting electromechanical properties to be discussed later. At temperatures above 120°C (248°F), the crystal structure is cubic. A unit cell of this structure is shown in Figure 4.15; Ba^{2+} ions are situated at all eight corners of the cube and a single Ti^{4+} is at the cube center, with O^{2-} ions located at the center of each of the six faces.

Table 4.5 summarizes the rock salt, cesium chloride, zinc blende, fluorite, and perovskite crystal structures in terms of cation–anion ratios and coordination numbers, and gives examples for each. Of course, many other ceramic crystal structures are possible.

4.14 CRYSTAL STRUCTURES FROM THE CLOSE PACKING OF ANIONS

It may be recalled (Section 4.8) that for metals, close-packed planes of atoms stacked on one another generate both FCC and HCP crystal structures. Similarly,

Table 4.5 Summary of Some Common Ceramic Crystal Structures

Structure Name	Structure Type	Anion Packing	Coordination Numbers		Examples
			Cation	Anion	
Rock salt (sodium chloride)	AX	FCC	6	6	NaCl, MgO, FeO
Cesium chloride	AX	Simple cubic	8	8	CsCl
Zinc blende (sphalerite)	AX	FCC	4	4	ZnS, SiC
Fluorite	AX_2	Simple cubic	8	4	CaF_2, UO_2, ThO_2
Perovskite	ABX_3	FCC	12(A) 6(B)	6	$BaTiO_3$, $SrZrO_3$, $SrSnO_3$
Spinel	AB_2X_4	FCC	4(A) 6(B)	4	$MgAl_2O_4$, $FeAl_2O_4$

Source: W. D. Kingery, H. K. Bowen, and D. R. Uhlmann, *Introduction to Ceramics,* 2nd edition. Copyright © 1976 by John Wiley & Sons, New York. Reprinted by permission of John Wiley & Sons, Inc.

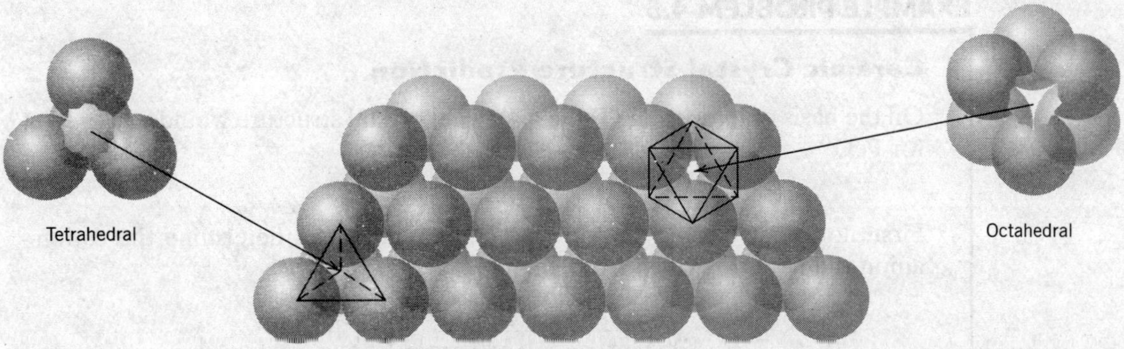

Figure 4.16 The stacking of one plane of close-packed (orange) spheres (anions) on top of another (blue spheres); the geometries of tetrahedral and octahedral positions between the planes are noted. (From W. G. Moffatt, G. W. Pearsall, and J. Wulff, *The Structure and Properties of Materials,* Vol. I, *Structure.* Copyright © 1964 by John Wiley & Sons, New York. Reprinted by permission of John Wiley & Sons, Inc.)

a number of ceramic crystal structures may be considered in terms of close-packed planes of ions, as well as unit cells. Ordinarily, the close-packed planes are composed of the large anions. As these planes are stacked atop each other, small interstitial sites are created between them in which the cations may reside.

These interstitial positions exist in two different types, as illustrated in Figure 4.16. Four atoms (three in one plane, and a single one in the adjacent plane) surround one type; this is termed a **tetrahedral position,** since straight lines drawn from the centers of the surrounding spheres form a four-sided tetrahedron. The other site type in Figure 4.16, involves six ion spheres, three in each of the two planes. Because an octahedron is produced by joining these six sphere centers, this site is called an **octahedral position.** Thus, the coordination numbers for cations filling tetrahedral and octahedral positions are 4 and 6, respectively. Furthermore, for each of these anion spheres, one octahedral and two tetrahedral positions will exist.

Ceramic crystal structures of this type depend on two factors: (1) the stacking of the close-packed anion layers (both FCC and HCP arrangements are possible, which correspond to *ABCABC* . . . and *ABABAB* . . . sequences, respectively), and (2) the manner in which the interstitial sites are filled with cations. For example, consider the rock salt crystal structure discussed above.The unit cell has cubic symmetry, and each cation (Na^+ ion) has six Cl^- ion nearest neighbors, as may be verified from Figure 4.11. That is, the Na^+ ion at the center has as nearest neighbors the six Cl^- ions that reside at the centers of each of the cube faces. The crystal structure, having cubic symmetry, may be considered in terms of an FCC array of close-packed planes of anions, and all planes are of the {111} type. The cations reside in octahedral positions because they have as nearest neighbors six anions. Furthermore, all octahedral positions are filled, since there is a single octahedral site per anion, and the ratio of anions to cations is 1:1. For this crystal structure, the relationship between the unit cell and close-packed anion plane stacking schemes is illustrated in Figure 4.17.

Other, but not all, ceramic crystal structures may be treated in a similar manner; included are the zinc blende and perovskite structures. The *spinel structure* is one of the $A_mB_nX_p$ types, which is found for magnesium aluminate or spinel ($MgAl_2O_4$).

EXAMPLE PROBLEM 4.5

Ceramic Crystal Structure Prediction

On the basis of ionic radii (Table 4.4), what crystal structure would you predict for FeO?

First, note that FeO is an AX-type compound. Next, determine the cation–anion radius ratio, which from Table 4.4 is

$$\frac{r_{Fe^{2+}}}{r_{O^{2-}}} = \frac{0.077\text{ nm}}{0.140\text{ nm}} = 0.550$$

This value lies between 0.414 and 0.732, and, therefore, from Table 4.4 the coordination number for the Fe^{2+} ion is 6; this is also the coordination number of O^{2-}, since there are equal numbers of cations and anions. The predicted crystal structure will be rock salt, which is the AX crystal structure having a coordination number of 6, as given in Table 4.5.

Concept Check 4.1

Table 4.4 gives the ionic radii for K^+ and O^{2-} as 0.138 and 0.140 nm, respectively.

(a) What would be the coordination number for each O^{2-} ion?

(b) Briefly describe the resulting crystal structure for K_2O.

(c) Explain why this is called the antifluorite structure.

[*The answer may be found in enclosed CD.*]

With this structure, the O^{2-} ions form an FCC lattice, whereas Mg^{2+} ions fill tetrahedral sites and Al^{3+} reside in octahedral positions. Magnetic ceramics, or ferrites, have a crystal structure that is a slight variant of this spinel structure, and the magnetic characteristics are affected by the occupancy of tetrahedral and octahedral positions (see Section 18.5).

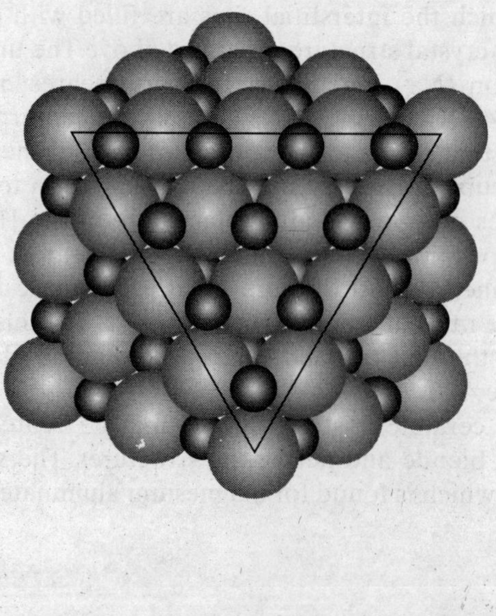

Figure 4.17 A section of the rock salt crystal structure from which a corner has been removed. The exposed plane of anions (green spheres inside the triangle) is a {111}-type plane; the cations (red spheres) occupy the interstitial octahedral positions.

4.15 CERAMIC DENSITY COMPUTATIONS

It is possible to compute the theoretical density of a crystalline ceramic material from unit cell data in a manner similar to that described in Section 4.5 for metals. In this case the density ρ may be determined using a modified form of Equation 4.5, as follows:

$$\rho = \frac{n'(\Sigma A_C + \Sigma A_A)}{V_C N_A} \tag{4.10}$$

where

n' = the number of formula units[2] within the unit cell

ΣA_C = the sum of the atomic weights of all cations in the formula unit

ΣA_A = the sum of the atomic weights of all anions in the formula unit

V_C = the unit cell volume

N_A = Avogadro's number, 6.023×10^{23} formula units/mol

EXAMPLE PROBLEM 4.6

Theoretical Density Calculation for Sodium Chloride

On the basis of crystal structure, compute the theoretical density for sodium chloride. How does this compare with its measured density?

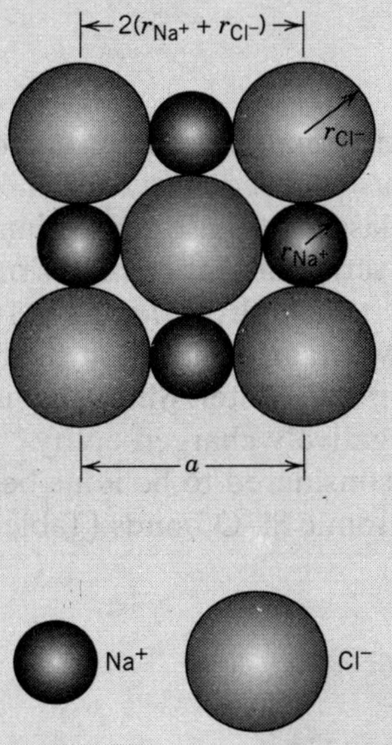

[2] By "formula unit" we mean all the ions that are included in the chemical formula unit. For example, for $BaTiO_3$, a formula unit consists of one barium ion, a titanium ion, and three oxygen ions.

Solution

The theoretical density may be determined using Equation 4.10 where n', the number of NaCl units per unit cell, is 4 because both sodium and chloride ions form FCC lattices. Furthermore,

$$\Sigma A_C = A_{Na} = 22.99 \text{ g/mol}$$
$$\Sigma A_A = A_{Cl} = 35.45 \text{ g/mol}$$

Since the unit cell is cubic, $V_C = a^3$, a being the unit cell edge length. For the face of the cubic unit cell shown below,

$$a = 2r_{Na^+} + 2r_{Cl^-}$$

r_{Na^+} and r_{Cl^-} being the sodium and chlorine ionic radii, given in Table 4.4 as 0.102 and 0.181 nm, respectively.
Thus,

$$V_C = a^3 = (2r_{Na^+} + 2r_{Cl^-})^3$$

And, finally,

$$\rho = \frac{n'(A_{Na} + A_{Cl})}{(2r_{Na^+} + 2r_{Cl^-})^3 N_A}$$
$$= \frac{4(22.99 + 35.45)}{[2(0.102 \times 10^{-7}) + 2(0.181 \times 10^{-7})]^3(6.023 \times 10^{23})}$$
$$= 2.14 \text{ g/cm}^3$$

This result compares very favorably with the experimental value of 2.16 g/cm^3.

4.16 SILICATE CERAMICS

Silicates are materials composed primarily of silicon and oxygen, the two most abundant elements in the earth's crust; consequently, the bulk of soils, rocks, clays, and sand come under the silicate classification. Rather than characterizing the crystal structures of these materials in terms of unit cells, it is more convenient to use various arrangements of an SiO_4^{4-} tetrahedron (Figure 4.18). Each atom of silicon is bonded to four oxygen atoms, which are situated at the corners of the tetrahedron; the silicon atom is positioned at the center. Since this is the basic unit of the silicates, it is often treated as a negatively charged entity.

Often the silicates are not considered to be ionic because there is a significant covalent character to the interatomic Si–O bonds (Table 4.2), which are directional

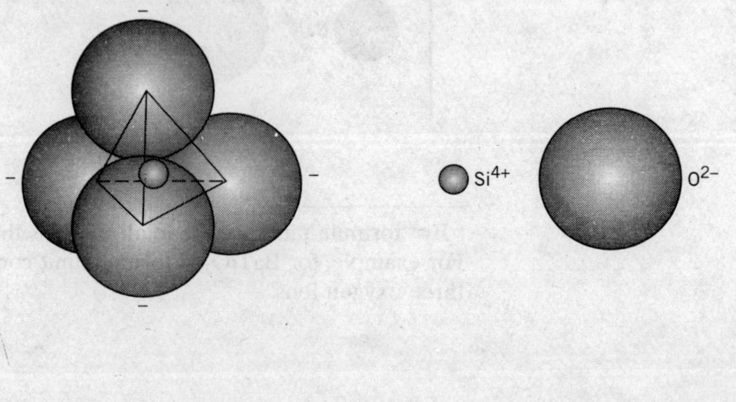

Figure 4.18 A silicon–oxygen (SiO_4^{4-}) tetrahedron.

and relatively strong. Regardless of the character of the Si–O bond, there is a −4 charge associated with every SiO_4^{4-} tetrahedron, since each of the four oxygen atoms requires an extra electron to achieve a stable electronic structure. Various silicate structures arise from the different ways in which the SiO_4^{4-} units can be combined into one-, two-, and three-dimensional arrangements.

Silica

Chemically, the most simple silicate material is silicon dioxide, or silica (SiO_2). Structurally, it is a three-dimensional network that is generated when every corner oxygen atom in each tetrahedron is shared by adjacent tetrahedra. Thus, the material is electrically neutral and all atoms have stable electronic structures. Under these circumstances the ratio of Si to O atoms is 1:2, as indicated by the chemical formula.

If these tetrahedra are arrayed in a regular and ordered manner, a crystalline structure is formed. There are three primary polymorphic crystalline forms of silica: quartz, cristobalite (Figure 4.19), and tridymite. Their structures are relatively complicated, and comparatively open; that is, the atoms are not closely packed together. As a consequence, these crystalline silicas have relatively low densities; for example, at room temperature quartz has a density of only 2.65 g/cm^3. The strength of the Si–O interatomic bonds is reflected in a relatively high melting temperature, 1710°C (3110°F).

Silica Glasses

Silica can also be made to exist as a noncrystalline solid or glass, having a high degree of atomic randomness, which is characteristic of the liquid; such a material is called *fused silica,* or *vitreous silica.* As with crystalline silica, the SiO_4^{4-} tetrahedron is the basic unit; beyond this structure, considerable disorder exists. The structures for crystalline and noncrystalline silica are compared schematically in Figure 3.10. Other oxides (e.g., B_2O_3 and GeO_2) may also form glassy structures (and polyhedral oxide structures similar to that shown in Figure 4.18); these materials, as well as SiO_2, are termed *network formers.*

The common inorganic glasses that are used for containers, windows, and so on are silica glasses to which have been added other oxides such as CaO and Na_2O. These oxides do not form polyhedral networks. Rather, their cations are incorporated within and modify the SiO_4^{4-} network; for this reason, these oxide additives are termed *network modifiers.* For example, Figure 4.20 is a schematic representation of the structure of a sodium–silicate glass. Still other oxides, such

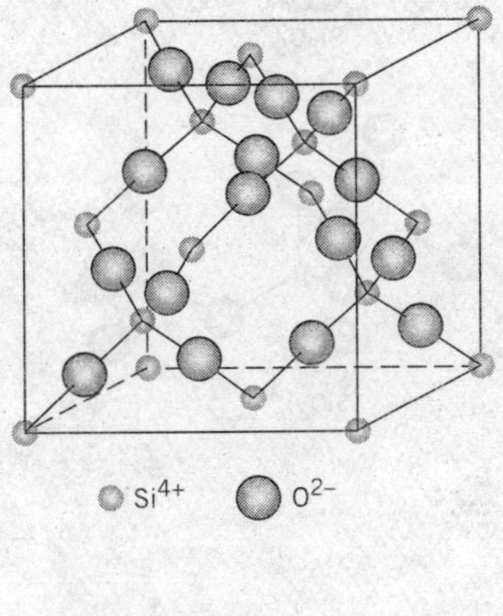

Figure 4.19 The arrangement of silicon and oxygen atoms in a unit cell of cristobalite, a polymorph of SiO_2.

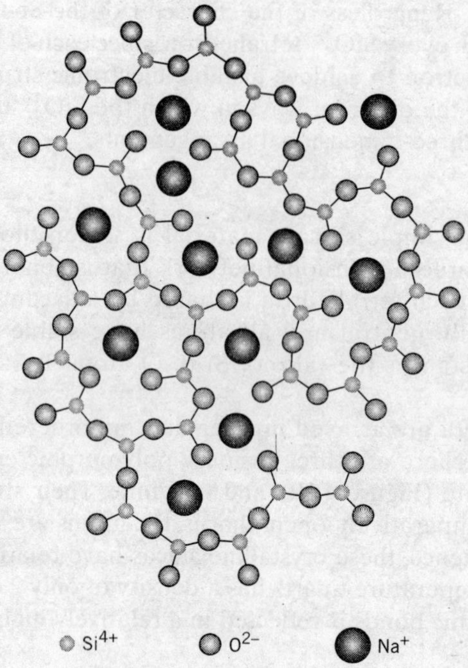

Figure 4.20 Schematic representation of ion positions in a sodium–silicate glass.

as TiO_2 and Al_2O_3, while not network formers, substitute for silicon and become part of and stabilize the network; these are called *intermediates.* From a practical perspective, the addition of these modifiers and intermediates lowers the melting point and viscosity of a glass, and makes it easier to form at lower temperatures (Section 12.14).

The Silicates

For the various silicate minerals, one, two, or three of the corner oxygen atoms of the SiO_4^{4-} tetrahedra are shared by other tetrahedra to form some rather complex structures. Some of these, represented in Figure 4.21, have formulas SiO_4^{4-},

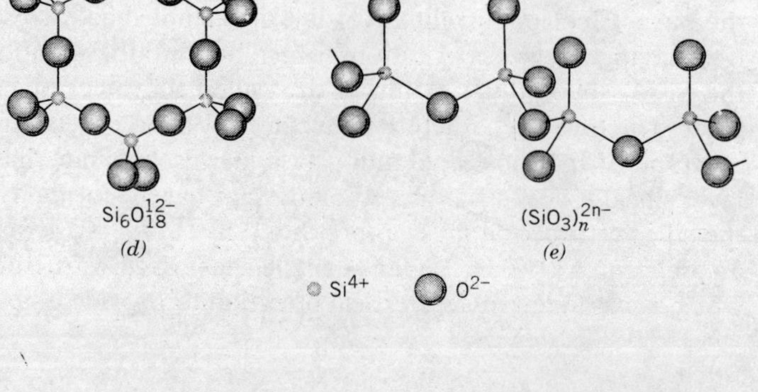

Figure 4.21 Five silicate ion structures formed from SiO_4^{4-} tetrahedra.

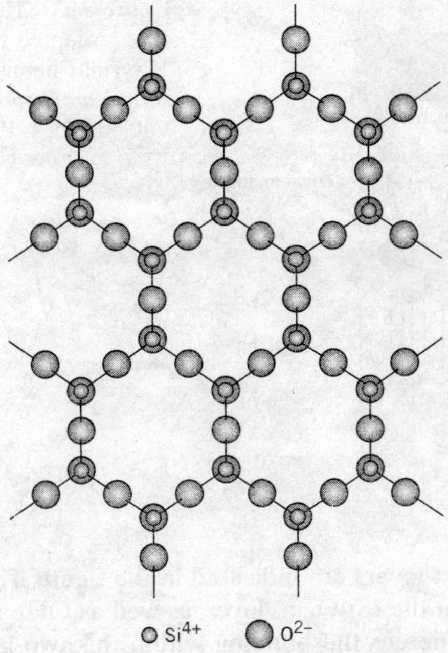

Figure 4.22 Schematic representation of the two-dimensional silicate sheet structure having a repeat unit formula of $(Si_2O_5)^{2-}$.

$Si_2O_7^{6-}$, $Si_3O_9^{6-}$, and so on; single-chain structures are also possible, as in Figure 4.21*e*. Positively charged cations such as Ca^{2+}, Mg^{2+}, and Al^{3+} serve two roles. First, they compensate the negative charges from the SiO_4^{4-} units so that charge neutrality is achieved; and second, these cations ionically bond the SiO_4^{4-} tetrahedra together.

Simple Silicates

Of these silicates, the most structurally simple ones involve isolated tetrahedra (Figure 4.21*a*). For example, forsterite (Mg_2SiO_4) has the equivalent of two Mg^{2+} ions associated with each tetrahedron in such a way that every Mg^{2+} ion has six oxygen nearest neighbors.

The $Si_2O_7^{6-}$ ion is formed when two tetrahedra share a common oxygen atom (Figure 4.21*b*). Akermanite ($Ca_2MgSi_2O_7$) is a mineral having the equivalent of two Ca^{2+} ions and one Mg^{2+} ion bonded to each $Si_2O_7^{6-}$ unit.

Layered Silicates

A two-dimensional sheet or layered structure can also be produced by the sharing of three oxygen ions in each of the tetrahedra (Figure 4.22); for this structure the repeating unit formula may be represented by $(Si_2O_5)^{2-}$. The net negative charge is associated with the unbonded oxygen atoms projecting out of the plane of the page. Electroneutrality is ordinarily established by a second planar sheet structure having an excess of cations, which bond to these unbonded oxygen atoms from the Si_2O_5 sheet. Such materials are called the sheet or layered silicates, and their basic structure is characteristic of the clays and other minerals.

One of the most common clay minerals, kaolinite, has a relatively simple two-layer silicate sheet structure. Kaolinite clay has the formula $Al_2(Si_2O_5)(OH)_4$ in which the silica tetrahedral layer, represented by $(Si_2O_5)^{2-}$, is made electrically neutral by an adjacent $Al_2(OH)_4^{2+}$ layer. A single sheet of this structure is shown in Figure 4.23, which is exploded in the vertical direction to provide a better perspective of the ion

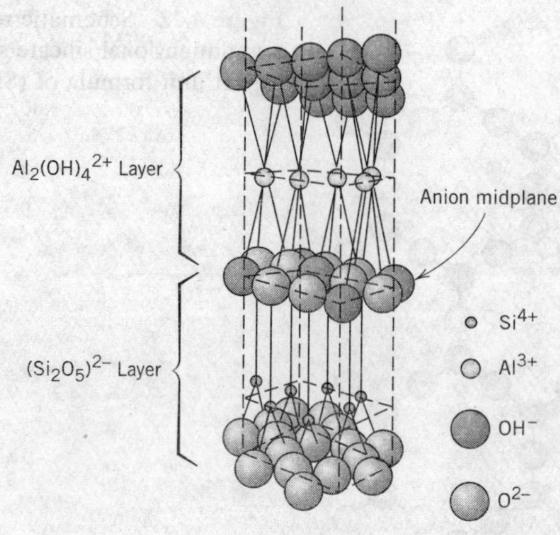

Figure 4.23 The structure of kaolinite clay. (Adapted from W. E. Hauth, "Crystal Chemistry of Ceramics," *American Ceramic Society Bulletin,* Vol. 30, No. 4, 1951, p. 140.)

positions; the two distinct layers are indicated in the figure. The midplane of anions consists of O^{2-} ions from the $(Si_2O_5)^{2-}$ layer, as well as OH^- ions that are a part of the $Al_2(OH)_4^{2+}$ layer. Whereas the bonding within this two-layered sheet is strong and intermediate ionic-covalent, adjacent sheets are only loosely bound to one another by weak van der Waals forces.

A crystal of kaolinite is made of a series of these double layers or sheets stacked parallel to each other, which form small flat plates typically less than 1 μm in diameter and nearly hexagonal. The chapter-opening photograph for this chapter is an electron micrograph of kaolinite crystals at a high magnification, showing the hexagonal crystal plates some of which are piled one on top of the other.

These silicate sheet structures are not confined to the clays; other minerals also in this group are talc $[Mg_3(Si_2O_5)_2(OH)_2]$ and the micas [e.g., muscovite, $KAl_3Si_3O_{10}(OH)_2$], which are important ceramic raw materials. As might be deduced from the chemical formulas, the structures for some silicates are among the most complex of all the inorganic materials.

4.17 CARBON

Carbon is an element that exists in various polymorphic forms, as well as in the amorphous state. This group of materials does not really fall within any one of the traditional metal, ceramic, polymer classification schemes. However, we choose to discuss these materials in this chapter since graphite, one of the polymorphic forms, is sometimes classified as a ceramic, and, in addition, the crystal structure of diamond, another polymorph, is similar to that of zinc blende, discussed in Section 4.11. Treatment of the carbon materials will focus on the structures and characteristics of graphite, diamond, the fullerenes, and carbon nanotubes, and, in addition, on their current and potential uses.

Diamond

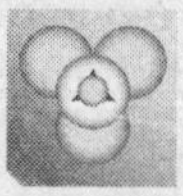

Diamond is a metastable carbon polymorph at room temperature and atmospheric pressure. Its crystal structure is a variant of the zinc blende, in which carbon atoms occupy all positions (both Zn and S), as indicated in the unit cell shown in Figure 4.24. Thus, each carbon bonds to four other carbons, and these bonds are totally covalent. This is appropriately called the *diamond cubic* crystal structure, which is also found for other Group IVA elements in the periodic table [e.g., germanium, silicon, and gray tin, below 13°C (55°F)].

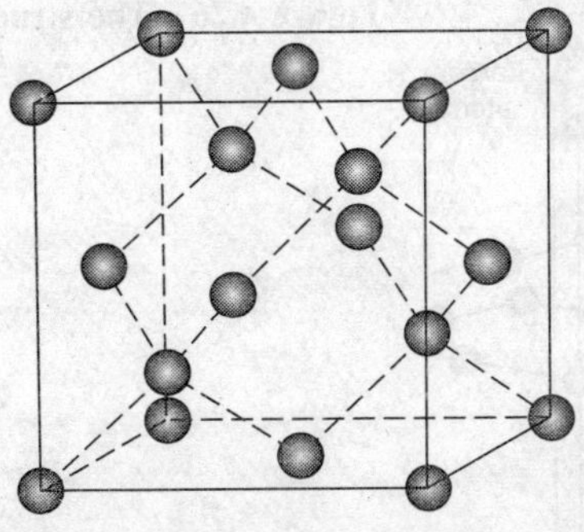

Figure 4.24 A unit cell for the diamond cubic crystal structure.

The physical properties of diamond make it an extremely attractive material. It is extremely hard (the hardest known material) and has a very low electrical conductivity; these characteristics are due to its crystal structure and the strong interatomic covalent bonds. Furthermore, it has an unusually high thermal conductivity for a nonmetallic material, is optically transparent in the visible and infrared regions of the electromagnetic spectrum, and has a high index of refraction. Relatively large diamond single crystals are used as gem stones. Industrially, diamonds are utilized to grind or cut other softer materials (Section 12.6). Techniques to produce synthetic diamonds have been developed, beginning in the mid-1950s, that have been refined to the degree that today a large proportion of the industrial-quality materials are man-made, in addition to some of those of gem quality.

Over the last several years, diamond in the form of thin films has been produced. Film growth techniques involve vapor-phase chemical reactions followed by the film deposition. Maximum film thicknesses are on the order of a millimeter. Furthermore, none of the films yet produced has the long-range crystalline regularity of natural diamond. The diamond is polycrystalline and may consist of very small and/or relatively large grains; in addition, amorphous carbon and graphite may be present. A scanning electron micrograph of the surface of a diamond thin film is shown in Figure 4.25. The

Figure 4.25 Scanning electron micrograph of a diamond thin film in which is shown numerous multifaceted microcrystals. 1000×. (Photograph courtesy of the Norton Company.)

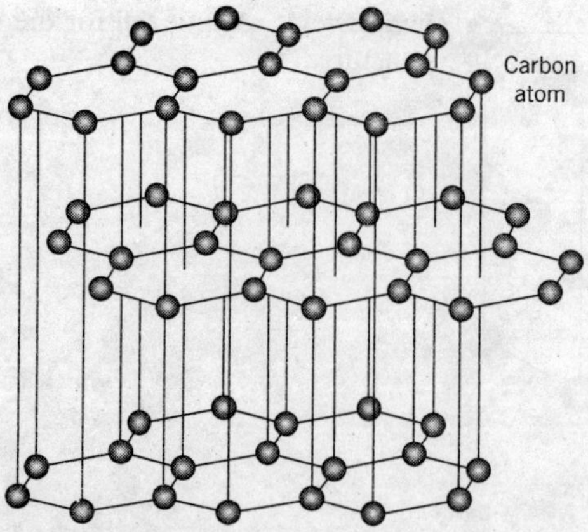

Figure 4.26 The structure of graphite.

mechanical, electrical, and optical properties of diamond films approach those of the bulk diamond material. These desirable properties have been and will continue to be exploited so as to create new and better products. For example, the surfaces of drills, dies, bearings, knives, and other tools have been coated with diamond films to increase surface hardness; some lenses and radomes have been made stronger while remaining transparent by the application of diamond coatings; coatings have also been applied to loudspeaker tweeters and to high-precision micrometers. Potential applications for these films include application to the surface of machine components such as gears, to optical recording heads and disks, and as substrates for semiconductor devices.

Graphite

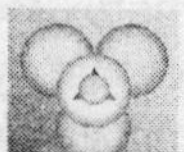

Another polymorph of carbon is graphite; it has a crystal structure (Figure 4.26) distinctly different from that of diamond and is also more stable than diamond at ambient temperature and pressure. The graphite structure is composed of layers of hexagonally arranged carbon atoms; within the layers, each carbon atom is bonded to three coplanar neighbor atoms by strong covalent bonds. The fourth bonding electron participates in a weak van der Waals type of bond between the layers. As a consequence of these weak interplanar bonds, interplanar cleavage is facile, which gives rise to the excellent lubricative properties of graphite. Also, the electrical conductivity is relatively high in crystallographic directions parallel to the hexagonal sheets.

Other desirable properties of graphite include the following: high strength and good chemical stability at elevated temperatures and in nonoxidizing atmospheres, high thermal conductivity, low coefficient of thermal expansion and high resistance to thermal shock, high adsorption of gases, and good machinability. Graphite is commonly used as heating elements for electric furnaces, as electrodes for arc welding, in metallurgical crucibles, in casting molds for metal alloys and ceramics, for high-temperature refractories and insulations, in rocket nozzles, in chemical reactor vessels, for electrical contacts, brushes and resistors, as electrodes in batteries, and in air purification devices.

Fullerenes

Another polymorphic form of carbon was discovered in 1985. It exists in discrete molecular form and consists of a hollow spherical cluster of sixty carbon atoms; a single molecule is denoted by C_{60}. Each molecule is composed of groups of carbon

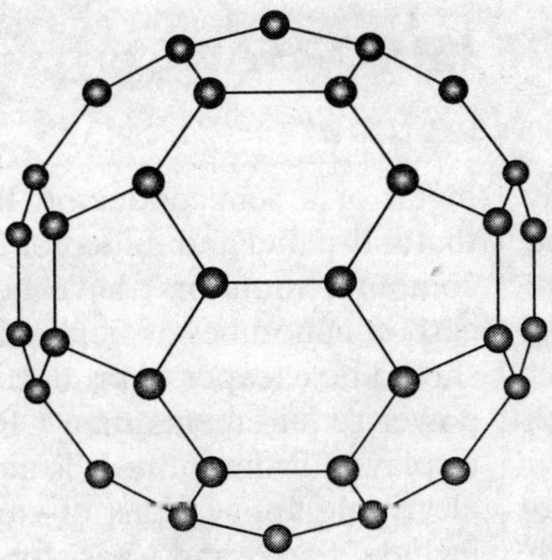

Figure 4.27 The structure of a C_{60} molecule.

atoms that are bonded to one another to form both hexagon (six-carbon atom) and pentagon (five-carbon atom) geometrical configurations. One such molecule, shown in Figure 4.27, is found to consist of 20 hexagons and 12 pentagons, which are arrayed such that no two pentagons share a common side; the molecular surface thus exhibits the symmetry of a soccer ball. The material composed of C_{60} molecules is known as *buckminsterfullerene,* named in honor of R. Buckminster Fuller, who invented the geodesic dome; each C_{60} is simply a molecular replica of such a dome-which is often referred to as "buckyball" for short. The term *fullerene* is used to denote the class of materials that are composed of this type of molecule.

Diamond and graphite are what may be termed *network solids,* in that all of the carbon atoms form primary bonds with adjacent atoms throughout the entirety of the solid. By way of contrast, the carbon atoms in buckminsterfullerene bond together so as to form these spherical molecules. In the solid state, the C_{60} units form a crystalline structure and pack together in a face-centered cubic array.

As a pure crystalline solid, this material is electrically insulating. However, with proper impurity additions, it can be made highly conductive and semiconductive.

Polymer Structures

4.18 POLYMER CRYSTALLINITY

The crystalline state may exist in polymeric materials. However, since it involves molecules instead of just atoms or ions, as with metals and ceramics, the atomic arrangements will be more complex for polymers. We think of **polymer crystallinity** as the packing of molecular chains to produce an ordered atomic array. Crystal structures may be specified in terms of unit cells, which are often quite complex. For example, Figure 4.29 shows the unit cell for polyethylene and its relationship to the molecular chain structure; this unit cell has orthorhombic geometry (Table 3.2). Of course, the chain molecules also extend beyond the unit cell shown in the figure.

Molecular substances having small molecules (e.g., water and methane) are normally either totally crystalline (as solids) or totally amorphous (as liquids). As a consequence of their size and often complexity, polymer molecules are often only partially crystalline (or semicrystalline), having crystalline regions dispersed within

MATERIALS OF IMPORTANCE

Carbon Nanotubes

Another molecular form of carbon has recently been discovered that has some unique and technologically promising properties. Its structure consists of a single sheet of graphite, rolled into a tube, both ends of which are capped with C_{60} fullerene hemispheres. This *carbon nanotube* is represented schematically in Figure 4.28. The *nano* prefix denotes that tube diameters are on the order of a nanometer (i.e., 100 nm or less). Each nanotube is a single molecule composed of millions of atoms; the length of this molecule is much greater (on the order of thousands of times greater) than its diameter. Multiple-walled carbon nanotubes consisting of concentric cylinders have also been found to exist.

These nanotubes are extremely strong and stiff, and relatively ductile. For single-walled nanotubes, tensile strengths range between 50 and 200 GPa (approximately an order of magnitude greater than for carbon fibers); this is the strongest known material. Elastic modulus values are on the order of one tetrapascal [TPa (1 TPa = 10^3 GPa)], with fracture strains between about 5% and 20%. Furthermore, nanotubes have relatively low densities. On the basis of these properties, the carbon nanotube has been termed the "ultimate fiber" and is extremely promising as a reinforcement in composite materials.

Carbon nanotubes also have unique and structure-sensitive electrical characteristics. Depending on the orientation of the hexagonal units in the graphene plane (i.e., tube wall) with the tube axis, the nanotube may behave electrically as either a metal or a semiconductor. It has been reported that flat-panel and full-color displays (i.e., TV and computer monitors) have been fabricated using carbon nanotubes as field emitters; these displays should be cheaper to produce and will have lower power requirements than CRT and liquid crystal displays. Furthermore, it is anticipated that future electronic applications of carbon nanotubes will include diodes and transistors.

An atomically resolved image of a carbon nanotube that was generated using a scanning tunneling microscope (a type of scanning probe microscope, Section 5.12). Note the dimensional scales (in the nanometer range) along the sides of the micrograph. (Micrograph courtesy of Vladimir K. Nevolin, Moscow Institute of Electronic Engineering.)

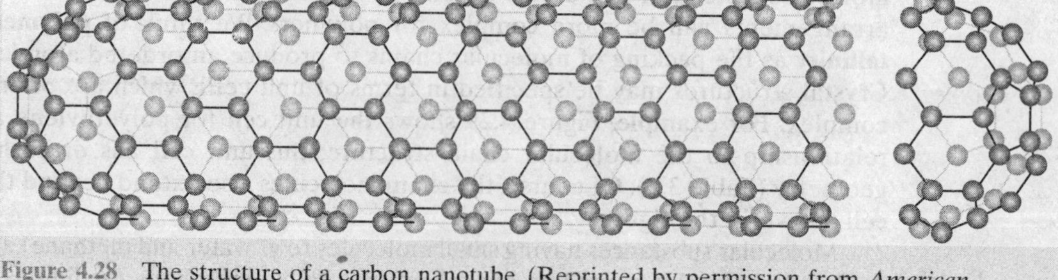

Figure 4.28 The structure of a carbon nanotube. (Reprinted by permission from *American Scientist*, magazine of Sigma Xi, The Scientific Research Society. Illustration by Aaron Cox/*American Scientist*.)

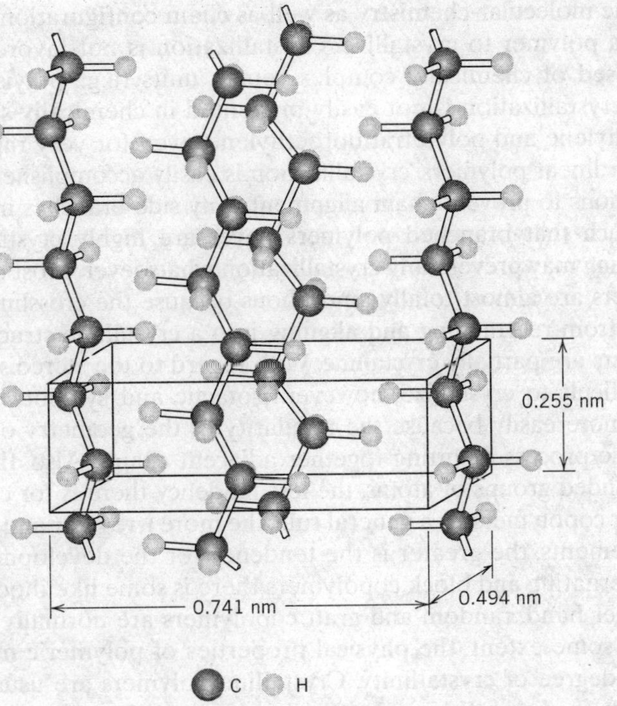

Figure 4.29 Arrangement of molecular chains in a unit cell for polyethylene. (Adapted from C. W. Bunn, *Chemical Crystallography,* Oxford University Press, Oxford, 1945, p. 233.)

the remaining amorphous material. Any chain disorder or misalignment will result in an amorphous region, a condition that is fairly common, since twisting, kinking, and coiling of the chains prevent the strict ordering of every segment of every chain. Other structural effects are also influential in determining the extent of crystallinity, as discussed below.

The degree of crystallinity may range from completely amorphous to almost entirely (up to about 95%) crystalline; in contrast, metal specimens are almost always entirely crystalline, whereas many ceramics are either totally crystalline or totally noncrystalline. Semicrystalline polymers are, in a sense, analogous to two-phase metal alloys, discussed previously.

The density of a crystalline polymer will be greater than an amorphous one of the same material and molecular weight, since the chains are more closely packed together for the crystalline structure. The degree of crystallinity by weight may be determined from accurate density measurements, according to

$$\%\,\text{crystallinity} = \frac{\rho_c(\rho_s - \rho_a)}{\rho_s(\rho_c - \rho_a)} \times 100 \tag{4.11}$$

where ρ_s is the density of a specimen for which the percent crystallinity is to be determined, ρ_a is the density of the totally amorphous polymer, and ρ_c is the density of the perfectly crystalline polymer. The values of ρ_a and ρ_c must be measured by other experimental means.

The degree of crystallinity of a polymer depends on the rate of cooling during solidification as well as on the chain configuration. During crystallization upon cooling through the melting temperature, the chains, which are highly random and entangled in the viscous liquid, must assume an ordered configuration. For this to occur, sufficient time must be allowed for the chains to move and align themselves.

The molecular chemistry as well as chain configuration also influence the ability of a polymer to crystallize. Crystallization is not favored in polymers that are composed of chemically complex repeat units (e.g., polyisoprene). On the other hand, crystallization is not easily prevented in chemically simple polymers such as polyethylene and polytetrafluoroethylene, even for very rapid cooling rates.

For linear polymers, crystallization is easily accomplished because there are few restrictions to prevent chain alignment. Any side branches interfere with crystallization, such that branched polymers never are highly crystalline; in fact, excessive branching may prevent any crystallization whatsoever. Most network and crosslinked polymers are almost totally amorphous because the crosslinks prevent the polymer chains from rearranging and aligning into a crystalline structure. A few crosslinked polymers are partially crystalline. With regard to the stereoisomers, atactic polymers are difficult to crystallize; however, isotactic and syndiotactic polymers crystallize much more easily because the regularity of the geometry of the side groups facilitates the process of fitting together adjacent chains. Also, the bulkier or larger the side-bonded groups of atoms, the less tendency there is for crystallization.

For copolymers, as a general rule, the more irregular and random the repeat unit arrangements, the greater is the tendency for the development of noncrystallinity. For alternating and block copolymers there is some likelihood of crystallization. On the other hand, random and graft copolymers are normally amorphous.

To some extent, the physical properties of polymeric materials are influenced by the degree of crystallinity. Crystalline polymers are usually stronger and more resistant to dissolution and softening by heat. Some of these properties are discussed in subsequent chapters.

Concept Check 4.2

(a) Compare the crystalline state in metals and polymers. **(b)** Compare the noncrystalline state as it applies to polymers and ceramic glasses.

[*The answer may be found in enclosed CD.*]

EXAMPLE PROBLEM 4.7

Computations of the Density and Percent Crystallinity of Polyethylene

(a) Compute the density of totally crystalline polyethylene. The orthorhombic unit cell for polyethylene is shown in Figure 4.29; also, the equivalent of two ethylene repeat units is contained within each unit cell.

(b) Using the answer to part (a), calculate the percent crystallinity of a branched polyethylene that has a density of 0.925 g/cm^3. The density for the totally amorphous material is 0.870 g/cm^3.

Solution

(a) Equation 4.5, utilized in this chapter to determine densities for metals, also applies to polymeric materials and is used to solve this problem. It takes the same form—viz.

$$\rho = \frac{nA}{V_C N_A}$$

where n represents the number of repeat units within the unit cell (for polyethylene $n = 2$), and A is the repeat unit molecular weight, which for polyethylene is

$$A = 2(A_C) + 4(A_H)$$
$$= (2)(12.01 \text{ g/mol}) + (4)(1.008 \text{ g/mol}) = 28.05 \text{ g/mol}$$

Also, V_C is the unit cell volume, which is just the product of the three unit cell edge lengths in Figure 14.10; or

$$V_C = (0.741 \text{ nm})(0.494 \text{ nm})(0.255 \text{ nm})$$
$$= (7.41 \times 10^{-8} \text{ cm})(4.94 \times 10^{-8} \text{ cm})(2.55 \times 10^{-8} \text{ cm})$$
$$= 9.33 \times 10^{-23} \text{ cm}^{-3}\text{/unit cell}$$

Now, substitution into Equation 4.5, of this value, values for n and A cited above, as well as N_A, leads to

$$\rho = \frac{nA}{V_C N_A}$$
$$= \frac{(2 \text{ repeat units/unit cell})(28.05 \text{ g/mol})}{(9.33 \times 10^{-23} \text{ cm}^{-3}\text{/unit cell})(6.023 \times 10^{23} \text{ repeat units/mol})}$$
$$= 0.998 \text{ g/cm}^3$$

(b) We now utilize Equation 4.11 to calculate the percent crystallinity of the branched polyethylene with $\rho_c = 0.998$ g/cm^3, $\rho_a = 0.870$ g/cm^3, and $\rho_s = 0.925$ g/cm^3. Thus,

$$\% \text{ crystallinity} = \frac{\rho_c(\rho_s - \rho_a)}{\rho_s(\rho_c - \rho_a)} \times 100$$
$$= \frac{0.998 \text{ g/cm}^3 \, (0.925 \text{ g/cm}^3 - 0.870 \text{ g/cm}^3)}{0.925 \text{ g/cm}^3 \, (0.998 \text{ g/cm}^3 - 0.870 \text{ g/cm}^3)} \times 100$$
$$= 46.4\%$$

4.19 POLYMER CRYSTALS

It has been proposed that a semicrystalline polymer consists of small crystalline regions (**crystallites**), each having a precise alignment, which are interspersed with amorphous regions composed of randomly oriented molecules. The structure of the crystalline regions may be deduced by examination of polymer single crystals, which may be grown from dilute solutions. These crystals are regularly shaped, thin platelets (or lamellae), approximately 10 to 20 nm thick, and on the order of 10 μm long. Frequently, these platelets will form a multilayered structure, like that shown in the electron micrograph of a single crystal of polyethylene, Figure 4.30. The molecular chains within each platelet fold back and forth on themselves, with folds occurring at the faces; this structure, aptly termed the **chain-folded model,** is illustrated schematically in Figure 4.31. Each platelet will consist of a number of molecules; however, the average chain length will be much greater than the thickness of the platelet.

Figure 4.30 Electron micrograph of a polyethylene single crystal. 20,000×. [From A. Keller, R. H. Doremus, B. W. Roberts, and D. Turnbull (Editors), *Growth and Perfection of Crystals.* General Electric Company and John Wiley & Sons, Inc., 1958, p. 498.]

Many bulk polymers that are crystallized from a melt are semicrystalline and form a **spherulite** structure. As implied by the name, each spherulite may grow to be roughly spherical in shape; one of them, as found in natural rubber, is shown in the transmission electron micrograph, the chapter-opening photograph for this chapter. The spherulite consists of an aggregate of ribbon-like chain-folded crystallites (lamellae) approximately 10 nm thick that radiate outward from a single nucleation site in the center. In this electron micrograph, these lamellae appear as thin white lines. The detailed structure of a spherulite is illustrated schematically in Figure 4.32. Shown here are the individual chain-folded lamellar crystals that are separated by amorphous material. Tie-chain molecules that act as connecting links between adjacent lamellae pass through these amorphous regions.

As the crystallization of a spherulitic structure nears completion, the extremities of adjacent spherulites begin to impinge on one another, forming more or less planar boundaries; prior to this time, they maintain their spherical shape. These boundaries are evident in Figure 4.33, which is a photomicrograph of polyethylene using cross-polarized light. A characteristic Maltese cross pattern appears within each spherulite. The bands or rings in the spherulite image result from twisting of the lamellar crystals as they extend like ribbons from the center.

Spherulites are considered to be the polymer analogue of grains in polycrystalline metals and ceramics. However, as discussed above, each spherulite is really composed of many different lamellar crystals and, in addition, some amorphous material. Polyethylene, polypropylene, poly(vinyl chloride), polytetrafluoroethylene, and nylon form a spherulitic structure when they crystallize from a melt.

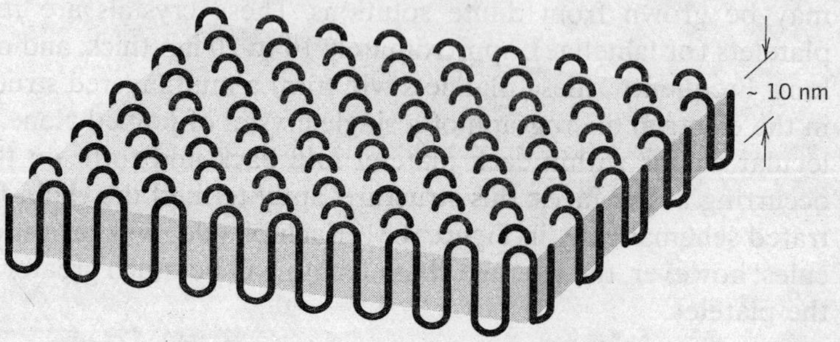

Figure 4.31 The chain-folded structure for a plate-shaped polymer crystallite.

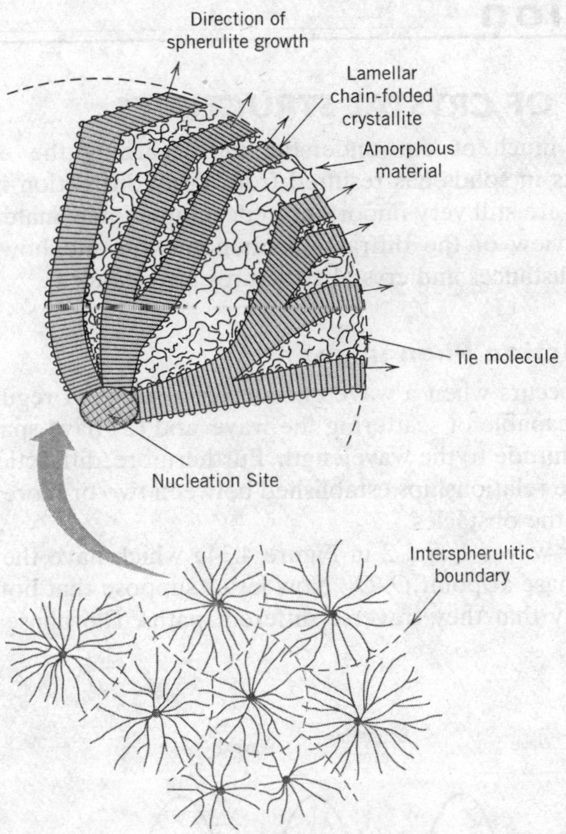

Figure 4.32 Schematic representation of the detailed structure of a spherulite.

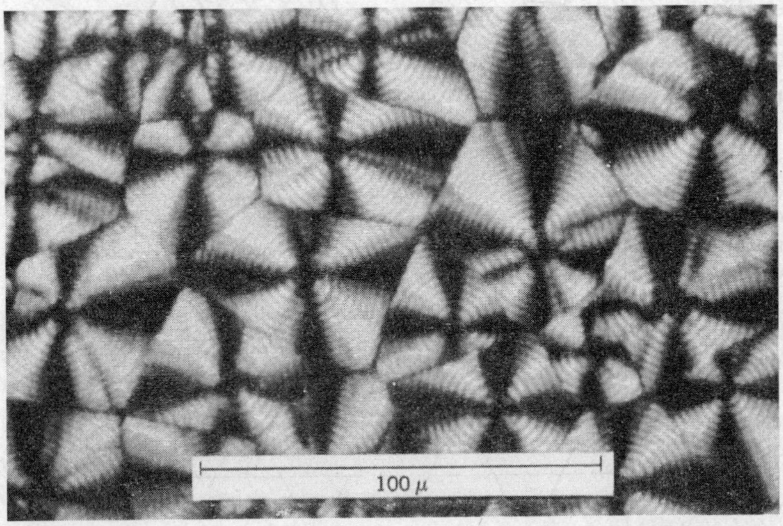

Figure 4.33 A transmission photomicrograph (using cross-polarized light) showing the spherulite structure of polyethylene. Linear boundaries form between adjacent spherulites, and within each spherulite appears a Maltese cross. 525×. (Courtesy F. P. Price, General Electric Company.)

X-Ray Diffraction

4.20 DETERMINATION OF CRYSTAL STRUCTURES

Historically, much of our understanding regarding the atomic and molecular arrangements in solids has resulted from x-ray diffraction investigations; furthermore, x-rays are still very important in developing new materials. We will now give a brief overview of the diffraction phenomenon and how, using x-rays, atomic interplanar distances and crystal structures are deduced.

The Diffraction Phenomenon

Diffraction occurs when a wave encounters a series of regularly spaced obstacles that (1) are capable of scattering the wave, and (2) have spacings that are comparable in magnitude to the wavelength. Furthermore, diffraction is a consequence of specific phase relationships established between two or more waves that have been scattered by the obstacles.

Consider waves 1 and 2 in Figure 4.34*a* which have the same wavelength (λ) and are in phase at point O–O'. Now let us suppose that both waves are scattered in such a way that they traverse different paths. The phase relationship between

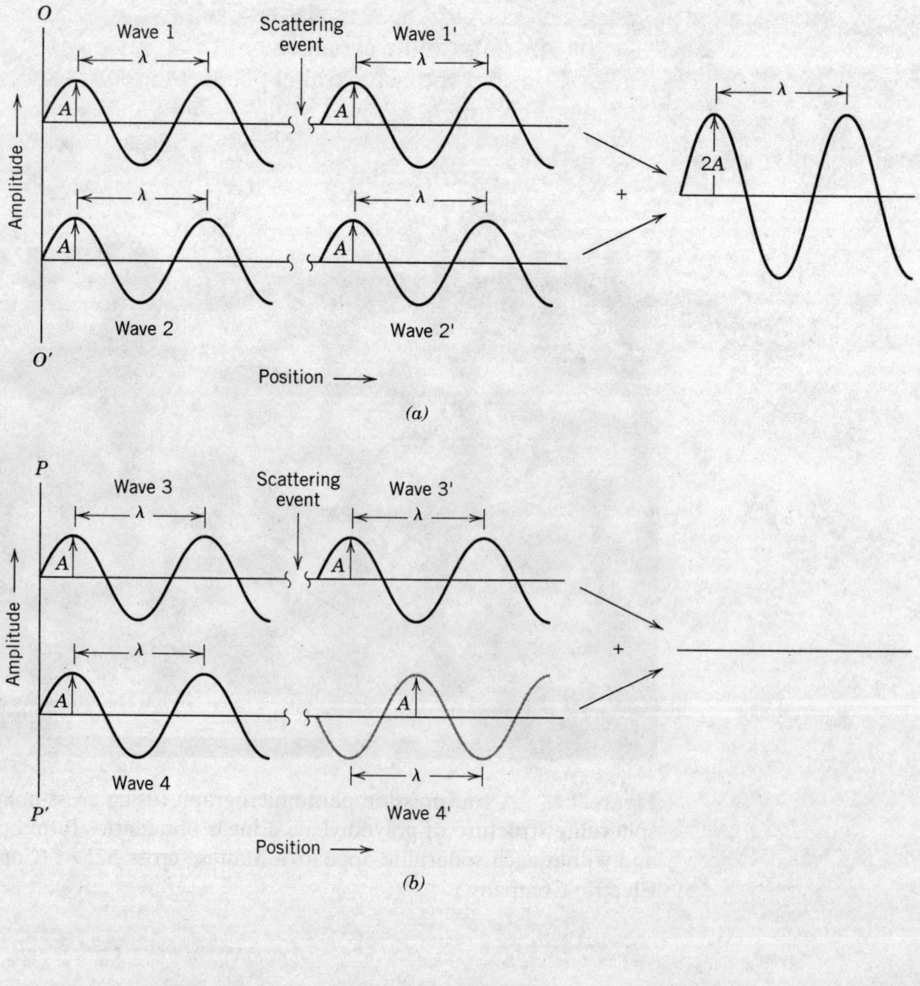

Figure 4.34 (*a*) Demonstration of how two waves (labeled 1 and 2) that have the same wavelength λ and remain in phase after a scattering event (waves 1′ and 2′) constructively interfere with one another. The amplitudes of the scattered waves add together in the resultant wave. (*b*) Demonstration of how two waves (labeled 3 and 4) that have the same wavelength and become out of phase after a scattering event (waves 3′ and 4′) destructively interfere with one another. The amplitudes of the two scattered waves cancel one another.

the scattered waves, which will depend upon the difference in path length, is important. One possibility results when this path length difference is an integral number of wavelengths. As noted in Figure 4.34*a*, these scattered waves (now labeled 1′ and 2′) are still in phase. They are said to mutually reinforce (or constructively interfere with) one another; and, when amplitudes are added, the wave shown on the right side of the figure results. This is a manifestation of **diffraction,** and we refer to a diffracted beam as one composed of a large number of scattered waves that mutually reinforce one another.

Other phase relationships are possible between scattered waves that will not lead to this mutual reinforcement. The other extreme is that demonstrated in Figure 4.34*b*, wherein the path length difference after scattering is some integral number of *half* wavelengths. The scattered waves are out of phase—that is, corresponding amplitudes cancel or annul one another, or destructively interfere (i.e., the resultant wave has zero amplitude), as indicated on the extreme right side of the figure. Of course, phase relationships intermediate between these two extremes exist, resulting in only partial reinforcement.

X-Ray Diffraction and Bragg's Law

X-rays are a form of electromagnetic radiation that have high energies and short wavelengths—wavelengths on the order of the atomic spacings for solids. When a beam of x-rays impinges on a solid material, a portion of this beam will be scattered in all directions by the electrons associated with each atom or ion that lies within the beam's path. Let us now examine the necessary conditions for diffraction of x-rays by a periodic arrangement of atoms.

Consider the two parallel planes of atoms A–A′ and B–B′ in Figure 4.35, which have the same *h*, *k*, and *l* Miller indices and are separated by the interplanar spacing d_{hkl}. Now assume that a parallel, monochromatic, and coherent (in-phase) beam of x-rays of wavelength λ is incident on these two planes at an angle θ. Two rays in this beam, labeled 1 and 2, are scattered by atoms *P* and *Q*. Constructive interference of the scattered rays 1′ and 2′ occurs also at an angle θ to the planes, if the path length difference between 1–*P*–1′ and 2–*Q*–2′ (i.e., $\overline{SQ} + \overline{QT}$) is equal to a whole number, *n*, of wavelengths. That is, the condition for diffraction is

$$n\lambda = \overline{SQ} + \overline{QT} \tag{4.12}$$

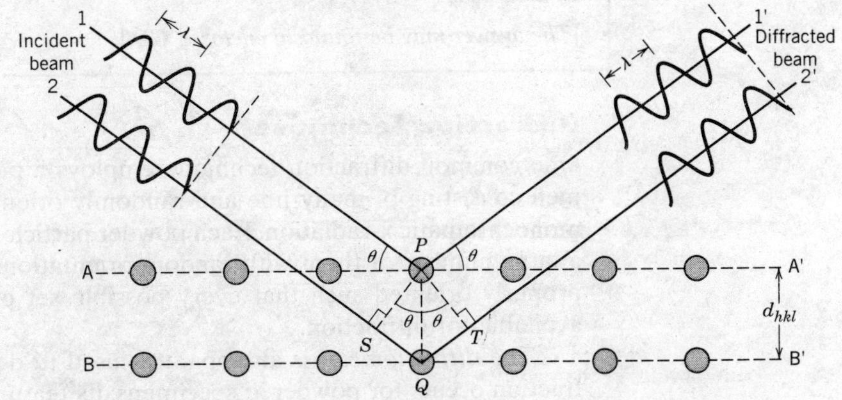

Figure 4.35 Diffraction of x-rays by planes of atoms (A–A′ and B–B′).

or

$$n\lambda = d_{hkl} \sin\theta + d_{hkl} \sin\theta$$
$$= 2d_{hkl} \sin\theta \tag{4.13}$$

Equation 4.13 is known as **Bragg's law;** also, n is the order of reflection, which may be any integer (1, 2, 3, . . .) consistent with $\sin\theta$ not exceeding unity. Thus, we have a simple expression relating the x-ray wavelength and interatomic spacing to the angle of the diffracted beam. If Bragg's law is not satisfied, then the interference will be nonconstructive in nature so as to yield a very low-intensity diffracted beam.

The magnitude of the distance between two adjacent and parallel planes of atoms (i.e., the interplanar spacing d_{hkl}) is a function of the Miller indices (h, k, and l) as well as the lattice parameter(s). For example, for crystal structures that have cubic symmetry,

$$d_{hkl} = \frac{a}{\sqrt{h^2 + k^2 + l^2}} \tag{4.14}$$

in which a is the lattice parameter (unit cell edge length). Relationships similar to Equation 4.14, but more complex, exist for the other six crystal systems noted in Table 3.1.

Bragg's law, Equation 4.13, is a necessary but not sufficient condition for diffraction by real crystals. It specifies when diffraction will occur for unit cells having atoms positioned only at cell corners. However, atoms situated at other sites (e.g., face and interior unit cell positions as with FCC and BCC) act as extra scattering centers, which can produce out-of-phase scattering at certain Bragg angles. The net result is the absence of some diffracted beams that, according to Equation 4.13, should be present. For example, for the BCC crystal structure, $h + k + l$ must be even if diffraction is to occur, whereas for FCC, h, k, and l must all be either odd or even.

Concept Check 4.3

For cubic crystals, as values of the planar indices h, k, and l increase, does the distance between adjacent and parallel planes (i.e., the interplanar spacing) increase or decrease? Why?

[*The answer may be found in enclosed CD.*]

Diffraction Techniques

One common diffraction technique employs a powdered or polycrystalline specimen consisting of many fine and randomly oriented particles that are exposed to monochromatic x-radiation. Each powder particle (or grain) is a crystal, and having a large number of them with random orientations ensures that some particles are properly oriented such that every possible set of crystallographic planes will be available for diffraction.

The *diffractometer* is an apparatus used to determine the angles at which diffraction occurs for powdered specimens; its features are represented schematically in Figure 4.36. A specimen S in the form of a flat plate is supported so that rotations about the axis labeled O are possible; this axis is perpendicular to the plane

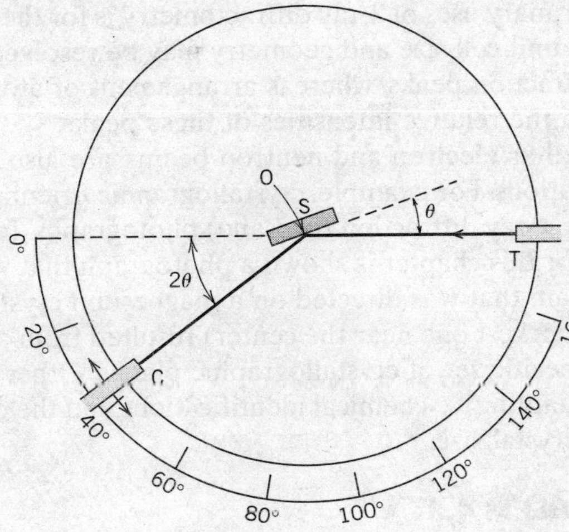

Figure 4.36 Schematic diagram of an x-ray diffractometer; T = x-ray source, S = specimen, C = detector, and O = the axis around which the specimen and detector rotate.

of the page. The monochromatic x-ray beam is generated at point T, and the intensities of diffracted beams are detected with a counter labeled C in the figure. The specimen, x-ray source, and counter are all coplanar.

The counter is mounted on a movable carriage that may also be rotated about the O axis; its angular position in terms of 2θ is marked on a graduated scale.[3] Carriage and specimen are mechanically coupled such that a rotation of the specimen through θ is accompanied by a 2θ rotation of the counter; this assures that the incident and reflection angles are maintained equal to one another (Figure 4.36). Collimators are incorporated within the beam path to produce a well-defined and focused beam. Utilization of a filter provides a near-monochromatic beam.

As the counter moves at constant angular velocity, a recorder automatically plots the diffracted beam intensity (monitored by the counter) as a function of 2θ; 2θ is termed the *diffraction angle,* which is measured experimentally. Figure 4.37 shows a diffraction pattern for a powdered specimen of lead. The high-intensity peaks result when the Bragg diffraction condition is satisfied by some set of crystallographic planes. These peaks are plane-indexed in the figure.

Other powder techniques have been devised wherein diffracted beam intensity and position are recorded on a photographic film instead of being measured by a counter.

Figure 4.37 Diffraction pattern for powdered lead. (Courtesy of Wesley L. Holman.)

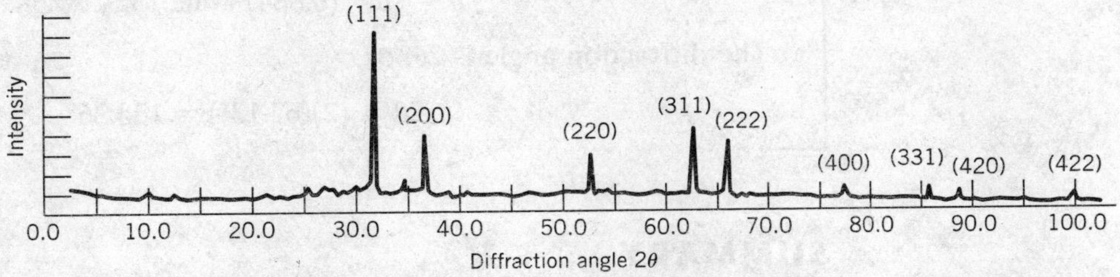

[3] Note that the symbol θ has been used in two different contexts for this discussion. Here, θ represents the angular locations of both x-ray source and counter relative to the specimen surface. Previously (e.g., Equation 4.13), it denoted the angle at which the Bragg criterion for diffraction is satisfied.

One of the primary uses of x-ray diffractometry is for the determination of crystal structure. The unit cell size and geometry may be resolved from the angular positions of the diffraction peaks, whereas arrangement of atoms within the unit cell is associated with the relative intensities of these peaks.

X-rays, as well as electron and neutron beams, are also used in other types of material investigations. For example, crystallographic orientations of single crystals are possible using x-ray diffraction (or Laue) photographs. In the (*a*) chapter-opening photograph for this chapter is shown a photograph that was generated using an incident x-ray beam that was directed on a magnesium crystal; each spot (with the exception of the darkest one near the center) resulted from an x-ray beam that was diffracted by a specific set of crystallographic planes. Other uses of x-rays include qualitative and quantitative chemical identifications and the determination of residual stresses and crystal size.

EXAMPLE PROBLEM 4.8

Interplanar Spacing and Diffraction Angle Computations

For BCC iron, compute (a) the interplanar spacing, and (b) the diffraction angle for the (220) set of planes. The lattice parameter for Fe is 0.2866 nm. Also, assume that monochromatic radiation having a wavelength of 0.1790 nm is used, and the order of reflection is 1.

Solution

(a) The value of the interplanar spacing d_{hkl} is determined using Equation 4.14, with $a = 0.2866$ nm, and $h = 2$, $k = 2$, and $l = 0$, since we are considering the (220) planes. Therefore,

$$d_{hkl} = \frac{a}{\sqrt{h^2 + k^2 + l^2}}$$

$$= \frac{0.2866 \text{ nm}}{\sqrt{(2)^2 + (2)^2 + (0)^2}} = 0.1013 \text{ nm}$$

(b) The value of θ may now be computed using Equation 4.13, with $n = 1$, since this is a first-order reflection:

$$\sin\theta = \frac{n\lambda}{2d_{hkl}} = \frac{(1)(0.1790 \text{ nm})}{(2)(0.1013 \text{ nm})} = 0.884$$

$$\theta = \sin^{-1}(0.884) = 62.13°$$

The diffraction angle is 2θ, or

$$2\theta = (2)(62.13°) = 124.26°$$

SUMMARY

Metallic Crystal Structures

Most common metals exist in at least one of three relatively simple crystal structures: face-centered cubic (FCC), body-centered cubic (BCC), and hexagonal close-packed (HCP). Two features of a crystal structure are coordination number (or number of nearest-neighbor atoms) and atomic packing factor (the fraction of solid sphere volume in the unit cell). Coordination number and atomic packing factor are the same for both FCC and HCP crystal structures, each of which may be generated by the stacking of close-packed planes of atoms.

Linear and Planar Densities

Crystallographic directional and planar equivalencies are related to atomic linear and planar densities, respectively. The atomic packing (i.e., planar density) of spheres in a crystallographic plane depends on the indices of the plane as well as the crystal structure. For a given crystal structure, planes having identical atomic packing yet different Miller indices belong to the same family.

Ceramic Crystal Structure

Both crystalline and noncrystalline states are possible for ceramics. The crystal structures of those materials for which the atomic bonding is predominantly ionic are determined by the charge magnitude and the radius of each kind of ion. Some of the simpler crystal structures are described in terms of unit cells; several of these were discussed (rock salt, cesium chloride, zinc blende, diamond cubic, graphite, fluorite, perovskite, and spinel structures).

Silicate Ceramics

For the silicates, structure is more conveniently represented by means of interconnecting SiO_4^{4-} tetrahedra. Relatively complex structures may result when other cations (e.g., Ca^{2+}, Mg^{2+}, Al^{3+}) and anions (e.g., OH^-) are added. The structures of silica (SiO_2), silica glass, and several of the simple and layered silicates were presented.

Carbon

The various forms of carbon—diamond, graphite, the fullerenes, and nanotubes—were also discussed. Diamond is a gem stone and, because of its hardness, is used to cut and grind softer materials. Furthermore, it is now being produced and utilized in thin films. The layered structure of graphite gives rise to its excellent lubricative properties and a relatively high electrical conductivity. Graphite is also known for its high strength and chemical stability at elevated temperatures and in nonoxidizing atmospheres. Fullerenes exist as hollow and spherical molecules composed of 60 carbon atoms. The recently discovered carbon nanotubes have extraordinary properties: high stiffnesses and strengths, low densities, and unusual electrical characteristics. Structurally, a nanotube is a graphite cylinder with fullerene hemispheres on its ends.

Polymer Crystallinity
Polymer Crystals

When the molecular chains are packed in an ordered atomic arrangement, the condition of crystallinity is said to exist. In addition to being entirely amorphous, polymers may also exhibit varying degrees of crystallinity; that is, crystalline regions are interdispersed within amorphous areas. Crystallinity is facilitated for polymers that are chemically simple and that have regular and symmetrical chain structures.

Many semicrystalline polymers form spherulites; each spherulite consists of a collection of ribbon-like chain-folded lamellar crystallites that radiate outward from its center.

X-Ray Diffraction: Determination of Crystal Structures

X-ray diffractometry is used for crystal structure and interplanar spacing determinations. A beam of x-rays directed on a crystalline material may experience diffraction (constructive interference) as a result of its interaction with a series of parallel atomic planes according to Bragg's law. Interplanar spacing is a function of the Miller indices and lattice parameter(s) as well as the crystal structure.

REFERENCES

Azaroff, L. F., *Elements of X-Ray Crystallography,* McGraw-Hill, New York, 1968. Reprinted by TechBooks, Marietta, OH, 1990.

Barsoum, M. W., *Fundamentals of Ceramics,* McGraw-Hill, New York, 1997.

Bowen, H. K., "Advanced Ceramics," *Scientific American,* Vol. 255, No. 4, October 1986, pp. 168–176.

Buerger, M. J., *Elementary Crystallography,* Wiley, New York, 1956.

Chiang, Y. M., D. P. Birnie, III, and W. D. Kingery, *Physical Ceramics: Principles for Ceramic Science and Engineering,* Wiley, New York, 1997.

Cullity, B. D., and S. R. Stock, *Elements of X-Ray Diffraction,* 3rd edition, Prentice Hall, Upper Saddle River, NJ, 2001.

Curl, R. F. and R. E. Smalley, "Fullerenes," *Scientific American,* Vol. 265, No. 4, October 1991, pp. 54–63.

Doremus, R. H., *Glass Science,* 2nd edition, Wiley, New York, 1994.

Engineered Materials Handbook, Vol. 4, *Ceramics and Glasses,* ASM International, Materials Park, OH, 1991.

Engineered Materials Handbook, Vol. 2, *Engineering Plastics,* ASM International, Materials Park, OH, 1988.

Hauth, W. E., "Crystal Chemistry in Ceramics," *American Ceramic Society Bulletin,* Vol. 30, 1951: No. 1, pp. 5–7; No. 2, pp. 47–49; No. 3, pp. 76–77; No. 4, pp. 137–142; No. 5, pp. 165–167; No. 6, pp. 203–205. A good overview of silicate structures.

Kingery, W. D., H. K. Bowen, and D. R. Uhlmann, *Introduction to Ceramics,* 2nd edition, Wiley, New York, 1976. Chapters 1–4, 14, and 15.

Norton, F. H., *Elements of Ceramics,* Addison-Wesley, 1974. Reprinted by TechBooks, Marietta, OH, 1991. Chapters 2 and 23.

QUESTIONS AND PROBLEMS

Metallic Crystal Structures

4.1 If the atomic radius of lead is 0.175 nm, calculate the volume of its unit cell in cubic meters.

4.2 Show for the body-centered cubic crystal structure that the unit cell edge length a and the atomic radius R are related through $a = 4R/\sqrt{3}$.

4.3 For the HCP crystal structure, show that the ideal c/a ratio is 1.633.

4.4 Show that the atomic packing factor for BCC is 0.68.

4.5 Show that the atomic packing factor for HCP is 0.74.

Density Computations

4.6 Molybdenum has a BCC crystal structure, an atomic radius of 0.1363 nm, and an atomic weight of 95.94 g/mol. Compute and compare its theoretical density with the experimental value found inside the front cover.

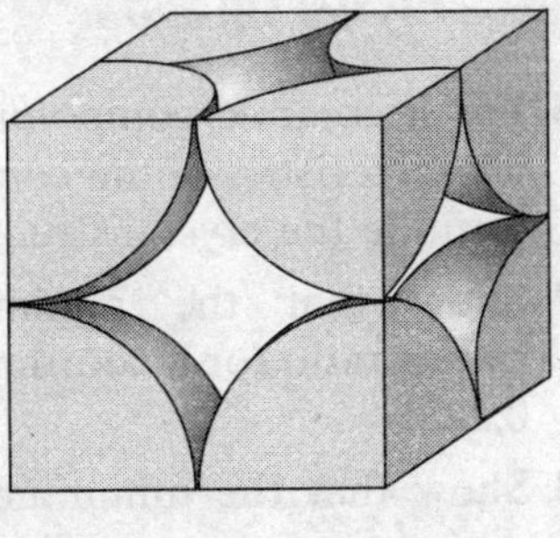

Figure 4.38 Hard-sphere unit cell representation of the simple cubic crystal structure.

4.7 Calculate the radius of a palladium atom, given that Pd has an FCC crystal structure, a density of 12.0 g/cm^3, and an atomic weight of 106.4 g/mol.

4.8 Calculate the radius of a tantalum atom, given that Ta has a BCC crystal structure, a density of 16.6 g/cm^3, and an atomic weight of 180.9 g/mol.

4.9 Some hypothetical metal has the simple cubic crystal structure shown in Figure 4.38. If its atomic weight is 74.5 g/mol and the atomic radius is 0.145 nm, compute its density.

4.10 Titanium has an HCP crystal structure and a density of 4.51 g/cm^3.

(a) What is the volume of its unit cell in cubic meters?

(b) If the c/a ratio is 1.58, compute the values of c and a.

4.11 Using atomic weight, crystal structure, and atomic radius data tabulated inside the front cover, compute the theoretical densities of aluminum, nickel, magnesium, and tungsten, and then compare these values with the measured densities listed in this same table. The c/a ratio for magnesium is 1.624.

4.12 Niobium has an atomic radius of 0.1430 nm and a density of 8.57 g/cm^3. Determine whether it has an FCC or BCC crystal structure.

4.13 Below are listed the atomic weight, density, and atomic radius for three hypothetical alloys. For each determine whether its crystal structure is FCC, BCC, or simple cubic and then justify your determination. A simple cubic unit cell is shown in Figure 4.38.

Alloy	*Atomic Weight (g/mol)*	*Density (g/cm^3)*	*Atomic Radius (nm)*
A	43.1	6.40	0.122
B	184.4	12.30	0.146
C	91.6	9.60	0.137

4.14 The unit cell for uranium has orthorhombic symmetry, with a, b, and c lattice parameters of 0.286, 0.587, and 0.495 nm, respectively. If its density, atomic weight, and atomic radius are 19.05 g/cm^3, 238.03 g/mol, and 0.1385 nm, respectively, compute the atomic packing factor.

4.15 Indium has a tetragonal unit cell for which the a and c lattice parameters are 0.459 and 0.495 nm, respectively.

(a) If the atomic packing factor and atomic radius are 0.693 and 0.1625 nm, respectively, determine the number of atoms in each unit cell.

(b) The atomic weight of indium is 114.82 g/mol; compute its theoretical density.

4.16 Beryllium has an HCP unit cell for which the ratio of the lattice parameters c/a is 1.568. If the radius of the Be atom is 0.1143 nm, **(a)** determine the unit cell volume, and **(b)** calculate the theoretical density of Be and compare it with the literature value.

4.17 Magnesium has an HCP crystal structure, a c/a ratio of 1.624, and a density of 1.74 g/cm^3. Compute the atomic radius for Mg.

4.18 Cobalt has an HCP crystal structure, an atomic radius of 0.1253 nm, and a c/a ratio of 1.623. Compute the volume of the unit cell for Co.

Atomic Arrangements

4.19 Sketch the atomic packing of **(a)** the (100) plane for the FCC crystal structure, and **(b)** the (111) plane for the BCC crystal structure (similar to Figures 4.4*b* and 4.5*b*).

4.20 Below are shown three different crystallographic planes for a unit cell of some hypothetical metal. The circles represent atoms:

(a) To what crystal system does the unit cell belong?

(b) What would this crystal structure be called?

(c) If the density of this metal is 18.91 g/cm^3, determine its atomic weight.

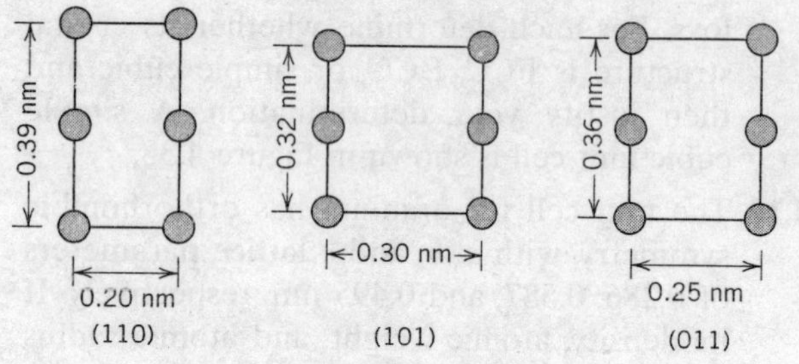

Linear and Planar Densities

4.21 **(a)** Derive linear density expressions for FCC [100] and [111] directions in terms of the atomic radius R.

(b) Compute and compare linear density values for these same two planes for copper.

4.22 **(a)** Derive linear density expressions for BCC [110] and [111] directions in terms of the atomic radius R.

(b) Compute and compare linear density values for these same two planes for iron.

4.23 **(a)** Derive planar density expressions for FCC (100) and (111) planes in terms of the atomic radius R.

(b) Compute and compare planar density values for these same two planes for aluminum.

4.24 **(a)** Derive planar density expressions for BCC (100) and (110) planes in terms of the atomic radius R.

(b) Compute and compare planar density values for these same two planes for molybdenum.

4.25 **(a)** Derive the planar density expression for the HCP (0001) plane in terms of the atomic radius R.

(b) Compute the planar density value for this same plane for titanium.

Ceramic Crystal Structures

4.26 For a ceramic compound, what are the two characteristics of the component ions that determine the crystal structure?

4.27 Show that the minimum cation-to-anion radius ratio for a coordination number of 4 is 0.225.

4.28 Show that the minimum cation-to-anion radius ratio for a coordination number of 6 is 0.414. [*Hint:* Use the NaCl crystal structure (Figure 4.11), and assume that anions and cations are just touching along cube edges and across face diagonals.]

4.29 Demonstrate that the minimum cation-to-anion radius ratio for a coordination number of 8 is 0.732.

4.30 On the basis of ionic charge and ionic radii given in Table 4.4, predict crystal structures for the following materials: **(a)** CaO, **(b)** MnS, **(c)** KBr, and **(d)** CsBr. Justify your selections.

4.31 Which of the cations in Table 4.4 would you predict to form fluorides having the cesium chloride crystal structure? Justify your choices.

4.32 Compute the atomic packing factor for the rock salt crystal structure in which $r_C/r_A = 0.414$.

4.33 The zinc blende crystal structure is one that may be generated from close-packed planes of anions.

(a) Will the stacking sequence for this structure be FCC or HCP? Why?

(b) Will cations fill tetrahedral or octahedral positions? Why?

(c) What fraction of the positions will be occupied?

4.34 The corundum crystal structure, found for Al_2O_3, consists of an HCP arrangement of O^{2-} ions; the Al^{3+} ions occupy octahedral positions.

(a) What fraction of the available octahedral positions are filled with Al^{3+} ions?

(b) Sketch two close-packed O^{2-} planes stacked in an AB sequence, and note octahedral positions that will be filled with the Al^{3+} ions.

4.35 Beryllium oxide (BeO) may form a crystal structure that consists of an HCP arrangement of O^{2-} ions. If the ionic radius of Be^{2+} is 0.035 nm, then

(a) Which type of interstitial site will the Be^{2+} ions occupy?

(b) What fraction of these available interstitial sites will be occupied by Be^{2+} ions?

4.36 Iron titanate, $FeTiO_3$, forms in the ilmenite crystal structure that consists of an HCP arrangement of O^{2-} ions.

(a) Which type of interstitial site will the Fe^{2+} ions occupy? Why?

(b) Which type of interstitial site will the Ti^{4+} ions occupy? Why?

(c) What fraction of the total tetrahedral sites will be occupied?

(d) What fraction of the total octahedral sites will be occupied?

4.37 Using the Molecule Definition Utility found in the CD enclosed with the book, generate (and print out) a three-dimensional unit cell for lead oxide, PbO, given the following: (1) The unit cell is tetragonal with $a = 0.397$ nm and $c = 0.502$ nm, (2) oxygen atoms are located at the following point coordinates:

000	001
100	101
010	011
110	111
$\frac{1}{2}\frac{1}{2}0$	$\frac{1}{2}\frac{1}{2}1$

and (3) Pb atoms are located at the following point coordinates:

$\frac{1}{2}$ 0 0.763	0 $\frac{1}{2}$ 0.237
$\frac{1}{2}$ 0 0.763	0 $\frac{1}{2}$ 0.237

4.38 Calculate the theoretical density of NiO, given that it has the rock salt crystal structure.

4.39 Iron oxide (FeO) has the rock salt crystal structure and a density of 5.70 g/cm^3.

(a) Determine the unit cell edge length.

(b) How does this result compare with the edge length as determined from the radii in Table 4.3, assuming that the Fe^{2+} and O^{2-} ions just touch each other along the edges?

4.40 Compute the theoretical density of diamond given that the C—C distance and bond angle are 0.154 nm and 109.5°, respectively. How does this value compare with the measured density?

4.41 Compute the theoretical density of ZnS given that the Zn—S distance and bond angle are 0.234 nm and 109.5°, respectively. How does this value compare with the measured density?

4.42 One crystalline form of silica (SiO_2) has a cubic unit cell, and from X-ray diffraction data it is known that the cell edge length is 0.700 nm. If the measured density is 2.32 g/cm^3, how many Si^{4+} and O^{2-} ions are there per unit cell?

4.43 (a) Using the ionic radii in Table 4.4, compute the theoretical density of CsCl. (*Hint:* Use a modification of the result of Problem 4.2.)

(b) The measured density is 3.99 g/cm^3. How do you explain the slight discrepancy between your calculated value and the measured one?

4.44 From the data in Table 4.4, compute the theoretical density of CaF_2, which has the fluorite structure.

4.45 A hypothetical AX type of ceramic material is known to have a density of 2.10 g/cm^3 and a unit cell of cubic symmetry with a cell edge length of 0.57 nm. The atomic weights of the A and X elements are 28.5 and 30.0 g/mol, respectively. On the basis of this information, which of the following crystal structures is (are) possible for this material: sodium chloride, cesium chloride, or zinc blende? Justify your choice(s).

4.46 The unit cell for Fe_3O_4 (FeO-Fe_2O_3) has cubic symmetry with a unit cell edge length of 0.839 nm. If the density of this material is 5.24 g/cm^3, compute its atomic packing factor. For this computation, you will need to use ionic radii listed in Table 4.4.

4.47 The unit cell for Al_2O_3 has hexagonal symmetry with lattice parameters $a = 0.4759$ nm and $c = 1.2989$ nm. If the density of this material is 3.99 g/cm^3, calculate its atomic packing factor. For this computation use ionic radii listed in Table 4.4.

4.48 Compute the atomic packing factor for the diamond cubic crystal structure (Figure 4.24). Assume that bonding atoms touch one another, that the angle between adjacent bonds is 109.5°, and that each atom internal to the unit cell is positioned $a/4$ of the distance away from the two nearest cell faces (a is the unit cell edge length).

4.49 Compute the atomic packing factor for cesium chloride using the ionic radii in Table 4.4 and assuming that the ions touch along the cube diagonals.

4.50 For each of the following crystal structures, represent the indicated plane in the manner of Figures 4.4 and 4.5, showing both anions and cations: **(a)** (100) plane for the cesium chloride crystal structure, **(b)** (200) plane for the cesium chloride crystal structure, **(c)** (111) plane for the diamond cubic crystal structure, and **(d)** (110) plane for the fluorite crystal structure.

Silicate Ceramics

4.51 In terms of bonding, explain why silicate materials have relatively low densities.

4.52 Determine the angle between covalent bonds in an SiO_4^{4-} tetrahedron.

Polymer Crystallinity

4.53 The density of totally crystalline nylon 6,6 at room temperature is 1.213 g/cm^3. Also, at room temperature the unit cell for this material is triclinic with lattice parameters

$$a = 0.497 \text{ nm} \qquad \alpha = 48.4°$$
$$b = 0.547 \text{ nm} \qquad \beta = 76.6°$$
$$c = 1.729 \text{ nm} \qquad \gamma = 62.5°$$

If the volume of a triclinic unit cell, V_{tri}, is a function of these lattice parameters as

$$V_{tri} = abc\sqrt{1 - \cos^2\alpha - \cos^2\beta - \cos^2\gamma + 2\cos\alpha\cos\beta\cos\gamma}$$

determine the number of repeat units per unit cell.

4.54 The density and associated percent crystallinity for two poly(ethylene terephthalate) materials are as follows:

ρ (g/cm³)	*Crystallinity (%)*
1.408	74.3
1.343	31.2

(a) Compute the densities of totally crystalline and totally amorphous poly(ethylene terephthalate).

(b) Determine the percent crystallinity of a specimen having a density of 1.382 g/cm^3.

4.55 The density and associated percent crystallinity for two polypropylene materials are as follows:

ρ (g/cm³)	*Crystallinity (%)*
0.904	62.8
0.895	54.4

(a) Compute the densities of totally crystalline and totally amorphous polypropylene.

b) Determine the density of a specimen having 74.6% crystallinity.

X-Ray Diffraction: Determination of Crystal Structures

4.56 Using the data for aluminum in Table 4.1, compute the interplanar spacing for the (110) set of planes.

4.57 Determine the expected diffraction angle for the first-order reflection from the (310) set of planes for BCC chromium when monochromatic radiation of wavelength 0.0711 nm is used.

4.58 Using the data for α-iron in Table 4.1, compute the interplanar spacings for the (111) and (211) sets of planes.

4.59 The metal rhodium has an FCC crystal structure. If the angle of diffraction for the (311) set of planes occurs at 36.12° (first-order reflection) when monochromatic x-radiation having a wavelength of 0.0711 nm is used, compute **(a)** the interplanar spacing for this set of planes, and **(b)** the atomic radius for a rhodium atom.

4.60 The metal niobium has a BCC crystal structure. If the angle of diffraction for the (211) set of planes occurs at 75.99° (first-order reflection) when monochromatic x-radiation having a wavelength of 0.1659 nm is used, compute (a) the interplanar spacing for this set of planes, and (b) the atomic radius for the niobium atom.

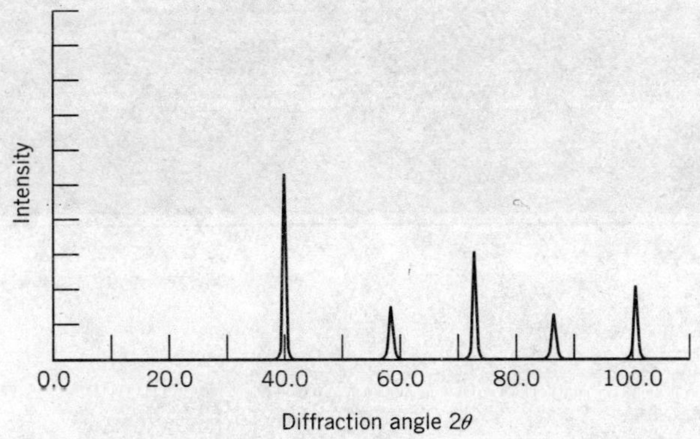

Figure 4.39 Diffraction pattern for powdered tungsten. (Courtesy of Wesley L. Holman.)

4.61 For which set of crystallographic planes will a first-order diffraction peak occur at a diffraction angle of 44.53° for FCC nickel when monochromatic radiation having a wavelength of 0.1542 nm is used?

4.62 Figure 4.37 shows an x-ray diffraction pattern for lead taken using a diffractometer and monochromatic x-radiation having a wavelength of 0.1542 nm; each diffraction peak on the pattern has been indexed. Compute the interplanar spacing for each set of planes indexed; also determine the lattice parameter of Pb for each of the peaks.

4.63 The diffraction peaks shown in Figure 4.37 are indexed according to the reflection rules for FCC (i.e., h, k, and l must all be either odd or even). Cite the h, k, and l indices of the first four diffraction peaks for BCC crystals consistent with $h + k + l$ being even.

4.64 Figure 4.39 shows the first five peaks of the x-ray diffraction pattern for tungsten, which has a BCC crystal structure; monochromatic x-radiation having a wavelength of 0.1542 nm was used.

(a) Index (i.e., give h, k, and l indices) for each of these peaks.

(b) Determine the interplanar spacing for each of the peaks.

(c) For each peak, determine the atomic radius for W and compare these with the value presented in Table 4.1.

DESIGN PROBLEM

Crystal Structures

4.D1 Gallium arsenide (GaAs) and indium arsenide (InAs) both have the zinc blende crystal structure and are soluble in each other at all concentrations. Determine the concentration in weight percent of InAs that must be added to GaAs to yield a unit cell edge length of 0.5820 nm. The densities of GaAs and InAs are 5.316 and 5.668 g/cm^3, respectively.

Chapter 5 Imperfections in Solids

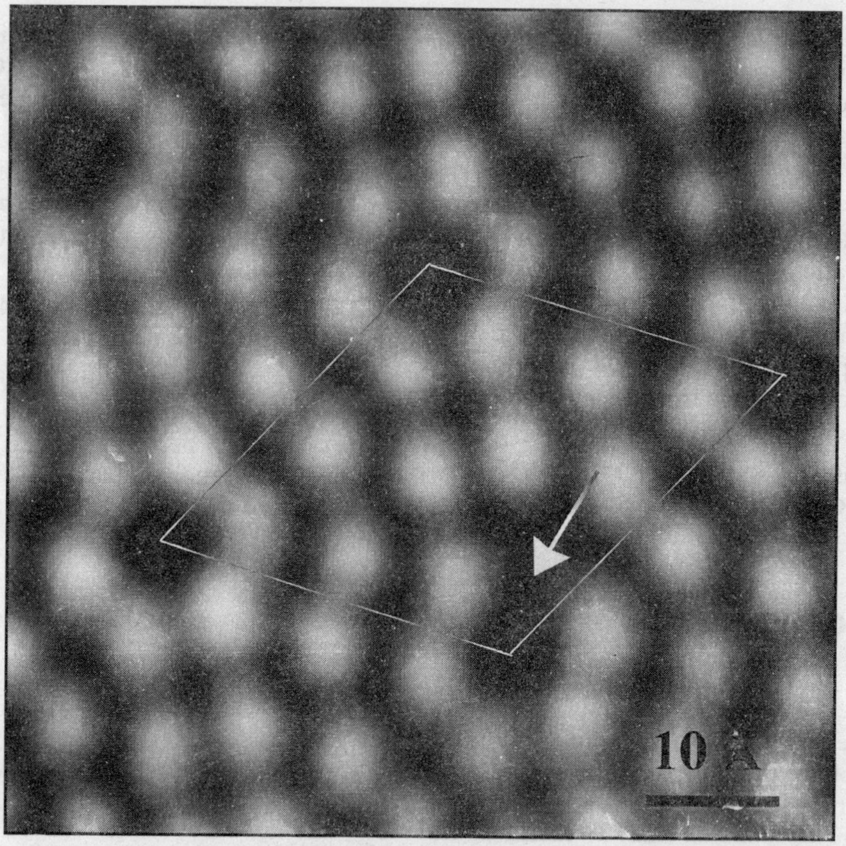

A scanning probe micrograph (generated using a scanning-tunneling microscope) that shows a (111)-type surface plane* for silicon. The arrow points to the location of a silicon atom that was removed using a tungsten nanotip probe. This site from which an atom is missing is the surface analogue of a vacancy defect—that is, a vacant lattice site within the bulk material. Approximately 20,000,000×. (Micrograph courtesy of D. Huang, Stanford University.)

---

*The plane shown here is termed a "Si(111)-7×7 reconstructed surface." The two-dimensional arrangement of atoms in a surface plane is different than the atomic arrangement for the equivalent plane within the interior of the material (i.e., the surface plane has been "reconstructed" by atomic displacements). The "7×7" notation pertains to the displacement magnitude. Furthermore, the diamond shape that has been drawn indicates a unit cell for this 7×7 structure.

Learning Objectives

After studying this chapter you should be able to do the following:

1. Describe both vacancy and self-interstitial crys talline defects.
2. Calculate the equilibrium number of vacancies in a material at some specified temperature, given the relevant constants.
3. Name the two types of solid solutions, and provide a brief written definition and/or schematic sketch of each.
4. Given the masses and atomic weights of two or more elements in a metal alloy, calculate the weight percent and atom percent for each element.
5. Name and describe eight different ionic point defects that are found in ceramic compounds.
6. For each of edge, screw, and mixed dislocations:
   (a) describe and make a drawing of the dislocation.
   (b) note the location of the dislocation line, and
   (c) indicate the direction along which the dislocation line extends.
7. Describe the atomic structure within the vicinity of (a) a grain boundary, and (b) a twin boundary.

5.1 INTRODUCTION

Thus far it has been tacitly assumed that perfect order exists throughout crystalline materials on an atomic scale. However, such an idealized solid does not exist; all contain large numbers of various defects or **imperfections.** As a matter of fact, many of the properties of materials are profoundly sensitive to deviations from crystalline perfection; the influence is not always adverse, and often specific characteristics are deliberately fashioned by the introduction of controlled amounts or numbers of particular defects, as detailed in succeeding chapters.

By "crystalline defect" is meant a lattice irregularity having one or more of its dimensions on the order of an atomic diameter. Classification of crystalline imperfections is frequently made according to geometry or dimensionality of the defect. Several different imperfections are discussed in this chapter, including **point defects** (those associated with one or two atomic positions), linear (or one-dimensional) defects, as well as interfacial defects, or boundaries, which are two-dimensional. Impurities in solids are also discussed, since impurity atoms may exist as point defects. Finally, techniques for the microscopic examination of defects and the structure of materials are briefly described.

Point Defects

5.2 VACANCIES AND SELF-INTERSTITIALS

The simplest of the point defects is a **vacancy,** or vacant lattice site, one normally occupied from which an atom is missing (Figure 5.1). All crystalline solids contain vacancies and, in fact, it is not possible to create such a material that is free of these defects. The necessity of the existence of vacancies is explained using principles of thermodynamics; in essence, the presence of vacancies increases the entropy (i.e., the randomness) of the crystal.

The equilibrium number of vacancies N_v for a given quantity of material depends on and increases with temperature according to

$$N_v = N \exp\left(-\frac{Q_v}{kT}\right) \tag{5.1}$$

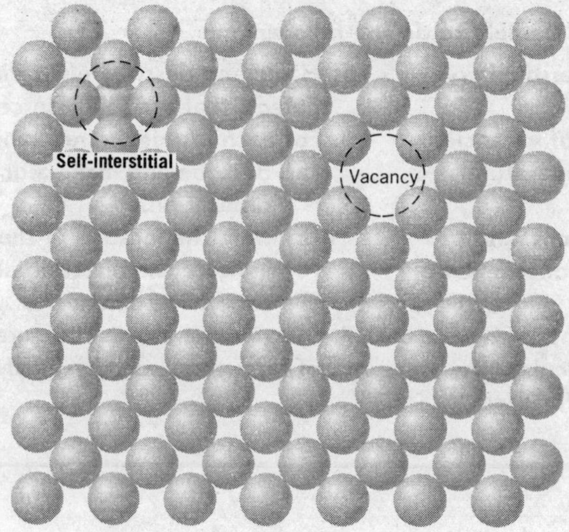

Figure 5.1 Two-dimensional representations of a vacancy and a self-interstitial. (Adapted from W. G. Moffatt, G. W. Pearsall, and J. Wulff, *The Structure and Properties of Materials,* Vol. I, *Structure,* p. 77. Copyright © 1964 by John Wiley & Sons, New York. Reprinted by permission of John Wiley & Sons, Inc.)

In this expression, N is the total number of atomic sites, Q_v is the energy required for the formation of a vacancy, T is the absolute temperature[1] in kelvins, and k is the gas or **Boltzmann's constant.** The value of k is 1.38×10^{-23} J/atom-K, or 8.62×10^{-5} eV/atom-K, depending on the units of Q_v.[2] Thus, the number of vacancies increases exponentially with temperature; that is, as T in Equation 5.1 increases, so also does the expression $\exp -(Q_v/kT)$. For most metals, the fraction of vacancies N_v/N just below the melting temperature is on the order of 10^{-4}; that is, one lattice site out of 10,000 will be empty. As ensuing discussions indicate, a number of other material parameters have an exponential dependence on temperature similar to that of Equation 5.1.

A **self-interstitial** is an atom from the crystal that is crowded into an interstitial site, a small void space that under ordinary circumstances is not occupied. This kind of defect is also represented in Figure 5.1. In metals, a self-interstitial introduces relatively large distortions in the surrounding lattice because the atom is substantially larger than the interstitial position in which it is situated. Consequently, the formation of this defect is not highly probable, and it exists in very small concentrations, which are significantly lower than for vacancies.

EXAMPLE PROBLEM 5.1

Number of Vacancies Computation at a Specified Temperature

Calculate the equilibrium number of vacancies per cubic meter for copper at 1000°C. The energy for vacancy formation is 0.9 eV/atom; the atomic weight and density (at 1000°C) for copper are 63.5 g/mol and 8.4 g/cm^3, respectively.

[1] Absolute temperature in kelvins (K) is equal to °C + 273.

[2] Boltzmann's constant per mole of atoms becomes the gas constant R; in such a case R = 8.31 J/mol-K.

Solution

This problem may be solved by using Equation 5.1; it is first necessary, however, to determine the value of N, the number of atomic sites per cubic meter for copper, from its atomic weight A_{Cu}, its density ρ, and Avogadro's number N_A, according to

$$N = \frac{N_A \rho}{A_{Cu}} \tag{5.2}$$

$$= \frac{(6.023 \times 10^{23} \text{ atoms/mol})(8.4 \text{ g/cm}^3)(10^6 \text{ cm}^3/\text{m}^3)}{63.5 \text{ g/mol}}$$

$$= 8.0 \times 10^{28} \text{ atoms/m}^3$$

Thus, the number of vacancics at 1000°C (1273 K) is equal to

$$N_v = N \exp\left(-\frac{Q_v}{kT}\right)$$

$$= (8.0 \times 10^{28} \text{ atoms/m}^3) \exp\left[-\frac{(0.9 \text{ eV})}{(8.62 \times 10^{-5} \text{ eV/K})(1273 \text{ K})}\right]$$

$$= 2.2 \times 10^{25} \text{ vacancies/m}^3$$

5.3 IMPURITIES IN SOLIDS

A pure metal consisting of only one type of atom just isn't possible; impurity or foreign atoms will always be present, and some will exist as crystalline point defects. In fact, even with relatively sophisticated techniques, it is difficult to refine metals to a purity in excess of 99.9999%. At this level, on the order of 10^{22} to 10^{23} impurity atoms will be present in one cubic meter of material. Most familiar metals are not highly pure; rather, they are **alloys,** in which impurity atoms have been added intentionally to impart specific characteristics to the material. Ordinarily, alloying is used in metals to improve mechanical strength and corrosion resistance. For example, sterling silver is a 92.5% silver–7.5% copper alloy. In normal ambient environments, pure silver is highly corrosion resistant, but also very soft. Alloying with copper significantly enhances the mechanical strength without depreciating the corrosion resistance appreciably.

The addition of impurity atoms to a metal will result in the formation of a **solid solution** and/or a new *second phase,* depending on the kinds of impurity, their concentrations, and the temperature of the alloy. The present discussion is concerned with the notion of a solid solution; treatment of the formation of a new phase is deferred to Chapter 7.

Several terms relating to impurities and solid solutions deserve mention. With regard to alloys, **solute** and **solvent** are terms that are commonly employed. "Solvent" represents the element or compound that is present in the greatest amount; on occasion, solvent atoms are also called *host atoms*. "Solute" is used to denote an element or compound present in a minor concentration.

Solid Solutions

A solid solution forms when, as the solute atoms are added to the host material, the crystal structure is maintained, and no new structures are formed. Perhaps it is

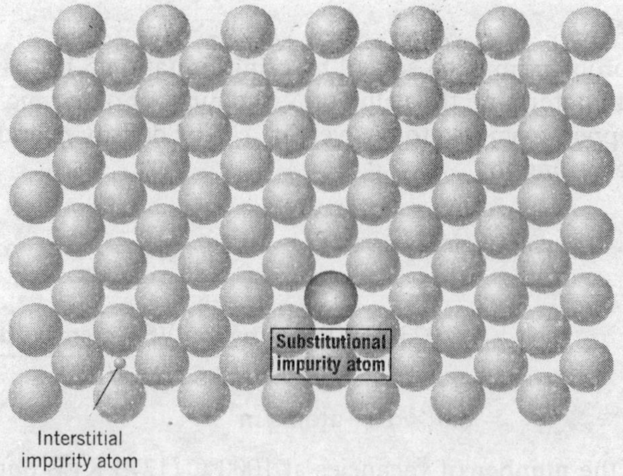

Figure 5.2 Two-dimensional schematic representations of substitutional and interstitial impurity atoms. (Adapted from W. G. Moffatt, G. W. Pearsall, and J. Wulff, *The Structure and Properties of Materials,* Vol. I, *Structure,* p. 77. Copyright © 1964 by John Wiley & Sons, New York. Reprinted by permission of John Wiley & Sons, Inc.)

useful to draw an analogy with a liquid solution. If two liquids, soluble in each other (such as water and alcohol) are combined, a liquid solution is produced as the molecules intermix, and its composition is homogeneous throughout. A solid solution is also compositionally homogeneous; the impurity atoms are randomly and uniformly dispersed within the solid.

Impurity point defects are found in solid solutions, of which there are two types: **substitutional** and **interstitial.** For the substitutional type, solute or impurity atoms replace or substitute for the host atoms (Figure 5.2). There are several features of the solute and solvent atoms that determine the degree to which the former dissolves in the latter, as follows:

1. *Atomic size factor*. Appreciable quantities of a solute may be accommodated in this type of solid solution only when the difference in atomic radii between the two atom types is less than about $\pm 15\%$. Otherwise the solute atoms will create substantial lattice distortions and a new phase will form.
2. *Crystal structure*. For appreciable solid solubility the crystal structures for metals of both atom types must be the same.
3. *Electronegativity*. The more electropositive one element and the more electronegative the other, the greater is the likelihood that they will form an intermetallic compound instead of a substitutional solid solution.
4. *Valences*. Other factors being equal, a metal will have more of a tendency to dissolve another metal of higher valency than one of a lower valency.

An example of a substitutional solid solution is found for copper and nickel. These two elements are completely soluble in one another at all proportions. With regard to the aforementioned rules that govern degree of solubility, the atomic radii for copper and nickel are 0.128 and 0.125 nm, respectively, both have the FCC crystal structure, and their electronegativities are 1.9 and 1.8 (Figure 2.7); finally, the most common valences are $+1$ for copper (although it sometimes can be $+2$) and $+2$ for nickel.

For interstitial solid solutions, impurity atoms fill the voids or interstices among the host atoms (see Figure 5.2). For metallic materials that have relatively high atomic packing factors, these interstitial positions are relatively small. Consequently, the atomic diameter of an interstitial impurity must be substantially smaller than that of the host atoms. Normally, the maximum allowable concentration of interstitial impurity atoms is low (less than 10%). Even very small impurity atoms are ordinarily larger than the interstitial sites, and as a consequence they introduce some lattice strains on the adjacent host atoms. Problem 5.5 calls for determination of the radii of impurity atoms (in terms of R, the host atom radius) that will just fit into interstitial positions without introducing any lattice strains for both FCC and BCC crystal structures.

Carbon forms an interstitial solid solution when added to iron; the maximum concentration of carbon is about 2%. The atomic radius of the carbon atom is much less than that for iron: 0.071 nm versus 0.124 nm. Solid solutions are also possible for ceramic materials, as discussed in Section 5.5.

5.4 SPECIFICATION OF COMPOSITION

It is often necessary to express the **composition** (or *concentration*)[3] of an alloy in terms of its constituent elements. The two most common ways to specify composition are weight (or mass) percent and atom percent. The basis for **weight percent** (wt%) is the weight of a particular element relative to the total alloy weight. For an alloy that contains two hypothetical atoms denoted by 1 and 2, the concentration of 1 in wt%, C_1, is defined as

$$C_1 = \frac{m_1}{m_1 + m_2} \times 100 \tag{5.3}$$

where m_1 and m_2 represent the weight (or mass) of elements 1 and 2, respectively. The concentration of 2 would be computed in an analogous manner.

The basis for **atom percent** (at%) calculations is the number of moles of an element in relation to the total moles of the elements in the alloy. The number of moles in some specified mass of a hypothetical element 1, n_{m1}, may be computed as follows:

$$n_{m1} = \frac{m_1'}{A_1} \tag{5.4}$$

Here, m_1' and A_1 denote the mass (in grams) and atomic weight, respectively, for element 1.

Concentration in terms of atom percent of element 1 in an alloy containing 1 and 2 atoms, C_1', is defined by[4]

$$C_1' = \frac{n_{m1}}{n_{m1} + n_{m2}} \times 100 \tag{5.5}$$

In like manner, the atom percent of 2 may be determined.

---

[3] The terms *composition* and *concentration* will be assumed to have the same meaning in this book (i.e., the relative content of a specific element or constituent in an alloy) and will be used interchangeably.

[4] In order to avoid confusion in notations and symbols that are being used in this section, we should point out that the prime (as in C_1' and m_1') is used to designate both composition, in atom percent, as well as mass of material in units of grams.

Atom percent computations also can be carried out on the basis of the number of atoms instead of moles, since one mole of all substances contains the same number of atoms.

Composition Conversions

Sometimes it is necessary to convert from one composition scheme to another—for example, from weight percent to atom percent. We will now present equations for making these conversions in terms of the two hypothetical elements 1 and 2. Using the convention of the previous section (i.e., weight percents denoted by C_1 and C_2, atom percents by C'_1 and C'_2, and atomic weights as A_1 and A_2), these conversion expressions are as follows:

$$C'_1 = \frac{C_1 A_2}{C_1 A_2 + C_2 A_1} \times 100 \tag{5.6a}$$

$$C'_2 = \frac{C_2 A_1}{C_1 A_2 + C_2 A_1} \times 100 \tag{5.6b}$$

$$C_1 = \frac{C'_1 A_1}{C'_1 A_1 + C'_2 A_2} \times 100 \tag{5.7a}$$

$$C_2 = \frac{C'_2 A_2}{C'_1 A_1 + C'_2 A_2} \times 100 \tag{5.7b}$$

Since we are considering only two elements, computations involving the preceding equations are simplified when it is realized that

$$C_1 + C_2 = 100 \tag{5.8a}$$

$$C'_1 + C'_2 = 100 \tag{5.8b}$$

In addition, it sometimes becomes necessary to convert concentration from weight percent to mass of one component per unit volume of material (i.e., from units of wt% to kg/m^3); this latter composition scheme is often used in diffusion computations (Section 6.3). Concentrations in terms of this basis will be denoted using a double prime (i.e., C''_1 and C''_2), and the relevant equations are as follows:

$$C''_1 = \left(\frac{C_1}{\dfrac{C_1}{\rho_1} + \dfrac{C_2}{\rho_2}} \right) \times 10^3 \tag{5.9a}$$

$$C''_2 = \left(\frac{C_2}{\dfrac{C_1}{\rho_1} + \dfrac{C_2}{\rho_2}} \right) \times 10^3 \tag{5.9b}$$

For density ρ in units of g/cm^3, these expressions yield C''_1 and C''_2 in kg/m^3.

Furthermore, on occasion we desire to determine the density and atomic weight of a binary alloy given the composition in terms of either weight percent or atom percent. If we represent alloy density and atomic weight by ρ_{ave} and A_{ave}, respectively, then

$$\rho_{ave} = \frac{100}{\dfrac{C_1}{\rho_1} + \dfrac{C_2}{\rho_2}} \tag{5.10a}$$

$$\rho_{ave} = \frac{C_1'A_1 + C_2'A_2}{\dfrac{C_1'A_1}{\rho_1} + \dfrac{C_2'A_2}{\rho_2}} \tag{5.10b}$$

$$A_{ave} = \frac{100}{\dfrac{C_1}{A_1} + \dfrac{C_2}{A_2}} \tag{5.11a}$$

$$A_{ave} = \frac{C_1'A_1 + C_2'A_2}{100} \tag{5.11b}$$

It should be noted that Equations 5.9 and 5.11 are not always exact. In their derivations, it is assumed that total alloy volume is exactly equal to the sum of the volumes of the individual elements. This normally is not the case for most alloys; however, it is a reasonably valid assumption and does not lead to significant errors for dilute solutions and over composition ranges where solid solutions exist.

EXAMPLE PROBLEM 5.2

Derivation of Composition-Conversion Equation

Derive Equation 5.6a.

Solution

To simplify this derivation, we will assume that masses are expressed in units of grams, and denoted with a prime (e.g., m_1'). Furthermore, the total alloy mass (in grams) M' is

$$M' = m_1' + m_2' \tag{5.12}$$

Using the definition of C_1' (Equation 5.5) and incorporating the expression for n_{m1}, Equation 5.4, and the analogous expression for n_{m2} yields

$$C_1' = \frac{n_{m1}}{n_{m1} + n_{m2}} \times 100$$

$$= \frac{\dfrac{m_1'}{A_1}}{\dfrac{m_1'}{A_1} + \dfrac{m_2'}{A_2}} \times 100 \tag{5.13}$$

Rearrangement of the mass-in-grams equivalent of Equation 5.3 leads to

$$m_1' = \frac{C_1M'}{100} \tag{5.14}$$

Substitution of this expression and its m_2' equivalent into Equation 5.13 gives

$$C_1' = \frac{\dfrac{C_1 M'}{100 A_1}}{\dfrac{C_1 M'}{100 A_1} + \dfrac{C_2 M'}{100 A_2}} \times 100 \tag{5.15}$$

Upon simplification we have

$$C_1' = \frac{C_1 A_2}{C_1 A_2 + C_2 A_1} \times 100$$

which is identical to Equation 5.6a.

EXAMPLE PROBLEM 5.3

Composition Conversion—From Weight Percent to Atom Percent

Determine the composition, in atom percent, of an alloy that consists of 97 wt% aluminum and 3 wt% copper.

Solution

If we denote the respective weight percent compositions as $C_{Al} = 97$ and $C_{Cu} = 3$, substitution into Equations 5.6a and 5.6b yields

$$\begin{aligned} C'_{Al} &= \frac{C_{Al} A_{Cu}}{C_{Al} A_{Cu} + C_{Cu} A_{Al}} \times 100 \\ &= \frac{(97)(63.55 \text{ g/mol})}{(97)(63.55 \text{ g/mol}) + (3)(26.98 \text{ g/mol})} \times 100 \\ &= 98.7 \text{ at\%} \end{aligned}$$

and

$$\begin{aligned} C'_{Cu} &= \frac{C_{Cu} A_{Al}}{C_{Cu} A_{Al} + C_{Al} A_{Cu}} \times 100 \\ &= \frac{(3)(26.98 \text{ g/mol})}{(3)(26.98 \text{ g/mol}) + (97)(63.55 \text{ g/mol})} \times 100 \\ &= 1.30 \text{ at\%} \end{aligned}$$

5.5 IMPERFECTIONS IN CERAMICS

Atomic Point Defects

Atomic defects involving host atoms may exist in ceramic compounds. As with metals, both vacancies and interstitials are possible; however, since ceramic materials contain ions of at least two kinds, defects for each ion type may occur. For example, in NaCl, Na interstitials and vacancies and Cl interstitials and vacancies may exist. It is highly improbable that there would be appreciable concentrations of anion interstitials. The anion is relatively large, and to fit into a small interstitial

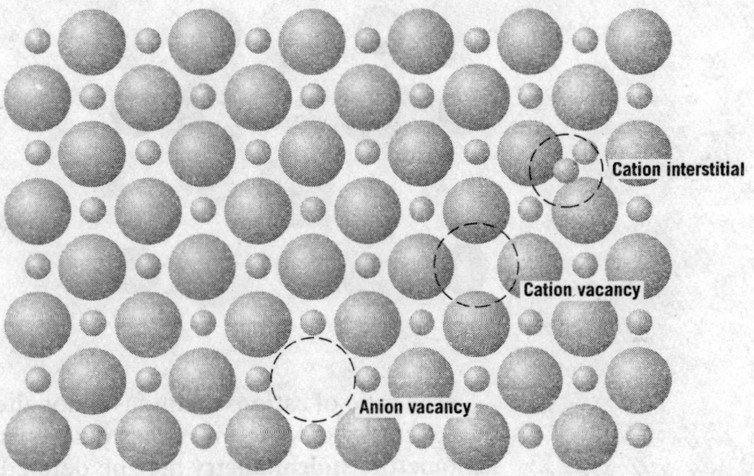

Figure 5.3 Schematic representations of cation and anion vacancies and a cation interstitial. (From W. G. Moffatt, G. W. Pearsall, and J. Wulff, *The Structure and Properties of Materials,* Vol. I, *Structure,* p. 78. Copyright © 1964 by John Wiley & Sons, New York. Reprinted by permission of John Wiley & Sons, Inc.)

position, substantial strains on the surrounding ions must be introduced. Anion and cation vacancies and a cation interstitial are represented in Figure 5.3.

The expression **defect structure** is often used to designate the types and concentrations of atomic defects in ceramics. Because the atoms exist as charged ions, when defect structures are considered, conditions of electroneutrality must be maintained. **Electroneutrality** is the state that exists when there are equal numbers of positive and negative charges from the ions. As a consequence, defects in ceramics do not occur alone. One such type of defect involves a cation–vacancy and a cation–interstitial pair. This is called a **Frenkel defect** (Figure 5.4). It might be thought of as being formed by a cation leaving its normal position and moving into an interstitial site. There is no change in charge because the cation maintains the same positive charge as an interstitial.

Another type of defect found in AX materials is a cation vacancy–anion vacancy pair known as a **Schottky defect,** also schematically diagrammed in Figure 5.4. This defect might be thought of as being created by removing one cation and one anion from the interior of the crystal and then placing them both at an external surface. Since both cations and anions have the same charge, and since for every anion vacancy there exists a cation vacancy, the charge neutrality of the crystal is maintained.

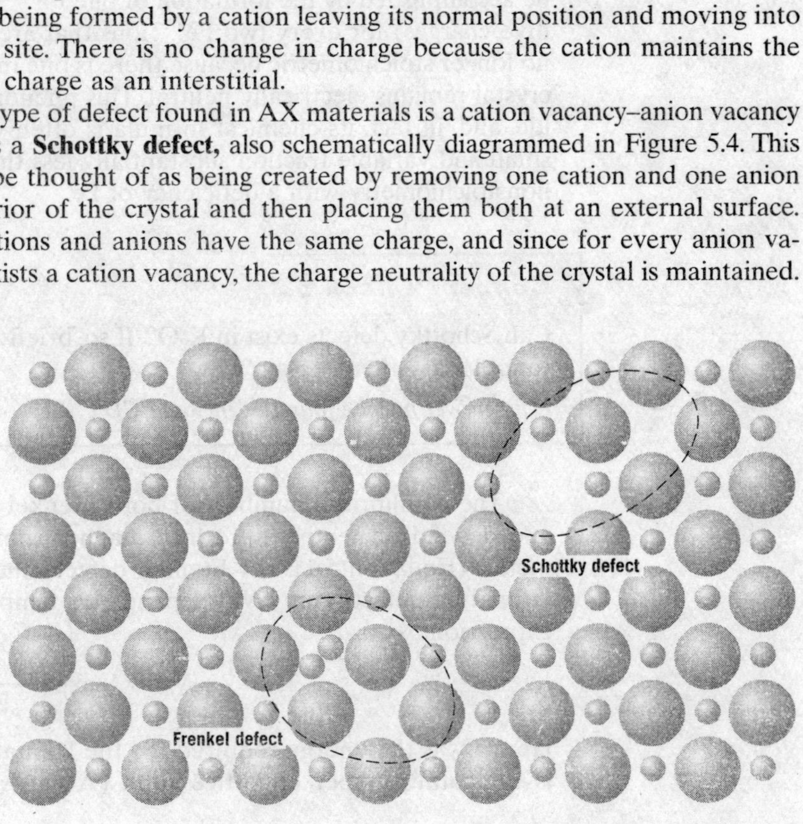

Figure 5.4 Schematic diagram showing Frenkel and Schottky defects in ionic solids. (From W. G. Moffatt, G. W. Pearsall, and J. Wulff, *The Structure and Properties of Materials,* Vol. I, *Structure,* p. 78. Copyright © 1964 by John Wiley & Sons, New York. Reprinted by permission of John Wiley & Sons, Inc.)

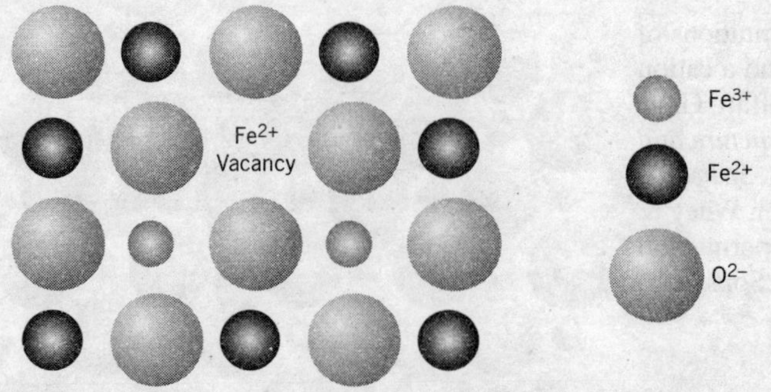

Figure 5.5 Schematic representation of an Fe^{2+} vacancy in FeO that results from the formation of two Fe^{3+} ions.

The ratio of cations to anions is not altered by the formation of either a Frenkel or a Schottky defect. If no other defects are present, the material is said to be stoichiometric. **Stoichiometry** may be defined as a state for ionic compounds wherein there is the exact ratio of cations to anions as predicted by the chemical formula. For example, NaCl is stoichiometric if the ratio of Na^+ ions to Cl^- ions is exactly 1:1. A ceramic compound is *nonstoichiometric* if there is any deviation from this exact ratio.

Nonstoichiometry may occur for some ceramic materials in which two valence (or ionic) states exist for one of the ion types. Iron oxide (wüstite, FeO) is one such material, for the iron can be present in both Fe^{2+} and Fe^{3+} states; the number of each of these ion types depends on temperature and the ambient oxygen pressure. The formation of an Fe^{3+} ion disrupts the electroneutrality of the crystal by introducing an excess +1 charge, which must be offset by some type of defect. This may be accomplished by the formation of one Fe^{2+} vacancy (or the removal of two positive charges) for every two Fe^{3+} ions that are formed (Figure 5.5). The crystal is no longer stoichiometric because there is one more O ion than Fe ion; however, the crystal remains electrically neutral. This phenomenon is fairly common in iron oxide, and, in fact, its chemical formula is often written as $Fe_{1-x}O$ (where x is some small and variable fraction substantially less than unity) to indicate a condition of nonstoichiometry with a deficiency of Fe.

Concept Check 5.1

Can Schottky defects exist in K_2O? If so, briefly describe this type of defect. If they cannot exist, then explain why.

[*The answer may be found in enclosed CD.*]

The equilibrium numbers of both Frenkel and Schottky defects increase with and depend on temperature in a manner similar to the number of vacancies in metals (Equation 5.1). For Frenkel defects, the number of cation-vacancy/cation-interstitial defect pairs (N_{fr}) depends on temperature according to the following expression:

$$N_{fr} = N \exp\left(-\frac{Q_{fr}}{2kT}\right) \tag{5.16}$$

Here Q_{fr} is the energy required for the formation of each Frenkel defect, and N is the total number of lattice sites. (Also, as in previous discussions, k and T

represent Boltzmann's constant and the absolute temperature, respectively.) The factor 2 is present in the denominator of the exponential because two defects (a missing cation and an interstitial cation) are associated with each Frenkel defect.

Similarly, for Schottky defects, in an AX-type compound, the equilibrium number (N_s) is a function of temperature as

$$N_s = N \exp\left(-\frac{Q_s}{2kT}\right) \tag{5.17}$$

where Q_s represents the Schottky defect energy of formation.

EXAMPLE PROBLEM 5.4

Computation of the Number of Schottky Defects in KCl

Calculate the number of Schottky defects per cubic meter in potassium chloride at 500°C. The energy required to form each Schottky defect is 2.6 eV, while the density for KCl (at 500°C) is 1.955 g/cm^3.

Solution

To solve this problem it is necessary to use Equation 5.17. However, we must first compute the value of N (the number of lattice sites per cubic meter); this is possible using a modified form of Equation 5.2—i.e.,

$$N = \frac{N_A \rho}{A_K + A_{Cl}} \tag{5.18}$$

where N_A is Avogadro's number (6.023×10^{23} atoms/mol), ρ is the density, and A_K and A_{Cl} are the atomic weights for potassium and chlorine (i.e., 39.10 and 35.45 g/mol), respectively. Therefore,

$$N = \frac{(6.023 \times 10^{23}\ \text{atoms/mol})(1.955\ \text{g/cm}^3)(10^6\ \text{cm}^3/\text{m}^3)}{39.10\ \text{g/mol} + 35.45\ \text{g/mol}}$$

$$= 1.58 \times 10^{28}\ \text{lattice sites/m}^3$$

Now, incorporating this value into Equation 5.17, leads to the following value for N_s

$$N_s = N \exp\left(-\frac{Q_s}{2kT}\right)$$

$$= (1.58 \times 10^{28}\ \text{lattice sites/m}^3) \exp\left[-\frac{2.6\ \text{eV}}{(2)(8.62 \times 10^{-5}\ \text{eV/K})(500 + 273\ \text{K})}\right]$$

$$= 5.31 \times 10^{19}\ \text{defects/m}^3$$

Impurities in Ceramics

Impurity atoms can form solid solutions in ceramic materials much as they do in metals. Solid solutions of both substitutional and interstitial types are possible. For an interstitial, the ionic radius of the impurity must be relatively small in comparison to the anion. Since there are both anions and cations, a substitutional impurity will substitute for the host ion to which it is most similar in an electrical sense: if

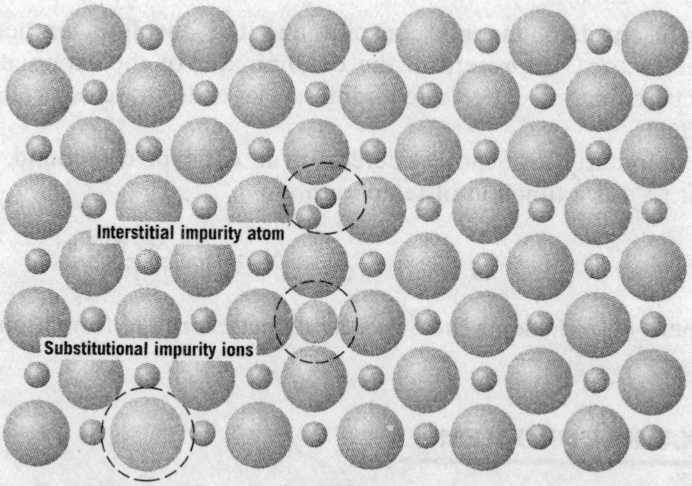

Figure 5.6 Schematic representations of interstitial, anion-substitutional, and cation-substitutional impurity atoms in an ionic compound. (Adapted from W. G. Moffatt, G. W. Pearsall, and J. Wulff, *The Structure and Properties of Materials,* Vol. I, *Structure,* p. 78. Copyright © 1964 by John Wiley & Sons, New York. Reprinted by permission of John Wiley & Sons, Inc.)

the impurity atom normally forms a cation in a ceramic material, it most probably will substitute for a host cation. For example, in sodium chloride, impurity Ca^{2+} and O^{2-} ions would most likely substitute for Na^+ and Cl^- ions, respectively. Schematic representations for cation and anion substitutional as well as interstitial impurities are shown in Figure 5.6. To achieve any appreciable solid solubility of substituting impurity atoms, the ionic size and charge must be very nearly the same as those of one of the host ions. For an impurity ion having a charge different from the host ion for which it substitutes, the crystal must compensate for this difference in charge so that electroneutrality is maintained with the solid. One way this is accomplished is by the formation of lattice defects—vacancies or interstitials of both ion types, as discussed above.

EXAMPLE PROBLEM 5.5

Determination of Possible Point Defect Types in NaCl Due to the Presence of Ca^{2+} Ions

If electroneutrality is to be preserved, what point defects are possible in NaCl when a Ca^{2+} substitutes for an Na^+ ion? How many of these defects exist for every Ca^{2+} ion?

Solution

Replacement of an Na^+ by a Ca^{2+} ion introduces one extra positive charge. Electroneutrality is maintained when either a single positive charge is eliminated or another single negative charge is added. Removal of a positive charge is accomplished by the formation of one Na^+ vacancy. Alternatively, a Cl^- interstitial will supply an additional negative charge, negating the effect of each Ca^{2+} ion. However, as mentioned above, the formation of this defect is highly unlikely.

Concept Check 5.2

What point defects are possible for MgO as an impurity in Al_2O_3? How many Mg^{2+} ions must be added to form each of these defects?

[The answer may be found in enclosed CD.]

Miscellaneous Imperfections

5.6 DISLOCATIONS—LINEAR DEFECTS

A *dislocation* is a linear or one-dimensional defect around which some of the atoms are misaligned. One type of dislocation is represented in Figure 5.7: an extra portion of a plane of atoms, or half-plane, the edge of which terminates within the crystal. This is termed an **edge dislocation;** it is a linear defect that centers around the line that is defined along the end of the extra half-plane of atoms. This is sometimes termed the **dislocation line,** which, for the edge dislocation in Figure 5.7, is perpendicular to the plane of the page. Within the region around the dislocation line there is some localized lattice distortion. The atoms above the dislocation line in Figure 5.7 are squeezed together, and those below are pulled apart; this is reflected in the slight curvature for the vertical planes of atoms as they bend around this extra half-plane. The magnitude of this distortion decreases with distance away from the dislocation line; at positions far removed, the crystal lattice is virtually perfect. Sometimes the edge dislocation in Figure 5.7 is represented by the symbol $\perp$, which also indicates the position of the dislocation line. An edge dislocation may also be formed by an extra half-plane of atoms that is included in the bottom portion of the crystal; its designation is a $\top$.

Another type of dislocation, called a **screw dislocation,** exists, which may be thought of as being formed by a shear stress that is applied to produce the distortion shown in Figure 5.8*a*: the upper front region of the crystal is shifted one atomic distance to the right relative to the bottom portion. The atomic distortion associated with a screw dislocation is also linear and along a dislocation line, line *AB* in Figure 5.8*b*. The screw dislocation derives its name from the spiral or helical path

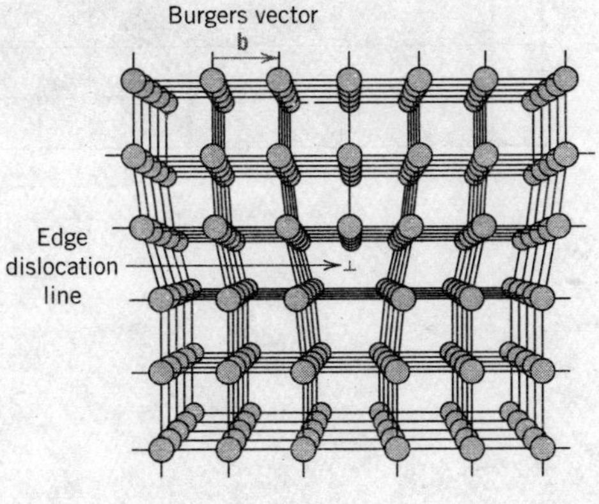

Figure 5.7 The atom positions around an edge dislocation; extra half-plane of atoms shown in perspective. (Adapted from A. G. Guy, *Essentials of Materials Science,* McGraw-Hill Book Company, New York, 1976, p. 153.)

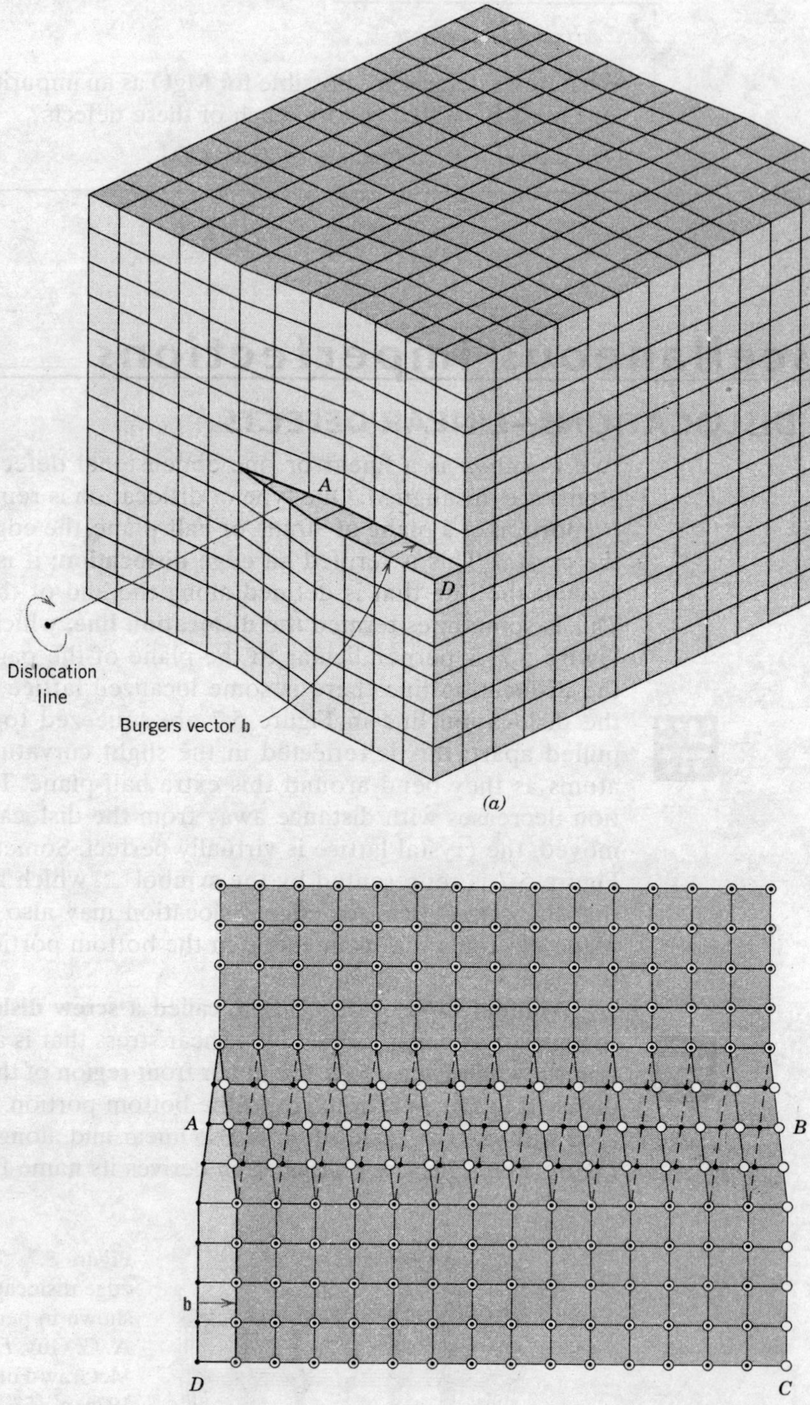

Figure 5.8 (*a*) A screw dislocation within a crystal. (*b*) The screw dislocation in (*a*) as viewed from above. The dislocation line extends along line *AB*. Atom positions above the slip plane are designated by open circles, those below by solid circles. [Figure (*b*) from W. T. Read, Jr., *Dislocations in Crystals,* McGraw-Hill Book Company, New York, 1953.]

or ramp that is traced around the dislocation line by the atomic planes of atoms. Sometimes the symbol ↻ is used to designate a screw dislocation.

Most dislocations found in crystalline materials are probably neither pure edge nor pure screw, but exhibit components of both types; these are termed **mixed dislocations.** All three dislocation types are represented schematically in Figure 5.9; the lattice distortion that is produced away from the two faces is mixed, having varying degrees of screw and edge character.

The magnitude and direction of the lattice distortion associated with a dislocation is expressed in terms of a **Burgers vector,** denoted by a **b**. Burgers vectors are indicated in Figures 5.7 and 5.8 for edge and screw dislocations, respectively. Furthermore, the nature of a dislocation (i.e., edge, screw, or mixed) is defined by the relative orientations of dislocation line and Burgers vector. For an edge, they are perpendicular (Figure 5.7), whereas for a screw, they are parallel (Figure 5.8); they are neither perpendicular nor parallel for a mixed dislocation. Also, even though a dislocation changes direction and nature within a crystal (e.g., from edge to mixed to screw), the Burgers vector will be the same at all points along its line. For example, all positions of the curved dislocation in Figure 5.9 will have the Burgers vector shown. For metallic materials, the Burgers vector for a dislocation will point in a close-packed crystallographic direction and will be of magnitude equal to the interatomic spacing.

As we note in Section 10.4, the permanent deformation of most crystalline materials is by the motion of dislocations. In addition, the Burgers vector is an element of the theory that has been developed to explain this type of deformation.

Dislocations can be observed in crystalline materials using electron-microscopic techniques. In Figure 5.10, a high-magnification transmission electron micrograph, the dark lines are the dislocations.

Virtually all crystalline materials contain some dislocations that were introduced during solidification, during plastic deformation, and as a consequence of thermal stresses that result from rapid cooling. Dislocations are involved in the plastic deformation of crystalline materials, both metals and ceramics, as discussed in Chapters 10 and 12. They have also been observed in polymeric materials, and are discussed in Section 5.10.

5.7 INTERFACIAL DEFECTS

Interfacial defects are boundaries that have two dimensions and normally separate regions of the materials that have different crystal structures and/or crystallographic orientations. These imperfections include external surfaces, grain boundaries, twin boundaries, stacking faults, and phase boundaries.

External Surfaces

One of the most obvious boundaries is the external surface, along which the crystal structure terminates. Surface atoms are not bonded to the maximum number of nearest neighbors, and are therefore in a higher energy state than the atoms at interior positions. The bonds of these surface atoms that are not satisfied give rise to a surface energy, expressed in units of energy per unit area (J/m^2 or erg/cm^2). To reduce this energy, materials tend to minimize, if at all possible, the total surface area. For example, liquids assume a shape having a minimum area—the droplets become spherical. Of course, this is not possible with solids, which are mechanically rigid.

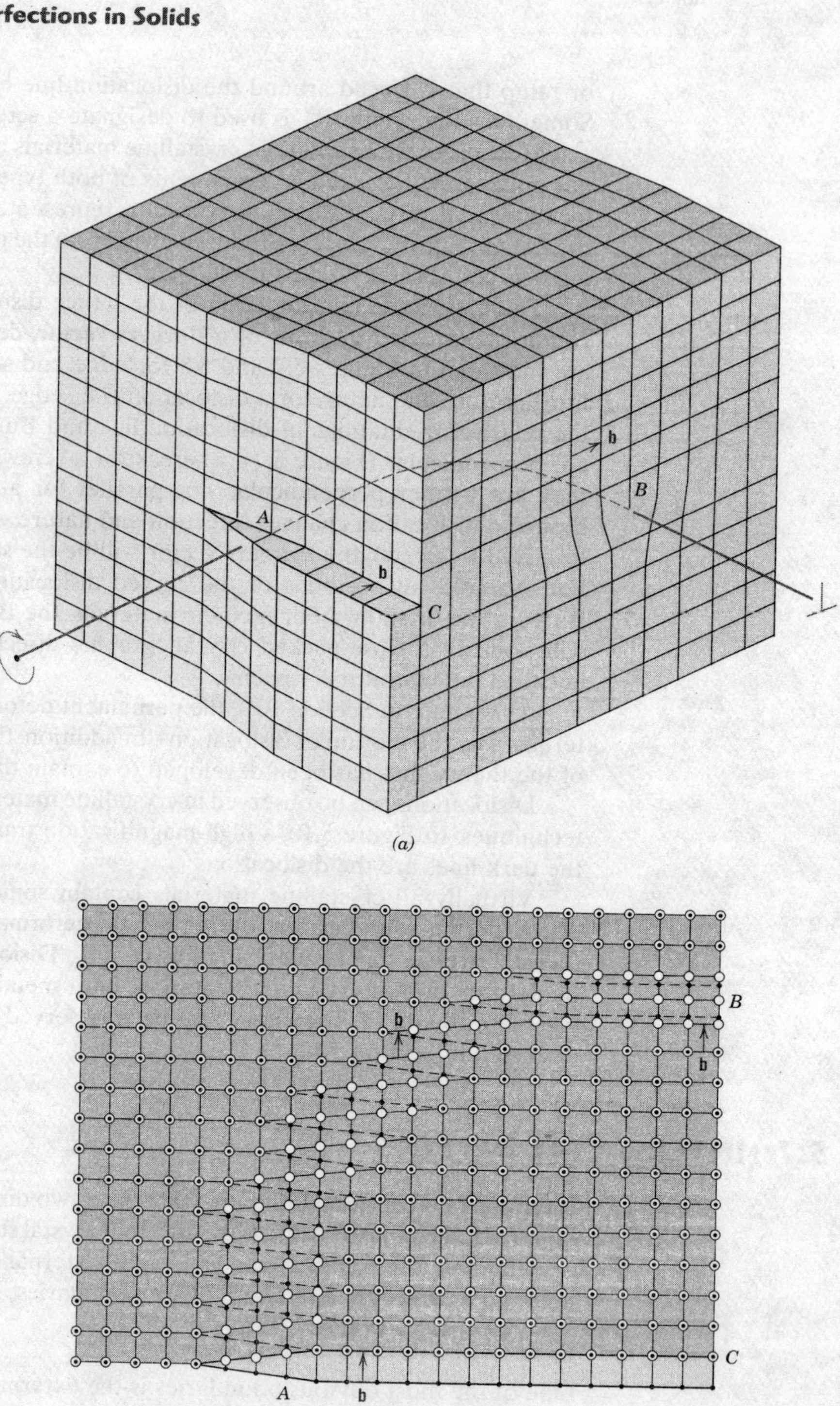

Figure 5.9 (*a*) Schematic representation of a dislocation that has edge, screw, and mixed character. (*b*) Top view, where open circles denote atom positions above the slip plane. Solid circles, atom positions below. At point *A*, the dislocation is pure screw, while at point *B*, it is pure edge. For regions in between where there is curvature in the dislocation line, the character is mixed edge and screw. [Figure (*b*) from W. T. Read, Jr., *Dislocations in Crystals,* McGraw-Hill Book Company, New York, 1953.]

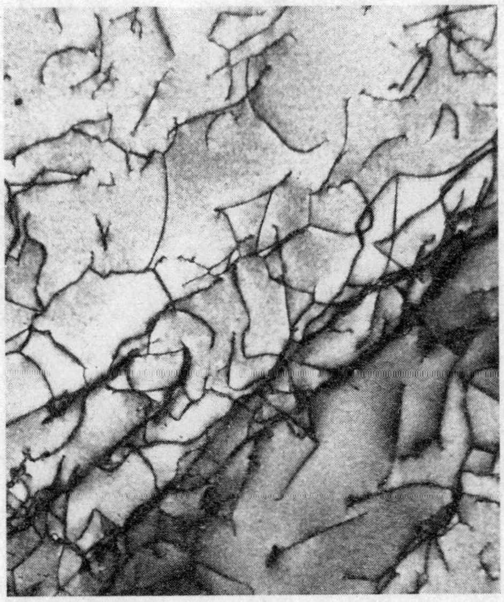

Figure 5.10 A transmission electron micrograph of a titanium alloy in which the dark lines are dislocations. 51,450×. (Courtesy of M. R. Plichta, Michigan Technological University.)

Grain Boundaries

Another interfacial defect, the grain boundary, was introduced in Section 3.9 as the boundary separating two small grains or crystals having different crystallographic orientations in polycrystalline materials. A grain boundary is represented schematically from an atomic perspective in Figure 5.11. Within the boundary region, which is probably just several atom distances wide, there is some atomic mismatch in a transition from the crystalline orientation of one grain to that of an adjacent one.

Various degrees of crystallographic misalignment between adjacent grains are possible (Figure 5.11). When this orientation mismatch is slight, on the order of a few degrees, then the term *small-* (or *low-*) *angle grain boundary* is used. These boundaries can be described in terms of dislocation arrays. One simple small-angle grain boundary is formed when edge dislocations are aligned in the manner of Figure 5.12.

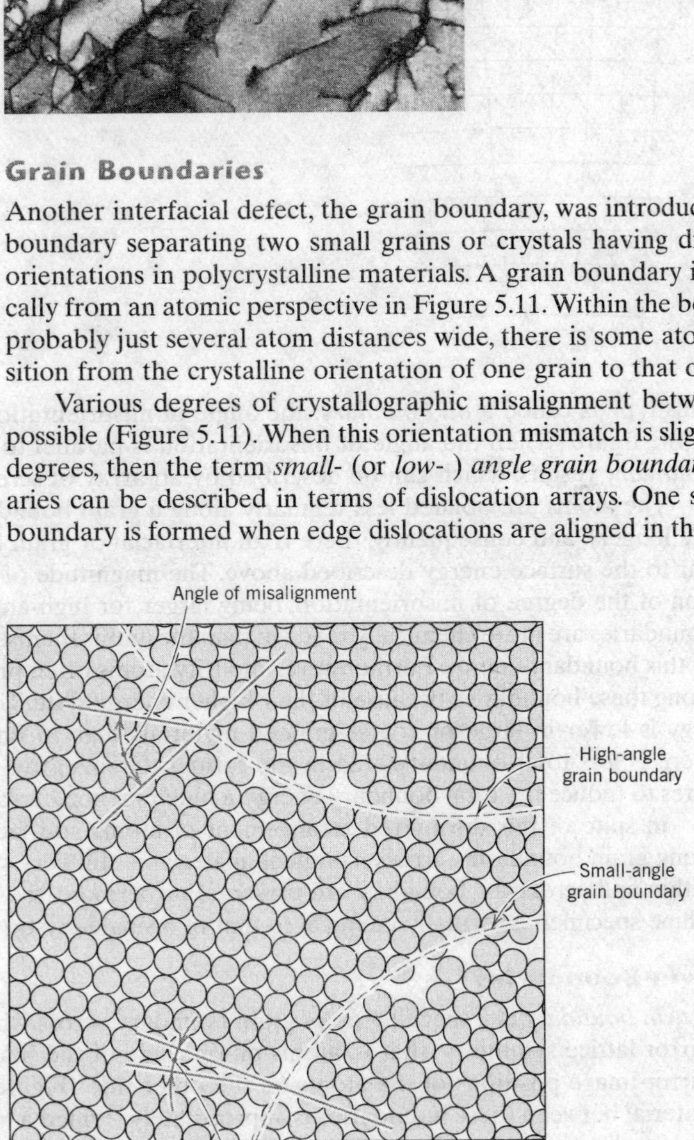

Figure 5.11 Schematic diagram showing small- and high-angle grain boundaries and the adjacent atom positions.

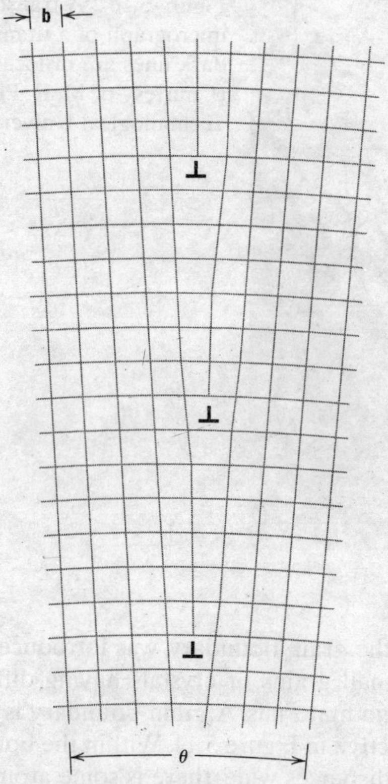

Figure 5.12 Demonstration of how a tilt boundary having an angle of misorientation θ results from an alignment of edge dislocations.

This type is called a *tilt boundary;* the angle of misorientation, θ, is also indicated in the figure. When the angle of misorientation is parallel to the boundary, a *twist boundary* results, which can be described by an array of screw dislocations.

The atoms are bonded less regularly along a grain boundary (e.g., bond angles are longer), and consequently, there is an interfacial or grain boundary energy similar to the surface energy described above. The magnitude of this energy is a function of the degree of misorientation, being larger for high-angle boundaries. Grain boundaries are more chemically reactive than the grains themselves as a consequence of this boundary energy. Furthermore, impurity atoms often preferentially segregate along these boundaries because of their higher energy state. The total interfacial energy is lower in large or coarse-grained materials than in fine-grained ones, since there is less total boundary area in the former. Grains grow at elevated temperatures to reduce the total boundary energy, a phenomenon explained in Section 10.13.

In spite of this disordered arrangement of atoms and lack of regular bonding along grain boundaries, a polycrystalline material is still very strong; cohesive forces within and across the boundary are present. Furthermore, the density of a polycrystalline specimen is virtually identical to that of a single crystal of the same material.

Twin Boundaries

A *twin boundary* is a special type of grain boundary across which there is a specific mirror lattice symmetry; that is, atoms on one side of the boundary are located in mirror-image positions of the atoms on the other side (Figure 5.13). The region of material between these boundaries is appropriately termed a *twin*. Twins result from atomic displacements that are produced from applied mechanical shear forces (mechanical twins), and also during annealing heat treatments following deforma-

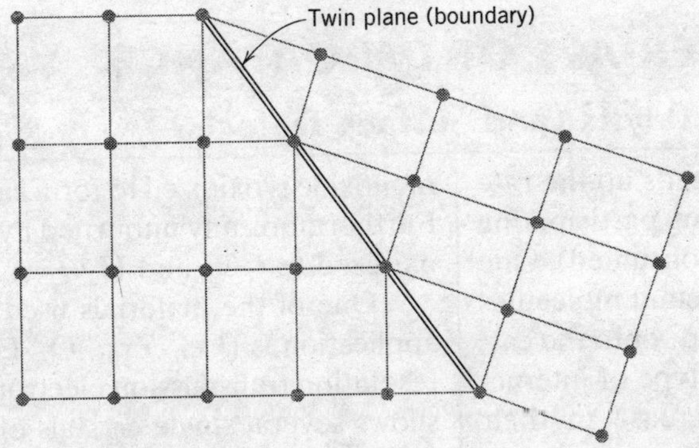

Figure 5.13 Schematic diagram showing a twin plane or boundary and the adjacent atom positions (colored circles).

tion (annealing twins). Twinning occurs on a definite crystallographic plane and in a specific direction, both of which depend on the crystal structure. Annealing twins are typically found in metals that have the FCC crystal structure, while mechanical twins are observed in BCC and HCP metals. The role of mechanical twins in the deformation process is discussed in Section 10.7. Annealing twins may be observed in the photomicrograph of the polycrystalline brass specimen shown in Figure 5.18*c*. The twins correspond to those regions having relatively straight and parallel sides and a different visual contrast than the untwinned regions of the grains within which they reside. An explanation for the variety of textural contrasts in this photomicrograph is provided in Section 5.12.

Miscellaneous Interfacial Defects

Other possible interfacial defects include stacking faults, phase boundaries, and ferromagnetic domain walls. Stacking faults are found in FCC metals when there is an interruption in the *ABCABCABC* . . . stacking sequence of close-packed planes (Section 4.8). Phase boundaries exist in multiphase materials (Section 7.3) across which there is a sudden change in physical and/or chemical characteristics. For ferromagnetic and ferrimagnetic materials, the boundary that separates regions having different directions of magnetization is termed a domain wall, which is discussed in Section 18.7.

Associated with each of the defects discussed in this section is an interfacial energy, the magnitude of which depends on boundary type, and which will vary from material to material. Normally, the interfacial energy will be greatest for external surfaces and least for domain walls.

Concept Check 5.3

The surface energy of a single crystal depends on crystallographic orientation. Does this surface energy increase or decrease with an increase in planar density. Why?

[*The answer may be found in enclosed CD.*]

5.8 BULK OR VOLUME DEFECTS

Other defects exist in all solid materials that are much larger than those heretofore discussed. These include pores, cracks, foreign inclusions, and other phases. They are normally introduced during processing and fabrication steps. Some of these defects and their effects on the properties of materials are discussed in subsequent chapters.

MATERIALS OF IMPORTANCE

Catalysts (and Surface Defects)

A *catalyst* is a substance that speeds up the rate of a chemical reaction without participating in the reaction itself (i.e., it is not consumed). One type of catalyst exists as a solid; reactant molecules in a gas or liquid phase are adsorbed[5] onto the catalytic surface, at which point some type of interaction occurs that promotes an increase in their chemical reactivity rate.

Adsorption sites on a catalyst are normally surface defects associated with planes of atoms; an interatomic/intermolecular bond is formed between a defect site and an adsorbed molecular species. Several types of surface defects, represented schematically in Figure 5.14, include ledges, kinks, terraces, vacancies, and individual adatoms (i.e., atoms adsorbed on the surface).

One important use of catalysts is in catalytic converters on automobiles, which reduce the emission of exhaust gas pollutants such as carbon monoxide (CO), nitrogen oxides (NO_x, where x is variable), and unburned hydrocarbons. Air is introduced into the exhaust emissions from the automobile engine; this mixture of gases then passes over the catalyst, which adsorbs on its surface molecules of CO, NO_x, and O_2. The NO_x dissociates into N and O atoms, whereas the O_2 dissociates into its atomic species. Pairs of nitrogen atoms combine to form N_2 molecules, and carbon monoxide is oxidized to form carbon dioxide (CO_2). Furthermore, any unburned hydrocarbons are also oxidized to CO_2 and H_2O.

One of the materials used as a catalyst in this application is $(Ce_{0.5}Zr_{0.5})O_2$. Figure 5.15 is a high-resolution transmission electron micrograph, which shows several single crystals of this material. Individual atoms are resolved in this micrograph as well as some of the defects presented in Figure 5.14. These surface defects act as adsorption sites for the atomic and molecular species noted in the previous paragraph. Consequently, dissociation, combination, and oxidation reactions involving these species are facilitated, such that the content of pollutant species (CO, NO_x, and unburned hydrocarbons) in the exhaust gas stream is reduced significantly.

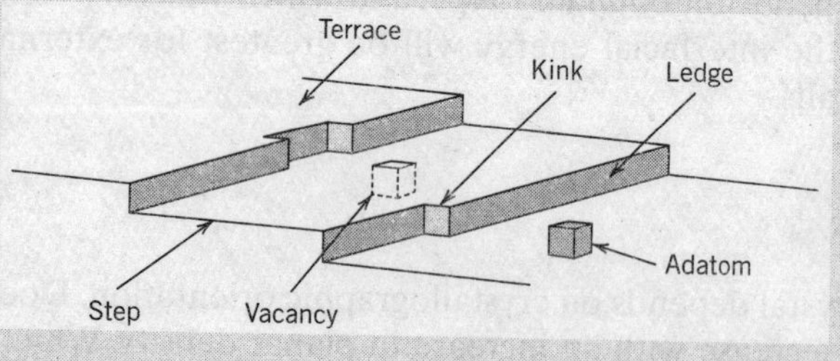

Figure 5.14 Schematic representations of surface defects that are potential adsorption sites for catalysis. Individual atom sites are represented as cubes. (From BOUDART, MICHEL, *KINETICS OF HETEROGENEOUS CATALYTIC REACTIONS*. © 1984 Princeton University Press. Reprinted by permission of Princeton University Press.)

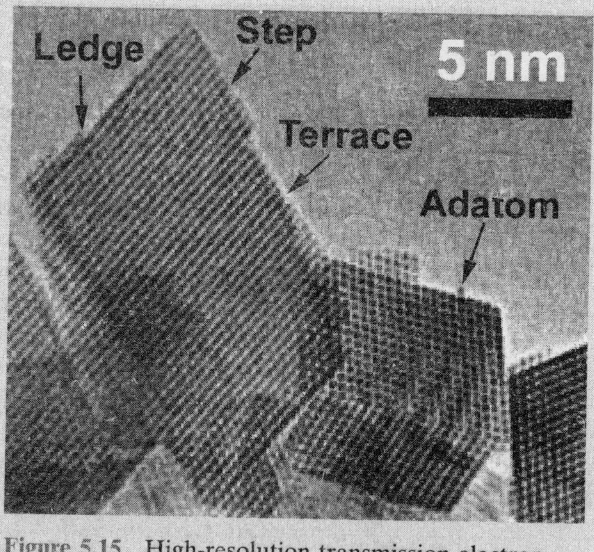

Figure 5.15 High-resolution transmission electron micrograph that shows single crystals of $(Ce_{0.5}Zr_{0.5})O_2$; this material is used in catalytic converters for automobiles. Surface defects represented schematically in Figure 5.10 are noted on the crystals. [From W. J. Stark, L. Mädler, M. Maciejewski, S. E. Pratsinis, A. Baiker, "Flame-Synthesis of Nanocrystalline Ceria/Zirconia: Effect of Carrier Liquid," *Chem. Comm.*, 588–589 (2003). Reproduced by permission of The Royal Society of Chemistry.]

[5] *Adsorption* is the adhesion of molecules of a gas or liquid to a solid surface. It should not be confused with *absorption* which is the assimilation of molecules into a solid or liquid.

5.9 ATOMIC VIBRATIONS

Every atom in a solid material is vibrating very rapidly about its lattice position within the crystal. In a sense, these **atomic vibrations** may be thought of as imperfections or defects. At any instant of time not all atoms vibrate at the same frequency and amplitude, nor with the same energy. At a given temperature there will exist a distribution of energies for the constituent atoms about an average energy. Over time the vibrational energy of any specific atom will also vary in a random manner. With rising temperature, this average energy increases, and, in fact, the temperature of a solid is really just a measure of the average vibrational activity of atoms and molecules. At room temperature, a typical vibrational frequency is on the order of 10^{13} vibrations per second, whereas the amplitude is a few thousandths of a nanometer.

Many properties and processes in solids are manifestations of this vibrational atomic motion. For example, melting occurs when the vibrations are vigorous enough to rupture large numbers of atomic bonds. A more detailed discussion of atomic vibrations and their influence on the properties of materials is presented in Chapter 19.

5.10 DEFECTS IN POLYMERS

The point defect concept is different in polymers than in metals (Section 5.2) and ceramics (Section 5.5) as a consequence of the chain-like macromolecules and the nature of the crystalline state for polymers. Point defects similar to those found in metals have been observed in crystalline regions of polymeric materials; these include vacancies and interstitial atoms and ions. Chain ends are considered to be defects because they are chemically dissimilar to normal chain units. Vacancies are also associated with the chain ends (Figure 5.16). However, additional defects can result from branches in the polymer chain or chain segments that emerge from the crystal. A chain section can leave a polymer crystal and reenter it at another point creating a loop, or can enter a second crystal to act as a tie molecule (see Figure 4.32). Screw dislocations also occur in polymer crystals (Figure 5.16).

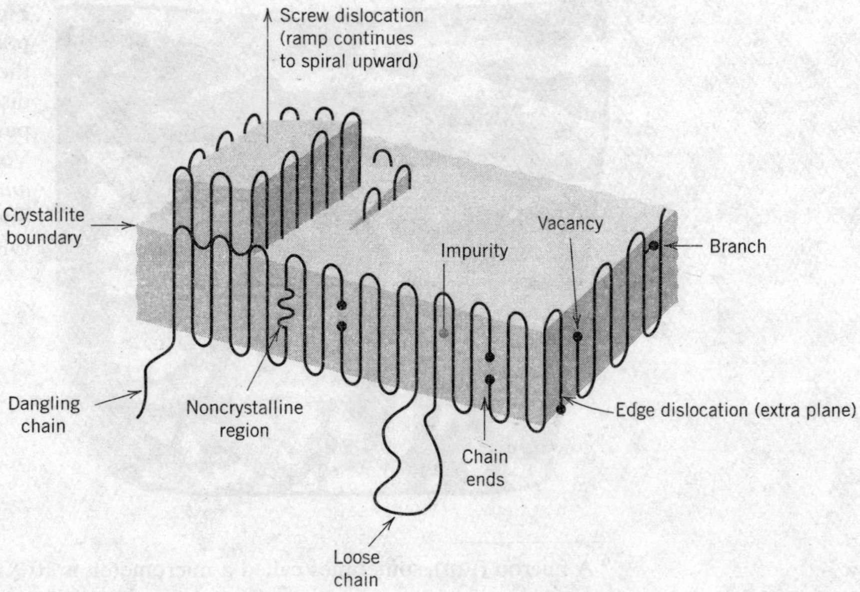

Figure 5.16 Schematic representation of defects in polymer crystallites.

Impurity atoms/ions or groups of atoms/ions may be incorporated in the molecular structure as interstitials; they may also be associated with main chains or as short side branches.

Furthermore, the surfaces of chain-folded layers (Figure 4.32) are considered to be interfacial defects, as are also boundaries between two adjacent crystalline regions.

Microscopic Examination

5.11 GENERAL

On occasion it is necessary or desirable to examine the structural elements and defects that influence the properties of materials. Some structural elements are of *macroscopic* dimensions; that is, they are large enough to be observed with the unaided eye. For example, the shape and average size or diameter of the grains for a polycrystalline specimen are important structural characteristics. Macroscopic grains are often evident on aluminum streetlight posts and also on highway guard rails. Relatively large grains having different textures are clearly visible on the surface of the sectioned lead ingot shown in Figure 5.17. However, in most materials the constituent grains are of *microscopic* dimensions, having diameters that may be on the order of microns,[6] and their details must be investigated using some type of microscope. Grain size and shape are only two features of what is termed the **microstructure;** these and other microstructural characteristics are discussed in subsequent chapters.

Optical, electron, and scanning probe microscopes are commonly used in **microscopy.** These instruments aid in investigations of the microstructural features of all material types. Some of these techniques employ photographic equipment in conjunction with the microscope; the photograph on which the image is recorded is called a **photomicrograph.** In addition, many microstructural images are computer generated and/or enhanced.

Microscopic examination is an extremely useful tool in the study and characterization of materials. Several important applications of microstructural examinations are as follows: to ensure that the associations between the properties and

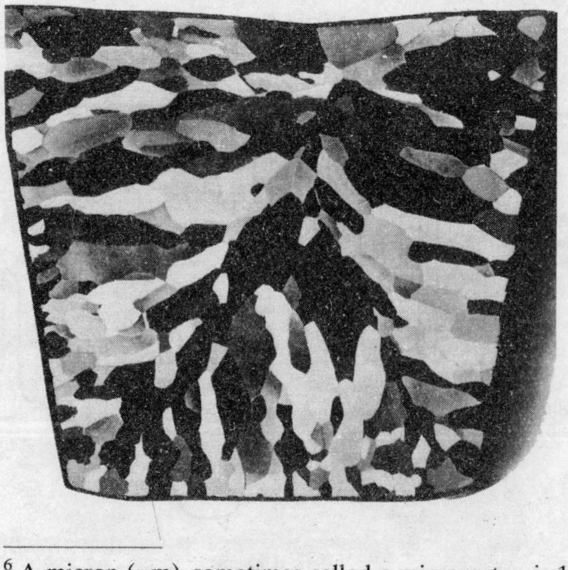

Figure 5.17 High-purity polycrystalline lead ingot in which the individual grains may be discerned. 0.7×. (Reproduced with permission from *Metals Handbook,* Vol. 9, 9th edition, *Metallography and Microstructures,* American Society for Metals, Metals Park, OH, 1985.)

[6] A micron (μm), sometimes called a micrometer, is 10^{-6} m.

structure (and defects) are properly understood, to predict the properties of materials once these relationships have been established, to design alloys with new property combinations, to determine whether or not a material has been correctly heat treated, and to ascertain the mode of mechanical fracture. Several techniques that are commonly used in such investigations are discussed next.

5.12 MICROSCOPIC TECHNIQUES

Optical Microscopy

With optical microscopy, the light microscope is used to study the microstructure; optical and illumination systems are its basic elements. For materials that are opaque to visible light (all metals and many ceramics and polymers), only the surface is subject to observation, and the light microscope must be used in a reflecting mode. Contrasts in the image produced result from differences in reflectivity of the various regions of the microstructure. Investigations of this type are often termed *metallographic,* since metals were first examined using this technique.

Normally, careful and meticulous surface preparations are necessary to reveal the important details of the microstructure. The specimen surface must first be ground and polished to a smooth and mirrorlike finish. This is accomplished by using successively finer abrasive papers and powders. The microstructure is revealed by a surface treatment using an appropriate chemical reagent in a procedure termed *etching*. The chemical reactivity of the grains of some single-phase materials depends on crystallographic orientation. Consequently, in a polycrystalline specimen, etching characteristics vary from grain to grain. Figure 5.18*b* shows how normally incident light is reflected by three etched surface grains, each having a different orientation. Figure 5.18*a* depicts the surface structure as it might appear when viewed with the microscope; the luster or texture of each grain depends on its reflectance properties. A photomicrograph of a polycrystalline specimen exhibiting these characteristics is shown in Figure 5.18*c*.

Also, small grooves form along grain boundaries as a consequence of etching. Since atoms along grain boundary regions are more chemically active, they dissolve at a greater rate than those within the grains. These grooves become discernible when viewed under a microscope because they reflect light at an angle different from that of the grains themselves; this effect is displayed in Figure 5.19*a*. Figure 5.19*b* is a photomicrograph of a polycrystalline specimen in which the grain boundary grooves are clearly visible as dark lines.

When the microstructure of a two-phase alloy is to be examined, an etchant is often chosen that produces a different texture for each phase so that the different phases may be distinguished from each other.

Electron Microscopy

The upper limit to the magnification possible with an optical microscope is approximately 2000 times. Consequently, some structural elements are too fine or small to permit observation using optical microscopy. Under such circumstances the electron microscope, which is capable of much higher magnifications, may be employed.

An image of the structure under investigation is formed using beams of electrons instead of light radiation. According to quantum mechanics, a high-velocity electron will become wave-like, having a wavelength that is inversely proportional to its velocity. When accelerated across large voltages, electrons can be made to

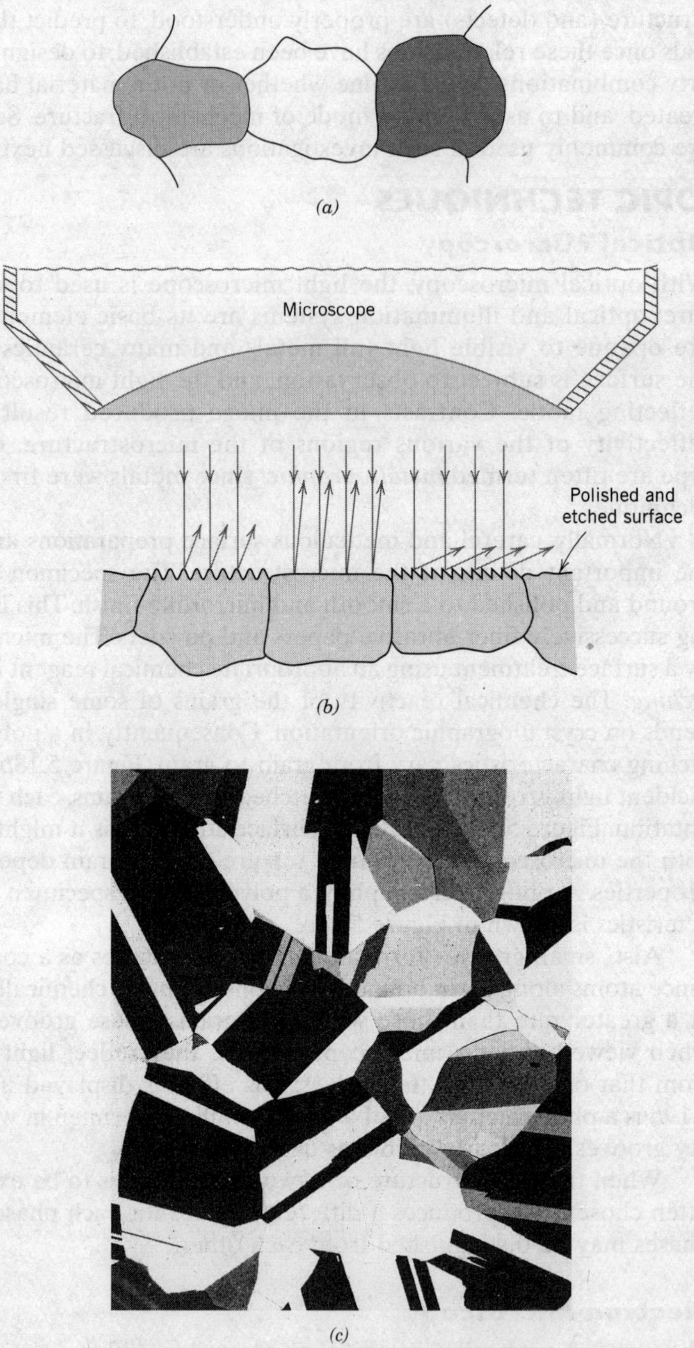

Figure 5.18
(*a*) Polished and etched grains as they might appear when viewed with an optical microscope. (*b*) Section taken through these grains showing how the etching characteristics and resulting surface texture vary from grain to grain because of differences in crystallographic orientation.
(*c*) Photomicrograph of a polycrystalline brass specimen. 60×. (Photomicrograph courtesy of J. E. Burke, General Electric Co.)

have wavelengths on the order of 0.003 nm (3 pm). High magnifications and resolving powers of these microscopes are consequences of the short wavelengths of electron beams. The electron beam is focused and the image formed with magnetic lenses; otherwise the geometry of the microscope components is essentially the same as with optical systems. Both transmission and reflection beam modes of operation are possible for electron microscopes.

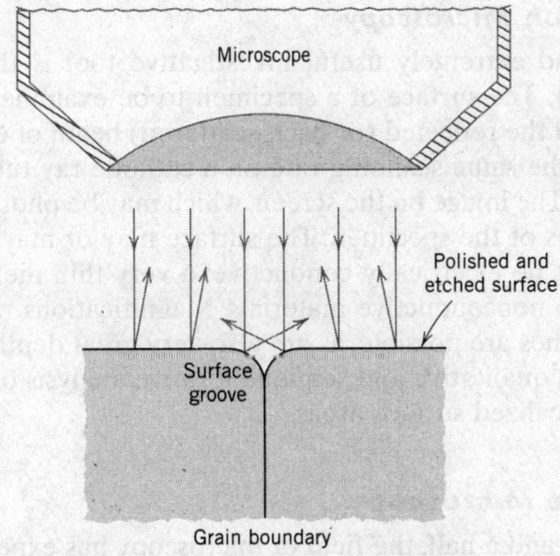

(a)

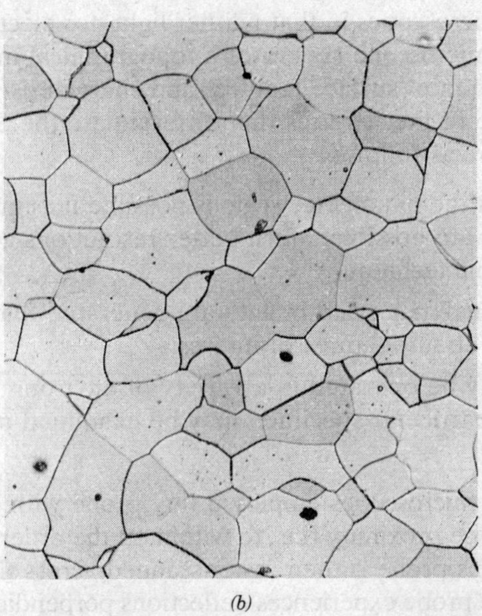

(b)

Figure 5.19 (*a*) Section of a grain boundary and its surface groove produced by etching; the light reflection characteristics in the vicinity of the groove are also shown. (*b*) Photomicrograph of the surface of a polished and etched polycrystalline specimen of an iron-chromium alloy in which the grain boundaries appear dark. 100×. [Photomicrograph courtesy of L. C. Smith and C. Brady, the National Bureau of Standards, Washington, DC (now the National Institute of Standards and Technology, Gaithersburg, MD.)]

Transmission Electron Microscopy

The image seen with a **transmission electron microscope (TEM)** is formed by an electron beam that passes through the specimen. Details of internal microstructural features are accessible to observation; contrasts in the image are produced by differences in beam scattering or diffraction produced between various elements of the microstructure or defect. Since solid materials are highly absorptive to electron beams, a specimen to be examined must be prepared in the form of a very thin foil; this ensures transmission through the specimen of an appreciable fraction of the incident beam. The transmitted beam is projected onto a fluorescent screen or a photographic film so that the image may be viewed. Magnifications approaching 1,000,000× are possible with transmission electron microscopy, which is frequently utilized in the study of dislocations.

Scanning Electron Microscopy

A more recent and extremely useful investigative tool is the **scanning electron microscope (SEM).** The surface of a specimen to be examined is scanned with an electron beam, and the reflected (or back-scattered) beam of electrons is collected, then displayed at the same scanning rate on a cathode ray tube (similar to a CRT television screen). The image on the screen, which may be photographed, represents the surface features of the specimen. The surface may or may not be polished and etched, but it must be electrically conductive; a very thin metallic surface coating must be applied to nonconductive materials. Magnifications ranging from 10 to in excess of 50,000 times are possible, as are also very great depths of field. Accessory equipment permits qualitative and semiquantitative analysis of the elemental composition of very localized surface areas.

Scanning Probe Microscopy

In the past decade and a half, the field of microscopy has experienced a revolution with the development of a new family of scanning probe microscopes. This **scanning probe microscope (SPM),** of which there are several varieties, differs from the optical and electron microscopes in that neither light nor electrons is used to form an image. Rather, the microscope generates a topographical map, on an atomic scale, that is a representation of surface features and characteristics of the specimen being examined. Some of the features that differentiate the SPM from other microscopic techniques are as follows:

- Examination on the nanometer scale is possible inasmuch as magnifications as high as $10^9\times$ are possible; much better resolutions are attainable than with other microscopic techniques.
- Three-dimensional magnified images are generated that provide topographical information about features of interest.
- Some SPMs may be operated in a variety of environments (e.g., vacuum, air, liquid); thus, a particular specimen may be examined in its most suitable environment.

Scanning probe microscopes employ a tiny probe with a very sharp tip that is brought into very close proximity (i.e., to within on the order of a nanometer) of the specimen surface. This probe is then raster-scanned across the plane of the surface. During scanning, the probe experiences deflections perpendicular to this plane, in response to electronic or other interactions between the probe and specimen surface. The in-surface-plane and out-of-plane motions of the probe are controlled by piezoelectric (Section 17.25) ceramic components that have nanometer resolutions. Furthermore, these probe movements are monitored electronically, and transferred to and stored in a computer, which then generates the three-dimensional surface image.

Specific scanning probe microscopic techniques differ from one another with regard to the type of interaction that is monitored. A scanning probe micrograph in which may be observed the atomic structure and a missing atom on the surface of silicon is shown in the chapter-opening photograph for this chapter.

These new SPMs, which allow examination of the surface of materials at the atomic and molecular level, have provided a wealth of information about a host of materials, from integrated circuit chips to biological molecules. Indeed, the advent of the SPMs has helped to usher in the era of nanomaterials—materials whose properties are designed by engineering atomic and molecular structures.

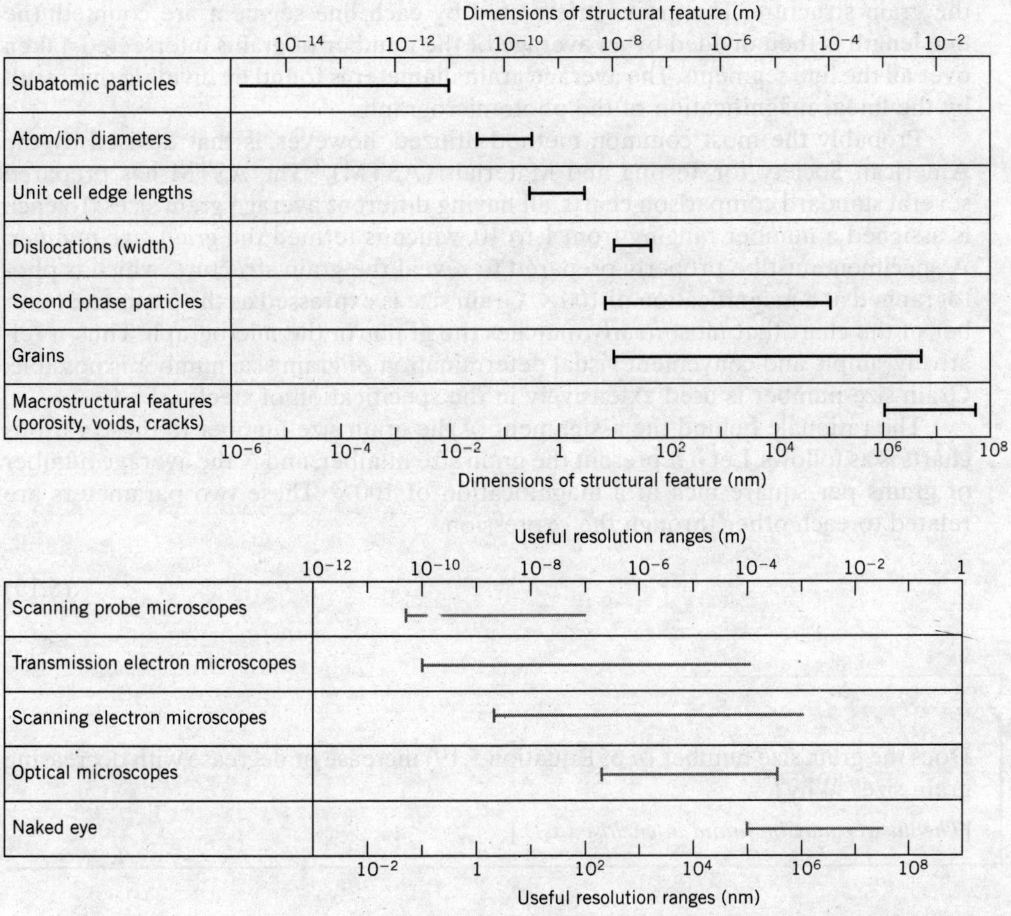

Figure 5.20 (*a*) Bar-chart showing size ranges for several structural features found in materials. (*b*) Bar-chart showing the useful resolution ranges for four microscopic techniques discussed in this chapter, in addition to the naked eye. (Courtesy of Prof. Sidnei Paciornik, DCMM PUC-Rio, Rio de Janeiro, Brazil, and Prof. Carlos Pérez Bergmann, Federal University of Rio Grande do Sul, Porto Alegre, Brazil.)

Figure 5.20*a* is a bar-chart showing dimensional size ranges for several types of structures found in materials (note that the axes are scaled logarithmically). Likewise, the useful dimensional resolution ranges for the several microscopic techniques discussed in this chapter (plus the naked eye) are presented in the bar-chart of Figure 5.20*b*. For three of these techniques (viz. SPM, TEM, and SEM), an upper resolution value is not imposed by the characteristics of the microscope, and, therefore, is somewhat arbitrary and not well defined. Furthermore, by comparing Figures 5.20*a* and 5.20*b*, it is possible to decide which microscopic technique(s) is (are) best suited for examination of each of the structure types.

5.13 GRAIN SIZE DETERMINATION

The **grain size** is often determined when the properties of a polycrystalline material are under consideration. In this regard, there exist a number of techniques by which size is specified in terms of average grain volume, diameter, or area. Grain size may be estimated by using an intercept method, described as follows. Straight lines all the same length are drawn through several photomicrographs that show the grain structure. The grains intersected by each line segment are counted; the line length is then divided by an average of the number of grains intersected, taken over all the line segments. The average grain diameter is found by dividing this result by the linear magnification of the photomicrographs.

Probably the most common method utilized, however, is that devised by the American Society for Testing and Materials (ASTM).[7] The ASTM has prepared several standard comparison charts, all having different average grain sizes. To each is assigned a number ranging from 1 to 10, which is termed the *grain size number*. A specimen must be properly prepared to reveal the grain structure, which is photographed at a magnification of 100×. Grain size is expressed as the grain size number of the chart that most nearly matches the grains in the micrograph. Thus, a relatively simple and convenient visual determination of grain size number is possible. Grain size number is used extensively in the specification of steels.

The rationale behind the assignment of the grain size number to these various charts is as follows. Let n represent the grain size number, and N the average number of grains per square inch at a magnification of 100×. These two parameters are related to each other through the expression

$$N = 2^{n-1} \tag{5.19}$$

Concept Check 5.4

Does the grain size number (n of Equation 5.19) increase or decrease with decreasing grain size? Why?

[*The answer may be found in enclosed CD.*]

EXAMPLE PROBLEM 5.6

Computations of ASTM Grain Size Number and Number of Grains Per Unit Area

(a) Determine the ASTM grain size number of a metal specimen if 55 grains per square inch are measured at a magnification of 100×.
(b) For this same specimen, how many grains per square inch will there be at a magnification of 85×?

Solution

(a) In order to determine the ASTM grain size number (n) it is necessary to employ Equation 5.19. Taking logarithms of both sides of this expression leads to

$$\log N = (n - 1) \log 2$$

And, solving for n yields

$$n = \frac{\log N}{\log 2} + 1$$

[7] ASTM Standard E 112, "Standard Methods for Estimating the Average Grain Size for Metals."

From the problem statement, $N = 45$, and, therefore

$$n = \frac{\log 45}{\log 2} + 1 = 6.5$$

(b) At magnifications other than 100×, use of the following modified form of Equation 5.19 is necessary:

$$N_M \left(\frac{M}{100}\right)^2 = 2^{n-1} \tag{5.20}$$

In this expression N_M = the number of grains per square inch at magnification M. In addition, the inclusion of the $(M/100)^2$ term makes use of the fact that, while magnification is a length parameter, area is expressed in terms of units of length squared. As a consequence, the number of grains per unit area increases with the square of the increase in magnification.

Solving Equation 5.17 for N_M, realizing that $M = 85$ and $n = 6.5$ leads to

$$N_M = 2^{n-1}\left(\frac{100}{M}\right)^2$$

$$= 2^{(6.5-1)}\left(\frac{100}{85}\right)^2 = 62.6 \text{ grains/in.}^2$$

SUMMARY

Vacancies and Self-Interstitials

All solid materials contain large numbers of imperfections or deviations from crystalline perfection. The several types of imperfection are categorized on the basis of their geometry and size. Point defects are those associated with one or two atomic positions, including vacancies (or vacant lattice sites), self-interstitials (host atoms that occupy interstitial sites), and impurity atoms.

Impurities in Solids

A solid solution may form when impurity atoms are added to a solid, in which case the original crystal structure is retained and no new phases are formed. For substitutional solid solutions, impurity atoms substitute for host atoms, and appreciable solubility is possible only when atomic diameters and electronegativities for both atom types are similar, when both elements have the same crystal structure, and when the impurity atoms have a valence that is the same as or less than the host material. Interstitial solid solutions form for relatively small impurity atoms that occupy interstitial sites among the host atoms.

Specification of Composition

Composition of an alloy may be specified in weight percent or atom percent. The basis for weight percent computations is the weight (or mass) of each alloy constituent relative to the total alloy weight. Atom percents are calculated in terms of the number of moles for each constituent relative to the total moles of all the elements in the alloy.

Imperfections in Ceramics

With regard to atomic point defects, interstitials and vacancies for each anion and cation type are possible. These imperfections often occur in pairs as Frenkel and Schottky defects to ensure that crystal electroneutrality is maintained. Addition of impurity atoms may result in the formation of substitutional or interstitial solid solutions. Any charge imbalance created by the impurity ions may be compensated by the generation of host ion vacancies or interstitials.

Dislocations—Linear Defects

Dislocations are one-dimensional crystalline defects of which there are two pure types: edge and screw. An edge may be thought of in terms of the lattice distortion along the end of an extra half-plane of atoms; a screw, as a helical planar ramp. For mixed dislocations, components of both pure edge and screw are found. The magnitude and direction of lattice distortion associated with a dislocation are specified by its Burgers vector. The relative orientations of Burgers vector and dislocation line are (1) perpendicular for edge, (2) parallel for screw, and (3) neither perpendicular nor parallel for mixed.

Interfacial Defects
Bulk or Volume Defects
Atomic Vibrations

Other imperfections include interfacial defects [external surfaces, grain boundaries (both small- and high-angle), twin boundaries, etc.], volume defects (cracks, pores, etc.), and atomic vibrations. Each type of imperfection has some influence on the properties of a material.

Defects in Polymers

Although the point defect state concept in polymers is different than metals and ceramics, vacancies, interstitial atoms, and impurity atoms/ions and groups of atoms/ions as interstitials have been found to exist in crystalline regions. Other defects include chains ends, dangling and loose chains, as well as dislocations.

Microscopic Techniques

Many of the important defects and structural elements of materials are of microscopic dimensions, and observation is possible only with the aid of a microscope. Both optical and electron microscopes are employed, usually in conjunction with photographic equipment. Transmissive and reflective modes are possible for each microscope type; preference is dictated by the nature of the specimen as well as the structural element or defect to be examined.

More recent scanning probe microscopic techniques have been developed that generate topographical maps representing the surface features and characteristics of the specimen. Examinations on the atomic and molecular levels are possible using these techniques.

Grain Size Determination

Grain size of polycrystalline materials is frequently determined using photomicrographic techniques. Two methods are commonly employed: intercept and standard comparison charts.

REFERENCES

ASM Handbook, Vol. 9, *Metallography and Microstructures,* ASM International, Materials Park, OH, 2004.

Brandon, D., and W. D. Kaplan, *Microstructural Characterization of Materials,* Wiley, New York, 1999.

DeHoff, R. T., and F. N. Rhines, *Quantitative Microscopy,* TechBooks, Marietta, OH, 1991.

Van Bueren, H. G., *Imperfections in Crystals,* North-Holland, Amsterdam (Wiley-Interscience, New York), 1960.

Vander Voort, G. F., *Metallography, Principles and Practice,* ASM International, Materials Park, OH, 1984.

QUESTIONS AND PROBLEMS

Vacancies and Self-Interstitials

5.1 Calculate the fraction of atom sites that are vacant for copper at its melting temperature of 1084°C (1357 K). Assume an energy for vacancy formation of 0.90 eV/atom.

5.2 Calculate the number of vacancies per cubic meter in gold at 900°C. The energy for vacancy formation is 0.98 eV/atom. Furthermore, the density and atomic weight for Au are 18.63 g/cm^3 (at 900°C) and 196.9 g/mol, respectively.

5.3 Calculate the energy for vacancy formation in silver, given that the equilibrium number of vacancies at 800°C (1073 K) is 3.6×10^{23} m^{-3}. The atomic weight and density (at 800°C) for silver are, respectively, 107.9 g/mol and 9.5 g/cm^3.

Impurities in Solids

5.4 Below, atomic radius, crystal structure, electronegativity, and the most common valence are tabulated, for several elements; for those that are nonmetals, only atomic radii are indicated.

Element	*Atomic Radius (nm)*	*Crystal Structure*	*Electro-negativity*	*Valence*
Ni	0.1246	FCC	1.8	+2
C	0.071			
H	0.046			
O	0.060			
Ag	0.1445	FCC	1.9	+1
Al	0.1431	FCC	1.5	+3
Co	0.1253	HCP	1.8	+2
Cr	0.1249	BCC	1.6	+3
Fe	0.1241	BCC	1.8	+2
Pt	0.1387	FCC	2.2	+2
Zn	0.1332	HCP	1.6	+2

Which of these elements would you expect to form the following with nickel:

(a) A substitutional solid solution having complete solubility

(b) A substitutional solid solution of incomplete solubility

(c) An interstitial solid solution

5.5 For both FCC and BCC crystal structures, there are two different types of interstitial sites. In each case, one site is larger than the other, and is normally occupied by impurity atoms. For FCC, this larger one is located at the center of each edge of the unit cell; it is termed an octahedral interstitial site. On the other hand, with BCC the larger site type is found at $0\,\frac{1}{2}\,\frac{1}{4}$ positions—that is, lying on {100} faces, and situated midway between two unit cell edges on this face and one-quarter of the distance between the other two unit cell edges; it is termed a tetrahedral interstitial site. For both FCC and BCC crystal structures, compute the radius r of an impurity atom that will just fit into one of these sites in terms of the atomic radius R of the host atom.

Specification of Composition

5.6 Derive the following equations:

(a) Equation 5.7a

(b) Equation 5.9a

(c) Equation 5.10a

(d) Equation 5.11b

5.7 What is the composition, in atom percent, of an alloy that consists of 92.5 wt% Ag and 7.5 wt% Cu?

5.8 What is the composition, in weight percent, of an alloy that consists of 5 at% Cu and 95 at% Pt?

5.9 Calculate the composition, in weight percent, of an alloy that contains 105 kg of iron, 0.2 kg of carbon, and 1.0 kg of chromium.

5.10 What is the composition, in atom percent, of an alloy that contains 33 g copper and 47 g zinc?

5.11 What is the composition, in atom percent, of an alloy that contains 44.5 lb_m of silver, 83.7 lb_m of gold, and 5.3 lb_m of Cu?

5.12 What is the composition, in atom percent, of an alloy that consists of 5.5 wt% Pb and 94.5 wt% Sn?

5.13 Convert the atom percent composition in Problem 5.11 to weight percent.

5.14 Calculate the number of atoms per cubic meter in lead.

5.15 The concentration of silicon in an iron-silicon alloy is 0.25 wt%. What is the concentration in kilograms of silicon per cubic meter of alloy?

5.16 Determine the approximate density of a Ti-6Al-4V titanium alloy that has a composition of 90 wt% Ti, 6 wt% Al, and 4 wt% V.

5.17 Calculate the unit cell edge length for an 80 wt% Ag-20 wt% Pd alloy. All of the palladium is in solid solution, the crystal structure for this alloy is FCC, and the room-temperature density of Pd is 12.02 g/cm^3.

5.18 Some hypothetical alloy is composed of 25 wt% of metal A and 75 wt% of metal B. If the densities of metals A and B are 6.17 and 8.00 g/cm^3, respectively, whereas their respective atomic weights are 171.3 and 162.0 g/mol, determine whether the crystal structure for this alloy is simple cubic, face-centered cubic, or body-centered cubic. Assume a unit cell edge length of 0.332 nm.

5.19 For a solid solution consisting of two elements (designated as 1 and 2), sometimes it is desirable to determine the number of atoms per cubic centimeter of one element in a solid solution, N_1, given the concentration of that element specified in weight percent, C_1. This computation is possible using the following expression:

$$N_1 = \frac{N_A C_1}{\dfrac{C_1 A_1}{\rho_1} + \dfrac{A_1}{\rho_2}(100 - C_1)} \tag{5.21}$$

where

N_A = Avogadro's number

ρ_1 and ρ_2 = densities of the two elements

A_1 = the atomic weight of element 1

Derive Equation 5.21 using Equation 5.2 and expressions contained in Section 5.4.

5.20 Molybdenum forms a substitutional solid solution with tungsten. Compute the number of molybdenum atoms per cubic centimeter for a molybdenum-tungsten alloy that contains 16.4 wt% Mo and 83.6 wt% W. The densities of pure molybdenum and tungsten are 10.22 and 19.30 g/cm^3, respectively.

5.21 Niobium forms a substitutional solid solution with vanadium. Compute the number of niobium atoms per cubic centimeter for a niobium-vanadium alloy that contains 24 wt% Nb and 76 wt% V. The densities of pure niobium and vanadium are 8.57 and 6.10 g/cm^3, respectively.

5.22 Sometimes it is desirable to be able to determine the weight percent of one element, C_1, that will produce a specified concentration in terms of the number of atoms per cubic centimeter, N_1, for an alloy composed of two types of atoms. This computation is possible using the following expression:

$$C_1 = \frac{100}{1 + \dfrac{N_A \rho_2}{N_1 A_1} - \dfrac{\rho_2}{\rho_1}} \tag{5.22}$$

where

N_A = Avogadro's number

ρ_1 and ρ_2 = densities of the two elements

A_1 and A_2 = the atomic weights of the two elements

Derive Equation 5.22 using Equation 5.2 and expressions contained in Section 5.4.

5.23 Gold forms a substitutional solid solution with silver. Compute the weight percent of gold that must be added to silver to yield an alloy that contains 5.5×10^{21} Au atoms per cubic centimeter. The densities of pure Au and Ag are 19.32 and 10.49 g/cm^3, respectively.

5.24 Germanium forms a substitutional solid solution with silicon. Compute the weight percent of germanium that must be added to silicon to yield an alloy that contains 2.43×10^{21} Ge atoms per cubic centimeter. The densities of pure Ge and Si are 5.32 and 2.33 g/cm^3, respectively.

5.25 Iron and vanadium both have the BCC crystal structure, and V forms a substitutional solid solution for concentrations up to approximately 20 wt% V at room temperature. Compute the unit cell edge length for a 90 wt% Fe–10 wt% V alloy.

Imperfections in Ceramics

5.26 Would you expect Frenkel defects for anions to exist in ionic ceramics in relatively large concentrations? Why or why not?

5.27 Calculate the fraction of lattice sites that are Schottky defects for cesium chloride at its melting temperature (645°C). Assume an energy for defect formation of 1.86 eV.

5.28 Calculate the number of Frenkel defects per cubic meter in silver chloride at 350°C. The energy for defect formation is 1.1 eV, while the density for AgCl is 5.50 g/cm^3 at (350°C).

5.29 Using the data given below that relate to the formation of Schottky defects in some oxide ceramic (having the chemical formula MO), determine the following:

(a) The energy for defect formation (in eV),

(b) the equilibrium number of Schottky defects per cubic meter at 1000°C, and

(c) the identity of the oxide (i.e., what is the metal M?)

T (°C)	ρ (g/cm^3)	N_s (m^{-3})
750	3.50	5.7×10^9
1000	3.45	?
1500	3.40	5.8×10^{17}

5.30 In your own words, briefly define the term "stoichiometric."

5.31 If cupric oxide (CuO) is exposed to reducing atmospheres at elevated temperatures, some of the Cu^{2+} ions will become Cu^{+}.

(a) Under these conditions, name one crystalline defect that you would expect to form in order to maintain charge neutrality.

(b) How many Cu^{+} ions are required for the creation of each defect?

(c) How would you express the chemical formula for this nonstoichiometric material?

5.32 **(a)** Suppose that CaO is added as an impurity to Li_2O. If the Ca^{2+} substitutes for Li^{+}, what kind of vacancies would you expect to form? How many of these vacancies are created for every Ca^{2+} added?

(b) Suppose that CaO is added as an impurity to $CaCl_2$. If the O^{2-} substitutes for Cl^{-}, what kind of vacancies would you expect to form? How many of these vacancies are created for every O^{2-} added?

Dislocations—Linear Defects

5.33 Cite the relative Burgers vector–dislocation line orientations for edge, screw, and mixed dislocations.

Interfacial Defects

5.34 For an FCC single crystal, would you expect the surface energy for a (100) plane to be greater or less than that for a (111) plane? Why? (*Note:* You may want to consult the solution to Problem 4.23 at the end of Chapter 4.)

5.35 For a BCC single crystal, would you expect the surface energy for a (100) plane to be greater or less than that for a (110) plane? Why? (*Note:* You may want to consult the solution to Problem 4.24 at the end of Chapter 4.)

5.36 **(a)** For a given material, would you expect the surface energy to be greater than, the same as, or less than the grain boundary energy? Why?

(b) The grain boundary energy of a small-angle grain boundary is less than for a high-angle one. Why is this so?

5.37 **(a)** Briefly describe a twin and a twin boundary.

(b) Cite the difference between mechanical and annealing twins.

5.38 For each of the following stacking sequences found in FCC metals, cite the type of planar defect that exists:

(a) . . . *A B C A B C B A C B A* . . .

(b) . . . *A B C A B C B C A B C* . . .

Now, copy the stacking sequences and indicate the position(s) of planar defect(s) with a vertical dashed line.

Grain Size Determination

5.39 **(a)** Using the intercept method, determine the average grain size, in millimeters, of the specimen whose microstructure is shown in Figure 5.19(*b*); use at least seven straight-line segments.

(b) Estimate the ASTM grain size number for this material.

5.40 **(a)** Employing the intercept technique, determine the average grain size for the steel specimen whose microstructure is shown in Figure 9.25(*a*); use at least seven straight-line segments.

(b) Estimate the ASTM grain size number for this material.

5.41 For an ASTM grain size of 6, approximately how many grains would there be per square inch at

(a) a magnification of 100, and

(b) without any magnification?

5.42 Determine the ASTM grain size number if 30 grains per square inch are measured at a magnification of 250.

5.43 Determine the ASTM grain size number if 25 grains per square inch are measured at a magnification of 75.

DESIGN PROBLEMS

Specification of Composition

5.D1 Aluminum–lithium alloys have been developed by the aircraft industry to reduce the weight and improve the performance of its aircraft. A commercial aircraft skin material having a density of 2.47 g/cm^3 is desired. Compute the concentration of Li (in wt%) that is required.

5.D2 Copper and platinum both have the FCC crystal structure, and Cu forms a substitutional solid solution for concentrations up to approximately 6 wt% Cu at room temperature. Determine the concentration in weight percent of Cu that must be added to platinum to yield a unit cell edge length of 0.390 nm.

Chapter 6 Diffusion

Photograph of a steel gear that has been "case hardened." The outer surface layer was selectively hardened by a high-temperature heat treatment during which carbon from the surrounding atmosphere diffused into the surface. The "case" appears as the dark outer rim of that segment of the gear that has been sectioned. Actual size. (Photograph courtesy of Surface Division Midland-Ross.)

Learning Objectives

After studying this chapter you should be able to do the following:

1. Describe the atomic mechanisms of diffusion in metallic, ionic and polymeric materials.
2. Distinguish between steady-state and nonsteady-state diffusion.
3. (a) Write Fick's first and second laws in equation form, and define all parameters.
   (b) Note the kind of diffusion for which each of these equations is normally applied.
4. Write the solution to Fick's second law for diffusion into a semi-infinite solid when the concentration of diffusing species at the surface is held constant. Define all parameters in this equation.
5. Calculate the diffusion coefficient for some material at a specified temperature, given the appropriate diffusion constants.

6.1 INTRODUCTION

Many reactions and processes that are important in the treatment of materials rely on the transfer of mass either within a specific solid (ordinarily on a microscopic level) or from a liquid, a gas, or another solid phase. This is necessarily accomplished by **diffusion,** the phenomenon of material transport by atomic motion. This chapter discusses the atomic mechanisms by which diffusion occurs, the mathematics of diffusion, and the influence of temperature and diffusing species on the rate of diffusion.

The phenomenon of diffusion may be demonstrated with the use of a *diffusion couple,* which is formed by joining bars of two different metals together so that there is intimate contact between the two faces; this is illustrated for copper and nickel in Figure 6.1, which includes schematic representations of atom positions and composition across the interface. This couple is heated for an extended period at an elevated temperature (but below the melting temperature of both metals), and cooled to room temperature. Chemical analysis will reveal a condition similar to that represented in Figure 6.2—namely, pure copper and nickel at the two extremities of the couple, separated by an alloyed region. Concentrations of both metals vary with position as shown

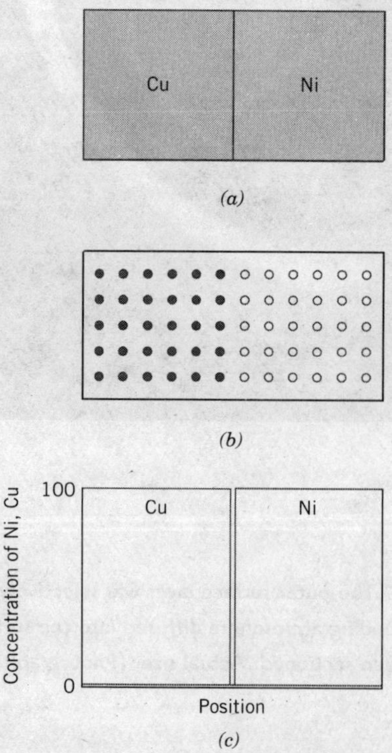

Figure 6.1 (*a*) A copper–nickel diffusion couple before a high-temperature heat treatment. (*b*) Schematic representations of Cu (closed circles) and Ni (open circles) atom locations within the diffusion couple. (*c*) Concentrations of copper and nickel as a function of position across the couple.

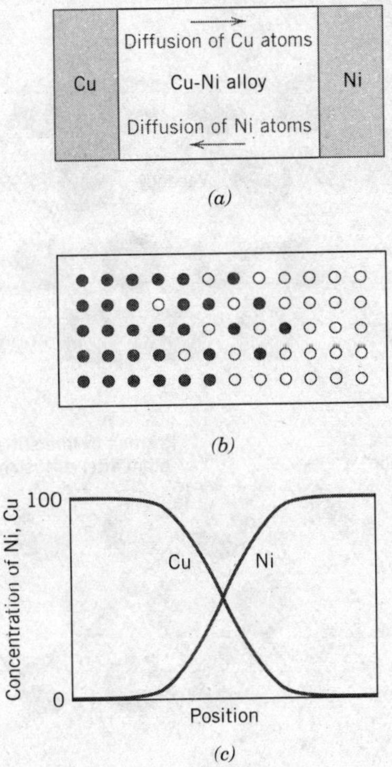

Figure 6.2 (*a*) A copper–nickel diffusion couple after a high-temperature heat treatment, showing the alloyed diffusion zone. (*b*) Schematic representations of Cu (closed circles) and Ni (open circles) atom locations within the couple. (*c*) Concentrations of copper and nickel as a function of position across the couple.

in Figure 6.2*c*. This result indicates that copper atoms have migrated or diffused into the nickel, and that nickel has diffused into copper. This process, whereby atoms of one metal diffuse into another, is termed **interdiffusion,** or **impurity diffusion.**

Interdiffusion may be discerned from a macroscopic perspective by changes in concentration which occur over time, as in the example for the Cu–Ni diffusion couple. There is a net drift or transport of atoms from high- to low-concentration regions. Diffusion also occurs for pure metals, but all atoms exchanging positions are of the same type; this is termed **self-diffusion.** Of course, self-diffusion is not normally subject to observation by noting compositional changes.

6.2 DIFFUSION MECHANISMS

From an atomic perspective, diffusion is just the stepwise migration of atoms from lattice site to lattice site. In fact, the atoms in solid materials are in constant motion, rapidly changing positions. For an atom to make such a move, two conditions must be met: (1) there must be an empty adjacent site, and (2) the atom must have sufficient energy to break bonds with its neighbor atoms and then cause some lattice distortion during the displacement. This energy is vibrational in nature (Section 5.9). At a specific temperature some small fraction of the total number of atoms is capable of diffusive motion, by virtue of the magnitudes of their vibrational energies. This fraction increases with rising temperature.

Several different models for this atomic motion have been proposed; of these possibilities, two dominate for metallic diffusion.

Vacancy Diffusion

One mechanism involves the interchange of an atom from a normal lattice position to an adjacent vacant lattice site or vacancy, as represented schematically in Figure 6.3*a*. This mechanism is aptly termed **vacancy diffusion.** Of course, this process necessitates the presence of vacancies, and the extent to which vacancy diffusion

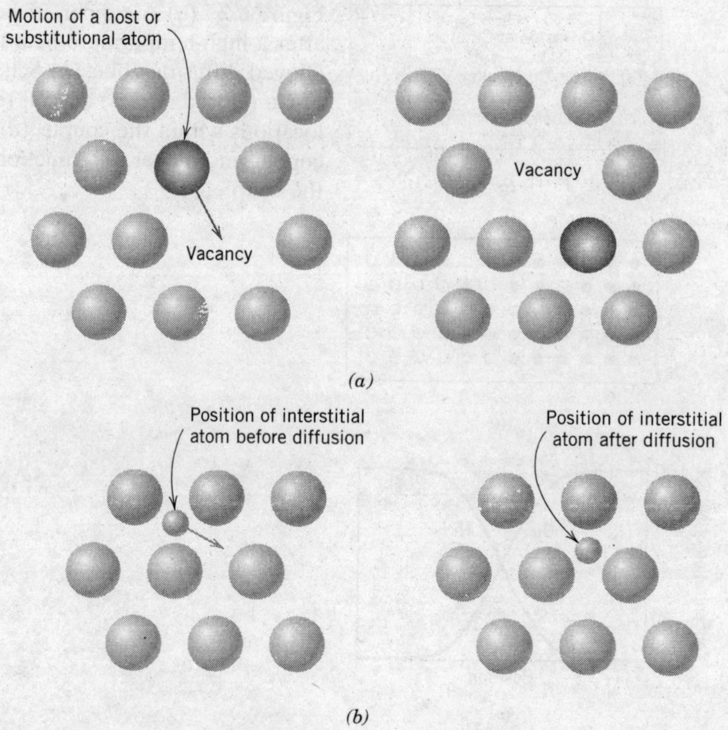

Figure 6.3 Schematic representations of (*a*) vacancy diffusion and (*b*) interstitial diffusion.

can occur is a function of the number of these defects that are present; significant concentrations of vacancies may exist in metals at elevated temperatures (Section 5.2). Since diffusing atoms and vacancies exchange positions, the diffusion of atoms in one direction corresponds to the motion of vacancies in the opposite direction. Both self-diffusion and interdiffusion occur by this mechanism; for the latter, the impurity atoms must substitute for host atoms.

Interstitial Diffusion

The second type of diffusion involves atoms that migrate from an interstitial position to a neighboring one that is empty. This mechanism is found for interdiffusion of impurities such as hydrogen, carbon, nitrogen, and oxygen, which have atoms that are small enough to fit into the interstitial positions. Host or substitutional impurity atoms rarely form interstitials and do not normally diffuse via this mechanism. This phenomenon is appropriately termed **interstitial diffusion** (Figure 6.3*b*).

In most metal alloys, interstitial diffusion occurs much more rapidly than diffusion by the vacancy mode, since the interstitial atoms are smaller and thus more mobile. Furthermore, there are more empty interstitial positions than vacancies; hence, the probability of interstitial atomic movement is greater than for vacancy diffusion.

6.3 STEADY-STATE DIFFUSION

Diffusion is a time-dependent process—that is, in a macroscopic sense, the quantity of an element that is transported within another is a function of time. Often it is necessary to know how fast diffusion occurs, or the rate of mass transfer. This rate is frequently expressed as a **diffusion flux** (J), defined as the mass (or, equivalently, the number of atoms) M diffusing through and perpendicular to a unit cross-sectional area of solid per unit of time. In mathematical form, this may be represented as

$$J = \frac{M}{At} \tag{6.1a}$$

where A denotes the area across which diffusion is occurring and t is the elapsed diffusion time. In differential form, this expression becomes

$$J = \frac{1}{A}\frac{dM}{dt} \tag{6.1b}$$

The units for J are kilograms or atoms per meter squared per second (kg/m^2-s or atoms/m^2-s).

If the diffusion flux does not change with time, a steady-state condition exists. One common example of **steady-state diffusion** is the diffusion of atoms of a gas through a plate of metal for which the concentrations (or pressures) of the diffusing species on both surfaces of the plate are held constant. This is represented schematically in Figure 6.4*a*.

When concentration C is plotted versus position (or distance) within the solid x, the resulting curve is termed the **concentration profile;** the slope at a particular point on this curve is the **concentration gradient:**

$$\text{concentration gradient} = \frac{dC}{dx} \tag{6.2a}$$

In the present treatment, the concentration profile is assumed to be linear, as depicted in Figure 6.4*b*, and

$$\text{concentration gradient} = \frac{\Delta C}{\Delta x} = \frac{C_A - C_B}{x_A - x_B} \tag{6.2b}$$

For diffusion problems, it is sometimes convenient to express concentration in terms of mass of diffusing species per unit volume of solid (kg/m^3 or g/cm^3).[1]

The mathematics of steady-state diffusion in a single (x) direction is relatively simple, in that the flux is proportional to the concentration gradient through the expression

$$J = -D\frac{dC}{dx} \tag{6.3}$$

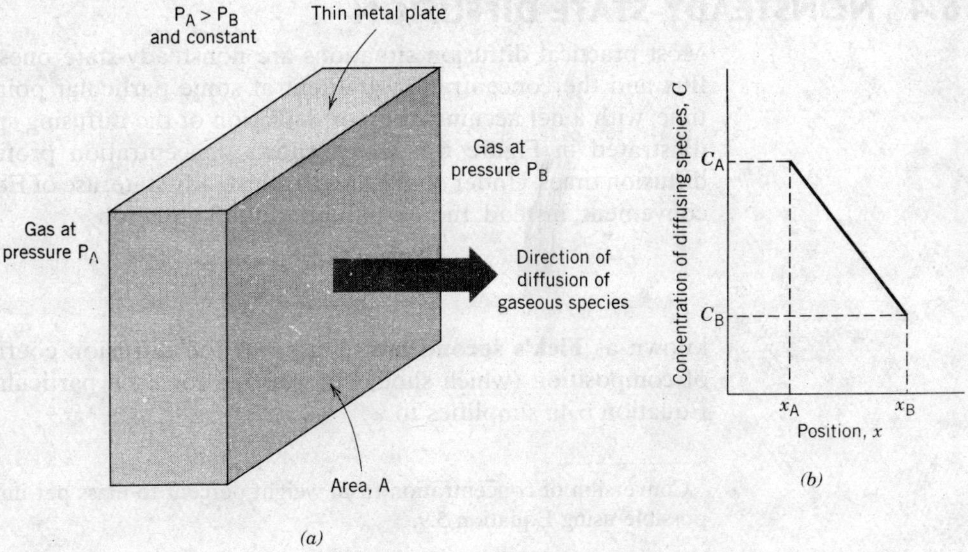

Figure 6.4 (*a*) Steady-state diffusion across a thin plate. (*b*) A linear concentration profile for the diffusion situation in (*a*).

The constant of proportionality D is called the **diffusion coefficient,** which is expressed in square meters per second. The negative sign in this expression indicates that the direction of diffusion is down the concentration gradient, from a high to a low concentration. Equation 6.3 is sometimes called **Fick's first law.**

Sometimes the term **driving force** is used in the context of what compels a reaction to occur. For diffusion reactions, several such forces are possible; but when diffusion is according to Equation 6.3, the concentration gradient is the driving force.

One practical example of steady-state diffusion is found in the purification of hydrogen gas. One side of a thin sheet of palladium metal is exposed to the impure gas composed of hydrogen and other gaseous species such as nitrogen, oxygen, and water vapor. The hydrogen selectively diffuses through the sheet to the opposite side, which is maintained at a constant and lower hydrogen pressure.

EXAMPLE PROBLEM 6.1

Diffusion Flux Computation

A plate of iron is exposed to a carburizing (carbon-rich) atmosphere on one side and a decarburizing (carbon-deficient) atmosphere on the other side at 700°C (1300°F). If a condition of steady state is achieved, calculate the diffusion flux of carbon through the plate if the concentrations of carbon at positions of 5 and 10 mm (5×10^{-3} and 10^{-2} m) beneath the carburizing surface are 1.2 and 0.8 kg/m^3, respectively. Assume a diffusion coefficient of 3×10^{-11} m^2/s at this temperature.

Solution

Fick's first law, Equation 6.3, is utilized to determine the diffusion flux. Substitution of the values above into this expression yields

$$J = -D\frac{C_A - C_B}{x_A - x_B} = -(3 \times 10^{-11}\ \text{m}^2/\text{s})\frac{(1.2 - 0.8)\ \text{kg/m}^3}{(5 \times 10^{-3} - 10^{-2})\ \text{m}}$$
$$= 2.4 \times 10^{-9}\ \text{kg/m}^2\text{-s}$$

6.4 NONSTEADY-STATE DIFFUSION

Most practical diffusion situations are nonsteady-state ones. That is, the diffusion flux and the concentration gradient at some particular point in a solid vary with time, with a net accumulation or depletion of the diffusing species resulting. This is illustrated in Figure 6.5, which shows concentration profiles at three different diffusion times. Under conditions of nonsteady state, use of Equation 6.3 is no longer convenient; instead, the partial differential equation

$$\frac{\partial C}{\partial t} = \frac{\partial}{\partial x}\left(D\frac{\partial C}{\partial x}\right) \tag{6.4a}$$

known as **Fick's second law,** is used. If the diffusion coefficient is independent of composition (which should be verified for each particular diffusion situation), Equation 6.4a simplifies to

---

[1] Conversion of concentration from weight percent to mass per unit volume (in kg/m^3) is possible using Equation 5.9.

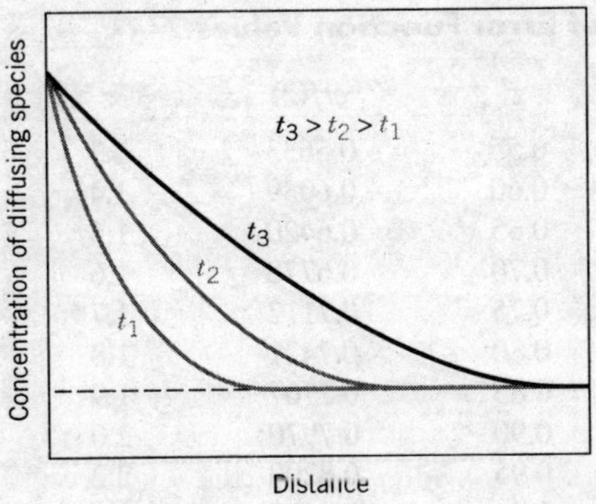

Figure 6.5 Concentration profiles for nonsteady-state diffusion taken at three different times, t_1, t_2, and t_3.

$$\frac{\partial C}{\partial t} = D\frac{\partial^2 C}{\partial x^2} \tag{6.4b}$$

Solutions to this expression (concentration in terms of both position and time) are possible when physically meaningful boundary conditions are specified. Comprehensive collections of these are given by Crank, and Carslaw and Jaeger (see References).

One practically important solution is for a semi-infinite solid[2] in which the surface concentration is held constant. Frequently, the source of the diffusing species is a gas phase, the partial pressure of which is maintained at a constant value. Furthermore, the following assumptions are made:

1. Before diffusion, any of the diffusing solute atoms in the solid are uniformly distributed with concentration of C_0.
2. The value of x at the surface is zero and increases with distance into the solid.
3. The time is taken to be zero the instant before the diffusion process begins.

These boundary conditions are simply stated as

For $t = 0$, $C = C_0$ at $0 \le x \le \infty$

For $t > 0$, $C = C_s$ (the constant surface concentration) at $x = 0$

$C = C_0$ at $x = \infty$

Application of these boundary conditions yields the solution[3]

$$\frac{C_x - C_0}{C_s - C_0} = 1 - \operatorname{erf}\left(\frac{x}{2\sqrt{Dt}}\right) \tag{6.5}$$

[2] A bar of solid is considered to be semi-infinite if none of the diffusing atoms reaches the bar end during the time over which diffusion takes place. A bar of length l is considered to be semi-infinite when $l > 10\sqrt{Dt}$.

[3] The solution to Fick's second law (Equation 6.4b) is given by

$$C_x = C(x, t) = A - B \operatorname{erf}\left(\frac{x}{2\sqrt{Dt}}\right)$$

Using the initial and boundary conditions and the relationships erf $(0) = 0$, erf $(+\infty) = +1$, erf $(-\infty) = -1$, erf $(-\theta) = -$erf (θ), the constants A and B can be determined.

Table 6.1 Tabulation of Error Function Values

z	erf(z)	z	erf(z)	z	erf(z)
0	0	0.55	0.5633	1.3	0.9340
0.025	0.0282	0.60	0.6039	1.4	0.9523
0.05	0.0564	0.65	0.6420	1.5	0.9661
0.10	0.1125	0.70	0.6778	1.6	0.9763
0.15	0.1680	0.75	0.7112	1.7	0.9838
0.20	0.2227	0.80	0.7421	1.8	0.9891
0.25	0.2763	0.85	0.7707	1.9	0.9928
0.30	0.3286	0.90	0.7970	2.0	0.9953
0.35	0.3794	0.95	0.8209	2.2	0.9981
0.40	0.4284	1.0	0.8427	2.4	0.9993
0.45	0.4755	1.1	0.8802	2.6	0.9998
0.50	0.5205	1.2	0.9103	2.8	0.9999

where C_x represents the concentration at depth x after time t. The expression $\mathrm{erf}(x/2\sqrt{Dt})$ is the Gaussian error function,[4] values of which are given in mathematical tables for various $x/2\sqrt{Dt}$ values; a partial listing is given in Table 6.1. The concentration parameters that appear in Equation 6.5 are noted in Figure 6.6, a concentration profile taken at a specific time. Equation 6.5 thus demonstrates the relationship between concentration, position, and time—namely, that C_x, being a function of the dimensionless parameter $x/\sqrt{Dt}$, may be determined at any time and position if the parameters C_0, C_s, and D are known.

Suppose that it is desired to achieve some specific concentration of solute, C_1, in an alloy; the left-hand side of Equation 6.5 now becomes

$$\frac{C_1 - C_0}{C_s - C_0} = \text{constant}$$

This being the case, the right-hand side of this same expression is also a constant, and subsequently

$$\frac{x}{2\sqrt{Dt}} = \text{constant} \tag{6.6a}$$

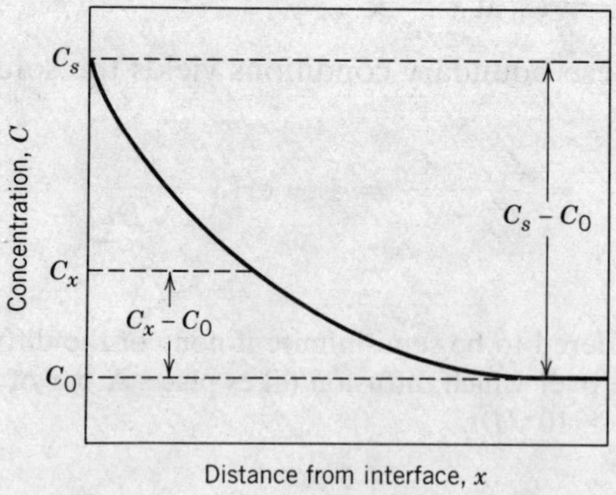

Figure 6.6 Concentration profile for nonsteady-state diffusion; concentration parameters relate to Equation 6.5.

[4] This Gaussian error function is defined by

$$\mathrm{erf}(z) = \frac{2}{\sqrt{\pi}} \int_0^z e^{-y^2}\, dy$$

where $x/2\sqrt{Dt}$ has been replaced by the variable z.

or

$$\frac{x^2}{Dt} = \text{constant} \tag{6.6b}$$

Some diffusion computations are thus facilitated on the basis of this relationship, as demonstrated in Example Problem 6.3.

EXAMPLE PROBLEM 6.2

Nonsteady-State Diffusion Time Computation I

For some applications, it is necessary to harden the surface of a steel (or iron-carbon alloy) above that of its interior. One way this may be accomplished is by increasing the surface concentration of carbon in a process termed **carburizing;** the steel piece is exposed, at an elevated temperature, to an atmosphere rich in a hydrocarbon gas, such as methane (CH_4).

Consider one such alloy that initially has a uniform carbon concentration of 0.25 wt% and is to be treated at 950°C (1750°F). If the concentration of carbon at the surface is suddenly brought to and maintained at 1.20 wt%, how long will it take to achieve a carbon content of 0.80 wt% at a position 0.5 mm below the surface? The diffusion coefficient for carbon in iron at this temperature is 1.6×10^{-11} m²/s; assume that the steel piece is semi-infinite.

Solution

Since this is a nonsteady-state diffusion problem in which the surface composition is held constant, Equation 6.5 is used. Values for all the parameters in this expression except time t are specified in the problem as follows:

$$C_0 = 0.25 \text{ wt\% C}$$
$$C_s = 1.20 \text{ wt\% C}$$
$$C_x = 0.80 \text{ wt\% C}$$
$$x = 0.50 \text{ mm} = 5 \times 10^{-4} \text{ m}$$
$$D = 1.6 \times 10^{-11} \text{ m}^2\text{/s}$$

Thus,

$$\frac{C_x - C_0}{C_s - C_0} = \frac{0.80 - 0.25}{1.20 - 0.25} = 1 - \text{erf}\left[\frac{(5 \times 10^{-4}\text{ m})}{2\sqrt{(1.6 \times 10^{-11}\text{ m}^2\text{/s})(t)}}\right]$$

$$0.4210 = \text{erf}\left(\frac{62.5 \text{ s}^{1/2}}{\sqrt{t}}\right)$$

We must now determine from Table 6.1 the value of z for which the error function is 0.4210. An interpolation is necessary, as

z	erf(z)
0.35	0.3794
z	0.4210
0.40	0.4284

$$\frac{z - 0.35}{0.40 - 0.35} = \frac{0.4210 - 0.3794}{0.4284 - 0.3794}$$

or

$$z = 0.392$$

Therefore,

$$\frac{62.5 \text{ s}^{1/2}}{\sqrt{t}} = 0.392$$

and solving for t,

$$t = \left(\frac{62.5 \text{ s}^{1/2}}{0.392}\right)^2 = 25{,}400 \text{ s} = 7.1 \text{ h}$$

EXAMPLE PROBLEM 6.3

Nonsteady-State Diffusion Time Computation II

The diffusion coefficients for copper in aluminum at 500 and 600°C are 4.8×10^{-14} and 6.3×10^{-13} m^2/s, respectively. Determine the approximate time at 500°C that will produce the same diffusion result (in terms of concentration of Cu at some specific point in Al) as a 10-h heat treatment at 600°C.

Solution

This is a diffusion problem in which Equation 6.6b may be employed. The composition in both diffusion situations will be equal at the same position (i.e., x is also a constant), thus

$$Dt = \text{constant} \tag{6.7}$$

at both temperatures. That is,

$$D_{500} t_{500} = D_{600} t_{600}$$

or

$$t_{500} = \frac{D_{600} t_{600}}{D_{500}} = \frac{(5.3 \times 10^{-13} \text{ m}^2/\text{s})(10 \text{ h})}{4.8 \times 10^{-14} \text{ m}^2/\text{s}} = 110.4 \text{ h}$$

6.5 FACTORS THAT INFLUENCE DIFFUSION

Diffusing Species

The magnitude of the diffusion coefficient D is indicative of the rate at which atoms diffuse. Coefficients, both self- and interdiffusion, for several metallic systems are listed in Table 6.2. The diffusing species as well as the host material influence the diffusion coefficient. For example, there is a significant difference in magnitude between self-diffusion and carbon interdiffusion in α iron at 500°C, the D value being greater for the carbon interdiffusion (3.0×10^{-21} vs. 2.4×10^{-12} m^2/s). This comparison also provides a contrast between rates of diffusion via vacancy and interstitial modes as discussed above. Self-diffusion occurs by a vacancy mechanism, whereas carbon diffusion in iron is interstitial.

Temperature

Temperature has a most profound influence on the coefficients and diffusion rates. For example, for the self-diffusion of Fe in α-Fe, the diffusion coefficient increases approximately six orders of magnitude (from 3.0×10^{-21} to 1.8×10^{-15} m^2/s) in rising temperature from 500 to 900°C (Table 6.2). The temperature dependence of

Table 6.2 A Tabulation of Diffusion Data

Diffusing Species	*Host Metal*	$D_0(m^2/s)$	*Activation Energy Q_d* *kJ/mol*	*eV/atom*	*Calculated Values* *T(°C)*	*D(m²/s)*
Fe	α-Fe (BCC)	2.8×10^{-4}	251	2.60	500 900	3.0×10^{-21} 1.8×10^{-15}
Fe	γ-Fe (FCC)	6.0×10^{-5}	284	2.94	900 1100	1.1×10^{-17} 7.8×10^{-16}
C	α-Fe	6.2×10^{-7}	80	0.83	500 900	2.4×10^{-12} 1.7×10^{-10}
C	γ-Fe	2.3×10^{-5}	148	1.53	900 1100	6.9×10^{-12} 6.3×10^{-11}
Cu	Cu	7.8×10^{-5}	211	2.19	500	4.2×10^{-19}
Zn	Cu	2.4×10^{-5}	189	1.96	500	4.0×10^{-18}
Al	Al	2.3×10^{-4}	144	1.49	500	4.2×10^{-14}
Cu	Al	6.5×10^{-5}	136	1.41	500	4.1×10^{-14}
Mg	Al	1.2×10^{-4}	131	1.35	500	1.9×10^{-13}
Cu	Ni	2.7×10^{-5}	256	2.65	500	1.3×10^{-22}

Source: E. A. Brandes and G. B. Brook (Editors), *Smithells Metals Reference Book,* 7th edition, Butterworth-Heinemann, Oxford, 1992.

the diffusion coefficients is

$$D = D_0 \exp\left(-\frac{Q_d}{RT}\right) \tag{6.8}$$

where

D_0 = a temperature-independent preexponential (m²/s)

Q_d = the **activation energy** for diffusion (J/mol or eV/atom)

R = the gas constant, 8.31 J/mol-K or 8.62×10^{-5} eV/atom-K

T = absolute temperature (K)

The activation energy may be thought of as that energy required to produce the diffusive motion of one mole of atoms. A large activation energy results in a relatively small diffusion coefficient. Table 6.2 also contains a listing of D_0 and Q_d values for several diffusion systems.

Taking natural logarithms of Equation 6.8 yields

$$\ln D = \ln D_0 - \frac{Q_d}{R}\left(\frac{1}{T}\right) \tag{6.9a}$$

or in terms of logarithms to the base 10

$$\log D = \log D_0 - \frac{Q_d}{2.3R}\left(\frac{1}{T}\right) \tag{6.9b}$$

Since D_0, Q_d, and R are all constants, Equation 6.9b takes on the form of an equation of a straight line:

$$y = b + mx$$

where y and x are analogous, respectively, to the variables log D and $1/T$. Thus, if log D is plotted versus the reciprocal of the absolute temperature, a straight line

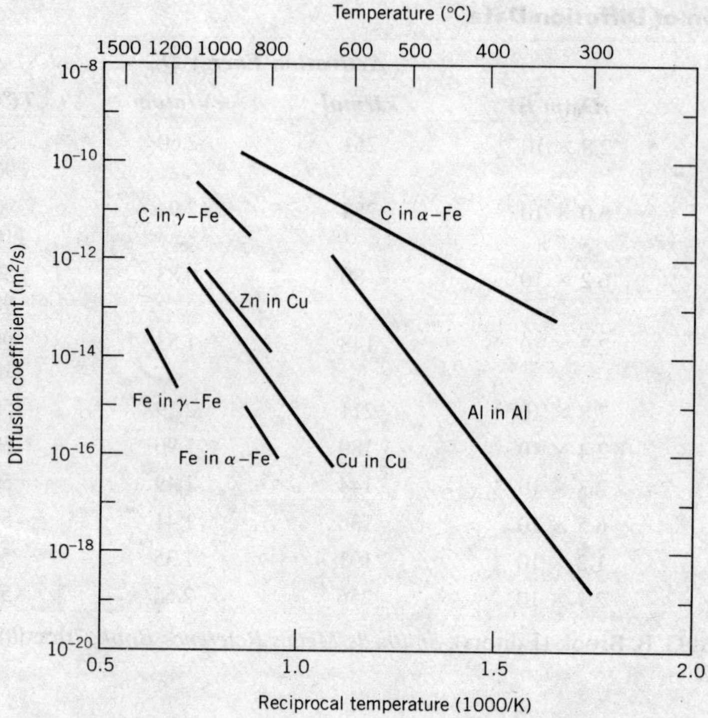

Figure 6.7 Plot of the logarithm of the diffusion coefficient versus the reciprocal of absolute temperature for several metals. [Data taken from E. A. Brandes and G. B. Brook (Editors), *Smithells Metals Reference Book,* 7th edition, Butterworth-Heinemann, Oxford, 1992.]

should result, having slope and intercept of $-Q_d/2.3R$ and log D_0, respectively. This is, in fact, the manner in which the values of Q_d and D_0 are determined experimentally. From such a plot for several alloy systems (Figure 6.7), it may be noted that linear relationships exist for all cases shown.

Concept Check 6.1

Rank the magnitudes of the diffusion coefficients from greatest to least for the following systems:

N in Fe at 700°C
Cr in Fe at 700°C
N in Fe at 900°C
Cr in Fe at 900°C

Now justify this ranking. (*Note:* Both Fe and Cr have the BCC crystal structure, and the atomic radii for Fe, Cr, and N are 0.124, 0.125, and 0.065 nm, respectively. You may also want to refer to Section 5.3.)

[*The answer may be found in enclosed CD.*]

Concept Check 6.2

Consider the self-diffusion of two hypothetical metals A and B. On a schematic graph of ln D versus $1/T$, plot (and label) lines for both metals given that $D_0(\text{A}) > D_0(\text{B})$ and also that $Q_d(\text{A}) > Q_d(\text{B})$.

[*The answer may be found in enclosed CD.*]

EXAMPLE PROBLEM 6.4

Diffusion Coefficient Determination

Using the data in Table 6.2, compute the diffusion coefficient for magnesium in aluminum at 550°C.

Solution

This diffusion coefficient may be determined by applying Equation 6.8; the values of D_0 and Q_d from Table 6.2 are 1.2×10^{-4} m²/s and 131 kJ/mol, respectively. Thus,

$$D = (1.2 \times 10^{-4}\ \text{m}^2/\text{s})\exp\left[-\frac{(131{,}000\ \text{J/mol})}{(8.31\ \text{J/mol-K})(550 + 273\ \text{K})}\right]$$

$$= 5.8 \times 10^{-13}\ \text{m}^2/\text{s}$$

EXAMPLE PROBLEM 6.5

Diffusion Coefficient Activation Energy and Preexponential Calculations

In Figure 6.8 is shown a plot of the logarithm (to the base 10) of the diffusion coefficient versus reciprocal of absolute temperature, for the diffusion of copper in gold. Determine values for the activation energy and the preexponential.

Solution

From Equation 6.9b the slope of the line segment in Figure 6.8 is equal to $-Q_d/2.3R$, and the intercept at $1/T = 0$ gives the value of $\log D_0$. Thus, the activation energy may be determined as

$$Q_d = -2.3R\,(\text{slope}) = -2.3R\left[\frac{\Delta(\log D)}{\Delta\left(\frac{1}{T}\right)}\right]$$

$$= -2.3R\left[\frac{\log D_1 - \log D_2}{\frac{1}{T_1} - \frac{1}{T_2}}\right]$$

where D_1 and D_2 are the diffusion coefficient values at $1/T_1$ and $1/T_2$, respectively. Let us arbitrarily take $1/T_1 = 0.8 \times 10^{-3}\,(\text{K})^{-1}$ and $1/T_2 = 1.1 \times 10^{-3}\,(\text{K})^{-1}$. We may now read the corresponding $\log D_1$ and $\log D_2$ values from the line segment in Figure 6.8.

[Before this is done, however, a parenthetic note of caution is offered. The vertical axis in Figure 6.8 is scaled logarithmically (to the base 10); however, the actual diffusion coefficient values are noted on this axis. For example, for $D = 10^{-14}$ m²/s, the logarithm of D is -14.0 *not* 10^{-14}. Furthermore, this logarithmic scaling affects the readings between decade values; for example, at a location midway between 10^{-14} and 10^{-15}, the value is not 5×10^{-15} but, rather, $10^{-14.5} = 3.2 \times 10^{-15}$].

Thus, from Figure 6.8, at $1/T_1 = 0.8 \times 10^{-3}\,(\text{K})^{-1}$, $\log D_1 = -12.40$, while for $1/T_2 = 1.1 \times 10^{-3}\,(\text{K})^{-1}$, $\log D_2 = -15.45$, and the activation energy, as

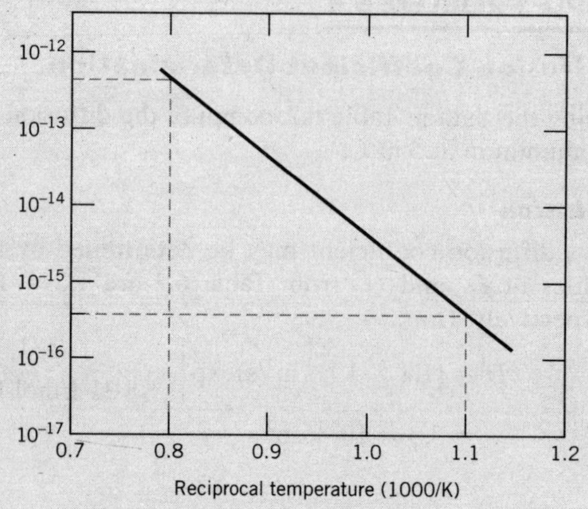

Figure 6.8 Plot of the logarithm of the diffusion coefficient versus the reciprocal of absolute temperature for the diffusion of copper in gold.

determined from the slope of the line segment in Figure 6.8 is

$$Q_d = -2.3R\left[\frac{\log D_1 - \log D_2}{\dfrac{1}{T_1} - \dfrac{1}{T_2}}\right]$$

$$= -2.3\,(8.31\text{ J/mol-K})\left[\frac{-12.40 - (-15.45)}{0.8 \times 10^{-3}\,(\text{K})^{-1} - 1.1 \times 10^{-3}\,(\text{K})^{-1}}\right]$$

$$= 194{,}000\text{ J/mol} = 194\text{ kJ/mol}$$

Now, rather than trying to make a graphical extrapolation to determine D_0, a more accurate value is obtained analytically using Equation 6.9b, and a specific value of D (or $\log D$) and its corresponding T (or $1/T$) from Figure 6.8. Since we know that $\log D = -15.45$ at $1/T = 1.1 \times 10^{-3}\,(\text{K})^{-1}$, then

$$\log D_0 = \log D + \frac{Q_d}{2.3R}\left(\frac{1}{T}\right)$$

$$= -15.45 + \frac{(194{,}000\text{ J/mol})(1.1 \times 10^{-3}\,[\text{K}]^{-1})}{(2.3)(8.31\text{ J/mol-K})}$$

$$= -4.28$$

Thus, $D_0 = 10^{-4.28}\text{ m}^2\text{/s} = 5.2 \times 10^{-5}\text{ m}^2\text{/s}$.

DESIGN EXAMPLE 6.1

Diffusion Temperature–Time Heat Treatment Specification

The wear resistance of a steel gear is to be improved by hardening its surface. This is to be accomplished by increasing the carbon content within an outer surface layer as a result of carbon diffusion into the steel; the carbon is to be supplied from an external carbon-rich gaseous atmosphere at an elevated and constant temperature. The initial carbon content of the steel is 0.20 wt%, whereas the surface concentration is to be maintained at 1.00 wt%. For this treatment to be effective, a carbon content of 0.60 wt% must be established at a position 0.75 mm below the surface. Specify an appropriate heat treatment in terms of temperature and time for temperatures between 900°C and 1050°C. Use data in Table 6.2 for the diffusion of carbon in γ-iron.

Solution

Since this is a nonsteady-state diffusion situation, let us first of all employ Equation 6.5, utilizing the following values for the concentration parameters:

$$C_0 = 0.20 \text{ wt\% C}$$
$$C_s = 1.00 \text{ wt\% C}$$
$$C_x = 0.60 \text{ wt\% C}$$

Therefore

$$\frac{C_x - C_0}{C_s - C_0} = \frac{0.60 - 0.20}{1.00 - 0.20} = 1 - \text{erf}\left(\frac{x}{2\sqrt{Dt}}\right)$$

and thus

$$0.5 = \text{erf}\left(\frac{x}{2\sqrt{Dt}}\right)$$

Using an interpolation technique as demonstrated in Example Problem 6.2 and the data presented in Table 6.1,

$$\frac{x}{2\sqrt{Dt}} = 0.4747 \tag{6.10}$$

The problem stipulates that $x = 0.75 \text{ mm} = 7.5 \times 10^{-4}$ m. Therefore

$$\frac{7.5 \times 10^{-4} \text{ m}}{2\sqrt{Dt}} = 0.4747$$

This leads to

$$Dt = 6.24 \times 10^{-7} \text{ m}^2$$

Furthermore, the diffusion coefficient depends on temperature according to Equation 6.8; and, from Table 6.2 for the diffusion of carbon in γ-iron, $D_0 = 2.3 \times 10^{-5}$ m^2/s and $Q_d = 148{,}000$ J/mol. Hence

$$Dt = D_0 \exp\left(-\frac{Q_d}{RT}\right)(t) = 6.24 \times 10^{-7} \text{ m}^2$$

$$(2.3 \times 10^{-5} \text{ m}^2\text{/s}) \exp\left[-\frac{148{,}000 \text{ J/mol}}{(8.31 \text{ J/mol-K})(T)}\right](t) = 6.24 \times 10^{-7} \text{ m}^2$$

and solving for the time t

$$t \text{ (in s)} = \frac{0.0271}{\exp\left(-\dfrac{17{,}810}{T}\right)}$$

Thus, the required diffusion time may be computed for some specified temperature (in K). Below are tabulated t values for four different temperatures that lie within the range stipulated in the problem.

Temperature (°C)	***Time***	
	s	***h***
900	106,400	29.6
950	57,200	15.9
1000	32,300	9.0
1050	19,000	6.3

MATERIAL OF IMPORTANCE

Aluminum for Integrated Circuit Interconnects

The heart of all computers and other electronic devices is the *integrated circuit* (or *IC*).[5] Each integrated circuit chip is a thin square wafer having dimensions on the order of 6 mm by 6 mm by 0.4 mm; furthermore, literally millions of interconnected electronic components and circuits are embedded in one of the chip faces. The base material for ICs is silicon, to which has been added very specific and extremely minute and controlled concentrations of impurities that are confined to very small and localized regions. For some ICs, the impurities are added using high-temperature diffusion heat treatments.

One important step in the IC fabrication process is the deposition of very thin and narrow conducting circuit paths to facilitate the passage of current from one device to another; these paths are called "interconnects," and several are shown in Figure 6.9, a scanning electron micrograph of an IC chip. Of course the material to be used for interconnects must have a high electrical conductivity—a metal, since, of all materials, metals have the highest conductivities. Table 6.3 cites values for silver, copper, gold, and aluminum, the most conductive metals.

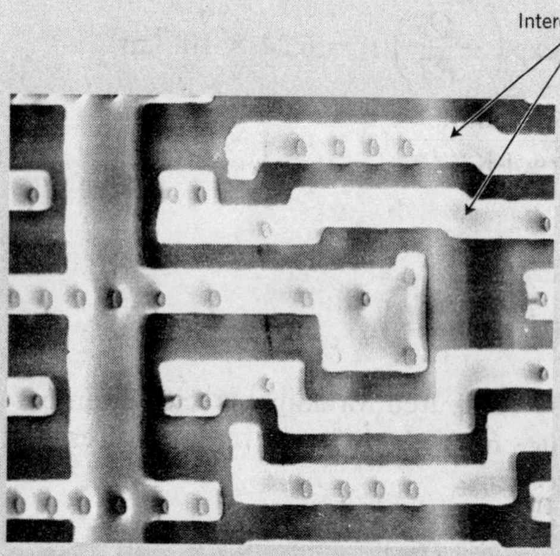

Figure 6.9 Scanning electron micrograph of an integrated circuit chip, on which is noted aluminum interconnect regions. Approximately 2000×. (Photograph courtesy of National Semiconductor Corporation.)

Table 6.3 Room-Temperature Electrical Conductivity Values for Silver, Copper, Gold, and Aluminum (the Four Most Conductive Metals)

Metal	*Electrical Conductivity* $[(ohm\text{-}meters)^{-1}]$
Silver	6.8×10^7
Copper	6.0×10^7
Gold	4.3×10^7
Aluminum	3.8×10^7

On the basis of these conductivities, and discounting material cost, Ag is the metal of choice, followed by Cu, Au, and Al.

Once these interconnects have been deposited, it is still necessary to subject the IC chip to other heat treatments, which may run as high as 500°C. If, during these treatments, there is significant diffusion of the interconnect metal into the silicon, the electrical functionality of the IC will be destroyed. Thus, since the extent of diffusion is dependent on the magnitude of the diffusion coefficient, it is necessary to select an interconnect metal that has a small value of D in silicon. Figure 6.10

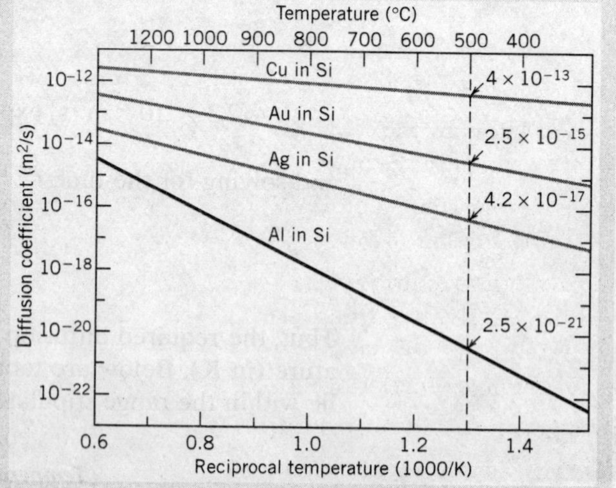

Figure 6.10 Logarithm of D-versus-$1/T$ (K) curves (lines) for the diffusion of copper, gold, silver, and aluminum in silicon. Also noted are D values at 500°C.

[5] Integrated circuits, their components and materials, are discussed in Section 17.15 and Sections 21.15 through 21.20.

plots the logarithm of D versus $1/T$ for the diffusion, into silicon, of copper, gold, silver, and aluminum. Also, a dashed vertical line has been constructed at 500°C, from which values of D, for the four metals are noted at this temperature. Here it may be seen that the diffusion coefficient for aluminum in silicon (2.5×10^{-21} m^2/s) is at least four orders of magnitude (i.e., a factor of 10^4) lower than the values for the other three metals.

Aluminum is indeed used for interconnects in some integrated circuits; even though its electrical conductivity is slightly lower than the values for silver, copper, and gold, its extremely low diffusion coefficient makes it the material of choice for this application. An aluminum-copper-silicon alloy (Al-4 wt% Cu-1.5 wt% Si) is sometimes also used for interconnects; it not only bonds easily to the surface of the chip, but is also more corrosion resistant than pure aluminum.

More recently, copper interconnects have also been used. However, it is first necessary to deposit a very thin layer of tantalum or tantalum nitride beneath the copper, which acts as a barrier to deter diffusion of Cu into the silicon.

6.6 OTHER DIFFUSION PATHS

Atomic migration may also occur along dislocations, grain boundaries, and external surfaces. These are sometimes called "*short-circuit*" *diffusion paths* inasmuch as rates are much faster than for bulk diffusion. However, in most situations short-circuit contributions to the overall diffusion flux are insignificant because the cross-sectional areas of these paths are extremely small.

6.7 DIFFUSION IN IONIC MATERIALS

For ionic compounds, the phenomenon of diffusion is more complicated than for metals inasmuch as it is necessary to consider the diffusive motion of two types of ions that have opposite charges. Diffusion in these materials usually occurs by a vacancy mechanism (Figure 6.3*a*). Also, as we noted in Section 5.5, in order to maintain charge neutrality in an ionic material, the following may be said about vacancies: (1) ion vacancies occur in pairs [as with Schottky defects (Figure 5.4)], (2) they form in nonstoichiometric compounds (Figure 5.5), and (3) they are created by substitutional impurity ions having different charge states than the host ions (Example Problem 5.5). In any event, associated with the diffusive motion of a single ion is a transference of electrical charge. In order to maintain localized charge neutrality in the vicinity of this moving ion, it is necessary that another species having an equal and opposite charge accompany the ion's diffusive motion. Possible charged species include another vacancy, an impurity atom, or an electronic carrier [i.e., a free electron or hole (Section 17.6)]. It follows that the rate of diffusion of these electrically charged couples is limited by the diffusion rate of the slowest moving species.

When an external electric field is applied across an ionic solid, the electrically charged ions migrate (i.e., diffuse) in response to forces that are brought to bear on them. As we discuss in Section 17.16, this ionic motion gives rise to an electric current. Furthermore, the electrical conductivity is a function of the diffusion coefficient (Equation 17.23). Consequently, much of the diffusion data for ionic solids come from electrical conductivity measurements.

6.8 DIFFUSION IN POLYMERIC MATERIALS

For polymeric materials, our interest is often in the diffusive motion of small foreign molecules (e.g., O_2, H_2O, CO_2, CH_4) between the molecular chains, rather than in the diffusive motion of chain atoms within the polymer structure. A polymer's permeability and absorption characteristics relate to the degree to which foreign substances diffuse into the material. Penetration of these foreign substances can lead to swelling and/or chemical reactions with the polymer molecules, and often a degradation of the material's mechanical and physical properties (Section 6.11).

Rates of diffusion are greater through amorphous regions than through crystalline regions; the structure of amorphous material is more "open." This diffusion mechanism may be considered to be analogous to interstitial diffusion in metals—that is, in polymers, diffusive movements occur through small voids between polymer chains from one open amorphous region to an adjacent open one.

Foreign molecule size also affects the diffusion rate: smaller molecules diffuse faster than larger ones. Furthermore, diffusion is more rapid for foreign molecules that are chemically inert than for those that react with the polymer.

One step in diffusion through a polymer membrane is the dissolution of the molecular species in the membrane material. This dissolution is a time-dependent process, and, if slower than the diffusive motion, may limit the overall rate of diffusion. Consequently, the diffusion properties of polymers are often characterized in terms of a *permeability coefficient* (denoted by P_M), where for the case of steady-state diffusion through a polymer membrane, Fick's first law (Equation 6.3), is modified as

$$J = P_M \frac{\Delta P}{\Delta x} \tag{6.11}$$

In this expression, J is the diffusion flux of gas through the membrane [(cm^3 STP)/(cm^2-s)], P_M is the permeability coefficient, Δx is the membrane thickness, and ΔP is the difference in pressure of the gas across the membrane. For small molecules in nonglassy polymers the permeability coefficient can be approximated as the product of the diffusion coefficient (D) and solubility of the diffusing species in the polymer (S)—i.e.,

$$P_M = DS \tag{6.12}$$

Table 6.4 presents the permeability coefficients of oxygen, nitrogen, carbon dioxide, and water vapor in several common polymers.[6]

For some applications, low permeability rates through polymeric materials are desirable, as with food and beverage packaging and automobile tires and inner tubes (see Sections 21.13 and 21.14). Polymer membranes are often used as filters, to selectively separate one chemical species from another (or others) (i.e., the desalinization of water). In such instances it is normally the case that the permeation rate of the substance to be filtered is significantly greater than for the other substance(s).

[6] The units for permeability coefficients in Table 6.4 are unusual, which are explained as follows: When the diffusing molecular species is in the gas phase, solubility is equal to

$$S = \frac{C}{P}$$

where C is the concentration of the diffusing species in the polymer [in units of (cm^3 STP)/cm^3 gas] and P is the partial pressure (in units of Pa). STP indicates that this is the volume of gas at standard temperature and pressure [273 K (0°C) and 101.3 kPa (1 atm)]. Thus, the units for S are (cm^3 STP)/Pa-cm^3. Since D is expressed in terms of cm^2/s, the units for the permeability coefficient are (cm^3 STP)(cm)/(cm^2-s-Pa).

Table 6.4 Permeability Coefficients P_M at 25°C for Oxygen, Nitrogen, Carbon Dioxide, and Water Vapor in a Variety of Polymers

		P_M [$\times 10^{-13}$ (cm^3 STP)(cm)/(cm^2-s-Pa)]			
Polymer	*Acronym*	O_2	N_2	CO_2	H_2O
Polyethylene (low density)	LDPE	2.2	0.73	9.5	68
Polyethylene (high density)	HDPE	0.30	0.11	0.27	9.0
Polypropylene	PP	1.2	0.22	6.4	38
Poly(vinyl chloride)	PVC	0.034	0.0089	0.012	206
Polystyrene	PS	2.0	0.59	7.9	840
poly(vinylidene chloride)	PVDC	0.0025	0.00044	0.015	7.0
Poly(ethylene terephthalate)	PET	0.044	0.011	0.23	—
Poly(ethyl methacrylate)	PEMA	0.89	0.17	3.8	2380

Source: Adapted from J. Brandrup, E. H. Immergut, E. A. Grulke, A. Abe, and D. R. Bloch (Editors), *Polymer Handbook,* 4th edition. Copyright © 1999 by John Wiley & Sons, New York. Reprinted by permission of John Wiley & Sons, Inc.

EXAMPLE PROBLEM 6.6

Computations of Diffusion Flux of Carbon Dioxide Through a Plastic Beverage Container and Beverage Shelf Life

The clear plastic bottles used for carbonated beverages (sometimes also called "soda," "pop," or "soda pop") are made from poly(ethylene terephthalate)(PET). The "fizz" in pop results from dissolved carbon dioxide (CO_2); and, because PET is permeable to CO_2, pop stored in PET bottles will eventually go "flat" (i.e., loose its fizz). A 20 oz. bottle of pop has a CO_2 pressure of about 400 kPa inside the bottle and the CO_2 pressure outside the bottle is 0.4 kPa.

(a) Assuming conditions of steady state, calculate the diffusion flux of CO_2 through the wall of the bottle.

(b) If the bottle must lose 750 (cm^3 STP) of CO_2 before the pop tastes flat, what is the shelf-life for a bottle of pop?

Note: Assume that each bottle has a surface area of 500 cm^2 and a wall thickness of 0.05 cm.

Solution

(a) This is a permeability problem in which Equation 6.11 is employed. The permeability coefficient of CO_2 through PET (Table 6.4) is 0.23×10^{-13} (cm^3 STP)(cm)/(cm^2-s-Pa). Thus, the diffusion flux is equal to

$$J = -P_M \frac{\Delta P}{\Delta x} = -P_M \frac{P_2 - P_1}{\Delta x}$$

$$= -0.23 \times 10^{-13} \frac{(\text{cm}^3\ \text{STP})(\text{cm})}{(\text{cm}^2)(\text{s})(\text{Pa})} \frac{(400\ \text{Pa} - 400{,}000\ \text{Pa})}{0.05\ \text{cm}}$$

$$= 1.8 \times 10^{-7}\,(\text{cm}^3\ \text{STP})/(\text{cm}^2\text{-s})$$

(b) The flow rate of CO_2 through the wall of the bottle $\dot{V}_{CO_2}$ is equal to

$$\dot{V}_{CO_2} = JA$$

where A is the surface area of the bottle (i.e., 500 cm^2); therefore,

$$\dot{V}_{CO_2} = [1.8 \times 10^{-7} (cm^3\ STP)/(cm^2\text{-}s)](500\ cm^2) = 9.0 \times 10^{-5} (cm^3\ STP)/s$$

The time it will take for a volume (V) of 750 (cm^3 STP) to escape is calculated as

$$\text{time} = \frac{V}{\dot{V}_{CO_2}} = \frac{750\ (cm^3\ STP)}{9.0 \times 10^{-5} (cm^3\ STP)/s} = 8.3 \times 10^6\ s$$
$$= 97\ \text{days (or about 3 months)}$$

SUMMARY

Diffusion Mechanisms

Solid-state diffusion is a means of mass transport within solid materials by stepwise atomic motion. The term "self-diffusion" refers to the migration of host atoms; for impurity atoms, the term "interdiffusion" is used. Two mechanisms are possible: vacancy and interstitial. For a given host metal, interstitial atomic species generally diffuse more rapidly.

Steady-State Diffusion
Nonsteady-State Diffusion

For steady-state diffusion, the concentration profile of the diffusing species is time independent, and the flux or rate is proportional to the negative of the concentration gradient according to Fick's first law. The mathematics for nonsteady state are described by Fick's second law, a partial differential equation. The solution for a constant surface composition boundary condition involves the Gaussian error function.

Factors That Influence Diffusion

The magnitude of the diffusion coefficient is indicative of the rate of atomic motion, being strongly dependent on and increasing exponentially with increasing temperature.

Diffusion in Ionic Materials

Diffusion in ionic materials normally occurs by a vacancy mechanism; localized charge neutrality is maintained by the coupled diffusive motion of a charged vacancy and some other charged entity.

Diffusion in Polymeric Materials

With regard to diffusion in polymers, small molecules of foreign substances diffuse between molecular chains, by an interstitial-type mechanism from one amorphous region to an adjacent one. Diffusion (or permeation) of gaseous species is often characterized in terms of the permeability coefficient, which is the product of the diffusion coefficient and solubility in the polymer. Permeation flow rates are expressed in terms of a modified form of Fick's first law.

REFERENCES

Gale, W. F. and T. C. Totemeier, (Editors), *Smithells Metals Reference Book,* 8th edition, Butterworth-Heinemann Ltd, Woburn, UK, 2004.

Carslaw, H. S. and J. C. Jaeger, *Conduction of Heat in Solids,* 2nd edition, Oxford University Press, Oxford, 1986.

Crank, J., *The Mathematics of Diffusion,* 2nd edition, Oxford University Press, Oxford, 1980.

Glicksman, M., *Diffusion in Solids,* Wiley-Interscience, New York, 2000.

Raghavan, V., *Introduction to Material Science and Engineering* 5th edition, Prentice-Hall India, New Delhi, 2005.

Shewmon, P. G., *Diffusion in Solids,* 2nd edition, The Minerals, Metals and Materials Society, Warrendale, PA, 1989.

QUESTIONS AND PROBLEMS

Introduction

6.1 Briefly explain the difference between self-diffusion and interdiffusion.

6.2 Self-diffusion involves the motion of atoms that are all of the same type; therefore it is not subject to observation by compositional changes, as with interdiffusion. Suggest one way in which self-diffusion may be monitored.

Diffusion Mechanisms

6.3 (a) Compare interstitial and vacancy atomic mechanisms for diffusion.

(b) Cite two reasons why interstitial diffusion is normally more rapid than vacancy diffusion.

Steady-State Diffusion

6.4 Briefly explain the concept of steady state as it applies to diffusion.

6.5 (a) Briefly explain the concept of a driving force.

(b) What is the driving force for steady-state diffusion?

6.6 The purification of hydrogen gas by diffusion through a palladium sheet was discussed in Section 6.3. Compute the number of kilograms of hydrogen that pass per hour through a 6-mm-thick sheet of palladium having an area of 0.25 m^2 at 600°C. Assume a diffusion coefficient of 1.7×10^{-8} m^2/s, that the concentrations at the high- and low-pressure sides of the plate are 2.0 and 0.4 kg of hydrogen per cubic meter of palladium, and that steady-state conditions have been attained.

6.7 A sheet of steel 2.5 mm thick has nitrogen atmospheres on both sides at 900°C and is permitted to achieve a steady-state diffusion condition. The diffusion coefficient for nitrogen in steel at this temperature is 1.2×10^{-10} m^2/s, and the diffusion flux is found to be 1.0×10^{-7} kg/m^2-s. Also, it is known that the concentration of nitrogen in the steel at the high-pressure surface is 2 kg/m^3. How far into the sheet from this high-pressure side will the concentration be 0.5 kg/m^3? Assume a linear concentration profile.

6.8 A sheet of BCC iron 2 mm thick was exposed to a carburizing gas atmosphere on one side and a decarburizing atmosphere on the other side at 675°C. After having reached steady state, the iron was quickly cooled to room temperature. The carbon concentrations at the two surfaces of the sheet were determined to be 0.015 and 0.0068 wt%. Compute the diffusion coefficient if the diffusion flux is 7.36×10^{-9} kg/m^2-s. *Hint:* Use Equation 5.9 to convert the concentrations from weight percent to kilograms of carbon per cubic meter of iron.

6.9 When α-iron is subjected to an atmosphere of nitrogen gas, the concentration of nitrogen in the iron, C_N (in weight percent), is a function of hydrogen pressure, p_{N_2}(in MPa), and absolute temperature (T) according to

$$C_N = 4.90 \times 10^{-3}\sqrt{p_{N_2}}\exp\left(-\frac{37.6\text{ kJ/mol}}{RT}\right) \tag{6.13}$$

Furthermore, the values of D_0 and Q_d for this diffusion system are 3.0×10^{-7} m^2/s and 76,150 J/mol, respectively. Consider a thin iron membrane 1.5 mm thick that is at 300°C.

Compute the diffusion flux through this membrane if the nitrogen pressure on one side of the membrane is 0.10 MPa (0.99 atm), and on the other side 6.0 MPa (49.3 atm).

Nonsteady-State Diffusion

6.10 Show that

$$C_x = \frac{B}{\sqrt{Dt}} \exp\left(-\frac{x^2}{4Dt}\right)$$

is also a solution to Equation 6.4b. The parameter B is a constant, being independent of both x and t.

6.11 Determine the carburizing time necessary to achieve a carbon concentration of 0.30 wt% at a position 4 mm into an iron–carbon alloy that initially contains 0.10 wt% C. The surface concentration is to be maintained at 0.90 wt% C, and the treatment is to be conducted at 1100°C. Use the diffusion data for γ-Fe in Table 6.2.

6.12 An FCC iron–carbon alloy initially containing 0.55 wt% C is exposed to an oxygen-rich and virtually carbon-free atmosphere at 1325 K (1052°C). Under these circumstances the carbon diffuses from the alloy and reacts at the surface with the oxygen in the atmosphere; that is, the carbon concentration at the surface position is maintained essentially at 0 wt% C. (This process of carbon depletion is termed *decarburization.*) (a) Find the solution to Fick's second law for this situation, and (b) At what position will the carbon concentration be 0.25 wt% after a 10-h treatment? The value of D at 1325 K is 4.3×10^{-11} m^2/s.

6.13 Nitrogen from a gaseous phase is to be diffused into pure iron at 675°C. If the surface concentration is maintained at 0.2 wt% N, what will be the concentration 2 mm from the surface after 25 h? The diffusion coefficient for nitrogen in iron at 675°C is 1.9×10^{-11} m^2/s.

6.14 Consider a diffusion couple composed of two semi-infinite solids of the same metal, and that each side of the diffusion couple has a different concentration of the same elemental impurity; furthermore, assume each impurity level is constant throughout its side of the diffusion couple. (a) For this situation, derive the solution to Fick's second law (assuming that the diffusion coefficient for the impurity is independent of concentration), using the general solution,

$$C(x, t) = A - B\, erf\left(\frac{x}{2\sqrt{Dt}}\right)$$

which is as follows:

$$C_x = \left(\frac{C_1 + C_2}{2}\right) - \left(\frac{C_1 - C_2}{2}\right) \operatorname{erf}\left(\frac{x}{2\sqrt{Dt}}\right) \qquad (6.14)$$

Use the initial conditions, when the $x = 0$ position is taken as the initial diffusion couple interface, then C_1 is the impurity concentration for $x < 0$; likewise, C_2 is the impurity content for $x > 0$.

(b) A diffusion couple composed of two platinum-gold alloys is formed; these alloys have compositions of 99.0 wt% Pt-1.0 wt% Au and 96.0 wt% Pt-4.0 wt% Au. Determine the time this diffusion couple must be heated at 1000°C (1273 K) in order for the composition to be 2.8 wt% Au at the 10 μm position into the 4.0 wt% Au side of the diffusion couple. Preexponential and activation energy values for Au diffusion in Pt are 1.3×10^{-5} m^2/s and 252,000 J/mol, respectively.

6.15 For a steel alloy it has been determined that a carburizing heat treatment of 15 h duration will raise the carbon concentration to 0.35 wt% at a point 2.0 mm from the surface. Estimate the time necessary to achieve the same concentration at a 6.0-mm position for an identical steel and at the same carburizing temperature.

Factors That Influence Diffusion

6.16 Cite the values of the diffusion coefficients for the interdiffusion of carbon in both α-iron (BCC) and γ-iron (FCC) at 900°C. Which is larger? Explain why this is the case.

6.17 Using the data in Table 6.2, compute the value of D for the diffusion of magnesium in aluminum at 400°C.

6.18 At what temperature will the diffusion coefficient for the diffusion of zinc in copper have a value of 2.6×10^{-16} m^2/s? Use the diffusion data in Table 6.2.

6.19 The preexponential and activation energy for the diffusion of chromium in nickel are 1.1×10^{-4} m^2/s and 272,000 J/mol, respectively. At what temperature will the diffusion coefficient have a value of 1.2×10^{-14} m^2/s?

6.20 The activation energy for the diffusion of copper in silver is 193,000 J/mol. Calculate the diffusion coefficient at 1200 K (927°C), given that D at 1000 K (727°C) is 1.0×10^{-14} m²/s.

6.21 The diffusion coefficients for nickel in iron are given at two temperatures:

T(K)	***D(m²/s)***
1473	2.2×10^{-15}
1673	4.8×10^{-14}

(a) Determine the values of D_0 and the activation energy Q_d.

(b) What is the magnitude of D at 1300°C (1573 K)?

6.22 The diffusion coefficients for carbon in nickel are given at two temperatures:

T(°C)	***D(m²/s)***
600	5.5×10^{-14}
700	3.9×10^{-13}

(a) Determine the values of D_0 and Q_d.

(b) What is the magnitude of D at 850°C?

6.23 Below is shown a plot of the logarithm (to the base 10) of the diffusion coefficient versus reciprocal of the absolute temperature, for the diffusion of gold in silver. Determine values for the activation energy and preexponential.

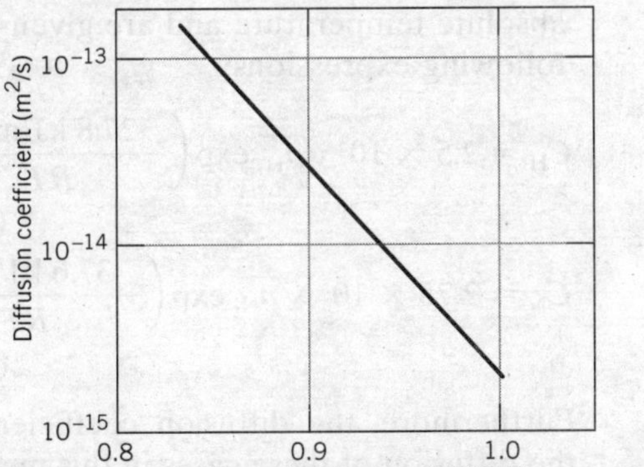

6.24 Carbon is allowed to diffuse through a steel plate 10 mm thick. The concentrations of carbon at the two faces are 0.85 and 0.40 kg C/cm³ Fe, which are maintained constant. If the preexponential and activation energy are 6.2×10^{-7} m²/s and 80,000 J/mol, respectively, compute the temperature at which the diffusion flux is 6.3×10^{-10} kg/m²-s.

6.25 The steady-state diffusion flux through a metal plate is 7.8×10^{-8} kg/m²-s at a temperature of 1200°C (1473 K) and when the concentration gradient is -500 kg/m⁴. Calculate the diffusion flux at 1000°C (1273 K) for the same concentration gradient and assuming an activation energy for diffusion of 145,000 J/mol.

6.26 At approximately what temperature would a specimen of γ-iron have to be carburized for 4 h to produce the same diffusion result as at 1000°C for 12 h?

6.27 **(a)** Calculate the diffusion coefficient for magnesium in aluminum at 450°C.

(b) What time will be required at 550°C to produce the same diffusion result (in terms of concentration at a specific point) as for 15 h at 450°C?

6.28 A copper–nickel diffusion couple similar to that shown in Figure 6.1*a* is fashioned. After a 500-h heat treatment at 1000°C (1273 K) the concentration of Ni is 3.0 wt% at the 1.0-mm position within the copper. At what temperature should the diffusion couple be heated to produce this same concentration (i.e., 3.0 wt% Ni) at a 2.0-mm position after 500 h? The preexponential and activation energy for the diffusion of Ni in Cu are 2.7×10^{-4} m²/s and 236,000 J/mol, respectively.

6.29 A diffusion couple similar to that shown in Figure 6.1*a* is prepared using two hypothetical metals A and B. After a 20-h heat treatment at 800°C (and subsequently cooling to room temperature) the concentration of B in A is 2.5 wt% at the 6.0-mm position within metal A. If another heat treatment is conducted on an identical diffusion couple, only at 1000°C for 20 h, at what position will the composition be 2.5 wt% B? Assume that the preexponential and activation energy for the diffusion coefficient are 1.5×10^{-4} m²/s and 125,000 J/mol, respectively.

6.30 The outer surface of a steel gear is to be hardened by increasing its carbon content; the carbon is to be supplied from an external carbon-rich atmosphere that is maintained at an elevated temperature. A diffusion heat treatment at 600°C (873 K) for 100 min increases the carbon concentration to 0.75 wt% at a position 0.5 mm below the surface. Estimate the diffusion time required at 900°C (1173 K) to achieve this same concentration also at a 0.5-mm position. Assume that the surface carbon content is the same for both heat treatments, which is maintained constant. Use the diffusion data in Table 6.2 for C diffusion in α-Fe.

6.31 An FCC iron–carbon alloy initially containing 0.10 wt% C is carburized at an elevated temperature and in an atmosphere wherein the surface carbon concentration is maintained at 1.10 wt%. If after 48 h the concentration of carbon is 0.30 wt% at a position 3.5 mm below the surface, determine the temperature at which the treatment was carried out.

Diffusion in Polymeric Materials

6.32 Consider the diffusion of oxygen through a low density polyethylene (LDPE) sheet 15 mm thick. The pressures of oxygen at the two faces are 2000 kPa and 150 kPa, which are maintained constant. Assuming conditions of steady state, what is the diffusion flux [in (cm^3 STP)/cm^2-s] at 298 K?

6.33 Carbon dioxide diffuses through a high density polyethylene (HDPE) sheet 50 mm thick at a rate of 2.2×10^{-8} (cm^3 STP)/cm^2-s at 325 K. The pressures of carbon dioxide at the two faces are 4000 kPa and 2500 kPa, which are maintained constant. Assuming conditions of steady state, what is the permeability coefficient at 325 K?

6.34 The permeability coefficient of a type of small gas molecule in a polymer is dependent on absolute temperature according to the following equation:

$$P_M = P_{M_0} \exp\left(-\frac{Q_p}{RT}\right)$$

where P_{M_0} and Q_p are constants for a given gas-polymer pair. Consider the diffusion of water through a polystyrene sheet 30 mm thick. The water vapor pressures at the two faces are 20 kPa and 1 kPa, which are maintained constant. Compute the diffusion flux [in (cm^3 STP)/cm^2-s] at 350 K? For this diffusion system

$$P_{M_0} = 9.0 \times 10^{-5} \text{ (cm}^3\text{ STP)/cm}^2\text{-s-Pa}$$
$$Q_p = 42.3 \text{ kJ/mol}$$

Also, assume a condition of steady state diffusion.

DESIGN PROBLEMS

Steady-State Diffusion (Factors That Influence Diffusion)

6.D1. It is desired to enrich the partial pressure of hydrogen in a hydrogen–nitrogen gas mixture for which the partial pressures of both gases are 0.1013 MPa (1 atm). It has been proposed to accomplish this by passing both gases through a thin sheet of some metal at an elevated temperature; inasmuch as hydrogen diffuses through the plate at a higher rate than does nitrogen, the partial pressure of hydrogen will be higher on the exit side of the sheet. The design calls for partial pressures of 0.051 MPa (0.5 atm) and 0.01013 MPa (0.1 atm), respectively, for hydrogen and nitrogen. The concentrations of hydrogen and nitrogen (C_H and C_N, in mol/m^3) in this metal are functions of gas partial pressures (p_{H_2} and p_{N_2}, in MPa) and absolute temperature and are given by the following expressions:

$$C_H = 2.5 \times 10^3 \sqrt{p_{H_2}} \exp\left(-\frac{27.8 \text{ kJ/mol}}{RT}\right) \tag{6.15a}$$

$$C_N = 2.75 \times 10^3 \sqrt{p_{N_2}} \exp\left(-\frac{37.6 \text{ kJ/mol}}{RT}\right) \tag{6.15b}$$

Furthermore, the diffusion coefficients for the diffusion of these gases in this metal are functions of the absolute temperature as follows:

$$D_H(\text{m}^2/\text{s}) = 1.4 \times 10^{-7} \exp\left(-\frac{13.4 \text{ kJ/mol}}{RT}\right) \tag{6.16a}$$

$$D_N(\text{m}^2/\text{s}) = 3.0 \times 10^{-7} \exp\left(-\frac{76.15 \text{ kJ/mol}}{RT}\right) \tag{6.16b}$$

Is it possible to purify hydrogen gas in this manner? If so, specify a temperature at which the process may be carried out, and also the thickness of metal sheet that would be required. If this procedure is not possible, then state the reason(s) why.

6.D2 A gas mixture is found to contain two diatomic A and B species (A_2 and B_2) for which the partial pressures of both are 0.1013 MPa (1 atm). This mixture is to be enriched in the partial pressure of the A species by passing both gases through a thin sheet of some metal at an elevated temperature. The resulting enriched mixture is to have a partial pressure of 0.051 MPa (0.5 atm) for gas A and 0.0203 MPa (0.2 atm) for gas B. The concentrations of A and B (C_A and C_B, in mol/m^3) are functions of gas partial pressures (p_{A_2} and p_{B_2}, in MPa) and absolute temperature according to the following expressions:

$$C_A = 1.5 \times 10^3 \sqrt{p_{A_2}} \exp\left(-\frac{20.0 \text{ kJ/mol}}{RT}\right) \quad (6.17a)$$

$$C_B = 2.0 \times 10^3 \sqrt{p_{B_2}} \exp\left(-\frac{27.0 \text{ kJ/mol}}{RT}\right) \quad (6.17b)$$

Furthermore, the diffusion coefficients for the diffusion of these gases in the metal are functions of the absolute temperature as follows:

$$D_A(\text{m}^2/\text{s}) = 5.0 \times 10^{-7} \exp\left(-\frac{13.0 \text{ kJ/mol}}{RT}\right) \quad (6.18a)$$

$$D_B(\text{m}^2/\text{s}) = 3.0 \times 10^{-6} \exp\left(-\frac{21.0 \text{ kJ/mol}}{RT}\right) \quad (6.18b)$$

Is it possible to purify the A gas in this manner? If so, specify a temperature at which the process may be carried out, and also the thickness of metal sheet that would be required. If this procedure is not possible, then state the reason(s) why.

Nonsteady-State Diffusion (Factors That Influence Diffusion)

6.D3 The wear resistance of a steel shaft is to be improved by hardening its surface. This is to be accomplished by increasing the nitrogen content within an outer surface layer as a result of nitrogen diffusion into the steel; the nitrogen is to be supplied from an external nitrogen-rich gas at an elevated and constant temperature. The initial nitrogen content of the steel is 0.0025 wt%, whereas the surface concentration is to be maintained at 0.45 wt%. For this treatment to be effective, a nitrogen content of 0.12 wt% must be established at a position 0.45 mm below the surface. Specify an appropriate heat treatment in terms of temperature and time for a temperature between 475°C and 625°C. The preexponential and activation energy for the diffusion of nitrogen in iron are 3×10^{-7} m^2/s and 76,150 J/mol, respectively, over this temperature range.

6.D4 The wear resistance of a steel gear is to be improved by hardening its surface, as described in Design Example 6.1. However, in this case the initial carbon content of the steel is 0.15 wt%, and a carbon content of 0.75 wt% is to be established at a position 0.65 mm below the surface. Furthermore, the surface concentration is to be maintained constant, but may be varied between 1.2 and 1.4 wt% C. Specify an appropriate heat treatment in terms of surface carbon concentration and time, and for a temperature between 1000°C and 1200°C.

Chapter 7 Phase Diagrams

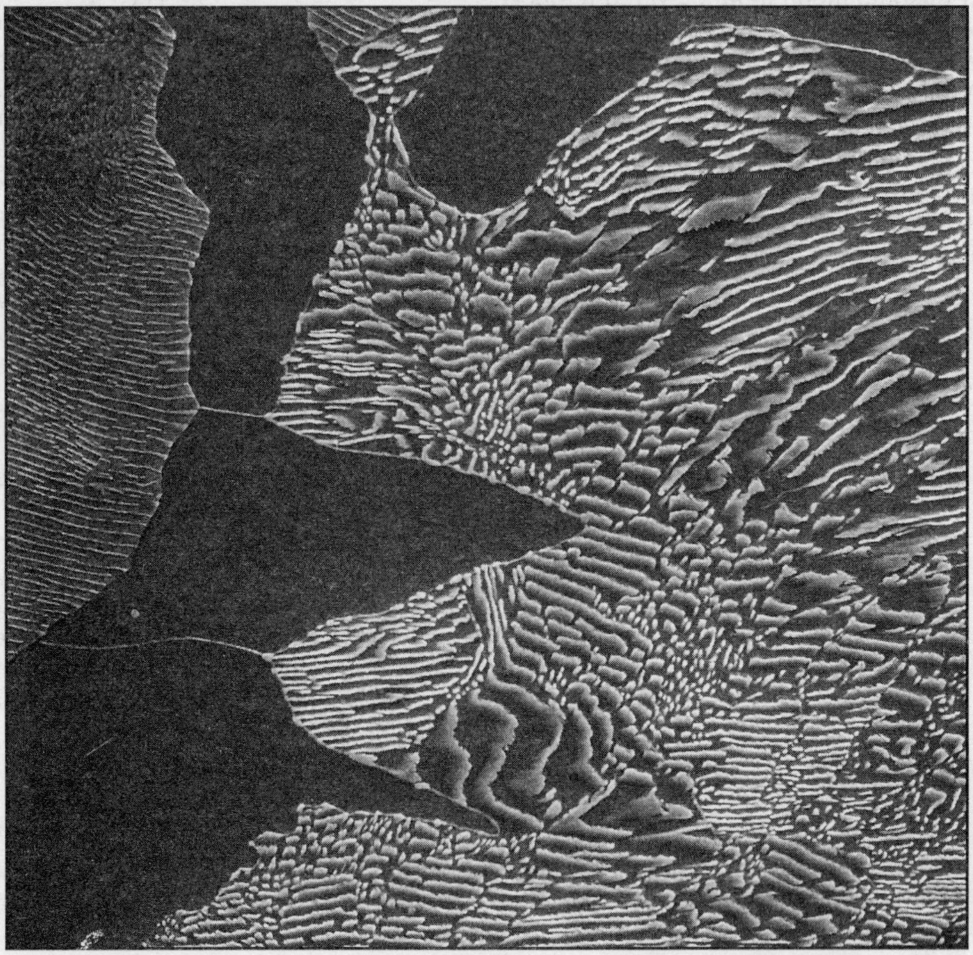

A scanning electron micrograph showing the microstructure of a plain carbon steel that contains 0.44 wt% C. The large dark areas are proeutectoid ferrite. Regions having the alternating light and dark lamellar structure are pearlite; the dark and light layers in the pearlite correspond, respectively, to ferrite and cementite phases. During etching of the surface prior to examination, the ferrite phase was preferentially dissolved; thus, the pearlite appears in topographical relief with cementite layers being elevated above the ferrite layers. 3000×. (Micrograph courtesy of Republic Steel Corporation.)

Learning Objectives

After studying this chapter you should be able to do the following:

1. (a) Schematically sketch simple isomorphous and eutectic phase diagrams.
   (b) On these diagrams label the various phase regions.
   (c) Label liquidus, solidus, and solvus lines.
2. Given a binary phase diagram, the composition of an alloy, its temperature, and assuming that the alloy is at equilibrium, determine
   (a) what phase(s) is (are) present,
   (b) the composition(s) of the phase(s), and
   (c) the mass fraction(s) of the phase(s).
3. For some given binary phase diagram, do the following:
   (a) locate the temperatures and compositions of all eutectic, eutectoid, peritectic, and congruent phase transformations; and
   (b) write reactions for all these transformations for either heating or cooling.
4. Given the composition of an iron–carbon alloy containing between 0.022 wt% C and 2.14 wt% C, be able to
   (a) specify whether the alloy is hypoeutectoid or hypereutectoid,
   (b) name the proeutectoid phase,
   (c) compute the mass fractions of proeutectoid phase and pearlite, and
   (d) make a schematic diagram of the microstructure at a temperature just below the eutectoid.

7.1 INTRODUCTION

The understanding of phase diagrams for alloy systems is extremely important because there is a strong correlation between microstructure and mechanical properties, and the development of microstructure of an alloy is related to the characteristics of its phase diagram. In addition, phase diagrams provide valuable information about melting, casting, crystallization, and other phenomena.

This chapter presents and discusses the following topics: (1) terminology associated with phase diagrams and phase transformations; (2) pressure–temperature phase diagrams for pure materials; (3) the interpretation of phase diagrams; (4) some of the common and relatively simple binary phase diagrams, including that for the iron–carbon system; and (5) the development of equilibrium microstructures, upon cooling, for several situations.

Definitions and Basic Concepts

It is necessary to establish a foundation of definitions and basic concepts relating to alloys, phases, and equilibrium before delving into the interpretation and utilization of phase diagrams. The term **component** is frequently used in this discussion; components are pure metals and/or compounds of which an alloy is composed. For example, in a copper–zinc brass, the components are Cu and Zn. *Solute* and *solvent,* which are also common terms, were defined in Section 5.3. Another term used in this context is **system,** which has two meanings. First, "system" may refer to a specific body of material under consideration (e.g., a ladle of molten steel). Or it may relate to the series of possible alloys consisting of the same components, but without regard to alloy composition (e.g., the iron–carbon system).

The concept of a solid solution was introduced in Section 5.3. By way of review, a solid solution consists of atoms of at least two different types; the solute atoms occupy either substitutional or interstitial positions in the solvent lattice, and the crystal structure of the solvent is maintained.

7.2 SOLUBILITY LIMIT

For many alloy systems and at some specific temperature, there is a maximum concentration of solute atoms that may dissolve in the solvent to form a solid solution; this is called a **solubility limit.** The addition of solute in excess of this solubility limit results in the formation of another solid solution or compound that has a distinctly different composition. To illustrate this concept, consider the sugar–water ($C_{12}H_{22}O_{11}$–H_2O) system. Initially, as sugar is added to water, a sugar–water solution or syrup forms. As more sugar is introduced, the solution becomes more concentrated, until the solubility limit is reached, or the solution becomes saturated with sugar. At this time the solution is not capable of dissolving any more sugar, and further additions simply settle to the bottom of the container. Thus, the system now consists of two separate substances: a sugar–water syrup liquid solution and solid crystals of undissolved sugar.

This solubility limit of sugar in water depends on the temperature of the water and may be represented in graphical form on a plot of temperature along the ordinate and composition (in weight percent sugar) along the abscissa, as shown in Figure 7.1. Along the composition axis, increasing sugar concentration is from left to right, and percentage of water is read from right to left. Since only two components are involved (sugar and water), the sum of the concentrations at any composition will equal 100 wt%. The solubility limit is represented as the nearly vertical line in the figure. For compositions and temperatures to the left of the solubility line, only the syrup liquid solution exists; to the right of the line, syrup and solid sugar coexist. The solubility limit at some temperature is the composition that corresponds to the intersection of the given temperature coordinate and the solubility limit line. For example, at 20°C the maximum solubility of sugar in water is 65 wt%. As Figure 7.1 indicates, the solubility limit increases slightly with rising temperature.

7.3 PHASES

Also critical to the understanding of phase diagrams is the concept of a **phase.** A phase may be defined as a homogeneous portion of a system that has uniform physical and chemical characteristics. Every pure material is considered to be a phase;

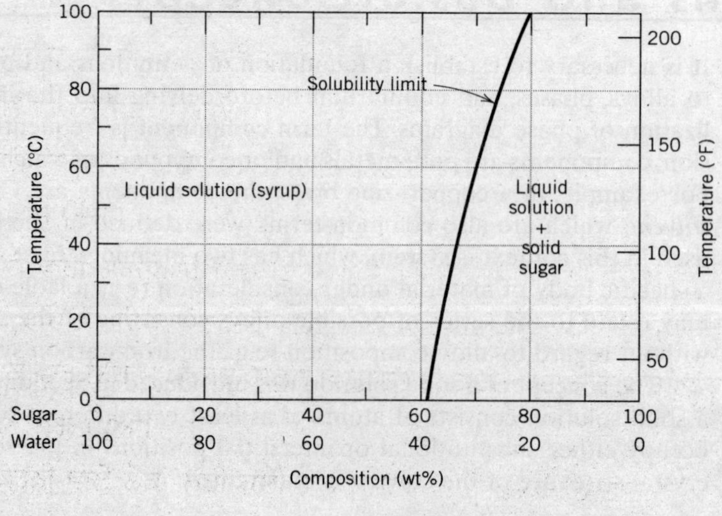

Figure 7.1 The solubility of sugar ($C_{12}H_{22}O_{11}$) in a sugar–water syrup.

so also is every solid, liquid, and gaseous solution. For example, the sugar–water syrup solution just discussed is one phase, and solid sugar is another. Each has different physical properties (one is a liquid, the other is a solid); furthermore, each is different chemically (i.e., has a different chemical composition); one is virtually pure sugar, the other is a solution of H_2O and $C_{12}H_{22}O_{11}$. If more than one phase is present in a given system, each will have its own distinct properties, and a boundary separating the phases will exist across which there will be a discontinuous and abrupt change in physical and/or chemical characteristics. When two phases are present in a system, it is not necessary that there be a difference in both physical and chemical properties; a disparity in one or the other set of properties is sufficient. When water and ice are present in a container, two separate phases exist; they are physically dissimilar (one is a solid, the other is a liquid) but identical in chemical makeup. Also, when a substance can exist in two or more polymorphic forms (e.g., having both FCC and BCC structures), each of these structures is a separate phase because their respective physical characteristics differ.

Sometimes, a single-phase system is termed "homogeneous." Systems composed of two or more phases are termed "mixtures" or "heterogeneous systems." Most metallic alloys and, for that matter, ceramic, polymeric, and composite systems are heterogeneous. Ordinarily, the phases interact in such a way that the property combination of the multiphase system is different from, and more attractive than, either of the individual phases.

7.4 MICROSTRUCTURE

Many times, the physical properties and, in particular, the mechanical behavior of a material depend on the microstructure. Microstructure is subject to direct microscopic observation, using optical or electron microscopes; this topic was touched on in Sections 5.11 and 5.12. In metal alloys, microstructure is characterized by the number of phases present, their proportions, and the manner in which they are distributed or arranged. The microstructure of an alloy depends on such variables as the alloying elements present, their concentrations, and the heat treatment of the alloy (i.e., the temperature, the heating time at temperature, and the rate of cooling to room temperature).

The procedure of specimen preparation for microscopic examination was briefly outlined in Section 5.12. After appropriate polishing and etching, the different phases may be distinguished by their appearance. For example, for a two-phase alloy, one phase may appear light and the other phase dark, as in the chapter-opening photograph for this chapter. When only a single phase or solid solution is present, the texture will be uniform, except for grain boundaries that may be revealed (Figure 5.17).

7.5 PHASE EQUILIBRIA

Equilibrium is another essential concept that is best described in terms of a thermodynamic quantity called the **free energy.** In brief, free energy is a function of the internal energy of a system, and also the randomness or disorder of the atoms or molecules (or entropy). A system is at equilibrium if its free energy is at a minimum under some specified combination of temperature, pressure, and composition. In a macroscopic sense, this means that the characteristics of the system do not change with time but persist indefinitely; that is, the system is stable. A change in temperature, pressure, and/or composition for a system in equilibrium will result in an increase in the free energy and in a possible spontaneous change to another state whereby the free energy is lowered.

The term **phase equilibrium,** often used in the context of this discussion, refers to equilibrium as it applies to systems in which more than one phase may exist. Phase equilibrium is reflected by a constancy with time in the phase characteristics of a system. Perhaps an example best illustrates this concept. Suppose that a sugar–water syrup is contained in a closed vessel and the solution is in contact with solid sugar at 20°C. If the system is at equilibrium, the composition of the syrup is 65 wt% $C_{12}H_{22}O_{11}$–35 wt% H_2O (Figure 7.1), and the amounts and compositions of the syrup and solid sugar will remain constant with time. If the temperature of the system is suddenly raised—say, to 100°C—this equilibrium or balance is temporarily upset in that the solubility limit has been increased to 80 wt% $C_{12}H_{22}O_{11}$ (Figure 7.1). Thus, some of the solid sugar will go into solution in the syrup. This will continue until the new equilibrium syrup concentration is established at the higher temperature.

This sugar–syrup example illustrates the principle of phase equilibrium using a liquid–solid system. In many metallurgical and materials systems of interest, phase equilibrium involves just solid phases. In this regard the state of the system is reflected in the characteristics of the microstructure, which necessarily include not only the phases present and their compositions but, in addition, the relative phase amounts and their spatial arrangement or distribution.

Free energy considerations and diagrams similar to Figure 7.1 provide information about the equilibrium characteristics of a particular system, which is important; but they do not indicate the time period necessary for the attainment of a new equilibrium state. It is often the case, especially in solid systems, that a state of equilibrium is never completely achieved because the rate of approach to equilibrium is extremely slow; such a system is said to be in a nonequilibrium or **metastable** state. A metastable state or microstructure may persist indefinitely, experiencing only extremely slight and almost imperceptible changes as time progresses. Often, metastable structures are of more practical significance than equilibrium ones. For example, some steel and aluminum alloys rely for their strength on the development of metastable microstructures during carefully designed heat treatments (Sections 8.5 and 10.14).

Thus not only is an understanding of equilibrium states and structures important, but also the speed or rate at which they are established and the factors that affect the rate must be considered. This chapter is devoted almost exclusively to equilibrium structures; the treatment of reaction rates and nonequilibrium structures is deferred to Chapter 8 and Section 10.14.

Concept Check 7.1

What is the difference between the states of phase equilibrium and metastability?

[*The answer may be found in enclosed CD.*]

7.6 ONE-COMPONENT (OR UNARY) PHASE DIAGRAMS

Much of the information about the control of the phase structure of a particular system is conveniently and concisely displayed in what is called a **phase diagram,** also often termed an *equilibrium diagram.* Now, there are three externally controllable parameters that will affect phase structure—viz. temperature, pressure, and composition—and phase diagrams are constructed when various combinations of these parameters are plotted against one another.

Perhaps the simplest and easiest type of phase diagram to understand is that for a one-component system, in which composition is held constant (i.e., the phase diagram is for a pure substance); this means that pressure and temperature are the variables. This one-component phase diagram (or *unary phase diagram*) [sometimes also called a *pressure–temperature* (or *P–T*) *diagram*] is represented as a two-dimensional plot of pressure (ordinate, or vertical axis) versus temperature (abscissa, or horizontal axis). Most often, the pressure axis is scaled logarithmically.

We illustrate this type of phase diagram and demonstrate its interpretation using as an example the one for H_2O, which is shown in Figure 7.2. Here it may be noted that regions for three different phases—solid, liquid, and vapor—are delineated on the plot. Each of the phases will exist under equilibrium conditions over the temperature–pressure ranges of its corresponding area. Furthermore, the three curves shown on the plot (labeled *aO*, *bO*, and *cO*) are phase boundaries; at any point on one of these curves, the two phases on either side of the curve are in equilibrium (or coexist) with one another. That is, equilibrium between solid and vapor phases is along curve *aO*—likewise for the solid-liquid, curve *bO*, and the liquid-vapor, curve *cO*. Also, upon crossing a boundary (as temperature and/or pressure is altered), one phase transforms to another. For example, at one atmosphere pressure, during heating the solid phase transforms to the liquid phase (i.e., melting occurs) at the point labeled 2 on Figure 7.2 (i.e., the intersection of the dashed horizontal line with the solid-liquid phase boundary); this point corresponds to a temperature of 0°C. Of course, the reverse transformation (liquid-to-solid, or solidification) takes place at the same point upon cooling. Similarly, at the intersection of the dashed line with the liquid-vapor phase boundary [point 3 (Figure 7.2), at 100°C] the liquid transforms to the vapor phase (or vaporizes) upon heating;

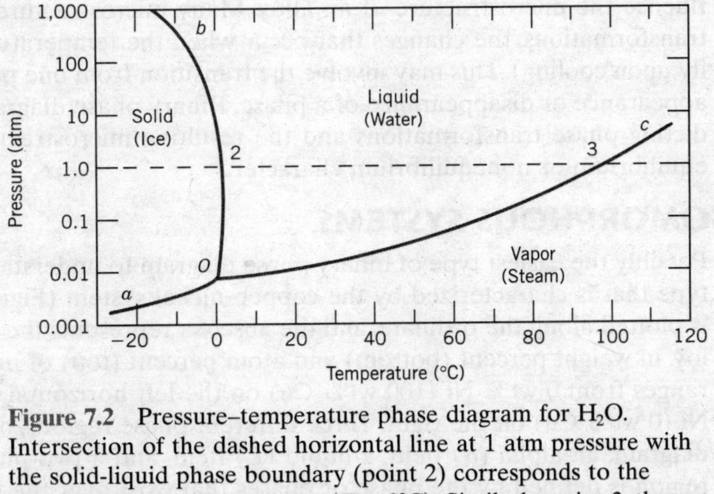

Figure 7.2 Pressure–temperature phase diagram for H_2O. Intersection of the dashed horizontal line at 1 atm pressure with the solid-liquid phase boundary (point 2) corresponds to the melting point at this pressure (T = 0°C). Similarly, point 3, the intersection with the liquid-vapor boundary, represents the boiling point (T = 100°C).

condensation occurs for cooling. And, finally, solid ice sublimes or vaporizes upon crossing the curve labeled *aO*.

As may also be noted from Figure 7.2, all three of the phase boundary curves intersect at a common point, which is labeled *O* (and for this H_2O system, at a temperature of 273.16 K and a pressure of 6.04×10^{-3} atm). This means that at this point only, all of the solid, liquid, and vapor phases are simultaneously in equilibrium with one another. Appropriately, this, and any other point on a *P–T* phase diagram where three phases are in equilibrium, is called a *triple point;* sometimes it is also termed an *invariant point* inasmuch as its position is distinct, or fixed by definite values of pressure and temperature. Any deviation from this point by a change of temperature and/or pressure will cause at least one of the phases to disappear.

Pressure-temperature phase diagrams for a number of substances have been determined experimentally, which also have solid, liquid, and vapor phase regions. In those instances when multiple solid phases (i.e., allotropes, Section 3.6) exist, there will appear a region on the diagram for each solid phase, and also other triple points. The pressure-temperature phase diagram for carbon (which includes phase regions for diamond and graphite) is shown on the front and back covers of this book.

Binary Phase Diagrams

Another type of extremely common phase diagram is one in which temperature and composition are variable parameters, and pressure is held constant—normally 1 atm. There are several different varieties; in the present discussion, we will concern ourselves with binary alloys—those that contain two components. If more than two components are present, phase diagrams become extremely complicated and difficult to represent. An explanation of the principles governing and the interpretation of phase diagrams can be demonstrated using binary alloys even though most alloys contain more than two components.

Binary phase diagrams are maps that represent the relationships between temperature and the compositions and quantities of phases at equilibrium, which influence the microstructure of an alloy. Many microstructures develop from phase transformations, the changes that occur when the temperature is altered (ordinarily upon cooling). This may involve the transition from one phase to another, or the appearance or disappearance of a phase. Binary phase diagrams are helpful in predicting phase transformations and the resulting microstructures, which may have equilibrium or nonequilibrium character.

7.7 BINARY ISOMORPHOUS SYSTEMS

Possibly the easiest type of binary phase diagram to understand and interpret is the type that is characterized by the copper–nickel system (Figure 7.3*a*). Temperature is plotted along the ordinate, and the abscissa represents the composition of the alloy, in weight percent (bottom) and atom percent (top) of nickel. The composition ranges from 0 wt% Ni (100 wt% Cu) on the left horizontal extremity to 100 wt% Ni (0 wt% Cu) on the right. Three different phase regions, or fields, appear on the diagram, an alpha (α) field, a liquid (*L*) field, and a two-phase $\alpha + L$ field. Each region is defined by the phase or phases that exist over the range of temperatures and compositions delimited by the phase boundary lines.

The liquid *L* is a homogeneous liquid solution composed of both copper and nickel. The α phase is a substitutional solid solution consisting of both Cu and Ni atoms, and

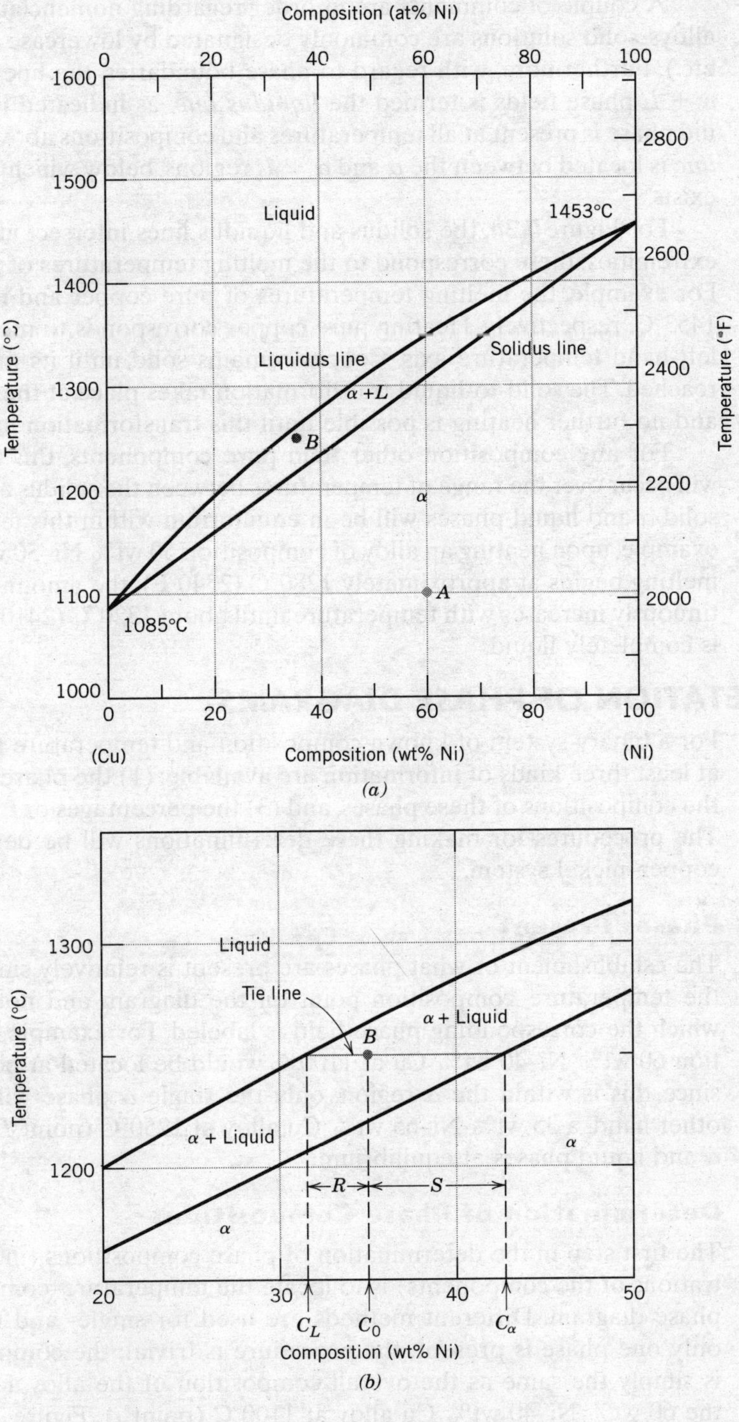

Figure 7.3 (*a*) The copper–nickel phase diagram. (*b*) A portion of the copper–nickel phase diagram for which compositions and phase amounts are determined at point *B*. (Adapted from *Phase Diagrams of Binary Nickel Alloys*, P. Nash, Editor, 1991. Reprinted by permission of ASM International, Materials Park, OH.)

having an FCC crystal structure. At temperatures below about 1080°C, copper and nickel are mutually soluble in each other in the solid state for all compositions. This complete solubility is explained by the fact that both Cu and Ni have the same crystal structure (FCC), nearly identical atomic radii and electronegativities, and similar valences, as discussed in Section 5.3. The copper–nickel system is termed **isomorphous** because of this complete liquid and solid solubility of the two components.

A couple of comments are in order regarding nomenclature. First, for metallic alloys, solid solutions are commonly designated by lowercase Greek letters (α, β, γ, etc.). Furthermore, with regard to phase boundaries, the line separating the L and $\alpha + L$ phase fields is termed the *liquidus line,* as indicated in Figure 7.3*a*; the liquid phase is present at all temperatures and compositions above this line. The *solidus line* is located between the α and $\alpha + L$ regions, below which only the solid α phase exists.

For Figure 7.3*a*, the solidus and liquidus lines intersect at the two composition extremities; these correspond to the melting temperatures of the pure components. For example, the melting temperatures of pure copper and nickel are 1085°C and 1453°C, respectively. Heating pure copper corresponds to moving vertically up the left-hand temperature axis. Copper remains solid until its melting temperature is reached. The solid-to-liquid transformation takes place at the melting temperature, and no further heating is possible until this transformation has been completed.

For any composition other than pure components, this melting phenomenon will occur over the range of temperatures between the solidus and liquidus lines; both solid α and liquid phases will be in equilibrium within this temperature range. For example, upon heating an alloy of composition 50 wt% Ni–50 wt% Cu (Figure 7.3*a*), melting begins at approximately 1280°C (2340°F); the amount of liquid phase continuously increases with temperature until about 1320°C (2410°F), at which the alloy is completely liquid.

7.8 INTERPRETATION OF PHASE DIAGRAMS

For a binary system of known composition and temperature that is at equilibrium, at least three kinds of information are available: (1) the phases that are present, (2) the compositions of these phases, and (3) the percentages or fractions of the phases. The procedures for making these determinations will be demonstrated using the copper–nickel system.

Phases Present

The establishment of what phases are present is relatively simple. One just locates the temperature–composition point on the diagram and notes the phase(s) with which the corresponding phase field is labeled. For example, an alloy of composition 60 wt% Ni–40 wt% Cu at 1100°C would be located at point *A* in Figure 7.3*a*; since this is within the α region, only the single α phase will be present. On the other hand, a 35 wt% Ni–65 wt% Cu alloy at 1250°C (point *B*) will consist of both α and liquid phases at equilibrium.

Determination of Phase Compositions

The first step in the determination of phase compositions (in terms of the concentrations of the components) is to locate the temperature–composition point on the phase diagram. Different methods are used for single- and two-phase regions. If only one phase is present, the procedure is trivial: the composition of this phase is simply the same as the overall composition of the alloy. For example, consider the 60 wt% Ni–40 wt% Cu alloy at 1100°C (point *A*, Figure 7.3*a*). At this composition and temperature, only the α phase is present, having a composition of 60 wt% Ni–40 wt% Cu.

For an alloy having composition and temperature located in a two-phase region, the situation is more complicated. In all two-phase regions (and in two-phase regions only), one may imagine a series of horizontal lines, one at every temperature; each of these is known as a **tie line,** or sometimes as an isotherm. These tie lines extend across the two-phase region and terminate at the phase boundary lines on either side. To compute the equilibrium concentrations of the two phases, the following procedure is used:

1. A tie line is constructed across the two-phase region at the temperature of the alloy.
2. The intersections of the tie line and the phase boundaries on either side are noted.
3. Perpendiculars are dropped from these intersections to the horizontal composition axis, from which the composition of each of the respective phases is read.

For example, consider again the 35 wt% Ni–65 wt% Cu alloy at 1250°C, located at point B in Figure 7.3*b* and lying within the $\alpha + L$ region. Thus, the problem is to determine the composition (in wt% Ni and Cu) for both the α and liquid phases. The tie line has been constructed across the $\alpha + L$ phase region, as shown in Figure 7.3*b*. The perpendicular from the intersection of the tie line with the liquidus boundary meets the composition axis at 31.5 wt% Ni–68.5 wt% Cu, which is the composition of the liquid phase, C_L. Likewise, for the solidus–tie line intersection, we find a composition for the α solid-solution phase, C_α, of 42.5 wt% Ni–57.5 wt% Cu.

Determination of Phase Amounts

The relative amounts (as fraction or as percentage) of the phases present at equilibrium may also be computed with the aid of phase diagrams. Again, the single- and two-phase situations must be treated separately. The solution is obvious in the single-phase region: Since only one phase is present, the alloy is composed entirely of that phase; that is, the phase fraction is 1.0 or, alternatively, the percentage is 100%. From the previous example for the 60 wt% Ni–40 wt% Cu alloy at 1100°C (point A in Figure 7.3*a*), only the α phase is present; hence, the alloy is completely or 100% α.

If the composition and temperature position is located within a two-phase region, things are more complex. The tie line must be utilized in conjunction with a procedure that is often called the **lever rule** (or the *inverse lever rule*), which is applied as follows:

1. The tie line is constructed across the two-phase region at the temperature of the alloy.
2. The overall alloy composition is located on the tie line.
3. The fraction of one phase is computed by taking the length of tie line from the overall alloy composition to the phase boundary for the *other* phase, and dividing by the total tie line length.
4. The fraction of the other phase is determined in the same manner.
5. If phase percentages are desired, each phase fraction is multiplied by 100. When the composition axis is scaled in weight percent, the phase fractions computed using the lever rule are mass fractions—the mass (or weight) of a specific phase divided by the total alloy mass (or weight). The mass of each phase is computed from the product of each phase fraction and the total alloy mass.

In the employment of the lever rule, tie line segment lengths may be determined either by direct measurement from the phase diagram using a linear scale, preferably graduated in millimeters, or by subtracting compositions as taken from the composition axis.

Consider again the example shown in Figure 7.3*b*, in which at 1250°C both α and liquid phases are present for a 35 wt% Ni–65 wt% Cu alloy. The problem is to compute the fraction of each of the α and liquid phases. The tie line has been constructed that was used for the determination of α and L phase compositions. Let the overall alloy composition be located along the tie line and denoted as C_0, and mass fractions be represented by W_L and W_α for the respective phases. From the lever rule, W_L may be computed according to

$$W_L = \frac{S}{R + S} \tag{7.1a}$$

or, by subtracting compositions,

$$W_L = \frac{C_\alpha - C_0}{C_\alpha - C_L} \tag{7.1b}$$

Composition need be specified in terms of only one of the constituents for a binary alloy; for the computation above, weight percent nickel will be used (i.e., $C_0 = 35$ wt% Ni, $C_\alpha = 42.5$ wt% Ni, and $C_L = 31.5$ wt% Ni), and

$$W_L = \frac{42.5 - 35}{42.5 - 31.5} = 0.68$$

Similarly, for the α phase,

$$W_\alpha = \frac{R}{R + S} \tag{7.2a}$$

$$= \frac{C_0 - C_L}{C_\alpha - C_L} \tag{7.2b}$$

$$= \frac{35 - 31.5}{42.5 - 31.5} = 0.32$$

Of course, identical answers are obtained if compositions are expressed in weight percent copper instead of nickel.

Thus, the lever rule may be employed to determine the relative amounts or fractions of phases in any two-phase region for a binary alloy if the temperature and composition are known and if equilibrium has been established. Its derivation is presented as an example problem.

It is easy to confuse the foregoing procedures for the determination of phase compositions and fractional phase amounts; thus, a brief summary is warranted. *Compositions* of phases are expressed in terms of weight percents of the components (e.g., wt% Cu, wt% Ni). For any alloy consisting of a single phase, the composition of that phase is the same as the total alloy composition. If two phases are present, the tie line must be employed, the extremities of which determine the compositions of the respective phases. With regard to *fractional phase amounts* (e.g., mass fraction of the α or liquid phase), when a single phase exists, the alloy is completely that phase. For a two-phase alloy, on the other hand, the lever rule is utilized, in which a ratio of tie line segment lengths is taken.

Concept Check 7.2

A copper–nickel alloy of composition 70 wt% Ni–30 wt% Cu is slowly heated from a temperature of 1300°C (2370°F).

(a) At what temperature does the first liquid phase form?

(b) What is the composition of this liquid phase?

(c) At what temperature does complete melting of the alloy occur?

(d) What is the composition of the last solid remaining prior to complete melting?

[The answer may be found in enclosed CD.]

Concept Check 7.3

Is it possible to have a copper–nickel alloy that, at equilibrium, consists of an α phase of composition 37 wt% Ni–63 wt% Cu, and also a liquid phase of composition 20 wt% Ni–80 wt% Cu? If so, what will be the approximate temperature of the alloy? If this is not possible, explain why.

[The answer may be found in enclosed CD.]

EXAMPLE PROBLEM 7.1

Lever Rule Derivation

Derive the lever rule.

Solution

Consider the phase diagram for copper and nickel (Figure 7.3*b*) and alloy of composition C_0 at 1250°C, and let C_α, C_L, W_α, and W_L represent the same parameters as above. This derivation is accomplished through two conservation-of-mass expressions. With the first, since only two phases are present, the sum of their mass fractions must be equal to unity; that is,

$$W_\alpha + W_L = 1 \tag{7.3}$$

For the second, the mass of one of the components (either Cu or Ni) that is present in both of the phases must be equal to the mass of that component in the total alloy, or

$$W_\alpha C_\alpha + W_L C_L = C_0 \tag{7.4}$$

Simultaneous solution of these two equations leads to the lever rule expressions for this particular situation, Equations 7.1b and 7.2b:

$$W_L = \frac{C_\alpha - C_0}{C_\alpha - C_L} \tag{7.1b}$$

$$W_\alpha = \frac{C_0 - C_L}{C_\alpha - C_L} \tag{7.2b}$$

For multiphase alloys, it is often more convenient to specify relative phase amount in terms of volume fraction rather than mass fraction. Phase volume fractions are preferred because they (rather than mass fractions) may be determined from examination of the microstructure; furthermore, the properties of a multiphase alloy may be estimated on the basis of volume fractions.

For an alloy consisting of α and β phases, the volume fraction of the α phase, V_α, is defined as

$$V_\alpha = \frac{v_\alpha}{v_\alpha + v_\beta} \tag{7.5}$$

where v_α and v_β denote the volumes of the respective phases in the alloy. Of course, an analogous expression exists for V_β, and, for an alloy consisting of just two phases, it is the case that $V_\alpha + V_\beta = 1$.

On occasion conversion from mass fraction to volume fraction (or vice versa) is desired. Equations that facilitate these conversions are as follows:

$$V_\alpha = \frac{\dfrac{W_\alpha}{\rho_\alpha}}{\dfrac{W_\alpha}{\rho_\alpha} + \dfrac{W_\beta}{\rho_\beta}} \tag{7.6a}$$

$$V_\beta = \frac{\dfrac{W_\beta}{\rho_\beta}}{\dfrac{W_\alpha}{\rho_\alpha} + \dfrac{W_\beta}{\rho_\beta}} \tag{7.6b}$$

and

$$W_\alpha = \frac{V_\alpha \rho_\alpha}{V_\alpha \rho_\alpha + V_\beta \rho_\beta} \tag{7.7a}$$

$$W_\beta = \frac{V_\beta \rho_\beta}{V_\alpha \rho_\alpha + V_\beta \rho_\beta} \tag{7.7b}$$

In these expressions, ρ_α and ρ_β are the densities of the respective phases; these may be determined approximately using Equations 5.10a and 5.10b.

When the densities of the phases in a two-phase alloy differ significantly, there will be quite a disparity between mass and volume fractions; conversely, if the phase densities are the same, mass and volume fractions are identical.

7.9 DEVELOPMENT OF MICROSTRUCTURE IN ISOMORPHOUS ALLOYS

Equilibrium Cooling

At this point it is instructive to examine the development of microstructure that occurs for isomorphous alloys during solidification. We first treat the situation in which the cooling occurs very slowly, in that phase equilibrium is continuously maintained.

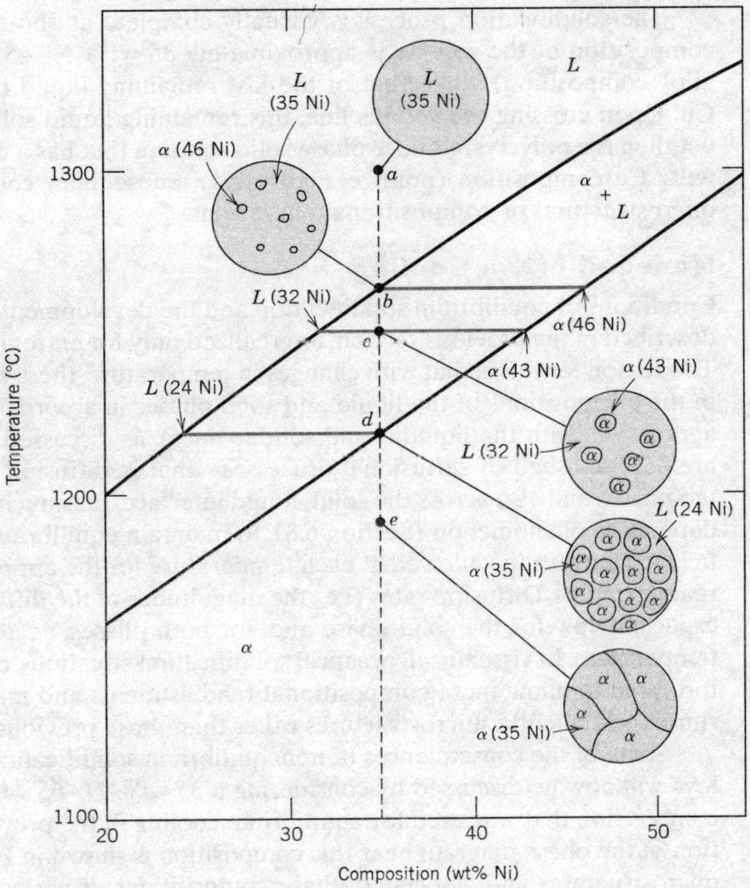

Figure 7.4 Schematic representation of the development of microstructure during the equilibrium solidification of a 35 wt% Ni–65 wt% Cu alloy.

Let us consider the copper–nickel system (Figure 7.3*a*), specifically an alloy of composition 35 wt% Ni–65 wt% Cu as it is cooled from 1300°C. The region of the Cu–Ni phase diagram in the vicinity of this composition is shown in Figure 7.4. Cooling of an alloy of the above composition corresponds to moving down the vertical dashed line. At 1300°C, point *a*, the alloy is completely liquid (of composition 35 wt% Ni–65 wt% Cu) and has the microstructure represented by the circle inset in the figure. As cooling begins, no microstructural or compositional changes will be realized until we reach the liquidus line (point *b*, ~1260°C). At this point, the first solid α begins to form, which has a composition dictated by the tie line drawn at this temperature [i.e., 46 wt% Ni–54 wt% Cu, noted as α(46 Ni)]; the composition of liquid is still approximately 35 wt% Ni–65 wt% Cu [*L*(35 Ni)], which is different from that of the solid α. With continued cooling, both compositions and relative amounts of each of the phases will change. The compositions of the liquid and α phases will follow the liquidus and solidus lines, respectively. Furthermore, the fraction of the α phase will increase with continued cooling. Note that the overall alloy composition (35 wt% Ni–65 wt% Cu) remains unchanged during cooling even though there is a redistribution of copper and nickel between the phases.

At 1250°C, point *c* in Figure 7.4, the compositions of the liquid and α phases are 32 wt% Ni–68 wt% Cu [*L*(32 Ni)] and 43 wt% Ni–57 wt% Cu [α(43 Ni)], respectively.

The solidification process is virtually complete at about 1220°C, point d; the composition of the solid α is approximately 35 wt% Ni–65 wt% Cu (the overall alloy composition) while that of the last remaining liquid is 24 wt% Ni–76 wt% Cu. Upon crossing the solidus line, this remaining liquid solidifies; the final product then is a polycrystalline α-phase solid solution that has a uniform 35 wt% Ni–65 wt% Cu composition (point e, Figure 7.4). Subsequent cooling will produce no microstructural or compositional alterations.

Nonequilibrium Cooling

Conditions of equilibrium solidification and the development of microstructures, as described in the previous section, are realized only for extremely slow cooling rates. The reason for this is that with changes in temperature, there must be readjustments in the compositions of the liquid and solid phases in accordance with the phase diagram (i.e., with the liquidus and solidus lines), as discussed. These readjustments are accomplished by diffusional processes—that is, diffusion in both solid and liquid phases and also across the solid–liquid interface. Inasmuch as diffusion is a time-dependent phenomenon (Section 6.3), to maintain equilibrium during cooling, sufficient time must be allowed at each temperature for the appropriate compositional readjustments. Diffusion rates (i.e., the magnitudes of the diffusion coefficients) are especially low for the solid phase and, for both phases, decrease with diminishing temperature. In virtually all practical solidification situations, cooling rates are much too rapid to allow these compositional readjustments and maintenance of equilibrium; consequently, microstructures other than those previously described develop.

Some of the consequences of nonequilibrium solidification for isomorphous alloys will now be discussed by considering a 35 wt% Ni–65 wt% Cu alloy, the same composition that was used for equilibrium cooling in the previous section. The portion of the phase diagram near this composition is shown in Figure 7.5; in addition, microstructures and associated phase compositions at various temperatures upon cooling are noted in the circular insets. To simplify this discussion it will be assumed that diffusion rates in the liquid phase are sufficiently rapid such that equilibrium is maintained in the liquid.

Let us begin cooling from a temperature of about 1300°C; this is indicated by point a' in the liquid region. This liquid has a composition of 35 wt% Ni–65 wt% Cu [noted as L(35 Ni) in the figure], and no changes occur while cooling through the liquid phase region (moving down vertically from point a'). At point b' (approximately 1260°C), α-phase particles begin to form, which, from the tie line constructed, have a composition of 46 wt% Ni–54 wt% Cu [α(46 Ni)].

Upon further cooling to point c' (about 1240°C), the liquid composition has shifted to 29 wt% Ni–71 wt% Cu; furthermore, at this temperature the composition of the α phase that solidified is 40 wt% Ni–60 wt% Cu [α(40 Ni)]. However, since diffusion in the solid α phase is relatively slow, the α phase that formed at point b' has not changed composition appreciably—that is, it is still about 46 wt% Ni—and the composition of the α grains has continuously changed with radial position, from 46 wt% Ni at grain centers to 40 wt% Ni at the outer grain perimeters. Thus, at point c', the *average composition* of the solid α grains that have formed would be some volume weighted average composition, lying between 46 and 40 wt% Ni. For the sake of argument, let us take this average composition to be 42 wt% Ni–58 wt% Cu [α(42 Ni)]. Furthermore, we would also find that, on the basis of lever-rule computations, a greater proportion of liquid is present for these nonequilibrium conditions than for equilibrium cooling. The implication of this nonequilibrium solidification phenomenon is that the solidus line on the phase diagram has been shifted to

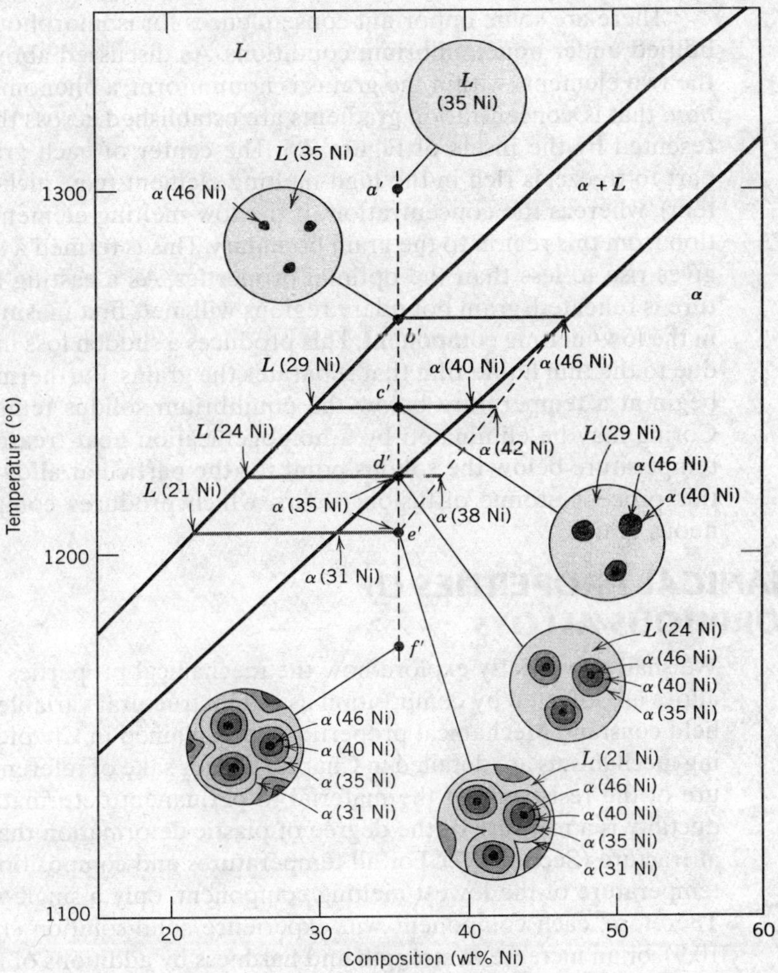

Figure 7.5 Schematic representation of the development of microstructure during the nonequilibrium solidification of a 35 wt% Ni–65 wt% Cu alloy.

higher Ni contents—to the average compositions of the α phase (e.g., 42 wt% Ni at 1240°C)—and is represented by the dashed line in Figure 7.5. There is no comparable alteration of the liquidus line inasmuch as it is assumed that equilibrium is maintained in the liquid phase during cooling because of sufficiently rapid diffusion rates.

At point *d*′ (~1220°C) and for equilibrium cooling rates, solidification should be completed. However, for this nonequilibrium situation, there is still an appreciable proportion of liquid remaining, and the α phase that is forming has a composition of 35 wt% Ni [α(35 Ni)]; also the *average* α-phase composition at this point is 38 wt% Ni [α(38 Ni)].

Nonequilibrium solidification finally reaches completion at point *e*′ (~1205°C). The composition of the last α phase to solidify at this point is about 31 wt% Ni; the *average* composition of the α phase at complete solidification is 35 wt% Ni. The inset at point *f*′ shows the microstructure of the totally solid material.

The degree of displacement of the nonequilibrium solidus curve from the equilibrium one will depend on rate of cooling. The slower the cooling rate, the smaller this displacement; that is, the difference between the equilibrium solidus and average solid composition is lower. Furthermore, if the diffusion rate in the solid phase is increased, this displacement will be diminished.

There are some important consequences for isomorphous alloys that have solidified under nonequilibrium conditions. As discussed above, the distribution of the two elements within the grains is nonuniform, a phenomenon termed *segregation;* that is, concentration gradients are established across the grains that are represented by the insets of Figure 7.5. The center of each grain, which is the first part to freeze, is rich in the high-melting element (e.g., nickel for this Cu–Ni system), whereas the concentration of the low-melting element increases with position from this region to the grain boundary. This is termed a *cored* structure, which gives rise to less than the optimal properties. As a casting having a cored structure is reheated, grain boundary regions will melt first inasmuch as they are richer in the low-melting component. This produces a sudden loss in mechanical integrity due to the thin liquid film that separates the grains. Furthermore, this melting may begin at a temperature below the equilibrium solidus temperature of the alloy. Coring may be eliminated by a homogenization heat treatment carried out at a temperature below the solidus point for the particular alloy composition. During this process, atomic diffusion occurs, which produces compositionally homogeneous grains.

7.10 MECHANICAL PROPERTIES OF ISOMORPHOUS ALLOYS

We shall now briefly explore how the mechanical properties of solid isomorphous alloys are affected by composition as other structural variables (e.g., grain size) are held constant. Mechanical properties are explained in Chapter 9 while strengthening mechanisms are detailed in Chapter 10. For sake of reference, strength is a measure of the resistance of the material to permanent deformation (Section 9.7) and ductility is a measure of the degree of plastic deformation that has been sustained at fracture (Section 9.7). For all temperatures and compositions below the melting temperature of the lowest-melting component, only a single solid phase will exist. Therefore, each component will experience solid-solution strengthening (Section 10.9), or an increase in strength and hardness by additions of the other component. This effect is demonstrated in Figure 7.6*a* as tensile strength versus composition for

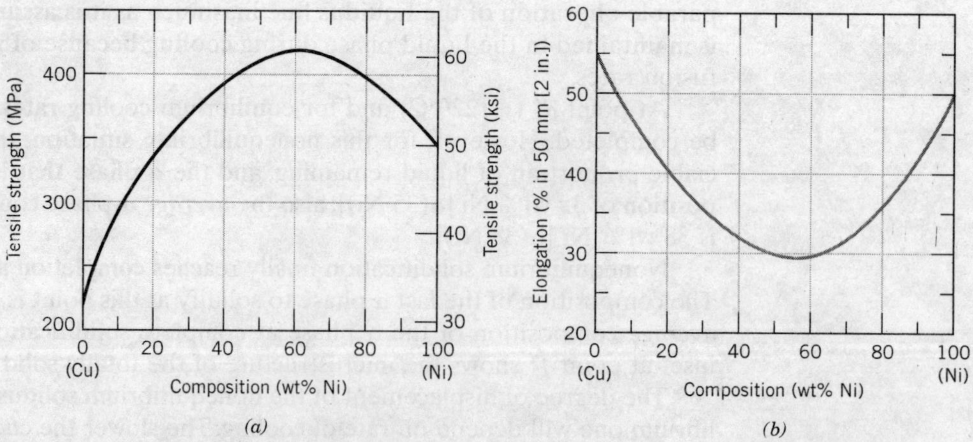

Figure 7.6 For the copper–nickel system, (*a*) tensile strength versus composition, and (*b*) ductility (%EL) versus composition at room temperature. A solid solution exists over all compositions for this system.

the copper–nickel system at room temperature; at some intermediate composition, the curve necessarily passes through a maximum. Plotted in Figure 7.6*b* is the ductility (%EL)–composition behavior, which is just the opposite of tensile strength; that is, ductility decreases with additions of the second component, and the curve exhibits a minimum.

7.11 BINARY EUTECTIC SYSTEMS

Another type of common and relatively simple phase diagram found for binary alloys is shown in Figure 7.7 for the copper–silver system; this is known as a binary eutectic phase diagram. A number of features of this phase diagram are important and worth noting. First, three single-phase regions are found on the diagram: α, β, and liquid. The α phase is a solid solution rich in copper; it has silver as the solute component and an FCC crystal structure. The β-phase solid solution also has an FCC structure, but copper is the solute. Pure copper and pure silver are also considered to be α and β phases, respectively.

Thus, the solubility in each of these solid phases is limited, in that at any temperature below line *BEG* only a limited concentration of silver will dissolve in copper (for the α phase), and similarly for copper in silver (for the β phase). The solubility limit for the α phase corresponds to the boundary line, labeled *CBA*, between the $\alpha/(\alpha + \beta)$ and $\alpha/(\alpha + L)$ phase regions; it increases with temperature to a maximum [8.0 wt% Ag at 779°C (1434°F)] at point *B*, and decreases back to zero at the melting temperature of pure copper, point *A* [1085°C (1985°F)]. At

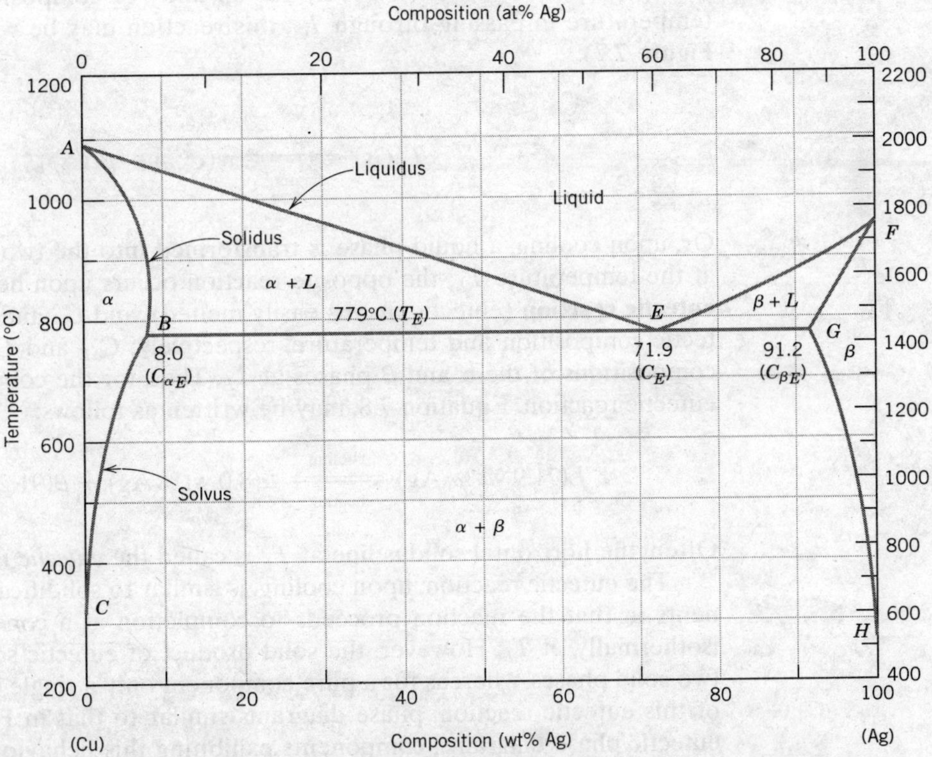

Figure 7.7 The copper–silver phase diagram. [Adapted from *Binary Alloy Phase Diagrams,* 2nd edition, Vol. 1, T. B. Massalski (Editor-in-Chief), 1990. Reprinted by permission of ASM International, Materials Park, OH.]

temperatures below 779°C (1434°F), the solid solubility limit line separating the α and $\alpha + \beta$ phase regions is termed a **solvus line;** the boundary AB between the α and $\alpha + L$ fields is the **solidus line,** as indicated in Figure 7.7. For the β phase, both solvus and solidus lines also exist, HG and GF, respectively, as shown. The maximum solubility of copper in the β phase, point G (8.8 wt% Cu), also occurs at 779°C (1434°F). This horizontal line BEG, which is parallel to the composition axis and extends between these maximum solubility positions, may also be considered a solidus line; it represents the lowest temperature at which a liquid phase may exist for any copper–silver alloy that is at equilibrium.

There are also three two-phase regions found for the copper–silver system (Figure 7.7): $\alpha + L$, $\beta + L$, and $\alpha + \beta$. The α- and β-phase solid solutions coexist for all compositions and temperatures within the $\alpha + \beta$ phase field; the α + liquid and β + liquid phases also coexist in their respective phase regions. Furthermore, compositions and relative amounts for the phases may be determined using tie lines and the lever rule as outlined previously.

As silver is added to copper, the temperature at which the alloys become totally liquid decreases along the **liquidus line,** line AE; thus, the melting temperature of copper is lowered by silver additions. The same may be said for silver: the introduction of copper reduces the temperature of complete melting along the other liquidus line, FE. These liquidus lines meet at the point E on the phase diagram, through which also passes the horizontal isotherm line BEG. Point E is called an **invariant point,** which is designated by the composition C_E and temperature T_E; for the copper–silver system, the values of C_E and T_E are 71.9 wt% Ag and 779°C (1434°F), respectively.

An important reaction occurs for an alloy of composition C_E as it changes temperature in passing through T_E; this reaction may be written as follows (per Figure 7.7):

$$L(C_E) \underset{\text{heating}}{\overset{\text{cooling}}{\rightleftharpoons}} \alpha(C_{\alpha E}) + \beta(C_{\beta E}) \tag{7.8}$$

Or, upon cooling, a liquid phase is transformed into the two solid α and β phases at the temperature T_E; the opposite reaction occurs upon heating. This is called a **eutectic reaction** (eutectic means easily melted), and C_E and T_E represent the eutectic composition and temperature, respectively; $C_{\alpha E}$ and $C_{\beta E}$ are the respective compositions of the α and β phases at T_E. Thus, for the copper–silver system, the eutectic reaction, Equation 7.8, may be written as follows:

$$L(71.9\text{ wt\% Ag}) \underset{\text{heating}}{\overset{\text{cooling}}{\rightleftharpoons}} \alpha(8.0\text{ wt\% Ag}) + \beta(91.2\text{ wt\% Ag})$$

Often, the horizontal solidus line at T_E is called the *eutectic isotherm.*

The eutectic reaction, upon cooling, is similar to solidification for pure components in that the reaction proceeds to completion at a constant temperature, or isothermally, at T_E. However, the solid product of eutectic solidification is always two solid phases, whereas for a pure component only a single phase forms. Because of this eutectic reaction, phase diagrams similar to that in Figure 7.7 are termed eutectic phase diagrams; components exhibiting this behavior comprise a eutectic system.

In the construction of binary phase diagrams, it is important to understand that one or at most two phases may be in equilibrium within a phase field. This holds true for the phase diagrams in Figures 7.3*a* and 7.7. For a eutectic system, three phases (α, β, and L) may be in equilibrium, but only at points along the eutectic isotherm. Another general rule is that single-phase regions are always separated from each other by a two-phase region that consists of the two single phases that it separates. For example, the $\alpha + \beta$ field is situated between the α and β single-phase regions in Figure 7.7.

Another common eutectic system is that for lead and tin; the phase diagram (Figure 7.8) has a general shape similar to that for copper–silver. For the lead–tin system the solid solution phases are also designated by α and β; in this case, α represents a solid solution of tin in lead and, for β, tin is the solvent and lead is the solute. The eutectic invariant point is located at 61.9 wt% Sn and 183°C (361°F). Of course, maximum solid solubility compositions as well as component melting temperatures will be different for the copper–silver and lead–tin systems, as may be observed by comparing their phase diagrams.

On occasion, low-melting-temperature alloys are prepared having near-eutectic compositions. A familiar example is the 60–40 solder, containing 60 wt% Sn and 40 wt% Pb. Figure 7.8 indicates that an alloy of this composition is completely molten at about 185°C (365°F), which makes this material especially attractive as a low-temperature solder, since it is easily melted.

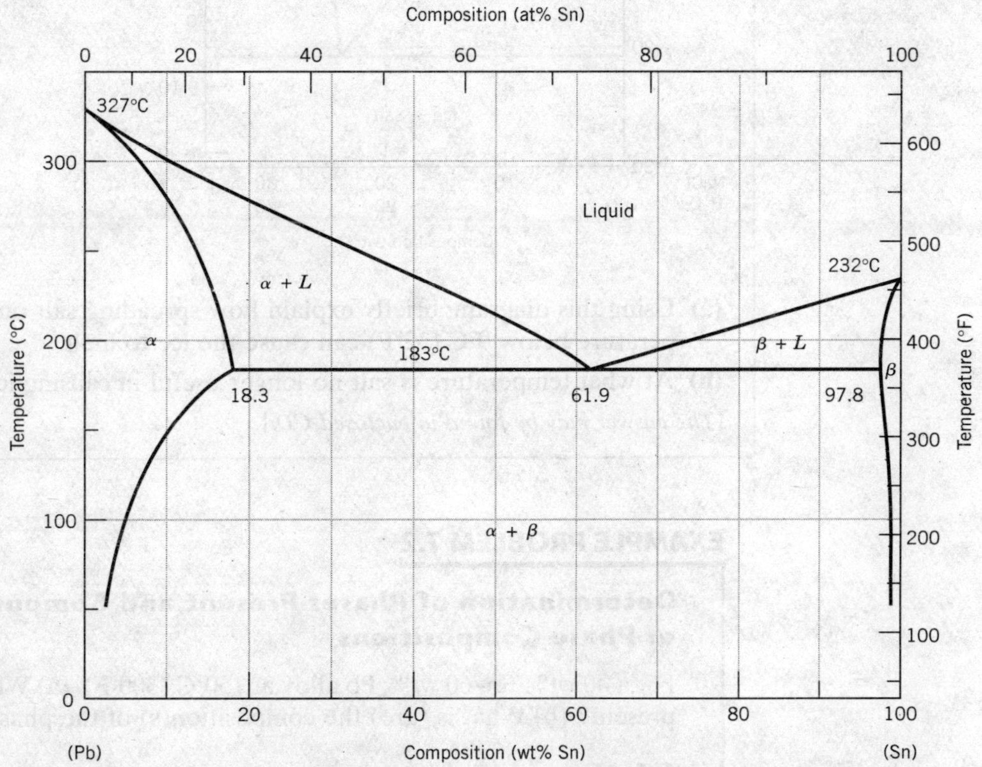

Figure 7.8 The lead–tin phase diagram. [Adapted from *Binary Alloy Phase Diagrams*, 2nd edition, Vol. 3, T. B. Massalski (Editor-in-Chief), 1990. Reprinted by permission of ASM International, Materials Park, OH.]

Concept Check 7.4

At 700°C (1290°F), what is the maximum solubility **(a)** of Cu in Ag? **(b)** Of Ag in Cu?

[The answer may be found in enclosed CD.]

Concept Check 7.5

Below is a portion of the H_2O–NaCl phase diagram:

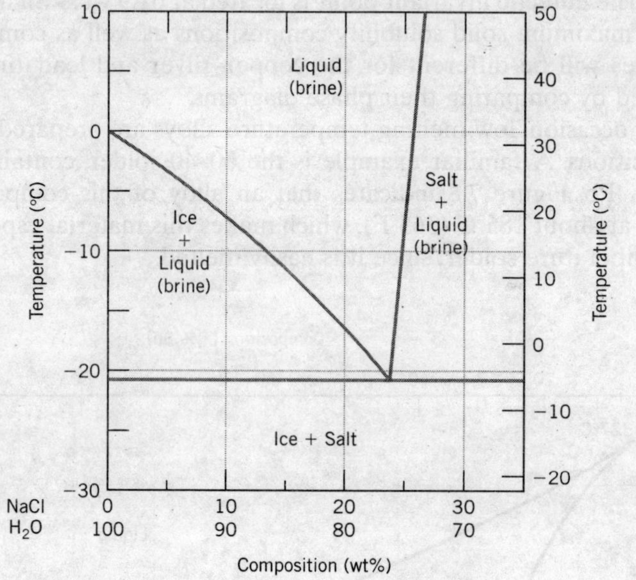

(a) Using this diagram, briefly explain how spreading salt on ice that is at a temperature below 0°C (32°F) can cause the ice to melt.

(b) At what temperature is salt no longer useful in causing ice to melt?

[The answer may be found in enclosed CD.]

EXAMPLE PROBLEM 7.2

Determination of Phases Present and Computation of Phase Compositions

For a 40 wt% Sn–60 wt% Pb alloy at 150°C (300°F), (a) What phase(s) is (are) present? (b) What is (are) the composition(s) of the phase(s)?

Solution

(a) Locate this temperature–composition point on the phase diagram (point *B* in Figure 7.9). Inasmuch as it is within the $\alpha + \beta$ region, both α and β phases will coexist.

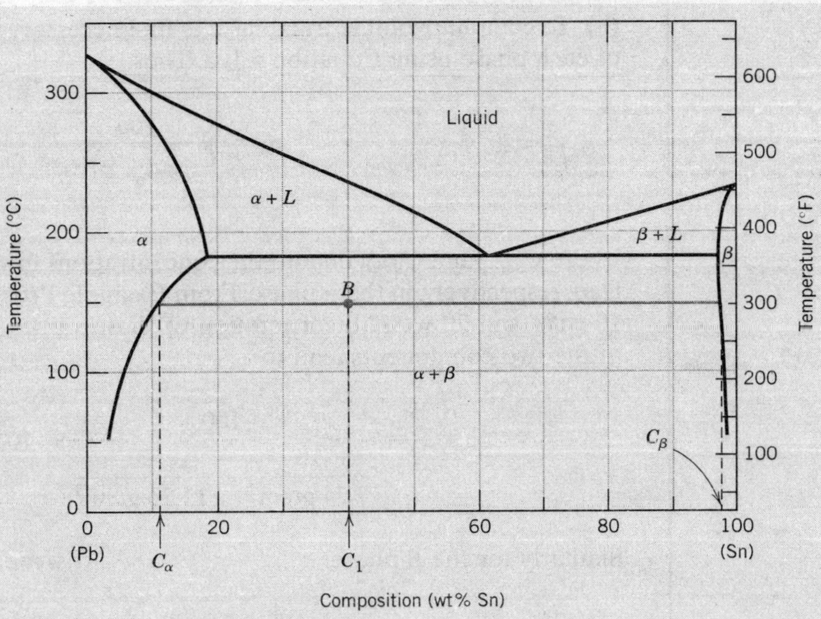

Figure 7.9 The lead–tin phase diagram. For a 40 wt% Sn–60 wt% Pb alloy at 150°C (point *B*), phase compositions and relative amounts are computed in Example Problems 7.2 and 7.3.

(b) Since two phases are present, it becomes necessary to construct a tie line across the $\alpha + \beta$ phase field at 150°C, as indicated in Figure 7.9. The composition of the α phase corresponds to the tie line intersection with the $\alpha/(\alpha + \beta)$ solvus phase boundary—about 10 wt% Sn–90 wt% Pb, denoted as C_α. Similarly for the β phase, which will have a composition of approximately 78 wt% Sn–2 wt% Pb (C_β).

EXAMPLE PROBLEM 7.3

Relative Phase Amount Determinations—Mass and Volume Fractions

For the lead–tin alloy in Example Problem 7.2, calculate the relative amount of each phase present in terms of (a) mass fraction and (b) volume fraction. At 150°C take the densities of Pb and Sn to be 11.23 and 7.24 g/cm^3, respectively.

Solution

(a) Since the alloy consists of two phases, it is necessary to employ the lever rule. If C_1 denotes the overall alloy composition, mass fractions may be computed by subtracting compositions, in terms of weight percent tin, as follows:

$$W_\alpha = \frac{C_\beta - C_1}{C_\beta - C_\alpha} = \frac{98 - 40}{98 - 10} = 0.66$$

$$W_\beta = \frac{C_1 - C_\alpha}{C_\beta - C_\alpha} = \frac{40 - 10}{98 - 10} = 0.34$$

(b) To compute volume fractions it is first necessary to determine the density of each phase using Equation 5.10a. Thus

$$\rho_\alpha = \frac{100}{\dfrac{C_{\text{Sn}(\alpha)}}{\rho_{\text{Sn}}} + \dfrac{C_{\text{Pb}(\alpha)}}{\rho_{\text{Pb}}}}$$

where $C_{\text{Sn}(\alpha)}$ and $C_{\text{Pb}(\alpha)}$ denote the concentrations in weight percent of tin and lead, respectively, in the α phase. From Example Problem 7.2, these values are 10 wt% and 70 wt%. Incorporation of these values along with the densities of the two components lead to

$$\rho_\alpha = \frac{100}{\dfrac{10}{7.24 \text{ g/cm}^3} + \dfrac{90}{11.23 \text{ g/cm}^3}} = 10.64 \text{ g/cm}^3$$

Similarly for the β phase:

$$\rho_\beta = \frac{100}{\dfrac{C_{\text{Sn}(\beta)}}{\rho_{\text{Sn}}} + \dfrac{C_{\text{Pb}(\beta)}}{\rho_{\text{Pb}}}}$$

$$= \frac{100}{\dfrac{98}{7.24 \text{ g/cm}^3} + \dfrac{2}{11.23 \text{ g/cm}^3}} = 7.29 \text{ g/cm}^3$$

Now it becomes necessary to employ Equations 7.6a and 7.6b to determine V_α and V_β as

$$V_\alpha = \frac{\dfrac{W_\alpha}{\rho_\alpha}}{\dfrac{W_\alpha}{\rho_\alpha} + \dfrac{W_\beta}{\rho_\beta}}$$

$$= \frac{\dfrac{0.66}{10.64 \text{ g/cm}^3}}{\dfrac{0.66}{10.64 \text{ g/cm}^3} + \dfrac{0.34}{7.29 \text{ g/cm}^3}} = 0.57$$

$$V_\beta = \frac{\dfrac{W_\beta}{\rho_\beta}}{\dfrac{W_\alpha}{\rho_\alpha} + \dfrac{W_\beta}{\rho_\beta}}$$

$$= \frac{\dfrac{0.34}{7.29 \text{ g/cm}^3}}{\dfrac{0.66}{10.64 \text{ g/cm}^3} + \dfrac{0.34}{7.29 \text{ g/cm}^3}} = 0.43$$

MATERIALS OF IMPORTANCE

Lead-Free Solders

Solders are metal alloys that are used to bond or join two or more components (usually other metal alloys). They are used extensively in the electronics industry to physically hold assemblies together; furthermore, they must allow expansion and contraction of the various components, must transmit electrical signals, and also dissipate any heat that is generated. The bonding action is accomplished by melting the solder material, allowing it to flow among and make contact with the components to be joined (which do not melt), and, finally, upon solidification, forming a physical bond with all of these components.

In the past, the vast majority of solders have been lead-tin alloys. These materials are reliable, inexpensive, and have relatively low melting temperatures. The most common lead–tin solder has a composition of 63 wt% Sn–37 wt% Pb. According to the lead–tin phase diagram, Figure 7.8, this composition is near the eutectic and has melting temperature of about 183°C, the lowest temperature possible with the existence of a liquid phase (at equilibrium) for the lead–tin system. It follows that this alloy is often called a "eutectic lead-tin solder."

Unfortunately, lead is a mildly toxic metal, and there is serious concern about the environmental impact of discarded lead-containing products that can leach into groundwater from landfills or pollute the air if incinerated. Consequently, in some countries legislation has been enacted that bans the use of lead-containing solders. This has forced the development of lead-free solders that, among other things, must have relatively low melting temperatures (or temperature ranges). Some of these are ternary alloys (i.e., composed of three metals), to include tin–silver–copper and tin–silver–bismuth solders. The compositions of several lead-free solders are listed in Table 7.1.

Of course, melting temperatures (or temperature ranges) are important in the development and selection of these new solder alloys, information that is available from phase diagrams. For example, the tin-bismuth phase diagram is presented in Figure 7.10. Here it may be noted that a eutectic exists at 57 wt% Bi and 139°C, which are indeed the composition and melting temperature of the Bi–Sn soldier in Table 7.1

Table 7.1 Compositions, Solidus Temperatures, and Liquidus Temperatures for Five Lead-Free Solders

Composition (wt%)	*Solidus Temperature (°C)*	*Liquidus Temperature (°C)*
52 In/48 Sn*	118	118
57 Bi/43 Sn*	139	139
91.8 Sn/3.4 Ag/ 4.8 Bi	211	213
95.5 Sn/3.8 Ag/ 0.7 Cu*	217	217
99.3 Sn/0.7 Cu*	227	227

*The compositions of these alloys are eutectic compositions; therefore, their solidus and liquidus temperatures are identical.

Source: Adapted from E. Bastow, "Solder Families and How They Work," *Advanced Materials & Processes,* Vol. 161, No. 12, M. W. Hunt (Editor-in-chief), ASM International, 2003, p. 28. Reprinted by permission of ASM International, Materials Park, OH.

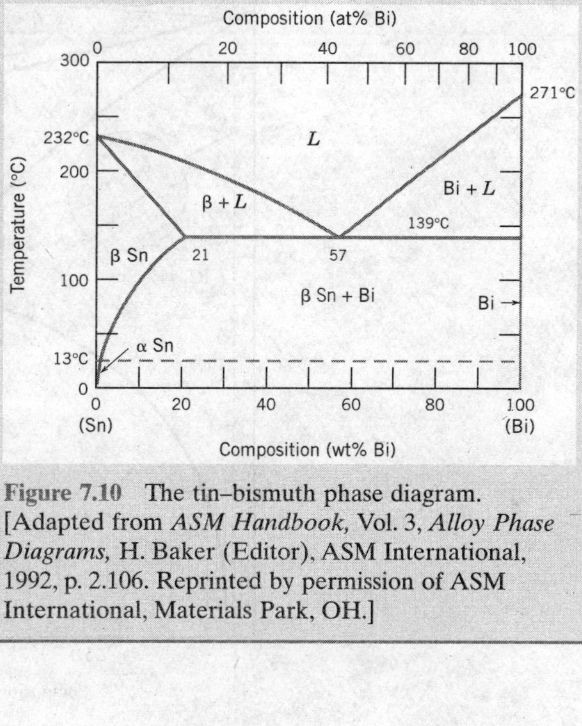

Figure 7.10 The tin–bismuth phase diagram. [Adapted from *ASM Handbook,* Vol. 3, *Alloy Phase Diagrams,* H. Baker (Editor), ASM International, 1992, p. 2.106. Reprinted by permission of ASM International, Materials Park, OH.]

7.12 DEVELOPMENT OF MICROSTRUCTURE IN EUTECTIC ALLOYS

Depending on composition, several different types of microstructures are possible for the slow cooling of alloys belonging to binary eutectic systems. These possibilities will be considered in terms of the lead–tin phase diagram, Figure 7.8.

The first case is for compositions ranging between a pure component and the maximum solid solubility for that component at room temperature [20°C (70°F)]. For the lead–tin system, this includes lead-rich alloys containing between 0 and about 2 wt% Sn (for the α phase solid solution), and also between approximately 79 wt% Sn and pure tin (for the β phase). For example, consider an alloy of composition C_1 (Figure 7.11) as it is slowly cooled from a temperature within the liquid-phase region, say, 350°C; this corresponds to moving down the dashed vertical line ww' in the figure. The alloy remains totally liquid and of composition C_1 until we cross the liquidus line at approximately 330°C, at which time the solid α phase begins to form. While passing through this narrow $\alpha + L$ phase region, solidification proceeds in the same manner as was described for the copper–nickel alloy in the preceding section; that is, with continued cooling more of the solid α forms. Furthermore, liquid- and solid-phase compositions are different, which follow along the liquidus and solidus phase boundaries, respectively. Solidification reaches completion at the point where ww' crosses the solidus line. The resulting alloy is polycrystalline with a uniform composition of C_1, and no subsequent changes will occur

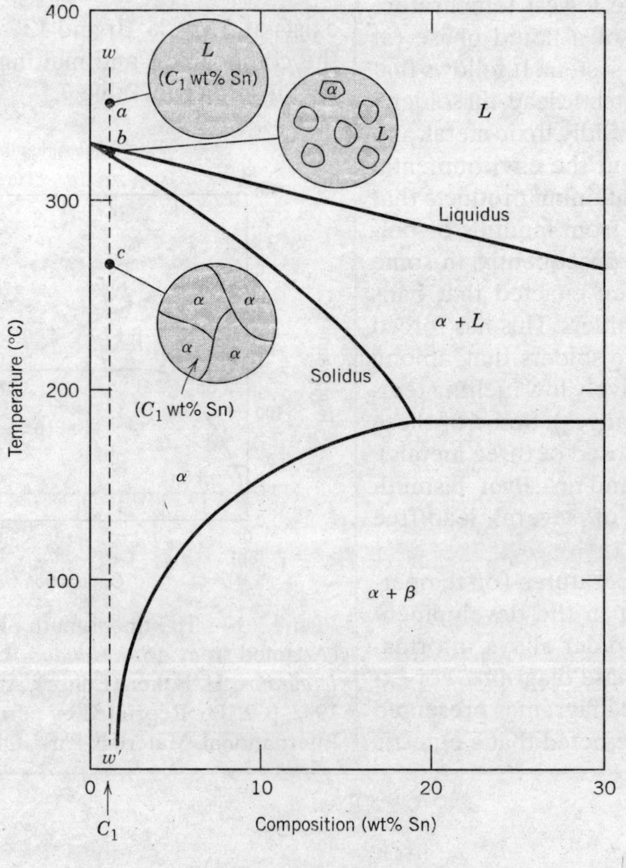

Figure 7.11 Schematic representations of the equilibrium microstructures for a lead–tin alloy of composition C_1 as it is cooled from the liquid-phase region.

upon cooling to room temperature. This microstructure is represented schematically by the inset at point c in Figure 7.11.

The second case considered is for compositions that range between the room temperature solubility limit and the maximum solid solubility at the eutectic temperature. For the lead–tin system (Figure 7.8), these compositions extend from about 2 wt% Sn to 18.3 wt% Sn (for lead-rich alloys) and from 77.8 wt% Sn to approximately 79 wt% Sn (for tin-rich alloys). Let us examine an alloy of composition C_2 as it is cooled along the vertical line xx' in Figure 7.12. Down to the intersection of xx' and the solvus line, changes that occur are similar to the previous case, as we pass through the corresponding phase regions (as demonstrated by the insets at points d, e, and f). Just above the solvus intersection, point f, the microstructure consists of α grains of composition C_2. Upon crossing the solvus line, the α solid solubility is exceeded, which results in the formation of small β-phase particles; these are indicated in the microstructure inset at point g. With continued cooling, these particles will grow in size because the mass fraction of the β phase increases slightly with decreasing temperature.

The third case involves solidification of the eutectic composition, 61.9 wt% Sn (C_3 in Figure 7.13). Consider an alloy having this composition that is cooled from a temperature within the liquid-phase region (e.g., 250°C) down the vertical line yy'

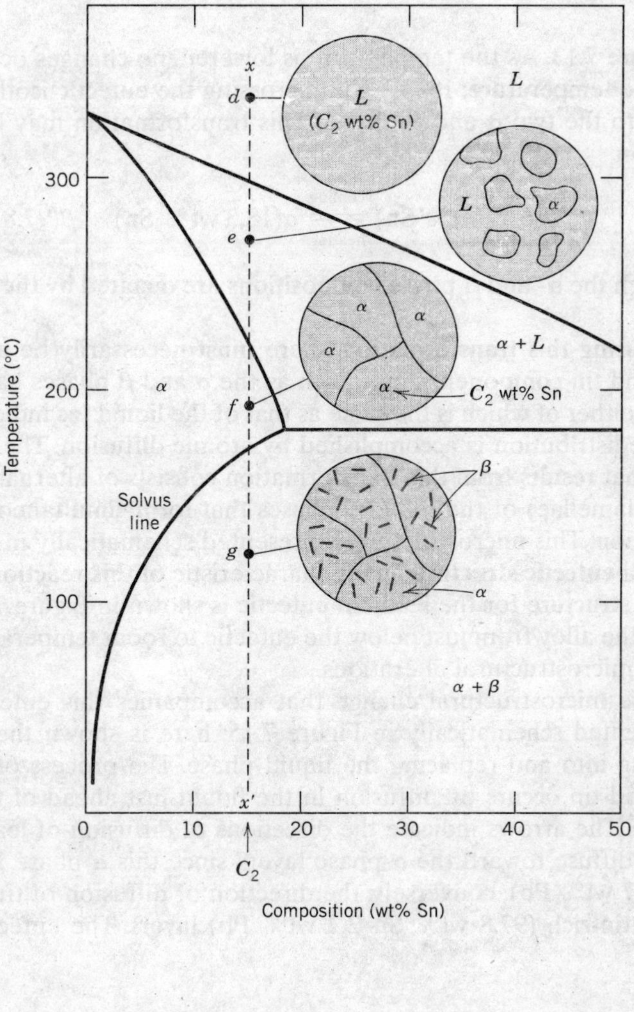

Figure 7.12 Schematic representations of the equilibrium microstructures for a lead–tin alloy of composition C_2 as it is cooled from the liquid-phase region.

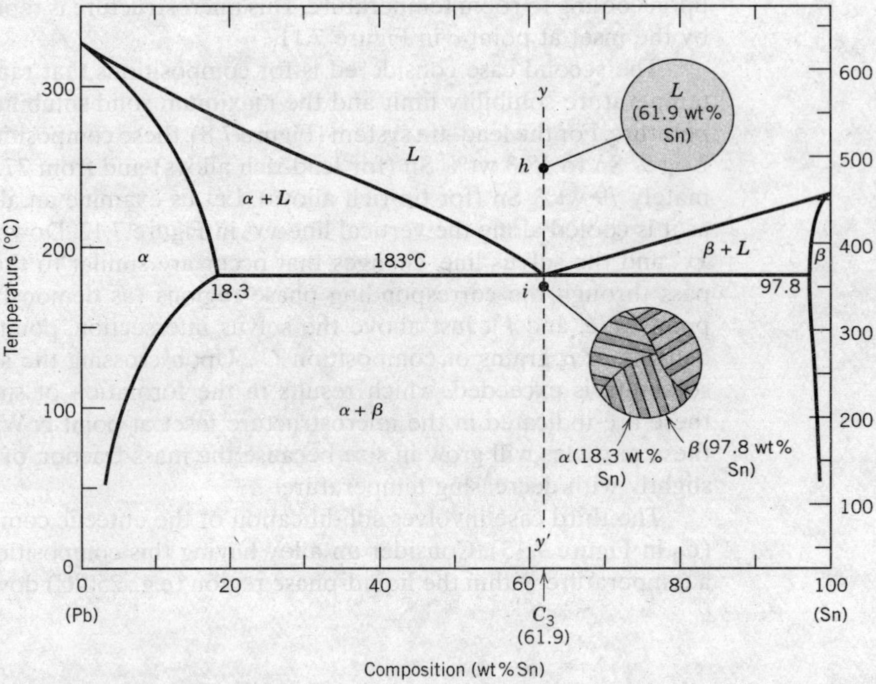

Figure 7.13 Schematic representations of the equilibrium microstructures for a lead–tin alloy of eutectic composition C_3 above and below the eutectic temperature.

in Figure 7.13. As the temperature is lowered, no changes occur until we reach the eutectic temperature, 183°C. Upon crossing the eutectic isotherm, the liquid transforms to the two α and β phases. This transformation may be represented by the reaction

$$L(61.9 \text{ wt\% Sn}) \underset{\text{heating}}{\overset{\text{cooling}}{\rightleftharpoons}} \alpha(18.3 \text{ wt\% Sn}) + \beta(97.8 \text{ wt\% Sn}) \tag{7.9}$$

in which the α- and β-phase compositions are dictated by the eutectic isotherm end points.

During this transformation, there must necessarily be a redistribution of the lead and tin components, inasmuch as the α and β phases have different compositions neither of which is the same as that of the liquid (as indicated in Equation 7.9). This redistribution is accomplished by atomic diffusion. The microstructure of the solid that results from this transformation consists of alternating layers (sometimes called lamellae) of the α and β phases that form simultaneously during the transformation. This microstructure, represented schematically in Figure 7.13, point i, is called a **eutectic structure** and is characteristic of this reaction. A photomicrograph of this structure for the lead–tin eutectic is shown in Figure 7.14. Subsequent cooling of the alloy from just below the eutectic to room temperature will result in only minor microstructural alterations.

The microstructural change that accompanies this eutectic transformation is represented schematically in Figure 7.15; here is shown the α-β layered eutectic growing into and replacing the liquid phase. The process of the redistribution of lead and tin occurs by diffusion in the liquid just ahead of the eutectic–liquid interface. The arrows indicate the directions of diffusion of lead and tin atoms; lead atoms diffuse toward the α-phase layers since this α phase is lead-rich (18.3 wt% Sn–81.7 wt% Pb); conversely, the direction of diffusion of tin is in the direction of the β, tin-rich (97.8 wt% Sn–2.2 wt% Pb) layers. The eutectic structure forms in

Figure 7.14 Photomicrograph showing the microstructure of a lead–tin alloy of eutectic composition. This microstructure consists of alternating layers of a lead-rich α-phase solid solution (dark layers), and a tin-rich β-phase solid solution (light layers). 375×. (Reproduced with permission from *Metals Handbook,* 7th edition, Vol. 7, *Metallography and Microstructures,* American Society for Metals, Materials Park, OH, 1985.)

these alternating layers because, for this lamellar configuration, atomic diffusion of lead and tin need only occur over relatively short distances.

The fourth and final microstructural case for this system includes all compositions other than the eutectic that, when cooled, cross the eutectic isotherm. Consider, for example, the composition C_4, Figure 7.16, which lies to the left of the eutectic; as the temperature is lowered, we move down the line zz', beginning at point j. The microstructural development between points j and l is similar to that for the second case, such that just prior to crossing the eutectic isotherm (point l), the α and liquid phases are present having compositions of approximately 18.3 and 61.9 wt% Sn, respectively, as determined from the appropriate tie line. As the temperature is lowered to just below the eutectic, the liquid phase, which is of the eutectic composition, will transform to the eutectic structure (i.e., alternating α and β lamellae); insignificant changes will occur with the α phase that formed during cooling through the $\alpha + L$ region. This microstructure is represented schematically by the inset at point m in Figure 7.16. Thus, the α phase will be present both in the eutectic structure and also as the phase that formed while cooling through the $\alpha + L$ phase field. To distinguish one α from the other, that which resides in the eutectic structure is called **eutectic** α, while the other that formed prior to crossing the eutectic isotherm is termed **primary** α; both are labeled in Figure 7.16. The photomicrograph in Figure 7.17 is of a lead–tin alloy in which both primary α and eutectic structures are shown.

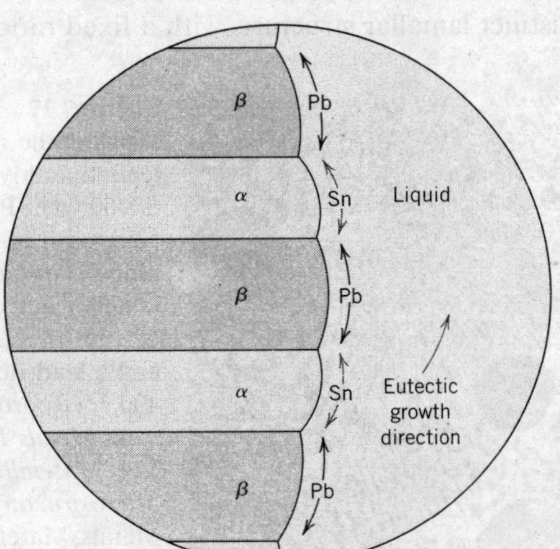

Figure 7.15 Schematic representation of the formation of the eutectic structure for the lead–tin system. Directions of diffusion of tin and lead atoms are indicated by blue and red arrows, respectively.

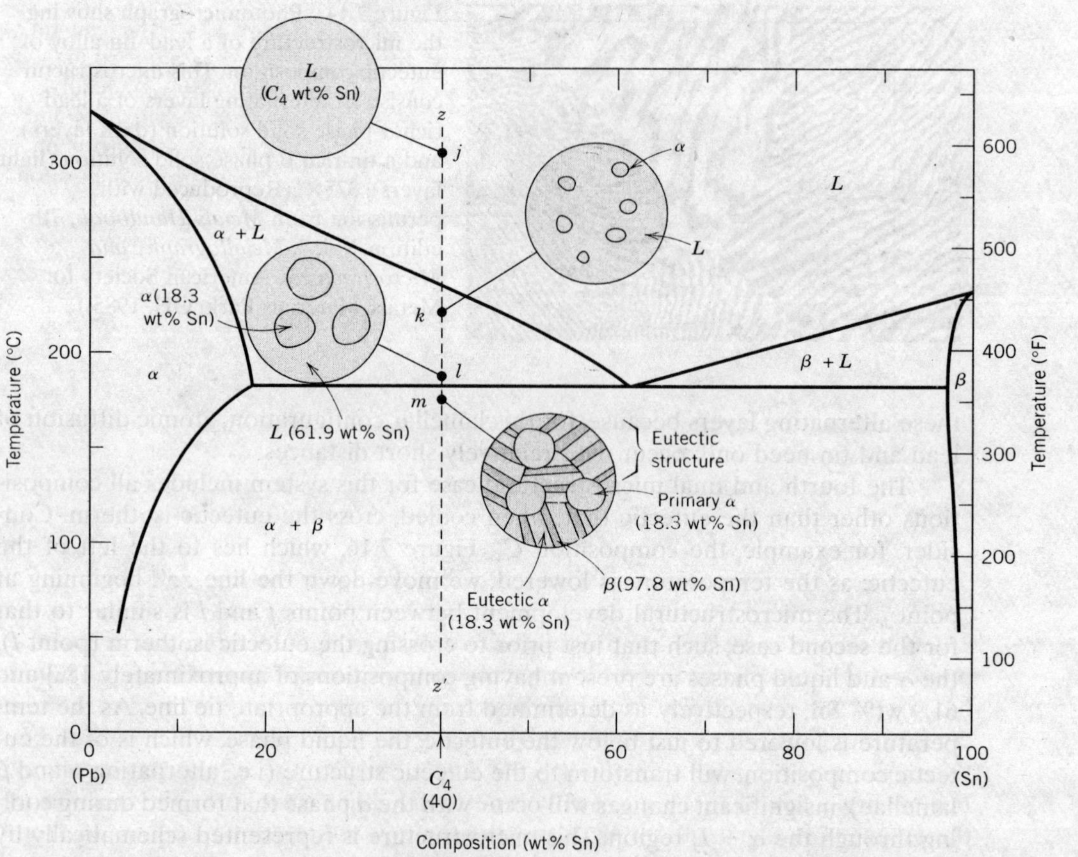

Figure 7.16 Schematic representations of the equilibrium microstructures for a lead–tin alloy of composition C_4 as it is cooled from the liquid-phase region.

In dealing with microstructures, it is sometimes convenient to use the term **microconstituent**—that is, an element of the microstructure having an identifiable and characteristic structure. For example, in the point *m* inset, Figure 7.16, there are two microconstituents—namely, primary α and the eutectic structure. Thus, the eutectic structure is a microconstituent even though it is a mixture of two phases, because it has a distinct lamellar structure, with a fixed ratio of the two phases.

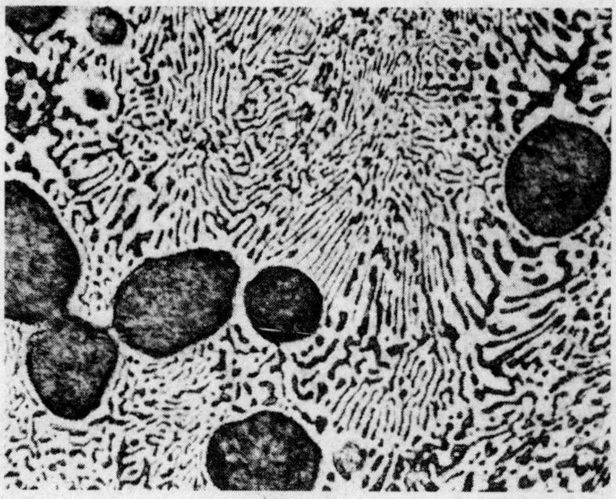

Figure 7.17 Photomicrograph showing the microstructure of a lead–tin alloy of composition 50 wt% Sn–50 wt% Pb. This microstructure is composed of a primary lead-rich α phase (large dark regions) within a lamellar eutectic structure consisting of a tin-rich β phase (light layers) and a lead-rich α phase (dark layers). 400×. (Reproduced with permission from *Metals Handbook,* 7th edition, Vol. 7, *Metallography and Microstructures,* American Society for Metals, Materials Park, OH, 1985.)

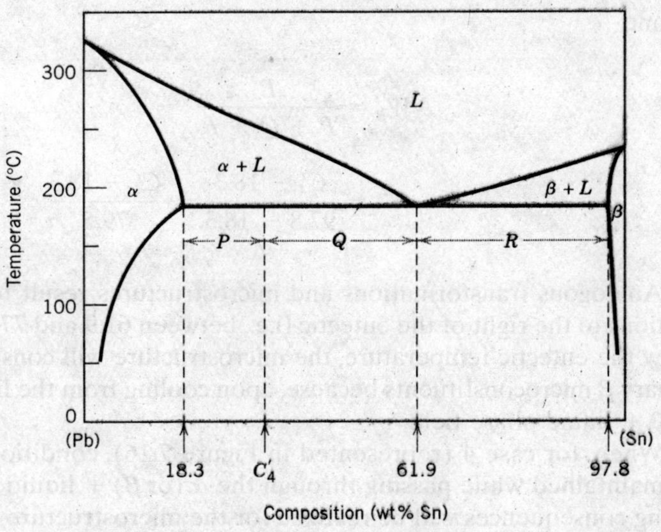

Figure 7.18 The lead–tin phase diagram used in computations for relative amounts of primary α and eutectic microconstituents for an alloy of composition C_4'.

It is possible to compute the relative amounts of both eutectic and primary α microconstituents. Since the eutectic microconstituent always forms from the liquid having the eutectic composition, this microconstituent may be assumed to have a composition of 61.9 wt% Sn. Hence, the lever rule is applied using a tie line between the α–(α + β) phase boundary (18.3 wt% Sn) and the eutectic composition. For example, consider the alloy of composition C_4' in Figure 7.18. The fraction of the eutectic microconstituent W_e is just the same as the fraction of liquid W_L from which it transforms, or

$$W_e = W_L = \frac{P}{P + Q}$$

$$= \frac{C_4' - 18.3}{61.9 - 18.3} = \frac{C_4' - 18.3}{43.6} \tag{7.10}$$

Furthermore, the fraction of primary α, $W_{\alpha'}$, is just the fraction of the α phase that existed prior to the eutectic transformation or, from Figure 7.18,

$$W_{\alpha'} = \frac{Q}{P + Q}$$

$$= \frac{61.9 - C_4'}{61.9 - 18.3} = \frac{61.9 - C_4'}{43.6} \tag{7.11}$$

The fractions of *total* α, W_α (both eutectic and primary), and also of total β, W_β, are determined by use of the lever rule and a tie line that extends *entirely across the α + β phase field*. Again, for an alloy having composition C_4',

$$W_\alpha = \frac{Q + R}{P + Q + R}$$

$$= \frac{97.8 - C_4'}{97.8 - 18.3} = \frac{97.8 - C_4'}{79.5} \tag{7.12}$$

and

$$W_\beta = \frac{P}{P + Q + R}$$

$$= \frac{C_4' - 18.3}{97.8 - 18.3} = \frac{C_4' - 18.3}{79.5} \tag{7.13}$$

Analogous transformations and microstructures result for alloys having compositions to the right of the eutectic (i.e., between 61.9 and 77.8 wt% Sn). However, below the eutectic temperature, the microstructure will consist of the eutectic and primary β microconstituents because, upon cooling from the liquid, we pass through the β + liquid phase field.

When, for case 4 (represented in Figure 7.16), conditions of equilibrium are not maintained while passing through the α (or β) + liquid phase region, the following consequences will be realized for the microstructure upon crossing the eutectic isotherm: (1) grains of the primary microconstituent will be cored, that is, have a nonuniform distribution of solute across the grains; and (2) the fraction of the eutectic microconstituent formed will be greater than for the equilibrium situation.

7.13 EQUILIBRIUM DIAGRAMS HAVING INTERMEDIATE PHASES OR COMPOUNDS

The isomorphous and eutectic phase diagrams discussed thus far are relatively simple, but those for many binary alloy systems are much more complex. The eutectic copper–silver and lead–tin phase diagrams (Figures 7.7 and 7.8) have only two solid phases, α and β; these are sometimes termed **terminal solid solutions,** because they exist over composition ranges near the concentration extremities of the phase diagram. For other alloy systems, **intermediate solid solutions** (or *intermediate phases*) may be found at other than the two composition extremes. Such is the case for the copper–zinc system. Its phase diagram (Figure 7.19) may at first appear formidable because there are some invariant points and reactions similar to the eutectic that have not yet been discussed. In addition, there are six different solid solutions—two terminal (α and η) and four intermediate (β, γ, δ, and ϵ). (The β' phase is termed an ordered solid solution, one in which the copper and zinc atoms are situated in a specific and ordered arrangement within each unit cell.) Some phase boundary lines near the bottom of Figure 7.19 are dashed to indicate that their positions have not been exactly determined. The reason for this is that at low temperatures, diffusion rates are very slow and inordinately long times are required for the attainment of equilibrium. Again, only single- and two-phase regions are found on the diagram, and the same rules outlined in Section 7.8 are utilized for computing phase compositions and relative amounts. The commercial brasses are copper-rich copper–zinc alloys; for example, cartridge brass has a composition of 70 wt% Cu–30 wt% Zn and a microstructure consisting of a single α phase.

For some systems, discrete intermediate compounds rather than solid solutions may be found on the phase diagram, and these compounds have distinct chemical formulas; for metal–metal systems, they are called **intermetallic compounds.** For example, consider the magnesium–lead system (Figure 7.20). The compound Mg_2Pb

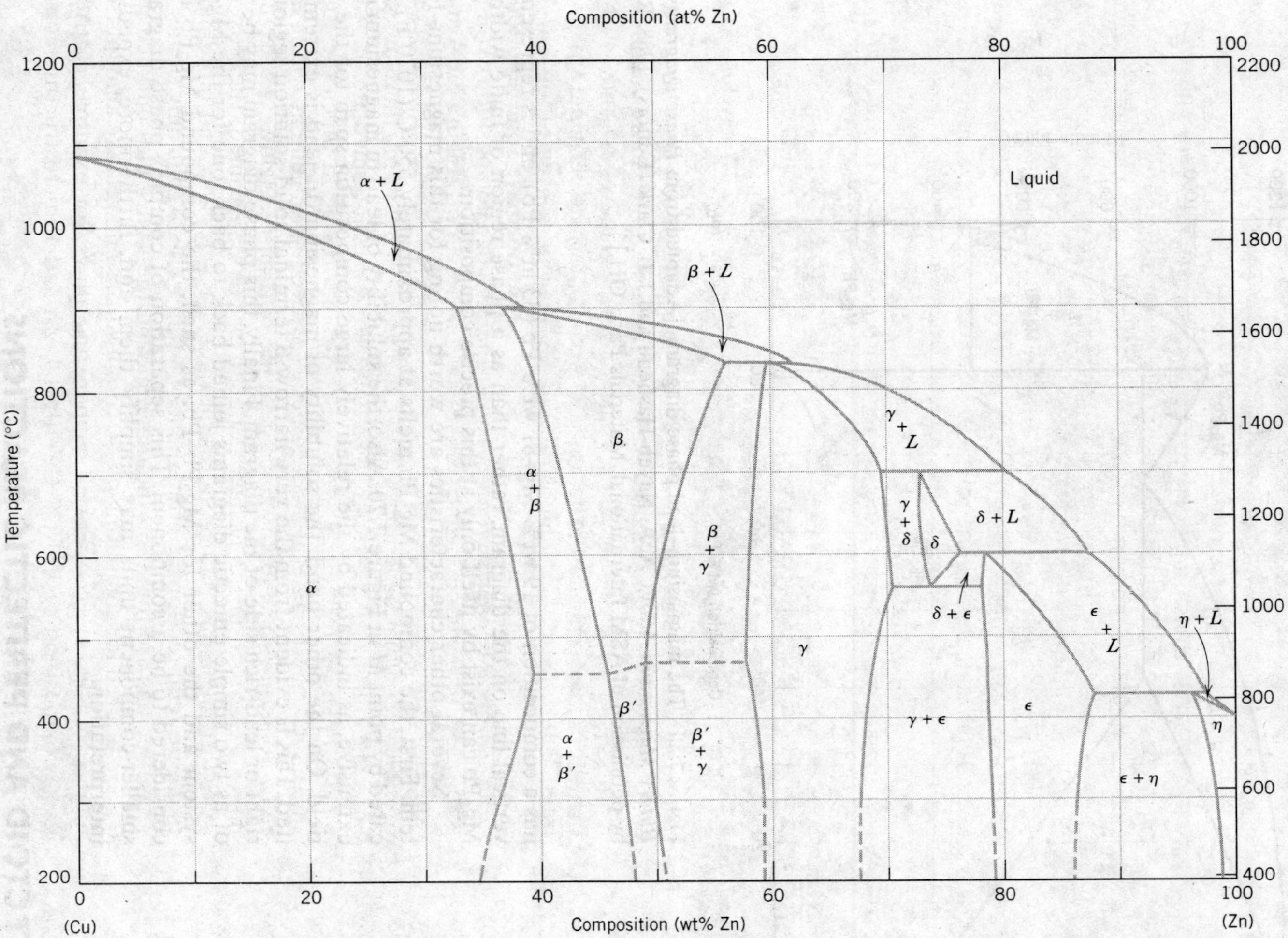

Figure 7.19 The copper–zinc phase diagram. [Adapted from *Binary Alloy Phase Diagrams,* 2nd edition, Vol. 2, T. B. Massalski (Editor-in-Chief), 1990. Reprinted by permission of ASM International, Materials Park, OH.]

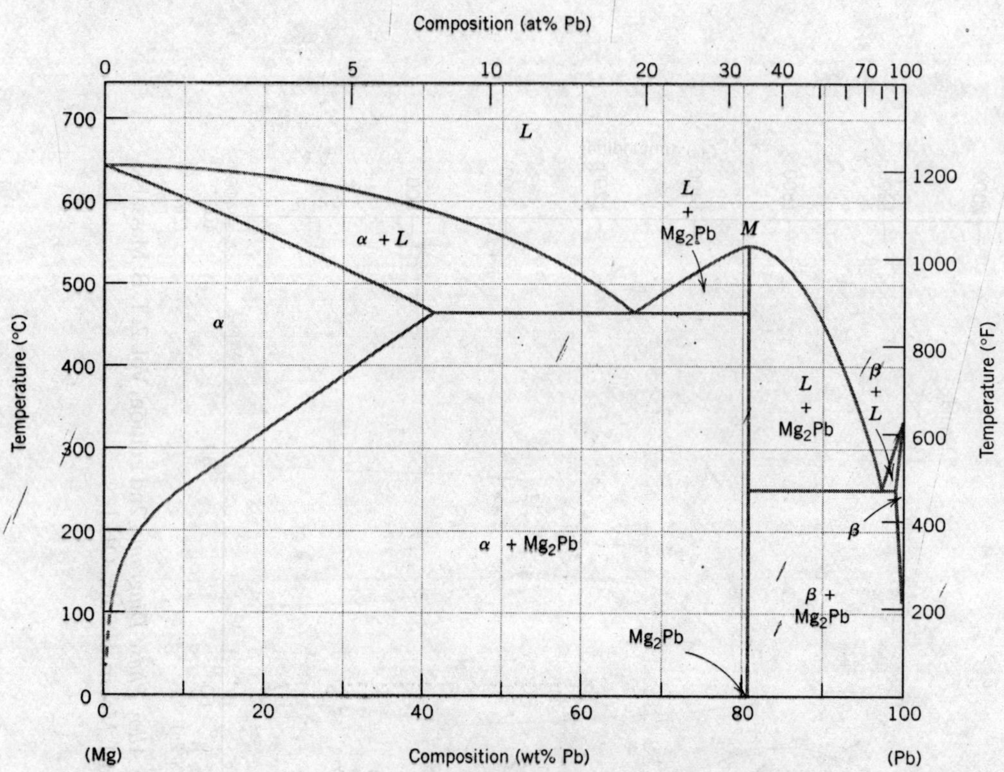

Figure 7.20 The magnesium–lead phase diagram. [Adapted from *Phase Diagrams of Binary Magnesium Alloys,* A. A. Nayeb-Hashemi and J. B. Clark (Editors), 1988. Reprinted by permission of ASM International, Materials Park, OH.]

has a composition of 19 wt% Mg–81 wt% Pb (33 at% Pb), and is represented as a vertical line on the diagram, rather than as a phase region of finite width; hence, Mg_2Pb can exist by itself only at this precise composition.

Several other characteristics are worth noting for this magnesium–lead system. First, the compound Mg_2Pb melts at approximately 550°C (1020°F), as indicated by point *M* in Figure 7.20. Also, the solubility of lead in magnesium is rather extensive, as indicated by the relatively large composition span for the α-phase field. On the other hand, the solubility of magnesium in lead is extremely limited. This is evident from the very narrow β terminal solid-solution region on the right or lead-rich side of the diagram. Finally, this phase diagram may be thought of as two simple eutectic diagrams joined back to back, one for the Mg–Mg_2Pb system and the other for Mg_2Pb–Pb; as such, the compound Mg_2Pb is really considered to be a component. This separation of complex phase diagrams into smaller-component units may simplify them and, furthermore, expedite their interpretation.

7.14 EUTECTOID AND PERITECTIC REACTIONS

In addition to the eutectic, other invariant points involving three different phases are found for some alloy systems. One of these occurs for the copper–zinc system (Figure 7.19) at 560°C (1040°F) and 74 wt% Zn–26 wt% Cu. A portion of the

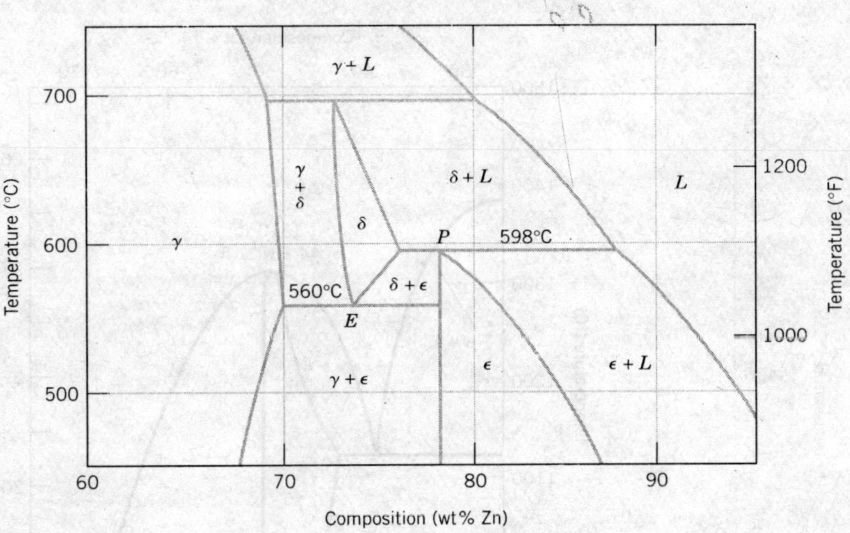

Figure 7.21 A region of the copper–zinc phase diagram that has been enlarged to show eutectoid and peritectic invariant points, labeled *E* (560°C, 74 wt% Zn) and *P* (598°C, 78.6 wt% Zn), respectively. [Adapted from *Binary Alloy Phase Diagrams*, 2nd edition, Vol. 2, T. B. Massalski (Editor-in-Chief), 1990. Reprinted by permission of ASM International, Materials Park, OH.]

phase diagram in this vicinity appears enlarged in Figure 7.21. Upon cooling, a solid δ phase transforms into two other solid phases (γ and ϵ) according to the reaction (per point *E*, Figure 7.21)

$$\delta \underset{\text{heating}}{\overset{\text{cooling}}{\rightleftharpoons}} \gamma + \epsilon \tag{7.14}$$

The reverse reaction occurs upon heating. It is called a **eutectoid** (or eutectic-like) **reaction,** and the invariant point (point *E*, Figure 7.21) and the horizontal tie line at 560°C are termed the *eutectoid* and *eutectoid isotherm,* respectively. The feature distinguishing "eutectoid" from "eutectic" is that one solid phase instead of a liquid transforms into two other solid phases at a single temperature. A eutectoid reaction is found in the iron–carbon system (Section 7.18) that is very important in the heat treating of steels.

The **peritectic reaction** is yet another invariant reaction involving three phases at equilibrium. With this reaction, upon heating, one solid phase transforms into a liquid phase and another solid phase. A peritectic exists for the copper–zinc system (Figure 7.21, point *P*) at 598°C (1108°F) and 78.6 wt% Zn–21.4 wt% Cu; this reaction is as follows (per point *P*, Figure 7.21):

$$\delta + L \underset{\text{heating}}{\overset{\text{cooling}}{\rightleftharpoons}} \epsilon \tag{7.15}$$

The low-temperature solid phase may be an intermediate solid solution (e.g., ϵ in the above reaction), or it may be a terminal solid solution. One of the latter peritectics exists at about 77 wt% Zn and 435°C (815°F) (see Figure 7.19), wherein the η phase, when heated, transforms to ϵ and liquid phases. Three other peritectics are found for the Cu–Zn system, the reactions of which involve β, δ, and γ intermediate solid solutions as the low-temperature phases that transform upon heating.

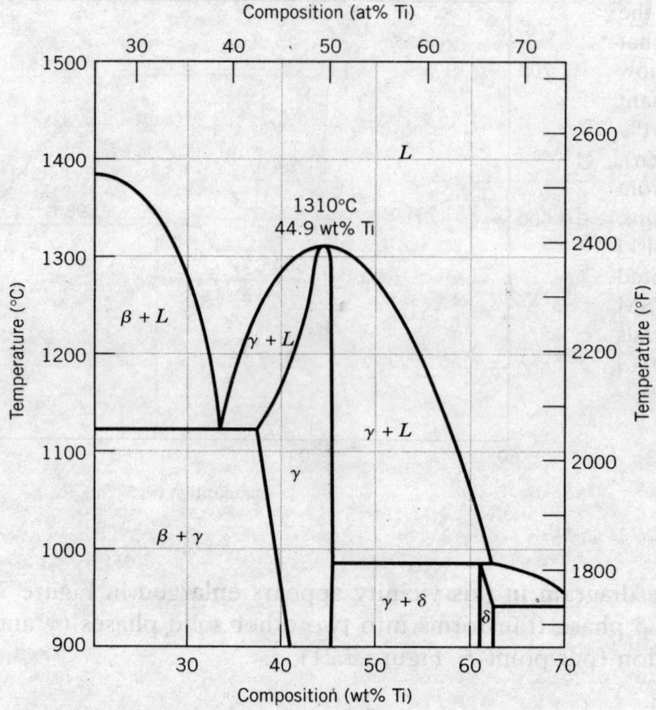

Figure 7.22 A portion of the nickel–titanium phase diagram on which is shown a congruent melting point for the γ-phase solid solution at 1310°C and 44.9 wt% Ti. [Adapted from *Phase Diagrams of Binary Nickel Alloys*, P. Nash (Editor), 1991. Reprinted by permission of ASM International, Materials Park, OH.]

7.15 CONGRUENT PHASE TRANSFORMATIONS

Phase transformations may be classified according to whether or not there is any change in composition for the phases involved. Those for which there are no compositional alterations are said to be **congruent transformations.** Conversely, for *incongruent transformations,* at least one of the phases will experience a change in composition. Examples of congruent transformations include allotropic transformations (Section 4.9) and melting of pure materials. Eutectic and eutectoid reactions, as well as the melting of an alloy that belongs to an isomorphous system, all represent incongruent transformations.

Intermediate phases are sometimes classified on the basis of whether they melt congruently or incongruently. The intermetallic compound Mg_2Pb melts congruently at the point designated M on the magnesium–lead phase diagram, Figure 7.20. Also, for the nickel–titanium system, Figure 7.22, there is a congruent melting point for the γ solid solution that corresponds to the point of tangency for the pairs of liquidus and solidus lines, at 1310°C and 44.9 wt% Ti. Furthermore, the peritectic reaction is an example of incongruent melting for an intermediate phase.

Concept Check 7.6

The figure on the next page is the hafnium–vanadium phase diagram, for which only single-phase regions are labeled. Specify temperature–composition points at which all eutectics, eutectoids, peritectics, and congruent phase transformations occur. Also, for each, write the reaction upon cooling. [Phase diagram from *ASM Handbook,* Vol. 3, *Alloy Phase Diagrams,* H. Baker (Editor), 1992, p. 2.244. Reprinted by permission of ASM International, Materials Park, OH.]

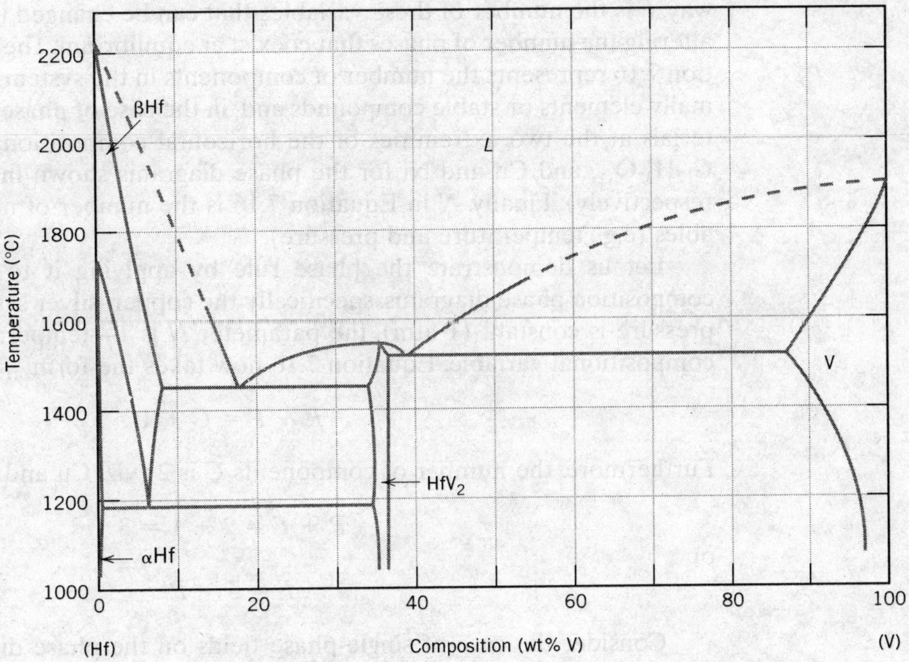

[*The answer may be found in enclosed CD.*]

7.16 CERAMIC AND TERNARY PHASE DIAGRAMS

It need not be assumed that phase diagrams exist only for metal–metal systems; in fact, phase diagrams that are very useful in the design and processing of ceramic systems have been experimentally determined for quite a number of these materials. Ceramic phase diagrams are discussed in Section 12.9.

Phase diagrams have also been determined for metallic (as well as ceramic) systems containing more than two components; however, their representation and interpretation may be exceedingly complex. For example, a ternary, or three-component, composition–temperature phase diagram in its entirety is depicted by a three-dimensional model. Portrayal of features of the diagram or model in two dimensions is possible but somewhat difficult.

7.17 THE GIBBS PHASE RULE

The construction of phase diagrams as well as some of the principles governing the conditions for phase equilibria are dictated by laws of thermodynamics. One of these is the **Gibbs phase rule,** proposed by the nineteenth-century physicist J. Willard Gibbs. This rule represents a criterion for the number of phases that will coexist within a system at equilibrium, and is expressed by the simple equation

$$P + F = C + N \tag{7.16}$$

where P is the number of phases present (the phase concept is discussed in Section 7.3). The parameter F is termed the *number of degrees of freedom* or the number of externally controlled variables (e.g., temperature, pressure, composition) which must be specified to completely define the state of the system. Expressed another way, F is the number of these variables that can be changed independently without altering the number of phases that coexist at equilibrium. The parameter C in Equation 7.16 represents the number of components in the system. Components are normally elements or stable compounds and, in the case of phase diagrams, are the materials at the two extremities of the horizontal compositional axis (e.g., H_2O and $C_{12}H_{22}O_{11}$, and Cu and Ni for the phase diagrams shown in Figures 7.1 and 7.3*a*, respectively). Finally, N in Equation 7.16 is the number of noncompositional variables (e.g., temperature and pressure).

Let us demonstrate the phase rule by applying it to binary temperature–composition phase diagrams, specifically the copper–silver system, Figure 7.7. Since pressure is constant (1 atm), the parameter N is 1—temperature is the only noncompositional variable. Equation 7.16 now takes the form

$$P + F = C + 1 \tag{7.17}$$

Furthermore, the number of components C is 2 (viz. Cu and Ag), and

$$P + F = 2 + 1 = 3$$

or

$$F = 3 - P$$

Consider the case of single-phase fields on the phase diagram (e.g., α, β, and liquid regions). Since only one phase is present, $P = 1$ and

$$\begin{aligned} F &= 3 - P \\ &= 3 - 1 = 2 \end{aligned}$$

This means that to completely describe the characteristics of any alloy that exists within one of these phase fields, we must specify two parameters; these are composition and temperature, which locate, respectively, the horizontal and vertical positions of the alloy on the phase diagram.

For the situation wherein two phases coexist, for example, $\alpha + L$, $\beta + L$, and $\alpha + \beta$ phase regions, Figure 7.7, the phase rule stipulates that we have but one degree of freedom since

$$\begin{aligned} F &= 3 - P \\ &= 3 - 2 = 1 \end{aligned}$$

Thus, it is necessary to specify either temperature or the composition of one of the phases to completely define the system. For example, suppose that we decide to specify temperature for the $\alpha + L$ phase region, say, T_1 in Figure 7.23. The compositions of the α and liquid phases (C_α and C_L) are thus dictated by the extremities of the tie line constructed at T_1 across the $\alpha + L$ field. Note that only the nature of the phases is important in this treatment and not the relative phase amounts. This is to say that the overall alloy composition could lie anywhere along this tie line constructed at temperature T_1 and still give C_α and C_L compositions for the respective α and liquid phases.

The second alternative is to stipulate the composition of one of the phases for this two-phase situation, which thereby fixes completely the state of the system. For example, if we specified C_α as the composition of the α phase that is in equilibrium with the liquid (Figure 7.23), then both the temperature of the alloy (T_1) and the composition of the liquid phase (C_L) are established, again by the tie line drawn across the $\alpha + L$ phase field so as to give this C_α composition.

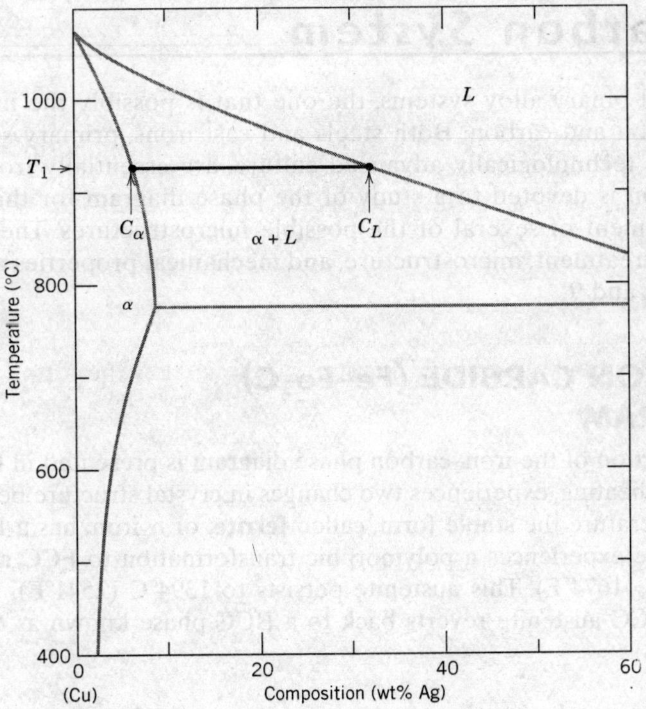

Figure 7.23 Enlarged copper-rich section of the Cu–Ag phase diagram in which the Gibbs phase rule for the coexistence of two phases (i.e., α and L) is demonstrated. Once the composition of either phase (i.e., C_α or C_L) or the temperature (i.e., T_1) is specified, values for the two remaining parameters are established by construction of the appropriate tie line.

For binary systems, when three phases are present, there are no degrees of freedom, since

$$F = 3 - P$$
$$= 3 - 3 = 0$$

This means that the compositions of all three phases as well as the temperature are fixed. This condition is met for a eutectic system by the eutectic isotherm; for the Cu–Ag system (Figure 7.7), it is the horizontal line that extends between points B and G. At this temperature, 779°C, the points at which each of the α, L, and β phase fields touch the isotherm line correspond to the respective phase compositions; namely, the composition of the α phase is fixed at 8.0 wt% Ag, that of the liquid at 71.9 wt% Ag, and that of the β phase at 71.2 wt% Ag. Thus, three-phase equilibrium will not be represented by a phase field, but rather by the unique horizontal isotherm line. Furthermore, all three phases will be in equilibrium for any alloy composition that lies along the length of the eutectic isotherm (e.g., for the Cu–Ag system at 779°C and compositions between 8.0 and 71.2 wt% Ag).

One use of the Gibbs phase rule is in analyzing for nonequilibrium conditions. For example, a microstructure for a binary alloy that developed over a range of temperatures and consisting of three phases is a nonequilibrium one; under these circumstances, three phases will exist only at a single temperature.

Concept Check 7.7

For a ternary system, three components are present; temperature is also a variable. What is the maximum number of phases that may be present for a ternary system, assuming that pressure is held constant?

[The answer may be found in enclosed CD.]

The Iron–Carbon System

Of all binary alloy systems, the one that is possibly the most important is that for iron and carbon. Both steels and cast irons, primary structural materials in every technologically advanced culture, are essentially iron–carbon alloys. This section is devoted to a study of the phase diagram for this system and the development of several of the possible microstructures. The relationships among heat treatment, microstructure, and mechanical properties are explored in Chapters 8 and 9.

7.18 THE IRON–IRON CARBIDE (Fe–Fe_3C) PHASE DIAGRAM

A portion of the iron–carbon phase diagram is presented in Figure 7.24. Pure iron, upon heating, experiences two changes in crystal structure before it melts. At room temperature the stable form, called **ferrite,** or α iron, has a BCC crystal structure. Ferrite experiences a polymorphic transformation to FCC **austenite,** or γ iron, at 912°C (1674°F). This austenite persists to 1394°C (2541°F), at which temperature the FCC austenite reverts back to a BCC phase known as δ ferrite, which finally

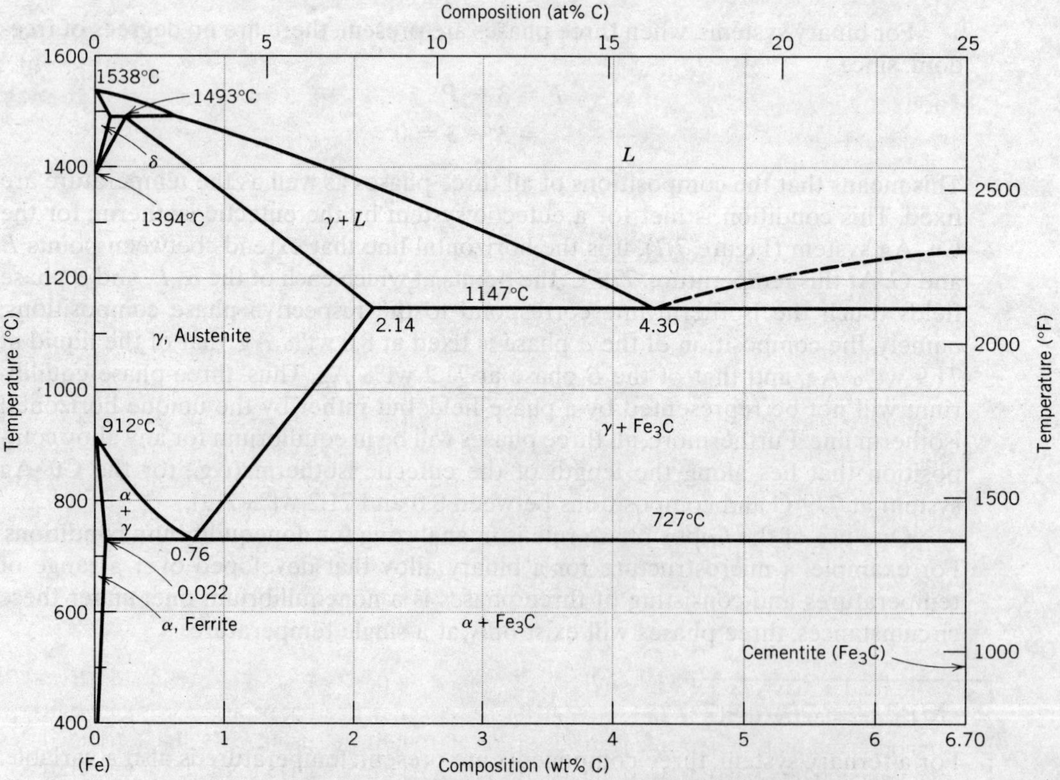

Figure 7.24 The iron–iron carbide phase diagram. [Adapted from *Binary Alloy Phase Diagrams,* 2nd edition, Vol. 1, T. B. Massalski (Editor-in-Chief), 1990. Reprinted by permission of ASM International, Materials Park, OH.]

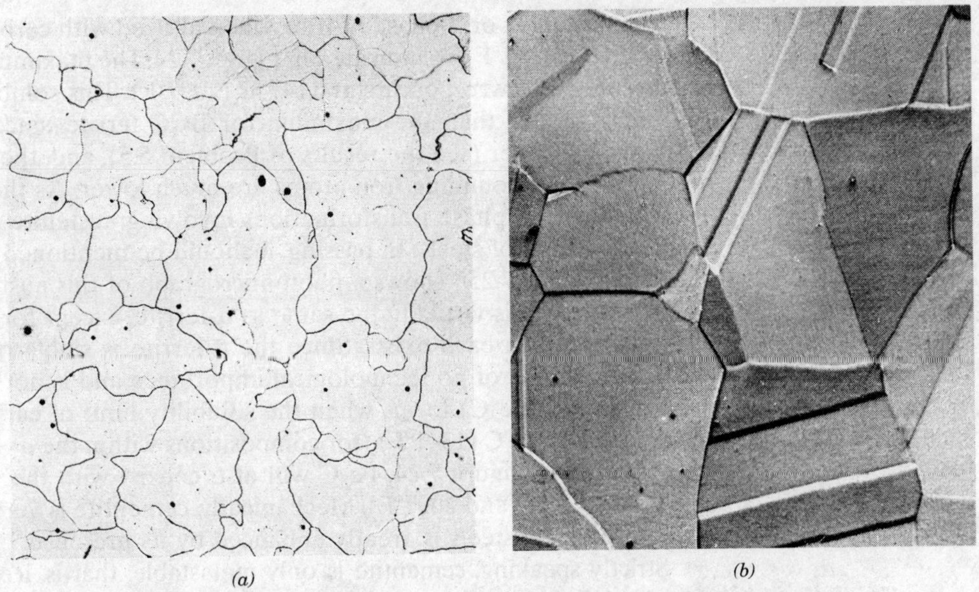

Figure 7.25 Photomicrographs of (*a*) α ferrite (90×) and (*b*) austenite (325×). (Copyright 1971 by United States Steel Corporation.)

melts at 1538°C (2800°F). All these changes are apparent along the left vertical axis of the phase diagram.[1]

The composition axis in Figure 7.24 extends only to 6.70 wt% C; at this concentration the intermediate compound iron carbide, or **cementite** (Fe_3C), is formed, which is represented by a vertical line on the phase diagram. Thus, the iron–carbon system may be divided into two parts: an iron-rich portion, as in Figure 7.24, and the other (not shown) for compositions between 6.70 and 100 wt% C (pure graphite). In practice, all steels and cast irons have carbon contents less than 6.70 wt% C; therefore, we consider only the iron–iron carbide system. Figure 7.24 would be more appropriately labeled the $Fe–Fe_3C$ phase diagram, since Fe_3C is now considered to be a component. Convention and convenience dictate that composition still be expressed in "wt% C" rather than "wt% Fe_3C"; 6.70 wt% C corresponds to 100 wt% Fe_3C.

Carbon is an interstitial impurity in iron and forms a solid solution with each of α and δ ferrites, and also with austenite, as indicated by the α, δ, and γ single-phase fields in Figure 7.24. In the BCC α ferrite, only small concentrations of carbon are soluble; the maximum solubility is 0.022 wt% at 727°C (1341°F). The limited solubility is explained by the shape and size of the BCC interstitial positions, which make it difficult to accommodate the carbon atoms. Even though present in relatively low concentrations, carbon significantly influences the mechanical properties of ferrite. This particular iron–carbon phase is relatively soft, may be made magnetic at temperatures below 768°C (1414°F), and has a density of 7.88 g/cm^3. Figure 7.25*a* is a photomicrograph of α ferrite.

[1] The reader may wonder why no β phase is found on the $Fe–Fe_3C$ phase diagram, Figure 7.24 (consistent with the α, β, γ, etc. labeling scheme described previously). Early investigators observed that the ferromagnetic behavior of iron disappears at 768°C and attributed this phenomenon to a phase transformation; the "β" label was assigned to the high-temperature phase. Later it was discovered that this loss of magnetism did not result from a phase transformation (see Section 20.6) and, therefore, the presumed β phase did not exist.

The austenite, or γ phase of iron, when alloyed with carbon alone, is not stable below 727°C (1341°F), as indicated in Figure 7.24. The maximum solubility of carbon in austenite, 2.14 wt%, occurs at 1147°C (2097°F). This solubility is approximately 100 times greater than the maximum for BCC ferrite, since the FCC interstitial positions are larger (see the results of Problem 5.5), and, therefore, the strains imposed on the surrounding iron atoms are much lower. As the discussions that follow demonstrate, phase transformations involving austenite are very important in the heat treating of steels. In passing, it should be mentioned that austenite is nonmagnetic. Figure 7.25*b* shows a photomicrograph of this austenite phase.

The δ ferrite is virtually the same as α ferrite, except for the range of temperatures over which each exists. Since the δ ferrite is stable only at relatively high temperatures, it is of no technological importance and is not discussed further.

Cementite (Fe_3C) forms when the solubility limit of carbon in α ferrite is exceeded below 727°C (1341°F) (for compositions within the $\alpha + Fe_3C$ phase region). As indicated in Figure 7.24, Fe_3C will also coexist with the γ phase between 727 and 1147°C (1341 and 2097°F). Mechanically, cementite is very hard and brittle; the strength of some steels is greatly enhanced by its presence.

Strictly speaking, cementite is only metastable; that is, it will remain as a compound indefinitely at room temperature. However, if heated to between 650 and 700°C (1200 and 1300°F) for several years, it will gradually change or transform into α iron and carbon, in the form of graphite, which will remain upon subsequent cooling to room temperature. Thus, the phase diagram in Figure 7.24 is not a true equilibrium one because cementite is not an equilibrium compound. However, inasmuch as the decomposition rate of cementite is extremely sluggish, virtually all the carbon in steel will be as Fe_3C instead of graphite, and the iron–iron carbide phase diagram is, for all practical purposes, valid. As will be seen in Section 9.2, addition of silicon to cast irons greatly accelerates this cementite decomposition reaction to form graphite.

The two-phase regions are labeled in Figure 7.24. It may be noted that one eutectic exists for the iron–iron carbide system, at 4.30 wt% C and 1147°C (2097°F); for this eutectic reaction,

$$L \underset{\text{heating}}{\overset{\text{cooling}}{\rightleftharpoons}} \gamma + Fe_3C \tag{7.18}$$

the liquid solidifies to form austenite and cementite phases. Of course, subsequent cooling to room temperature will promote additional phase changes.

It may be noted that a eutectoid invariant point exists at a composition of 0.76 wt% C and a temperature of 727°C (1341°F). This eutectoid reaction may be represented by

$$\gamma(0.76\text{ wt\% C}) \underset{\text{heating}}{\overset{\text{cooling}}{\rightleftharpoons}} \alpha(0.022\text{ wt\% C}) + Fe_3C\ (6.7\text{ wt\% C}) \tag{7.19}$$

or, upon cooling, the solid γ phase is transformed into α iron and cementite. (Eutectoid phase transformations were addressed in Section 7.14.) The eutectoid phase changes described by Equation 7.19 are very important, being fundamental to the heat treatment of steels, as explained in subsequent discussions.

Ferrous alloys are those in which iron is the prime component, but carbon as well as other alloying elements may be present. In the classification scheme of ferrous alloys based on carbon content, there are three types: iron, steel, and cast iron. Commercially pure iron contains less than 0.008 wt% C and, from the phase diagram, is composed almost exclusively of the ferrite phase at room temperature. The iron–carbon alloys that contain between 0.008 and 2.14 wt% C are classified as steels. In most steels the microstructure consists of both α and Fe_3C phases. Upon cooling to room temperature, an alloy within this composition range must pass through at least a portion of the γ-phase field; distinctive microstructures are subsequently produced, as discussed below. Although a steel alloy may contain as much as 2.14 wt% C, in practice, carbon concentrations rarely exceed 1.0 wt%. The properties and various classifications of steels are treated in Section 9.2. Cast irons are classified as ferrous alloys that contain between 2.14 and 6.70 wt% C. However, commercial cast irons normally contain less than 4.5 wt% C. These alloys are discussed further also in Section 9.2.

7.19 DEVELOPMENT OF MICROSTRUCTURE IN IRON–CARBON ALLOYS

Several of the various microstructures that may be produced in steel alloys and their relationships to the iron–iron carbon phase diagram are now discussed, and it is shown that the microstructure that develops depends on both the carbon content and heat treatment. This discussion is confined to very slow cooling of steel alloys, in which equilibrium is continuously maintained. A more detailed exploration of the influence of heat treatment on microstructure, and ultimately on the mechanical properties of steels, is contained in Chapter 8.

Phase changes that occur upon passing from the γ region into the $\alpha + Fe_3C$ phase field (Figure 7.24) are relatively complex and similar to those described for the eutectic systems in Section 7.12. Consider, for example, an alloy of eutectoid composition (0.76 wt% C) as it is cooled from a temperature within the γ phase region, say, 800°C—that is, beginning at point *a* in Figure 7.26 and moving down the

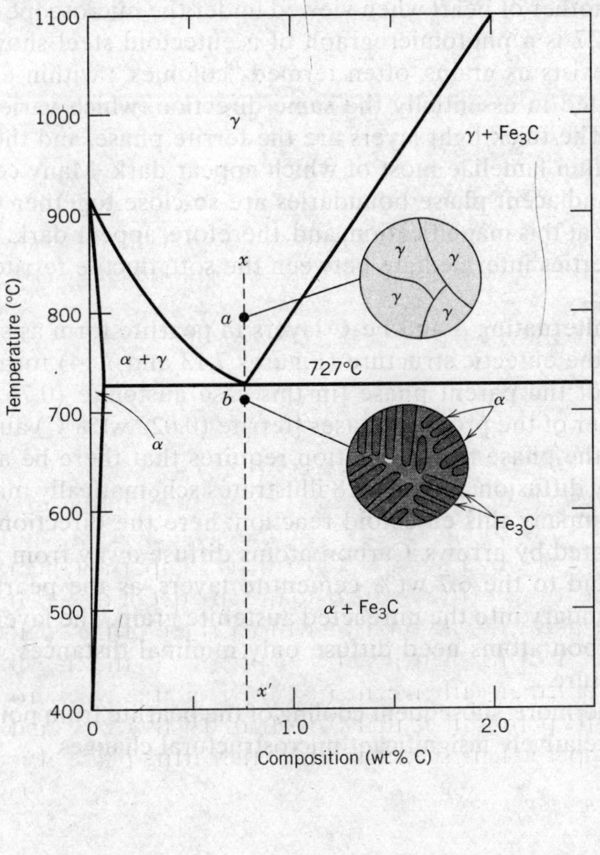

Figure 7.26 Schematic representations of the microstructures for an iron–carbon alloy of eutectoid composition (0.76 wt% C) above and below the eutectoid temperature.

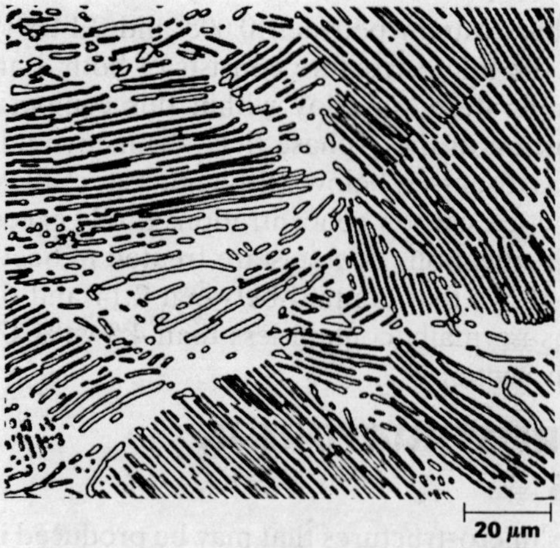

Figure 7.27 Photomicrograph of a eutectoid steel showing the pearlite microstructure consisting of alternating layers of α ferrite (the light phase) and Fe_3C (thin layers most of which appear dark). 500×. (Reproduced with permission from *Metals Handbook*, 7th edition, Vol. 7, *Metallography and Microstructures*, American Society for Metals, Materials Park, OH, 1985.)

vertical line xx'. Initially, the alloy is composed entirely of the austenite phase having a composition of 0.76 wt% C and corresponding microstructure, also indicated in Figure 7.26. As the alloy is cooled, there will occur no changes until the eutectoid temperature (727°C) is reached. Upon crossing this temperature to point b, the austenite transforms according to Equation 7.19.

The microstructure for this eutectoid steel that is slowly cooled through the eutectoid temperature consists of alternating layers or lamellae of the two phases (α and Fe_3C) that form simultaneously during the transformation. In this case, the relative layer thickness is approximately 8 to 1. This microstructure, represented schematically in Figure 7.26, point b, is called **pearlite** because it has the appearance of mother of pearl when viewed under the microscope at low magnifications. Figure 7.27 is a photomicrograph of a eutectoid steel showing the pearlite. The pearlite exists as grains, often termed "colonies"; within each colony the layers are oriented in essentially the same direction, which varies from one colony to another. The thick light layers are the ferrite phase, and the cementite phase appears as thin lamellae most of which appear dark. Many cementite layers are so thin that adjacent phase boundaries are so close together that they are indistinguishable at this magnification, and, therefore, appear dark. Mechanically, pearlite has properties intermediate between the soft, ductile ferrite and the hard, brittle cementite.

The alternating α and Fe_3C layers in pearlite form as such for the same reason that the eutectic structure (Figures 7.13 and 7.14) forms—because the composition of the parent phase [in this case austenite (0.76 wt% C)] is different from either of the product phases [ferrite (0.022 wt% C) and cementite (6.7 wt% C)], and the phase transformation requires that there be a redistribution of the carbon by diffusion. Figure 7.28 illustrates schematically microstructural changes that accompany this eutectoid reaction; here the directions of carbon diffusion are indicated by arrows. Carbon atoms diffuse away from the 0.022 wt% ferrite regions and to the 6.7 wt% cementite layers, as the pearlite extends from the grain boundary into the unreacted austenite grain. The layered pearlite forms because carbon atoms need diffuse only minimal distances with the formation of this structure.

Furthermore, subsequent cooling of the pearlite from point b in Figure 7.26 will produce relatively insignificant microstructural changes.

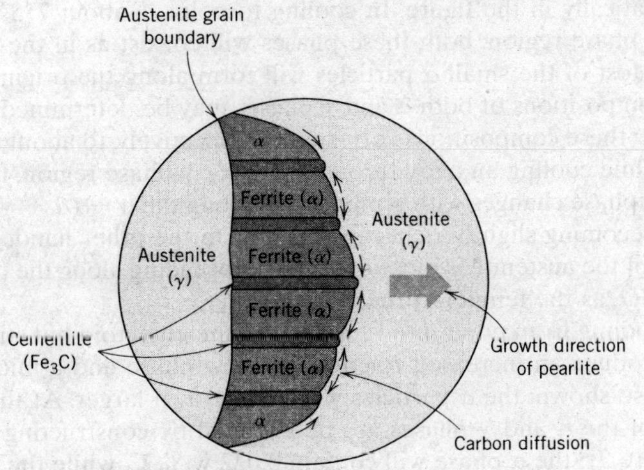

Figure 7.28 Schematic representation of the formation of pearlite from austenite; direction of carbon diffusion indicated by arrows.

Hypoeutectoid Alloys

Microstructures for iron–iron carbide alloys having other than the eutectoid composition are now explored; these are analogous to the fourth case described in Section 7.12 and illustrated in Figure 7.16 for the eutectic system. Consider a composition C_0 to the left of the eutectoid, between 0.022 and 0.76 wt% C; this is termed a **hypoeutectoid** (less than eutectoid) **alloy.** Cooling an alloy of this composition is represented by moving down the vertical line yy' in Figure 7.29. At about 875°C, point c, the microstructure will consist entirely of grains of the γ phase, as shown

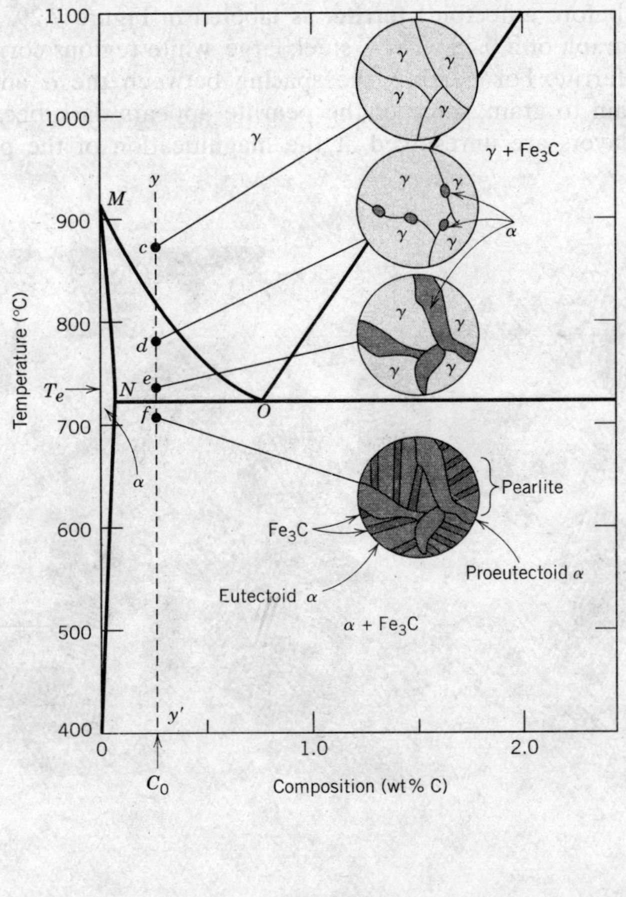

Figure 7.29 Schematic representations of the microstructures for an iron–carbon alloy of hypoeutectoid composition C_0 (containing less than 0.76 wt% C) as it is cooled from within the austenite phase region to below the eutectoid temperature.

schematically in the figure. In cooling to point d, about 775°C, which is within the $\alpha + \gamma$ phase region, both these phases will coexist as in the schematic microstructure. Most of the small α particles will form along the original γ grain boundaries. The compositions of both α and γ phases may be determined using the appropriate tie line; these compositions correspond, respectively, to about 0.020 and 0.40 wt% C.

While cooling an alloy through the $\alpha + \gamma$ phase region, the composition of the ferrite phase changes with temperature along the $\alpha - (\alpha + \gamma)$ phase boundary, line MN, becoming slightly richer in carbon. On the other hand, the change in composition of the austenite is more dramatic, proceeding along the $(\alpha + \gamma) - \gamma$ boundary, line MO, as the temperature is reduced.

Cooling from point d to e, just above the eutectoid but still in the $\alpha + \gamma$ region, will produce an increased fraction of the α phase and a microstructure similar to that also shown: the α particles will have grown larger. At this point, the compositions of the α and γ phases are determined by constructing a tie line at the temperature T_e; the α phase will contain 0.022 wt% C, while the γ phase will be of the eutectoid composition, 0.76 wt% C.

As the temperature is lowered just below the eutectoid, to point f, all the γ phase that was present at temperature T_e (and having the eutectoid composition) will transform to pearlite, according to the reaction in Equation 7.19. There will be virtually no change in the α phase that existed at point e in crossing the eutectoid temperature—it will normally be present as a continuous matrix phase surrounding the isolated pearlite colonies. The microstructure at point f will appear as the corresponding schematic inset of Figure 7.29. Thus the ferrite phase will be present both in the pearlite and also as the phase that formed while cooling through the $\alpha + \gamma$ phase region. The ferrite that is present in the pearlite is called *eutectoid ferrite,* whereas the other, that formed above T_e, is termed **proeutectoid** (meaning pre- or before eutectoid) **ferrite,** as labeled in Figure 7.29. Figure 7.30 is a photomicrograph of a 0.38 wt% C steel; large, white regions correspond to the proeutectoid ferrite. For pearlite, the spacing between the α and Fe_3C layers varies from grain to grain; some of the pearlite appears dark because the many close-spaced layers are unresolved at the magnification of the photomicrograph. The

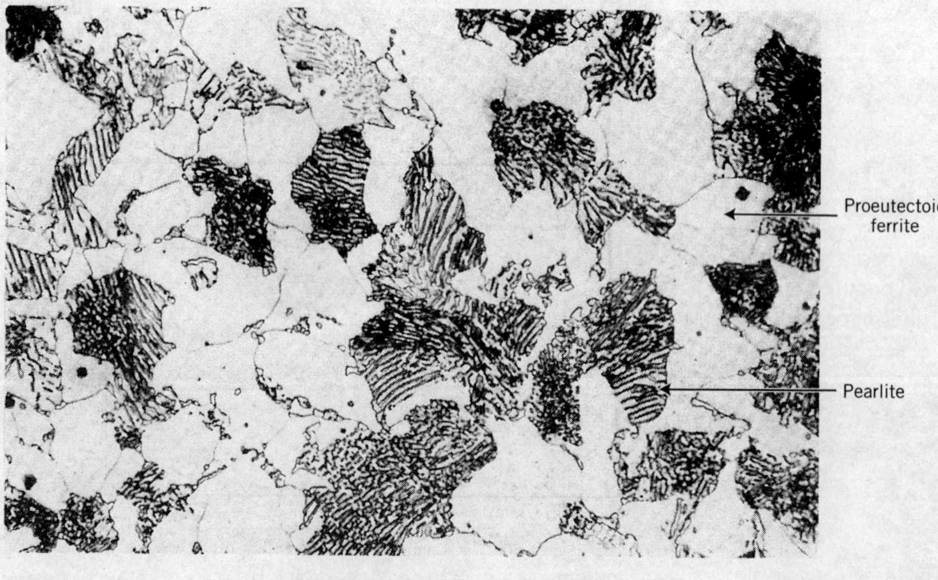

Figure 7.30 Photomicrograph of a 0.38 wt% C steel having a microstructure consisting of pearlite and proeutectoid ferrite. 635×. (Photomicrograph courtesy of Republic Steel Corporation.)

chapter-opening photograph for this chapter is a scanning electron micrograph of a hypoeutectoid (0.44 wt% C) steel in which may also be seen both pearlite and proeutectoid ferrite, only at a higher magnification. Note also that two microconstituents are present in these micrographs—proeutectoid ferrite and pearlite—which will appear in all hypoeutectoid iron–carbon alloys that are slowly cooled to a temperature below the eutectoid.

The relative amounts of the proeutectoid α and pearlite may be determined in a manner similar to that described in Section 7.12 for primary and eutectic microconstituents. We use the lever rule in conjunction with a tie line that extends from the $\alpha - (\alpha + Fe_3C)$ phase boundary (0.022 wt% C) to the eutectoid composition (0.76 wt% C), inasmuch as pearlite is the transformation product of austenite having this composition. For example, let us consider an alloy of composition C_0' in Figure 7.31. Thus, the fraction of pearlite, W_p, may be determined according to

$$W_p = \frac{T}{T + U}$$

$$= \frac{C_0' - 0.022}{0.76 - 0.022} = \frac{C_0' - 0.022}{0.74} \qquad (7.20)$$

Furthermore, the fraction of proeutectoid α, $W_{\alpha'}$, is computed as follows:

$$W_{\alpha'} = \frac{U}{T + U}$$

$$= \frac{0.76 - C_0'}{0.76 - 0.022} = \frac{0.76 - C_0'}{0.74} \qquad (7.21)$$

Of course, fractions of both total α (eutectoid and proeutectoid) and cementite are determined using the lever rule and a tie line that extends across the entirety of the $\alpha + Fe_3C$ phase region, from 0.022 to 6.7 wt% C.

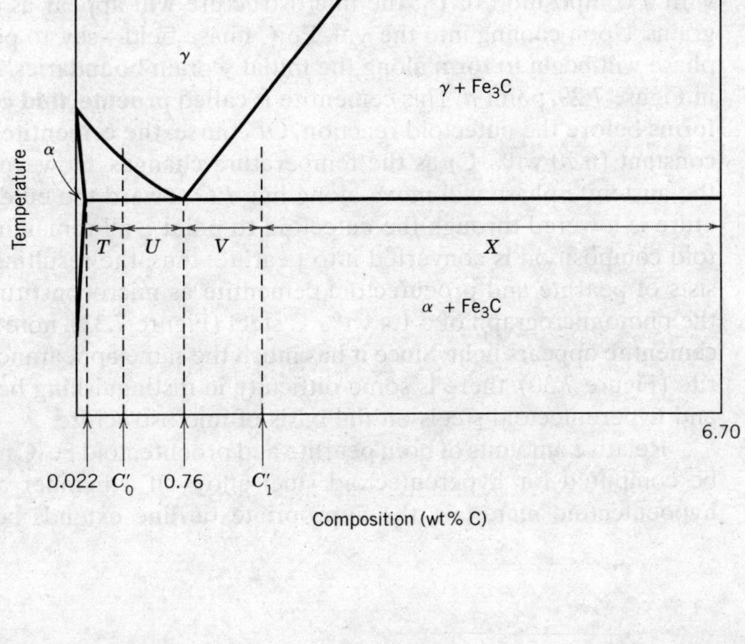

Figure 7.31 A portion of the $Fe–Fe_3C$ phase diagram used in computations for relative amounts of proeutectoid and pearlite microconstituents for hypoeutectoid (C_0') and hypereutectoid (C_1') compositions.

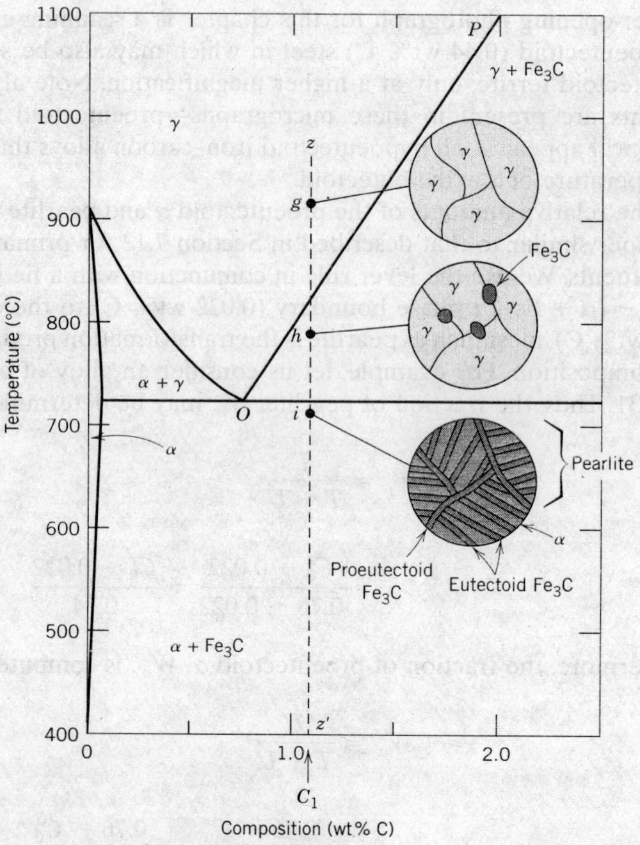

Figure 7.32 Schematic representations of the microstructures for an iron–carbon alloy of hypereutectoid composition C_1 (containing between 0.76 and 2.14 wt% C), as it is cooled from within the austenite phase region to below the eutectoid temperature.

Hypereutectoid Alloys

Analogous transformations and microstructures result for **hypereutectoid alloys,** those containing between 0.76 and 2.14 wt% C, which are cooled from temperatures within the γ phase field. Consider an alloy of composition C_1 in Figure 7.32 that, upon cooling, moves down the line zz'. At point g only the γ phase will be present with a composition of C_1; the microstructure will appear as shown, having only γ grains. Upon cooling into the $\gamma + Fe_3C$ phase field—say, to point h—the cementite phase will begin to form along the initial γ grain boundaries, similar to the α phase in Figure 7.29, point d. This cementite is called **proeutectoid cementite**—that which forms before the eutectoid reaction. Of course, the cementite composition remains constant (6.70 wt% C) as the temperature changes. However, the composition of the austenite phase will move along line PO toward the eutectoid. As the temperature is lowered through the eutectoid to point i, all remaining austenite of eutectoid composition is converted into pearlite; thus, the resulting microstructure consists of pearlite and proeutectoid cementite as microconstituents (Figure 7.32). In the photomicrograph of a 1.4 wt% C steel (Figure 7.33), note that the proeutectoid cementite appears light. Since it has much the same appearance as proeutectoid ferrite (Figure 7.30), there is some difficulty in distinguishing between hypoeutectoid and hypereutectoid steels on the basis of microstructure.

Relative amounts of both pearlite and proeutectoid Fe_3C microconstituents may be computed for hypereutectoid steel alloys in a manner analogous to that for hypoeutectoid materials; the appropriate tie line extends between 0.76 and 6.70

Figure 7.33 Photomicrograph of a 1.4 wt% C steel having a microstructure consisting of a white proeutectoid cementite network surrounding the pearlite colonies. 1000×. (Copyright 1971 by United States Steel Corporation.)

wt% C. Thus, for an alloy having composition C_1' in Figure 7.31, fractions of pearlite W_p and proeutectoid cementite $W_{Fe_3C'}$ are determined from the following lever rule expressions:

$$W_p = \frac{X}{V + X} = \frac{6.70 - C_1'}{6.70 - 0.76} = \frac{6.70 - C_1'}{5.94} \tag{7.22}$$

and

$$W_{Fe_3C'} = \frac{V}{V + X} = \frac{C_1' - 0.76}{6.70 - 0.76} = \frac{C_1' - 0.76}{5.94} \tag{7.23}$$

Concept Check 7.8

Briefly explain why a proeutectoid phase (ferrite or cementite) forms along austenite grain boundaries. *Hint*: Consult Section 5.7.

[*The answer may be found in enclosed CD.*]

EXAMPLE PROBLEM 7.4

Determination of Relative Amounts of Ferrite, Cementite, and Pearlite Microconstituents

For a 79.65 wt% Fe–0.35 wt% C alloy at a temperature just below the eutectoid, determine the following:

(a) The fractions of total ferrite and cementite phases

(b) The fractions of the proeutectoid ferrite and pearlite

(c) The fraction of eutectoid ferrite

Solution

(a) This part of the problem is solved by application of the lever rule expressions employing a tie line that extends all the way across the $\alpha + Fe_3C$ phase field. Thus, C_0' is 0.35 wt% C, and

$$W_\alpha = \frac{6.70 - 0.35}{6.70 - 0.022} = 0.95$$

and

$$W_{Fe_3C} = \frac{0.35 - 0.022}{6.70 - 0.022} = 0.05$$

(b) The fractions of proeutectoid ferrite and pearlite are determined by using the lever rule and a tie line that extends only to the eutectoid composition (i.e., Equations 7.20 and 7.21). Or

$$W_p = \frac{0.35 - 0.022}{0.76 - 0.022} = 0.44$$

and

$$W_{\alpha'} = \frac{0.76 - 0.35}{0.76 - 0.022} = 0.56$$

(c) All ferrite is either as proeutectoid or eutectoid (in the pearlite). Therefore, the sum of these two ferrite fractions will equal the fraction of total ferrite; that is,

$$W_{\alpha'} + W_{\alpha e} = W_\alpha$$

where $W_{\alpha e}$ denotes the fraction of the total alloy that is eutectoid ferrite. Values for W_α and $W_{\alpha'}$ were determined in parts (a) and (b) as 0.95 and 0.56, respectively. Therefore,

$$W_{\alpha e} = W_\alpha - W_{\alpha'} = 0.95 - 0.56 = 0.39$$

Nonequilibrium Cooling

In this discussion on the microstructural development of iron–carbon alloys it has been assumed that, upon cooling, conditions of metastable equilibrium[2] have been continuously maintained; that is, sufficient time has been allowed at each new temperature for any necessary adjustment in phase compositions and relative amounts as predicted from the Fe–Fe_3C phase diagram. In most situations these cooling rates are impractically slow and really unnecessary; in fact, on many occasions nonequilibrium conditions are desirable. Two nonequilibrium effects of practical importance are (1) the occurrence of phase changes or transformations at temperatures other than those predicted by phase boundary lines on the phase diagram, and (2) the

[2] The term "metastable equilibrium" is used in this discussion inasmuch as Fe_3C is only a metastable compound.

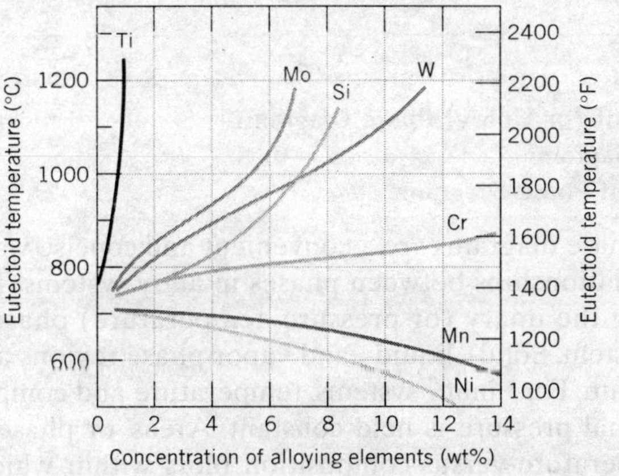

Figure 7.34 The dependence of eutectoid temperature on alloy concentration for several alloying elements in steel. (From Edgar C. Bain, *Functions of the Alloying Elements in Steel,* American Society for Metals, 1939, p. 127.)

existence at room temperature of nonequilibrium phases that do not appear on the phase diagram. Both are discussed in the next chapter.

7.20 THE INFLUENCE OF OTHER ALLOYING ELEMENTS

Additions of other alloying elements (Cr, Ni, Ti, etc.) bring about rather dramatic changes in the binary iron–iron carbide phase diagram, Figure 7.24. The extent of these alterations of the positions of phase boundaries and the shapes of the phase fields depends on the particular alloying element and its concentration. One of the important changes is the shift in position of the eutectoid with respect to temperature and to carbon concentration. These effects are illustrated in Figures 7.34 and 7.35, which plot the eutectoid temperature and eutectoid composition (in wt% C) as a function of concentration for several other alloying elements. Thus, other alloy additions alter not only the temperature of the eutectoid reaction but also the relative fractions of pearlite and the proeutectoid phase that form. Steels are normally alloyed for other reasons, however—usually either to improve their corrosion resistance or to render them amenable to heat treatment (see Section 23.5).

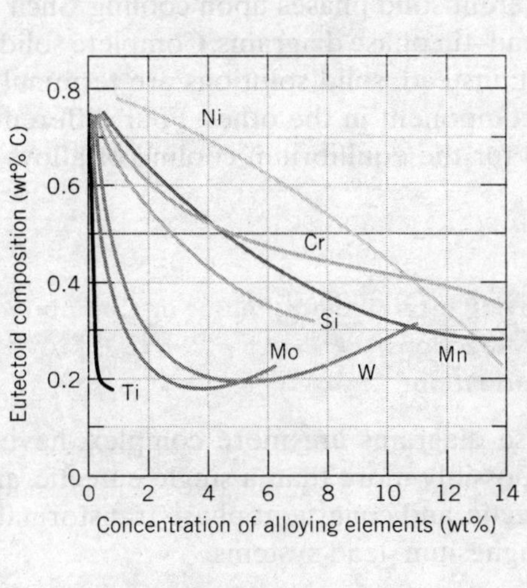

Figure 7.35 The dependence of eutectoid composition (wt% C) on alloy concentration for several alloying elements in steel. (From Edgar C. Bain, *Functions of the Alloying Elements in Steel,* American Society for Metals, 1939, p. 127.)

SUMMARY

Phase Equilibria
One-Component (or Unary) Phase Diagrams
Binary Phase Diagrams
Interpretation of Phase Diagrams

Equilibrium phase diagrams are a convenient and concise way of representing the most stable relationships between phases in alloy systems. This discussion began by considering the unary (or pressure–temperature) phase diagram for a one-component system. Solid-, liquid-, and vapor-phase regions are found on this type of phase diagram. For binary systems, temperature and composition are variables, whereas external pressure is held constant. Areas, or phase regions, are defined on these temperature-versus-composition plots within which either one or two phases exist. For an alloy of specified composition and at a known temperature, the phases present, their compositions, and relative amounts under equilibrium conditions may be determined. Within two-phase regions, tie lines and the lever rule must be used for phase composition and mass fraction computations, respectively.

Binary Isomorphous Systems
Development of Microstructure in Isomorphous Alloys
Mechanical Properties of Isomorphous Alloys

Several different kinds of phase diagram were discussed for metallic systems. Isomorphous diagrams are those for which there is complete solubility in the solid phase; the copper–nickel system displays this behavior. Also discussed for alloys belonging to isomorphous systems were the development of microstructure for both cases of equilibrium and nonequilibrium cooling, and the dependence of mechanical characteristics on composition.

Binary Eutectic Systems
Development of Microstructure in Eutectic Alloys

In a eutectic reaction, as found in some alloy systems, a liquid phase transforms isothermally to two different solid phases upon cooling. Such a reaction is noted on the copper–silver and lead–tin phase diagrams. Complete solid solubility for all compositions does not exist; instead, solid solutions are terminal—there is only a limited solubility of each component in the other. Four different kinds of microstructures that may develop for the equilibrium cooling of alloys belonging to eutectic systems were discussed.

Equilibrium Diagrams Having Intermediate Phases or Compounds
Eutectoid and Peritectic Reactions
Congruent Phase Transformations

Other equilibrium phase diagrams are more complex, having intermediate compounds and/or phases, possibly more than a single eutectic, and other reactions including eutectoid, peritectic, and congruent phase transformations. These are found for copper–zinc and magnesium–lead systems.

The Gibbs Phase Rule

The Gibbs phase rule was introduced; it is a simple equation that relates the number of phases present in a system at equilibrium with the number of degrees of freedom, the number of components, and the number of noncompositional variables.

The Iron–Iron Carbide (Fe–Fe_3C) Phase Diagram
Development of Microstructure in Iron–Carbon Alloys

Considerable attention was given to the iron–carbon system, and specifically, the iron–iron carbide phase diagram, which technologically is one of the most important. The development of microstructure in many iron–carbon alloys and steels depends on the eutectoid reaction in which the FCC austenite phase of composition 0.76 wt% C transforms isothermally to the BCC α ferrite phase (0.022 wt% C) and the intermetallic compound, cementite (Fe_3C). The microstructural product of an iron–carbon alloy of eutectoid composition is pearlite, a microconstituent consisting of alternating layers of ferrite and cementite. The microstructures of alloys having carbon contents less than the eutectoid (hypoeutectoid) are comprised of a proeutectoid ferrite phase in addition to pearlite. On the other hand, pearlite and proeutectoid cementite constitute the microconstituents for hypereutectoid alloys—those with carbon contents in excess of the eutectoid composition.

REFERENCES

ASM Handbook, Vol. 3, *Alloy Phase Diagrams,* ASM International, Materials Park, OH, 1992.

ASM Handbook, Vol. 7, *Metallography and Microstructures,* ASM International, Materials Park, OH, 2004.

Hansen, M. and K. Anderko, *Constitution of Binary Alloys,* 2nd edition, McGraw-Hill, New York, 1958. *First Supplement* (R. P. Elliott), 1965. *Second Supplement* (F. A. Shunk), 1969. Reprinted by Genium Publishing Corp., Schenectady, NY.

Massalski, T. B., H. Okamoto, P. R. Subramanian, and L. Kacprzak (Editors), *Binary Phase Diagrams,* 2nd edition, ASM International, Materials Park, OH, 1990. Three volumes. Also on CD with updates.

Okamoto, H., *Desk Handbook: Phase Diagrams for Binary Alloys,* ASM International, Materials Park, OH, 2000.

Petzow, G., *Ternary Alloys, A Comprehensive Compendium of Evaluated Constitutional Data and Phase Diagrams,* Wiley, New York, 1988–1995. Fifteen volumes.

Villars, P., A. Prince, and H. Okamoto (Editors), *Handbook of Ternary Alloy Phase Diagrams,* ASM International, Materials Park, OH, 1995. Ten volumes. Also on CD.

QUESTIONS AND PROBLEMS

Solubility Limit

7.1 Consider the sugar–water phase diagram of Figure 7.1.

(a) How much sugar will dissolve in 1000 g of water at 80°C (176°F)?

(b) If the saturated liquid solution in part (a) is cooled to 20°C (68°F), some of the sugar will precipitate out as a solid. What will be the composition of the saturated liquid solution (in wt% sugar) at 20°C?

(c) How much of the solid sugar will come out of solution upon cooling to 20°C?

7.2 At 100°C, what is the maximum solubility (a) of Pb in Sn? (b) of Sn in Pb?

Microstructure

7.3 Cite three variables that determine the microstructure of an alloy.

Phase Equilibria

7.4 What thermodynamic condition must be met for a state of equilibrium to exist?

One-Component (or Unary) Phase Diagrams

7.5 Consider a specimen of ice that is at −25°C and 10 atm pressure. Using Figure 7.2, the pressure–temperature phase diagram for H_2O, determine the pressure to which the specimen must be raised or lowered to cause it (a) to melt, and (b) to sublime.

7.6 At a pressure of 0.1 atm, determine (a) the melting temperature for ice, and (b) the boiling temperature for water.

Binary Isomorphous Systems

7.7 Given here are the solidus and liquidus temperatures for the copper–gold system. Construct the phase diagram for this system and label each region.

Composition (wt% Au)	*Solidus Temperature (°C)*	*Liquidus Temperature (°C)*
0	1085	1085
20	1019	1042
40	972	996
60	934	946
80	911	911
90	928	942
95	974	984
100	1064	1064

Interpretation of Phase Diagrams (Binary Isomorphous Systems) (Binary Eutectic Systems) (Equilibrium Diagrams Having Intermediate Phases or Compounds)

7.8 Cite the phases that are present and the phase compositions for the following alloys:

(a) 15 wt% Sn–85 wt% Pb at 100°C (212°F)

(b) 25 wt% Pb–75 wt% Mg at 425°C (800°F)

(c) 85 wt% Ag–15 wt% Cu at 800°C (1470°F)

(d) 55 wt% Zn–45 wt% Cu at 600°C (1110°F)

(e) 1.25 kg Sn and 14 kg Pb at 200°C (390°F)

(f) 7.6 lb_m Cu and 144.4 lb_m Zn at 600°C (1110°F)

(g) 21.7 mol Mg and 35.4 mol Pb at 350°C (660°F)

(h) 4.2 mol Cu and 1.1 mol Ag at 900°C (1650°F)

7.9 Is it possible to have a copper–silver alloy that, at equilibrium, consists of a β phase of composition 72 wt% Ag–8 wt% Cu, and also a liquid phase of composition 76 wt% Ag–24 wt% Cu? If so, what will be the approximate temperature of the alloy? If this is not possible, explain why.

7.10 Is it possible to have a copper–silver alloy that, at equilibrium, consists of an α phase of composition 4 wt% Ag–96 wt% Cu, and also a β phase of composition 75 wt% Ag–5 wt% Cu? If so, what will be the approximate temperature of the alloy? If this is not possible, explain why.

7.11 A lead–tin alloy of composition 30 wt% Sn–70 wt% Pb is slowly heated from a temperature of 150°C (300°F).

(a) At what temperature does the first liquid phase form?

(b) What is the composition of this liquid phase?

(c) At what temperature does complete melting of the alloy occur?

(d) What is the composition of the last solid remaining prior to complete melting?

7.12 A 50 wt% Ni–50 wt% Cu alloy is slowly cooled from 1400°C (2550°F) to 1200°C (2190°F).

(a) At what temperature does the first solid phase form?

(b) What is the composition of this solid phase?

(c) At what temperature does the liquid solidify?

(d) What is the composition of this last remaining liquid phase?

7.13 For an alloy of composition 52 wt% Zn–48 wt% Cu, cite the phases present and their mass fractions at the following temperatures: 1000°C, 800°C, 500°C, and 300°C.

7.14 Determine the relative amounts (in terms of mass fractions) of the phases for the alloys and temperatures given in Problem 7.8.

7.15 A 2.0-kg specimen of an 85 wt% Pb–15 wt% Sn alloy is heated to 200°C (390°F); at this temperature it is entirely an α-phase solid solution (Figure 7.8). The alloy is to be melted to the extent that 50% of the specimen is liquid, the remainder being the α phase. This may be accomplished by heating the alloy or changing its composition while holding the temperature constant.

(a) To what temperature must the specimen be heated?

(b) How much tin must be added to the 2.0-kg specimen at 200°C to achieve this state?

7.16 A magnesium–lead alloy of mass 7.5 kg consists of a solid α phase that has a composition just slightly below the solubility limit at 300°C (570°F).

(a) What mass of lead is in the alloy?

(b) If the alloy is heated to 400°C (750°F), how much more lead may be dissolved in the α phase without exceeding the solubility limit of this phase?

7.17 A 65 wt% Ni–35 wt% Cu alloy is heated to a temperature within the α + liquid-phase region. If the composition of the α phase is 70 wt% Ni, determine:

(a) The temperature of the alloy

(b) The composition of the liquid phase

(c) The mass fractions of both phases

7.18 A 40 wt% Pb–60 wt% Mg alloy is heated to a temperature within the α + liquid-phase region. If the mass fraction of each phase is 0.5, then estimate:

(a) The temperature of the alloy

(b) The compositions of the two phases

7.19 For alloys of two hypothetical metals A and B, there exist an α, A-rich phase and a β, B-rich phase. From the mass fractions of both phases for two different alloys provided in the table below, (which are at the same temperature), determine the composition of the phase boundary (or solubility limit) for both α and β phases at this temperature.

Alloy Composition	*Fraction α Phase*	*Fraction β Phase*
70 wt% A–30 wt% B	0.78	0.22
35 wt% A–65 wt% B	0.36	0.64

7.20 A hypothetical A–B alloy of composition 40 wt% B–60 wt% A at some temperature is found to consist of mass fractions of 0.66 and 0.34 for the α and β phases, respectively. If the composition of the α phase is 13 wt% B–87 wt% A, what is the composition of the β phase?

7.21 Is it possible to have a copper–silver alloy of composition 20 wt% Ag–80 wt% Cu that, at equilibrium, consists of α and liquid phases having mass fractions $W_\alpha = 0.80$ and $W_L = 0.20$? If so, what will be the approximate temperature of the alloy? If such an alloy is not possible, explain why.

7.22 For 5.7 kg of a magnesium–lead alloy of composition 50 wt% Pb–50 wt% Mg, is it possible, at equilibrium, to have α and Mg_2Pb phases with respective masses of 5.13 and 0.57 kg? If so, what will be the approximate temperature of the alloy? If such an alloy is not possible, then explain why.

7.23 Derive Equations 7.6a and 7.7a, which may be used to convert mass fraction to volume fraction, and vice versa.

7.24 Determine the relative amounts (in terms of volume fractions) of the phases for the alloys and temperatures given in Problems 7.8a, b, and d. Given here are the approximate densities of the various metals at the alloy temperatures:

Metal	*Temperature (°C)*	*Density (g/cm³)*
Cu	600	8.68
Mg	425	1.68
Pb	100	11.27
Pb	425	10.96
Sn	100	7.29
Zn	600	6.67

Development of Microstructure in Isomorphous Alloys

7.25 **(a)** Briefly describe the phenomenon of coring and why it occurs.

(b) Cite one undesirable consequence of coring.

Mechanical Properties of Isomorphous Alloys

7.26 It is desirable to produce a copper–nickel alloy that has a minimum noncold-worked tensile strength of 380 MPa (55,000 psi) and a ductility of at least 45%EL. Is such an alloy possible? If so, what must be its composition? If this is not possible, then explain why.

Binary Eutectic Systems

7.27 A 60 wt% Pb–40 wt% Mg alloy is rapidly quenched to room temperature from an elevated temperature in such a way that the high-temperature microstructure is preserved. This microstructure is found to consist of the α phase and Mg_2Pb, having respective mass fractions of 0.42 and 0.58. Determine the approximate temperature from which the alloy was quenched.

Development of Microstructure in Eutectic Alloys

7.28 Briefly explain why, upon solidification, an alloy of eutectic composition forms a microstructure consisting of alternating layers of the two solid phases.

7.29 What is the difference between a phase and a microconstituent?

7.30 Is it possible to have a magnesium–lead alloy in which the mass fractions of primary α and total α are 0.60 and 0.85, respectively, at 460°C (860°F)? Why or why not?

7.31 For 2.8 kg of a lead–tin alloy, is it possible to have the masses of primary β and total β of 2.21 kg and 2.53 kg, respectively, at 180°C (355°F)? Why or why not?

7.32 For a lead–tin alloy of composition 80 wt% Sn–20 wt% Pb and at 180°C (355°F) do the following:

(a) Determine the mass fractions of α and β phases.

(b) Determine the mass fractions of primary β and eutectic microconstituents.

(c) Determine the mass fraction of eutectic β.

7.33 The microstructure of a copper–silver alloy at 775°C (1425°F) consists of primary α and eutectic structures. If the mass fractions of these two microconstituents are 0.73 and 0.27, respectively, determine the composition of the alloy.

7.34 Consider the hypothetical eutectic phase diagram for metals A and B, which is similar to that for the lead–tin system, Figure 7.8. Assume that: (1) α and β phases exist at the A and B extremities of the phase diagram, respectively; (2) the eutectic composition is 36 wt% A–64 wt% B; and (3) the composition of the α phase at the eutectic temperature is 88 wt% A–12 wt% B. Determine the composition of an alloy that will yield primary β and total β mass fractions of 0.367 and 0.768, respectively.

7.35 For a 64 wt% Zn–36 wt% Cu alloy, make schematic sketches of the microstructure that would be observed for conditions of very slow cooling at the following temperatures: 900°C (1650°F), 820°C (1510°F), 750°C (1380°F), and 600°C (1100°F). Label all phases and indicate their approximate compositions.

7.36 For a 76 wt% Pb–24 wt% Mg alloy, make schematic sketches of the microstructure that would be observed for conditions of very slow cooling at the following temperatures: 575°C (1070°F), 500°C (930°F), 450°C (840°F), and 300°C (570°F). Label all phases and indicate their approximate compositions.

7.37 For a 52 wt% Zn–48 wt% Cu alloy, make schematic sketches of the microstructure that would be observed for conditions of very slow cooling at the following temperatures: 950°C (1740°F), 860°C (1580°F), 800°C (1470°F), and 600°C (1100°F). Label all phases and indicate their approximate compositions.

7.38 On the basis of the photomicrograph (i.e., the relative amounts of the microconstituents) for the lead–tin alloy shown in Figure 7.17 and the Pb–Sn phase diagram (Figure 7.8), estimate the composition of the alloy, and then compare this estimate with the composition given in the figure legend of Figure 7.17. Make the following assumptions: (1) the area fraction of each phase and microconstituent in the photomicrograph is equal to its volume fraction; (2) the densities of the α and β phases as well as the eutectic structure are 11.2, 7.3, and 8.7 g/cm^3, respectively; and (3) this photomicrograph represents the equilibrium microstructure at 180°C (355°F).

7.39 The room-temperature tensile strengths of pure copper and pure silver are 209 MPa and 125 MPa, respectively.

(a) Make a schematic graph of the room-temperature tensile strength versus composition for all compositions between pure copper and pure silver. (*Hint:* you may want to consult Sections 7.10 and 7.11, as well as Equation 7.24 in Problem 7.64.)

(b) On this same graph schematically plot tensile strength versus composition at 600°C.

(c) Explain the shapes of these two curves, as well as any differences between them.

Equilibrium Diagrams Having Intermediate Phases or Compounds

7.40 Two intermetallic compounds, A_3B and AB_3, exist for elements A and B. If the compositions for A_3B and AB_3 are 71.0 wt% A–7.0 wt% B and 53.0 wt% A–47.0 wt% B, respectively, and element A is zirconium, identify element B.

Congruent Phase Transformations
Binary Eutectic Systems
Equilibrium Diagrams Having Intermediate Phases or Compounds
Eutectoid and Peritectic Reactions

7.41 What is the principal difference between congruent and incongruent phase transformations?

7.42 Figure 7.36 is the tin–gold phase diagram, for which only single-phase regions are labeled. Specify temperature–composition points at which all eutectics, eutectoids, peritectics, and congruent phase transformations occur. Also, for each, write the reaction upon cooling.

7.43 Figure 7.37 is a portion of the copper–aluminum phase diagram for which only single-phase regions are labeled. Specify temperature–composition points at which all eutectics, eutectoids, peritectics, and congruent phase transformations occur. Also, for each, write the reaction upon cooling.

7.44 Construct the hypothetical phase diagram for metals A and B between room temperature (20°C) and 700°C given the following information:

- The melting temperature of metal A is 480°C.
- The maximum solubility of B in A is 4 wt% B, which occurs at 420°C.
- The solubility of B in A at room temperature is 0 wt% B.
- One eutectic occurs at 420°C and 18 wt% B–82 wt% A.

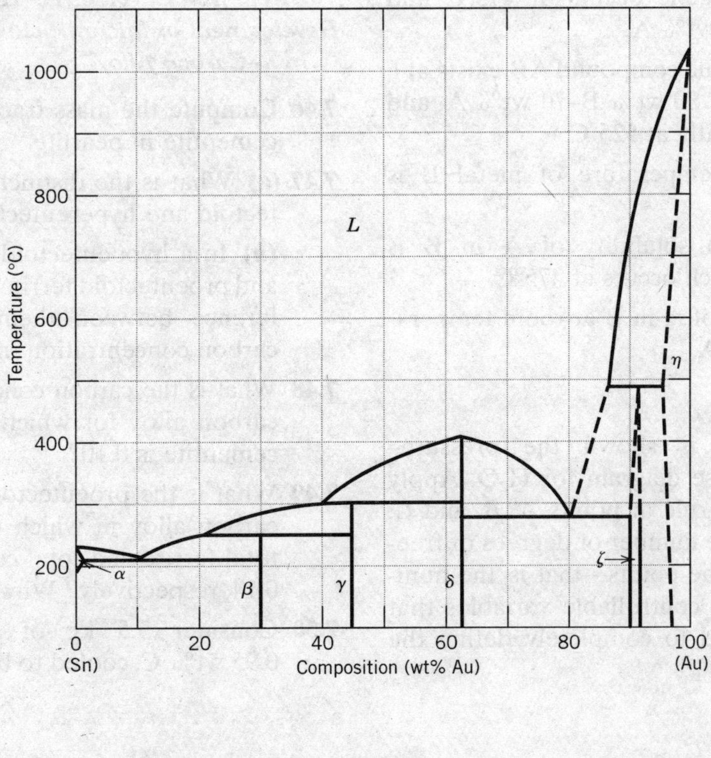

Figure 7.36 The tin–gold phase diagram. (Adapted with permission from *Metals Handbook,* 8th edition, Vol. 8, *Metallography, Structures and Phase Diagrams,* American Society for Metals, Metals Park, OH, 1973.)

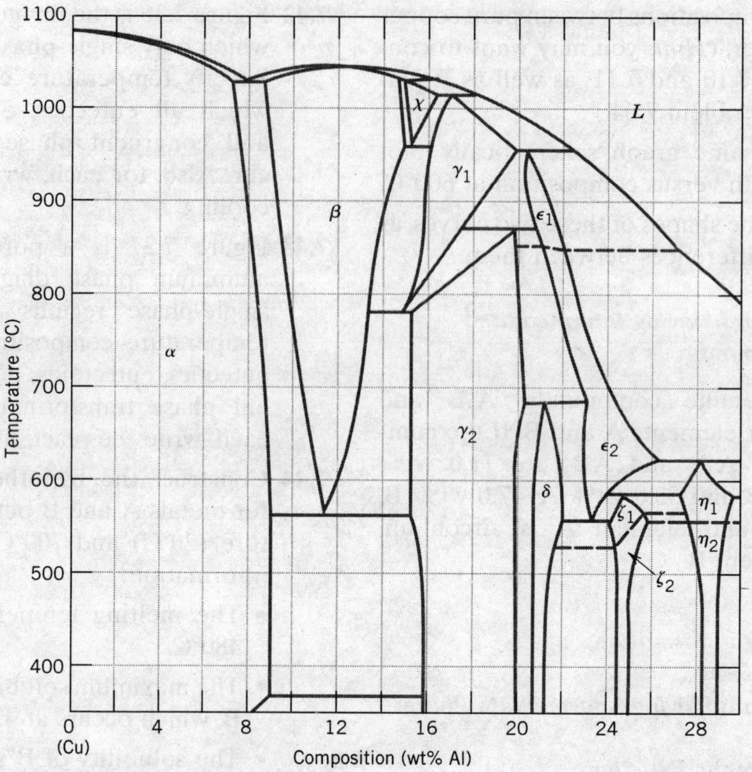

Figure 7.37 The copper–aluminum phase diagram. (Adapted with permission from *Metals Handbook,* 8th edition, Vol. 8, *Metallography Structures and Phase Diagrams,* American Society for Metals, Metals Park, OH, 1973.)

- A second eutectic occurs at 475°C and 42 wt% B–58 wt% A.
- The intermetallic compound AB exists at a composition of 30 wt% B–70 wt% A, and melts congruently at 525°C.
- The melting temperature of metal B is 600°C.
- The maximum solubility of A in B is 13 wt% A, which occurs at 475°C.
- The solubility of A in B at room temperature is 3 wt% A.

The Gibbs Phase Rule

7.45 In Figure 7.38 is shown the pressure–temperature phase diagram for H_2O. Apply the Gibbs phase rule at points *A*, *B*, and *C*; that is, specify the number of degrees of freedom at each of the points—that is, the number of externally controllable variables that need be specified to completely define the system.

The Iron–Iron Carbide (Fe–Fe_3C) Phase Diagram Development of Microstructure in Iron–Carbon Alloys

7.46 Compute the mass fractions of α ferrite and cementite in pearlite.

7.47 **(a)** What is the distinction between hypoeutectoid and hypereutectoid steels?

(b) In a hypoeutectoid steel, both eutectoid and proeutectoid ferrite exist. Explain the difference between them. What will be the carbon concentration in each?

7.48 What is the carbon concentration of an iron–carbon alloy for which the fraction of total cementite is 0.10?

7.49 What is the proeutectoid phase for an iron–carbon alloy in which the mass fractions of total ferrite and total cementite are 0.86 and 0.14, respectively? Why?

7.50 Consider 3.5 kg of austenite containing 0.95 wt% C, cooled to below 727°C (1341°F).

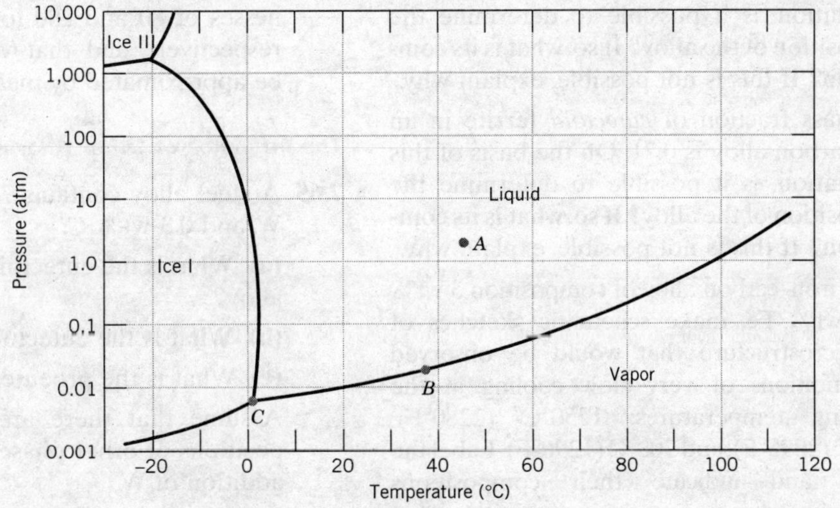

Figure 7.38 Logarithm pressure-versus-temperature phase diagram for H_2O.

(a) What is the proeutectoid phase?

(b) How many kilograms each of total ferrite and cementite form?

(c) How many kilograms each of pearlite and the proeutectoid phase form?

(d) Schematically sketch and label the resulting microstructure.

7.51 Consider 6.0 kg of austenite containing 0.45 wt% C, cooled to below 727°C (1341°F).

(a) What is the proeutectoid phase?

(b) How many kilograms each of total ferrite and cementite form?

(c) How many kilograms each of pearlite and the proeutectoid phase form?

(d) Schematically sketch and label the resulting microstructure.

7.52 Compute the mass fractions of proeutectoid ferrite and pearlite that form in an iron–carbon alloy containing 0.35 wt% C.

7.53 The microstructure of an iron–carbon alloy consists of proeutectoid ferrite and pearlite; the mass fractions of these two microconstituents are 0.174 and 0.826, respectively. Determine the concentration of carbon in this alloy.

7.54 The mass fractions of total ferrite and total cementite in an iron–carbon alloy are 0.91 and 0.09, respectively. Is this a hypoeutectoid or hypereutectoid alloy? Why?

7.55 The microstructure of an iron–carbon alloy consists of proeutectoid cementite and pearlite; the mass fractions of these microconstituents are 0.11 and 0.89, respectively. Determine the concentration of carbon in this alloy.

7.56 Consider 1.5 kg of a 79.7 wt% Fe–0.3 wt% C alloy that is cooled to a temperature just below the eutectoid.

(a) How many kilograms of proeutectoid ferrite form?

(b) How many kilograms of eutectoid ferrite form?

(c) How many kilograms of cementite form?

7.57 Compute the maximum mass fraction of proeutectoid cementite possible for a hypereutectoid iron–carbon alloy.

7.58 Is it possible to have an iron–carbon alloy for which the mass fractions of total cementite and proeutectoid ferrite are 0.057 and 0.36, respectively? Why or why not?

7.59 Is it possible to have an iron–carbon alloy for which the mass fractions of total ferrite and pearlite are 0.860 and 0.969, respectively? Why or why not?

7.60 Compute the mass fraction of eutectoid cementite in an iron–carbon alloy that contains 1.00 wt% C.

7.61 The mass fraction of *eutectoid* cementite in an iron–carbon alloy is 0.109. On the basis of this information, is it possible to determine the composition of the alloy? If so, what is its composition? If this is not possible, explain why.

7.62 The mass fraction of *eutectoid* ferrite in an iron–carbon alloy is 0.71. On the basis of this information, is it possible to determine the composition of the alloy? If so, what is its composition? If this is not possible, explain why.

7.63 For an iron–carbon alloy of composition 3 wt% C–97 wt% Fe, make schematic sketches of the microstructure that would be observed for conditions of very slow cooling at the following temperatures: 1250°C (2280°F), 1145°C (2095°F), and 700°C (1290°F). Label the phases and indicate their compositions (approximate).

7.64 Often, the properties of multiphase alloys may be approximated by the relationship

$$E\,(\text{alloy}) = E_\alpha V_\alpha + E_\beta V_\beta \qquad (7.24)$$

where E represents a specific property (modulus of elasticity, hardness, etc.), and V is the volume fraction. The subscripts α and β denote the existing phases or microconstituents. Employ the relationship above to determine the approximate Brinell hardness of a 79.75 wt% Fe–0.25 wt% C alloy. Assume Brinell hardnesses of 80 and 280 for ferrite and pearlite, respectively, and that volume fractions may be approximated by mass fractions.

The Influence of Other Alloying Elements

7.65 A steel alloy contains 75.7 wt% Fe, 4.0 wt% W, and 0.3 wt% C.

(a) What is the eutectoid temperature of this alloy?

(b) What is the eutectoid composition?

(c) What is the proeutectoid phase?

Assume that there are no changes in the positions of other phase boundaries with the addition of W.

7.66 A steel alloy is known to contain 73.65 wt% Fe, 6.0 wt% Mn, and 0.35 wt% C.

(a) What is the approximate eutectoid temperature of this alloy?

(b) What is the proeutectoid phase when this alloy is cooled to a temperature just below the eutectoid?

(c) Compute the relative amounts of the proeutectoid phase and pearlite. Assume that there are no alterations in the positions of other phase boundaries with the addition of Mn.

Chapter 8 Phase Transformations

A photomicrograph of a pearlitic steel that has partially transformed to spheroidite. 2000×. (Courtesy of United States Steel Corporation.)

Learning Objectives

After careful study of this chapter you should be able to do the following:

1. Make a schematic fraction transformation-versus-logarithm of time plot for a typical solid–solid transformation; cite the equation that describes this behavior.
2. Briefly describe the microstructure for each of the following microconstituents that are found in steel alloys: fine pearlite, coarse pearlite, spheroidite, bainite, martensite, and tempered martensite.
3. Cite the general mechanical characteristics for each of the following microconstituents: fine pearlite, coarse pearlite, spheroidite, bainite, martensite, and tempered martensite. Now, in terms of microstructure (or crystal structure), briefly explain these behaviors.
4. Given the isothermal transformation (or continuous cooling transformation) diagram for some iron–carbon alloy, design a heat treatment that will produce a specified microstructure.

8.1 INTRODUCTION

One reason for the versatility of metallic materials lies in the wide range of mechanical properties they possess, which are accessible to management by various means. Three strengthening mechanisms will be discussed in Chapter 10—namely, grain size refinement, solid-solution strengthening, and strain hardening. Additional techniques are available wherein the mechanical properties are reliant on the characteristics of the microstructure.

The development of microstructure in both single- and two-phase alloys ordinarily involves some type of phase transformation—an alteration in the number and/or character of the phases. The first portion of this chapter is devoted to a brief discussion of some of the basic principles relating to transformations involving solid phases. Inasmuch as most phase transformations do not occur instantaneously, consideration is given to the dependence of reaction progress on time, or the **transformation rate.** This is followed by a discussion of the development of two-phase microstructures for iron–carbon alloys. Modified phase diagrams are introduced that permit determination of the microstructure that results from a specific heat treatment. Finally, other microconstituents in addition to pearlite are presented, and, for each, the mechanical properties are discussed.

Phase Transformations

8.2 BASIC CONCEPTS

A variety of **phase transformations** are important in the processing of materials, and usually they involve some alteration of the microstructure. For purposes of this discussion, these transformations are divided into three classifications. In one group are simple diffusion-dependent transformations in which there is no change in either the number or composition of the phases present. These include solidification of a pure metal, allotropic transformations, and, recrystallization and grain growth (see Sections 10.12 and 10.13).

In another type of diffusion-dependent transformation, there is some alteration in phase compositions and often in the number of phases present; the final microstructure ordinarily consists of two phases. The eutectoid reaction, described by Equation 7.19, is of this type; it receives further attention in Section 8.5.

The third kind of transformation is diffusionless, wherein a metastable phase is produced. As discussed in Section 8.5, a martensitic transformation, which may be induced in some steel alloys, falls into this category.

8.3 THE KINETICS OF PHASE TRANSFORMATIONS

With phase transformations, normally at least one new phase is formed that has different physical/chemical characteristics and/or a different structure than the parent phase. Furthermore, most phase transformations do not occur instantaneously. Rather, they begin by the formation of numerous small particles of the new phase(s), which increase in size until the transformation has reached completion. The progress of a phase transformation may be broken down into two distinct stages: **nucleation** and **growth.** Nucleation involves the appearance of very small particles, or nuclei of the new phase (often consisting of only a few hundred atoms), which are capable of growing. During the growth stage these nuclei increase in size, which results in the disappearance of some (or all) of the parent phase. The transformation reaches completion if the growth of these new phase particles is allowed to proceed until the equilibrium fraction is attained. We now discuss the mechanics of these two processes, and how they relate to solid-state transformations.

Nucleation

There are two types of nucleation: *homogeneous* and *heterogeneous*. The distinction between them is made according to the site at which nucleating events occur. For the homogeneous type, nuclei of the new phase form uniformly throughout the parent phase, whereas for the heterogeneous type, nuclei form preferentially at structural inhomogeneities, such as container surfaces, insoluble impurities, grain boundaries, dislocations, and so on. We begin by discussing homogeneous nucleation because its description and theory are simpler to treat. These principles are then extended to a discussion of the heterogeneous type.

Homogeneous Nucleation

A discussion of the theory of nucleation involves a thermodynamic parameter called **free energy** (or *Gibbs free energy*), G. In brief, free energy is a function of other thermodynamic parameters, of which one is the internal energy of the system (i.e., the *enthalpy, H*), and another is a measurement of the randomness or disorder of the atoms or molecules (i.e., the *entropy, S*). It is not our purpose here to provide a detailed discussion of the principles of thermodynamics as they apply to materials systems. However, relative to phase transformations, an important thermodynamic parameter is the change in free energy ΔG; a transformation will occur spontaneously only when ΔG has a negative value.

For the sake of simplicity, let us first consider the solidification of a pure material, assuming that nuclei of the solid phase form in the interior of the liquid as atoms cluster together so as to form a packing arrangement similar to that found in the solid phase. Furthermore, it will be assumed that each nucleus is spherical in geometry and has a radius r. This situation is represented schematically in Figure 8.1.

There are two contributions to the total free energy change that accompany a solidification transformation. The first is the free energy difference between the solid and liquid phases, or the volume free energy, ΔG_v. Its value will be negative if the temperature is below the equilibrium solidification temperature, and the magnitude of its contribution is the product of ΔG_v and the volume of the spherical nucleus (i.e., $\frac{4}{3}\pi r^3$). The second energy contribution results from the formation of the

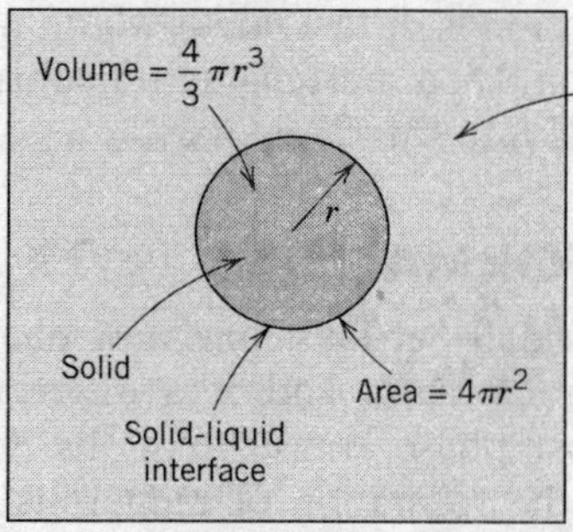

Figure 8.1 Schematic diagram showing the nucleation of a spherical solid particle in a liquid.

solid–liquid phase boundary during the solidification transformation. Associated with this boundary is a surface free energy, γ, which is positive; furthermore, the magnitude of this contribution is the product of γ and the surface area of the nucleus (i.e., $4\pi r^2$). Finally, the total free energy change is equal to the sum of these two contributions—that is,

$$\Delta G = \tfrac{4}{3}\pi r^3 \Delta G_v + 4\pi r^2 \gamma \tag{8.1}$$

These volume, surface, and total free energy contributions are plotted schematically as a function of nucleus radius in Figures 8.2*a* and 8.2*b*. Here (Figure 8.2*a*) it will be noted that for the curve corresponding to the first term on the right-hand side of Equation 8.1, the free energy (which is negative) decreases with the third power of r. Furthermore, for the curve resulting from the second term in Equation 8.1, energy values are positive and increase with the square of the radius. Consequently, the curve associated with the sum of both terms (Figure 8.2*b*) first increases, passes through a maximum, and finally decreases. In a physical sense, this means that as a solid particle begins to form as atoms in the liquid cluster together, its free energy first increases. If this cluster reaches a size corresponding to the critical radius r^*, then growth will continue with the accompaniment of a decrease

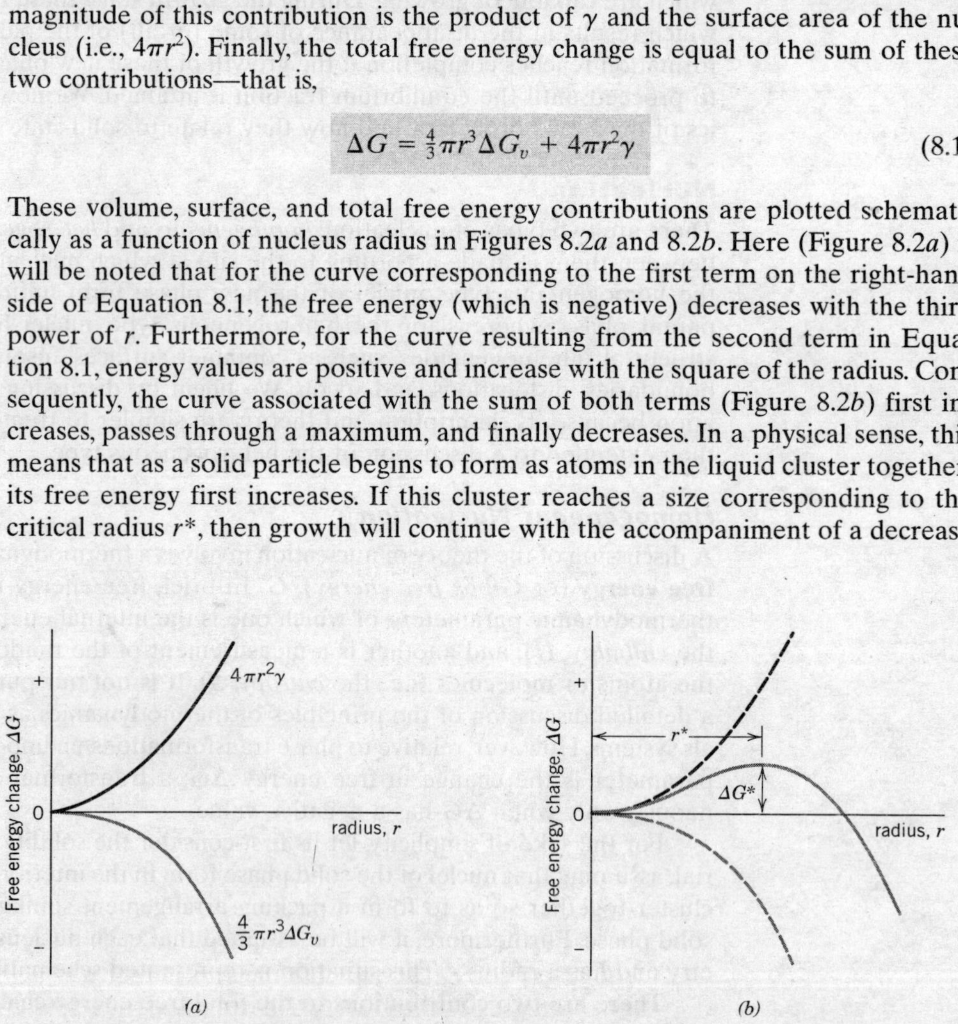

Figure 8.2 (*a*) Schematic curves for volume free energy and surface free energy contributions to the total free energy change attending the formation of a spherical embryo/nucleus during solidification. (*b*) Schematic plot of free energy versus embryo/nucleus radius, on which is shown the critical free energy change (ΔG^*) and the critical nucleus radius (r^*).

in free energy. On the other hand, a cluster of radius less than the critical will shrink and redissolve. This subcritical particle is an *embryo,* whereas the particle of radius greater than r^* is termed a *nucleus*. A critical free energy, ΔG^*, occurs at the critical radius and, consequently, at the maximum of the curve in Figure 8.2*b*. This ΔG^* corresponds to an *activation free energy,* which is the free energy required for the formation of a stable nucleus. Equivalently, it may be considered an energy barrier to the nucleation process.

Since r^* and ΔG^* appear at the maximum on the free energy-versus-radius curve of Figure 8.2*b*, derivation of expressions for these two parameters is a simple matter. For r^*, we differentiate the ΔG equation (Equation 8.1) with respect to r, set the resulting expression equal to zero, and then solve for r ($= r^*$). That is,

$$\frac{d(\Delta G)}{dr} = \tfrac{4}{3}\pi \Delta G_v (3r^2) + 4\pi\gamma(2r) = 0 \tag{8.2}$$

which leads to the result

$$r^* = -\frac{2\gamma}{\Delta G_v} \tag{8.3}$$

Now, substitution of this expression for r^* into Equation 8.1 yields the following expression for ΔG^*:

$$\Delta G^* = \frac{16\pi\gamma^3}{3(\Delta G_v)^2} \tag{8.4}$$

This volume free energy change ΔG_v is the driving force for the solidification transformation, and its magnitude is a function of temperature. At the equilibrium solidification temperature T_m, the value of ΔG_v is zero, and with diminishing temperature its value becomes increasingly more negative.

It can be shown that ΔG_v is a function of temperature as

$$\Delta G_v = \frac{\Delta H_f (T_m - T)}{T_m} \tag{8.5}$$

where ΔH_f is the latent heat of fusion (i.e., the heat given up during solidification), and T_m and the temperature T are in Kelvin. Substitution of this expression for ΔG_v into Equations 8.3 and 8.4 yields

$$r^* = \left(-\frac{2\gamma T_m}{\Delta H_f}\right)\left(\frac{1}{T_m - T}\right) \tag{8.6}$$

and

$$\Delta G^* = \left(\frac{16\pi\gamma^3 T_m^2}{3\Delta H_f^2}\right)\frac{1}{(T_m - T)^2} \tag{8.7}$$

Thus, from these two equations, both the critical radius r^* and the activation free energy ΔG^* decrease as temperature T decreases. (The γ and ΔH_f parameters in these expressions are relatively insensitive to temperature changes.) Figure 8.3, a schematic ΔG-versus-r plot that shows curves for two different temperatures, illustrates these relationships. Physically, this means that with a lowering of temperature at temperatures below the equilibrium solidification temperature (T_m), nucleation occurs more

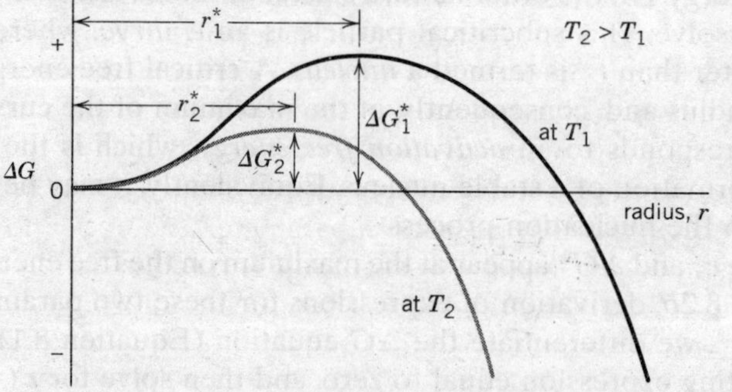

Figure 8.3 Schematic free-energy-versus-embryo/nucleus-radius curves for two different temperatures. The critical free energy change (ΔG^*) and critical nucleus radius (r^*) are indicated for each temperature.

readily. Furthermore, the number of stable nuclei n^* (having radii greater than r^*) is a function of temperature as

$$n^* = K_1 \exp\left(-\frac{\Delta G^*}{kT}\right) \tag{8.8}$$

where the constant K_1 is related to the total number of nuclei of the solid phase. For the exponential term of this expression, changes in temperature have a greater effect on the magnitude of the ΔG^* term in the numerator than the T term in the denominator. Consequently, as the temperature is lowered below T_m the exponential term in Equation 8.8 also decreases such that the magnitude of n^* increases. This temperature dependence (n^* versus T) is represented in the schematic plot of Figure 8.4*a*.

There is another important temperature-dependent step that is involved in and also influences nucleation: the clustering of atoms by short-range diffusion during the formation of nuclei. The influence of temperature on the rate of diffusion (i.e., magnitude of the diffusion coefficient, D) is given in Equation 6.8. Furthermore, this diffusion effect is related to the frequency at which atoms from the liquid attach themselves to the solid nucleus, ν_d. Or, the dependence of ν_d on temperature is the same as for the diffusion coefficient—namely,

$$\nu_d = K_2 \exp\left(-\frac{Q_d}{kT}\right) \tag{8.9}$$

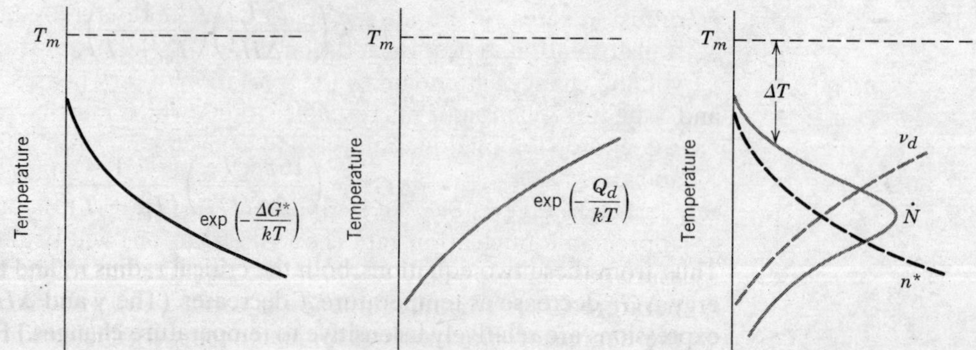

Figure 8.4 For solidification, schematic plots of (*a*) number of stable nuclei versus temperature, (*b*) frequency of atomic attachment versus temperature, and (*c*) nucleation rate versus temperature (also shown are curves for parts *a* and *b*).

where Q_d is a temperature-independent parameter—the activation energy for diffusion—and K_2 is a temperature-independent constant. Thus, from Equation 8.9 a diminishment of temperature results in a reduction in ν_d. This effect, represented by the curve shown in Figure 8.4*b*, is just the reverse of that for n^* as discussed above.

The principles and concepts just developed are now extended to a discussion of another important nucleation parameter, the nucleation rate $\dot{N}$ (which has units of nuclei per unit volume per second). This rate is simply proportional to the product of n^* (Equation 8.8) and ν_d (Equation 8.9); that is,

$$\dot{N} = K_3 n^* \nu_d = K_1 K_2 K_3 \left[\exp\left(-\frac{\Delta G^*}{kT}\right) \exp\left(-\frac{Q_d}{kT}\right) \right] \tag{8.10}$$

Here K_3 is the number of atoms on a nucleus surface. Figure 8.4*c* schematically plots nucleation rate as a function of temperature and, in addition, the curves of Figures 8.4*a* and 8.4*b* from which the $\dot{N}$ curve is derived. Note (Figure 8.4*c*) that, with a lowering of temperature from below T_m, the nucleation rate first increases, achieves a maximum, and subsequently diminishes.

The shape of this $\dot{N}$ curve is explained as follows: for the upper region of the curve (a sudden and dramatic increase in $\dot{N}$ with decreasing T), ΔG^* is greater than Q_d, which means that the $\exp(-\Delta G^*/kT)$ term of Equation 8.10 is much smaller than $\exp(-Q_d/kT)$. In other words, the nucleation rate is suppressed at high temperatures due to a small activation driving force. With continued diminishment of temperature, there comes a point at which ΔG^* becomes smaller than the temperature-independent Q_d with the result that $\exp(-Q_d/kT) < \exp(-\Delta G^*/kT)$, or that, at lower temperatures, a low atomic mobility suppresses the nucleation rate. This accounts for the shape of the lower curve segment (a precipitous reduction of $\dot{N}$ with a continued diminishment of temperature). Furthermore, the $\dot{N}$ curve of Figure 8.4*c* necessarily passes through a maximum over the intermediate temperature range where values for ΔG^* and Q_d are of approximately the same magnitude.

Several qualifying comments are in order regarding the above discussion. First, although we assumed a spherical shape for nuclei, this method may be applied to any shape with the same final result. Furthermore, this treatment may be utilized for types of transformations other than solidification (i.e., liquid–solid)—for example, solid–vapor and solid–solid. However, magnitudes of ΔG_v and γ, in addition to diffusion rates of the atomic species, will undoubtedly differ among the various transformation types. In addition, for solid–solid transformations, there may be volume changes attendant to the formation of new phases. These changes may lead to the introduction of microscopic strains, which must be taken into account in the ΔG expression of Equation 8.1, and, consequently, will affect the magnitudes of r^* and ΔG^*.

From Figure 8.4*c* it is apparent that during the cooling of a liquid, an appreciable nucleation rate (i.e., solidification) will begin only after the temperature has been lowered to below the equilibrium solidification (or melting) temperature (T_m). This phenomenon is termed *supercooling* (or *undercooling*), and the degree of supercooling for homogeneous nucleation may be significant (on the order of several hundred degrees Kelvin) for some systems. In Table 8.1 is tabulated, for several materials, typical degrees of supercooling for homogeneous nucleation.

Table 8.1 Degree of Supercooling (ΔT) Values (Homogeneous Nucleation) for Several Metals

Metal	ΔT (°C)
Antimony	135
Germanium	227
Silver	227
Gold	230
Copper	236
Iron	295
Nickel	319
Cobalt	330
Palladium	332

Source: D. Turnbull and R. E. Cech, "Microscopic Observation of the Solidification of Small Metal Droplets," *J. Appl. Phys.*, **21,** 808 (1950).

EXAMPLE PROBLEM 8.1

Computation of Critical Nucleus Radius and Activation Free Energy

(a) For the solidification of pure gold, calculate the critical radius r^* and the activation free energy ΔG^* if nucleation is homogeneous. Values for the latent heat of fusion and surface free energy are -1.16×10^9 J/m^3 and 0.132 J/m^2, respectively. Use the supercooling value found in Table 8.1.

(b) Now calculate the number of atoms found in a nucleus of critical size. Assume a lattice parameter of 0.413 nm for solid gold at its melting temperature.

Solution

(a) In order to compute the critical radius, we employ Equation 8.6, using the melting temperature of 1064°C for gold, assuming a supercooling value of 230°C (Table 8.1), and realizing that ΔH_f is negative. Hence

$$r^* = \left(-\frac{2\gamma T_m}{\Delta H_f}\right)\left(\frac{1}{T_m - T}\right)$$

$$= \left[-\frac{(2)(0.132 \text{ J/m}^2)(1064 + 273 \text{ K})}{-1.16 \times 10^9 \text{ J/m}^3}\right]\left(\frac{1}{230 \text{ K}}\right)$$

$$= 1.32 \times 10^{-9} \text{ m} = 1.32 \text{ nm}$$

For computation of the activation free energy, Equation 8.7 is employed. Thus

$$\Delta G^* = \left(\frac{16\pi\gamma^3 T_m^2}{3\Delta H_f^2}\right)\frac{1}{(T_m - T)^2}$$

$$= \left[\frac{(16)(\pi)(0.132 \text{ J/m}^2)^3(1064 + 273 \text{ K})^2}{(3)(-1.16 \times 10^9 \text{ J/m}^3)^2}\right]\left[\frac{1}{(230 \text{ K})^2}\right]$$

$$= 9.64 \times 10^{-19} \text{ J}$$

(b) In order to compute the number of atoms in a nucleus of critical size (assuming a spherical nucleus of radius r^*), it is first necessary to determine the number of unit cells, which we then multiply by the number of atoms per unit cell. The number of unit cells found in this critical nucleus is just the ratio of critical nucleus and unit cell volumes. Inasmuch as gold has the FCC crystal structure (and a cubic unit cell), its unit cell volume is just a^3, where a is the lattice parameter (i.e., unit cell edge length); its value is 0.413 nm, as cited in the problem statement. Therefore, the number of unit cells found in a radius of critical size is just

$$\text{\# unit cells/particle} = \frac{\text{critical nucleus volume}}{\text{unit cell volume}} = \frac{\frac{4}{3}\pi r^{*3}}{a^3} \tag{8.11}$$

$$= \frac{\left(\frac{4}{3}\right)(\pi)(1.32\text{ nm})^3}{(0.413\text{ nm})^3} = 137\text{ unit cells}$$

Inasmuch as there is the equivalence of four atoms per FCC unit cell (Section 4.2), the total number of atoms per critical nucleus is just

$$(137\text{ unit cells/critical nucleus})(4\text{ atoms/unit cell}) = 548\text{ atoms/critical nucleus}$$

Heterogeneous Nucleation

Although levels of supercooling for homogeneous nucleation may be significant (on occasion several hundred degrees Celsius), in practical situations they are often on the order of only several degrees Celsius. The reason for this is that the activation energy (i.e., energy barrier) for nucleation (ΔG^* of Equation 8.4) is lowered when nuclei form on preexisting surfaces or interfaces, since the surface free energy (γ of Equation 8.4) is reduced. In other words, it is easier for nucleation to occur at surfaces and interfaces than at other sites. Again, this type of nucleation is termed *heterogeneous*.

In order to understand this phenomenon, let us consider the nucleation, on a flat surface, of a solid particle from a liquid phase. It is assumed that both the liquid and solid phases "wet" this flat surface, that is, both of these phases spread out and cover the surface; this configuration is depicted schematically in Figure 8.5. Also noted in the figure are three interfacial energies (represented as vectors) that exist at two-phase boundaries—γ_{SL}, γ_{SI}, and γ_{IL}—as well as the wetting angle θ (the angle between the γ_{SI} and γ_{SL} vectors). Taking a surface tension force balance in the plane of the flat surface leads to the following expression:

$$\gamma_{IL} = \gamma_{SI} + \gamma_{SL}\cos\theta \tag{8.12}$$

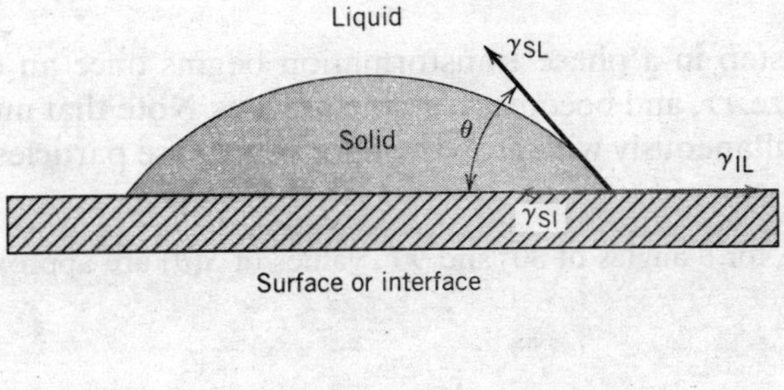

Figure 8.5 Heterogeneous nucleation of a solid from a liquid. The solid–surface (γ_{SI}), solid–liquid (γ_{SL}), and liquid–surface (γ_{IL}) interfacial energies are represented by vectors. The wetting angle (θ) is also shown.

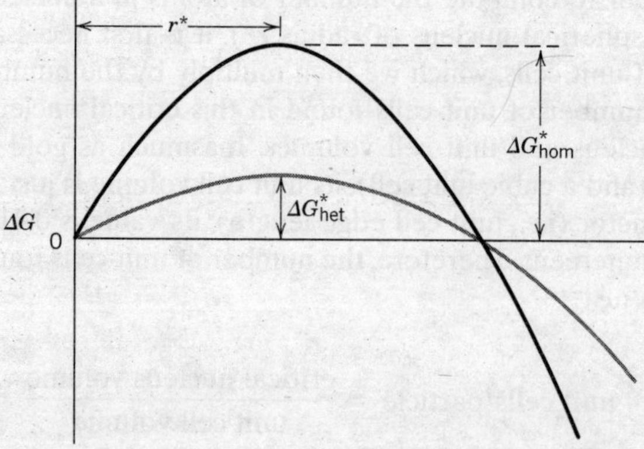

Figure 8.6 Schematic free-energy-versus-embryo/nucleus-radius plot on which are presented curves for both homogeneous and heterogeneous nucleation. Critical free energies and the critical radius are also shown.

Now, using a somewhat involved procedure similar to the one presented above for homogeneous nucleation (which we have chosen to omit), it is possible to derive equations for r^* and ΔG^*; these are as follows:

$$r^* = -\frac{2\gamma_{SL}}{\Delta G_v} \tag{8.13}$$

$$\Delta G^* = \left(\frac{16\pi\gamma_{SL}^3}{3\Delta G_v^2}\right) S(\theta) \tag{8.14}$$

The $S(\theta)$ term of this last equation is a function only of θ (i.e., the shape of the nucleus), which will have a numerical value between zero and unity.[1]

From Equation 8.13, it is important to note that the critical radius r^* for heterogeneous nucleation is the same as for homogeneous, inasmuch as γ_{SL} is the same surface energy as γ in Equation 8.3. It is also evident that the activation energy barrier for heterogeneous nucleation (Equation 8.14) is smaller than the homogeneous barrier (Equation 8.4) by an amount corresponding to the value of this $S(\theta)$ function, or

$$\Delta G^*_{het} = \Delta G^*_{hom} S(\theta) \tag{8.15}$$

Figure 8.6, a schematic graph of ΔG versus nucleus radius, plots curves for both types of nucleation, and indicates the difference in the magnitudes of ΔG^*_{het} and ΔG^*_{hom}, in addition to the constancy of r^*. This lower ΔG^* for heterogeneous means that a smaller energy must be overcome during the nucleation process (than for homogeneous), and, therefore, heterogeneous nucleation occurs more readily (Equation 8.10). In terms of the nucleation rate, the $\dot{N}$ versus T curve (Figure 8.4*c*) is shifted to higher temperatures for heterogeneous. This effect is represented in Figure 8.7, which also shows that a much smaller degree of supercooling (ΔT) is required for heterogeneous nucleation.

Growth

The growth step in a phase transformation begins once an embryo has exceeded the critical size, r^*, and becomes a stable nucleus. Note that nucleation will continue to occur simultaneously with growth of the new phase particles; of course, nucleation

[1] For example, for θ angles of 30° and 90°, values of $S(\theta)$ are approximately 0.01 and 0.5, respectively.

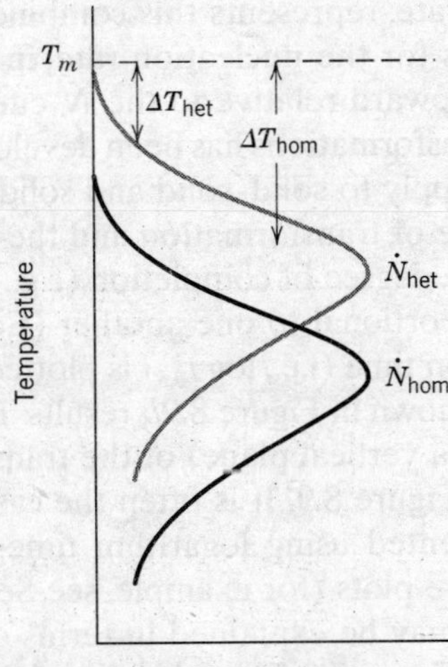

Figure 8.7 Nucleation rate versus temperature for both homogeneous and heterogeneous nucleation. Degree of supercooling (ΔT) for each is also shown.

cannot occur in regions that have already transformed to the new phase. Furthermore, the growth process will cease in any region where particles of the new phase meet, since here the transformation will have reached completion.

Particle growth occurs by long-range atomic diffusion, which normally involves several steps—for example, diffusion through the parent phase, across a phase boundary, and then into the nucleus. Consequently, the growth rate $\dot{G}$ is determined by the rate of diffusion, and its temperature dependence is the same as for the diffusion coefficient (Equation 6.8)—namely,

$$\dot{G} = C \exp\left(-\frac{Q}{kT}\right) \tag{8.16}$$

where Q (the activation energy) and C (a preexponential) are independent of temperature.[2] The temperature dependence of $\dot{G}$ is represented by one of the curves in Figure 8.8; also shown is a curve for the nucleation rate, $\dot{N}$ (again, almost always the rate for heterogeneous nucleation). Now, at a specific temperature, the overall transformation rate is equal to some product of $\dot{N}$ and $\dot{G}$. The third curve of

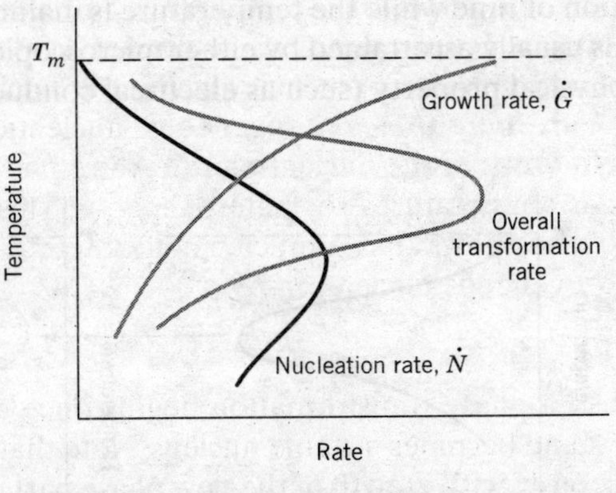

Figure 8.8 Schematic plot showing curves for nucleation rate ($\dot{N}$), growth rate ($\dot{G}$), and overall transformation rate versus temperature.

---

[2] Processes the rates of which depend on temperature as $\dot{G}$ in Equation (8.16) are sometimes termed **thermally activated.** Also, a rate equation of this form (i.e., having the exponential temperature dependence) is termed an *Arrhenius rate equation.*

Figure 8.8, which is for the total rate, represents this combined effect. The general shape of this curve is the same as for the nucleation rate, in that it has a peak or maximum that has been shifted upward relative to the $\dot{N}$ curve.

Whereas this treatment on transformations has been developed for solidification, the same general principles also apply to solid–solid and solid–gas transformations.

As we shall see below, the rate of transformation and the time required for the transformation to proceed to some degree of completion (e.g., time to 50% reaction completion, $t_{0.5}$) are inversely proportional to one another (Equation 8.18). Thus, if the logarithm of this transformation time (i.e., log $t_{0.5}$) is plotted versus temperature, a curve having the general shape shown in Figure 8.9*b* results. This "C-shaped" curve is a virtual mirror image (through a vertical plane) of the transformation rate curve of Figure 8.8, as demonstrated in Figure 8.9. It is often the case that the kinetics of phase transformations are represented using logarithm time- (to some degree of transformation) versus-temperature plots (for example, see Section 8.5).

Several physical phenomena may be explained in terms of the transformation rate-versus-temperature curve of Figure 8.8. First, the size of the product phase particles will depend on transformation temperature. For example, for transformations that occur at temperatures near to T_m, corresponding to low nucleation and high growth rates, few nuclei form that grow rapidly. Thus, the resulting microstructure will consist of few and relatively large phase particles (e.g., coarse grains). Conversely, for transformations at lower temperatures, nucleation rates are high and growth rates low, which results in many small particles (e.g., fine grains).

Also, from Figure 8.8, when a material is cooled very rapidly through the temperature range encompassed by the transformation rate curve to a relatively low temperature where the rate is extremely low, it is possible to produce nonequilibrium phase structures (for example, see Sections 8.5 and 10.14).

Kinetic Considerations of Solid-State Transformations

The previous discussion of this section has centered on the temperature dependences of nucleation, growth, and transformation rates. The *time* dependence of rate (which is often termed the **kinetics** of a transformation) is also an important consideration, often in the heat treatment of materials. Also, since many transformations of interest to materials scientists and engineers involve only solid phases, we have decided to devote the following discussion to the kinetics of solid-state transformations.

With many kinetic investigations, the fraction of reaction that has occurred is measured as a function of time while the temperature is maintained constant. Transformation progress is usually ascertained by either microscopic examination or measurement of some physical property (such as electrical conductivity) the magnitude

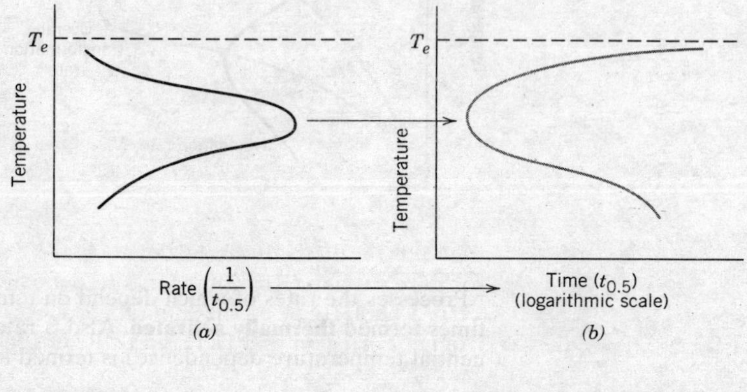

Figure 8.9 Schematic plots of (*a*) transformation rate versus temperature, and (*b*) logarithm time [to some degree (e.g., 0.5 fraction) of transformation] versus temperature. The curves in both (*a*) and (*b*) are generated from the same set of data—i.e., for horizontal axes, the time [scaled logarithmically in the (*b*) plot] is just the reciprocal of the rate from plot (*a*).

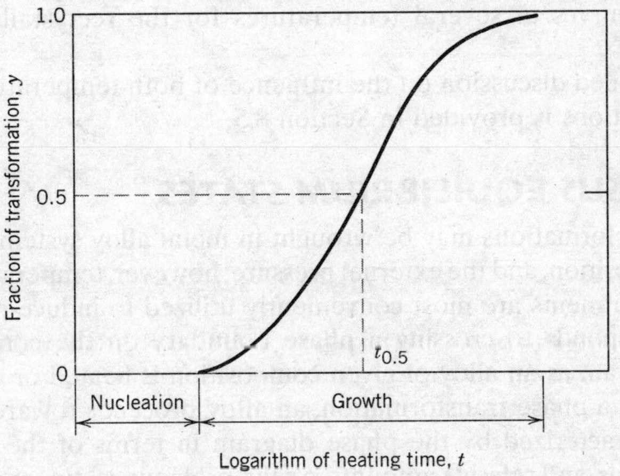

Figure 8.10 Plot of fraction reacted versus the logarithm of time typical of many solid-state transformations in which temperature is held constant.

of which is distinctive of the new phase. Data are plotted as the fraction of transformed material versus the logarithm of time; an S-shaped curve similar to that in Figure 8.10 represents the typical kinetic behavior for most solid-state reactions. Nucleation and growth stages are also indicated in the figure.

For solid-state transformations displaying the kinetic behavior in Figure 8.10, the fraction of transformation y is a function of time t as follows:

$$y = 1 - \exp(-kt^n) \tag{8.17}$$

where k and n are time-independent constants for the particular reaction. The above expression is often referred to as the *Avrami equation*.

By convention, the rate of a transformation is taken as the reciprocal of time required for the transformation to proceed halfway to completion, $t_{0.5}$, or

$$\text{rate} = \frac{1}{t_{0.5}} \tag{8.18}$$

Temperature will have a profound influence on the kinetics and thus on the rate of a transformation. This is demonstrated in Figure 8.11, where y-versus-log t

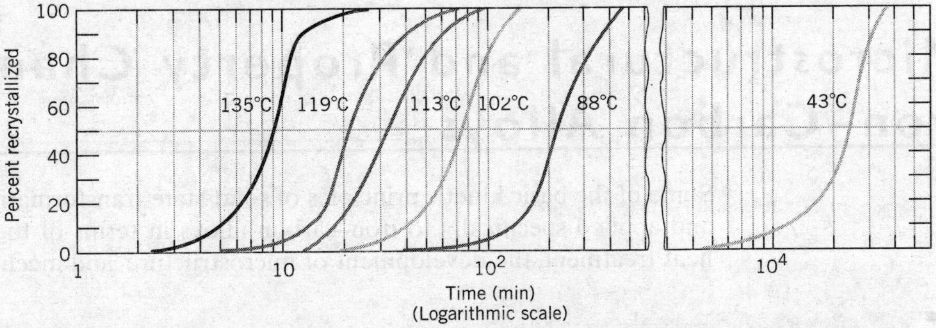

Figure 8.11 Percent recrystallization as a function of time and at constant temperature for pure copper. (Reprinted with permission from *Metallurgical Transactions,* Vol. 188, 1950, a publication of The Metallurgical Society of AIME, Warrendale, PA. Adapted from B. F. Decker and D. Harker, "Recrystallization in Rolled Copper," *Trans. AIME,* **188,** 1950, p. 888.)

S-shaped curves at several temperatures for the recrystallization of copper are shown.

A detailed discussion on the influence of both temperature and time on phase transformations is provided in Section 8.5.

8.4 METASTABLE VERSUS EQUILIBRIUM STATES

Phase transformations may be wrought in metal alloy systems by varying temperature, composition, and the external pressure; however, temperature changes by means of heat treatments are most conveniently utilized to induce phase transformations. This corresponds to crossing a phase boundary on the composition-temperature phase diagram as an alloy of given composition is heated or cooled.

During a phase transformation, an alloy proceeds toward an equilibrium state that is characterized by the phase diagram in terms of the product phases, their compositions, and relative amounts. As the previous section noted, most phase transformations require some finite time to go to completion, and the speed or rate is often important in the relationship between the heat treatment and the development of microstructure. One limitation of phase diagrams is their inability to indicate the time period required for the attainment of equilibrium.

The rate of approach to equilibrium for solid systems is so slow that true equilibrium structures are rarely achieved. When phase transformations are induced by temperature changes, equilibrium conditions are maintained only if heating or cooling is carried out at extremely slow and unpractical rates. For other than equilibrium cooling, transformations are shifted to lower temperatures than indicated by the phase diagram; for heating, the shift is to higher temperatures. These phenomena are termed **supercooling** and **superheating,** respectively. The degree of each depends on the rate of temperature change; the more rapid the cooling or heating, the greater the supercooling or superheating. For example, for normal cooling rates the iron–carbon eutectoid reaction is typically displaced 10 to 20°C (18 to 36°F) below the equilibrium transformation temperature.[3]

For many technologically important alloys, the preferred state or microstructure is a metastable one, intermediate between the initial and equilibrium states; on occasion, a structure far removed from the equilibrium one is desired. It thus becomes imperative to investigate the influence of time on phase transformations. This kinetic information is, in many instances, of greater value than a knowledge of the final equilibrium state.

Microstructural and Property Changes in Iron–Carbon Alloys

Some of the basic kinetic principles of solid-state transformations are now extended and applied specifically to iron–carbon alloys in terms of the relationships among heat treatment, the development of microstructure, and mechanical properties. This

[3] It is important to note that the treatments relating to the kinetics of phase transformations in Section 8.3 are constrained to the condition of constant temperature. By way of contrast, the discussion of this section pertains to phase transformations that occur with changing temperature. This same distinction exists between Sections 8.5 (Isothermal Transformation Diagrams) and 8.6 (Continuous Cooling Transformation Diagrams).

system has been chosen because it is familiar and because a wide variety of microstructures and mechanical properties are possible for iron–carbon (or steel) alloys.

8.5 ISOTHERMAL TRANSFORMATION DIAGRAMS

Pearlite

Consider again the iron–iron carbide eutectoid reaction

$$\gamma(0.76 \text{ wt\% C}) \underset{\text{heating}}{\overset{\text{cooling}}{\rightleftharpoons}} \alpha(0.022 \text{ wt\% C}) + Fe_3C(6.70 \text{ wt\% C}) \tag{8.19}$$

which is fundamental to the development of microstructure in steel alloys. Upon cooling, austenite, having an intermediate carbon concentration, transforms to a ferrite phase, having a much lower carbon content, and also cementite, with a much higher carbon concentration. Pearlite is one microstructural product of this transformation (Figure 7.27), and the mechanism of pearlite formation was discussed previously (Section 7.19) and demonstrated in Figure 7.28.

Temperature plays an important role in the rate of the austenite-to-pearlite transformation. The temperature dependence for an iron–carbon alloy of eutectoid composition is indicated in Figure 8.12, which plots S-shaped curves of the percentage transformation versus the logarithm of time at three different temperatures. For each curve, data were collected after rapidly cooling a specimen composed of 100% austenite to the temperature indicated; that temperature was maintained constant throughout the course of the reaction.

A more convenient way of representing both the time and temperature dependence of this transformation is in the bottom portion of Figure 8.13. Here, the vertical and horizontal axes are, respectively, temperature and the logarithm of time. Two solid curves are plotted; one represents the time required at each temperature for the initiation or start of the transformation; the other is for the transformation conclusion. The dashed curve corresponds to 50% of transformation completion. These curves were generated from a series of plots of the percentage transformation versus the logarithm of time taken over a range of temperatures. The S-shaped curve [for 675°C (1247°F)], in the upper portion of Figure 8.13, illustrates how the data transfer is made.

In interpreting this diagram, note first that the eutectoid temperature [727°C (1341°F)] is indicated by a horizontal line; at temperatures above the eutectoid and

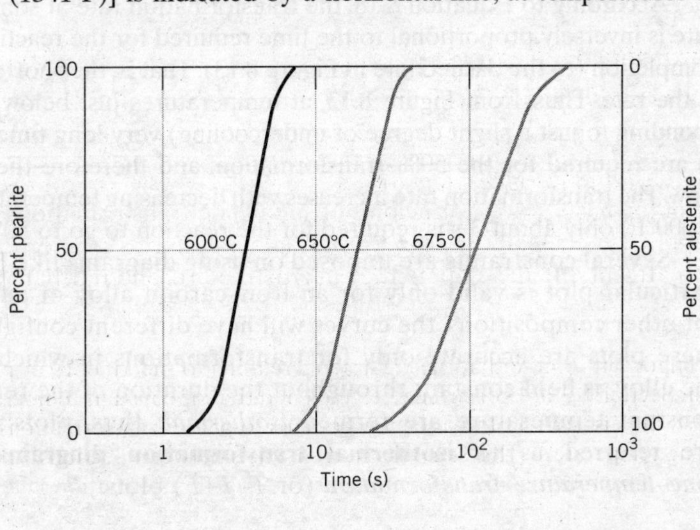

Figure 8.12 For an iron–carbon alloy of eutectoid composition (0.76 wt% C), isothermal fraction reacted versus the logarithm of time for the austenite-to-pearlite transformation.

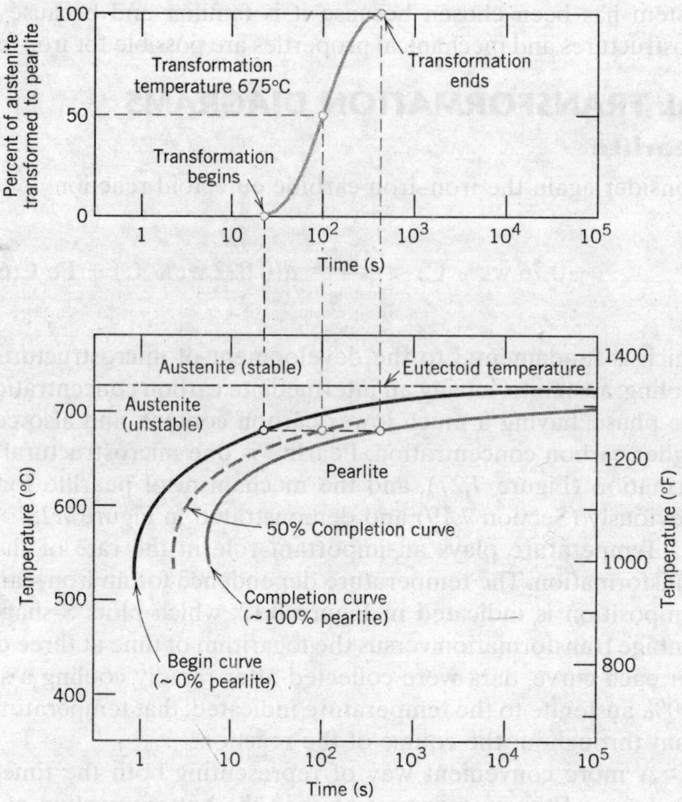

Figure 8.13 Demonstration of how an isothermal transformation diagram (bottom) is generated from percentage transformation-versus-logarithm of time measurements (top). [Adapted from H. Boyer, (Editor), *Atlas of Isothermal Transformation and Cooling Transformation Diagrams,* American Society for Metals, 1977, p. 369.]

for all times, only austenite will exist, as indicated in the figure. The austenite-to-pearlite transformation will occur only if an alloy is supercooled to below the eutectoid; as indicated by the curves, the time necessary for the transformation to begin and then end depends on temperature. The start and finish curves are nearly parallel, and they approach the eutectoid line asymptotically. To the left of the transformation start curve, only austenite (which is unstable) will be present, whereas to the right of the finish curve, only pearlite will exist. In between, the austenite is in the process of transforming to pearlite, and thus both microconstituents will be present.

According to Equation 8.18, the transformation rate at some particular temperature is inversely proportional to the time required for the reaction to proceed to 50% completion (to the dashed line in Figure 8.13). That is, the shorter this time, the higher is the rate. Thus, from Figure 8.13, at temperatures just below the eutectoid (corresponding to just a slight degree of undercooling) very long times (on the order of 10^5 s) are required for the 50% transformation, and therefore the reaction rate is very slow. The transformation rate increases with decreasing temperature such that at 540°C (1000°F) only about 3 s is required for the reaction to go to 50% completion.

Several constraints are imposed on using diagrams like Figure 8.13. First, this particular plot is valid only for an iron–carbon alloy of eutectoid composition; for other compositions, the curves will have different configurations. In addition, these plots are accurate only for transformations in which the temperature of the alloy is held constant throughout the duration of the reaction. Conditions of constant temperature are termed *isothermal;* thus, plots such as Figure 8.13 are referred as to **isothermal transformation diagrams,** or sometimes as *time–temperature–transformation* (or *T–T–T*) plots.

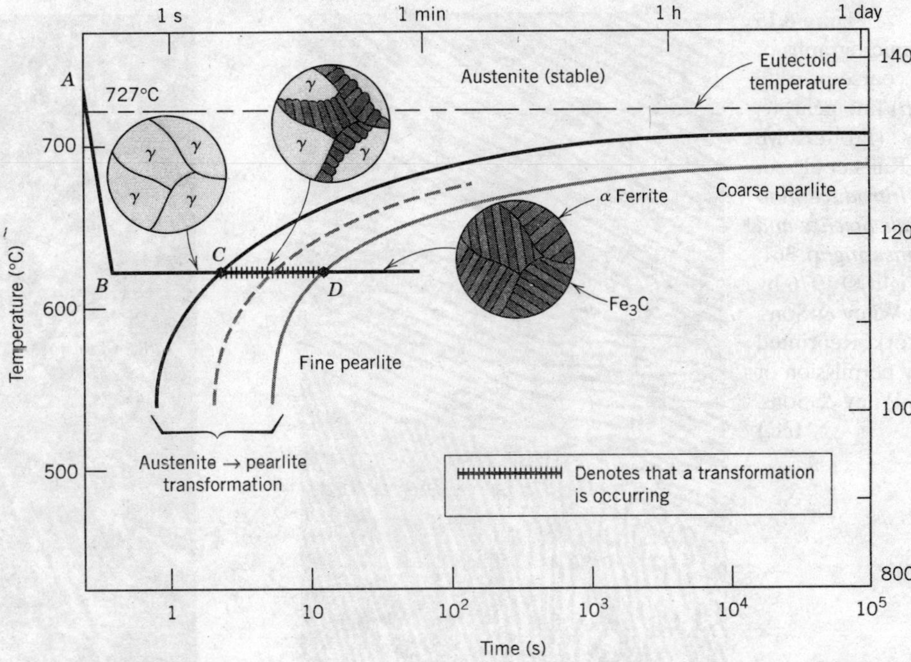

Figure 8.14 Isothermal transformation diagram for a eutectoid iron–carbon alloy, with superimposed isothermal heat treatment curve (*ABCD*). Microstructures before, during, and after the austenite-to-pearlite transformation are shown. [Adapted from H. Boyer (Editor), *Atlas of Isothermal Transformation and Cooling Transformation Diagrams*, American Society for Metals, 1977, p. 28.]

An actual isothermal heat treatment curve (*ABCD*) is superimposed on the isothermal transformation diagram for a eutectoid iron–carbon alloy in Figure 8.14. Very rapid cooling of austenite to a temperature is indicated by the near-vertical line *AB*, and the isothermal treatment at this temperature is represented by the horizontal segment *BCD*. Of course, time increases from left to right along this line. The transformation of austenite to pearlite begins at the intersection, point *C* (after approximately 3.5 s), and has reached completion by about 15 s, corresponding to point *D*. Figure 8.14 also shows schematic microstructures at various times during the progression of the reaction.

The thickness ratio of the ferrite and cementite layers in pearlite is approximately 8 to 1. However, the absolute layer thickness depends on the temperature at which the isothermal transformation is allowed to occur. At temperatures just below the eutectoid, relatively thick layers of both the α-ferrite and Fe_3C phases are produced; this microstructure is called **coarse pearlite,** and the region at which it forms is indicated to the right of the completion curve on Figure 8.14. At these temperatures, diffusion rates are relatively high, such that during the transformation illustrated in Figure 7.28 carbon atoms can diffuse relatively long distances, which results in the formation of thick lamellae. With decreasing temperature, the carbon diffusion rate decreases, and the layers become progressively thinner. The thin-layered structure produced in the vicinity of 540°C is termed **fine pearlite;** this is also indicated in Figure 8.14. To be discussed in Section 8.7 is the dependence of mechanical properties on lamellar thickness. Photomicrographs of coarse and fine pearlite for a eutectoid composition are shown in Figure 8.15.

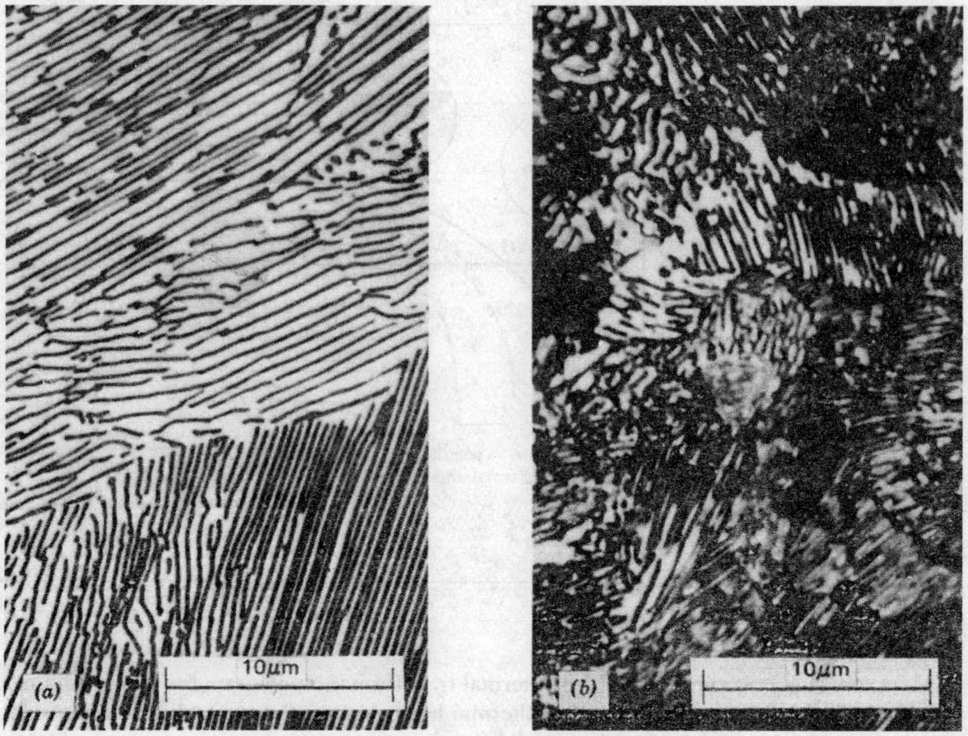

Figure 8.15 Photomicrographs of (*a*) coarse pearlite and (*b*) fine pearlite. 3000×. (From K. M. Ralls et al., *An Introduction to Materials Science and Engineering,* p. 361. Copyright © 1976 by John Wiley & Sons, New York. Reprinted by permission of John Wiley & Sons, Inc.)

For iron–carbon alloys of other compositions, a proeutectoid phase (either ferrite or cementite) will coexist with pearlite, as discussed in Section 7.19. Thus additional curves corresponding to a proeutectoid transformation also must be included on the isothermal transformation diagram. A portion of one such diagram for a 1.13 wt% C alloy is shown in Figure 8.16.

Bainite

In addition to pearlite, other microconstituents that are products of the austenitic transformation exist; one of these is called **bainite.** The microstructure of bainite consists of ferrite and cementite phases, and thus diffusional processes are involved

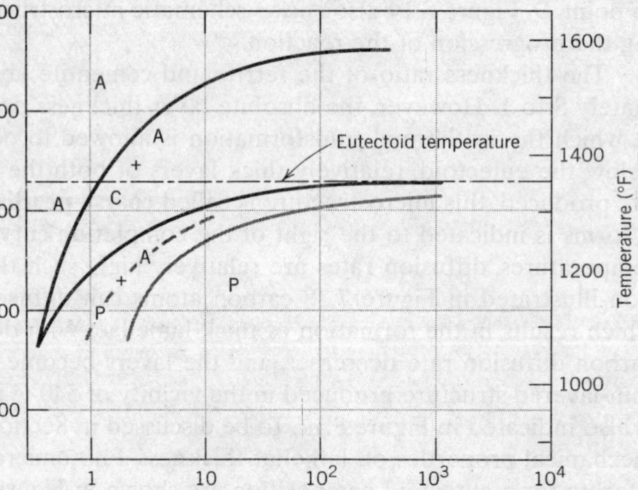

Figure 8.16 Isothermal transformation diagram for a 1.13 wt% C iron–carbon alloy: A, austenite; C, proeutectoid cementite; P, pearlite. [Adapted from H. Boyer (Editor), *Atlas of Isothermal Transformation and Cooling Transformation Diagrams,* American Society for Metals, 1977, p. 33.]

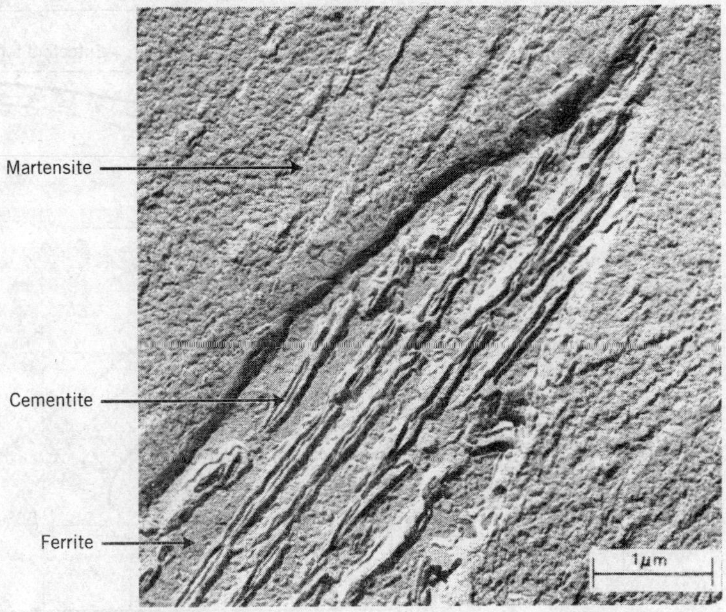

Figure 8.17 Transmission electron micrograph showing the structure of bainite. A grain of bainite passes from lower left to upper right-hand corners, which consists of elongated and needle-shaped particles of Fe_3C within a ferrite matrix. The phase surrounding the bainite is martensite. (Reproduced with permission from *Metals Handbook,* 8th edition, Vol. 8, *Metallography, Structures and Phase Diagrams,* American Society for Metals, Materials Park, OH, 1973.)

in its formation. Bainite forms as needles or plates, depending on the temperature of the transformation; the microstructural details of bainite are so fine that their resolution is possible only using electron microscopy. Figure 8.17 is an electron micrograph that shows a grain of bainite (positioned diagonally from lower left to upper right); it is composed of a ferrite matrix and elongated particles of Fe_3C; the various phases in this micrograph have been labeled. In addition, the phase that surrounds the needle is martensite, the topic to which a subsequent section is addressed. Furthermore, no proeutectoid phase forms with bainite.

The time–temperature dependence of the bainite transformation may also be represented on the isothermal transformation diagram. It occurs at temperatures below those at which pearlite forms; begin-, end-, and half-reaction curves are just extensions of those for the pearlitic transformation, as shown in Figure 8.18, the isothermal transformation diagram for an iron–carbon alloy of eutectoid composition that has been extended to lower temperatures. All three curves are C-shaped and have a "nose" at point *N*, where the rate of transformation is a maximum. As may be noted, whereas pearlite forms above the nose [i.e., over the temperature range of about 540 to 727°C (1000 to 1341°F)], at temperatures between about 215 and 540°C (420 and 1000°F), bainite is the transformation product.

It should also be noted that pearlitic and bainitic transformations are really competitive with each other, and once some portion of an alloy has transformed to either pearlite or bainite, transformation to the other microconstituent is not possible without reheating to form austenite.

Spheroidite

If a steel alloy having either pearlitic or bainitic microstructures is heated to, and left at, a temperature below the eutectoid for a sufficiently long period of time—for example, at about 700°C (1300°F) for between 18 and 24 h—yet another microstructure will form. It is called **spheroidite** (Figure 8.19). Instead of the alternating ferrite and cementite lamellae (pearlite), or the microstructure observed for bainite, the Fe_3C phase appears as sphere-like particles embedded in a continuous α phase matrix. This transformation has occurred by additional carbon diffusion with

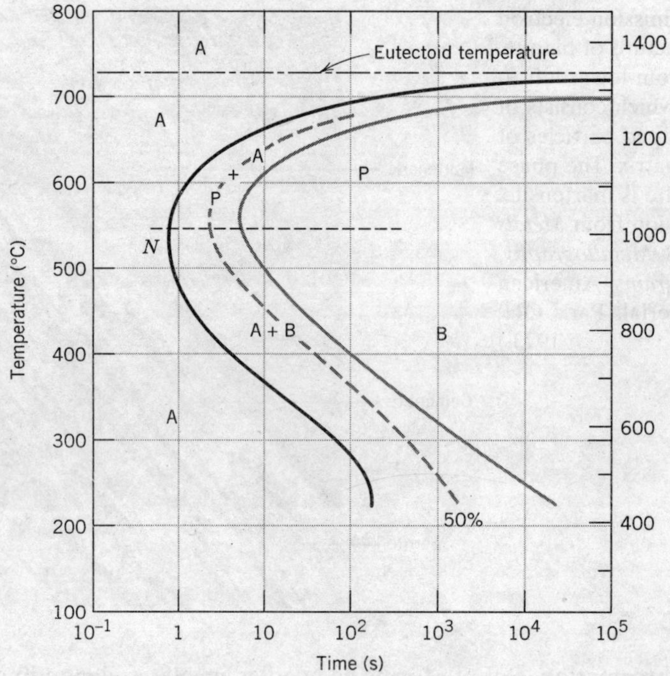

Figure 8.18 Isothermal transformation diagram for an iron–carbon alloy of eutectoid composition, including austenite-to-pearlite (A–P) and austenite-to-bainite (A–B) transformations. [Adapted from H. Boyer (Editor), *Atlas of Isothermal Transformation and Cooling Transformation Diagrams,* American Society for Metals, 1977, p. 28.]

no change in the compositions or relative amounts of ferrite and cementite phases. The chapter-opening photograph for this chapter is a photomicrograph that shows a pearlitic steel that has partially transformed to spheroidite. The driving force for this transformation is the reduction in α–Fe_3C phase boundary area. The kinetics of spheroidite formation are not included on isothermal transformation diagrams.

Concept Check 8.1

Which is the more stable, the pearlitic or the spheroiditic microstructure? Why?

[*The answer may be found in enclosed CD.*]

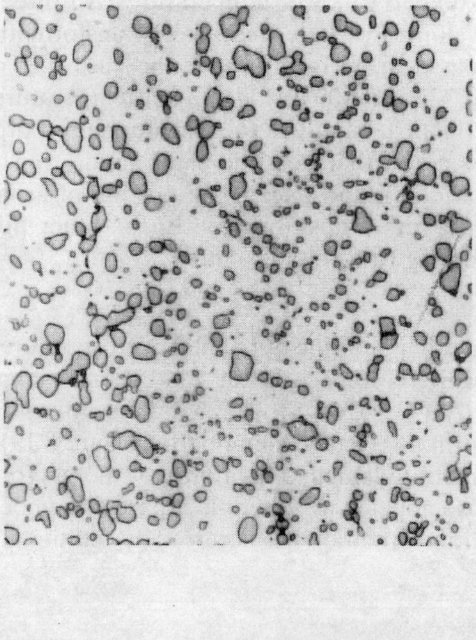

Figure 8.19 Photomicrograph of a steel having a spheroidite microstructure. The small particles are cementite; the continuous phase is α ferrite. 1000×. (Copyright 1971 by United States Steel Corporation.)

Martensite

Yet another microconstituent or phase called **martensite** is formed when austenitized iron–carbon alloys are rapidly cooled (or quenched) to a relatively low temperature (in the vicinity of the ambient). Martensite is a nonequilibrium single-phase structure that results from a diffusionless transformation of austenite. It may be thought of as a transformation product that is competitive with pearlite and bainite. The martensitic transformation occurs when the quenching rate is rapid enough to prevent carbon diffusion. Any diffusion whatsoever will result in the formation of ferrite and cementite phases.

The martensitic transformation is not well understood. However, large numbers of atoms experience cooperative movements, in that there is only a slight displacement of each atom relative to its neighbors. This occurs in such a way that the FCC austenite experiences a polymorphic transformation to a body-centered tetragonal (BCT) martensite. A unit cell of this crystal structure (Figure 8.20) is simply a body-centered cube that has been elongated along one of its dimensions; this structure is distinctly different from that for BCC ferrite. All the carbon atoms remain as interstitial impurities in martensite; as such, they constitute a supersaturated solid solution that is capable of rapidly transforming to other structures if heated to temperatures at which diffusion rates become appreciable. Many steels, however, retain their martensitic structure almost indefinitely at room temperature.

The martensitic transformation is not, however, unique to iron–carbon alloys. It is found in other systems and is characterized, in part, by the diffusionless transformation.

Since the martensitic transformation does not involve diffusion, it occurs almost instantaneously; the martensite grains nucleate and grow at a very rapid rate—the velocity of sound within the austenite matrix. Thus the martensitic transformation rate, for all practical purposes, is time independent.

Martensite grains take on a plate-like or needle-like appearance, as indicated in Figure 8.21. The white phase in the micrograph is austenite (retained austenite) that did not transform during the rapid quench. As already mentioned, martensite as well as other microconstituents (e.g., pearlite) can coexist.

Being a nonequilibrium phase, martensite does not appear on the iron–iron carbide phase diagram (Figure 7.24). The austenite-to-martensite transformation is, however, represented on the isothermal transformation diagram. Since the martensitic transformation is diffusionless and instantaneous, it is not depicted in this diagram as the pearlitic and bainitic reactions are. The beginning of this transformation is represented by a horizontal line designated M(start) (Figure 8.22). Two other horizontal and dashed lines, labeled M(50%) and M(90%), indicate percentages of the austenite-to-martensite transformation. The temperatures at which these lines are located vary with alloy composition but, nevertheless, must be relatively

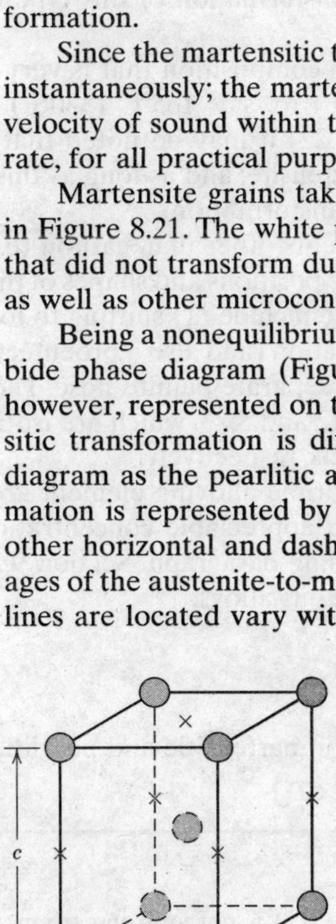

Figure 8.20 The body-centered tetragonal unit cell for martensitic steel showing iron atoms (circles) and sites that may be occupied by carbon atoms (crosses). For this tetragonal unit cell, $c > a$.

Figure 8.21 Photomicrograph showing the martensitic microstructure. The needle-shaped grains are the martensite phase, and the white regions are austenite that failed to transform during the rapid quench. 1220×. (Photomicrograph courtesy of United States Steel Corporation.)

low because carbon diffusion must be virtually nonexistent.[4] The horizontal and linear character of these lines indicates that the martensitic transformation is independent of time; it is a function only of the temperature to which the alloy is quenched or rapidly cooled. A transformation of this type is termed an **athermal transformation.**

Consider an alloy of eutectoid composition that is very rapidly cooled from a temperature above 727°C (1341°F) to, say, 165°C (330°F). From the isothermal transformation diagram (Figure 8.22) it may be noted that 50% of the austenite will immediately transform to martensite; and as long as this temperature is maintained, there will be no further transformation.

The presence of alloying elements other than carbon (e.g., Cr, Ni, Mo, and W) may cause significant changes in the positions and shapes of the curves in the isothermal transformation diagrams. These include (1) shifting to longer times the nose of the austenite-to-pearlite transformation (and also a proeutectoid phase nose, if such exists), and (2) the formation of a separate bainite nose. These alterations may be observed by comparing Figures 8.22 and 8.23, which are isothermal transformation diagrams for carbon and alloy steels, respectively.

Steels in which carbon is the prime alloying element are termed **plain carbon steels,** whereas **alloy steels** contain appreciable concentrations of other elements, including those cited in the preceding paragraph. Section 9.2 tells more about the classification and properties of ferrous alloys.

Concept Check 8.2

Cite two major differences between martensitic and pearlitic transformations.

[*The answer may be found in enclosed CD.*]

---

[4] The alloy that is the subject of Figure 8.21 is not an iron-carbon alloy of eutectoid composition; furthermore, its 100% martensite transformation temperature lies below the ambient. Since the photomicrograph was taken at room temperature, some austenite (i.e., the retained austenite) is present, having not transformed to martensite.

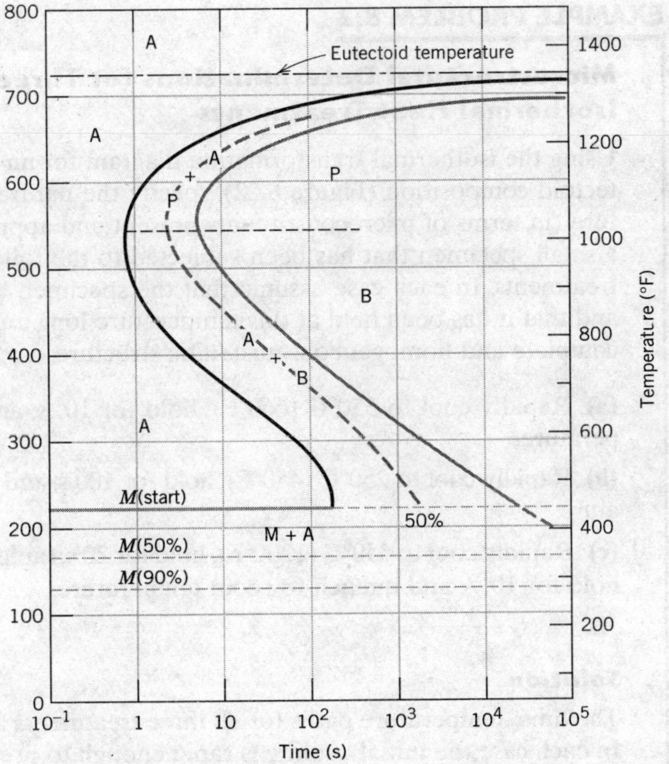

Figure 8.22 The complete isothermal transformation diagram for an iron–carbon alloy of eutectoid composition: A, austenite; B, bainite; M, martensite; P, pearlite.

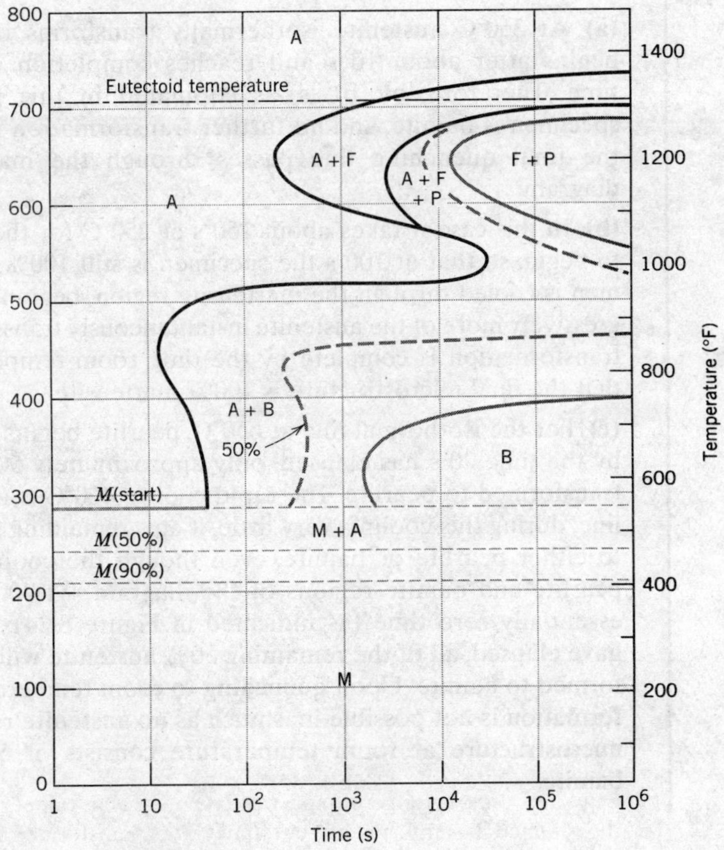

Figure 8.23 Isothermal transformation diagram for an alloy steel (type 4340): A, austenite; B, bainite; P, pearlite; M, martensite; F, proeutectoid ferrite. [Adapted from H. Boyer (Editor), *Atlas of Isothermal Transformation and Cooling Transformation Diagrams,* American Society for Metals, 1977, p. 181.]

EXAMPLE PROBLEM 8.2

Microstructural Determinations for Three Isothermal Heat Treatments

Using the isothermal transformation diagram for an iron–carbon alloy of eutectoid composition (Figure 8.22), specify the nature of the final microstructure (in terms of microconstituents present and approximate percentages) of a small specimen that has been subjected to the following time–temperature treatments. In each case assume that the specimen begins at 760°C (1400°F) and that it has been held at this temperature long enough to have achieved a complete and homogeneous austenitic structure.

(a) Rapidly cool to 350°C (660°F), hold for 10^4 s, and quench to room temperature.

(b) Rapidly cool to 250°C (480°F), hold for 100 s, and quench to room temperature.

(c) Rapidly cool to 650°C (1200°F), hold for 20 s, rapidly cool to 400°C (750°F), hold for 10^3 s, and quench to room temperature.

Solution

The time–temperature paths for all three treatments are shown in Figure 8.24. In each case the initial cooling is rapid enough to prevent any transformation from occurring.

(a) At 350°C austenite isothermally transforms to bainite; this reaction begins after about 10 s and reaches completion at about 500 s elapsed time. Therefore, by 10^4 s, as stipulated in this problem, 100% of the specimen is bainite, and no further transformation is possible, even though the final quenching line passes through the martensite region of the diagram.

(b) In this case it takes about 150 s at 250°C for the bainite transformation to begin, so that at 100 s the specimen is still 100% austenite. As the specimen is cooled through the martensite region, beginning at about 215°C, progressively more of the austenite instantaneously transforms to martensite. This transformation is complete by the time room temperature is reached, such that the final microstructure is 100% martensite.

(c) For the isothermal line at 650°C, pearlite begins to form after about 7 s; by the time 20 s has elapsed, only approximately 50% of the specimen has transformed to pearlite. The rapid cool to 400°C is indicated by the vertical line; during this cooling, very little, if any, remaining austenite will transform to either pearlite or bainite, even though the cooling line passes through pearlite and bainite regions of the diagram. At 400°C, we begin timing at essentially zero time (as indicated in Figure 8.24); thus, by the time 10^3 s have elapsed, all of the remaining 50% austenite will have completely transformed to bainite. Upon quenching to room temperature, any further transformation is not possible inasmuch as no austenite remains; and so the final microstructure at room temperature consists of 50% pearlite and 50% bainite.

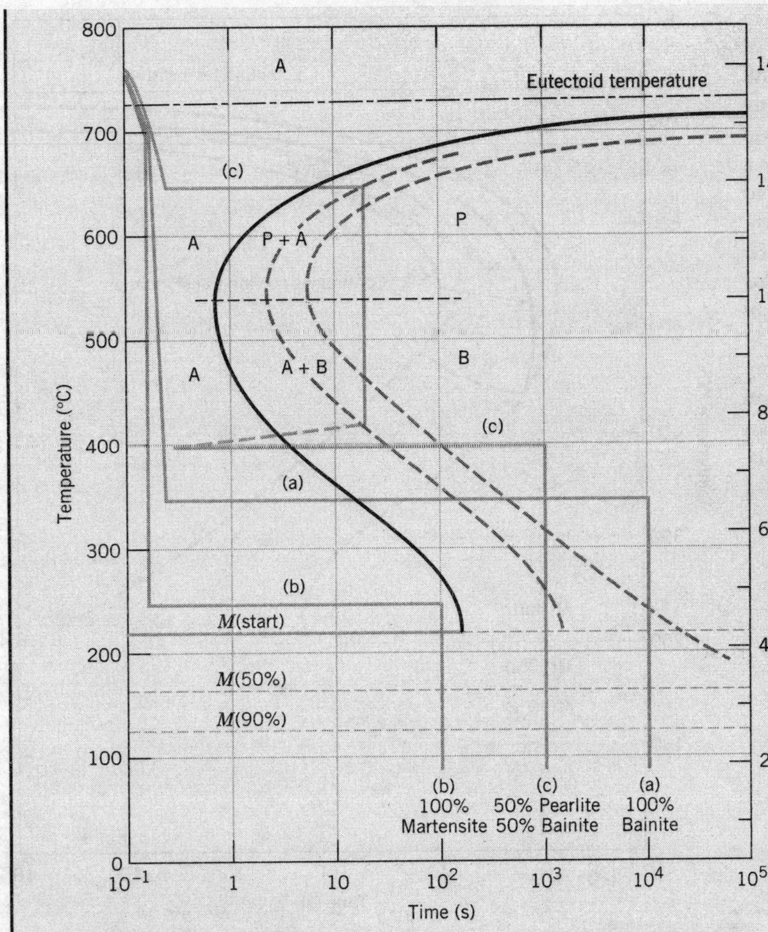

Figure 8.24 Isothermal transformation diagram for an iron–carbon alloy of eutectoid composition and the isothermal heat treatments (a), (b), and (c) in Example Problem 8.2.

Concept Check 8.3

Make a copy of the isothermal transformation diagram for an iron-carbon alloy of eutectoid composition (Figure 8.22) and then sketch and label on this diagram a time-temperature path that will produce 100% fine pearlite.

[The answer may be found in enclosed CD.]

8.6 CONTINUOUS COOLING TRANSFORMATION DIAGRAMS

Isothermal heat treatments are not the most practical to conduct because an alloy must be rapidly cooled to and maintained at an elevated temperature from a higher temperature above the eutectoid. Most heat treatments for steels involve the continuous cooling of a specimen to room temperature. An isothermal transformation diagram is valid only for conditions of constant temperature; this diagram must be modified for transformations that occur as the temperature is constantly changing.

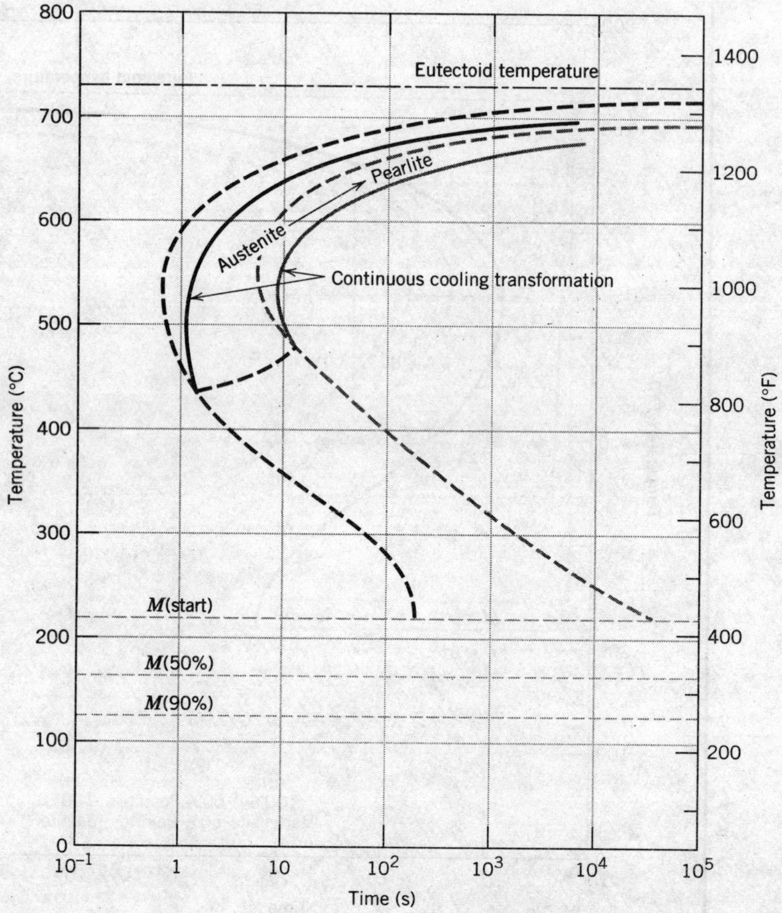

Figure 8.25 Superimposition of isothermal and continuous cooling transformation diagrams for a eutectoid iron–carbon alloy. [Adapted from H. Boyer (Editor), *Atlas of Isothermal Transformation and Cooling Transformation Diagrams,* American Society for Metals, 1977, p. 376.]

For continuous cooling, the time required for a reaction to begin and end is delayed. Thus the isothermal curves are shifted to longer times and lower temperatures, as indicated in Figure 8.25 for an iron–carbon alloy of eutectoid composition. A plot containing such modified beginning and ending reaction curves is termed a **continuous cooling transformation** (*CCT*) **diagram.** Some control may be maintained over the rate of temperature change depending on the cooling environment. Two cooling curves corresponding to moderately fast and slow rates are superimposed and labeled in Figure 8.26, again for a eutectoid steel. The transformation starts after a time period corresponding to the intersection of the cooling curve with the beginning reaction curve and concludes upon crossing the completion transformation curve. The microstructural products for the moderately rapid and slow cooling rate curves in Figure 8.26 are fine and coarse pearlite, respectively.

Normally, bainite will not form when an alloy of eutectoid composition or, for that matter, any plain carbon steel is continuously cooled to room temperature. This is because all the austenite will have transformed to pearlite by the time the bainite transformation has become possible. Thus, the region representing the austenite–pearlite transformation terminates just below the nose (Figure 8.26) as indicated by the curve *AB*. For any cooling curve passing through *AB* in Figure 8.26, the transformation ceases at the point of intersection; with continued cooling, the unreacted austenite begins transforming to martensite upon crossing the *M*(start) line.

With regard to the representation of the martensitic transformation, the *M*(start), *M*(50%), and *M*(90%) lines occur at identical temperatures for both isothermal and

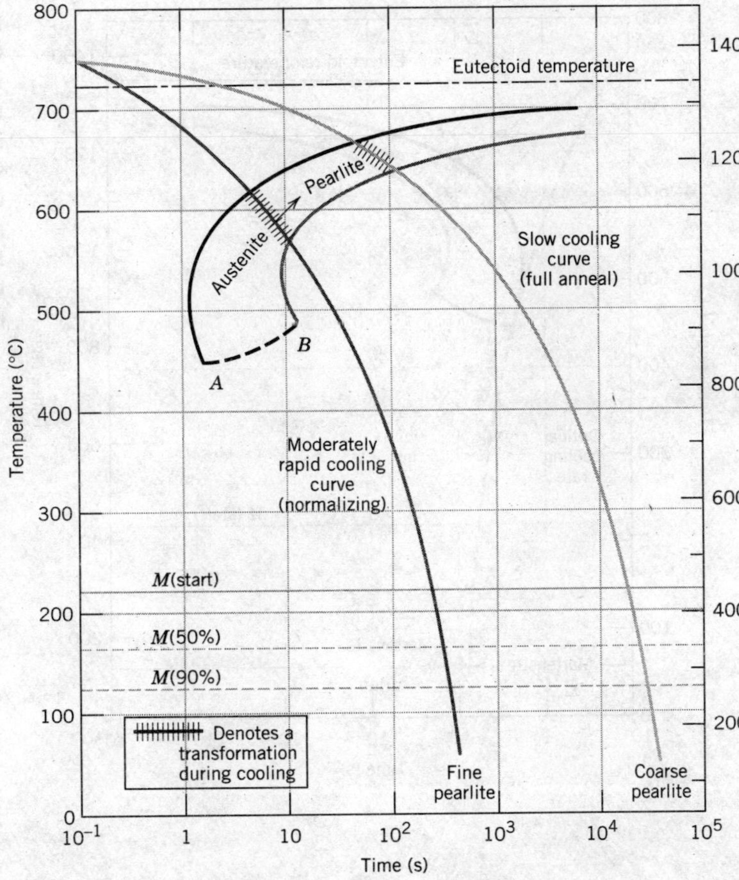

Figure 8.26 Moderately rapid and slow cooling curves superimposed on a continuous cooling transformation diagram for a eutectoid iron–carbon alloy.

continuous cooling transformation diagrams. This may be verified for an iron–carbon alloy of eutectoid composition by comparison of Figures 8.22 and 8.25.

For the continuous cooling of a steel alloy, there exists a critical quenching rate, which represents the minimum rate of quenching that will produce a totally martensitic structure. This critical cooling rate, when included on the continuous transformation diagram, will just miss the nose at which the pearlite transformation begins, as illustrated in Figure 8.27. As the figure also shows, only martensite will exist for quenching rates greater than the critical; in addition, there will be a range of rates over which both pearlite and martensite are produced. Finally, a totally pearlitic structure develops for low cooling rates.

Carbon and other alloying elements also shift the pearlite (as well as the proeutectoid phase) and bainite noses to longer times, thus decreasing the critical cooling rate. In fact, one of the reasons for alloying steels is to facilitate the formation of martensite so that totally martensitic structures can develop in relatively thick cross sections. Figure 8.28 shows the continuous cooling transformation diagram for the same alloy steel for which the isothermal transformation diagram is presented in Figure 8.23. The presence of the bainite nose accounts for the possibility of formation of bainite for a continuous cooling heat treatment. Several cooling curves superimposed on Figure 8.28 indicate the critical cooling rate, and also how the transformation behavior and final microstructure are influenced by the rate of cooling.

Interestingly enough, the critical cooling rate is diminished even by the presence of carbon. In fact, iron–carbon alloys containing less than about 0.25 wt% carbon are not normally heat treated to form martensite because quenching rates too

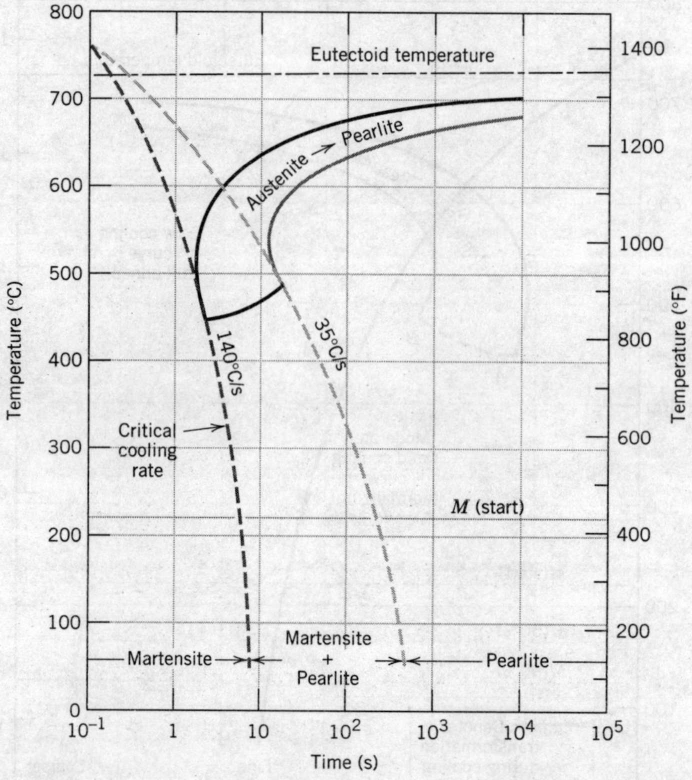

Figure 8.27 Continuous cooling transformation diagram for a eutectoid iron–carbon alloy and superimposed cooling curves, demonstrating the dependence of the final microstructure on the transformations that occur during cooling.

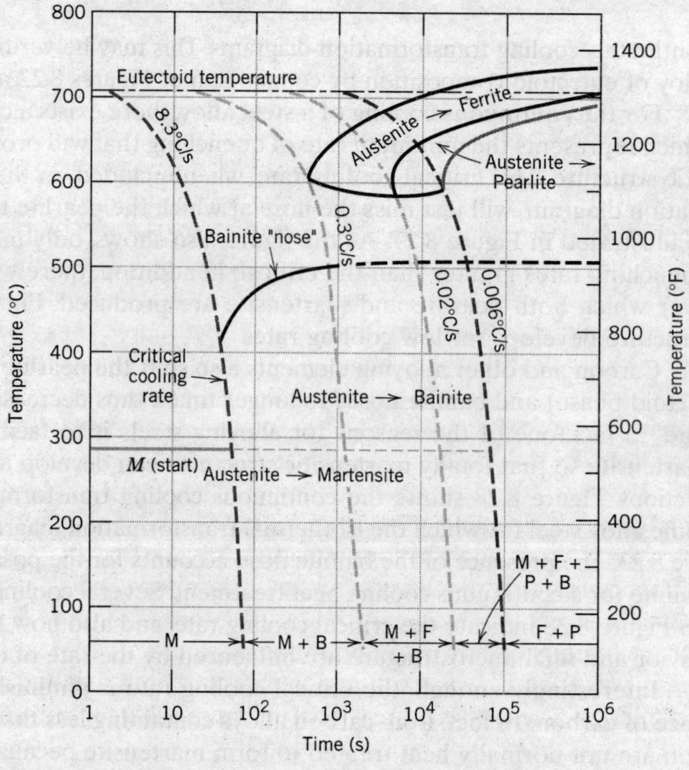

Figure 8.28 Continuous cooling transformation diagram for an alloy steel (type 4340) and several superimposed cooling curves demonstrating dependence of the final microstructure of this alloy on the transformations that occur during cooling. [Adapted from H. E. McGannon (Editor), *The Making, Shaping and Treating of Steel,* 9th edition, United States Steel Corporation, Pittsburgh, 1971, p. 1096.]

rapid to be practical are required. Other alloying elements that are particularly effective in rendering steels heat treatable are chromium, nickel, molybdenum, manganese, silicon, and tungsten; however, these elements must be in solid solution with the austenite at the time of quenching.

In summary, isothermal and continuous cooling transformation diagrams are, in a sense, phase diagrams in which the parameter of time is introduced. Each is experimentally determined for an alloy of specified composition, the variables being temperature and time. These diagrams allow prediction of the microstructure after some time period for constant temperature and continuous cooling heat treatments, respectively.

Concept Check 8.4

Briefly describe the simplest continuous cooling heat treatment procedure that would be used to convert a 4340 steel from (martensite + bainite) to (ferrite + pearlite).

[*The answer may be found in enclosed CD.*]

8.7 MECHANICAL BEHAVIOR OF IRON–CARBON ALLOYS

We shall now discuss the mechanical behavior of iron–carbon alloys having the microstructures discussed heretofore—namely, fine and coarse pearlite, spheroidite, bainite, and martensite. For all but martensite, two phases are present (i.e., ferrite and cementite), and so an opportunity is provided to explore several mechanical property-microstructure relationships that exist for these alloys.

Mechanical properties will be explained in Chapter 9. The concepts of strength, hardness and ductility are explained in detail in Chapter 9. For sake of reference, these concepts are described briefly here. Strength is a measure of the resistance of the material to permanent deformation (Section 9.7). Hardness is a meassure of a material's resistance to localized plastic deformation (Section 9.8). Tensile strength and hardness are roughly proportional, since both are indicators of a material's resistance to permanent deformation. Ductility is a measure of the degree of plastic deformation that has been sustained at fracture (Section 9.7). The ability of a metal to plastically deform depends on the ability of dislocations to move (Sections 10.2 through 10.6). By reducing the mobility of dislocations, the mechanical strength and hardness may be enhanced. The mechanisms of strengthening of metals are detailed in Chapter 10. Virtually all strengthening techniques rely on the simple principle of restricting or hindering dislocation motion, which renders a material harder and stronger.

Pearlite

Cementite is much harder but more brittle than ferrite. Thus, increasing the fraction of Fe_3C in a steel alloy while holding other microstructural elements constant will result in a harder and stronger material. This is demonstrated in Figure 8.29*a*, in which the tensile and yield strengths as well as the Brinell hardness number are plotted as a function of the weight percent carbon (or equivalently as the percentage of Fe_3C) for steels that are composed of fine pearlite. All three parameters increase with increasing carbon concentration. Inasmuch as cementite is more brittle, increasing its content will result in a decrease in both ductility and toughness (or impact energy). These effects are shown in Figure 8.29*b* for the same fine pearlitic steels.

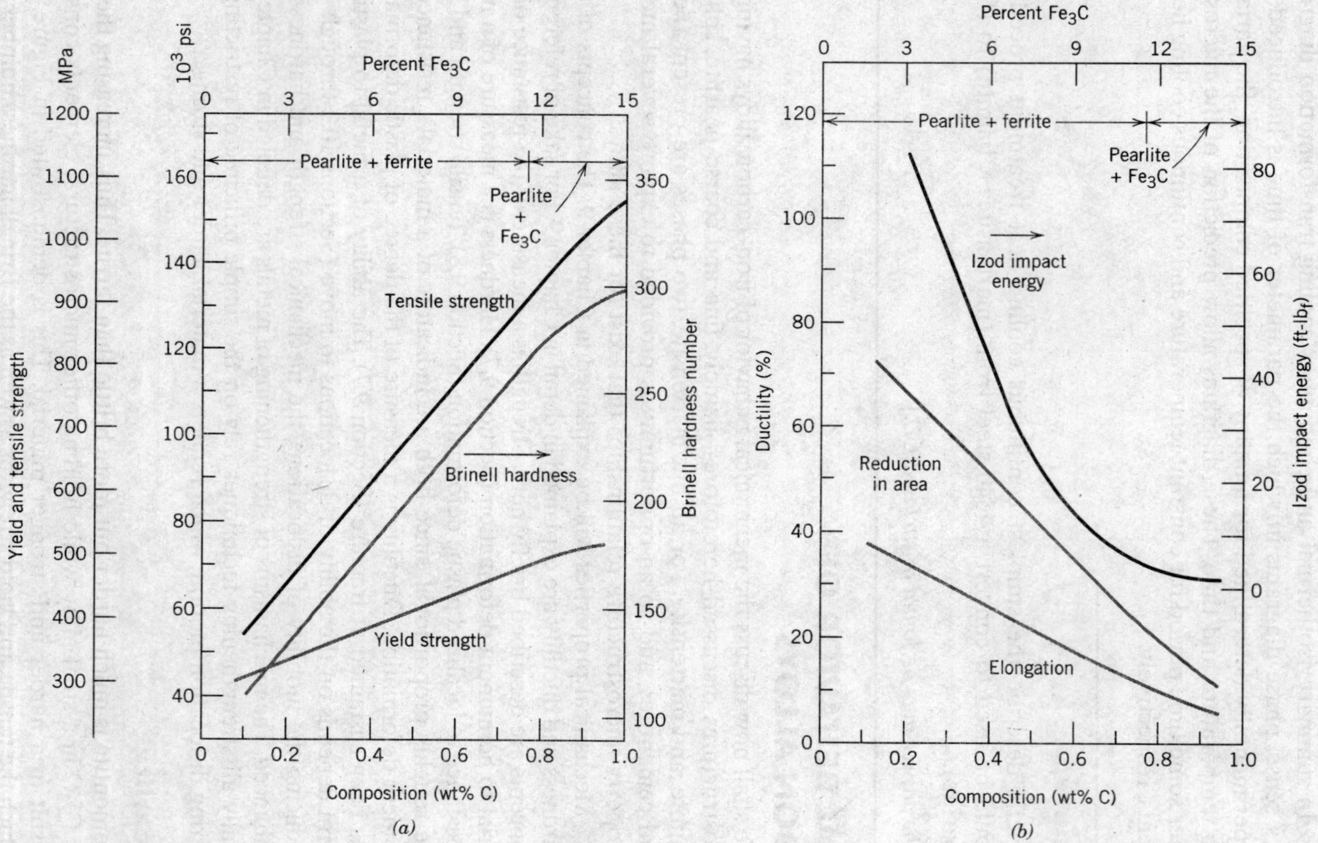

Figure 8.29 (*a*) Yield strength, tensile strength, and Brinell hardness versus carbon concentration for plain carbon steels having microstructures consisting of fine pearlite. (*b*) Ductility (%EL and %RA) and Izod impact energy versus carbon concentration for plain carbon steels having microstructures consisting of fine pearlite. [Data taken from *Metals Handbook: Heat Treating,* Vol. 4, 9th edition, V. Masseria (Managing Editor), American Society for Metals, 1981, p. 9.]

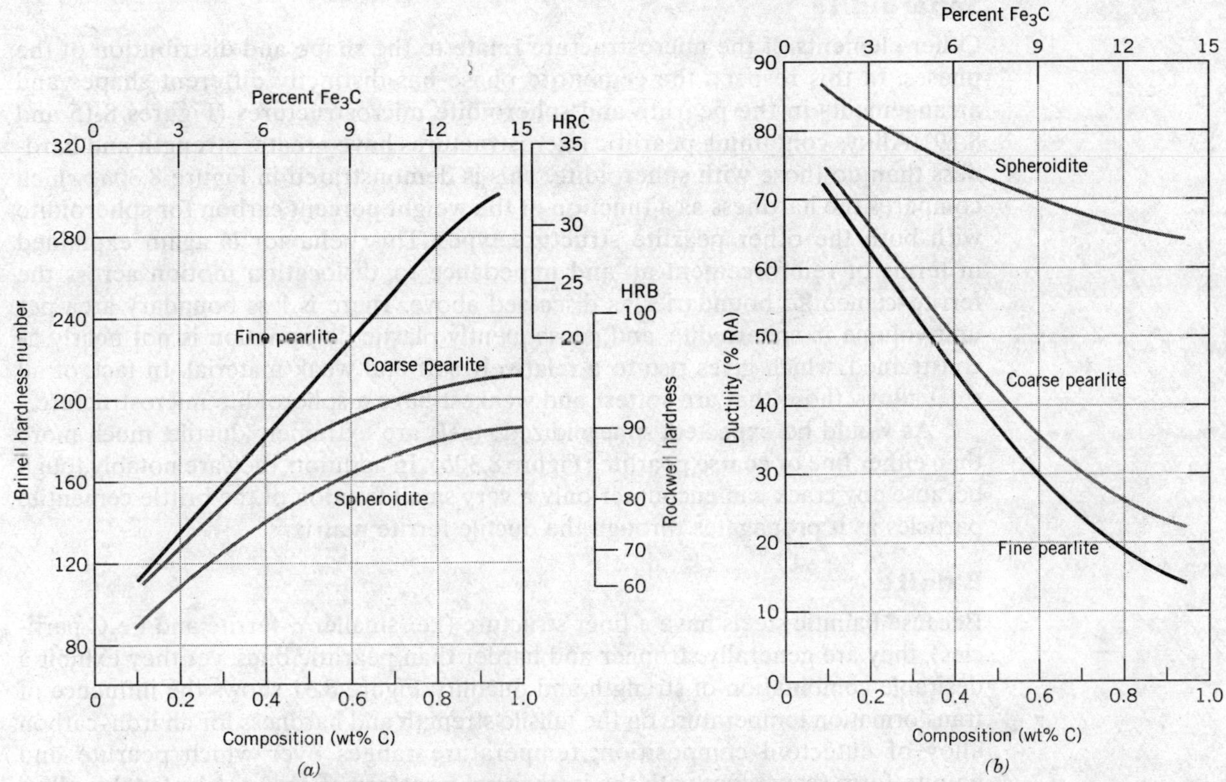

Figure 8.30 (*a*) Brinell and Rockwell hardness as a function of carbon concentration for plain carbon steels having fine and coarse pearlite as well as spheroidite microstructures. (*b*) Ductility (%RA) as a function of carbon concentration for plain carbon steels having fine and coarse pearlite as well as spheroidite microstructures. (Data taken from *Metals Handbook: Heat Treating,* Vol. 4, 9th edition, V. Masseria, Managing Editor, American Society for Metals, 1981, pp. 9 and 17.)

The layer thickness of each of the ferrite and cementite phases in the microstructure also influences the mechanical behavior of the material. Fine pearlite is harder and stronger than coarse pearlite, as demonstrated in Figure 8.30*a*, which plots hardness versus the carbon concentration.

The reasons for this behavior relate to phenomena that occur at the α–Fe_3C phase boundaries. First, there is a large degree of adherence between the two phases across a boundary. Therefore, the strong and rigid cementite phase severely restricts deformation of the softer ferrite phase in the regions adjacent to the boundary; thus the cementite may be said to reinforce the ferrite. The degree of this reinforcement is substantially higher in fine pearlite because of the greater phase boundary area per unit volume of material. In addition, phase boundaries serve as barriers to dislocation motion in much the same way as grain boundaries (Section 10.8). For fine pearlite there are more boundaries through which a dislocation must pass during plastic deformation. Thus, the greater reinforcement and restriction of dislocation motion in fine pearlite account for its greater hardness and strength.

Coarse pearlite is more ductile than fine pearlite, as illustrated in Figure 8.30*b*, which plots percentage reduction in area versus carbon concentration for both microstructure types. This behavior results from the greater restriction to plastic deformation of the fine pearlite.

Spheroidite

Other elements of the microstructure relate to the shape and distribution of the phases. In this respect, the cementite phase has distinctly different shapes and arrangements in the pearlite and spheroidite microstructures (Figures 8.15 and 8.19). Alloys containing pearlitic microstructures have greater strength and hardness than do those with spheroidite. This is demonstrated in Figure 8.30*a*, which compares the hardness as a function of the weight percent carbon for spheroidite with both the other pearlite structure types. This behavior is again explained in terms of reinforcement at, and impedance to, dislocation motion across the ferrite–cementite boundaries as discussed above. There is less boundary area per unit volume in spheroidite, and consequently plastic deformation is not nearly as constrained, which gives rise to a relatively soft and weak material. In fact, of all steel alloys, those that are softest and weakest have a spheroidite microstructure.

As would be expected, spheroidized steels are extremely ductile, much more than either fine or coarse pearlite (Figure 8.30*b*). In addition, they are notably tough because any crack can encounter only a very small fraction of the brittle cementite particles as it propagates through the ductile ferrite matrix.

Bainite

Because bainitic steels have a finer structure (i.e., smaller α-ferrite and Fe_3C particles), they are generally stronger and harder than pearlitic ones; yet they exhibit a desirable combination of strength and ductility. Figure 8.31 shows the influence of transformation temperature on the tensile strength and hardness for an iron–carbon alloy of eutectoid composition; temperature ranges over which pearlite and bainite form (consistent with the isothermal transformation diagram for this alloy, Figure 8.18) are noted at the top of Figure 8.31.

Martensite

Of the various microstructures that may be produced for a given steel alloy, martensite is the hardest and strongest and, in addition, the most brittle; it has, in fact, negligible ductility. Its hardness is dependent on the carbon content, up to about 0.6 wt% as demonstrated in Figure 8.32, which plots the hardness of martensite and fine pearlite as a function of weight percent carbon. In contrast to pearlitic steels, strength and hardness of martensite are not thought to be related to microstructure. Rather,

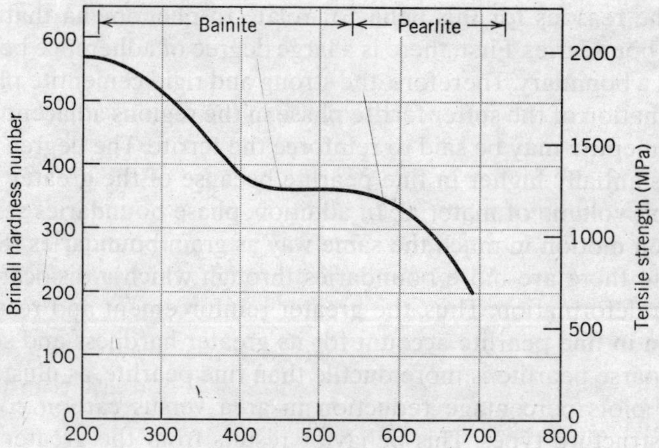

Figure 8.31 Brinell hardness and tensile strength (at room temperature) as a function of isothermal transformation temperature for an iron–carbon alloy of eutectoid composition, taken over the temperature range at which bainitic and pearlitic microstructures form. (Adapted from E. S. Davenport, "Isothermal Transformation in Steels," *Trans. ASM,* **27**, 1939, p. 847. Reprinted by permission of ASM International.)

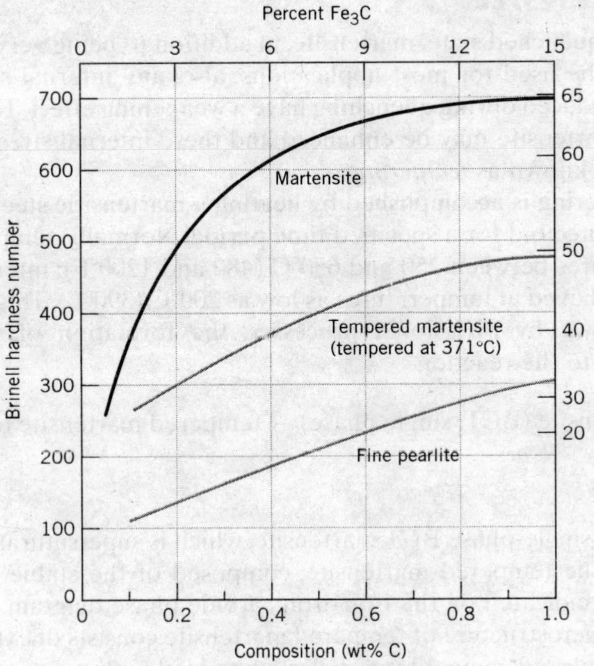

Figure 8.32 Hardness (at room temperature) as a function of carbon concentration for plain carbon martensitic, tempered martensitic [tempered at 371°C (700°F)], and pearlitic steels. (Adapted from Edgar C. Bain, *Functions of the Alloying Elements in Steel,* American Society for Metals, 1939, p. 36; and R. A. Grange, C. R. Hribal, and L. F. Porter, *Metall. Trans. A,* Vol. 8A, p. 1776.)

these properties are attributed to the effectiveness of the interstitial carbon atoms in hindering dislocation motion (as a solid-solution effect, Section 10.9), and to the relatively few slip systems (along which dislocations move) for the BCT structure.

Austenite is slightly denser than martensite, and therefore, during the phase transformation upon quenching, there is a net volume increase. Consequently, relatively large pieces that are rapidly quenched may crack as a result of internal stresses; this becomes a problem especially when the carbon content is greater than about 0.5 wt%.

Concept Check 8.5

Rank the following iron-carbon alloys and associated microstructures from the highest to the lowest tensile strength:

0.25 wt% C with spheroidite

0.25 wt% C with coarse pearlite

0.6 wt% C with fine pearlite, and

0.6 wt% C with coarse pearlite.

Justify this ranking.

[*The answer may be found in enclosed CD.*]

Concept Check 8.6

For a eutectoid steel, describe an isothermal heat treatment that would be required to produce a specimen having a hardness of 93 HRB.

[*The answer may be found in enclosed CD.*]

8.8 TEMPERED MARTENSITE

In the as-quenched state, martensite, in addition to being very hard, is so brittle that it cannot be used for most applications; also, any internal stresses that may have been introduced during quenching have a weakening effect. The ductility and toughness of martensite may be enhanced and these internal stresses relieved by a heat treatment known as *tempering*.

Tempering is accomplished by heating a martensitic steel to a temperature below the eutectoid for a specified time period. Normally, tempering is carried out at temperatures between 250 and 650°C (480 and 1200°F); internal stresses, however, may be relieved at temperatures as low as 200°C (390°F). This tempering heat treatment allows, by diffusional processes, the formation of **tempered martensite,** according to the reaction

$$\text{martensite (BCT, single phase)} \rightarrow \text{tempered martensite } (\alpha + \text{Fe}_3\text{C phases}) \tag{8.20}$$

where the single-phase BCT martensite, which is supersaturated with carbon, transforms to the tempered martensite, composed of the stable ferrite and cementite phases, as indicated on the iron–iron carbide phase diagram.

The microstructure of tempered martensite consists of extremely small and uniformly dispersed cementite particles embedded within a continuous ferrite matrix. This is similar to the microstructure of spheroidite except that the cementite particles are much, much smaller. An electron micrograph showing the microstructure of tempered martensite at a very high magnification is presented in Figure 8.33.

Tempered martensite may be nearly as hard and strong as martensite, but with substantially enhanced ductility and toughness. For example, on the hardness-versus-weight percent carbon plot of Figure 8.32 is included a curve for tempered martensite. The hardness and strength may be explained by the large ferrite–cementite phase boundary area per unit volume that exists for the very fine and numerous cementite particles. Again, the hard cementite phase reinforces the ferrite matrix along the boundaries, and these boundaries also act as barriers to dislocation motion during plastic deformation. The continuous ferrite phase is also very ductile and relatively tough, which accounts for the improvement of these two properties for tempered martensite.

The size of the cementite particles influences the mechanical behavior of tempered martensite; increasing the particle size decreases the ferrite–cementite phase

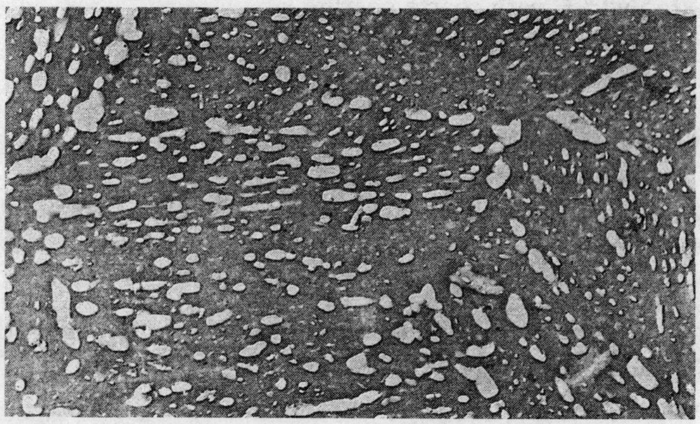

Figure 8.33 Electron micrograph of tempered martensite. Tempering was carried out at 594°C (1100°F). The small particles are the cementite phase; the matrix phase is α-ferrite. 9300×. (Copyright 1971 by United States Steel Corporation.)

boundary area and, consequently, results in a softer and weaker material yet one that is tougher and more ductile. Furthermore, the tempering heat treatment determines the size of the cementite particles. Heat treatment variables are temperature and time, and most treatments are constant-temperature processes. Since carbon diffusion is involved in the martensite-tempered martensite transformation, increasing the temperature will accelerate diffusion, the rate of cementite particle growth, and, subsequently, the rate of softening. The dependence of tensile and yield strength and ductility on tempering temperature for an alloy steel is shown in Figure 8.34. Before tempering, the material was quenched in oil to produce the martensitic structure; the tempering time at each temperature was 1 h. This type of tempering data is ordinarily provided by the steel manufacturer.

The time dependence of hardness at several different temperatures is presented in Figure 8.35 for a water-quenched steel of eutectoid composition; the time scale is logarithmic. With increasing time the hardness decreases, which corresponds to the growth and coalescence of the cementite particles. At temperatures approaching the eutectoid [700°C (1300°F)] and after several hours, the microstructure will have become spheroiditic (Figure 8.19), with large cementite spheroids embedded within the continuous ferrite phase. Correspondingly, overtempered martensite is relatively soft and ductile.

Concept Check 8.7

A steel alloy is quenched from a temperature within the austenite phase region into water at room temperature so as to form martensite; the alloy is subsequently tempered at an elevated temperature which is held constant.

(a) Make a schematic plot showing how room-temperature ductility varies with the logarithm of tempering time at the elevated temperature. (Be sure to label your axes.)

(b) Superimpose and label on this same plot the room-temperature behavior resulting from tempering at a higher temperature and briefly explain the difference in behavior between these two temperatures.

[*The answer may be found in enclosed CD.*]

Temper Embrittlement

The tempering of some steels may result in a reduction of toughness as measured by impact tests (Section 11.6); this is termed *temper embrittlement*. The phenomenon occurs when the steel is tempered at a temperature above about 575°C (1070°F) followed by slow cooling to room temperature, or when tempering is carried out at between approximately 375 and 575°C (700 and 1070°F). Steel alloys that are susceptible to temper embrittlement have been found to contain appreciable concentrations of the alloying elements manganese, nickel, or chromium and, in addition, one or more of antimony, phosphorus, arsenic, and tin as impurities in relatively low concentrations. The presence of these alloying elements and impurities shifts the ductile-to-brittle transition to significantly higher temperatures; the ambient temperature thus lies below this transition in the brittle regime. It has been observed that crack propagation of these embrittled materials is intergranular (Figure 11.7); that is, the fracture path is along the grain boundaries of the precursor austenite phase. Furthermore, alloy and impurity elements have been found to preferentially segregate in these regions.

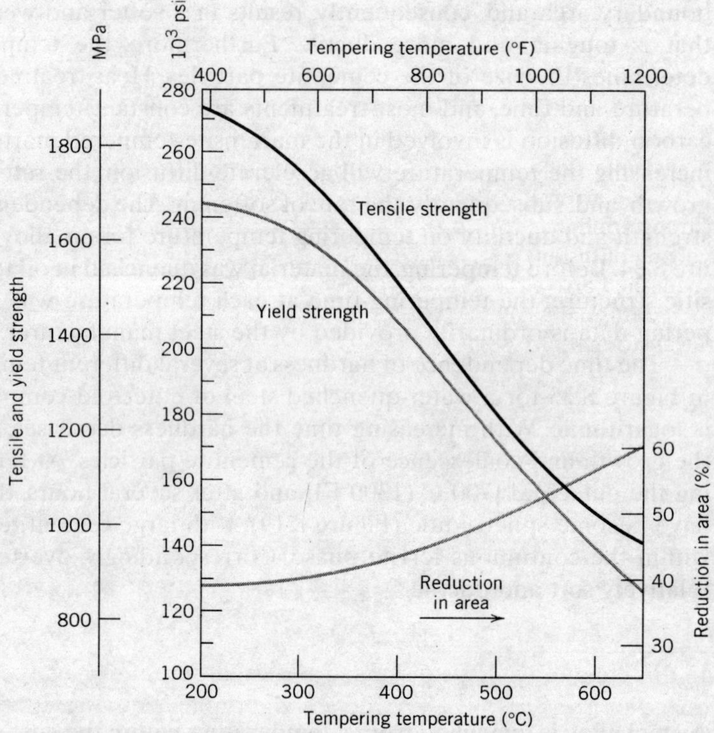

Figure 8.34 Tensile and yield strengths and ductility (%RA) (at room temperature) versus tempering temperature for an oil-quenched alloy steel (type 4340). (Adapted from figure furnished courtesy Republic Steel Corporation.)

Temper embrittlement may be avoided by (1) compositional control, and/or (2) tempering above 575°C or below 375°C, followed by quenching to room temperature. Furthermore, the toughness of steels that have been embrittled may be improved significantly by heating to about 600°C (1100°F) and then rapidly cooling to below 300°C (570°F).

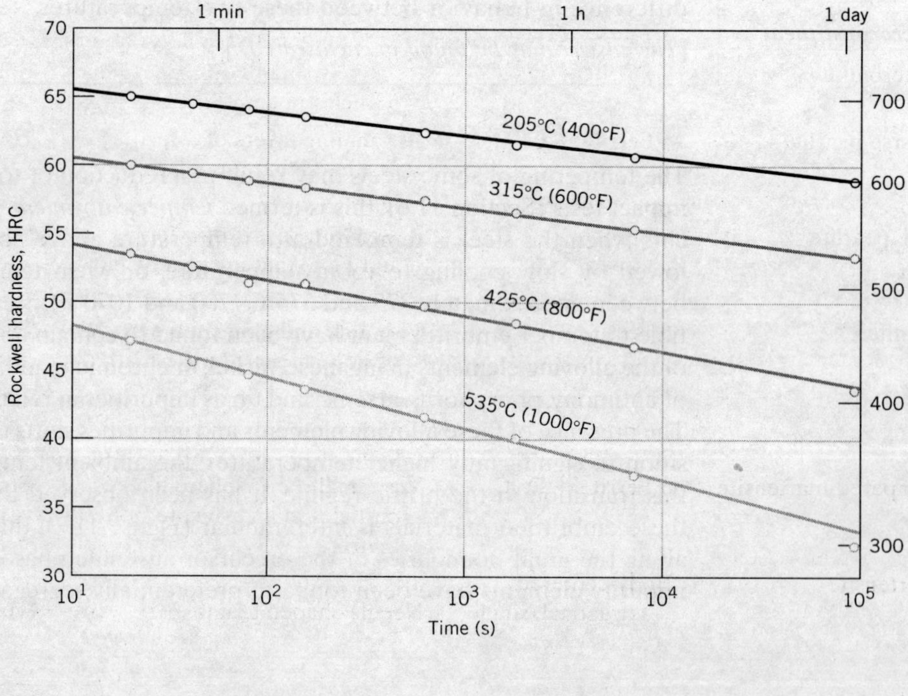

Figure 8.35 Hardness (at room temperature) versus tempering time for a water-quenched eutectoid plain carbon (1080) steel. (Adapted from Edgar C. Bain, *Functions of the Alloying Elements in Steel,* American Society for Metals, 1939, p. 233.)

Figure 8.36 Possible transformations involving the decomposition of austenite. Solid arrows, transformations involving diffusion; dashed arrow, diffusionless transformation.

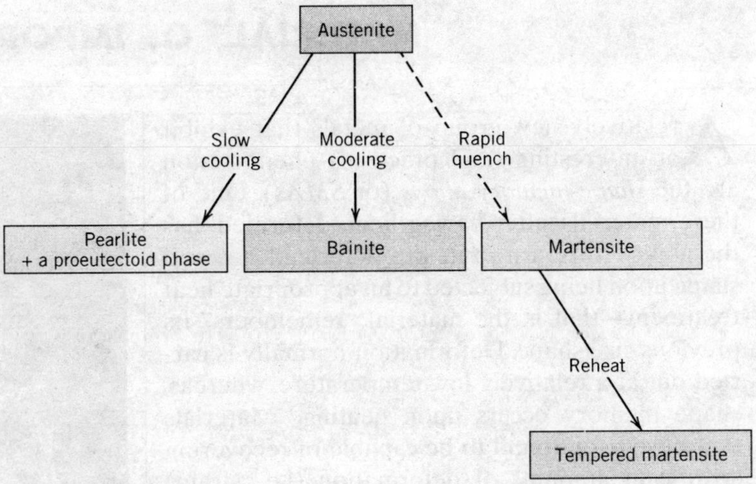

8.9 REVIEW OF PHASE TRANSFORMATIONS AND MECHANICAL PROPERTIES FOR IRON–CARBON ALLOYS

In this chapter we have discussed several different microstructures that may be produced in iron–carbon alloys depending on heat treatment. Figure 8.36 summarizes the transformation paths that produce these various microstructures. Here, it is assumed that pearlite, bainite, and martensite result from continuous cooling treatments; furthermore, the formation of bainite is only possible for alloy steels (not plain carbon ones) as outlined above.

Furthermore, microstructural characteristics and mechanical properties of the several microconstituents for iron–carbon alloys are summarized in Table 8.2.

Table 8.2 Summary of Microstructures and Mechanical Properties for Iron–Carbon Alloys

Microconstituent	*Phases Present*	*Arrangement of Phases*	*Mechanical Properties (Relative)*
Spheroidite	α Ferrite + Fe_3C	Relatively small Fe_3C sphere-like particles in an α-ferrite matrix	Soft and ductile
Coarse pearlite	α Ferrite + Fe_3C	Alternating layers of α ferrite and Fe_3C that are relatively thick	Harder and stronger than spheroidite, but not as ductile as spheroidite
Fine pearlite	α Ferrite + Fe_3C	Alternating layers of α ferrite and Fe_3C that are relatively thin	Harder and stronger than coarse pearlite, but not as ductile as coarse pearlite
Bainite	α Ferrite + Fe_3C	Very fine and elongated particles of Fe_3C in an α-ferrite matrix	Hardness and strength greater than fine pearlite; hardness less than martensite; ductility greater than martensite
Tempered martensite	α Ferrite + Fe_3C	Very small Fe_3C sphere-like particles in an α-ferrite matrix	Strong; not as hard as martensite, but much more ductile than martensite
Martensite	Body-centered tetragonal, single phase	Needle-shaped grains	Very hard and very brittle

MATERIALS OF IMPORTANCE

Shape-Memory Alloys

A relatively new group of metals that exhibit an interesting (and practical) phenomenon are the *shape-memory alloys* (or *SMAs*). One of these materials, after having been deformed, has the ability to return to its pre-deformed size and shape upon being subjected to an appropriate heat treatment—that is, the material "remembers" its previous size/shape. Deformation normally is carried out at a relatively low temperature, whereas, shape memory occurs upon heating.[5] Materials that have been found to be capable of recovering significant amounts of deformation (i.e., strain) are nickel–titanium alloys (Nitinol,[6] is their tradename), and some copper-base alloys (viz. Cu–Zn–Al and Cu–Al–Ni alloys).

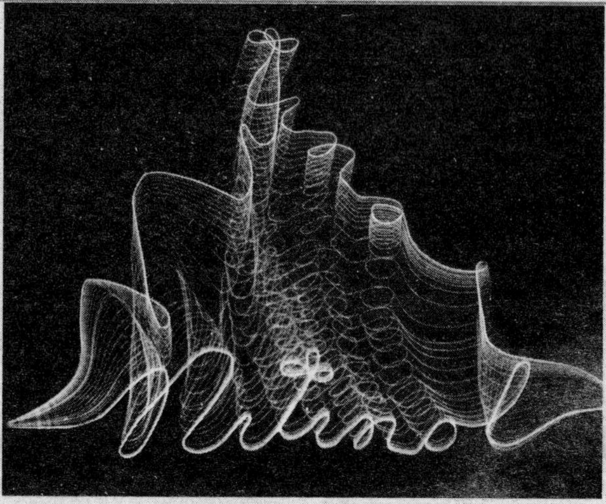

Time-lapse photograph that demonstrates the shape-memory effect. A wire of a shape-memory alloy (Nitinol) has been bent and treated such that its memory shape spells the word "Nitinol". The wire is then deformed and, upon heating (by passage of an electric current), springs back to its pre-deformed shape; this shape recovery process is recorded on the photograph. [Photograph courtesy the Naval Surface Warfare Center (previously the Naval Ordnance Laboratory)].

A shape memory alloy is polymorphic (Section 4.9)—that is, it may have two crystal structures (or phases), and the shape-memory effect involves phase transformations between them. One phase (termed an austenite phase) has a body-centered cubic structure that exists at elevated temperatures; its structure is represented schematically by the inset shown at stage 1 of Figure 8.37. Upon cooling, the austenite transforms spontaneously to a martensite phase, which is similar to the martensitic transformation for the iron–carbon system (Section 8.5)—that is, it is diffusionless, involves an orderly shift of large groups of atoms, occurs very rapidly, and the degree of transformation is dependent on temperature; temperatures at which the transformation begins and ends are indicated by "M_s" and "M_f" labels on the left vertical axis of Figure 4.9. In addition, this martensite is heavily twinned,[7] as represented schematically by the stage 2 inset, Figure 8.37. Under the influence of an applied stress, deformation of martensite (i.e., the passage from stage 2 to stage 3, Figure 8.37) occurs by the migration of twin boundaries—some twinned regions grow while others shrink; this deformed martensitic structure is represented by the stage 3 inset. Furthermore, when the stress is removed, the deformed shape is retained at this temperature. And, finally, upon subsequent heating to the initial temperature, the material reverts back to (i.e., "remembers") its original size and shape (stage 4). This stage 3–stage 4 process is accompanied by a phase transformation from the deformed martensite to the original high-temperature austenite phase. For these shape memory alloys, the martensite-to-austenite transformation occurs over a temperature range, between temperatures denoted by "A_s" (austenite start) and "A_f" (austenite finish) labels on the right vertical axis of

[5] Alloys that demonstrate this phenomenon only upon heating are said to have a *one-way* shape memory. Some of these materials experience size/shape changes on both heating and cooling; these are termed *two-way* shape memory alloys. In this discussion, we discuss the mechanism for only the one-way shape-memory.

[6] "Nitinol" is really an acronym for *ni*ckel-*ti*tanium *N*aval *O*rdnance *L*aboratory, where this alloy was discovered.

[7] The phenomenon of twinning is described in Section 10.7.

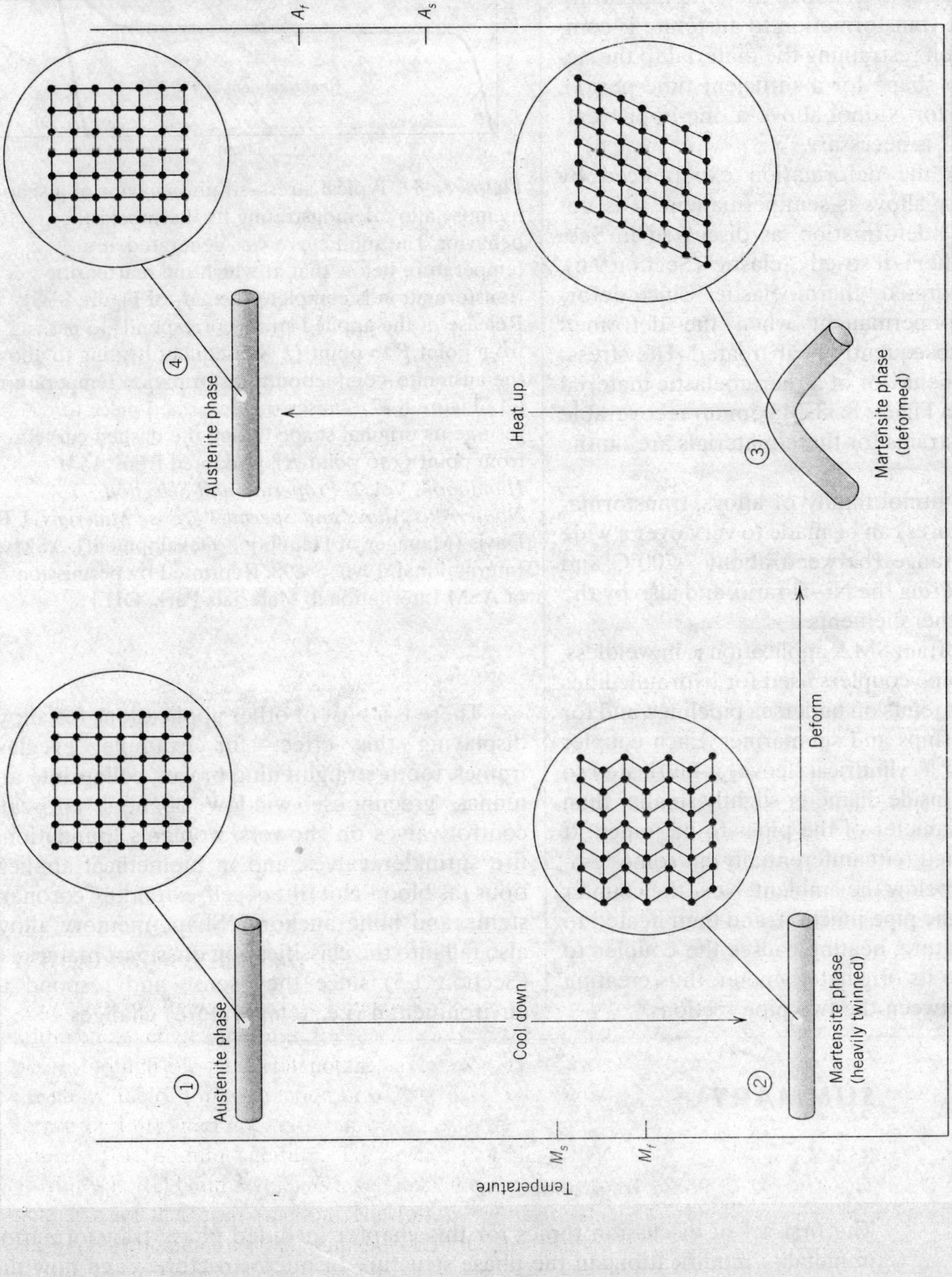

Figure 8.37 Diagram illustrating the shape memory effect. The insets are schematic representations of the crystal structure at the four stages. M_s and M_f denote temperatures at which the martensitic transformation begins and ends. Likewise for the austenite transformation, A_s and A_f represent beginning and end transformation temperatures. (Adapted from BALL, Philip; *MADE TO MEASURE*. © 1997 Princeton University Press. Reprinted by permission of Princeton University Press.)

Figure 8.37. Of course, this deformation–transformation cycle may be repeated for the shape-memory material.

The original shape (to be remembered) is created by heating to well above the A_f temperature (such that the transformation to austenite is complete), and then restraining the material to the desired memory shape for a sufficient time period. For example, for Nitinol alloys, a one-hour treatment at 500°C is necessary.

Although the deformation experienced by shape-memory alloys is semipermanent, it is not truly "plastic" deformation, as discussed in Section 9.7—neither is it strictly "elastic" (Section 9.6). Rather, it is termed "thermoelastic," since deformation is nonpermanent when the deformed material is subsequently heat treated. The stress-versus-strain behavior of a thermoelastic material is presented in Figure 8.38. Maximum recoverable deformation strains for these materials are on the order of 8%.

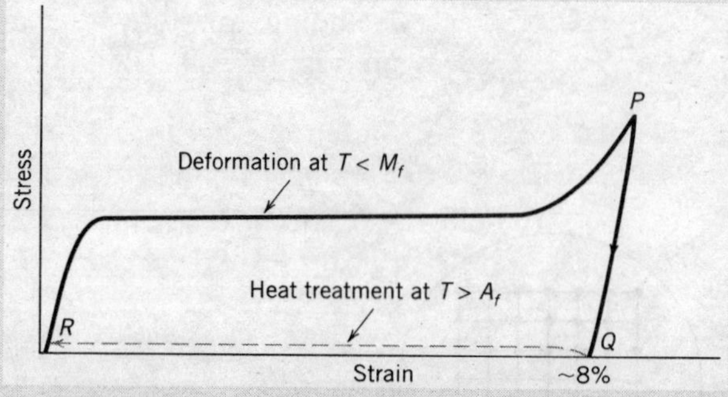

Figure 8.38 Typical stress–strain behavior of a shape-memory alloy, demonstrating its thermoelastic behavior. The solid curve was generated at a temperature below that at which the martensitic transformation is complete (i.e., M_f of Figure 8.37). Release of the applied stress corresponds to passing from point P to point Q. Subsequent heating to above the austenite–completion transformation temperature (A_f, Figure 8.37), causes the deformed piece to resume its original shape (along the dashed curve from point Q to point R). [Adapted from *ASM Handbook,* Vol. 2, *Properties and Selection: Nonferrous Alloys and Special-Purpose Materials,* J. R. Davis (Manager of Handbook Development), ASM International, 1990, p. 898. Reprinted by permission of ASM International, Materials Park, OH.]

For this Nitinol family of alloys, transformation temperatures can be made to vary over a wide temperature range (between about −200°C and 110°C), by altering the Ni–Ti ratio, and also by the addition of other elements.

One important SMA application is in weldless, shrink-to-fit pipe couplers used for hydraulic lines on aircraft, for joints on undersea pipelines, and for plumbing on ships and submarines. Each coupler (in the form of a cylindrical sleeve) is fabricated so as to have an inside diameter slightly smaller than the outside diameter of the pipes to be joined. It is then stretched (circumferentially) at some temperature well below the ambient. Next the coupler is fitted over the pipe junction, and then heated to room temperature; heating causes the coupler to shrink back to its original diameter, thus creating a tight seal between the two pipe sections.

There is a host of other applications for alloys displaying this effect—for example, eyeglass frames, tooth-straightening braces, collapsible antennas, greenhouse window openers, antiscald control valves on showers, women's foundations, fire sprinkler valves, and in biomedical applications (as blood-clot filters, self-extending coronary stents, and bone anchors). Shape-memory alloys also fall into the classification of "smart materials" (Section 1.5) since they sense and respond to environmental (i.e., temperature) changes.

SUMMARY

Basic Concepts
The Kinetics of Phase Transformations

The first set of discussion topics for this chapter included phase transformations in metals—modifications in the phase structure or microstructure—and how they affect mechanical properties. Nucleation and growth processes, which are involved in the production of a new phase, were discussed, in addition to the temperature dependence of phase transformation rate. Other kinetic principles were treated, including, for solid-state transformations, the dependence of fraction of transformation on time.

Metastable Versus Equilibrium States
Isothermal Transformation Diagrams
Continuous Cooling Transformation Diagrams
Mechanical Behavior of Iron–Carbon Alloys
Tempered Martensite

As a practical matter, phase diagrams are severely restricted relative to transformations in multiphase alloys, because they provide no information as to phase transformation rates. The element of time is incorporated into both isothermal transformation and continuous cooling transformation diagrams; transformation progress as a function of temperature and elapsed time is expressed for a specific alloy at constant temperature and for continuous cooling treatments, respectively. Diagrams of both types were presented for iron–carbon steel alloys, and their utility with regard to the prediction of microstructural products was discussed.

Several microconstituents are possible for steels, the formation of which depends on composition and heat treatment. These microconstituents include fine and coarse pearlite, and bainite, which are composed of ferrite and cementite phases and result from the decomposition of austenite via diffusional processes. A spheroidite microstructure (also consisting of ferrite and cementite phases) may be produced when a steel specimen composed of any of the preceding microstructures is heat treated at a temperature just below the eutectoid. The mechanical characteristics of pearlitic, bainitic, and spheroiditic steels were compared and also explained in terms of their microconstituents.

Martensite, yet another transformation product in steels, results when austenite is cooled very rapidly. It is a metastable and single-phase structure that may be produced in steels by a diffusionless and almost instantaneous transformation of austenite. Transformation progress is dependent on temperature rather than time, and may be represented on both isothermal and continuous cooling transformation diagrams. Furthermore, alloying element additions retard the formation rate of pearlite and bainite, thus rendering the martensitic transformation more competitive. Mechanically, martensite is extremely hard; applicability, however, is limited by its brittleness. A tempering heat treatment increases the ductility at some sacrifice of strength and hardness. During tempering, martensite transforms to tempered martensite, which consists of the equilibrium ferrite and cementite phases. Embrittlement of some steel alloys results when specific alloying and impurity elements are present, and upon tempering within a definite temperature range.

REFERENCES

Atkins, M., *Atlas of Continuous Cooling Transformation Diagrams for Engineering Steels,* British Steel Corporation, Sheffield, England, 1980.

Atlas of Isothermal Transformation and Cooling Transformation Diagrams, ASM International, Materials Park, OH, 1977.

Brooks, C. R., *Principles of the Heat Treatment of Plain Carbon and Low Alloy Steels,* ASM International, Materials Park, OH, 1996.

Jena, A. K. and M. C. Chaturvedi, *Phase Transformation in Materials*, Prentice Hall, New Jersey, 1992.

Porter, D. A. and K. E. Easterling, *Phase Transformations in Metals and Alloys,* Chapman and Hall, New York, 1992.

Shewmon, P. G., *Transformations in Metals,* McGraw-Hill, New York, 1969. Reprinted by Williams Book Company, Tulsa, OK.

Vander Voort, G. (Editor), *Atlas of Time–Temperature Diagrams for Irons and Steels,* ASM International, Materials Park, OH, 1991.

Vander Voort, G. (Editor), *Atlas of Time–Temperature Diagrams for Nonferrous Alloys,* ASM International, Materials Park, OH, 1991.

QUESTIONS AND PROBLEMS

The Kinetics of Phase Transformations

8.1 Name the two stages involved in the formation of particles of a new phase. Briefly describe each.

8.2 **(a)** Rewrite the expression for the total free energy change for nucleation (Equation 8.1) for the case of a cubic nucleus of edge length a (instead of a sphere of radius r). Now differentiate this expression with respect to a (per Equation 8.2) and solve for both the critical cube edge length, a^*, and also ΔG^*.

(b) Is ΔG^* greater for a cube or a sphere? Why?

8.3 If ice homogeneously nucleates at $-40°C$, calculate the critical radius given values of -3.1×10^8 J/m^3 and 25×10^{-3} J/m^2, respectively, for the latent heat of fusion and the surface free energy.

8.4 **(a)** For the solidification of nickel, calculate the critical radius r^* and the activation free energy ΔG^* if nucleation is homogeneous. Values for the latent heat of fusion and surface free energy are -2.53×10^9 J/m^3 and 0.255 J/m^2, respectively. Use the supercooling value found in Table 8.1.

(b) Now calculate the number of atoms found in a nucleus of critical size. Assume a lattice parameter of 0.360 nm for solid nickel at its melting temperature.

8.5 **(a)** Assume for the solidification of nickel (Problem 8.4) that nucleation is homogeneous, and the number of stable nuclei is 10^6 nuclei per cubic meter. Calculate the critical radius and the number of stable nuclei that exist at the following degrees of supercooling: 200 K and 300 K.

(b) What is significant about the magnitudes of these critical radii and the numbers of stable nuclei?

8.6 For some transformation having kinetics that obey the Avrami equation (Equation 8.17), the parameter n is known to have a value of 1.5. If, after 125 s, the reaction is 25% complete, how long (total time) will it take the transformation to go to 90% completion?

8.7 Compute the rate of some reaction that obeys Avrami kinetics, assuming that the constants n and k have values of 2.0 and 5×10^{-4}, respectively, for time expressed in seconds.

8.8 It is known that the kinetics of recrystallization for some alloy obey the Avrami equation, and that the value of n in the exponential is 5.0. If, at some temperature, the fraction recrystallized is 0.30 after 100 min, determine the rate of recrystallization at this temperature.

8.9 The kinetics of the austenite-to-pearlite transformation obey the Avrami relationship. Using the fraction transformed–time data given here, determine the total time required for 95% of the austenite to transform to pearlite:

Fraction Transformed	*Time (s)*
0.2	280
0.6	425

8.10 The fraction recrystallized–time data for the recrystallization at 350°C of a previously deformed aluminum are tabulated here. Assuming that the kinetics of this process obey the Avrami relationship, determine the fraction recrystallized after a total time of 116.8 min.

Fraction Recrystallized	*Time (min)*
0.30	95.2
0.80	126.6

8.11 **(a)** From the curves shown in Figure 8.11 and using Equation 8.18, determine the rate of recrystallization for pure copper at the several temperatures.

(b) Make a plot of ln(rate) versus the reciprocal of temperature (in K^{-1}), and determine the activation energy for this recrystallization process. (See Section 6.5.)

(c) By extrapolation, estimate the length of time required for 50% recrystallization at room temperature, 20°C (293 K).

8.12 Determine values for the constants n and k (Equation 8.17) for the recrystallization of copper (Figure 8.11) at 119°C.

Metastable Versus Equilibrium States

8.13 In terms of heat treatment and the development of microstructure, what are two major limitations of the iron–iron carbide phase diagram?

8.14 **(a)** Briefly describe the phenomena of superheating and supercooling.

(b) Why do these phenomena occur?

Isothermal Transformation Diagrams

8.15 Suppose that a steel of eutectoid composition is cooled to 675°C (1250°F) from 760°C (1400°F) in less than 0.5 s and held at this temperature.

(a) How long will it take for the austenite-to-pearlite reaction to go to 50% completion? To 100% completion?

(b) Estimate the hardness of the alloy that has completely transformed to pearlite.

8.16 Briefly cite the differences between pearlite, bainite, and spheroidite relative to microstructure and mechanical properties.

8.17 What is the driving force for the formation of spheroidite?

8.18 Using the isothermal transformation diagram for an iron–carbon alloy of eutectoid composition (Figure 8.22), specify the nature of the final microstructure (in terms of microconstituents present and approximate percentages of each) of a small specimen that has been subjected to the following time–temperature treatments. In each case assume that the specimen begins at 760°C (1400°F) and that it has been held at this temperature long enough to have achieved a complete and homogeneous austenitic structure.

(a) Cool rapidly to 350°C (660°F), hold for 10^3 s, then quench to room temperature.

(b) Rapidly cool to 625°C (1160°F), hold for 10 s, then quench to room temperature.

(c) Rapidly cool to 600°C (1110°F), hold for 4 s, rapidly cool to 450°C (840°F), hold for 10 s, then quench to room temperature.

(d) Reheat the specimen in part (c) to 700°C (1290°F) for 20 h.

(e) Rapidly cool to 300°C (570°F), hold for 20 s, then quench to room temperature in water. Reheat to 425°C (800°F) for 10^3 s and slowly cool to room temperature.

(f) Cool rapidly to 665°C (1230°F), hold for 10^3 s, then quench to room temperature.

(g) Rapidly cool to 575°C (1065°F), hold for 20 s, rapidly cool to 350°C (660°F), hold for 100 s, then quench to room temperature.

(h) Rapidly cool to 350°C (660°F), hold for 150 s, then quench to room temperature.

8.19 Make a copy of the isothermal transformation diagram for an iron–carbon alloy of eutectoid composition (Figure 8.22) and then sketch and label time–temperature paths on this diagram to produce the following microstructures:

(a) 100% coarse pearlite

(b) 50% martensite and 50% austenite

(c) 50% coarse pearlite, 25% bainite, and 25% martensite

8.20 Using the isothermal transformation diagram for a 1.13 wt% C steel alloy (Figure 8.39), determine the final microstructure (in terms of just the microconstituents present) of a small specimen that has been subjected to the following time–temperature treatments. In each case assume that the specimen begins at 920°C (1690°F) and that it has been held at this temperature long enough to have achieved a complete and homogeneous austenitic structure.

(a) Rapidly cool to 250°C (480°F), hold for 10^3 s, then quench to room temperature.

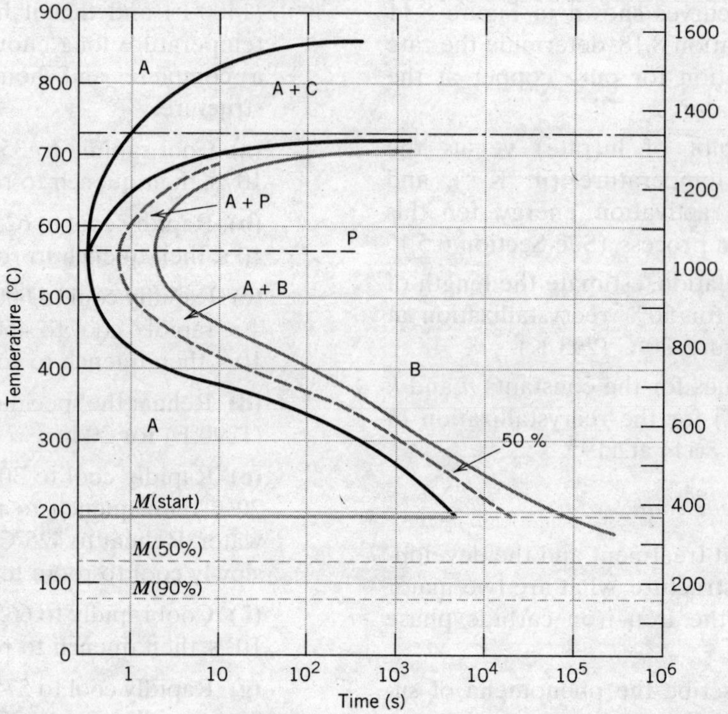

Figure 8.39 Isothermal transformation diagram for a 1.13 wt% C iron–carbon alloy: A, austenite; B, bainite; C, proeutectoid cementite; M, martensite; P, pearlite. [Adapted from H. Boyer (Editor), *Atlas of Isothermal Transformation and Cooling Transformation Diagrams,* American Society for Metals, 1977, p. 33.]

(b) Rapidly cool to 775°C (1430°F), hold for 500 s, then quench to room temperature.

(c) Rapidly cool to 400°C (750°F), hold for 500 s, then quench to room temperature.

(d) Rapidly cool to 700°C (1290°F), hold at this temperature for 10^5 s, then quench to room temperature.

(e) Rapidly cool to 650°C (1200°F), hold at this temperature for 3 s, rapidly cool to 400°C (750°F), hold for 25 s, then quench to room temperature.

(f) Rapidly cool to 350°C (660°F), hold for 300 s, then quench to room temperature.

(g) Rapidly cool to 675°C (1250°F), hold for 7 s, then quench to room temperature.

(h) Rapidly cool to 600°C (1110°F), hold at this temperature for 7 s, rapidly cool to 450°C (840°F), hold at this temperature for 4 s, then quench to room temperature.

8.21 For parts a, c, d, f, and h of Problem 8.20, determine the approximate percentages of the microconstituents that form.

8.22 Make a copy of the isothermal transformation diagram for a 1.13 wt% C iron–carbon alloy (Figure 8.39), and then on this diagram sketch and label time–temperature paths to produce the following microstructures:

(a) 6.2% proeutectoid cementite and 93.8% coarse pearlite

(b) 50% fine pearlite and 50% bainite

(c) 100% martensite

(d) 100% tempered martensite

Continuous Cooling Transformation Diagrams

8.23 Name the microstructural products of eutectoid iron–carbon alloy (0.76 wt% C) specimens that are first completely transformed to austenite, then cooled to room temperature at the following rates: **(a)** 1°C/s, **(b)** 20°C/s, **(c)** 50°C/s, and **(d)** 175°C/s.

8.24 Figure 8.40 shows the continuous cooling transformation diagram for a 0.35 wt% C iron–carbon alloy. Make a copy of this figure and then sketch and label continuous cooling curves to yield the following microstructures:

(a) Fine pearlite and proeutectoid ferrite

(b) Martensite

(c) Martensite and proeutectoid ferrite

(d) Coarse pearlite and proeutectoid ferrite

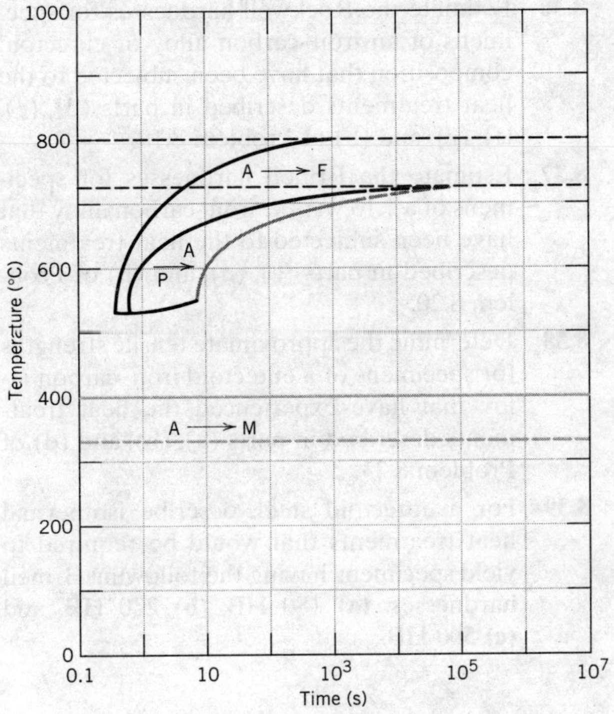

Figure 8.40 Continuous cooling transformation diagram for a 0.35 wt% C iron–carbon alloy.

(e) Martensite, fine pearlite, and proeutectoid ferrite

8.25 Cite two important differences between continuous cooling transformation diagrams for plain carbon and alloy steels.

8.26 Briefly explain why there is no bainite transformation region on the continuous cooling transformation diagram for an iron–carbon alloy of eutectoid composition.

8.27 Name the microstructural products of 4340 alloy steel specimens that are first completely transformed to austenite, then cooled to room temperature at the following rates: **(a)** 0.005°C/s, **(b)** 0.05°C/s, **(c)** 0.5°C/s, and **(d)** 5°C/s.

8.28 Briefly describe the simplest continuous cooling heat treatment procedure that would be used in converting a 4340 steel from one microstructure to another.

(a) (Martensite + ferrite + bainite) to (martensite + ferrite + pearlite + bainite)

(b) (Martensite + ferrite + bainite) to spheroidite

(c) (Martensite + bainite + ferrite) to tempered martensite

8.29 On the basis of diffusion considerations, explain why fine pearlite forms for the moderate cooling of austenite through the eutectoid temperature, whereas coarse pearlite is the product for relatively slow cooling rates.

Mechanical Behavior of Iron–Carbon Alloys
Tempered Martensite

8.30 Briefly explain why fine pearlite is harder and stronger than coarse pearlite, which in turn is harder and stronger than spheroidite.

8.31 Cite two reasons why martensite is so hard and brittle.

8.32 Rank the following iron–carbon alloys and associated microstructures from the hardest to the softest: **(a)** 0.25 wt% C with coarse pearlite, **(b)** 0.80 wt% C with spheroidite, **(c)** 0.25 wt% C with spheroidite, and **(d)** 0.80 wt% C with fine pearlite. Justify this ranking.

8.33 Briefly explain why the hardness of tempered martensite diminishes with tempering time (at constant temperature) and with increasing temperature (at constant tempering time).

8.34 Briefly describe the simplest heat treatment procedure that would be used in converting a 0.76 wt% C steel from one microstructure to the other, as follows:

(a) Martensite to spheroidite

(b) Spheroidite to martensite

(c) Bainite to pearlite

(d) Pearlite to bainite

(e) Spheroidite to pearlite

(f) Pearlite to spheroidite

(g) Tempered martensite to martensite

(h) Bainite to spheroidite

8.35 (a) Briefly describe the microstructural difference between spheroidite and tempered martensite.

(b) Explain why tempered martensite is much harder and stronger.

8.36 Estimate the Rockwell hardnesses for specimens of an iron–carbon alloy of eutectoid composition that have been subjected to the heat treatments described in parts (d), (e), (f), (g), and (h) of Problem 8.18.

8.37 Estimate the Brinell hardnesses for specimens of a 1.13 wt% C iron–carbon alloy that have been subjected to the heat treatments described in parts (a), (d), and (h) of Problem 8.20.

8.38 Determine the approximate tensile strengths for specimens of a eutectoid iron–carbon alloy that have experienced the heat treatments described in parts (a), (b), and (d) of Problem 8.23.

8.39 For a eutectoid steel, describe isothermal heat treatments that would be required to yield specimens having the following Brinell hardnesses: **(a)** 180 HB, **(b)** 220 HB, and **(c)** 500 HB.

DESIGN PROBLEMS

Continuous Cooling Transformation Diagrams
Mechanical Behavior of Iron–Carbon Alloys

8.D1 Is it possible to produce an iron–carbon alloy of eutectoid composition that has a minimum hardness of 200 HB and a minimum ductility of 25% RA? If so, describe the continuous cooling heat treatment to which the alloy would be subjected to achieve these properties. If it is not possible, explain why.

8.D2 Is it possible to produce an iron–carbon alloy that has a minimum tensile strength of 620 MPa (90,000 psi) and a minimum ductility of 50% RA? If so, what will be its composition and microstructure (coarse and fine pearlites and spheroidite are alternatives)? If this is not possible, explain why.

8.D3 It is desired to produce an iron–carbon alloy that has a minimum hardness of 200 HB and a minimum ductility of 35% RA. Is such an alloy possible? If so, what will be its composition and microstructure (coarse and fine pearlites and spheroidite are alternatives)? If this is not possible, explain why.

Tempered Martensite

8.D4 **(a)** For a 1080 steel that has been water quenched, estimate the tempering time at 535°C (1000°F) to achieve a hardness of 45 HRC.

(b) What will be the tempering time at 425°C (800°F) necessary to attain the same hardness?

8.D5 An alloy steel (4340) is to be used in an application requiring a minimum tensile strength of 1515 MPa (220,000 psi) and a minimum ductility of 40% RA. Oil quenching followed by tempering is to be used. Briefly describe the tempering heat treatment.

8.D6 Is it possible to produce an oil-quenched and tempered 4340 steel that has a minimum yield strength of 1240 MPa (180,000 psi) and a ductility of at least 50% RA? If this is possible, describe the tempering heat treatment. If it is not possible, then explain why.

Chapter 9 Mechanical Properties of Metals

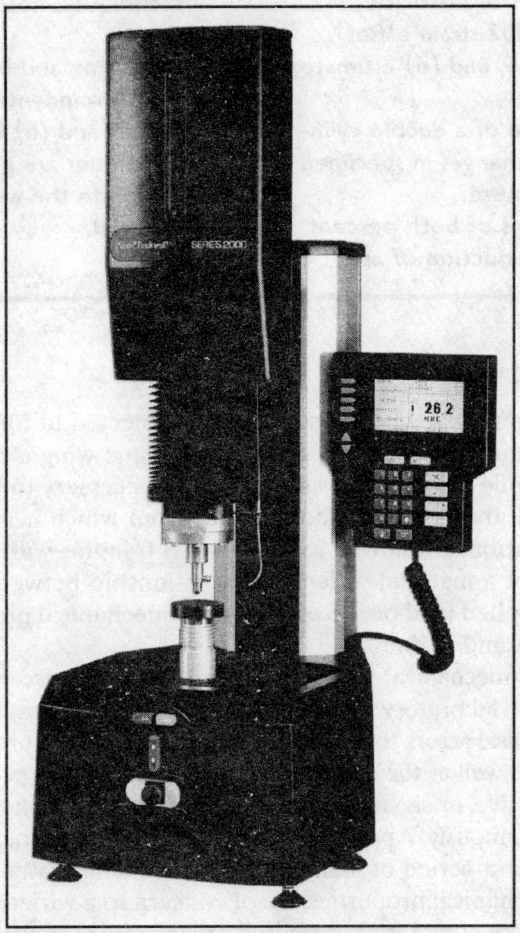

A modern Rockwell hardness tester. (Photograph courtesy of Wilson Instruments Division, Instron Corporation, originator of the Rockwell® Hardness Tester.)

Learning Objectives

After studying this chapter you should be able to do the following:

1. Name different kinds of steels, cast irons and non-ferrous alloys, and, for each, cite distinctive properties, and typical uses.
2. State the purposes of and describe procedures for different annealing treatments.
3. Define engineering stress and engineering strain.
4. State Hooke's law, and note the conditions under which it is valid.
5. Define Poisson's ratio.
6. Given an engineering stress–strain diagram, determine (a) the modulus of elasticity, (b) the yield strength (0.002 strain offset), and (c) the tensile strength, and (d) estimate the percent elongation.
7. For the tensile deformation of a ductile cylindrical specimen, describe changes in specimen profile to the point of fracture.
8. Compute ductility in terms of both percent elongation and percent reduction of area for a material that is loaded in tension to fracture.
9. Give brief definitions of and the units for modulus of resilience and toughness (static).
10. For a specimen being loaded in tension, given the applied load, the instantaneous cross-sectional dimensions, as well as original and instantaneous lengths, be able to compute true stress and true strain values.
11. Name the two most common hardness-testing techniques; note two differences between them.
12. (a) Name and briefly describe the two different microindentation hardness testing techniques, and (b) cite situations for which these techniques are generally used.
13. Compute the working stress for a ductile material.

9.1 INTRODUCTION

Many materials, when in service, are subjected to forces or loads; examples include the aluminum alloy from which an airplane wing is constructed and the steel in an automobile axle. In such situations it is necessary to know the characteristics of the material and to design the member from which it is made such that any resulting deformation will not be excessive and fracture will not occur. The mechanical behavior of a material reflects the relationship between its response or deformation to an applied load or force. Important mechanical properties are strength, hardness, ductility, and stiffness.

The mechanical properties of materials are ascertained by performing carefully designed laboratory experiments that replicate as nearly as possible the service conditions. Factors to be considered include the nature of the applied load and its duration, as well as the environmental conditions. It is possible for the load to be tensile, compressive, or shear, and its magnitude may be constant with time, or it may fluctuate continuously. Application time may be only a fraction of a second, or it may extend over a period of many years. Service temperature may be an important factor.

Mechanical properties are of concern to a variety of parties (e.g., producers and consumers of materials, research organizations, government agencies) that have differing interests. Consequently, it is imperative that there be some consistency in the manner in which tests are conducted, and in the interpretation of their results. This consistency is accomplished by using standardized testing techniques. Establishment and publication of these standards are often coordinated by professional societies. In the United States the most active organization is the American Society for Testing and Materials (ASTM). Its *Annual Book of ASTM Standards* (http://www.astm.org) comprises numerous volumes, which are issued and updated yearly; a large number of these standards relate to mechanical testing techniques. Several of these are referenced by footnote in this and subsequent chapters.

The role of structural engineers is to determine stresses and stress distributions within members that are subjected to well-defined loads. This may be accomplished by experimental testing techniques and/or by theoretical and mathematical stress analyses. These topics are treated in traditional stress analysis and strength of materials texts.

Materials and metallurgical engineers, on the other hand, are concerned with producing and fabricating materials to meet service requirements as predicted by these stress analyses. This necessarily involves an understanding of the relationships between the microstructure (i.e., internal features) of materials and their mechanical properties.

Materials are frequently chosen for structural applications because they have desirable combinations of mechanical characteristics. The present discussion is confined primarily to the mechanical behavior of metals; polymers and ceramics are treated separately because they are, to a large degree, mechanically dissimilar to metals. This chapter discusses the stress–strain behavior of metals and the related mechanical properties, and also examines other important mechanical characteristics. Discussions of the microscopic aspects of deformation mechanisms and methods to strengthen and regulate the mechanical behavior of metals are deferred to later chapters.

Often a materials problem is really one of selecting the material that has the right combination of characteristics for a specific application. Therefore, the people who are involved in the decision making should have some knowledge of the available options. The first portion of this chapter provides an abbreviated overview of some of the commercial alloys, their general properties, and limitations.

Types of Metal Alloys

Metal alloys, by virtue of composition, are often grouped into two classes—ferrous and nonferrous. Ferrous alloys, those in which iron is the principal constituent, include steels and cast irons. These alloys and their characteristics are the first topics of discussion of this section. The nonferrous ones—all alloys that are not iron based—are treated next.

9.2 FERROUS ALLOYS

Ferrous alloys—those of which iron is the prime constituent—are produced in larger quantities than any other metal type. They are especially important as engineering construction materials. Their widespread use is accounted for by three factors: (1) iron-containing compounds exist in abundant quantities within the earth's crust; (2) metallic iron and steel alloys may be produced using relatively economical extraction, refining, alloying, and fabrication techniques; and (3) ferrous alloys are extremely versatile, in that they may be tailored to have a wide range of mechanical and physical properties. The principal disadvantage of many ferrous alloys is their susceptibility to corrosion. This section discusses compositions, microstructures, and properties of a number of different classes of steels and cast irons. A taxonomic classification scheme for the various ferrous alloys is presented in Figure 9.1.

Steels

Steels are iron–carbon alloys that may contain appreciable concentrations of other alloying elements; there are thousands of alloys that have different compositions

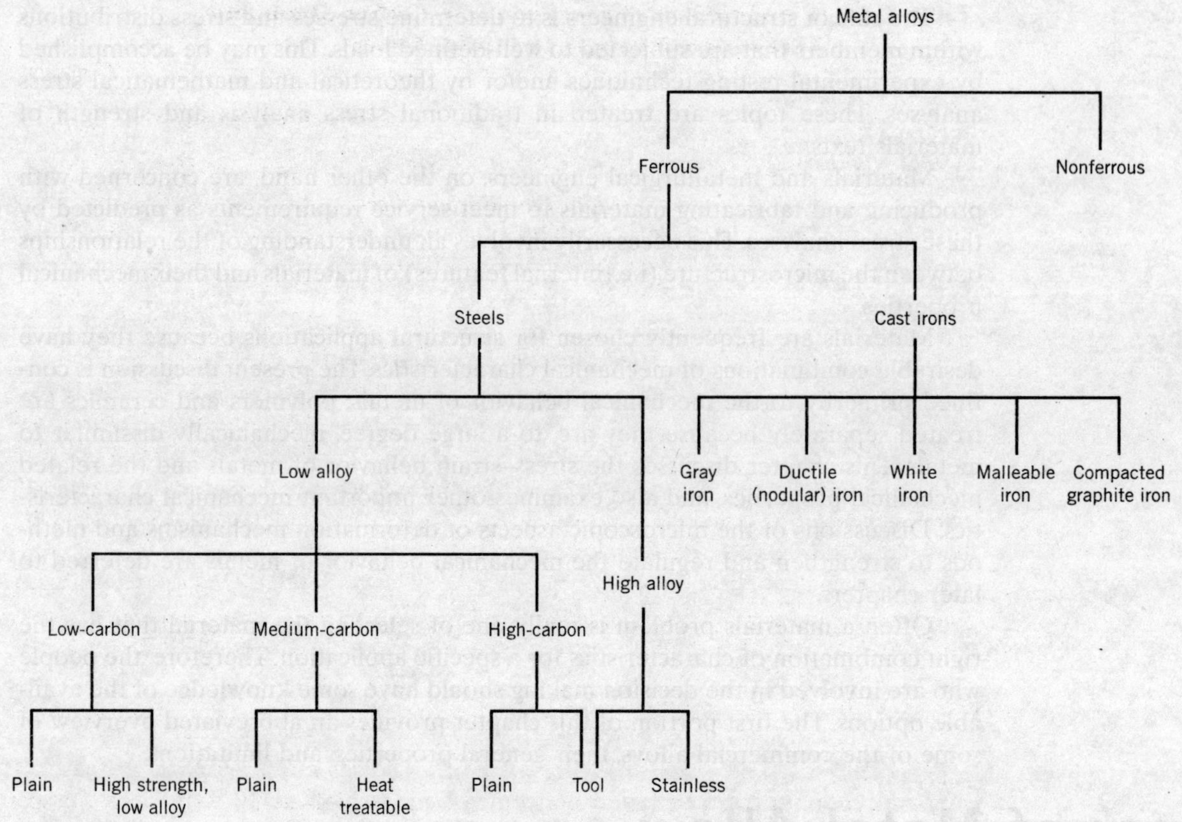

Figure 9.1 Classification scheme for the various ferrous alloys.

and/or heat treatments. The mechanical properties are sensitive to the content of carbon, which is normally less than 1.0 wt%. Some of the more common steels are classified according to carbon concentration—namely, into low-, medium-, and high-carbon types. Subclasses also exist within each group according to the concentration of other alloying elements. **Plain carbon steels** contain only residual concentrations of impurities other than carbon and a little manganese. For **alloy steels,** more alloying elements are intentionally added in specific concentrations.

Low-Carbon Steels

Of all the different steels, those produced in the greatest quantities fall within the low-carbon classification. These generally contain less than about 0.25 wt% C and are unresponsive to heat treatments intended to form martensite; strengthening is accomplished by cold work. Microstructures consist of ferrite and pearlite constituents. As a consequence, these alloys are relatively soft and weak but have outstanding ductility and toughness; in addition, they are machinable, weldable, and, of all steels, are the least expensive to produce. Typical applications include automobile body components, structural shapes (I-beams, channel and angle iron), and sheets that are used in pipelines, buildings, bridges, and tin cans. Tables 9.1a and 9.1b present the compositions and mechanical properties of several plain low-carbon steels. They typically have a yield strength of 275 MPa (40,000 psi), tensile strengths between 415 and 550 MPa (60,000 and 80,000 psi), and a ductility of 25% EL.

Table 9.1a Compositions of Five Plain Low-Carbon Steels and Three High-Strength, Low-Alloy Steels

Designation[a]		*Composition (wt%)*[b]		
AISI/SAE or ASTM Number	*UNS Number*	*C*	*Mn*	*Other*
		Plain Low-Carbon Steels		
1010	G10100	0.10	0.45	
1020	G10200	0.20	0.45	
A36	K02600	0.29	1.00	0.20 Cu (min)
A516 Grade 70	K02700	0.31	1.00	0.25 Si
		High-Strength, Low-Alloy Steels		
A440	K12810	0.28	1.35	0.30 Si (max), 0.20 Cu (min)
A633 Grade E	K12002	0.22	1.35	0.30 Si, 0.08 V, 0.02 N, 0.03 Nb
A656 Grade 1	K11804	0.18	1.60	0.60 Si, 0.1 V, 0.20 Al, 0.015 N

[a] The codes used by the American Iron and Steel Institute (AISI), the Society of Automotive Engineers (SAE), and the American Society for Testing and Materials (ASTM), and in the Uniform Numbering System (UNS) are explained in the text.

[b] Also a maximum of 0.04 wt% P, 0.05 wt% S, and 0.30 wt% Si (unless indicated otherwise).

Source: Adapted from *Metals Handbook: Properties and Selection: Irons and Steels*, Vol. 1, 9th edition, B. Bardes (Editor), American Society for Metals, 1978, pp. 185, 407.

Another group of low-carbon alloys are the **high-strength, low-alloy (HSLA) steels.** They contain other alloying elements such as copper, vanadium, nickel, and molybdenum in combined concentrations as high as 10 wt%, and possess higher strengths than the plain low-carbon steels. Most may be strengthened by heat treatment, giving tensile strengths in excess of 480 MPa (70,000 psi); in ad-

Table 9.1b Mechanical Characteristics of Hot-Rolled Material and Typical Applications for Various Plain Low-Carbon and High-Strength, Low-Alloy Steels

AISI/SAE or ASTM Number	*Tensile Strength (MPa)*	*Yield Strength (MPa)*	*Ductility (%EL in 50 mm)*	*Typical Applications*
		Plain Low-Carbon Steels		
1010	325	180	28	Automobile panels, nails, and wire
1020	380	205	25	Pipe; structural and sheet steel
A36	400	220	23	Structural (bridges and buildings)
A516 Grade 70	485	260	21	Low-temperature pressure vessels
		High-Strength, Low-Alloy Steels		
A440	435	290	21	Structures that are bolted or riveted
A633 Grade E	520	380	23	Structures used at low ambient temperatures
A656 Grade 1	655	552	15	Truck frames and railway cars

dition, they are ductile, formable, and machinable. Several are listed in Table 9.1. In normal atmospheres, the HSLA steels are more resistant to corrosion than the plain carbon steels, which they have replaced in many applications where structural strength is critical (e.g., bridges, towers, support columns in high-rise buildings, and pressure vessels).

Medium-Carbon Steels

The medium-carbon steels have carbon concentrations between about 0.25 and 0.60 wt%. These alloys may be heat treated by austenitizing, quenching, and then tempering to improve their mechanical properties. They are most often utilized in the tempered condition, having microstructures of tempered martensite. The plain medium-carbon steels have low hardenabilities (Section 23.5) and can be successfully heat treated only in very thin sections and with very rapid quenching rates. Additions of chromium, nickel, and molybdenum improve the capacity of these alloys to be heat treated (Section 23.5), giving rise to a variety of strength–ductility combinations. These heat-treated alloys are stronger than the low-carbon steels, but at a sacrifice of ductility and toughness. Applications include railway wheels and tracks, gears, crankshafts, and other machine parts and high-strength structural components calling for a combination of high strength, wear resistance, and toughness.

The compositions of several of these alloyed medium-carbon steels are presented in Table 9.2a. Some comment is in order regarding the designation schemes that are also included. The Society of Automotive Engineers (SAE), the American

Table 9.2a AISI/SAE and UNS Designation Systems and Composition Ranges for Plain Carbon Steel and Various Low-Alloy Steels

		Composition Ranges (wt% of Alloying Elements in Addition to C)[b]			
AISI/SAE Designation[a]	*UNS Designation*	*Ni*	*Cr*	*Mo*	*Other*
10xx, Plain carbon	G10xx0				
11xx, Free machining	G11xx0				0.08–0.33S
12xx, Free machining	G12xx0				0.10–0.35S, 0.04–0.12P
13xx	G13xx0				1.60–1.90Mn
40xx	G40xx0			0.20–0.30	
41xx	G41xx0		0.80–1.10	0.15–0.25	
43xx	G43xx0	1.65–2.00	0.40–0.90	0.20–0.30	
46xx	G46xx0	0.70–2.00		0.15–0.30	
48xx	G48xx0	3.25–3.75		0.20–0.30	
51xx	G51xx0		0.70–1.10		
61xx	G61xx0		0.50–1.10		0.10–0.15V
86xx	G86xx0	0.40–0.70	0.40–0.60	0.15–0.25	
92xx	G92xx0				1.80–2.20Si

[a] The carbon concentration, in weight percent times 100, is inserted in the place of "xx" for each specific steel.

[b] Except for 13xx alloys, manganese concentration is less than 1.00 wt%.
Except for 12xx alloys, phosphorus concentration is less than 0.35 wt%.
Except for 11xx and 12xx alloys, sulfur concentration is less than 0.04 wt%.
Except for 92xx alloys, silicon concentration varies between 0.15 and 0.35 wt%.

Iron and Steel Institute (AISI), and the American Society for Testing and Materials (ASTM) are responsible for the classification and specification of steels as well as other alloys. The AISI/SAE designation for these steels is a four-digit number: the first two digits indicate the alloy content; the last two give the carbon concentration. For plain carbon steels, the first two digits are 1 and 0; alloy steels are designated by other initial two-digit combinations (e.g., 13, 41, 43). The third and fourth digits represent the weight percent carbon multiplied by 100. For example, a 1060 steel is a plain carbon steel containing 0.60 wt% C.

A unified numbering system (UNS) is used for uniformly indexing both ferrous and nonferrous alloys. Each UNS number consists of a single-letter prefix followed by a five-digit number. The letter is indicative of the family of metals to which an alloy belongs. The UNS designation for these alloys begins with a G, followed by the AISI/SAE number; the fifth digit is a zero. Table 9.2b contains the mechanical characteristics and typical applications of several of these steels, which have been quenched and tempered.

High-Carbon Steels

The high-carbon steels, normally having carbon contents between 0.60 and 1.4 wt%, are the hardest, strongest, and yet least ductile of the carbon steels. They are almost always used in a hardened and tempered condition and, as such, are especially wear resistant and capable of holding a sharp cutting edge. The tool and die steels are high-carbon alloys, usually containing chromium, vanadium, tungsten, and molybdenum. These alloying elements combine with carbon to form very hard and wear-resistant carbide compounds (e.g., $Cr_{23}C_6$, V_4C_3, and WC). Some tool steel compositions and their applications are listed in Table 9.3. These steels are utilized as cutting tools and dies for forming and shaping materials, as well as in knives, razors, hacksaw blades, springs, and high-strength wire.

Table 9.2b Typical Applications and Mechanical Property Ranges for Oil-Quenched and Tempered Plain Carbon and Alloy Steels

AISI Number	*UNS Number*	*Tensile Strength (MPa)*	*Yield Strength (MPa)*	*Ductility (%EL in 50 mm)*	*Typical Applications*
			Plain Carbon Steels		
1040	G10400	605–780	430–585	33–19	Crankshafts, bolts
1080[a]	G10800	800–1310	480–980	24–13	Chisels, hammers
1095[a]	G10950	760–1280	510–830	26–10	Knives, hacksaw blades
			Alloy Steels		
4063	G40630	786–2380	710–1770	24–4	Springs, hand tools
4340	G43400	980–1960	895–1570	21–11	Bushings, aircraft tubing
6150	G61500	815–2170	745–1860	22–7	Shafts, pistons, gears

[a] Classified as high-carbon steels.

Table 9.3 Designations, Compositions, and Applications for Six Tool Steels

AISI Number	UNS Number	Composition (wt%)[a] C	Cr	Ni	Mo	W	V	Typical Applications
M1	T11301	0.85	3.75	0.30 max	8.70	1.75	1.20	Drills, saws; lathe and planer tools
A2	T30102	1.00	5.15	0.30 max	1.15	—	0.35	Punches, embossing dies
D2	T30402	1.50	12	0.30 max	0.95	—	1.10 max	Cutlery, drawing dies
O1	T31501	0.95	0.50	0.30 max	—	0.50	0.30 max	Shear blades, cutting tools
S1	T41901	0.50	1.40	0.30 max	0.50 max	2.25	0.25	Pipe cutters, concrete drills
W1	T72301	1.10	0.15 max	0.20 max	0.10 max	0.15 max	0.10 max	Blacksmith tools, woodworking tools

[a] The balance of the composition is iron. Manganese concentrations range between 0.10 and 1.4 wt%, depending on alloy; silicon concentrations between 0.20 and 1.2 wt% depending on alloy.

Source: Adapted from *ASM Handbook,* Vol. 1, *Properties and Selection: Irons, Steels, and High-Performance Alloys,* 1990. Reprinted by permission of ASM International, Materials Park, OH.

Stainless Steels

The **stainless steels** are highly resistant to corrosion (rusting) in a variety of environments, especially the ambient atmosphere. Their predominant alloying element is chromium; a concentration of at least 11 wt% Cr is required. Corrosion resistance may also be enhanced by nickel and molybdenum additions.

Stainless steels are divided into three classes on the basis of the predominant phase constituent of the microstructure—martensitic, ferritic, or austenitic. Table 9.4 lists several stainless steels, by class, along with composition, typical mechanical properties, and applications. A wide range of mechanical properties combined with excellent resistance to corrosion make stainless steels very versatile in their applicability.

Martensitic stainless steels are capable of being heat treated in such a way that martensite is the prime microconstituent. Additions of alloying elements in significant concentrations produce dramatic alterations in the iron–iron carbide phase diagram (Figure 7.24). For austenitic stainless steels, the austenite (or γ) phase field is extended to room temperature. Ferritic stainless steels are composed of the α ferrite (BCC) phase. Austenitic and ferritic stainless steels are hardened and strengthened by cold work because they are not heat treatable. The austenitic stainless steels are the most corrosion resistant because of the high chromium contents and also the nickel additions; and they are produced in the largest quantities. Both martensitic and ferritic stainless steels are magnetic; the austenitic stainlesses are not.

Some stainless steels are frequently used at elevated temperatures and in severe environments because they resist oxidation and maintain their mechanical integrity under such conditions; the upper temperature limit in oxidizing atmospheres is about 1000°C (1800°F). Equipment employing these steels includes gas turbines, high-temperature steam boilers, heat-treating furnaces, aircraft, missiles, and nuclear power generating units. Also included in Table 9.4 is one ultrahigh-strength stainless steel (17-7PH), which is unusually strong and corrosion resistant. Strengthening is accomplished by precipitation-hardening heat treatments (Section 10.9).

Table 9.4 Designations, Compositions, Mechanical Properties, and Typical Applications for Austenitic, Ferritic, Martensitic, and Precipitation-Hardenable Stainless Steels

				Mechanical Properties			
AISI Number	*UNS Number*	*Composition (wt%)*[a]	*Condition*[b]	*Tensile Strength (MPa)*	*Yield Strength (MPa)*	*Ductility (%EL in 50 mm)*	*Typical Applications*
			Ferritic				
409	S40900	0.08 C, 9.0 Cr, 1.0 Mn, 0.50 Ni, 0.75 Ti	Annealed	380	205	20	Automotive exhaust components, tanks for agricultural sprays
446	S44600	0.20 C, 25 Cr, 1.5 Mn	Annealed	515	275	20	Valves (high temperature), glass molds, combustion chambers
			Austenitic				
304	S30400	0.08 C, 19 Cr, 9 Ni, 2.0 Mn	Annealed	515	205	40	Chemical and food processing equipment, cryogenic vessels
316L	S31603	0.03 C, 17 Cr, 12 Ni, 2.5 Mo, 2.0 Mn	Annealed	485	170	40	Welding construction
			Martensitic				
410	S41000	0.15 C, 12.5 Cr, 1.0 Mn	Annealed Q & T	485 825	275 620	20 12	Rifle barrels, cutlery, jet engine parts
440A	S44002	0.70 C, 17 Cr, 0.75 Mo, 1.0 Mn	Annealed Q & T	725 1790	415 1650	20 5	Cutlery, bearings, surgical tools
			Precipitation Hardenable				
17-7PH	S17700	0.09 C, 17 Cr, 7 Ni, 1.0 Al, 1.0 Mn	Precipitation hardened	1450	1310	1–6	Springs, knives, pressure vessels

[a] The balance of the composition is iron.

[b] Q & T denotes quenched and tempered.

Source: Adapted from *ASM Handbook*, Vol. 1, *Properties and Selection: Irons, Steels, and High-Performance Alloys*, 1990. Reprinted by permission of ASM International, Materials Park, OH.

Concept Check 9.1

Briefly explain why ferritic and austenitic stainless steels are not heat treatable. *Hint:* you may want to consult the first portion of Section 9.3.

[The answer may be found in enclosed CD.]

Cast Irons

Generically, **cast irons** are a class of ferrous alloys with carbon contents above 2.14 wt%; in practice, however, most cast irons contain between 3.0 and 4.5 wt% C and, in addition, other alloying elements. A reexamination of the iron–iron carbide phase diagram (Figure 7.24) reveals that alloys within this composition range become completely liquid at temperatures between approximately 1150 and 1300°C (2100 and 2350°F), which is considerably lower than for steels. Thus, they are easily melted and amenable to casting. Furthermore, some cast irons are very brittle, and casting is the most convenient fabrication technique.

Cementite (Fe_3C) is a metastable compound, and under some circumstances it can be made to dissociate or decompose to form α ferrite and graphite, according to the reaction

$$Fe_3C \rightarrow 3Fe\ (\alpha) + C\ (\text{graphite}) \tag{9.1}$$

Thus, the true equilibrium diagram for iron and carbon is not that presented in Figure 7.24, but rather as shown in Figure 9.2. The two diagrams are virtually identical on the iron-rich side (e.g., eutectic and eutectoid temperatures for the Fe–Fe_3C system are 1147 and 727°C, respectively, as compared to 1153 and 740°C for Fe–C); however, Figure 9.2 extends to 100 wt% carbon such that graphite is the carbon-rich phase, instead of cementite at 9.7 wt% C (Figure 7.24).

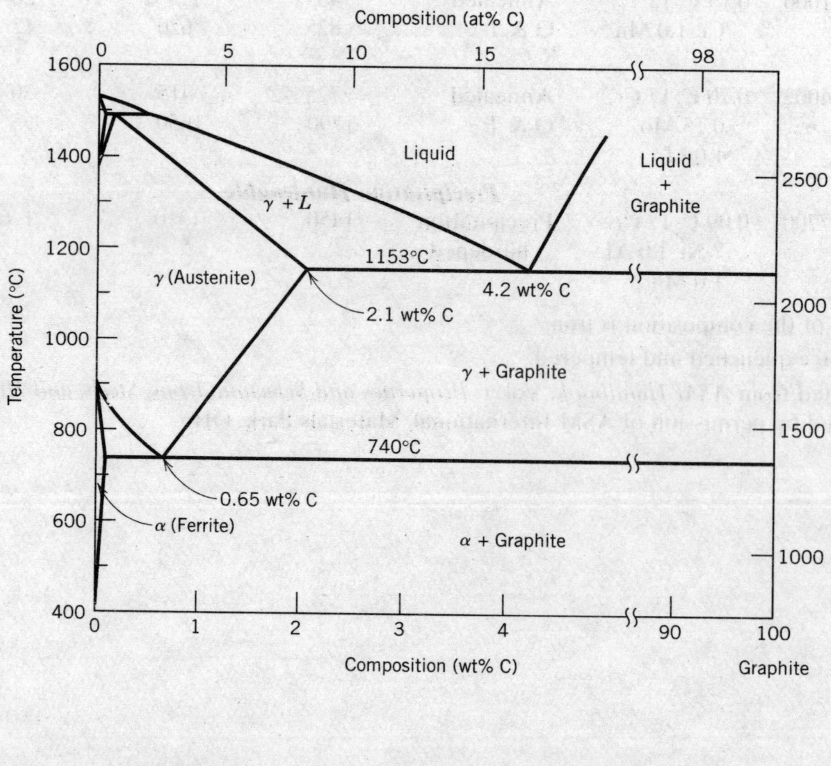

Figure 9.2 The true equilibrium iron–carbon phase diagram with graphite instead of cementite as a stable phase. [Adapted from *Binary Alloy Phase Diagrams,* T. B. Massalski, (Editor-in-Chief), 1990. Reprinted by permission of ASM International, Materials Park, OH.]

This tendency to form graphite is regulated by the composition and rate of cooling. Graphite formation is promoted by the presence of silicon in concentrations greater than about 1 wt%. Also, slower cooling rates during solidification favor graphitization (the formation of graphite). For most cast irons, the carbon exists as graphite, and both microstructure and mechanical behavior depend on composition and heat treatment. The most common cast iron types are gray, nodular, white, malleable, and compacted graphite.

Gray Iron

The carbon and silicon contents of **gray cast irons** vary between 2.5 and 4.0 wt% and 1.0 and 3.0 wt%, respectively. For most of these cast irons, the graphite exists in the form of flakes (similar to corn flakes), which are normally surrounded by an α-ferrite or pearlite matrix; the microstructure of a typical gray iron is shown in Figure 9.3*a*. Because of these graphite flakes, a fractured surface takes on a gray appearance, hence its name.

Mechanically, gray iron is comparatively weak and brittle in tension as a consequence of its microstructure; the tips of the graphite flakes are sharp and pointed, and may serve as points of stress concentration when an external tensile stress is applied. Strength and ductility are much higher under compressive loads. Typical mechanical properties and compositions of several of the common gray cast irons

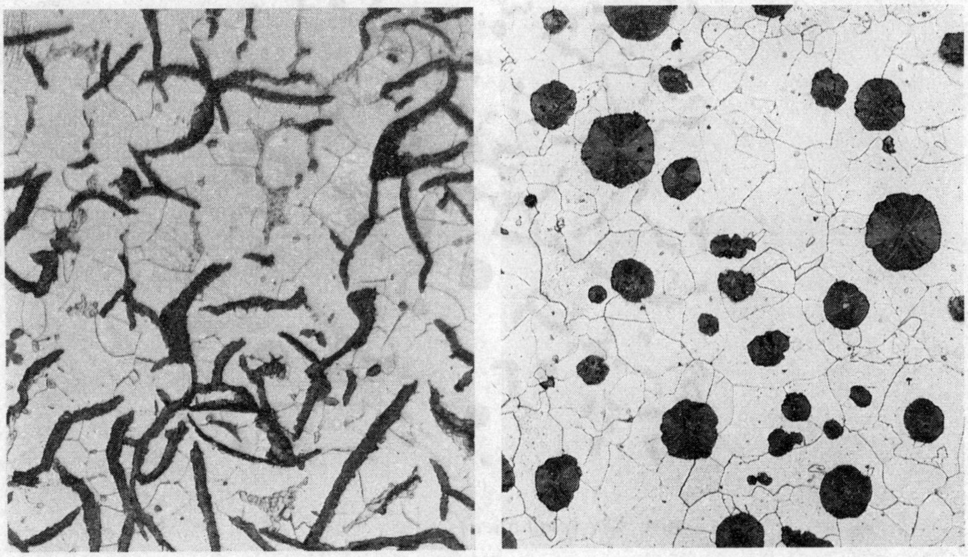

(*a*) (*b*)

Figure 9.3 Optical photomicrographs of various cast irons. (*a*) Gray iron: the dark graphite flakes are embedded in an α-ferrite matrix. 500×. (*b*) Nodular (ductile) iron: the dark graphite nodules are surrounded by an α-ferrite matrix. 200×. (*c*) White iron: the light cementite regions are surrounded by pearlite, which has the ferrite–cementite layered structure. 400×. (*d*) Malleable iron: dark graphite rosettes (temper carbon) in an α-ferrite matrix. 150×. (*e*) Compacted graphite iron: dark graphite worm-like particles are embedded within an α-ferrite matrix. 100×. [Figures (*a*) and (*b*) courtesy of C. H. Brady and L. C. Smith, National Bureau of Standards, Washington, DC (now the National Institute of Standards and Technology, Gaithersburg, MD). Figure (*c*) courtesy of Amcast Industrial Corporation. Figure (*d*) reprinted with permission of the Iron Castings Society, Des Plaines, IL. Figure (*e*) courtesy of SinterCast, Ltd.]

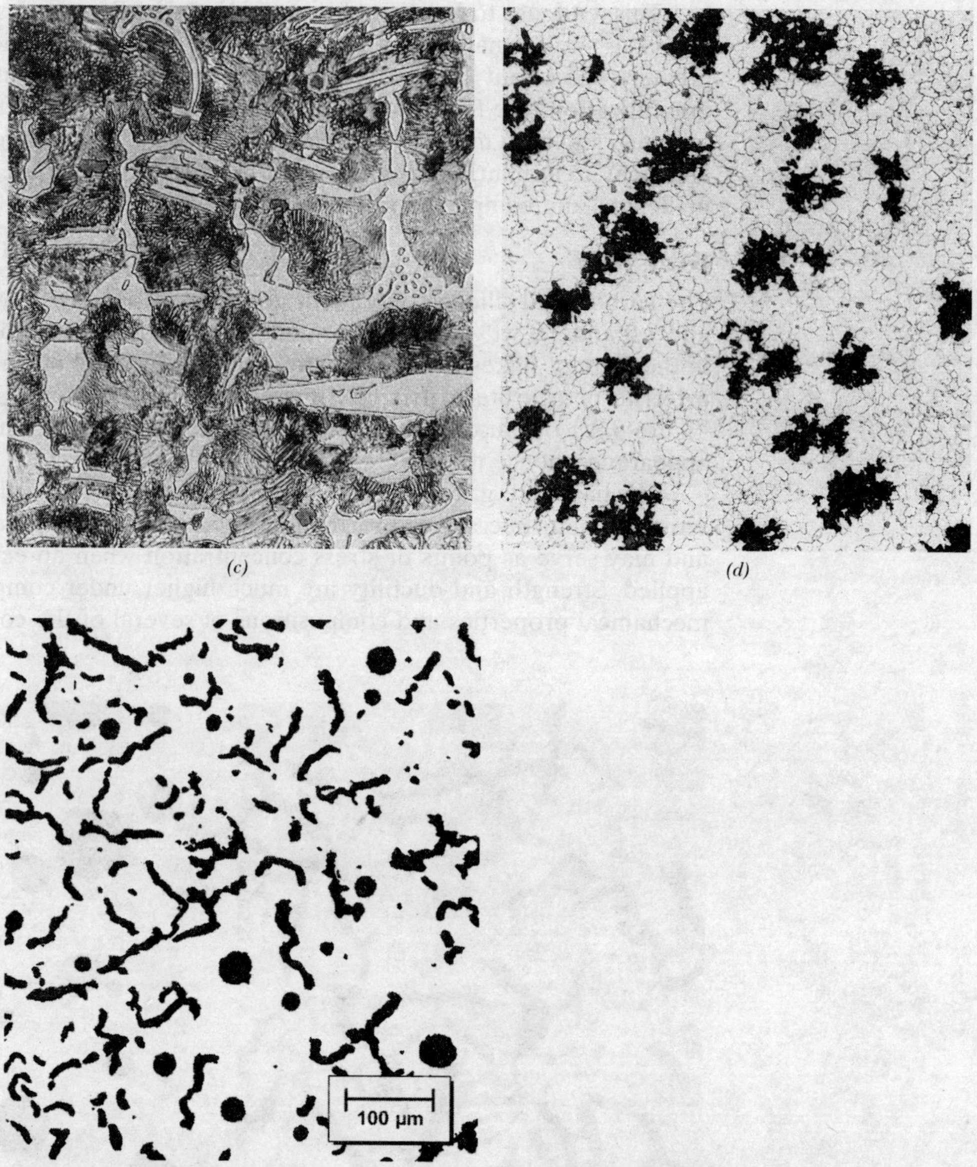

(c) (d) (e)

Figure 9.3 (*continued*)

are listed in Table 9.5. Gray irons do have some desirable characteristics and, in fact, are utilized extensively. They are very effective in damping vibrational energy; this is represented in Figure 9.4, which compares the relative damping capacities of steel and gray iron. Base structures for machines and heavy equipment that are exposed to vibrations are frequently constructed of this material. In addition, gray irons exhibit a high resistance to wear. Furthermore, in the molten state they have a high fluidity at casting temperature, which permits casting pieces having intricate shapes; also, casting shrinkage is low. Finally, and perhaps most important, gray cast irons are among the least expensive of all metallic materials.

Gray irons having microstructures different from that shown in Figure 9.3*a* may be generated by adjustment of composition and/or by using an appropriate

Table 9.5 Designations, Minimum Mechanical Properties, Approximate Compositions, and Typical Applications for Various Gray, Nodular, Malleable, and Compacted Graphite Cast Irons

Grade	UNS Number	Composition (wt%)[a]	Matrix Structure	Mechanical Properties: Tensile Strength (MPa)	Mechanical Properties: Yield Strength (MPa)	Mechanical Properties: Ductility (%EL in 50 mm)	Typical Applications
				Gray Iron			
SAE G1800	F10004	3.40–3.7 C, 2.55 Si, 0.7 Mn	Ferrite + Pearlite	124	—	—	Miscellaneous soft iron castings in which strength is not a primary consideration
SAE G2500	F10005	3.2–3.5 C, 2.20 Si, 0.8 Mn	Ferrite + Pearlite	173	—	—	Small cylinder blocks, cylinder heads, pistons, clutch plates, transmission cases
SAE G4000	F10008	3.0–3.3 C, 2.0 Si, 0.8 Mn	Pearlite	276	—	—	Diesel engine castings, liners, cylinders, and pistons
				Ductile (Nodular) Iron			
ASTM A536							
60–40–18	F32800	3.5–3.8 C, 2.0–2.8 Si, 0.05 Mg, <0.20 Ni, <0.10 Mo	Ferrite	414	276	18	Pressure-containing parts such as valve and pump bodies
100–70–03	F34800		Pearlite	689	483	3	High-strength gears and machine components
120–90–02	F36200		Tempered martensite	827	621	2	Pinions, gears, rollers, slides
				Malleable Iron			
32510	F22200	2.3–2.7 C, 1.0–1.75 Si, <0.55 Mn	Ferrite	345	224	10	General engineering service at normal and elevated temperatures
45006	F23131	2.4–2.7 C, 1.25–1.55 Si, <0.55 Mn	Ferrite + Pearlite	448	310	6	
				Compacted Graphite Iron			
ASTM A842							
Grade 250	—	3.1–4.0 C, 1.7–3.0 Si, 0.015–0.035 Mg, 0.06–0.13 Ti	Ferrite	250	175	3	Diesel engine blocks, exhaust manifolds, brake discs for high-speed trains
Grade 450	—		Pearlite	450	315	1	

[a] The balance of the composition is iron.

Source: Adapted from *ASM Handbook,* Vol. 1, *Properties and Selection: Irons, Steels, and High-Performance Alloys,* 1990. Reprinted by permission of ASM International, Materials Park, OH.

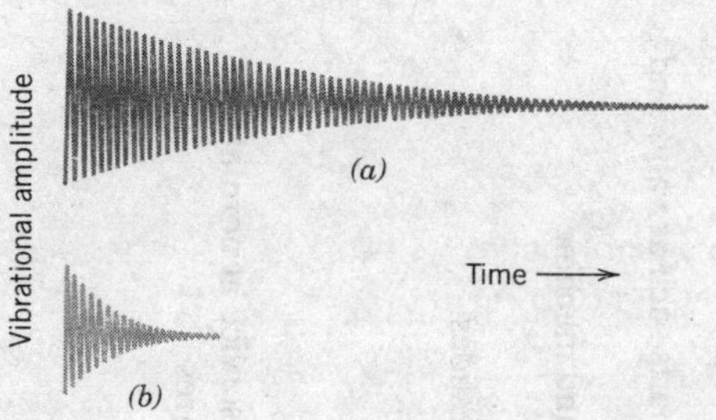

Figure 9.4 Comparison of the relative vibrational damping capacities of (*a*) steel and (*b*) gray cast iron. (From *Metals Engineering Quarterly,* February 1961. Copyright 1961 American Society for Metals.)

treatment. For example, lowering the silicon content or increasing the cooling rate may prevent the complete dissociation of cementite to form graphite (Equation 9.1). Under these circumstances the microstructure consists of graphite flakes embedded in a pearlite matrix. Figure 9.5 compares schematically the several cast iron microstructures obtained by varying the composition and heat treatment.

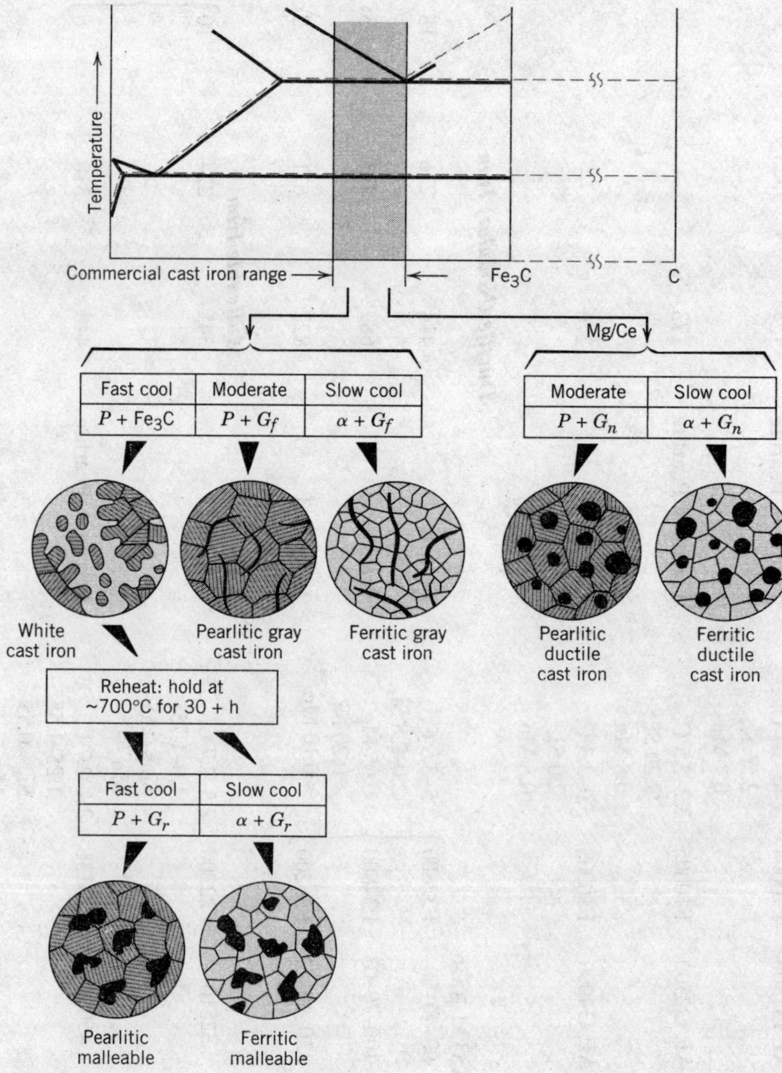

Figure 9.5 From the iron–carbon phase diagram, composition ranges for commercial cast irons. Also shown are schematic microstructures that result from a variety of heat treatments. G_f, flake graphite; G_r, graphite rosettes; G_n, graphite nodules; P, pearlite; α, ferrite. (Adapted from W. G. Moffatt, G. W. Pearsall, and J. Wulff, *The Structure and Properties of Materials,* Vol. I, *Structure,* p. 195. Copyright © 1964 by John Wiley & Sons, New York. Reprinted by permission of John Wiley & Sons, Inc.)

Ductile (or Nodular) Iron

Adding a small amount of magnesium and/or cerium to the gray iron before casting produces a distinctly different microstructure and set of mechanical properties. Graphite still forms, but as nodules or sphere-like particles instead of flakes. The resulting alloy is called **nodular** or **ductile iron,** and a typical microstructure is shown in Figure 9.3*b*. The matrix phase surrounding these particles is either pearlite or ferrite, depending on heat treatment (Figure 9.5); it is normally pearlite for an as-cast piece. However, a heat treatment for several hours at about 700°C (1300°F) will yield a ferrite matrix as in this photomicrograph. Castings are stronger and much more ductile than gray iron, as a comparison of their mechanical properties in Table 9.5 shows. In fact, ductile iron has mechanical characteristics approaching those of steel. For example, ferritic ductile irons have tensile strengths ranging between 380 and 480 MPa (55,000 and 70,000 psi), and ductilities (as percent elongation) from 10% to 20%. Typical applications for this material include valves, pump bodies, crankshafts, gears, and other automotive and machine components.

White Iron and Malleable Iron

For low-silicon cast irons (containing less than 1.0 wt% Si) and rapid cooling rates, most of the carbon exists as cementite instead of graphite, as indicated in Figure 9.5. A fracture surface of this alloy has a white appearance, and thus it is termed **white cast iron.** An optical photomicrograph showing the microstructure of white iron is presented in Figure 9.3*c*. Thick sections may have only a surface layer of white iron that was "chilled" during the casting process; gray iron forms at interior regions, which cool more slowly. As a consequence of large amounts of the cementite phase, white iron is extremely hard but also very brittle, to the point of being virtually unmachinable. Its use is limited to applications that necessitate a very hard and wear-resistant surface, without a high degree of ductility—for example, as rollers in rolling mills. Generally, white iron is used as an intermediary in the production of yet another cast iron, **malleable iron.**

Heating white iron at temperatures between 800 and 900°C (1470 and 1650°F) for a prolonged time period and in a neutral atmosphere (to prevent oxidation) causes a decomposition of the cementite, forming graphite, which exists in the form of clusters or rosettes surrounded by a ferrite or pearlite matrix, depending on cooling rate, as indicated in Figure 9.5. A photomicrograph of a ferritic malleable iron is presented in Figure 9.3*d*. The microstructure is similar to that for nodular iron (Figure 9.3*b*), which accounts for relatively high strength and appreciable ductility or malleability. Some typical mechanical characteristics are also listed in Table 9.5. Representative applications include connecting rods, transmission gears, and differential cases for the automotive industry, and also flanges, pipe fittings, and valve parts for railroad, marine, and other heavy-duty services.

Gray and ductile cast irons are produced in approximately the same amounts; however, white and malleable cast irons are produced in smaller quantities.

Concept Check 9.2

It is possible to produce cast irons that consist of a martensite matrix in which graphite is embedded in either flake, nodule, or rosette form. Briefly describe the treatment necessary to produce each of these three microstructures.

[*The answer may be found in enclosed CD.*]

Compacted Graphite Iron

A relatively recent addition to the family of cast irons is **compacted graphite iron** (abbreviated *CGI*). As with gray, ductile, and malleable irons, carbon exists as graphite, which formation is promoted by the presence of silicon. Silicon content ranges between 1.7 and 3.0 wt%, whereas carbon concentration is normally between 3.1 and 4.0 wt%. Two CGI materials are included in Table 9.5.

Microstructurally, the graphite in CGI alloys has a worm-like (or vermicular) shape; a typical CGI microstructure is shown in the optical micrograph of Figure 9.3*e*. In a sense, this microstructure is intermediate between that of gray iron (Figure 9.3*a*) and ductile (nodular) iron (Figure 9.3*b*), and, in fact, some of the graphite (less than 20%) may be as nodules. However, sharp edges (characteristic of graphite flakes) should be avoided; the presence of this feature leads to a reduction in fracture and fatigue resistance of the material. Magnesium and/or cerium is also added, but concentrations are lower than for ductile iron. The chemistries of CGIs are more complex than for the other cast iron types; compositions of magnesium, cerium, and other additives must be controlled so as to produce a microstructure that consists of the worm-like graphite particles, while at the same time limiting the degree of graphite nodularity, and preventing the formation of graphite flakes. Furthermore, depending on heat treatment, the matrix phase will be pearlite and/or ferrite.

As with the other types of cast irons, the mechanical properties of CGIs are related to microstructure: graphite particle shape as well as the matrix phase/microconstituent. An increase in degree of nodularity of the graphite particles leads to enhancements of both strength and ductility. Furthermore, CGIs with ferritic matrices have lower strengths and higher ductilities than those with pearlitic matrices. Tensile and yield strengths for compacted graphite irons are comparable to values for ductile and malleable irons, yet are greater than those observed for the higher-strength gray irons (Table 9.5). In addition, ductilities for CGIs are intermediate between values for gray and ductile irons; also, moduli of elasticity range between 140 and 165 GPa (20×10^6 and 24×10^6 psi).

Compared to the other cast iron types, desirable characteristics of CGIs include the following:

- Higher thermal conductivity
- Better resistance to thermal shock (i.e., fracture resulting from rapid temperature changes)
- Lower oxidation at elevated temperatures

Compacted graphite irons are now being used in a number of important applications—these include: diesel engine blocks, exhaust manifolds, gearbox housings, brake discs for high-speed trains, and flywheels.

9.3 NONFERROUS ALLOYS

Steel and other ferrous alloys are consumed in exceedingly large quantities because they have such a wide range of mechanical properties, may be fabricated with relative ease, and are economical to produce. However, they have some distinct limitations, chiefly: (1) a relatively high density, (2) a comparatively low electrical conductivity, and (3) an inherent susceptibility to corrosion in some common environments. Thus, for many applications it is advantageous or even necessary to utilize other alloys having more suitable property combinations. Alloy systems are classified either according to the base metal or according to some specific characteristic that a group of alloys share. This section discusses the following metal and alloy systems: copper, aluminum, magnesium, and titanium alloys, the refractory metals, the superalloys, the noble metals, and miscellaneous alloys, including those that have nickel, lead, tin, zirconium, and zinc as base metals.

On occasion, a distinction is made between cast and wrought alloys. Alloys that are so brittle that forming or shaping by appreciable deformation is not possible ordinarily are cast; these are classified as *cast alloys*. On the other hand, those that are amenable to mechanical deformation are termed **wrought alloys.**

In addition, the heat treatability of an alloy system is mentioned frequently. "Heat treatable" designates an alloy whose mechanical strength is improved by precipitation hardening (Section 10.14) or a martensitic transformation (normally the former), both of which involve specific heat-treating procedures.

Copper and Its Alloys

Copper and copper-based alloys, possessing a desirable combination of physical properties, have been utilized in quite a variety of applications since antiquity. Unalloyed copper is so soft and ductile that it is difficult to machine; also, it has an almost unlimited capacity to be cold worked. Furthermore, it is highly resistant to corrosion in diverse environments including the ambient atmosphere, seawater, and some industrial chemicals. The mechanical and corrosion-resistance properties of copper may be improved by alloying. Most copper alloys cannot be hardened or strengthened by heat-treating procedures; consequently, cold working and/or solid-solution alloying must be utilized to improve these mechanical properties.

The most common copper alloys are the **brasses** for which zinc, as a substitutional impurity, is the predominant alloying element. As may be observed for the copper–zinc phase diagram (Figure 7.19), the α phase is stable for concentrations up to approximately 35 wt% Zn. This phase has an FCC crystal structure, and α brasses are relatively soft, ductile, and easily cold worked. Brass alloys having a higher zinc content contain both α and β' phases at room temperature. The β' phase has an ordered BCC crystal structure and is harder and stronger than the α phase; consequently, $\alpha + \beta'$ alloys are generally hot worked.

Some of the common brasses are yellow, naval, and cartridge brass, muntz metal, and gilding metal. The compositions, properties, and typical uses of several of these alloys are listed in Table 9.6. Some of the common uses for brass alloys include costume jewelry, cartridge casings, automotive radiators, musical instruments, electronic packaging, and coins.

The **bronzes** are alloys of copper and several other elements, including tin, aluminum, silicon, and nickel. These alloys are somewhat stronger than the brasses, yet they still have a high degree of corrosion resistance. Table 9.6 contains several of the bronze alloys, their compositions, properties, and applications. Generally they are utilized when, in addition to corrosion resistance, good tensile properties are required.

The most common heat-treatable copper alloys are the beryllium coppers. They possess a remarkable combination of properties: tensile strengths as high as 1400 MPa (200,000 psi), excellent electrical and corrosion properties, and wear resistance when properly lubricated; they may be cast, hot worked, or cold worked. High strengths are attained by precipitation-hardening heat treatments (Section 10.14). These alloys are costly because of the beryllium additions, which range between 1.0 and 2.5 wt%. Applications include jet aircraft landing gear bearings and bushings, springs, and surgical and dental instruments. One of these alloys (C17200) is included in Table 9.6.

Table 9.6 Compositions, Mechanical Properties, and Typical Applications for Eight Copper Alloys

Alloy Name	*UNS Number*	*Composition (wt%)*[a]	*Condition*	*Mechanical Properties* *Tensile Strength (MPa)*	*Yield Strength (MPa)*	*Ductility (% EL in 50 mm)*	*Typical Applications*
			Wrought Alloys				
Electrolytic tough pitch	C11000	0.04 O	Annealed	220	69	45	Electrical wire, rivets, screening, gaskets, pans, nails, roofing
Beryllium copper	C17200	1.9 Be, 0.20 Co	Precipitation hardened	1140–1310	690–860	4–10	Springs, bellows, firing pins, bushings, valves, diaphragms
Cartridge brass	C26000	30 Zn	Annealed	300	75	68	Automotive radiator cores, ammunition components, lamp fixtures, flashlight shells, kickplates
			Cold-worked (H04 hard)	525	435	8	
Phosphor bronze, 5% A	C51000	5 Sn, 0.2 P	Annealed	325	130	64	Bellows, clutch disks, diaphragms, fuse clips, springs, welding rods
			Cold-worked (H04 hard)	560	515	10	
Copper–nickel, 30%	C71500	30 Ni	Annealed	380	125	36	Condenser and heat-exchanger components, saltwater piping
			Cold-worked (H02 hard)	515	485	15	
			Cast Alloys				
Leaded yellow brass	C85400	29 Zn, 3 Pb, 1 Sn	As cast	234	83	35	Furniture hardware, radiator fittings, light fixtures, battery clamps
Tin bronze	C90500	10 Sn, 2 Zn	As cast	310	152	25	Bearings, bushings, piston rings, steam fittings, gears
Aluminum bronze	C95400	4 Fe, 11 Al	As cast	586	241	18	Bearings, gears, worms, bushings, valve seats and guards, pickling hooks

[a] The balance of the composition is copper.

Source: Adapted from *ASM Handbook*, Vol. 2, *Properties and Selection: Nonferrous Alloys and Special-Purpose Materials,* 1990. Reprinted by permission of ASM International, Materials Park, OH.

Concept Check 9.3

What is the main difference between brass and bronze?

[*The answer may be found in enclosed CD.*]

Aluminum and Its Alloys

Aluminum and its alloys are characterized by a relatively low density (2.7 g/cm^3 as compared to 7.9 g/cm^3 for steel), high electrical and thermal conductivities, and a resistance to corrosion in some common environments, including the ambient atmosphere. Many of these alloys are easily formed by virtue of high ductility; this is evidenced by the thin aluminum foil sheet into which the relatively pure material may be rolled. Since aluminum has an FCC crystal structure, its ductility is retained even at very low temperatures. The chief limitation of aluminum is its low melting temperature [660°C (1220°F)], which restricts the maximum temperature at which it can be used.

The mechanical strength of aluminum may be enhanced by cold work and by alloying; however, both processes tend to diminish resistance to corrosion. Principal alloying elements include copper, magnesium, silicon, manganese, and zinc. Nonheat-treatable alloys consist of a single phase, for which an increase in strength is achieved by solid-solution strengthening. Others are rendered heat treatable (capable of being precipitation hardened) as a result of alloying. In several of these alloys precipitation hardening is due to the precipitation of two elements other than aluminum, to form an intermetallic compound such as $MgZn_2$.

Generally, aluminum alloys are classified as either cast or wrought. Composition for both types is designated by a four-digit number that indicates the principal impurities, and in some cases, the purity level. For cast alloys, a decimal point is located between the last two digits. After these digits is a hyphen and the basic **temper designation**—a letter and possibly a one- to three-digit number, which indicates the mechanical and/or heat treatment to which the alloy has been subjected. For example, F, H, and O represent, respectively, the as-fabricated, strain-hardened, and annealed states; T3 means that the alloy was solution heat treated, cold worked, and then naturally aged (age hardened). A solution heat treatment followed by artificial aging is indicated by T9. The compositions, properties, and applications of several wrought and cast alloys are contained in Table 9.7. Some of the more common applications of aluminum alloys include aircraft structural parts, beverage cans, bus bodies, and automotive parts (engine blocks, pistons, and manifolds).

Recent attention has been given to alloys of aluminum and other low-density metals (e.g., Mg and Ti) as engineering materials for transportation, to effect reductions in fuel consumption. An important characteristic of these materials is **specific strength,** which is quantified by the tensile strength–specific gravity ratio. Even though an alloy of one of these metals may have a tensile strength that is inferior to a more dense material (such as steel), on a weight basis it will be able to sustain a larger load.

A generation of new aluminum–lithium alloys have been developed recently for use by the aircraft and aerospace industries. These materials have relatively low densities (between about 2.5 and 2.6 g/cm^3), high specific moduli (elastic modulus-specific gravity ratios), and excellent fatigue and low-temperature toughness properties. Furthermore, some of them may be precipitation hardened. However, these materials are more costly to manufacture than the conventional aluminum alloys because special processing techniques are required as a result of lithium's chemical reactivity.

Concept Check 9.4

Explain why, under some circumstances, it is not advisable to weld a structure that is fabricated with a 3003 aluminum alloy. *Hint:* you may want to consult Section 10.12.

[*The answer may be found in enclosed CD.*]

Table 9.7 Compositions, Mechanical Properties, and Typical Applications for Several Common Aluminum Alloys

				Mechanical Properties			
Aluminum Association Number	*UNS Number*	*Composition (wt%)[a]*	*Condition (Temper Designation)*	*Tensile Strength (MPa)*	*Yield Strength (MPa)*	*Ductility (%EL in 50 mm)*	*Typical Applications/ Characteristics*
			Wrought, Nonheat-Treatable Alloys				
1100	A91100	0.12 Cu	Annealed (O)	90	35	35–45	Food/chemical handling and storage equipment, heat exchangers, light reflectors
3003	A93003	0.12 Cu, 1.2 Mn, 0.1 Zn	Annealed (O)	110	40	30–40	Cooking utensils, pressure vessels and piping
5052	A95052	2.5 Mg, 0.25 Cr	Strain hardened (H32)	230	195	12–18	Aircraft fuel and oil lines, fuel tanks, appliances, rivets, and wire
			Wrought, Heat-Treatable Alloys				
2024	A92024	4.4 Cu, 1.5 Mg, 0.6 Mn	Heat treated (T4)	470	325	20	Aircraft structures, rivets, truck wheels, screw machine products
6061	A96061	1.0 Mg, 0.6 Si, 0.30 Cu, 0.20 Cr	Heat treated (T4)	240	145	22–25	Trucks, canoes, railroad cars, furniture, pipelines
7075	A97075	5.6 Zn, 2.5 Mg, 1.6 Cu, 0.23 Cr	Heat treated (T6)	570	505	11	Aircraft structural parts and other highly stressed applications
			Cast, Heat-Treatable Alloys				
295.0	A02950	4.5 Cu, 1.1 Si	Heat treated (T4)	221	110	8.5	Flywheel and rear-axle housings, bus and aircraft wheels, crankcases
359.0	A03560	7.0 Si, 0.3 Mg	Heat treated (T6)	228	164	3.5	Aircraft pump parts, automotive transmission cases, water-cooled cylinder blocks
			Aluminum–Lithium Alloys				
2090	—	2.7 Cu, 0.25 Mg, 2.25 Li, 0.12 Zr	Heat treated, cold worked (T83)	455	455	5	Aircraft structures and cryogenic tankage structures
8090	—	1.3 Cu, 0.95 Mg, 2.0 Li, 0.1 Zr	Heat treated, cold worked (T651)	465	360	—	Aircraft structures that must be highly damage tolerant

[a] The balance of the composition is aluminum.

Source: Adapted from *ASM Handbook*, Vol. 2, *Properties and Selection: Nonferrous Alloys and Special-Purpose Materials*, 1990. Reprinted by permission of ASM International, Materials Park, OH.

Magnesium and Its Alloys

Perhaps the most outstanding characteristic of magnesium is its density, 1.7 g/cm^3, which is the lowest of all the structural metals; therefore, its alloys are used where light weight is an important consideration (e.g., in aircraft components). Magnesium has an HCP crystal structure, is relatively soft, and has a low elastic modulus: 45 GPa (6.5×10^6 psi). At room temperature magnesium and its alloys are difficult to deform; in fact, only small degrees of cold work may be imposed without annealing. Consequently, most fabrication is by casting or hot working at temperatures between 200 and 350°C (400 and 650°F). Magnesium, like aluminum, has a moderately low melting temperature [651°C (1204°F)]. Chemically, magnesium alloys are relatively unstable and especially susceptible to corrosion in marine environments. On the other hand, corrosion or oxidation resistance is reasonably good in the normal atmosphere; it is believed that this behavior is due to impurities rather than being an inherent characteristic of Mg alloys. Fine magnesium powder ignites easily when heated in air; consequently, care should be exercised when handling it in this state.

These alloys are also classified as either cast or wrought, and some of them are heat treatable. Aluminum, zinc, manganese, and some of the rare earths are the major alloying elements. A composition–temper designation scheme similar to that for aluminum alloys is also used. Table 9.8 lists several common magnesium alloys, their compositions, properties, and applications. These alloys are used in aircraft and missile applications, as well as in luggage. Furthermore, in the last several years the demand for magnesium alloys has increased dramatically in a host of different industries. For many applications, magnesium alloys have replaced engineering plastics that have comparable densities inasmuch as the magnesium materials are stiffer, more recyclable, and less costly to produce. For example, magnesium is now employed in a variety of hand-held devices (e.g., chain saws, power tools, hedge clippers), in automobiles (e.g., steering wheels and columns, seat frames, transmission cases), and in audio-video-computer-communications equipment (e.g., laptop computers, camcorders, TV sets, cellular telephones).

Concept Check 9.5

On the basis of melting temperature, oxidation resistance, yield strength, and degree of brittleness, discuss whether it would be advisable to hot work or to cold work (a) aluminum alloys, and (b) magnesium alloys. *Hint:* you may want to consult Sections 10.10 and 10.12.

[*The answer may be found in enclosed CD.*]

Titanium and Its Alloys

Titanium and its alloys are relatively new engineering materials that possess an extraordinary combination of properties. The pure metal has a relatively low density (4.5 g/cm^3), a high melting point [1668°C (3035°F)], and an elastic modulus of 107 GPa (15.5×10^6 psi). Titanium alloys are extremely strong; room temperature tensile strengths as high as 1400 MPa (200,000 psi) are attainable, yielding remarkable specific strengths. Furthermore, the alloys are highly ductile and easily forged and machined.

The major limitation of titanium is its chemical reactivity with other materials at elevated temperatures. This property has necessitated the development of

Table 9.8 Compositions, Mechanical Properties, and Typical Applications for Six Common Magnesium Alloys

ASTM Number	UNS Number	Composition (wt%)[a]	Condition	Mechanical Properties: Tensile Strength (MPa)	Yield Strength (MPa)	Ductility (%EL in 50 mm)	Typical Applications
			Wrought Alloys				
AZ31B	M11311	3.0 Al, 1.0 Zn, 0.2 Mn	As extruded	262	200	15	Structures and tubing, cathodic protection
HK31A	M13310	3.0 Th, 0.6 Zr	Strain hardened, partially annealed	255	200	9	High strength to 315°C (600°F)
ZK60A	M16600	5.5 Zn, 0.45 Zr	Artificially aged	350	285	11	Forgings of maximum strength for aircraft
			Cast Alloys				
AZ91D	M11916	9.0 Al, 0.15 Mn, 0.7 Zn	As cast	230	150	3	Die-cast parts for automobiles, luggage, and electronic devices
AM60A	M10600	9.0 Al, 0.13 Mn	As cast	220	130	6	Automotive wheels
AS41A	M10410	4.3 Al, 1.0 Si, 0.35 Mn	As cast	210	140	6	Die castings requiring good creep resistance

[a] The balance of the composition is magnesium.

Source: Adapted from *ASM Handbook*, Vol. 2, *Properties and Selection: Nonferrous Alloys and Special-Purpose Materials,* 1990. Reprinted by permission of ASM International, Materials Park, OH.

nonconventional refining, melting, and casting techniques; consequently, titanium alloys are quite expensive. In spite of this high temperature reactivity, the corrosion resistance of titanium alloys at normal temperatures is unusually high; they are virtually immune to air, marine, and a variety of industrial environments. Table 9.9 presents several titanium alloys along with their typical properties and applications. They are commonly utilized in airplane structures, space vehicles, surgical implants, and in the petroleum and chemical industries.

The Refractory Metals

Metals that have extremely high melting temperatures are classified as the refractory metals. Included in this group are niobium (Nb), molybdenum (Mo), tungsten (W), and tantalum (Ta). Melting temperatures range between 2468°C (4474°F) for niobium and 3410°C (6170°F), the highest melting temperature of any metal, for tungsten. Interatomic bonding in these metals is extremely strong, which accounts for the melting temperatures, and, in addition, large elastic moduli and high strengths and hardnesses, at ambient as well as elevated temperatures. The

Table 9.9 Compositions, Mechanical Properties, and Typical Applications for Several Common Titanium Alloys

				Average Mechanical Properties			
Alloy Type	*Common Name (UNS Number)*	*Composition (wt%)*	*Condition*	*Tensile Strength (MPa)*	*Yield Strength (MPa)*	*Ductility (%EL in 50 mm)*	*Typical Applications*
Commercially pure	Unalloyed (R50500)	99.1 Ti	Annealed	484	414	25	Jet engine shrouds, cases and airframe skins, corrosion-resistant equipment for marine and chemical processing industries
α	Ti-5Al-2.5Sn (R54520)	5 Al, 2.5 Sn, balance Ti	Annealed	826	784	16	Gas turbine engine casings and rings; chemical processing equipment requiring strength to temperatures of 480°C (900°F)
Near α	Ti-8Al-1Mo-1V (R54810)	8 Al, 1 Mo, 1 V, balance Ti	Annealed (duplex)	950	890	15	Forgings for jet engine components (compressor disks, plates, and hubs)
α-β	Ti-6Al-4V (R56400)	6 Al, 4 V, balance Ti	Annealed	947	877	14	High-strength prosthetic implants, chemical-processing equipment, airframe structural components
α-β	Ti-6Al-6V-2Sn (R56620)	6 Al, 2 Sn, 6 V, 0.75 Cu, balance Ti	Annealed	1050	985	14	Rocket engine case airframe applications and high-strength airframe structures
β	Ti-10V-2Fe-3Al	10 V, 2 Fe, 3 Al, balance Ti	Solution + aging	1223	1150	10	Best combination of high strength and toughness of any commercial titanium alloy; used for applications requiring uniformity of tensile properties at surface and center locations; high-strength airframe components

Source: Adapted from *ASM Handbook,* Vol. 2, *Properties and Selection: Nonferrous Alloys and Special-Purpose Materials,* 1990. Reprinted by permission of ASM International, Materials Park, OH.

applications of these metals are varied. For example, tantalum and molybdenum are alloyed with stainless steel to improve its corrosion resistance. Molybdenum alloys are utilized for extrusion dies and structural parts in space vehicles; incandescent light filaments, x-ray tubes, and welding electrodes employ tungsten alloys. Tantalum is immune to chemical attack by virtually all environments at temperatures below 150°C, and is frequently used in applications requiring such a corrosion-resistant material.

The Superalloys

The superalloys have superlative combinations of properties. Most are used in aircraft turbine components, which must withstand exposure to severely oxidizing environments and high temperatures for reasonable time periods. Mechanical integrity under these conditions is critical; in this regard, density is an important consideration because centrifugal stresses are diminished in rotating members when the density is reduced. These materials are classified according to the predominant metal in the alloy, which may be cobalt, nickel, or iron. Other alloying elements include the refractory metals (Nb, Mo, W, Ta), chromium, and titanium. In addition to turbine applications, these alloys are utilized in nuclear reactors and petrochemical equipment.

The Noble Metals

The noble or precious metals are a group of eight elements that have some physical characteristics in common. They are expensive (precious) and are superior or notable (noble) in properties—that is, characteristically soft, ductile, and oxidation resistant. The noble metals are silver, gold, platinum, palladium, rhodium, ruthenium, iridium, and osmium; the first three are most common and are used extensively in jewelry. Silver and gold may be strengthened by solid-solution alloying with copper; sterling silver is a silver–copper alloy containing approximately 7.5 wt% Cu. Alloys of both silver and gold are employed as dental restoration materials; also, some integrated circuit electrical contacts are of gold. Platinum is used for chemical laboratory equipment, as a catalyst (especially in the manufacture of gasoline), and in thermocouples to measure elevated temperatures.

Miscellaneous Nonferrous Alloys

The discussion above covers the vast majority of nonferrous alloys; however, a number of others are found in a variety of engineering applications, and a brief exposure of these is worthwhile.

Nickel and its alloys are highly resistant to corrosion in many environments, especially those that are basic (alkaline). Nickel is often coated or plated on some metals that are susceptible to corrosion as a protective measure. Monel, a nickel-based alloy containing approximately 65 wt% Ni and 28 wt% Cu (the balance iron), has very high strength and is extremely corrosion resistant; it is used in pumps, valves, and other components that are in contact with some acid and petroleum solutions. As already mentioned, nickel is one of the principal alloying elements in stainless steels and one of the major constituents in the superalloys.

Lead, tin, and their alloys find some use as engineering materials. Both are mechanically soft and weak, have low melting temperatures, are quite resistant to many corrosion environments, and have recrystallization temperatures below room temperature. Some common solders are lead–tin alloys, which have low melting temperatures. Applications for lead and its alloys include x-ray shields and storage batteries. The primary use of tin is as a very thin coating on the inside of plain

MATERIALS OF INTEREST

Metal Alloys Used for Euro Coins

On January 1st, 2002 the euro became the single legal currency in twelve European countries; since that date, several other nations have also joined the European monetary union, and have adopted the euro as their official currency. Euro coins are minted in eight different denominations: 2 and 1 euros, as well as 50, 20, 10, 5, 2, and 1 cent euros. Each coin has a common design on one face, whereas the reverse face design is one of several chosen by the monetary union countries. Several of these coins are shown in the photograph below.

In deciding which metal alloys to use for these coins, a number of issues were considered; most of them centered on material properties.

- The ability to distinguish a coin of one denomination from that of another denomination is important. This may be accomplished by having coins of different sizes, different colors, and different shapes. With regard to color, alloys must be chosen that retain their distinctive colors, which means that they do not easily tarnish in the air and other commonly encountered environments.
- Security is an important issue—that is, producing coins that are difficult to counterfeit. Most vending machines use electrical conductivity to identify coins, to prevent false coins from being used. This means that each coin must have its own unique "electronic signature," which depends on its alloy composition.

Photograph showing 1 euro, 2 euro, 20 cent euro, and 50 cent euro coins. (Photograph courtesy of Outokumpu Copper.)

- The alloys chosen must be "coinable" or easy to mint—that is, sufficiently soft and ductile to allow design reliefs to be stamped into the coin surfaces.
- Also, the alloys must be wear resistant (i.e., hard and strong) for long-term use, and so that the reliefs stamped into the coin surfaces are retained. Of course, strain-hardening (Section 10.10) occurs during the stamping operation which enhances hardness.
- High degrees of corrosion resistance in common environments are required for the alloys selected, to ensure minimal material losses over the lifetimes of the coins.
- It is highly desirable to use alloys of a base metal (or metals) that retains (retain) its (their) intrinsic value(s).
- Alloy recyclability is another requirement for the alloy(s) used.
- The alloy(s) from which the coins are made should also provide for human health—that is, have antibacterial characteristics so undesirable microorganisms will not grow on their surfaces.

Copper was selected as the base metal for all euro coins, inasmuch as it and its alloys satisfy the above criteria. Several different copper alloys and alloy combinations are used for the eight different coins. These are as follows:

- 2 euro coin: This coin is termed "bimetallic"—it consists of an outer ring and an inner disk. For the outer ring, a 75Cu–25Ni alloy is used, which has a silver color. The inner disk is composed of a three-layer structure—high-purity nickel that is clad on both sides with a nickel brass alloy (75Cu–20Zn–5Ni); this alloy has a gold color.
- 1 euro coin: This coin is also bimetallic, whereas the alloys used for its outer ring and inner disk are reversed from those for the 2 euro.
- 50, 20, and 10 euro cent pieces: These coins are made of a "Nordic Gold" alloy—89Cu–5Al–5Zn–1Sn.
- 5, 2, and 1 euro cent pieces: Copper-plated steels are used for these coins.

carbon steel cans (tin cans) that are used for food containers; this coating inhibits chemical reactions between the steel and the food products.

Unalloyed zinc also is a relatively soft metal having a low melting temperature and a subambient recrystallization temperature. Chemically, it is reactive in a number of common environments and, therefore, susceptible to corrosion. Galvanized steel is just plain carbon steel that has been coated with a thin zinc layer; the zinc preferentially corrodes and protects the steel (Section 16.9). Typical applications of galvanized steel are familiar (sheet metal, fences, screen, screws, etc.). Common applications of zinc alloys include padlocks, plumbing fixtures, automotive parts (door handles and grilles), and office equipment.

Although zirconium is relatively abundant in the earth's crust, it was not until quite recent times that commercial refining techniques were developed. Zirconium and its alloys are ductile and have other mechanical characteristics that are comparable to those of titanium alloys and the austenitic stainless steels. However, the primary asset of these alloys is their resistance to corrosion in a host of corrosive media, including superheated water. Furthermore, zirconium is transparent to thermal neutrons, so that its alloys have been used as cladding for uranium fuel in water-cooled nuclear reactors. In terms of cost, these alloys are also often the materials of choice for heat exchangers, reactor vessels, and piping systems for the chemical-processing and nuclear industries. They are also used in incendiary ordnance and in sealing devices for vacuum tubes.

In Appendix B is tabulated a wide variety of properties (e.g., density, elastic modulus, yield and tensile strengths, electrical resistivity, coefficient of thermal expansion, etc.) for a large number of metals and alloys.

9.4 THERMAL PROCESSING OF METALS

Earlier chapters have discussed a number of phenomena that occur in metals and alloys at elevated temperatures—for example, the decomposition of austenite. Other important phenomena like recrystallization and precipitation hardening are explained in Chapter 10. These are effective in altering the mechanical characteristics when appropriate heat treatments or thermal processes are employed. In fact, the use of heat treatments on commercial alloys is an exceedingly common practice. Therefore, we consider next the details of one of these processes, namely, annealing procedures.

The term **annealing** refers to a heat treatment in which a material is exposed to an elevated temperature for an extended time period and then slowly cooled. Ordinarily, annealing is carried out to (1) relieve stresses; (2) increase softness, ductility, and toughness; and/or (3) produce a specific microstructure. A variety of annealing heat treatments are possible; they are characterized by the changes that are induced, which many times are microstructural and are responsible for the alteration of the mechanical properties.

Any annealing process consists of three stages: (1) heating to the desired temperature, (2) holding or "soaking" at that temperature, and (3) cooling, usually to room temperature. Time is an important parameter in these procedures. During heating and cooling, there exist temperature gradients between the outside and interior portions of the piece; their magnitudes depend on the size and geometry of the piece. If the rate of temperature change is too great, temperature gradients and internal stresses may be induced that may lead to warping or even cracking. Also, the actual annealing time must be long enough to allow for any necessary transformation reactions. Annealing temperature is also an important consideration; annealing may be accelerated by increasing the temperature, since diffusional processes are normally involved.

Process Annealing

Process annealing is a heat treatment that is used to negate the effects of cold work—that is, to soften and increase the ductility of a previously strain-hardened metal. It is commonly utilized during fabrication procedures that require extensive plastic deformation, to allow a continuation of deformation without fracture or excessive energy consumption. Recovery and recrystallization processes are allowed to occur. Ordinarily a fine-grained microstructure is desired, and therefore, the heat treatment is terminated before appreciable grain growth has occurred. Surface oxidation or scaling may be prevented or minimized by annealing at a relatively low temperature (but above the recrystallization temperature) or in a nonoxidizing atmosphere.

Stress Relief

Internal residual stresses may develop in metal pieces in response to the following: (1) plastic deformation processes such as machining and grinding; (2) nonuniform cooling of a piece that was processed or fabricated at an elevated temperature, such as a weld or a casting; and (3) a phase transformation that is induced upon cooling wherein parent and product phases have different densities. Distortion and warpage may result if these residual stresses are not removed. They may be eliminated by a **stress relief** annealing heat treatment in which the piece is heated to the recommended temperature, held there long enough to attain a uniform temperature, and finally cooled to room temperature in air. The annealing temperature is ordinarily a relatively low one such that effects resulting from cold working and other heat treatments are not affected.

Annealing of Ferrous Alloys

Several different annealing procedures are employed to enhance the properties of steel alloys. However, before they are discussed, some comment relative to the labeling of phase boundaries is necessary. Figure 9.6 shows the portion of the iron–iron carbide phase diagram in the vicinity of the eutectoid. The horizontal line at the eutectoid temperature, conventionally labeled A_1, is termed the **lower critical temperature,** below which, under equilibrium conditions, all austenite will have transformed into ferrite and cementite phases. The phase boundaries denoted as A_3 and A_{cm} represent the **upper critical temperature** lines, for hypoeutectoid and hypereutectoid steels, respectively. For temperatures and compositions above these boundaries, only the austenite phase will prevail. As explained in Section 7.20, other alloying elements will shift the eutectoid and the positions of these phase boundary lines.

Normalizing

Steels that have been plastically deformed by, for example, a rolling operation, consist of grains of pearlite (and most likely a proeutectoid phase), which are irregularly shaped and relatively large, but vary substantially in size. An annealing heat treatment called **normalizing** is used to refine the grains (i.e., to decrease the average grain size) and produce a more uniform and desirable size distribution; fine-grained pearlitic steels are tougher than coarse-grained ones. Normalizing is accomplished

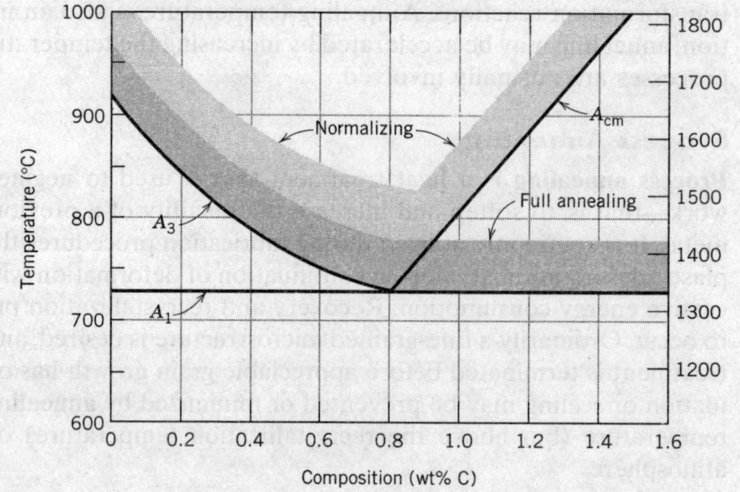

Figure 9.6 The iron–iron carbide phase diagram in the vicinity of the eutectoid, indicating heat-treating temperature ranges for plain carbon steels. (Adapted from G. Krauss, *Steels: Heat Treatment and Processing Principles,* ASM International, 1990, page 108.)

by heating at least 55°C (100°F) above the upper critical temperature—that is, above A_3 for compositions less than the eutectoid (0.76 wt% C), and above A_{cm} for compositions greater than the eutectoid as represented in Figure 9.6. After sufficient time has been allowed for the alloy to completely transform to austenite—a procedure termed **austenitizing**—the treatment is terminated by cooling in air. A normalizing cooling curve is superimposed on the continuous cooling transformation diagram (Figure 8.26).

Full Anneal

A heat treatment known as **full annealing** is often utilized in low- and medium-carbon steels that will be machined or will experience extensive plastic deformation during a forming operation. In general, the alloy is treated by heating to a temperature of about 50°C above the A_3 line (to form austenite) for compositions less than the eutectoid, or, for compositions in excess of the eutectoid, 50°C above the A_1 line (to form austenite and Fe_3C phases), as noted in Figure 9.6. The alloy is then furnace cooled; that is, the heat-treating furnace is turned off and both furnace and steel cool to room temperature at the same rate, which takes several hours. The microstructural product of this anneal is coarse pearlite (in addition to any proeutectoid phase) that is relatively soft and ductile. The full-anneal cooling procedure (also shown in Figure 8.26) is time consuming; however, a microstructure having small grains and a uniform grain structure results.

Spheroidizing

Medium- and high-carbon steels having a microstructure containing even coarse pearlite may still be too hard to conveniently machine or plastically deform. These steels, and in fact any steel, may be heat treated or annealed to develop the spheroidite structure as described in Section 8.5. Spheroidized steels have a maximum softness and ductility and are easily machined or deformed. The **spheroidizing** heat treatment, during which there is a coalescence of the Fe_3C to form the spheroid particles (see the chapter-opening photograph for Chapter 8), can take place by several methods, as follows:

- Heating the alloy at a temperature just below the eutectoid [line A_1 in Figure 9.6, or at about 700°C (1300°F)] in the α + Fe_3C region of the phase diagram.

If the precursor microstructure contains pearlite, spheroidizing times will ordinarily range between 15 and 25 h.

- Heating to a temperature just above the eutectoid temperature, and then either cooling very slowly in the furnace, or holding at a temperature just below the eutectoid temperature.
- Heating and cooling alternately within about ±50°C of the A_1 line of Figure 9.6.

To some degree, the rate at which spheroidite forms depends on prior microstructure. For example, it is slowest for pearlite, and the finer the pearlite, the more rapid the rate. Also, prior cold work increases the spheroidizing reaction rate.

Still other annealing treatments are possible. For example, glasses are annealed, as outlined in Section 12.16, to remove residual internal stresses that render the material excessively weak. In addition, microstructural alterations and the attendant modification of mechanical properties of cast irons, as discussed in Section 9.2, result from what are in a sense annealing treatments.

Deformation

9.5 CONCEPTS OF STRESS AND STRAIN

If a load is static or changes relatively slowly with time and is applied uniformly over a cross section or surface of a member, the mechanical behavior may be ascertained by a simple stress–strain test; these are most commonly conducted for metals at room temperature. There are three principal ways in which a load may be applied: namely, tension, compression, and shear (Figures 9.7*a*, *b*, *c*). In engineering practice many loads are torsional rather than pure shear; this type of loading is illustrated in Figure 9.7*d*.

Tension Tests[1]

One of the most common mechanical stress–strain tests is performed in *tension*. As will be seen, the tension test can be used to ascertain several mechanical properties of materials that are important in design. A specimen is deformed, usually to fracture, with a gradually increasing tensile load that is applied uniaxially along the long axis of a specimen. A standard tensile specimen is shown in Figure 9.8. Normally, the cross section is circular, but rectangular specimens are also used. This "dogbone" specimen configuration was chosen so that, during testing, deformation is confined to the narrow center region (which has a uniform cross section along its length), and, also, to reduce the likelihood of fracture at the ends of the specimen. The standard diameter is approximately 12.8 mm (0.5 in.), whereas the reduced section length should be at least four times this diameter; 60 mm ($2\frac{1}{4}$ in.) is common. Gauge length is used in ductility computations, as discussed in Section 9.7; the standard value is 50 mm (2.0 in.). The specimen is mounted by its ends into the holding grips of the testing apparatus (Figure 9.9). The tensile testing machine is designed to elongate the specimen at a constant rate, and to continuously and simultaneously measure the instantaneous applied load (with a load cell) and the resulting elongations (using an extensometer). A stress–strain test typically takes

[1] ASTM Standards E 8 and E 8M, "Standard Test Methods for Tension Testing of Metallic Materials."

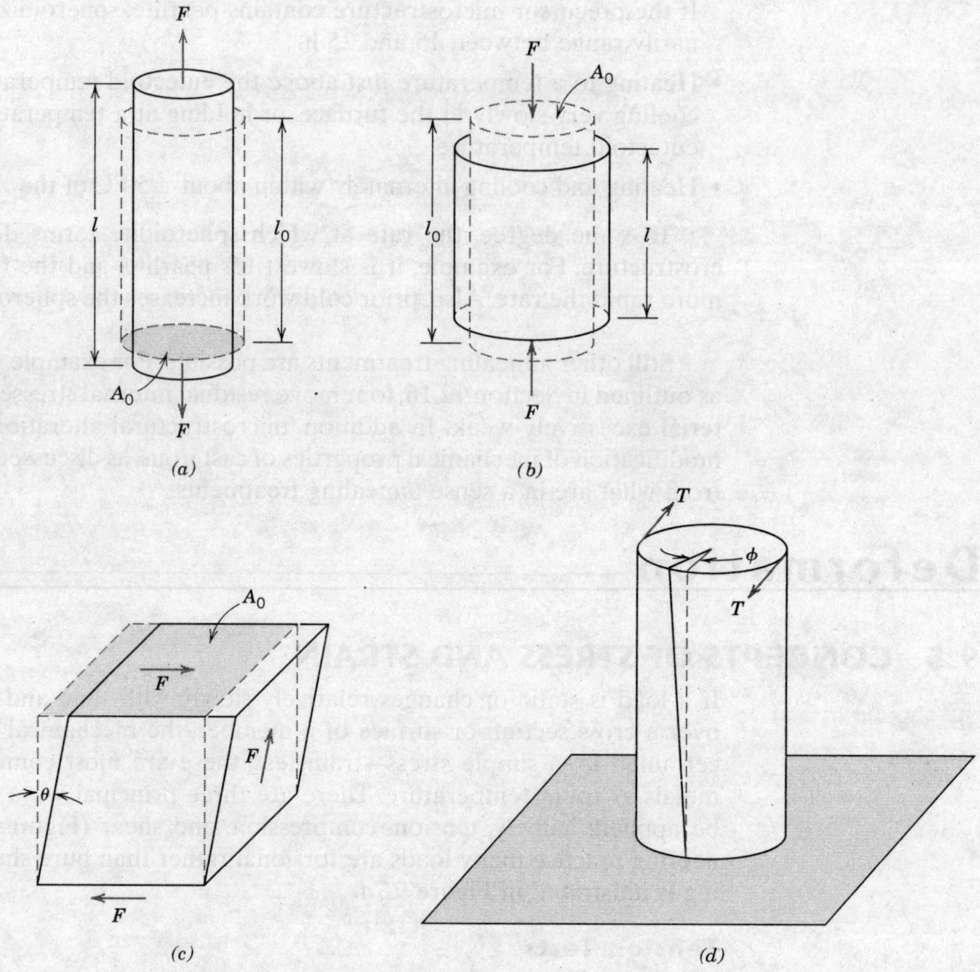

Figure 9.7 (*a*) Schematic illustration of how a tensile load produces an elongation and positive linear strain. Dashed lines represent the shape before deformation; solid lines, after deformation. (*b*) Schematic illustration of how a compressive load produces contraction and a negative linear strain. (*c*) Schematic representation of shear strain γ, where $\gamma = \tan\theta$. (*d*) Schematic representation of torsional deformation (i.e., angle of twist ϕ) produced by an applied torque T.

several minutes to perform and is destructive; that is, the test specimen is permanently deformed and usually fractured.

The output of such a tensile test is recorded (usually on a computer) as load or force versus elongation. These load–deformation characteristics are dependent on the specimen size. For example, it will require twice the load to produce the same elongation if the cross-sectional area of the specimen is doubled. To minimize these geometrical factors, load and elongation are normalized to the respective parameters of **engineering stress** and **engineering strain.** Engineering stress σ is defined by the relationship

$$\sigma = \frac{F}{A_0} \tag{9.1}$$

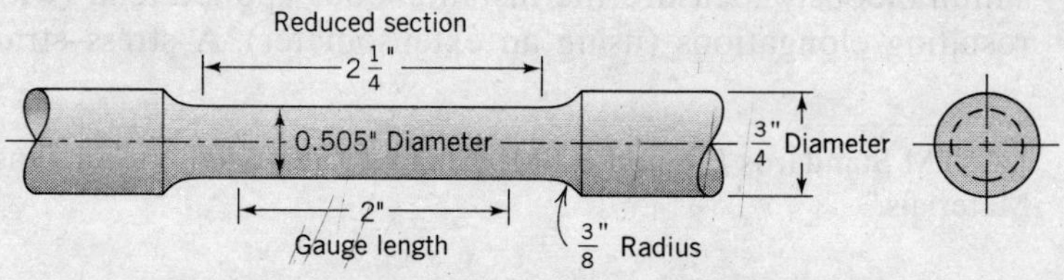

Figure 9.8 A standard tensile specimen with circular cross section.

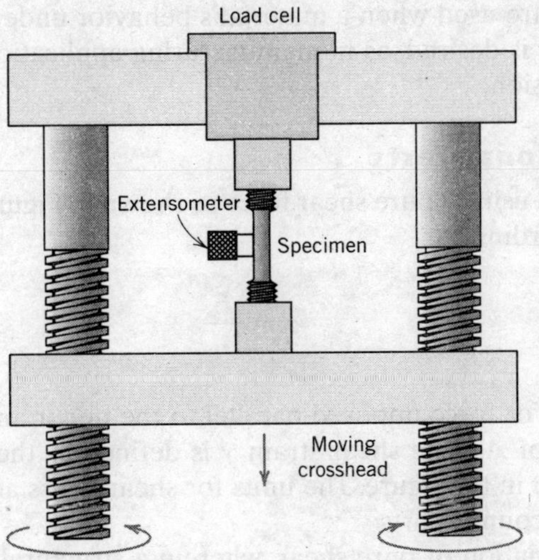

Figure 9.9 Schematic representation of the apparatus used to conduct tensile stress–strain tests. The specimen is elongated by the moving crosshead; load cell and extensometer measure, respectively, the magnitude of the applied load and the elongation. (Adapted from H. W. Hayden, W. G. Moffatt, and J. Wulff, *The Structure and Properties of Materials,* Vol. III, *Mechanical Behavior,* p. 2. Copyright © 1965 by John Wiley & Sons, New York. Reprinted by permission of John Wiley & Sons, Inc.)

in which F is the instantaneous load applied perpendicular to the specimen cross section, in units of newtons (N) or pounds force (lb_f), and A_0 is the original cross-sectional area before any load is applied (m^2 or $in.^2$). The units of engineering stress (referred to subsequently as just stress) are megapascals, MPa (SI) (where 1 MPa $= 10^6$ N/m^2), and pounds force per square inch, psi (Customary U.S.).[2]

Engineering strain ϵ is defined according to

$$\epsilon = \frac{l_i - l_0}{l_0} = \frac{\Delta l}{l_0} \tag{9.2}$$

in which l_0 is the original length before any load is applied, and l_i is the instantaneous length. Sometimes the quantity $l_i - l_0$ is denoted as Δl, and is the deformation elongation or change in length at some instant, as referenced to the original length. Engineering strain (subsequently called just strain) is unitless, but meters per meter or inches per inch are often used; the value of strain is obviously independent of the unit system. Sometimes strain is also expressed as a percentage, in which the strain value is multiplied by 100.

Compression Tests[3]

Compression stress–strain tests may be conducted if in-service forces are of this type. A compression test is conducted in a manner similar to the tensile test, except that the force is compressive and the specimen contracts along the direction of the stress. Equations 9.1 and 9.2 are utilized to compute compressive stress and strain, respectively. By convention, a compressive force is taken to be negative, which yields a negative stress. Furthermore, since l_0 is greater than l_i, compressive strains computed from Equation 9.2 are necessarily also negative. Tensile tests are more common because they are easier to perform; also, for most materials used in structural applications, very little additional information is obtained from compressive tests.

---

[2] Conversion from one system of stress units to the other is accomplished by the relationship 145 psi = 1 MPa.

[3] ASTM Standard E 9, "Standard Test Methods of Compression Testing of Metallic Materials at Room Temperature."

Compressive tests are used when a material's behavior under large and permanent (i.e., plastic) strains is desired, as in manufacturing applications, or when the material is brittle in tension.

Shear and Torsional Tests[4]

For tests performed using a pure shear force as shown in Figure 9.7*c*, the shear stress τ is computed according to

$$\tau = \frac{F}{A_0} \tag{9.3}$$

where F is the load or force imposed parallel to the upper and lower faces, each of which has an area of A_0. The shear strain γ is defined as the tangent of the strain angle θ, as indicated in the figure. The units for shear stress and strain are the same as for their tensile counterparts.

Torsion is a variation of pure shear, wherein a structural member is twisted in the manner of Figure 9.7*d*; torsional forces produce a rotational motion about the longitudinal axis of one end of the member relative to the other end. Examples of torsion are found for machine axles and drive shafts, and also for twist drills. Torsional tests are normally performed on cylindrical solid shafts or tubes. A shear stress τ is a function of the applied torque T, whereas shear strain γ is related to the angle of twist, ϕ in Figure 9.7*d*.

Geometric Considerations of the Stress State

Stresses that are computed from the tensile, compressive, shear, and torsional force states represented in Figure 9.7 act either parallel or perpendicular to planar faces of the bodies represented in these illustrations. Note that the stress state is a function of the orientations of the planes upon which the stresses are taken to act. For example, consider the cylindrical tensile specimen of Figure 9.10 that is subjected to a tensile stress σ applied parallel to its axis. Furthermore, consider also the plane p-p' that is oriented at some arbitrary angle θ relative to the plane of the specimen end-face. Upon this plane p-p', the applied stress is no longer a pure tensile one. Rather, a more complex stress state is present that consists of a tensile (or normal) stress σ' that acts normal to the p-p' plane and, in addition, a shear stress τ' that acts parallel to this plane; both of these stresses are represented in the figure. Using mechanics of materials principles,[5] it is possible to develop equations for σ' and τ' in terms of σ and θ, as follows:

$$\sigma' = \sigma \cos^2 \theta = \sigma\left(\frac{1 + \cos 2\theta}{2}\right) \tag{9.4a}$$

$$\tau' = \sigma \sin \theta \cos \theta = \sigma\left(\frac{\sin 2\theta}{2}\right) \tag{9.4b}$$

These same mechanics principles allow the transformation of stress components from one coordinate system to another coordinate system that has a different orientation. Such treatments are beyond the scope of the present discussion.

---

[4] ASTM Standard E 143, "Standard Test for Shear Modulus."

[5] See, for example, W. F. Riley, L. D. Sturges, and D. H. Morris, *Mechanics of Materials*, 5th edition, John Wiley & Sons, New York, 1999.

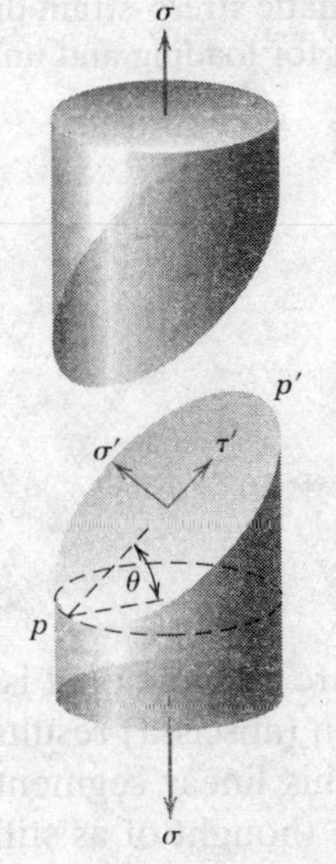

Figure 9.10 Schematic representation showing normal (σ') and shear (τ') stresses that act on a plane oriented at an angle θ relative to the plane taken perpendicular to the direction along which a pure tensile stress (σ) is applied.

9.6 ELASTIC DEFORMATION

Stress-Strain Behavior

The degree to which a structure deforms or strains depends on the magnitude of an imposed stress. For most metals that are stressed in tension and at relatively low levels, stress and strain are proportional to each other through the relationship

$$\sigma = E\epsilon \tag{9.5}$$

This is known as Hooke's law, and the constant of proportionality E (GPa)[6] is the **modulus of elasticity**, or *Young's modulus*. For most typical metals the magnitude of this modulus ranges between 45 GPa, for magnesium, and 407 GPa, for tungsten. Modulus of elasticity values for several metals at room temperature are presented in Table 9.10.

Table 9.10 Room-Temperature Elastic and Shear Moduli, and Poisson's Ratio for Various Metal Alloys

Metal Alloy	*Modulus of Elasticity (GPa)*	*Shear Modulus (GPa)*	*Poisson's Ratio*
Aluminum	69	25	0.33
Brass	97	37	0.34
Copper	110	46	0.34
Magnesium	45	17	0.29
Nickel	207	76	0.31
Steel	207	83	0.30
Titanium	107	45	0.34
Tungsten	407	160	0.28

[6] The SI unit for the modulus of elasticity is gigapascal, GPa, where 1 GPa = 10^9 N/m^2 = 10^3 MPa.

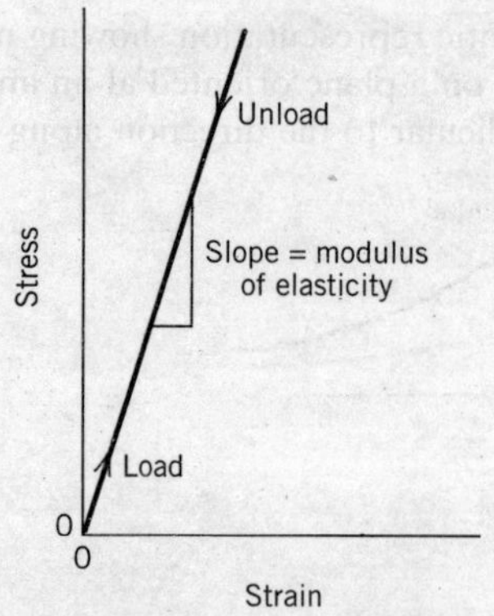

Figure 9.11 Schematic stress–strain diagram showing linear elastic deformation for loading and unloading cycles.

Deformation in which stress and strain are proportional is called **elastic deformation;** a plot of stress (ordinate) versus strain (abscissa) results in a linear relationship, as shown in Figure 9.11. The slope of this linear segment corresponds to the modulus of elasticity E. This modulus may be thought of as stiffness, or a material's resistance to elastic deformation. The greater the modulus, the stiffer the material, or the smaller the elastic strain that results from the application of a given stress. The modulus is an important design parameter used for computing elastic deflections.

Elastic deformation is nonpermanent, which means that when the applied load is released, the piece returns to its original shape. As shown in the stress–strain plot (Figure 9.11), application of the load corresponds to moving from the origin up and along the straight line. Upon release of the load, the line is traversed in the opposite direction, back to the origin.

There are some materials (e.g., gray cast iron, concrete, and many polymers) for which this elastic portion of the stress–strain curve is not linear (Figure 9.12); hence, it is not possible to determine a modulus of elasticity as described above. For this nonlinear behavior, either *tangent* or *secant modulus* is normally used. Tangent modulus is taken as the slope of the stress–strain curve at some specified level of stress, while secant modulus represents the slope of a secant drawn from the origin to some given point of the σ–ϵ curve. The determination of these moduli is illustrated in Figure 9.12.

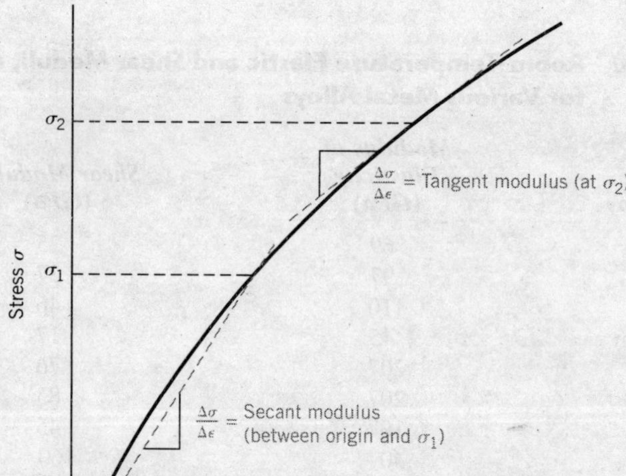

Figure 9.12 Schematic stress–strain diagram showing non-linear elastic behavior, and how secant and tangent moduli are determined.

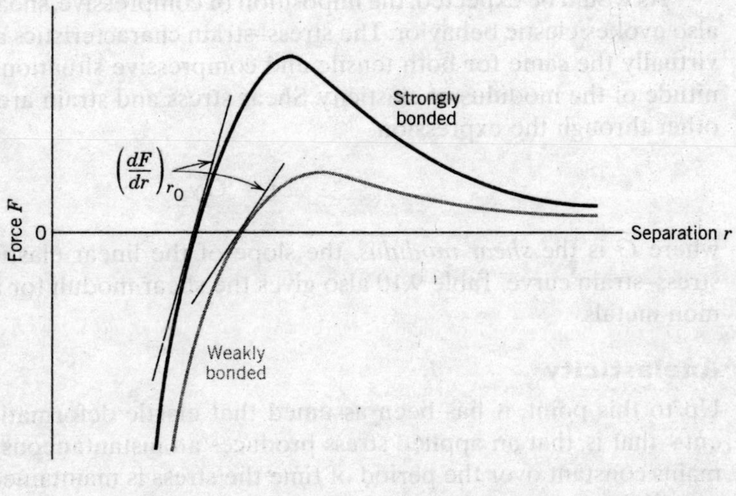

Figure 9.13 Force versus interatomic separation for weakly and strongly bonded atoms. The magnitude of the modulus of elasticity is proportional to the slope of each curve at the equilibrium interatomic separation r_0.

On an atomic scale, macroscopic elastic strain is manifested as small changes in the interatomic spacing and the stretching of interatomic bonds. As a consequence, the magnitude of the modulus of elasticity is a measure of the resistance to separation of adjacent atoms, that is, the interatomic bonding forces. Furthermore, this modulus is proportional to the slope of the interatomic force–separation curve (Figure 2.8*a*) at the equilibrium spacing:

$$E \propto \left(\frac{dF}{dr}\right)_{r_0} \tag{9.6}$$

Figure 9.13 shows the force–separation curves for materials having both strong and weak interatomic bonds; the slope at r_0 is indicated for each.

Values of the modulus of elasticity for ceramic materials are about the same as for metals; for polymers they are lower (Figure 1.4). These differences are a direct consequence of the different types of atomic bonding in the three materials types. Furthermore, with increasing temperature, the modulus of elasticity diminishes, as is shown for several metals in Figure 9.14.

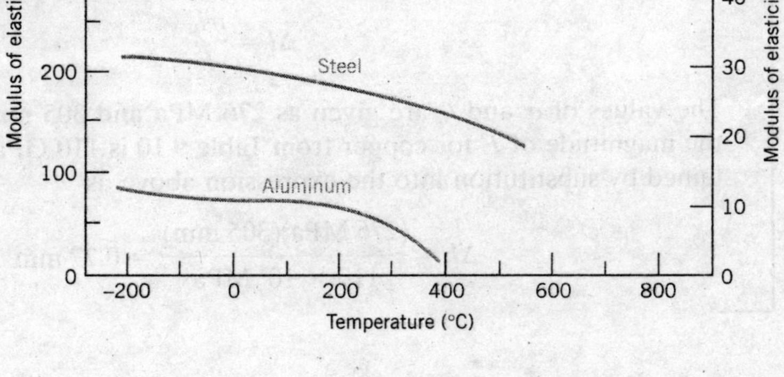

Figure 9.14 Plot of modulus of elasticity versus temperature for tungsten, steel, and aluminum. (Adapted from K. M. Ralls, T. H. Courtney, and J. Wulff, *Introduction to Materials Science and Engineering*. Copyright © 1976 by John Wiley & Sons, New York. Reprinted by permission of John Wiley & Sons, Inc.)

As would be expected, the imposition of compressive, shear, or torsional stresses also evokes elastic behavior. The stress–strain characteristics at low stress levels are virtually the same for both tensile and compressive situations, to include the magnitude of the modulus of elasticity. Shear stress and strain are proportional to each other through the expression

$$\tau = G\gamma \tag{9.7}$$

where G is the *shear modulus,* the slope of the linear elastic region of the shear stress–strain curve. Table 9.10 also gives the shear moduli for a number of the common metals.

Anelasticity

Up to this point, it has been assumed that elastic deformation is time independent—that is, that an applied stress produces an instantaneous elastic strain that remains constant over the period of time the stress is maintained. It has also been assumed that upon release of the load the strain is totally recovered—that is, that the strain immediately returns to zero. In most engineering materials, however, there will also exist a time-dependent elastic strain component. That is, elastic deformation will continue after the stress application, and upon load release some finite time is required for complete recovery. This time-dependent elastic behavior is known as **anelasticity,** and it is due to time-dependent microscopic and atomistic processes that are attendant to the deformation. For metals the anelastic component is normally small and is often neglected. However, for some polymeric materials its magnitude is significant; in this case it is termed *viscoelastic behavior,* which is the discussion topic of Section 14.4.

EXAMPLE PROBLEM 9.1

Elongation (Elastic) Computation

A piece of copper originally 305 mm long is pulled in tension with a stress of 276 MPa. If the deformation is entirely elastic, what will be the resultant elongation?

Solution

Since the deformation is elastic, strain is dependent on stress according to Equation 9.5. Furthermore, the elongation Δl is related to the original length l_0 through Equation 9.2. Combining these two expressions and solving for Δl yields

$$\sigma = \epsilon E = \left(\frac{\Delta l}{l_0}\right)E$$

$$\Delta l = \frac{\sigma l_0}{E}$$

The values of σ and l_0 are given as 276 MPa and 305 mm, respectively, and the magnitude of E for copper from Table 9.10 is 110 GPa. Elongation is obtained by substitution into the expression above as

$$\Delta l = \frac{(276\text{ MPa})(305\text{ mm})}{110 \times 10^3\text{ MPa}} = 0.77\text{ mm}$$

Elastic Properties of Materials

When a tensile stress is imposed on a metal specimen, an elastic elongation and accompanying strain ϵ_z result in the direction of the applied stress (arbitrarily taken to be the z direction), as indicated in Figure 9.15. As a result of this elongation, there will be constrictions in the lateral (x and y) directions perpendicular to the applied stress; from these contractions, the compressive strains ϵ_x and ϵ_y may be determined. If the applied stress is uniaxial (only in the z direction), and the material is isotropic, then $\epsilon_x = \epsilon_y$. A parameter termed **Poisson's ratio** ν is defined as the ratio of the lateral and axial strains, or

$$\nu = -\frac{\epsilon_x}{\epsilon_z} = -\frac{\epsilon_y}{\epsilon_z} \tag{9.8}$$

The negative sign is included in the expression so that ν will always be positive, since ϵ_x and ϵ_z will always be of opposite sign. Theoretically, Poisson's ratio for isotropic materials should be $\frac{1}{4}$; furthermore, the maximum value for ν (or that value for which there is no net volume change) is 0.50. For many metals and other alloys, values of Poisson's ratio range between 0.25 and 0.35. Table 9.10 shows ν values for several common metallic materials.

For isotropic materials, shear and elastic moduli are related to each other and to Poisson's ratio according to

$$E = 2G(1 + \nu) \tag{9.9}$$

In most metals G is about $0.4E$; thus, if the value of one modulus is known, the other may be approximated.

Many materials are elastically anisotropic; that is, the elastic behavior (e.g., the magnitude of E) varies with crystallographic direction (see Table 3.2). For these materials the elastic properties are completely characterized only by the specification of several elastic constants, their number depending on characteristics of the crystal

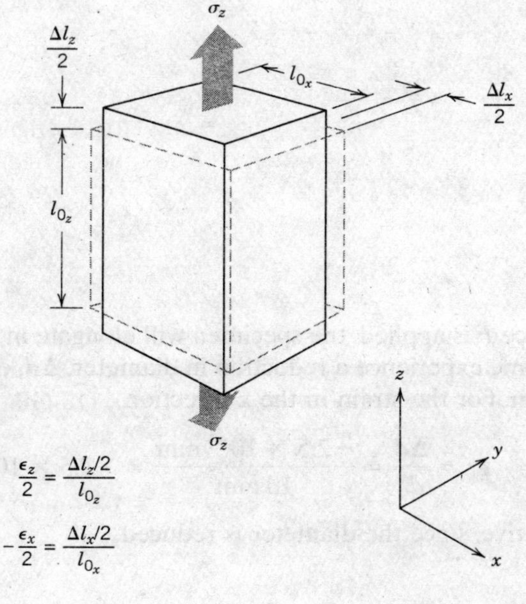

Figure 9.15 Axial (z) elongation (positive strain) and lateral (x and y) contractions (negative strains) in response to an imposed tensile stress. Solid lines represent dimensions after stress application; dashed lines, before.

structure. Even for isotropic materials, for complete characterization of the elastic properties, at least two constants must be given. Since the grain orientation is random in most polycrystalline materials, these may be considered to be isotropic; inorganic ceramic glasses are also isotropic. The remaining discussion of mechanical behavior assumes isotropy and polycrystallinity because such is the character of most engineering materials.

EXAMPLE PROBLEM 9.2

Computation of Load to Produce Specified Diameter Change

A tensile stress is to be applied along the long axis of a cylindrical brass rod that has a diameter of 10 mm. Determine the magnitude of the load required to produce a 2.5×10^{-3} mm change in diameter if the deformation is entirely elastic.

Solution

This deformation situation is represented in the accompanying drawing.

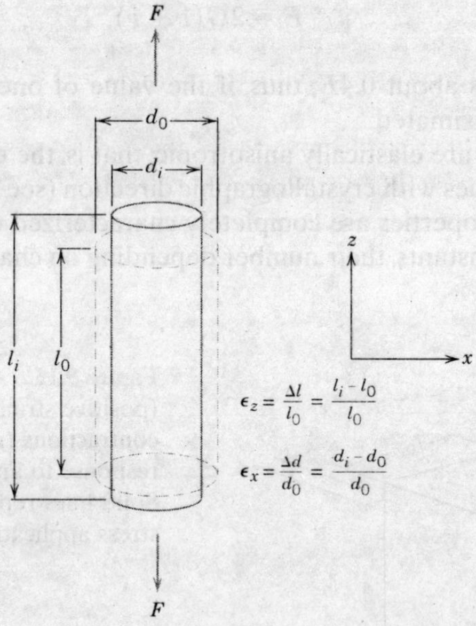

When the force F is applied, the specimen will elongate in the z direction and at the same time experience a reduction in diameter, Δd, of 2.5×10^{-3} mm in the x direction. For the strain in the x direction,

$$\epsilon_x = \frac{\Delta d}{d_0} = \frac{-2.5 \times 10^{-3}\text{ mm}}{10\text{ mm}} = -2.5 \times 10^{-4}$$

which is negative, since the diameter is reduced.

It next becomes necessary to calculate the strain in the z direction using Equation 9.8. The value for Poisson's ratio for brass is 0.34 (Table 9.10), and thus

$$\epsilon_z = -\frac{\epsilon_x}{\nu} = -\frac{(-2.5 \times 10^{-4})}{0.34} = 7.35 \times 10^{-4}$$

The applied stress may now be computed using Equation 9.5 and the modulus of elasticity, given in Table 9.10 as 97 GPa, as

$$\sigma = \epsilon_z E = (7.35 \times 10^{-4})(97 \times 10^3 \text{ MPa}) = 71.3 \text{ MPa}$$

Finally, from Equation 9.1, the applied force may be determined as

$$F = \sigma A_0 = \sigma\left(\frac{d_0}{2}\right)^2 \pi$$

$$= (71.3 \times 10^6 \text{ N/m}^2)\left(\frac{10 \times 10^{-3} \text{ m}}{2}\right)^2 \pi = 5600 \text{ N}$$

9.7 PLASTIC DEFORMATION

For most metallic materials, elastic deformation persists only to strains of about 0.005. As the material is deformed beyond this point, the stress is no longer proportional to strain (Hooke's law, Equation 9.5, ceases to be valid), and permanent, nonrecoverable, or **plastic deformation** occurs. Figure 9.16a plots schematically the tensile stress–strain behavior into the plastic region for a typical metal. The transition from elastic to plastic is a gradual one for most metals; some curvature results at the onset of plastic deformation, which increases more rapidly with rising stress.

From an atomic perspective, plastic deformation corresponds to the breaking of bonds with original atom neighbors and then reforming bonds with new neighbors

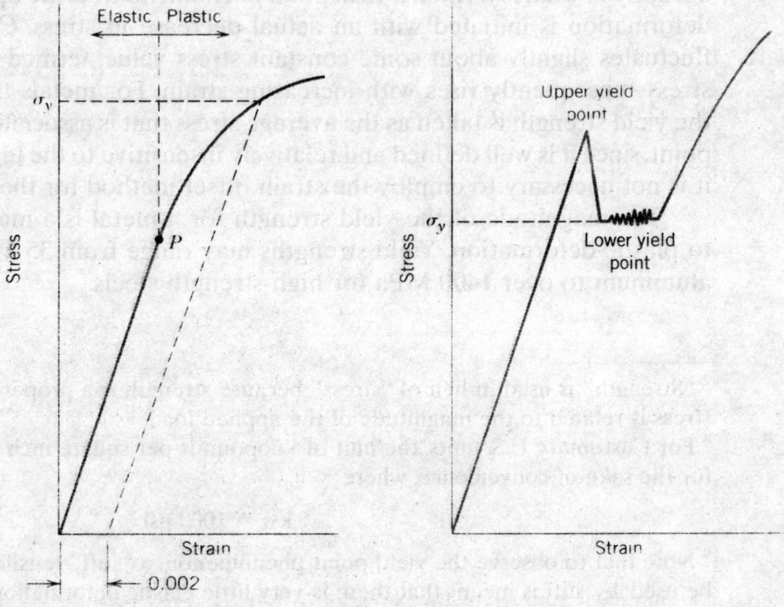

Figure 9.16 (a) Typical stress–strain behavior for a metal showing elastic and plastic deformations, the proportional limit P, and the yield strength σ_y, as determined using the 0.002 strain offset method. (b) Representative stress–strain behavior found for some steels demonstrating the yield point phenomenon.

as large numbers of atoms or molecules move relative to one another; upon removal of the stress they do not return to their original positions. The mechanism of this deformation is different for crystalline and amorphous materials. For crystalline solids, deformation is accomplished by means of a process called slip, which involves the motion of dislocations as discussed in Section 10.2. Plastic deformation in noncrystalline solids (as well as liquids) occurs by a viscous flow mechanism, which is outlined in Section 12.12.

Tensile Properties

Yielding and Yield Strength

Most structures are designed to ensure that only elastic deformation will result when a stress is applied. A structure or component that has plastically deformed, or experienced a permanent change in shape, may not be capable of functioning as intended. It is therefore desirable to know the stress level at which plastic deformation begins, or where the phenomenon of **yielding** occurs. For metals that experience this gradual elastic–plastic transition, the point of yielding may be determined as the initial departure from linearity of the stress–strain curve; this is sometimes called the **proportional limit**, as indicated by point P in Figure 9.16*a*. In such cases the position of this point may not be determined precisely. As a consequence, a convention has been established wherein a straight line is constructed parallel to the elastic portion of the stress–strain curve at some specified strain offset, usually 0.002. The stress corresponding to the intersection of this line and the stress–strain curve as it bends over in the plastic region is defined as the **yield strength** σ_y.[7] This is demonstrated in Figure 9.16*a*. Of course, the units of yield strength are MPa or psi.[8]

For those materials having a nonlinear elastic region (Figure 9.12), use of the strain offset method is not possible, and the usual practice is to define the yield strength as the stress required to produce some amount of strain (e.g., $\epsilon = 0.005$).

Some steels and other materials exhibit the tensile stress–strain behavior as shown in Figure 9.16*b*. The elastic–plastic transition is very well defined and occurs abruptly in what is termed a *yield point phenomenon*. At the upper yield point, plastic deformation is initiated with an actual decrease in stress. Continued deformation fluctuates slightly about some constant stress value, termed the lower yield point; stress subsequently rises with increasing strain. For metals that display this effect, the yield strength is taken as the average stress that is associated with the lower yield point, since it is well defined and relatively insensitive to the testing procedure.[9] Thus, it is not necessary to employ the strain offset method for these materials.

The magnitude of the yield strength for a metal is a measure of its resistance to plastic deformation. Yield strengths may range from 35 MPa for a low-strength aluminum to over 1400 MPa for high-strength steels.

[7] "Strength" is used in lieu of "stress" because strength is a property of the metal, whereas stress is related to the magnitude of the applied load.

[8] For Customary U.S. units, the unit of kilopounds per square inch (ksi) is sometimes used for the sake of convenience, where

$$1 \text{ ksi} = 1000 \text{ psi}$$

[9] Note that to observe the yield point phenomenon, a "stiff" tensile-testing apparatus must be used; by stiff is meant that there is very little elastic deformation of the machine during loading.

Concept Check 9.6

Cite the primary differences between elastic, anelastic, and plastic deformation behaviors.

[The answer may be found in enclosed CD.]

Tensile Strength

After yielding, the stress necessary to continue plastic deformation in metals increases to a maximum, point *M* in Figure 9.17, and then decreases to the eventual fracture, point *F*. The **tensile strength** *TS* (MPa) is the stress at the maximum on the engineering stress–strain curve (Figure 9.17). This corresponds to the maximum stress that can be sustained by a structure in tension; if this stress is applied and maintained, fracture will result. All deformation up to this point is uniform throughout the narrow region of the tensile specimen. However, at this maximum stress, a small constriction or neck begins to form at some point, and all subsequent deformation is confined at this neck, as indicated by the schematic specimen insets in Figure 9.17. This phenomenon is termed "necking," and fracture ultimately occurs at the neck. The fracture strength corresponds to the stress at fracture.

Tensile strengths may vary anywhere from 50 MPa for an aluminum to as high as 3000 MPa for the high-strength steels. Ordinarily, when the strength of a metal is cited for design purposes, the yield strength is used. This is because by the time a stress corresponding to the tensile strength has been applied, often a structure has experienced so much plastic deformation that it is useless. Furthermore, fracture strengths are not normally specified for engineering design purposes.

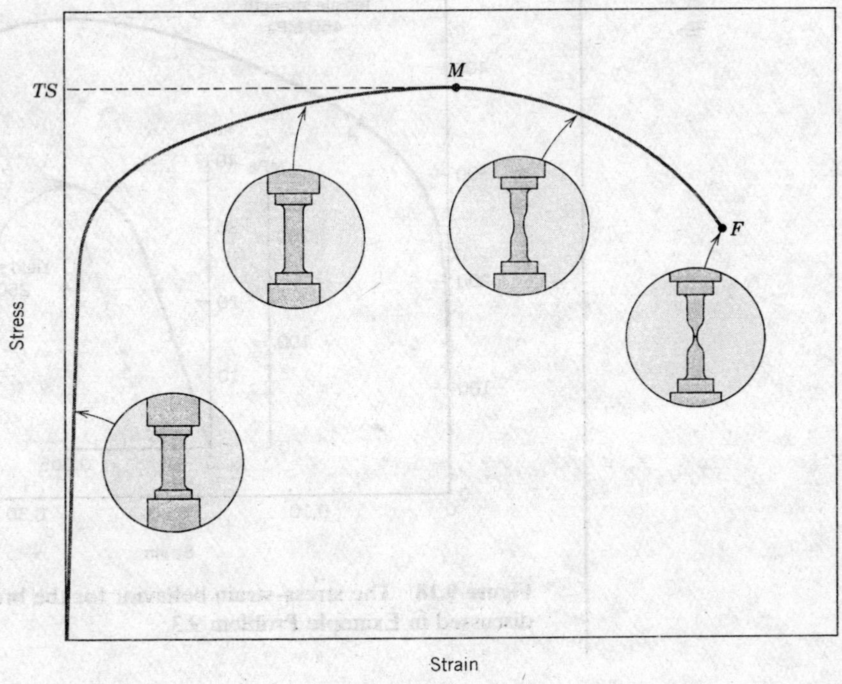

Figure 9.17 Typical engineering stress–strain behavior to fracture, point *F*. The tensile strength *TS* is indicated at point *M*. The circular insets represent the geometry of the deformed specimen at various points along the curve.

EXAMPLE PROBLEM 9.3

Mechanical Property Determinations from Stress–Strain Plot

From the tensile stress–strain behavior for the brass specimen shown in Figure 9.18, determine the following:

(a) The modulus of elasticity

(b) The yield strength at a strain offset of 0.002

(c) The maximum load that can be sustained by a cylindrical specimen having an original diameter of 12.8 mm

(d) The change in length of a specimen originally 250 mm long that is subjected to a tensile stress of 345 MPa

Solution

(a) The modulus of elasticity is the slope of the elastic or initial linear portion of the stress–strain curve. The strain axis has been expanded in the inset, Figure 9.18, to facilitate this computation. The slope of this linear region is the rise over the run, or the change in stress divided by the corresponding change in strain; in mathematical terms,

$$E = \text{slope} = \frac{\Delta\sigma}{\Delta\epsilon} = \frac{\sigma_2 - \sigma_1}{\epsilon_2 - \epsilon_1} \tag{9.10}$$

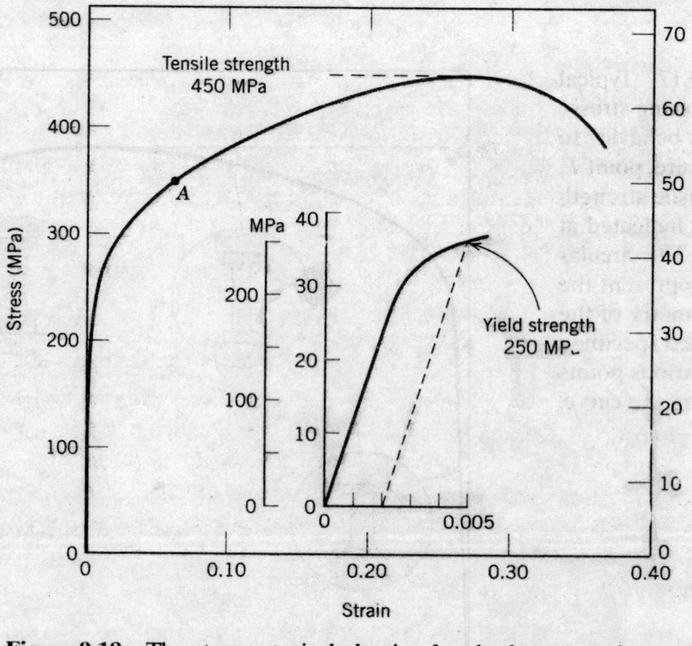

Figure 9.18 The stress–strain behavior for the brass specimen discussed in Example Problem 9.3.

Inasmuch as the line segment passes through the origin, it is convenient to take both σ_1 and ϵ_1 as zero. If σ_2 is arbitrarily taken as 150 MPa, then ϵ_2 will have a value of 0.0019. Therefore,

$$E = \frac{(150 - 0)\ \text{MPa}}{0.0016 - 0} = 93.8\ \text{GPa}$$

which is very close to the value of 97 GPa given for brass in Table 9.10.

(b) The 0.002 strain offset line is constructed as shown in the inset; its intersection with the stress–strain curve is at approximately 250 MPa, which is the yield strength of the brass.

(c) The maximum load that can be sustained by the specimen is calculated by using Equation 9.1, in which σ is taken to be the tensile strength, from Figure 9.18, 450 MPa. Solving for F, the maximum load, yields

$$F = \sigma A_0 = \sigma\left(\frac{d_0}{2}\right)^2 \pi$$

$$= (450 \times 10^6\ \text{N/m}^2)\left(\frac{12.8 \times 10^{-3}\ \text{m}}{2}\right)^2 \pi = 57{,}900\ \text{N}$$

(d) To compute the change in length, Δl, in Equation 9.2, it is first necessary to determine the strain that is produced by a stress of 345 MPa. This is accomplished by locating the stress point on the stress–strain curve, point A, and reading the corresponding strain from the strain axis, which is approximately 0.09. Inasmuch as $l_0 = 250$ mm, we have

$$\Delta l = \epsilon l_0 = (0.06)(250\ \text{mm}) = 15\ \text{mm}$$

Ductility

Ductility is another important mechanical property. It is a measure of the degree of plastic deformation that has been sustained at fracture. A material that experiences very little or no plastic deformation upon fracture is termed *brittle*. The tensile stress–strain behaviors for both ductile and brittle materials are schematically illustrated in Figure 9.19.

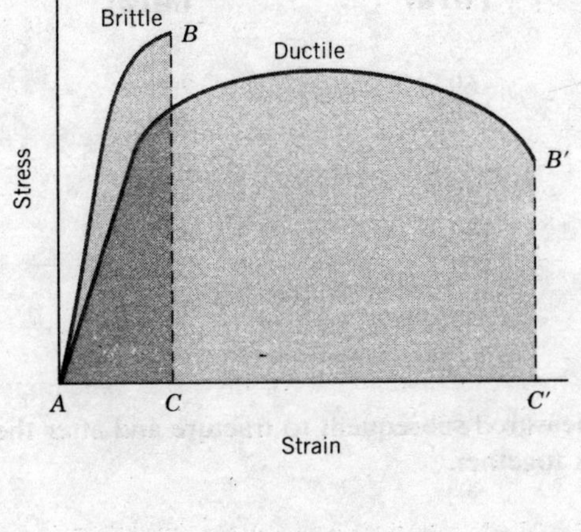

Figure 9.19 Schematic representations of tensile stress–strain behavior for brittle and ductile materials loaded to fracture.

Ductility may be expressed quantitatively as either *percent elongation* or *percent reduction in area*. The percent elongation %EL is the percentage of plastic strain at fracture, or

$$\%\text{EL} = \left(\frac{l_f - l_0}{l_0}\right) \times 100 \tag{9.11}$$

where l_f is the fracture length[10] and l_0 is the original gauge length as above. Inasmuch as a significant proportion of the plastic deformation at fracture is confined to the neck region, the magnitude of %EL will depend on specimen gauge length. The shorter l_0, the greater is the fraction of total elongation from the neck and, consequently, the higher the value of %EL. Therefore, l_0 should be specified when percent elongation values are cited; it is commonly 50 mm.

Percent reduction in area %RA is defined as

$$\%\text{RA} = \left(\frac{A_0 - A_f}{A_0}\right) \times 100 \tag{9.12}$$

where A_0 is the original cross-sectional area and A_f is the cross-sectional area at the point of fracture.[10] Percent reduction in area vaues are independent of both l_0 and A_0. Furthermore, for a given material the magnitudes of %EL and %RA will, in general, be different. Most metals possess at least a moderate degree of ductility at room temperature; however, some become brittle as the temperature is lowered (Section 11.6).

A knowledge of the ductility of materials is important for at least two reasons. First, it indicates to a designer the degree to which a structure will deform plastically before fracture. Second, it specifies the degree of allowable deformation during fabrication operations. We sometimes refer to relatively ductile materials as being "forgiving," in the sense that they may experience local deformation without fracture should there be an error in the magnitude of the design stress calculation.

Brittle materials are *approximately* considered to be those having a fracture strain of less than about 5%.

Thus, several important mechanical properties of metals may be determined from tensile stress–strain tests. Table 9.2 presents some typical room-temperature values of

Table 9.11 Typical Mechanical Properties of Several Metals and Alloys in an Annealed State

Metal Alloy	*Yield Strength (MPa)*	*Tensile Strength (MPa)*	*Ductility, (%EL in 50 mm)*
Aluminum	35	90	40
Copper	69	200	45
Brass (70Cu–30Zn)	75	300	68
Iron	130	262	45
Nickel	138	480	40
Steel (1020)	180	380	25
Titanium	450	520	25
Molybdenum	565	655	35

[10] Both l_f and A_f are measured subsequent to fracture and after the two broken ends have been repositioned back together.

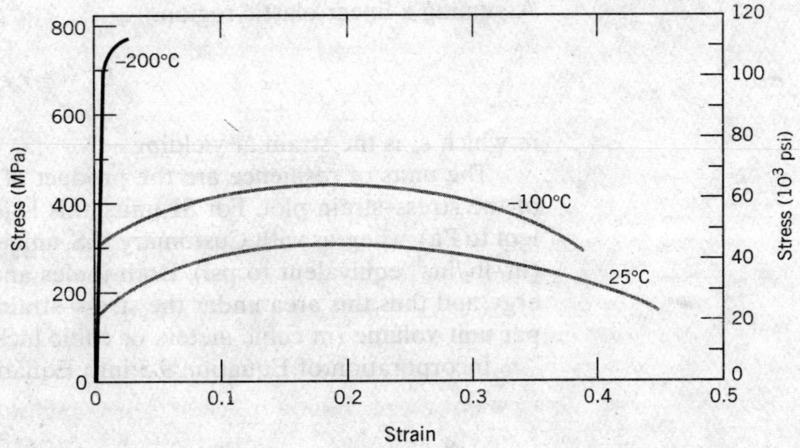

Figure 9.20 Engineering stress–strain behavior for iron at three temperatures.

yield strength, tensile strength, and ductility for several of the common metals. These properties are sensitive to any prior deformation, the presence of impurities, and/or any heat treatment to which the metal has been subjected. The modulus of elasticity is one mechanical parameter that is insensitive to these treatments. As with modulus of elasticity, the magnitudes of both yield and tensile strengths decline with increasing temperature; just the reverse holds for ductility—it usually increases with temperature. Figure 9.20 shows how the stress–strain behavior of iron varies with temperature.

Resilience

Resilience is the capacity of a material to absorb energy when it is deformed elastically and then, upon unloading, to have this energy recovered. The associated property is the *modulus of resilience,* U_r, which is the strain energy per unit volume required to stress a material from an unloaded state up to the point of yielding.

Computationally, the modulus of resilience for a specimen subjected to a uniaxial tension test is just the area under the engineering stress–strain curve taken to yielding (Figure 9.21), or

$$U_r = \int_0^{\epsilon_y} \sigma \, d\epsilon \tag{9.13a}$$

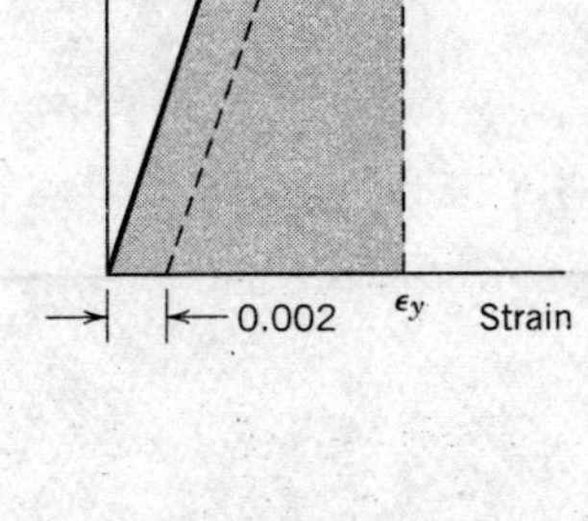

Figure 9.21 Schematic representation showing how modulus of resilience (corresponding to the shaded area) is determined from the tensile stress–strain behavior of a material.

Assuming a linear elastic region,

$$U_r = \tfrac{1}{2}\sigma_y \epsilon_y \tag{9.13b}$$

in which ϵ_y is the strain at yielding.

The units of resilience are the product of the units from each of the two axes of the stress–strain plot. For SI units, this is joules per cubic meter (J/m^3, equivalent to Pa), whereas with Customary U.S. units it is inch-pounds force per cubic inch (in.-lb$_f$/in.^{3}, equivalent to psi). Both joules and inch-pounds force are units of energy, and thus this area under the stress–strain curve represents energy absorption per unit volume (in cubic meters or cubic inches) of material.

Incorporation of Equation 9.5 into Equation 9.13b yields

$$U_r = \tfrac{1}{2}\sigma_y \epsilon_y = \tfrac{1}{2}\sigma_y \left(\frac{\sigma_y}{E}\right) = \frac{\sigma_y^2}{2E} \tag{9.14}$$

Thus, resilient materials are those having high yield strengths and low moduli of elasticity; such alloys would be used in spring applications.

Toughness

Toughness is a mechanical term that is used in several contexts; loosely speaking, it is a measure of the ability of a material to absorb energy up to fracture. Specimen geometry as well as the manner of load application are important in toughness determinations. For dynamic (high strain rate) loading conditions and when a notch (or point of stress concentration) is present, *notch toughness* is assessed by using an impact test, as discussed in Section 11.9. Furthermore, fracture toughness is a property indicative of a material's resistance to fracture when a crack is present (Section 11.5).

For the static (low strain rate) situation, toughness may be ascertained from the results of a tensile stress–strain test. It is the area under the σ–ϵ curve up to the point of fracture. The units for toughness are the same as for resilience (i.e., energy per unit volume of material). For a material to be tough, it must display both strength and ductility; often, ductile materials are tougher than brittle ones. This is demonstrated in Figure 9.19, in which the stress–strain curves are plotted for both material types. Hence, even though the brittle material has higher yield and tensile strengths, it has a lower toughness than the ductile one, by virtue of lack of ductility; this is deduced by comparing the areas ABC and $AB'C'$ in Figure 9.19.

Concept Check 9.7

Of those metals listed in Table 9.12,

(a) Which will experience the greatest percent reduction in area? Why?

(b) Which is the strongest? Why?

(c) Which is the stiffest? Why?

[*The answer may be found in enclosed CD.*]

Table 9.12 Tensile Stress–Strain Data for Several Hypothetical Metals to be Used with Concept Checks 9.2 and 9.4

Material	*Yield Strength (MPa)*	*Tensile Strength (MPa)*	*Strain at Fracture*	*Fracture Strength (MPa)*	*Elastic Modulus (GPa)*
A	310	340	0.23	265	210
B	100	120	0.40	105	150
C	415	550	0.15	500	310
D	700	850	0.14	720	210
E	Fractures before yielding			650	350

True Stress and Strain

From Figure 9.17, the decline in the stress necessary to continue deformation past the maximum, point M, seems to indicate that the metal is becoming weaker. This is not at all the case; as a matter of fact, it is increasing in strength. However, the cross-sectional area is decreasing rapidly within the neck region, where deformation is occurring. This results in a reduction in the load-bearing capacity of the specimen. The stress, as computed from Equation 9.1, is on the basis of the original cross-sectional area before any deformation, and does not take into account this reduction in area at the neck.

Sometimes it is more meaningful to use a true stress–true strain scheme. **True stress** σ_T is defined as the load F divided by the instantaneous cross-sectional area A_i over which deformation is occurring (i.e., the neck, past the tensile point), or

$$\sigma_T = \frac{F}{A_i} \tag{9.15}$$

Furthermore, it is occasionally more convenient to represent strain as **true strain** ϵ_T, defined by

$$\epsilon_T = \ln \frac{l_i}{l_0} \tag{9.16}$$

If no volume change occurs during deformation—that is, if

$$A_i l_i = A_0 l_0 \tag{9.17}$$

true and engineering stress and strain are related according to

$$\sigma_T = \sigma(1 + \epsilon) \tag{9.18a}$$

$$\epsilon_T = \ln(1 + \epsilon) \tag{9.18b}$$

Equations 9.18a and 9.18b are valid only to the onset of necking; beyond this point true stress and strain should be computed from actual load, cross-sectional area, and gauge length measurements.

A schematic comparison of engineering and true stress–strain behaviors is made in Figure 9.22. It is worth noting that the true stress necessary to sustain increasing strain continues to rise past the tensile point M'.

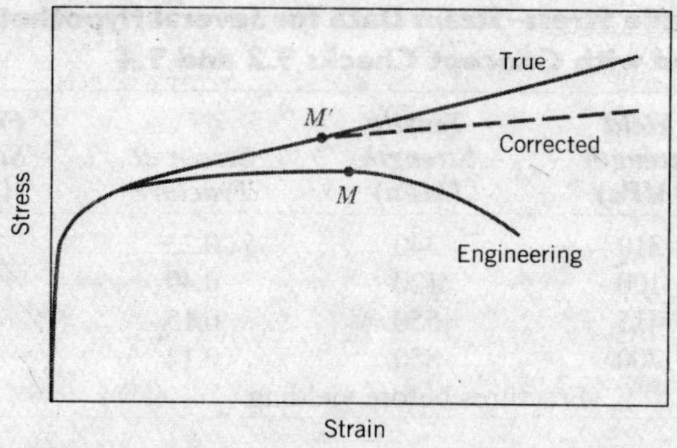

Figure 9.22 A comparison of typical tensile engineering stress–strain and true stress–strain behaviors. Necking begins at point M on the engineering curve, which corresponds to M' on the true curve. The "corrected" true stress–strain curve takes into account the complex stress state within the neck region.

Coincident with the formation of a neck is the introduction of a complex stress state within the neck region (i.e., the existence of other stress components in addition to the axial stress). As a consequence, the correct stress (*axial*) within the neck is slightly lower than the stress computed from the applied load and neck cross-sectional area. This leads to the "corrected" curve in Figure 9.22.

For some metals and alloys the region of the true stress–strain curve from the onset of plastic deformation to the point at which necking begins may be approximated by

$$\sigma_T = K\epsilon_T^n \tag{9.19}$$

In this expression, K and n are constants; these values will vary from alloy to alloy, and will also depend on the condition of the material (i.e., whether it has been plastically deformed, heat treated, etc.). The parameter n is often termed the *strain-hardening exponent* and has a value less than unity. Values of n and K for several alloys are contained in Table 9.13.

Table 9.13 Tabulation of *n* and *K* Values (Equation 9.19) for Several Alloys

Material	*n*	*K (MPa)*
Low-carbon steel (annealed)	0.21	600
4340 steel alloy (tempered @ 315°C)	0.12	2650
304 stainless steel (annealed)	0.44	1400
Copper (annealed)	0.44	530
Naval brass (annealed)	0.21	585
2024 aluminum alloy (heat treated—T3)	0.17	780
AZ-31B magnesium alloy (annealed)	0.16	450

EXAMPLE PROBLEM 9.4

Ductility and True-Stress-At-Fracture Computations

A cylindrical specimen of steel having an original diameter of 12.8 mm is tensile tested to fracture and found to have an engineering fracture strength σ_f of 460 MPa. If its cross-sectional diameter at fracture is 10.7 mm, determine:

(a) The ductility in terms of percent reduction in area

(b) The true stress at fracture

Solution

(a) Ductility is computed using Equation 9.12, as

$$\%\,\text{RA} = \frac{\left(\frac{12.8\text{ mm}}{2}\right)^2\pi - \left(\frac{10.7\text{ mm}}{2}\right)^2\pi}{\left(\frac{12.8\text{ mm}}{2}\right)^2\pi} \times 100$$

$$= \frac{128.7\text{ mm}^2 - 89.9\text{ mm}^2}{128.7\text{ mm}^2} \times 100 = 30\%$$

(b) True stress is defined by Equation 9.15, where in this case the area is taken as the fracture area A_f. However, the load at fracture must first be computed from the fracture strength as

$$F = \sigma_f A_0 = (460 \times 10^6\text{ N/m}^2)(128.7\text{ mm}^2)\left(\frac{1\text{ m}^2}{10^6\text{ mm}^2}\right) = 59{,}200\text{ N}$$

Thus, the true stress is calculated as

$$\sigma_T = \frac{F}{A_f} = \frac{59{,}200\text{ N}}{(89.9\text{ mm}^2)\left(\frac{1\text{ m}^2}{10^6\text{ mm}^2}\right)}$$

$$= 6.6 \times 10^8\text{ N/m}^2 = 660\text{ MPa}$$

EXAMPLE PROBLEM 9.5

Calculation of Strain-Hardening Exponent

Compute the strain-hardening exponent n in Equation 9.19 for an alloy in which a true stress of 415 MPa produces a true strain of 0.10; assume a value of 1035 MPa for K.

Solution

This requires some algebraic manipulation of Equation 9.19 so that n becomes the dependent parameter. This is accomplished by taking logarithms and rearranging. Solving for n yields

$$n = \frac{\log \sigma_T - \log K}{\log \epsilon_T}$$

$$= \frac{\log(415\text{ MPa}) - \log(1035\text{ MPa})}{\log(0.1)} = 0.40$$

Elastic Recovery after Plastic Deformation

Upon release of the load during the course of a stress–strain test, some fraction of the total deformation is recovered as elastic strain. This behavior is demonstrated in Figure 9.23, a schematic engineering stress–strain plot. During the unloading cycle, the curve traces a near straight-line path from the point of unloading (point *D*), and its slope is virtually identical to the modulus of elasticity, or parallel to the initial elastic portion of the curve. The magnitude of this elastic strain, which is regained during unloading, corresponds to the strain recovery, as shown in Figure 9.23. If the load is reapplied, the curve will traverse essentially the same linear portion in the direction opposite to unloading; yielding will again occur at the unloading stress level where the unloading began. There will also be an elastic strain recovery associated with fracture.

Compressive, Shear, and Torsional Deformation

Of course, metals may experience plastic deformation under the influence of applied compressive, shear, and torsional loads. The resulting stress–strain behavior into the plastic region will be similar to the tensile counterpart (Figure 9.16*a*: yielding and the associated curvature). However, for compression, there will be no maximum, since necking does not occur; furthermore, the mode of fracture will be different from that for tension.

Concept Check 9.8

Make a schematic plot showing the tensile engineering stress–strain behavior for a typical metal alloy to the point of fracture. Now superimpose on this plot a schematic compressive engineering stress–strain curve for the same alloy. Explain any differences between the two curves.

[*The answer may be found in enclosed CD.*]

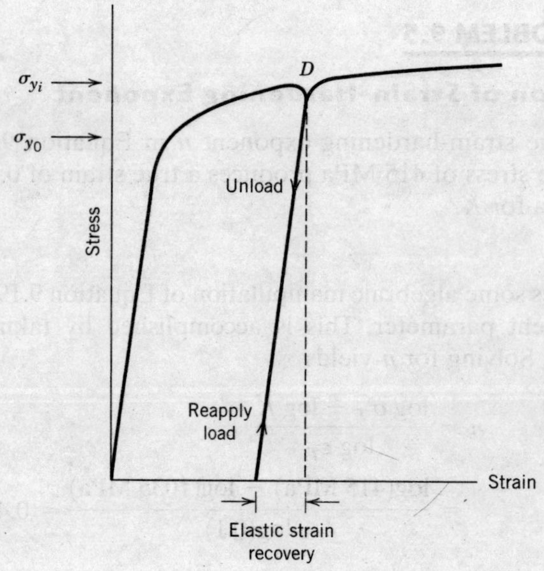

Figure 9.23 Schematic tensile stress–strain diagram showing the phenomena of elastic strain recovery and strain hardening. The initial yield strength is designated as σ_{y0}; σ_{yi} is the yield strength after releasing the load at point *D*, and then upon reloading.

9.8 HARDNESS

Another mechanical property that may be important to consider is **hardness**, which is a measure of a material's resistance to localized plastic deformation (e.g., a small dent or a scratch). Early hardness tests were based on natural minerals with a scale constructed solely on the ability of one material to scratch another that was softer. A qualitative and somewhat arbitrary hardness indexing scheme was devised, termed the Mohs scale, which ranged from 1 on the soft end for talc to 10 for diamond. Quantitative hardness techniques have been developed over the years in which a small indenter is forced into the surface of a material to be tested, under controlled conditions of load and rate of application. The depth or size of the resulting indentation is measured, which in turn is related to a hardness number; the softer the material, the larger and deeper is the indentation, and the lower the hardness index number. Measured hardnesses are only relative (rather than absolute), and care should be exercised when comparing values determined by different techniques.

Hardness tests are performed more frequently than any other mechanical test for several reasons:

1. They are simple and inexpensive—ordinarily no special specimen need be prepared, and the testing apparatus is relatively inexpensive.
2. The test is nondestructive—the specimen is neither fractured nor excessively deformed; a small indentation is the only deformation.
3. Other mechanical properties often may be estimated from hardness data, such as tensile strength (see Figure 9.25).

Rockwell Hardness Tests[11]

The Rockwell tests constitute the most common method used to measure hardness because they are so simple to perform and require no special skills. Several different scales may be utilized from possible combinations of various indenters and different loads, which permit the testing of virtually all metal alloys (as well as some polymers). Indenters include spherical and hardened steel balls having diameters of $\frac{1}{16}$, $\frac{1}{8}$, $\frac{1}{4}$, and $\frac{1}{2}$ in. (1.588, 3.175, 9.350, and 12.70 mm), and a conical diamond (Brale) indenter, which is used for the hardest materials.

With this system, a hardness number is determined by the difference in depth of penetration resulting from the application of an initial minor load followed by a larger major load; utilization of a minor load enhances test accuracy. On the basis of the magnitude of both major and minor loads, there are two types of tests: Rockwell and superficial Rockwell. For Rockwell, the minor load is 10 kg, whereas major loads are 60, 100, and 150 kg. Each scale is represented by a letter of the alphabet; several are listed with the corresponding indenter and load in Tables 9.14 and 9.15a. For superficial tests, 3 kg is the minor load; 15, 30, and 45 kg are the possible major load values. These scales are identified by a 15, 30, or 45 (according to load), followed by N, T, W, X, or Y, depending on indenter. Superficial tests are frequently performed on thin specimens. Table 9.6b presents several superficial scales.

When specifying Rockwell and superficial hardnesses, both hardness number and scale symbol must be indicated. The scale is designated by the symbol HR

[11] ASTM Standard E 18, "Standard Test Methods for Rockwell Hardness and Rockwell Superficial Hardness of Metallic Materials."

Table 9.14 Hardness-Testing Techniques

Test	Indenter	Shape of Indentation: Side View	Shape of Indentation: Top View	Load	Formula for Hardness Number[a]
Brinell	10-mm sphere of steel or tungsten carbide	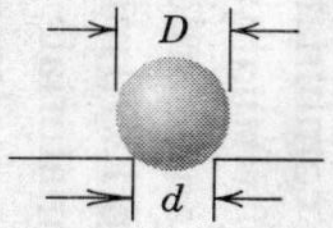	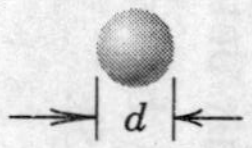	P	$HB = \frac{2P}{\pi D[D - \sqrt{D^2 - d^2}]}$
Vickers microhardness	Diamond pyramid			P	$HV = 1.854P/d_1^2$
Knoop microhardness	Diamond pyramid	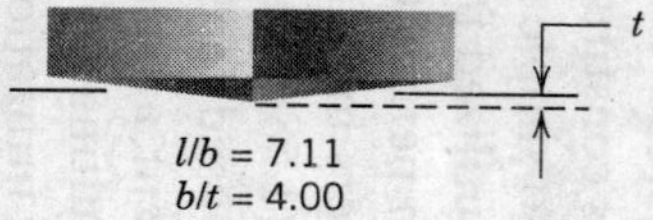	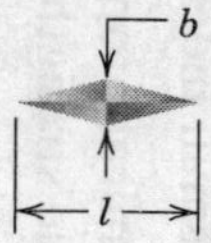	P	$HK = 14.2P/l^2$
Rockwell and Superficial Rockwell	Diamond cone; $\frac{1}{16}, \frac{1}{8}, \frac{1}{4}, \frac{1}{2}$ in. diameter steel spheres	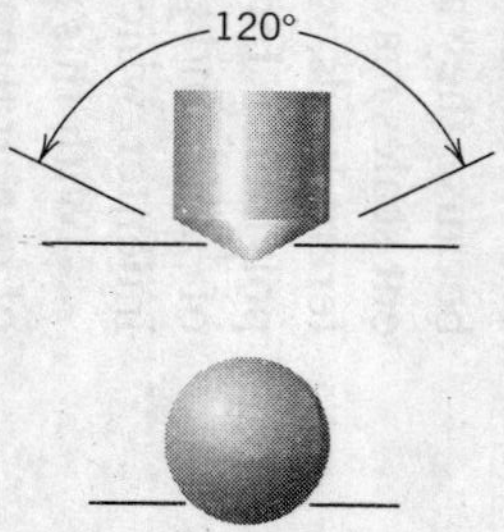		60 kg, 100 kg, 150 kg } Rockwell 15 kg, 30 kg, 45 kg } Superficial Rockwell	

[a] For the hardness formulas given, P (the applied load) is in kg, while D, d, d_1, and l are all in mm.

Source: Adapted from H. W. Hayden, W. G. Moffatt, and J. Wulff, *The Structure and Properties of Materials,* Vol. III, *Mechanical Behavior*. Copyright © 1965 by John Wiley & Sons, New York. Reprinted by permission of John Wiley & Sons, Inc.

Table 9.15a Rockwell Hardness Scales

Scale Symbol	*Indenter*	*Major Load (kg)*
A	Diamond	60
B	$\frac{1}{16}$-in. ball	100
C	Diamond	150
D	Diamond	100
E	$\frac{1}{8}$-in. ball	100
F	$\frac{1}{16}$-in. ball	60
G	$\frac{1}{16}$-in. ball	150
H	$\frac{1}{8}$-in. ball	60
K	$\frac{1}{8}$-in. ball	150

Table 9.15b Superficial Rockwell Hardness Scales

Scale Symbol	*Indenter*	*Major Load (kg)*
15N	Diamond	15
30N	Diamond	30
45N	Diamond	45
15T	$\frac{1}{16}$-in. ball	15
30T	$\frac{1}{16}$-in. ball	30
45T	$\frac{1}{16}$-in. ball	45
15W	$\frac{1}{8}$-in. ball	15
30W	$\frac{1}{8}$-in. ball	30
45W	$\frac{1}{8}$-in. ball	45

followed by the appropriate scale identification.[12] For example, 80 HRB represents a Rockwell hardness of 80 on the B scale, and 60 HR30W indicates a superficial hardness of 60 on the 30W scale.

For each scale, hardnesses may range up to 130; however, as hardness values rise above 100 or drop below 20 on any scale, they become inaccurate; and because the scales have some overlap, in such a situation it is best to utilize the next harder or softer scale.

Inaccuracies also result if the test specimen is too thin, if an indentation is made too near a specimen edge, or if two indentations are made too close to one another. Specimen thickness should be at least ten times the indentation depth, whereas allowance should be made for at least three indentation diameters between the center of one indentation and the specimen edge, or to the center of a second indentation. Furthermore, testing of specimens stacked one on top of another is not recommended. Also, accuracy is dependent on the indentation being made into a smooth flat surface.

The modern apparatus for making Rockwell hardness measurements (see the chapter-opening photograph for this chapter) is automated and very simple to use; hardness is read directly, and each measurement requires only a few seconds.

The modern testing apparatus also permits a variation in the time of load application. This variable must also be considered in interpreting hardness data.

[12] Rockwell scales are also frequently designated by an R with the appropriate scale letter as a subscript, for example, R_C denotes the Rockwell C scale.

Brinell Hardness Tests[13]

In Brinell tests, as in Rockwell measurements, a hard, spherical indenter is forced into the surface of the metal to be tested. The diameter of the hardened steel (or tungsten carbide) indenter is 10.00 mm (0.394 in.). Standard loads range between 500 and 3000 kg in 500-kg increments; during a test, the load is maintained constant for a specified time (between 10 and 30 s). Harder materials require greater applied loads. The Brinell hardness number, HB, is a function of both the magnitude of the load and the diameter of the resulting indentation (see Table 9.14).[14] This diameter is measured with a special low-power microscope, utilizing a scale that is etched on the eyepiece. The measured diameter is then converted to the appropriate HB number using a chart; only one scale is employed with this technique.

Semiautomatic techniques for measuring Brinell hardness are available. These employ optical scanning systems consisting of a digital camera mounted on a flexible probe, which allows positioning of the camera over the indentation. Data from the camera are transferred to a computer that analyzes the indentation, determines its size, and then calculates the Brinell hardness number. For this technique, surface finish requirements are normally more stringent that for manual measurements.

Maximum specimen thickness as well as indentation position (relative to specimen edges) and minimum indentation spacing requirements are the same as for Rockwell tests. In addition, a well-defined indentation is required; this necessitates a smooth flat surface in which the indentation is made.

Knoop and Vickers Microindentation Hardness Tests[15]

Two other hardness-testing techniques are Knoop (pronounced *nūp*) and Vickers (sometimes also called diamond pyramid). For each test a very small diamond indenter having pyramidal geometry is forced into the surface of the specimen. Applied loads are much smaller than for Rockwell and Brinell, ranging between 1 and 1000 g. The resulting impression is observed under a microscope and measured; this measurement is then converted into a hardness number (Table 9.14). Careful specimen surface preparation (grinding and polishing) may be necessary to ensure a well-defined indentation that may be accurately measured. The Knoop and Vickers hardness numbers are designated by HK and HV, respectively,[16] and hardness scales for both techniques are approximately equivalent. Knoop and Vickers are referred to as microindentation-testing methods on the basis of indenter size. Both are well suited for measuring the hardness of small, selected specimen regions; furthermore, Knoop is used for testing brittle materials such as ceramics.

The modern microindentation hardness-testing equipment has been automated by coupling the indenter apparatus to an image analyzer that incorporates a computer and software package. The software controls important system functions to include indent location, indent spacing, computation of hardness values, and plotting of data.

---

[13] ASTM Standard E 10, "Standard Test Method for Brinell Hardness of Metallic Materials."
[14] The Brinell hardness number is also represented by BHN.
[15] ASTM Standard E 92, "Standard Test Method for Vickers Hardness of Metallic Materials," and ASTM Standard E 384, "Standard Test for Microhardness of Materials."
[16] Sometimes KHN and VHN are used to denote Knoop and Vickers hardness numbers, respectively.

Other hardness-testing techniques are frequently employed but will not be discussed here; these include ultrasonic microhardness, dynamic (Scleroscope), durometer (for plastic and elastomeric materials), and scratch hardness tests. These are described in references provided at the end of the chapter.

Hardness Conversion

The facility to convert the hardness measured on one scale to that of another is most desirable. However, since hardness is not a well-defined material property, and because of the experimental dissimilarities among the various techniques, a comprehensive conversion scheme has not been devised. Hardness conversion data have been determined experimentally and found to be dependent on material type and characteristics. The most reliable conversion data exist for steels, some of which are presented in Figure 9.24 for Knoop, Brinell, and two Rockwell scales; the Mohs scale is also included. Detailed conversion tables for various other metals and

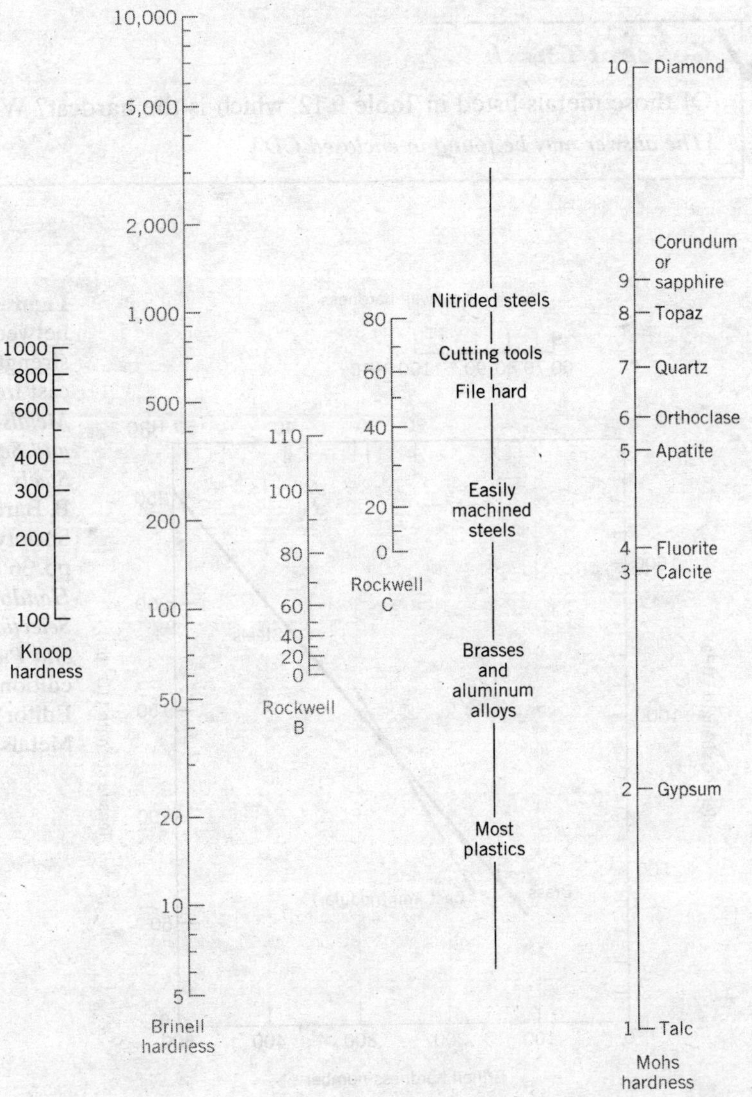

Figure 9.24 Comparison of several hardness scales. (Adapted from G. F. Kinney, *Engineering Properties and Applications of Plastics,* p. 202. Copyright © 1957 by John Wiley & Sons, New York. Reprinted by permission of John Wiley & Sons, Inc.)

alloys are contained in ASTM Standard E 140, "Standard Hardness Conversion Tables for Metals." In light of the preceding discussion, care should be exercised in extrapolation of conversion data from one alloy system to another.

Correlation Between Hardness and Tensile Strength

Both tensile strength and hardness are indicators of a metal's resistance to plastic deformation. Consequently, they are roughly proportional, as shown in Figure 9.25, for tensile strength as a function of the HB for cast iron, steel, and brass. The same proportionality relationship does not hold for all metals, as Figure 9.25 indicates. As a rule of thumb for most steels, the HB and the tensile strength are related according to

$$TS(\text{MPa}) = 3.45 \times \text{HB} \tag{9.20a}$$

$$TS(\text{psi}) = 500 \times \text{HB} \tag{9.20b}$$

Concept Check 9.9

Of those metals listed in Table 9.12, which is the hardest? Why?

[*The answer may be found in enclosed CD.*]

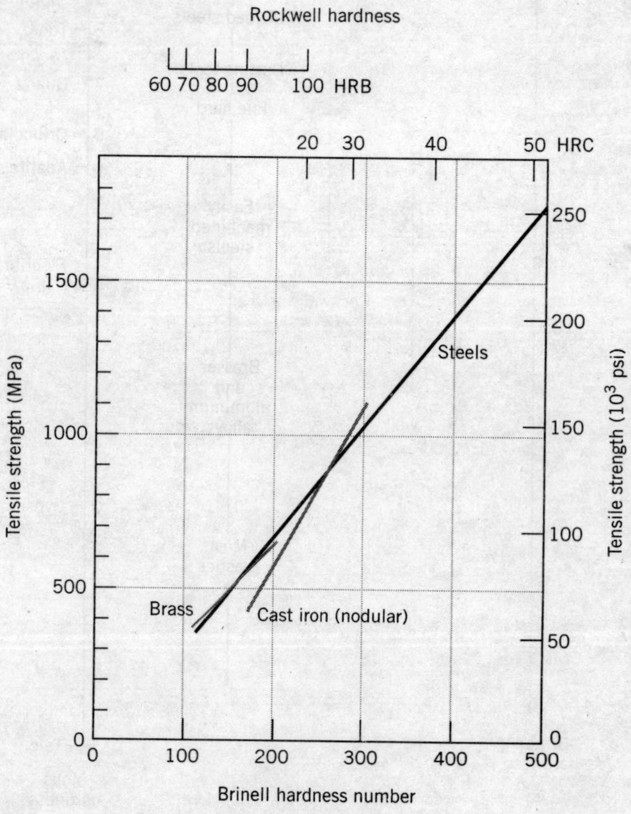

Figure 9.25 Relationships between hardness and tensile strength for steel, brass, and cast iron. [Data taken from *Metals Handbook: Properties and Selection: Irons and Steels,* Vol. 1, 9th edition, B. Bardes (Editor), American Society for Metals, 1978, pp. 36 and 461; and *Metals Handbook: Properties and Selection: Nonferrous Alloys and Pure Metals,* Vol. 2, 9th edition, H. Baker (Managing Editor), American Society for Metals, 1979, p. 327.]

Property Variability and Design/Safety Factors

9.9 VARIABILITY OF MATERIAL PROPERTIES

At this point it is worthwhile to discuss an issue that sometimes proves troublesome to many engineering students—namely, that measured material properties are not exact quantities. That is, even if we have a most precise measuring apparatus and a highly controlled test procedure, there will always be some scatter or variability in the data that are collected from specimens of the same material. For example, consider a number of identical tensile samples that are prepared from a single bar of some metal alloy, which samples are subsequently stress–strain tested in the same apparatus. We would most likely observe that each resulting stress–strain plot is slightly different from the others. This would lead to a variety of modulus of elasticity, yield strength, and tensile strength values. A number of factors lead to uncertainties in measured data. These include the test method, variations in specimen fabrication procedures, operator bias, and apparatus calibration. Furthermore, inhomogeneities may exist within the same lot of material, and/or slight compositional and other differences from lot to lot. Of course, appropriate measures should be taken to minimize the possibility of measurement error, and also to mitigate those factors that lead to data variability.

It should also be mentioned that scatter exists for other measured material properties such as density, electrical conductivity, and coefficient of thermal expansion.

It is important for the design engineer to realize that scatter and variability of materials properties are inevitable and must be dealt with appropriately. On occasion, data must be subjected to statistical treatments and probabilities determined. For example, instead of asking the question, "What is the fracture strength of this alloy?" the engineer should become accustomed to asking the question, "What is the probability of failure of this alloy under these given circumstances?"

It is often desirable to specify a typical value and degree of dispersion (or scatter) for some measured property; such is commonly accomplished by taking the average and the standard deviation, respectively.

Computation of Average and Standard Deviation Values

An average value is obtained by dividing the sum of all measured values by the number of measurements taken. In mathematical terms, the average $\bar{x}$ of some parameter x is

$$\bar{x} = \frac{\sum_{i=1}^{n} x_i}{n} \tag{9.21}$$

where n is the number of observations or measurements and x_i is the value of a discrete measurement.

Furthermore, the standard deviation s is determined using the following expression:

$$s = \left[\frac{\sum_{i=1}^{n} (x_i - \bar{x})^2}{n - 1} \right]^{1/2} \tag{9.22}$$

where x_i, $\bar{x}$, and n are defined above. A large value of the standard deviation corresponds to a high degree of scatter.

EXAMPLE PROBLEM 9.6

Average and Standard Deviation Computations

The following tensile strengths were measured for four specimens of the same steel alloy:

Sample Number	*Tensile Strength (MPa)*
1	520
2	512
3	515
4	522

(a) Compute the average tensile strength.

(b) Determine the standard deviation.

Solution

(a) The average tensile strength ($\overline{TS}$) is computed using Equation 9.21 with $n = 4$:

$$\overline{TS} = \frac{\sum_{i=1}^{4} (TS)_i}{4}$$

$$= \frac{520 + 512 + 515 + 522}{4}$$

$$= 517 \text{ MPa}$$

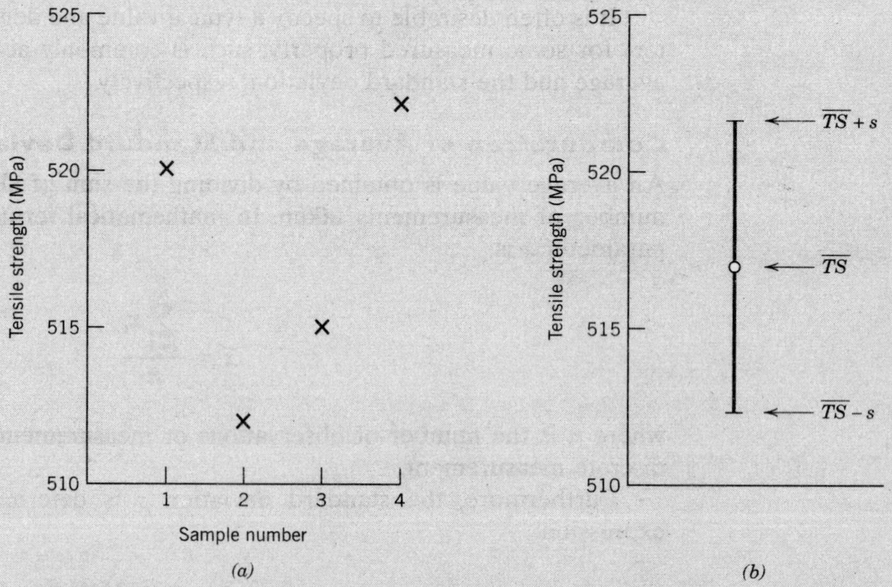

Figure 9.26 (*a*) Tensile strength data associated with Example Problem 9.9. (*b*) The manner in which these data could be plotted. The data point corresponds to the average value of the tensile strength ($\overline{TS}$); error bars that indicate the degree of scatter correspond to the average value plus and minus the standard deviation ($\overline{TS} \pm s$).

(b) For the standard deviation, using Equation 9.22,

$$s = \left[\frac{\sum_{i=1}^{4} \{(TS)_i - \overline{TS}\}^2}{4 - 1} \right]^{1/2}$$

$$= \left[\frac{(520 - 517)^2 + (512 - 517)^2 + (515 - 517)^2 + (522 - 517)^2}{4 - 1} \right]^{1/2}$$

$$= 4.6 \text{ MPa}$$

Figure 9.26 presents the tensile strength by specimen number for this example problem and also how the data may be represented in graphical form. The tensile strength data point (Figure 9.26*b*) corresponds to the average value $\overline{TS}$, whereas scatter is depicted by error bars (short horizontal lines) situated above and below the data point symbol and connected to this symbol by vertical lines. The upper error bar is positioned at a value of the average value plus the standard deviation ($\overline{TS} + s$), whereas the lower error bar corresponds to the average minus the standard deviation ($\overline{TS} - s$).

9.10 DESIGN/SAFETY FACTORS

There will always be uncertainties in characterizing the magnitude of applied loads and their associated stress levels for in-service applications; ordinarily load calculations are only approximate. Furthermore, as noted in the previous section, virtually all engineering materials exhibit a variability in their measured mechanical properties. Consequently, design allowances must be made to protect against unanticipated failure. One way this may be accomplished is by establishing, for the particular application, a **design stress,** denoted as σ_d. For static situations and when ductile materials are used, σ_d is taken as the calculated stress level σ_c (on the basis of the estimated maximum load) multiplied by a *design factor,* N'; that is,

$$\sigma_d = N'\sigma_c \tag{9.23}$$

where N' is greater than unity. Thus, the material to be used for the particular application is chosen so as to have a yield strength at least as high as this value of σ_d.

Alternatively, a **safe stress** or *working stress,* σ_w, is used instead of design stress. This safe stress is based on the yield strength of the material and is defined as the yield strength divided by a *factor of safety,* N, or

$$\sigma_w = \frac{\sigma_y}{N} \tag{9.24}$$

Utilization of design stress (Equation 9.23) is usually preferred since it is based on the anticipated maximum applied stress instead of the yield strength of the material; normally there is a greater uncertainty in estimating this stress level than in the specification of the yield strength. However, in the discussion of this text, we are concerned with factors that influence the yield strengths of metal alloys and not in the determination of applied stresses; therefore, the succeeding discussion will deal with working stresses and factors of safety.

The choice of an appropriate value of N is necessary. If N is too large, then component overdesign will result; that is, either too much material or an alloy having a higher-than-necessary strength will be used. Values normally range between 1.2 and 4.0. Selection of N will depend on a number of factors, including economics, previous experience, the accuracy with which mechanical forces and material properties may be determined, and, most important, the consequences of failure in terms of loss of life and/or property damage.

DESIGN EXAMPLE 9.1

Specification of Support Post Diameter

A tensile-testing apparatus is to be constructed that must withstand a maximum load of 220,000 N. The design calls for two cylindrical support posts, each of which is to support half of the maximum load. Furthermore, plain-carbon (1045) steel ground and polished shafting rounds are to be used; the minimum yield and tensile strengths of this alloy are 310 MPa and 565 MPa, respectively. Specify a suitable diameter for these support posts.

Solution

The first step in this design process is to decide on a factor of safety, N, which then allows determination of a working stress according to Equation 9.24. In addition, to ensure that the apparatus will be safe to operate, we also want to minimize any elastic deflection of the rods during testing; therefore, a relatively conservative factor of safety is to be used, say $N = 5$. Thus, the working stress σ_w is just

$$\sigma_w = \frac{\sigma_y}{N}$$

$$= \frac{310 \text{ MPa}}{5} = 62 \text{ MPa}$$

From the definition of stress, Equation 9.1,

$$A_0 = \left(\frac{d}{2}\right)^2 \pi = \frac{F}{\sigma_w}$$

where d is the rod diameter and F is the applied force; furthermore, each of the two rods must support half of the total force or 110,000 N. Solving for d leads to

$$d = 2\sqrt{\frac{F}{\pi \sigma_w}}$$

$$= 2\sqrt{\frac{110{,}000 \text{ N}}{\pi(62 \times 10^6 \text{ N/m}^2)}}$$

$$= 4.75 \times 10^{-2} \text{ m} = 47.5 \text{ mm}$$

Therefore, the diameter of each of the two rods should be 47.5 mm.

SUMMARY

Ferrous Alloys

This chapter began with a discussion of the various types of metal alloys. With regard to composition, metals and alloys are classified as either ferrous or nonferrous. Ferrous alloys (steels and cast irons) are those in which iron is the prime constituent. Most steels contain less than 1.0 wt% C, and, in addition, other alloying elements, which render them susceptible to heat treatment (and an enhancement of mechanical properties) and/or more corrosion resistant. Plain low-carbon steels and high-strength low-alloy, medium-carbon, tool, and stainless steels are the most common types.

Cast irons contain a higher carbon content, normally between 3.0 and 4.5 wt% C, and other alloying elements, notably silicon. For these materials, most of the carbon exists in graphite form rather than combined with iron as cementite. Gray, ductile (or nodular), malleable, and compacted graphite irons are the four most widely used cast irons; the latter three are reasonably ductile.

Nonferrous Alloys

All other alloys fall within the nonferrous category, which is further subdivided according to base metal or some distinctive characteristic that is shared by a group of alloys. The compositions, typical properties, and applications of copper, aluminum, magnesium, titanium, nickel, lead, tin, zirconium, and zinc alloys, as well as the refractory metals, the superalloys, and the noble metals were discussed.

Annealing Processes

The final sections of this chapter were devoted to discussions of some of the heat treatments that are used to fashion the mechanical properties of metal alloys. The exposure to an elevated temperature for an extended time period followed by cooling to room temperature at a relatively slow rate is termed annealing; several specific annealing treatments were discussed briefly. During process annealing, a cold-worked piece is rendered softer yet more ductile as a consequence of recrystallization. Internal residual stresses that have been introduced are eliminated during a stress-relief anneal. For ferrous alloys, normalizing is used to refine and improve the grain structure. Fabrication characteristics may also be enhanced by full anneal and spheroidizing treatments that produce microstructures consisting of coarse pearlite and spheroidite, respectively.

Concepts of Stress and Strain
Stress–Strain Behavior
Elastic Properties of Materials
True Stress and Strain

A number of the important mechanical properties of materials, predominantly metals, have been discussed in this chapter. Concepts of stress and strain were first introduced. Stress is a measure of an applied mechanical load or force, normalized to take into account cross-sectional area. Two different stress parameters were defined—engineering stress and true stress. Strain represents the amount of deformation induced by a stress; both engineering and true strains are used.

Some of the mechanical characteristics of metals can be ascertained by simple stress–strain tests. There are four test types: tension, compression, torsion, and shear.

Tensile are the most common. A material that is stressed first undergoes elastic, or nonpermanent, deformation, wherein stress and strain are proportional. The constant of proportionality is the modulus of elasticity for tension and compression, and is the shear modulus when the stress is shear. Poisson's ratio represents the negative ratio of transverse and longitudinal strains.

Tensile Properties

The phenomenon of yielding occurs at the onset of plastic or permanent deformation; yield strength is determined by a strain offset method from the stress–strain behavior, which is indicative of the stress at which plastic deformation begins. Tensile strength corresponds to the maximum tensile stress that may be sustained by a specimen, whereas percents elongation and reduction in area are measures of ductility—the amount of plastic deformation that has occurred at fracture. Resilience is the capacity of a material to absorb energy during elastic deformation; modulus of resilience is the area beneath the engineering stress–strain curve up to the yield point. Also, static toughness represents the energy absorbed during the fracture of a material, and is taken as the area under the entire engineering stress–strain curve. Ductile materials are normally tougher than brittle ones.

Hardness

Hardness is a measure of the resistance to localized plastic deformation. In several popular hardness-testing techniques (Rockwell, Brinell, Knoop, and Vickers) a small indenter is forced into the surface of the material, and an index number is determined on the basis of the size or depth of the resulting indentation. For many metals, hardness and tensile strength are approximately proportional to each other.

Variability of Material Properties

Measured mechanical properties (as well as other material properties) are not exact and precise quantities, in that there will always be some scatter for the measured data. Typical material property values are commonly specified in terms of averages, whereas magnitudes of scatter may be expressed as standard deviations.

Design/Safety Factors

As a result of uncertainties in both measured mechanical properties and inservice applied stresses, design or safe stresses are normally utilized for design purposes. For ductile materials, safe stress is the ratio of the yield strength and the factor of safety.

REFERENCES

ASM Handbook, Vol. 1, *Properties and Selection: Irons, Steels,* and *High-Performance Alloys,* ASM International, Materials Park, OH, 1990.

ASM Handbook, Vol. 2, *Properties and Selection: Nonferrous Alloys and Special-Purpose Materials,* ASM International, Materials Park, OH, 1991.

ASM Handbook, Vol. 4, *Heat Treating,* ASM International, Materials Park, OH, 1991.

ASM Handbook, Vol. 8, *Mechanical Testing and Evaluation,* ASM International, Materials Park, OH, 2000.

Boyer, H. E. (Editor), *Atlas of Stress–Strain Curves,* 2nd edition, ASM International, Materials Park, OH, 2002.

Brooks, C. R., *Principles of the Heat Treatment of Plain Carbon and Low Alloy Steels,* ASM International, Materials Park, OH, 1995.

Chandler, H. (Editor), *Hardness Testing,* 2nd edition, ASM International, Materials Park, OH, 2000.

Courtney, T. H., *Mechanical Behavior of Materials,* 2nd edition, McGraw-Hill Higher Education, Burr Ridge, IL, 2000.

Davis, J. R., *Cast Irons,* ASM International, Materials Park, OH, 1999.

Davis, J. R. (Editor), *Tensile Testing,* 2nd edition, ASM International, Materials Park, OH, 2004.

Dieter, G. E., *Mechanical Metallurgy,* 3rd edition, McGraw-Hill Book Company, New York, 1989.

Dowling, N. E., *Mechanical Behavior of Materials,* 2nd edition, Prentice Hall PTR, Paramus, NJ, 1998.

Frick, J., (Editor), *Woldman's Engineering Alloys,* 9th edition, ASM International, Materials Park, OH, 2000.

Henkel, D. P. and A. W. Pense, *Structures and Properties of Engineering Materials,* 5th edition, McGraw-Hill, New York, 2001.

McClintock, F. A. and A. S. Argon, *Mechanical Behavior of Materials,* Addison-Wesley Publishing Co., Reading, MA, 1969. Reprinted by CBLS Publishers, Marietta, OH, 1993.

Metals and Alloys in the Unified Numbering System, 10th edition, Society of Automotive Engineers, and American Society for Testing and Materials, Warrendale, PA, 2005.

Meyers, M. A. and K. K. Chawla, *Mechanical Behavior of Materials,* Prentice Hall PTR, Paramus, NJ, 1999.

Worldwide Guide to Equivalent Irons and Steels, 4th edition, ASM International, Materials Park, OH, 2000.

Worldwide Guide to Equivalent Nonferrous Metals and Alloys, 4th edition, ASM International, Materials Park, OH, 2001.

QUESTIONS AND PROBLEMS

Ferrous Alloys

9.1 **(a)** List the four classifications of steels. **(b)** For each, briefly describe the properties and typical applications.

9.2 **(a)** Cite three reasons why ferrous alloys are used so extensively. **(b)** Cite three characteristics of ferrous alloys that limit their utilization.

9.3 What is the function of alloying elements in tool steels?

9.4 Compute the volume percent of graphite V_{Gr} in a 2.5 wt% C cast iron, assuming that all the carbon exists as the graphite phase. Assume densities of 7.9 and 2.3 g/cm^3 for ferrite and graphite, respectively.

9.5 On the basis of microstructure, briefly explain why gray iron is brittle and weak in tension.

9.6 Compare gray and malleable cast irons with respect to **(a)** composition and heat treatment, **(b)** microstructure, and **(c)** mechanical characteristics.

9.7 Compare white and nodular cast irons with respect to **(a)** composition and heat treatment, **(b)** microstructure, and **(c)** mechanical characteristics.

9.8 Is it possible to produce malleable cast iron in pieces having large cross-sectional dimensions? Why or why not?

Nonferrous Alloys

9.9 What is the principal difference between wrought and cast alloys?

9.10 Why must rivets of a 2017 aluminum alloy be refrigerated before they are used?

9.11 What is the chief difference between heat-treatable and non-heat-treatable alloys?

9.12 Give the distinctive features, limitations, and applications of the following alloy groups: titanium alloys, refractory metals, superalloys, and noble metals.

Annealing Processes

9.13 In your own words describe the following heat treatment procedures for steels and, for each, the intended final microstructure: full annealing, normalizing, quenching, and tempering.

9.14 Cite three sources of internal residual stresses in metal components. What are two possible adverse consequences of these stresses?

9.15 Give the approximate minimum temperature at which it is possible to austenitize each of the following iron–carbon alloys during a normalizing heat treatment: **(a)** 0.15 wt% C, **(b)** 0.50 wt% C, and **(c)** 1.10 wt% C.

9.16 Give the approximate temperature at which it is desirable to heat each of the following iron–carbon alloys during a full anneal Ωheat treatment: **(a)** 0.20 wt% C, **(b)** 0.60 wt% C, **(c)** 0.76 wt% C, and **(d)** 0.95 wt% C.

9.17 What is the purpose of a spheroidizing heat treatment? On what classes of alloys is it normally used?

Concepts of Stress and Strain

9.18 Using mechanics of materials principles (i.e., equations of mechanical equilibrium applied to a free-body diagram), derive Equations 9.4a and 9.4b.

9.19 **(a)** Equations 9.4a and 9.4b are expressions for normal (σ') and shear (τ') stresses, respectively, as a function of the applied tensile stress (σ) and the inclination angle of the plane on which these stresses are taken (θ of Figure 9.4). Make a plot on which is presented the orientation parameters of these expressions (i.e., $\cos^2\theta$ and $\sin\theta\cos\theta$) versus θ.

(b) From this plot, at what angle of inclination is the normal stress a maximum?

(c) Also, at what inclination angle is the shear stress a maximum?

Stress–Strain Behavior

9.20 A specimen of copper having a rectangular cross section 15.2 mm × 19.1 mm is pulled in tension with 44,500 N force, producing only elastic deformation. Calculate the resulting strain.

9.21 A cylindrical specimen of a nickel alloy having an elastic modulus of 207 GPa and an original diameter of 10.2 mm will experience only elastic deformation when a tensile load of 8900 N is applied. Compute the maximum length of the specimen before deformation if the maximum allowable elongation is 0.25 mm.

9.22 An aluminum bar 125 mm long and having a square cross section 19.5 mm on an edge is pulled in tension with a load of 66,700 N, and experiences an elongation of 0.43 mm. Assuming that the deformation is entirely elastic, calculate the modulus of elasticity of the aluminum.

9.23 Consider a cylindrical nickel wire 2.0 mm in diameter and 3×10^4 mm long. Calculate its elongation when a load of 300 N is applied. Assume that the deformation is totally elastic.

9.24 For a brass alloy, the stress at which plastic deformation begins is 345 MPa, and the modulus of elasticity is 103 GPa.

(a) What is the maximum load that may be applied to a specimen with a cross-sectional area of 130 mm^2 without plastic deformation?

(b) If the original specimen length is 76 mm, what is the maximum length to which it may be stretched without causing plastic deformation?

9.25 A cylindrical rod of steel (E = 207 GPa) having a yield strength of 310 MPa is to be subjected to a load of 11,100 N. If the length of the rod is 500 mm, what must be the diameter to allow an elongation of 0.38 mm?

9.26 Consider a cylindrical specimen of a steel alloy (Figure 9.27) 8.5 mm in diameter and 80 mm long that is pulled in tension. Determine its elongation when a load of 65,250 N is applied.

9.27 Figure 9.28 shows, for a gray cast iron, the tensile engineering stress–strain curve in the elastic region. Determine **(a)** the tangent modulus at 25 MPa, and **(b)** the secant modulus taken to 35 MPa.

9.28 As noted in Section 3.10, for single crystals of some substances, the physical properties are anisotropic; that is, they are dependent on crystallographic direction. One such property is the modulus of elasticity. For cubic single crystals, the modulus of elasticity in a general $[uvw]$ direction, E_{uvw}, is described by the relationship

$$\frac{1}{E_{uvw}} = \frac{1}{E_{\langle 100\rangle}} - 3\left(\frac{1}{E_{\langle 100\rangle}} - \frac{1}{E_{\langle 111\rangle}}\right)(\alpha^2\beta^2 + \beta^2\gamma^2 + \gamma^2\alpha^2)$$

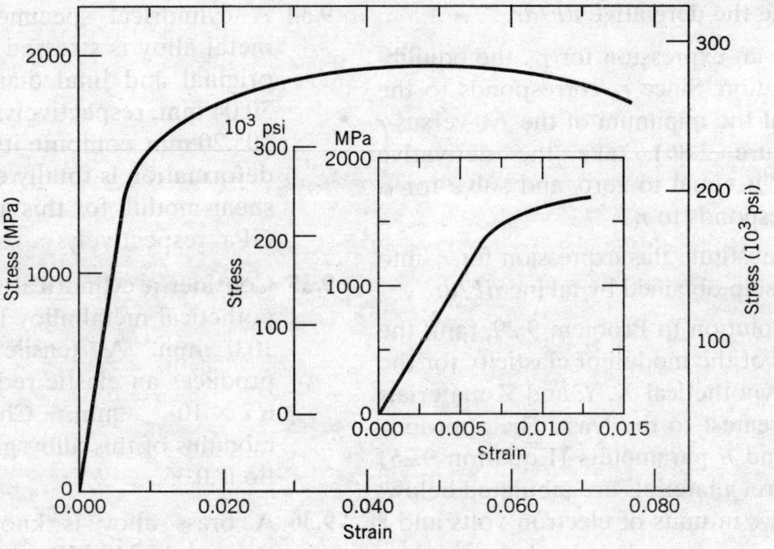

Figure 9.27 Tensile stress–strain behavior for an alloy steel.

where $E_{\langle 100 \rangle}$ and $E_{\langle 111 \rangle}$ are the moduli of elasticity in [100] and [111] directions, respectively; α, β, and γ are the cosines of the angles between [uvw] and the respective [100], [010], and [001] directions. Verify that the $E_{\langle 110 \rangle}$ values for aluminum, copper, and iron in Table 3.3 are correct.

9.29 In Section 2.6 it was noted that the net bonding energy E_N between two isolated positive and negative ions is a function of interionic distance r as follows:

$$E_N = -\frac{A}{r} + \frac{B}{r^n} \qquad (9.25)$$

where A, B, and n are constants for the particular ion pair. Equation 9.25 is also valid for the bonding energy between adjacent ions in solid materials. The modulus of elasticity E is proportional to the slope of the interionic force–separation curve at the equilibrium interionic separation; that is,

$$E \propto \left(\frac{dF}{dr}\right)_{r_0}$$

Derive an expression for the dependence of the modulus of elasticity on these A, B, and n parameters (for the two-ion system) using the following procedure:

1. Establish a relationship for the force F as a function of r, realizing that

$$F = \frac{dE_N}{dr}$$

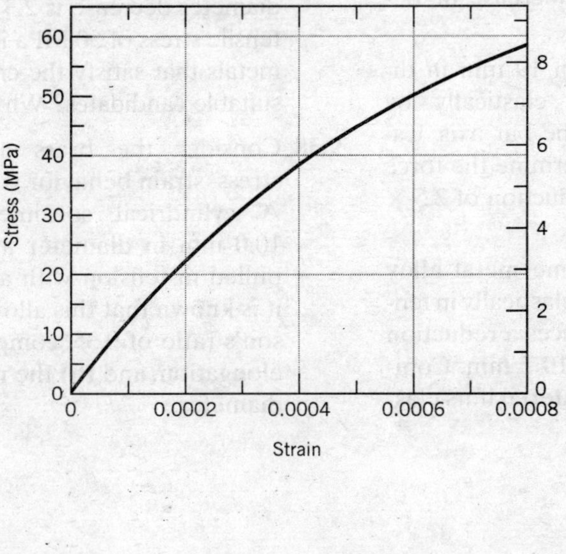

Figure 9.28 Tensile stress–strain behavior for a gray cast iron.

2. Now take the derivative dF/dr.

3. Develop an expression for r_0, the equilibrium separation. Since r_0 corresponds to the value of r at the minimum of the E_N-versus-r curve (Figure 2.8*b*), take the derivative dE_N/dr, set it equal to zero, and solve for r, which corresponds to r_0.

4. Finally, substitute this expression for r_0 into the relationship obtained by taking dF/dr.

9.30 Using the solution to Problem 9.29, rank the magnitudes of the moduli of elasticity for the following hypothetical X, Y, and Z materials from the greatest to the least. The appropriate A, B, and n parameters (Equation 9.25) for these three materials are tabulated below; they yield E_N in units of electron volts and r in nanometers:

Material	*A*	*B*	*n*
X	1.5	7.0×10^{-6}	8
Y	2.0	1.0×10^{-5}	9
Z	3.5	4.0×10^{-6}	7

Elastic Properties of Materials

9.31 A cylindrical specimen of steel having a diameter of 15.2 mm and length of 250 mm is deformed elastically in tension with a force of 48,900 N. Using the data contained in Table 9.10, determine the following:

(a) The amount by which this specimen will elongate in the direction of the applied stress.

(b) The change in diameter of the specimen. Will the diameter increase or decrease?

9.32 A cylindrical bar of aluminum 19 mm in diameter is to be deformed elastically by application of a force along the bar axis. Using the data in Table 9.10, determine the force that will produce an elastic reduction of 2.5×10^{-3} mm in the diameter.

9.33 A cylindrical specimen of some metal alloy 10 mm in diameter is stressed elastically in tension. A force of 15,000 N produces a reduction in specimen diameter of 7×10^{-3} mm. Compute Poisson's ratio for this material if its elastic modulus is 100 GPa.

9.34 A cylindrical specimen of a hypothetical metal alloy is stressed in compression. If its original and final diameters are 30.00 and 30.04 mm, respectively, and its final length is 105.20 mm, compute its original length if the deformation is totally elastic. The elastic and shear moduli for this alloy are 65.5 and 25.4 GPa, respectively.

9.35 Consider a cylindrical specimen of some hypothetical metal alloy that has a diameter of 10.0 mm. A tensile force of 1500 N produces an elastic reduction in diameter of 6.7×10^{-4} mm. Compute the elastic modulus of this alloy, given that Poisson's ratio is 0.35.

9.36 A brass alloy is known to have a yield strength of 240 MPa, a tensile strength of 310 MPa, and an elastic modulus of 110 GPa. A cylindrical specimen of this alloy 15.2 mm in diameter and 380 mm long is stressed in tension and found to elongate 1.9 mm. On the basis of the information given, is it possible to compute the magnitude of the load that is necessary to produce this change in length? If so, calculate the load. If not, explain why.

9.37 A cylindrical metal specimen 15.0 mm in diameter and 150 mm long is to be subjected to a tensile stress of 50 MPa; at this stress level the resulting deformation will be totally elastic.

(a) If the elongation must be less than 0.072 mm, which of the metals in Table 9.1 are suitable candidates? Why?

(b) If, in addition, the maximum permissible diameter decrease is 2.3×10^{-3} mm when the tensile stress of 50 MPa is applied, which of the metals that satisfy the criterion in part (a) are suitable candidates? Why?

9.38 Consider the brass alloy for which the stress–strain behavior is shown in Figure 9.12. A cylindrical specimen of this material 10.0 mm in diameter and 101.6 mm long is pulled in tension with a force of 10,000 N. If it is known that this alloy has a value for Poisson's ratio of 0.35, compute **(a)** the specimen elongation, and **(b)** the reduction in specimen diameter.

9.39 A cylindrical rod 120 mm long and having a diameter of 15.0 mm is to be deformed using a tensile load of 35,000 N. It must not experience either plastic deformation or a diameter reduction of more than 1.2×10^{-2} mm. Of the materials listed below, which are possible candidates? Justify your choice(s).

Material	*Modulus of Elasticity (GPa)*	*Yield Strength (MPa)*	*Poisson's Ratio*
Aluminum alloy	70	250	0.33
Titanium alloy	105	850	0.36
Steel alloy	205	550	0.27
Magnesium alloy	45	170	0.35

9.40 A cylindrical rod 500 mm long, having a diameter of 12.7 mm, is to be subjected to a tensile load. If the rod is to experience neither plastic deformation nor an elongation of more than 1.3 mm when the applied load is 29,000 N, which of the four metals or alloys listed below are possible candidates? Justify your choice(s).

Material	*Modulus of Elasticity (GPa)*	*Yield Strength (MPa)*	*Tensile Strength (MPa)*
Aluminum alloy	70	255	420
Brass alloy	100	345	420
Copper	110	210	275
Steel alloy	207	450	550

Tensile Properties

9.41 Figure 9.27 shows the tensile engineering stress–strain behavior for a steel alloy.

(a) What is the modulus of elasticity?

(b) What is the proportional limit?

(c) What is the yield strength at a strain offset of 0.002?

(d) What is the tensile strength?

9.42 A cylindrical specimen of a brass alloy having a length of 100 mm must elongate only 5 mm when a tensile load of 100,000 N is applied. Under these circumstances what must be the radius of the specimen? Consider this brass alloy to have the stress–strain behavior shown in Figure 9.18.

9.43 A load of 140,000 N is applied to a cylindrical specimen of a steel alloy (displaying the stress–strain behavior shown in Figure 9.27) that has a cross-sectional diameter of 10 mm.

(a) Will the specimen experience elastic and/or plastic deformation? Why?

(b) If the original specimen length is 500 mm, how much will it increase in length when this load is applied?

9.44 A bar of a steel alloy that exhibits the stress–strain behavior shown in Figure 9.27 is subjected to a tensile load; the specimen is 375 mm long and of square cross section 5.5 mm on a side.

(a) Compute the magnitude of the load necessary to produce an elongation of 2.25 mm.

(b) What will be the deformation after the load has been released?

9.45 A cylindrical specimen of stainless steel having a diameter of 12.8 mm and a gauge length of 50.800 mm is pulled in tension. Use the load–elongation characteristics tabulated below to complete parts (a) through (f).

Load (N)	*Length (mm)*
0	50.800
12,700	50.825
25,400	50.851
38,100	50.876
50,800	50.902
76,200	50.952
89,100	51.003
92,700	51.054
102,500	51.181
107,800	51.308
119,400	51.562
128,300	51.816
149,700	52.832
159,000	53.848
160,400	54.356
159,500	54.864
151,500	55.880
124,700	59.642
	Fracture

(a) Plot the data as engineering stress versus engineering strain.

(b) Compute the modulus of elasticity.

(c) Determine the yield strength at a strain offset of 0.002.

(d) Determine the tensile strength of this alloy.

(e) What is the approximate ductility, in percent elongation?

(f) Compute the modulus of resilience.

9.46 A specimen of magnesium having a rectangular cross section of dimensions 3.2 mm × 19.1 mm is deformed in tension. Using the load–elongation data tabulated as follows, complete parts (a) through (f).

Load (N)	*Length (mm)*
0	63.50
1380	63.53
2780	63.56
5630	63.62
7430	63.70
8140	63.75
9870	64.14
12,850	65.41
14,100	69.68
14,340	67.95
13,830	69.22
12,500	70.49
Fracture	

(a) Plot the data as engineering stress versus engineering strain.

(b) Compute the modulus of elasticity.

(c) Determine the yield strength at a strain offset of 0.002.

(d) Determine the tensile strength of this alloy.

(e) Compute the modulus of resilience.

(f) What is the ductility, in percent elongation?

9.47 A cylindrical metal specimen having an original diameter of 12.8 mm and gauge length of 50.80 mm is pulled in tension until fracture occurs. The diameter at the point of fracture is 8.13 mm, and the fractured gauge length is 74.17 mm. Calculate the ductility in terms of percent reduction in area and percent elongation.

9.48 Calculate the moduli of resilience for the materials having the stress–strain behaviors shown in Figures 9.18 and 9.27.

9.49 Determine the modulus of resilience for each of the following alloys:

Material	*Yield Strength (MPa)*
Steel alloy	830
Brass alloy	380
Aluminum alloy	275
Titanium alloy	690

Use modulus of elasticity values in Table 9.10.

9.50 A steel alloy to be used for a spring application must have a modulus of resilience of at least 2.07 MPa. What must be its minimum yield strength?

True Stress and Strain

9.51 Show that Equations 9.18a and 9.18b are valid when there is no volume change during deformation.

9.52 Demonstrate that Equation 9.16, the expression defining true strain, may also be represented by

$$\epsilon_T = \ln\left(\frac{A_0}{A_i}\right)$$

when specimen volume remains constant during deformation. Which of these two expressions is more valid during necking? Why?

9.53 Using the data in Problem 9.45 and Equations 9.15, 9.16, and 9.18a, generate a true stresÍs–true strain plot for stainless steel. Equation 9.18a becomes invalid past the point at which necking begins; therefore, measured diameters are given below for the last three data points, which should be used in true stress computations.

Load (N)	*Length (mm)*	*Diameter (mm)*
159,500	54.864	12.22
151,500	55.880	9.80
124,700	59.642	10.65

9.54 A tensile test is performed on a metal specimen, and it is found that a true plastic strain of 0.16 is produced when a true stress of 500 MPa is applied; for the same metal, the value of K in Equation 9.19 is 825 MPa. Calculate the true strain that results from the application of a true stress of 600 MPa.

9.55 For some metal alloy, a true stress of 345 MPa produces a plastic true strain of 0.02. How much will a specimen of this material elongate when a true stress of 415 MPa is applied if the original length is 500 mm? Assume a value of 0.22 for the strain-hardening exponent, *n*.

9.56 The following true stresses produce the corresponding true plastic strains for a brass alloy:

True Stress (MPa)	*True Strain*
415	0.15
485	0.25

What true stress is necessary to produce a true plastic strain of 0.21?

9.57 For a brass alloy, the following engineering stresses produce the corresponding plastic engineering strains, prior to necking:

Engineering Stress (MPa)	*Engineering Strain*
315	0.105
340	0.220

On the basis of this information, compute the *engineering* stress necessary to produce an *engineering* strain of 0.28.

9.58 Find the toughness (or energy to cause fracture) for a metal that experiences both elastic and plastic deformation. Assume Equation 9.5 for elastic deformation, that the modulus of elasticity is 103 GPa, and that elastic deformation terminates at a strain of 0.007. For plastic deformation, assume that the relationship between stress and strain is described by Equation 9.19, in which the values for K and n are 1520 MPa and 0.15, respectively. Furthermore, plastic deformation occurs between strain values of 0.007 and 0.60, at which point fracture occurs.

9.59 For a tensile test, it can be demonstrated that necking begins when

$$\frac{d\sigma_T}{d\epsilon_T} = \sigma_T \qquad (9.26)$$

Using Equation 9.19, determine the value of the true strain at this onset of necking.

9.60 Taking the logarithm of both sides of Equation 9.19 yields

$$\log \sigma_T = \log K + n \log \epsilon_T \qquad (9.27)$$

Thus, a plot of $\log \sigma_T$ versus $\log \epsilon_T$ in the plastic region to the point of necking should yield a straight line having a slope of n and an intercept (at $\log \sigma_T = 0$) of $\log K$.

Using the appropriate data tabulated in Problem 9.45, make a plot of $\log \sigma_T$ versus $\log \epsilon_T$ and determine the values of n and K. It will be necessary to convert engineering stresses and strains to true stresses and strains using Equations 9.18a and 9.18b.

Elastic Recovery After Plastic Deformation

9.61 A cylindrical specimen of a brass alloy 10.0 mm in diameter and 120.0 mm long is pulled in tension with a force of 11,750 N; the force is subsequently released.

(a) Compute the final length of the specimen at this time. The tensile stress–strain behavior for this alloy is shown in Figure 9.18.

(b) Compute the final specimen length when the load is increased to 23,500 N and then released.

9.62 A steel alloy specimen having a rectangular cross section of dimensions 19 mm × 3.2 mm has the stress–strain behavior shown in Figure 9.27. If this specimen is subjected to a tensile force of 110,000 N then

(a) Determine the elastic and plastic strain values.

(b) If its original length is 610 mm, what will be its final length after the load in part (a) is applied and then released?

Hardness

9.63 (a) A 10-mm-diameter Brinell hardness indenter produced an indentation 2.50 mm in diameter in a steel alloy when a load of 1000 kg was used. Compute the HB of this material.

(b) What will be the diameter of an indentation to yield a hardness of 300 HB when a 500-kg load is used?

9.64 Estimate the Brinell and Rockwell hardnesses for the following:

(a) The naval brass for which the stress–strain behavior is shown in Figure 9.18.

(b) The steel alloy for which the stress–strain behavior is shown in Figure 9.27.

9.65 Using the data represented in Figure 9.25, specify equations relating tensile strength and Brinell hardness for brass and nodular cast iron, similar to Equations 9.20a and 9.20b for steels.

Variability of Material Properties

9.66 Cite five factors that lead to scatter in measured material properties.

9.67 Below are tabulated a number of Rockwell G hardness values that were measured on a single steel specimen. Compute average and standard deviation hardness values.

47.3	48.7	47.1
52.1	50.0	50.4
45.6	49.2	45.9
49.9	48.3	49.4
47.6	51.1	48.5
50.4	49.7	49.7

Design/Safety Factors

9.68 Upon what three criteria are factors of safety based?

9.69 Determine working stresses for the two alloys that have the stress–strain behaviors shown in Figures 9.18 and 9.27.

DESIGN PROBLEMS

Ferrous Alloys
Nonferrous Alloys

9.D1 Below is a list of metals and alloys:

Plain carbon steel	Magnesium
Brass	Zinc
Gray cast iron	Tool steel
Platinum	Aluminum
Stainless steel	Tungsten
Titanium alloy	

Select from this list the one metal or alloy that is best suited for each of the following applications, and cite at least one reason for your choice:

(a) The block of an internal combustion engine

(b) Condensing heat exchanger for steam

(c) Jet engine turbofan blades

(d) Drill bit

(e) Cryogenic (i.e., very low temperature) container

(f) As a pyrotechnic (i.e., in flares and fireworks)

(g) High-temperature furnace elements to be used in oxidizing atmospheres

9.D2 A group of new materials are the metallic glasses (or amorphous metals). Write an essay about these materials in which you address the following issues: (1) compositions of some of the common metallic glasses, (2) characteristics of these materials that make them technologically attractive, (3) characteristics that limit their utilization, (4) current and potential uses, and (5) at least one technique that is used to produce metallic glasses.

9.D3 Of the following alloys, pick the one(s) that may be strengthened by heat treatment, cold work, or both: 410 stainless steel, 4340 steel, F10004 cast iron, C26000 cartridge brass, 359.0 aluminum, ZK60A magnesium, R56400 titanium, 1100 aluminum, and zinc.

9.D4 A structural member 250 mm long must be able to support a load of 44,400 N without experiencing any plastic deformation. Given the following data for brass, steel, aluminum, and titanium, rank them from least to greatest weight in accordance with these criteria.

Alloy	*Yield Strength (MPa)*	*Density (g/cm^3)*
Brass	345	8.5
Steel	690	7.9
Aluminum	275	2.7
Titanium	480	4.5

9.D5 Discuss whether it would be advisable to hot work or cold work the following metals and alloys on the basis of melting temperature, oxidation resistance, yield strength, and degree of brittleness: platinum, molybdenum, lead, 304 stainless steel, and copper.

9.D6 A large tower is to be supported by a series of steel wires; it is estimated that the load on each wire will be 13,300 N. Determine the minimum required wire diameter, assuming a factor of safety of 2 and a yield strength of 860 MPa for the steel.

9.D7 **(a)** Gaseous hydrogen at a constant pressure of 0.658 MPa (5 atm) is to flow within the inside of a thin-walled cylindrical tube of nickel that has a radius of 0.125 m. The temperature of the tube is to be 350°C and the pressure of hydrogen outside of the tube will be maintained at 0.0127 MPa (0.125 atm). Calculate the minimum wall thickness if the diffusion flux is to be no greater than 1.25×10^{-7} mol/m^2-s. The concentration of hydrogen in the nickel, C_H (in moles hydrogen per m^3 of Ni) is a function of hydrogen pressure, P_{H_2} (in MPa) and absolute temperature (T) according to

$$C_H = 30.8\sqrt{p_{H_2}}\exp\left(-\frac{12.3 \text{ kJ/mol}}{RT}\right) \quad (9.28)$$

Furthermore, the diffusion coefficient for the diffusion of H in Ni depends on temperature as

$$D_H(\text{m}^2/\text{s}) = 4.76 \times 10^{-7}\exp\left(-\frac{39.56 \text{ kJ/mol}}{RT}\right) \quad (9.29)$$

(b) For thin-walled cylindrical tubes that are pressurized, the circumferential stress is a function of the pressure difference across the wall (Δp), cylinder radius (r), and tube thickness (Δx) as

$$\sigma = \frac{r\Delta p}{4\Delta x} \quad (9.30)$$

Compute the circumferential stress to which the walls of this pressurized cylinder are exposed.

(c) The room-temperature yield strength of Ni is 100 MPa and, furthermore, σ_y diminishes about 5 MPa for every 50°C rise in temperature. Would you expect the wall thickness computed in part (b) to be suitable for this Ni cylinder at 350°C? Why or why not?

(d) If this thickness is found to be suitable, compute the minimum thickness that could be used without any deformation of the tube walls. How much would the diffusion flux increase with this reduction in thickness? On the other hand, if the thickness determined in part (c) is found to be unsuitable, then specify a minimum thickness that you would use. In this case, how much of a diminishment in diffusion flux would result?

9.D8 Consider the steady-state diffusion of hydrogen through the walls of a cylindrical nickel tube as described in Problem 9.D7. One design calls for a diffusion flux of 2.5×10^{-8} mol/m^2-s, a tube radius of 0.100 m, and inside and outside pressures of 1.015 MPa (10 atm) and 0.01015 MPa (0.1 atm), respectively; the maximum allowable temperature is 300°C. Specify a suitable temperature and wall thickness to give this diffusion flux and yet ensure that the tube walls will not experience any permanent deformation.

Chapter 10 Dislocations and Strengthening Mechanisms in Metals

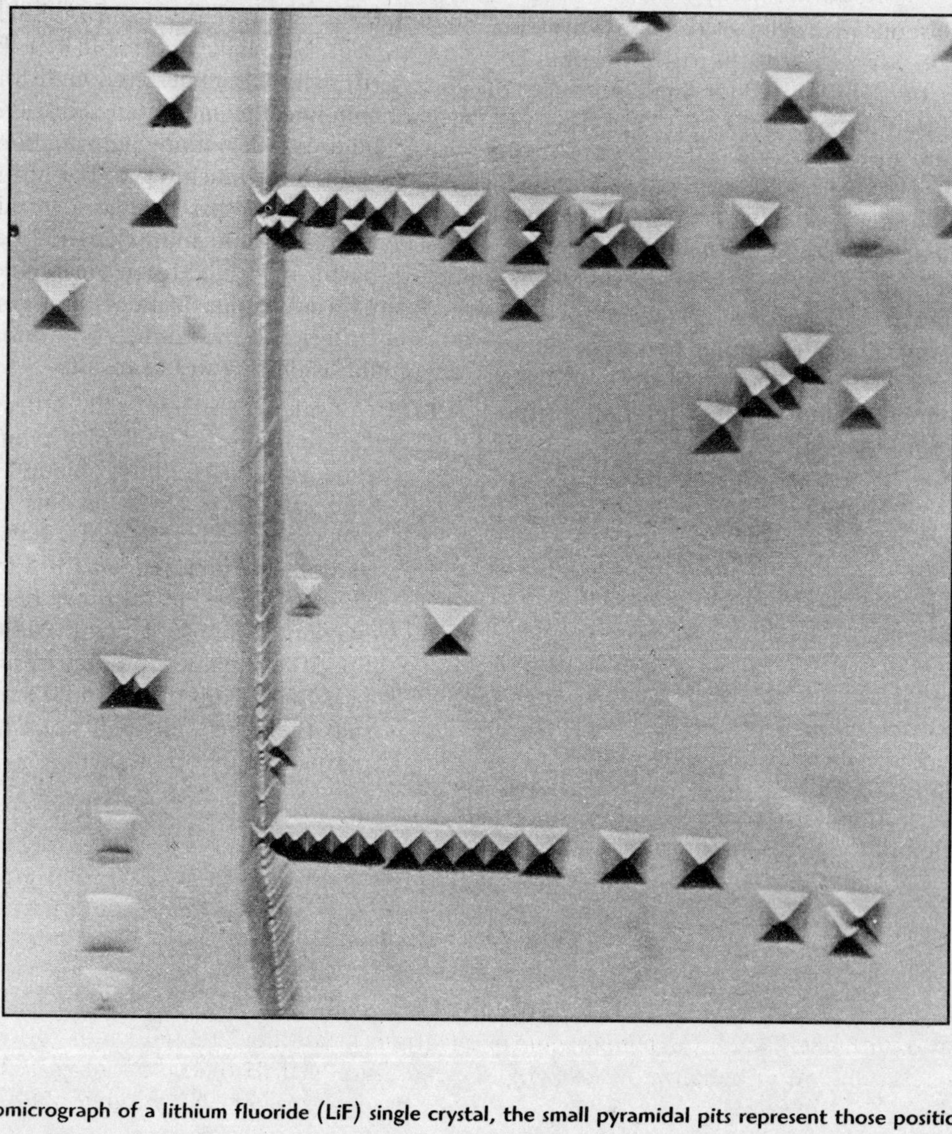

In this photomicrograph of a lithium fluoride (LiF) single crystal, the small pyramidal pits represent those positions at which dislocations intersect the surface. The surface was polished and then chemically treated; these "etch pits" result from localized chemical attack around the dislocations and indicate the distribution of the dislocations. 750×. (Photomicrograph courtesy of W. G. Johnston, General Electric Co.)

Learning Objectives

After studying this chapter you should be able to do the following:

1. **Describe edge and screw dislocation motion from an atomic perspective.**
2. **Describe how plastic deformation occurs by the motion of edge and screw dislocations in response to applied shear stresses.**
3. **Define slip system and cite one example.**
4. **Describe how the grain structure of a polycrystalline metal is altered when it is plastically deformed.**
5. **Explain how grain boundaries impede dislocation motion and why a metal having small grains is stronger than one having large grains.**
6. **Describe and explain solid-solution strengthening for substitutional impurity atoms in terms of lattice strain interactions with dislocations.**
7. **Describe and explain the phenomenon of strain hardening (or cold working) in terms of dislocations and strain field interactions.**
8. **Describe recrystallization in terms of both the alteration of microstructure and mechanical characteristics of the material.**
9. **Describe the phenomenon of grain growth from both macroscopic and atomic perspectives.**
10. **Using a phase diagram, describe and explain the two heat treatments that are used to precipitation harden a metal alloy.**
11. **Make a schematic plot of room-temperature strength (or hardness) versus the logarithm of time for a precipitation heat treatment at constant temperature. Explain the shape of this curve in terms of the mechanism of precipitation hardening.**

10.1 INTRODUCTION

Chapter 9 explained that materials may experience two kinds of deformation: elastic and plastic. Plastic deformation is permanent, and strength and hardness are measures of a material's resistance to this deformation. On a microscopic scale, plastic deformation corresponds to the net movement of large numbers of atoms in response to an applied stress. During this process, interatomic bonds must be ruptured and then reformed. In crystalline solids, plastic deformation most often involves the motion of dislocations, linear crystalline defects that were introduced in Section 5.6. This chapter discusses the characteristics of dislocations and their involvement in plastic deformation. Twinning, another process by which some metals plastically deform, is also treated. In addition, and probably most importantly, several techniques are presented for strengthening single-phase metals, the mechanisms of which are described in terms of dislocations. Finally, the latter sections of this chapter are concerned with recovery and recrystallization—processes that occur in plastically deformed metals, normally at elevated temperatures—and, in addition, grain growth.

Dislocations and Plastic Deformation

Early materials studies led to the computation of the theoretical strengths of perfect crystals, which were many times greater than those actually measured. During the 1930s it was theorized that this discrepancy in mechanical strengths could be explained by a type of linear crystalline defect that has since come to be known as a dislocation. It was not until the 1950s, however, that the existence of such dislocation defects was established by direct observation with the electron microscope. Since then, a theory of dislocations has evolved that explains many of the physical and mechanical phenomena in metals [as well as crystalline ceramics (Section 12.12)].

10.2 BASIC CONCEPTS

Edge and screw are the two fundamental dislocation types. In an edge dislocation, localized lattice distortion exists along the end of an extra half-plane of atoms, which also defines the dislocation line (Figure 5.7). A screw dislocation may be thought of as resulting from shear distortion; its dislocation line passes through the center of a spiral, atomic plane ramp (Figure 5.8). Many dislocations in crystalline materials have both edge and screw components; these are mixed dislocations (Figure 5.9).

Plastic deformation corresponds to the motion of large numbers of dislocations. An edge dislocation moves in response to a shear stress applied in a direction perpendicular to its line; the mechanics of dislocation motion are represented in Figure 10.1. Let the initial extra half-plane of atoms be plane *A*. When the shear stress is applied as indicated (Figure 10.1*a*), plane *A* is forced to the right; this in turn pushes the top halves of planes *B*, *C*, *D*, and so on, in the same direction. If the applied shear stress is of sufficient magnitude, the interatomic bonds of plane *B* are severed along the shear plane, and the upper half of plane *B* becomes the extra half-plane as plane *A* links up with the bottom half of plane *B* (Figure 10.1*b*). This process is subsequently repeated for the other planes, such that the extra half-plane, by discrete steps, moves from left to right by successive and repeated breaking of bonds and shifting by interatomic distances of upper half-planes. Before and after the movement of a dislocation through some particular region of the crystal, the atomic arrangement is ordered and perfect; it is only during the passage of the extra half-plane that the lattice structure is disrupted. Ultimately this extra half-plane may emerge from the right surface of the crystal, forming an edge that is one atomic distance wide; this is shown in Figure 10.1*c*.

The process by which plastic deformation is produced by dislocation motion is termed **slip;** the crystallographic plane along which the dislocation line traverses is the *slip plane,* as indicated in Figure 10.1. Macroscopic plastic deformation simply corresponds to permanent deformation that results from the movement of dislocations, or slip, in response to an applied shear stress, as represented in Figure 10.2*a*.

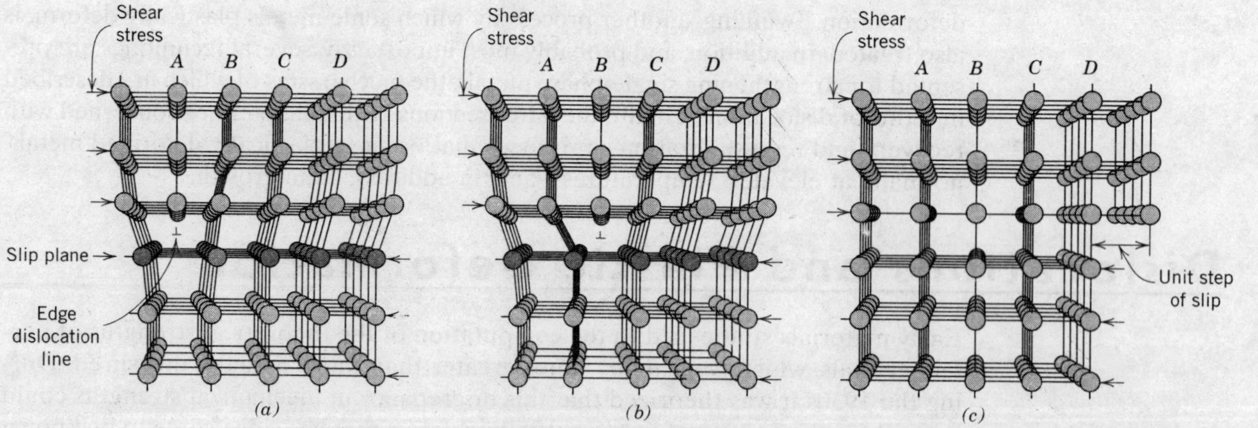

Figure 10.1 Atomic rearrangements that accompany the motion of an edge dislocation as it moves in response to an applied shear stress. (*a*) The extra half-plane of atoms is labeled *A*. (*b*) The dislocation moves one atomic distance to the right as *A* links up to the lower portion of plane *B*; in the process, the upper portion of *B* becomes the extra half-plane. (*c*) A step forms on the surface of the crystal as the extra half-plane exits. (Adapted from A. G. Guy, *Essentials of Materials Science,* McGraw-Hill Book Company, New York, 1976, p. 153.)

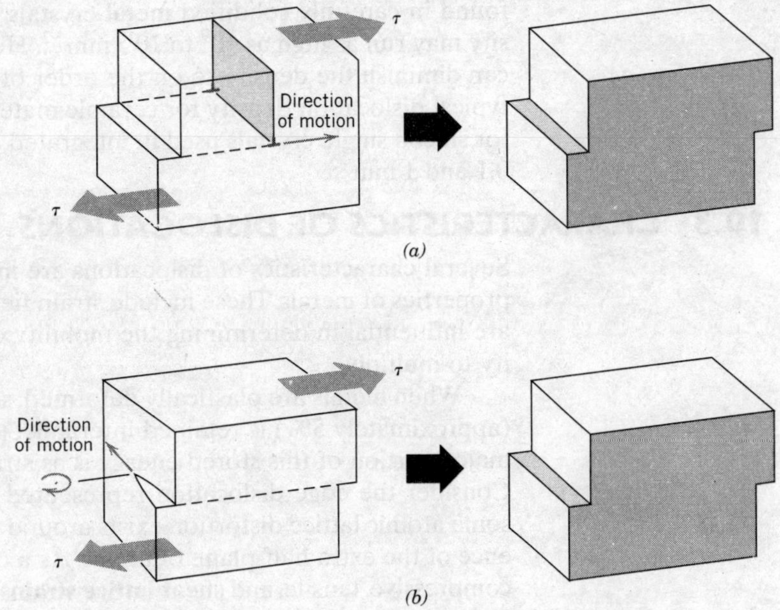

Figure 10.2 The formation of a step on the surface of a crystal by the motion of (*a*) an edge dislocation and (*b*) a screw dislocation. Note that for an edge, the dislocation line moves in the direction of the applied shear stress τ; for a screw, the dislocation line motion is perpendicular to the stress direction. (Adapted from H. W. Hayden, W. G. Moffatt, and J. Wulff, *The Structure and Properties of Materials*, Vol. III, *Mechanical Behavior*, p. 70. Copyright © 1965 by John Wiley & Sons, New York. Reprinted by permission of John Wiley & Sons, Inc.)

Dislocation motion is analogous to the mode of locomotion employed by a caterpillar (Figure 10.3). The caterpillar forms a hump near its posterior end by pulling in its last pair of legs a unit leg distance. The hump is propelled forward by repeated lifting and shifting of leg pairs. When the hump reaches the anterior end, the entire caterpillar has moved forward by the leg separation distance. The caterpillar hump and its motion correspond to the extra half-plane of atoms in the dislocation model of plastic deformation.

The motion of a screw dislocation in response to the applied shear stress is shown in Figure 10.2*b*; the direction of movement is perpendicular to the stress direction. For an edge, motion is parallel to the shear stress. However, the net plastic deformation for the motion of both dislocation types is the same (see Figure 10.2). The direction of motion of the mixed dislocation line is neither perpendicular nor parallel to the applied stress, but lies somewhere in between.

All metals and alloys contain some dislocations that were introduced during solidification, during plastic deformation, and as a consequence of thermal stresses that result from rapid cooling. The number of dislocations, or **dislocation density** in a material, is expressed as the total dislocation length per unit volume or, equivalently, the number of dislocations that intersect a unit area of a random section. The units of dislocation density are millimeters of dislocation per cubic millimeter or just per square millimeter. Dislocation densities as low as 10^3 mm^{-2} are typically

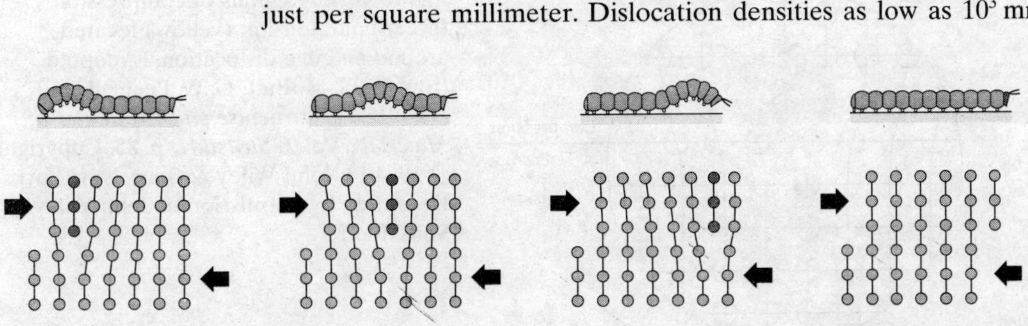

Figure 10.3 Representation of the analogy between caterpillar and dislocation motion.

found in carefully solidified metal crystals. For heavily deformed metals, the density may run as high as 10^9 to 10^{10} mm^{-2}. Heat treating a deformed metal specimen can diminish the density to on the order of 10^5 to 10^6 mm^{-2}. By way of contrast, a typical dislocation density for ceramic materials is between 10^2 and 10^4 mm^{-2}; also, for silicon single crystals used in integrated circuits the value normally lies between 0.1 and 1 mm^{-2}.

10.3 CHARACTERISTICS OF DISLOCATIONS

Several characteristics of dislocations are important with regard to the mechanical properties of metals. These include strain fields that exist around dislocations, which are influential in determining the mobility of the dislocations, as well as their ability to multiply.

When metals are plastically deformed, some fraction of the deformation energy (approximately 5%) is retained internally; the remainder is dissipated as heat. The major portion of this stored energy is as strain energy associated with dislocations. Consider the edge dislocation represented in Figure 10.4. As already mentioned, some atomic lattice distortion exists around the dislocation line because of the presence of the extra half-plane of atoms. As a consequence, there are regions in which compressive, tensile, and shear **lattice strains** are imposed on the neighboring atoms. For example, atoms immediately above and adjacent to the dislocation line are squeezed together. As a result, these atoms may be thought of as experiencing a compressive strain relative to atoms positioned in the perfect crystal and far removed from the dislocation; this is illustrated in Figure 10.4. Directly below the half-plane, the effect is just the opposite; lattice atoms sustain an imposed tensile strain, which is as shown. Shear strains also exist in the vicinity of the edge dislocation. For a screw dislocation, lattice strains are pure shear only. These lattice distortions may be considered to be strain fields that radiate from the dislocation line. The strains extend into the surrounding atoms, and their magnitude decreases with radial distance from the dislocation.

The strain fields surrounding dislocations in close proximity to one another may interact such that forces are imposed on each dislocation by the combined interactions of all its neighboring dislocations. For example, consider two edge dislocations that have the same sign and the identical slip plane, as represented in Figure 10.5*a*. The compressive and tensile strain fields for both lie on the same side of the slip plane; the strain field interaction is such that there exists between these two isolated dislocations a mutual repulsive force that tends to move them apart. On the other hand, two dislocations of opposite sign and having the same slip plane will be attracted to one another, as indicated in Figure 10.5*b*, and

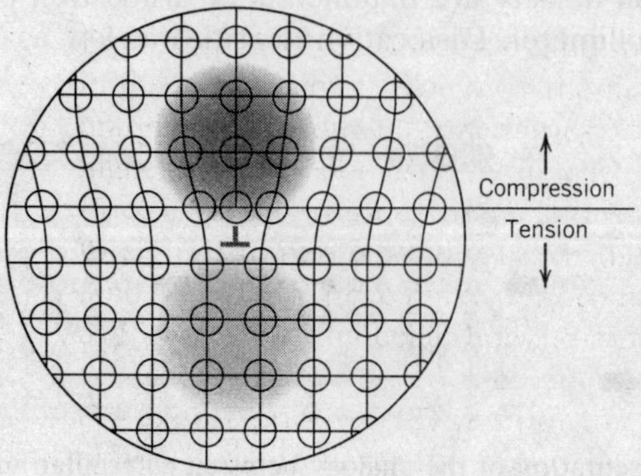

Figure 10.4 Regions of compression (green) and tension (yellow) located around an edge dislocation. (Adapted from W. G. Moffatt, G. W. Pearsall, and J. Wulff, *The Structure and Properties of Materials,* Vol. I, *Structure,* p. 85. Copyright © 1964 by John Wiley & Sons, New York. Reprinted by permission of John Wiley & Sons, Inc.)

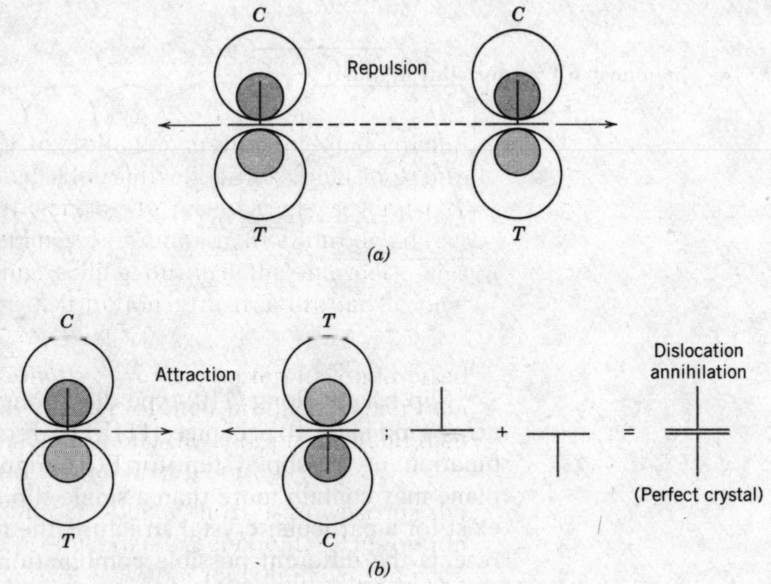

Figure 10.5 (*a*) Two edge dislocations of the same sign and lying on the same slip plane exert a repulsive force on each other; *C* and *T* denote compression and tensile regions, respectively. (*b*) Edge dislocations of opposite sign and lying on the same slip plane exert an attractive force on each other. Upon meeting, they annihilate each other and leave a region of perfect crystal. (Adapted from H. W. Hayden, W. G. Moffatt, and J. Wulff, *The Structure and Properties of Materials,* Vol. III, *Mechanical Behavior,* p. 75. Copyright © 1965 by John Wiley & Sons, New York. Reprinted by permission of John Wiley & Sons.)

dislocation annihilation will occur when they meet. That is, the two extra half-planes of atoms will align and become a complete plane. Dislocation interactions are possible between edge, screw, and/or mixed dislocations, and for a variety of orientations. These strain fields and associated forces are important in the strengthening mechanisms for metals.

During plastic deformation, the number of dislocations increases dramatically. We know that the dislocation density in a metal that has been highly deformed may be as high as 10^{10} mm^{-2}. One important source of these new dislocations is existing dislocations, which multiply; furthermore, grain boundaries, as well as internal defects and surface irregularities such as scratches and nicks, which act as stress concentrations, may serve as dislocation formation sites during deformation.

10.4 SLIP SYSTEMS

Dislocations do not move with the same degree of ease on all crystallographic planes of atoms and in all crystallographic directions. Ordinarily there is a preferred plane, and in that plane there are specific directions along which dislocation motion occurs. This plane is called the *slip plane;* it follows that the direction of movement is called the *slip direction.* This combination of the slip plane and the slip direction is termed the **slip system.** The slip system depends on the crystal structure of the metal and is such that the atomic distortion that accompanies the motion of a dislocation is a minimum. For a particular crystal structure, the slip plane is the plane that has the most dense atomic packing—that is, has the greatest planar density. The slip direction corresponds to the direction, in this plane, that is most closely packed with atoms—that is, has the highest linear density. Planar and linear atomic densities were discussed in Section 4.7.

Consider, for example, the FCC crystal structure, a unit cell of which is shown in Figure 10.6*a*. There is a set of planes, the {111} family, all of which are closely packed. A (111)-type plane is indicated in the unit cell; in Figure 10.6*b*, this plane is positioned within the plane of the page, in which atoms are now represented as touching nearest neighbors.

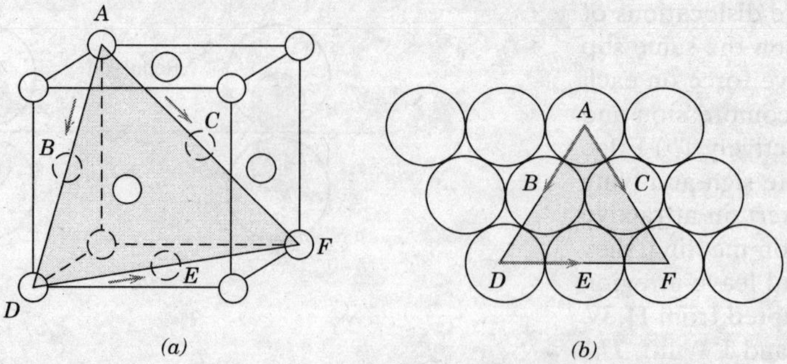

Figure 10.6 (*a*) A {111} ⟨110⟩ slip system shown within an FCC unit cell. (*b*) The (111) plane from (*a*) and three ⟨110⟩ slip directions (as indicated by arrows) within that plane comprise possible slip systems.

Slip occurs along ⟨110⟩-type directions within the {111} planes, as indicated by arrows in Figure 10.6. Hence, {111}⟨110⟩ represents the slip plane and direction combination, or the slip system for FCC. Figure 10.6*b* demonstrates that a given slip plane may contain more than a single slip direction. Thus, several slip systems may exist for a particular crystal structure; the number of independent slip systems represents the different possible combinations of slip planes and directions. For example, for face-centered cubic, there are 12 slip systems: four unique {111} planes and, within each plane, three independent ⟨110⟩ directions.

The possible slip systems for BCC and HCP crystal structures are listed in Table 10.1. For each of these structures, slip is possible on more than one family of planes (e.g., {110}, {211}, and {321} for BCC). For metals having these two crystal structures, some slip systems are often operable only at elevated temperatures.

Metals with FCC or BCC crystal structures have a relatively large number of slip systems (at least 12). These metals are quite ductile because extensive plastic deformation is normally possible along the various systems. Conversely, HCP metals, having few active slip systems, are normally quite brittle.

The Burgers vector concept was introduced in Section 5.6, and denoted by a **b** for edge, screw, and mixed dislocations in Figures 5.7, 5.8, and 5.9, respectively. With regard to the process of slip, a Burgers vector's direction corresponds to a dislocation's slip direction, whereas its magnitude is equal to the unit slip distance (or interatomic separation in this direction). Of course, both the direction and the magnitude of **b** will depend on crystal structure, and it is convenient to specify a Burgers vector in terms of unit cell edge length (a) and crystallographic direction indices.

Table 10.1 Slip Systems for Face-Centered Cubic, Body-Centered Cubic, and Hexagonal Close-Packed Metals

Metals	*Slip Plane*	*Slip Direction*	*Number of Slip Systems*
	Face-Centered Cubic		
Cu, Al, Ni, Ag, Au	{111}	$\langle 1\bar{1}0\rangle$	12
	Body-Centered Cubic		
α-Fe, W, Mo	{110}	$\langle \bar{1}11\rangle$	12
α-Fe, W	{211}	$\langle \bar{1}11\rangle$	12
α-Fe, K	{321}	$\langle \bar{1}11\rangle$	24
	Hexagonal Close-Packed		
Cd, Zn, Mg, Ti, Be	{0001}	$\langle 11\bar{2}0\rangle$	3
Ti, Mg, Zr	$\{10\bar{1}0\}$	$\langle 11\bar{2}0\rangle$	3
Ti, Mg	$\{10\bar{1}1\}$	$\langle 11\bar{2}0\rangle$	6

Burgers vectors for face-centered cubic, body-centered cubic, and hexagonal close-packed crystal structures are given as follows:

$$\mathbf{b}(\text{FCC}) = \frac{a}{2}\langle 110 \rangle \tag{10.1a}$$

$$\mathbf{b}(\text{BCC}) = \frac{a}{2}\langle 111 \rangle \tag{10.1b}$$

$$\mathbf{b}(\text{HCP}) = \frac{a}{3}\langle 11\bar{2}0 \rangle \tag{10.1c}$$

Concept Check 10.1

Which of the following is the slip system for the simple cubic crystal structure? Why?

$\{100\}\langle 110 \rangle$
$\{110\}\langle 110 \rangle$
$\{100\}\langle 010 \rangle$
$\{110\}\langle 111 \rangle$

(*Note:* a unit cell for the simple cubic crystal structure is shown in Figure 4.38.)
[*The answer may be found in enclosed CD.*]

10.5 SLIP IN SINGLE CRYSTALS

A further explanation of slip is simplified by treating the process in single crystals, then making the appropriate extension to polycrystalline materials. As mentioned previously, edge, screw, and mixed dislocations move in response to shear stresses applied along a slip plane and in a slip direction. As noted in Section 9.5, even though an applied stress may be pure tensile (or compressive), shear components exist at all but parallel or perpendicular alignments to the stress direction (Equation 9.4b). These are termed **resolved shear stresses,** and their magnitudes depend not only on the applied stress, but also on the orientation of both the slip plane and direction within that plane. Let ϕ represent the angle between the normal to the slip plane and the applied stress direction, and λ the angle between the slip and stress directions, as indicated in Figure 10.7; it can then be shown that for the resolved shear stress τ_R

$$\tau_R = \sigma \cos \phi \cos \lambda \tag{10.2}$$

where σ is the applied stress. In general, $\phi + \lambda \neq 90°$, since it need not be the case that the tensile axis, the slip plane normal, and the slip direction all lie in the same plane.

A metal single crystal has a number of different slip systems that are capable of operating. The resolved shear stress normally differs for each one because the orientation of each relative to the stress axis (ϕ and λ angles) also differs. However, one slip system is generally oriented most favorably—that is, has the largest resolved shear stress, $\tau_R(\text{max})$:

$$\tau_R(\text{max}) = \sigma(\cos \phi \cos \lambda)_{\text{max}} \tag{10.3}$$

In response to an applied tensile or compressive stress, slip in a single crystal commences on the most favorably oriented slip system when the resolved shear stress reaches some critical value, termed the **critical resolved shear stress** τ_{crss}; it represents the minimum shear stress required to initiate slip, and is a property of the

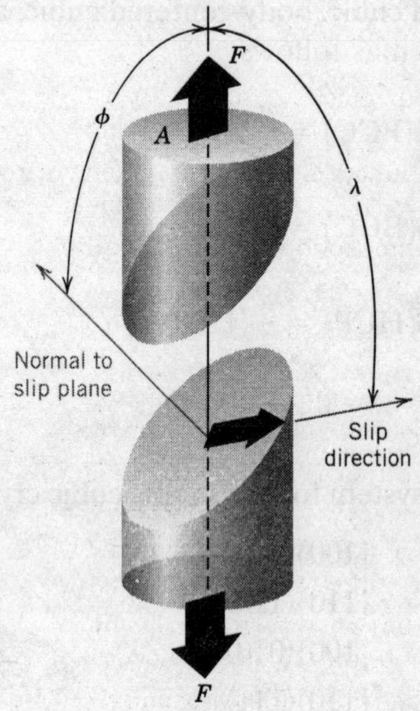

Figure 10.7 Geometrical relationships between the tensile axis, slip plane, and slip direction used in calculating the resolved shear stress for a single crystal.

material that determines when yielding occurs. The single crystal plastically deforms or yields when $\tau_R(\max) = \tau_{crss}$, and the magnitude of the applied stress required to initiate yielding (i.e., the yield strength σ_y) is

$$\sigma_y = \frac{\tau_{crss}}{(\cos\phi\cos\lambda)_{max}} \tag{10.4}$$

The minimum stress necessary to introduce yielding occurs when a single crystal is oriented such that $\phi = \lambda = 45°$; under these conditions,

$$\sigma_y = 2\tau_{crss} \tag{10.5}$$

For a single-crystal specimen that is stressed in tension, deformation will be as in Figure 10.8, where slip occurs along a number of equivalent and most favorably oriented planes and directions at various positions along the specimen length. This slip deformation forms as small steps on the surface of the single crystal that are parallel to one another and loop around the circumference of the specimen as indicated in Figure 10.8. Each step results from the movement of a large number of

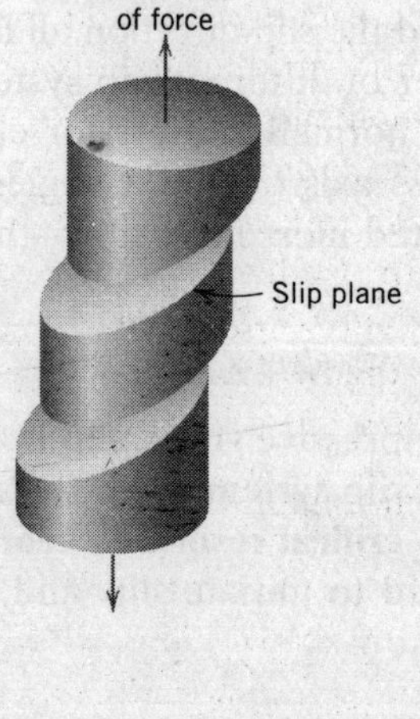

Figure 10.8 Macroscopic slip in a single crystal.

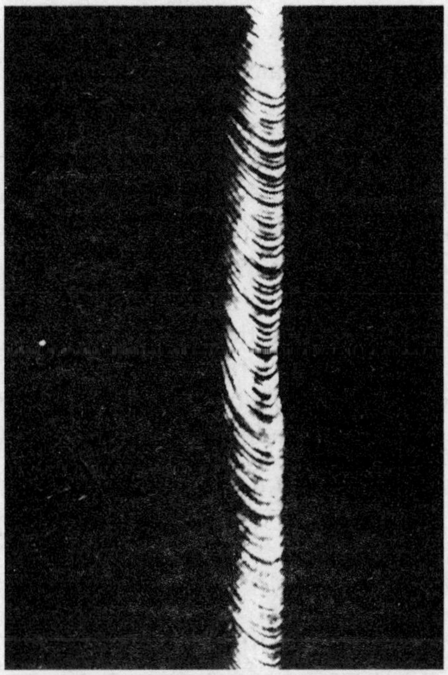

Figure 10.9 Slip in a zinc single crystal. (From C. F. Elam, *The Distortion of Metal Crystals,* Oxford University Press, London, 1935.)

dislocations along the same slip plane. On the surface of a polished single crystal specimen, these steps appear as lines, which are called *slip lines*. A zinc single crystal that has been plastically deformed to the degree that these slip markings are discernible is shown in Figure 10.9.

With continued extension of a single crystal, both the number of slip lines and the slip step width will increase. For FCC and BCC metals, slip may eventually begin along a second slip system, the system that is next most favorably oriented with the tensile axis. Furthermore, for HCP crystals having few slip systems, if the stress axis for the most favorable slip system is either perpendicular to the slip direction ($\lambda = 90°$) or parallel to the slip plane ($\phi = 90°$), the critical resolved shear stress will be zero. For these extreme orientations the crystal ordinarily fractures rather than deforming plastically.

Concept Check 10.2

Explain the difference between resolved shear stress and critical resolved shear stress.

[*The answer may be found in enclosed CD.*]

EXAMPLE PROBLEM 10.1

Resolved Shear Stress and Stress-to-Initiate-Yielding Computations

Consider a single crystal of BCC iron oriented such that a tensile stress is applied along a [010] direction.

(a) Compute the resolved shear stress along a (110) plane and in a $[\bar{1}11]$ direction when a tensile stress of 52 MPa is applied.

(b) If slip occurs on a (110) plane and in a $[\bar{1}11]$ direction, and the critical resolved shear stress is 30 MPa, calculate the magnitude of the applied tensile stress necessary to initiate yielding.

Solution

(a) A BCC unit cell along with the slip direction and plane as well as the direction of the applied stress are shown in the accompanying diagram. In order to solve this problem we must use Equation 10.2. However, it is first necessary to determine values for ϕ and λ, where, from the diagram below, ϕ is the angle between the normal to the (110) slip plane (i.e., the [110] direction) and the [010] direction, and λ represents the angle between $[\bar{1}11]$ and [010] directions. In general, for cubic unit cells, an angle θ between directions 1 and 2, represented by $[u_1v_1w_1]$ and $[u_2v_2w_2]$, respectively, is equal to

$$\theta = \cos^{-1}\left[\frac{u_1u_2 + v_1v_2 + w_1w_2}{\sqrt{(u_1^2 + v_1^2 + w_1^2)(u_2^2 + v_2^2 + w_2^2)}}\right] \tag{10.6}$$

For the determination of the value of ϕ, let $[u_1v_1w_1]$ = [110] and $[u_2v_2w_2]$ = [010] such that

$$\phi = \cos^{-1}\left\{\frac{(1)(0) + (1)(1) + (0)(0)}{\sqrt{[(1)^2 + (1)^2 + (0)^2][(0)^2 + (1)^2 + (0)^2]}}\right\}$$

$$= \cos^{-1}\left(\frac{1}{\sqrt{2}}\right) = 45°$$

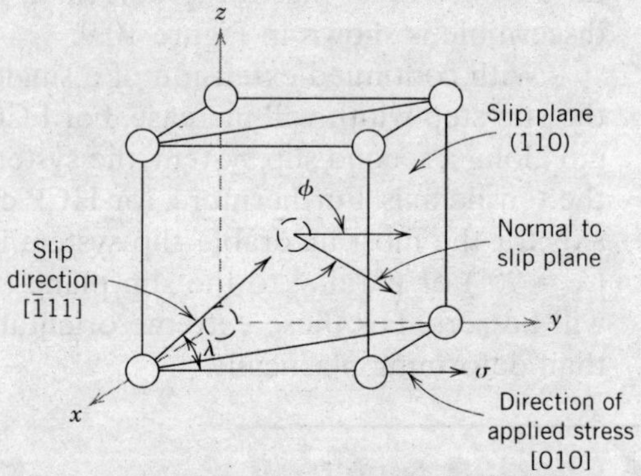

However, for λ, we take $[u_1v_1w_1] = [\bar{1}11]$ and $[u_2v_2w_2]$ = [010], and

$$\lambda = \cos^{-1}\left[\frac{(-1)(0) + (1)(1) + (1)(0)}{\sqrt{[(-1)^2 + (1)^2 + (1)^2][(0)^2 + (1)^2 + (0)^2]}}\right]$$

$$= \cos^{-1}\left(\frac{1}{\sqrt{3}}\right) = 54.7°$$

Thus, according to Equation 10.2,

$$\tau_R = \sigma \cos\phi \cos\lambda = (52\text{ MPa})(\cos 45°)(\cos 54.7°)$$

$$= (52\text{ MPa})\left(\frac{1}{\sqrt{2}}\right)\left(\frac{1}{\sqrt{3}}\right)$$

$$= 21.3\text{ MPa}$$

(b) The yield strength σ_y may be computed from Equation 10.4; ϕ and λ will be the same as for part (a), and

$$\sigma_y = \frac{30 \text{ MPa}}{(\cos 45°)(\cos 54.7°)} = 73.4 \text{ MPa}$$

10.6 PLASTIC DEFORMATION OF POLYCRYSTALLINE MATERIALS

Deformation and slip in polycrystalline materials is somewhat more complex. Because of the random crystallographic orientations of the numerous grains, the direction of slip varies from one grain to another. For each, dislocation motion occurs along the slip system that has the most favorable orientation, as defined above. This is exemplified by a photomicrograph of a polycrystalline copper specimen that has been plastically deformed (Figure 10.10); before deformation the surface was polished. Slip lines[1] are visible, and it appears that two slip systems operated for most of the grains, as evidenced by two sets of parallel yet intersecting sets of lines. Furthermore, variation in grain orientation is indicated by the difference in alignment of the slip lines for the several grains.

Gross plastic deformation of a polycrystalline specimen corresponds to the comparable distortion of the individual grains by means of slip. During deformation, mechanical integrity and coherency are maintained along the grain boundaries; that is, the grain boundaries usually do not come apart or open up. As a consequence, each individual grain is constrained, to some degree, in the shape it may assume by its neighboring grains. The manner in which grains distort as a result of gross plastic deformation is indicated in Figure 10.11. Before deformation the grains are equiaxed, or have approximately the same dimension in all directions. For this particular deformation, the grains become elongated along the direction in which the specimen was extended.

Polycrystalline metals are stronger than their single-crystal equivalents, which means that greater stresses are required to initiate slip and the attendant yielding. This is, to a large degree, also a result of geometrical constraints that are imposed on the grains during deformation. Even though a single grain may be favorably oriented with the applied stress for slip, it cannot deform until the adjacent and less favorably oriented grains are capable of slip also; this requires a higher applied stress level.

10.7 DEFORMATION BY TWINNING

In addition to slip, plastic deformation in some metallic materials can occur by the formation of mechanical twins, or *twinning*. The concept of a twin was introduced in Section 5.7; that is, a shear force can produce atomic displacements such that on one side of a plane (the twin boundary), atoms are located in mirror-image positions of atoms on the other side. The manner in which this is accomplished is demonstrated

[1] These slip lines are microscopic ledges produced by dislocations (Figure 10.1c) that have exited from a grain and appear as lines when viewed with a microscope. They are analogous to the macroscopic steps found on the surfaces of deformed single crystals (Figures 10.8 and 10.9).

Figure 10.10 Slip lines on the surface of a polycrystalline specimen of copper that was polished and subsequently deformed. 173×. [Photomicrograph courtesy of C. Brady, National Bureau of Standards (now the National Institute of Standards and Technology, Gaithersburg, MD).]

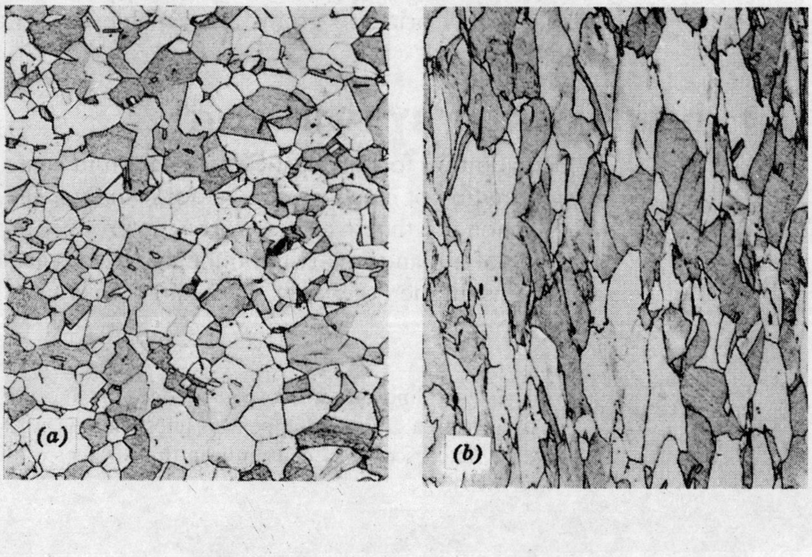

Figure 10.11 Alteration of the grain structure of a polycrystalline metal as a result of plastic deformation. (*a*) Before deformation the grains are equiaxed. (*b*) The deformation has produced elongated grains. 170×. (From W. G. Moffatt, G. W. Pearsall, and J. Wulff, *The Structure and Properties of Materials,* Vol. I, *Structure,* p. 140. Copyright © 1964 by John Wiley & Sons, New York. Reprinted by permission of John Wiley & Sons, Inc.)

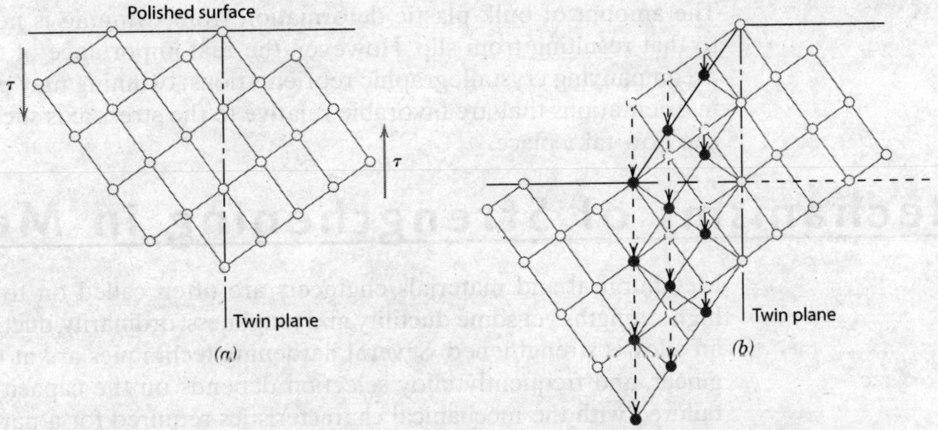

Figure 10.12 Schematic diagram showing how twinning results from an applied shear stress τ. In (*b*), open circles represent atoms that did not change position; dashed and solid circles represent original and final atom positions, respectively. (From G. E. Dieter, *Mechanical Metallurgy,* 3rd edition. Copyright © 1986 by McGraw-Hill Book Company, New York. Reproduced with permission of McGraw-Hill Book Company.)

in Figure 10.12. Here, open circles represent atoms that did not move, and dashed and solid circles represent original and final positions, respectively, of atoms within the twinned region. As may be noted in this figure, the displacement magnitude within the twin region (indicated by arrows) is proportional to the distance from the twin plane. Furthermore, twinning occurs on a definite crystallographic plane and in a specific direction that depend on crystal structure. For example, for BCC metals, the twin plane and direction are (112) and [111], respectively.

Slip and twinning deformations are compared in Figure 10.13 for a single crystal that is subjected to a shear stress τ. Slip ledges are shown in Figure 10.13*a*, the formation of which was described in Section 10.5; for twinning, the shear deformation is homogeneous (Figure 10.13*b*). These two processes differ from each other in several respects. First, for slip, the crystallographic orientation above and below the slip plane is the same both before and after the deformation; for twinning, there will be a reorientation across the twin plane. In addition, slip occurs in distinct atomic spacing multiples, whereas the atomic displacement for twinning is less than the interatomic separation.

Mechanical twinning occurs in metals that have BCC and HCP crystal structures, at low temperatures, and at high rates of loading (shock loading), conditions under which the slip process is restricted; that is, there are few operable slip systems.

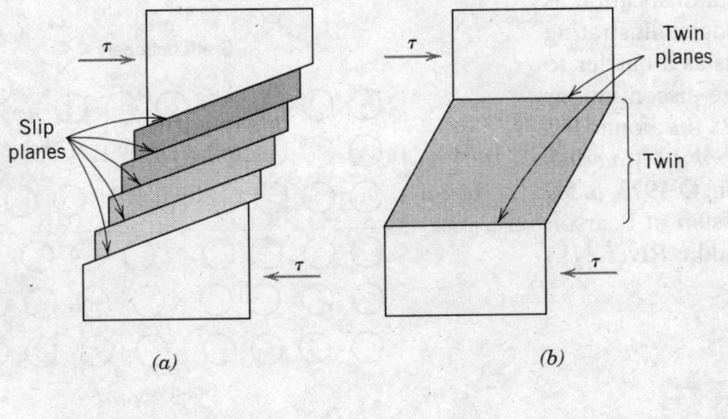

Figure 10.13 For a single crystal subjected to a shear stress τ, (*a*) deformation by slip; (*b*) deformation by twinning.

The amount of bulk plastic deformation from twinning is normally small relative to that resulting from slip. However, the real importance of twinning lies with the accompanying crystallographic reorientations; twinning may place new slip systems in orientations that are favorable relative to the stress axis such that the slip process can now take place.

Mechanisms of Strengthening in Metals

Metallurgical and materials engineers are often called on to design alloys having high strengths yet some ductility and toughness; ordinarily, ductility is sacrificed when an alloy is strengthened. Several hardening techniques are at the disposal of an engineer, and frequently alloy selection depends on the capacity of a material to be tailored with the mechanical characteristics required for a particular application.

Important to the understanding of strengthening mechanisms is the relation between dislocation motion and mechanical behavior of metals. Because macroscopic plastic deformation corresponds to the motion of large numbers of dislocations, *the ability of a metal to plastically deform depends on the ability of dislocations to move.* Since hardness and strength (both yield and tensile) are related to the ease with which plastic deformation can be made to occur, by reducing the mobility of dislocations, the mechanical strength may be enhanced; that is, greater mechanical forces will be required to initiate plastic deformation. In contrast, the more unconstrained the dislocation motion, the greater is the facility with which a metal may deform, and the softer and weaker it becomes. Virtually all strengthening techniques rely on this simple principle: *restricting or hindering dislocation motion renders a material harder and stronger.*

The present discussion is confined to strengthening mechanisms for single-phase metals, by grain size reduction, solid-solution alloying, and strain hardening. Deformation and strengthening of multiphase alloys are more complicated, involving concepts beyond the scope of the present discussion; Chapter 8 and Section 10.14 treat techniques that are used to strengthen multiphase alloys.

10.8 STRENGTHENING BY GRAIN SIZE REDUCTION

The size of the grains, or average grain diameter, in a polycrystalline metal influences the mechanical properties. Adjacent grains normally have different crystallographic orientations and, of course, a common grain boundary, as indicated in Figure 10.14. During plastic deformation, slip or dislocation motion must take place

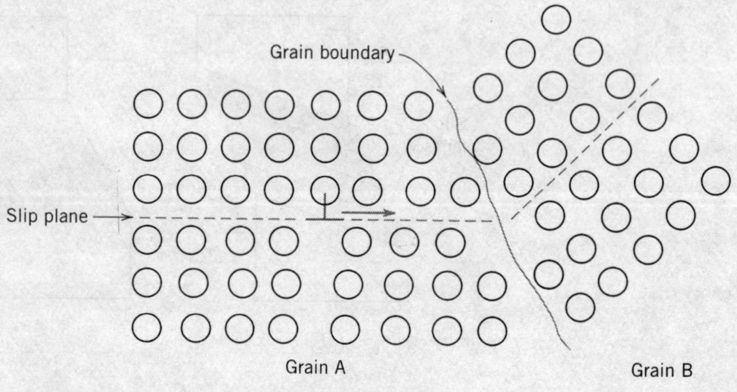

Figure 10.14 The motion of a dislocation as it encounters a grain boundary, illustrating how the boundary acts as a barrier to continued slip. Slip planes are discontinuous and change directions across the boundary. (From Van Vlack, *A Textbook of Materials Technology,* 1st edition, © 1973, p. 53. Adapted by permission of Pearson Education, Inc., Upper Saddle River, NJ.)

across this common boundary—say, from grain A to grain B in Figure 10.14. The grain boundary acts as a barrier to dislocation motion for two reasons:

1. Since the two grains are of different orientations, a dislocation passing into grain B will have to change its direction of motion; this becomes more difficult as the crystallographic misorientation increases.
2. The atomic disorder within a grain boundary region will result in a discontinuity of slip planes from one grain into the other.

It should be mentioned that, for high-angle grain boundaries, it may not be the case that dislocations traverse grain boundaries during deformation; rather, dislocations tend to "pile up" (or back up) at grain boundaries. These pile-ups introduce stress concentrations ahead of their slip planes, which generate new dislocations in adjacent grains.

A fine-grained material (one that has small grains) is harder and stronger than one that is coarse grained, since the former has a greater total grain boundary area to impede dislocation motion. For many materials, the yield strength σ_y varies with grain size according to

$$\sigma_y = \sigma_0 + k_y d^{-1/2} \tag{10.7}$$

In this expression, termed the *Hall-Petch equation, d* is the average grain diameter, and σ_0 and k_y are constants for a particular material. Note that Equation 10.7 is not valid for both very large (i.e., coarse) grain and extremely fine grain polycrystalline materials. Figure 10.15 demonstrates the yield strength dependence on grain size for a brass alloy. Grain size may be regulated by the rate of solidification from the liquid phase, and also by plastic deformation followed by an appropriate heat treatment, as discussed in Section 10.13.

It should also be mentioned that grain size reduction improves not only strength, but also the toughness of many alloys.

Small-angle grain boundaries (Section 5.7) are not effective in interfering with the slip process because of the slight crystallographic misalignment across the boundary. On the other hand, twin boundaries (Section 5.7) will effectively block slip and increase the strength of the material. Boundaries between two different

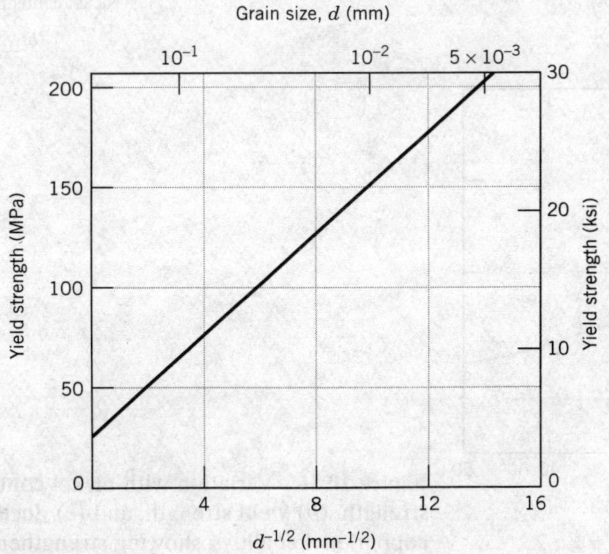

Figure 10.15 The influence of grain size on the yield strength of a 70 Cu–30 Zn brass alloy. Note that the grain diameter increases from right to left and is not linear. (Adapted from H. Suzuki, "The Relation Between the Structure and Mechanical Properties of Metals," Vol. II, *National Physical Laboratory, Symposium No. 15,* 1963, p. 524.)

phases are also impediments to movements of dislocations; this is important in the strengthening of more complex alloys. The sizes and shapes of the constituent phases significantly affect the mechanical properties of multiphase alloys; these are the topics of discussion in Sections 8.7, 8.8, and 15.1.

10.9 SOLID-SOLUTION STRENGTHENING

Another technique to strengthen and harden metals is alloying with impurity atoms that go into either substitutional or interstitial solid solution. Accordingly, this is called **solid-solution strengthening.** High-purity metals are almost always softer and weaker than alloys composed of the same base metal. Increasing the concentration of the impurity results in an attendant increase in tensile and yield strengths, as indicated in Figures 10.16*a* and 10.16*b* for nickel in copper; the dependence of ductility on nickel concentration is presented in Figure 10.16*c*.

Alloys are stronger than pure metals because impurity atoms that go into solid solution ordinarily impose lattice strains on the surrounding host atoms. Lattice strain field interactions between dislocations and these impurity atoms result, and, consequently, dislocation movement is restricted. For example, an impurity atom that is smaller than a host atom for which it substitutes exerts tensile strains on the surrounding crystal lattice, as illustrated in Figure 10.17*a*. Conversely, a larger substitutional atom imposes compressive strains in its vicinity (Figure 10.18*a*). These

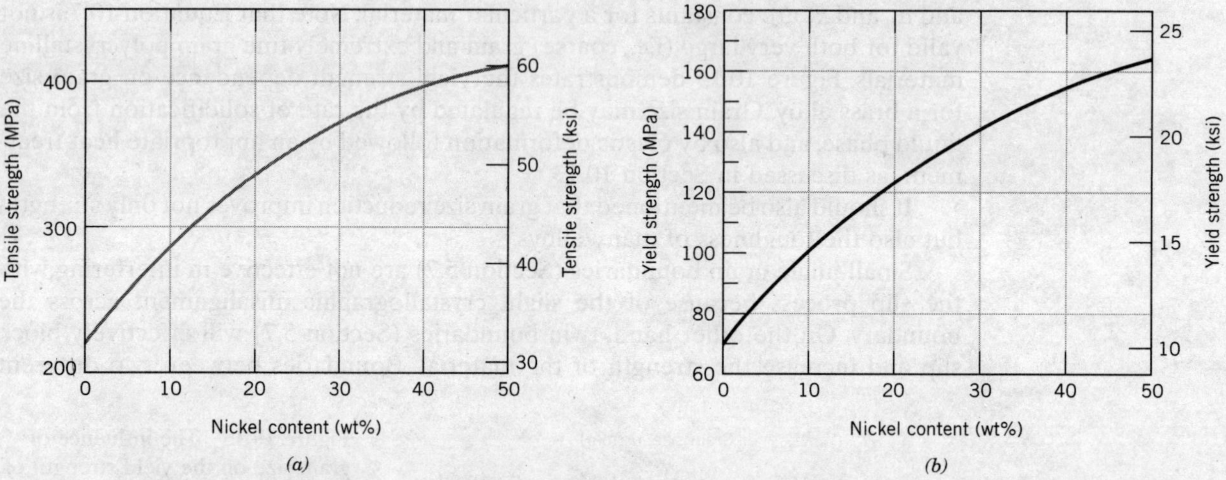

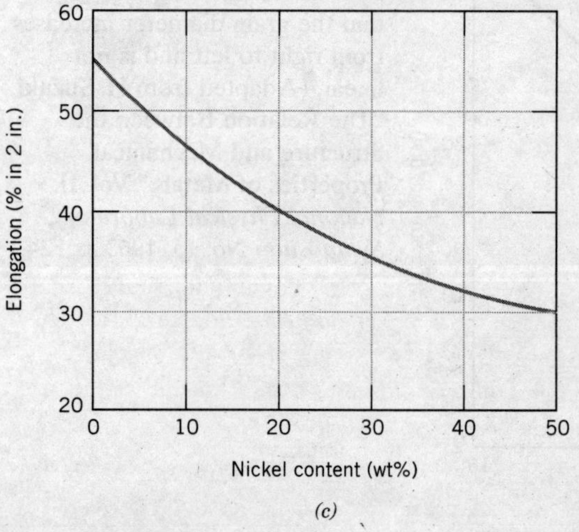

Figure 10.16 Variation with nickel content of (*a*) tensile strength, (*b*) yield strength, and (*c*) ductility (%EL) for copper–nickel alloys, showing strengthening.

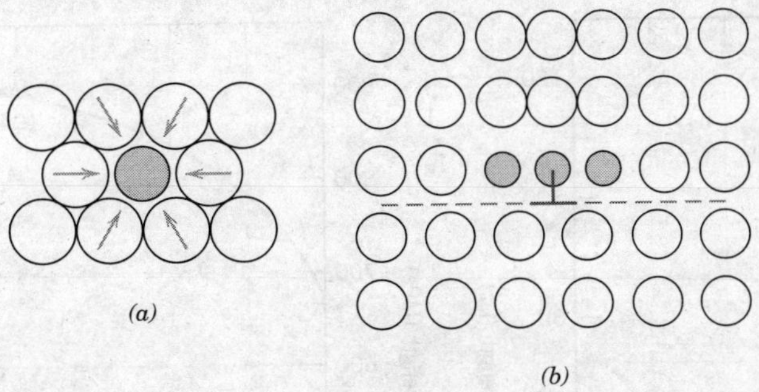

Figure 10.17 (*a*) Representation of tensile lattice strains imposed on host atoms by a smaller substitutional impurity atom. (*b*) Possible locations of smaller impurity atoms relative to an edge dislocation such that there is partial cancellation of impurity–dislocation lattice strains.

solute atoms tend to diffuse to and segregate around dislocations in a way so as to reduce the overall strain energy—that is, to cancel some of the strain in the lattice surrounding a dislocation. To accomplish this, a smaller impurity atom is located where its tensile strain will partially nullify some of the dislocation's compressive strain. For the edge dislocation in Figure 10.17*b*, this would be adjacent to the dislocation line and above the slip plane. A larger impurity atom would be situated as in Figure 10.18*b*.

The resistance to slip is greater when impurity atoms are present because the overall lattice strain must increase if a dislocation is torn away from them. Furthermore, the same lattice strain interactions (Figures 10.17*b* and 10.18*b*) will exist between impurity atoms and dislocations that are in motion during plastic deformation. Thus, a greater applied stress is necessary to first initiate and then continue plastic deformation for solid-solution alloys, as opposed to pure metals; this is evidenced by the enhancement of strength and hardness.

10.10 STRAIN HARDENING

Strain hardening is the phenomenon whereby a ductile metal becomes harder and stronger as it is plastically deformed. Sometimes it is also called *work hardening*, or, because the temperature at which deformation takes place is "cold" relative to the absolute melting temperature of the metal, **cold working.** Most metals strain harden at room temperature.

It is sometimes convenient to express the degree of plastic deformation as *percent cold work* rather than as strain. Percent cold work (%CW) is defined as

$$\%\,\mathrm{CW} = \left(\frac{A_0 - A_d}{A_0}\right) \times 100 \tag{10.8}$$

where A_0 is the original area of the cross section that experiences deformation, and A_d is the area after deformation.

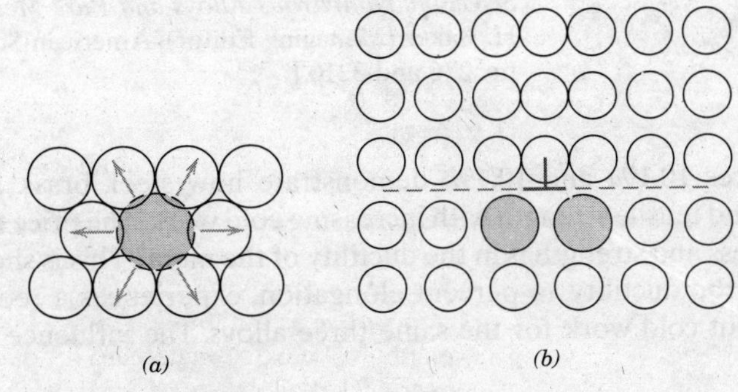

Figure 10.18 (*a*) Representation of compressive strains imposed on host atoms by a larger substitutional impurity atom. (*b*) Possible locations of larger impurity atoms relative to an edge dislocation such that there is partial cancellation of impurity–dislocation lattice strains.

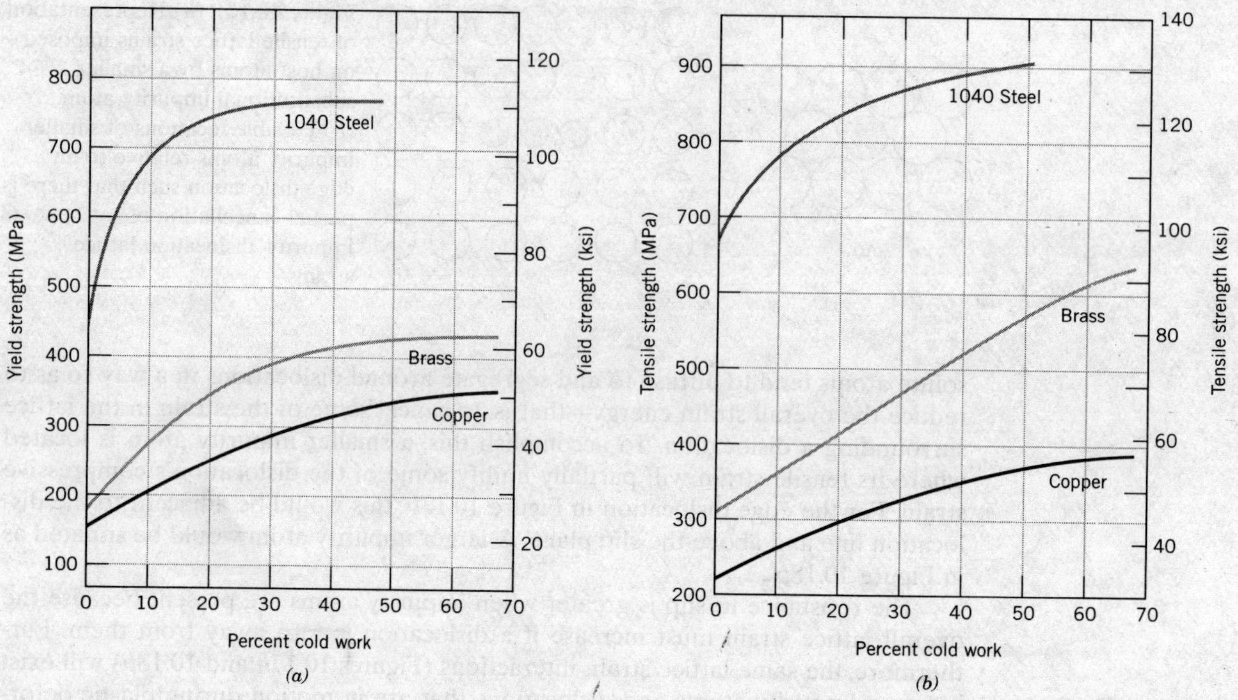

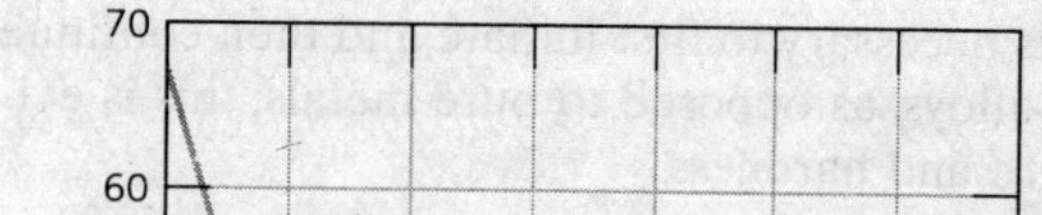

Figure 10.19 For 1040 steel, brass, and copper, (*a*) the increase in yield strength, (*b*) the increase in tensile strength, and (*c*) the decrease in ductility (%EL) with percent cold work. [Adapted from *Metals Handbook: Properties and Selection: Irons and Steels,* Vol. 1, 9th edition, B. Bardes (Editor), American Society for Metals, 1978, p. 226; and *Metals Handbook: Properties and Selection: Nonferrous Alloys and Pure Metals,* Vol. 2, 9th edition, H. Baker (Managing Editor), American Society for Metals, 1979, pp. 276 and 3210.]

Figures 10.19*a* and 10.19*b* demonstrate how steel, brass, and copper increase in yield and tensile strength with increasing cold work. The price for this enhancement of hardness and strength is in the ductility of the metal. This is shown in Figure 10.19*c*, in which the ductility, in percent elongation, experiences a reduction with increasing percent cold work for the same three alloys. The influence of cold work on the

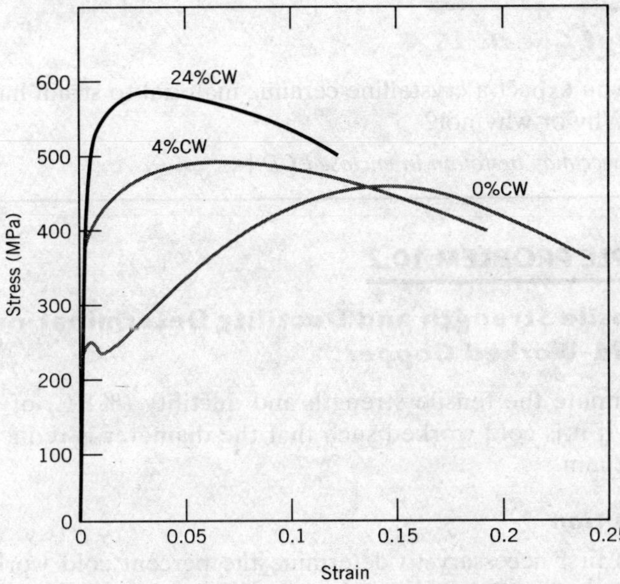

Figure 10.20 The influence of cold work on the stress–strain behavior of a low-carbon steel; curves are shown for 0% CW, 4% CW, and 24% CW.

stress–strain behavior of a low-carbon steel is shown in Figure 10.20; here stress–strain curves are plotted at 0% CW, 4% CW, and 24% CW.

Strain hardening is demonstrated in a stress–strain diagram presented earlier (Figure 9.23). Initially, the metal with yield strength σ_{y_0} is plastically deformed to point D. The stress is released, then reapplied with a resultant new yield strength, σ_{y_i}. The metal has thus become stronger during the process because σ_{y_i} is greater than σ_{y_0}.

The strain-hardening phenomenon is explained on the basis of dislocation–dislocation strain field interactions similar to those discussed in Section 10.3. The dislocation density in a metal increases with deformation or cold work, due to dislocation multiplication or the formation of new dislocations, as noted previously. Consequently, the average distance of separation between dislocations decreases—the dislocations are positioned closer together. On the average, dislocation–dislocation strain interactions are repulsive. The net result is that the motion of a dislocation is hindered by the presence of other dislocations. As the dislocation density increases, this resistance to dislocation motion by other dislocations becomes more pronounced. Thus, the imposed stress necessary to deform a metal increases with increasing cold work.

Strain hardening is often utilized commercially to enhance the mechanical properties of metals during fabrication procedures. The effects of strain hardening may be removed by an annealing heat treatment, as discussed in Section 9.4.

In passing, for the mathematical expression relating true stress and strain, Equation 9.25, the parameter n is called the *strain-hardening exponent,* which is a measure of the ability of a metal to strain harden; the larger its magnitude, the greater the strain hardening for a given amount of plastic strain.

Concept Check 10.3

When making hardness measurements, what will be the effect of making an indentation very close to a preexisting indentation? Why?

[*The answer may be found in enclosed CD.*]

Concept Check 10.4

Would you expect a crystalline ceramic material to strain harden at room temperature? Why or why not?

[*The answer may be found in enclosed CD.*]

EXAMPLE PROBLEM 10.2

Tensile Strength and Ductility Determinations for Cold-Worked Copper

Compute the tensile strength and ductility (%EL) of a cylindrical copper rod if it is cold worked such that the diameter is reduced from 15.2 mm to 12.2 mm.

Solution

It is first necessary to determine the percent cold work resulting from the deformation. This is possible using Equation 10.8:

$$\%\,\text{CW} = \frac{\left(\dfrac{15.2\ \text{mm}}{2}\right)^2 \pi - \left(\dfrac{12.2\ \text{mm}}{2}\right)^2 \pi}{\left(\dfrac{15.2\ \text{mm}}{2}\right)^2 \pi} \times 100 = 35.6\%$$

The tensile strength is read directly from the curve for copper (Figure 10.19*b*) as 340 MPa. From Figure 10.19*c*, the ductility at 35.6%CW is about 7%EL.

In summary, we have just discussed the three mechanisms that may be used to strengthen and harden single-phase metal alloys: strengthening by grain size reduction, solid-solution strengthening, and strain hardening. Of course they may be used in conjunction with one another; for example, a solid-solution strengthened alloy may also be strain hardened.

It should also be noted that the strengthening effects due to grain size reduction and strain hardening can be eliminated or at least reduced by an elevated-temperature heat treatment (Sections 10.12 and 10.13). Conversely, solid-solution strengthening is unaffected by heat treatment.

Recovery, Recrystallization, and Grain Growth

As outlined in the preceding paragraphs of this chapter, plastically deforming a polycrystalline metal specimen at temperatures that are low relative to its absolute melting temperature produces microstructural and property changes that include (1) a change in grain shape (Section 10.6), (2) strain hardening (Section 10.10), and (3) an increase in dislocation density (Section 10.3). Some fraction of the energy expended in deformation is stored in the metal as strain energy, which is associated with tensile, compressive, and shear zones around the newly created dislocations (Section 10.3).

Furthermore, other properties such as electrical conductivity (Section 17.8) and corrosion resistance may be modified as a consequence of plastic deformation.

These properties and structures may revert back to the precold-worked states by appropriate heat treatment (sometimes termed an annealing treatment). Such restoration results from two different processes that occur at elevated temperatures: *recovery* and *recrystallization,* which may be followed by *grain growth.*

10.11 RECOVERY

During **recovery,** some of the stored internal strain energy is relieved by virtue of dislocation motion (in the absence of an externally applied stress), as a result of enhanced atomic diffusion at the elevated temperature. There is some reduction in the number of dislocations, and dislocation configurations (similar to that shown in Figure 5.12) are produced having low strain energies. In addition, physical properties such as electrical and thermal conductivities and the like are recovered to their precold-worked states.

10.12 RECRYSTALLIZATION

Even after recovery is complete, the grains are still in a relatively high strain energy state. **Recrystallization** is the formation of a new set of strain-free and equiaxed grains (i.e., having approximately equal dimensions in all directions) that have low dislocation densities and are characteristic of the precold-worked condition. The driving force to produce this new grain structure is the difference in internal energy between the strained and unstrained material. The new grains form as very small nuclei and grow until they completely consume the parent material, processes that involve short-range diffusion. Several stages in the recrystallization process are represented in Figures 10.21*a* to 10.21*d*; in these photomicrographs, the small

(*a*) (*b*)

Figure 10.21 Photomicrographs showing several stages of the recrystallization and grain growth of brass. (*a*) Cold-worked (33% CW) grain structure. (*b*) Initial stage of recrystallization after heating 3 s at 580°C (1075°F); the very small grains are those that have recrystallized. (*c*) Partial replacement of cold-worked grains by recrystallized ones (4 s at 580°C). (*d*) Complete recrystallization (8 s at 580°C). (*e*) Grain growth after 15 min at 580°C. (*f*) Grain growth after 10 min at 700°C (1290°F). All photomicrographs 75×. (Photomicrographs courtesy of J. E. Burke, General Electric Company.)

(c) (d) (e) (f)

Figure 10.21 (*continued*)

speckled grains are those that have recrystallized. Thus, recrystallization of cold-worked metals may be used to refine the grain structure.

Also, during recrystallization, the mechanical properties that were changed as a result of cold working are restored to their precold-worked values; that is, the metal becomes softer, weaker, yet more ductile. Some heat treatments are designed to allow recrystallization to occur with these modifications in the mechanical characteristics (Section 9.4).

Recrystallization is a process the extent of which depends on both time and temperature. The degree (or fraction) of recrystallization increases with time, as may be noted in the photomicrographs shown in Figures 10.21*a–d*. The explicit

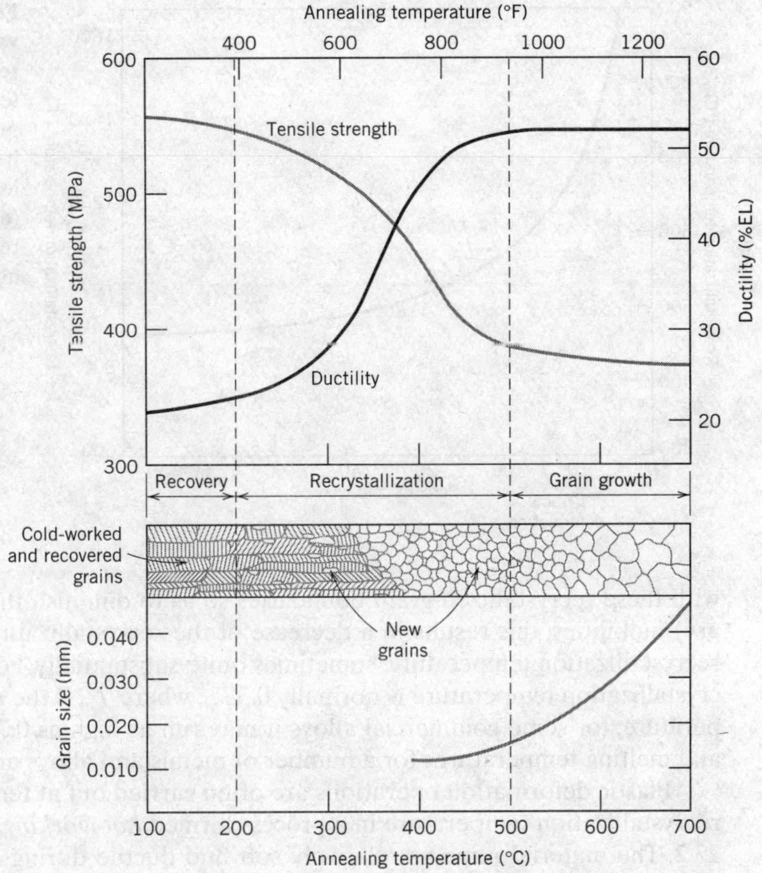

Figure 10.22 The influence of annealing temperature (for an annealing time of 1 h) on the tensile strength and ductility of a brass alloy. Grain size as a function of annealing temperature is indicated. Grain structures during recovery, recrystallization, and grain growth stages are shown schematically. (Adapted from G. Sachs and K. R. Van Horn, *Practical Metallurgy, Applied Metallurgy and the Industrial Processing of Ferrous and Nonferrous Metals and Alloys,* American Society for Metals, 1940, p. 139.)

time dependence of recrystallization is addressed in more detail near the end of Section 8.3.

The influence of temperature is demonstrated in Figure 10.22, which plots tensile strength and ductility (at room temperature) of a brass alloy as a function of the temperature and for a constant heat treatment time of 1 h. The grain structures found at the various stages of the process are also presented schematically.

The recrystallization behavior of a particular metal alloy is sometimes specified in terms of a **recrystallization temperature,** the temperature at which recrystallization just reaches completion in 1 h. Thus, the recrystallization temperature for the brass alloy of Figure 10.22 is about 450°C (850°F). Typically, it is between one-third and one-half of the absolute melting temperature of a metal or alloy and depends on several factors, including the amount of prior cold work and the purity of the alloy. Increasing the percentage of cold work enhances the rate of recrystallization, with the result that the recrystallization temperature is lowered, and approaches a constant or limiting value at high deformations; this effect is shown in Figure 10.23. Furthermore, it is this limiting or minimum recrystallization temperature that is normally specified in the literature. There exists some critical degree of cold work below which recrystallization cannot be made to occur, as shown in the figure; normally, this is between 2% and 20% cold work.

Recrystallization proceeds more rapidly in pure metals than in alloys. During recrystallization, grain-boundary motion occurs as the new grain nuclei form and then grow. It is believed that impurity atoms preferentially segregate at and interact

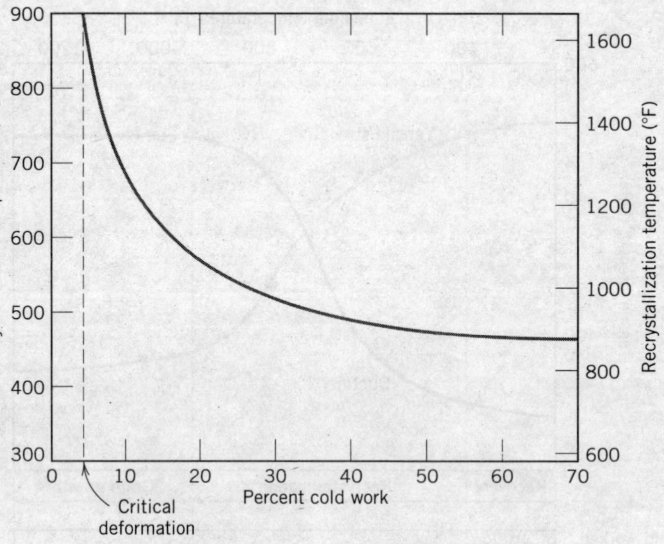

Figure 10.23 The variation of recrystallization temperature with percent cold work for iron. For deformations less than the critical (about 5% CW), recrystallization will not occur.

with these recrystallized grain boundaries so as to diminish their (i.e., grain boundary) mobilities; this results in a decrease of the recrystallization rate and raises the recrystallization temperature, sometimes quite substantially. For pure metals, the recrystallization temperature is normally $0.3T_m$, where T_m is the absolute melting temperature; for some commercial alloys it may run as high as $0.7T_m$. Recrystallization and melting temperatures for a number of metals and alloys are listed in Table 10.2.

Plastic deformation operations are often carried out at temperatures above the recrystallization temperature in a process termed *hot working,* described in Section 23.2. The material remains relatively soft and ductile during deformation because it does not strain harden, and thus large deformations are possible.

Concept Check 10.5

Briefly explain why some metals (i.e., lead and tin) do not strain harden when deformed at room temperature.

[*The answer may be found in enclosed CD.*]

Table 10.2 Recrystallization and Melting Temperatures for Various Metals and Alloys

Metal	*Recrystallization Temperature (°C)*	*Melting Temperature (°C)*
Lead	−4	327
Tin	−4	232
Zinc	10	420
Aluminum (99.999 wt%)	80	660
Copper (99.999 wt%)	120	1085
Brass (60 Cu–40 Zn)	475	900
Nickel (99.99 wt%)	370	1455
Iron	450	1538
Tungsten	1200	3410

Concept Check 10.6

Would you expect it to be possible for ceramic materials to experience recrystallization? Why or why not?

[*The answer may be found in enclosed CD.*]

DESIGN EXAMPLE 10.1

Description of Diameter Reduction Procedure

A cylindrical rod of noncold-worked brass having an initial diameter of 6.4 mm is to be cold worked by drawing such that the cross-sectional area is reduced. It is required to have a cold-worked yield strength of at least 345 MPa and a ductility in excess of 20%EL; in addition, a final diameter of 5.1 mm is necessary. Describe the manner in which this procedure may be carried out.

Solution

Let us first consider the consequences (in terms of yield strength and ductility) of cold working in which the brass specimen diameter is reduced from 6.4 mm (designated by d_0) to 5.1 mm (d_i). The %CW may be computed from Equation 10.8 as

$$\%\text{CW} = \frac{\left(\dfrac{d_0}{2}\right)^2 \pi - \left(\dfrac{d_i}{2}\right)^2 \pi}{\left(\dfrac{d_0}{2}\right)^2 \pi} \times 100$$

$$= \frac{\left(\dfrac{6.4 \text{ mm}}{2}\right)^2 \pi - \left(\dfrac{5.1 \text{ mm}}{2}\right)^2 \pi}{\left(\dfrac{6.4 \text{ mm}}{2}\right)^2 \pi} \times 100 = 36.5\%\text{CW}$$

From Figures 10.19*a* and 10.19*c*, a yield strength of 410 MPa and a ductility of 8%EL are attained from this deformation. According to the stipulated criteria, the yield strength is satisfactory; however, the ductility is too low.

Another processing alternative is a partial diameter reduction, followed by a recrystallization heat treatment in which the effects of the cold work are nullified. The required yield strength, ductility, and diameter are achieved through a second drawing step.

Again, reference to Figure 10.19*a* indicates that 20%CW is required to give a yield strength of 345 MPa. On the other hand, from Figure 10.19*c*, ductilities greater than 20%EL are possible only for deformations of 23%CW or less. Thus during the final drawing operation, deformation must be between 20%CW and 23%CW. Let's take the average of these extremes, 21.5%CW, and then calculate the final diameter for the first drawing d'_0, which becomes the original diameter for the second drawing. Again, using Equation 10.8,

$$21.5\%\text{CW} = \frac{\left(\dfrac{d'_0}{2}\right)^2 \pi - \left(\dfrac{5.1 \text{ mm}}{2}\right)^2 \pi}{\left(\dfrac{d'_0}{2}\right)^2 \pi} \times 100$$

Now, solving for d'_0 from the expression above gives

$$d'_0 = 5.8 \text{ mm}$$

10.13 GRAIN GROWTH

After recrystallization is complete, the strain-free grains will continue to grow if the metal specimen is left at the elevated temperature (Figures 10.21*d–f*); this phenomenon is called **grain growth.** Grain growth does not need to be preceded by recovery and recrystallization; it may occur in all polycrystalline materials, metals and ceramics alike.

An energy is associated with grain boundaries, as explained in Section 5.7. As grains increase in size, the total boundary area decreases, yielding an attendant reduction in the total energy; this is the driving force for grain growth.

Grain growth occurs by the migration of grain boundaries. Obviously, not all grains can enlarge, but large ones grow at the expense of small ones that shrink. Thus, the average grain size increases with time, and at any particular instant there will exist a range of grain sizes. Boundary motion is just the short-range diffusion of atoms from one side of the boundary to the other. The directions of boundary movement and atomic motion are opposite to each other, as shown in Figure 10.24.

For many polycrystalline materials, the grain diameter d varies with time t according to the relationship

$$d^n - d_0^n = Kt \tag{10.9}$$

where d_0 is the initial grain diameter at $t = 0$, and K and n are time-independent constants; the value of n is generally equal to or greater than 2.

The dependence of grain size on time and temperature is demonstrated in Figure 10.25, a plot of the logarithm of grain size as a function of the logarithm of time for a brass alloy at several temperatures. At lower temperatures the curves are linear. Furthermore, grain growth proceeds more rapidly as temperature increases; that is, the curves are displaced upward to larger grain sizes. This is explained by the enhancement of diffusion rate with rising temperature.

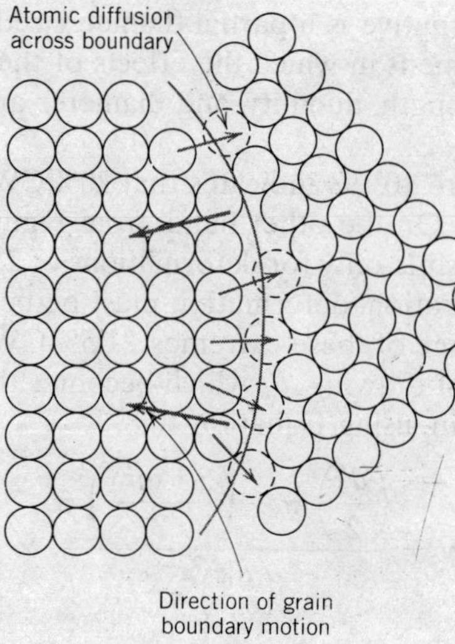

Figure 10.24 Schematic representation of grain growth via atomic diffusion. (From Van Vlack, Lawrence H., *Elements of Materials Science and Engineering*, © 1989, p. 221. Adapted by permission of Pearson Education, Inc., Upper Saddle River, NJ.)

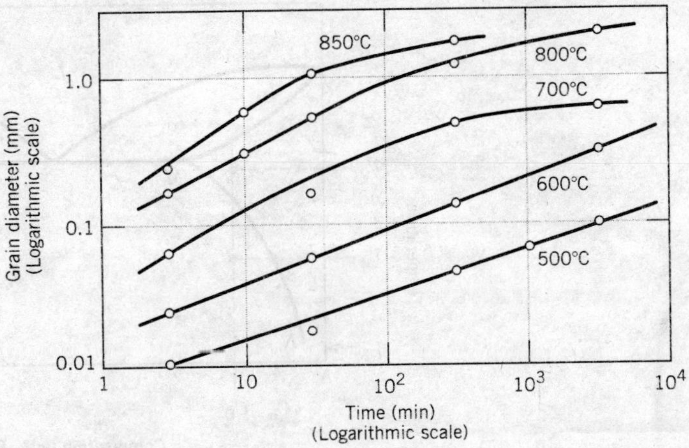

Figure 10.25 The logarithm of grain diameter versus the logarithm of time for grain growth in brass at several temperatures. (From J. E. Burke, "Some Factors Affecting the Rate of Grain Growth in Metals." Reprinted with permission from *Metallurgical Transactions,* Vol. 180, 1949, a publication of The Metallurgical Society of AIME, Warrendale, Pennsylvania.)

The mechanical properties at room temperature of a fine-grained metal are usually superior (i.e., higher strength and toughness) to those of coarse-grained ones. If the grain structure of a single-phase alloy is coarser than that desired, refinement may be accomplished by plastically deforming the material, then subjecting it to a recrystallization heat treatment, as described above.

10.14 PRECIPITATION HARDENING

The strength and hardness of some metal alloys may be enhanced by the formation of extremely small uniformly dispersed particles of a second phase within the original phase matrix; this must be accomplished by phase transformations that are induced by appropriate heat treatments. The process is called **precipitation hardening** because the small particles of the new phase are termed "precipitates." "Age hardening" is also used to designate this procedure because the strength develops with time, or as the alloy ages. Examples of alloys that are hardened by precipitation treatments include aluminum–copper, copper–beryllium, copper–tin, and magnesium–aluminum; some ferrous alloys are also precipitation hardenable.

Precipitation hardening and the treating of steel to form tempered martensite are totally different phenomena, even though the heat treatment procedures are similar; therefore, the processes should not be confused. The principal difference lies in the mechanisms by which hardening and strengthening are achieved. These should become apparent as precipitation hardening is explained.

Heat Treatments

Inasmuch as precipitation hardening results from the development of particles of a new phase, an explanation of the heat treatment procedure is facilitated by use of a phase diagram. Even though, in practice, many precipitation-hardenable alloys contain two or more alloying elements, the discussion is simplified by reference to a binary system. The phase diagram must be of the form shown for the hypothetical A–B system in Figure 10.26.

Two requisite features must be displayed by the phase diagrams of alloy systems for precipitation hardening: an appreciable maximum solubility of one component in the other, on the order of several percent; and a solubility limit that rapidly decreases in concentration of the major component with temperature reduction. Both these conditions are satisfied by this hypothetical phase diagram (Figure 10.26). The maximum solubility corresponds to the composition at point *M*. In

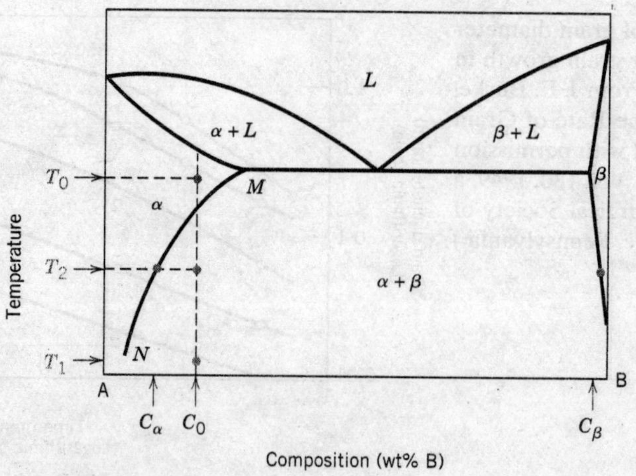

Figure 10.26 Hypothetical phase diagram for a precipitation-hardenable alloy of composition C_0.

addition, the solubility limit boundary between the α and $\alpha + \beta$ phase fields diminishes from this maximum concentration to a very low B content in A at point N. Furthermore, the composition of a precipitation-hardenable alloy must be less than the maximum solubility. These conditions are necessary but *not* sufficient for precipitation hardening to occur in an alloy system. An additional requirement is discussed below.

Solution Heat Treating

Precipitation hardening is accomplished by two different heat treatments. The first is a **solution heat treatment** in which all solute atoms are dissolved to form a single-phase solid solution. Consider an alloy of composition C_0 in Figure 10.26. The treatment consists of heating the alloy to a temperature within the α phase field—say, T_0—and waiting until all the β phase that may have been present is completely dissolved. At this point, the alloy consists only of an α phase of composition C_0. This procedure is followed by rapid cooling or quenching to temperature T_1, which for many alloys is room temperature, to the extent that any diffusion and the accompanying formation of any of the β phase are prevented. Thus, a nonequilibrium situation exists in which only the α-phase solid solution supersaturated with B atoms is present at T_1; in this state the alloy is relatively soft and weak. Furthermore, for most alloys diffusion rates at T_1 are extremely slow, such that the single α phase is retained at this temperature for relatively long periods.

Precipitation Heat Treating

For the second or **precipitation heat treatment,** the supersaturated α solid solution is ordinarily heated to an intermediate temperature T_2 (Figure 10.26) within the $\alpha + \beta$ two-phase region, at which temperature diffusion rates become appreciable. The β precipitate phase begins to form as finely dispersed particles of composition C_β, which process is sometimes termed "aging." After the appropriate aging time at T_2, the alloy is cooled to room temperature; normally, this cooling rate is not an important consideration. Both solution and precipitation heat treatments are represented on the temperature-versus-time plot, Figure 10.27. The character of these β particles, and subsequently the strength and hardness of the alloy, depend on both the precipitation temperature T_2 and the aging time at this temperature. For some alloys, aging occurs spontaneously at room temperature over extended time periods.

The dependence of the growth of the precipitate β particles on time and temperature under isothermal heat treatment conditions may be represented by

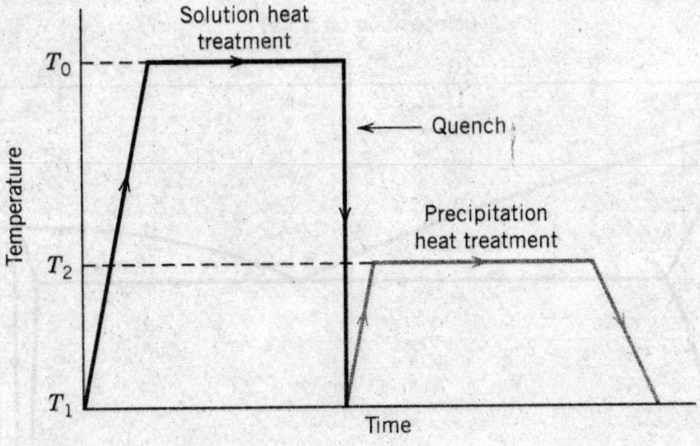

Figure 10.27 Schematic temperature-versus-time plot showing both solution and precipitation heat treatments for precipitation hardening.

C-shaped curves similar to those in Figure 8.18 for the eutectoid transformation in steels. However, it is more useful and convenient to present the data as tensile strength, yield strength, or hardness at room temperature as a function of the logarithm of aging time, at constant temperature T_2. The behavior for a typical precipitation-hardenable alloy is represented schematically in Figure 10.28. With increasing time, the strength or hardness increases, reaches a maximum, and finally diminishes. This reduction in strength and hardness that occurs after long time periods is known as **overaging.** The influence of temperature is incorporated by the superposition, on a single plot, of curves at a variety of temperatures.

Mechanism of Hardening

Precipitation hardening is commonly employed with high-strength aluminum alloys. Although a large number of these alloys have different proportions and combinations of alloying elements, the mechanism of hardening has perhaps been studied most extensively for the aluminum–copper alloys. Figure 10.29 presents the aluminum-rich portion of the aluminum–copper phase diagram. The α phase is a substitutional solid solution of copper in aluminum, whereas the intermetallic compound $CuAl_2$ is designated the θ phase. For an aluminum–copper alloy of, say, composition 96 wt% Al–4 wt% Cu, in the development of this equilibrium θ phase during the precipitation heat treatment, several transition phases are first formed in a specific sequence. The mechanical properties are influenced by the character of the particles of these transition phases. During the initial hardening stage (at short times, Figure 10.28), copper atoms cluster together in very small and thin discs that are only one or two atoms thick and approximately 25 atoms in diameter; these form at countless positions within the α phase. The clusters, sometimes called zones, are so small that they are really not regarded as distinct precipitate particles. However, with time and the subsequent diffusion of copper atoms, zones become

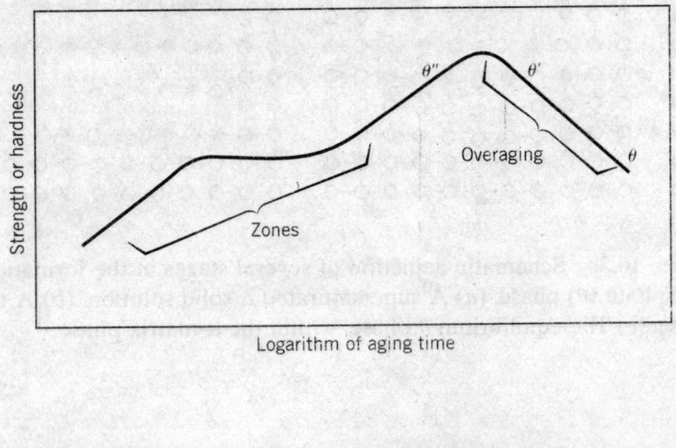

Figure 10.28 Schematic diagram showing strength and hardness as a function of the logarithm of aging time at constant temperature during the precipitation heat treatment.

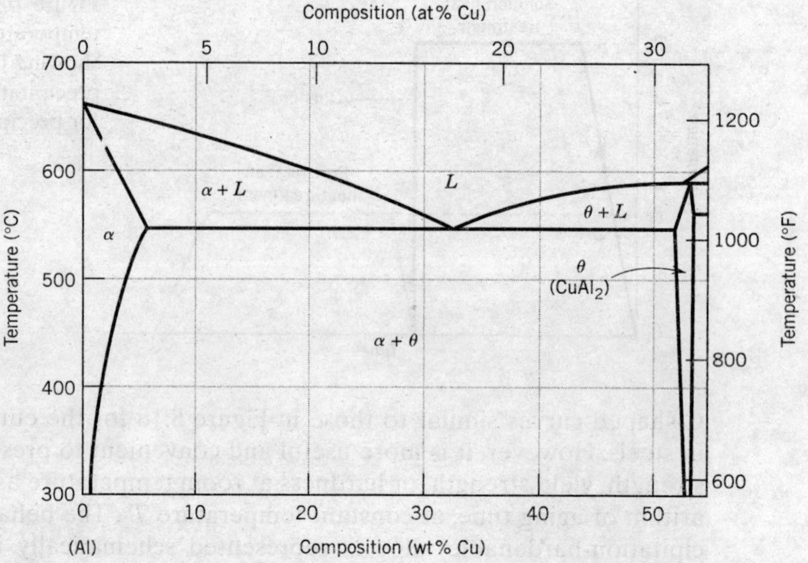

Figure 10.29 The aluminum-rich side of the aluminum–copper phase diagram. (Adapted from J. L. Murray, *International Metals Review*, **30**, 5, 1985. Reprinted by permission of ASM International.)

particles as they increase in size. These precipitate particles then pass through two transition phases (denoted as θ'' and θ'), before the formation of the equilibrium θ phase (Figure 10.30*c*). Transition phase particles for a precipitation-hardened 7150 aluminum alloy are shown in the electron micrograph of Figure 10.31.

The strengthening and hardening effects shown in Figure 10.28 result from the innumerable particles of these transition and metastable phases. As noted in the figure, maximum strength coincides with the formation of the θ'' phase, which may be preserved upon cooling the alloy to room temperature. Overaging results from continued particle growth and the development of θ' and θ phases.

The strengthening process is accelerated as the temperature is increased. This is demonstrated in Figure 10.32*a*, a plot of yield strength versus the logarithm of time for a 2014 aluminum alloy at several different precipitation temperatures. Ideally, temperature and time for the precipitation heat treatment should be designed to produce a hardness or strength in the vicinity of the maximum. Associated with an increase in strength is a reduction in ductility, which is demonstrated in Figure 10.32*b* for the same 2014 aluminum alloy at the several temperatures.

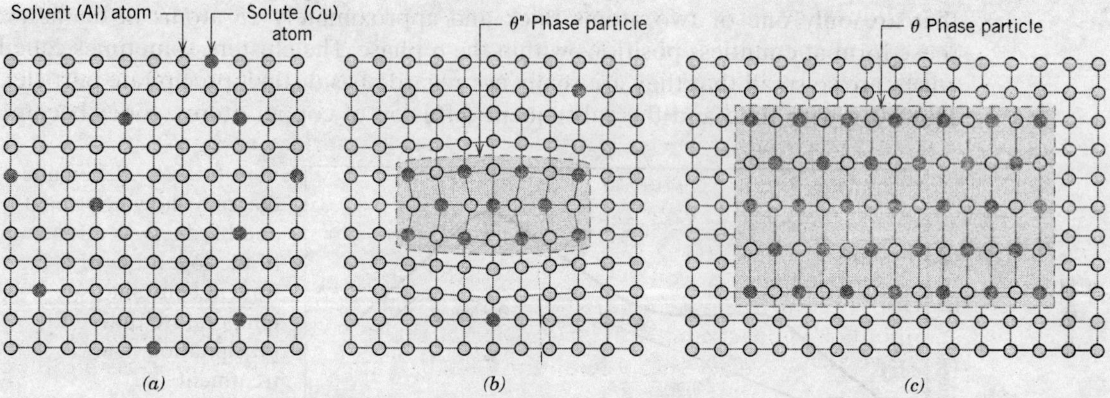

Figure 10.30 Schematic depiction of several stages in the formation of the equilibrium precipitate (θ) phase. (*a*) A supersaturated α solid solution. (*b*) A transition, θ'', precipitate phase. (*c*) The equilibrium θ phase, within the α-matrix phase.

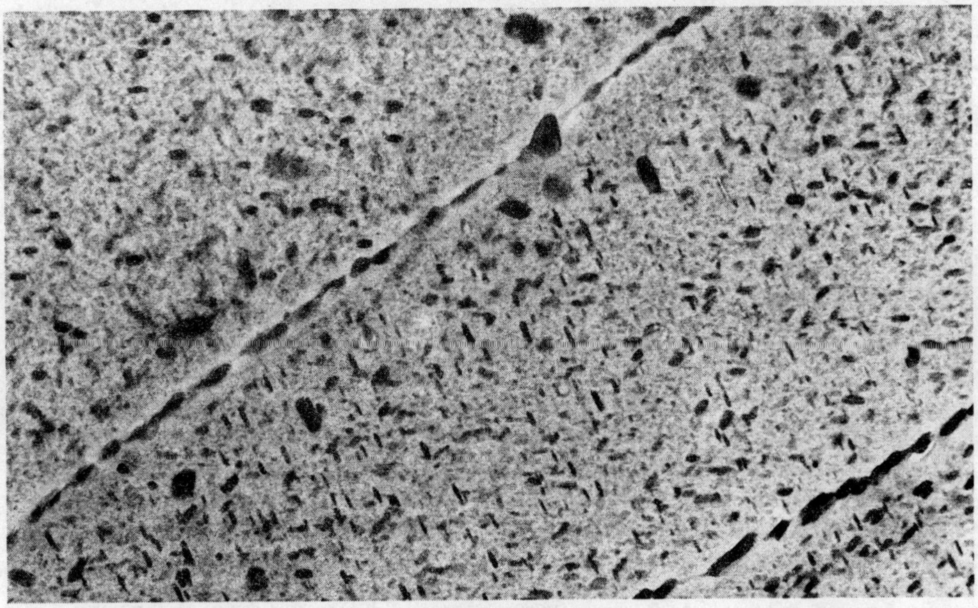

Figure 10.31 A transmission electron micrograph showing the microstructure of a 7150-T651 aluminum alloy (6.2Zn, 2.3Cu, 2.3Mg, 0.12Zr, the balance Al) that has been precipitation hardened. The light matrix phase in the micrograph is an aluminum solid solution. The majority of the small plate-shaped dark precipitate particles are a transition η' phase, the remainder being the equilibrium η ($MgZn_2$) phase. Note that grain boundaries are "decorated" by some of these particles. 90,000×. (Courtesy of G. H. Narayanan and A. G. Miller, Boeing Commercial Airplane Company.)

Not all alloys that satisfy the aforementioned conditions relative to composition and phase diagram configuration are amenable to precipitation hardening. In addition, lattice strains must be established at the precipitate–matrix interface. For aluminum–copper alloys, there is a distortion of the crystal lattice structure around and within the vicinity of particles of these transition phases (Figure 10.30*b*). During plastic deformation, dislocation motions are effectively impeded as a result of these distortions, and, consequently, the alloy becomes harder and stronger. As the θ phase forms, the resultant overaging (softening and weakening) is explained by a reduction in the resistance to slip that is offered by these precipitate particles.

Alloys that experience appreciable precipitation hardening at room temperature and after relatively short time periods must be quenched to and stored under refrigerated conditions. Several aluminum alloys that are used for rivets exhibit this behavior. They are driven while still soft, then allowed to age harden at the normal ambient temperature. This is termed **natural aging; artificial aging** is carried out at elevated temperatures.

Concept Check 10.7

Is it possible to produce a precipitation hardened 2014 aluminum alloy having a minimum yield strength of 350 MPa (50,000 psi) and a ductility of at least 18%EL? If so, specify the precipitation heat treatment. If it is not possible then explain why.

[*The answer may be found in enclosed CD.*]

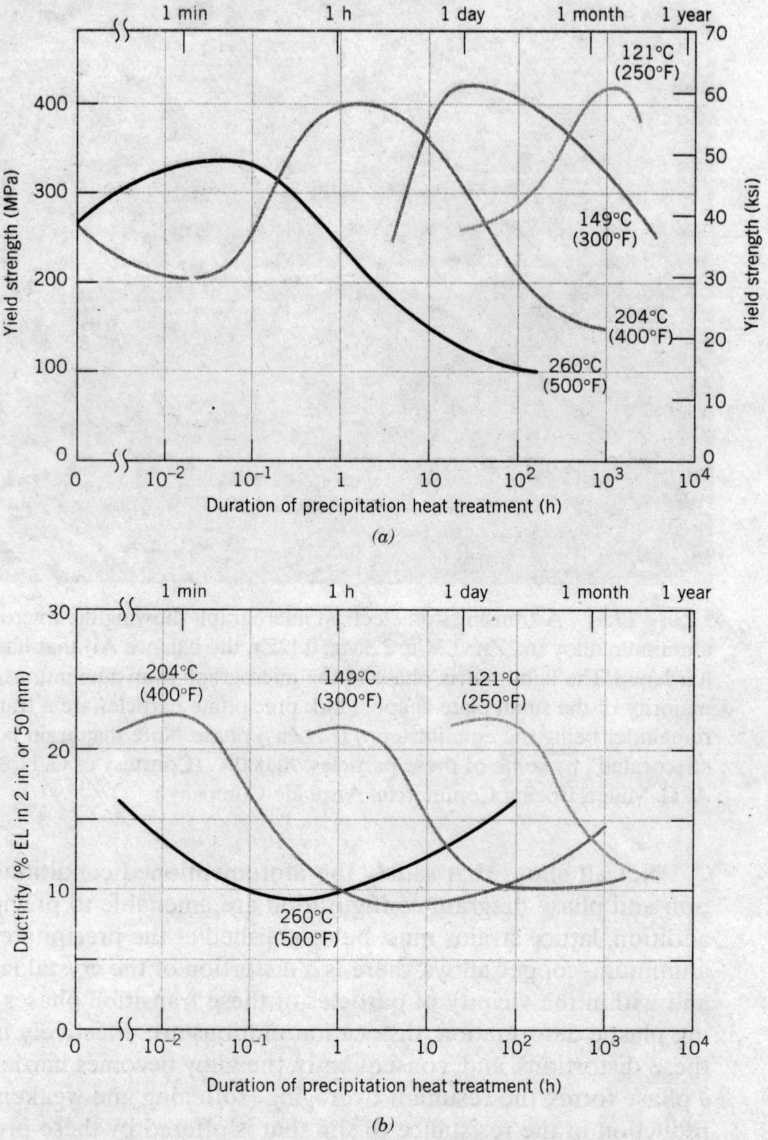

Figure 10.32 The precipitation hardening characteristics of a 2014 aluminum alloy (0.9 wt% Si, 4.4 wt% Cu, 0.8 wt% Mn, 0.5 wt% Mg) at four different aging temperatures: (*a*) yield strength, and (*b*) ductility (%EL). [Adapted from *Metals Handbook: Properties and Selection: Nonferrous Alloys and Pure Metals*, Vol. 2, 9th edition, H. Baker (Managing Editor), American Society for Metals, 1979, p. 41.]

Miscellaneous Considerations

The combined effects of strain hardening and precipitation hardening may be employed in high-strength alloys. The order of these hardening procedures is important in the production of alloys having the optimum combination of mechanical properties. Normally, the alloy is solution heat treated and then quenched. This is followed by cold working and finally by the precipitation-hardening heat treatment. In the final treatment, little strength loss is sustained as a result of recrystallization. If the alloy is precipitation hardened before cold working, more energy must be expended in its deformation; in addition, cracking may also result because of the reduction in ductility that accompanies the precipitation hardening.

Most precipitation-hardened alloys are limited in their maximum service temperatures. Exposure to temperatures at which aging occurs may lead to a loss of strength due to overaging.

SUMMARY

Basic Concepts
Slip Systems

On a microscopic level, plastic deformation corresponds to the motion of dislocations in response to an externally applied shear stress, a process termed "slip." Slip occurs on specific crystallographic planes and within these planes only in certain directions. A slip system represents a slip plane–slip direction combination, and operable slip systems depend on the crystal structure of the material.

Slip in Single Crystals

The critical resolved shear stress is the minimum shear stress required to initiate dislocation motion; the yield strength of a single crystal depends on both the magnitude of the critical resolved shear stress and the orientation of slip components relative to the direction of the applied stress.

Plastic Deformation of Polycrystalline Materials

For polycrystalline materials, slip occurs within each grain along the slip systems that are most favorably oriented with the applied stress; furthermore, during deformation, grains change shape in such a manner that coherency at the grain boundaries is maintained.

Deformation by Twinning

Under some circumstances limited plastic deformation may occur in BCC and HCP metals by mechanical twinning. Normally, twinning is important to the degree that accompanying crystallographic reorientations make the slip process more favorable.

Characteristics of Dislocations
Strengthening by Grain Size Reduction
Solid-Solution Strengthening
Strain Hardening

Since the ease with which a material is capable of plastic deformation is a function of dislocation mobility, restricting dislocation motion increases hardness and strength. On the basis of this principle, three different strengthening mechanisms were discussed. Grain boundaries serve as barriers to dislocation motion; thus refining the grain size of a polycrystalline material renders it harder and stronger. Solid-solution strengthening results from lattice strain interactions between impurity atoms and dislocations. Finally, as a material is plastically deformed, the dislocation density increases, as does also the extent of repulsive dislocation–dislocation strain field interactions; strain hardening is just the enhancement of strength with increased plastic deformation.

Recovery
Recrystallization
Grain Growth

The microstructural and mechanical characteristics of a plastically deformed metal specimen may be restored to their predeformed states by an appropriate heat treatment, during which recovery, recrystallization, and grain growth processes are allowed to occur. During recovery there is a reduction in dislocation density and alterations in dislocation configurations. Recrystallization is the formation of a new set of grains that are strain free; in addition, the material becomes softer and more ductile. Grain growth is the increase in average grain size of polycrystalline materials, which proceeds by grain boundary motion.

Precipitation Hardening

Some alloys are amenable to precipitation hardening—that is, to strengthening by the formation of very small particles of a second, or precipitate, phase. Control of particle size, and subsequently the strength, is accomplished by two heat treatments. For the second or precipitation treatment at constant temperature, strength increases with time to a maximum and decreases during overaging. This process is accelerated with rising temperature. The strengthening phenomenon is explained in terms of an increased resistance to dislocation motion by lattice strains, which are established in the vicinity of these microscopically small precipitate particles.

REFERENCES

Hirth, J. P., and J. Lothe, *Theory of Dislocations,* 2nd edition, Wiley-Interscience, New York, 1982. Reprinted by Krieger, Melbourne, FL, 1992.

Hull, D., *Introduction to Dislocations,* 3rd edition, Butterworth-Heinemann, Woburn, UK, 1984.

Read, W. T., Jr., *Dislocations in Crystals,* McGraw-Hill, New York, 1953.

Weertman, J., and J. R. Weertman, *Elementary Dislocation Theory,* Macmillan, New York, 1964. Reprinted by Oxford University Press, New York, 1992.

QUESTIONS AND PROBLEMS

Basic Concepts

Characteristics of Dislocations

10.1 To provide some perspective on the dimensions of atomic defects, consider a metal specimen that has a dislocation density of 10^5 mm^{-2}. Suppose that all the dislocations in 1000 mm^3 (1 cm^3) were somehow removed and linked end to end. How far (in miles) would this chain extend? Now suppose that the density is increased to 10^9 mm^{-2} by cold working. What would be the chain length of dislocations in 1000 mm^3 of material?

10.2 Consider two edge dislocations of opposite sign and having slip planes that are separated by several atomic distances as indicated in the diagram. Briefly describe the defect that results when these two dislocations become aligned with each other.

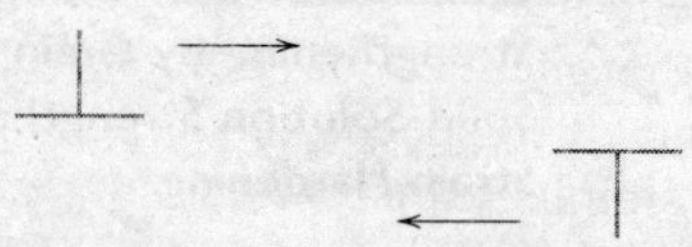

10.3 Is it possible for two screw dislocations of opposite sign to annihilate each other? Explain your answer.

10.4 For each of edge, screw, and mixed dislocations, cite the relationship between the direction of the applied shear stress and the direction of dislocation line motion.

Slip Systems

10.5 **(a)** Define a slip system.

(b) Do all metals have the same slip system? Why or why not?

10.6 **(a)** Compare planar densities (Section 4.7 and Problem 4.23) for the (100), (110), and (111) planes for FCC.

(b) Compare planar densities (Problem 4.24) for the (100), (110), and (111) planes for BCC.

10.7 One slip system for the BCC crystal structure is $\{110\}\langle 111\rangle$. In a manner similar to Figure 10.6*b*, sketch a $\{110\}$-type plane for the BCC structure, representing atom positions with circles. Now, using arrows, indicate two different $\langle 111\rangle$ slip directions within this plane.

10.8 One slip system for the HCP crystal structure is $\{0001\}\langle 11\bar{2}0\rangle$. In a manner similar to Figure 10.6b, sketch a $\{0001\}$-type plane for the HCP structure and, using arrows, indicate three different $\langle 11\bar{2}0\rangle$ slip directions within this plane. You might find Figure 3.6 helpful.

10.9 Equations 10.1a and 10.1b, expressions for Burgers vectors for FCC and BCC crystal structures, are of the form

$$\mathbf{b} = \frac{a}{2}\langle uvw\rangle$$

where a is the unit cell edge length. Also, since the magnitudes of these Burgers vectors may be determined from the following equation:

$$|\mathbf{b}| = \frac{a}{2}(u^2 + v^2 + w^2)^{1/2} \qquad (10.10)$$

determine values of $|\mathbf{b}|$ for copper and iron. You may want to consult Table 4.1.

10.10 **(a)** In the manner of Equations 10.1a, 10.1b, and 10.1c, specify the Burgers vector for the simple cubic crystal structure. Its unit cell is shown in Figure 4.38. Also, simple cubic is the crystal structure for the edge dislocation of Figure 5.7, and for its motion as presented in Figure 10.1. You may also want to consult the answer to Concept Check 10.1.

(b) On the basis of Equation 10.10, formulate an expression for the magnitude of the Burgers vector, $|\mathbf{b}|$, for simple cubic.

Slip in Single Crystals

10.11 Sometimes $\cos\phi \cos\lambda$ in Equation 10.2 is termed the *Schmid factor*. Determine the magnitude of the Schmid factor for an FCC single crystal oriented with its [120] direction parallel to the loading axis.

10.12 Consider a metal single crystal oriented such that the normal to the slip plane and the slip direction are at angles of 60° and 35°, respectively, with the tensile axis. If the critical resolved shear stress is 6.2 MPa, will an applied stress of 12 MPa cause the single crystal to yield? If not, what stress will be necessary?

10.13 A single crystal of zinc is oriented for a tensile test such that its slip plane normal makes an angle of 65° with the tensile axis. Three possible slip directions make angles of 30°, 48°, and 78° with the same tensile axis.

(a) Which of these three slip directions is most favored?

(b) If plastic deformation begins at a tensile stress of 2.5 MPa, determine the critical resolved shear stress for zinc.

10.14 Consider a single crystal of nickel oriented such that a tensile stress is applied along a [001] direction. If slip occurs on a (111) plane and in a $[\bar{1}01]$ direction, and is initiated at an applied tensile stress of 13.9 MPa, compute the critical resolved shear stress.

10.15 A single crystal of a metal that has the FCC crystal structure is oriented such that a tensile stress is applied parallel to the [100] direction. If the critical resolved shear stress for this material is 0.5 MPa, calculate the magnitude(s) of applied stress(es) necessary to cause slip to occur on the (111) plane in each of the $[1\bar{1}0]$, $[10\bar{1}]$, and $[0\bar{1}1]$ directions.

10.16 **(a)** A single crystal of a metal that has the BCC crystal structure is oriented such that a tensile stress is applied in the [100] direction. If the magnitude of this stress is 4.0 MPa, compute the resolved shear stress in the $[1\bar{1}1]$ direction on each of the (110), (011), and $(10\bar{1})$ planes.

(b) On the basis of these resolved shear stress values, which slip system(s) is (are) most favorably oriented?

10.17 Consider a single crystal of some hypothetical metal that has the BCC crystal structure and is oriented such that a tensile stress is applied along a [121] direction. If slip occurs on a (101) plane and in a [111] direction, compute the stress at which the crystal yields if its critical resolved shear stress is 2.4 MPa.

10.18 The critical resolved shear stress for copper is 0.48 MPa. Determine the maximum possible yield strength for a single crystal of Cu pulled in tension.

Deformation by Twinning

10.19 List four major differences between deformation by twinning and deformation by slip relative to mechanism, conditions of occurrence, and final result.

Strengthening by Grain Size Reduction

10.20 Briefly explain why small-angle grain boundaries are not as effective in interfering with the slip process as are high-angle grain boundaries.

10.21 Briefly explain why HCP metals are typically more brittle than FCC and BCC metals.

10.22 Describe in your own words the three strengthening mechanisms discussed in this chapter (i.e., grain size reduction, solid-solution strengthening, and strain hardening). Be sure to explain how dislocations are involved in each of the strengthening techniques.

10.23 **(a)** From the plot of yield strength versus (grain diameter)$^{-1/2}$ for a 70 Cu–30 Zn cartridge brass, Figure 10.15, determine values for the constants σ_0 and k_y in Equation 10.10.

(b) Now predict the yield strength of this alloy when the average grain diameter is 2.0×10^{-3} mm.

10.24 The lower yield point for an iron that has an average grain diameter of 1×10^{-2} mm is 230 MPa. At a grain diameter of 6×10^{-3} mm, the yield point increases to 275 MPa. At what grain diameter will the lower yield point be 310 MPa?

10.25 If it is assumed that the plot in Figure 10.15 is for noncold-worked brass, determine the grain size of the alloy in Figure 10.19; assume its composition is the same as the alloy in Figure 10.15.

Solid-Solution Strengthening

10.26 In the manner of Figures 10.17*b* and 10.18*b*, indicate the location in the vicinity of an edge dislocation at which an interstitial impurity atom would be expected to be situated. Now briefly explain in terms of lattice strains why it would be situated at this position.

Strain Hardening

10.27 **(a)** Show, for a tensile test, that

$$\%\,\text{CW} = \left(\frac{\epsilon}{\epsilon + 1}\right) \times 100$$

if there is no change in specimen volume during the deformation process (i.e., $A_0 l_0 = A_d l_d$).

(b) Using the result of part (a), compute the percent cold work experienced by naval brass (for which the stress–strain behavior is shown in Figure 9.18) when a stress of 415 MPa is applied.

10.28 Two previously undeformed cylindrical specimens of an alloy are to be strain hardened by reducing their cross-sectional areas (while maintaining their circular cross sections). For one specimen, the initial and deformed radii are 15 mm and 12 mm, respectively. The second specimen, with an initial radius of 11 mm, must have the same deformed hardness as the first specimen; compute the second specimen's radius after deformation.

10.29 Two previously undeformed specimens of the same metal are to be plastically deformed by reducing their cross-sectional areas. One has a circular cross section, and the other is rectangular; during deformation the circular cross section is to remain circular, and the rectangular is to remain as such. Their original and deformed dimensions are as follows:

	Circular (diameter, mm)	*Rectangular (mm)*
Original dimensions	18.0	20 × 50
Deformed dimensions	15.9	13.7 × 55.1

Which of these specimens will be the hardest after plastic deformation, and why?

10.30 A cylindrical specimen of cold-worked copper has a ductility (%EL) of 15%. If its cold-worked radius is 6.4 mm, what was its radius before deformation?

10.31 (a) What is the approximate ductility (%EL) of a brass that has a yield strength of 345 MPa?

(b) What is the approximate Brinell hardness of a 1040 steel having a yield strength of 620 MPa?

10.32 Experimentally, it has been observed for single crystals of a number of metals that the critical resolved shear stress τ_{crss} is a function of the dislocation density ρ_D as

$$\tau_{crss} = \tau_0 + A\sqrt{\rho_D}$$

where τ_0 and A are constants. For copper, the critical resolved shear stress is 0.69 MPa at a dislocation density of 10^4 mm^{-2}. If it is known that the value of τ_0 for copper is 0.069 MPa, compute the τ_{crss} at a dislocation density of 10^6 mm^{-2}.

Recovery
Recrystallization
Grain Growth

10.33 Briefly cite the differences between recovery and recrystallization processes.

10.34 Estimate the fraction of recrystallization from the photomicrograph in Figure 10.21*c*.

10.35 Explain the differences in grain structure for a metal that has been cold worked and one that has been cold worked and then recrystallized.

10.36 (a) What is the driving force for recrystallization?

(b) For grain growth?

10.37 (a) From Figure 10.25, compute the length of time required for the average grain diameter to increase from 0.03 to 0.3 mm at 600°C for this brass material.

(b) Repeat the calculation at 700°C.

10.38 The average grain diameter for a brass material was measured as a function of time at 650°C, which is tabulated below at two different times:

Time (min)	*Grain Diameter (mm)*
40	5.6×10^{-2}
100	8.0×10^{-2}

(a) What was the original grain diameter?

(b) What grain diameter would you predict after 200 min at 650°C?

10.39 An undeformed specimen of some alloy has an average grain diameter of 0.050 mm. You are asked to reduce its average grain diameter to 0.020 mm. Is this possible? If so, explain the procedures you would use and name the processes involved. If it is not possible, explain why.

10.40 Grain growth is strongly dependent on temperature (i.e., rate of grain growth increases with increasing temperature), yet temperature is not explicitly given as a part of Equation 10.9.

(a) Into which of the parameters in this expression would you expect temperature to be included?

(b) On the basis of your intuition, cite an explicit expression for this temperature dependence.

10.41 An uncold-worked brass specimen of average grain size 0.01 mm has a yield strength of 150 MPa. Estimate the yield strength of this alloy after it has been heated to 500°C for 1000 s, if it is known that the value of σ_0 is 25 MPa.

Precipitation Hardening

10.42 Compare precipitation hardening (Section 10.14) and the hardening of steel by quenching and tempering (Sections 8.5, 8.6, and 8.8) with regard to

(a) The total heat treatment procedure

(b) The microstructures that develop

(c) How the mechanical properties change during the several heat treatment stages

10.43 What is the principal difference between natural and artificial aging processes?

DESIGN PROBLEMS

Strain Hardening
Recrystallization

10.D1 Determine whether or not it is possible to cold work steel so as to give a minimum Brinell hardness of 240, and at the same time have a ductility of at least 15%EL. Justify your decision.

10.D2 Determine whether or not it is possible to cold work brass so as to give a minimum Brinell hardness of 150, and at the same time have a ductility of at least 20%EL. Justify your decision.

10.D3 A cylindrical specimen of cold-worked steel has a Brinell hardness of 240.

(a) Estimate its ductility in percent elongation.

(b) If the specimen remained cylindrical during deformation and its original radius was 10 mm, determine its radius after deformation.

10.D4 It is necessary to select a metal alloy for an application that requires a yield strength of at least 310 MPa while maintaining a minimum ductility (%EL) of 27%. If the metal may be cold worked, decide which of the following are candidates: copper, brass, and a 1040 steel. Why?

10.D5 A cylindrical rod of 1040 steel originally 11.4 mm in diameter is to be cold worked by drawing; the circular cross section will be maintained during deformation. A cold-worked tensile strength in excess of 825 MPa and a ductility of at least 12%EL are desired. Furthermore, the final diameter must be 8.9 mm. Explain how this may be accomplished.

10.D6 A cylindrical rod of brass originally 10.2 mm in diameter is to be cold worked by drawing; the circular cross section will be maintained during deformation. A cold-worked yield strength in excess of 380 MPa and a ductility of at least 15%EL are desired. Furthermore, the final diameter must be 10.6 mm. Explain how this may be accomplished.

10.D7 A cylindrical brass rod having a minimum tensile strength of 450 MPa, a ductility of at least 13%EL, and a final diameter of 12.7 mm is desired. Some 19.0 mm diameter brass stock that has been cold worked 35% is available. Describe the procedure you would follow to obtain this material. Assume that brass experiences cracking at 65%CW.

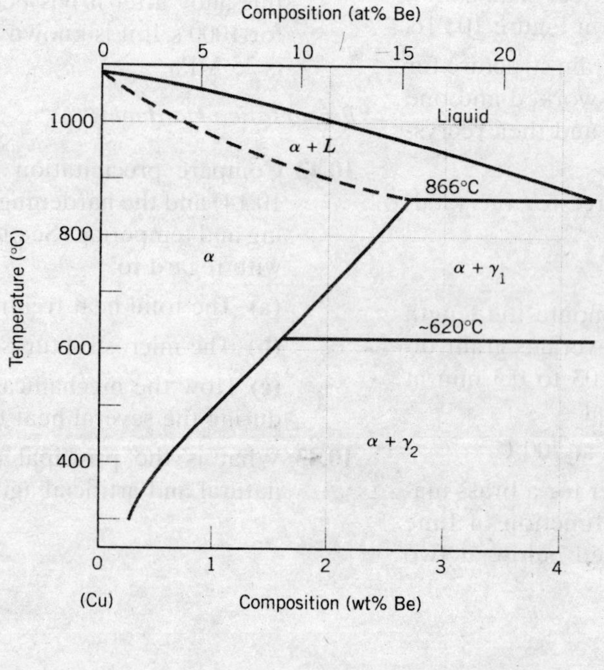

Figure 10.33 The copper-rich side of the copper–beryllium phase diagram. [Adapted from *Binary Alloy Phase Diagrams*, 2nd edition, Vol. 2, T. B. Massalski (Editor-in-Chief), 1990. Reprinted by permission of ASM International, Materials Park, OH.]

Precipitation Hardening

10.D8 Copper-rich copper–beryllium alloys are precipitation hardenable. After consulting the portion of the phase diagram (Figure 10.33), do the following:

(a) Specify the range of compositions over which these alloys may be precipitation hardened.

(b) Briefly describe the heat-treatment procedures (in terms of temperatures) that would be used to precipitation harden an alloy having a composition of your choosing, yet lying within the range given for part (a).

10.D9 A solution heat-treated 2014 aluminum alloy is to be precipitation hardened to have a minimum yield strength of 345 MPa and a ductility of at least 12%EL. Specify a practical precipitation heat treatment in terms of temperature and time that would give these mechanical characteristics. Justify your answer.

10.D10 Is it possible to produce a precipitation hardened 2014 aluminum alloy having a minimum yield strength of 380 MPa and a ductility of at least 15%EL? If so, specify the precipitation heat treatment. If it is not possible then explain why.

Chapter 11 Failure of Metals

An oil tanker that fractured in a brittle manner by crack propagation around its girth. (Photography by Neal Boenzi. Reprinted with permission from *The New York Times*.)

Learning Objectives

After studying this chapter you should be able to do the following:

1. **Describe the mechanism of crack propagation for both ductile and brittle modes of fracture.**
2. **Explain why the strengths of brittle materials are much lower than predicted by theoretical calculations.**
3. **Define fracture toughness in terms of (a) a brief statement, and (b) an equation; define all parameters in this equation.**
4. **Make a distinction between *fracture toughness* and *plane strain fracture toughness.***
5. **Name and describe the two impact fracture testing techniques.**
6. **Define fatigue and specify the conditions under which it occurs.**
7. **From a fatigue plot for some material, determine (a) the fatigue lifetime (at a specified stress level), and (b) the fatigue strength (at a specified number of cycles).**
8. **Define creep and specify the conditions under which it occurs.**
9. **Given a creep plot for some material, determine (a) the steady-state creep rate, and (b) the rupture lifetime.**

11.1 INTRODUCTION

The failure of engineering materials is almost always an undesirable event for several reasons; these include human lives that are put in jeopardy, economic losses, and the interference with the availability of products and services. Even though the causes of failure and the behavior of materials may be known, prevention of failures is difficult to guarantee. The usual causes are improper materials selection and processing and inadequate design of the component or its misuse. It is the responsibility of the engineer to anticipate and plan for possible failure and, in the event that failure does occur, to assess its cause and then take appropriate preventive measures against future incidents.

The following topics are addressed in this chapter: simple fracture (both ductile and brittle modes), fundamentals of fracture mechanics, impact fracture testing, the ductile-to-brittle transition, fatigue, and creep. These discussions include failure mechanisms, testing techniques, and methods by which failure may be prevented or controlled.

Concept Check 11.1

Cite two situations in which the possibility of failure is part of the design of a component or product.

[*The answer may be found in enclosed CD.*]

Fracture

11.2 FUNDAMENTALS OF FRACTURE

Simple fracture is the separation of a body into two or more pieces in response to an imposed stress that is static (i.e., constant or slowly changing with time) and at temperatures that are low relative to the melting temperature of the material. The applied stress may be tensile, compressive, shear, or torsional; the present discussion will be confined to fractures that result from uniaxial tensile loads. For engineering materials, two fracture modes are possible: **ductile** and **brittle.** Classification is based on the ability of a material to experience plastic deformation. Ductile materials typically exhibit substantial plastic deformation with high energy absorption before fracture. On the other hand, there is normally little or no plastic deformation with low energy absorption accompanying a brittle fracture. The tensile stress–strain behaviors of both fracture types may be reviewed in Figure 9.19.

"Ductile"and "brittle" are relative terms; whether a particular fracture is one mode or the other depends on the situation. Ductility may be quantified in terms of percent elongation (Equation 9.11) and percent reduction in area (Equation 9.12). Furthermore, ductility is a function of temperature of the material, the strain rate, and the stress state. The disposition of normally ductile materials to fail in a brittle manner is discussed in Section 11.6.

Any fracture process involves two steps—crack formation and propagation—in response to an imposed stress. The mode of fracture is highly dependent on the mechanism of crack propagation. Ductile fracture is characterized by extensive plastic deformation in the vicinity of an advancing crack. Furthermore, the process proceeds relatively slowly as the crack length is extended. Such a crack is often said to be *stable*. That is, it resists any further extension unless there is an increase in the applied stress. In addition, there will ordinarily be evidence of appreciable gross deformation at the fracture surfaces (e.g., twisting and tearing). On the other hand, for brittle fracture, cracks may spread extremely rapidly, with very little accompanying plastic deformation. Such cracks may be said to be *unstable,* and crack propagation, once started, will continue spontaneously without an increase in magnitude of the applied stress.

Ductile fracture is almost always preferred for two reasons. First, brittle fracture occurs suddenly and catastrophically without any warning; this is a consequence of the spontaneous and rapid crack propagation. On the other hand, for ductile fracture, the presence of plastic deformation gives warning that fracture is imminent, allowing preventive measures to be taken. Second, more strain energy is required to induce ductile fracture inasmuch as ductile materials are generally tougher. Under the action of an applied tensile stress, most metal alloys are ductile, whereas ceramics are notably brittle, and polymers may exhibit both types of fracture.

11.3 DUCTILE FRACTURE

Ductile fracture surfaces will have their own distinctive features on both macroscopic and microscopic levels. Figure 11.1 shows schematic representations for two characteristic macroscopic fracture profiles. The configuration shown in Figure 11.1*a* is found for extremely soft metals, such as pure gold and lead at room temperature, and other metals, polymers, and inorganic glasses at elevated temperatures. These highly ductile materials neck down to a point fracture, showing virtually 100% reduction in area.

The most common type of tensile fracture profile for ductile metals is that represented in Figure 11.1*b*, where fracture is preceded by only a moderate amount of

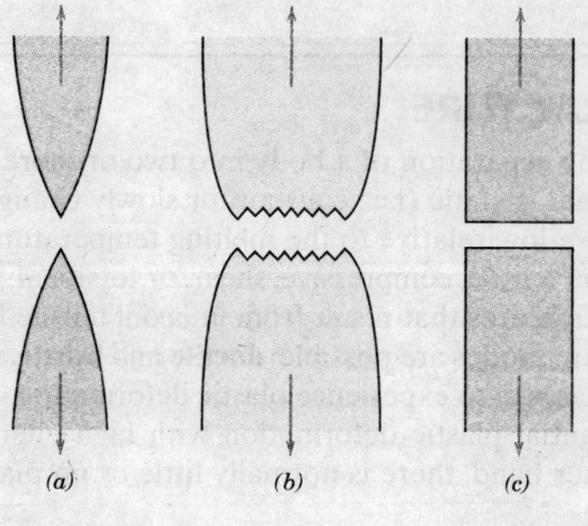

Figure 11.1 (*a*) Highly ductile fracture in which the specimen necks down to a point. (*b*) Moderately ductile fracture after some necking. (*c*) Brittle fracture without any plastic deformation.

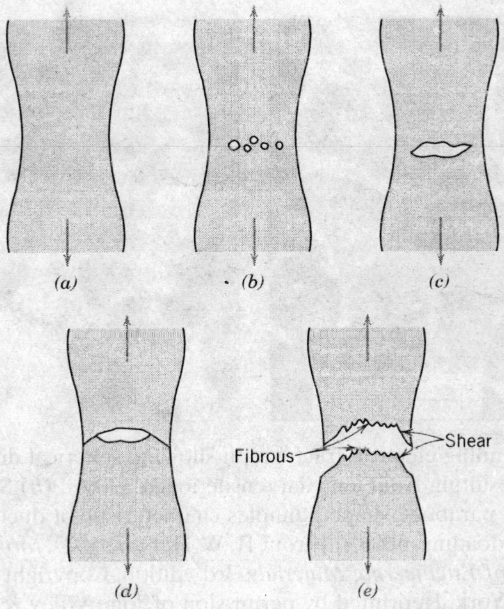

Figure 11.2 Stages in the cup-and-cone fracture. (*a*) Initial necking. (*b*) Small cavity formation. (*c*) Coalescence of cavities to form a crack. (*d*) Crack propagation. (*e*) Final shear fracture at a 45° angle relative to the tensile direction. (From K. M. Ralls, T. H. Courtney, and J. Wulff, *Introduction to Materials Science and Engineering,* p. 4611. Copyright © 1976 by John Wiley & Sons, New York. Reprinted by permission of John Wiley & Sons, Inc.)

necking. The fracture process normally occurs in several stages (Figure 11.2). First, after necking begins, small cavities, or microvoids, form in the interior of the cross section, as indicated in Figure 11.2*b*. Next, as deformation continues, these microvoids enlarge, come together, and coalesce to form an elliptical crack, which has its long axis perpendicular to the stress direction. The crack continues to grow in a direction parallel to its major axis by this microvoid coalescence process (Figure 11.2*c*). Finally, fracture ensues by the rapid propagation of a crack around the outer perimeter of the neck (Figure 11.2*d*), by shear deformation at an angle of about 45° with the tensile axis—this is the angle at which the shear stress is a maximum. Sometimes a fracture having this characteristic surface contour is termed a *cup-and-cone fracture* because one of the mating surfaces is in the form of a cup, the other like a cone. In this type of fractured specimen (Figure 11.3*a*), the central interior region of the surface has an irregular and fibrous appearance, which is indicative of plastic deformation.

Fractographic Studies

Much more detailed information regarding the mechanism of fracture is available from microscopic examination, normally using scanning electron microscopy. Studies

Figure 11.3 (*a*) Cup-and-cone fracture in aluminum. (*b*) Brittle fracture in a mild steel.

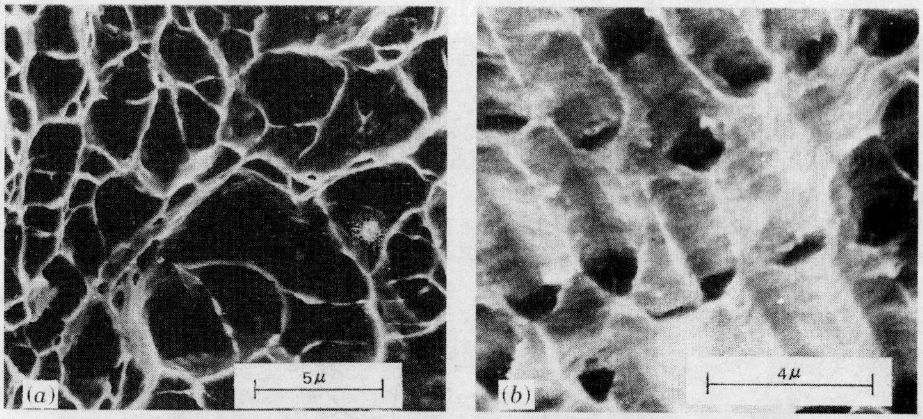

Figure 11.4 (*a*) Scanning electron fractograph showing spherical dimples characteristic of ductile fracture resulting from uniaxial tensile loads. 3300×. (*b*) Scanning electron fractograph showing parabolic-shaped dimples characteristic of ductile fracture resulting from shear loading. 5000×. (From R. W. Hertzberg, *Deformation and Fracture Mechanics of Engineering Materials,* 3rd edition. Copyright © 1989 by John Wiley & Sons, New York. Reprinted by permission of John Wiley & Sons, Inc.)

of this type are termed *fractographic*. The scanning electron microscope is preferred for fractographic examinations since it has a much better resolution and depth of field than does the optical microscope; these characteristics are necessary to reveal the topographical features of fracture surfaces.

When the fibrous central region of a cup-and-cone fracture surface is examined with the electron microscope at a high magnification, it will be found to consist of numerous spherical "dimples" (Figure 11.4*a*); this structure is characteristic of fracture resulting from uniaxial tensile failure. Each dimple is one half of a microvoid that formed and then separated during the fracture process. Dimples also form on the 45° shear lip of the cup-and-cone fracture. However, these will be elongated or C-shaped, as shown in Figure 11.4*b*. This parabolic shape may be indicative of shear failure. Furthermore, other microscopic fracture surface features are also possible. Fractographs such as those shown in Figures 11.4*a* and 11.4*b* provide valuable information in the analyses of fracture, such as the fracture mode, the stress state, and the site of crack initiation.

11.4 BRITTLE FRACTURE

Brittle fracture takes place without any appreciable deformation, and by rapid crack propagation. The direction of crack motion is very nearly perpendicular to the direction of the applied tensile stress and yields a relatively flat fracture surface, as indicated in Figure 11.1*c*.

Fracture surfaces of materials that failed in a brittle manner will have their own distinctive patterns; any signs of gross plastic deformation will be absent. For example, in some steel pieces, a series of V-shaped "chevron" markings may form near the center of the fracture cross section that point back toward the crack initiation site (Figure 11.5*a*). Other brittle fracture surfaces contain lines or ridges that radiate from the origin of the crack in a fanlike pattern (Figure 11.5*b*). Often, both of these marking patterns will be sufficiently coarse to be discerned with the naked eye. For very hard and fine-grained metals, there will be no discernible fracture pattern. Brittle fracture in amorphous materials, such as ceramic glasses, yields a relatively shiny and smooth surface.

(a)

(b)

Figure 11.5 (*a*) Photograph showing V-shaped "chevron" markings characteristic of brittle fracture. Arrows indicate origin of crack. Approximately actual size. (*b*) Photograph of a brittle fracture surface showing radial fan-shaped ridges. Arrow indicates origin of crack. Approximately 2×. [(*a*) From R. W. Hertzberg, *Deformation and Fracture Mechanics of Engineering Materials,* 3rd edition. Copyright © 1989 by John Wiley & Sons, New York. Reprinted by permission of John Wiley & Sons, Inc. Photograph courtesy of Roger Slutter, Lehigh University. (*b*) Reproduced with permission from D. J. Wulpi, *Understanding How Components Fail,* American Society for Metals, Materials Park, OH, 1985.]

For most brittle crystalline materials, crack propagation corresponds to the successive and repeated breaking of atomic bonds along specific crystallographic planes (Figure 11.6*a*); such a process is termed *cleavage*. This type of fracture is said to be **transgranular** (or *transcrystalline*), because the fracture cracks pass through the grains. Macroscopically, the fracture surface may have a grainy or faceted texture (Figure 11.3*b*), as a result of changes in orientation of the cleavage planes from grain to grain. This cleavage feature is shown at a higher magnification in the scanning electron micrograph of Figure 11.6*b*.

In some alloys, crack propagation is along grain boundaries (Figure 11.7*a*); this fracture is termed **intergranular.** Figure 11.7*b* is a scanning electron micrograph

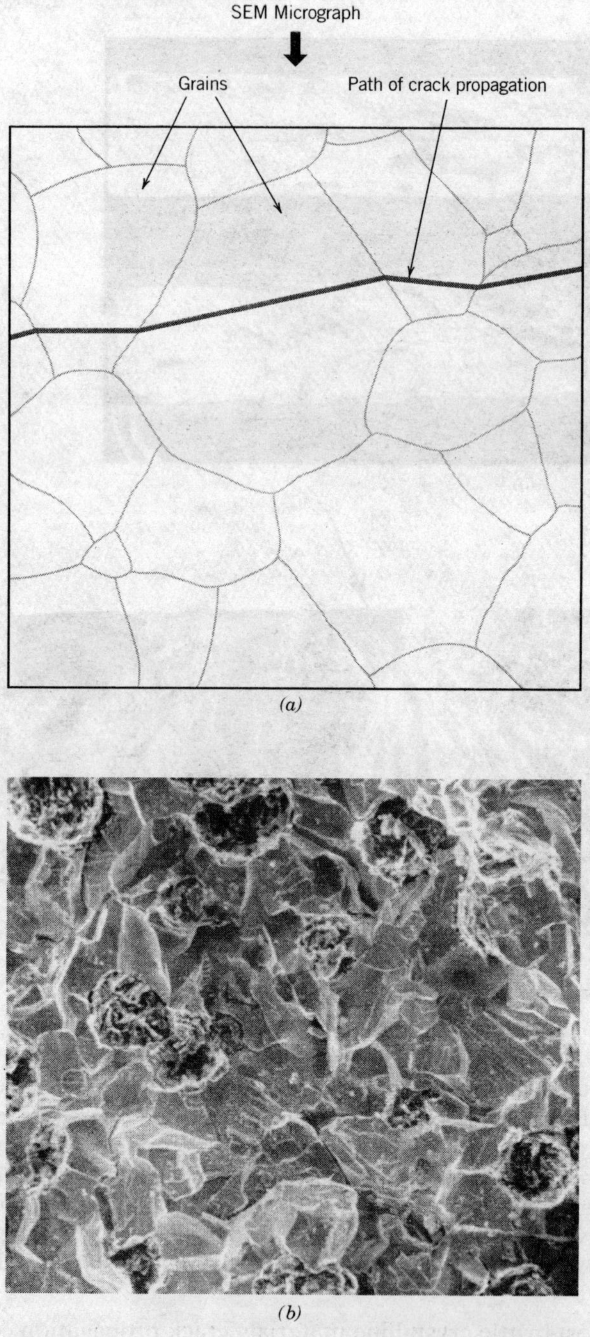

Figure 11.6 (*a*) Schematic cross-section profile showing crack propagation through the interior of grains for transgranular fracture. (*b*) Scanning electron fractograph of ductile cast iron showing a transgranular fracture surface. Magnification unknown. [Figure (*b*) from V. J. Colangelo and F. A. Heiser, *Analysis of Metallurgical Failure of metalss,* 2nd edition. Copyright © 1987 by John Wiley & Sons, New York. Reprinted by permission of John Wiley & Sons, Inc.]

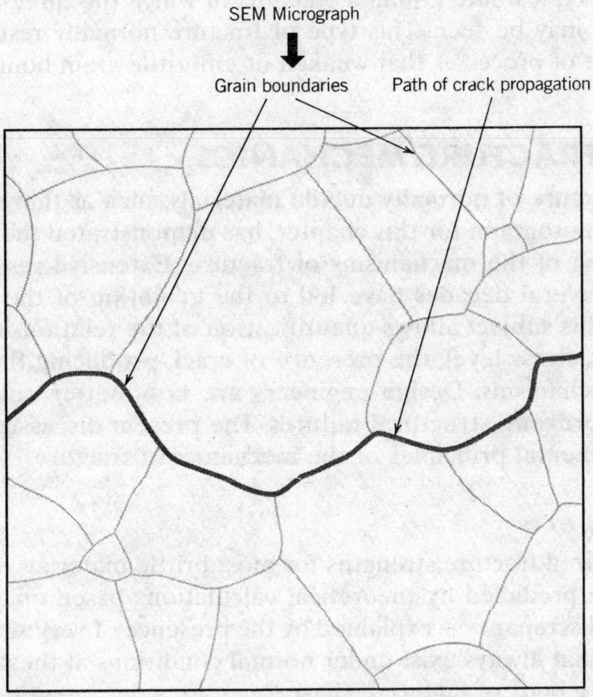

(a)

(b)

Figure 11.7 (*a*) Schematic cross-section profile showing crack propagation along grain boundaries for intergranular fracture. (*b*) Scanning electron fractograph showing an intergranular fracture surface. 50×. [Figure (*b*) reproduced with permission from *ASM Handbook*, Vol. 12, *Fractography*, ASM International, Materials Park, OH, 1987.]

showing a typical intergranular fracture, in which the three-dimensional nature of the grains may be seen. This type of fracture normally results subsequent to the occurrence of processes that weaken or embrittle grain boundary regions.

11.5 PRINCIPLES OF FRACTURE MECHANICS

Brittle fracture of normally ductile materials, such as that shown in the chapter-opening photograph for this chapter, has demonstrated the need for a better understanding of the mechanisms of fracture. Extensive research endeavors over the past several decades have led to the evolution of the field of **fracture mechanics.** This subject allows quantification of the relationships between material properties, stress level, the presence of crack-producing flaws, and crack propagation mechanisms. Design engineers are now better equipped to anticipate, and thus prevent, structural failures. The present discussion centers on some of the fundamental principles of the mechanics of fracture.

Stress Concentration

The measured fracture strengths for most brittle materials are significantly lower than those predicted by theoretical calculations based on atomic bonding energies. This discrepancy is explained by the presence of very small, microscopic flaws or cracks that always exist under normal conditions at the surface and within the interior of a body of material. These flaws are a detriment to the fracture strength because an applied stress may be amplified or concentrated at the tip, the magnitude of this amplification depending on crack orientation and geometry. This phenomenon is demonstrated in Figure 11.8, a stress profile across a cross section containing an internal crack. As indicated by this profile, the magnitude of this localized stress diminishes with distance away from the crack tip. At positions far

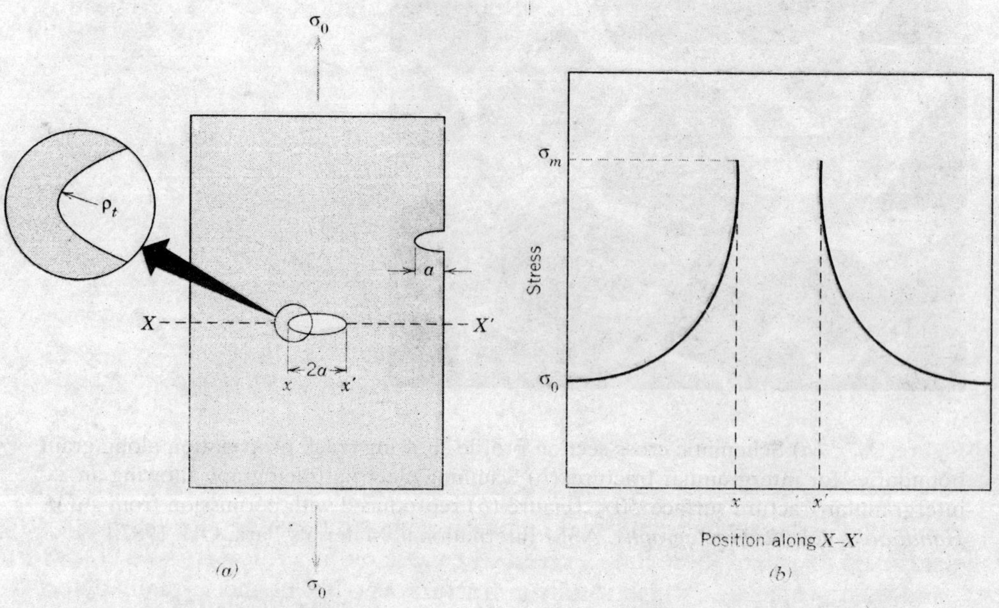

Figure 11.8 (*a*) The geometry of surface and internal cracks. (*b*) Schematic stress profile along the line X–X' in (*a*), demonstrating stress amplification at crack tip positions.

removed, the stress is just the nominal stress σ_0, or the applied load divided by the specimen cross-sectional area (perpendicular to this load). Due to their ability to amplify an applied stress in their locale, these flaws are sometimes called **stress raisers.**

If it is assumed that a crack is similar to an elliptical hole through a plate, and is oriented perpendicular to the applied stress, the maximum stress, σ_m, occurs at the crack tip and may be approximated by

$$\sigma_m = 2\sigma_0\left(\frac{a}{\rho_t}\right)^{1/2} \tag{11.1}$$

where σ_0 is the magnitude of the nominal applied tensile stress, ρ_t is the radius of curvature of the crack tip (Figure 11.8*a*), and a represents the length of a surface crack, or half of the length of an internal crack. For a relatively long microcrack that has a small tip radius of curvature, the factor $(a/\rho_t)^{1/2}$ may be very large. This will yield a value of σ_m that is many times the value of σ_0.

Sometimes the ratio σ_m/σ_0 is denoted as the *stress concentration factor* K_t:

$$K_t = \frac{\sigma_m}{\sigma_0} = 2\left(\frac{a}{\rho_t}\right)^{1/2} \tag{11.2}$$

which is simply a measure of the degree to which an external stress is amplified at the tip of a crack.

By way of comment, it should be said that stress amplification is not restricted to these microscopic defects; it may occur at macroscopic internal discontinuities (e.g., voids), at sharp corners, and at notches in large structures.

Furthermore, the effect of a stress raiser is more significant in brittle than in ductile materials. For a ductile material, plastic deformation ensues when the maximum stress exceeds the yield strength. This leads to a more uniform distribution of stress in the vicinity of the stress raiser and to the development of a maximum stress concentration factor less than the theoretical value. Such yielding and stress redistribution do not occur to any appreciable extent around flaws and discontinuities in brittle materials; therefore, essentially the theoretical stress concentration will result.

Using principles of fracture mechanics, it is possible to show that the critical stress σ_c required for crack propagation in a brittle material is described by the expression

$$\sigma_c = \left(\frac{2E\gamma_s}{\pi a}\right)^{1/2} \tag{11.3}$$

where

E = modulus of elasticity

γ_s = specific surface energy

a = one half the length of an internal crack

All brittle materials contain a population of small cracks and flaws that have a variety of sizes, geometries, and orientations. When the magnitude of a tensile stress at the tip of one of these flaws exceeds the value of this critical stress, a crack forms and then propagates, which results in fracture. Very small and virtually defect-free metallic and ceramic whiskers have been grown with fracture strengths that approach their theoretical values.

EXAMPLE PROBLEM 11.1

Maximum Flaw Length Computation

A relatively large plate of a glass is subjected to a tensile stress of 40 MPa. If the specific surface energy and modulus of elasticity for this glass are 0.3 J/m^2 and 69 GPa, respectively, determine the maximum length of a surface flaw that is possible without fracture.

Solution

To solve this problem it is necessary to employ Equation 11.3. Rearrangement of this expression such that a is the dependent variable, and realizing that $\sigma = 40$ MPa, $\gamma_s = 0.3$ J/m^2, and $E = 69$ GPa leads to

$$a = \frac{2E\gamma_s}{\pi\sigma^2}$$

$$= \frac{(2)(69 \times 10^9 \text{ N/m}^2)(0.3 \text{ N/m})}{\pi(40 \times 10^6 \text{ N/m}^2)^2}$$

$$= 8.2 \times 10^{-6} \text{ m} = 0.0082 \text{ mm} = 8.2\ \mu\text{m}$$

Fracture Toughness

Furthermore, using fracture mechanical principles, an expression has been developed that relates this critical stress for crack propagation (σ_c) and crack length (a) as

$$K_c = Y\sigma_c\sqrt{\pi a} \tag{11.4}$$

In this expression K_c is the **fracture toughness,** a property that is a measure of a material's resistance to brittle fracture when a crack is present. Worth noting is that K_c has the unusual units of MPa$\sqrt{\text{m}}$ or psi$\sqrt{\text{in.}}$ (alternatively, ksi$\sqrt{\text{in.}}$). Furthermore, Y is a dimensionless parameter or function that depends on both crack and specimen sizes and geometries, as well as the manner of load application.

Relative to this Y parameter, for planar specimens containing cracks that are much shorter than the specimen width, Y has a value of approximately unity. For example, for a plate of infinite width having a through-thickness crack (Figure 11.9a),

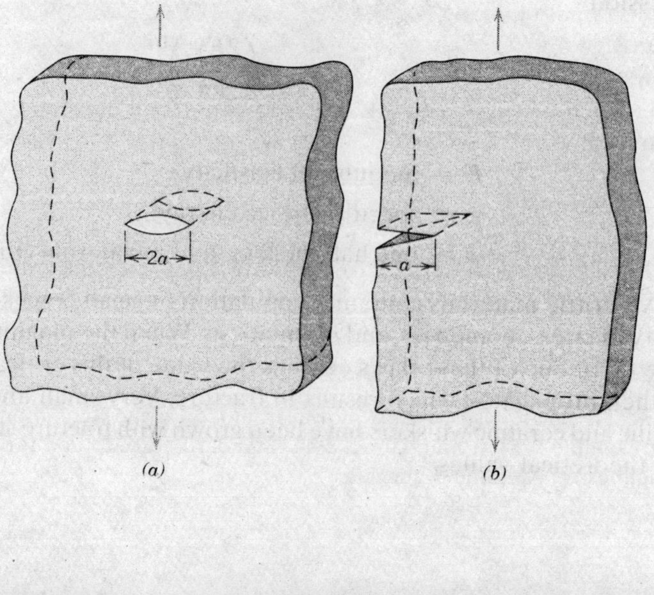

Figure 11.9 Schematic representations of (a) an interior crack in a plate of infinite width, and (b) an edge crack in a plate of semi-infinite width.

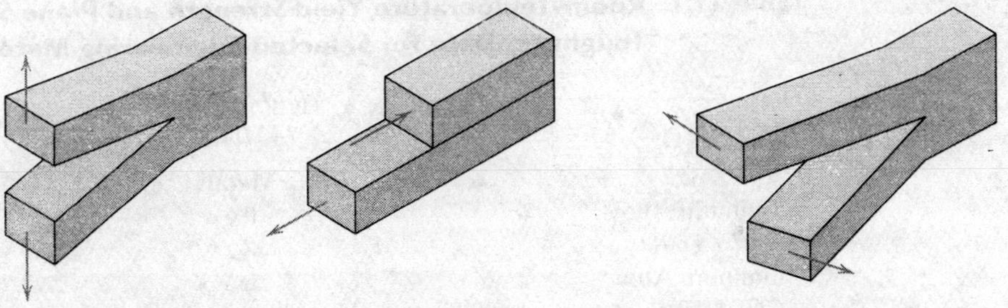

(a) (b) (c)

Figure 11.10 The three modes of crack surface displacement. (*a*) Mode I, opening or tensile mode; (*b*) mode II, sliding mode; and (*c*) mode III, tearing mode.

$Y = 1.0$; whereas for a plate of semi-infinite width containing an edge crack of length a (Figure 11.9*b*), $Y \cong 1.1$. Mathematical expressions for Y have been determined for a variety of crack-specimen geometries; these expressions are often relatively complex.

For relatively thin specimens, the value of K_c will depend on specimen thickness. However, when specimen thickness is much greater than the crack dimensions, K_c becomes independent of thickness; under these conditions a condition of **plane strain** exists. By plane strain we mean that when a load operates on a crack in the manner represented in Figure 11.9*a*, there is no strain component perpendicular to the front and back faces. The K_c value for this thick-specimen situation is known as the **plane strain fracture toughness** K_{Ic}; furthermore, it is also defined by

$$K_{Ic} = Y\sigma\sqrt{\pi a} \tag{11.5}$$

K_{Ic} is the fracture toughness cited for most situations. The I (i.e., Roman numeral "one") subscript for K_{Ic} denotes that the plane strain fracture toughness is for mode I crack displacement, as illustrated in Figure 11.10*a*.[1]

Brittle materials, for which appreciable plastic deformation is not possible in front of an advancing crack, have low K_{Ic} values and are vulnerable to catastrophic failure. On the other hand, K_{Ic} values are relatively large for ductile materials. Fracture mechanics is especially useful in predicting catastrophic failure in materials having intermediate ductilities. Plane strain fracture toughness values for a number of different materials are presented in Table 11.1 (and Figure 1.6); a more extensive list of K_{Ic} values is contained in Table B.5, Appendix B.

The plane strain fracture toughness K_{Ic} is a fundamental material property that depends on many factors, the most influential of which are temperature, strain rate, and microstructure. The magnitude of K_{Ic} diminishes with increasing strain rate and decreasing temperature. Furthermore, an enhancement in yield strength wrought by solid solution or dispersion additions or by strain hardening generally produces a corresponding decrease in K_{Ic}. Furthermore, K_{Ic} normally increases with reduction in grain size as composition and other microstructural variables are maintained constant. Yield strengths are included for some of the materials listed in Table 11.1.

Several different testing techniques are used to measure K_{Ic}.[2] Virtually any specimen size and shape consistent with mode I crack displacement may be utilized,

---

[1] Two other crack displacement modes denoted by II and III and as illustrated in Figures 11.10*b* and 11.10*c* are also possible; however, mode I is most commonly encountered.

[2] See for example ASTM Standard E 399, "Standard Test Method for Plane Strain Fracture Toughness of Metallic Materials."

Table 11.1 Room-Temperature Yield Strength and Plane Strain Fracture Toughness Data for Selected Engineering Materials

Material	*Yield Strength (MPa)*	K_{Ic} ($MPa\sqrt{m}$)
	Metals	
Aluminum Alloy[a] (7075-T651)	495	24
Aluminum Alloy[a] (2024-T3)	345	44
Titanium Alloy[a] (Ti-6Al-4V)	910	55
Alloy Steel[a] (4340 tempered @ 260°C)	1640	50.0
Alloy Steel[a] (4340 tempered @ 425°C)	1420	87.4
	Ceramics	
Concrete	—	0.2–1.4
Soda-Lime Glass	—	0.7–0.8
Aluminum Oxide	—	2.7–5.0
	Polymers	
Polystyrene (PS)	—	0.7–1.1
Poly(methyl methacrylate) (PMMA)	53.8–73.1	0.7–1.6
Polycarbonate (PC)	62.1	2.2

[a] **Source:** Reprinted with permission, *Advanced Materials and Processes*, ASM International, © 1990.

and accurate values will be realized provided that the Y scale parameter in Equation 11.5 has been properly determined.

Design Using Fracture Mechanics

According to Equations 11.4 and 11.5, three variables must be considered relative to the possibility for fracture of some structural component—namely, the fracture toughness (K_c) or plane strain fracture toughness (K_{Ic}), the imposed stress (σ), and the flaw size (a)—assuming, of course, that Y has been determined. When designing a component, it is first important to decide which of these variables are constrained by the application and which are subject to design control. For example, material selection (and hence K_c or K_{Ic}) is often dictated by factors such as density (for lightweight applications) or the corrosion characteristics of the environment. Or, the allowable flaw size is either measured or specified by the limitations of available flaw detection techniques. It is important to realize, however, that once any combination of two of the above parameters is prescribed, the third becomes fixed (Equations 11.4 and 11.5). For example, assume that K_{Ic} and the magnitude of a are specified by application constraints; therefore, the design (or critical) stress σ_c must be

$$\sigma_c = \frac{K_{Ic}}{Y\sqrt{\pi a}} \tag{11.6}$$

Table 11.2 A List of Several Common Nondestructive Testing (NDT) Techniques

Technique	*Defect Location*	*Defect Size Sensitivity (mm)*	*Testing Location*
Scanning electron microscopy (SEM)	Surface	>0.001	Laboratory
Dye penetrant	Surface	0.025–0.25	Laboratory/in-field
Ultrasonics	Subsurface	>0.050	Laboratory/in-field
Optical microscopy	Surface	0.1–0.5	Laboratory
Visual inspection	Surface	>0.1	Laboratory/in-field
Acoustic emission	Surface/subsurface	>0.1	Laboratory/in-field
Radiography (X-ray/gamma ray)	Subsurface	>2% of specimen thickness	Laboratory/in-field

On the other hand, if stress level and plane strain fracture toughness are fixed by the design situation, then the maximum allowable flaw size a_c is

$$a_c = \frac{1}{\pi}\left(\frac{K_{Ic}}{\sigma Y}\right)^2 \tag{11.7}$$

A number of nondestructive test (NDT) techniques have been developed that permit detection and measurement of both internal and surface flaws.[3] Such techniques are used to examine structural components that are in service for defects and flaws that could lead to premature failure; in addition, NDTs are used as a means of quality control for manufacturing processes. As the name implies, these techniques must not destroy the material/structure being examined. Furthermore, some testing methods must be conducted in a laboratory setting; others may be adapted for use in the field. Several commonly employed NDT techniques and their characteristics are listed in Table 11.2.

One important example of the use of NDT is for the detection of cracks and leaks in the walls of oil pipelines in remote areas such as Alaska. Ultrasonic analysis is utilized in conjunction with a "robotic analyzer" that can travel relatively long distances within a pipeline.

DESIGN EXAMPLE 11.1

Material Specification for a Pressurized Spherical Tank

Consider the thin-walled spherical tank of radius r and thickness t (Figure 11.11) that may be used as a pressure vessel.

(a) One design of such a tank calls for yielding of the wall material prior to failure as a result of the formation of a crack of critical size and its subsequent rapid propagation. Thus, plastic distortion of the wall may be observed and the pressure within the tank released before the occurrence of catastrophic failure. Consequently, materials having large critical crack lengths are desired. On the basis

[3] Sometimes the terms nondestructive evaluation (NDE) and nondestructive inspection (NDI) are also used for these techniques.

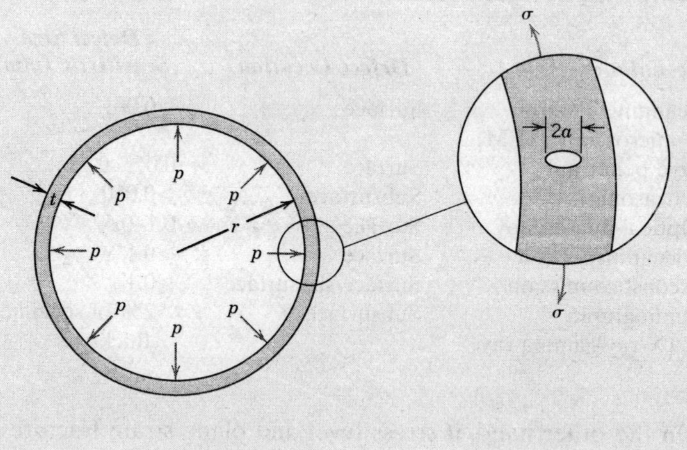

Figure 11.11 Schematic diagram showing the cross section of a spherical tank that is subjected to an internal pressure p, and that has a radial crack of length $2a$ in its wall.

of this criterion, rank the metal alloys listed in Table B.5, Appendix B, as to critical crack size, from longest to shortest.

(b) An alternative design that is also often utilized with pressure vessels is termed *leak-before-break.* Using principles of fracture mechanics, allowance is made for the growth of a crack through the thickness of the vessel wall prior to the occurrence of rapid crack propagation (Figure 11.11). Thus, the crack will completely penetrate the wall without catastrophic failure, allowing for its detection by the leaking of pressurized fluid. With this criterion the critical crack length a_c (i.e., one-half of the total internal crack length) is taken to be equal to the pressure vessel thickness t. Allowance for $a_c = t$ instead of $a_c = t/2$ assures that fluid leakage will occur prior to the buildup of dangerously high pressures. Using this criterion, rank the metal alloys in Table B.5, Appendix B as to the maximum allowable pressure.

For this spherical pressure vessel, the circumferential wall stress σ is a function of the pressure p in the vessel and the radius r and wall thickness t according to

$$\sigma = \frac{pr}{2t} \tag{11.8}$$

For both parts (a) and (b) assume a condition of plane strain.

Solution

(a) For the first design criterion, it is desired that the circumferential wall stress be less than the yield strength of the material. Substitution of σ_y for σ in Equation 11.5, and incorporation of a factor of safety N leads to

$$K_{Ic} = Y\left(\frac{\sigma_y}{N}\right)\sqrt{\pi a_c} \tag{11.9}$$

where a_c is the critical crack length. Solving for a_c yields the following expression:

$$a_c = \frac{N^2}{Y^2\pi}\left(\frac{K_{Ic}}{\sigma_y}\right)^2 \tag{11.10}$$

Therefore, the critical crack length is proportional to the square of the K_{Ic}-σ_y ratio, which is the basis for the ranking of the metal alloys in Table B.5. The

Table 11.3 Ranking of Several Metal Alloys Relative to Critical Crack Length (Yielding Criterion) for a Thin-Walled Spherical Pressure Vessel

Material	$\left(\frac{K_{Ic}}{\sigma_y}\right)^2$ *(mm)*
Medium carbon (1040) steel	43.1
AZ31B magnesium	19.6
2024 aluminum (T3)	16.3
Ti-5Al-2.5Sn titanium	6.6
4140 steel (tempered @ 482°C)	5.3
4340 steel (tempered @ 425°C)	3.8
Ti-6Al-4V titanium	3.7
17-7PH steel	3.4
7075 aluminum (T651)	2.4
4140 steel (tempered @ 370°C)	1.6
4340 steel (tempered @ 260°C)	0.93

ranking is provided in Table 11.3, where it may be seen that the medium carbon (1040) steel with the largest ratio has the longest critical crack length, and, therefore, is the most desirable material on the basis of this criterion.

(b) As stated previously, the leak-before-break criterion is just met when one-half of the internal crack length is equal to the thickness of the pressure vessel—that is, when $a = t$. Substitution of $a = t$ into Equation 11.5 gives

$$K_{Ic} = Y\sigma\sqrt{\pi t} \tag{11.11}$$

and, from Equation 11.8

$$t = \frac{pr}{2\sigma} \tag{11.12}$$

The stress is replaced by the yield strength, inasmuch as the tank should be designed to contain the pressure without yielding; furthermore, substitution of Equation 11.12 into Equation 11.11, after some rearrangement, yields the following expression:

$$p = \frac{2}{Y^2\pi r}\left(\frac{K_{Ic}^2}{\sigma_y}\right) \tag{11.13}$$

Hence, for some given spherical vessel of radius r, the maximum allowable pressure consistent with this leak-before-break criterion is proportional to K_{Ic}^2/σ_y. The same several materials are ranked according to this ratio in Table 11.4; as may be noted, the medium carbon steel will contain the greatest pressures.

Of the 11 metal alloys that are listed in Table B.5, the medium carbon steel ranks first according to both yielding and leak-before-break criteria. For these reasons, many pressure vessels are constructed of medium carbon steels, when temperature extremes and corrosion need not be considered.

Table 11.4 Ranking of Several Metal Alloys Relative to Maximum Allowable Pressure (Leak-Before-Break Criterion) for a Thin-Walled Spherical Pressure Vessel

Material	$\frac{K_{Ic}^2}{\sigma_y}$ *(MPa-m)*
Medium carbon (1040) steel	11.2
4140 steel (tempered @ 482°C)	6.1
Ti-5Al-2.5Sn titanium	5.8
2024 aluminum (T3)	5.6
4340 steel (tempered @ 425°C)	5.4
17-7PH steel	4.4
AZ31B magnesium	3.9
Ti-6Al-4V titanium	3.3
4140 steel (tempered @ 370°C)	2.4
4340 steel (tempered @ 260°C)	1.5
7075 aluminum (T651)	1.2

11.6 IMPACT FRACTURE TESTING

Prior to the advent of fracture mechanics as a scientific discipline, impact testing techniques were established so as to ascertain the fracture characteristics of materials. It was realized that the results of laboratory tensile tests could not be extrapolated to predict fracture behavior; for example, under some circumstances normally ductile metals fracture abruptly and with very little plastic deformation. Impact test conditions were chosen to represent those most severe relative to the potential for fracture—namely, (1) deformation at a relatively low temperature, (2) a high strain rate (i.e., rate of deformation), and (3) a triaxial stress state (which may be introduced by the presence of a notch).

Impact Testing Techniques

Two standardized tests,[4] the **Charpy** and **Izod,** were designed and are still used to measure the **impact energy,** sometimes also termed *notch toughness*. The Charpy V-notch (CVN) technique is most commonly used in the United States. For both Charpy and Izod, the specimen is in the shape of a bar of square cross section, into which a V-notch is machined (Figure 11.12*a*). The apparatus for making V-notch impact tests is illustrated schematically in Figure 11.12*b*. The load is applied as an impact blow from a weighted pendulum hammer that is released from a cocked position at a fixed height *h*. The specimen is positioned at the base as shown. Upon release, a knife edge mounted on the pendulum strikes and fractures the specimen at the notch, which acts as a point of stress concentration for this high-velocity

[4] ASTM Standard E 23, "Standard Test Methods for Notched Bar Impact Testing of Metallic Materials."

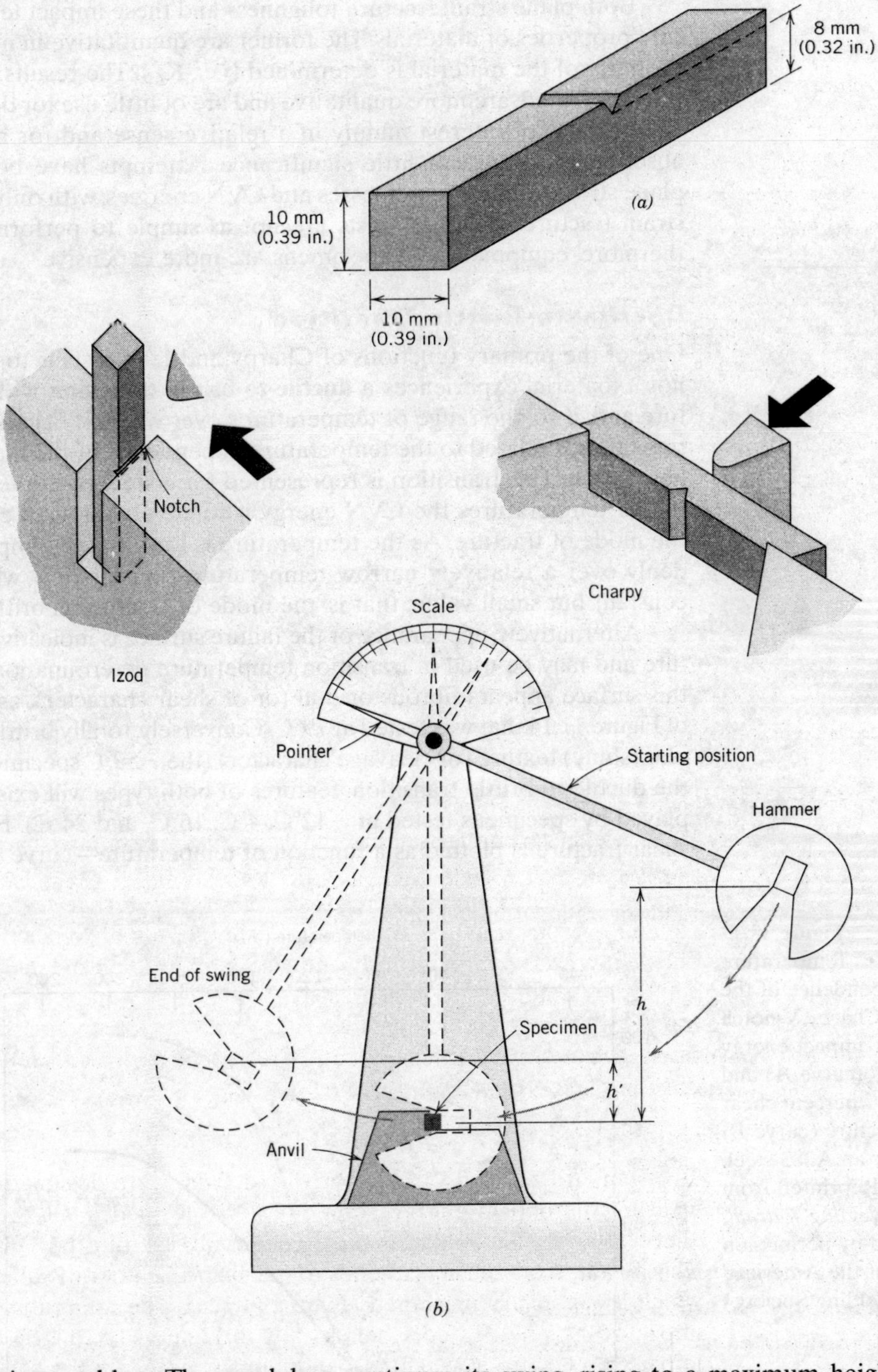

Figure 11.12 (*a*) Specimen used for Charpy and Izod impact tests. (*b*) A schematic drawing of an impact testing apparatus. The hammer is released from fixed height *h* and strikes the specimen; the energy expended in fracture is reflected in the difference between *h* and the swing height *h*′. Specimen placements for both Charpy and Izod tests are also shown. [Figure (*b*) adapted from H. W. Hayden, W. G. Moffatt, and J. Wulff, *The Structure and Properties of Materials,* Vol. III, *Mechanical Behavior,* p. 13. Copyright © 1965 by John Wiley & Sons, New York. Reprinted by permission of John Wiley & Sons, Inc.]

impact blow. The pendulum continues its swing, rising to a maximum height *h*′, which is lower than *h*. The energy absorption, computed from the difference between *h* and *h*′, is a measure of the impact energy. The primary difference between the Charpy and Izod techniques lies in the manner of specimen support, as illustrated in Figure 11.12*b*. Furthermore, these are termed impact tests in light of the manner of load application. Variables including specimen size and shape as well as notch configuration and depth influence the test results.

Both plane strain fracture toughness and these impact tests determine the fracture properties of materials. The former are quantitative in nature, in that a specific property of the material is determined (i.e., K_{Ic}). The results of the impact tests, on the other hand, are more qualitative and are of little use for design purposes. Impact energies are of interest mainly in a relative sense and for making comparisons—absolute values are of little significance. Attempts have been made to correlate plane strain fracture toughnesses and CVN energies, with only limited success. Plane strain fracture toughness tests are not as simple to perform as impact tests; furthermore, equipment and specimens are more expensive.

Ductile-to-Brittle Transition

One of the primary functions of Charpy and Izod tests is to determine whether or not a material experiences a **ductile-to-brittle transition** with decreasing temperature and, if so, the range of temperatures over which it occurs. The ductile-to-brittle transition is related to the temperature dependence of the measured impact energy absorption. This transition is represented for a steel by curve *A* in Figure 11.13. At higher temperatures the CVN energy is relatively large, in correlation with a ductile mode of fracture. As the temperature is lowered, the impact energy drops suddenly over a relatively narrow temperature range, below which the energy has a constant but small value; that is, the mode of fracture is brittle.

Alternatively, appearance of the failure surface is indicative of the nature of fracture and may be used in transition temperature determinations. For ductile fracture this surface appears fibrous or dull (or of shear character), as in the steel specimen of Figure 11.14 that was tested at 79°C. Conversely, totally brittle surfaces have a granular (shiny) texture (or cleavage character) (the −59°C specimen, Figure 11.14). Over the ductile-to-brittle transition, features of both types will exist (in Figure 11.14, displayed by specimens tested at −12°C, 4°C, 16°C, and 24°C). Frequently, the percent shear fracture is plotted as a function of temperature—curve *B* in Figure 11.13.

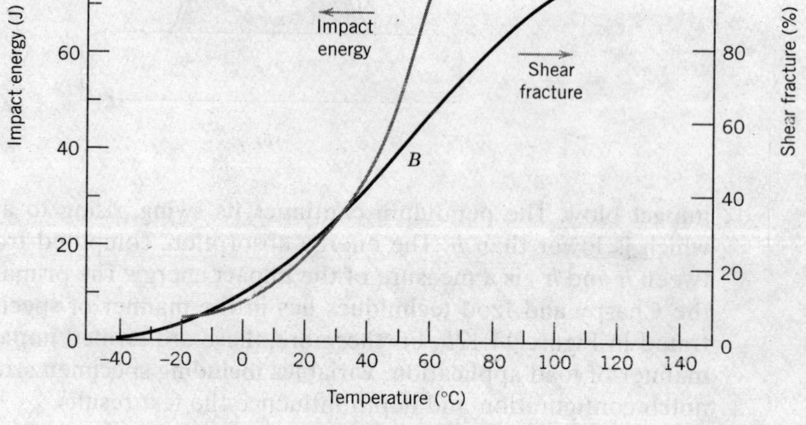

Figure 11.13 Temperature dependence of the Charpy V-notch impact energy (curve *A*) and percent shear fracture (curve *B*) for an A283 steel. (Reprinted from *Welding Journal.* Used by permission of the American Welding Society.)

Figure 11.14 Photograph of fracture surfaces of A36 steel Charpy V-notch specimens tested at indicated temperatures (in °C). (From R. W. Hertzberg, *Deformation and Fracture Mechanics of Engineering Materials*, 3rd edition, Fig. 9.6, p. 329. Copyright © 1989 by John Wiley & Sons, Inc., New York. Reprinted by permission of John Wiley & Sons, Inc.)

For many alloys there is a range of temperatures over which the ductile-to-brittle transition occurs (Figure 11.13); this presents some difficulty in specifying a single ductile-to-brittle transition temperature. No explicit criterion has been established, and so this temperature is often defined as that temperature at which the CVN energy assumes some value (e.g., 20 J or 15 ft-lb$_f$), or corresponding to some given fracture appearance (e.g., 50% fibrous fracture). Matters are further complicated inasmuch as a different transition temperature may be realized for each of these criteria. Perhaps the most conservative transition temperature is that at which the fracture surface becomes 100% fibrous; on this basis, the transition temperature is approximately 110°C (230°F) for the steel alloy that is the subject of Figure 11.13.

Structures constructed from alloys that exhibit this ductile-to-brittle behavior should be used only at temperatures above the transition temperature, to avoid brittle and catastrophic failure. Classic examples of this type of failure occurred, with disastrous consequences, during World War II when a number of welded transport ships, away from combat, suddenly and precipitously split in half. The vessels were constructed of a steel alloy that possessed adequate ductility according to room-temperature tensile tests. The brittle fractures occurred at relatively low ambient temperatures, at about 4°C (40°F), in the vicinity of the transition temperature of the alloy. Each fracture crack originated at some point of stress concentration, probably a sharp corner or fabrication defect, and then propagated around the entire girth of the ship.

In addition to the ductile-to-brittle transition represented in Figure 11.13, two other general types of impact energy-versus-temperature behavior have been observed; these are represented schematically by the upper and lower curves of Figure 11.15.

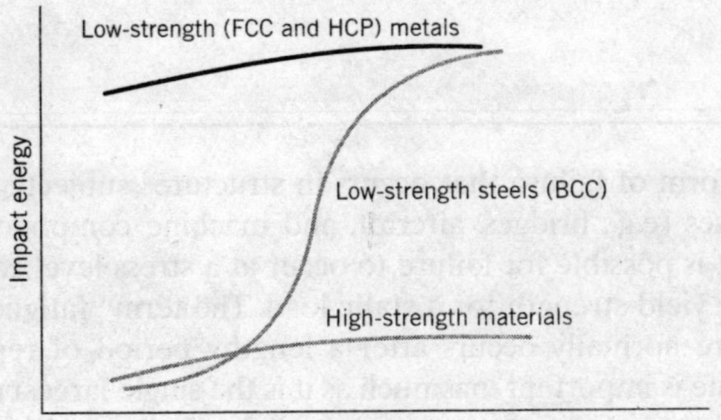

Figure 11.15 Schematic curves for the three general types of impact energy-versus-temperature behavior.

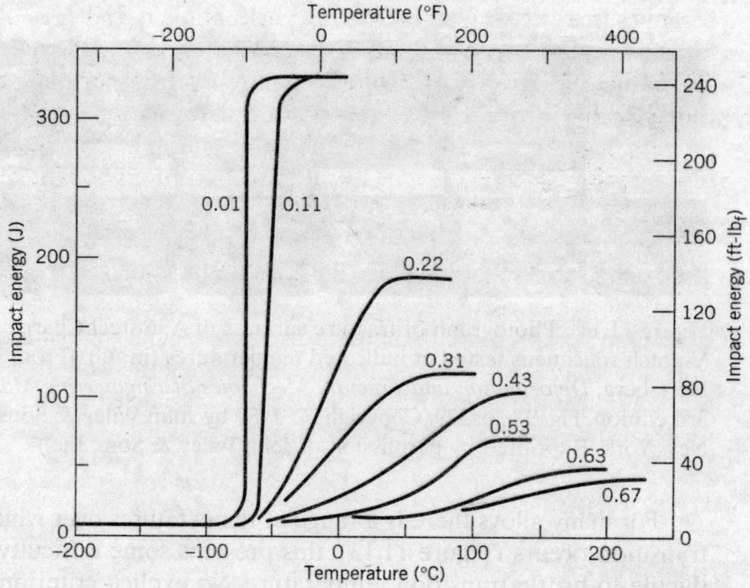

Figure 11.16 Influence of carbon content on the Charpy V-notch energy-versus-temperature behavior for steel. (Reprinted with permission from ASM International, Metals Park, OH 44073-9989, USA; J. A. Reinbolt and W. J. Harris, Jr., "Effect of Alloying Elements on Notch Toughness of Pearlitic Steels," *Transactions of ASM*, Vol. 43, 1951.)

Here it may be noted that low-strength FCC metals (some aluminum and copper alloys) and most HCP metals do not experience a ductile-to-brittle transition (corresponding to the upper curve of Figure 11.15), and retain high impact energies (i.e., remain ductile) with decreasing temperature. For high-strength materials (e.g., high-strength steels and titanium alloys), the impact energy is also relatively insensitive to temperature (the lower curve of Figure 11.15); however, these materials are also very brittle, as reflected by their low impact energy values. And, of course, the characteristic ductile-to-brittle transition is represented by the middle curve of Figure 11.15. As noted, this behavior is typically found in low-strength steels that have the BCC crystal structure.

For these low-strength steels, the transition temperature is sensitive to both alloy composition and microstructure. For example, decreasing the average grain size results in a lowering of the transition temperature. Hence, refining the grain size both strengthens (Section 10.8) and toughens steels. In contrast, increasing the carbon content, while increasing the strength of steels, also raises the CVN transition of steels, as indicated in Figure 11.16.

Most ceramics and polymers also experience a ductile-to-brittle transition. For ceramic materials, the transition occurs only at elevated temperatures, ordinarily in excess of 1000°C (1850°F). This behavior as related to polymers is discussed in Section 14.6.

Fatigue

Fatigue is a form of failure that occurs in structures subjected to dynamic and fluctuating stresses (e.g., bridges, aircraft, and machine components). Under these circumstances it is possible for failure to occur at a stress level considerably lower than the tensile or yield strength for a static load. The term "fatigue" is used because this type of failure normally occurs after a lengthy period of repeated stress or strain cycling. Fatigue is important inasmuch as it is the single largest cause of failure in metals, estimated to comprise approximately 90% of all metallic failures; polymers and ceramics (except for glasses) are also susceptible to this type of failure. Furthermore, fatigue is catastrophic and insidious, occurring very suddenly and without warning.

Fatigue failure is brittlelike in nature even in normally ductile metals, in that there is very little, if any, gross plastic deformation associated with failure. The process occurs by the initiation and propagation of cracks, and ordinarily the fracture surface is perpendicular to the direction of an applied tensile stress.

11.7 CYCLIC STRESSES

The applied stress may be axial (tension-compression), flexural (bending), or torsional (twisting) in nature. In general, three different fluctuating stress–time modes are possible. One is represented schematically by a regular and sinusoidal time dependence in Figure 11.17*a*, wherein the amplitude is symmetrical about a mean zero stress level, for example, alternating from a maximum tensile stress (σ_{max}) to a minimum compressive stress (σ_{min}) of equal magnitude; this is referred to as a *reversed stress cycle.*

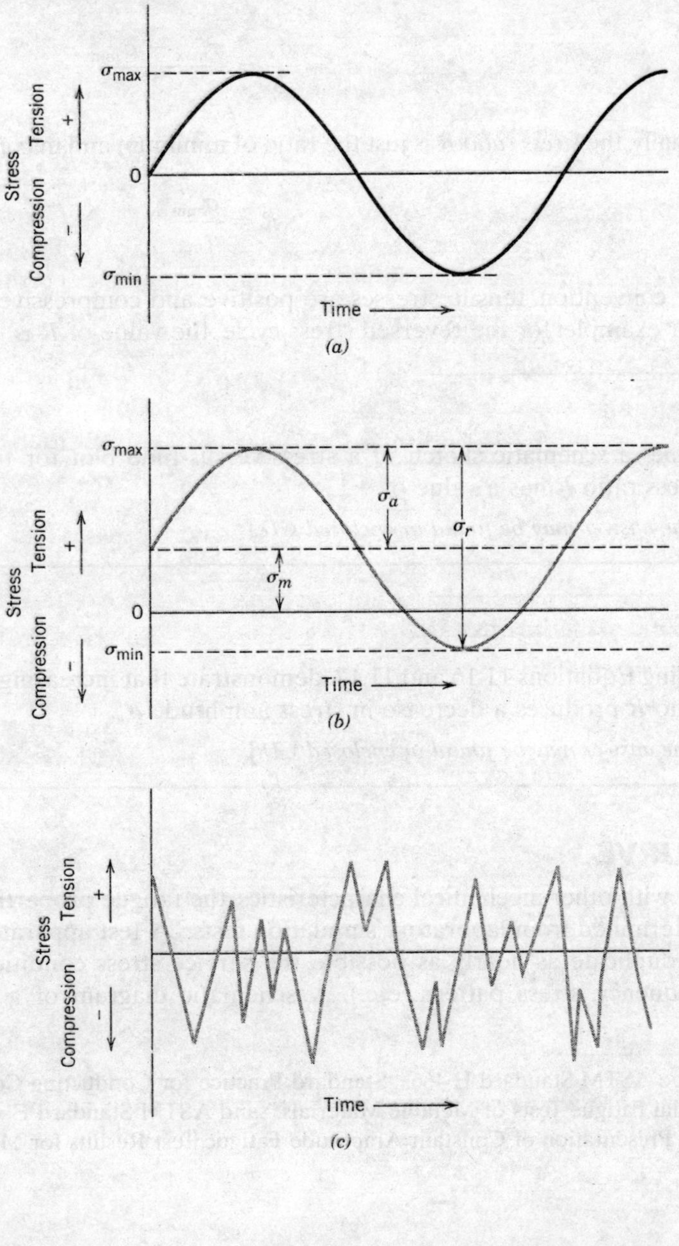

Figure 11.17 Variation of stress with time that accounts for fatigue failure of metalss. (*a*) Reversed stress cycle, in which the stress alternates from a maximum tensile stress (+) to a maximum compressive stress (−) of equal magnitude. (*b*) Repeated stress cycle, in which maximum and minimum stresses are asymmetrical relative to the zero-stress level; mean stress σ_m, range of stress σ_r, and stress amplitude σ_a are indicated. (*c*) Random stress cycle.

Another type, termed *repeated stress cycle,* is illustrated in Figure 11.17*b*; the maxima and minima are asymmetrical relative to the zero stress level. Finally, the stress level may vary randomly in amplitude and frequency, as exemplified in Figure 11.17*c*.

Also indicated in Figure 11.17*b* are several parameters used to characterize the fluctuating stress cycle. The stress amplitude alternates about a *mean stress* σ_m, defined as the average of the maximum and minimum stresses in the cycle, or

$$\sigma_m = \frac{\sigma_{max} + \sigma_{min}}{2} \tag{11.14}$$

Furthermore, the *range of stress* σ_r is just the difference between σ_{max} and σ_{min}—namely,

$$\sigma_r = \sigma_{max} - \sigma_{min} \tag{11.15}$$

Stress amplitude σ_a is just one half of this range of stress, or

$$\sigma_a = \frac{\sigma_r}{2} = \frac{\sigma_{max} - \sigma_{min}}{2} \tag{11.16}$$

Finally, the *stress ratio R* is just the ratio of minimum and maximum stress amplitudes:

$$R = \frac{\sigma_{min}}{\sigma_{max}} \tag{11.17}$$

By convention, tensile stresses are positive and compressive stresses are negative. For example, for the reversed stress cycle, the value of R is -1.

Concept Check 11.2

Make a schematic sketch of a stress-versus-time plot for the situation when the stress ratio R has a value of $+1$.

[The answer may be found in enclosed CD.]

Concept Check 11.3

Using Equations 11.16 and 11.17, demonstrate that increasing the value of the stress ratio R produces a decrease in stress amplitude σ_a.

[The answer may be found in enclosed CD.]

11.8 THE *S–N* CURVE

As with other mechanical characteristics, the fatigue properties of materials can be determined from laboratory simulation tests.[5] A test apparatus should be designed to duplicate as nearly as possible the service stress conditions (stress level, time frequency, stress pattern, etc.). A schematic diagram of a rotating-bending test

[5] See ASTM Standard E 466, "Standard Practice for Conducting Constant Amplitude Axial Fatigue Tests of Metallic Materials," and ASTM Standard E 468, "Standard Practice for Presentation of Constant Amplitude Fatigue Test Results for Metallic Materials."

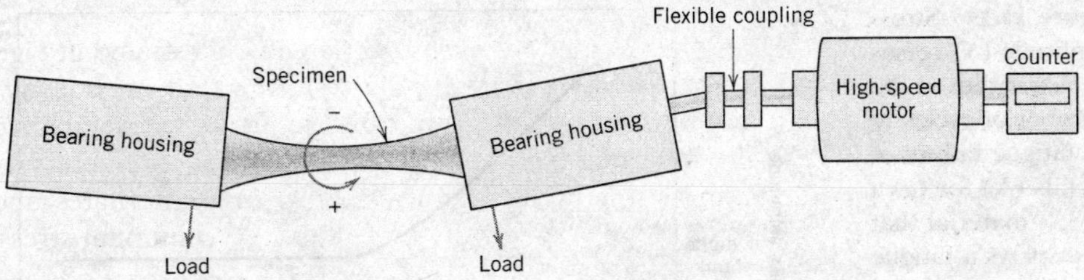

Figure 11.18 Schematic diagram of fatigue-testing apparatus for making rotating-bending tests. (From Keyser, *Materials Science in Engineering,* 4th Edition, © 1986, p. 811. Adapted by permission of Pearson Education, Inc., Upper Saddle River, NJ.)

apparatus, commonly used for fatigue testing, is shown in Figure 11.18; the compression and tensile stresses are imposed on the specimen as it is simultaneously bent and rotated. Tests are also frequently conducted using an alternating uniaxial tension-compression stress cycle.

A series of tests are commenced by subjecting a specimen to the stress cycling at a relatively large maximum stress amplitude (σ_{max}), usually on the order of two-thirds of the static tensile strength; the number of cycles to failure is counted. This procedure is repeated on other specimens at progressively decreasing maximum stress amplitudes. Data are plotted as stress S versus the logarithm of the number N of cycles to failure for each of the specimens. The values of S are normally taken as stress amplitudes (σ_a, Equation 11.16); on occasion, σ_{max} or σ_{min} values may be used.

Two distinct types of S–N behavior are observed, which are represented schematically in Figure 11.19. As these plots indicate, the higher the magnitude of the stress, the smaller the number of cycles the material is capable of sustaining before failure. For some ferrous (iron base) and titanium alloys, the S–N curve (Figure 11.19*a*) becomes horizontal at higher N values; or there is a limiting stress level, called the **fatigue limit** (also sometimes the *endurance limit*), below which fatigue failure will not occur. This fatigue limit represents the largest value of fluctuating stress that will *not* cause failure for essentially an infinite number of cycles. For many steels, fatigue limits range between 35% and 60% of the tensile strength.

Most nonferrous alloys (e.g., aluminum, copper, magnesium) do not have a fatigue limit, in that the S–N curve continues its downward trend at increasingly greater N values (Figure 11.19*b*). Thus, fatigue will ultimately occur regardless of the magnitude of the stress. For these materials, the fatigue response is specified as **fatigue strength,** which is defined as the stress level at which failure will occur for some specified number of cycles (e.g., 10^7 cycles). The determination of fatigue strength is also demonstrated in Figure 11.19*b*.

Another important parameter that characterizes a material's fatigue behavior is **fatigue life** N_f. It is the number of cycles to cause failure at a specified stress level, as taken from the S–N plot (Figure 11.19*b*).

Unfortunately, there always exists considerable scatter in fatigue data—that is, a variation in the measured N value for a number of specimens tested at the same stress level. This variation may lead to significant design uncertainties when fatigue life and/or fatigue limit (or strength) are being considered. The scatter in results is a consequence of the fatigue sensitivity to a number of test and material parameters that are impossible to control precisely. These parameters include specimen fabrication and surface preparation, metallurgical variables, specimen alignment in the apparatus, mean stress, and test frequency.

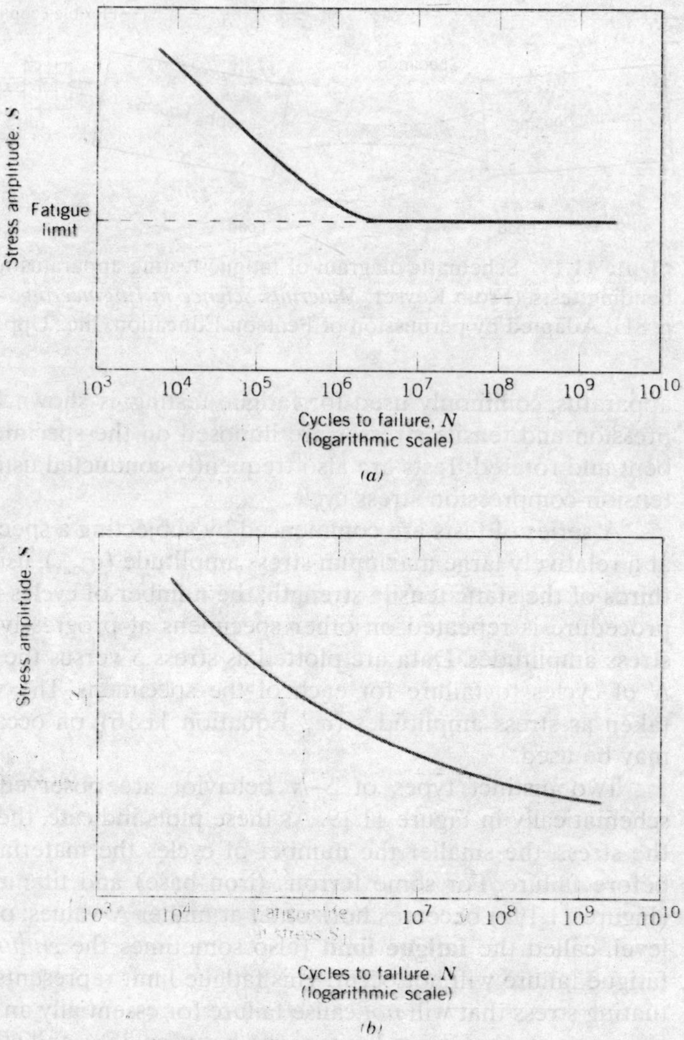

Figure 11.19 Stress amplitude (S) versus logarithm of the number of cycles to fatigue failure of metals (N) for (a) a material that displays a fatigue limit, and (b) a material that does not display a fatigue limit.

Fatigue S–N curves similar to those shown in Figure 11.19 represent "best fit" curves that have been drawn through average-value data points. It is a little unsettling to realize that approximately one-half of the specimens tested actually failed at stress levels lying nearly 25% below the curve (as determined on the basis of statistical treatments).

Several statistical techniques have been developed to specify fatigue life and fatigue limit in terms of probabilities. One convenient way of representing data treated in this manner is with a series of constant probability curves, several of which are plotted in Figure 11.20. The P value associated with each curve represents the probability of failure. For example, at a stress of 200 MPa, we would expect 1% of the specimens to fail at about 10^6 cycles and 50% to fail at about 2×10^7 cycles, and so on. Remember that S–N curves represented in the literature are normally average values, unless noted otherwise.

The fatigue behaviors represented in Figures 11.19a and 11.19b may be classified into two domains. One is associated with relatively high loads that produce not only elastic strain but also some plastic strain during each cycle. Consequently, fatigue lives are relatively short: this domain is termed *low-cycle fatigue* and occurs

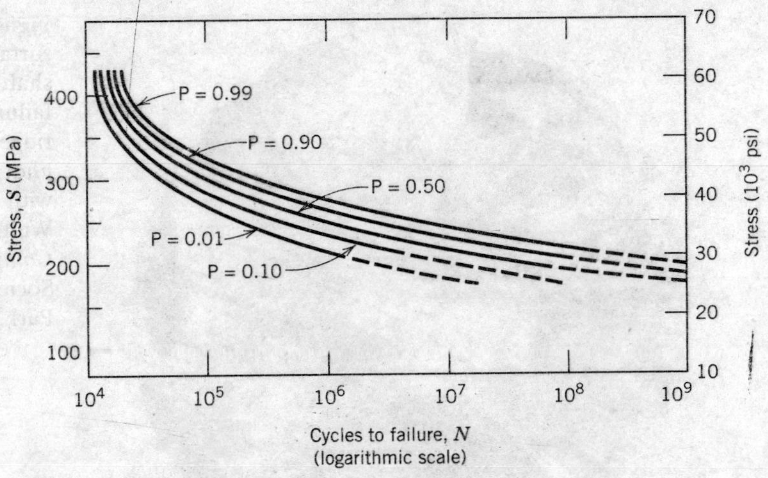

Figure 11.20 Fatigue *S–N* probability of failure of metals curves for a 7075-T6 aluminum alloy; *P* denotes the probability of failure of metals. (From G. M. Sinclair and T. J. Dolan, *Trans. ASME*, **75,** 1953, p. 867. Reprinted with permission of the American Society of Mechanical Engineers.)

at less than about 10^4 to 10^5 cycles. For lower stress levels wherein deformations are totally elastic, longer lives result. This is called *high-cycle fatigue* inasmuch as relatively large numbers of cycles are required to produce fatigue failure. High-cycle fatigue is associated with fatigue lives greater than about 10^4 to 10^5 cycles.

11.9 CRACK INITIATION AND PROPAGATION

The process of fatigue failure is characterized by three distinct steps: (1) crack initiation, wherein a small crack forms at some point of high stress concentration; (2) crack propagation, during which this crack advances incrementally with each stress cycle; and (3) final failure, which occurs very rapidly once the advancing crack has reached a critical size. Cracks associated with fatigue failure almost always initiate (or nucleate) on the surface of a component at some point of stress concentration. Crack nucleation sites include surface scratches, sharp fillets, keyways, threads, dents, and the like. In addition, cyclic loading can produce microscopic surface discontinuities resulting from dislocation slip steps that may also act as stress raisers, and therefore as crack initiation sites.

The region of a fracture surface that formed during the crack propagation step may be characterized by two types of markings termed *beachmarks* and *striations*. Both of these features indicate the position of the crack tip at some point in time and appear as concentric ridges that expand away from the crack initiation site(s), frequently in a circular or semicircular pattern. Beachmarks (sometimes also called "clamshell marks") are of macroscopic dimensions (Figure 11.21), and may be observed with the unaided eye. These markings are found for components that experienced interruptions during the crack propagation stage—for example, a machine that operated only during normal work-shift hours. Each beachmark band represents a period of time over which crack growth occurred.

On the other hand, fatigue striations are microscopic in size and subject to observation with the electron microscope (either TEM or SEM). Figure 11.22 is an electron fractograph that shows this feature. Each striation is thought to represent the advance distance of a crack front during a single load cycle. Striation width depends on, and increases with, increasing stress range.

At this point it should be emphasized that although both beachmarks and striations are fatigue fracture surface features having similar appearances, they are

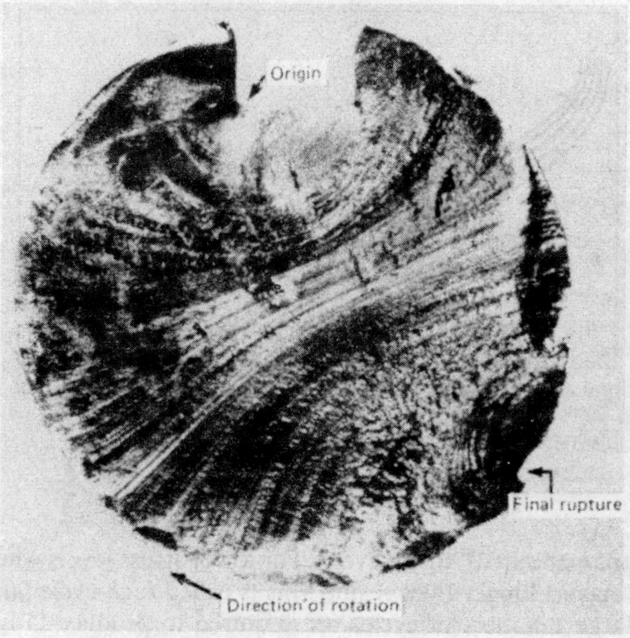

Figure 11.21 Fracture surface of a rotating steel shaft that experienced fatigue failure of metals. Beachmark ridges are visible in the photograph. (Reproduced with permission from D. J. Wulpi, *Understanding How Components Fail,* American Society for Metals, Materials Park, OH, 1985.)

nevertheless different, both in origin and size. There may be literally thousands of striations within a single beachmark.

Often the cause of failure may be deduced after examination of the failure surfaces. The presence of beachmarks and/or striations on a fracture surface confirms that the cause of failure was fatigue. Nevertheless, the absence of either or both does not exclude fatigue as the cause of failure.

One final comment regarding fatigue failure surfaces: Beachmarks and striations will not appear on that region over which the rapid failure occurs. Rather, the

Figure 11.22 Transmission electron fractograph showing fatigue striations in aluminum. Magnification unknown. (From V. J. Colangelo and F. A. Heiser, *Analysis of Metallurgical Failure of metalss,* 2nd edition. Copyright © 1987 by John Wiley & Sons, New York. Reprinted by permission of John Wiley & Sons, Inc.)

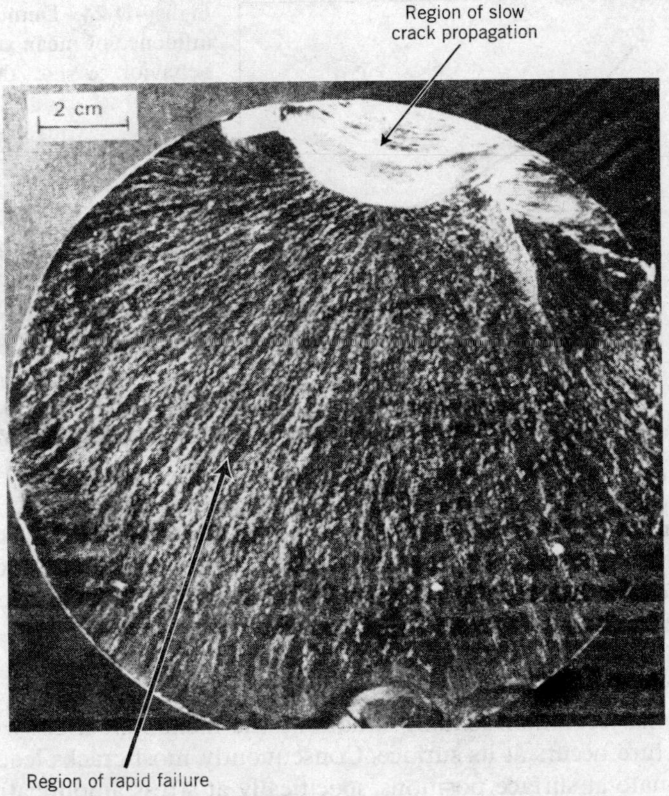

Figure 11.23 Fatigue failure of metals surface. A crack formed at the top edge. The smooth region also near the top corresponds to the area over which the crack propagated slowly. Rapid failure of metals occurred over the area having a dull and fibrous texture (the largest area). Approximately 0.5×. [Reproduced by permission from *Metals Handbook: Fractography and Atlas of Fractographs,* Vol. 9, 8th edition, H. E. Boyer (Editor), American Society for Metals, 1974.]

rapid failure may be either ductile or brittle; evidence of plastic deformation will be present for ductile, and absent for brittle, failure. This region of failure may be noted in Figure 11.23.

Concept Check 11.4

Surfaces for some steel specimens that have failed by fatigue have a bright crystalline or grainy appearance. Laymen may explain the failure by saying that the metal crystallized while in service. Offer a criticism for this explanation.

[*The answer may be found in enclosed CD.*]

11.10 FACTORS THAT AFFECT FATIGUE LIFE

As mentioned in Section 11.8, the fatigue behavior of engineering materials is highly sensitive to a number of variables. Some of these factors include mean stress level, geometrical design, surface effects, and metallurgical variables, as well as the environment. This section is devoted to a discussion of these factors and, in addition, to measures that may be taken to improve the fatigue resistance of structural components.

Mean Stress

The dependence of fatigue life on stress amplitude is represented on the *S–N* plot. Such data are taken for a constant mean stress σ_m, often for the reversed cycle

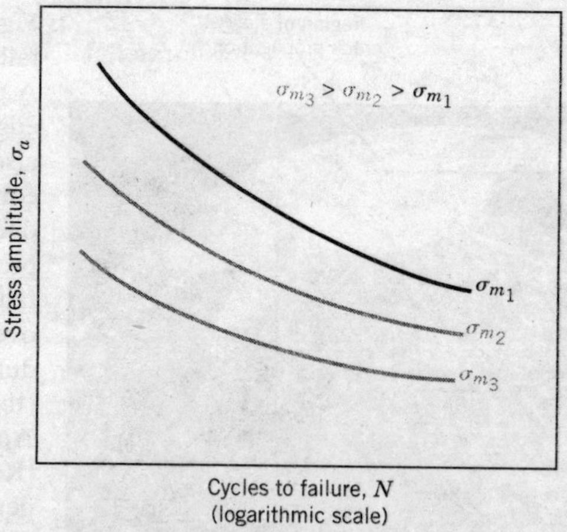

Figure 11.24 Demonstration of the influence of mean stress σ_m on S–N fatigue behavior.

situation ($\sigma_m = 0$). Mean stress, however, will also affect fatigue life; this influence may be represented by a series of S–N curves, each measured at a different σ_m, as depicted schematically in Figure 11.24. As may be noted, increasing the mean stress level leads to a decrease in fatigue life.

Surface Effects

For many common loading situations, the maximum stress within a component or structure occurs at its surface. Consequently, most cracks leading to fatigue failure originate at surface positions, specifically at stress amplification sites. Therefore, it has been observed that fatigue life is especially sensitive to the condition and configuration of the component surface. Numerous factors influence fatigue resistance, the proper management of which will lead to an improvement in fatigue life. These include design criteria as well as various surface treatments.

Design Factors

The design of a component can have a significant influence on its fatigue characteristics. Any notch or geometrical discontinuity can act as a stress raiser and fatigue crack initiation site; these design features include grooves, holes, keyways, threads, and so on. The sharper the discontinuity (i.e., the smaller the radius of curvature), the more severe the stress concentration. The probability of fatigue failure may be reduced by avoiding (when possible) these structural irregularities, or by making design modifications whereby sudden contour changes leading to sharp corners are eliminated—for example, calling for rounded fillets with large radii of curvature at the point where there is a change in diameter for a rotating shaft (Figure 11.25).

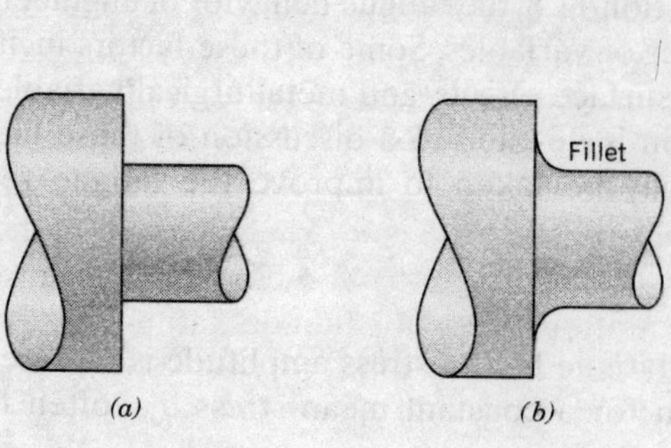

Figure 11.25 Demonstration of how design can reduce stress amplification. (*a*) Poor design: sharp corner. (*b*) Good design: fatigue lifetime improved by incorporating rounded fillet into a rotating shaft at the point where there is a change in diameter.

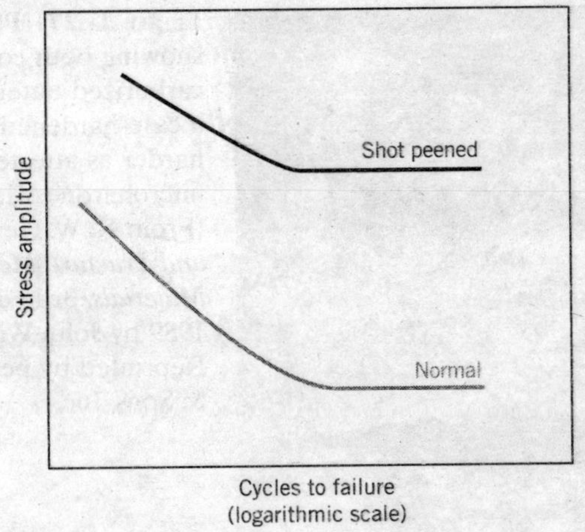

Figure 11.26 Schematic *S–N* fatigue curves for normal and shot-peened steel.

Surface Treatments

During machining operations, small scratches and grooves are invariably introduced into the workpiece surface by cutting tool action. These surface markings can limit the fatigue life. It has been observed that improving the surface finish by polishing will enhance fatigue life significantly.

One of the most effective methods of increasing fatigue performance is by imposing residual compressive stresses within a thin outer surface layer. Thus, a surface tensile stress of external origin will be partially nullified and reduced in magnitude by the residual compressive stress. The net effect is that the likelihood of crack formation and therefore of fatigue failure is reduced.

Residual compressive stresses are commonly introduced into ductile metals mechanically by localized plastic deformation within the outer surface region. Commercially, this is often accomplished by a process termed *shot peening*. Small, hard particles (shot) having diameters within the range of 0.1 to 1.0 mm are projected at high velocities onto the surface to be treated. The resulting deformation induces compressive stresses to a depth of between one-quarter and one-half of the shot diameter. The influence of shot peening on the fatigue behavior of steel is demonstrated schematically in Figure 11.26.

Case hardening is a technique by which both surface hardness and fatigue life are enhanced for steel alloys. This is accomplished by a carburizing or nitriding process whereby a component is exposed to a carbonaceous or nitrogenous atmosphere at an elevated temperature. A carbon- or nitrogen-rich outer surface layer (or "case") is introduced by atomic diffusion from the gaseous phase. The case is normally on the order of 1 mm deep and is harder than the inner core of material. (The influence of carbon content on hardness for Fe–C alloys is demonstrated in Figure 8.29*a*.) The improvement of fatigue properties results from increased hardness within the case, as well as the desired residual compressive stresses the formation of which attends the carburizing or nitriding process. A carbon-rich outer case may be observed for the gear shown in the chapter-opening photograph for Chapter 6; it appears as a dark outer rim within the sectioned segment. The increase in case hardness is demonstrated in the photomicrograph appearing in Figure 11.27. The dark and elongated diamond shapes are Knoop microhardness indentations. The upper indentation, lying within the carburized layer, is smaller than the core indentation.

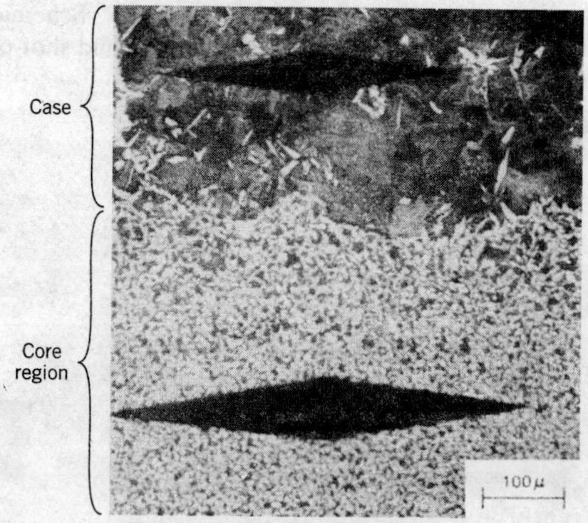

Figure 11.27 Photomicrograph showing both core (bottom) and carburized outer case (top) regions of a case-hardened steel. The case is harder as attested by the smaller microhardness indentation. 100×. (From R. W. Hertzberg, *Deformation and Fracture Mechanics of Engineering Materials,* 3rd edition. Copyright © 1989 by John Wiley & Sons, New York. Reprinted by permission of John Wiley & Sons, Inc.)

11.11 ENVIRONMENTAL EFFECTS

Environmental factors may also affect the fatigue behavior of materials. A few brief comments will be given relative to two types of environment-assisted fatigue failure: thermal fatigue and corrosion fatigue.

Thermal fatigue is normally induced at elevated temperatures by fluctuating thermal stresses; mechanical stresses from an external source need not be present. The origin of these thermal stresses is the restraint to the dimensional expansion and/or contraction that would normally occur in a structural member with variations in temperature. The magnitude of a thermal stress developed by a temperature change ΔT is dependent on the coefficient of thermal expansion α_l and the modulus of elasticity E according to

$$\sigma = \alpha_l E \, \Delta T \tag{11.18}$$

(The topics of thermal expansion and thermal stresses are discussed in Sections 19.3 and 19.5.) Of course, thermal stresses will not arise if this mechanical restraint is absent. Therefore, one obvious way to prevent this type of fatigue is to eliminate, or at least reduce, the restraint source, thus allowing unhindered dimensional changes with temperature variations, or to choose materials with appropriate physical properties.

Failure that occurs by the simultaneous action of a cyclic stress and chemical attack is termed **corrosion fatigue.** Corrosive environments have a deleterious influence and produce shorter fatigue lives. Even the normal ambient atmosphere will affect the fatigue behavior of some materials. Small pits may form as a result of chemical reactions between the environment and material, which serve as points of stress concentration and therefore as crack nucleation sites. In addition, crack propagation rate is enhanced as a result of the corrosive environment. The nature of the stress cycles will influence the fatigue behavior; for example, lowering the load application frequency leads to longer periods during which the opened crack is in contact with the environment and to a reduction in the fatigue life.

Several approaches to corrosion fatigue prevention exist. On one hand, we can take measures to reduce the rate of corrosion by some of the techniques discussed in Chapter 16—for example, apply protective surface coatings, select a more corrosion-resistant material, and reduce the corrosiveness of the environment. And/or it might be advisable to take actions to minimize the probability of normal fatigue failure, as outlined above—for example, reduce the applied tensile stress level and impose residual compressive stresses on the surface of the member.

Creep

Materials are often placed in service at elevated temperatures and exposed to static mechanical stresses (e.g., turbine rotors in jet engines and steam generators that experience centrifugal stresses, and high-pressure steam lines). Deformation under such circumstances is termed **creep.** Defined as the time-dependent and permanent deformation of materials when subjected to a constant load or stress, creep is normally an undesirable phenomenon and is often the limiting factor in the lifetime of a part. It is observed in all materials types; for metals it becomes important only for temperatures greater than about $0.4T_m$ (T_m = absolute melting temperature). Amorphous polymers, which include plastics and rubbers, are especially sensitive to creep deformation as discussed in Section 14.4.

11.12 GENERALIZED CREEP BEHAVIOR

A typical creep test[6] consists of subjecting a specimen to a constant load or stress while maintaining the temperature constant; deformation or strain is measured and plotted as a function of elapsed time. Most tests are the constant load type, which yield information of an engineering nature; constant stress tests are employed to provide a better understanding of the mechanisms of creep.

Figure 11.28 is a schematic representation of the typical constant load creep behavior of metals. Upon application of the load there is an instantaneous deformation, as indicated in the figure, which is mostly elastic. The resulting creep curve consists of three regions, each of which has its own distinctive strain–time feature. *Primary* or *transient creep* occurs first, typified by a continuously decreasing creep rate; that is, the slope of the curve diminishes with time. This suggests that the material is experiencing an increase in creep resistance or strain hardening (Section 10.10)—deformation becomes more difficult as the material is strained. For *secondary creep,* sometimes termed *steady-state creep,* the rate is constant; that is, the plot becomes linear. This is often the stage of creep that is of the longest duration. The constancy of creep rate is explained on the basis of a balance between the competing processes of strain hardening and recovery, recovery (Section 10.11) being the process whereby a material becomes softer and retains its ability to experience deformation. Finally, for *tertiary creep,* there is an acceleration of the rate and ultimate failure. This failure is frequently termed *rupture* and results from microstructural and/or metallurgical changes; for example, grain boundary separation, and the formation of internal cracks, cavities, and voids. Also, for tensile loads, a neck may form at some point within the deformation region. These all lead to a decrease in the effective cross-sectional area and an increase in strain rate.

[6] ASTM Standard E 139, "Standard Practice for Conducting Creep, Creep-Rupture, and Stress-Rupture Tests of Metallic Materials."

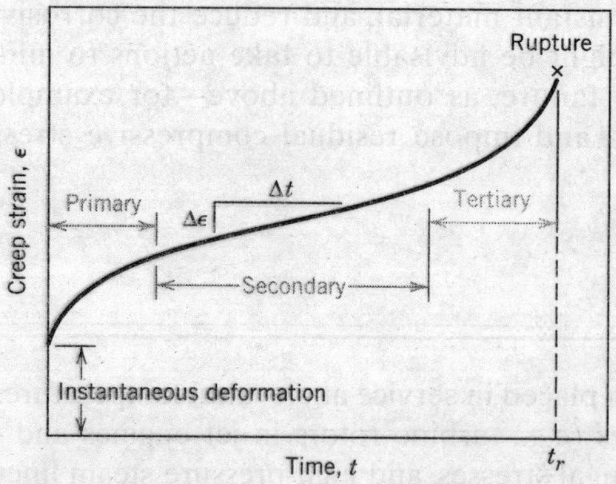

Figure 11.28 Typical creep curve of strain versus time at constant stress and constant elevated temperature. The minimum creep rate $\Delta\epsilon/\Delta t$ is the slope of the linear segment in the secondary region. Rupture lifetime t_r is the total time to rupture.

For metallic materials most creep tests are conducted in uniaxial tension using a specimen having the same geometry as for tensile tests (Figure 9.8). On the other hand, uniaxial compression tests are more appropriate for brittle materials; these provide a better measure of the intrinsic creep properties inasmuch as there is no stress amplification and crack propagation, as with tensile loads. Compressive test specimens are usually right cylinders or parallelepipeds having length-to-diameter ratios ranging from about 2 to 4. For most materials creep properties are virtually independent of loading direction.

Possibly the most important parameter from a creep test is the slope of the secondary portion of the creep curve ($\Delta\epsilon/\Delta t$ in Figure 11.28); this is often called the minimum or *steady-state creep rate* $\dot{\epsilon}_s$. It is the engineering design parameter that is considered for long-life applications, such as a nuclear power plant component that is scheduled to operate for several decades, and when failure or too much strain are not options. On the other hand, for many relatively short-life creep situations (e.g., turbine blades in military aircraft and rocket motor nozzles), *time to rupture,* or the *rupture lifetime* t_r, is the dominant design consideration; it is also indicated in Figure 11.28. Of course, for its determination, creep tests must be conducted to the point of failure; these are termed *creep rupture* tests. Thus, a knowledge of these creep characteristics of a material allows the design engineer to ascertain its suitability for a specific application.

Concept Check 11.5

Superimpose on the same strain-versus-time plot schematic creep curves for both constant tensile stress and constant tensile load, and explain the differences in behavior.

[*The answer may be found in enclosed CD.*]

11.13 STRESS AND TEMPERATURE EFFECTS

Both temperature and the level of the applied stress influence the creep characteristics (Figure 11.29). At a temperature substantially below $0.4T_m$, and after the initial deformation, the strain is virtually independent of time. With either increasing stress or temperature, the following will be noted: (1) the instantaneous strain at the time of stress application increases, (2) the steady-state creep rate is increased, and (3) the rupture lifetime is diminished.

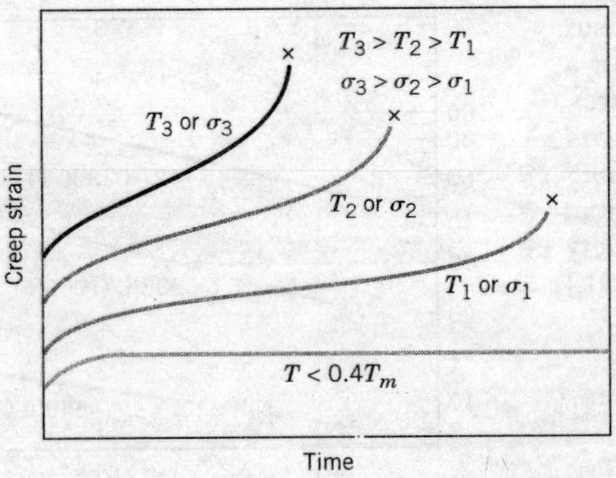

Figure 11.29 Influence of stress σ and temperature T on creep behavior.

The results of creep rupture tests are most commonly presented as the logarithm of stress versus the logarithm of rupture lifetime. Figure 11.30 is one such plot for a nickel alloy in which a linear relationship can be seen to exist at each temperature. For some alloys and over relatively large stress ranges, nonlinearity in these curves is observed.

Empirical relationships have been developed in which the steady-state creep rate as a function of stress and temperature is expressed. Its dependence on stress can be written

$$\dot{\epsilon}_s = K_1\sigma^n \tag{11.19}$$

where K_1 and n are material constants. A plot of the logarithm of $\dot{\epsilon}_s$ versus the logarithm of σ yields a straight line with slope of n; this is shown in Figure 11.31 for a nickel alloy at three temperatures. Clearly, a straight line segment is drawn at each temperature.

Now, when the influence of temperature is included,

$$\dot{\epsilon}_s = K_2\sigma^n \exp\left(-\frac{Q_c}{RT}\right) \tag{11.20}$$

where K_2 and Q_c are constants; Q_c is termed the activation energy for creep.

Figure 11.30 Stress (logarithmic scale) versus rupture lifetime (logarithmic scale) for a low carbon–nickel alloy at three temperatures. [From *Metals Handbook: Properties and Selection: Stainless Steels, Tool Materials and Special-Purpose Metals,* Vol. 3, 9th edition, D. Benjamin (Senior Editor), American Society for Metals, 1980, p. 130.]

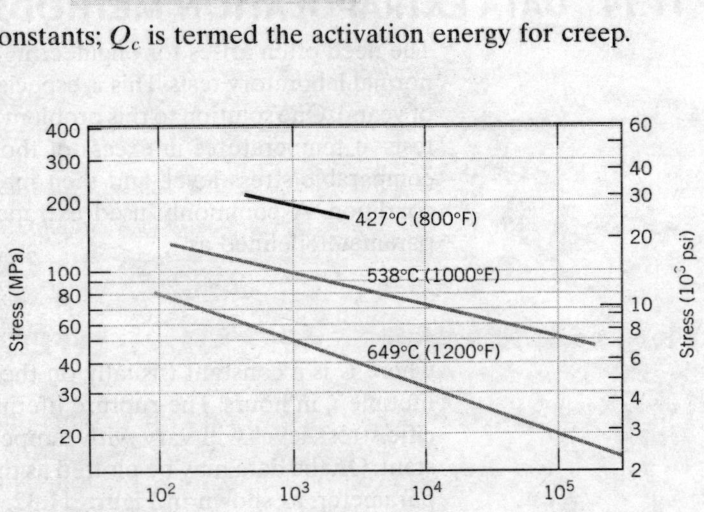

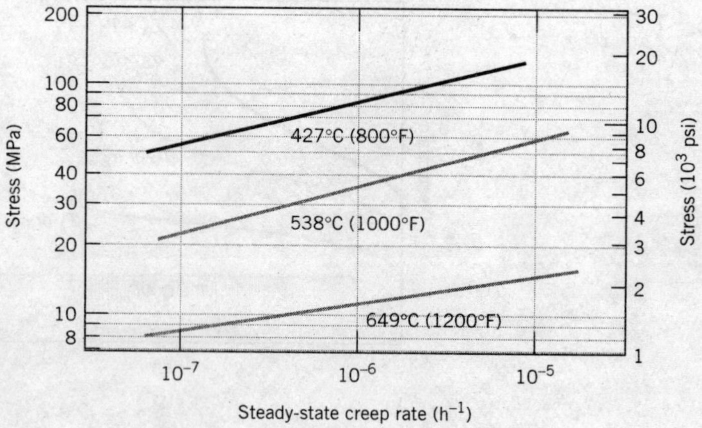

Figure 11.31 Stress (logarithmic scale) versus steady-state creep rate (logarithmic scale) for a low carbon–nickel alloy at three temperatures. [From *Metals Handbook: Properties and Selection: Stainless Steels, Tool Materials and Special-Purpose Metals,* Vol. 3, 9th edition, D. Benjamin (Senior Editor), American Society for Metals, 1980, p. 131.]

Several theoretical mechanisms have been proposed to explain the creep behavior for various materials; these mechanisms involve stress-induced vacancy diffusion, grain boundary diffusion, dislocation motion, and grain boundary sliding. Each leads to a different value of the stress exponent n in Equation 11.19. It has been possible to elucidate the creep mechanism for a particular material by comparing its experimental n value with values predicted for the various mechanisms. In addition, correlations have been made between the activation energy for creep (Q_c) and the activation energy for diffusion (Q_d, Equation 6.8).

Creep data of this nature are represented pictorially for some well-studied systems in the form of stress–temperature diagrams, which are termed *deformation mechanism maps.* These maps indicate stress–temperature regimes (or areas) over which various mechanisms operate. Constant strain rate contours are often also included. Thus, for some creep situation, given the appropriate deformation mechanism map and any two of the three parameters—temperature, stress level, and creep strain rate—the third parameter may be determined.

11.14 DATA EXTRAPOLATION METHODS

The need often arises for engineering creep data that are impractical to collect from normal laboratory tests. This is especially true for prolonged exposures (on the order of years). One solution to this problem involves performing creep and/or creep rupture tests at temperatures in excess of those required, for shorter time periods, and at a comparable stress level, and then making a suitable extrapolation to the in-service condition. A commonly used extrapolation procedure employs the Larson–Miller parameter, defined as

$$T(C + \log t_r) \tag{11.21}$$

where C is a constant (usually on the order of 20), for T in Kelvin and the rupture lifetime t_r in hours. The rupture lifetime of a given material measured at some specific stress level will vary with temperature such that this parameter remains constant. Or, the data may be plotted as the logarithm of stress versus the Larson–Miller parameter, as shown in Figure 11.32. Utilization of this technique is demonstrated in the following design example.

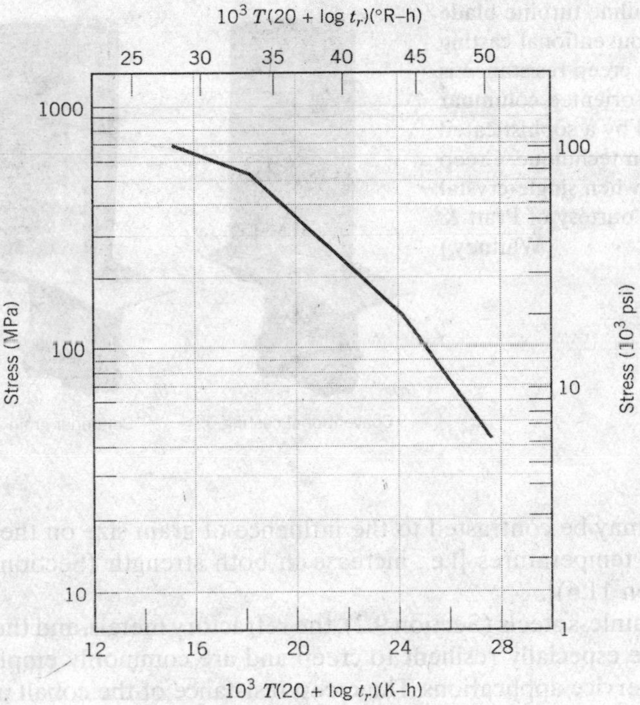

Figure 11.32 Logarithm stress versus the Larson–Miller parameter for an S-590 iron. (From F. R. Larson and J. Miller, *Trans. ASME,* **74,** 765, 1952. Reprinted by permission of ASME.)

DESIGN EXAMPLE 11.2

Rupture Lifetime Prediction

Using the Larson–Miller data for S-590 iron shown in Figure 11.32, predict the time to rupture for a component that is subjected to a stress of 140 MPa at 800°C (1073 K).

Solution

From Figure 11.32, at 140 MPa the value of the Larson–Miller parameter is 24.0×10^3, for T in K and t_r in h; therefore,

$$24.0 \times 10^3 = T(20 + \log t_r)$$
$$= 1073(20 + \log t_r)$$

and, solving for the time,

$$22.37 = 20 + \log t_r$$
$$t_r = 233 \text{ h (9.7 days)}$$

11.15 ALLOYS FOR HIGH-TEMPERATURE USE

There are several factors that affect the creep characteristics of metals. These include melting temperature, elastic modulus, and grain size. In general, the higher the melting temperature, the greater the elastic modulus, and the larger the grain size, the better is a material's resistance to creep. Relative to grain size, smaller grains permit more grain-boundary sliding, which results in higher creep rates. This

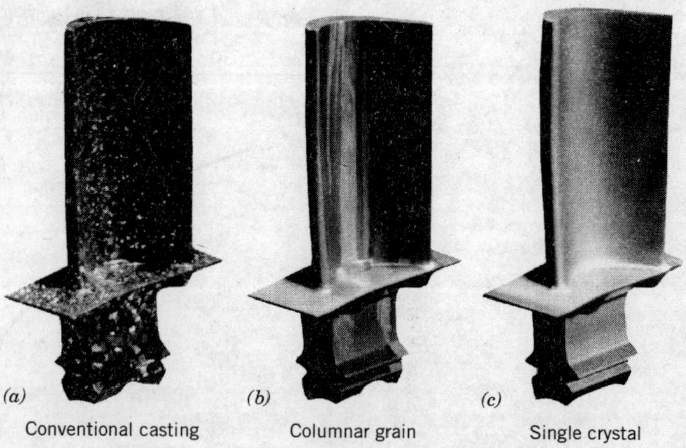

Figure 11.33 (*a*) Polycrystalline turbine blade that was produced by a conventional casting technique. High-temperature creep resistance is improved as a result of an oriented columnar grain structure (*b*) produced by a sophisticated directional solidification technique. Creep resistance is further enhanced when single-crystal blades (*c*) are used. (Courtesy of Pratt & Whitney.)

effect may be contrasted to the influence of grain size on the mechanical behavior at low temperatures [i.e., increase in both strength (Section 10.8) and toughness (Section 11.6)].

Stainless steels (Section 9.2), the refractory metals, and the superalloys (Section 9.3) are especially resilient to creep and are commonly employed in high-temperature service applications. The creep resistance of the cobalt and nickel superalloys is enhanced by solid-solution alloying, and also by the addition of a dispersed phase that is virtually insoluble in the matrix. In addition, advanced processing techniques have been utilized; one such technique is directional solidification, which produces either highly elongated grains or single-crystal components (Figure 11.33). Another is the controlled unidirectional solidification of alloys having specially designed compositions wherein two-phase composites result.

SUMMARY

Fundamentals of Fracture
Ductile Fracture

Fracture, in response to tensile loading and at relatively low temperatures, may occur by ductile and brittle modes, both of which involve the formation and propagation of cracks. For ductile fracture, evidence will exist of gross plastic deformation at the fracture surface. In tension, highly ductile metals will neck down to essentially a point fracture; cup-and-cone mating fracture surfaces result for moderate ductility. Cracks in ductile materials are said to be stable (i.e., resist extension without an increase in applied stress); and inasmuch as fracture is noncatastrophic, this fracture mode is almost always preferred.

Brittle Fracture

For brittle fracture, cracks are unstable, and the fracture surface is relatively flat and perpendicular to the direction of the applied tensile load. Chevron and ridge-like patterns are possible, which indicate the direction of crack propagation. Transgranular (through-grain) and intergranular (between-grain) fractures are found in brittle polycrystalline materials.

Principles of Fracture Mechanics

The significant discrepancy between actual and theoretical fracture strengths of brittle materials is explained by the existence of small flaws that are capable of amplifying an applied tensile stress in their vicinity, leading ultimately to crack formation. Fracture ensues when the theoretical cohesive strength is exceeded at the tip of one of these flaws.

The fracture toughness of a material is indicative of its resistance to brittle fracture when a crack is present. It depends on specimen thickness, and, for relatively thick specimens (i.e., conditions of plane strain), is termed the plane strain fracture toughness. This parameter is the one normally cited for design purposes; its value is relatively large for ductile materials (and small for brittle ones), and is a function of microstructure, strain rate, and temperature. With regard to designing against the possibility of fracture, consideration must be given to material (its fracture toughness), the stress level, and the flaw size detection limit.

Impact Fracture Testing

Qualitatively, the fracture behavior of materials may be determined using Charpy and Izod impact testing techniques. On the basis of the temperature dependence of measured impact energy (or appearance of the fracture surface), it is possible to ascertain whether or not a material experiences a ductile-to-brittle transition and the temperature range over which such a transition occurs. Low-strength steel alloys typify this behavior, and, for structural applications, should be used at temperatures in excess of the transition range. Furthermore, low-strength FCC metals, most HCP metals, and high-strength materials do not experience this ductile-to-brittle transition.

Cyclic Stresses (Fatigue)
The *S–N* Curve

Fatigue is a common type of catastrophic failure wherein the applied stress level fluctuates with time. Test data are plotted as stress versus the logarithm of the number of cycles to failure. For many metals and alloys, stress diminishes continuously with increasing number of cycles at failure; fatigue strength and fatigue life are the parameters used to characterize the fatigue behavior of these materials. On the other hand, for other metals/alloys, at some point, stress ceases to decrease with, and becomes independent of, the number of cycles; the fatigue behavior of these materials is expressed in terms of fatigue limit.

Crack Initiation and Propagation

The processes of fatigue crack initiation and propagation were discussed. Cracks normally nucleate on the surface of a component at some point of stress concentration. Two characteristic fatigue surface features are beachmarks and striations. Beachmarks form on components that experience applied stress interruptions; they normally may be observed with the naked eye. Fatigue striations are of microscopic dimensions, and each is thought to represent the crack tip advance distance over a single load cycle.

Factors That Affect Fatigue Life

Measures that may be taken to extend fatigue life include: (1) reducing the mean stress level; (2) eliminating sharp surface discontinuities; (3) improving the surface finish by polishing; (4) imposing surface residual compressive stresses by shot peening; and (5) case hardening by using a carburizing or nitriding process.

Environmental Effects

The fatigue behavior of materials may also be affected by the environment. Thermal stresses may be induced in components that are exposed to elevated temperature fluctuations and when thermal expansion and/or contraction is restrained; fatigue for these conditions is termed thermal fatigue. The presence of a chemically active environment may lead to a reduction in fatigue life for corrosion fatigue.

Generalized Creep Behavior

The time-dependent plastic deformation of materials subjected to a constant load (or stress) and temperatures greater than about $0.4T_m$ is termed creep. A typical creep curve (strain versus time) will normally exhibit three distinct regions. For transient (or primary) creep, the rate (or slope) diminishes with time. The plot becomes linear (i.e., creep rate is constant) in the steady-state (or secondary) region. And finally, deformation accelerates for tertiary creep, just prior to failure (or rupture). Important design parameters available from such a plot include the steady-state creep rate (slope of the linear region) and rupture lifetime.

Stress and Temperature Effects

Both temperature and applied stress level influence creep behavior. Increasing either of these parameters produces the following effects: (1) an increase in the instantaneous initial deformation; (2) an increase in the steady-state creep rate; and (3) a diminishment of the rupture lifetime. Analytical expressions were presented which relate $\dot{\epsilon}_s$ to both temperature and stress.

Data Extrapolation Methods

Extrapolation of creep test data to lower temperature—longer time regimes is possible using the Larson–Miller parameter.

Alloys for High-Temperature Use

Metal alloys that are especially resistant to creep have high elastic moduli and melting temperatures; these include the superalloys, the stainless steels, and the refractory metals. Various processing techniques are employed to improve the creep properties of these materials.

REFERENCES

ASM Handbook, Vol. 11, *Failure Analysis and Prevention,* ASM International, Materials Park, OH, 1986.

ASM Handbook, Vol. 12, *Fractography,* ASM International, Materials Park, OH, 1987.

ASM Handbook, Vol. 19, *Fatigue and Fracture,* ASM International, Materials Park, OH, 1996.

Boyer, H. E. (Editor), *Atlas of Creep and Stress–Rupture Curves,* ASM International, Materials Park, OH, 1988.

Boyer, H. E. (Editor), *Atlas of Fatigue Curves,* ASM International, Materials Park, OH, 1986.

Colangelo, V. J. and F. A. Heiser, *Analysis of Metallurgical Failures,* 2nd edition, Wiley, New York, 1987.

Collins, J. A., *Failure of Materials in Mechanical Design,* 2nd edition, Wiley, New York, 1993.
Courtney, T. H., *Mechanical Behavior of Materials,* 2nd edition, McGraw-Hill, New York, 2000.
Dieter, G. E., *Mechanical Metallurgy,* 3rd edition, McGraw-Hill, New York, 1986.
Esaklul, K. A., *Handbook of Case Histories in Failure Analysis,* ASM International, Materials Park, OH, 1992 and 1993. In two volumes.
Fatigue Data Book: Light Structural Alloys, ASM International, Materials Park, OH, 1995.
Hertzberg, R. W., *Deformation and Fracture Mechanics of Engineering Materials,* 4th edition, Wiley, New York, 1996.
Stevens, R. I., A. Fatemi, R. R. Stevens, and H. O. Fuchs, *Metal Fatigue in Engineering,* 2nd edition, Wiley, New York, 2000.
Tetelman, A. S. and A. J. McEvily, *Fracture of Structural Materials,* Wiley, New York, 1967. Reprinted by Books on Demand, Ann Arbor, MI.
Wulpi, D. J., *Understanding How Components Fail,* 2nd edition, ASM International, Materials Park, OH, 1999.

QUESTIONS AND PROBLEMS

Principles of Fracture Mechanics

11.1 What is the magnitude of the maximum stress that exists at the tip of an internal crack having a radius of curvature of 1.9×10^{-4} mm and a crack length of 3.8×10^{-2} mm when a tensile stress of 140 MPa is applied?

11.2 Estimate the theoretical fracture strength of a brittle material if it is known that fracture occurs by the propagation of an elliptically shaped surface crack of length 0.5 mm and having a tip radius of curvature of 5×10^{-3} mm, when a stress of 1035 MPa is applied.

11.3 If the specific surface energy for aluminum oxide is 0.90 J/m^2, using data contained in Table 12.3, compute the critical stress required for the propagation of an internal crack of length 0.40 mm.

11.4 An MgO component must not fail when a tensile stress of 13.5 MPa is applied. Determine the maximum allowable surface crack length if the surface energy of MgO is 1.0 J/m^2. Data found in Table 12.3 may prove helpful.

11.5 A specimen of a 4340 steel alloy with a plane strain fracture toughness of 54.8 MPa$\sqrt{\text{m}}$ is exposed to a stress of 1030 MPa. Will this specimen experience fracture if it is known that the largest surface crack is 0.5 mm long? Why or why not? Assume that the parameter Y has a value of 1.0.

11.6 Some aircraft component is fabricated from an aluminum alloy that has a plane strain fracture toughness of 40 MPa$\sqrt{\text{m}}$. It has been determined that fracture results at a stress of 300 MPa when the maximum (or critical) internal crack length is 4.0 mm. For this same component and alloy, will fracture occur at a stress level of 260 MPa when the maximum internal crack length is 6.0 mm? Why or why not?

11.7 Suppose that a wing component on an aircraft is fabricated from an aluminum alloy that has a plane strain fracture toughness of 26 MPa$\sqrt{\text{m}}$. It has been determined that fracture results at a stress of 112 MPa when the maximum internal crack length is 11.6 mm. For this same component and alloy, compute the stress level at which fracture will occur for a critical internal crack length of 6.0 mm.

11.8 A large plate is fabricated from a steel alloy that has a plane strain fracture toughness of 82.4 MPa$\sqrt{\text{m}}$. If, during service use, the plate is exposed to a tensile stress of 345 MPa, determine the minimum length of a surface crack that will lead to fracture. Assume a value of 1.0 for Y.

11.9 Calculate the maximum internal crack length allowable for a Ti-6Al-4V titanium alloy (Table 11.1) component that is loaded to a stress one-half of its yield strength. Assume that the value of Y is 1.50.

11.10 A structural component in the form of a wide plate is to be fabricated from a steel alloy that has a plane strain fracture toughness of 98.9 MPa$\sqrt{m}$ and a yield strength of 860 MPa. The flaw size resolution limit of the flaw detection apparatus is 3.0 mm. If the design stress is one-half of the yield strength and the value of Y is 1.0, determine whether or not a critical flaw for this plate is subject to detection.

11.11 After consultation of other references, write a brief report on one or two nondestructive test techniques that are used to detect and measure internal and/or surface flaws in metal alloys.

Impact Fracture Testing

11.12 Following is tabulated data that were gathered from a series of Charpy impact tests on a tempered 4340 steel alloy.

Temperature (°C)	*Impact Energy (J)*
0	105
−25	104
−50	103
−75	97
−100	63
−113	40
−125	34
−150	28
−175	25
−200	24

(a) Plot the data as impact energy versus temperature.

(b) Determine a ductile-to-brittle transition temperature as that temperature corresponding to the average of the maximum and minimum impact energies.

(c) Determine a ductile-to-brittle transition temperature as that temperature at which the impact energy is 50 J.

11.13 Following is tabulated data that were gathered from a series of Charpy impact tests on a commercial low-carbon steel alloy.

Temperature (°C)	*Impact Energy (J)*
50	76
40	76
30	71
20	58
10	38
0	23
−10	14
−20	9
−30	5
−40	1.5

(a) Plot the data as impact energy versus temperature.

(b) Determine a ductile-to-brittle transition temperature as that temperature corresponding to the average of the maximum and minimum impact energies.

(c) Determine a ductile-to-brittle transition temperature as that temperature at which the impact energy is 20 J.

Cyclic Stresses (Fatigue)
The S–N Curve

11.14 A fatigue test was conducted in which the mean stress was 70 MPa, and the stress amplitude was 210 MPa.

(a) Compute the maximum and minimum stress levels.

(b) Compute the stress ratio.

(c) Compute the magnitude of the stress range.

11.15 A cylindrical 1045 steel bar (Figure 11.34) is subjected to repeated compression-tension stress cycling along its axis. If the load amplitude is 66,700 N, compute the minimum allowable bar diameter to ensure that fatigue failure will not occur. Assume a safety factor of 2.0.

11.16 A 6.4 mm diameter cylindrical rod fabricated from a 2014-T6 aluminum alloy (Figure 11.34) is subjected to reversed tension-compression load cycling along its axis. If the maximum tensile and compressive loads are +5340 N and −5340 N, respectively, determine its fatigue life. Assume that the stress plotted in Figure 11.34 is stress amplitude.

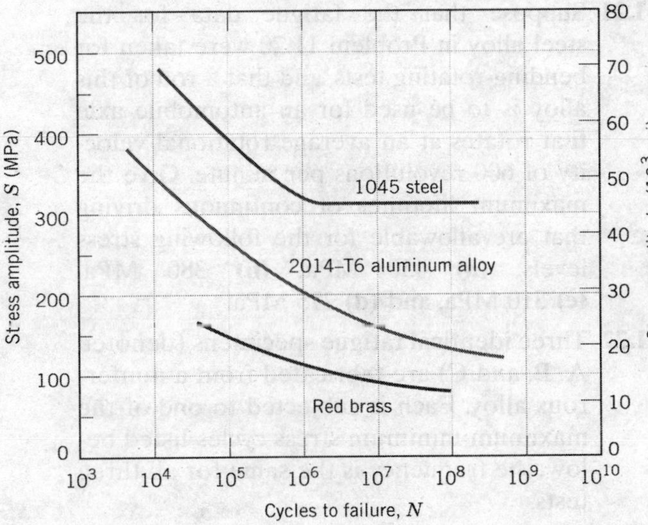

Figure 11.34 Stress magnitude S versus the logarithm of the number N of cycles to fatigue failure of metals for red brass, an aluminum alloy, and a plain carbon steel. (Adapted from H. W. Hayden, W. G. Moffatt, and J. Wulff, *The Structure and Properties of Materials,* Vol. III, *Mechanical Behavior,* p. 15. Copyright © 1965 by John Wiley & Sons, New York. Reprinted by permission of John Wiley & Sons, Inc. Also adapted from *ASM Handbook,* Vol. 2, *Properties and Selection: Nonferrous Alloys and Special-Purpose Materials,* 1990. Reprinted by permission of ASM International.)

11.17 A 15.2 mm diameter cylindrical rod fabricated from a 2014-T6 aluminum alloy (Figure 11.34) is subjected to a repeated tension-compression load cycling along its axis. Compute the maximum and minimum loads that will be applied to yield a fatigue life of 1.0×10^8 cycles. Assume that the stress plotted on the vertical axis is stress amplitude, and data were taken for a mean stress of 35 MPa.

11.18 The fatigue data for a brass alloy are given as follows:

Stress Amplitude (MPa)	***Cycles to Failure***
170	3.7×10^4
148	1.0×10^5
130	3.0×10^5
114	1.0×10^6
92	1.0×10^7
80	1.0×10^8
74	1.0×10^9

(a) Make an S–N plot (stress amplitude versus logarithm cycles to failure) using these data.

(b) Determine the fatigue strength at 4×10^6 cycles.

(c) Determine the fatigue life for 120 MPa.

11.19 Suppose that the fatigue data for the brass alloy in Problem 11.18 were taken from bending-rotating tests, and that a rod of this alloy is to be used for an automobile axle that rotates at an average rotational velocity of 1800 revolutions per minute. Give the maximum torsional stress amplitude possible for each of the following lifetimes of the rod: **(a)** 1 year, **(b)** 1 month, **(c)** 1 day, and **(d)** 1 hour.

11.20 The fatigue data for a steel alloy are given as follows:

Stress Amplitude (MPa)	***Cycles to Failure***
470	10^4
440	3×10^4
390	10^5
350	3×10^5
310	10^6
290	3×10^6
290	10^7
290	10^8

(a) Make an S–N plot (stress amplitude versus logarithm cycles to failure) using these data.

(b) What is the fatigue limit for this alloy?

(c) Determine fatigue lifetimes at stress amplitudes of 415 MPa and 275 MPa.

(d) Estimate fatigue strengths at 2×10^4 and 6×10^5 cycles.

11.21 Suppose that the fatigue data for the steel alloy in Problem 11.20 were taken for bending-rotating tests, and that a rod of this alloy is to be used for an automobile axle that rotates at an average rotational velocity of 600 revolutions per minute. Give the maximum lifetimes of continuous driving that are allowable for the following stress levels: **(a)** 450 MPa, **(b)** 380 MPa, **(c)** 310 MPa, and **(d)** 275 MPa.

11.22 Three identical fatigue specimens (denoted A, B, and C) are fabricated from a nonferrous alloy. Each is subjected to one of the maximum-minimum stress cycles listed below; the frequency is the same for all three tests.

Specimen	σ_{max} *(MPa)*	σ_{min} *(MPa)*
A	+450	−150
B	+300	−300
C	+500	−200

(a) Rank the fatigue lifetimes of these three specimens from the longest to the shortest.

(b) Now justify this ranking using a schematic *S–N* plot.

11.23 Cite five factors that may lead to scatter in fatigue life data.

Crack Initiation and Propagation Factors That Affect Fatigue Life

11.24 Briefly explain the difference between fatigue striations and beachmarks both in terms of **(a)** size and **(b)** origin.

11.25 List four measures that may be taken to increase the resistance to fatigue of a metal alloy.

Generalized Creep Behavior

11.26 Give the approximate temperature at which creep deformation becomes an important consideration for each of the following metals: tin, molybdenum, iron, gold, zinc, and chromium.

11.27 The following creep data were taken on an aluminum alloy at 480°C and a constant stress of 2.75 MPa. Plot the data as strain versus time, then determine the steady-state or minimum creep rate. *Note:* The initial and instantaneous strain is not included.

Time (min)	*Strain*	*Time (min)*	*Strain*
0	0.00	18	0.82
2	0.22	20	0.88
4	0.34	22	0.95
6	0.41	24	1.03
8	0.48	26	1.12
10	0.55	28	1.22
12	0.62	30	1.36
14	0.68	32	1.53
16	0.75	34	1.77

Stress and Temperature Effects

11.28 A specimen 1015 mm long of a low carbon–nickel alloy (Figure 11.31) is to be exposed to a tensile stress of 70 MPa at 427°C. Determine its elongation after 10,000 h. Assume that the total of both instantaneous and primary creep elongations is 1.3 mm.

11.29 For a cylindrical low carbon–nickel alloy specimen (Figure 11.31) originally 19 mm in diameter and 635 mm long, what tensile load is necessary to produce a total elongation of 6.44 mm after 5000 h at 538°C? Assume that the sum of instantaneous and primary creep elongations is 1.8 mm.

11.30 If a component fabricated from a low carbon–nickel alloy (Figure 11.30) is to be exposed to a tensile stress of 31 MPa at 649°C, estimate its rupture lifetime.

11.31 A cylindrical component constructed from a low carbon–nickel alloy (Figure 11.30) has a diameter of 19.1 mm. Determine the maximum load that may be applied for it to survive 10,000 h at 538°C.

11.32 From Equation 11.19, if the logarithm of $\dot{\epsilon}_s$ is plotted versus the logarithm of σ, then a straight line should result, the slope of which is the stress exponent n. Using Figure 11.31, determine the value of n for the low carbon–nickel alloy at each of the three temperatures.

11.33 (a) Estimate the activation energy for creep (i.e., Q_c in Equation 11.20) for the low carbon–nickel alloy having the steady-state creep behavior shown in Figure 11.31. Use data taken at a stress level of 55 MPa and temperatures of 427°C and 538°C. Assume that the stress exponent n is independent of temperature. (b) Estimate $\dot{\epsilon}_s$ at 649°C (922 K).

11.34 Steady-state creep rate data are given here for some alloy taken at 200°C (473 K):

$\dot{\epsilon}_s$ (h^{-1})	σ(*MPa*)
2.5×10^{-3}	55
2.4×10^{-2}	69

If it is known that the activation energy for creep is 140,000 J/mol, compute the steady-state creep rate at a temperature of 250°C (523 K) and a stress level of 48 MPa.

11.35 Steady-state creep data taken for an iron at a stress level of 140 MPa are given here:

$\dot{\epsilon}_s$ (h^{-1})	*T* (*K*)
6.6×10^{-4}	1090
11.8×10^{-2}	1200

If it is known that the value of the stress exponent *n* for this alloy is 11.5, compute the steady-state creep rate at 1300 K and a stress level of 83 MPa.

Alloys for High-Temperature Use

11.36 Cite three metallurgical/processing techniques that are employed to enhance the creep resistance of metal alloys.

DESIGN PROBLEMS

11.D1 Each student (or group of students) is to obtain an object/structure/component that has failed. It may come from your home, an automobile repair shop, a machine shop, etc. Conduct an investigation to determine the cause and type of failure (i.e., simple fracture, fatigue, creep). In addition, propose measures that can be taken to prevent future incidents of this type of failure. Finally, submit a report that addresses the above issues.

Principles of Fracture Mechanics

11.D2 **(a)** For the thin-walled spherical tank discussed in Design Example 11.1, on the basis of critical crack size criterion [as addressed in part (a)], rank the following polymers from longest to shortest critical crack length: nylon 6,6 (50% relative humidity), polycarbonate, poly(ethylene terephthalate), and poly(methyl methacrylate). Comment on the magnitude range of the computed values used in the ranking relative to those tabulated for metal alloys as provided in Table 11.3. For these computations, use data contained in Tables B.4 and B.5 in Appendix B.

(b) Now rank these same four polymers relative to maximum allowable pressure according to the leak-before-break criterion, as described in the (b) portion of Design Example 11.1. As above, comment on these values in relation to those for the metal alloys that are tabulated in Table 11.4.

Data Extrapolation Methods

11.D3 An S-590 iron component (Figure 11.32) must have a creep rupture lifetime of at least 20 days at 650°C (923 K). Compute the maximum allowable stress level.

11.D4 Consider an S-590 iron component (Figure 11.32) that is subjected to a stress of 55 MPa. At what temperature will the rupture lifetime be 200 h?

11.D5 For an 18-8 Mo stainless steel (Figure 11.35), predict the time to rupture for a component that is subjected to a stress of 100 MPa at 600°C (873 K).

11.D6 Consider an 18-8 Mo stainless steel component (Figure 11.35) that is exposed to a temperature of 650°C (923 K). What is the maximum allowable stress level for a rupture lifetime of 1 year? 15 years?

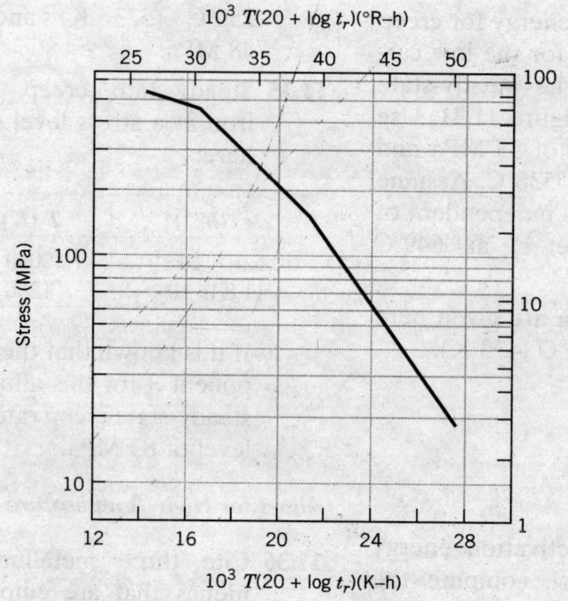

Figure 11.35 Logarithm stress versus the Larson–Miller parameter for an 18-8 Mo stainless steel. (From F. R. Larson and J. Miller, *Trans. ASME,* **74,** 765, 1952. Reprinted by permission of ASME.)

Chapter 12 Applications and Properties of Ceramics

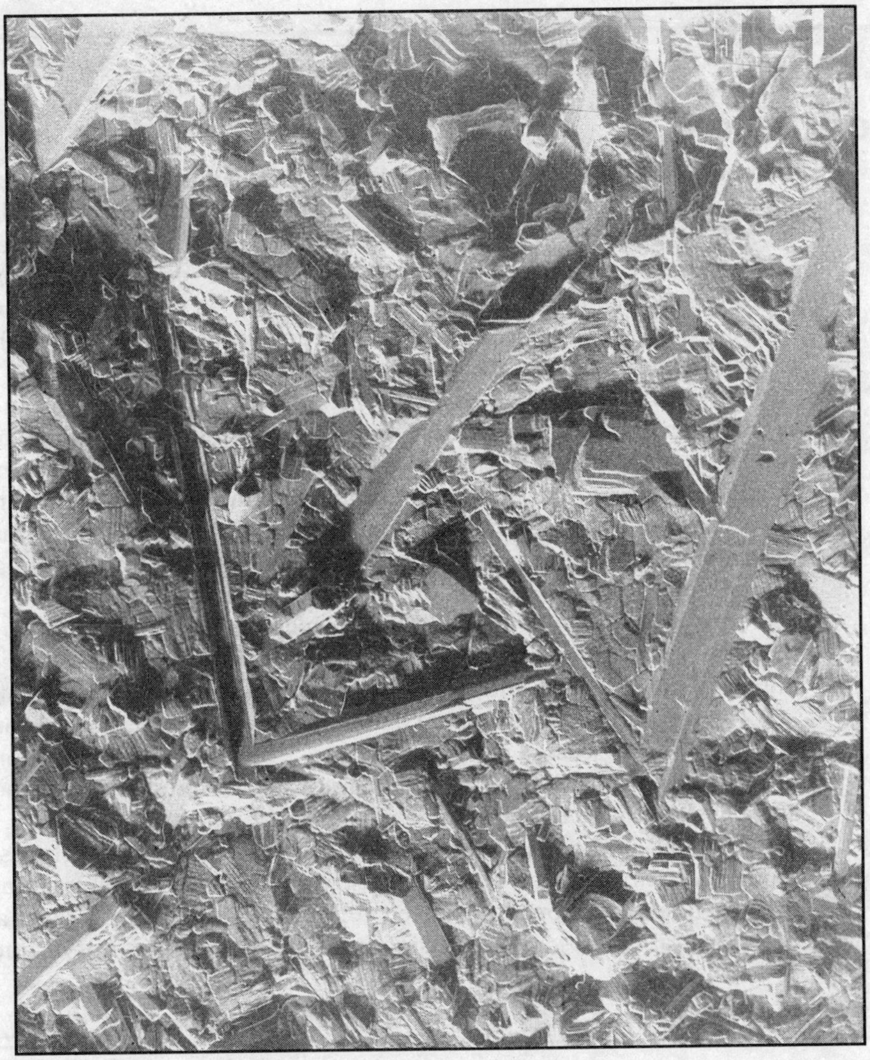

Scanning electron micrograph showing the microstructure of a glass–ceramic material. The long acicular blade-shaped particles yield a material with unusual strength and toughness. 65,000×. (Photograph courtesy of L. R. Pinckney and G. J. Fine of Corning Incorporated.)

Learning Objectives

After careful study of this chapter you should be able to do the following:

1. Describe the process that is used to produce glass–ceramics.
2. Name the two types of clay products, and then give two examples of each.
3. Cite three important requirements that normally must be met by refractory ceramics and abrasive ceramics.
4. Describe the mechanism by which cement hardens when water is added.
5. Briefly explain why there is normally significant scatter in the fracture strength for identical specimens of the same ceramic material.
6. Compute the flexural strength of ceramic rod specimens that have been bent to fracture in three-point loading.
7. On the basis of slip considerations, explain why crystalline ceramic materials are normally brittle.
8. Briefly describe and explain the procedure by which glass pieces are thermally tempered.

12.1 INTRODUCTION

Ceramic materials were discussed briefly in Chapter 1, which noted that they are inorganic and nonmetallic materials. Most ceramics are compounds between metallic and nonmetallic elements for which the interatomic bonds are either totally ionic, or predominantly ionic but having some covalent character. The term "ceramic" comes from the Greek word *keramikos,* which means "burnt stuff," indicating that desirable properties of these materials are normally achieved through a high-temperature heat treatment process called firing.

Up until the past 60 or so years, the most important materials in this class were termed the "traditional ceramics," those for which the primary raw material is clay; products considered to be traditional ceramics are china, porcelain, bricks, tiles, and, in addition, glasses and high-temperature ceramics. Of late, significant progress has been made in understanding the fundamental character of these materials and of the phenomena that occur in them that are responsible for their unique properties. Consequently, a new generation of these materials has evolved, and the term "ceramic" has taken on a much broader meaning. To one degree or another, these new materials have a rather dramatic effect on our lives; electronic, computer, communication, aerospace, and a host of other industries rely on their use.

The types of crystal structure and atomic point defect that are found in ceramic materials were discussed in Chapters 4 and 5, respectively. Applications for this class of materials are treated at the begining of this chapter. Some of their mechanical and physical characteristics are detailed at the end of the chapter. Most ceramic materials fall into an application-classification scheme that includes the following groups: glasses, structural clay products, whitewares, refractories, abrasives, cements, and the newly developed advanced ceramics. Figure 12.1 presents a taxonomy of these several types; some discussion is devoted to each in this chapter.

Types and Applications of Ceramics

12.2 GLASSES

The glasses are a familiar group of ceramics; containers, lenses, and fiberglass represent typical applications. As already mentioned, they are noncrystalline silicates containing other oxides, notably CaO, Na_2O, K_2O, and Al_2O_3, which influence the glass properties. A typical soda–lime glass consists of approximately 70 wt% SiO_2,

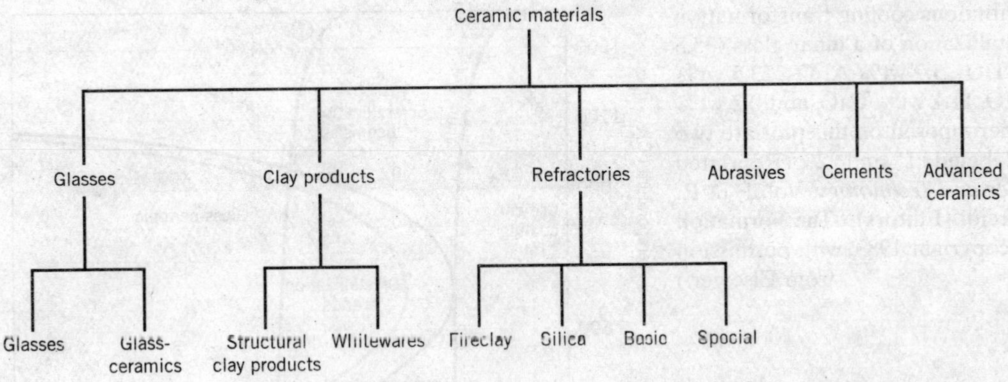

Figure 12.1 Classification of ceramic materials on the basis of application.

the balance being mainly Na_2O (soda) and CaO (lime). The compositions of several common glass materials are contained in Table 12.1. Possibly the two prime assets of these materials are their optical transparency and the relative ease with which they may be fabricated.

12.3 GLASS–CERAMICS

Most inorganic glasses can be made to transform from a noncrystalline state to one that is crystalline by the proper high-temperature heat treatment. This process is called **crystallization,** and the product is a fine-grained polycrystalline material which is often called a **glass–ceramic.** The formation of these small glass-ceramic grains is, in a sense, a phase transformation, which involves nucleation and growth stages. As a consequence, the kinetics (i.e., the rate) of crystallization may be described using the same principles that were applied to phase transformations for metal systems in Section 8.3. For example, dependence of degree of transformation on temperature and time may be expressed using isothermal transformation and continuous cooling transformation diagrams (Sections 8.5 and 8.6). The continuous

Table 12.1 Compositions and Characteristics of Some of the Common Commercial Glasses

	Composition (wt%)						
Glass Type	SiO_2	Na_2O	CaO	Al_2O_3	B_2O_3	***Other***	***Characteristics and Applications***
Fused silica	>99.5						High melting temperature, very low coefficient of expansion (thermally shock resistant)
96% Silica (Vycor™)	96				4		Thermally shock and chemically resistant—laboratory ware
Borosilicate (Pyrex™)	81	3.5		2.5	13		Thermally shock and chemically resistant—ovenware
Container (soda–lime)	74	16	5	1		4MgO	Low melting temperature, easily worked, also durable
Fiberglass	55		16	15	10	4MgO	Easily drawn into fibers—glass–resin composites
Optical flint	54	1				37PbO, $8K_2O$	High density and high index of refraction—optical lenses
Glass–ceramic (Pyroceram™)	43.5	14		30	5.5	$6.5TiO_2$, $0.5As_2O_3$	Easily fabricated; strong; resists thermal shock—ovenware

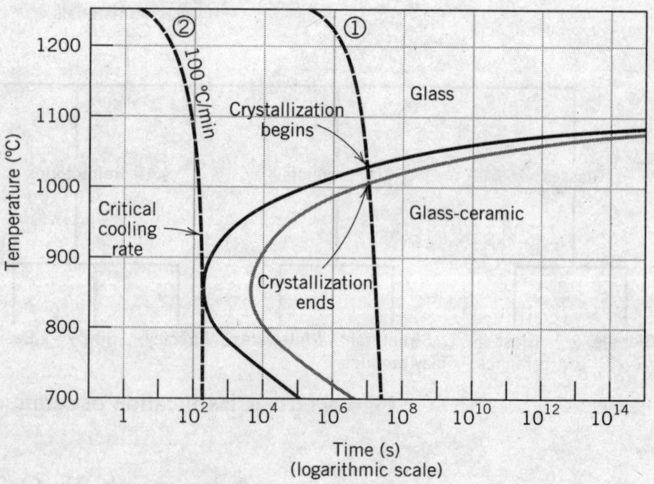

Figure 12.2 Continuous cooling transformation diagram for the crystallization of a lunar glass (35.5 wt% SiO_2, 14.3 wt% TiO_2, 3.7 wt% Al_2O_3, 23.5 wt% FeO, 11.6 wt% MgO, 11.1 wt% CaO, and 0.2 wt% Na_2O). Also superimposed on this plot are two cooling curves, labeled "1" and "2". (Reprinted from *Glass: Science and Technology,* Vol. 1, D. R. Uhlmann and N. J. Kreidl (Editors), "The Formation of Glasses," p. 22, copyright 1983, with permission from Elsevier.)

cooling transformation diagram for the crystallization of a lunar glass is presented in Figure 12.2; the begin- and end-transformation curves on this plot have the same general shape as those for an iron–carbon alloy of eutectoid composition (Figure 8.25). Also included are two continuous cooling curves, which are labeled "1" and "2"; the cooling rate represented by curve 2 is much greater than that for curve 1. As also noted on this plot, for the continuous cooling path represented by curve 1, crystallization begins at its intersection with the upper curve, and progresses as time increases and temperature continues to decrease; upon crossing the lower curve, all of the original glass has crystallized. The other cooling curve (curve 2) just misses the nose of the crystallization start curve. It represents a critical cooling rate (for this glass, 100°C/min)—that is, the minimum cooling rate for which the final room-temperature product is 100% glass; for cooling rates less than this, some glass-ceramic material will form.

A nucleating agent (frequently titanium dioxide) is often added to the glass to promote crystallization. The presence of a nucleating agent shifts the begin and end transformation curves to shorter times.

Properties and Applications of Glass–Ceramics

Glass-ceramic materials have been designed to have the following characteristics: relatively high mechanical strengths; low coefficients of thermal expansion (to avoid thermal shock); relatively high temperature capabilities; good dielectric properties (for electronic packaging applications); and good biological compatibility. Some glass–ceramics may be made optically transparent; others are opaque. Possibly the most attractive attribute of this class of materials is the ease with which they may be fabricated; conventional glass-forming techniques may be used conveniently in the mass production of nearly pore-free ware.

Glass–ceramics are manufactured commercially under the trade names of Pyroceram™, Corningware™, Cercor™, and Vision™. The most common uses for these materials are as ovenware, tableware, oven windows, and rangetops—primarily because of their strength and excellent resistance to thermal shock. They also serve as electrical insulators and as substrates for printed circuit boards, and are used for architectural cladding, and for heat exchangers and regenerators. A typical glass–ceramic is also included in Table 12.1, and the microstructure of a commercial material is shown in the chapter opening photograph for this chapter.

Concept Check 12.1

Briefly explain why glass–ceramics may not be transparent. *Hint:* you may want to consult Chapter 20.

[*The answer may be found in enclosed CD.*]

12.4 CLAY PRODUCTS

One of the most widely used ceramic raw materials is clay. This inexpensive ingredient, found naturally in great abundance, often is used as mined without any upgrading of quality. Another reason for its popularity lies in the ease with which clay products may be formed; when mixed in the proper proportions, clay and water form a plastic mass that is very amenable to shaping. The formed piece is dried to remove some of the moisture, after which it is fired at an elevated temperature to improve its mechanical strength.

Most of the clay-based products fall within two broad classifications: the **structural clay products** and the **whitewares.** Structural clay products include building bricks, tiles, and sewer pipes—applications in which structural integrity is important. The whiteware ceramics become white after the high-temperature **firing.** Included in this group are porcelain, pottery, tableware, china, and plumbing fixtures (sanitary ware). In addition to clay, many of these products also contain nonplastic ingredients, which influence the changes that take place during the drying and firing processes, and the characteristics of the finished piece (Section 23.7).

12.5 REFRACTORIES

Another important class of ceramics that are utilized in large tonnages is the **refractory ceramics.** The salient properties of these materials include the capacity to withstand high temperatures without melting or decomposing, and the capacity to remain unreactive and inert when exposed to severe environments. In addition, the ability to provide thermal insulation is often an important consideration. Refractory materials are marketed in a variety of forms, but bricks are the most common. Typical applications include furnace linings for metal refining, glass manufacturing, metallurgical heat treatment, and power generation.

Of course, the performance of a refractory ceramic, to a large degree, depends on its composition. On this basis, there are several classifications—namely, fireclay, silica, basic, and special refractories. Compositions for a number of commercial refractories are listed in Table 12.2. For many commercial materials, the raw ingredients consist of both large (or grog) particles and fine particles, which may have different compositions. Upon firing, the fine particles normally are involved in the formation of a bonding phase, which is responsible for the increased strength of the brick; this phase may be predominantly either glassy or crystalline. The service temperature is normally below that at which the refractory piece was fired.

Porosity is one microstructural variable that must be controlled to produce a suitable refractory brick. Strength, load-bearing capacity, and resistance to attack by corrosive materials all increase with porosity reduction. At the same time, thermal insulation characteristics and resistance to thermal shock are diminished. Of course, the optimum porosity depends on the conditions of service.

Table 12.2 Compositions of Five Common Ceramic Refractory Materials

Refractory Type	*Composition (wt%)* Al_2O_3	SiO_2	MgO	Cr_2O_3	Fe_2O_3	CaO	TiO_2	*Apparent Porosity (%)*
Fireclay	25–45	70–50	0–1		0–1	0–1	1–2	10–25
High-alumina fireclay	90–50	10–45	0–1		0–1	0–1	1–4	18–25
Silica	0.2	96.3	0.6			2.2		25
Periclase	1.0	3.0	90.0	0.3	3.0	2.5		22
Periclase–chrome ore	9.0	5.0	73.0	8.2	2.0	2.2		21

Source: From W. D. Kingery, H. K. Bowen, and D. R. Uhlmann, *Introduction to Ceramics,* 2nd edition. Copyright © 1976 by John Wiley & Sons, New York. Reprinted by permission of John Wiley & Sons, Inc.

Fireclay Refractories

The primary ingredients for the fireclay refractories are high-purity fireclays, alumina and silica mixtures usually containing between 25 and 45 wt% alumina. According to the SiO_2–Al_2O_3 phase diagram (Section 12.9), over this composition range the highest temperature possible without the formation of a liquid phase is 1587°C (2890°F). Below this temperature the equilibrium phases present are mullite and silica (cristobalite). During refractory service use, the presence of a small amount of a liquid phase may be allowable without compromising mechanical integrity. Above 1587°C the fraction of liquid phase present will depend on refractory composition. Upgrading the alumina content will increase the maximum service temperature, allowing for the formation of a small amount of liquid.

Fireclay bricks are used principally in furnace construction, to confine hot atmospheres, and to thermally insulate structural members from excessive temperatures. For fireclay brick, strength is not ordinarily an important consideration, because support of structural loads is usually not required. Some control is normally maintained over the dimensional accuracy and stability of the finished product.

Silica Refractories

The prime ingredient for silica refractories, sometimes termed acid refractories, is silica. These materials, well known for their high-temperature load-bearing capacity, are commonly used in the arched roofs of steel- and glass-making furnaces; for these applications, temperatures as high as 1650°C (3000°F) may be realized. Under these conditions some small portion of the brick will actually exist as a liquid. The presence of even small concentrations of alumina has an adverse influence on the performance of these refractories, which may be explained by the silica–alumina phase diagram (Section 12.9). Since the eutectic composition (7.7 wt% Al_2O_3) is very near the silica extremity of the phase diagram, even small additions of Al_2O_3 lower the liquidus temperature significantly, which means that substantial amounts of liquid may be present at temperatures in excess of 1600°C (2910°F). Thus, the alumina content should be held to a minimum, normally to between 0.2 and 1.0 wt%.

These refractory materials are also resistant to slags that are rich in silica (called acid slags) and are often used as containment vessels for them. On the other hand, they are readily attacked by slags composed of a high proportion of CaO and/or MgO (basic slags), and contact with these oxide materials should be avoided.

Basic Refractories

The refractories that are rich in periclase, or magnesia (MgO), are termed basic; they may also contain calcium, chromium, and iron compounds. The presence of silica is deleterious to their high-temperature performance. Basic refractories are especially resistant to attack by slags containing high concentrations of MgO and CaO, and find extensive use in some steel-making open hearth furnaces.

Special Refractories

There are yet other ceramic materials that are used for rather specialized refractory applications. Some of these are relatively high-purity oxide materials, many of which may be produced with very little porosity. Included in this group are alumina, silica, magnesia, beryllia (BeO), zirconia (ZrO_2), and mullite ($3Al_2O_3$–$2SiO_2$). Others include carbide compounds, in addition to carbon and graphite. Silicon carbide (SiC) has been used for electrical resistance heating elements, as a crucible material, and in internal furnace components. Carbon and graphite are very refractory, but find limited application because they are susceptible to oxidation at temperatures in excess of about 800°C (1470°F). As would be expected, these specialized refractories are relatively expensive.

Concept Check 12.2

Upon consideration of the SiO_2–Al_2O_3 phase diagram (Section 12.9) for the following pair of compositions, which would you judge to be the more desirable refractory? Justify your choice.

20 wt% Al_2O_3–80 wt% SiO_2
25 wt% Al_2O_3–75 wt% SiO_2

[*The answer may be found in enclosed CD.*]

12.6 ABRASIVES

Abrasive ceramics are used to wear, grind, or cut away other material, which necessarily is softer. Therefore, the prime requisite for this group of materials is hardness or wear resistance; in addition, a high degree of toughness is essential to ensure that the abrasive particles do not easily fracture. Furthermore, high temperatures may be produced from abrasive frictional forces, so some refractoriness is also desirable.

Diamonds, both natural and synthetic, are utilized as abrasives; however, they are relatively expensive. The more common ceramic abrasives include silicon carbide, tungsten carbide (WC), aluminum oxide (or corundum), and silica sand.

Abrasives are used in several forms—bonded to grinding wheels, as coated abrasives, and as loose grains. In the first case, the abrasive particles are bonded to a wheel by means of a glassy ceramic or an organic resin. The surface structure should contain some porosity; a continual flow of air currents or liquid coolants within the pores that surround the refractory grains prevents excessive heating. Figure 12.3 shows the microstructure of a bonded abrasive, revealing abrasive grains, the bonding phase, and pores.

Coated abrasives are those in which an abrasive powder is coated on some type of paper or cloth material; sandpaper is probably the most familiar example. Wood, metals, ceramics, and plastics are all frequently ground and polished using this form of abrasive.

Figure 12.3 Photomicrograph of an aluminum oxide bonded ceramic abrasive. The light regions are the Al_2O_3 abrasive grains; the gray and dark areas are the bonding phase and porosity, respectively. 100×. (From W. D. Kingery, H. K. Bowen, and D. R. Uhlmann, *Introduction to Ceramics,* 2nd edition, p. 568. Copyright © 1976 by John Wiley & Sons. Reprinted by permission of John Wiley & Sons, Inc.)

Grinding, lapping, and polishing wheels often employ loose abrasive grains that are delivered in some type of oil- or water-based vehicle. Diamonds, corundum, silicon carbide, and rouge (an iron oxide) are used in loose form over a variety of grain size ranges.

12.7 CEMENTS

Several familiar ceramic materials are classified as inorganic **cements:** cement, plaster of paris, and lime, which, as a group, are produced in extremely large quantities. The characteristic feature of these materials is that when mixed with water, they form a paste that subsequently sets and hardens. This trait is especially useful in that solid and rigid structures having just about any shape may be expeditiously formed. Also, some of these materials act as a bonding phase that chemically binds particulate aggregates into a single cohesive structure. Under these circumstances, the role of the cement is similar to that of the glassy bonding phase that forms when clay products and some refractory bricks are fired. One important difference, however, is that the cementitious bond develops at room temperature.

Of this group of materials, portland cement is consumed in the largest tonnages. It is produced by grinding and intimately mixing clay and lime-bearing minerals in the proper proportions, and then heating the mixture to about 1400°C (2550°F) in a rotary kiln; this process, sometimes called **calcination,** produces physical and chemical changes in the raw materials. The resulting "clinker" product is then ground into a very fine powder to which is added a small amount of gypsum ($CaSO_4$–$2H_2O$) to retard the setting process. This product is portland cement. The properties of portland cement, including setting time and final strength, to a large degree depend on its composition.

Several different constituents are found in portland cement, the principal ones being tricalcium silicate ($3CaO$–SiO_2) and dicalcium silicate ($2CaO$–SiO_2). The setting and hardening of this material result from relatively complicated hydration reactions that occur among the various cement constituents and the water that is added. For example, one hydration reaction involving dicalcium silicate is as follows:

$$2CaO\text{–}SiO_2 + xH_2O = 2CaO\text{–}SiO_2\text{–}xH_2O \tag{12.1}$$

where x is variable and depends on how much water is available. These hydrated products are in the form of complex gels or crystalline substances that form the cementitious bond. Hydration reactions begin just as soon as water is added to the cement. These are first manifested as setting (i.e., the stiffening of the once-plastic paste), which takes place soon after mixing, usually within several hours. Hardening of the mass follows as a result of further hydration, a relatively slow process that may continue for as long as several years. It should be emphasized that the process by which cement hardens is not one of drying but, rather, of hydration in which water actually participates in a chemical bonding reaction.

Portland cement is termed a hydraulic cement because its hardness develops by chemical reactions with water. It is used primarily in mortar and concrete to bind, into a cohesive mass, aggregates of inert particles (sand and/or gravel); these are considered to be composite materials (see Section 15.2). Other cement materials, such as lime, are nonhydraulic; that is, compounds other than water (e.g., CO_2) are involved in the hardening reaction.

Concept Check 12.3

Explain why it is important to grind cement into a fine powder.

[*The answer may be found in enclosed CD.*]

12.8 ADVANCED CERAMICS

Although the traditional ceramics discussed previously account for the bulk of the production, the development of new and what are termed "advanced ceramics" has begun and will continue to establish a prominent niche in our advanced technologies. In particular, electrical, magnetic, and optical properties and property combinations unique to ceramics have been exploited in a host of new products; some of these are discussed in Chapters 17, 18, and 20. Furthermore, advanced ceramics are utilized in optical fiber communications systems, in microelectromechanical systems (MEMS), as ball bearings, and in applications that exploit the piezoelectric behavior of a number of ceramic materials. Each of these will now be discussed.

Microelectromechanical Systems (MEMS)

Microelectromechanical systems (abbreviated *MEMS*) are miniature "smart" systems (Section 1.5) consisting of a multitude of mechanical devices that are integrated with large numbers of electrical elements on a substrate of silicon. The mechanical components are microsensors and microactuators. Microsensors collect environmental information by measuring mechanical, thermal, chemical, optical, and/or magnetic phenomena. The microelectronic components then process this sensory input, and subsequently render decisions that direct responses from the microactuator devices—devices that perform such responses as positioning, moving, pumping, regulating, and filtering. These actuating devices include beams, pits, gears, motors, and membranes, which are of microscopic dimensions, on the order of microns in size. Figure 12.4 is a scanning electron micrograph of a linear rack gear reduction drive MEMS.

The processing of MEMS is virtually the same as that used for the production of silicon-based integrated circuits; this includes photolithographic, ion implantation, etching, and deposition technologies, which are well established. In addition, some mechanical components are fabricated using micromachining techniques. MEMS components are very sophisticated, reliable, and miniscule in size. Furthermore, since the above fabrication techniques involve batch operations, the MEMS technology is very economical and cost effective.

Figure 12.4 Scanning electron micrograph showing a linear rack gear reduction drive MEMS. This gear chain converts rotational motion from the top-left gear to linear motion to drive the linear track (lower-right). Approximately 100×. (Courtesy Sandia National Laboratories, SUMMiT* Technologies, www.mems.sandia.gov.)

There are some limitations to the use of silicon in MEMS. Silicon has a low fracture toughness (~0.90 MPa$\sqrt{m}$), a relatively low softening temperature (600°C), and is highly active to the presence of water and oxygen. Consequently, research is currently being conducted into using ceramic materials—which are tougher, more refractory, and more inert—for some MEMS components, especially high-speed devices and nanoturbines. Those ceramic materials being considered are amorphous silicon carbonitrides (silicon carbide–silicon nitride alloys), which may be produced using metal organic precursors. In addition, fabrication of these ceramic MEMS will undoubtedly involve some of the traditional techniques discussed later in this chapter.

One example of a practical MEMS application is an accelerometer (accelerator/decelerator sensor) that is used in the deployment of air-bag systems in automobile crashes. For this application the important microelectronic component is a free-standing microbeam. Compared to conventional air-bag systems, the MEMS units are smaller, lighter, more reliable, and are produced at a considerable cost reduction.

Potential MEMS applications include electronic displays, data storage units, energy conversion devices, chemical detectors (for hazardous chemical and biological agents, and drug screening), and microsystems for DNA amplification and identification. There are undoubtedly many yet unforeseen uses of this MEMS technology, which will have a profound impact on our society in the future; these will probably overshadow the effects of microelectronic integrated circuits during the past three decades.

Optical Fibers

One new and advanced ceramic material that is a critical component in our modern optical communications systems is the **optical fiber.** The optical fiber is made of extremely high-purity silica, which must be free of even minute levels of contaminants and other defects that absorb, scatter, and attenuate a light beam. Very advanced and sophisticated processing techniques have been developed to produce fibers that meet the rigid restrictions required for this application. A discussion of optical fibers and their role in communications is provided in Section 20.14.

Ceramic Ball Bearings

Another new and interesting application of ceramic materials is in bearings. A bearing consists of balls and races that are in contact with and rub against one

MATERIALS OF IMPORTANCE

Piezoelectric Ceramics

A few ceramic materials (as well as some polymers) exhibit the unusual phenomenon of piezoelectricity[1]—electric polarization[2] (i.e., an electric field or voltage) is induced in the ceramic crystal when a mechanical strain (dimensional change) is imposed on it. The inverse piezoelectric effect is also displayed by this group of materials; that is, a mechanical strain results from the imposition of an electrical field.

Piezoelectric materials may be utilized as transducers between electrical and mechanical energies. One of the early uses of piezoelectric ceramics was in sonar, wherein underwater objects (e.g., submarines) are detected and their positions determined using an ultrasonic emitting and receiving system. A piezoelectric crystal is caused to oscillate by an electrical signal, which produces high-frequency mechanical vibrations that are transmitted through the water. Upon encountering an object, these signals are reflected back, and another piezoelectric material receives this reflected vibrational energy, which it then converts back into an electrical signal. Distance from the ultrasonic source and reflecting body is determined from the elapsed time between sending and receiving events.

More recently, the utilization of piezoelectric devices has grown dramatically as a consequence of increases in automatization and consumer attraction to modern sophisticated gadgets. Applications that employ piezoelectric devices are found in the automotive, computer, commercial/consumer, and medical sectors. Some of these applications are as follows: automotive—wheel balances, seat belt buzzers, tread-wear indicators, keyless door entry, and airbag sensors; computer—microactuators for hard disks and notebook transformers; commercial/consumer—ink-jet printing heads, strain gauges, ultrasonic welders, and smoke detectors; medical—insulin pumps, ultrasonic therapy, and ultrasonic cataract-removal devices.

Commonly used piezoelectric ceramics include barium titanate ($BaTiO_3$), lead titanate ($PbTiO_3$), lead zirconate–titanate (PZT) [$Pb(Zr,Ti)O_3$], and potassium niobate ($KNbO_3$).

[1] The piezoelectric phenomenon is described in more detail in Section 17.25.

[2] Electric polarization (explained in Sections 17.19 and 17.20) is the alignment of electric dipoles (Section 2.7) in a common direction, which gives rise to an electric field that is oriented in this same direction.

another when in use. In the past, both ball and race components traditionally have been made of bearing steels that are very hard, extremely corrosion resistant, and may be polished to a very smooth surface finish. Over the past decade or so silicon nitride (Si_3N_4) balls have begun replacing steel balls in a number of applications, since several properties of Si_3N_4 make it a more desirable material. In most instances races are still made of steel, because its tensile strength is superior to that of silicon nitride. This combination of ceramic balls and steel races is termed a *hybrid bearing*.

Since the density of Si_3N_4 is much less than steel (3.2 versus 7.8 g/cm^3) hybrid bearings weigh less than conventional ones; thus, centrifugal loading is less in the hybrids, with the result that they may operate at higher speeds (20% to 40% higher). Furthermore, the modulus of elasticity of silicon nitride is higher than for bearing steels (320 GPa versus about 200 GPa). Thus, the Si_3N_4 balls are more rigid, and experience lower deformations while in use, which leads to reductions in noise and vibration levels. Lifetimes for the hybrid bearings are greater than for steel bearings—normally three to five times greater. The longer life is a consequence of the higher hardness of Si_3N_4 (75 to 80 HRC as compared to 58 to 64 HRC for bearing steels) and silicon nitride's superior compressive strength (3000 MPa versus 900 MPa), which results in lower wear rates. In addition, less heat is generated using the hybrid bearings, because the coefficient of friction of Si_3N_4 is approximately 30% that of steel; this leads to an increase in grease life. In addition, lower lubrication levels are required than for the all-steel bearings. Ceramic materials are inherently more corrosion resistant than metal alloys; thus, the silicon nitride balls may be used in more corrosive environments and at higher operating temperatures. Finally, because Si_3N_4 is an electrical insulator (bearing steels are much more electrically conductive), the ceramic bearings are immune to arcing damage.

Some of the applications that employ these hybrid bearings include inline skates, bicycles, electric motors, machine tool spindles, precision medical hand tools (e.g., high-speed dental drills and surgical saws), and textile, food processing, and chemical equipment.

It should also be mentioned that all-ceramic bearings (having both ceramic races and balls) are now being utilized on a limited basis in applications where a high degree of corrosion resistance is required.

A significant research effort has gone into the development of this silicon nitride bearing material. Some of the challenges that were encountered are as follows: processing/fabrication techniques to yield a pore-free material, fabrication of spherical pieces that require a minimum of machining, and a polishing/lapping technique to produce a smoother surface finish than steel balls

12.9 CERAMIC PHASE DIAGRAMS

Phase diagrams have been experimentally determined for a large number of ceramic systems. For binary or two-component phase diagrams, it is frequently the case that the two components are compounds that share a common element, often oxygen. These diagrams may have configurations similar to metal–metal systems, and they are interpreted in the same way. For a review of the interpretation of phase diagrams, the reader is referred to Section 7.8.

The Al_2O_3–Cr_2O_3 System

One of the relatively simple ceramic phase diagrams is that found for the aluminum oxide–chromium oxide system, Figure 12.5. This diagram has the same form as the isomorphous copper–nickel phase diagram (Figure 7.3*a*), consisting of single liquid and single solid phase regions separated by a two-phase solid–liquid region having the shape of a blade. The Al_2O_3–Cr_2O_3 solid solution is a substitutional one in which Al^{3+} substitutes for Cr^{3+}, and vice versa. It exists for all compositions below the melting point of Al_2O_3 inasmuch as both aluminum and chromium ions have the same charge as well as similar radii (0.053 and 0.062 nm, respectively). Furthermore, both Al_2O_3 and Cr_2O_3 have the same crystal structure.

The MgO–Al_2O_3 System

The phase diagram for the magnesium oxide–aluminum oxide system (Figure 12.6) is similar in many respects to the lead–magnesium diagram (Figure 7.20). There exists an intermediate phase, or better, a compound called *spinel,* which has the chemical formula $MgAl_2O_4$ (or MgO–Al_2O_3). Even though spinel is a distinct compound [of composition 50 mol% Al_2O_3–50 mol% MgO (72 wt% Al_2O_3–28 wt% MgO)], it is represented on the phase diagram as a single-phase field rather than as a vertical line, as for Mg_2Pb (Figure 7.20); that is, there is a range of compositions over which spinel is a stable compound. Thus, spinel is nonstoichiometric for other than the 50 mol% Al_2O_3–50 mol% MgO composition. Furthermore, there is limited solubility of Al_2O_3 in MgO below about 1400°C (2550°F) at the left-hand extremity of Figure 12.6, which is due primarily to the differences in charge and

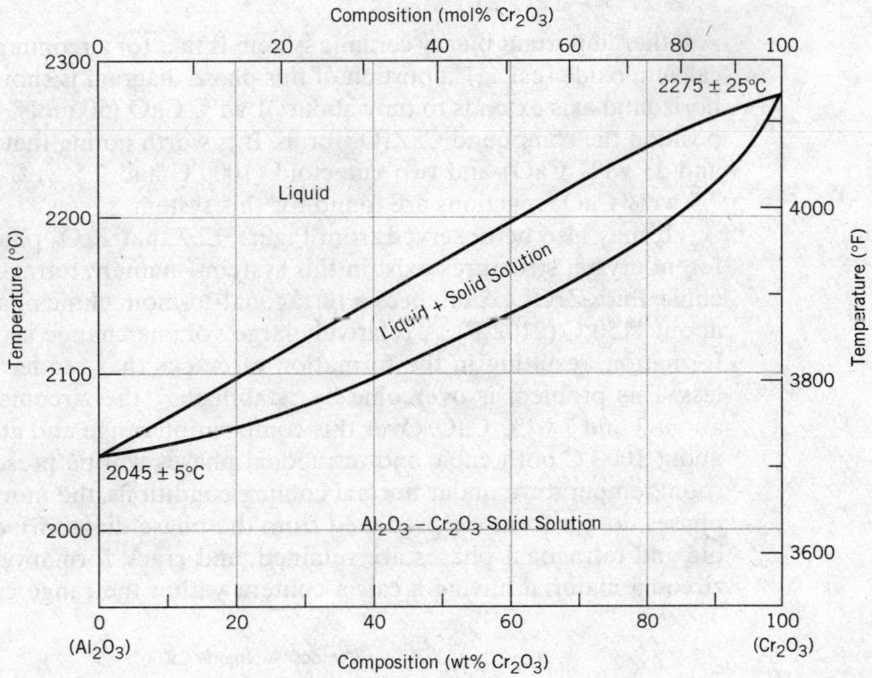

Figure 12.5 The aluminum oxide–chromium oxide phase diagram. (Adapted from E. N. Bunting, "Phase Equilibria in the System Cr_2O_3–Al_2O_3," *Bur. Standards J. Research,* **6**, 1931, p. 948.)

radii of the Mg^{2+} and Al^{3+} ions (0.072 versus 0.053 nm). For the same reasons, MgO is virtually insoluble in Al_2O_3, as evidenced by a lack of a terminal solid solution on the right-hand side of the phase diagram. Also, two eutectics are found, one on either side of the spinel phase field, and stoichiometric spinel melts congruently at about 2100°C (3800°F).

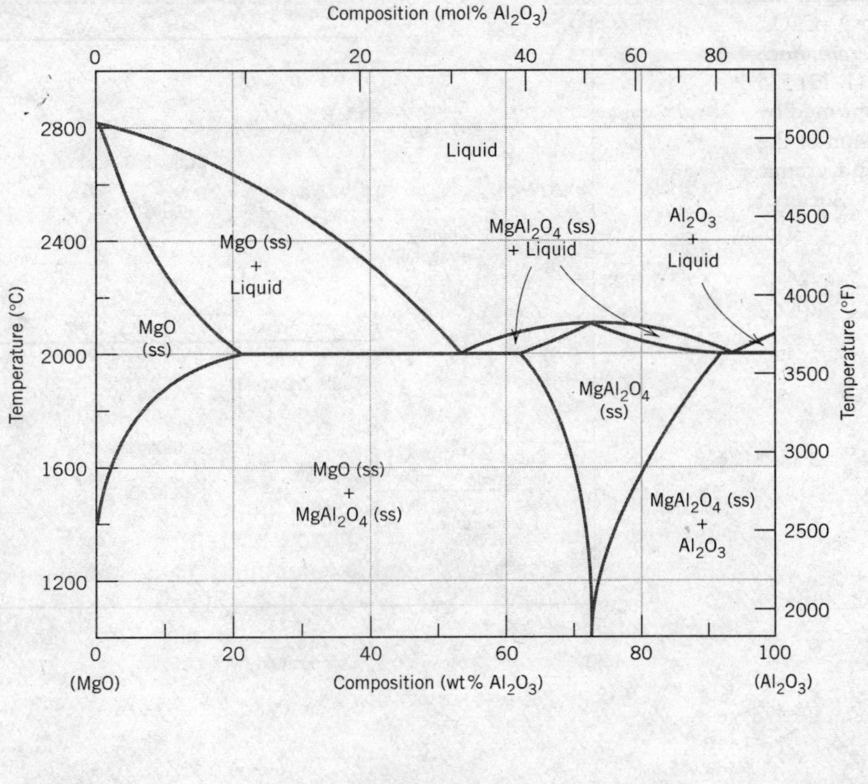

Figure 12.6 The magnesium oxide–aluminum oxide phase diagram; *ss* denotes solid solution. (Adapted from B. Hallstedt, "Thermodynamic Assessment of the System MgO–Al_2O_3," *J. Am. Ceram. Soc.,* **75** [6] 1502 (1992). Reprinted by permission of the American Ceramic Society.)

The ZrO_2–CaO System

Another important binary ceramic system is that for zirconium oxide (zirconia) and calcium oxide (calcia); a portion of this phase diagram is shown in Figure 12.7. The horizontal axis extends to only about 31 wt% CaO (50 mol% CaO), at which composition the compound $CaZrO_3$ forms. It is worth noting that one eutectic (2250°C and 23 wt% CaO) and two eutectoid (1000°C and 2.5 wt% CaO, and 850°C and 7.5 wt% CaO) reactions are found for this system.

It may also be observed from Figure 12.7 that ZrO_2 phases having three different crystal structures exist in this system—namely, tetragonal, monoclinic, and cubic. Pure ZrO_2 experiences a tetragonal-to-monoclinic phase transformation at about 1150°C (2102°F). A relatively large volume change accompanies this transformation, resulting in the formation of cracks that render a ceramic ware useless. This problem is overcome by "stabilizing" the zirconia by adding between about 3 and 7 wt% CaO. Over this composition range and at temperatures above about 1000°C both cubic and tetragonal phases will be present. Upon cooling to room temperature under normal cooling conditions, the monoclinic and $CaZr_4O_9$ phases do not form (as predicted from the phase diagram); consequently, the cubic and tetragonal phases are retained, and crack formation is circumvented. A zirconia material having a calcia content within the range cited above is termed

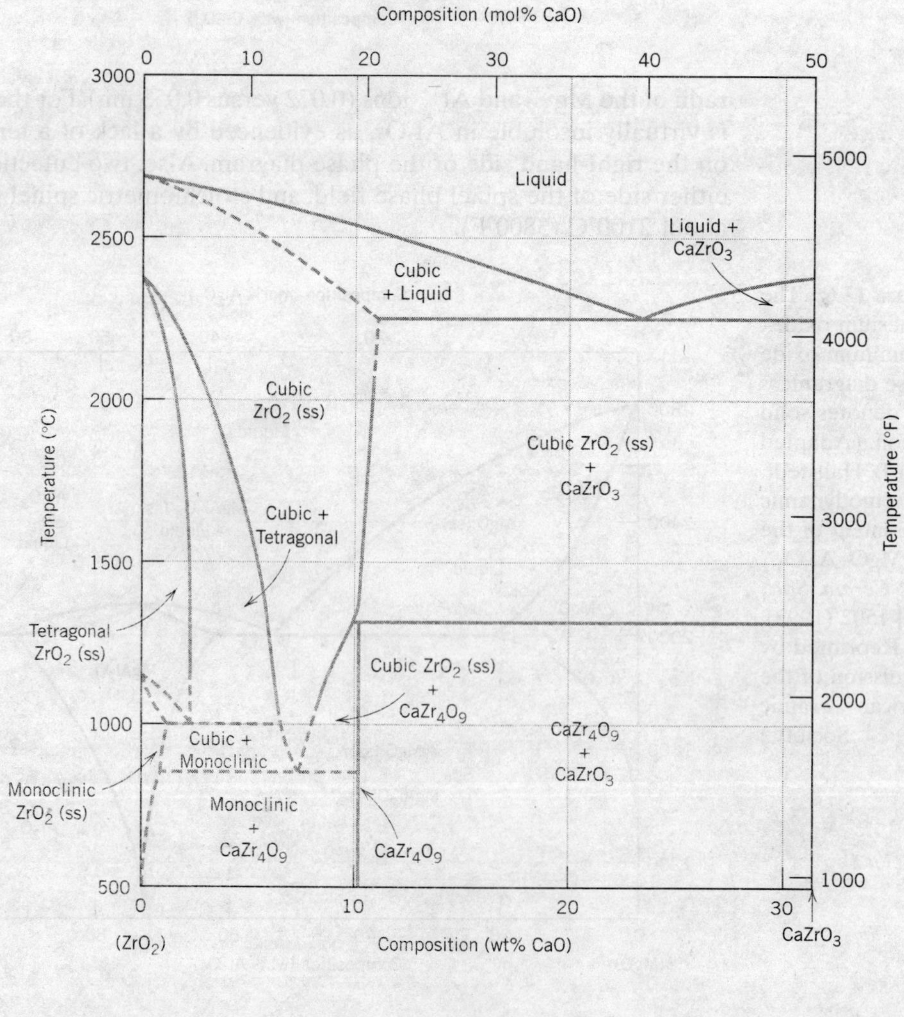

Figure 12.7 A portion of the zirconia–calcia phase diagram; *ss* denotes solid solution. (Adapted from V. S. Stubican and S. P. Ray, "Phase Equilibria and Ordering in the System ZrO_2–CaO," *J. Am. Ceram. Soc.*, **60** [11–12] 535 (1977). Reprinted by permission of the American Ceramic Society.)

a *partially stabilized zirconia,* or *PSZ*. Yttrium oxide (Y_2O_3) and magnesium oxide are also used as stabilizing agents. Furthermore, for higher stabilizer contents, only the cubic phase may be retained at room temperature; such a material is fully stabilized.

The SiO_2–Al_2O_3 System

Commercially, the silica–alumina system is an important one since the principal constituents of many ceramic refractories are these two materials. Figure 12.8 shows the SiO_2–Al_2O_3 phase diagram. The polymorphic form of silica that is stable at these temperatures is termed *cristobalite,* the unit cell for which is shown in Figure 4.9. Silica and alumina are not mutually soluble in one another, which is evidenced by the absence of terminal solid solutions at both extremities of the phase diagram. Also, it may be noted that the intermediate compound *mullite,* $3Al_2O_3$–$2SiO_2$, exists, which is represented as a narrow phase field in Figure 12.8; furthermore, mullite melts incongruently at 1890°C (3435°F). A single eutectic exists at 1587°C (2890°F) and 7.7 wt% Al_2O_3. In Section 12.5, refractory ceramic materials, the prime constituents for which are silica and alumina, are discussed.

Concept Check 12.4

(a) For the SiO_2–Al_2O_3 system, what is the maximum temperature that is possible without the formation of a liquid phase? **(b)** At what composition or over what range of compositions will this maximum temperature be achieved?

[The answer may be found in enclosed CD.]

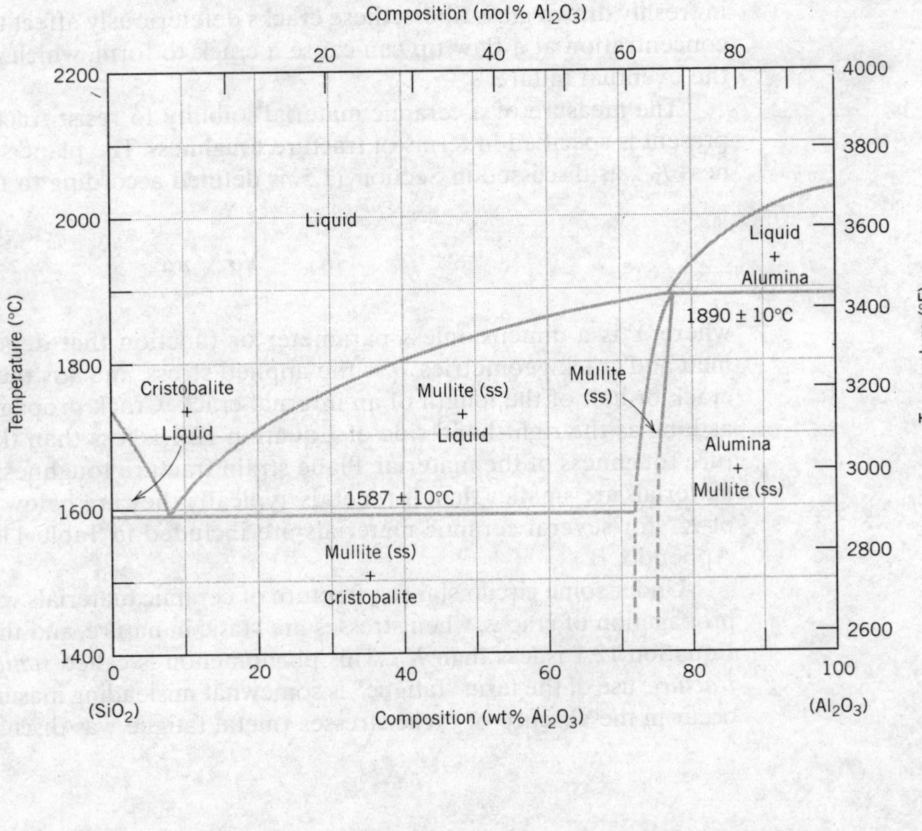

Figure 12.8 The silica–alumina phase diagram. (Adapted from F. J. Klug, S. Prochazka, and R. H. Doremus, "Alumina–Silica Phase Diagram in the Mullite Region," *J. Am. Ceram. Soc.,* **70** [10] 758 (1987). Reprinted by permission of the American Ceramic Society.)

Mechanical Properties

Ceramic materials are somewhat limited in applicability by their mechanical properties, which in many respects are inferior to those of metals. The principal drawback is a disposition to catastrophic fracture in a brittle manner with very little energy absorption.

12.10 BRITTLE FRACTURE OF CERAMICS

At room temperature, both crystalline and noncrystalline ceramics almost always fracture before any plastic deformation can occur in response to an applied tensile load. The topics of brittle fracture and fracture mechanics, as discussed previously in Sections 11.4 and 11.5, also relate to the fracture of ceramic materials; they will be reviewed briefly in this context.

The brittle fracture process consists of the formation and propagation of cracks through the cross section of material in a direction perpendicular to the applied load. Crack growth in crystalline ceramics may be either transgranular (i.e., through the grains) or intergranular (i.e., along grain boundaries); for transgranular fracture, cracks propagate along specific crystallographic (or cleavage) planes, planes of high atomic density.

The measured fracture strengths of ceramic materials are substantially lower than predicted by theory from interatomic bonding forces. This may be explained by very small and omnipresent flaws in the material that serve as stress raisers—points at which the magnitude of an applied tensile stress is amplified. The degree of stress amplification depends on crack length and tip radius of curvature according to Equation 8.1, being greatest for long and pointed flaws. These stress raisers may be minute surface or interior cracks (microcracks), internal pores, and grain corners, which are virtually impossible to eliminate or control. For example, even moisture and contaminants in the atmosphere can introduce surface cracks in freshly drawn glass fibers; these cracks deleteriously affect the strength. A stress concentration at a flaw tip can cause a crack to form, which may propagate until the eventual failure.

The measure of a ceramic material's ability to resist fracture when a crack is present is specified in terms of fracture toughness. The plane strain fracture toughness K_{Ic}, as discussed in Section 11.5, is defined according to the expression

$$K_{Ic} = Y\sigma\sqrt{\pi a} \tag{12.1}$$

where Y is a dimensionless parameter or function that depends on both specimen and crack geometries, σ is the applied stress, and a is the length of a surface crack or half of the length of an internal crack. Crack propagation will not occur as long as the right-hand side of Equation 12.1 is less than the plane strain fracture toughness of the material. Plane strain fracture toughness values for ceramic materials are smaller than for metals; typically they are below 10 MPa$\sqrt{\text{m}}$. Values of K_{Ic} for several ceramic materials are included in Table 11.1 and Table B.5 of Appendix B.

Under some circumstances, fracture of ceramic materials will occur by the slow propagation of cracks, when stresses are static in nature, and the right-hand side of Equation 12.1 is less than K_{Ic}. This phenomenon is called *static fatigue,* or *delayed fracture;* use of the term "fatigue" is somewhat misleading inasmuch as fracture may occur in the absence of cyclic stresses (metal fatigue was discussed in Chapter 11).

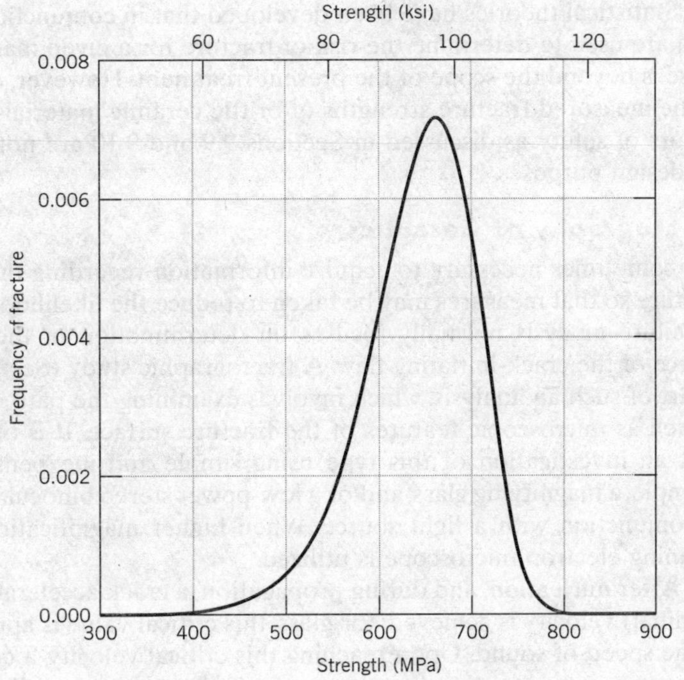

Figure 12.9 The frequency distribution of observed fracture strengths for a silicon nitride material.

It has been observed that this type of fracture is especially sensitive to environmental conditions, specifically when moisture is present in the atmosphere. Relative to mechanism, a stress–corrosion process probably occurs at the crack tips. That is, the combination of an applied tensile stress and atmospheric moisture at crack tips causes ionic bonds to rupture; this leads to a sharpening and lengthening of the cracks until, ultimately, one crack grows to a size capable of rapid propagation according to Equation 11.3. Furthermore, the duration of stress application preceding fracture diminishes with increasing stress. Consequently, when specifying the static fatigue strength, the time of stress application should also be stipulated. Silicate glasses are especially susceptible to this type of fracture; it has also been observed in other ceramic materials to include porcelain, portland cement, high-alumina ceramics, barium titanate, and silicon nitride.

There is usually considerable variation and scatter in the fracture strength for many specimens of a specific brittle ceramic material. A distribution of fracture strengths for a silicon nitride material is shown in Figure 12.9. This phenomenon may be explained by the dependence of fracture strength on the probability of the existence of a flaw that is capable of initiating a crack. This probability varies from specimen to specimen of the same material and depends on fabrication technique and any subsequent treatment. Specimen size or volume also influences fracture strength; the larger the specimen, the greater is this flaw existence probability, and the lower the fracture strength.

For compressive stresses, there is no stress amplification associated with any existent flaws. For this reason, brittle ceramics display much higher strengths in compression than in tension (on the order of a factor of 10), and they are generally utilized when load conditions are compressive. Also, the fracture strength of a brittle ceramic may be enhanced dramatically by imposing residual compressive stresses at its surface. One way this may be accomplished is by thermal tempering (see Section 12.16).

Statistical theories have been developed that in conjunction with experimental data are used to determine the risk of fracture for a given material; a discussion of these is beyond the scope of the present treatment. However, due to the dispersion in the measured fracture strengths of brittle ceramic materials, average values and factors of safety as discussed in Sections 9.9 and 9.10 are not normally employed for design purposes.

Fractography of Ceramics

It is sometimes necessary to acquire information regarding the cause of a ceramic fracture so that measures may be taken to reduce the likelihood of future incidents. A failure analysis normally focuses on determination of the location, type, and source of the crack-initiating flaw. A fractographic study (Section 11.3) is normally a part of such an analysis, which involves examining the path of crack propagation as well as microscopic features of the fracture surface. It is often possible to conduct an investigation of this type using simple and inexpensive equipment—for example, a magnifying glass, and/or a low-power stereo binocular optical microscope in conjunction with a light source. When higher magnifications are required the scanning electron microscope is utilized.

After nucleation, and during propagation, a crack accelerates until a critical (or terminal) velocity is achieved; for glass, this critical value is approximately one-half of the speed of sound. Upon reaching this critical velocity, a crack may branch (or bifurcate), a process that may be successively repeated until a family of cracks is produced. Typical crack configurations for four common loading schemes are shown in Figure 12.10. The site of nucleation can often be traced back to the point where a set of cracks converges or comes together. Furthermore, rate of crack acceleration increases with increasing stress level; correspondingly degree of branching also increases with rising stress. For example, from experience we know that when a large rock strikes (and probably breaks) a window, more crack branching results [i.e., more and smaller cracks form (or more broken fragments are produced)] than for a small pebble impact.

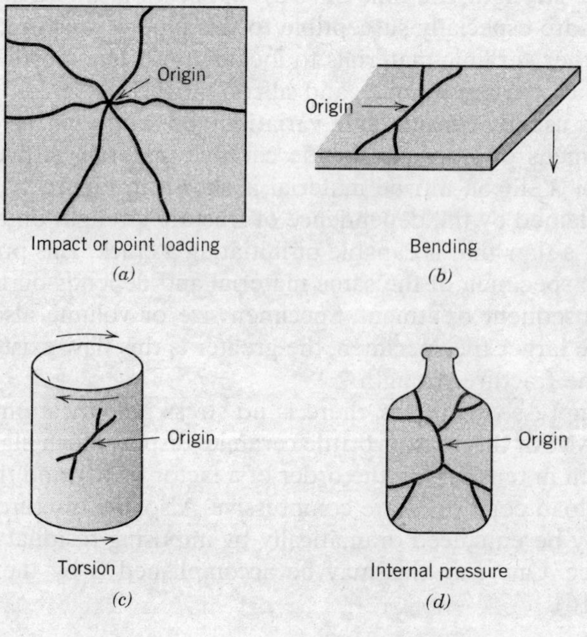

Figure 12.10 For brittle ceramic materials, schematic representations of crack origins and configurations that result from (*a*) impact (point contact) loading, (*b*) bending, (*c*) torsional loading, and (*d*) internal pressure. (From D. W. Richerson, *Modern Ceramic Engineering,* 2nd edition, Marcel Dekker, Inc., New York, 1992. Reprinted from *Modern Ceramic Engineering,* 2nd edition, p. 681, by courtesy of Marcel Dekker, Inc.)

During propagation, a crack interacts with the microstructure of the material, with the stress, as well as with elastic waves that are generated; these interactions produce distinctive features on the fracture surface. Furthermore, these features provide important information on where the crack initiated, and the source of the crack-producing defect. In addition, measurement of the approximate fracture-producing stress may be useful; stress magnitude is indicative of whether the ceramic piece was excessively weak, or the in-service stress was greater than anticipated.

Several microscopic features normally found on the crack surfaces of failed ceramic pieces are shown in the schematic diagram of Figure 12.11 and also the photomicrograph in Figure 12.12. The crack surface that formed during the initial acceleration stage of propagation is flat and smooth, and appropriately termed the *mirror* region (Figure 12.11). For glass fractures, this mirror region is extremely flat and highly reflective; on the other hand, for polycrystalline ceramics, the flat mirror surfaces are rougher and have a granular texture. The outer perimeter of the mirror region is roughly circular, with the crack origin at its center.

Upon reaching its critical velocity, the crack begins to branch—that is, the crack surface changes propagation direction. At this time there is a roughening of the crack interface on a microscopic scale, and the formation of two more surface features—*mist* and *hackle;* these are also noted in Figures 12.11 and 12.12. The mist is a faint annular region just outside the mirror; it is often not discernible for polycrystalline ceramic pieces. And beyond the mist is the hackle, which has an even rougher texture. The hackle is composed of a set of striations or lines that radiate away from the crack source in the direction of crack propagation; furthermore, they intersect near the crack initiation site, and may be used to pinpoint its location.

Qualitative information regarding the magnitude of the fracture-producing stress is available from measurement of the mirror radius (r_m in Figure 12.11). This radius is a function of the acceleration rate of a newly formed crack—that is, the greater this acceleration rate, the sooner the crack reaches its critical velocity, and the smaller the mirror radius. Furthermore, the acceleration rate increases with

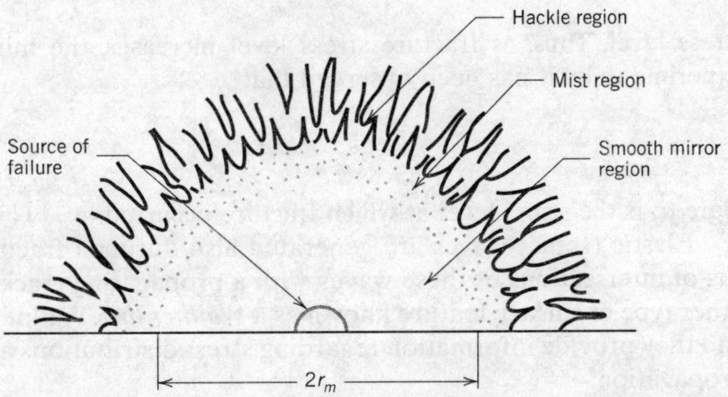

Figure 12.11 Schematic diagram that shows typical features observed on the fracture surface of a brittle ceramic. (Adapted from J. J. Mecholsky, R. W. Rice, and S. W. Freiman, "Prediction of Fracture Energy and Flaw Size in Glasses from Measurements of Mirror Size," *J. Am. Ceram. Soc.*, **57** [10] 440 (1974). Reprinted with permission of The American Ceramic Society, *www.ceramics.org*. Copyright 1974. All rights reserved.)

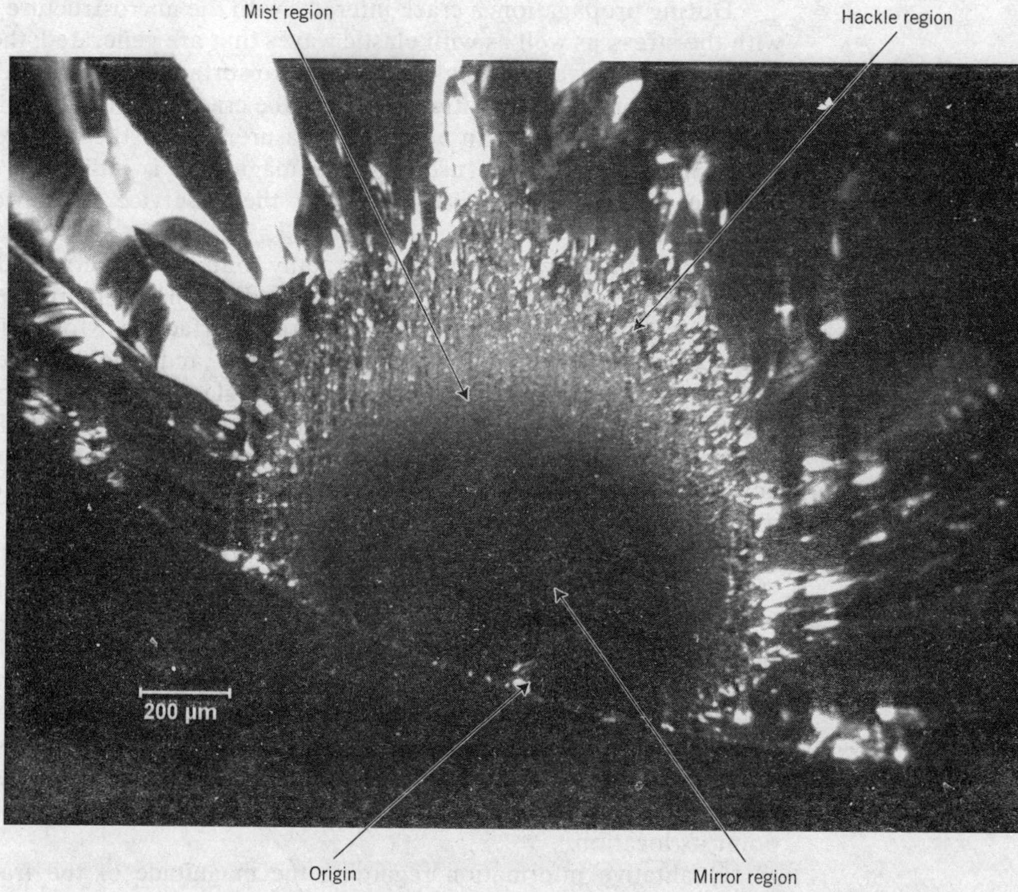

Figure 12.12 Photomicrograph of the fracture surface of a 6 mm-diameter fused silica rod that was fractured in four-point bending. Features typical of this kind of fracture are noted—i.e., the origin, as well as mirror, mist, and hackle regions. 500×. (Courtesy of George Quinn, National Institute of Standards and Technology, Gaithersburg, MD.)

stress level. Thus, as fracture stress level increases, the mirror radius decreases; experimentally it has been observed that

$$\sigma_f \propto \frac{1}{r_m^{0.5}} \tag{12.2}$$

Here σ_f is the stress level at which fracture occurred.

Elastic (sonic) waves are generated also during a fracture event, and the locus of intersections of these waves with a propagating crack front give rise to another type of surface feature known as a *Wallner line*. Wallner lines are arc shaped, and they provide information regarding stress distributions and directions of crack propagation.

12.11 STRESS–STRAIN BEHAVIOR

Flexural Strength

The stress–strain behavior of brittle ceramics is not usually ascertained by a tensile test as outlined in Section 9.5, for three reasons. First, it is difficult to

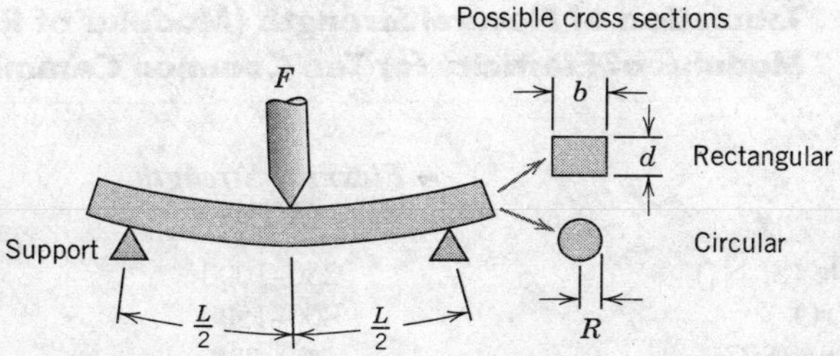

σ = stress = $\frac{Mc}{I}$

where M = maximum bending moment
c = distance from center of specimen to outer fibers
I = moment of inertia of cross section
F = applied load

	M	c	I	σ
Rectangular	$\frac{FL}{4}$	$\frac{d}{2}$	$\frac{bd^3}{12}$	$\frac{3FL}{2bd^2}$
Circular	$\frac{FL}{4}$	R	$\frac{\pi R^4}{4}$	$\frac{FL}{\pi R^3}$

Figure 12.13 A three-point loading scheme for measuring the stress–strain behavior and flexural strength of brittle ceramics, including expressions for computing stress for rectangular and circular cross sections.

prepare and test specimens having the required geometry. Second, it is difficult to grip brittle materials without fracturing them; and third, ceramics fail after only about 0.1% strain, which necessitates that tensile specimens be perfectly aligned to avoid the presence of bending stresses, which are not easily calculated. Therefore, a more suitable transverse bending test is most frequently employed, in which a rod specimen having either a circular or rectangular cross section is bent until fracture using a three- or four-point loading technique;[2] the three-point loading scheme is illustrated in Figure 12.13. At the point of loading, the top surface of the specimen is placed in a state of compression, while the bottom surface is in tension. Stress is computed from the specimen thickness, the bending moment, and the moment of inertia of the cross section; these parameters are noted in Figure 12.13 for rectangular and circular cross sections. The maximum tensile stress (as determined using these stress expressions) exists at the bottom specimen surface directly below the point of load application. Since the tensile strengths of ceramics are about one-tenth of their compressive strengths, and since fracture occurs on the tensile specimen face, the flexure test is a reasonable substitute for the tensile test.

The stress at fracture using this flexure test is known as the **flexural strength,** *modulus of rupture, fracture strength,* or the *bend strength,* an important mechanical parameter for brittle ceramics. For a rectangular cross section, the flexural strength σ_{fs} is equal to

$$\sigma_{fs} = \frac{3F_f L}{2bd^2} \tag{12.3a}$$

[2] ASTM Standard C1161, "Standard Test Method for Flexural Strength of Advanced Ceramics at Ambient Temperature."

Table 12.3 Tabulation of Flexural Strength (Modulus of Rupture) and Modulus of Elasticity for Ten Common Ceramic Materials

Material	*Flexural Strength (MPa)*	*Modulus of Elasticity (GPa)*
Silicon nitride (Si_3N_4)	250–1000	304
Zirconia[a] (ZrO_2)	800–1500	205
Silicon carbide (SiC)	100–820	345
Aluminum oxide (Al_2O_3)	275–700	393
Glass-ceramic (Pyroceram)	247	120
Mullite ($3Al_2O_3$-$2SiO_2$)	185	145
Spinel ($MgAl_2O_4$)	110–245	260
Magnesium oxide (MgO)	105[b]	225
Fused silica (SiO_2)	110	73
Soda-lime glass	69	69

[a] Partially stabilized with 3 mol% Y_2O_3.

[b] Sintered and containing approximately 5% porosity.

where F_f is the load at fracture, L is the distance between support points, and the other parameters are as indicated in Figure 12.13. When the cross section is circular, then

$$\sigma_{fs} = \frac{F_f L}{\pi R^3} \tag{12.3b}$$

where R is the specimen radius.

Characteristic flexural strength values for several ceramic materials are given in Table 12.3. Furthermore, σ_{fs} will depend on specimen size; as explained above, with increasing specimen volume (that is, specimen volume exposed to a tensile stress) there is an increase in the probability of the existence of a crack-producing flaw and, consequently, a decrease in flexural strength. In addition, the magnitude of flexural strength for a specific ceramic material will be greater than its fracture strength measured from a tensile test. This phenomenon may be explained by differences in specimen volume that are exposed to tensile stresses: the entirety of a tensile specimen is under tensile stress, whereas only some volume fraction of a flexural specimen is subjected to tensile stresses—those regions in the vicinity of the specimen surface opposite to the point of load application (see Figure 12.13).

Elastic Behavior

The elastic stress–strain behavior for ceramic materials using these flexure tests is similar to the tensile test results for metals: a linear relationship exists between stress and strain. Figure 12.14 compares the stress–strain behavior to fracture for aluminum oxide and glass. Again, the slope in the elastic region is the modulus of elasticity; the range of moduli of elasticity for ceramic materials is between about 70 and 500 GPa, being slightly higher than for metals. Table 12.5 lists values for several ceramic materials. A more comprehensive tabulation is contained in Table B.2 of Appendix B. Also, from Figure 12.14 note that neither material experiences plastic deformation prior to fracture.

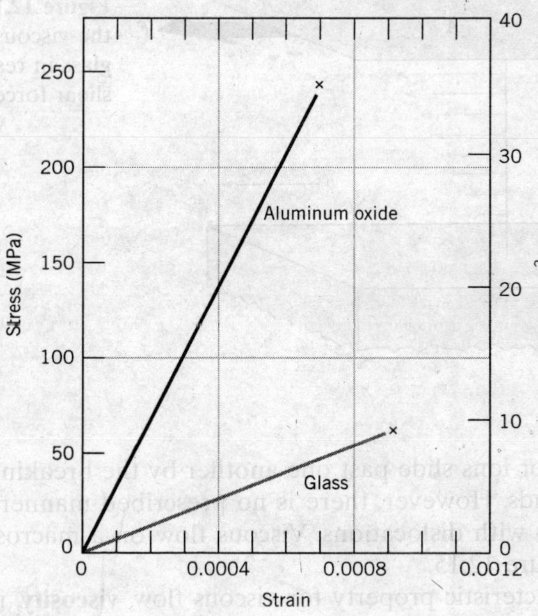

Figure 12.14 Typical stress–strain behavior to fracture for aluminum oxide and glass.

12.12 MECHANISMS OF PLASTIC DEFORMATION

Although at room temperature most ceramic materials suffer fracture before the onset of plastic deformation, a brief exploration into the possible mechanisms is worthwhile. Plastic deformation is different for crystalline and noncrystalline ceramics; however, each is discussed.

Crystalline Ceramics

For crystalline ceramics, plastic deformation occurs, as with metals, by the motion of dislocations (Chapter 10). One reason for the hardness and brittleness of these materials is the difficulty of slip (or dislocation motion). For crystalline ceramic materials for which the bonding is predominantly ionic, there are very few slip systems (crystallographic planes and directions within those planes) along which dislocations may move. This is a consequence of the electrically charged nature of the ions. For slip in some directions, ions of like charge are brought into close proximity to one another; because of electrostatic repulsion, this mode of slip is very restricted, to the extent that plastic deformation in ceramics is rarely measurable at room temperature. By way of contrast, in metals, since all atoms are electrically neutral, considerably more slip systems are operable and, consequently, dislocation motion is much more facile.

On the other hand, for ceramics in which the bonding is highly covalent, slip is also difficult and they are brittle for the following reasons: (1) the covalent bonds are relatively strong, (2) there are also limited numbers of slip systems, and (3) dislocation structures are complex.

Noncrystalline Ceramics

Plastic deformation does not occur by dislocation motion for noncrystalline ceramics because there is no regular atomic structure. Rather, these materials deform by *viscous flow,* the same manner in which liquids deform; the rate of deformation is proportional to the applied stress. In response to an applied shear

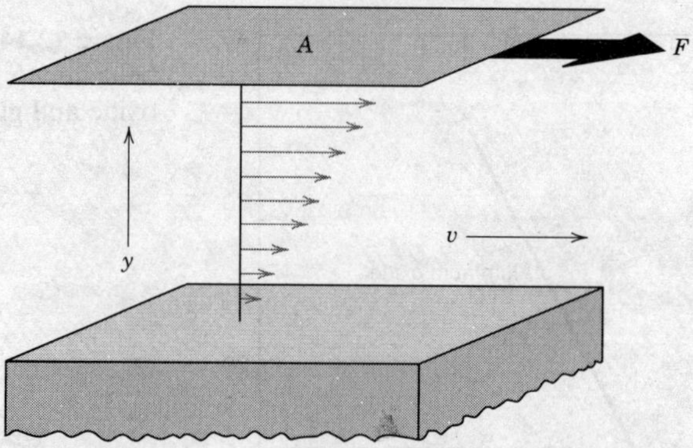

Figure 12.15 Representation of the viscous flow of a liquid or fluid glass in response to an applied shear force.

stress, atoms or ions slide past one another by the breaking and reforming of interatomic bonds. However, there is no prescribed manner or direction in which this occurs, as with dislocations. Viscous flow on a macroscopic scale is demonstrated in Figure 12.15.

The characteristic property for viscous flow, **viscosity,** is a measure of a noncrystalline material's resistance to deformation. For viscous flow in a liquid that originates from shear stresses imposed by two flat and parallel plates, the viscosity η is the ratio of the applied shear stress τ and the change in velocity dv with distance dy in a direction perpendicular to and away from the plates, or

$$\eta = \frac{\tau}{dv/dy} = \frac{F/A}{dv/dy} \tag{12.4}$$

This scheme is represented in Figure 12.15.

The units for viscosity are poises (P) and pascal-seconds (Pa-s); 1 P = 1 dyne-s/cm^2, and 1 Pa-s = 1 N-s/m^2. Conversion from one system of units to the other is according to

$$10 \text{ P} = 1 \text{ Pa-s}$$

Liquids have relatively low viscosities; for example, the viscosity of water at room temperature is about 10^{-3} Pa-s. On the other hand, glasses have extremely large viscosities at ambient temperatures, which is accounted for by strong interatomic bonding. As the temperature is raised, the magnitude of the bonding is diminished, the sliding motion or flow of the atoms or ions is facilitated, and subsequently there is an attendant decrease in viscosity. A discussion of the temperature dependence of viscosity for glasses is deferred to Section 12.14.

12.13 MISCELLANEOUS MECHANICAL CONSIDERATIONS

Influence of Porosity

For some ceramic fabrication techniques, the precursor material is in the form of a powder. Subsequent to compaction or forming of these powder particles into the desired shape, pores or void spaces will exist between the powder particles. During the ensuing heat treatment, much of this porosity will be eliminated; however, it is often the case that this pore elimination process is incomplete and some residual porosity will remain. Any residual porosity will have a deleterious influence on both the elastic properties and strength. For example, it has been observed for some ce-

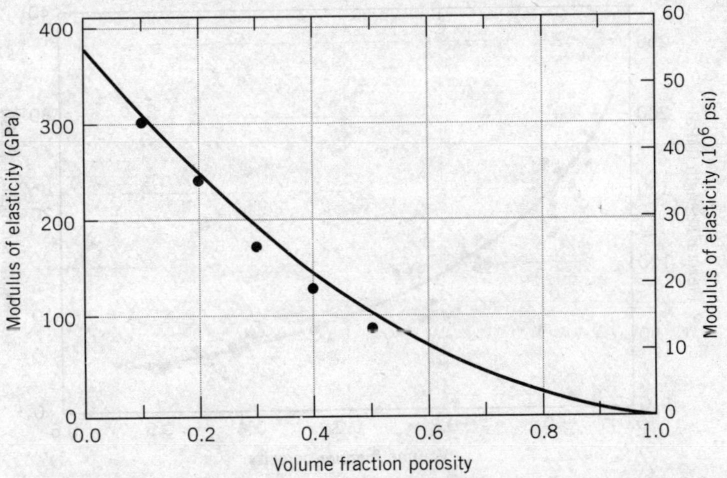

Figure 12.16 The influence of porosity on the modulus of elasticity for aluminum oxide at room temperature. The curve drawn is according to Equation 12.5. (From R. L. Coble and W. D. Kingery, "Effect of Porosity on Physical Properties of Sintered Alumina," *J. Am. Ceram. Soc.,* **39,** 11, Nov. 1956, p. 381. Reprinted by permission of the American Ceramic Society.)

ramic materials that the magnitude of the modulus of elasticity E decreases with volume fraction porosity P according to

$$E = E_0(1 - 1.9P + 0.9P^2) \tag{12.5}$$

where E_0 is the modulus of elasticity of the nonporous material. The influence of volume fraction porosity on the modulus of elasticity for aluminum oxide is shown in Figure 12.16; the curve represented in the figure is according to Equation 12.5.

Porosity is deleterious to the flexural strength for two reasons: (1) pores reduce the cross-sectional area across which a load is applied, and (2) they also act as stress concentrators—for an isolated spherical pore, an applied tensile stress is amplified by a factor of 2. The influence of porosity on strength is rather dramatic; for example, it is not uncommon that 10 vol% porosity will decrease the flexural strength by 50% from the measured value for the nonporous material. The degree of the influence of pore volume on flexural strength is demonstrated in Figure 12.17, again for aluminum oxide. Experimentally it has been shown that the flexural strength decreases exponentially with volume fraction porosity (P) as

$$\sigma_{fs} = \sigma_0 \exp(-nP) \tag{12.6}$$

In this expression σ_0 and n are experimental constants.

Hardness

One beneficial mechanical property of ceramics is their hardness, which is often utilized when an abrasive or grinding action is required; in fact, the hardest known materials are ceramics. A listing of a number of different ceramic materials according to Knoop hardness is contained in Table 12.4. Only ceramics having Knoop hardnesses of about 1000 or greater are utilized for their abrasive characteristics.

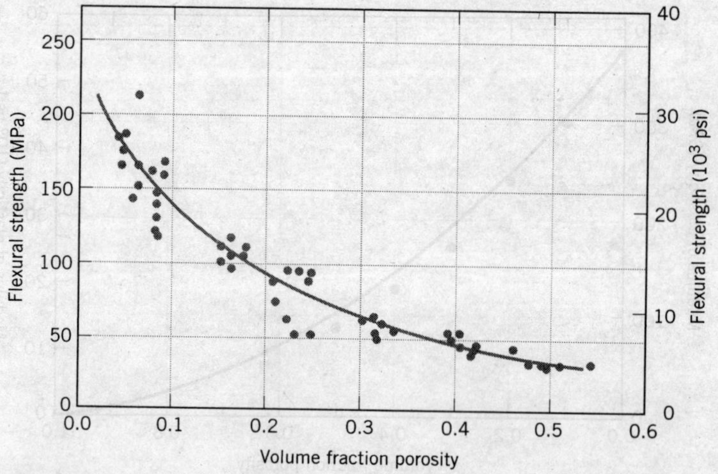

Figure 12.17 The influence of porosity on the flexural strength for aluminum oxide at room temperature. (From R. L. Coble and W. D. Kingery, "Effect of Porosity on Physical Properties of Sintered Alumina," *J. Am. Ceram. Soc.,* **39,** 11, Nov. 1956, p. 382. Reprinted by permission of the American Ceramic Society.)

Creep

Often ceramic materials experience creep deformation as a result of exposure to stresses (usually compressive) at elevated temperatures. In general, the time–deformation creep behavior of ceramics is similar to that of metals (Section 11.12); however, creep occurs at higher temperatures in ceramics. High-temperature compressive creep tests are conducted on ceramic materials to ascertain creep deformation as a function of temperature and stress level.

Other Properties

12.14 GLASS PROPERTIES

Some of the temperature-sensitive properties of glass materials will be presented. Glassy, or noncrystalline, materials do not solidify in the same sense as do those that are crystalline. Upon cooling, a glass becomes more and more viscous in a continuous manner with decreasing temperature; there is no definite temperature at which the liquid transforms to a solid as with crystalline materials. In fact, one

Table 12.4 Approximate Knoop Hardness (100 g load) for Seven Ceramic Materials

Material	*Approximate Knoop Hardness*
Diamond (carbon)	7000
Boron carbide (B_4C)	2800
Silicon carbide (SiC)	2500
Tungsten carbide (WC)	2100
Aluminum oxide (Al_2O_3)	2100
Quartz (SiO_2)	800
Glass	550

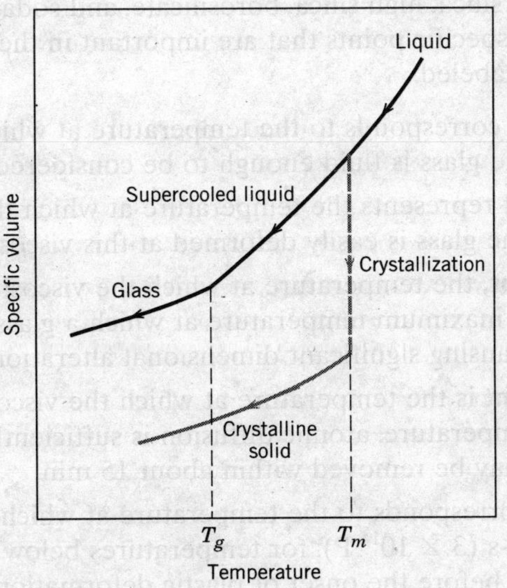

Figure 12.18 Contrast of specific volume-versus-temperature behavior of crystalline and noncrystalline materials. Crystalline materials solidify at the melting temperature T_m. Characteristic of the noncrystalline state is the glass transition temperature T_g.

of the distinctions between crystalline and noncrystalline materials lies in the dependence of specific volume (or volume per unit mass, the reciprocal of density) on temperature, as illustrated in Figure 12.18. For crystalline materials, there is a discontinuous decrease in volume at the melting temperature T_m. However, for glassy materials, volume decreases continuously with temperature reduction; a slight decrease in slope of the curve occurs at what is called the **glass transition temperature,** or *fictive* temperature, T_g. Below this temperature, the material is considered to be a glass; above, it is first a supercooled liquid, and finally a liquid.

Also important in glass-forming operations are the viscosity–temperature characteristics of the glass. Figure 12.19 plots the logarithm of viscosity versus the

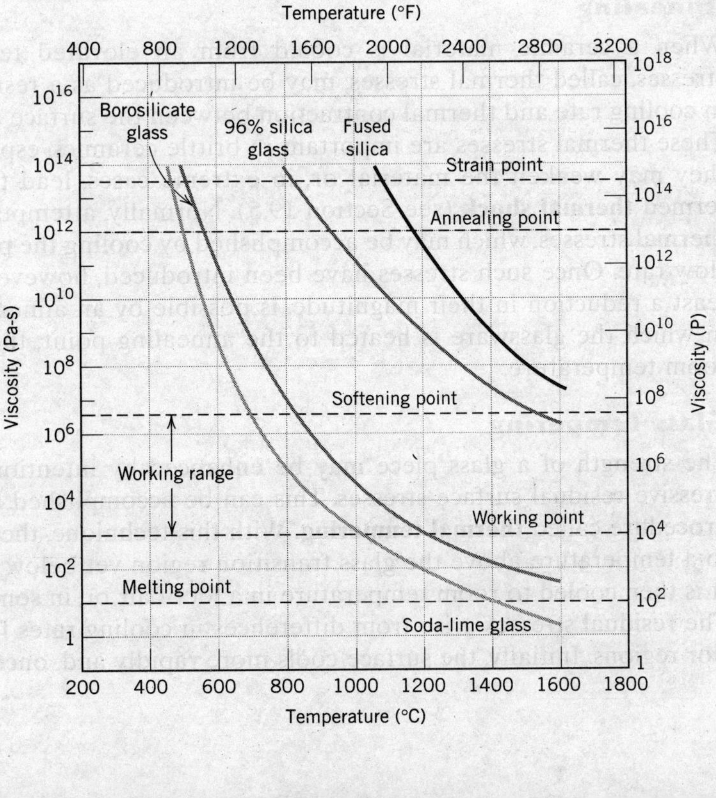

Figure 12.19 Logarithm of viscosity versus temperature for fused silica and three silica glasses. (From E. B. Shand, *Engineering Glass,* Modern Materials, Vol. 6, Academic Press, New York, 1968, p. 262.)

temperature for fused silica, high silica, borosilicate, and soda–lime glasses. On the viscosity scale several specific points that are important in the fabrication and processing of glasses are labeled:

1. The **melting point** corresponds to the temperature at which the viscosity is 10 Pa-s (100 P); the glass is fluid enough to be considered a liquid.
2. The **working point** represents the temperature at which the viscosity is 10^3 Pa-s (10^4 P); the glass is easily deformed at this viscosity.
3. The **softening point,** the temperature at which the viscosity is 4×10^6 Pa-s (4×10^7 P), is the maximum temperature at which a glass piece may be handled without causing significant dimensional alterations.
4. The **annealing point** is the temperature at which the viscosity is 10^{12} Pa-s (10^{13} P); at this temperature, atomic diffusion is sufficiently rapid that any residual stresses may be removed within about 15 min.
5. The **strain point** corresponds to the temperature at which the viscosity becomes 3×10^{13} Pa-s (3×10^{14} P); for temperatures below the strain point, fracture will occur before the onset of plastic deformation. The glass transition temperature will be above the strain point.

Most glass-forming operations are carried out within the working range—between the working and softening temperatures.

Of course, the temperature at which each of these points occurs depends on glass composition. For example, the softening points for soda–lime and 96% silica glasses from Figure 12.19 are about 700 and 1550°C (1300 and 2825°F), respectively. That is, forming operations may be carried out at significantly lower temperatures for the soda–lime glass. The formability of a glass is tailored to a large degree by its composition.

12.15 HEAT TREATMENT OF GLASSES

Annealing

When a ceramic material is cooled from an elevated temperature, internal stresses, called thermal stresses, may be introduced as a result of the difference in cooling rate and thermal contraction between the surface and interior regions. These thermal stresses are important in brittle ceramics, especially glasses, since they may weaken the material or, in extreme cases, lead to fracture, which is termed **thermal shock** (see Section 19.5). Normally, attempts are made to avoid thermal stresses, which may be accomplished by cooling the piece at a sufficiently slow rate. Once such stresses have been introduced, however, elimination, or at least a reduction in their magnitude, is possible by an annealing heat treatment in which the glassware is heated to the annealing point, then slowly cooled to room temperature.

Glass Tempering

The strength of a glass piece may be enhanced by intentionally inducing compressive residual surface stresses. This can be accomplished by a heat treatment procedure called **thermal tempering.** With this technique, the glassware is heated to a temperature above the glass transition region yet below the softening point. It is then cooled to room temperature in a jet of air or, in some cases, an oil bath. The residual stresses arise from differences in cooling rates for surface and interior regions. Initially, the surface cools more rapidly and, once having dropped to

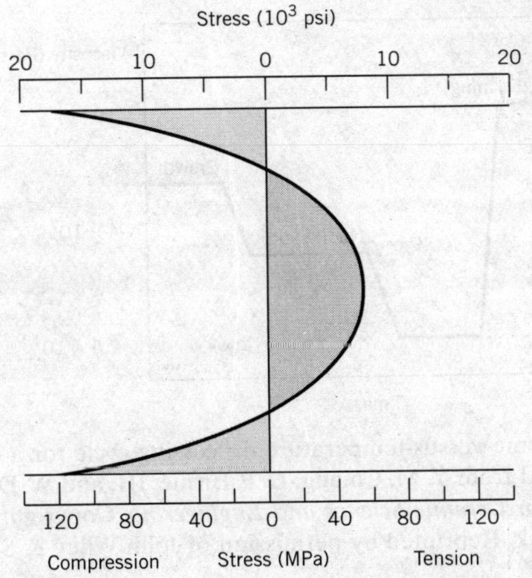

Figure 12.20 Room-temperature residual stress distribution over the cross section of a tempered glass plate. (From W. D. Kingery, H. K. Bowen, and D. R. Uhlmann, *Introduction to Ceramics,* 2nd edition. Copyright © 1976 by John Wiley & Sons, New York. Reprinted by permission of John Wiley & Sons, Inc.)

a temperature below the strain point, becomes rigid. At this time, the interior, having cooled less rapidly, is at a higher temperature (above the strain point) and, therefore, is still plastic. With continued cooling, the interior attempts to contract to a greater degree than the now rigid exterior will allow. Thus, the inside tends to draw in the outside, or to impose inward radial stresses. As a consequence, after the glass piece has cooled to room temperature, it sustains compressive stresses on the surface, with tensile stresses at interior regions. The room-temperature stress distribution over a cross section of a glass plate is represented schematically in Figure 12.20.

The failure of ceramic materials almost always results from a crack that is initiated at the surface by an applied tensile stress. To cause fracture of a tempered glass piece, the magnitude of an externally applied tensile stress must be great enough to first overcome the residual compressive surface stress and, in addition, to stress the surface in tension sufficiently to initiate a crack, which may then propagate. For an untempered glass, a crack will be introduced at a lower external stress level, and, consequently, the fracture strength will be smaller.

Tempered glass is used for applications in which high strength is important; these include large doors and eyeglass lenses.

Concept Check 12.5

How does the thickness of a glassware affect the magnitude of the thermal stresses that may be introduced? Why?

[*The answer may be found in enclosed CD.*]

12.16 HEAT TREATMENT OF GLASS CERAMICS

The first stage in the fabrication of a glass-ceramic ware is forming it into the desired shape as a glass. Forming techniques used are the same as for glass pieces, as described previously—viz. pressing and drawing. Conversion of the glass into a

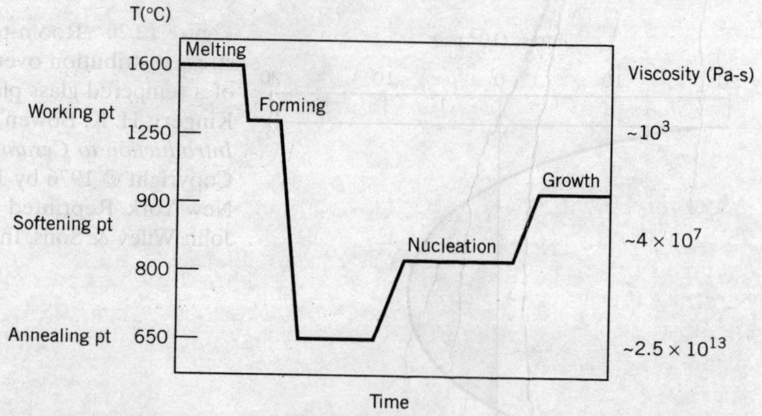

Figure 12.21 Typical time-versus-temperature processing cycle for a Li_2O–Al_2O_3–SiO_2 glass–ceramic. (Adapted from Y. M. Chiang, D. P. Birnie, III, and W. D. Kingery, *Physical Ceramics—Principles for Ceramic Science and Engineering*. Copyright © 1997 by John Wiley & Sons, New York. Reprinted by permission of John Wiley & Sons, Inc.)

glass–ceramic (i.e., crystallation, Section 12.3) is accomplished by appropriate heat treatments. One such set of heat treatments for a Li_2O–Al_2O_2–SiO_2 glass–ceramic is detailed in the time-versus-temperature plot of Figure 12.21. After melting and forming operations, nucleation and growth of the crystalline phase particles are carried out isothermally at two different temperatures.

SUMMARY

Glasses
Glass–Ceramics

This chapter began by discussing the various types of ceramic materials. The familiar glass materials are noncrystalline silicates that contain other oxides; the most desirable trait of these materials is their optical transparency. Glass–ceramics are initially fabricated as a glass, then crystallized.

Clay Products

Clay is the principal component of the whitewares and structural clay products. Other ingredients may be added, such as feldspar and quartz, which influence the changes that occur during firing.

Refractories

The materials that are employed at elevated temperatures and often in reactive environments are the refractory ceramics; on occasion, their ability to thermally insulate is also utilized. On the basis of composition and application, the four main subdivisions are fireclay, silica, basic, and special.

Abrasives

The abrasive ceramics, being hard and tough, are utilized to cut, grind, and polish other softer materials. Diamond, silicon carbide, tungsten carbide, corundum, and silica sand are the most common examples. The abrasives may be employed in the form of loose grains, bonded to an abrasive wheel, or coated on paper or a fabric.

Cements

When mixed with water, inorganic cements form a paste that is capable of assuming just about any desired shape. Subsequent setting or hardening is a result of chemical reactions involving the cement particles and occurs at the ambient temperature. For hydraulic cements, of which portland cement is the most common, the chemical reaction is one of hydration.

Advanced Ceramics

Many of our modern technologies utilize and will continue to utilize advanced ceramics because of their unique mechanical, chemical, electrical, magnetic, and optical properties and property combinations. The following advanced ceramic materials were discussed briefly: piezoelectric ceramics, microelectromechanical systems (MEMS), and ceramic ball bearings.

Ceramic Phase Diagrams

Phase diagrams for the Al_2O_3–Cr_2O_3, MgO–Al_2O_3, ZrO_2–CaO, and SiO_2–Al_2O_3 systems were discussed. These diagrams are especially useful in assessing the high-temperature performance of ceramic materials.

Brittle Fracture of Ceramics
Stress–Strain Behavior

At room temperature, virtually all ceramics are brittle. Microcracks, the presence of which is very difficult to control, result in amplification of applied tensile stresses and account for relatively low fracture strengths (flexural strengths). This amplification does not occur with compressive loads, and, consequently, ceramics are stronger in compression. Fractographic analysis of the fracture surface of a ceramic material may reveal the location and source of the crack-producing flaw, as well as the magnitude of the fracture stress. Representative strengths of ceramic materials are determined by performing transverse bending tests to fracture.

Mechanisms of Plastic Deformation

Any plastic deformation of crystalline ceramics is a result of dislocation motion; the brittleness of these materials is explained, in part, by the limited number of operable slip systems. The mode of plastic deformation for noncrystalline materials is by viscous flow; a material's resistance to deformation is expressed as viscosity. At room temperature, the viscosities of many noncrystalline ceramics are extremely high.

Miscellaneous Mechanical Considerations

Many ceramic bodies contain residual porosity, which is deleterious to both their moduli of elasticity and fracture strengths. In addition to their inherent brittleness, ceramic materials are distinctively hard. Also, since these materials are frequently utilized at elevated temperatures and under applied loads, creep characteristics are important.

Heat Treatment of Glasses and Glass–Ceramics

Since glasses are formed at elevated temperatures, the temperature–viscosity behavior is an important consideration. Melting, working, softening, annealing, and strain points represent temperatures that correspond to specific viscosity values. Knowledge of these points is important in the fabrication and processing of a glass of given composition. After fabrication, glasses may be annealed and/or tempered to improve mechanical characteristics.

REFERENCES

Barsoum, M. W., *Fundamentals of Ceramics,* McGraw-Hill, New York, 1997.

Bergeron, C. G. and S. H. Risbud, *Introduction to Phase Equilibria in Ceramics,* American Ceramic Society, Columbus, OH, 1984.

Bowen, H. K., "Advanced Ceramics," *Scientific American,* Vol. 255, No. 4, October 1986, pp. 168–176.

Chiang, Y. M., D. P. Birnie, III, and W. D. Kingery, *Physical Ceramics: Principles for Ceramic Science and Engineering,* Wiley, New York, 1997.

Davidge, R. W., *Mechanical Behaviour of Ceramics,* Cambridge University Press, Cambridge, 1979. Reprinted by TechBooks, Marietta, OH, 1988.

Doremus, R. H., *Glass Science,* 2nd edition, Wiley, New York, 1994.

Engineered Materials Handbook, Vol. 4, *Ceramics and Glasses,* ASM International, Materials Park, OH, 1991.

Green, D. J., *An Introduction to the Mechanical Properties of Ceramics,* Cambridge University Press, Cambridge, 1998.

Hewlett, P. C., *Lea's Chemistry of Cement & Concrete,* 4th edition, Butterworth-Heinemann, Woburn, UK, 2004.

Kingery, W. D., H. K. Bowen, and D. R. Uhlmann, *Introduction to Ceramics,* 2nd edition, Wiley, New York, 1976. Chapters 1–4, 10, 11, 14, 15, and 16.

Norton, F. H., *Elements of Ceramics,* Addison-Wesley, 1974. Reprinted by TechBooks, Marietta, OH, 1991. Chapters 2 and 23.

Norton, F. H., *Refractories,* 4th edition. Reprinted by TechBooks, Marietta, OH, 1985.

Phase Equilibria Diagrams (for Ceramists), American Ceramic Society, Westerville, OH. In fourteen volumes, published between 1964 and 2005. Also on CD-ROM.

Reed, J. S., *Principles of Ceramic Processing,* 2nd edition, Wiley, New York, 1995.

Richerson, D. W., *The Magic of Ceramics,* American Ceramic Society, Westerville, OH, 2000.

Richerson, D. W., *Modern Ceramic Engineering,* 2nd edition, Marcel Dekker, New York, 1992.

Tooley, F. V. (Editor), *Handbook of Glass Manufacture,* Ashlee, New York, 1985. In two volumes.

Wachtman, J. B., *Mechanical Properties of Ceramics,* Wiley, New York, 1996.

QUESTIONS AND PROBLEMS

Glasses
Glass–Ceramics

12.1 Cite the two desirable characteristics of glasses.

12.2 (a) What is crystallization?

(b) Cite two properties that may be improved by crystallization.

Refractories

12.3 For refractory ceramic materials, cite three characteristics that improve with and two characteristics that are adversely affected by increasing porosity.

12.4 Find the maximum temperature to which the following two magnesia–alumina refractory materials may be heated before a liquid phase will appear.

(a) A spinel-bonded magnesia material of composition 88.5 wt% MgO–11.5 wt% Al_2O_3.

(b) A magnesia–alumina spinel of composition 25 wt% MgO–75 wt% Al_2O_3. Consult Figure 12.6.

12.5 Upon consideration of the SiO_2–Al_2O_3 phase diagram, Figure 12.8, for each pair of the following list of compositions, which would you judge to be the more desirable refractory? Justify your choices.

(a) 99.8 wt% SiO_2–0.2 wt% Al_2O_3 and 99.0 wt% SiO_2–1.0 wt% Al_2O_3

(b) 70 wt% Al_2O_3–30 wt% SiO_2 and 74 wt% Al_2O_3–26 wt% SiO_2

(c) 90 wt% Al_2O_3–10 wt% SiO_2 and 95 wt% Al_2O_3–5 wt% SiO_2

12.6 Compute the mass fractions of liquid in the following fireclay refractory materials at 1600°C (2910°F):

(a) 25 wt% Al_2O_3–75 wt% SiO_2

(b) 45 wt% Al_2O_3–55 wt% SiO_2

12.7 For the MgO–Al_2O_3 system, what is the maximum temperature that is possible without the formation of a liquid phase? At what composition or over what range of compositions will this maximum temperature be achieved?

Cements

12.8 Compare the manner in which the aggregate particles become bonded together in clay-based mixtures during firing and in cements during setting.

Ceramic Phase Diagrams

12.9 For the ZrO_2–CaO system (Figure 12.7), write all eutectic and eutectoid reactions for cooling.

12.10 From Figure 12.6, the phase diagram for the MgO–Al_2O_3 system, it may be noted that the spinel solid solution exists over a range of compositions, which means that it is nonstoichiometric at compositions other than 50 mol% MgO–50 mol% Al_2O_3.

(a) The maximum nonstoichiometry on the Al_2O_3-rich side of the spinel phase field exists at about 2000°C (3630°F) corresponding to approximately 82 mol% (92 wt%) Al_2O_3. Determine the type of vacancy defect that is produced and the percentage of vacancies that exist at this composition.

(b) The maximum nonstoichiometry on the MgO-rich side of the spinel phase field exists at about 2000°C (3630°F) corresponding to approximately 39 mol% (62 wt%) Al_2O_3. Determine the type of vacancy defect that is produced and the percentage of vacancies that exist at this composition.

12.11 When kaolinite clay $[Al_2(Si_2O_5)(OH)_4]$ is heated to a sufficiently high temperature, chemical water is driven off.

(a) Under these circumstances, what is the composition of the remaining product (in weight percent Al_2O_3)?

(b) What are the liquidus and solidus temperatures of this material?

Brittle Fracture of Ceramics

12.12 Briefly explain **(a)** why there may be significant scatter in the fracture strength for some given ceramic material, and **(b)** why fracture strength increases with decreasing specimen size.

12.13 The tensile strength of brittle materials may be determined using a variation of Equation 11.1. Compute the critical crack tip radius for a glass specimen that experiences tensile fracture at an applied stress of 70 MPa. Assume a critical surface crack length of 10^{-2} mm and a theoretical fracture strength of $E/10$, where E is the modulus of elasticity.

12.14 The fracture strength of glass may be increased by etching away a thin surface layer. It is believed that the etching may alter surface crack geometry (i.e., reduce crack length and increase the tip radius). Compute the ratio of the etched and original crack-tip radii for a fourfold increase in fracture strength if half of the crack length is removed.

Stress–Strain Behavior

12.15 A three-point bending test is performed on a spinel ($MgAl_2O_4$) specimen having a rectangular cross section of height d 3.8 mm and width b 9 mm; the distance between support points is 25 mm.

(a) Compute the flexural strength if the load at fracture is 350 N.

(b) The point of maximum deflection Δy occurs at the center of the specimen and is described by

$$\Delta y = \frac{FL^3}{48\,EI}$$

where E is the modulus of elasticity and I is the cross-sectional moment of inertia. Compute Δy at a load of 310 N.

12.16 A circular specimen of MgO is loaded using a three-point bending mode. Compute the minimum possible radius of the specimen without fracture, given that the applied load is 5560 N, the flexural strength is 105 MPa, and the separation between load points is 45 mm.

12.17 A three-point bending test was performed on an aluminum oxide specimen having a circular cross section of radius 5.0 mm; the specimen fractured at a load of 3000 N when the distance between the support points was 40 mm. Another test is to be performed on a specimen of this same material, but one that has a square cross section of 15 mm length on each edge. At what load would you expect this specimen to fracture if the support point separation is maintained at 40 mm?

12.18 (a) A three-point transverse bending test is conducted on a cylindrical specimen of aluminum oxide having a reported flexural strength of 300 MPa. If the specimen radius is 5.0 mm and the support point separation distance is 15.0 mm, predict whether or not you would expect the specimen to fracture when a load of 7500 N is applied? Justify your prediction.

(b) Would you be 100% certain of the prediction in part (a)? Why or why not?

Mechanisms of Plastic Deformation

12.19 Cite one reason why ceramic materials are, in general, harder yet more brittle than metals.

Miscellaneous Mechanical Considerations

12.20 The modulus of elasticity for spinel ($MgAl_2O_4$) having 5 vol% porosity is 240 GPa.

(a) Compute the modulus of elasticity for the nonporous material.

(b) Compute the modulus of elasticity for 15 vol% porosity.

12.21 The modulus of elasticity for titanium carbide (TiC) having 5 vol% porosity is 310 GPa.

(a) Compute the modulus of elasticity for the nonporous material.

(b) At what volume percent porosity will the modulus of elasticity be 240 GPa?

12.22 Using the data in Table 12.3, do the following:

(a) Determine the flexural strength for nonporous MgO assuming a value of 3.75 for n in Equation 12.6.

(b) Compute the volume fraction porosity at which the flexural strength for MgO is 74 MPa.

12.23 The flexural strength and associated volume fraction porosity for two specimens of the same ceramic material are as follows:

σ_{fs} *(MPa)*	P
70	0.10
60	0.15

(a) Compute the flexural strength for a completely nonporous specimen of this material.

(b) Compute the flexural strength for a 0.20 volume fraction porosity.

Heat Treatment of Glasses and Glass–Ceramics

12.24 Soda and lime are added to a glass batch in the form of soda ash (Na_2CO_3) and limestone ($CaCO_3$). During heating, these two ingredients decompose to give off carbon dioxide (CO_2), the resulting products being soda and lime. Compute the weight of soda ash and limestone that must be added to 125 kg of quartz (SiO_2) to yield a glass of composition 78 wt% SiO_2, 17 wt% Na_2O, and 5 wt% CaO.

12.25 What is the distinction between glass transition temperature and melting temperature?

12.26 Compare the temperatures at which soda–lime, borosilicate, 96% silica, and fused silica may be annealed.

12.27 Compare the softening points for 96% silica, borosilicate, and soda–lime glasses.

12.28 The viscosity η of a glass varies with temperature according to the relationship

$$\eta = A \exp\left(\frac{Q_{vis}}{RT}\right)$$

where Q_{vis} is the energy of activation for viscous flow, A is a temperature-independent constant, and R and T are, respectively, the gas constant and the absolute temperature. A plot of ln η versus $1/T$ should be nearly linear, and with a slope of Q_{vis}/R. Using the data in Figure 12.19, **(a)** make such a plot for the soda-lime glass, and **(b)** determine the activation energy between temperatures of 900 and 1600°C.

12.29 For many viscous materials, the viscosity η may be defined in terms of the expression

$$\eta = \frac{\sigma}{d\epsilon/dt}$$

where σ and $d\epsilon/dt$ are, respectively, the tensile stress and the strain rate. A cylindrical specimen of a borosilicate glass of diameter 4 mm and length 125 mm is subjected to a tensile force of 2 N along its axis. If its deformation is to be less than 2.5 mm over a week's time, using Figure 12.19, determine the maximum temperature to which the specimen may be heated.

12.30 **(a)** Explain why residual thermal stresses are introduced into a glass piece when it is cooled.

(b) Are thermal stresses introduced upon heating? Why or why not?

12.31 Borosilicate glasses and fused silica are resistant to thermal shock. Why is this so?

12.32 In your own words, briefly describe what happens as a glass piece is thermally tempered.

12.33 Glass pieces may also be strengthened by chemical tempering. With this procedure, the glass surface is put in a state of compression by exchanging some of the cations near the surface with other cations having a larger diameter. Suggest one type of cation that, by replacing Na^+, will induce chemical tempering in a soda–lime glass.

DESIGN PROBLEMS

12.D1 Some of our modern kitchen cookware is made of ceramic materials.

(a) List at least three important characteristics required of a material to be used for this application.

(b) Make a comparison of three ceramic materials as to their relative properties and, in addition, to cost.

(c) On the basis of this comparison, select the material most suitable for the cookware.

Stress–Strain Behavior

12.D2 It is necessary to select a ceramic material to be stressed using a three-point loading scheme (Figure 12.13). The specimen must have a circular cross section, a radius of 3.8 mm, and must not experience fracture or a deflection of more than 0.021 mm at its center when a load of 445 N is applied. If the distance between support points is 50.8 mm, which of the materials in Table 12.5 are candidates? The magnitude of the centerpoint deflection may be computed using the equation supplied in Problem 12.15.

Chapter 13 Structures of Polymers

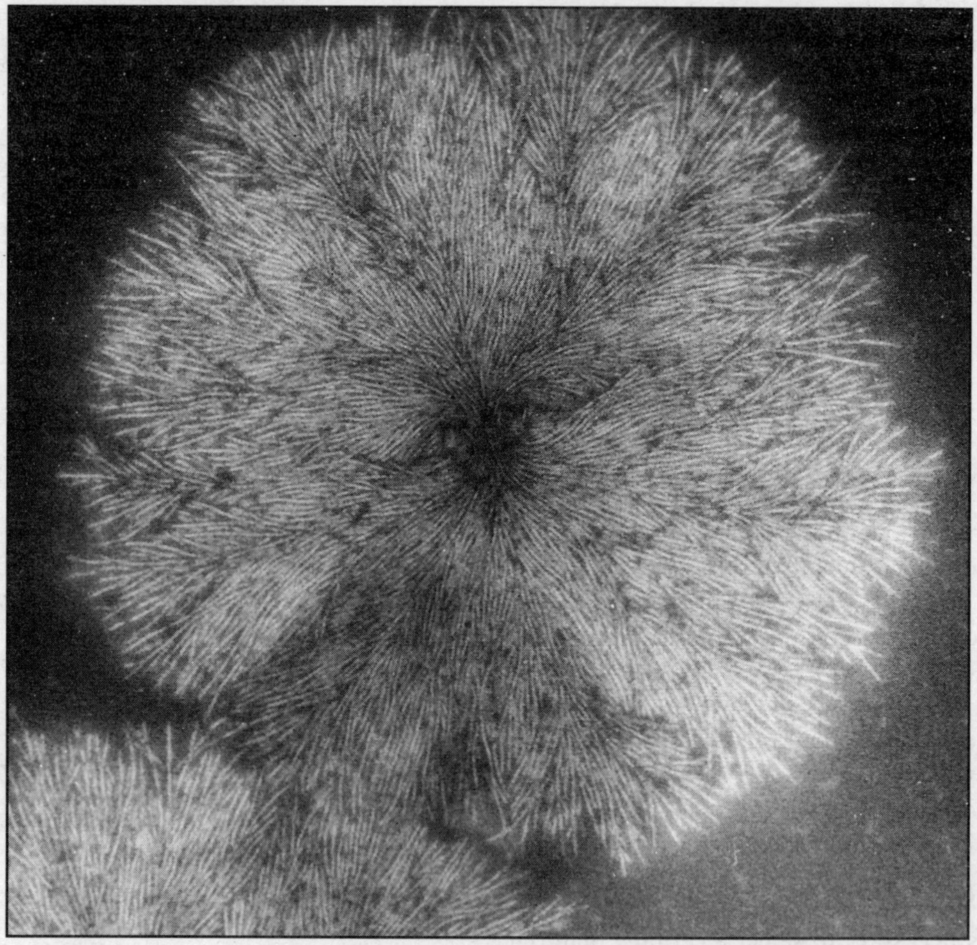

Transmission electron micrograph showing the spherulite structure in a natural rubber specimen. Chain-folded lamellar crystallites approximately 10 nm thick extend in radial directions from the center; they appear as white lines in the micrograph. 30,000×. (Photograph supplied by P. J. Phillips. First published in R. Bartnikas and R. M. Eichhorn, *Engineering Dielectrics,* Vol. IIA, *Electrical Properties of Solid Insulating Materials: Molecular Structure and Electrical Behavior,* 1983. Copyright ASTM, 1916 Race Street, Philadelphia, PA 19103. Reprinted with permission.)

Learning Objectives

After careful study of this chapter you should be able to do the following:

1. Describe a typical polymer molecule in terms of its chain structure and, in addition, how the molecule may be generated from repeat units.
2. Draw repeat units for polyethylene, poly(vinyl chloride), polytetrafluoroethylene, polypropylene, and polystyrene.
3. Calculate number-average and weight-average molecular weights, and degree of polymerization for a specified polymer.
4. Name and briefly describe:
   (a) the four general types of polymer molecular structures,
   (b) the three types of stereoisomers,
   (c) the two kinds of geometrical isomers,
   (d) the four types of copolymers.
5. Cite the differences in behavior and molecular structure for thermoplastic and thermosetting polymers.

13.1 INTRODUCTION

Naturally occurring polymers—those derived from plants and animals—have been used for many centuries; these materials include wood, rubber, cotton, wool, leather, and silk. Other natural polymers such as proteins, enzymes, starches, and cellulose are important in biological and physiological processes in plants and animals. Modern scientific research tools have made possible the determination of the molecular structures of this group of materials, and the development of numerous polymers, which are synthesized from small organic molecules. Many of our useful plastics, rubbers, and fiber materials are synthetic polymers. In fact, since the conclusion of World War II, the field of materials has been virtually revolutionized by the advent of synthetic polymers. The synthetics can be produced inexpensively, and their properties may be managed to the degree that many are superior to their natural counterparts. In some applications metal and wood parts have been replaced by plastics, which have satisfactory properties and may be produced at a lower cost.

As with metals and ceramics, the properties of polymers are intricately related to the structural elements of the material. This chapter explores molecular and crystal structures of polymers; Chapter 14 discusses the relationships between structure and some of the physical and chemical properties, along with typical applications and forming methods.

13.2 HYDROCARBON MOLECULES

Since most polymers are organic in origin, we briefly review some of the basic concepts relating to the structure of their molecules. First, many organic materials are *hydrocarbons;* that is, they are composed of hydrogen and carbon. Furthermore, the intramolecular bonds are covalent. Each carbon atom has four electrons that may participate in covalent bonding, whereas every hydrogen atom has only one bonding electron. A single covalent bond exists when each of the two bonding atoms contributes one electron, as represented schematically in Figure 2.10 for a molecule of methane (CH_4). Double and triple bonds between two carbon atoms involve the sharing of two and three pairs of electrons, respectively. For example, in ethylene, which has the chemical formula C_2H_4, the two carbon atoms are doubly bonded together, and each is also singly bonded to two hydrogen atoms, as represented by the structural formula

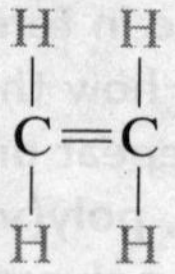

where — and = denote single and double covalent bonds, respectively. An example of a triple bond is found in acetylene, C_2H_2:

$$H-C\equiv C-H$$

Molecules that have double and triple covalent bonds are termed **unsaturated.** That is, each carbon atom is not bonded to the maximum (four) other atoms; as such, it is possible for another atom or group of atoms to become attached to the original molecule. Furthermore, for a **saturated** hydrocarbon, all bonds are single ones, and no new atoms may be joined without the removal of others that are already bonded.

Some of the simple hydrocarbons belong to the paraffin family; the chainlike paraffin molecules include methane (CH_4), ethane (C_2H_6), propane (C_3H_8), and butane (C_4H_{10}). Compositions and molecular structures for paraffin molecules are contained in Table 13.1. The covalent bonds in each molecule are strong, but only weak hydrogen and van der Waals bonds exist between molecules, and thus these hydrocarbons have relatively low melting and boiling points. However, boiling temperatures rise with increasing molecular weight (Table 13.1).

Hydrocarbon compounds with the same composition may have different atomic arrangements, a phenomenon termed **isomerism.** For example, there are two isomers for butane; normal butane has the structure

Table 13.1 Compositions and Molecular Structures for Some of the Paraffin Compounds: C_nH_{2n+2}

Name	*Composition*	*Structure*	*Boiling Point (°C)*
Methane	CH_4	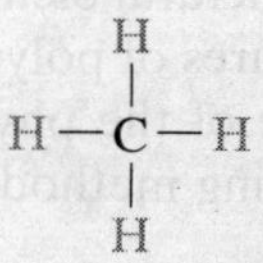	−164
Ethane	C_2H_6	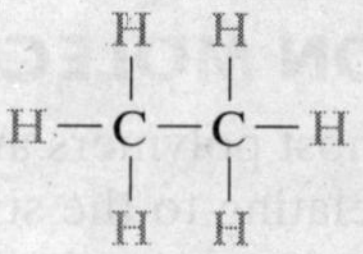	−88.6
Propane	C_3H_8	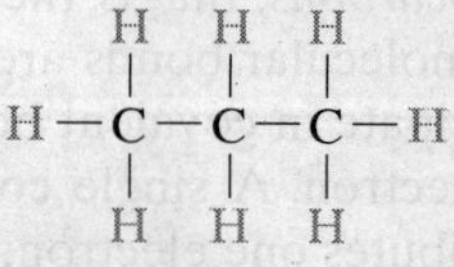	−42.1
Butane	C_4H_{10}		−0.5
Pentane	C_5H_{12}		36.1
Hexane	C_6H_{14}		69.0

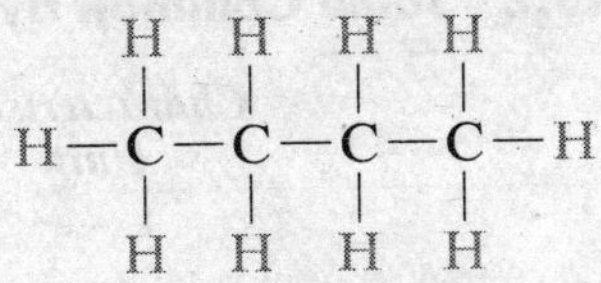

whereas a molecule of isobutane is represented as follows:

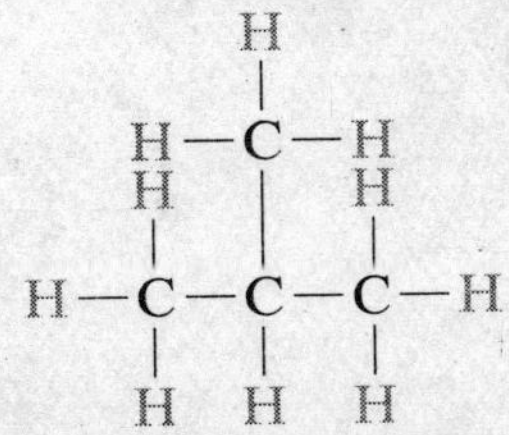

Some of the physical properties of hydrocarbons will depend on the isomeric state; for example, the boiling temperatures for normal butane and isobutane are −0.5 and −12.3°C (31.1 and 9.9°F), respectively.

There are numerous other organic groups, many of which are involved in polymer structures. Several of the more common groups are presented in Table 13.2, where R and R′ represent organic groups such as CH_3, C_2H_5, and C_6H_5 (methyl, ethyl, and phenyl).

Concept Check 13.1

Differentiate between polymorphism (see Chapter 4) and isomerism.

[*The answer may be found in enclosed CD.*]

13.3 POLYMER MOLECULES

The molecules in polymers are gigantic in comparison to the hydrocarbon molecules already discussed; because of their size they are often referred to as **macromolecules.** Within each molecule, the atoms are bound together by covalent interatomic bonds. For carbon chain polymers, the backbone of each chain is a string of carbon atoms. Many times each carbon atom singly bonds to two adjacent carbons atoms on either side, represented schematically in two dimensions as follows:

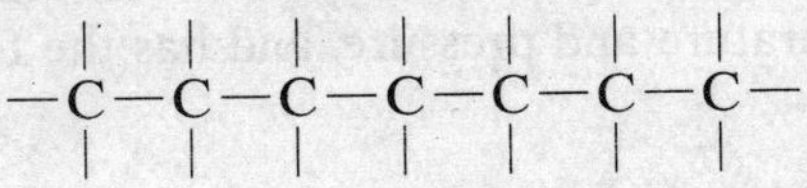

Each of the two remaining valence electrons for every carbon atom may be involved in side-bonding with atoms or radicals that are positioned adjacent to the chain. Of course, both chain and side double bonds are also possible.

These long molecules are composed of structural entities called **repeat units,** which are successively repeated along the chain.[1] The term **monomer** refers to the small molecule from which a polymer is synthesized. Hence, monomer and repeat unit mean different things, but sometimes the term monomer or monomer unit is used instead of the more proper term repeat unit.

---

[1] A repeat unit is also sometimes called a mer. "Mer" originates from the Greek word *meros,* which means part; the term **polymer** was coined to mean "many mers."

Table 13.2 Some Common Hydrocarbon Groups

Family	*Characteristic Unit*		*Representative Compound*
Alcohols	R—OH	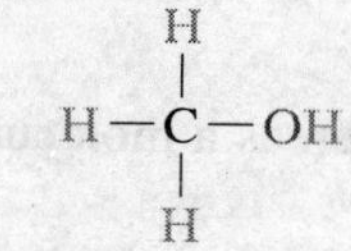	Methyl alcohol
Ethers	R—O—R′	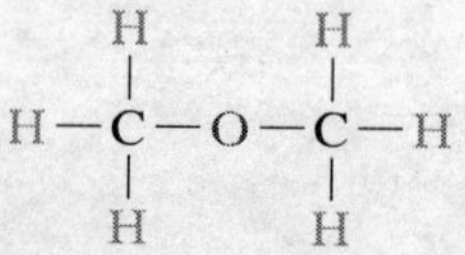	Dimethyl ether
Acids	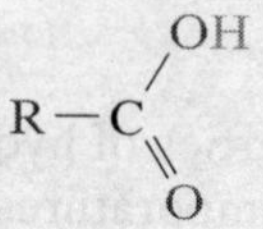	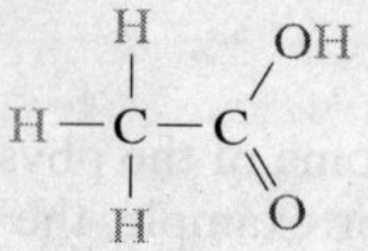	Acetic acid
Aldehydes	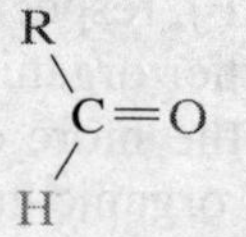	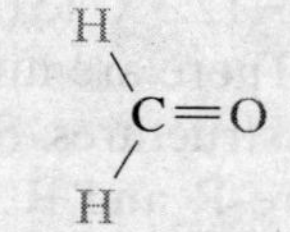	Formaldehyde
Aromatic hydrocarbons		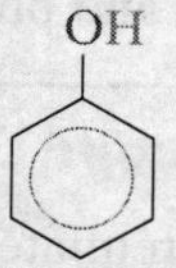	Phenol

[a] The simplified structure 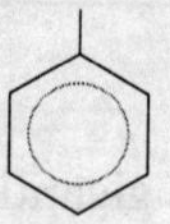 denotes a phenyl group, 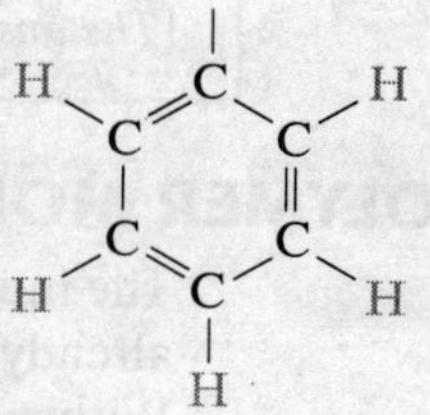

13.4 THE CHEMISTRY OF POLYMER MOLECULES

Consider again the hydrocarbon ethylene (C_2H_4), which is a gas at ambient temperature and pressure, and has the following molecular structure:

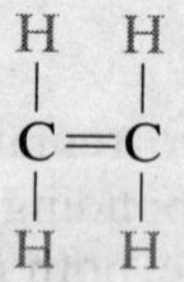

If the ethylene gas is reacted under appropriate conditions, it will transform to polyethylene (PE), which is a solid polymeric material. This process begins when an active center is formed by the reaction between an initiator or catalyst species (R·) and the ethylene monomer, as follows:

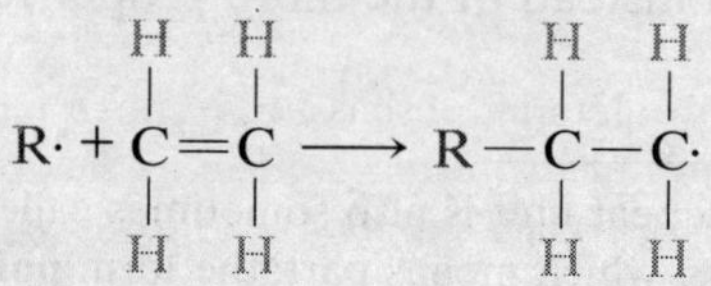

(13.1)

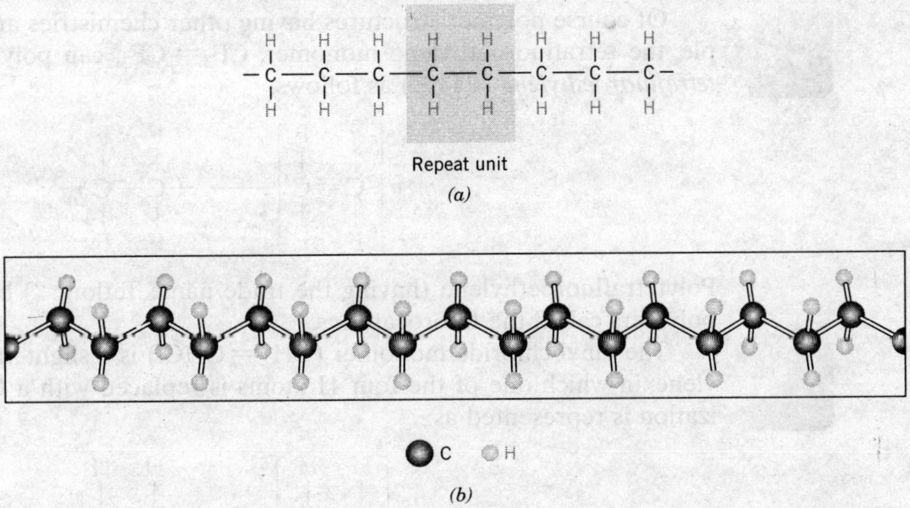

Figure 13.1 For polyethylene, (*a*) a schematic representation of repeat unit and chain structures, and (*b*) a perspective of the molecule, indicating the zigzag backbone structure.

The polymer chain then forms by the sequential addition of monomer units to this active growing chain molecule. The active site, or unpaired electron (denoted by ·), is transferred to each successive end monomer as it is linked to the chain. This may be represented schematically as follows:

$$\mathrm{R{-}\overset{\displaystyle H}{\underset{\displaystyle H}{\overset{|}{\underset{|}{C}}}}{-}\overset{\displaystyle H}{\underset{\displaystyle H}{\overset{|}{\underset{|}{C}}}}\cdot + \overset{\displaystyle H}{\underset{\displaystyle H}{\overset{|}{\underset{|}{C}}}}{=}\overset{\displaystyle H}{\underset{\displaystyle H}{\overset{|}{\underset{|}{C}}}} \longrightarrow R{-}\overset{\displaystyle H}{\underset{\displaystyle H}{\overset{|}{\underset{|}{C}}}}{-}\overset{\displaystyle H}{\underset{\displaystyle H}{\overset{|}{\underset{|}{C}}}}{-}\overset{\displaystyle H}{\underset{\displaystyle H}{\overset{|}{\underset{|}{C}}}}{-}\overset{\displaystyle H}{\underset{\displaystyle H}{\overset{|}{\underset{|}{C}}}}\cdot} \tag{13.2}$$

The final result, after the addition of many ethylene monomer units, is the polyethylene molecule;[2] a portion of one such molecule and the polyethylene repeat unit are shown in Figure 13.1*a*. This polyethylene chain structure can also be represented as

$$\mathrm{-\!\!\left(\overset{\displaystyle H}{\underset{\displaystyle H}{\overset{|}{\underset{|}{C}}}}{-}\overset{\displaystyle H}{\underset{\displaystyle H}{\overset{|}{\underset{|}{C}}}}\right)\!\!-_{n}}$$

or alternatively as

$$-\!\!\left(CH_2 - CH_2\right)\!\!-_{n}$$

Here the repeat units are enclosed in parentheses, and the subscript n indicates the number of times it repeats.[3]

The representation in Figure 13.1*a* is not strictly correct in that the angle between the singly bonded carbon atoms is not 180° as shown, but rather close to 109°. A more accurate three-dimensional model is one in which the carbon atoms form a zigzag pattern (Figure 13.1*b*), the C—C bond length being 0.154 nm. In this discussion, depiction of polymer molecules is frequently simplified using the linear chain model shown in Figure 13.1*a*.

---

[2] A more detailed discussion of polymerization reactions including both addition and condensation mechanisms is given in Section 14.20.

[3] Chain ends/end-groups (i.e., the Rs in Equation 13.2) are not normally represented in chain structures.

Of course polymer structures having other chemistries are possible. For example, the tetrafluoroethylene monomer, $CF_2{=}CF_2$, can polymerize to form *polytetrafluoroethylene* (PTFE) as follows:

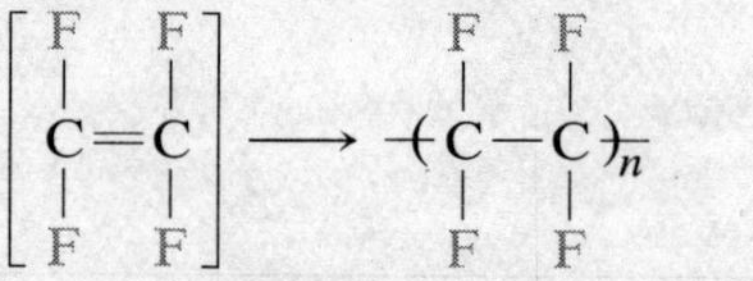

(13.3)

Polytetrafluoroethylene (having the trade name Teflon™) belongs to a family of polymers called the fluorocarbons.

The vinyl chloride monomer ($CH_2{=}CHCl$) is a slight variant of that for ethylene, in which one of the four H atoms is replaced with a Cl atom. Its polymerization is represented as

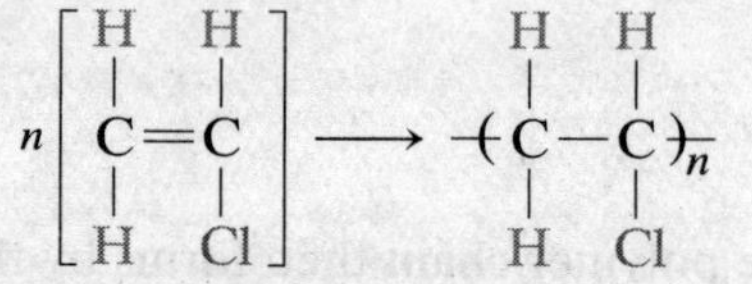

(13.4)

and leads to *poly(vinyl chloride)* (PVC), another common polymer.

Some polymers may be represented using the following generalized form:

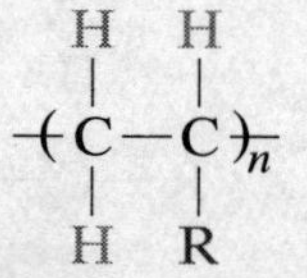

where the "R" depicts either an atom [i.e., H or Cl, for polyethylene or poly(vinyl chloride), respectively], or an organic group such as CH_3, C_2H_5, and C_6H_5 (methyl, ethyl, and phenyl). For example, when R represents a CH_3 group, the polymer is *polypropylene* (PP). Poly(vinyl chloride) and polypropylene chain structures are also represented in Figure 13.2. Table 13.3 lists repeat units for some of the more common polymers; as may be noted, some of them—for example, nylon, polyester, and polycarbonate—are relatively complex. Repeat units for a large number of relatively common polymers are given in Appendix D.

When all the repeating units along a chain are of the same type, the resulting polymer is called a **homopolymer.** Chains may be composed of two or more different repeat units, in what are termed **copolymers** (see Section 13.10).

The monomers discussed thus far have an active bond that may react to form two covalent bonds with other monomers forming a two-dimensional chain-like molecular structure, as indicated above for ethylene. Such a monomer is termed **bifunctional.** In general, the **functionality** is the number of bonds that a given monomer can form. For example, monomers such as phenol–formaldehyde (Table 13.3), are **trifunctional;** they have three active bonds, from which a three-dimensional molecular network structure results.

Concept Check 13.2

On the basis of the structures presented in the previous section, sketch the repeat unit structure for poly(vinyl fluoride).

[The answer may be found in enclosed CD.]

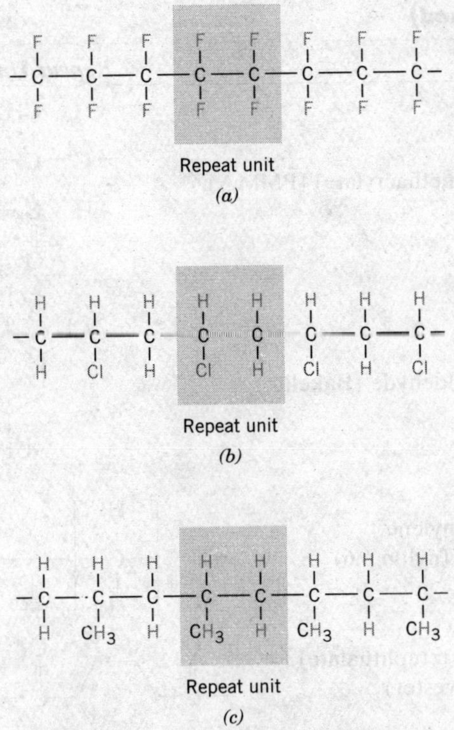

Figure 13.2 Repeat unit and chain structures for (*a*) polytetrafluoroethylene, (*b*) poly(vinyl chloride), and (*c*) polypropylene.

Table 13.3 A Listing of Repeat Units for 10 of the More Common Polymeric Materials

Polymer	*Repeat Unit*
Polyethylene (PE)	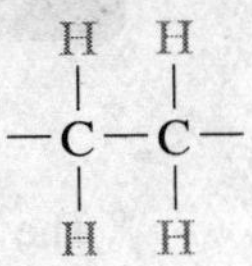
Poly(vinyl chloride) (PVC)	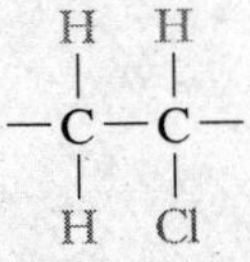
Polytetrafluoroethylene (PTFE)	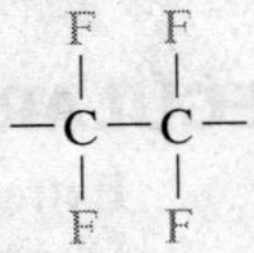
Polypropylene (PP)	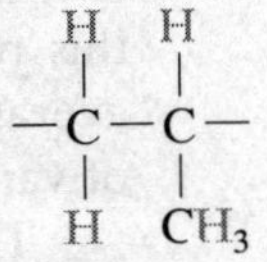
Polystyrene (PS)	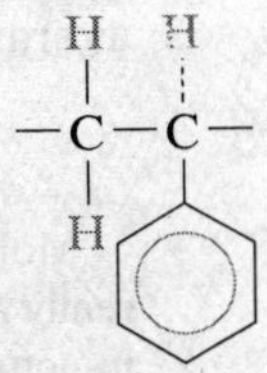

(*Continued*)

Table 13.3 (Continued)

Polymer		*Repeat Unit*
	Poly(methyl methacrylate) (PMMA)	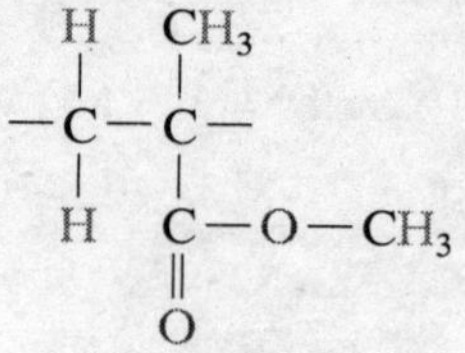
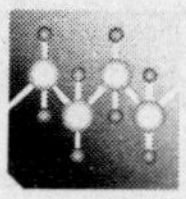	Phenol-formaldehyde (Bakelite)	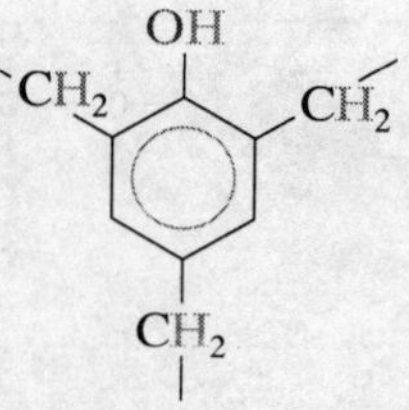
	Poly(hexamethylene adipamide) (nylon 6,6)	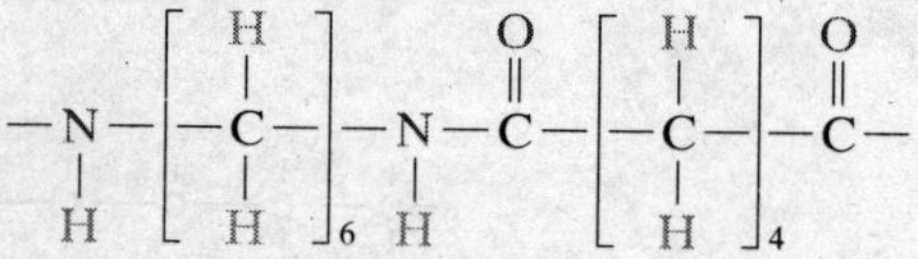
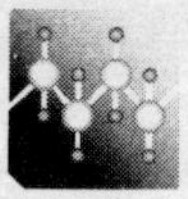	Poly(ethylene terephthalate) (PET, a polyester)	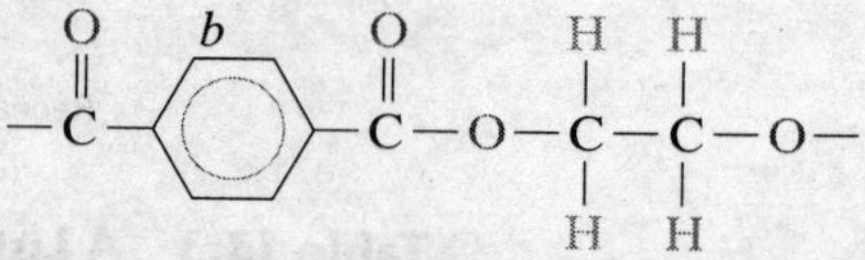
	Polycarbonate (PC)	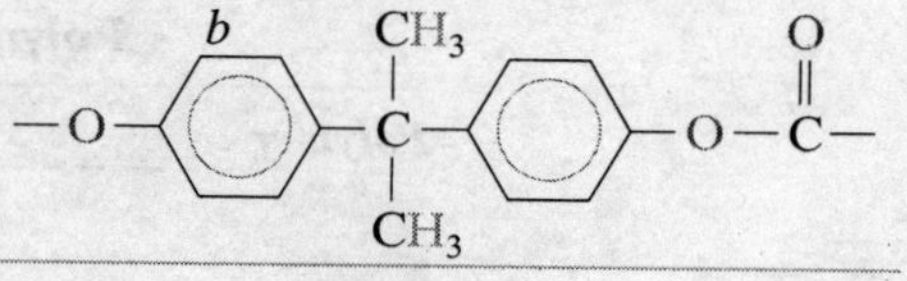

[b] The 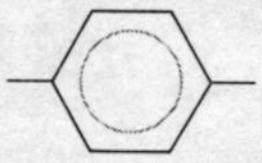 symbol in the backbone chain denotes an aromatic ring as 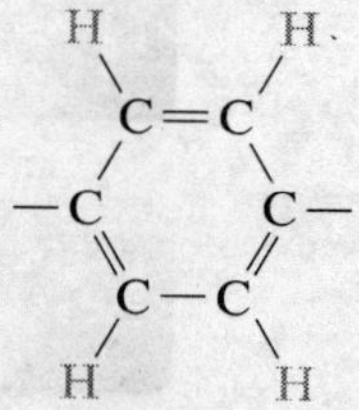

13.5 MOLECULAR WEIGHT

Extremely large molecular weights[4] are observed in polymers with very long chains. During the polymerization process not all polymer chains will grow to the same length; this results in a distribution of chain lengths or molecular weights. Ordinarily, an average molecular weight is specified, which may be determined by the measurement of various physical properties such as viscosity and osmotic pressure.

There are several ways of defining average molecular weight. The number-average molecular weight $\overline{M}_n$ is obtained by dividing the chains into a series of size

[4] "Molecular mass," "molar mass," and "relative molecular mass" are sometimes used and are really more appropriate terms than "molecular weight" in the context of the present discussion—in actual fact, we are dealing with masses and not weights. However, molecular weight is most commonly found in the polymer literature, and thus will be used throughout this book.

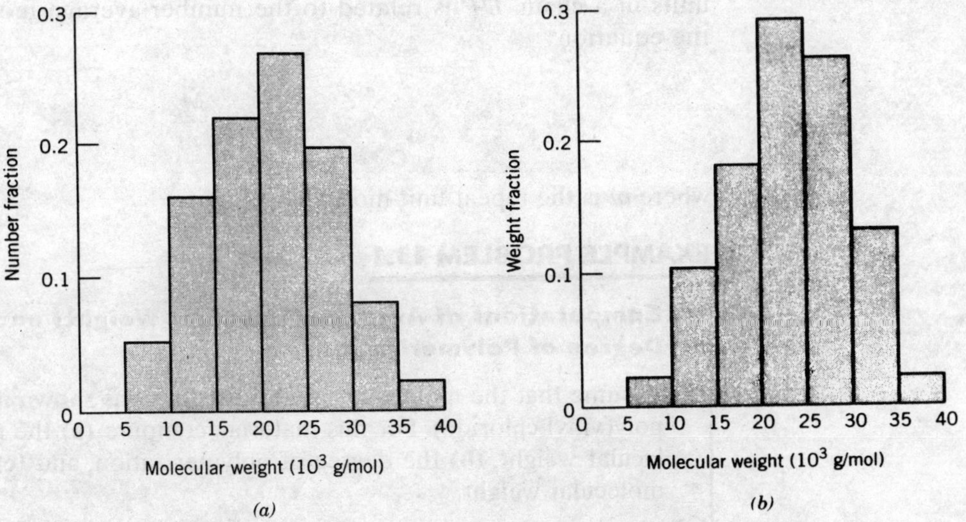

Figure 13.3 Hypothetical polymer molecule size distributions on the basis of (*a*) number and (*b*) weight fractions of molecules.

ranges and then determining the number fraction of chains within each size range (Figure 13.3*a*). The number-average molecular weight is expressed as

$$\overline{M}_n = \Sigma x_i M_i \tag{13.5a}$$

where M_i represents the mean (middle) molecular weight of size range i, and x_i is the fraction of the total number of chains within the corresponding size range.

A weight-average molecular weight $\overline{M}_w$ is based on the weight fraction of molecules within the various size ranges (Figure 13.3*b*). It is calculated according to

$$\overline{M}_w = \Sigma w_i M_i \tag{13.5b}$$

where, again, M_i is the mean molecular weight within a size range, whereas w_i denotes the weight fraction of molecules within the same size interval. Computations for both number-average and weight-average molecular weights are carried out in Example Problem 13.1. A typical molecular weight distribution along with these molecular weight averages is shown in Figure 13.4.

An alternate way of expressing average chain size of a polymer is as the **degree of polymerization,** DP, which represents the average number of repeat

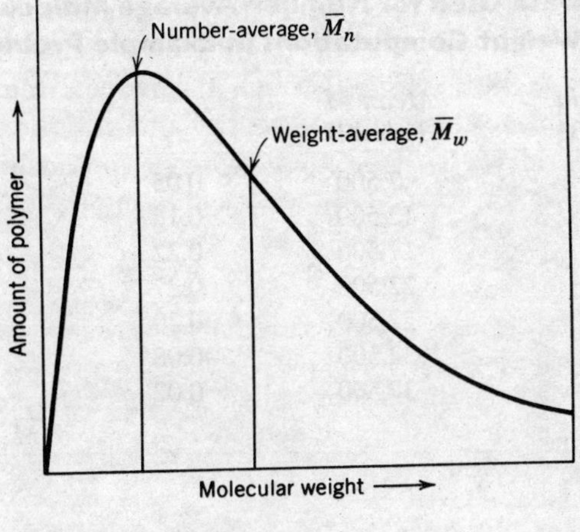

Figure 13.4 Distribution of molecular weights for a typical polymer.

units in a chain. DP is related to the number-average molecular weight $\overline{M}_n$ by the equation

$$DP = \frac{\overline{M}_n}{m} \tag{13.6}$$

where m is the repeat unit molecular weight.

EXAMPLE PROBLEM 13.1

Computations of Average Molecular Weights and Degree of Polymerization

Assume that the molecular weight distributions shown in Figure 13.3 are for poly(vinyl chloride). For this material, compute **(a)** the number-average molecular weight, **(b)** the degree of polymerization, and **(c)** the weight-average molecular weight.

Solution

(a) The data necessary for this computation, as taken from Figure 13.3*a*, are presented in Table 13.4a. According to Equation 13.5a, summation of all the x_iM_i products (from the right-hand column) yields the number-average molecular weight, which in this case is 21,150 g/mol.

(b) To determine the degree of polymerization (Equation 13.6), it is first necessary to compute the repeat unit molecular weight. For PVC, each repeat unit consists of two carbon atoms, three hydrogen atoms, and a single chlorine atom (Table 13.3). Furthermore, the atomic weights of C, H, and Cl are, respectively, 12.01, 1.01, and 35.45 g/mol. Thus, for PVC

$$\begin{aligned} m &= 2(12.01 \text{ g/mol}) + 3(1.01 \text{ g/mol}) + 35.45 \text{ g/mol} \\ &= 62.50 \text{ g/mol} \end{aligned}$$

and

$$DP = \frac{\overline{M}_n}{m} = \frac{21{,}150 \text{ g/mol}}{62.50 \text{ g/mol}} = 338$$

(c) Table 13.4b shows the data for the weight-average molecular weight, as taken from Figure 13.3*b*. The w_iM_i products for the size intervals are tabulated in the right-hand column. The sum of these products (Equation 13.5b) yields a value of 23,200 g/mol for $\overline{M}_w$.

Table 13.4a Data Used for Number-Average Molecular Weight Computations in Example Problem 13.1

Molecular Weight Range (g/mol)	*Mean M_i (g/mol)*	x_i	x_iM_i
5,000–10,000	7,500	0.05	375
10,000–15,000	12,500	0.16	2000
15,000–20,000	17,500	0.22	3850
20,000–25,000	22,500	0.27	6075
25,000–30,000	27,500	0.20	5500
30,000–35,000	32,500	0.08	2600
35,000–40,000	37,500	0.02	750
			$\overline{M}_n$ = 21,150

Table 13.4b Data Used for Weight-Average Molecular Weight Computations in Example Problem 13.1

Molecular Weight Range (g/mol)	*Mean M_i (g/mol)*	w_i	w_iM_i
5,000–10,000	7,500	0.02	150
10,000–15,000	12,500	0.10	1250
15,000–20,000	17,500	0.18	3150
20,000–25,000	22,500	0.29	6525
25,000–30,000	27,500	0.26	7150
30,000–35,000	32,500	0.13	4225
35,000–40,000	37,500	0.02	750
			$\overline{M}_w$ = 23,200

Many polymer properties are affected by the length of the polymer chains. For example, the melting or softening temperature increases with increasing molecular weight (for $\overline{M}$ up to about 100,000 g/mol). At room temperature, polymers with very short chains (having molecular weights on the order of 100 g/mol) exist as liquids or gases. Those with molecular weights of approximately 1000 g/mol are waxy solids (such as paraffin wax) and soft resins. Solid polymers (sometimes termed *high polymers*), which are of prime interest here, commonly have molecular weights ranging between 10,000 and several million g/mol. Thus, the same polymer material can have quite different properties if it is produced with a different molecular weight. Other properties that depend on molecular weight include elastic modulus and strength (see Chapter 14).

13.6 MOLECULAR SHAPE

Previously, polymer molecules have been shown as linear chains, neglecting the zigzag arrangement of the backbone atoms (Figure 13.1*b*). Single chain bonds are capable of rotating and bending in three dimensions. Consider the chain atoms in Figure 13.5*a*; a third carbon atom may lie at any point on the cone of revolution and still subtend about a 109° angle with the bond between the other two atoms. A straight chain segment results when successive chain atoms are positioned as in Figure 13.5*b*. On the other hand, chain bending and twisting are possible when there is a rotation of the chain atoms into other positions, as illustrated in Figure 13.5*c*.[5] Thus, a single chain molecule composed of many chain atoms might assume a shape similar to that represented schematically in Figure 13.6, having a multitude of bends, twists, and kinks.[6] Also indicated in this figure is the end-to-end distance of the polymer chain *r*; this distance is much smaller than the total chain length.

Polymers consist of large numbers of molecular chains, each of which may bend, coil, and kink in the manner of Figure 13.6. This leads to extensive intertwining and entanglement of neighboring chain molecules, a situation similar to a heavily tangled fishing line. These random coils and molecular entanglements are responsible

[5] For some polymers, rotation of carbon backbone atoms within the cone may be hindered by bulky side group elements on neighboring chains.

[6] The term *conformation* is often used in reference to the physical outline of a molecule, or molecular shape, that can only be altered by rotation of chain atoms about single bonds.

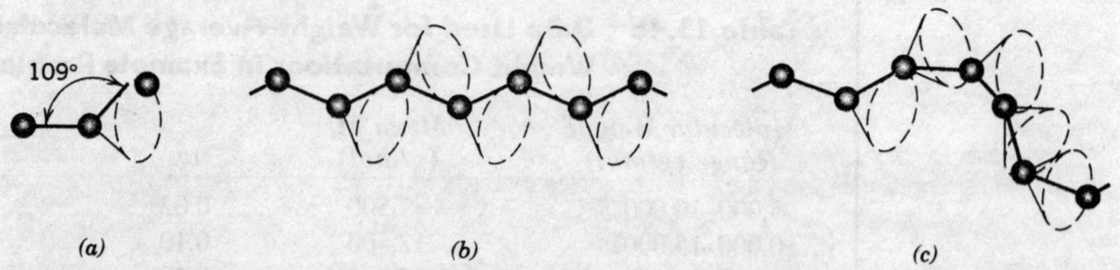

Figure 13.5 Schematic representations of how polymer chain shape is influenced by the positioning of backbone carbon atoms (gray circles). For (*a*), the rightmost atom may lie anywhere on the dashed circle and still subtend a 109° angle with the bond between the other two atoms. Straight and twisted chain segments are generated when the backbone atoms are situated as in (*b*) and (*c*), respectively. (From *Science and Engineering of Materials,* 3rd edition by Askeland. © 1994. Reprinted with permission of Nelson, a division of Thomson Learning: www.thomsonrights.com. Fax 800 730-2215.)

for a number of important characteristics of polymers, to include the large elastic extensions displayed by the rubber materials.

Some of the mechanical and thermal characteristics of polymers are a function of the ability of chain segments to experience rotation in response to applied stresses or thermal vibrations. Rotational flexibility is dependent on repeat unit structure and chemistry. For example, the region of a chain segment that has a double bond (C=C) is rotationally rigid. Also, introduction of a bulky or large side group of atoms restricts rotational movement. For example, polystyrene molecules, which have a phenyl side group (Table 13.3), are more resistant to rotational motion than are polyethylene chains.

13.7 MOLECULAR STRUCTURE

The physical characteristics of a polymer depend not only on its molecular weight and shape but also on differences in the structure of the molecular chains. Modern polymer synthesis techniques permit considerable control over various structural possibilities. This section discusses several molecular structures including linear, branched, crosslinked, and network, in addition to various isomeric configurations.

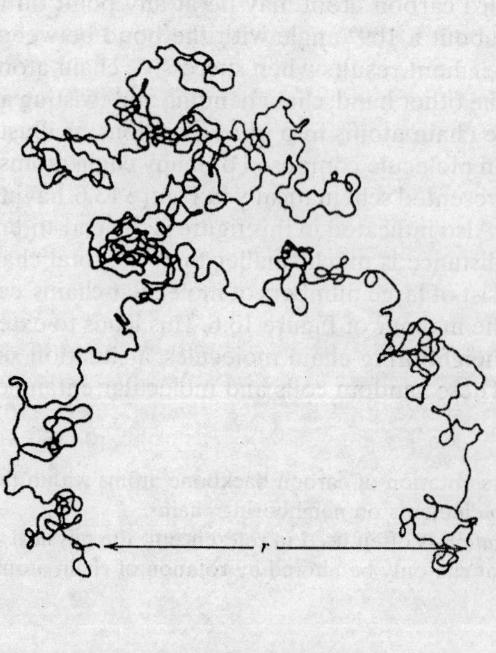

Figure 13.6 Schematic representation of a single polymer chain molecule that has numerous random kinks and coils produced by chain bond rotations. (From L. R. G. Treloar, *The Physics of Rubber Elasticity,* 2nd edition, Oxford University Press, Oxford, 1958, p. 47.)

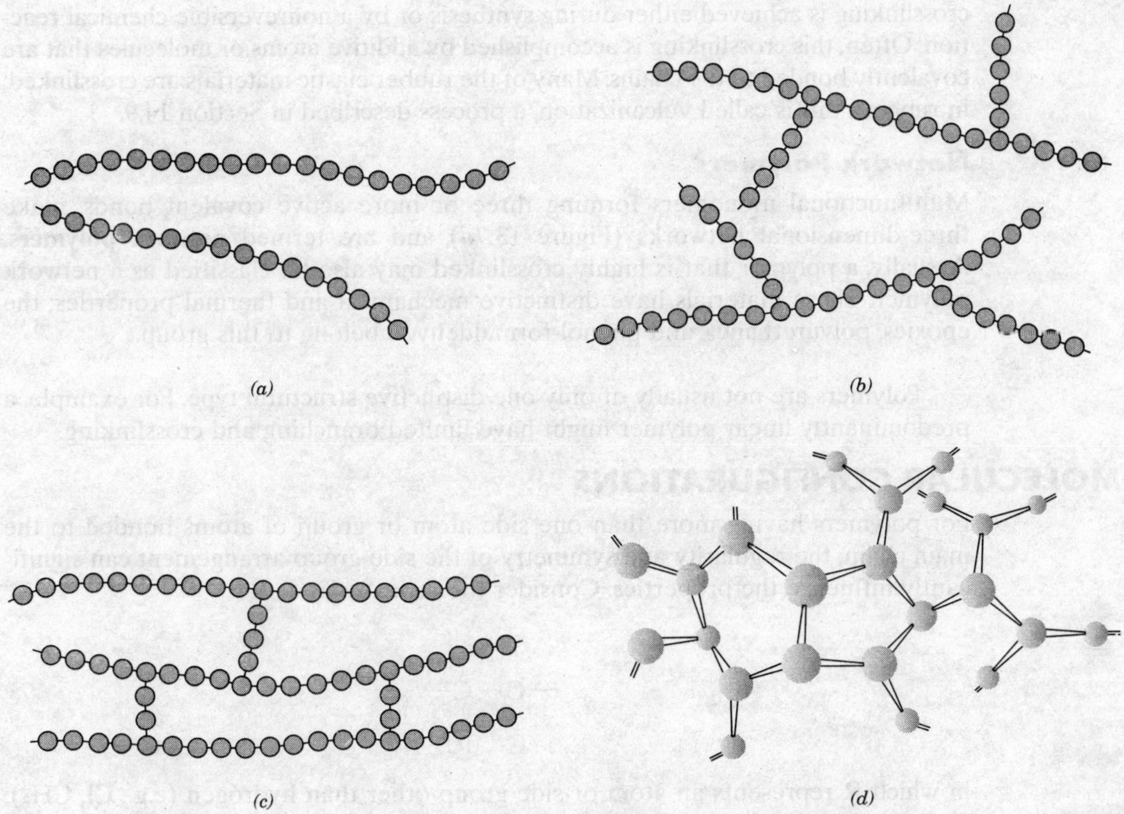

Figure 13.7 Schematic representations of (*a*) linear, (*b*) branched, (*c*) crosslinked, and (*d*) network (three-dimensional) molecular structures. Circles designate individual repeat units.

Linear Polymers

Linear polymers are those in which the repeat units are joined together end to end in single chains. These long chains are flexible and may be thought of as a mass of spaghetti, as represented schematically in Figure 13.7*a*, where each circle represents a repeat unit. For linear polymers, there may be extensive van der Waals and hydrogen bonding between the chains. Some of the common polymers that form with linear structures are polyethylene, poly(vinyl chloride), polystyrene, poly(methyl methacrylate), nylon, and the fluorocarbons.

Branched Polymers

Polymers may be synthesized in which side-branch chains are connected to the main ones, as indicated schematically in Figure 13.7*b*; these are fittingly called **branched polymers.** The branches, considered to be part of the main-chain molecule, may result from side reactions that occur during the synthesis of the polymer. The chain packing efficiency is reduced with the formation of side branches, which results in a lowering of the polymer density. Those polymers that form linear structures may also be branched. For example, high density polyethylene (HDPE) is primarily a linear polymer, while low density polyethylene (LDPE) contains short chain branches.

Crosslinked Polymers

In **crosslinked polymers,** adjacent linear chains are joined one to another at various positions by covalent bonds, as represented in Figure 13.7*c*. The process of crosslinking is achieved either during synthesis or by a nonreversible chemical reaction. Often, this crosslinking is accomplished by additive atoms or molecules that are covalently bonded to the chains. Many of the rubber elastic materials are crosslinked; in rubbers, this is called vulcanization, a process described in Section 14.9.

Network Polymers

Multifunctional monomers forming three or more active covalent bonds, make three-dimensional networks (Figure 13.7*d*) and are termed **network polymers.** Actually, a polymer that is highly crosslinked may also be classified as a network polymer. These materials have distinctive mechanical and thermal properties; the epoxies, polyurethanes, and phenol-formaldehyde belong to this group.

Polymers are not usually of only one distinctive structural type. For example, a predominantly linear polymer might have limited branching and crosslinking.

13.8 MOLECULAR CONFIGURATIONS

For polymers having more than one side atom or group of atoms bonded to the main chain, the regularity and symmetry of the side group arrangement can significantly influence the properties. Consider the repeat unit

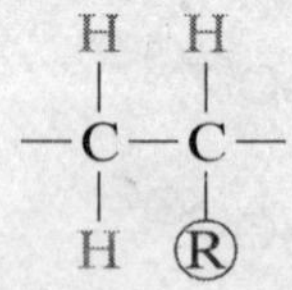

in which R represents an atom or side group other than hydrogen (e.g., Cl, CH_3). One arrangement is possible when the R side groups of successive repeat units are bound to alternate carbon atoms as follows:

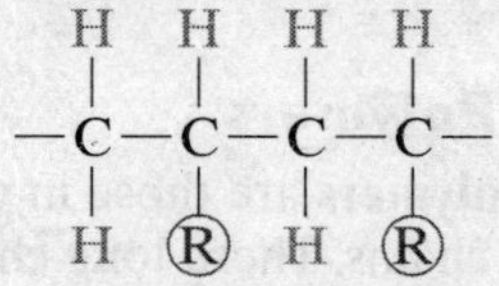

This is designated as a head-to-tail configuration.[7] Its complement, the head-to-head configuration, occurs when R groups are bound to adjacent chain atoms:

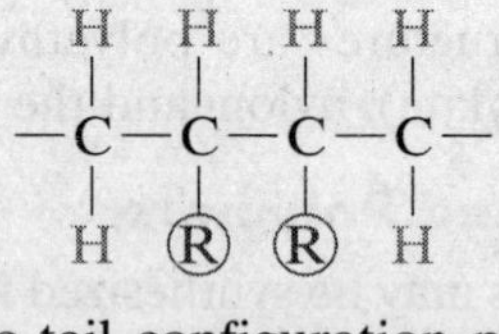

In most polymers, the head-to-tail configuration predominates; often a polar repulsion occurs between R groups for the head-to-head configuration.

Isomerism (Section 13.2) is also found in polymer molecules, wherein different atomic configurations are possible for the same composition. Two isomeric subclasses, stereoisomerism and geometrical isomerism, are topics of discussion in the succeeding sections.

---

[7] The term *configuration* is used in reference to arrangements of units along the axis of the chain, or atom positions that are not alterable except by the breaking and then reforming of primary bonds.

Stereoisomerism

Stereoisomerism denotes the situation in which atoms are linked together in the same order (head-to-tail) but differ in their spatial arrangement. For one stereoisomer, all the R groups are situated on the same side of the chain as follows:

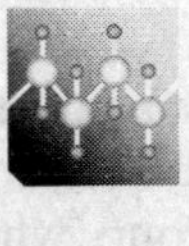

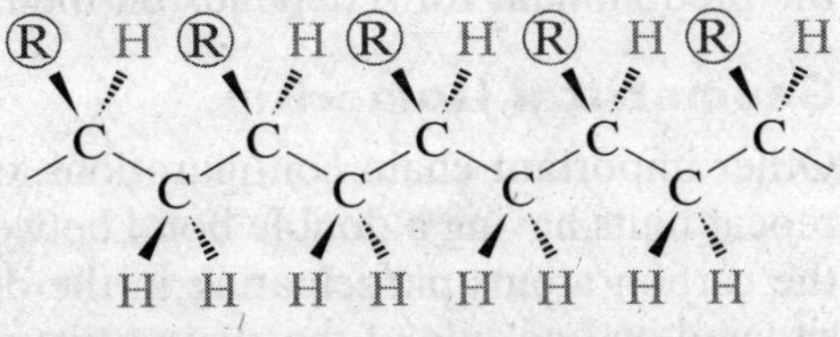

This is called an **isotactic configuration.** This diagram shows the zigzag pattern of the carbon chain atoms. Furthermore, representation of the structural geometry in three dimensions is important, as indicated by the wedge-shaped bonds; solid wedges represent bonds that project out of the plane of the page, dashed ones represent bonds that project into the page.[8]

In a **syndiotactic configuration,** the R groups alternate sides of the chain:[9]

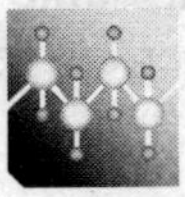

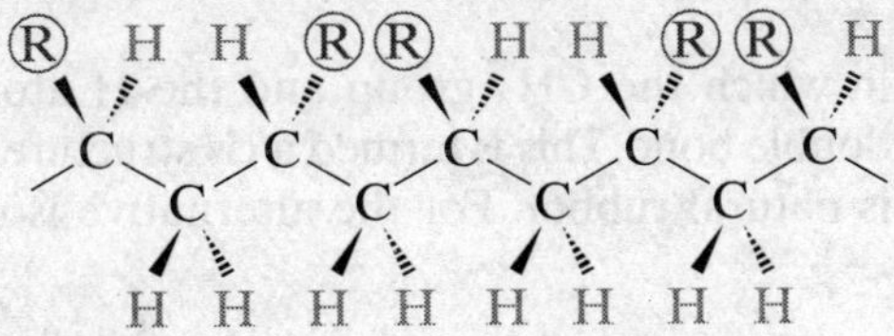

and for random positioning.

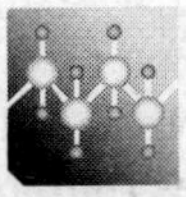

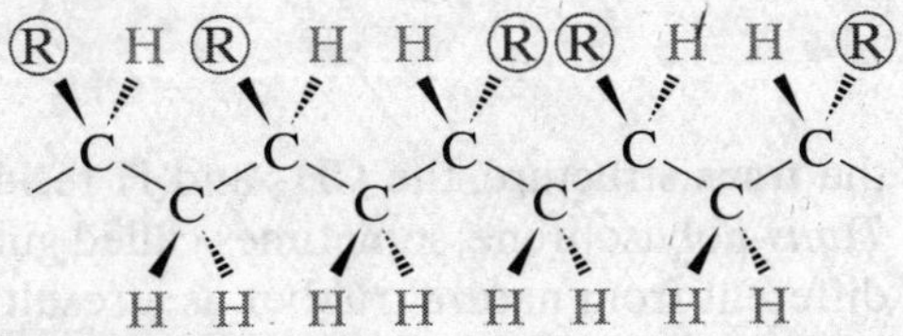

the term **atactic configuration** is used.[10]

---

[8] The isotactic configuration is sometimes represented using the following linear (i.e., nonzigzag) and two-dimensional schematic:

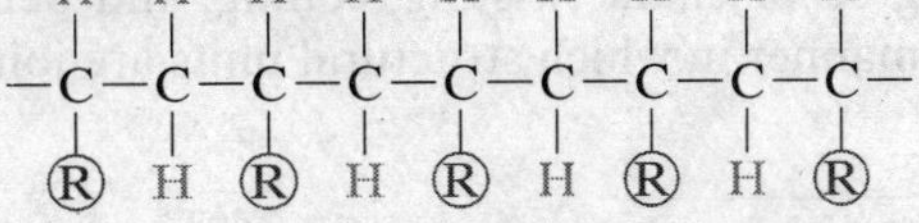

[9] The linear and two-dimensional schematic for syndiotactic is represented as

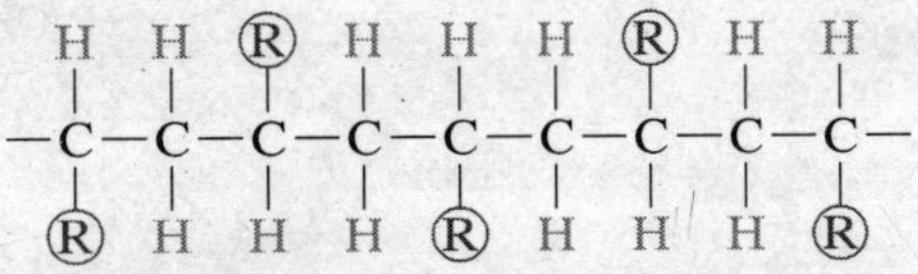

[10] For atactic the linear and two-dimensional schematic is

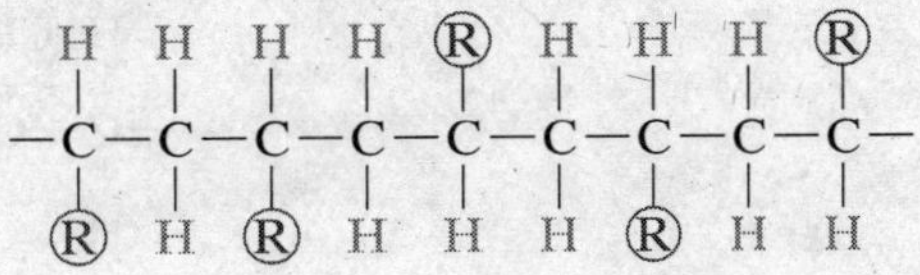

Conversion from one stereoisomer to another (e.g., isotactic to syndiotactic) is not possible by a simple rotation about single chain bonds; these bonds must first be severed, and then, after the appropriate rotation, they are reformed.

In reality, a specific polymer does not exhibit just one of these configurations; the predominant form depends on the method of synthesis.

Geometrical Isomerism

Other important chain configurations, or geometrical isomers, are possible within repeat units having a double bond between chain carbon atoms. Bonded to each of the carbon atoms participating in the double bond is a side group, which may be situated on one side of the chain or its opposite. Consider the isoprene repeat unit having the structure

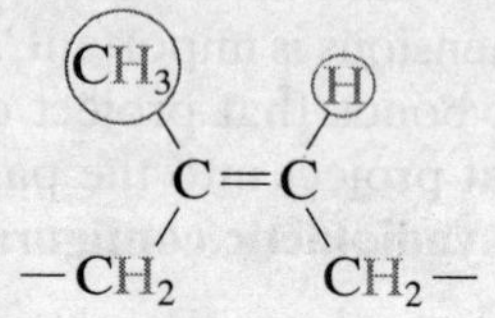

in which the CH_3 group and the H atom are positioned on the same side of the double bond. This is termed a **cis** structure, and the resulting polymer, *cis*-polyisoprene, is natural rubber. For the alternative isomer

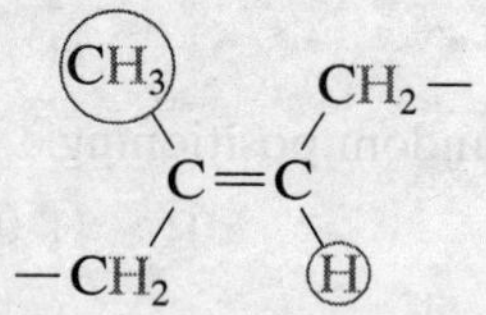

the **trans** structure, the CH_3 and H reside on opposite sides of the double bond.[11] *Trans*-polyisoprene, sometimes called gutta percha, has properties that are distinctly different from natural rubber as a result of this configurational alteration. Conversion of trans to cis, or vice versa, is not possible by a simple chain bond rotation because the chain double bond is extremely rigid.

Summarizing the preceding sections, polymer molecules may be characterized in terms of their size, shape, and structure. Molecular size is specified in terms of molecular weight (or degree of polymerization). Molecular shape relates to the degree of chain twisting, coiling, and bending. Molecular structure depends on the manner in which structural units are joined together. Linear, branched, crosslinked,

[11] For cis-isoprene the linear chain representation is as follows:

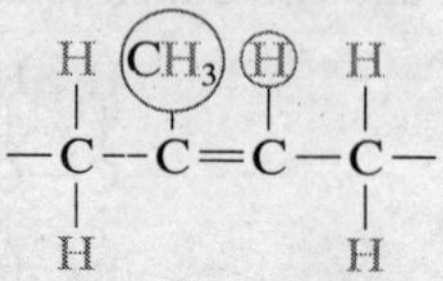

whereas the linear schematic for the trans structure is

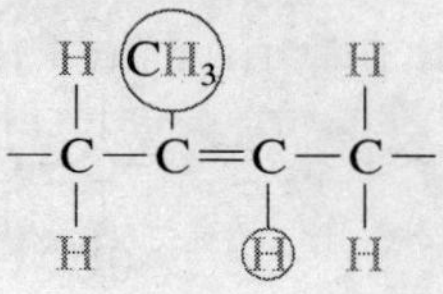

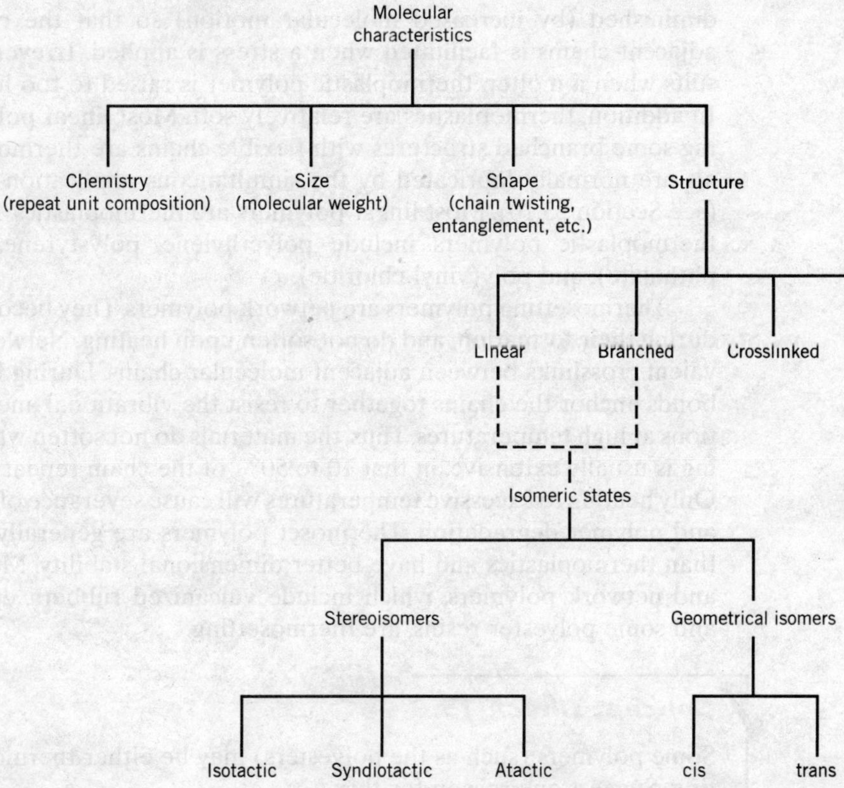

Figure 13.8 Classification scheme for the characteristics of polymer molecules.

and network structures are all possible, in addition to several isomeric configurations (isotactic, syndiotactic, atactic, cis, and trans). These molecular characteristics are presented in the taxonomic chart, Figure 13.8. Note that some of the structural elements are not mutually exclusive of one another, and, in fact, it may be necessary to specify molecular structure in terms of more than one. For example, a linear polymer may also be isotactic.

Concept Check 13.3

What is the difference between *configuration* and *conformation* in relation to polymer chains?

[*The answer may be found in enclosed CD.*]

13.9 THERMOPLASTIC AND THERMOSETTING POLYMERS

The response of a polymer to mechanical forces at elevated temperatures is related to its dominant molecular structure. In fact, one classification scheme for these materials is according to behavior with rising temperature. *Thermoplastics* (or **thermoplastic polymers**) and *thermosets* (or **thermosetting polymers**) are the two subdivisions. Thermoplastics soften when heated (and eventually liquefy) and harden when cooled—processes that are totally reversible and may be repeated. On a molecular level, as the temperature is raised, secondary bonding forces are diminished (by increased molecular motion) so that the relative movement of adjacent chains is facilitated when a stress is applied. Irreversible degradation results when a molten thermoplastic polymer is raised to too high of a temperature. In addition, thermoplastics are relatively soft. Most linear polymers and those having some branched structures with flexible chains are thermoplastic. These materials are normally fabricated by the simultaneous application of heat and pressure (see Section 23.10). Most linear polymers are thermoplastics. Examples of common thermoplastic polymers include polyethylene, polystyrene, poly(ethylene terephthalate), and poly(vinyl chloride).

Thermosetting polymers are network polymers. They become permanently hard during their formation, and do not soften upon heating. Network polymers have covalent crosslinks between adjacent molecular chains. During heat treatments, these bonds anchor the chains together to resist the vibrational and rotational chain motions at high temperatures. Thus, the materials do not soften when heated. Crosslinking is usually extensive, in that 10 to 50% of the chain repeat units are crosslinked. Only heating to excessive temperatures will cause severance of these crosslink bonds and polymer degradation. Thermoset polymers are generally harder and stronger than thermoplastics and have better dimensional stability. Most of the crosslinked and network polymers, which include vulcanized rubbers, epoxies, and phenolics and some polyester resins, are thermosetting.

Concept Check 13.4

Some polymers (such as the polyesters) may be either thermoplastic or thermosetting. Suggest one reason for this.

[*The answer may be found in enclosed CD.*]

13.10 COPOLYMERS

Polymer chemists and scientists are continually searching for new materials that can be easily and economically synthesized and fabricated, with improved properties or better property combinations than are offered by the homopolymers previously discussed. One group of these materials are the copolymers.

Consider a copolymer that is composed of two repeat units as represented by ● and ○ in Figure 13.9. Depending on the polymerization process and the relative fractions of these repeat unit types, different sequencing arrangements along the polymer chains are possible. For one, as depicted in Figure 13.9*a*, the two different units are randomly dispersed along the chain in what is termed a **random copolymer.** For an **alternating copolymer,** as the name suggests, the two repeat units alternate chain positions, as illustrated in Figure 13.9*b*. A **block copolymer** is one in which identical repeat units are clustered in blocks along the chain (Figure 13.9*c*). Finally, homopolymer side branches of one type may be grafted to homopolymer main chains that are composed of a different repeat unit; such a material is termed a **graft copolymer** (Figure 13.9*d*).

When calculating the degree of polymerization for a copolymer, the value m in Equation 13.7 is replaced with the average value $\overline{m}$ that is determined from

Average repeat unit molecular weight for a copolymer

$$\overline{m} = \Sigma f_j m_j \tag{13.7}$$

In this expression, f_j and m_j are, respectively, the mole fraction and molecular weight of repeat unit j in the polymer chain.

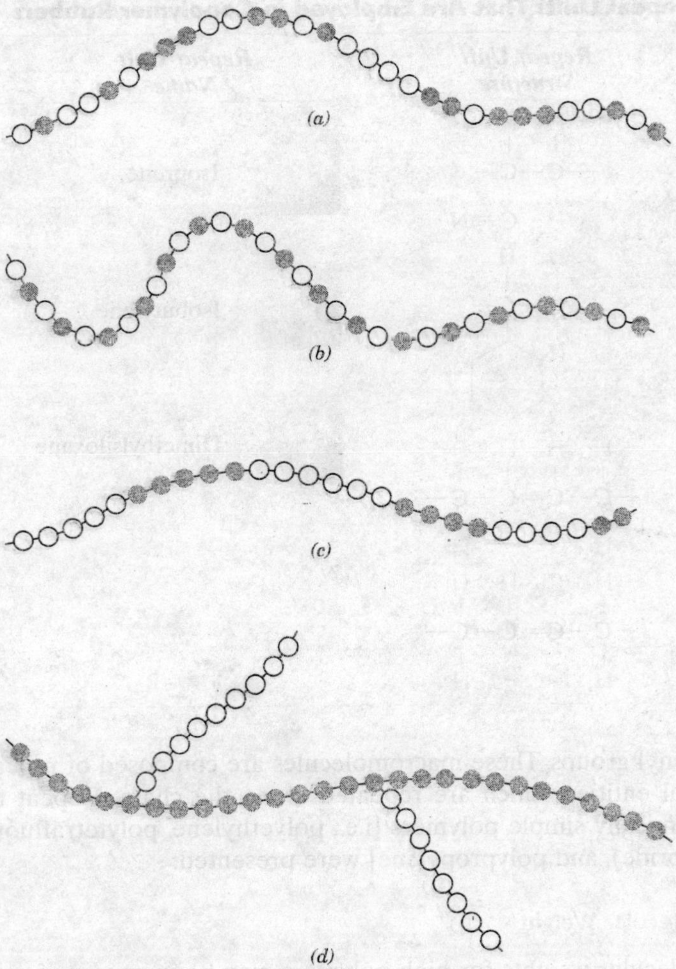

Figure 13.9 Schematic representations of (*a*) random, (*b*) alternating, (*c*) block, and (*d*) graft copolymers. The two different repeat unit types are designated by blue and red circles.

Synthetic rubbers, discussed in Section 14.16, are often copolymers; chemical repeat units that are employed in some of these rubbers are contained in Table 13.5. Styrene–butadiene rubber (SBR) is a common random copolymer from which automobile tires are made. Nitrile rubber (NBR) is another random copolymer composed of acrylonitrile and butadiene. It is also highly elastic and, in addition, resistant to swelling in organic solvents; gasoline hoses are made of NBR. Impact modified polystyrene is a block copolymer that consists of alternating blocks of styrene and butadiene. The rubbery isoprene blocks act to slow cracks propagating through the material.

SUMMARY

Hydrocarbon Molecules
Polymer Molecules
The Chemistry of Polymer Molecules

Most polymeric materials are composed of very large molecular chains with side-groups of various atoms (O, Cl, etc.) or organic groups such as methyl, ethyl, or

Table 13.5 Chemical Repeat Units That Are Employed in Copolymer Rubbers

Repeat Unit Name	*Repeat Unit Structure*	*Repeat Unit Name*	*Repeat Unit Structure*
Acrylonitrile	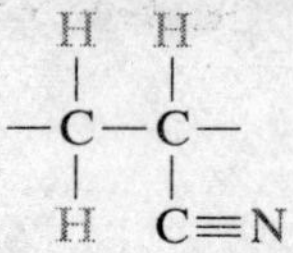	Isoprene	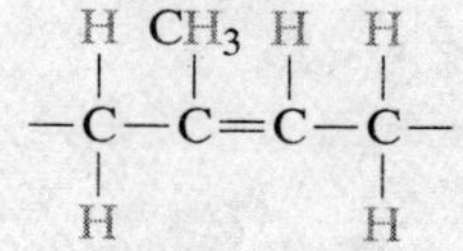
Styrene	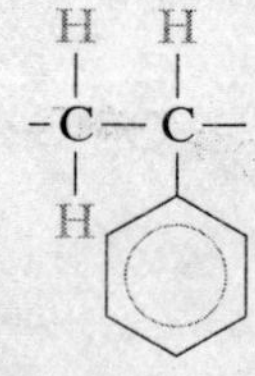	Isobutylene	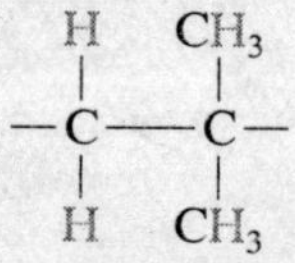
Butadiene	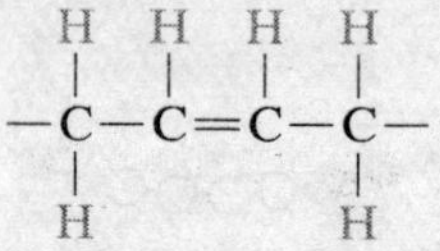	Dimethylsiloxane	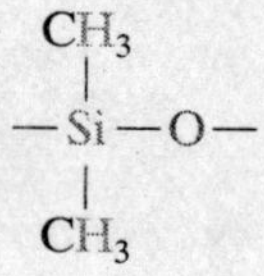
Chloroprene	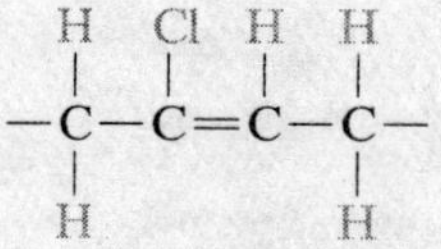		

phenyl groups. These macromolecules are composed of repeat units, smaller structural entities, which are repeated along the chain. Repeat units for some of the chemically simple polymers [i.e., polyethylene, polytetrafluoroethylene, poly(vinyl chloride), and polypropylene] were presented.

Molecular Weight

Molecular weights for high polymers may be in excess of a million. Since all molecules are not of the same size, there is a distribution of molecular weights. Molecular weight is often expressed in terms of number and weight averages. Chain length may also be specified by degree of polymerization, the number of repeat units per average molecule.

Molecular Shape
Molecular Structure
Molecular Configurations
Copolymers

Several molecular characteristics that have an influence on the properties of polymers were discussed. Molecular entanglements occur when the chains assume twisted, coiled, and kinked shapes or contours. With regard to molecular structure, linear, branched, crosslinked, and network structures are possible, in addition to isotactic, syndiotactic, and atactic stereoisomers, and the cis and trans geometrical isomers. The copolymers include random, alternating, block, and graft types.

Thermoplastic and Thermosetting Polymers

With regard to behavior at elevated temperatures, polymers are classified as either thermoplastic or thermosetting. The former have linear and branched structures; they soften when heated and harden when cooled. In contrast, thermosets, once having hardened, will not soften upon heating; their structures are crosslinked and network.

REFERENCES

Baer, E., "Advanced Polymers," *Scientific American,* Vol. 255, No. 4, October 1986, pp. 178–190.

Carraher, C. E., Jr., *Seymour/Carraher's Polymer Chemistry,* 6th edition, Marcel Dekker, New York, 2003.

Cowie, J. M. G., *Polymers: Chemistry and Physics of Modern Materials,* 2nd edition, Chapman and Hall (USA), New York, 1991.

Engineered Materials Handbook, Vol. 2, *Engineering Plastics,* ASM International, Materials Park, OH, 1988.

McCrum, N. G., C. P. Buckley, and C. B. Bucknall, *Principles of Polymer Engineering,* 2nd edition, Oxford University Press, Oxford, 1997. Chapters 0–6.

Rodriguez, F., C. Cohen, C. K. Ober, and L. Archer, *Principles of Polymer Systems,* 5th edition, Taylor & Francis, New York, 2003.

Rosen, S. L., *Fundamental Principles of Polymeric Materials,* 2nd edition, Wiley, New York, 1993.

Rudin, A., *The Elements of Polymer Science and Engineering,* 2nd edition, Academic Press, San Diego, 1998.

Sperling, L. H., *Introduction to Physical Polymer Science.* 3rd edition, Wiley, New York, 2001.

Young, R. J., and P. Lovell, *Introduction to Polymers,* 2nd edition, Chapman and Hall, New York, 1991.

QUESTIONS AND PROBLEMS

Hydrocarbon Molecules
Polymer Molecules
The Chemistry of Polymer Molecules

13.1 On the basis of the structures presented in this chapter, sketch repeat unit structures for the following polymers: **(a)** polychlorotrifluoroethylene, and **(b)** poly(vinyl alcohol).

Molecular Weight

13.2 Compute repeat unit molecular weights for the following: **(a)** polytetrafluoroethylene, **(b)** poly(methyl methacrylate), **(c)** nylon 6,6, and **(d)** poly(ethylene terephthalate).

13.3 The number-average molecular weight of a polystyrene is 500,000 g/mol. Compute the degree of polymerization.

13.4 **(a)** Compute the repeat unit molecular weight of polypropylene.

(b) Compute the number-average molecular weight for a polypropylene for which the degree of polymerization is 15,000.

13.5 Below, molecular weight data for a polytetrafluoroethylene material are tabulated. Compute **(a)** the number-average molecular weight, **(b)** the weight-average molecular weight, and **(c)** the degree of polymerization.

Molecular Weight Range (g/mol)	x_i	w_i
10,000–20,000	0.03	0.01
20,000–30,000	0.09	0.04
30,000–40,000	0.15	0.11
40,000–50,000	0.25	0.23
50,000–60,000	0.22	0.24
60,000–70,000	0.14	0.18
70,000–80,000	0.08	0.12
80,000–90,000	0.04	0.07

13.6 Molecular weight data for some polymer are tabulated here. Compute **(a)** the number-average molecular weight, and **(b)** the weight-average molecular weight. **(c)** If it is known that this material's degree of polymerization is 477, which one of the polymers listed in Table 13.3 is this polymer? Why?

Molecular Weight Range (g/mol)	x_i	w_i
8,000–20,000	0.05	0.02
20,000–32,000	0.15	0.08
32,000–44,000	0.21	0.17
44,000–56,000	0.28	0.29
56,000–68,000	0.18	0.23
68,000–80,000	0.10	0.16
80,000–92,000	0.03	0.05

13.7 Is it possible to have a poly(vinyl chloride) homopolymer with the following molecular weight data, and a degree of polymerization of 1120? Why or why not?

Molecular Weight Range (g/mol)	w_i	x_i
8,000–20,000	0.02	0.05
20,000–32,000	0.08	0.15
32,000–44,000	0.17	0.21
44,000–56,000	0.29	0.28
56,000–68,000	0.23	0.18
68,000–80,000	0.16	0.10
80,000–92,000	0.05	0.03

13.8 High-density polyethylene may be chlorinated by inducing the random substitution of chlorine atoms for hydrogen.

(a) Determine the concentration of Cl (in wt%) that must be added if this substitution occurs for 8% of all the original hydrogen atoms.

(b) In what ways does this chlorinated polyethylene differ from poly(vinyl chloride)?

Molecular Shape

13.9 For a linear polymer molecule, the total chain length L depends on the bond length between chain atoms d, the total number of bonds in the molecule N, and the angle between adjacent backbone chain atoms θ, as follows:

$$L = Nd \sin\left(\frac{\theta}{2}\right) \quad (13.8)$$

Furthermore, the average end-to-end distance for a series of polymer molecules r in Figure 13.6 is equal to

$$r = d\sqrt{N} \quad (13.9)$$

A linear polyethylene has a number-average molecular weight of 300,000 g/mol; compute average values of L and r for this material.

13.10 Using the definitions for total chain molecule length, L (Equation 13.11) and average chain end-to-end distance r (Equation 13.9), for a linear polytetrafluoroethylene determine:

(a) the number-average molecular weight for L = 2000 nm;

(b) the number-average molecular weight for r = 15 nm.

Molecular Configurations

13.11 Sketch portions of a linear polypropylene molecule that are **(a)** syndiotactic, **(b)** atactic, and **(c)** isotactic.

13.12 Sketch cis and trans structures for **(a)** butadiene, and **(b)** chloroprene.

Thermoplastic and Thermosetting Polymers

13.13 Make comparisons of thermoplastic and thermosetting polymers **(a)** on the basis of mechanical characteristics upon heating, and **(b)** according to possible molecular structures.

13.14 **(a)** Is it possible to grind up and reuse phenol-formaldehyde? Why or why not?

(b) Is it possible to grind up and reuse polypropylene? Why or why not?

Copolymers

13.15 Sketch the repeat structure for each of the following alternating copolymers: **(a)** poly(ethylene-propylene), **(b)** poly(butadiene-styrene), and **(c)** poly(isobutylene-isoprene).

13.16 The number-average molecular weight of a poly(acrylonitrile-butadiene) alternating copolymer is 1,000,000 g/mol; determine the average number of acrylonitrile and butadiene repeat units per molecule.

13.17 Calculate the number-average molecular weight of a random poly(isobutylene-isoprene) copolymer in which the fraction of isobutylene repeat units is 0.25; assume that this concentration corresponds to a degree of polymerization of 1500.

13.18 An alternating copolymer is known to have a number-average molecular weight of 100,000 g/mol and a degree of polymerization of 2210. If one of the repeat units is ethylene, which of styrene, propylene, tetrafluoroethylene, and vinyl chloride is the other repeat unit? Why?

13.19 **(a)** Determine the ratio of butadiene to acrylonitrile repeat units in a copolymer having a number-average molecular weight of 250,000 g/mol and a degree of polymerization of 4640.

(b) Which type(s) of copolymer(s) will this copolymer be, considering the following possibilities: random, alternating, graft, and block? Why?

13.20 Crosslinked copolymers consisting of 35 wt% ethylene and 65 wt% propylene may have elastic properties similar to those for natural rubber. For a copolymer of this composition, determine the fraction of both repeat unit types.

13.21 A random poly(styrene-butadiene) copolymer has a number-average molecular weight of 350,000 g/mol and a degree of polymerization of 5000. Compute the fraction of styrene and butadiene repeat units in this copolymer.

Polymer Crystallinity (Molecular Structure)

13.22 Explain briefly why the tendency of a polymer to crystallize decreases with increasing molecular weight.

13.23 For each of the following pairs of polymers, do the following: (1) state whether or not it is possible to determine whether one polymer is more likely to crystallize than the other; (2) if it is possible, note which is the more likely and then cite reason(s) for your choice; and (3) if it is not possible to decide, then state why.

(a) Linear and atactic poly(vinyl chloride); linear and isotactic polypropylene.

(b) Linear and syndiotactic polypropylene; crosslinked *cis*-isoprene.

(c) Network phenol-formaldehyde; linear and isotactic polystyrene.

(d) Block poly(acrylonitrile-isoprene) copolymer; graft poly(chloroprene-isobutylene) copolymer.

Chapter 14 Characteristics and Applications of Polymers

Photograph of several billiard balls that are made of phenol-formaldehyde (Bakelite). The Materials of Importance piece that follows Section 14.15 discusses the invention of phenol-formaldehyde and its replacement of ivory for billiard balls. (Photography by S. Tanner.)

Learning Objectives

After careful study of this chapter you should be able to do the following:

1. **Make schematic plots of the three characteristic stress–strain behaviors observed for polymeric materials.**
2. **Describe/sketch the various stages in the elastic and plastic deformations of a semicrystalline (spherulitic) polymer.**
3. **Discuss the influence of the following factors on polymer tensile modulus and/or strength: (a) molecular weight, (b) degree of crystallinity, (c) predeformation, and (d) heat treating of undeformed materials.**
4. **Describe the molecular mechanism by which elastomeric polymers deform elastically.**
5. **List four characteristics or structural components of a polymer that affect both its melting and glass-transition temperatures.**
6. **Cite the seven different polymer application types and, for each, note its general characteristics.**
7. **Briefly describe addition and condensation polymerization mechanisms.**
8. **Name the five types of polymer additives and, for each, indicate how it modifies the properties.**

14.1 INTRODUCTION

This chapter discusses some of the characteristics important to polymeric materials and, in addition, the various types and processing techniques.

Mechanical Behavior of Polymers

14.2 STRESS–STRAIN BEHAVIOR

The mechanical properties of polymers are specified with many of the same parameters that are used for metals—that is, modulus of elasticity, and yield and tensile strengths. For many polymeric materials, the simple stress–strain test is employed for the characterization of some of these mechanical parameters.[1] The mechanical characteristics of polymers, for the most part, are highly sensitive to the rate of deformation (strain rate), the temperature, and the chemical nature of the environment (the presence of water, oxygen, organic solvents, etc.). Some modifications of the testing techniques and specimen configurations used for metals (Chapter 9) are necessary with polymers, especially for the highly elastic materials, such as rubbers.

Three typically different types of stress–strain behavior are found for polymeric materials, as represented in Figure 14.1. Curve *A* illustrates the stress–strain character for a brittle polymer, inasmuch as it fractures while deforming elastically. The behavior for a plastic material, curve *B*, is similar to that for many metallic materials; the initial deformation is elastic, which is followed by yielding and a region of plastic deformation. Finally, the deformation displayed by curve *C* is totally elastic; this rubber-like elasticity (large recoverable strains produced at low stress levels) is displayed by a class of polymers termed the **elastomers.**

Modulus of elasticity (termed *tensile modulus* or sometimes just *modulus* for polymers) and ductility in percent elongation are determined for polymers in the

[1] ASTM Standard D 638, "Standard Test Method for Tensile Properties of Plastics."

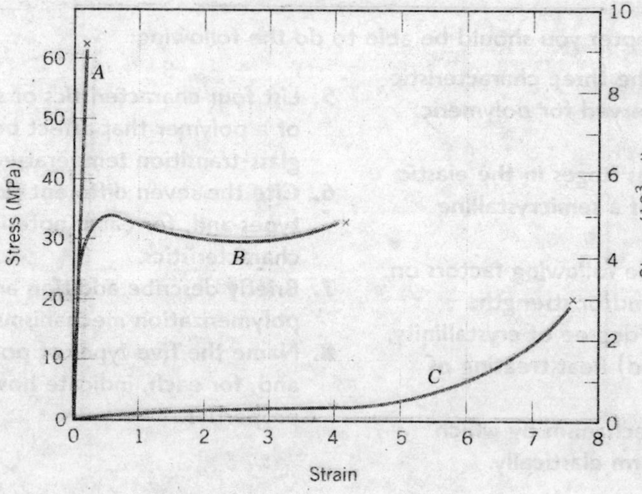

Figure 14.1 The stress–strain behavior for brittle (curve *A*), plastic (curve *B*), and highly elastic (elastomeric) (curve *C*) polymers.

same manner as for metals (Section 9.7). For plastic polymers (curve *B*, Figure 14.1), the yield point is taken as a maximum on the curve, which occurs just beyond the termination of the linear-elastic region (Figure 14.2). The stress at this maximum is the yield strength (σ_y). Furthermore, tensile strength (*TS*) corresponds to the stress at which fracture occurs (Figure 14.2): *TS* may be greater than or less than σ_y. Strength, for these plastic polymers, is normally taken as tensile strength. Table 14.1 gives these mechanical properties for several polymeric materials; more comprehensive lists are provided in Tables B.2, B.3, and B.4, Appendix B.

Polymers are, in many respects, mechanically dissimilar to metals (Figures 1.4, 1.5, and 1.6). For example, the modulus for highly elastic polymeric materials may be as low as 7 MPa, but may run as high as 4 GPa for some of the very stiff polymers; modulus values for metals are much larger and range between 48 and 410 GPa. Maximum tensile strengths for polymers are about 100 MPa—for some metal alloys 4100 MPa. And, whereas metals rarely elongate plastically to more than 100%, some highly elastic polymers may experience elongations to greater than 1000%.

In addition, the mechanical characteristics of polymers are much more sensitive to temperature changes near room temperature. Consider the stress–strain behavior for poly(methyl methacrylate) (Plexiglas) at several temperatures between 4 and

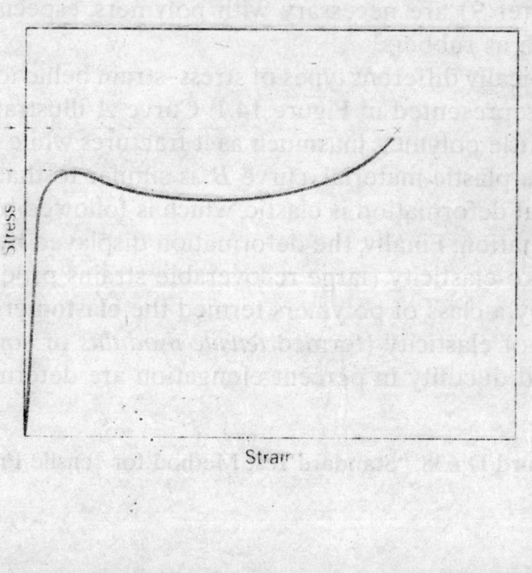

Figure 14.2 Schematic stress–strain curve for a plastic polymer showing how yield and tensile strengths are determined.

Table 14.1 Room-Temperature Mechanical Characteristics of Some of the More Common Polymers

Material	*Specific Gravity*	*Tensile Modulus (GPa)*	*Tensile Strength (MPa)*	*Yield Strength (MPa)*	*Elongation at Break (%)*
Polyethylene (low density)	0.917–0.932	0.17–0.28	8.3–31.4	9.0–14.5	100–650
Polyethylene (high density)	0.952–0.965	1.06–1.09	22.1–31.0	26.2–33.1	10–1200
Poly(vinyl chloride)	1.30–1.58	2.4–4.1	40.7–51.7	40.7–44.8	40–80
Polytetrafluoroethylene	2.14–2.20	0.40–0.55	20.7–34.5	—	200–400
Polypropylene	0.90–0.91	1.14–1.55	31–41.4	31.0–37.2	100–600
Polystyrene	1.04–1.05	2.28–3.28	35.9–51.7	—	1.2–2.5
Poly(methyl methacrylate)	1.17–1.20	2.24–3.24	48.3–72.4	53.8–73.1	2.0–5.5
Phenol-formaldehyde	1.24–1.32	2.76–4.83	34.5–62.1	—	1.5–2.0
Nylon 6,6	1.13–1.15	1.58–3.80	75.9–94.5	44.8–82.8	15–300
Polyester (PET)	1.29–1.40	2.8–4.1	48.3–72.4	59.3	30–300
Polycarbonate	1.20	2.38	62.8–72.4	62.1	110–150

Source: *Modern Plastics Encyclopedia '96*. Copyright 1995, The McGraw-Hill Companies. Reprinted with permission.

60°C (Figure 14.3). It should be noted that increasing the temperature produces (1) a decrease in elastic modulus, (2) a reduction in tensile strength, and (3) an enhancement of ductility—at 4°C the material is totally brittle, while there is considerable plastic deformation at both 50 and 60°C.

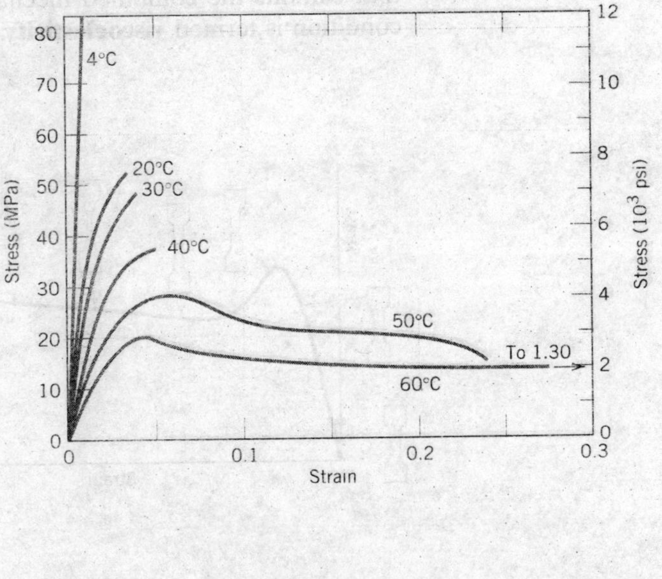

Figure 14.3 The influence of temperature on the stress–strain characteristics of poly(methyl methacrylate). (From T. S. Carswell and H. K. Nason, "Effect of Environmental Conditions on the Mechanical Properties of Organic Plastics," *Symposium on Plastics*, American Society for Testing and Materials, Philadelphia, 1944. Copyright, ASTM, 1916 Race Street, Philadelphia, PA 19103. Reprinted with permission.)

The influence of strain rate on the mechanical behavior may also be important. In general, decreasing the rate of deformation has the same influence on the stress–strain characteristics as increasing the temperature; that is, the material becomes softer and more ductile.

14.3 MACROSCOPIC DEFORMATION

Some aspects of the macroscopic deformation of semicrystalline polymers deserve our attention. The tensile stress–strain curve for a semicrystalline material, which was initially undeformed, is shown in Figure 14.4; also included in the figure are schematic representations of the specimen profiles at various stages of deformation. Both upper and lower yield points are evident on the curve, which are followed by a near horizontal region. At the upper yield point, a small neck forms within the gauge section of the specimen. Within this neck, the chains become oriented (i.e., chain axes become aligned parallel to the elongation direction, a condition that is represented schematically in Figure 14.13*d*), which leads to localized strengthening. Consequently, there is a resistance to continued deformation at this point, and specimen elongation proceeds by the propagation of this neck region along the gauge length; the chain orientation phenomenon (Figure 14.13*d*) accompanies this neck extension. This tensile behavior may be contrasted to that found for ductile metals (Section 9.7), wherein once a neck has formed, all subsequent deformation is confined to within the neck region.

Concept Check 14.1

When citing the ductility as percent elongation for semicrystalline polymers, it is not necessary to specify the specimen gauge length, as is the case with metals. Why is this so?

[*The answer may be found in enclosed CD.*]

14.4 VISCOELASTIC DEFORMATION

An amorphous polymer may behave like a glass at low temperatures, a rubbery solid at intermediate temperatures [above the glass transition temperature (Section 14.12)], and a viscous liquid as the temperature is further raised. For relatively small deformations, the mechanical behavior at low temperatures may be elastic; that is, in conformity to Hooke's law, $\sigma = E\epsilon$. At the highest temperatures, viscous or liquid-like behavior prevails. For intermediate temperatures the polymer is a rubbery solid that exhibits the combined mechanical characteristics of these two extremes; the condition is termed **viscoelasticity.**

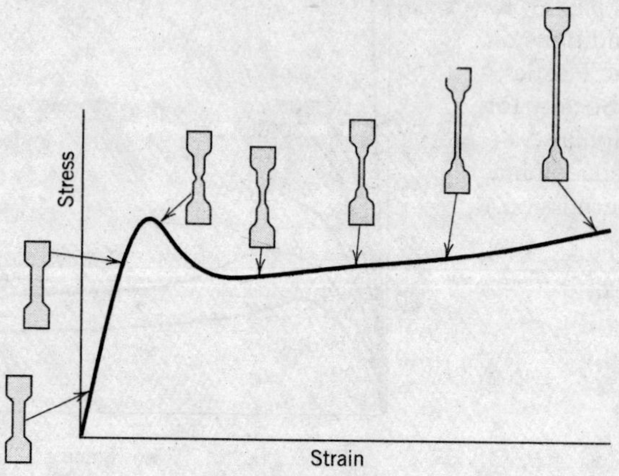

Figure 14.4 Schematic tensile stress–strain curve for a semicrystalline polymer. Specimen contours at several stages of deformation are included. (From Jerold M. Schultz, *Polymer Materials Science,* copyright © 1974, p. 488. Reprinted by permission of Prentice Hall, Inc., Englewood Cliffs, NJ.)

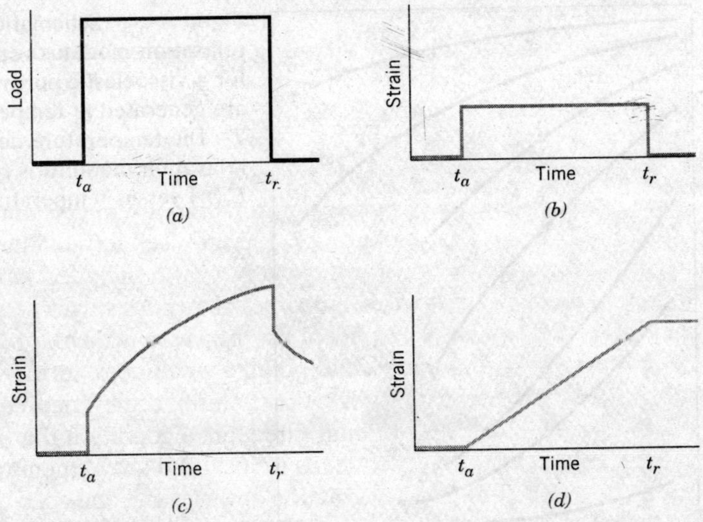

Figure 14.5 (*a*) Load versus time, where load is applied instantaneously at time t_a and released at t_r. For the load–time cycle in (*a*), the strain-versus-time responses are for totally elastic (*b*), viscoelastic (*c*), and viscous (*d*) behaviors.

Elastic deformation is instantaneous, which means that total deformation (or strain) occurs the instant the stress is applied or released (i.e., the strain is independent of time). In addition, upon release of the external stress, the deformation is totally recovered—the specimen assumes its original dimensions. This behavior is represented in Figure 14.5*b* as strain versus time for the instantaneous load–time curve, shown in Figure 14.5*a*.

By way of contrast, for totally viscous behavior, deformation or strain is not instantaneous; that is, in response to an applied stress, deformation is delayed or dependent on time. Also, this deformation is not reversible or completely recovered after the stress is released. This phenomenon is demonstrated in Figure 14.5*d*.

For the intermediate viscoelastic behavior, the imposition of a stress in the manner of Figure 14.5*a* results in an instantaneous elastic strain, which is followed by a viscous, time-dependent strain, a form of anelasticity (Section 9.6); this behavior is illustrated in Figure 14.5*c*.

A familiar example of these viscoelastic extremes is found in a silicone polymer that is sold as a novelty and known by some as "silly putty." When rolled into a ball and dropped onto a horizontal surface, it bounces elastically—the rate of deformation during the bounce is very rapid. On the other hand, if pulled in tension with a gradually increasing applied stress, the material elongates or flows like a highly viscous liquid. For this and other viscoelastic materials, the rate of strain determines whether the deformation is elastic or viscous.

Viscoelastic Relaxation Modulus

The viscoelastic behavior of polymeric materials is dependent on both time and temperature; several experimental techniques may be used to measure and quantify this behavior. *Stress relaxation* measurements represent one possibility. With these tests, a specimen is initially strained rapidly in tension to a predetermined and relatively low strain level. The stress necessary to maintain this strain is measured as a function of time, while temperature is held constant. Stress is found to decrease with time due to molecular relaxation processes that take place within the polymer. We may define a **relaxation modulus** $E_r(t)$, a time-dependent elastic modulus for viscoelastic polymers, as

$$E_r(t) = \frac{\sigma(t)}{\epsilon_0} \tag{14.1}$$

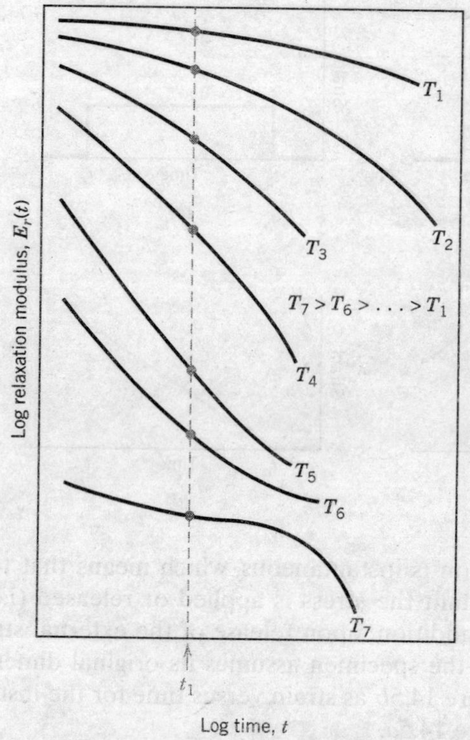

Figure 14.6 Schematic plot of logarithm of relaxation modulus versus logarithm of time for a viscoelastic polymer; isothermal curves are generated at temperatures T_1 through T_7. The temperature dependence of the relaxation modulus is represented as log $E_r(t_1)$ versus temperature.

where $\sigma(t)$ is the measured time-dependent stress and ϵ_0 is the strain level, which is maintained constant.

Furthermore, the magnitude of the relaxation modulus is a function of temperature; and to more fully characterize the viscoelastic behavior of a polymer, isothermal stress relaxation measurements must be conducted over a range of temperatures. Figure 14.6 is a schematic log $E_r(t)$-versus-log time plot for a polymer that exhibits viscoelastic behavior. Curves generated at a variety of temperatures are included. Key features of this plot are that (1) the magnitude of $E_r(t)$ decreases with time (corresponding to the decay of stress, Equation 14.1), and (2) the curves are displaced to lower $E_r(t)$ levels with increasing temperature.

To represent the influence of temperature, data points are taken at a specific time from the log $E_r(t)$-versus-log time plot—for example, t_1 in Figure 14.6—and then cross-plotted as log $E_r(t_1)$ versus temperature. Figure 14.7 is such a plot for an amorphous (atactic) polystyrene; in this case, t_1 was arbitrarily taken 10 s after the load application. Several distinct regions may be noted on the curve shown in this figure. At the lowest temperatures, in the glassy region, the material is rigid and brittle, and the value of $E_r(10)$ is that of the elastic modulus, which initially is virtually independent of temperature. Over this temperature range, the strain–time characteristics are as represented in Figure 14.5*b*. On a molecular level, the long molecular chains are essentially frozen in position at these temperatures.

As the temperature is increased, $E_r(10)$ drops abruptly by about a factor of 10^3 within a 20°C (35°F) temperature span; this is sometimes called the leathery, or glass transition region, and the glass transition temperature (T_g, Section 14.13) lies near the upper temperature extremity; for polystyrene (Figure 14.7), T_g = 100°C (212°F). Within this temperature region, a polymer specimen will be leathery; that is, deformation will be time dependent and not totally recoverable on release of an applied load, characteristics that are depicted in Figure 14.5*c*.

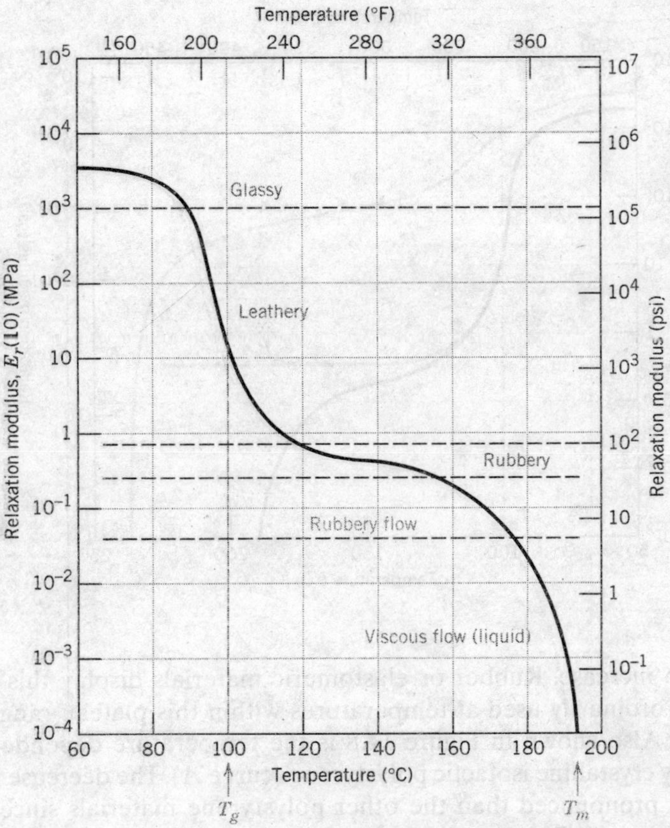

Figure 14.7 Logarithm of the relaxation modulus versus temperature for amorphous polystyrene, showing the five different regions of viscoelastic behavior. (From A. V. Tobolsky, *Properties and Structures of Polymers.* Copyright © 1960 by John Wiley & Sons, New York. Reprinted by permission of John Wiley & Sons, Inc.)

Within the rubbery plateau temperature region (Figure 14.7), the material deforms in a rubbery manner; here, both elastic and viscous components are present, and deformation is easy to produce because the relaxation modulus is relatively low.

The final two high-temperature regions are rubbery flow and viscous flow. Upon heating through these temperatures, the material experiences a gradual transition to a soft rubbery state, and finally to a viscous liquid. In the rubbery flow region, the polymer is a very viscous liquid that exhibits both elastic and viscous flow components. Within the viscous flow region, the modulus decreases dramatically with increasing temperature; again, the strain–time behavior is as represented in Figure 14.5*d*. From a molecular standpoint, chain motion intensifies so greatly that for viscous flow, the chain segments experience vibration and rotational motion largely independent of one another. At these temperatures, any deformation is entirely viscous and essentially no elastic behavior occurs.

Normally, the deformation behavior of a viscous polymer is specified in terms of viscosity, a measure of a material's resistance to flow by shear forces. Viscosity is discussed for the inorganic glasses in Section 12.12.

The rate of stress application also influences the viscoelastic characteristics. Increasing the loading rate has the same influence as lowering temperature.

The log $E_r(10)$-versus-temperature behavior for polystyrene materials having several molecular configurations is plotted in Figure 14.8. The curve for the amorphous material (curve C) is the same as in Figure 14.7. For a lightly crosslinked atactic polystyrene (curve B), the rubbery region forms a plateau that extends to the temperature at which the polymer decomposes; this material will not experience melting. For increased crosslinking, the magnitude of the plateau $E_r(10)$ value will

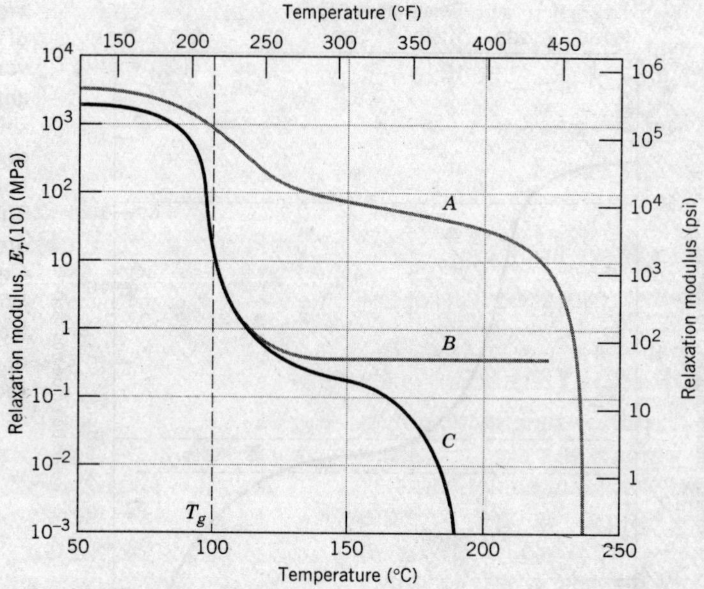

Figure 14.8 Logarithm of the relaxation modulus versus temperature for crystalline isotactic (curve A), lightly crosslinked atactic (curve B), and amorphous (curve C) polystyrene. (From A. V. Tobolsky, *Properties and Structures of Polymers.* Copyright © 1960 by John Wiley & Sons, New York. Reprinted by permission of John Wiley & Sons, Inc.)

also increase. Rubber or elastomeric materials display this type of behavior and are ordinarily used at temperatures within this plateau range.

Also shown in Figure 14.8 is the temperature dependence for an almost totally crystalline isotactic polystyrene (curve A). The decrease in $E_r(10)$ at T_g is much less pronounced than the other polystyrene materials since only a small volume fraction of this material is amorphous and experiences the glass transition. Furthermore, the relaxation modulus is maintained at a relatively high value with increasing temperature until its melting temperature T_m is approached. From Figure 14.8, the melting temperature of this isotactic polystyrene is about 240°C (460°F).

Viscoelastic Creep

Many polymeric materials are susceptible to time-dependent deformation when the stress level is maintained constant; such deformation is termed *viscoelastic creep.* This type of deformation may be significant even at room temperature and under modest stresses that lie below the yield strength of the material. For example, automobile tires may develop flat spots on their contact surfaces when the automobile is parked for prolonged time periods. Creep tests on polymers are conducted in the same manner as for metals (Chapter 11); that is, a stress (normally tensile) is applied instantaneously and is maintained at a constant level while strain is measured as a function of time. Furthermore, the tests are performed under isothermal conditions. Creep results are represented as a time-dependent *creep modulus* $E_c(t)$, defined by[2]

$$E_c(t) = \frac{\sigma_0}{\epsilon(t)} \tag{14.2}$$

wherein σ_0 is the constant applied stress and $\epsilon(t)$ is the time-dependent strain. The creep modulus is also temperature sensitive and diminishes with increasing temperature.

[2] *Creep compliance,* $J_c(t)$, the reciprocal of the creep modulus, is also sometimes used in this context.

With regard to the influence of molecular structure on the creep characteristics, as a general rule the susceptibility to creep decreases [i.e., $E_c(t)$ increases] as the degree of crystallinity increases.

Concept Check 14.2

An amorphous polystyrene that is deformed at 120°C will exhibit which of the behaviors shown in Figure 14.5?

[*The answer may be found in enclosed CD.*]

14.5 FRACTURE OF POLYMERS

The fracture strengths of polymeric materials are low relative to those of metals and ceramics. As a general rule, the mode of fracture in thermosetting polymers (heavily crosslinked networks) is brittle. In simple terms, during the fracture process, cracks form at regions where there is a localized stress concentration (i.e., scratches, notches, and sharp flaws). As with metals (Section 11.5), the stress is amplified at the tips of these cracks leading to crack propagation and fracture. Covalent bonds in the network or crosslinked structure are severed during fracture.

For thermoplastic polymers, both ductile and brittle modes are possible, and many of these materials are capable of experiencing a ductile-to-brittle transition. Factors that favor brittle fracture are a reduction in temperature, an increase in strain rate, the presence of a sharp notch, increased specimen thickness, and any modification of the polymer structure that raises the glass transition temperature (T_g) (see Section 14.14). Glassy thermoplastics are brittle below their glass transition temperatures. However, as the temperature is raised, they become ductile in the vicinity of their T_gs and experience plastic yielding prior to fracture. This behavior is demonstrated by the stress–strain characteristics of poly(methyl methacrylate) in Figure 14.3. At 4°C, PMMA is totally brittle, whereas at 60°C it becomes extremely ductile.

One phenomenon that frequently precedes fracture in some thermoplastic polymers is *crazing*. Associated with crazes are regions of very localized plastic deformation, which lead to the formation of small and interconnected microvoids (Figure 14.9*a*).

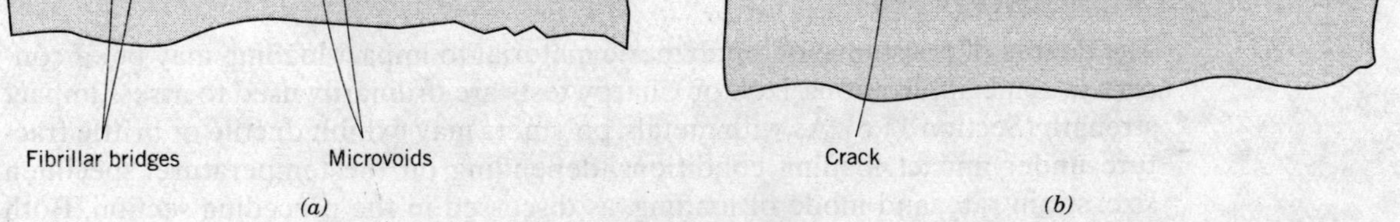

Figure 14.9 Schematic drawings of (*a*) a craze showing microvoids and fibrillar bridges, and (*b*) a craze followed by a crack. (From J. W. S. Hearle, *Polymers and Their Properties*, Vol. 1, *Fundamentals of Structure and Mechanics*, Ellis Horwood, Ltd., Chichester, West Sussex, England, 1982.)

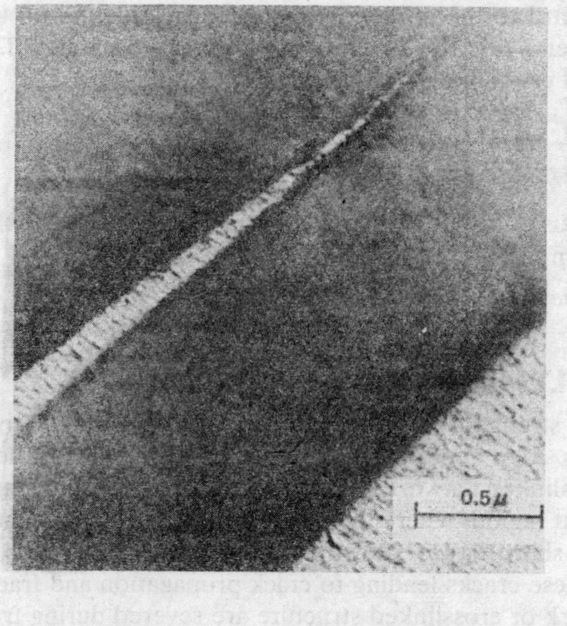

Figure 14.10 Photomicrograph of a craze in poly(phenylene oxide). (From R. P. Kambour and R. E. Robertson, "The Mechanical Properties of Plastics," in *Polymer Science, A Materials Science Handbook,* A. D. Jenkins, Editor. Reprinted with permission of Elsevier Science Publishers.)

Fibrillar bridges form between these microvoids wherein molecular chains become oriented as in Figure 14.13*d*. If the applied tensile load is sufficient, these bridges elongate and break, causing the microvoids to grow and coalesce. As the microvoids coalesce, cracks begin to form, as demonstrated in Figure 14.9*b*. A craze is different from a crack in that it can support a load across its face. Furthermore, this process of craze growth prior to cracking absorbs fracture energy and effectively increases the fracture toughness of the polymer. In glassy polymers, the cracks propagate with little craze formation resulting in low fracture toughnesses. Crazes form at highly stressed regions associated with scratches, flaws, and molecular inhomogeneities; in addition, they propagate perpendicular to the applied tensile stress, and typically are 5 μm or less thick. Figure 14.10 is a photomicrograph in which a craze is shown.

Principles of fracture mechanics developed in Section 11.5 also apply to brittle and quasi-brittle polymers; the susceptibility of these materials to fracture when a crack is present may be expressed in terms of the plane strain fracture toughness. The magnitude of K_{Ic} will depend on characteristics of the polymer (i.e., molecular weight, percent crystallinity, etc.) as well as temperature, strain rate, and the external environment. Representative values of K_{Ic} for several polymers are included in Table 11.1 and Table B.5, Appendix B.

14.6 MISCELLANEOUS MECHANICAL CHARACTERISTICS

Impact Strength

The degree of resistance of a polymeric material to impact loading may be of concern in some applications. Izod or Charpy tests are ordinarily used to assess impact strength (Section 11.6). As with metals, polymers may exhibit ductile or brittle fracture under impact loading conditions, depending on the temperature, specimen size, strain rate, and mode of loading, as discussed in the preceding section. Both semicrystalline and amorphous polymers are brittle at low temperatures, and both have relatively low impact strengths. However, they experience a ductile-to-brittle transition over a relatively narrow temperature range, similar to that shown for

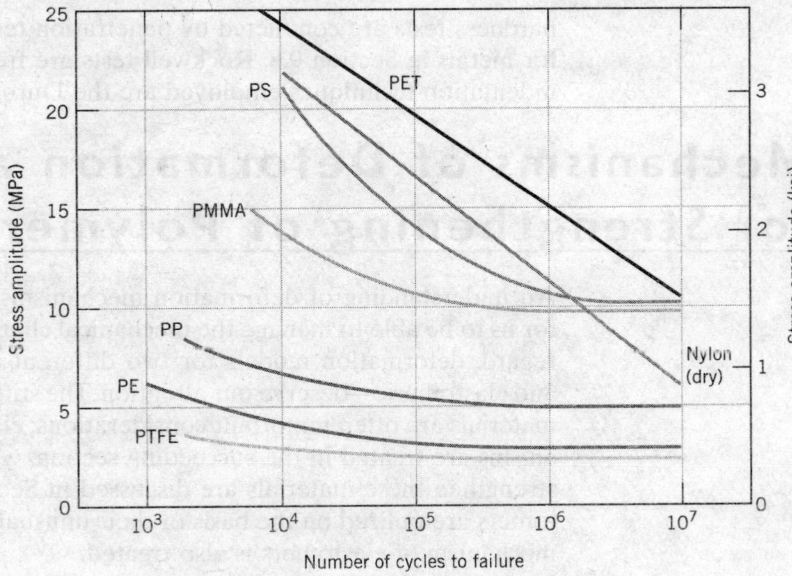

Figure 14.11 Fatigue curves (stress amplitude versus the number of cycles to failure) for poly(ethylene terephthalate) (PET), nylon, polystyrene (PS), poly(methyl methacrylate) (PMMA), polypropylene (PP), polyethylene (PE), and polytetrafluoroethylene (PTFE). The testing frequency was 30 Hz. (From M. N. Riddell, "A Guide to Better Testing of Plastics," *Plast. Eng.*, Vol. 30, No. 4, p. 78, 1974.)

a steel in Figure 11.13. Of course, impact strength undergoes a gradual decrease at still higher temperatures as the polymer begins to soften. Ordinarily, the two impact characteristics most sought after are a high impact strength at the ambient temperature and a ductile-to-brittle transition temperature that lies below room temperature.

Fatigue

Polymers may experience fatigue failure under conditions of cyclic loading. As with metals, fatigue occurs at stress levels that are low relative to the yield strength. Fatigue testing in polymers has not been nearly as extensive as with metals; however, fatigue data are plotted in the same manner for both types of material, and the resulting curves have the same general shape. Fatigue curves for several common polymers are shown in Figure 14.11, as stress versus the number of cycles to failure (on a logarithmic scale). Some polymers have a fatigue limit (a stress level at which the stress at failure becomes independent of the number of cycles); others do not appear to have such a limit. As would be expected, fatigue strengths and fatigue limits for polymeric materials are much lower than for metals.

The fatigue behavior of polymers is much more sensitive to loading frequency than for metals. Cycling polymers at high frequencies and/or relatively large stresses can cause localized heating; consequently, failure may be due to a softening of the material rather than as a result of typical fatigue processes.

Tear Strength and Hardness

Other mechanical properties that are sometimes influential in the suitability of a polymer for some particular application include tear resistance and hardness. The ability to resist tearing is an important property of some plastics, especially those used for thin films in packaging. *Tear strength,* the mechanical parameter that is measured, is the energy required to tear apart a cut specimen that has a standard geometry. The magnitude of tensile and tear strengths are related.

As with metals, hardness represents a material's resistance to scratching, penetration, marring, and so on. Polymers are softer than metals and ceramics, and most hardness tests are conducted by penetration techniques similar to those described for metals in Section 9.8. Rockwell tests are frequently used for polymers.[3] Other indentation techniques employed are the Durometer and Barcol.[4]

Mechanisms of Deformation and for Strengthening of Polymers

An understanding of deformation mechanisms of polymers is important in order for us to be able to manage the mechanical characteristics of these materials. In this regard, deformation models for two different types of polymers—semicrystalline and elastomeric—deserve our attention. The stiffness and strength of semicrystalline materials are often important considerations; elastic and plastic deformation mechanisms are treated in the succeeding section, whereas methods used to stiffen and strengthen these materials are discussed in Section 14.8. On the other hand, elastomers are utilized on the basis of their unusual elastic properties; the deformation mechanism of elastomers is also treated.

14.7 DEFORMATION OF SEMICRYSTALLINE POLYMERS

Many semicrystalline polymers in bulk form will have the spherulitic structure described in Section 14.19. By way of review, let us repeat here that each spherulite consists of numerous chain-folded ribbons, or lamellae, that radiate outward from the center. Separating these lamellae are areas of amorphous material (Figure 4.32); adjacent lamellae are connected by tie chains that pass through these amorphous regions.

Mechanism of Elastic Deformation

As with other material types, elastic deformation of polymers occurs at relatively low stress levels on the stress-strain curve (Figure 14.1). The onset of elastic deformation for semicrystalline polymers results from chain molecules in amorphous regions elongating in the direction of the applied tensile stress. This process is represented schematically for two adjacent chain-folded lamellae and the interlamellar amorphous material as Stage 1 in Figure 14.12. Continued deformation in the second stage occurs by changes in both amorphous and lamellar crystalline regions. Amorphous chains continue to align and become elongated; in addition, there is bending and stretching of the strong chain covalent bonds within the lamellar crystallites. This leads to a slight, reversible increase in the lamellar crystallite thickness as indicated by Δt in Figure 14.12*c*.

Inasmuch as semicrystalline polymers are composed of both crystalline and amorphous regions, they may, in a sense, be considered composite materials. As such, the elastic modulus may be taken as some combination of the moduli of crystalline and amorphous phases.

Mechanism of Plastic Deformation

The transition from elastic to plastic deformation occurs in Stage 3 of Figure 14.13. (Note that Figure 14.12*c* is identical to Figure 14.13*a*.) During Stage 3, adjacent

[3] ASTM Standard D 785, "Rockwell Hardness of Plastics and Electrical Insulating Materials."
[4] ASTM Standard D 2240, "Standard Test Method for Rubber Property—Durometer Hardness;" and ASTM Standard D 2583, "Standard Test Method for Indentation of Rigid Plastics by Means of a Barcol Impressor."

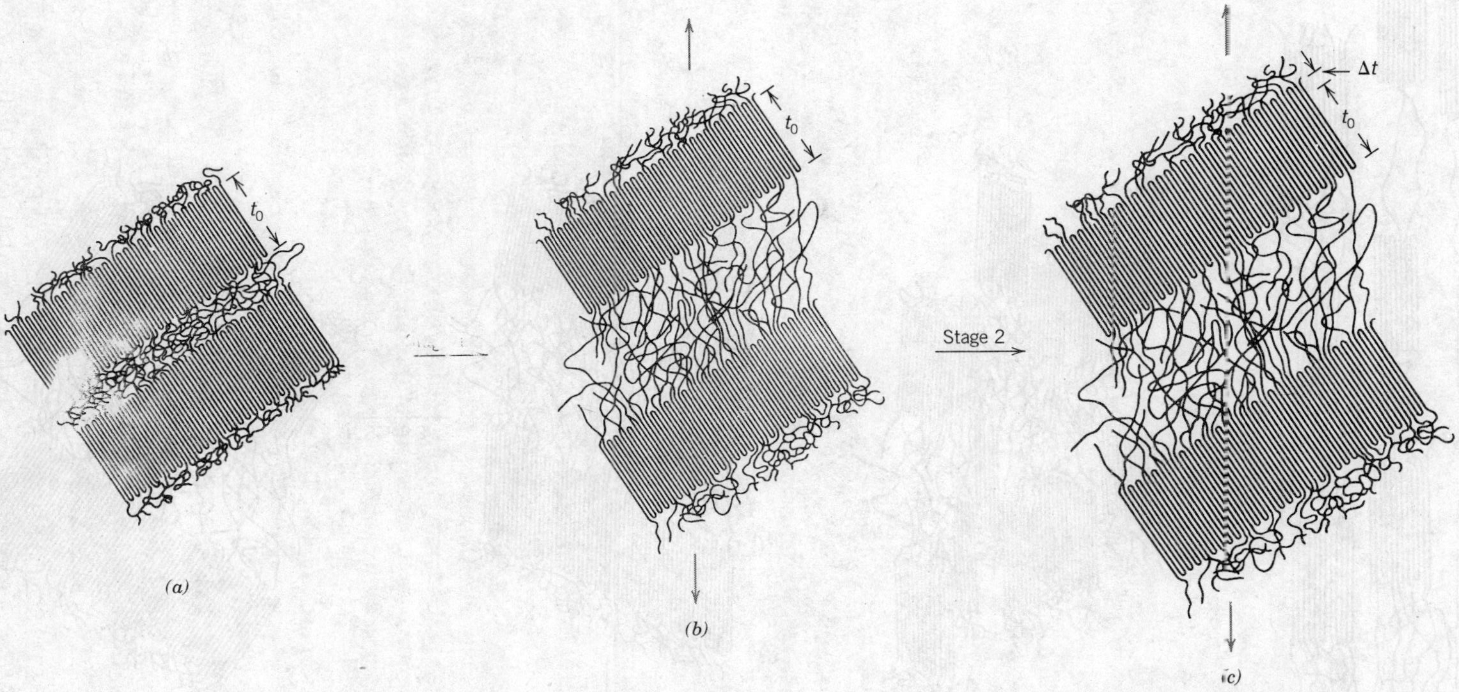

Figure 14.12 Stages in the elastic deformation of a semicrystalline polymer. (*a*) Two adjacent chain-folded lamellae and interlamellar amorphous material before deformation. (*b*) Elongation of amorphous tie chains during the first stage of deformation. (*c*) Increase in lamellar crystallite thickness (which is reversible) due to bending and stretching of chains in crystallite regions. (From Schultz, Jerold M., *Polymer Materials Science*, 1st edition, © 1974, pp. 500, 501. Adapted by permission of Pearson Education, Inc., Upper Saddle River, NJ.)

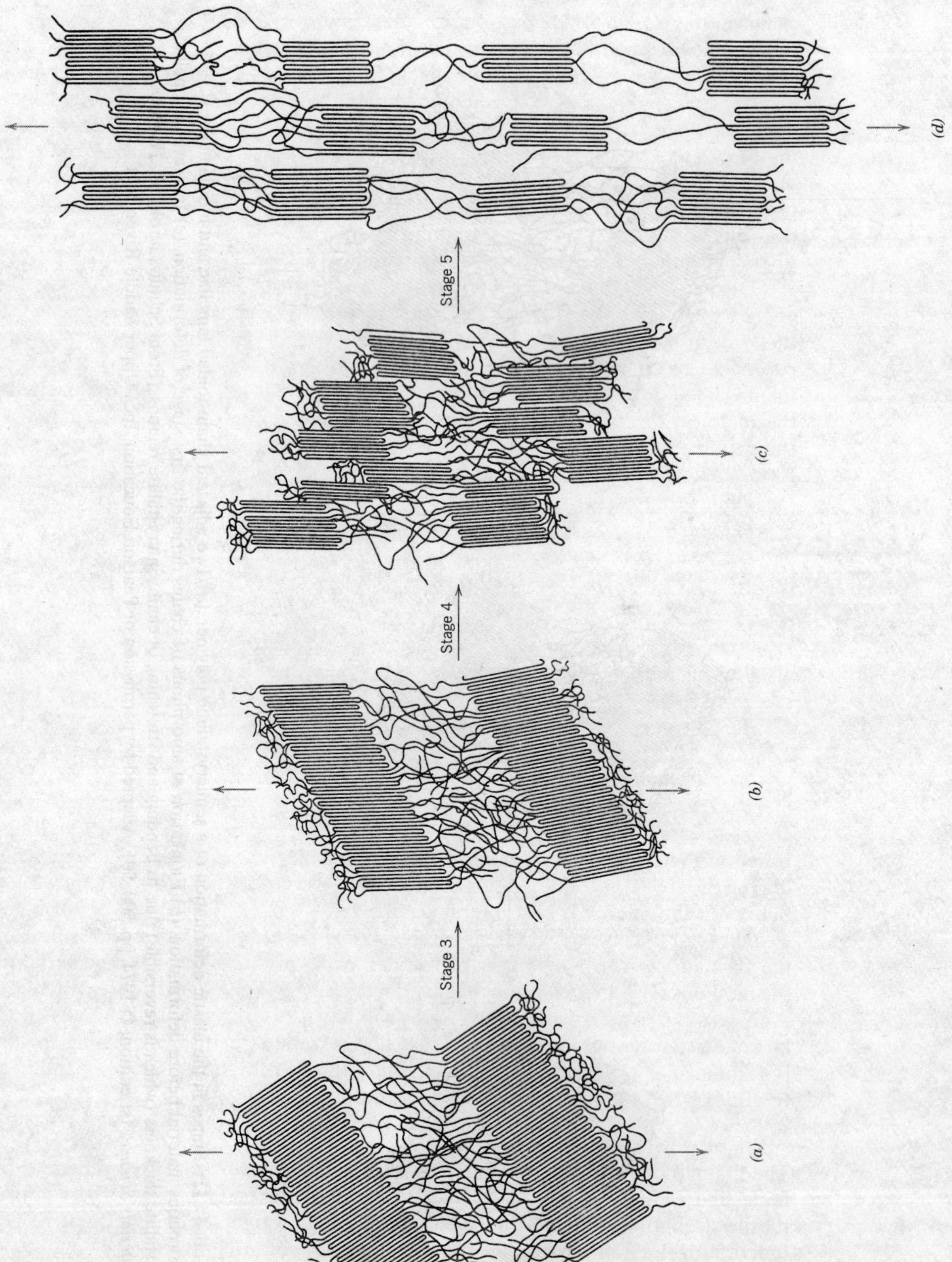

Figure 14.13 Stages in the plastic deformation of a semicrystalline polymer. (*a*) Two adjacent chain-folded lamellae and interlamellar amorphous material after elastic deformation (also shown as Figure 14.12*c*). (*b*) Tilting of lamellar chain folds. (*c*) Separation of crystalline block segments. (*d*) Orientation of block segments and tie chains with the tensile axis in the final plastic deformation stage. (From Schultz, Jerold M., *Polymer Materials Science*, 1st edition, © 1974, pp. 500, 501. Adapted by permission of Pearson Education, Inc., Upper Saddle River, NJ.)

chains in the lamellae slide past one another (Figure 14.13*b*); this results in tilting of the lamellae so that the chain folds become more aligned with the tensile axis. Any chain displacement is resisted by relatively weak secondary or van der Waals bonds.

Crystalline block segments separate from the lamellae, in Stage 4 (Figure 14.13*c*), with the segments attached to one another by tie chains. In the final stage, Stage 5, the blocks and tie chains become oriented in the direction of the tensile axis (Figure 14.13*d*). Thus, appreciable tensile deformation of semicrystalline polymers produces a highly oriented structure. This process of orientation is referred to as **drawing,** and is commonly used to improve the mechanical properties of polymer fibers and films (this is discussed in more detail in Section 14.24).

During deformation the spherulites experience shape changes for moderate levels of elongation. However, for large deformations, the spherulitic structure is virtually destroyed. Also, to a degree, the processes represented in Figure 14.13 are reversible. That is, if deformation is terminated at some arbitrary stage, and the specimen is heated to an elevated temperature near its melting point (i.e., is annealed), the material will recrystallize to again form a spherulitic structure. Furthermore, the specimen will tend to shrink back, in part, to the dimensions it had prior to deformation. The extent of this shape and structural recovery will depend on the annealing temperature and also the degree of elongation.

14.8 FACTORS THAT INFLUENCE THE MECHANICAL PROPERTIES OF SEMICRYSTALLINE POLYMERS

A number of factors influence the mechanical characteristics of polymeric materials. For example, we have already discussed the effects of temperature and strain rate on stress–strain behavior (Section 14.2, Figure 14.3). Again, increasing the temperature or diminishing the strain rate leads to a decrease in the tensile modulus, a reduction in tensile strength, and an enhancement of ductility.

In addition, several structural/processing factors have decided influences on the mechanical behavior (i.e., strength and modulus) of polymeric materials. An increase in strength results whenever any restraint is imposed on the process illustrated in Figure 14.13; for example, extensive chain entanglements or a significant degree of intermolecular bonding inhibit relative chain motions. It should be noted that even though secondary intermolecular (e.g., van der Waals) bonds are much weaker than the primary covalent ones, significant intermolecular forces result from the formation of large numbers of van der Waals interchain bonds. Furthermore, the modulus rises as both the secondary bond strength and chain alignment increase. As a result, polymers with polar groups will have stronger secondary bonds and a larger elastic modulus. We now discuss how several structural/processing factors [viz. molecular weight, degree of crystallinity, predeformation (drawing), and heat treating] affect the mechanical behavior of polymers.

Molecular Weight

The magnitude of the tensile modulus does not seem to be directly influenced by molecular weight. On the other hand, for many polymers it has been observed that tensile strength increases with increasing molecular weight. Mathematically, *TS* is a function of the number-average molecular weight according to

$$TS = TS_{\infty} - \frac{A}{\overline{M}_n} \tag{14.3}$$

where TS_∞ is the tensile strength at infinite molecular weight and A is a constant. The behavior described by this equation is explained by increased chain entanglements with rising $\overline{M}_n$.

Degree of Crystallinity

For a specific polymer, the degree of crystallinity can have a rather significant influence on the mechanical properties, since it affects the extent of the intermolecular secondary bonding. For crystalline regions in which molecular chains are closely packed in an ordered and parallel arrangement, extensive secondary bonding ordinarily exists between adjacent chain segments. This secondary bonding is much less prevalent in amorphous regions, by virtue of the chain misalignment. As a consequence, for semicrystalline polymers, tensile modulus increases significantly with degree of crystallinity. For example, for polyethylene, the modulus increases approximately an order of magnitude as the crystallinity fraction is raised from 0.3 to 0.6.

Furthermore, increasing the crystallinity of a polymer generally enhances its strength; in addition, the material tends to become more brittle. The influence of chain chemistry and structure (branching, stereoisomerism, etc.) on degree of crystallinity was discussed in Chapter 4.

The effects of both percent crystallinity and molecular weight on the physical state of polyethylene are represented in Figure 14.14.

Predeformation by Drawing

On a commercial basis, one of the most important techniques used to improve mechanical strength and tensile modulus is to permanently deform the polymer in tension. This procedure is sometimes termed *drawing,* and corresponds to the neck extension process illustrated schematically in Figure 14.4. In terms of property alterations, drawing is the polymer analog of strain hardening in metals. It is an important stiffening and strengthening technique that is employed in the production of fibers and films. During drawing the molecular chains slip past one another and become highly oriented; for semicrystalline materials the chains assume conformations similar to that represented schematically in Figure 14.13*d*.

Degrees of strengthening and stiffening will depend on the extent of deformation (or extension) of the material. Furthermore, the properties of drawn polymers are highly anisotropic. For those materials drawn in uniaxial tension, tensile modulus and strength values are significantly greater in the direction of deformation than in other directions. Tensile modulus in the direction of drawing may be enhanced by up to approximately a factor of three relative to the undrawn material. At an angle

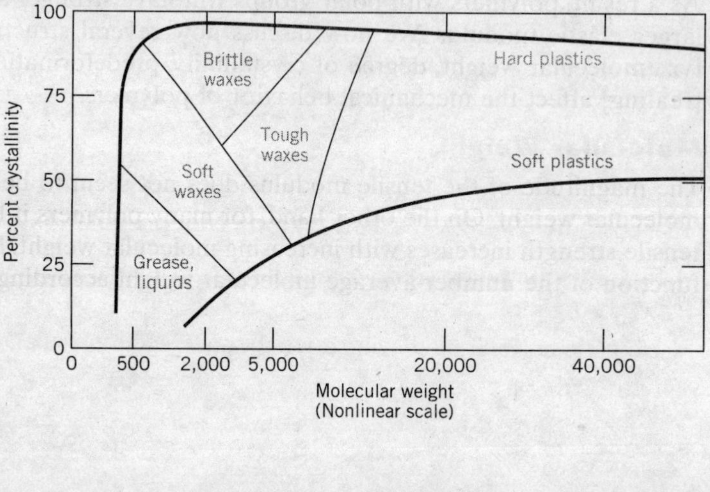

Figure 14.14 The influence of degree of crystallinity and molecular weight on the physical characteristics of polyethylene. (From R. B. Richards, "Polyethylene—Structure, Crystallinity and Properties," *J. Appl. Chem.,* **1,** 370, 1951.)

of 45° from the tensile axis the modulus is a minimum; at this orientation the modulus has a value on the order of one-fifth that of the undrawn polymer.

Tensile strength parallel to the direction of orientation may be improved by a factor of at least two to five relative to that of the unoriented material. On the other hand, perpendicular to the alignment direction, tensile strength is reduced by on the order of one-third to one-half.

For an amorphous polymer that is drawn at an elevated temperature, the oriented molecular structure is retained only when the material is quickly cooled to the ambient; this procedure gives rise to the strengthening and stiffening effects described in the previous paragraph. On the other hand, if, after stretching, the polymer is held at the temperature of drawing, molecular chains relax and assume random conformations characteristic of the predeformed state; as a consequence, drawing will have no effect on the mechanical characteristics of the material.

Heat Treating

Heat treating (or annealing) of semicrystalline polymers can lead to an increase in the percent crystallinity, and crystallite size and perfection, as well as modifications of the spherulite structure. For undrawn materials that are subjected to constant-time heat treatments, increasing the annealing temperature leads to the following: (1) an increase in tensile modulus, (2) an increase in yield strength, and (3) a reduction in ductility. Note that these annealing effects are opposite to those typically observed for metallic materials (Section 7.12)—i.e., weakening, softening, and enhanced ductility.

For some polymer fibers that have been drawn, the influence of annealing on the tensile modulus is contrary to that for undrawn materials—that is, modulus decreases with increased annealing temperature due to a loss of chain orientation and strain-induced crystallinity.

Concept Check 14.3

For the following pair of polymers, do the following: (1) state whether or not it is possible to decide if one polymer has a higher tensile modulus than the other; (2) if this is possible, note which has the higher tensile modulus and then cite the reason(s) for your choice; and (3) if it is not possible to decide, then state why not.

- Syndiotactic polystyrene having a number-average molecular weight of 400,000 g/mol
- Isotactic polystyrene having a number-average molecular weight of 650,000 g/mol.

[*The answer may be found in enclosed CD.*]

Concept Check 14.4

For the following pair of polymers, do the following: (1) state whether or not it is possible to decide if one polymer has a higher tensile strength than the other; (2) if this is possible, note which has the higher tensile strength and then cite the reason(s) for your choice; and (3) if it is not possible to decide, then state why not.

- Syndiotactic polystyrene having a number-average molecular weight of 600,000 g/mol
- Isotactic polystyrene having a number-average molecular weight of 500,000 g/mol.

[*The answer may be found in enclosed CD.*]

MATERIALS OF IMPORTANCE

Shrink-Wrap Polymer Films

An interesting application of heat treatment in polymers is the shrink-wrap used in packaging. Shrink-wrap is a polymer film, usually made of poly(vinyl chloride), polyethylene, or polyolefin (a multilayer sheet with alternating layers of polyethylene and polypropylene). It is initially plastically deformed (cold drawn) by about 20-300% to provide a prestretched (aligned) film. The film is wrapped around an object to be packaged and sealed at the edges. When heated to about 100 to 150°C, this prestretched material shrinks to recover 80-90% of its initial deformation, which gives a tightly stretched, wrinkle-free, transparent polymer film. For example, CDs and many other objects that you purchase are packaged in shrink-wrap.

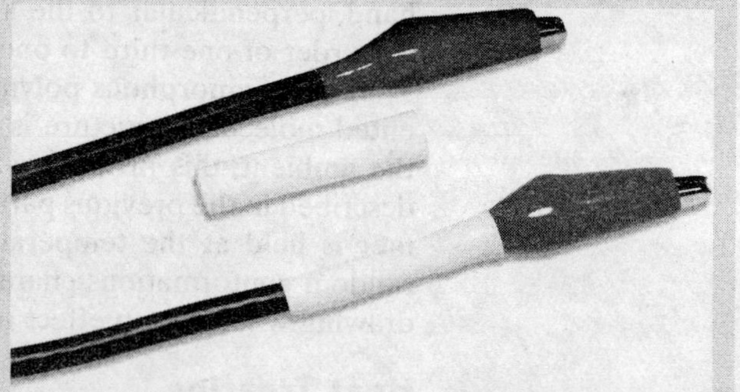

Photograph showing (from top to bottom) an electrical connection, a piece of as-received polymer shrink-tubing, and the constricted tubing around the junction—application of heat to the tubing caused its diameter to shrink. (Photography by S. Tanner.)

14.9 DEFORMATION OF ELASTOMERS

One of the fascinating properties of the elastomeric materials is their rubber-like elasticity. That is, they have the ability to be deformed to quite large deformations, and then elastically spring back to their original form. This results from crosslinks in the polymer that provide a force to restore the chains to their undeformed conformations. Elastomeric behavior was probably first observed in natural rubber; however, the past few years have brought about the synthesis of a large number of elastomers with a wide variety of properties. Typical stress–strain characteristics of elastomeric materials are displayed in Figure 14.1, curve *C*. Their moduli of elasticity are quite small and, furthermore, vary with strain since the stress–strain curve is nonlinear.

In an unstressed state, an elastomer will be amorphous and composed of crosslinked molecular chains that are highly twisted, kinked, and coiled. Elastic deformation, upon application of a tensile load, is simply the partial uncoiling, untwisting, and straightening, and the resultant elongation of the chains in the stress direction, a phenomenon represented in Figure 14.15. Upon release of the stress,

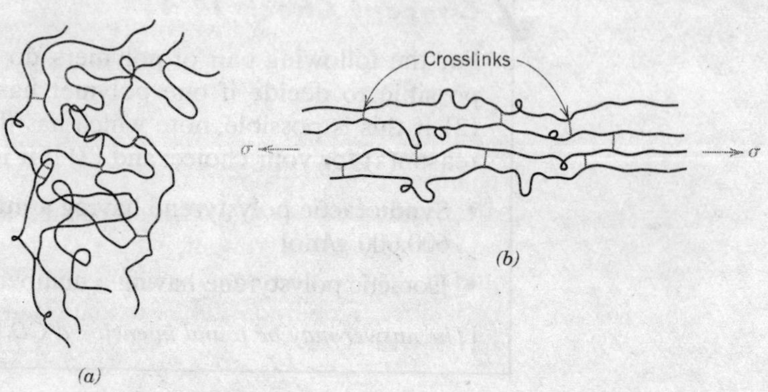

Figure 14.15 Schematic representation of crosslinked polymer chain molecules (*a*) in an unstressed state and (*b*) during elastic deformation in response to an applied tensile stress. (Adapted from Z. D. Jastrzebski, *The Nature and Properties of Engineering Materials*, 3rd edition. Copyright © 1987 by John Wiley & Sons, New York. Reprinted by permission of John Wiley & Sons, Inc.)

the chains spring back to their prestressed conformations, and the macroscopic piece returns to its original shape.

Part of the driving force for elastic deformation is a thermodynamic parameter called *entropy,* which is a measure of the degree of disorder within a system; entropy increases with increasing disorder. As an elastomer is stretched and the chains straighten and become more aligned, the system becomes more ordered. From this state, the entropy increases if the chains return to their original kinked and coiled contours. Two intriguing phenomena result from this entropic effect. First, when stretched, an elastomer experiences a rise in temperature; second, the modulus of elasticity increases with increasing temperature, which is opposite to the behavior found in other materials (see Figure 9.14).

Several criteria must be met for a polymer to be elastomeric: (1) It must not easily crystallize; elastomeric materials are amorphous, having molecular chains that are naturally coiled and kinked in the unstressed state. (2) Chain bond rotations must be relatively free for the coiled chains to readily respond to an applied force. (3) For elastomers to experience relatively large elastic deformations, the onset of plastic deformation must be delayed. Restricting the motions of chains past one another by crosslinking accomplishes this objective. The crosslinks act as anchor points between the chains and prevent chain slippage from occurring; the role of crosslinks in the deformation process is illustrated in Figure 14.15. Crosslinking in many elastomers is carried out in a process called vulcanization, to be discussed below. (4) Finally, the elastomer must be above its glass transition temperature (Section 14.13). The lowest temperature at which rubber-like behavior persists for many of the common elastomers is between −50 and −90°C (−60 and −130°F). Below its glass transition temperature, an elastomer becomes brittle such that its stress–strain behavior resembles curve *A* in Figure 14.1.

Vulcanization

The crosslinking process in elastomers is called **vulcanization,** which is achieved by a nonreversible chemical reaction, ordinarily carried out at an elevated temperature. In most vulcanizing reactions, sulfur compounds are added to the heated elastomer; chains of sulfur atoms bond with adjacent polymer backbone chains and crosslink them, which is accomplished according to the following reaction:

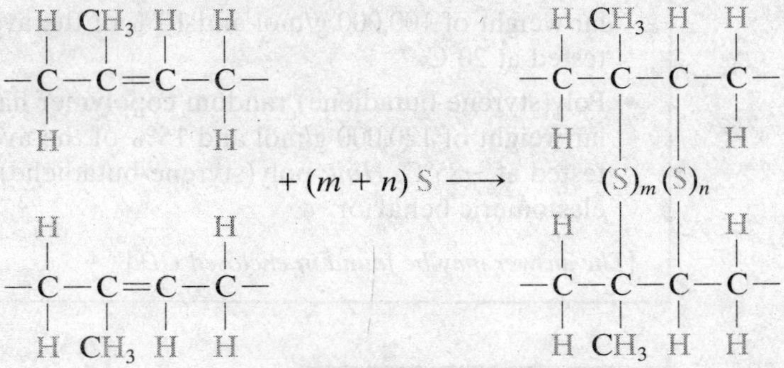

(14.4)

in which the two crosslinks shown consist of *m* and *n* sulfur atoms. Crosslink main chain sites are carbon atoms that were doubly bonded before vulcanization but, after vulcanization, have become singly bonded.

Unvulcanized rubber, which contains very few crosslinks, is soft and tacky and has poor resistance to abrasion. Modulus of elasticity, tensile strength, and resistance to degradation by oxidation are all enhanced by vulcanization. The magnitude of the modulus of elasticity is directly proportional to the density of the

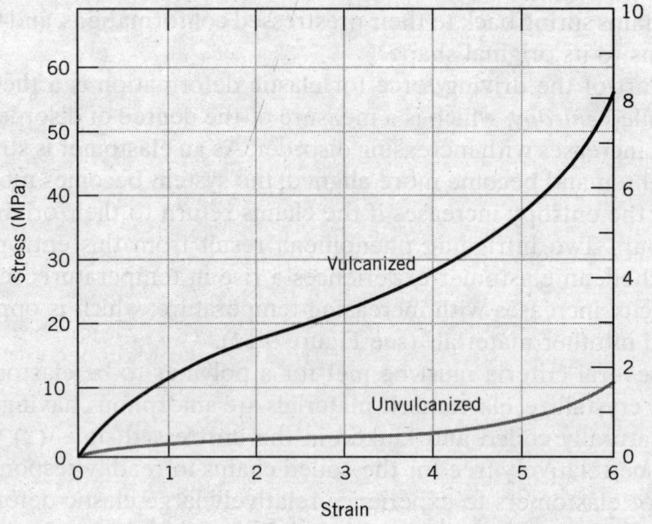

Figure 14.16 Stress–strain curves to 600% elongation for unvulcanized and vulcanized natural rubber.

crosslinks. Stress–strain curves for vulcanized and unvulcanized natural rubber are presented in Figure 14.16. To produce a rubber that is capable of large extensions without rupture of the primary chain bonds, there must be relatively few crosslinks, and these must be widely separated. Useful rubbers result when about 1 to 5 parts (by weight) of sulfur are added to 100 parts of rubber. This corresponds to about one crosslink for every 10 to 20 repeat units. Increasing the sulfur content further hardens the rubber and also reduces its extensibility. Also, since they are crosslinked, elastomeric materials are thermosetting in nature.

Concept Check 14.5

For the following pair of polymers, plot and label schematic stress–strain curves on the same graph.

- Poly(styrene-butadiene) random copolymer having a number-average molecular weight of 100,000 g/mol and 10% of the available sites crosslinked and tested at 20°C
- Poly(styrene-butadiene) random copolymer having a number-average molecular weight of 120,000 g/mol and 15% of the available sites crosslinked and tested at −85°C. *Hint:* poly(styrene-butadiene) copolymers may exhibit elastomeric behavior.

[*The answer may be found in enclosed CD.*]

Concept Check 14.6

In terms of molecular structure, explain why phenol-formaldehyde (Bakelite) will not be an elastomer. (The molecular structure for phenol-formaldehyde is presented in Table 13.3.)

[*The answer may be found in enclosed CD.*]

Crystallization, Melting, and Glass Transition Phenomena in Polymers

Three phenomena that are important with respect to the design and processing of polymeric materials are crystallization, melting, and the glass transition. Crystallization is the process by which, upon cooling, an ordered (i.e., crystalline) solid phase is produced from a liquid melt having a highly random molecular structure. The melting transformation is the reverse process that occurs when a polymer is heated. The glass-transition phenomenon occurs with amorphous or noncrystallizable polymers that, when cooled from a liquid melt, become rigid solids yet retain the disordered molecular structure that is characteristic of the liquid state. Of course, alterations of physical and mechanical properties attend crystallization, melting, and the glass transition. Furthermore, for semicrystalline polymers, crystalline regions will experience melting (and crystallization), while noncrystalline areas pass through the glass transition.

14.10 CRYSTALLIZATION

An understanding of the mechanism and kinetics of polymer crystallization is important because the degree of crystallinity influences the mechanical and thermal properties of these materials. The crystallization of a molten polymer occurs by nucleation and growth processes, topics discussed in the context of phase transformations for metals in Section 10.3. For polymers, upon cooling through the melting temperature, nuclei form wherein small regions of the tangled and random molecules become ordered and aligned in the manner of chain-folded layers, Figure 13.12. At temperatures in excess of the melting temperature, these nuclei are unstable due to the thermal atomic vibrations that tend to disrupt the ordered molecular arrangements. Subsequent to nucleation and during the crystallization growth stage, nuclei grow by the continued ordering and alignment of additional molecular chain segments; that is, the chain-folded layers remain the same thickness, but increase in lateral dimensions, or for spherulitic structures (Figure 13.13) there is an increase in spherulite radius.

The time dependence of crystallization is the same as for many solid-state transformations—Figure 8.10; that is, a sigmoidal-shaped curve results when fraction transformation (i.e., fraction crystallized) is plotted versus the logarithm of time (at constant temperature). Such a plot is presented in Figure 14.17 for the crystallization of polypropylene at three temperatures. Mathematically, fraction crystallized y is a function of time t according to the Avrami equation, Equation 8.17, as

$$y = 1 - \exp(-kt^n) \tag{8.17}$$

where k and n are time-independent constants, whose values depend on the crystallizing system. Normally, the extent of crystallization is measured by specimen volume changes since there will be a difference in volume for liquid and crystallized phases. Rate of crystallization may be specified in the same manner as for the transformations discussed in Section 8.3, and according to Equation 8.18; that is, rate is equal to the reciprocal of time required for crystallization to proceed to 50% completion. This rate is dependent on crystallization temperature (Figure 14.17) and also on the molecular weight of the polymer; rate decreases with increasing molecular weight.

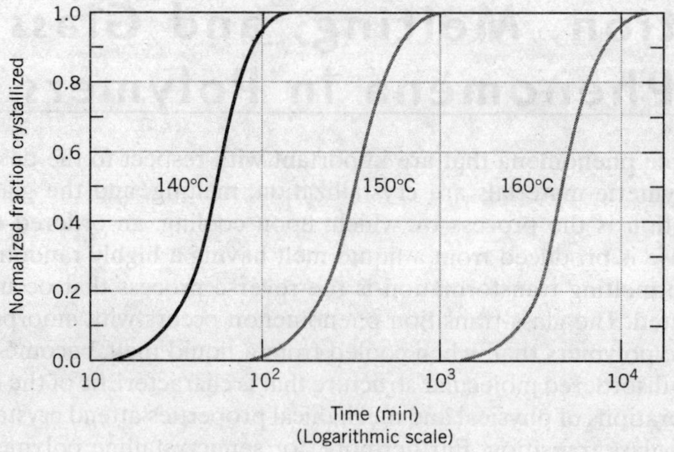

Figure 14.17 Plot of normalized fraction crystallized versus the logarithm of time for polypropylene at constant temperatures of 140°C, 150°C, and 160°C. (Adapted from P. Parrini and G. Corrieri, *Makromol. Chem.*, **62**, 83, 1963. Reprinted by permission of Hüthig & Wepf Publishers, Zug, Switzerland.)

For polypropylene (as well as any polymer), the attainment of 100% crystallinity is not possible. Therefore, in Figure 14.17, the vertical axis is scaled as "normalized fraction crystallized." A value of 1.0 for this parameter corresponds to the highest level of crystallization that is achieved during the tests, which, in reality, is less than complete crystallization.

14.11 MELTING

The melting of a polymer crystal corresponds to the transformation of a solid material, having an ordered structure of aligned molecular chains, to a viscous liquid in which the structure is highly random. This phenomenon occurs, upon heating, at the **melting temperature,** T_m. There are several features distinctive to the melting of polymers that are not normally observed with metals and ceramics; these are consequences of the polymer molecular structures and lamellar crystalline morphology. First of all, melting of polymers takes place over a range of temperatures; this phenomenon is discussed in more detail below. In addition, the melting behavior depends on the history of the specimen, in particular the temperature at which it crystallized. The thickness of chain-folded lamellae will depend on crystallization temperature; the thicker the lamellae, the higher the melting temperature. Impurities in the polymer and imperfections in the crystals also decrease the melting temperature. Finally, the apparent melting behavior is a function of the rate of heating; increasing this rate results in an elevation of the melting temperature.

As a previous section notes, polymeric materials are responsive to heat treatments that produce structural and property alterations. An increase in lamellar thickness may be induced by annealing just below the melting temperature. Annealing also raises the melting temperature by decreasing the vacancies and other imperfections in polymer crystals and increasing crystallite thickness.

14.12 THE GLASS TRANSITION

The glass transition occurs in amorphous (or glassy) and semicrystalline polymers, and is due to a reduction in motion of large segments of molecular chains with decreasing temperature. Upon cooling, the glass transition corresponds to the gradual transformation from a liquid to a rubbery material, and finally, to a rigid solid.

The temperature at which the polymer experiences the transition from rubbery to rigid states is termed the **glass transition temperature,** T_g. Of course, this sequence of events occurs in the reverse order when a rigid glass at a temperature below T_g is heated. In addition, abrupt changes in other physical properties accompany this glass transition: for example, stiffness (Figure 14.7), heat capacity, and coefficient of thermal expansion.

14.13 MELTING AND GLASS TRANSITION TEMPERATURES

Melting and glass transition temperatures are important parameters relative to in-service applications of polymers. They define, respectively, the upper and lower temperature limits for numerous applications, especially for semicrystalline polymers. The glass transition temperature may also define the upper use temperature for glassy amorphous materials. Furthermore, T_m and T_g also influence the fabrication and processing procedures for polymers and polymer-matrix composites. These issues are discussed in succeeding sections of this chapter.

The temperatures at which melting and/or the glass transition occur for a polymer are determined in the same manner as for ceramic materials—from a plot of specific volume (the reciprocal of density) versus temperature. Figure 14.18 is such a plot, where curves A and C, for amorphous and crystalline polymers, respectively, have the same configurations as their ceramic counterparts (Figure 12.19).[5] For the crystalline material, there is a discontinuous change in specific volume at the melting temperature T_m. The curve for the totally amorphous material is continuous but experiences a slight decrease in slope at the glass transition temperature, T_g. The behavior is intermediate between these extremes for a semicrystalline polymer (curve B) in that both melting and glass transition phenomena are observed; T_m and T_g are properties of the respective crystalline and amorphous phases in this

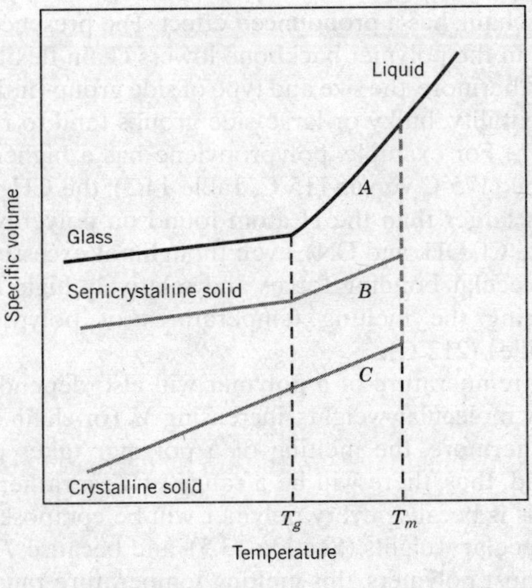

Figure 14.18 Specific volume versus temperature, upon cooling from the liquid melt, for totally amorphous (curve A), semicrystalline (curve B), and crystalline (curve C) polymers.

[5] It should be noted that no engineering polymer is 100% crystalline; curve C is included in Figure 14.18 to illustrate the extreme behavior that would be displayed by a totally crystalline material.

Table 14.2 Melting and Glass Transition Temperatures for Some of the More Common Polymeric Materials

Material	*Glass Transition Temperature (°C)*	*Melting Temperature (°C)*
Polyethylene (low density)	−110	115
Polytetrafluoroethylene	−97	327
Polyethylene (high density)	−90	137
Polypropylene	−18	175
Nylon 6,6	57	265
Polyester (PET)	69	265
Poly(vinyl chloride)	87	212
Polystyrene	100	240
Polycarbonate	150	265

semicrystalline material. As discussed above, the behaviors represented in Figure 14.18 will depend on the rate of cooling or heating. Representative melting and glass transition temperatures of a number of polymers are contained in Table 14.2 and Appendix E.

14.14 FACTORS THAT INFLUENCE MELTING AND GLASS TRANSITION TEMPERATURES

Melting Temperature

During melting of a polymer there will be a rearrangement of the molecules in the transformation from ordered to disordered molecular states. Molecular chemistry and structure will influence the ability of the polymer chain molecules to make these rearrangements and, therefore, will also affect the melting temperature.

Chain stiffness, which is controlled by the ease of rotation about the chemical bonds along the chain, has a pronounced effect. The presence of double bonds and aromatic groups in the polymer backbone lowers chain flexibility and causes an increase in T_m. Furthermore, the size and type of side groups influence chain rotational freedom and flexibility; bulky or large side groups tend to restrict molecular rotation and raise T_m. For example, polypropylene has a higher melting temperature than polyethylene (175°C versus 115°C, Table 14.2); the CH_3 methyl side group for polypropylene is larger than the H atom found on polyethylene. The presence of polar groups (viz. Cl, OH, and CN), even though not excessively large, leads to significant intermolecular bonding forces and relatively high T_ms. This may be verified by comparing the melting temperatures of polypropylene (175°C) and poly(vinyl chloride) (212°C).

The melting temperature of a polymer will also depend on molecular weight. At relatively low molecular weights, increasing $\overline{M}$ (or chain length) raises T_m (Figure 14.19). Furthermore, the melting of a polymer takes place over a range of temperatures, and, thus, there will be a range of T_ms, rather than a single melting temperature. This is because every polymer will be composed of molecules having a variety of molecular weights (Section 13.5), and because T_m depends on molecular weight. For most polymers, this melting temperature range will normally be on the order of several degrees Celsius. Those melting temperatures cited in Table 14.2 and Appendix E are near the high ends of these ranges.

Degree of branching will also affect the melting temperature of a polymer. The introduction of side branches introduces defects into the crystalline material and

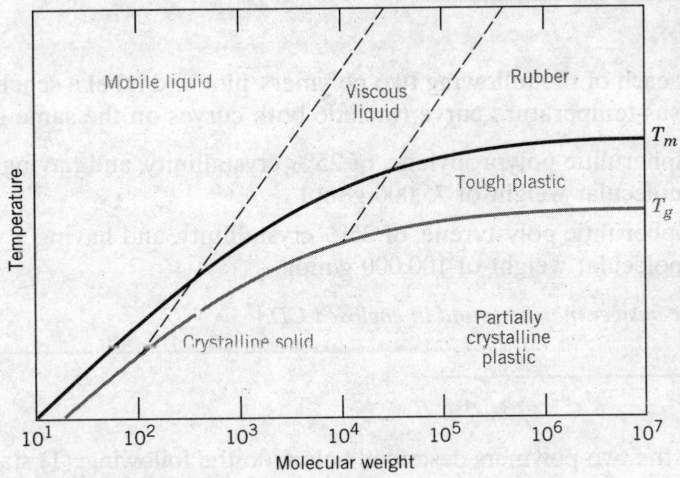

Figure 14.19 Dependence of polymer properties as well as melting and glass transition temperatures on molecular weight. (From F. W. Billmeyer, Jr., *Textbook of Polymer Science,* 3rd edition. Copyright © 1984 by John Wiley & Sons, New York. Reprinted by permission of John Wiley & Sons, Inc.)

lowers the melting temperature. High-density polyethylene, being a predominately linear polymer, has a higher melting temperature (137°C, Table 14.2) than low-density polyethylene (115°C) which has some branching.

Glass Transition Temperature

Upon heating through the glass transition temperature, the amorphous solid polymer transforms from a rigid to a rubbery state. Correspondingly, the molecules that are virtually frozen in position below T_g begin to experience rotational and translational motions above T_g. Thus, the value of the glass transition temperature will depend on molecular characteristics that affect chain stiffness; most of these factors and their influences are the same as for the melting temperature, as discussed above. Again, chain flexibility is diminished and T_g is increased by the presence of the following:

1. Bulky side groups; from Table 14.2, the respective values for polypropylene and polystyrene are −18°C and 100°C.
2. Polar groups; for example, the T_g values for poly(vinyl chloride) and polypropylene are 87°C and −18°C, respectively.
3. Double bonds and aromatic groups in the backbone, which tend to stiffen the polymer chain.

Increasing the molecular weight also tends to raise the glass transition temperature, as noted in Figure 14.19. A small amount of branching will tend to lower T_g; on the other hand, a high density of branches reduces chain mobility, and elevates the glass transition temperature. Some amorphous polymers are crosslinked, which has been observed to elevate T_g; crosslinks restrict molecular motion. With a high density of crosslinks, molecular motion is virtually disallowed; long-range molecular motion is prevented, to the degree that these polymers do not experience a glass transition or its accompanying softening.

From the preceding discussion it is evident that essentially the same molecular characteristics raise and lower both melting and glass transition temperatures. Normally the value of T_g lies somewhere between 0.5 and $0.8T_m$ (in Kelvin). Consequently, for a homopolymer, it is not possible to independently vary both T_m and T_g. A greater degree of control over these two parameters is possible by the synthesis and utilization of copolymeric materials.

Concept Check 14.7

For each of the following two polymers, plot and label a schematic specific volume-versus-temperature curve (include both curves on the same graph):

- Spherulitic polypropylene, of 25% crystallinity, and having a weight-average molecular weight of 75,000 g/mol
- Spherulitic polystyrene, of 25% crystallinity, and having a weight-average molecular weight of 100,000 g/mol.

[*The answer may be found in enclosed CD.*]

Concept Check 14.8

For the two polymers described below, do the following: (1) state whether or not it is possible to determine whether one polymer has a higher melting temperature than the other; (2) if it is possible, note which has the higher melting temperature and then cite reason(s) for your choice; and (3) if it is not possible to decide, then state why not.

- Isotactic polystyrene that has a density of 1.12 g/cm^3 and a weight-average molecular weight of 150,000 g/mol
- Syndiotactic polystyrene that has a density of 1.10 g/cm^3 and a weight-average molecular weight of 125,000 g/mol.

[*The answer may be found in enclosed CD.*]

Polymer Types

There are many different polymeric materials that are familiar to us and find a wide variety of applications; in fact, one way of classifying them is according to their end-use. Within this scheme the various polymer types include plastics, elastomers (or rubbers), fibers, coatings, adhesives, foams, and films. Depending on its properties, a particular polymer may be used in two or more of these application categories. For example, a plastic, if crosslinked and utilized above its glass transition temperature, may make a satisfactory elastomer. Or a fiber material may be used as a plastic if it is not drawn into filaments. This portion of the chapter includes a brief discussion of each of these types of polymer.

14.15 PLASTICS

Possibly the largest number of different polymeric materials come under the plastic classification. **Plastics** are materials that have some structural rigidity under load, and are used in general-purpose applications. Polyethylene, polypropylene, poly(vinyl chloride), polystyrene, and the fluorocarbons, epoxies, phenolics, and polyesters may all be classified as plastics. They have a wide variety of combinations of properties. Some plastics are very rigid and brittle (Figure 14.1, curve *A*). Others are flexible, exhibiting both elastic and plastic deformations when stressed, and sometimes experiencing considerable deformation before fracture (Figure 14.1, curve *B*).

Polymers falling within this classification may have any degree of crystallinity, and all molecular structures and configurations (linear, branched, isotactic, etc.) are possible. Plastic materials may be either thermoplastic or thermosetting; in fact, this is the manner in which they are usually subclassified. However, to be considered plastics, linear or branched polymers must be used below their glass transition temperatures (if amorphous) or below their melting temperatures (if semicrystalline), or must be crosslinked enough to maintain their shape. The trade names, characteristics, and typical applications for a number of plastics are given in Table 14.3.

Several plastics exhibit especially outstanding properties. For applications in which optical transparency is critical, polystyrene and poly(methyl methacrylate) are especially well suited; however, it is imperative that the material be highly amorphous or, if semicrystalline, have very small crystallites. The fluorocarbons have a low coefficient of friction and are extremely resistant to attack by a host of chemicals, even at relatively high temperatures. They are utilized as coatings on nonstick cookware, in bearings and bushings, and for high-temperature electronic components.

Table 14.3 Trade Names, Characteristics, and Typical Applications for a Number of Plastic Materials

Material Type	*Trade Names*	*Major Application Characteristics*	*Typical Applications*
		Thermoplastics	
Acrylonitrile-butadiene-styrene (ABS)	Abson Cycolac Kralastic Lustran Novodur Tybrene	Outstanding strength and toughness, resistant to heat distortion; good electrical properties; flammable and soluble in some organic solvents	Refrigerator linings, lawn and garden equipment, toys, highway safety devices
Acrylics [poly(methyl methacrylate)]	Acrylite Diakon Lucite Plexiglas	Outstanding light transmission and resistance to weathering; only fair mechanical properties	Lenses, transparent aircraft enclosures, drafting equipment, outdoor signs
Fluorocarbons (PTFE or TFE)	Teflon Fluon Halar Hostaflon TF Neoflon	Chemically inert in almost all environments, excellent electrical properties; low coefficient of friction; may be used to 260°C (500°F); relatively weak and poor cold-flow properties	Anticorrosive seals, chemical pipes and valves, bearings, antiadhesive coatings, high-temperature electronic parts
Polyamides (nylons)	Nylon Baylon Durethan Herox Nomex Ultramid Zytel	Good mechanical strength, abrasion resistance, and toughness; low coefficient of friction; absorbs water and some other liquids	Bearings, gears, cams, bushings, handles, and jacketing for wires and cables
Polycarbonates	Calibre Iupilon Lexan Makrolon Merlon	Dimensionally stable; low water absorption; transparent; very good impact resistance and ductility; chemical resistance not outstanding	Safety helmets, lenses, light globes, base for photographic film
Polyethylene	Alathon Alkathene Fortiflex Hi-fax Petrothene Rigidex Rotothene Zendel	Chemically resistant and electrically insulating; tough and relatively low coefficient of friction; low strength and poor resistance to weathering	Flexible bottles, toys, tumblers, battery parts, ice trays, film wrapping materials

Table 14.3 (*Continued*)

Material Type	*Trade Names*	*Major Application Characteristics*	*Typical Applications*
Polypropylene	Herculon Meraklon Moplen Poly-pro Pro-fax Propak Propathene	Resistant to heat distortion; excellent electrical properties and fatigue strength; chemically inert; relatively inexpensive; poor resistance to UV light	Sterilizable bottles, packaging film, TV cabinets, luggage
Polystyrene	Carinex Dylene Hostyren Lustrex Styron Vestyron	Excellent electrical properties and optical clarity; good thermal and dimensional stability; relatively inexpensive	Wall tile, battery cases, toys, indoor lighting panels, appliance housings
Vinyls	Darvic Exon Geon Pliovic Saran Tygon Vista	Good low-cost, general-purpose materials; ordinarily rigid, but may be made flexible with plasticizers; often copolymerized; susceptible to heat distortion	Floor coverings, pipe, electrical wire insulation, garden hose, phonograph records
Polyester (PET or PETE)	Celanar Dacron Eastapak Hylar Melinex Mylar Petra	One of the toughest of plastic films; excellent fatigue and tear strength, and resistance to humidity, acids, greases, oils, and solvents	Magnetic recording tapes, clothing, automotive tire cords, beverage containers
		Thermosetting Polymers	
Epoxies	Araldite Epikote Epon Epi-rez Lekutherm Lytex	Excellent combination of mechanical properties and corrosion resistance; dimensionally stable; good adhesion; relatively inexpensive; good electrical properties	Electrical moldings, sinks, adhesives, protective coatings, used with fiberglass laminates
Phenolics	Bakelite Amberol Arofene Durite Resinox	Excellent thermal stability to over 150°C (300°F); may be compounded with a large number of resins, fillers, etc.; inexpensive	Motor housings, telephones, auto distributors, electrical fixtures
Polyesters	Aropol Baygal Derakane Laminac Selectron	Excellent electrical properties and low cost; can be formulated for room- or high-temperature use; often fiber reinforced	Helmets, fiberglass boats, auto body components, chairs, fans

Source: Adapted from C. A. Harper (Editor), *Handbook of Plastics and Elastomers.* Copyright © 1975 by McGraw-Hill Book Company. Reproduced with permission.

MATERIAL OF IMPORTANCE

Phenolic Billiard Balls

Up until about 1912 virtually all billiard balls were made of ivory that came only from the tusks of elephants. For a ball to roll true, it needed to be fashioned from high-quality ivory that came from the center of flaw-free tusks—on the order of one tusk in fifty had the requisite consistency of density. At this time, ivory was becoming scarce and expensive as more and more elephants were being killed (and billiards was becoming popular). Also, there was then (and still is) a serious concern about reductions in elephant populations (and their ultimate extinction) due to ivory hunters, and some countries had imposed (and still impose) severe restrictions on the importation of ivory and ivory products.

Consequently, substitutes for ivory were sought for billiard balls. For example, one early alternative was a pressed mixture of wood pulp and bone dust; this material proved quite unsatisfactory. The most suitable replacement (which is still being used for billiard balls today) is one of the first man-made polymers—phenol-formaldehyde, sometimes also called "phenolic".

The invention of this material is one of the important and interesting events in the annals of man-made polymers. The discoverer of the process for synthesizing phenol-formaldehyde was Leo Baekeland. As a young and very bright Ph.D. chemist, he immigrated from Belgium to the United States in the early 1900s. Shortly after his arrival, he began research into creating a synthetic shellac, to replace the natural material, which was relatively expensive to manufacture; shellac was (and is still) used as a lacquer, a wood preservative, and as an electrical insulator in the then-emerging electrical industry. His efforts eventually led to the discovery that a suitable substitute could be synthesized by reacting phenol [or carbolic acid (C_6H_5OH), a white crystalline material] with formaldehyde (HCHO, a colorless and poisonous gas) under controlled conditions of heat and pressure. The product of this reaction was a liquid that subsequently hardened into a transparent and amber-colored solid. Baekeland named his new material "Bakelite"; today we use the generic names "phenol-formaldehyde" or just "phenolic". Shortly after its discovery, Bakelite was found to be the ideal synthetic material for billiard balls (per the chapter-opening photograph for this chapter).

Phenol-formaldehyde is a thermosetting polymer, and has a number of desirable properties: for a polymer it is very heat resistant and hard, is less brittle than many of the ceramic materials, is very stable and unreactive with most common solutions and solvents, and doesn't easily chip, fade, or discolor. Furthermore, it is a relatively inexpensive material, and modern phenolics can be produced having a large variety of colors. The elastic characteristics of this polymer are very similar to those of ivory, and when phenolic billiard balls collide, they make the same clicking sound as ivory balls. Other uses of this important polymeric material are found in Table 14.3.

14.16 ELASTOMERS

The characteristics of and deformation mechanism for elastomers were treated previously (Section 14.9). The present discussion, therefore, focuses on the types of elastomeric materials.

Table 14.4 lists properties and applications of common elastomers; these properties are typical and, of course, depend on the degree of vulcanization and on whether any reinforcement is used. Natural rubber is still utilized to a large degree because it has an outstanding combination of desirable properties. However, the most important synthetic elastomer is SBR, which is used predominantly in automobile tires, reinforced with carbon black. NBR, which is highly resistant to degradation and swelling, is another common synthetic elastomer.

Table 14.4 Tabulation of Important Characteristics and Typical Applications for Five Commercial Elastomers

Chemical Type	*Trade (Common) Names*	*Elongation (%)*	*Useful Temperature Range (°C)*	*Major Application Characteristics*	*Typical Applications*
Natural polyisoprene	Natural rubber (NR)	500–760	−60 to 120	Excellent physical properties; good resistance to cutting, gouging, and abrasion; low heat, ozone, and oil resistance; good electrical properties	Pneumatic tires and tubes; heels and soles; gaskets
Styrene-butadiene copolymer	GRS, Buna S (SBR)	450–500	−60 to 120	Good physical properties; excellent abrasion resistance; not oil, ozone, or weather resistant; electrical properties good, but not outstanding	Same as natural rubber
Acrylonitrile-butadiene copolymer	Buna A, Nitrile (NBR)	400–600	−50 to 150	Excellent resistance to vegetable, animal, and petroleum oils; poor low-temperature properties; electrical properties not outstanding	Gasoline, chemical, and oil hose; seals and O-rings; heels and soles
Chloroprene	Neoprene (CR)	100–800	−50 to 105	Excellent ozone, heat, and weathering resistance; good oil resistance; excellent flame resistance; not as good in electrical applications as natural rubber	Wire and cable; chem. tank linings; belts, hoses, seals, and gaskets
Polysiloxane	Silicone (VMQ)	100–800	−115 to 315	Excellent resistance to high and low temperatures; low strength; excellent electrical properties	High- and low-temperature insulation; seals, diaphragms; tubing for food and medical uses

Sources: Adapted from C. A. Harper (Editor), *Handbook of Plastics and Elastomers.* Copyright © 1975 by McGraw-Hill Book Company, reproduced with permission; and Materials Engineering's *Materials Selector,* copyright Penton/IPC.

For many applications (e.g., automobile tires), the mechanical properties of even vulcanized rubbers are not satisfactory in terms of tensile strength, abrasion and tear resistance, and stiffness. These characteristics may be further improved by additives such as carbon black (Section 15.2).

Finally, some mention should be made of the silicone rubbers. For these materials, the backbone chain is made of alternating silicon and oxygen atoms:

$$\left(\begin{array}{c} R \\ | \\ \mathrm{Si} - \mathrm{O} \\ | \\ R \end{array}\right)_n$$

where R and R′ represent side-bonded atoms such as hydrogen or groups of atoms such as CH_3. For example, polydimethylsiloxane has the repeat unit

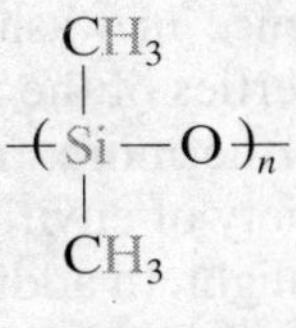

Of course, as elastomers, these materials are crosslinked.

The silicone elastomers possess a high degree of flexibility at low temperatures [to −90°C (−130°F)] and yet are stable to temperatures as high as 250°C (480°F). In addition, they are resistant to weathering and lubricating oils, which makes them particularly desirable for applications in automobile engine compartments. Biocompatibility is another of their assets, and, therefore, they are often employed in medical applications such as blood tubing. A further attractive characteristic is that some silicone rubbers vulcanize at room temperature (RTV rubbers).

Concept Check 14.9

During the winter months, the temperature in some parts of Alaska may go as low as −55°C (−65°F). Of the elastomers natural isoprene, styrene-butadiene, acrylonitrile-butadiene, chloroprene, and polysiloxane, which would be suitable for automobile tires under these conditions? Why?

[*The answer may be found in enclosed CD.*]

Concept Check 14.10

Silicone polymers may be prepared to exist as liquids at room temperature. Cite differences in molecular structure between them and the silicone elastomers. *Hint:* You may want to consult Sections 13.5 and 14.9.

[*The answer may be found in enclosed CD.*]

14.17 FIBERS

The **fiber** polymers are capable of being drawn into long filaments having at least a 100:1 length-to-diameter ratio. Most commercial fiber polymers are utilized in the textile industry, being woven or knit into cloth or fabric. In addition, the aramid fibers are employed in composite materials, Section 15.8. To be useful as a textile material, a fiber polymer must have a host of rather restrictive physical and chemical properties. While in use, fibers may be subjected to a variety of mechanical deformations—stretching, twisting, shearing, and abrasion. Consequently, they must have a high tensile strength (over a relatively wide temperature range) and a high modulus of elasticity, as well as abrasion resistance. These properties are governed by the chemistry of the polymer chains and also by the fiber drawing process.

The molecular weight of fiber materials should be relatively high or the molten material will be too weak and will break during the drawing process. Also, because the tensile strength increases with degree of crystallinity, the structure and configuration of the chains should allow the production of a highly crystalline polymer. That translates into a requirement for linear and unbranched chains that are symmetrical and have regular repeat units. Polar groups in the polymer also improve the fiber-forming properties by increasing both crystallinity and the intermolecular forces between the chains.

Convenience in washing and maintaining clothing depends primarily on the thermal properties of the fiber polymer, that is, its melting and glass transition temperatures. Furthermore, fiber polymers must exhibit chemical stability to a rather extensive variety of environments, including acids, bases, bleaches, dry cleaning solvents, and sunlight. In addition, they must be relatively nonflammable and amenable to drying.

14.18 MISCELLANEOUS APPLICATIONS

Coatings

Coatings are frequently applied to the surface of materials to serve one or more of the following functions: (1) to protect the item from the environment that may produce corrosive or deteriorative reactions; (2) to improve the item's appearance; and (3) to provide electrical insulation. Many of the ingredients in coating materials are polymers, the majority of which are organic in origin. These organic coatings fall into several different classifications, as follows: paint, varnish, enamel, lacquer, and shellac.

Many common coatings are *latexes*. A latex is a stable suspension of small insoluble polymer particles dispersed in water. These materials have become increasingly popular because they don't contain large quantities of organic solvents that are emitted into the environment—that is, they have low volatile organic compound (VOC) emissions. VOCs react in the atmosphere to produce smog. Large users of coatings such as automobile manufacturers continue to reduce their VOC emissions to comply with environmental regulations.

Adhesives

An **adhesive** is a substance used to bond together the surfaces of two solid materials (termed "adherends"). There are two types of bonding mechanisms: mechanical and chemical. For mechanical there is actual penetration of the adhesive into surface pores and crevices. Chemical bonding involves intermolecular forces between the adhesive and adherend, which forces may be covalent and/or van der Waals; degree of van der Waals bonding is enhanced when the adhesive material contains polar groups.

Although natural adhesives (animal glue, casein, starch, and rosin) are still used for many applications, a host of new adhesive materials based on synthetic polymers have been developed; these include polyurethanes, polysiloxanes (silicones), epoxies, polyimides, acrylics, and rubber materials. Adhesives may be used to join a large variety of materials—viz. metals, ceramics, polymers, composites, skin, etc.—and the choice of which adhesive to use will depend on such factors as (1) the materials to be bonded and their porosities; (2) the required adhesive properties (i.e., whether the bond is to be temporary or permanent); (3) maximum/minimum exposure temperatures; and (4) processing conditions.

For all but the pressure-sensitive adhesives (discussed below), the adhesive material is applied as a low-viscosity liquid, so as to cover evenly and completely the adherend surfaces, and allow for maximum bonding interactions. The actual bonding joint forms as the adhesive undergoes a liquid-to-solid transition (or cures), which may be accomplished through either a physical process (e.g., crystallization, solvent evaporation) or a chemical process [e.g., addition polymerization, condensation polymerization (Section 14.20), vulcanization]. Characteristics of a sound joint should include high shear, peel, and fracture strengths.

Adhesive bonding offers some advantages over other joining technologies (e.g., riveting, bolting, and welding) including lighter weight, the ability to join dissimilar materials and thin components, better fatigue resistance, and lower manufacturing costs. Furthermore, it is the technology of choice when exact positioning of components as well as processing speed are essential. The chief drawback of adhesive joints is service temperature limitation; polymers maintain their mechanical integrity only at relatively low temperatures, and strength decreases rapidly with increasing temperature. The maximum temperature possible for continuous use for some of the newly-developed polymers is 300°C. Adhesive joints are found in a large number applications, especially in the aerospace, automotive, and construction industries, in packaging, and some household goods.

A special class of this group of materials is the pressure-sensitive adhesives (or self-adhesive materials), such as those found on self-stick tapes, labels, and postage stamps. These materials are designed to adhere to just about any surface by making contact and with the application of slight pressure. Unlike the adhesives described above, bonding action does not result from a physical transformation or a chemical reaction. Rather, these materials contain polymer tackifying resins; during detachment of the two bonding surfaces, small fibrils form that are attached to the surfaces and tend to hold them together. Polymers used for pressure-sensitive adhesives include the acrylics, styrenic block copolymers (Section 14.19), and natural rubber.

Films

Polymeric materials have found widespread use in the form of thin *films*. Films having thicknesses between 0.025 and 0.125 mm (0.001 and 0.005 in.) are fabricated and used extensively as bags for packaging food products and other merchandise, as textile products, and a host of other uses. Important characteristics of the materials produced and used as films include low density, a high degree of flexibility, high tensile and tear strengths, resistance to attack by moisture and other chemicals, and low permeability to some gases, especially water vapor (Section 13.14). Some of the polymers that meet these criteria and are manufactured in film form are polyethylene, polypropylene, cellophane, and cellulose acetate.

Foams

Foams are plastic materials that contain a relatively high volume percentage of small pores and trapped gas bubbles. Both thermoplastic and thermosetting materials are used as foams; these include polyurethane, rubber, polystyrene, and poly(vinyl chloride). Foams are commonly used as cushions in automobiles and furniture as well as in packaging and thermal insulation. The foaming process is often carried out by incorporating into the batch of material a blowing agent that, upon heating, decomposes with the liberation of a gas. Gas bubbles are generated throughout the now-fluid mass, which remain in the solid upon cooling and give rise to a sponge-like structure. The same effect is produced by dissolving an inert gas into a molten polymer under high pressure. When the pressure is rapidly reduced, the gas comes out of solution and forms bubbles and pores that remain in the solid as it cools.

14.19 ADVANCED POLYMERIC MATERIALS

A number of new polymers having unique and desirable combinations of properties have been developed over the past several years; many have found niches in new technologies and/or have satisfactorily replaced other materials. Some of these include ultrahigh molecular weight polyethylene, liquid crystal polymers, and thermoplastic elastomers. Each of these will now be discussed.

Ultrahigh Molecular Weight Polyethylene

Ultrahigh molecular weight polyethylene (*UHMWPE*) is a linear polyethylene that has an extremely high molecular weight. Its typical $\overline{M}_w$ is approximately 4×10^6 g/mol, which is an order of magnitude (i.e., factor of ten) greater than that of high-density polyethylene. In fiber form, UHMWPE is highly aligned and has the trade name Spectra™. Some of the extraordinary characteristics of this material are as follows:

1. An extremely high impact resistance
2. Outstanding resistance to wear and abrasion
3. A very low coefficient of friction
4. A self-lubricating and nonstick surface
5. Very good chemical resistance to normally encountered solvents
6. Excellent low-temperature properties
7. Outstanding sound damping and energy absorption characteristics
8. Electrically insulating and excellent dielectric properties

However, since this material has a relatively low melting temperature, its mechanical properties diminish rapidly with increasing temperature.

This unusual combination of properties leads to numerous and diverse applications for this material, including bullet-proof vests, composite military helmets, fishing line, ski-bottom surfaces, golf ball cores, bowling alley and ice skating rink surfaces, biomedical prostheses (Section 21.12), blood filters, marking pen nibs, bulk material handling equipment (for coal, grain, cement, gravel, etc.), bushings, pump impellers, and valve gaskets.

Liquid Crystal Polymers

The **liquid crystal polymers** (*LCP*s) are a group of chemically complex and structurally distinct materials that have unique properties and are utilized in diverse applications. Discussion of the chemistry of these materials is beyond the scope of this book. Suffice it to say that LCPs are composed of extended, rod-shaped, and rigid molecules. In terms of molecular arrangement, these materials do not fall within any of conventional liquid, amorphous, crystalline, or semicrystalline classifications, but may be considered as a new state of matter—the liquid crystalline state, being neither crystalline nor liquid. In the melt (or liquid) condition, whereas other polymer molecules are randomly oriented, LCP molecules can become aligned in highly ordered configurations. As solids, this molecular alignment remains, and, in addition, the molecules form in domain structures having characteristic intermolecular spacings. A schematic comparison of liquid crystals, amorphous polymers, and semicrystalline polymers in both melt and solid states is illustrated in Figure 14.20. Furthermore, there are three types of liquid crystals, based on orientation and positional ordering—smectic, nematic, and cholesteric; distinctions among these types are also beyond the scope of this discussion.

The principal use of liquid crystal polymers is in *liquid crystal displays* (*LCD*s) on digital watches, flat-panel computer monitors and televisions, and other digital displays. Here cholesteric types of LCPs are employed which, at room temperature, are fluid liquids, transparent, and optically anisotropic. The displays are composed of two sheets of glass between which is sandwiched the liquid crystal material. The outer face of each glass sheet is coated with a transparent and electrically conductive film; in addition, the character-forming number/letter

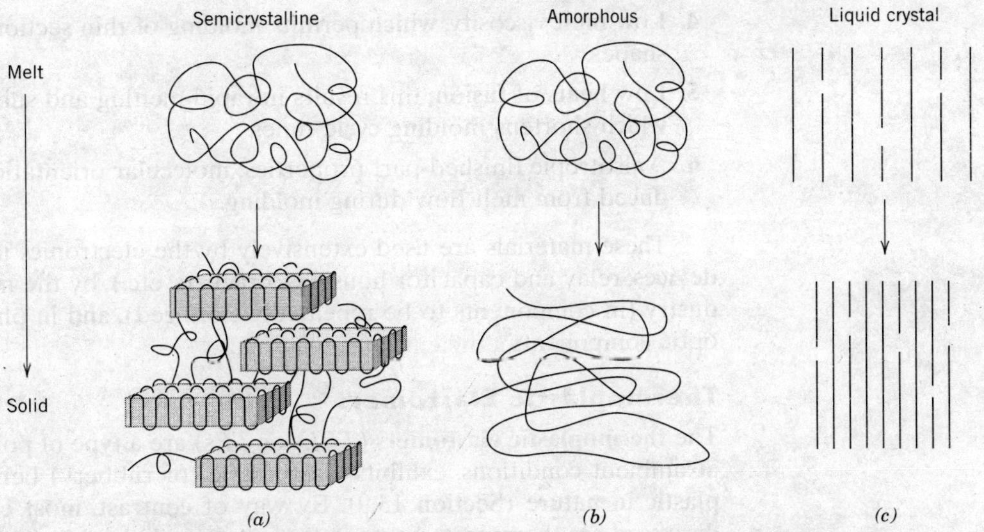

Figure 14.20 Schematic representations of the molecular structures in both melt and solid states for (*a*) semicrystalline, (*b*) amorphous, and (*c*) liquid crystal polymers. (Adapted from G. W. Calundann and M. Jaffe, "Anisotropic Polymers, Their Synthesis and Properties," Chapter VII in *Proceedings of the Robert A. Welch Foundation Conferences on Polymer Research*, 26th Conference, Synthetic Polymers, Nov. 1982.)

elements are etched into this film on the side that is to be viewed. A voltage applied through the conductive films (and thus between these two glass sheets) over one of these character-forming regions causes a disruption of the orientation of the LCP molecules in this region, a darkening of this LCP material, and, in turn, the formation of a visible character.

Some of the nematic type of liquid crystal polymers are rigid solids at room temperature and, on the basis of an outstanding combination of properties and processing characteristics, have found widespread use in a variety of commercial applications. For example, these materials exhibit the following behaviors:

1. Excellent thermal stability; they may be used to temperatures as high as 230°C (450°F).
2. Stiff and strong; their tensile moduli range between 10 and 24 GPa (1.4×10^6 and 3.5×10^6 psi), while tensile strengths are from 125 to 255 MPa (18,000 to 37,000 psi).
3. High impact strengths, which are retained upon cooling to relatively low temperatures.
4. Chemical inertness to a wide variety of acids, solvents, bleaches, etc.
5. Inherent flame resistance and combustion products that are relatively nontoxic.

The thermal stability and chemical inertness of these materials are explained by extremely high intermolecular interactions.

The following may be said about their processing and fabrication characteristics:

1. All conventional processing techniques available for thermoplastic materials may be used.
2. Extremely low shrinkage and warpage take place during molding.
3. Exceptional dimensional repeatability from part to part.

4. Low melt viscosity, which permits molding of thin sections and/or complex shapes.
5. Low heats of fusion; this results in rapid melting and subsequent cooling, which shortens molding cycle times.
6. Anisotropic finished-part properties; molecular orientation effects are produced from melt flow during molding.

These materials are used extensively by the electronics industry (interconnect devices, relay and capacitor housings, brackets, etc.), by the medical equipment industry (in components to be repeatedly sterilized), and in photocopiers and fiber-optic components.

Thermoplastic Elastomers

The **thermoplastic elastomers** (*TPE*s or *TE*s) are a type of polymeric material that, at ambient conditions, exhibits elastomeric (or rubbery) behavior, yet is thermoplastic in nature (Section 13.9). By way of contrast, most elastomers heretofore discussed are thermosets, because they are crosslinked during vulcanization. Of the several varieties of TPEs, one of the best known and widely used is a block copolymer consisting of block segments of a hard and rigid thermoplastic (commonly styrene [S]), that alternate with block segments of a soft and flexible elastic material (often butadiene [B] or isoprene [I]). For a common TPE, hard polymerized segments are located at chain ends, whereas each soft central region consists of polymerized butadiene or isoprene units. These TPEs are frequently termed *styrenic block copolymers,* and chain chemistries for the two (S-B-S and S-I-S) types are shown in Figure 14.21

At ambient temperatures, the soft, amorphous, central (butadiene or isoprene) segments impart the rubbery, elastomeric behavior to the material. Furthermore, for temperatures below the T_m of the hard (styrene) component, hard chain-end segments from numerous adjacent chains aggregate together to form rigid crystalline domain regions. These domains are "physical crosslinks" that act as anchor points so as to restrict soft-chain segment motions; they function in much the same way as "chemical crosslinks" for the thermoset elastomers. A schematic illustration for the structure of this TPE type is presented in Figure 14.22.

The tensile modulus of this TPE material is subject to alteration; increasing the number of soft-component blocks per chain will lead to a decrease in modulus and, therefore, a diminishment of stiffness. Furthermore, the useful temperature range lies between T_g of the soft and flexible component and T_m of the hard, rigid one. For the styrenic block copolymers this range is between about −70°C and 100°C.

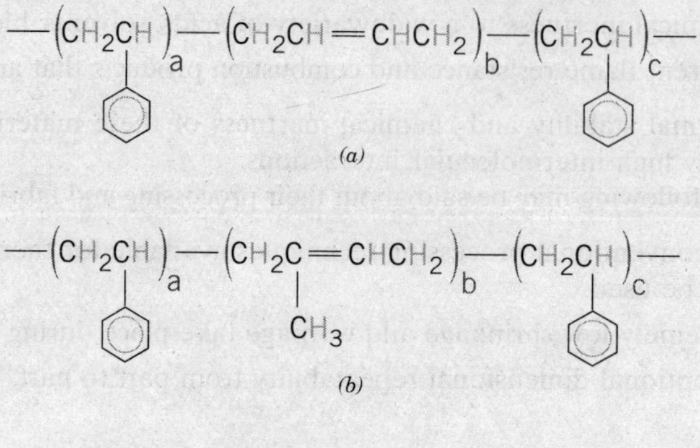

Figure 14.21 Representations of the chain chemistries for (*a*) styrene-butadiene-styrene (S-B-S), and (*b*) styrene-isoprene-styrene (S-I-S) thermoplastic elastomers.

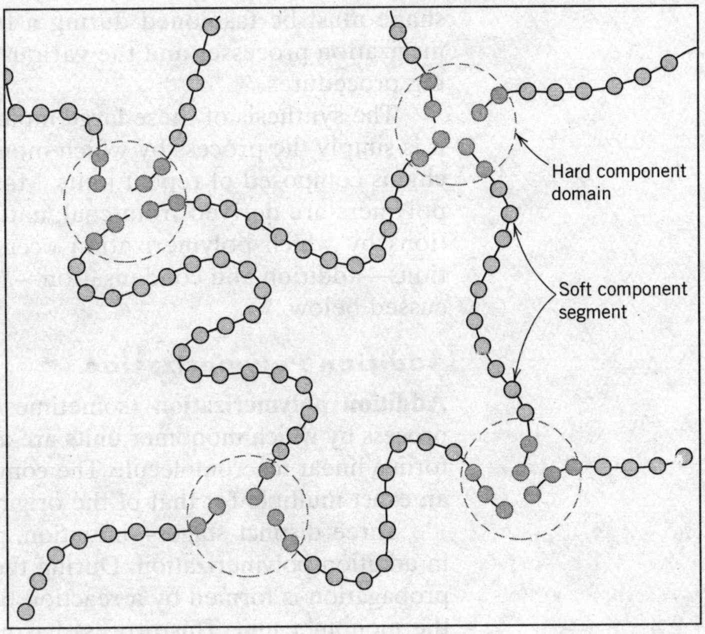

Figure 14.22 Schematic representation of the molecular structure for a thermoplastic elastomer. This structure consists of "soft" (i.e., butadiene or isoprene) repeat unit center-chain segments and "hard" (i.e., styrene) domains (chain ends), which act as physical crosslinks at room temperature. (From *The Science and Engineering of Materials,* fifth edition by ASKELAND/PHULE. © 2006. Reprinted with permission of Nelson, a division of Thomson Learning: www.thomsonrights.com. Fax 800 730-2214.)

In addition to the styrenic block copolymers, there are other types of TPEs, including thermoplastic olefins, copolyesters, thermoplastic polyurethanes, and elastomeric polyamides.

The chief advantage of the TPEs over the thermoset elastomers is that upon heating above T_m of the hard phase, they melt (i.e., the physical crosslinks disappear), and, therefore, they may be processed by conventional thermoplastic forming techniques [e.g., blow molding, injection molding, etc. (Section 14.22)]; thermoset polymers do not experience melting, and, consequently, forming is normally more difficult. Furthermore, since the melting-solidification process is reversible and repeatable for thermoplastic elastomers, TPE parts may be reformed into other shapes. In other words, they are recyclable; thermoset elastomers are, to a large degree, nonrecyclable. Scrap that is generated during forming procedures may also be recycled, which results in lower production costs than with thermosets. In addition, tighter controls may be maintained on part dimensions for TPEs, and TPEs have lower densities.

In quite a variety of applications, the thermoplastic elastomers have replaced the conventional thermoset elastomers. Typical uses for the TPEs include automotive exterior trim (bumpers, fascia, etc.), automotive underhood components (electrical insulation and connectors, and gaskets), shoe soles and heels, sporting goods (e.g., bladders for footballs and soccer balls), medical barrier films and protective coatings, and as components in sealants, caulking, and adhesives.

14.20 POLYMERIZATION

The large macromolecules of the commercially useful polymers must be synthesized from substances having smaller molecules in a process termed polymerization. Furthermore, the properties of a polymer may be modified and enhanced by the inclusion of additive materials. Finally, a finished piece having a desired shape must be fashioned during a forming operation. This section treats polymerization processes and the various forms of additives, as well as specific forming procedures.

The synthesis of these large molecules (polymers) is termed polymerization; it is simply the process by which monomers are linked together to generate long chains composed of repeat units. Most generally, the raw materials for synthetic polymers are derived from coal, natural gas, and petroleum products. The reactions by which polymerization occur are grouped into two general classifications—addition and condensation—according to the reaction mechanism, as discussed below.

Addition Polymerization

Addition polymerization (sometimes called *chain reaction polymerization*) is a process by which monomer units are attached one at a time in chainlike fashion to form a linear macromolecule. The composition of the resultant product molecule is an exact multiple for that of the original reactant monomer.

Three distinct stages—initiation, propagation, and termination—are involved in addition polymerization. During the initiation step, an active center capable of propagation is formed by a reaction between an initiator (or catalyst) species and the monomer unit. This process has already been demonstrated for polyethylene (Equation 13.1), which is repeated as follows:

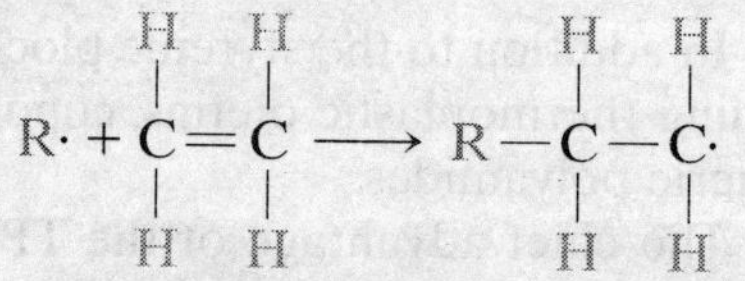
(14.5)

Again, R· represents the active initiator, and · is an unpaired electron.

Propagation involves the linear growth of the polymer chain by the sequential addition of monomer units to this active growing chain molecule. This may be represented, again for polyethylene, as follows:

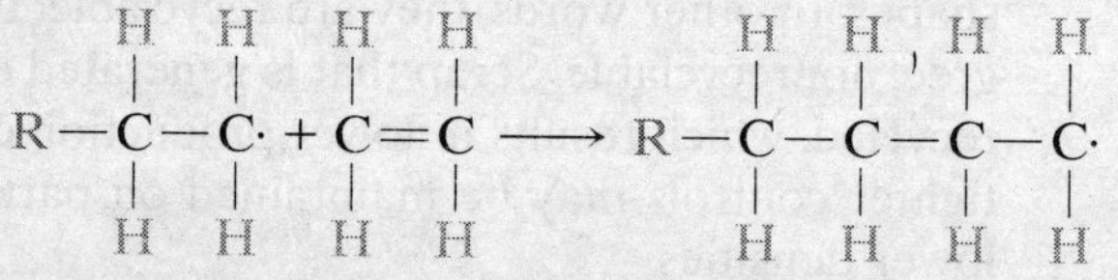
(14.6)

Chain growth is relatively rapid; the period required to grow a molecule consisting of, say, 1000 repeat units is on the order of 10^{-2} to 10^{-3} s.

Propagation may end or terminate in different ways. First, the active ends of two propagating chains may link together to form one molecule according to the following reaction:[6]

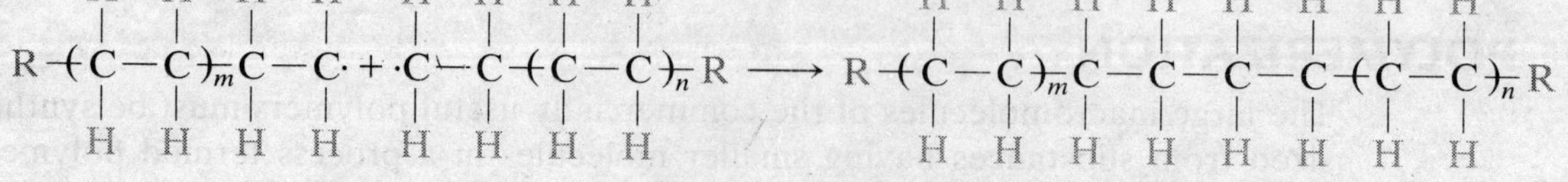
(14.7)

[6] This type of termination reaction is referred to as *combination*.

The other termination possibility involves two growing molecules that react to form two "dead chains" as[7]

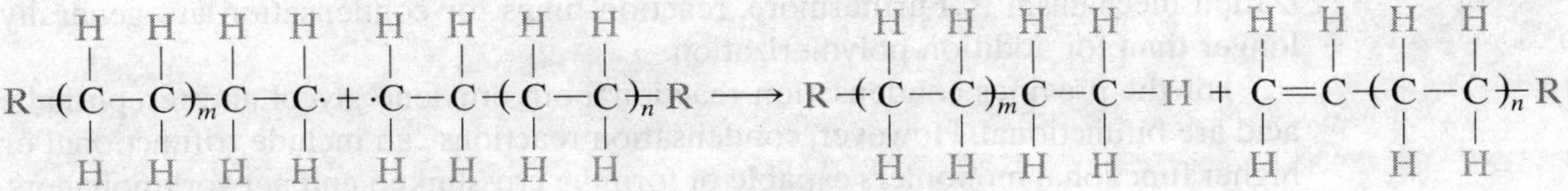

(14.8)

thus terminating the growth of each chain.

Molecular weight is governed by the relative rates of initiation, propagation, and termination. Ordinarily, they are controlled to ensure the production of a polymer having the desired degree of polymerization.

Addition polymerization is used in the synthesis of polyethylene, polypropylene, poly(vinyl chloride), and polystyrene, as well as many of the copolymers.

Concept Check 14.11

Cite whether the molecular weight of a polymer that is synthesized by addition polymerization is relatively high, medium, or relatively low for the following situations:

(a) Rapid initiation, slow propagation, and rapid termination.

(b) Slow initiation, rapid propagation, and slow termination.

(c) Rapid initiation, rapid propagation, and slow termination.

(d) Slow initiation, slow propagation, and rapid termination.

[*The answer may be found in enclosed CD.*]

Condensation Polymerization

Condensation (or *step reaction*) **polymerization** is the formation of polymers by stepwise intermolecular chemical reactions that may involve more than one monomer species. There is usually a small molecular weight byproduct such as water that is eliminated (or condensed). No reactant species has the chemical formula of the repeat unit, and the intermolecular reaction occurs every time a repeat unit is formed. For example, consider the formation of the polyester, poly(ethylene terephthalate) (PET), from the reaction between ethylene glycol and terephthalic acid; the intermolecular reaction is as follows:

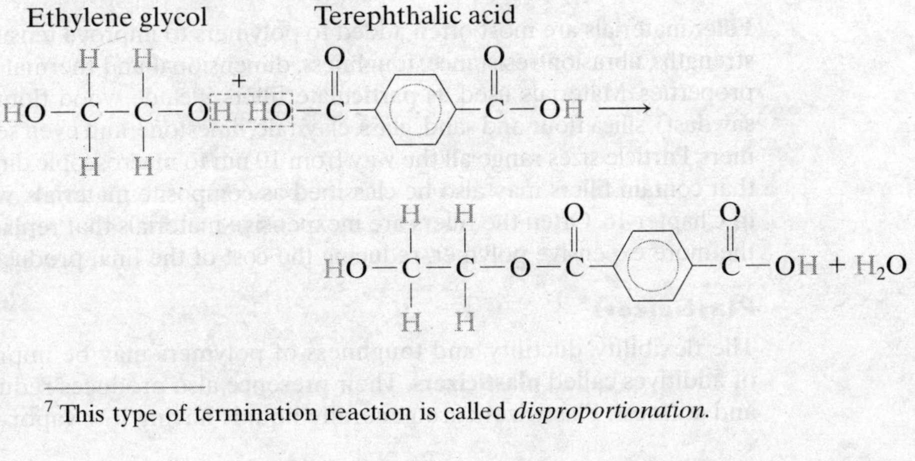

(14.9)

[7] This type of termination reaction is called *disproportionation*.

This stepwise process is successively repeated, producing a linear molecule. The chemistry of the specific reaction is not important but the condensation polymerization mechanism is. Furthermore, reaction times for condensation are generally longer than for addition polymerization.

For the previous condensation reaction, both ethylene glycol and terephthalic acid are bifunctional. However, condensation reactions can include trifunctional or higher functional monomers capable of forming crosslinked and network polymers. The thermosetting polyesters and phenol-formaldehyde, the nylons, and the polycarbonates are produced by condensation polymerization. Some polymers, such as nylon, may be polymerized by either technique.

Concept Check 14.12

Nylon 6,6 may be formed by means of a condensation polymerization reaction in which hexamethylene diamine [NH_2—$(CH_2)_6$—NH_2] and adipic acid react with one another with the formation of water as a byproduct. Write out this reaction in the manner of Equation 14.9. *Note:* the structure for adipic acid is

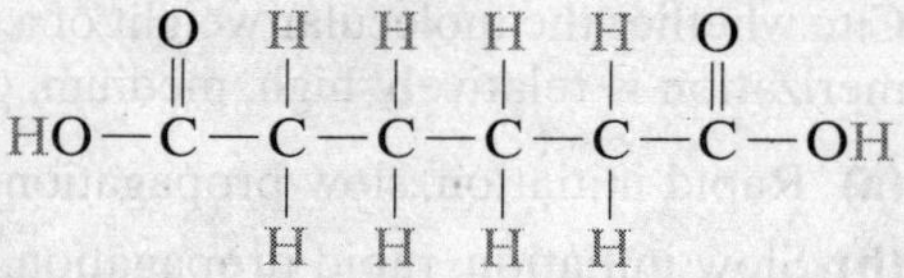

[The answer may be found in enclosed CD.]

14.21 POLYMER ADDITIVES

Most of the properties of polymers discussed earlier in this chapter are intrinsic ones—that is, characteristic of or fundamental to the specific polymer. Some of these properties are related to and controlled by the molecular structure. Many times, however, it is necessary to modify the mechanical, chemical, and physical properties to a much greater degree than is possible by the simple alteration of this fundamental molecular structure. Foreign substances called *additives* are intentionally introduced to enhance or modify many of these properties, and thus render a polymer more serviceable. Typical additives include filler materials, plasticizers, stabilizers, colorants, and flame retardants.

Fillers

Filler materials are most often added to polymers to improve tensile and compressive strengths, abrasion resistance, toughness, dimensional and thermal stability, and other properties. Materials used as particulate fillers include wood flour (finely powdered sawdust), silica flour and sand, glass, clay, talc, limestone, and even some synthetic polymers. Particle sizes range all the way from 10 nm to macroscopic dimensions. Polymers that contain fillers may also be classified as composite materials, which are discussed in Chapter 16. Often the fillers are inexpensive materials that replace some volume of the more expensive polymer, reducing the cost of the final product.

Plasticizers

The flexibility, ductility, and toughness of polymers may be improved with the aid of additives called **plasticizers.** Their presence also produces reductions in hardness and stiffness. Plasticizers are generally liquids having low vapor pressures and low molecular weights. The small plasticizer molecules occupy positions between the large polymer chains, effectively increasing the interchain distance with a reduction in the secondary intermolecular bonding. Plasticizers are commonly used in polymers that are intrinsically brittle at room temperature, such as poly(vinyl chloride) and some of the acetate copolymers. The plasticizer lowers the glass transition temperature, so that at ambient conditions the polymers may be used in applications requiring some degree of pliability and ductility. These applications include thin sheets or films, tubing, raincoats, and curtains.

Concept Check 14.13

(a) Why must the vapor pressure of a plasticizer be relatively low?

(b) How will the crystallinity of a polymer be affected by the addition of a plasticizer? Why?

(c) How does the addition of a plasticizer influence the tensile strength of a polymer? Why?

[*The answer may be found in enclosed CD.*]

Stabilizers

Some polymeric materials, under normal environmental conditions, are subject to rapid deterioration, generally in terms of mechanical integrity. Additives that counteract deteriorative processes are called **stabilizers.**

One common form of deterioration results from exposure to light [in particular ultraviolet (UV) radiation]. Ultraviolet radiation interacts with and causes a severance of some of the covalent bonds along the molecular chains, which may also result in some crosslinking. There are two primary approaches to UV stabilization. The first is to add a UV absorbent material, often as a thin layer at the surface. This essentially acts as a sunscreen and blocks out the UV radiation before it can penetrate into and damage the polymer. The second approach is to add materials that react with the bonds broken by UV radiation before they can participate in other reactions that lead to additional polymer damage.

Another important type of deterioration is oxidation (Section 16.12). It is a consequence of the chemical interaction between oxygen [as either diatomic oxygen (O_2) or ozone (O_3)] and the polymer molecules. Stabilizers that protect against oxidation either consume oxygen before it reaches the polymer, and/or they prevent the occurrence of oxidation reactions that would further damage the material.

Colorants

Colorants impart a specific color to a polymer; they may be added in the form of dyes or pigments. The molecules in a dye actually dissolve in the polymer. Pigments are filler materials that do not dissolve, but remain as a separate phase; normally they have a small particle size and a refractive index near to that of the parent polymer. Others may impart opacity as well as color to the polymer.

Flame Retardants

The flammability of polymeric materials is a major concern, especially in the manufacture of textiles and children's toys. Most polymers are flammable in their pure form; exceptions include those containing significant contents of chlorine and/or fluorine, such as poly(vinyl chloride) and polytetrafluoroethylene. The flammability resistance of the remaining combustible polymers may be enhanced by additives called **flame retardants.** These retardants may function by interfering with the combustion process through the gas phase, or by initiating a different combustion reaction that generates less heat, thereby reducing the temperature; this causes a slowing or cessation of burning.

SUMMARY

Stress–Strain Behavior

On the basis of stress–strain behavior, polymers fall within three general classifications: brittle, plastic, and highly elastic. These materials are neither as strong nor as stiff as metals, and their mechanical properties are sensitive to changes in temperature and strain rate. However, their high flexibilities, low densities, and resistance to corrosion make them the materials of choice for many applications.

Viscoelastic Deformation

Viscoelastic mechanical behavior, being intermediate between totally elastic and totally viscous, is displayed by a number of polymeric materials. It is characterized by the relaxation modulus, a time-dependent modulus of elasticity. The magnitude of the relaxation modulus is very sensitive to temperature; critical to the in-service temperature range for elastomers is this temperature dependence.

Fracture of Polymers

Fracture strengths of polymeric materials are low relative to metals and ceramics. Both brittle and ductile fracture modes are possible, and some thermoplastic materials experience a ductile-to-brittle transition with a lowering of temperature, an increase in strain rate, and/or an alteration of specimen thickness or geometry. In some thermoplastics, the crack-formation process may be preceded by crazing; crazing can lead to an increase in ductility and toughness of the material.

Deformation of Semicrystalline Polymers

During the elastic deformation of a semicrystalline polymer having a spherulitic structure that is stressed in tension, the molecules in amorphous regions elongate in the stress direction. In addition, molecules in crystallites experience bending and stretching, which causes a slight increase in lamellar thickness.

The mechanism of plastic deformation for spherulitic polymers was also presented. Tensile deformation occurs in several stages as both amorphous tie chains and chain-folded block segments (which separate from the ribbon-like lamellae) become oriented with the tensile axis. Also, during deformation the shapes of spherulites are altered (for moderate deformations); relatively large degrees of deformation lead to a complete destruction of the spherulites to form highly aligned structures. Furthermore, the predeformed spherulitic structure and macroscopic shape may be partially restored by annealing at an elevated temperature below the polymer's melting temperature.

Factors That Influence the Mechanical Properties of Semicrystalline Polymers

The mechanical behavior of a polymer will be influenced by both in-service and structural/processing factors. With regard to the former, increasing the temperature and/or diminishing the strain rate leads to reductions in tensile modulus and tensile strength and an enhancement of ductility. In addition, other factors that affect the mechanical properties include molecular weight, degree of crystallinity, predeformation drawing, and heat treating. The influence of each of these factors was discussed.

Deformation of Elastomers

Large elastic extensions are possible for the elastomeric materials that are amorphous and lightly crosslinked. Deformation corresponds to the unkinking and uncoiling of chains in response to an applied tensile stress. Crosslinking is often achieved during a vulcanization process. Many of the elastomers are copolymers, whereas the silicone elastomers are really inorganic materials.

Crystallization
Melting
The Glass Transition
Melting and Glass Transition Temperatures
Factors That Influence Melting and Glass Transition Temperatures

The molecular mechanics of crystallization, melting, and the glass transition were discussed. The manner in which melting and glass transition temperatures are determined was outlined; these parameters are important relative to the temperature range over which a particular polymer may be utilized and processed. The magnitudes of T_m and T_g increase with increasing chain stiffness; stiffness is enhanced by the presence of chain double bonds and side groups that are either bulky or polar. Molecular weight and degree of branching also affect T_m and T_g.

Plastics

The various types and applications of polymeric materials were also discussed. Plastic materials are perhaps the most widely used group of polymers, which include the following: polyethylene, polypropylene, poly(vinyl chloride), polystyrene, and the fluorocarbons, epoxies, phenolics, and polyesters.

Fibers

Many polymeric materials may be spun into fibers, which are used primarily in textiles. Mechanical, thermal, and chemical characteristics of these materials are especially critical.

Miscellaneous Applications

Other miscellaneous applications that employ polymers include coatings, adhesives, films, and foams.

Advanced Polymeric Materials

Also discussed were three advanced polymeric materials: ultrahigh molecular weight polyethylene, liquid crystal polymers, and thermoplastic elastomers. These materials have unusual properties and are used in a host of high-technology applications.

Polymerization
Polymer Additives

The final sections of this chapter treated synthesis and fabrication techniques for polymeric materials. Synthesis of large molecular weight polymers is attained by polymerization, of which there are two types: addition and condensation. The properties of polymers may be further modified by using additives; these include fillers, plasticizers, stabilizers, colorants, and flame retardants.

REFERENCES

Billmeyer, F. W., Jr., *Textbook of Polymer Science,* 3rd edition, Wiley-Interscience, New York, 1984.

Carraher, C. E., Jr., *Seymour/Carraher's Polymer Chemistry,* 6th edition, Marcel Dekker, New York, 2003.

Engineered Materials Handbook, Vol. 2, *Engineering Plastics,* ASM International, Metals Park, OH, 1988.

Harper, C. A. (Editor), *Handbook of Plastics, Elastomers and Composites,* 3rd edition, McGraw-Hill Professional Book Group, New York, 1996.

Landel, R. F. (Editor), *Mechanical Properties of Polymers and Composites,* 2nd edition, Marcel Dekker, New York, 1994.

McCrum, N. G., C. P. Buckley, and C. B. Bucknall, *Principles of Polymer Engineering,* 2nd edition, Oxford University Press, Oxford, 1997. Chapters 7–8.

Muccio, E. A., *Plastic Part Technology,* ASM International, Materials Park, OH, 1991.

Muccio, E. A., *Plastics Processing Technology,* ASM International, Materials Park, OH, 1994.

Powell, P. C., and A. J. Housz, *Engineering with Polymers,* 2nd edition, Nelson Thornes, Cheltenham, UK, 1998.

Rosen, S. L., *Fundamental Principles of Polymeric Materials,* 2nd edition, Wiley, New York, 1993.

Rudin, A., *The Elements of Polymer Science and Engineering,* 2nd edition, Academic Press, San Diego, 1998.

Strong, A. B., *Plastics: Materials and Processing,* 3rd edition, Prentice Hall PTR, Paramus, IL, 2006.

Tobolsky, A. V., *Properties and Structures of Polymers,* Wiley, New York, 1960. Advanced treatment.

Ward, I. M. and J. Sweeney, *An Introduction to the Mechanical Properties of Solid Polymers,* 2nd edition, John Wiley & Sons, Hoboken, NJ, 2004.

QUESTIONS AND PROBLEMS

Stress–Strain Behavior

14.1 From the stress–strain data for poly(methyl methacrylate) shown in Figure 14.3, determine the modulus of elasticity and tensile strength at room temperature (20°C), and compare these values with those given in Table 14.1.

Viscoelastic Deformation

14.2 In your own words, briefly describe the phenomenon of viscoelasticity.

14.3 For some viscoelastic polymers that are subjected to stress relaxation tests, the stress decays with time according to

$$\sigma(t) = \sigma(0) \exp\left(-\frac{t}{\tau}\right) \qquad (14.10)$$

where $\sigma(t)$ and $\sigma(0)$ represent the time-dependent and initial (i.e., time = 0) stresses, respectively, and t and τ denote elapsed time and the relaxation time; τ is a time-independent constant characteristic of the material. A specimen of some viscoelastic polymer with the stress relaxation that obeys Equation 14.10 was suddenly pulled in tension to a measured strain of 0.5; the stress necessary to maintain this constant strain was measured as a function of time. Determine $E_r(10)$ for this material if the initial stress level was 3.5 MPa, which dropped to 0.5 MPa after 30 s.

14.4 In Figure 14.23, the logarithm of $E_r(t)$ versus the logarithm of time is plotted for PMMA at a variety of temperatures. Make a plot of log $E_r(10)$ versus temperature and then estimate its T_g.

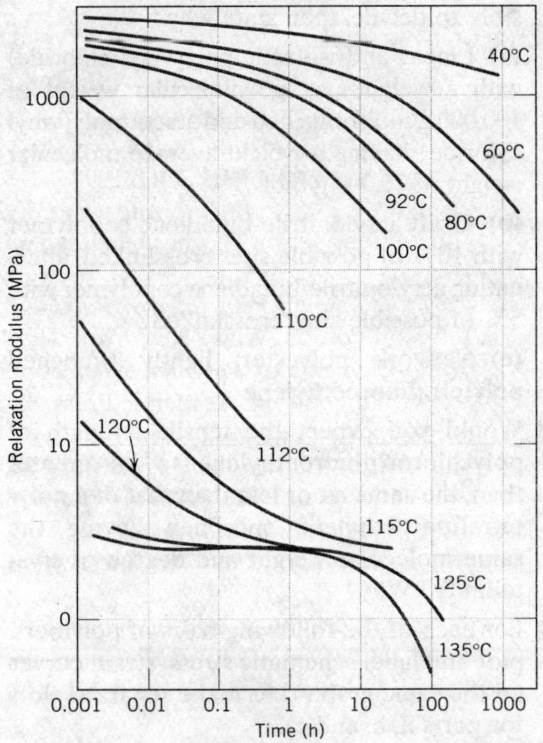

Figure 14.23 Logarithm of relaxation modulus versus logarithm of time for poly(methyl methacrylate) between 40 and 135°C. (From J. R. McLoughlin and A. V. Tobolsky, *J. Colloid Sci.,* **7,** 555, 1952. Reprinted with permission.)

14.5 On the basis of the curves in Figure 14.5, sketch schematic strain–time plots for the following polystyrene materials at the specified temperatures:

(a) Crystalline at 70°C

(b) Amorphous at 180°C

(c) Crosslinked at 180°C

(d) Amorphous at 100°C

14.6 (a) Contrast the manner in which stress relaxation and viscoelastic creep tests are conducted.

(b) For each of these tests, cite the experimental parameter of interest and how it is determined.

14.7 Make two schematic plots of the logarithm of relaxation modulus versus temperature for an amorphous polymer (curve *C* in Figure 14.8).

(a) On one of these plots demonstrate how the behavior changes with increasing molecular weight.

(b) On the other plot, indicate the change in behavior with increasing crosslinking.

Fracture of Polymers
Miscellaneous Mechanical Characteristics

14.8 For thermoplastic polymers, cite five factors that favor brittle fracture.

14.9 (a) Compare the fatigue limits for PMMA (Figure 14.11) and the steel alloy for which fatigue data are given in Problem 11.20.

(b) Compare the fatigue strengths at 10^6 cycles for nylon 6 (Figure 14.11) and 2014-T6 aluminum (Figure 11.34).

Deformation of Semicrystalline Polymers
(Deformation of Elastomers)

14.10 In your own words, describe the mechanisms by which semicrystalline polymers **(a)** elastically deform and **(b)** plastically deform, and **(c)** by which elastomers elastically deform.

Factors That Influence the Mechanical Properties of Semicrystalline Polymers
Deformation of Elastomers

14.11 Briefly explain how each of the following influences the tensile modulus of a semicrystalline polymer and why:

(a) Molecular weight

(b) Degree of crystallinity

(c) Deformation by drawing

(d) Annealing of an undeformed material

(f) Annealing of a drawn material

14.12 Briefly explain how each of the following influences the tensile or yield strength of a semicrystalline polymer and why:

(a) Molecular weight

(b) Degree of crystallinity

(c) Deformation by drawing

(d) Annealing of an undeformed material

14.13 Normal butane and isobutane have boiling temperatures of −0.5 and −12.3°C (31.1 and 9.9°F), respectively. Briefly explain this behavior on the basis of their molecular structures, as presented in Section 13.2.

14.14 The tensile strength and number-average molecular weight for two poly(methyl methacrylate) materials are as follows:

Tensile Strength (MPa)	*Number-Average Molecular Weight (g/mol)*
50	30,000
150	50,000

Estimate the tensile strength at a number-average molecular weight of 40,000 g/mol.

14.15 The tensile strength and number-average molecular weight for two polyethylene materials are as follows:

Tensile Strength (MPa)	*Number-Average Molecular Weight (g/mol)*
90	20,000
180	40,000

Estimate the number-average molecular weight that is required to give a tensile strength of 140 MPa.

14.16 For each of the following pairs of polymers, do the following: (1) state whether or not it is possible to decide whether one polymer has a higher tensile modulus than the other; (2) if this is possible, note which has the higher tensile modulus and then cite the reason(s) for your choice; and (3) if it is not possible to decide, then state why.

(a) Branched and atactic poly(vinyl chloride) with a weight-average molecular weight of 100,000 g/mol; linear and isotactic poly(vinyl chloride) having a weight-average molecular weight of 75,000 g/mol

(b) Random styrene-butadiene copolymer with 5% of possible sites crosslinked; block styrene-butadiene copolymer with 10% of possible sites crosslinked

(c) Branched polyethylene with a number-average molecular weight of 100,000 g/mol; atactic polypropylene with a number-average molecular weight of 150,000 g/mol

14.17 For each of the following pairs of polymers, do the following: (1) state whether or not it is possible to decide whether one polymer has a higher tensile strength than the other; (2) if this is possible, note which has the higher tensile strength and then cite the reason(s) for your choice; and (3) if it is not possible to decide, then state why.

(a) Linear and isotactic poly(vinyl chloride) with a weight-average molecular weight of 100,000 g/mol; branched and atactic poly(vinyl chloride) having a weight-average molecular weight of 75,000 g/mol

(b) Graft acrylonitrile-butadiene copolymer with 10% of possible sites crosslinked; alternating acrylonitrile-butadiene copolymer with 5% of possible sites crosslinked

(c) Network polyester; lightly branched polytetrafluoroethylene

14.18 Would you expect the tensile strength of polychlorotrifluoroethylene to be greater than, the same as, or less than that of a polytetrafluoroethylene specimen having the same molecular weight and degree of crystallinity? Why?

14.19 For each of the following pairs of polymers, plot and label schematic stress–strain curves on the same graph (i.e., make separate plots for parts a, b, and c).

(a) Polyisoprene having a number-average molecular weight of 100,000 g/mol and 10% of available sites crosslinked; polyisoprene having a number-average molecular weight of 100,000 g/mol and 20% of available sites crosslinked

(b) Syndiotactic polypropylene having a weight-average molecular weight of 100,000 g/mol; atactic polypropylene having a weight-average molecular weight of 75,000 g/mol

(c) Branched polyethylene having a number-average molecular weight of 90,000 g/mol; heavily crosslinked polyethylene having a number-average molecular weight of 90,000 g/mol

14.20 List the two molecular characteristics that are essential for elastomers.

14.21 Which of the following would you expect to be elastomers and which thermosetting polymers at room temperature? Justify each choice.

(a) Linear and highly crystalline polyethylene

(b) Phenol-formaldehyde

(c) Heavily crosslinked polyisoprene having a glass-transition temperature of 50°C

(d) Lightly crosslinked polyisoprene having a glass-transition temperature of −60°C

(e) Linear and partially amorphous poly(vinyl chloride)

14.22 Fifteen kilogram of polychloroprene is vulcanized with 5.2 kg sulfur. What fraction of the possible crosslink sites is bonded to sulfur crosslinks, assuming that, on the average, 5.5 sulfur atoms participate ineach crosslink?

14.23 Compute the weight percent sulfur that must be added to completely crosslink an alternating acrylonitrile-butadiene copolymer, assuming that four sulfur atoms participate in each crosslink.

14.24 The vulcanization of polyisoprene is accomplished with sulfur atoms according to Equation 14.4. If 45.3 wt% sulfur is combined with polyisoprene, how many crosslinks will be associated with each isoprene repeat unit if it is assumed that, on the average, five sulfur atoms participate in each crosslink?

14.25 For the vulcanization of polyisoprene, compute the weight percent of sulfur that must be added to ensure that 10% of possible sites will be crosslinked; assume that, on the average, 3.5 sulfur atoms are associated with each crosslink.

14.26 Demonstrate, in a manner similar to Equation 14.4, how vulcanization may occur in a chloroprene rubber.

Crystallization

14.27 Determine values for the constants n and k (Equation 8.17) for the crystallization of polypropylene (Figure 14.17) at 150°C.

Melting and Glass Transition Temperatures

14.28 Name the following polymer(s) that would be suitable for the fabrication of cups to contain hot coffee: polyethylene, polypropylene, poly(vinyl chloride), PET polyester, and polycarbonate. Why?

14.29 Of those polymers listed in Table 14.2, which polymer(s) would be best suited for use as ice cube trays? Why?

Factors That Influence Melting and Glass Transition Temperatures

14.30 For each of the following pairs of polymers, plot and label schematic specific volume versus temperature curves on the same graph (i.e., make separate plots for parts a, b, and c).

(a) Linear polyethylene with a weight-average molecular weight of 75,000 g/mol; branched polyethylene with a weight-average molecular weight of 50,000 g/mol

(b) Spherulitic poly(vinyl chloride), of 50% crystallinity, and having a degree of polymerization of 5000; spherulitic polypropylene, of 50% crystallinity, and degree of polymerization of 10,000

(c) Totally amorphous polystyrene having a degree of polymerization of 7000; totally amorphous polypropylene having a degree of polymerization of 7000

14.31 For each of the following pairs of polymers, do the following: (1) state whether or not it is possible to determine whether one polymer has a higher melting temperature than the other; (2) if it is possible, note which has the higher melting temperature and then cite reason(s) for your choice; and (3) if it is not possible to decide, then state why.

(a) Branched polyethylene having a number-average molecular weight of 850,000 g/mol; linear polyethylene having a number-average molecular weight of 850,000 g/mol

(b) Polytetrafluoroethylene having a density of 2.14 g/cm^3 and a weight-average molecular weight of 600,000 g/mol; PTFE having a density of 2.20 g/cm^3 and a weight-average molecular weight of 600,000 g/mol

(c) Linear and syndiotactic poly(vinyl chloride) having a number-average molecular weight of 500,000 g/mol; linear polyethylene having a number-average molecular weight of 225,000 g/mol

(d) Linear and syndiotactic polypropylene having a weight-average molecular weight of 500,000 g/mol; linear and atactic polypropylene having a weight-average molecular weight of 750,000 g/mol

14.32 Make a schematic plot showing how the modulus of elasticity of an amorphous polymer depends on the glass transition temperature. Assume that molecular weight is held constant.

Elastomers

Fibers

Miscellaneous Applications

14.33 Briefly explain the difference in molecular chemistry between silicone polymers and other polymeric materials.

14.34 List two important characteristics for polymers that are to be used in fiber applications.

14.35 Cite five important characteristics for polymers that are to be used in thin-film applications.

Polymerization

14.36 Cite the primary differences between addition and condensation polymerization techniques.

14.37 **(a)** How much ethylene glycol must be added to 20.0 kg of terephthalic acid to produce a linear chain structure of poly(ethylene terephthalate) according to Equation 14.9?

(b) What is the mass of the resulting polymer?

14.38 Nylon 6,6 may be formed by means of a condensation polymerization reaction in which hexamethylene diamine [NH_2—$(CH_2)_6$—NH_2] and adipic acid react with one another with the formation of water as a byproduct. What masses of hexamethylene diamine and adipic acid are necessary to yield 20 kg of completely linear nylon 6,6? (*Note:* the chemical equation for this reaction is the answer to Concept Check 14.12.)

Polymer Additives

14.39 What is the distinction between dye and pigment colorants?

DESIGN QUESTIONS

14.D1 **(a)** List several advantages and disadvantages of using transparent polymeric materials for eyeglass lenses.

(b) Cite four properties (in addition to being transparent) that are important for this application.

(c) Note three polymers that may be candidates for eyeglass lenses, and then tabulate values of the properties noted in part (b) for these three materials.

14.D2 Write an essay on polymeric materials that are used in the packaging of food products and drinks. Include a list of the general requisite characteristics of materials that are used for these applications. Now cite a specific material that is utilized for each of three different container types and the rationale for each choice.

14.D3 Write an essay on the replacement of metallic automobile components by polymers and composite materials. Address the following issues: (1) Which automotive components (e.g., crankshaft) now use polymers and/or composites? (2) Specifically what materials (e.g., high-density polyethylene) are now being used? (3) What are the reasons for these replacements?

Chapter 15 Composite Materials

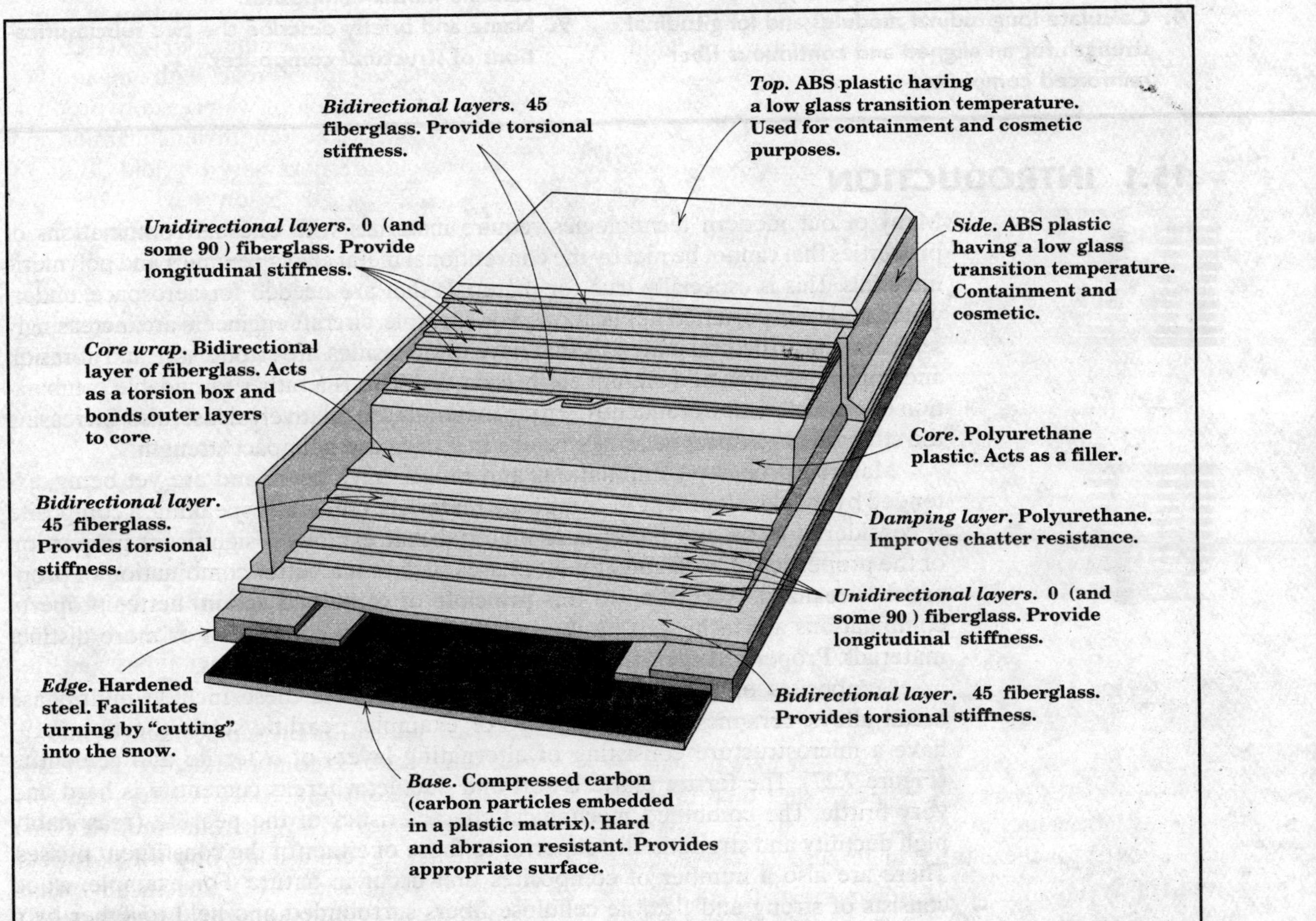

One relatively complex composite structure is the modern ski. In this illustration, a cross section of a high-performance snow ski, are shown the various components. The function of each component is noted, as well as the material that is used in its construction. (Courtesy of Evolution Ski Company, Salt Lake City, Utah.)

Learning Objectives

After careful study of this chapter you should be able to do the following:

1. **Name the three main divisions of composite materials, and cite the distinguishing feature of each.**
2. **Cite the difference in strengthening mechanism for large-particle and dispersion-strengthened particle-reinforced composites.**
3. **Distinguish the three different types of fiber-reinforced composites on the basis of fiber length and orientation; comment on the distinctive mechanical characteristics for each type.**
4. **Calculate longitudinal modulus and longitudinal strength for an aligned and continuous fiber-reinforced composite.**
5. **Compute longitudinal strengths for discontinuous and aligned fibrous composite materials.**
6. **Note the three common fiber reinforcements used in polymer-matrix composites, and, for each, cite both desirable characteristics and limitations.**
7. **Cite the desirable features of metal-matrix composites.**
8. **Note the primary reason for the creation of ceramic-matrix composites.**
9. **Name and briefly describe the two subclassifications of structural composites.**

15.1 INTRODUCTION

Many of our modern technologies require materials with unusual combinations of properties that cannot be met by the conventional metal alloys, ceramics, and polymeric materials. This is especially true for materials that are needed for aerospace, underwater, and transportation applications. For example, aircraft engineers are increasingly searching for structural materials that have low densities, are strong, stiff, and abrasion and impact resistant, and are not easily corroded. This is a rather formidable combination of characteristics. Frequently, strong materials are relatively dense; also, increasing the strength or stiffness generally results in a decrease in impact strength.

Material property combinations and ranges have been, and are yet being, extended by the development of composite materials. Generally speaking, a composite is considered to be any multiphase material that exhibits a significant proportion of the properties of both constituent phases such that a better combination of properties is realized. According to this **principle of combined action,** better property combinations are fashioned by the judicious combination of two or more distinct materials. Property trade-offs are also made for many composites.

Composites of sorts have already been discussed; these include multiphase metal alloys, ceramics, and polymers. For example, pearlitic steels (Section 7.19) have a microstructure consisting of alternating layers of α ferrite and cementite (Figure 7.27). The ferrite phase is soft and ductile, whereas cementite is hard and very brittle. The combined mechanical characteristics of the pearlite (reasonably high ductility and strength) are superior to those of either of the constituent phases. There are also a number of composites that occur in nature. For example, wood consists of strong and flexible cellulose fibers surrounded and held together by a stiffer material called lignin. Also, bone is a composite of the strong yet soft protein collagen and the hard, brittle mineral apatite.

A composite, in the present context, is a multiphase material that is *artificially made,* as opposed to one that occurs or forms naturally. In addition, the constituent phases must be chemically dissimilar and separated by a distinct interface. Thus, most metallic alloys and many ceramics do not fit this definition because their multiple phases are formed as a consequence of natural phenomena.

In designing composite materials, scientists and engineers have ingeniously combined various metals, ceramics, and polymers to produce a new generation of

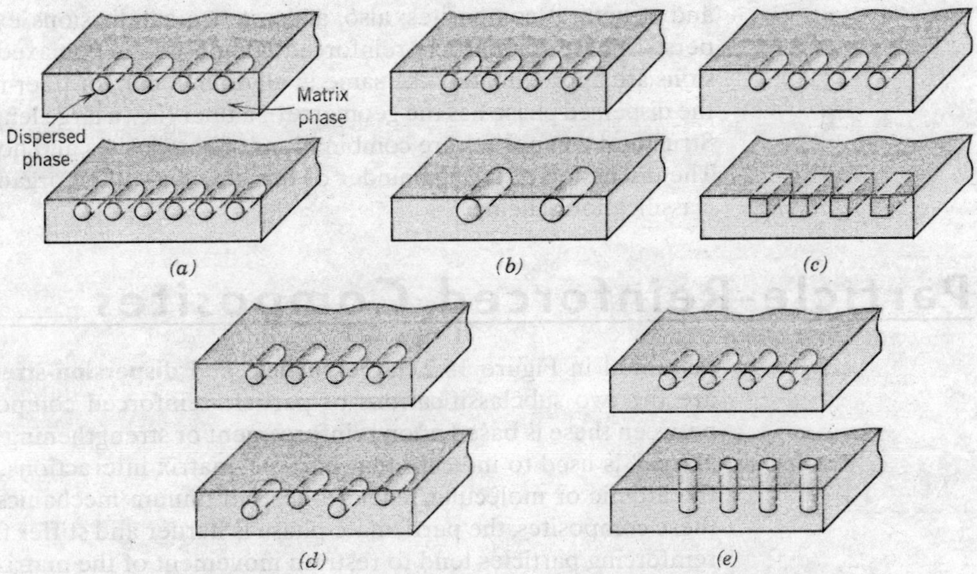

Figure 15.1 Schematic representations of the various geometrical and spatial characteristics of particles of the dispersed phase that may influence the properties of composites: (*a*) concentration, (*b*) size, (*c*) shape, (*d*) distribution, and (*e*) orientation. (From Richard A. Flinn and Paul K. Trojan, *Engineering Materials and Their Applications,* 4th edition. Copyright © 1990 by John Wiley & Sons, Inc. Adapted by permission of John Wiley & Sons, Inc.)

extraordinary materials. Most composites have been created to improve combinations of mechanical characteristics such as stiffness, toughness, and ambient and high-temperature strength.

Many composite materials are composed of just two phases; one is termed the **matrix,** which is continuous and surrounds the other phase, often called the **dispersed phase.** The properties of composites are a function of the properties of the constituent phases, their relative amounts, and the geometry of the dispersed phase. "Dispersed phase geometry" in this context means the shape of the particles and the particle size, distribution, and orientation; these characteristics are represented in Figure 15.1.

One simple scheme for the classification of composite materials is shown in Figure 15.2, which consists of three main divisions: particle-reinforced, fiber-reinforced,

Figure 15.2 A classification scheme for the various composite types discussed in this chapter.

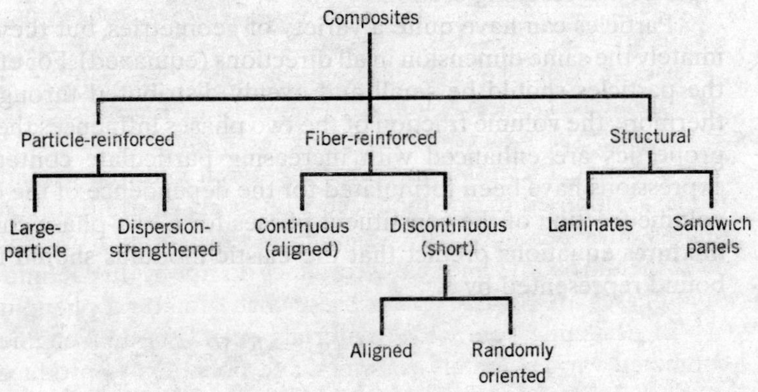

and structural composites; also, at least two subdivisions exist for each. The dispersed phase for particle-reinforced composites is equiaxed (i.e., particle dimensions are approximately the same in all directions); for fiber-reinforced composites, the dispersed phase has the geometry of a fiber (i.e., a large length-to-diameter ratio). Structural composites are combinations of composites and homogeneous materials. The discussion of the remainder of this chapter will be organized according to this classification scheme.

Particle-Reinforced Composites

As noted in Figure 15.2, **large-particle** and **dispersion-strengthened composites** are the two subclassifications of particle-reinforced composites. The distinction between these is based upon reinforcement or strengthening mechanism. The term "large" is used to indicate that particle–matrix interactions cannot be treated on the atomic or molecular level; rather, continuum mechanics is used. For most of these composites, the particulate phase is harder and stiffer than the matrix. These reinforcing particles tend to restrain movement of the matrix phase in the vicinity of each particle. In essence, the matrix transfers some of the applied stress to the particles, which bear a fraction of the load. The degree of reinforcement or improvement of mechanical behavior depends on strong bonding at the matrix–particle interface.

For dispersion-strengthened composites, particles are normally much smaller, with diameters between 0.01 and 0.1 μm (10 and 100 nm). Particle–matrix interactions that lead to strengthening occur on the atomic or molecular level. The mechanism of strengthening is similar to that for precipitation hardening discussed in Section 10.14. Whereas the matrix bears the major portion of an applied load, the small dispersed particles hinder or impede the motion of dislocations. Thus, plastic deformation is restricted such that yield and tensile strengths, as well as hardness, improve.

15.2 LARGE-PARTICLE COMPOSITES

Some polymeric materials to which fillers have been added (Section 14.21) are really large-particle composites. Again, the fillers modify or improve the properties of the material and/or replace some of the polymer volume with a less expensive material—the filler.

Another familiar large-particle composite is concrete, which is composed of cement (the matrix), and sand and gravel (the particulates). Concrete is the discussion topic of a succeeding section.

Particles can have quite a variety of geometries, but they should be of approximately the same dimension in all directions (equiaxed). For effective reinforcement, the particles should be small and evenly distributed throughout the matrix. Furthermore, the volume fraction of the two phases influences the behavior; mechanical properties are enhanced with increasing particulate content. Two mathematical expressions have been formulated for the dependence of the elastic modulus on the volume fraction of the constituent phases for a two-phase composite. These **rule of mixtures** equations predict that the elastic modulus should fall between an upper bound represented by

$$E_c(u) = E_m V_m + E_p V_p \tag{15.1}$$

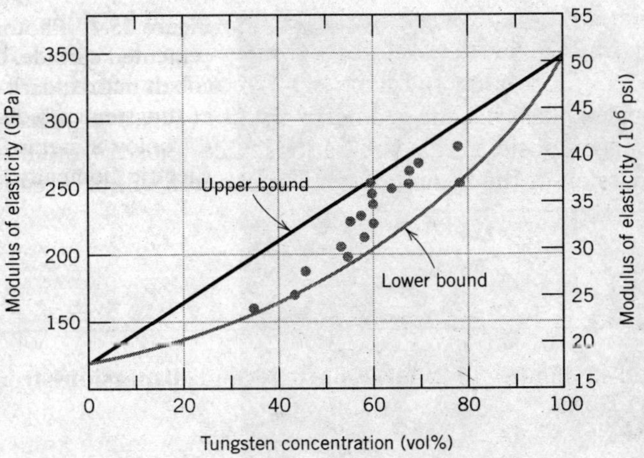

Figure 15.3 Modulus of elasticity versus volume percent tungsten for a composite of tungsten particles dispersed within a copper matrix. Upper and lower bounds are according to Equations 15.1 and 15.2; experimental data points are included. (From R. H. Krock, *ASTM Proceedings*, Vol. 63, 1963. Copyright ASTM, 1916 Race Street, Philadelphia, PA 19103. Reprinted with permission.)

and a lower bound, or limit,

$$E_c(l) = \frac{E_m E_p}{V_m E_p + V_p E_m} \tag{15.2}$$

In these expressions, E and V denote the elastic modulus and volume fraction, respectively, whereas the subscripts c, m, and p represent composite, matrix, and particulate phases. Figure 15.3 plots upper- and lower-bound E_c-versus-V_p curves for a copper–tungsten composite, in which tungsten is the particulate phase; experimental data points fall between the two curves. Equations analogous to 15.1 and 15.2 for fiber-reinforced composites are derived in Section 15.5.

Large-particle composites are utilized with all three material types (metals, polymers, and ceramics). The **cermets** are examples of ceramic–metal composites. The most common cermet is the cemented carbide, which is composed of extremely hard particles of a refractory carbide ceramic such as tungsten carbide (WC) or titanium carbide (TiC), embedded in a matrix of a metal such as cobalt or nickel. These composites are utilized extensively as cutting tools for hardened steels. The hard carbide particles provide the cutting surface but, being extremely brittle, are not themselves capable of withstanding the cutting stresses. Toughness is enhanced by their inclusion in the ductile metal matrix, which isolates the carbide particles from one another and prevents particle-to-particle crack propagation. Both matrix and particulate phases are quite refractory, to withstand the high temperatures generated by the cutting action on materials that are extremely hard. No single material could possibly provide the combination of properties possessed by a cermet. Relatively large volume fractions of the particulate phase may be utilized, often exceeding 90 vol%; thus the abrasive action of the composite is maximized. A photomicrograph of a WC–Co cemented carbide is shown in Figure 15.4.

Both elastomers and plastics are frequently reinforced with various particulate materials. Our use of many of the modern rubbers would be severely restricted without reinforcing particulate materials such as carbon black. Carbon black consists of very small and essentially spherical particles of carbon, produced by the combustion of natural gas or oil in an atmosphere that has only a limited air supply. When added to vulcanized rubber, this extremely inexpensive material enhances tensile strength, toughness, and tear and abrasion resistance. Automobile tires contain on the order of 15 to 30 vol% of carbon black. For the carbon black to provide significant

Figure 15.4 Photomicrograph of a WC–Co cemented carbide. Light areas are the cobalt matrix; dark regions, the particles of tungsten carbide. 100×. (Courtesy of Carboloy Systems Department, General Electric Company.)

reinforcement, the particle size must be extremely small, with diameters between 20 and 50 nm; also, the particles must be evenly distributed throughout the rubber and must form a strong adhesive bond with the rubber matrix. Particle reinforcement using other materials (e.g., silica) is much less effective because this special interaction between the rubber molecules and particle surfaces does not exist. Figure 15.5 is an electron micrograph of a carbon black-reinforced rubber.

Concrete

Concrete is a common large-particle composite in which both matrix and dispersed phases are ceramic materials. Since the terms "concrete" and "cement" are sometimes incorrectly interchanged, perhaps it is appropriate to make a distinction between them. In a broad sense, concrete implies a composite material consisting of an aggregate of particles that are bound together in a solid body by some type of binding medium, that is, a cement. The two most familiar concretes are those made with portland and

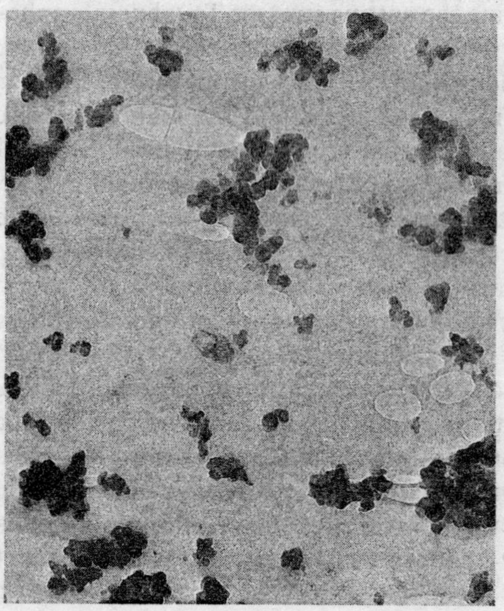

Figure 15.5 Electron micrograph showing the spherical reinforcing carbon black particles in a synthetic rubber tire tread compound. The areas resembling water marks are tiny air pockets in the rubber. 80,000×. (Courtesy of Goodyear Tire & Rubber Company.)

asphaltic cements, where the aggregate is gravel and sand. Asphaltic concrete is widely used primarily as a paving material, whereas portland cement concrete is employed extensively as a structural building material. Only the latter is treated in this discussion.

Portland Cement Concrete

The ingredients for this concrete are portland cement, a fine aggregate (sand), a coarse aggregate (gravel), and water. The process by which portland cement is produced and the mechanism of setting and hardening were discussed very briefly in Section 12.7. The aggregate particles act as a filler material to reduce the overall cost of the concrete product because they are cheap, whereas cement is relatively expensive. To achieve the optimum strength and workability of a concrete mixture, the ingredients must be added in the correct proportions. Dense packing of the aggregate and good interfacial contact are achieved by having particles of two different sizes; the fine particles of sand should fill the void spaces between the gravel particles. Ordinarily these aggregates comprise between 60% and 80% of the total volume. The amount of cement–water paste should be sufficient to coat all the sand and gravel particles, otherwise the cementitious bond will be incomplete. Furthermore, all the constituents should be thoroughly mixed. Complete bonding between cement and the aggregate particles is contingent upon the addition of the correct quantity of water. Too little water leads to incomplete bonding, and too much results in excessive porosity; in either case the final strength is less than the optimum.

The character of the aggregate particles is an important consideration. In particular, the size distribution of the aggregates influences the amount of cement–water paste required. Also, the surfaces should be clean and free from clay and silt, which prevent the formation of a sound bond at the particle surface.

Portland cement concrete is a major material of construction, primarily because it can be poured in place and hardens at room temperature, and even when submerged in water. However, as a structural material, there are some limitations and disadvantages. Like most ceramics, portland cement concrete is relatively weak and extremely brittle; its tensile strength is approximately 10 to 15 times smaller than its compressive strength. Also, large concrete structures can experience considerable thermal expansion and contraction with temperature fluctuations. In addition, water penetrates into external pores, which can cause severe cracking in cold weather as a consequence of freeze–thaw cycles. Most of these inadequacies may be eliminated or at least improved by reinforcement and/or the incorporation of additives.

Reinforced Concrete

The strength of portland cement concrete may be increased by additional reinforcement. This is usually accomplished by means of steel rods, wires, bars (rebar), or mesh, which are embedded into the fresh and uncured concrete. Thus, the reinforcement renders the hardened structure capable of supporting greater tensile, compressive, and shear stresses. Even if cracks develop in the concrete, considerable reinforcement is maintained.

Steel serves as a suitable reinforcement material because its coefficient of thermal expansion is nearly the same as that of concrete. In addition, steel is not rapidly corroded in the cement environment, and a relatively strong adhesive bond is formed between it and the cured concrete. This adhesion may be enhanced by the incorporation of contours into the surface of the steel member, which permits a greater degree of mechanical interlocking.

Portland cement concrete may also be reinforced by mixing into the fresh concrete fibers of a high-modulus material such as glass, steel, nylon, and polyethylene.

Care must be exercised in utilizing this type of reinforcement, since some fiber materials experience rapid deterioration when exposed to the cement environment.

Still another reinforcement technique for strengthening concrete involves the introduction of residual compressive stresses into the structural member; the resulting material is called **prestressed concrete.** This method utilizes one characteristic of brittle ceramics—namely, that they are stronger in compression than in tension. Thus, to fracture a prestressed concrete member, the magnitude of the precompressive stress must be exceeded by an applied tensile stress.

In one such prestressing technique, high-strength steel wires are positioned inside the empty molds and stretched with a high tensile force, which is maintained constant. After the concrete has been placed and allowed to harden, the tension is released. As the wires contract, they put the structure in a state of compression because the stress is transmitted to the concrete via the concrete–wire bond that is formed.

Another technique is also utilized in which stresses are applied after the concrete hardens; it is appropriately called *posttensioning.* Sheet metal or rubber tubes are situated inside and pass through the concrete forms, around which the concrete is cast. After the cement has hardened, steel wires are fed through the resulting holes, and tension is applied to the wires by means of jacks attached and abutted to the faces of the structure. Again, a compressive stress is imposed on the concrete piece, this time by the jacks. Finally, the empty spaces inside the tubing are filled with a grout to protect the wire from corrosion.

Concrete that is prestressed should be of a high quality, with a low shrinkage and a low creep rate. Prestressed concretes, usually prefabricated, are commonly used for highway and railway bridges.

15.3 DISPERSION-STRENGTHENED COMPOSITES

Metals and metal alloys may be strengthened and hardened by the uniform dispersion of several volume percent of fine particles of a very hard and inert material. The dispersed phase may be metallic or nonmetallic; oxide materials are often used. Again, the strengthening mechanism involves interactions between the particles and dislocations within the matrix, as with precipitation hardening. The dispersion strengthening effect is not as pronounced as with precipitation hardening; however, the strengthening is retained at elevated temperatures and for extended time periods because the dispersed particles are chosen to be unreactive with the matrix phase. For precipitation-hardened alloys, the increase in strength may disappear upon heat treatment as a consequence of precipitate growth or dissolution of the precipitate phase.

The high-temperature strength of nickel alloys may be enhanced significantly by the addition of about 3 vol% of thoria (ThO_2) as finely dispersed particles; this material is known as thoria-dispersed (or TD) nickel. The same effect is produced in the aluminum–aluminum oxide system. A very thin and adherent alumina coating is caused to form on the surface of extremely small (0.1 to 0.2 μm thick) flakes of aluminum, which are dispersed within an aluminum metal matrix; this material is termed sintered aluminum powder (SAP).

Concept Check 15.1

Cite the general difference in strengthening mechanism between large-particle and dispersion-strengthened particle-reinforced composites.

[*The answer may be found in enclosed CD.*]

Fiber-Reinforced Composites

Technologically, the most important composites are those in which the dispersed phase is in the form of a fiber. Design goals of **fiber-reinforced composites** often include high strength and/or stiffness on a weight basis. These characteristics are expressed in terms of **specific strength** and **specific modulus** parameters, which correspond, respectively, to the ratios of tensile strength to specific gravity and modulus of elasticity to specific gravity. Fiber-reinforced composites with exceptionally high specific strengths and moduli have been produced that utilize low-density fiber and matrix materials.

As noted in Figure 15.2, fiber-reinforced composites are subclassified by fiber length. For short fiber, the fibers are too short to produce a significant improvement in strength.

15.4 INFLUENCE OF FIBER LENGTH

The mechanical characteristics of a fiber-reinforced composite depend not only on the properties of the fiber, but also on the degree to which an applied load is transmitted to the fibers by the matrix phase. Important to the extent of this load transmittance is the magnitude of the interfacial bond between the fiber and matrix phases. Under an applied stress, this fiber–matrix bond ceases at the fiber ends, yielding a matrix deformation pattern as shown schematically in Figure 15.6; in other words, there is no load transmittance from the matrix at each fiber extremity.

Some critical fiber length is necessary for effective strengthening and stiffening of the composite material. This critical length l_c is dependent on the fiber diameter d and its ultimate (or tensile) strength σ_f^*, and on the fiber–matrix bond strength (or the shear yield strength of the matrix, whichever is smaller) τ_c according to

$$l_c = \frac{\sigma_f^* d}{2\tau_c} \tag{15.3}$$

For a number of glass and carbon fiber–matrix combinations, this critical length is on the order of 1 mm, which ranges between 20 and 150 times the fiber diameter.

When a stress equal to σ_f^* is applied to a fiber having just this critical length, the stress–position profile shown in Figure 15.7*a* results; that is, the maximum fiber load is achieved only at the axial center of the fiber. As fiber length l increases, the fiber reinforcement becomes more effective; this is demonstrated in Figure 15.7*b*, a stress–axial position profile for $l > l_c$ when the applied stress is equal to the fiber strength. Figure 15.7*c* shows the stress–position profile for $l < l_c$.

Fibers for which $l \gg l_c$ (normally $l > 15l_c$) are termed *continuous; discontinuous* or *short fibers* have lengths shorter than this. For discontinuous fibers of lengths

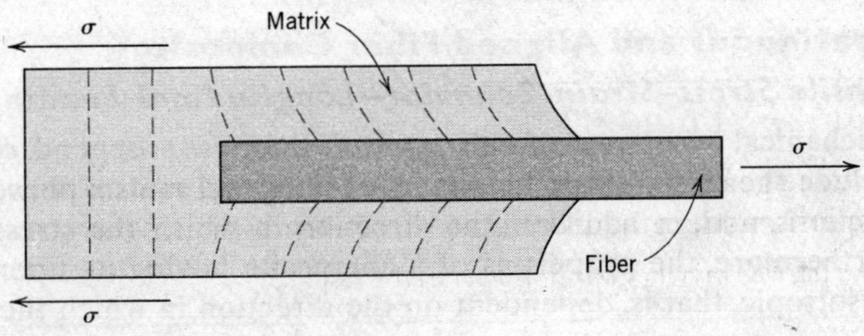

Figure 15.6 The deformation pattern in the matrix surrounding a fiber that is subjected to an applied tensile load.

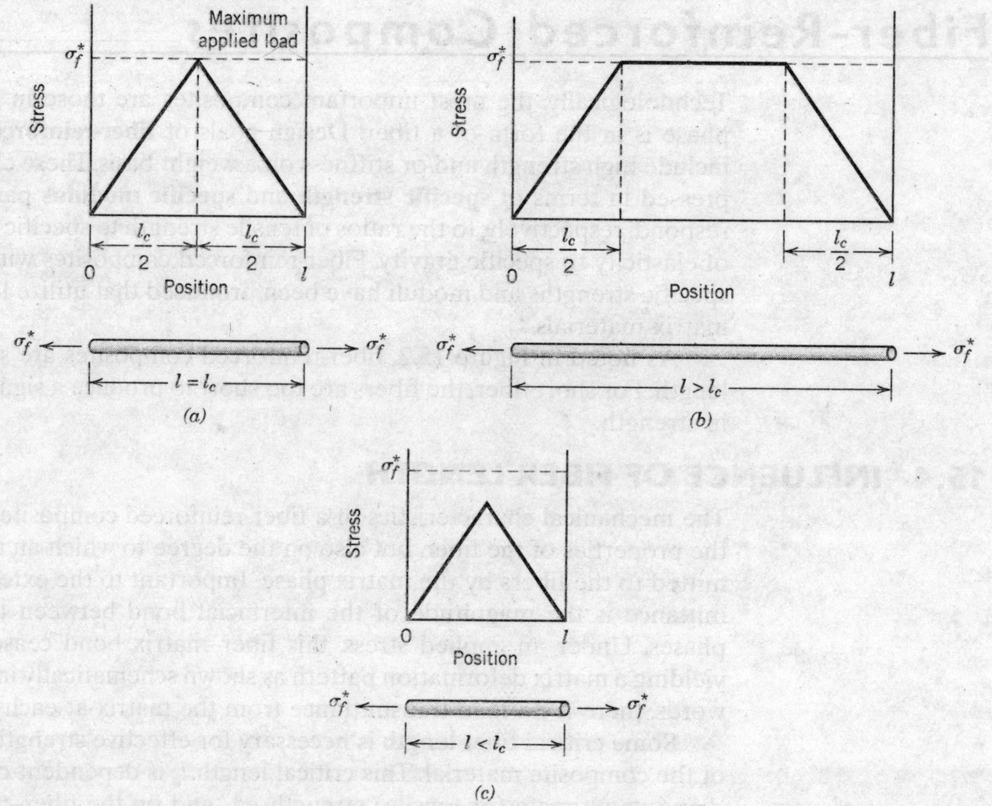

Figure 15.7 Stress–position profiles when fiber length l (*a*) is equal to the critical length l_c, (*b*) is greater than the critical length, and (*c*) is less than the critical length for a fiber-reinforced composite that is subjected to a tensile stress equal to the fiber tensile strength σ_f^*.

significantly less than l_c, the matrix deforms around the fiber such that there is virtually no stress transference and little reinforcement by the fiber. These are essentially the particulate composites as described above. To affect a significant improvement in strength of the composite, the fibers must be continuous.

15.5 INFLUENCE OF FIBER ORIENTATION AND CONCENTRATION

The arrangement or orientation of the fibers relative to one another, the fiber concentration, and the distribution all have a significant influence on the strength and other properties of fiber-reinforced composites. With respect to orientation, two extremes are possible: (1) a parallel alignment of the longitudinal axis of the fibers in a single direction, and (2) a totally random alignment. Continuous fibers are normally aligned (Figure 15.8*a*), whereas discontinuous fibers may be aligned (Figure 15.8*b*), randomly oriented (Figure 15.8*c*), or partially oriented. Better overall composite properties are realized when the fiber distribution is uniform.

Continuous and Aligned Fiber Composites

Tensile Stress–Strain Behavior—Longitudinal Loading

Mechanical responses of this type of composite depend on several factors to include the stress–strain behaviors of fiber and matrix phases, the phase volume fractions, and, in addition, the direction in which the stress or load is applied. Furthermore, the properties of a composite having its fibers aligned are highly anisotropic, that is, dependent on the direction in which they are measured. Let

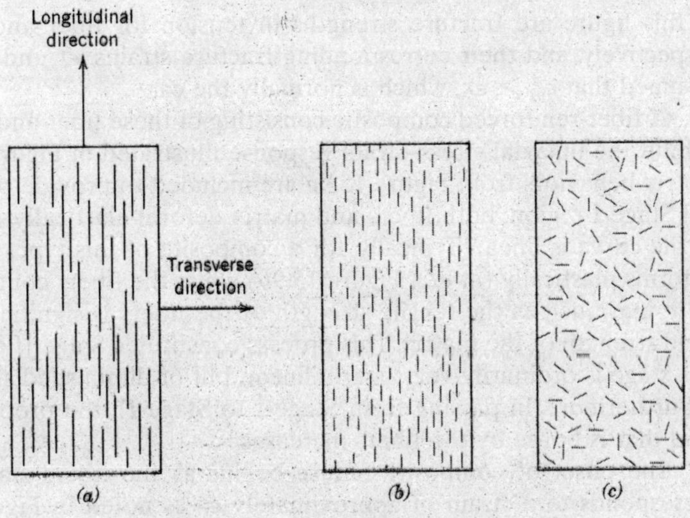

Figure 15.8 Schematic representations of (*a*) continuous and aligned, (*b*) discontinuous and aligned, and (*c*) discontinuous and randomly oriented fiber-reinforced composites.

us first consider the stress–strain behavior for the situation wherein the stress is applied along the direction of alignment, the **longitudinal direction,** which is indicated in Figure 15.8*a*.

To begin, assume the stress versus strain behaviors for fiber and matrix phases that are represented schematically in Figure 15.9*a*; in this treatment we consider the fiber to be totally brittle and the matrix phase to be reasonably ductile. Also indicated

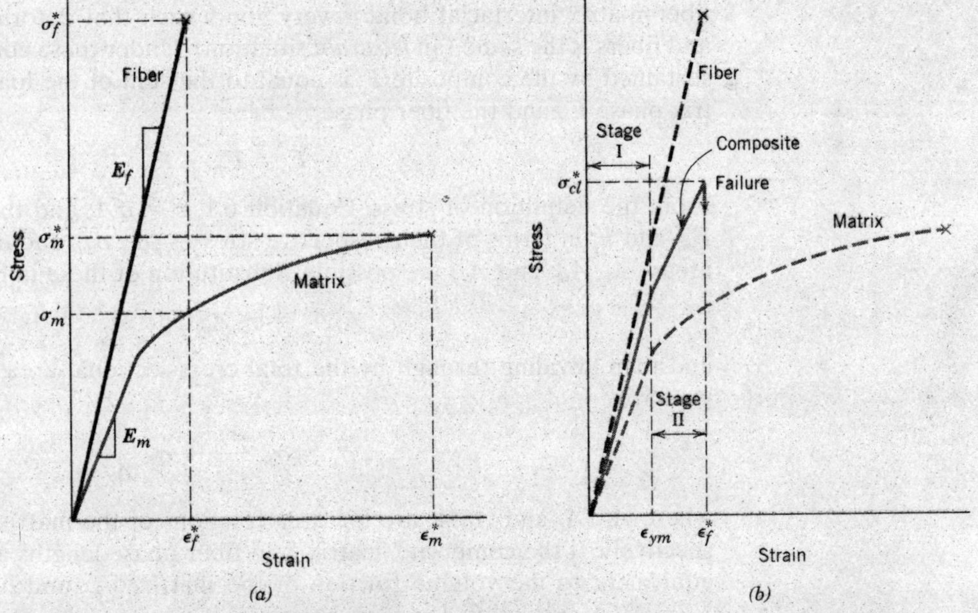

Figure 15.9 (*a*) Schematic stress–strain curves for brittle fiber and ductile matrix materials. Fracture stresses and strains for both materials are noted. (*b*) Schematic stress–strain curve for an aligned fiber-reinforced composite that is exposed to a uniaxial stress applied in the direction of alignment; curves for the fiber and matrix materials shown in part (*a*) are also superimposed.

in this figure are fracture strengths in tension for fiber and matrix, σ_f^* and σ_m^*, respectively, and their corresponding fracture strains, ϵ_f^* and ϵ_m^*; furthermore, it is assumed that $\epsilon_m^* > \epsilon_f^*$, which is normally the case.

A fiber-reinforced composite consisting of these fiber and matrix materials will exhibit the uniaxial stress–strain response illustrated in Figure 15.9*b*; the fiber and matrix behaviors from Figure 15.9*a* are included to provide perspective. In the initial Stage I region, both fibers and matrix deform elastically; normally this portion of the curve is linear. Typically, for a composite of this type, the matrix yields and deforms plastically (at ϵ_{ym}, Figure 15.9*b*) while the fibers continue to stretch elastically, inasmuch as the tensile strength of the fibers is significantly higher than the yield strength of the matrix. This process constitutes Stage II as noted in the figure; this stage is ordinarily very nearly linear, but of diminished slope relative to Stage I. Furthermore, in passing from Stage I to Stage II, the proportion of the applied load that is borne by the fibers increases.

The onset of composite failure begins as the fibers start to fracture, which corresponds to a strain of approximately ϵ_f^* as noted in Figure 15.9*b*. Composite failure is not catastrophic for a couple of reasons. First, not all fibers fracture at the same time, since there will always be considerable variations in the fracture strength of brittle fiber materials (Section 12.10). In addition, even after fiber failure, the matrix is still intact inasmuch as $\epsilon_f^* < \epsilon_m^*$ (Figure 15.9*a*). Thus, these fractured fibers, which are shorter than the original ones, are still embedded within the intact matrix, and consequently are capable of sustaining a diminished load as the matrix continues to plastically deform.

Elastic Behavior—Longitudinal Loading

Let us now consider the elastic behavior of a continuous and oriented fibrous composite that is loaded in the direction of fiber alignment. First, it is assumed that the fiber–matrix interfacial bond is very good, such that deformation of both matrix and fibers is the same (an *isostrain* situation). Under these conditions, the total load sustained by the composite F_c is equal to the sum of the loads carried by the matrix phase F_m and the fiber phase F_f, or

$$F_c = F_m + F_f \tag{15.4}$$

From the definition of stress, Equation 6.1, $F = \sigma A$; and thus expressions for F_c, F_m, and F_f in terms of their respective stresses (σ_c, σ_m, and σ_f) and cross-sectional areas (A_c, A_m, and A_f) are possible. Substitution of these into Equation 15.4 yields

$$\sigma_c A_c = \sigma_m A_m + \sigma_f A_f \tag{15.5}$$

and then, dividing through by the total cross-sectional area of the composite, A_c, we have

$$\sigma_c = \sigma_m \frac{A_m}{A_c} + \sigma_f \frac{A_f}{A_c} \tag{15.6}$$

where A_m/A_c and A_f/A_c are the area fractions of the matrix and fiber phases, respectively. If the composite, matrix, and fiber phase lengths are all equal, A_m/A_c is equivalent to the volume fraction of the matrix, V_m, and likewise for the fibers, $V_f = A_f/A_c$. Equation 15.6 now becomes

$$\sigma_c = \sigma_m V_m + \sigma_f V_f \tag{15.7}$$

The previous assumption of an isostrain state means that

$$\epsilon_c = \epsilon_m = \epsilon_f \tag{15.8}$$

and when each term in Equation 15.7 is divided by its respective strain,

$$\frac{\sigma_c}{\epsilon_c} = \frac{\sigma_m}{\epsilon_m} V_m + \frac{\sigma_f}{\epsilon_f} V_f \tag{15.9}$$

Furthermore, if composite, matrix, and fiber deformations are all elastic, then $\sigma_c/\epsilon_c = E_c$, $\sigma_m/\epsilon_m = E_m$, and $\sigma_f/\epsilon_f = E_f$, the E's being the moduli of elasticity for the respective phases. Substitution into Equation 15.9 yields an expression for the modulus of elasticity of a continuous and aligned fibrous composite *in the direction of alignment* (or *longitudinal direction*), E_{cl}, as

$$E_{cl} = E_m V_m + E_f V_f \tag{15.10a}$$

or

$$E_{cl} = E_m(1 - V_f) + E_f V_f \tag{15.10b}$$

since the composite consists of only matrix and fiber phases; that is, $V_m + V_f = 1$.

Thus, E_{cl} is equal to the volume-fraction weighted average of the moduli of elasticity of the fiber and matrix phases. Other properties, including density, also have this dependence on volume fractions. Equation 15.10*a* is the fiber analogue of Equation 15.1, the upper bound for particle-reinforced composites.

It can also be shown, for longitudinal loading, that the ratio of the load carried by the fibers to that carried by the matrix is

$$\frac{F_f}{F_m} = \frac{E_f V_f}{E_m V_m} \tag{15.11}$$

The demonstration is left as a homework problem.

EXAMPLE PROBLEM 15.1

Property Determinations for a Glass Fiber-Reinforced Composite—Longitudinal Direction

A continuous and aligned glass fiber-reinforced composite consists of 40 vol% of glass fibers having a modulus of elasticity of 69 GPa and 60 vol% of a polyester resin that, when hardened, displays a modulus of 3.4 GPa.

(a) Compute the modulus of elasticity of this composite in the longitudinal direction.

(b) If the cross-sectional area is 250 mm^2 and a stress of 50 MPa is applied in this longitudinal direction, compute the magnitude of the load carried by each of the fiber and matrix phases.

(c) Determine the strain that is sustained by each phase when the stress in part (b) is applied.

Solution

(a) The modulus of elasticity of the composite is calculated using Equation 15.10a:

$$E_{cl} = (3.4\ \text{GPa})(0.6) + (69\ \text{GPa})(0.4) = 30\ \text{GPa}$$

(b) To solve this portion of the problem, first find the ratio of fiber load to matrix load, using Equation 15.11; thus,

$$\frac{F_f}{F_m} = \frac{(69 \text{ GPa})(0.4)}{(3.4 \text{ GPa})(0.6)} = 13.5$$

or $F_f = 13.5\ F_m$.

In addition, the total force sustained by the composite F_c may be computed from the applied stress σ and total composite cross-sectional area A_c according to

$$F_c = A_c\sigma = (250 \text{ mm}^2)(50 \text{ MPa}) = 12{,}500 \text{ N}$$

However, this total load is just the sum of the loads carried by fiber and matrix phases; that is,

$$F_c = F_f + F_m = 12{,}500 \text{ N}$$

Substitution for F_f from the above yields

$$13.5\ F_m + F_m = 12{,}500 \text{ N}$$

or

$$F_m = 860 \text{ N}$$

whereas

$$F_f = F_c - F_m = 12{,}500 \text{ N} - 860 \text{ N} = 11{,}640 \text{ N}$$

Thus, the fiber phase supports the vast majority of the applied load.

(c) The stress for both fiber and matrix phases must first be calculated. Then, by using the elastic modulus for each (from part a), the strain values may be determined.

For stress calculations, phase cross-sectional areas are necessary:

$$A_m = V_m A_c = (0.6)(250 \text{ mm}^2) = 150 \text{ mm}^2$$

and

$$A_f = V_f A_c = (0.4)(250 \text{ mm}^2) = 100 \text{ mm}^2$$

Thus,

$$\sigma_m = \frac{F_m}{A_m} = \frac{860 \text{ N}}{150 \text{ mm}^2} = 5.73 \text{ MPa}$$

$$\sigma_f = \frac{F_f}{A_f} = \frac{11{,}640 \text{ N}}{100 \text{ mm}^2} = 116.4 \text{ MPa}$$

Finally, strains are computed as

$$\epsilon_m = \frac{\sigma_m}{E_m} = \frac{5.73 \text{ MPa}}{3.4 \times 10^3 \text{ MPa}} = 1.69 \times 10^{-3}$$

$$\epsilon_f = \frac{\sigma_f}{E_f} = \frac{116.4 \text{ MPa}}{69 \times 10^3 \text{ MPa}} = 1.69 \times 10^{-3}$$

Therefore, strains for both matrix and fiber phases are identical, which they should be, according to Equation 15.8 in the previous development.

Elastic Behavior—Transverse Loading

A continuous and oriented fiber composite may be loaded in the **transverse direction;** that is, the load is applied at a 90° angle to the direction of fiber alignment as shown in Figure 15.8*a*. For this situation the stress σ to which the composite as well as both phases are exposed is the same, or

$$\sigma_c = \sigma_m = \sigma_f = \sigma \tag{15.12}$$

This is termed an *isostress* state. Also, the strain or deformation of the entire composite ϵ_c is

$$\epsilon_c = \epsilon_m V_m + \epsilon_f V_f \tag{15.13}$$

but, since $\epsilon = \sigma / E$,

$$\frac{\sigma}{E_{ct}} = \frac{\sigma}{E_m} V_m + \frac{\sigma}{E_f} V_f \tag{15.14}$$

where E_{ct} is the modulus of elasticity in the transverse direction. Now, dividing through by σ yields

$$\frac{1}{E_{ct}} = \frac{V_m}{E_m} + \frac{V_f}{E_f} \tag{15.15}$$

which reduces to

$$E_{ct} = \frac{E_m E_f}{V_m E_f + V_f E_m} = \frac{E_m E_f}{(1 - V_f)E_f + V_f E_m} \tag{15.16}$$

Equation 15.16 is analogous to the lower-bound expression for particulate composites, Equation 15.2.

EXAMPLE PROBLEM 15.2

Elastic Modulus Determination for a Glass Fiber-Reinforced Composite—Transverse Direction

Compute the elastic modulus of the composite material described in Example Problem 15.1, but assume that the stress is applied perpendicular to the direction of fiber alignment.

Solution

According to Equation 15.16,

$$E_{ct} = \frac{(3.4 \text{ GPa})(69 \text{ GPa})}{(0.6)(69 \text{ GPa}) + (0.4)(3.4 \text{ GPa})}$$
$$= 5.5 \text{ GPa}$$

This value for E_{ct} is slightly greater than that of the matrix phase but, from Example Problem 15.1a, only approximately one-fifth of the modulus of elasticity along the fiber direction (E_{cl}), which indicates the degree of anisotropy of continuous and oriented fiber composites.

Table 15.1 Typical Longitudinal and Transverse Tensile Strengths for Three Unidirectional Fiber-Reinforced Composites. The Fiber Content for Each Is Approximately 50 Vol%

Material	*Longitudinal Tensile Strength (MPa)*	*Transverse Tensile Strength (MPa)*
Glass–polyester	700	20
Carbon (high modulus)–epoxy	1000	35
Kevlar™–epoxy	1200	20

Source: D. Hull and T. W. Clyne, *An Introduction to Composite Materials,* 2nd edition, Cambridge University Press, 1996, p. 179.

Longitudinal Tensile Strength

We now consider the strength characteristics of continuous and aligned fiber-reinforced composites that are loaded in the longitudinal direction. Under these circumstances, strength is normally taken as the maximum stress on the stress–strain curve, Figure 15.9*b*; often this point corresponds to fiber fracture, and marks the onset of composite failure. Table 15.1 lists typical longitudinal tensile strength values for three common fibrous composites. Failure of this type of composite material is a relatively complex process, and several different failure modes are possible. The mode that operates for a specific composite will depend on fiber and matrix properties, and the nature and strength of the fiber–matrix interfacial bond.

If we assume that $\epsilon_f^* < \epsilon_m^*$ (Figure 15.9*a*), which is the usual case, then fibers will fail before the matrix. Once the fibers have fractured, the majority of the load that was borne by the fibers is now transferred to the matrix. This being the case, it is possible to adapt the expression for the stress on this type of composite, Equation 15.7, into the following expression for the longitudinal strength of the composite, σ_{cl}^*:

$$\sigma_{cl}^* = \sigma_m'(1 - V_f) + \sigma_f^* V_f \tag{15.17}$$

Here σ_m' is the stress in the matrix at fiber failure (as illustrated in Figure 15.9*a*) and, as previously, σ_f^* is the fiber tensile strength.

Transverse Tensile Strength

The strengths of continuous and unidirectional fibrous composites are highly anisotropic, and such composites are normally designed to be loaded along the high-strength, longitudinal direction. However, during in-service applications transverse tensile loads may also be present. Under these circumstances, premature failure may result inasmuch as transverse strength is usually extremely low—it sometimes lies below the tensile strength of the matrix. Thus, in actual fact, the reinforcing effect of the fibers is a negative one. Typical transverse tensile strengths for three unidirectional composites are contained in Table 15.1.

Whereas longitudinal strength is dominated by fiber strength, a variety of factors will have a significant influence on the transverse strength; these factors include properties of both the fiber and matrix, the fiber–matrix bond strength, and the presence of voids. Measures that have been employed to improve the transverse strength of these composites usually involve modifying properties of the matrix.

Concept Check 15.2

In the table below are listed four hypothetical aligned fiber-reinforced composites (labeled A through D), along with their characteristics. On the basis of these data, rank the four composites from highest to lowest strength in the longitudinal direction, and then justify your ranking.

Composite	*Fiber Type*	*Vol. Fraction Fibers*	*Fiber Strength (MPa)*	*Ave. Fiber Length (mm)*	*Critical Length (mm)*
A	glass	0.20	3.5×10^3	8	0.70
B	glass	0.35	3.5×10^3	12	0.75
C	carbon	0.40	5.5×10^3	8	0.40
D	carbon	0.30	5.5×10^3	8	0.50

[The answer may be found in enclosed CD.]

Discontinuous and Aligned Fiber Composites

Even though reinforcement efficiency is lower for discontinuous than for continuous fibers, discontinuous and aligned fiber composites (Figure 15.8*b*) are becoming increasingly more important in the commercial market. Chopped glass fibers are used most extensively; however, carbon and aramid discontinuous fibers are also employed. These short fiber composites can be produced having moduli of elasticity and tensile strengths that approach 90% and 50%, respectively, of their continuous fiber counterparts.

For a discontinuous and aligned fiber composite having a uniform distribution of fibers and in which $l > l_c$, the longitudinal strength (σ^*_{cd}) is given by the relationship

$$\sigma^*_{cd} = \sigma^*_f V_f \left(1 - \frac{l_c}{2l}\right) + \sigma'_m(1 - V_f) \tag{15.18}$$

where σ^*_f and σ'_m represent, respectively, the fracture strength of the fiber and the stress in the matrix when the composite fails (Figure 15.9*a*).

If the fiber length is less than critical ($l < l_c$), then the longitudinal strength ($\sigma^*_{cd'}$) is given by

$$\sigma^*_{cd'} = \frac{l\tau_c}{d} V_f + \sigma'_m(1 - V_f) \tag{15.19}$$

where d is the fiber diameter and τ_c is the smaller of either the fiber–matrix bond strength or the matrix shear yield strength.

Discontinuous and Randomly Oriented Fiber Composites

Normally, when the fiber orientation is random, short and discontinuous fibers are used; reinforcement of this type is schematically demonstrated in Figure 15.8*c*. Under these circumstances, a "rule-of-mixtures" expression for the elastic modulus similar to Equation 15.10*a* may be utilized, as follows:

$$E_{cd} = KE_f V_f + E_m V_m \tag{15.20}$$

Table 15.2 Properties of Unreinforced and Reinforced Polycarbonates with Randomly Oriented Glass Fibers

		Fiber Reinforcement (vol%)		
Property	*Unreinforced*	*20*	*30*	*40*
Specific gravity	1.19–1.22	1.35	1.43	1.52
Tensile strength (MPa)	59–62	110	131	159
Modulus of elasticity (GPa)	2.24–2.345	5.93	8.62	11.6
Elongation (%)	90–115	4–6	3–5	3–5
Impact strength, notched Izod (lb_f/in.)	12–16	2.0	2.0	2.5

Source: Adapted from Materials Engineering's *Materials Selector,* copyright © Penton/IPC.

In this expression, K is a fiber efficiency parameter that depends on V_f and the E_f/E_m ratio. Of course, its magnitude will be less than unity, usually in the range 0.1 to 0.6. Thus, for random fiber reinforcement (as with oriented), the modulus increases in some proportion of the volume fraction of fiber. Table 15.2, which gives some of the mechanical properties of unreinforced and reinforced polycarbonates for discontinuous and randomly oriented glass fibers, provides an idea of the magnitude of the reinforcement that is possible.

By way of summary, then, aligned fibrous composites are inherently anisotropic, in that the maximum strength and reinforcement are achieved along the alignment (longitudinal) direction. In the transverse direction, fiber reinforcement is virtually nonexistent: fracture usually occurs at relatively low tensile stresses. For other stress orientations, composite strength lies between these extremes. The efficiency of fiber reinforcement for several situations is presented in Table 15.3; this efficiency is taken to be unity for an oriented fiber composite in the alignment direction, and zero perpendicular to it.

When multidirectional stresses are imposed within a single plane, aligned layers that are fastened together one on top of another at different orientations are frequently utilized. These are termed *laminar composites,* which are discussed in Section 15.14.

Table 15.3 Reinforcement Efficiency of Fiber-Reinforced Composites for Several Fiber Orientations and at Various Directions of Stress Application

Fiber Orientation	*Stress Direction*	*Reinforcement Efficiency*
All fibers parallel	Parallel to fibers	1
	Perpendicular to fibers	0
Fibers randomly and uniformly distributed within a specific plane	Any direction in the plane of the fibers	$\frac{3}{8}$
Fibers randomly and uniformly distributed within three dimensions in space	Any direction	$\frac{1}{5}$

Source: H. Krenchel, *Fibre Reinforcement,* Copenhagen: Akademisk Forlag, 1964 [33].

Applications involving totally multidirectional applied stresses normally use discontinuous fibers, which are randomly oriented in the matrix material. Table 15.3 shows that the reinforcement efficiency is only one-fifth that of an aligned composite in the longitudinal direction; however, the mechanical characteristics are isotropic.

Consideration of orientation and fiber length for a particular composite will depend on the level and nature of the applied stress as well as fabrication cost. Production rates for short-fiber composites (both aligned and randomly oriented) are rapid, and intricate shapes can be formed that are not possible with continuous fiber reinforcement. Furthermore, fabrication costs are considerably lower than for continuous and aligned; fabrication techniques applied to short-fiber composite materials include compression, injection, and extrusion molding, which are described for unreinforced polymers in Section 23.10.

Concept Check 15.3

Cite one desirable characteristic and one less desirable characteristic for each of (1) discontinuous-oriented, and (2) discontinuous-randomly oriented fiber-reinforced composites.

[*The answer may be found in enclosed CD.*]

15.6 THE FIBER PHASE

An important characteristic of most materials, especially brittle ones, is that a small-diameter fiber is much stronger than the bulk material. As discussed in Section 12.10, the probability of the presence of a critical surface flaw that can lead to fracture diminishes with decreasing specimen volume, and this feature is used to advantage in the fiber-reinforced composites. Also, the materials used for reinforcing fibers have high tensile strengths.

On the basis of diameter and character, fibers are grouped into three different classifications: *whiskers, fibers,* and *wires*. **Whiskers** are very thin single crystals that have extremely large length-to-diameter ratios. As a consequence of their small size, they have a high degree of crystalline perfection and are virtually flaw free, which accounts for their exceptionally high strengths; they are among the strongest known materials. In spite of these high strengths, whiskers are not utilized extensively as a reinforcement medium because they are extremely expensive. Moreover, it is difficult and often impractical to incorporate whiskers into a matrix. Whisker materials include graphite, silicon carbide, silicon nitride, and aluminum oxide; some mechanical characteristics of these materials are given in Table 15.4.

Materials that are classified as **fibers** are either polycrystalline or amorphous and have small diameters; fibrous materials are generally either polymers or ceramics (e.g., the polymer aramids, glass, carbon, boron, aluminum oxide, and silicon carbide). Table 15.4 also presents some data on a few materials that are used in fiber form.

Fine wires have relatively large diameters; typical materials include steel, molybdenum, and tungsten. Wires are utilized as a radial steel reinforcement in automobile tires, in filament-wound rocket casings, and in wire-wound high-presure hoses.

Table 15.4 Characteristics of Several Fiber-Reinforcement Materials

Material	*Specific Gravity*	*Tensile Strength (GPa)*	*Specific Strength (GPa)*	*Modulus of Elasticity (GPa)*	*Specific Modulus (GPa)*
		Whiskers			
Graphite	2.2	20	9.1	700	318
Silicon nitride	3.2	5–7	1.56–2.2	350–380	109–118
Aluminum oxide	4.0	10–20	2.5–5.0	700–1500	175–375
Silicon carbide	3.2	20	6.25	480	150
		Fibers			
Aluminum oxide	3.95	1.38	0.35	379	96
Aramid (Kevlar 49™)	1.44	3.6–4.1	2.5–2.85	131	91
Carbon[a]	1.78–2.15	1.5–4.8	0.70–2.70	228–724	106–407
E-glass	2.58	3.45	1.34	72.5	28.1
Boron	2.57	3.6	1.40	400	156
Silicon carbide	3.0	3.9	1.30	400	133
UHMWPE (Spectra 900™)	0.97	2.6	2.68	117	121
		Metallic Wires			
High-strength steel	7.9	2.39	0.30	210	26.6
Molybdenum	10.2	2.2	0.22	324	31.8
Tungsten	19.3	2.89	0.15	407	21.1

[a] The term "carbon" instead of "graphite" is used to denote these fibers, since they are composed of crystalline graphite regions, and also of noncrystalline material and areas of crystal misalignment.

15.7 THE MATRIX PHASE

The **matrix phase** of fibrous composites may be a metal, polymer, or ceramic. In general, metals and polymers are used as matrix materials because some ductility is desirable; for ceramic-matrix composites (Section 15.10), the reinforcing component is added to improve fracture toughness. The discussion of this section will focus on polymer and metal matrices.

For fiber-reinforced composites, the matrix phase serves several functions. First, it binds the fibers together and acts as the medium by which an externally applied stress is transmitted and distributed to the fibers; only a very small proportion of an applied load is sustained by the matrix phase. Furthermore, the matrix material should be ductile. In addition, the elastic modulus of the fiber should be much higher than that of the matrix. The second function of the matrix is to protect the individual fibers from surface damage as a result of mechanical abrasion or chemical reactions with the environment. Such interactions may introduce surface flaws capable of forming cracks, which may lead to failure at low tensile stress levels. Finally, the matrix separates the fibers and, by virtue of its relative softness and plasticity, prevents the propagation of brittle cracks from fiber to fiber, which could result in catastrophic failure; in other words, the matrix phase serves as a barrier to crack propagation. Even though some of the individual fibers fail, total composite fracture will not occur until large numbers of adjacent fibers, once having failed, form a cluster of critical size.

It is essential that adhesive bonding forces between fiber and matrix be high to minimize fiber pull-out. In fact, bonding strength is an important consideration in the choice of the matrix–fiber combination. The ultimate strength of the composite depends to a large degree on the magnitude of this bond; adequate bonding is essential to maximize the stress transmittance from the weak matrix to the strong fibers.

15.8 POLYMER-MATRIX COMPOSITES

Polymer-matrix composites (*PMCs*) consist of a polymer resin[1] as the matrix, with fibers as the reinforcement medium. These materials are used in the greatest diversity of composite applications, as well as in the largest quantities, in light of their room-temperature properties, ease of fabrication, and cost. In this section the various classifications of PMCs are discussed according to reinforcement type (i.e., glass, carbon, and aramid), along with their applications and the various polymer resins that are employed.

Glass Fiber-Reinforced Polymer (GFRP) Composites

Fiberglass is simply a composite consisting of glass fibers, either continuous or discontinuous, contained within a polymer matrix; this type of composite is produced in the largest quantities. The composition of the glass that is most commonly drawn into fibers (sometimes referred to as *E-glass*) is contained in Table 12.1; fiber diameters normally range between 3 and 20 μm. Glass is popular as a fiber reinforcement material for several reasons:

1. It is easily drawn into high-strength fibers from the molten state.
2. It is readily available and may be fabricated into a glass-reinforced plastic economically using a wide variety of composite-manufacturing techniques.
3. As a fiber it is relatively strong, and when embedded in a plastic matrix, it produces a composite having a very high specific strength.
4. When coupled with the various plastics, it possesses a chemical inertness that renders the composite useful in a variety of corrosive environments.

The surface characteristics of glass fibers are extremely important because even minute surface flaws can deleteriously affect the tensile properties, as discussed in Section 12.10. Surface flaws are easily introduced by rubbing or abrading the surface with another hard material. Also, glass surfaces that have been exposed to the normal atmosphere for even short time periods generally have a weakened surface layer that interferes with bonding to the matrix. Newly drawn fibers are normally coated during drawing with a "size," a thin layer of a substance

[1] The term "resin" is used in this context to denote a high-molecular-weight reinforcing plastic.

that protects the fiber surface from damage and undesirable environmental interactions. This size is ordinarily removed prior to composite fabrication and replaced with a "coupling agent" or finish that produces a chemical bond between the fiber and matrix.

There are several limitations to this group of materials. In spite of having high strengths, they are not very stiff and do not display the rigidity that is necessary for some applications (e.g., as structural members for airplanes and bridges). Most fiberglass materials are limited to service temperatures below 200°C; at higher temperatures, most polymers begin to flow or to deteriorate. Service temperatures may be extended to approximately 300°C by using high-purity fused silica for the fibers and high-temperature polymers such as the polyimide resins.

Many fiberglass applications are familiar: automotive and marine bodies, plastic pipes, storage containers, and industrial floorings. The transportation industries are utilizing increasing amounts of glass fiber-reinforced plastics in an effort to decrease vehicle weight and boost fuel efficiencies. A host of new applications are being used or currently investigated by the automotive industry.

Carbon Fiber-Reinforced Polymer (CFRP) Composites

Carbon is a high-performance fiber material that is the most commonly used reinforcement in advanced (i.e., nonfiberglass) polymer-matrix composites. The reasons for this are as follows:

1. Carbon fibers have the highest specific modulus and specific strength of all reinforcing fiber materials.
2. They retain their high tensile modulus and high strength at elevated temperatures; high-temperature oxidation, however, may be a problem.
3. At room temperature, carbon fibers are not affected by moisture or a wide variety of solvents, acids, and bases.
4. These fibers exhibit a diversity of physical and mechanical characteristics, allowing composites incorporating these fibers to have specific engineered properties.
5. Fiber and composite manufacturing processes have been developed that are relatively inexpensive and cost effective.

Use of the term "carbon fiber" may seem perplexing since carbon is an element, and, as noted in Section 4.17, the stable form of crystalline carbon at ambient conditions is graphite, having the structure represented in Figure 4.26. Carbon fibers are not totally crystalline, but are composed of both graphitic and noncrystalline regions; these areas of noncrystallinity are devoid of the three-dimensional ordered arrangement of hexagonal carbon networks that is characteristic of graphite (Figure 4.26).

Manufacturing techniques for producing carbon fibers are relatively complex and will not be discussed. However, three different organic precursor materials are used: rayon, polyacrylonitrile (PAN), and pitch. Processing technique will vary from precursor to precursor, as will also the resultant fiber characteristics.

One classification scheme for carbon fibers is by tensile modulus; on this basis the four classes are standard, intermediate, high, and ultrahigh moduli. Furthermore, fiber diameters normally range between 4 and 10 μm; both continuous and chopped forms are available. In addition, carbon fibers are normally coated with a protective epoxy size that also improves adhesion with the polymer matrix.

Carbon-reinforced polymer composites are currently being utilized extensively in sports and recreational equipment (fishing rods, golf clubs), filament-wound rocket motor cases, pressure vessels, and aircraft structural components—both military and commercial, fixed wing and helicopters (e.g., as wing, body, stabilizer, and rudder components).

Aramid Fiber-Reinforced Polymer Composites

Aramid fibers are high-strength, high-modulus materials that were introduced in the early 1970s. They are especially desirable for their outstanding strength-to-weight ratios, which are superior to metals. Chemically, this group of materials is known as poly(paraphenylene terephthalamide). There are a number of aramid materials; trade names for two of the most common are Kevlar™ and Nomex™. For the former, there are several grades (viz. Kevlar 29, 49, and 149) that have different mechanical behaviors. During synthesis, the rigid molecules are aligned in the direction of the fiber axis, as liquid crystal domains (Section 14.19); the repeat unit and the mode of chain alignment are represented in Figure 15.10. Mechanically, these fibers have longitudinal tensile strengths and tensile moduli (Table 15.4) that are higher than other polymeric fiber materials; however, they are relatively weak in compression. In addition, this material is known for its toughness, impact resistance, and resistance to creep and fatigue failure. Even though the aramids are thermoplastics, they are, nevertheless, resistant to combustion and stable to relatively high temperatures; the temperature range over which they retain their high mechanical properties is between −200 and 200°C. Chemically, they are susceptible to degradation by strong acids and bases, but they are relatively inert in other solvents and chemicals.

The aramid fibers are most often used in composites having polymer matrices; common matrix materials are the epoxies and polyesters. Since the fibers are relatively flexible and somewhat ductile, they may be processed by most common textile operations. Typical applications of these aramid composites are in ballistic products (bulletproof vests and armor), sporting goods, tires, ropes, missile cases, pressure vessels, and as a replacement for asbestos in automotive brake and clutch linings, and gaskets.

The properties of continuous and aligned glass-, carbon-, and aramid-fiber reinforced epoxy composites are included in Table 15.5. Thus, a comparison of the mechanical characteristics of these three materials may be made in both longitudinal and transverse directions.

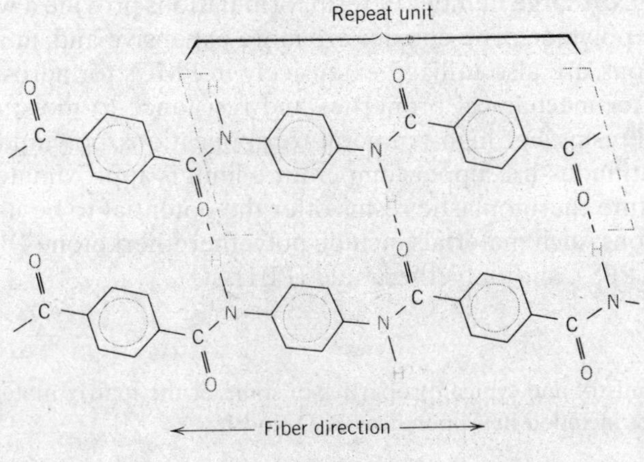

Figure 15.10 Schematic representation of repeat unit and chain structures for aramid (Kevlar) fibers. Chain alignment with the fiber direction and hydrogen bonds that form between adjacent chains are also shown. [From F. R. Jones (Editor), *Handbook of Polymer-Fibre Composites.* Copyright © 1994 by Addison-Wesley Longman. Reprinted with permission.]

Table 15.5 Properties of Continuous and Aligned Glass-, Carbon-, and Aramid-Fiber Reinforced Epoxy-Matrix Composites in Longitudinal and Transverse Directions. In All Cases the Fiber Volume Fraction Is 0.60

Property	*Glass (E-glass)*	*Carbon (High Strength)*	*Aramid (Kevlar 49)*
Specific gravity	2.1	1.6	1.4
Tensile modulus			
Longitudinal (GPa)	45	145	76
Transverse (GPa)	12	10	5.5
Tensile strength			
Longitudinal (MPa)	1020	1240	1380
Transverse (MPa)	40	41	30
Ultimate tensile strain			
Longitudinal	2.3	0.9	1.8
Transverse	0.4	0.4	0.5

Source: Adapted from R. F. Floral and S. T. Peters, "Composite Structures and Technologies," tutorial notes, 1989.

Other Fiber Reinforcement Materials

Glass, carbon, and the aramids are the most common fiber reinforcements incorporated in polymer matrices. Other fiber materials that are used to much lesser degrees are boron, silicon carbide, and aluminum oxide; tensile moduli, tensile strengths, specific strengths, and specific moduli of these materials in fiber form are contained in Table 15.4. Boron fiber-reinforced polymer composites have been used in military aircraft components, helicopter rotor blades, and some sporting goods. Silicon carbide and aluminum oxide fibers are utilized in tennis rackets, circuit boards, military armor, and rocket nose cones.

Polymer Matrix Materials

The roles assumed by the polymer matrix are outlined in Section 15.7. In addition, the matrix often determines the maximum service temperature, since it normally softens, melts, or degrades at a much lower temperature than the fiber reinforcement.

The most widely utilized and least expensive polymer resins are the polyesters and vinyl esters;[2] these matrix materials are used primarily for glass fiber-reinforced composites. A large number of resin formulations provide a wide range of properties for these polymers. The epoxies are more expensive and, in addition to commercial applications, are also utilized extensively in PMCs for aerospace applications; they have better mechanical properties and resistance to moisture than the polyesters and vinyl resins. For high-temperature applications, polyimide resins are employed; their continuous-use, upper-temperature limit is approximately 230°C. Finally, high-temperature thermoplastic resins offer the potential to be used in future aerospace applications; such materials include polyetheretherketone (PEEK), poly(phenylene sulfide) (PPS), and polyetherimide (PEI).

[2] The chemistry and typical properties of some of the matrix materials discussed in this section are included in Appendices B, D, and E.

DESIGN EXAMPLE 15.1

Design of a Tubular Composite Shaft

A tubular composite shaft is to be designed that has an outside diameter of 70 mm, an inside diameter of 50 mm and a length of 1.0 m; such is represented schematically in Figure 15.11. The mechanical characteristic of prime importance is bending stiffness in terms of the longitudinal modulus of elasticity; strength and fatigue resistance are not significant parameters for this application when filament composites are utilized. Stiffness is to be specified as maximum allowable deflection in bending; when subjected to three-point bending as in Figure 12.13 (i.e., support points at both tube extremities and load application at the longitudinal midpoint), a load of 1000 N is to produce an elastic deflection of no more than 0.35 mm at the mid-point position.

Continuous fibers that are oriented parallel to the tube axis will be used; possible fiber materials are glass, and carbon in standard-, intermediate-, and high-modulus grades. The matrix material is to be an epoxy resin, and the maximum allowable fiber volume fraction is 0.60.

This design problem calls for us to do the following:

(a) Decide which of the four fiber materials, when embedded in the epoxy matrix, meet the stipulated criteria.

(b) Of these possibilities, select the one fiber material that will yield the lowest-cost composite material (assuming fabrication costs are the same for all fibers).

Elastic modulus, density, and cost data for the fiber and matrix materials are contained in Table 15.6.

Solution

(a) It first becomes necessary to determine the required longitudinal modulus of elasticity for this composite material, consistent with the stipulated criteria. This computation necessitates the use of the three-point deflection expression

$$\Delta y = \frac{FL^3}{48\,EI} \tag{15.21}$$

in which Δy is the midpoint deflection, F is the applied force, L is the support point separation distance, E is the modulus of elasticity, and I is the cross-sectional

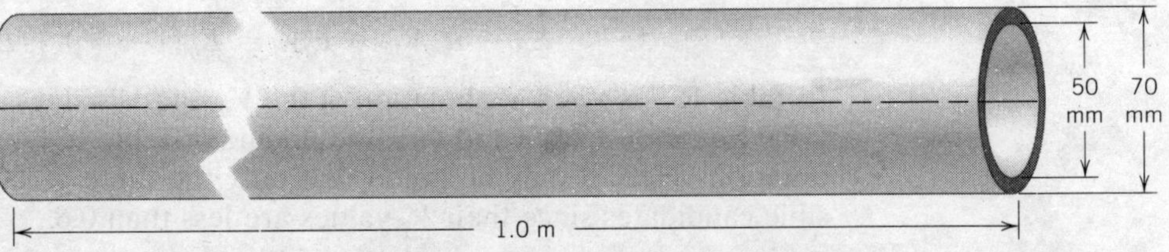

Figure 15.11 Schematic representation of a tubular composite shaft, the subject of Design Example 15.1.

Table 15.6 Elastic Modulus, Density, and Cost Data for Glass and Various Carbon Fibers, and Epoxy Resin

Material	*Elastic Modulus (GPa)*	*Density (g/cm^3)*	*Cost (\$/kg)*
Glass fibers	72.5	2.58	2.50
Carbon fibers (standard modulus)	230	1.80	35.00
Carbon fibers (intermediate modulus)	285	1.80	70.00
Carbon fibers (high modulus)	400	1.80	175.00
Epoxy resin	2.4	1.14	9.00

moment of inertia. For a tube having inside and outside diameters of d_i and d_o, respectively,

$$I = \frac{\pi}{64}(d_o^4 - d_i^4) \tag{15.22}$$

and

$$E = \frac{4FL^3}{3\pi \Delta y (d_o^4 - d_i^4)} \tag{15.23}$$

For this shaft design,

$$F = 1000 \text{ N}$$
$$L = 1.0 \text{ m}$$
$$\Delta y = 0.35 \text{ mm}$$
$$d_o = 70 \text{ mm}$$
$$d_i = 50 \text{ mm}$$

Thus, the required longitudinal modulus of elasticity for this shaft is

$$E = \frac{4(1000 \text{ N})(1.0 \text{ m})^3}{3\pi(0.35 \times 10^{-3} \text{ m})[(70 \times 10^{-3} \text{ m})^4 - (50 \times 10^{-3} \text{ m})^4]}$$
$$= 69.3 \text{ GPa}$$

The next step is to determine the fiber and matrix volume fractions for each of the four candidate fiber materials. This is possible using the rule-of-mixtures expression, Equation 15.10b:

$$E_{cs} = E_m V_m + E_f V_f = E_m(1 - V_f) + E_f V_f$$

In Table 15.7 is given a tabulation of the V_m and V_f values required for $E_{cs} = 69.3$ GPa; Equation 15.10b and the moduli data in Table 15.6 were used in these computations. Here it may be noted that only the three carbon fiber types are possible candidates since their V_f values are less than 0.6.

(b) At this point it becomes necessary to determine the volume of fibers and matrix for each of the three carbon types. The total tube volume V_c in centimeters is

$$V_c = \frac{\pi L}{4}(d_o^2 - d_i^2) \tag{15.24}$$

$$= \frac{\pi(100 \text{ cm})}{4}[(7.0 \text{ cm})^2 - (5.0 \text{ cm})^2]$$

$$= 1885 \text{ cm}^3$$

Table 15.7 Fiber and Matrix Volume Fractions for Three Carbon Fiber Types as Required to Give a Composite Modulus of 69.3 GPa

Fiber Type	V_f	V_m
Glass	0.954	0.046
Carbon (standard modulus)	0.293	0.707
Carbon (intermediate modulus)	0.237	0.763
Carbon (high modulus)	0.168	0.832

Thus, fiber and matrix volumes result from products of this value and the V_f and V_m values cited in Table 15.7. These volume values are presented in Table 15.8, which are then converted into masses using densities (Table 15.6), and finally into material costs, from the per unit mass cost (also given in Table 15.6).

As may be noted in Table 15.8, the material of choice (i.e., the least expensive) is the standard-modulus carbon-fiber composite; the relatively low cost per unit mass of this fiber material offsets its relatively low modulus of elasticity and required high volume fraction.

Table 15.8 Fiber and Matrix Volumes, Masses, and Costs and Total Material Cost for Three Carbon Fiber-Epoxy-Matrix Composites

Fiber Type	*Fiber Volume* (cm^3)	*Fiber Mass (kg)*	*Fiber Cost ($)*	*Matrix Volume* (cm^3)	*Matrix Mass (kg)*	*Matrix Cost ($)*	*Total Cost ($)*
Carbon (standard modulus)	552	0.994	34.80	1333	1.520	13.70	48.50
Carbon (intermediate modulus)	447	0.805	56.35	1438	1.639	14.75	71.10
Carbon (high modulus)	317	0.571	99.90	1568	1.788	15.10	115.00

15.9 METAL-MATRIX COMPOSITES

As the name implies, for **metal-matrix composites** (*MMC*s) the matrix is a ductile metal. These materials may be utilized at higher service temperatures than their base metal counterparts; furthermore, the reinforcement may improve specific stiffness, specific strength, abrasion resistance, creep resistance, thermal conductivity, and dimensional stability. Some of the advantages of these materials over the polymer-matrix composites include higher operating temperatures, nonflammability, and greater resistance to degradation by organic fluids. Metal-matrix composites are much more expensive than PMCs, and, therefore, their (MMC) use is somewhat restricted.

The superalloys, as well as alloys of aluminum, magnesium, titanium, and copper, are employed as matrix materials. The reinforcement may be in the form of particulates, both continuous and discontinuous fibers, and whiskers; concentrations normally range between 10 and 60 vol%. Continuous fiber materials include carbon, silicon carbide, boron, aluminum oxide, and the refractory metals. On the other hand, discontinuous reinforcements consist primarily of silicon carbide whiskers, chopped fibers of aluminum oxide and carbon, and particulates of silicon carbide and aluminum oxide. In a sense, the cermets (Section 15.2) fall within this MMC scheme. In Table 15.9 are presented the properties of several common metal-matrix, continuous and aligned fiber-reinforced composites.

Some matrix–reinforcement combinations are highly reactive at elevated temperatures. Consequently, composite degradation may be caused by high-temperature processing or by subjecting the MMC to elevated temperatures during service. This problem is commonly resolved either by applying a protective surface coating to the reinforcement or by modifying the matrix alloy composition.

Normally the processing of MMCs involves at least two steps: consolidation or synthesis (i.e., introduction of reinforcement into the matrix), followed by a shaping operation. A host of consolidation techniques are available, some of which are relatively sophisticated; discontinuous fiber MMCs are amenable to shaping by standard metal-forming operations (e.g., forging, extrusion, rolling).

Automobile manufacturers have recently begun to use MMCs in their products. For example, some engine components have been introduced consisting of an aluminum-alloy matrix that is reinforced with aluminum oxide and carbon fibers; this MMC is light in weight and resists wear and thermal distortion. Metal-matrix composites are also employed in driveshafts (that have higher rotational speeds and reduced vibrational noise levels), extruded stabilizer bars, and forged suspension and transmission components.

The aerospace industry also uses MMCs. Structural applications include advanced aluminum alloy metal-matrix composites; boron fibers are used as the reinforcement for the Space Shuttle Orbiter, and continuous graphite fibers for the Hubble Telescope.

The high-temperature creep and rupture properties of some of the superalloys (Ni- and Co-based alloys) may be enhanced by fiber reinforcement using refractory metals such as tungsten. Excellent high-temperature oxidation resistance and

Table 15.9 Properties of Several Metal-Matrix Composites Reinforced with Continuous and Aligned Fibers

Fiber	*Matrix*	*Fiber Content (vol%)*	*Density (g/cm^3)*	*Longitudinal Tensile Modulus (GPa)*	*Longitudinal Tensile Strength (MPa)*
Carbon	6061 Al	41	2.44	320	620
Boron	6061 Al	48	—	207	1515
SiC	6061 Al	50	2.93	230	1480
Alumina	380.0 Al	24	—	120	340
Carbon	AZ31 Mg	38	1.83	300	510
Borsic	Ti	45	3.68	220	1270

Source: Adapted from J. W. Weeton, D. M. Peters, and K. L. Thomas, *Engineers' Guide to Composite Materials,* ASM International, Materials Park, OH, 1987.

impact strength are also maintained. Designs incorporating these composites permit higher operating temperatures and better efficiencies for turbine engines.

15.10 CERAMIC-MATRIX COMPOSITES

As discussed in Chapter 12, ceramic materials are inherently resilient to oxidation and deterioration at elevated temperatures; were it not for their disposition to brittle fracture, some of these materials would be ideal candidates for use in high-temperature and severe-stress applications, specifically for components in automobile and aircraft gas turbine engines. Fracture toughness values for ceramic materials are low and typically lie between 1 and 5 MPa$\sqrt{m}$, Table 11.1 and Table B.5, Appendix B. By way of contrast, K_{Ic} values for mostmetals are much higher (15 to greater than 150 MPa$\sqrt{m}$).

The fracture toughnesses of ceramics have been improved significantly by the development of a new generation of **ceramic-matrix composites** (*CMCs*)—particulates, fibers, or whiskers of one ceramic material that have been embedded into a matrix of another ceramic. Ceramic-matrix composite materials have extended fracture toughnesses to between about 6 and 20 MPa$\sqrt{m}$.

In essence, this improvement in the fracture properties results from interactions between advancing cracks and dispersed phase particles. Crack initiation normally occurs with the matrix phase, whereas crack propagation is impeded or hindered by the particles, fibers, or whiskers. Several techniques are utilized to retard crack propagation, which are discussed as follows.

One particularly interesting and promising toughening technique employs a phase transformation to arrest the propagation of cracks and is aptly termed *transformation toughening.* Small particles of partially stabilized zirconia (Section 12.9) are dispersed within the matrix material, often Al_2O_3 or ZrO_2 itself. Typically, CaO, MgO, Y_2O_3, and CeO are used as stabilizers. Partial stabilization allows retention of the metastable tetragonal phase at ambient conditions rather than the stable monoclinic phase; these two phases are noted on the ZrO_2–$ZrCaO_3$ phase diagram, Figure 12.7. The stress field in front of a propagating crack causes these metastably retained tetragonal particles to undergo transformation to the stable monoclinic phase. Accompanying this transformation is a slight particle volume increase, and the net result is that compressive stresses are established on the crack surfaces near the crack tip that tend to pinch the crack shut, thereby arresting its growth. This process is demonstrated schematically in Figure 15.12.

Other recently developed toughening techniques involve the utilization of ceramic whiskers, often SiC or Si_3N_4. These whiskers may inhibit crack propagation by (1) deflecting crack tips, (2) forming bridges across crack faces, (3) absorbing energy during pull-out as the whiskers debond from the matrix, and/or (4) causing a redistribution of stresses in regions adjacent to the crack tips.

In general, increasing fiber content improves strength and fracture toughness; this is demonstrated in Table 15.10 for SiC whisker-reinforced alumina. Furthermore, there is a considerable reduction in the scatter of fracture strengths for whisker-reinforced ceramics relative to their unreinforced counterparts. In addition, these CMCs exhibit improved high-temperature creep behavior and resistance to thermal shock (i.e., failure resulting from sudden changes in temperature).

Ceramic-matrix composites may be fabricated using hot pressing, hot isostatic pressing, and liquid phase sintering techniques. Relative to applications, SiC whisker-reinforced aluminas are being utilized as cutting tool inserts for machining hard metal alloys; tool lives for these materials are greater than for cemented carbides (Section 15.2).

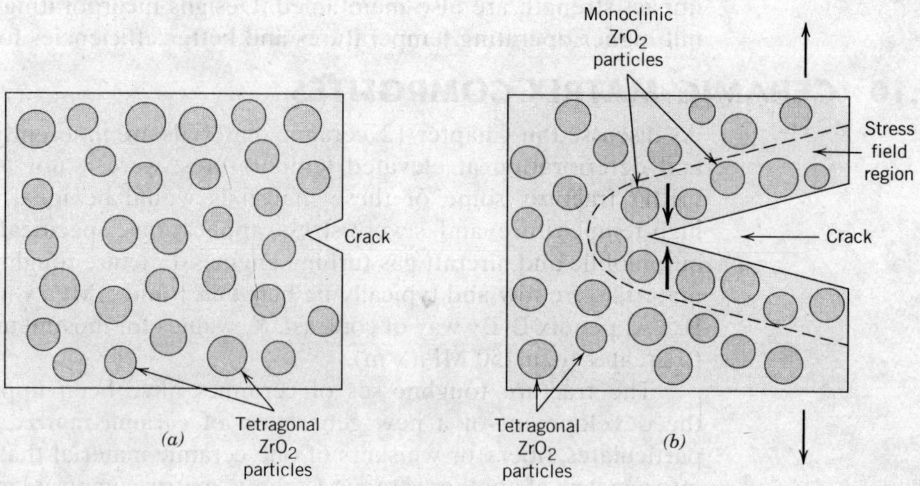

Figure 15.12 Schematic demonstration of transformation toughening. (*a*) A crack prior to inducement of the ZrO_2 particle phase transformation. (*b*) Crack arrestment due to the stress-induced phase transformation.

15.11 CARBON–CARBON COMPOSITES

One of the most advanced and promising engineering material is the carbon fiber-reinforced carbon-matrix composite, often termed a **carbon–carbon composite;** as the name implies, both reinforcement and matrix are carbon. These materials are relatively new and expensive and, therefore, are not currently being utilized extensively. Their desirable properties include high-tensile moduli and tensile strengths that are retained to temperatures in excess of 2000°C, resistance to creep, and relatively large fracture toughness values. Furthermore, carbon–carbon composites have low coefficients of thermal expansion and relatively high thermal conductivities; these characteristics, coupled with high strengths, give rise to a relatively low susceptibility to thermal shock. Their major drawback is a propensity to high-temperature oxidation.

The carbon–carbon composites are employed in rocket motors, as friction materials in aircraft and high-performance automobiles, for hot-pressing molds, in components for advanced turbine engines, and as ablative shields for re-entry vehicles.

The primary reason that these composite materials are so expensive is the relatively complex processing techniques that are employed. Preliminary procedures are similar to those used for carbon-fiber, polymer-matrix composites. That is, the continuous carbon fibers are laid down having the desired two- or three-dimensional pattern; these fibers are then impregnated with a liquid polymer resin, often

Table 15.10 Room Temperature Fracture Strengths and Fracture Toughnesses for Various SiC Whisker Contents in Al_2O_3

Whisker Content (vol%)	*Fracture Strength (MPa)*	*Fracture Toughness ($MPa\sqrt{m}$)*
0	—	4.5
10	455 ± 55	7.1
20	655 ± 135	7.5–9.0
40	850 ± 130	6.0

Source: Adapted from *Engineered Materials Handbook,* Vol. 1, *Composites,* C. A. Dostal (Senior Editor), ASM International, Materials Park, OH, 1987.

a phenolic; the workpiece is next formed into the final shape, and the resin is allowed to cure. At this time the matrix resin is "pyrolyzed," that is, converted into carbon by heating in an inert atmosphere; during pyrolysis, molecular components consisting of oxygen, hydrogen, and nitrogen are driven off, leaving behind large carbon chain molecules. Subsequent heat treatments at higher temperatures will cause this carbon matrix to densify and increase in strength. The resulting composite, then, consists of the original carbon fibers that remained essentially unaltered, which are contained in this pyrolyzed carbon matrix.

15.12 HYBRID COMPOSITES

A relatively new fiber reinforced composite is the **hybrid,** which is obtained by using two or more different kinds of fibers in a single matrix; hybrids have a better all-around combination of properties than composites containing only a single fiber type. A variety of fiber combinations and matrix materials are used, but in the most common system, both carbon and glass fibers are incorporated into a polymeric resin. The carbon fibers are strong and relatively stiff and provide a low-density reinforcement; however, they are expensive. Glass fibers are inexpensive and lack the stiffness of carbon. The glass–carbon hybrid is stronger and tougher, has a higher impact resistance, and may be produced at a lower cost than either of the comparable all-carbon or all-glass reinforced plastics.

There are a number of ways in which the two different fibers may be combined, which will ultimately affect the overall properties. For example, the fibers may all be aligned and intimately mixed with one another; or laminations may be constructed consisting of layers, each of which consists of a single fiber type, alternating one with another. In virtually all hybrids the properties are anisotropic.

When hybrid composites are stressed in tension, failure is usually noncatastrophic (i.e., does not occur suddenly). The carbon fibers are the first to fail, at which time the load is transferred to the glass fibers. Upon failure of the glass fibers, the matrix phase must sustain the applied load. Eventual composite failure concurs with that of the matrix phase.

Principal applications for hybrid composites are lightweight land, water, and air transport structural components, sporting goods, and lightweight orthopedic components.

Structural Composites

A **structural composite** is normally composed of both homogeneous and composite materials, the properties of which depend not only on the properties of the constituent materials but also on the geometrical design of the various structural elements. Laminar composites and sandwich panels are two of the most common structural composites; only a relatively superficial examination is offered here for them.

15.13 LAMINAR COMPOSITES

A **laminar composite** is composed of two-dimensional sheets or panels that have a preferred high-strength direction such as is found in wood and continuous and aligned fiber-reinforced plastics. The layers are stacked and subsequently cemented together such that the orientation of the high-strength direction varies with each successive layer (Figure 15.13). For example, adjacent wood sheets in plywood are

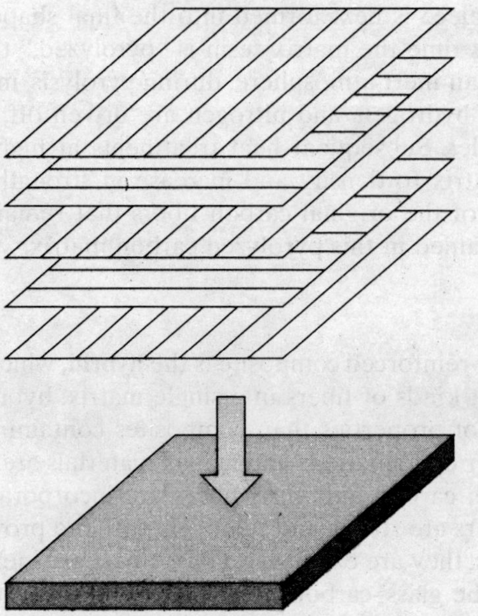

Figure 15.13 The stacking of successive oriented, fiber-reinforced layers for a laminar composite.

aligned with the grain direction at right angles to each other. Laminations may also be constructed using fabric material such as cotton, paper, or woven glass fibers embedded in a plastic matrix. Thus a laminar composite has relatively high strength in a number of directions in the two-dimensional plane; however, the strength in any given direction is, of course, lower than it would be if all the fibers were oriented in that direction. One example of a relatively complex laminated structure is the modern ski (see the chapter-opening illustration for this chapter).

15.14 SANDWICH PANELS

Sandwich panels, considered to be a class of structural composites, are designed to be light-weight beams or panels having relatively high stiffnesses and strengths. A sandwich panel consists of two outer sheets, or faces, that are separated by and adhesively bonded to a thicker core (Figure 15.14). The outer sheets are made of a relatively stiff and strong material, typically aluminum alloys, fiber-reinforced plastics, titanium, steel, or plywood; they impart high stiffness and strength to the structure, and must be thick enough to withstand tensile and compressive stresses that result from loading. The core material is lightweight, and normally has a low modulus of elasticity. Core materials typically fall within three categories: rigid polymeric foams (i.e., phenolics, epoxy, polyurethanes), wood (i.e., balsa wood), and honeycombs (see below).

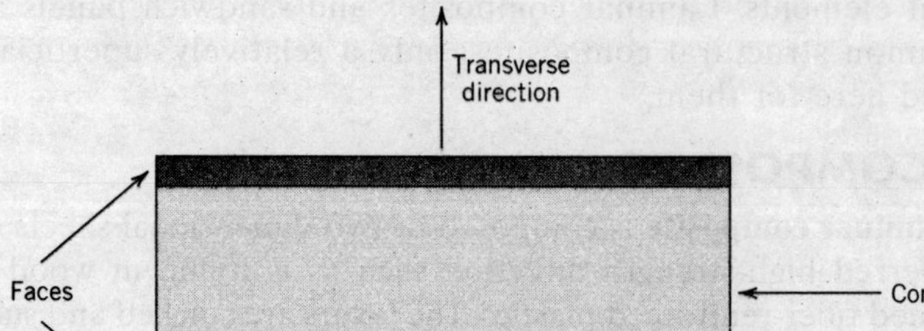

Figure 15.14 Schematic diagram showing the cross section of a sandwich panel.

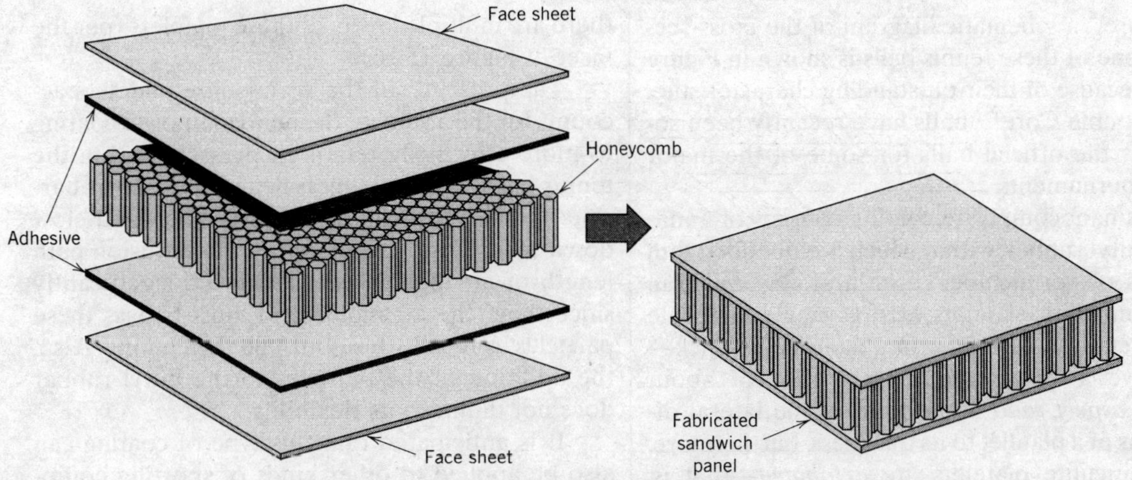

Figure 15.15 Schematic diagram showing the construction of a honeycomb core sandwich panel. (Reprinted with permission from *Engineered Materials Handbook,* Vol. 1, *Composites,* ASM International, Metals Park, OH, 1987.)

Structurally, the core serves several functions. First of all, it provides continuous support for the faces. In addition, it must have sufficient shear strength to withstand transverse shear stresses, and also be thick enough to provide high shear stiffness (to resist buckling of the panel). (It should be noted that tensile and compressive stresses on the core are much lower than on the faces.)

Another popular core consists of a "honeycomb" structure—thin foils that have been formed into interlocking hexagonal cells, with axes oriented perpendicular to the face planes; Figure 15.15 shows a cutaway view of a honeycomb core sandwich panel. The honeycomb material is normally either an aluminum alloy or aramid polymer. Strength and stiffness of honeycomb structures depend on cell size, cell wall thickness, and the material from which the honeycomb is made.

Sandwich panels are used in a wide variety of applications including roofs, floors, and walls of buildings; and, in aerospace and aircraft (i.e., for wings, fuselage, and tailplane skins).

MATERIALS OF IMPORTANCE

Nanocomposites in Tennis Balls

Nanocomposites—composites that consist of nanosized particles embedded in some type of matrix—are a group of promising new materials, that will undoubtedly become infused with some of our modern technologies. In fact, one type of nanocomposite is currently being used in high-performance tennis balls. These balls retain their original pressure and bounce twice as long as conventional ones. Air permeation through the walls of the ball is inhibited by a factor of two due to the presence of a flexible and very thin (10 to 50 μm) nanocomposite barrier coating that covers the

[4] This coating was developed by InMat Inc., and is called Air D-Fense™. Wilson Sporting Goods has incorporated this coating in its Double Core™ tennis balls.

[5] Vermiculite is one member of the layered silicates group that is discussed in Section 4.16.

inner core;[4] a schematic diagram of the cross-section of one of these tennis balls is shown in Figure 15.16. Because of their outstanding characteristics, these Double Core™ balls have recently been selected as the official balls for some of the major tennis tournaments.

This nanocomposite coating consists of a matrix of butyl rubber, within which is embedded thin platelets of vermiculite,[5] a natural clay mineral. The vermiculite platelets exist as single-molecule thin sheets—on the order of a nanometer thick—that have a very large aspect ratio (of about 10,000); *aspect ratio* is the ratio of the lateral dimensions of a platelet to its thickness. Furthermore, the vermiculite platelets are *exfoliated*—that is, they remain separated from one another. Also, within the butyl rubber, the vermiculite platelets are aligned such that all their lateral axes lie in the same plane; and throughout this barrier coating there are multiple layers of these platelets (per the inset of Figure 15.16).

The presence of the vermiculite platelets accounts for the ability of the nanocomposite coating to more effectively retain air pressure within the tennis balls. These platelets act as multi-layer barriers to the diffusion of air molecules, and slow down the diffusion rate; that is, the diffusion path length of air molecules is enhanced significantly since they (the air molecules) must bypass these particles as they diffuse through the coating. Also, the addition of the particles to the butyl rubber does not diminish its flexibility.

It is anticipated that this type of coating can also be applied to other kinds of sporting equipment (i.e., soccer balls, footballs, bicycle tires), as well as to automobile tires (which would be lighter in weight and more recyclable).

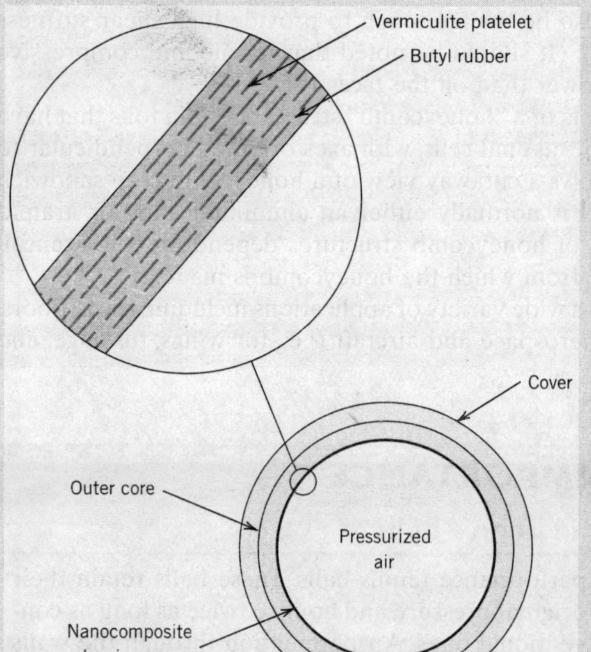

Figure 15.16 Schematic diagram showing the cross-section of a high-performance Double Core™ tennis ball. The inset drawing presents a detailed view of the nanocomposite coating that acts as a barrier to air permeation.

Photograph of a can of Double Core™ tennis balls and an individual ball. (Photograph courtesy of Wilson Sporting Goods Company.)

SUMMARY

Introduction

Composites are artificially produced multiphase materials having a desirable combination of the best properties of the constituent phases. Usually, one phase (the matrix) is continuous and completely surrounds the other (the dispersed phase). In this discussion, composites were classified as particle-reinforced, fiber-reinforced, and structural.

Large-Particle Composites
Dispersion-Strengthened Composites

Large-particle and dispersion-strengthened composites fall within the particle-reinforced classification. For dispersion strengthening, improved strength is achieved by extremely small particles of the dispersed phase, which inhibit dislocation motion; that is, the strengthening mechanism involves interactions that may be treated on the atomic level. The particle size is normally greater with large-particle composites, whose mechanical characteristics are enhanced by reinforcement action.

Concrete, a type of large-particle composite, consists of an aggregate of particles bonded together with cement. In the case of portland cement concrete, the aggregate consists of sand and gravel; the cementitious bond develops as a result of chemical reactions between the portland cement and water. The mechanical strength of this concrete may be improved by reinforcement methods (e.g., embedment into the fresh concrete of steel rods, wires, etc.). Additional reinforcement is possible by the imposition of residual compressive stresses using prestressing and posttensioning techniques.

Influence of Fiber Length
The Fiber Phase

Of the several composite types, the potential for reinforcement efficiency is greatest for those that are fiber reinforced. With these composites an applied load is transmitted to and distributed among the fibers via the matrix phase, which in most cases is at least moderately ductile. Significant reinforcement is possible only if the matrix–fiber bond is strong. On the basis of diameter, fiber reinforcements are classified as whiskers, fibers, or wires. Since reinforcement discontinues at the fiber extremities, reinforcement efficiency depends on fiber length. For each fiber–matrix combination, there exists some critical length; the length of continuous fibers greatly exceeds this critical value, whereas shorter fibers are discontinuous.

Influence of Fiber Orientation and Concentration

Fiber arrangement is also crucial relative to composite characteristics. The mechanical properties of continuous and aligned fiber composites are highly anisotropic. In the alignment direction, reinforcement and strength are a maximum; perpendicular to the alignment, they are a minimum. The stress–strain behavior for longitudinal loading was discussed. Composite rule-of-mixture expressions for the modulus in both longitudinal and transverse orientations were developed; in addition, an equation for longitudinal strength was also cited.

For short and discontinuous fibrous composites, the fibers may be either aligned or randomly oriented. Significant strengths and stiffnesses are possible for aligned short-fiber composites in the longitudinal direction. Despite some limitations on reinforcement efficiency, the properties of randomly oriented short-fiber composites are isotropic.

Polymer-Matrix Composites
Metal-Matrix Composites
Ceramic-Matrix Composites
Carbon-Carbon Composites
Hybrid Composites

Fibrous-reinforced composites are sometimes classified according to matrix type; within this scheme are three classifications: polymer-, metal-, and ceramic-matrix. Polymer-matrix are the most common, which may be reinforced with glass, carbon, and aramid fibers. Service temperatures are higher for metal-matrix composites, which also utilize a variety of fiber and whisker types. The objective of many polymer- and metal-matrix composites is a high specific strength and/or specific modulus, which requires matrix materials having low densities. With ceramic-matrix composites, the design goal is increased fracture toughness. This is achieved by interactions between advancing cracks and dispersed phase particles; transformation toughening is one such technique for improving K_{Ic}. Other more advanced composites are carbon–carbon (carbon fibers embedded in a pyrolyzed carbon matrix) and the hybrids (containing at least two different fiber types).

Laminar Composites
Sandwich Panels

Two general kinds of structural composites were discussed: the laminar composites and sandwich panels. The properties of laminar composites are virtually isotropic in a two-dimensional plane. This is made possible with several sheets of a highly anisotropic composite, which are cemented onto one another such that the high-strength direction is varied with each successive layer. Sandwich panels consist of two strong and stiff sheet faces that are separated by a core material or structure. These structures combine relatively high strengths and stiffnesses with low densities.

REFERENCES

Agarwal, B. D. and L. J. Broutman, *Analysis and Performance of Fiber Composites,* 2nd edition, Wiley, New York, 1990.

Ashbee, K. H., *Fundamental Principles of Fiber Reinforced Composites,* 2nd edition, Technomic Publishing Company, Lancaster, PA, 1993.

ASM Handbook, Vol. 21, *Composites,* ASM International, Materials Park, OH, 2001.

Chawla, K. K., *Composite Materials Science and Engineering,* 2nd edition, Springer-Verlag, New York, 1998.

Chou, T. W., R. L. McCullough, and R. B. Pipes, "Composites," *Scientific American,* Vol. 255, No. 4, October 1986, pp. 192–203.

Hollaway, L. (Editor), *Handbook of Polymer Composites for Engineers,* Technomic Publishing Company, Lancaster, PA, 1994.

Hull, D. and T. W. Clyne, *An Introduction to Composite Materials,* 2nd edition, Cambridge University Press, New York, 1996.

Mallick, P. K., *Fiber-Reinforced Composites, Materials, Manufacturing, and Design,* 2nd edition, Marcel Dekker, New York, 1993.

Peters, S. T., *Handbook of Composites,* 2nd edition, Springer-Verlag, New York, 1998.

Strong, A. B., *Fundamentals of Composites: Materials, Methods, and Applications,* Society of Manufacturing Engineers, Dearborn, MI, 1989.

Woishnis, W. A. (Editor), *Engineering Plastics and Composites,* 2nd edition, ASM International, Materials Park, OH, 1993.

QUESTIONS AND PROBLEMS

Large-Particle Composites

15.1 The mechanical properties of cobalt may be improved by incorporating fine particles of tungsten carbide (WC). Given that the moduli of elasticity of these materials are, respectively, 200 GPa and 700 GPa, plot modulus of elasticity versus the volume percent of WC in Co from 0 to 100 vol%, using both upper- and lower-bound expressions.

15.2 Estimate the maximum and minimum thermal conductivity values for a cermet that contains 90 vol% titanium carbide (TiC) particles in a nickel matrix. Assume thermal conductivities of 27 and 67 W/m-K for TiC and Ni, respectively.

15.3 A large-particle composite consisting of tungsten particles within a copper matrix is to be prepared. If the volume fractions of tungsten and copper are 0.70 and 0.30, respectively, estimate the upper limit for the specific stiffness of this composite given the data that follow.

	Specific Gravity	*Modulus of Elasticity (GPa)*
Copper	8.9	110
Tungsten	19.3	407

15.4 (a) What is the distinction between cement and concrete?

(b) Cite three important limitations that restrict the use of concrete as a structural material.

(c) Briefly explain three techniques that are utilized to strengthen concrete by reinforcement.

Dispersion-Strengthened Composites

15.5 Cite one similarity and two differences between precipitation hardening and dispersion strengthening.

Influence of Fiber Length

15.6 For some glass fiber–epoxy matrix combination, the critical fiber length–fiber diameter ratio is 40. Using the data in Table 15.4, determine the fiber–matrix bond strength.

15.7 (a) For a fiber-reinforced composite, the efficiency of reinforcement η is dependent on fiber length l according to

$$\eta = \frac{l - 2x}{l}$$

where x represents the length of the fiber at each end that does not contribute to the load transfer. Make a plot of η versus l to $l = 50$ mm assuming that $x = 1.25$ mm.

(b) What length is required for a 0.90 efficiency of reinforcement?

Influence of Fiber Orientation and Concentration

15.8 A continuous and aligned fiber-reinforced composite is to be produced consisting of 45 vol% aramid fibers and 55 vol% of a polycarbonate matrix; mechanical characteristics of these two materials are as follows:

	Modulus of Elasticity (GPa)	*Tensile Strength (MPa)*
Aramid fiber	131	3600
Polycarbonate	2.4	65

Also, the stress on the polycarbonate matrix when the aramid fibers fail is 35 MPa.

For this composite, compute

(a) the longitudinal tensile strength, and

(b) the longitudinal modulus of elasticity

15.9 Is it possible to produce a continuous and oriented aramid fiber–epoxy matrix composite having longitudinal and transverse moduli of elasticity of 35 GPa and 5.17 GPa, respectively? Why or why not? Assume that the elastic modulus of the epoxy is 3.4 GPa.

15.10 For a continuous and oriented fiber-reinforced composite, the moduli of elasticity in the longitudinal and transverse directions are 33.1 and 3.66 GPa, respectively. If the volume fraction of fibers is 0.30, determine the moduli of elasticity of fiber and matrix phases.

15.11 **(a)** Verify that Equation 15.11, the expression for the fiber load–matrix load ratio (F_f/F_m), is valid.

(b) What is the F_f/F_c ratio in terms of E_f, E_m, and V_f?

15.12 In an aligned and continuous carbon fiber-reinforced nylon 6,6 composite, the fibers are to carry 97% of a load applied in the longitudinal direction.

(a) Using the data provided, determine the volume fraction of fibers that will be required.

(b) What will be the tensile strength of this composite? Assume that the matrix stress at fiber failure is 50 MPa.

	Modulus of Elasticity (GPa)	*Tensile Strength (MPa)*
Carbon fiber	260	4000
Nylon 6,6	2.8	76

15.13 Assume that the composite described in Problem 15.8 has a cross-sectional area of 480 mm^2 and is subjected to a longitudinal load of 53,400 N.

(a) Calculate the fiber–matrix load ratio.

(b) Calculate the actual loads carried by both fiber and matrix phases.

(c) Compute the magnitude of the stress on each of the fiber and matrix phases.

(d) What strain is experienced by the composite?

15.14 A continuous and aligned fibrous reinforced composite having a cross-sectional area of 970 mm^2 is subjected to an external tensile load. If the stresses sustained by the fiber and matrix phases are 215 MPa and 5.38 MPa, respectively, the force sustained by the fiber phase is 76,800 N, and the total longitudinal composite strain is 1.56×10^{-3}, then determine

(a) the force sustained by the matrix phase

(b) the modulus of elasticity of the composite material in the longitudinal direction, and

(c) the moduli of elasticity for fiber and matrix phases.

15.15 Compute the longitudinal strength of an aligned carbon fiber–epoxy matrix composite having a 0.20 volume fraction of fibers, assuming the following: (1) an average fiber diameter of 6×10^{-3} mm, (2) an average fiber length of 8.0 mm, (3) a fiber fracture strength of 4.5 GPa, (4) a fiber–matrix bond strength of 75 MPa, (5) a matrix stress at composite failure of 6.0 MPa, and (6) a matrix tensile strength of 60 MPa.

15.16 It is desired to produce an aligned carbon fiber–epoxy matrix composite having a longitudinal tensile strength of 500 MPa. Calculate the volume fraction of fibers necessary if (1) the average fiber diameter and length are 0.01 mm and 0.5 mm, respectively; (2) the fiber fracture strength is 4.0 GPa; (3) the fiber–matrix bond strength is 25 MPa; and (4) the matrix stress at composite failure is 7.0 MPa.

15.17 Compute the longitudinal tensile strength of an aligned glass fiber–epoxy matrix composite in which the average fiber diameter and length are 0.015 mm and 2.0 mm, respectively, and the volume fraction of fibers is 0.25. Assume that (1) the fiber–matrix bond strength is 100 MPa, (2) the fracture strength of the fibers is 3500 MPa, and (3) the matrix stress at composite failure is 5.5 MPa.

15.18 **(a)** From the moduli of elasticity data in Table 15.2 for glass fiber-reinforced polycarbonate composites, determine the value of the fiber efficiency parameter for each of 20, 30, and 40 vol% fibers.

(b) Estimate the modulus of elasticity for 50 vol% glass fibers.

The Fiber Phase

The Matrix Phase

15.19 For a polymer-matrix fiber-reinforced composite,

(a) List three functions of the matrix phase.

(b) Compare the desired mechanical characteristics of matrix and fiber phases.

(c) Cite two reasons why there must be a strong bond between fiber and matrix at their interface.

15.20 **(a)** What is the distinction between matrix and dispersed phases in a composite material?

(b) Contrast the mechanical characteristics of matrix and dispersed phases for fiber-reinforced composites.

Polymer–Matrix Composites

15.21 **(a)** Calculate and compare the specific longitudinal strengths of the glass-fiber, carbon-fiber, and aramid-fiber reinforced epoxy composites in Table 15.5 with the following alloys: cold-rolled 17-7PH stainless steel, normalized 1040 plain-carbon steel, 7075-T6 aluminum alloy, cold-worked (H04 temper) C26000 cartridge brass, extruded AZ31B magnesium alloy, and annealed Ti-5Al–2.5Sn titanium alloy.

(b) Compare the specific moduli of the same three fiber-reinforced epoxy composites with the same metal alloys. Densities (i.e., specific gravities), tensile strengths, and moduli of elasticity for these metal alloys may be found in Tables B.1, B.4, and B.2, respectively, in Appendix B.

15.22 **(a)** List four reasons why glass fibers are most commonly used for reinforcement.

(b) Why is the surface perfection of glass fibers so important?

(c) What measures are taken to protect the surface of glass fibers?

15.23 Cite the distinction between carbon and graphite.

15.24 **(a)** Cite several reasons why fiberglass-reinforced composites are utilized extensively.

(b) Cite several limitations of this type of composite.

Hybrid Composites

15.25 **(a)** What is a hybrid composite?

(b) List two important advantages of hybrid composites over normal fiber composites.

15.26 **(a)** Write an expression for the modulus of elasticity for a hybrid composite in which all fibers of both types are oriented in the same direction.

(b) Using this expression, compute the longitudinal modulus of elasticity of a hybrid composite consisting of aramid and glass fibers in volume fractions of 0.25 and 0.35, respectively, within a polyester resin matrix (E_m = 4.0 GPa).

15.27 Derive a generalized expression analogous to Equation 15.16 for the transverse modulus of elasticity of an aligned hybrid composite consisting of two types of continuous fibers.

Laminar Composites
Sandwich Panels

15.28 Briefly describe laminar composites. What is the prime reason for fabricating these materials?

15.29 **(a)** Briefly describe sandwich panels.

(b) What is the prime reason for fabricating these structural composites?

(c) What are the functions of the faces and the core?

DESIGN PROBLEMS

15.D1 Composite materials are now being utilized extensively in sports equipment.

(a) List at least four different sports implements that are made of, or contain composites.

(b) For one of these implements, write an essay in which you do the following: (1) Cite the materials that are used for matrix and dispersed phases, and, if possible, the proportions of each phase; (2) note the nature of the dispersed phase (i.e., continuous fibers); and (3) describe the process by which the implement is fabricated.

Influence of Fiber Orientation and Concentration

15.D2 It is desired to produce an aligned and continuous fiber-reinforced epoxy composite having a maximum of 40 vol% fibers. In addition, a minimum longitudinal modulus of elasticity of 55 GPa is required, as well as a minimum tensile strength of 1200 MPa. Of E-glass, carbon (PAN standard modulus), and aramid fiber materials, which are possible candidates and why? The epoxy has a modulus of elasticity of 3.1 GPa and a tensile strength of 69 MPa. In addition, assume the following stress levels on the epoxy matrix at fiber failure: E-glass—70 MPa; carbon (PAN standard modulus)—30 MPa; and aramid—50 MPa. Other fiber data are contained in Tables B.2 and B.4 in Appendix B. For aramid fibers, use the minimum of the range of strength values.

15.D3 It is desired to produce a continuous and oriented carbon fiber-reinforced epoxy having a modulus of elasticity of at least 69 GPa in the direction of fiber alignment. The maximum permissible specific gravity is 1.40. Given the following data, is such a composite possible? Why or why not? Assume that composite specific gravity may be determined using a relationship similar to Equation 15.10a.

	Specific Gravity	*Modulus of Elasticity (GPa)*
Carbon fiber	1.80	260
Epoxy	1.25	2.4

15.D4 It is desired to fabricate a continuous and aligned glass fiber-reinforced polyester having a tensile strength of at least 1250 MPa in the longitudinal direction. The maximum possible specific gravity is 1.80. Using the following data, determine whether such a composite is possible. Justify your decision. Assume a value of 20 MPa for the stress on the matrix at fiber failure.

	Specific Gravity	*Tensile Strength (MPa)*
Glass fiber	2.50	3500
Polyester	1.35	50

15.D5 It is necessary to fabricate an aligned and discontinuous glass fiber–epoxy matrix composite having a longitudinal tensile strength of 1200 MPa using a 0.35 volume fraction of fibers. Compute the required fiber fracture strength assuming that the average fiber diameter and length are 0.015 mm and 5.0 mm, respectively. The fiber–matrix bond strength is 80 MPa, and the matrix stress at composite failure is 6.55 MPa.

15.D6 A tubular shaft similar to that shown in Figure 15.11 is to be designed that has an outside diameter of 100 mm and a length of 1.25 m. The mechanical characteristic of prime importance is bending stiffness in terms of the longitudinal modulus of elasticity. Stiffness is to be specified as maximum allowable deflection in bending; when subjected to three-point bending as in Figure 12.13, a load of 1700 N is to produce an elastic deflection of no more than 0.20 mm at the midpoint position.

Continuous fibers that are oriented parallel to the tube axis will be used; possible fiber materials are glass, and carbon in standard-, intermediate-, and high-modulus grades. The matrix material is to be an epoxy resin, and fiber volume fraction is 0.40.

(a) Decide which of the four fiber materials are possible candidates for this application, and for each candidate determine the required inside diameter consistent with the above criteria.

(b) For each candidate, determine the required cost, and on this basis, specify the fiber that would be the least expensive to use.

Elastic modulus, density, and cost data for the fiber and matrix materials are contained in Table 15.6.

Chapter 16 Corrosion and Degradation

Photograph showing a bar of steel that has been bent into a "horseshoe" shape using a nut-and-bolt assembly. While immersed in seawater, stress corrosion cracks formed along the bend at those regions where the tensile stresses are the greatest. (Photograph courtesy of F. L. LaQue. From F. L. LaQue, *Marine Corrosion, Causes and Prevention.* Copyright © 1975 by John Wiley & Sons, Inc. Reprinted by permission of John Wiley & Sons, Inc.)

Learning Objectives

After careful study of this chapter you should be able to do the following:

1. Distinguish between oxidation and reduction electrochemical reactions.
2. Describe the following: galvanic couple, standard half-cell, and standard hydrogen electrode.
3. Compute the cell potential and write the spontaneous electrochemical reaction direction for two pure metals that are electrically connected and also submerged in solutions of their respective ions.
4. Determine metal oxidation rate given the reaction current density.
5. Name and briefly describe the two different types of polarization, and specify the conditions under which each is rate controlling.
6. For each of the eight forms of corrosion and hydrogen embrittlement, describe the nature of the deteriorative process, and then note the proposed mechanism.
7. List five measures that are commonly used to prevent corrosion.
8. Explain why ceramic materials are, in general, very resistant to corrosion.
9. For polymeric materials discuss (a) two degradation processes that occur when they are exposed to liquid solvents, and (b) the causes and consequences of molecular chain bond rupture.

16.1 INTRODUCTION

To one degree or another, most materials experience some type of interaction with a large number of diverse environments. Often, such interactions impair a material's usefulness as a result of the deterioration of its mechanical properties (e.g., ductility and strength), other physical properties, or appearance. Occasionally, to the chagrin of a design engineer, the degradation behavior of a material for some application is ignored, with adverse consequences.

Deteriorative mechanisms are different for the three material types. In metals, there is actual material loss either by dissolution **(corrosion)** or by the formation of nonmetallic scale or film (*oxidation*). Ceramic materials are relatively resistant to deterioration, which usually occurs at elevated temperatures or in rather extreme environments; the process is frequently also called corrosion. For polymers, mechanisms and consequences differ from those for metals and ceramics, and the term **degradation** is most frequently used. Polymers may dissolve when exposed to a liquid solvent, or they may absorb the solvent and swell; also, electromagnetic radiation (primarily ultraviolet) and heat may cause alterations in their molecular structures.

The deterioration of each of these material types is discussed in this chapter, with special regard to mechanism, resistance to attack by various environments, and measures to prevent or reduce degradation.

Corrosion of Metals

Corrosion is defined as the destructive and unintentional attack of a metal; it is electrochemical and ordinarily begins at the surface. The problem of metallic corrosion is one of significant proportions; in economic terms, it has been estimated that approximately 5% of an industrialized nation's income is spent on corrosion prevention and the maintenance or replacement of products lost or contaminated as a result of corrosion reactions. The consequences of corrosion are all too common. Familiar examples include the rusting of automotive body panels and radiator and exhaust components.

Corrosion processes are occasionally used to advantage. For example, etching procedures, as discussed in Section 5.12, make use of the selective chemical reactivity of grain boundaries or various microstructural constituents.

16.2 ELECTROCHEMICAL CONSIDERATIONS

For metallic materials, the corrosion process is normally electrochemical, that is, a chemical reaction in which there is transfer of electrons from one chemical species to another. Metal atoms characteristically lose or give up electrons in what is called an **oxidation** reaction. For example, the hypothetical metal M that has a valence of n (or n valence electrons) may experience oxidation according to the reaction

$$M \longrightarrow M^{n+} + ne^- \tag{16.1}$$

in which M becomes an $n+$ positively charged ion and in the process loses its n valence electrons; e^- is used to symbolize an electron. Examples in which metals oxidize are

$$Fe \longrightarrow Fe^{2+} + 2e^- \tag{16.2a}$$

$$Al \longrightarrow Al^{3+} + 3e^- \tag{16.2b}$$

The site at which oxidation takes place is called the **anode;** oxidation is sometimes called an anodic reaction.

The electrons generated from each metal atom that is oxidized must be transferred to and become a part of another chemical species in what is termed a **reduction** reaction. For example, some metals undergo corrosion in acid solutions, which have a high concentration of hydrogen (H^+) ions; the H^+ ions are reduced as follows:

$$2H^+ + 2e^- \longrightarrow H_2 \tag{16.3}$$

and hydrogen gas (H_2) is evolved.

Other reduction reactions are possible, depending on the nature of the solution to which the metal is exposed. For an acid solution having dissolved oxygen, reduction according to

$$O_2 + 4H^+ + 4e^- \longrightarrow 2H_2O \tag{16.4}$$

will probably occur. Or, for a neutral or basic aqueous solution in which oxygen is also dissolved,

$$O_2 + 2H_2O + 4e^- \longrightarrow 4(OH^-) \tag{16.5}$$

Any metal ions present in the solution may also be reduced; for ions that can exist in more than one valence state (multivalent ions), reduction may occur by

$$M^{n+} + e^- \longrightarrow M^{(n-1)+} \tag{16.6}$$

in which the metal ion decreases its valence state by accepting an electron. Or a metal may be totally reduced from an ionic to a neutral metallic state according to

$$M^{n+} + ne^- \longrightarrow M \tag{16.7}$$

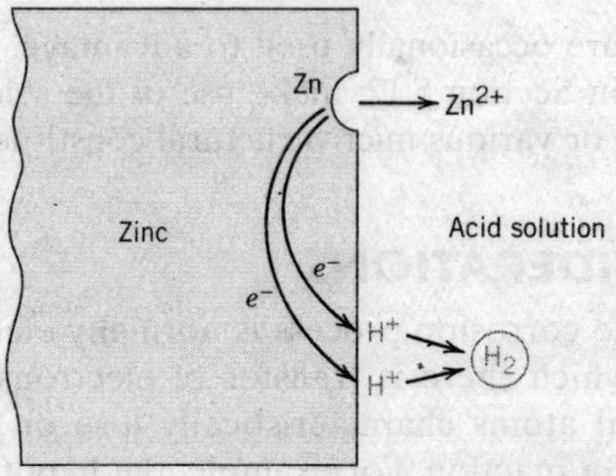

Figure 16.1 The electrochemical reactions associated with the corrosion of zinc in an acid solution. (From M. G. Fontana, *Corrosion Engineering,* 3rd edition. Copyright © 1986 by McGraw-Hill Book Company. Reproduced with permission.)

The location at which reduction occurs is called the **cathode.** Furthermore, it is possible for two or more of the reduction reactions above to occur simultaneously.

An overall electrochemical reaction must consist of at least one oxidation and one reduction reaction, and will be the sum of them; often the individual oxidation and reduction reactions are termed *half-reactions.* There can be no net electrical charge accumulation from the electrons and ions; that is, the total rate of oxidation must equal the total rate of reduction, or all electrons generated through oxidation must be consumed by reduction.

For example, consider zinc metal immersed in an acid solution containing H^+ ions. At some regions on the metal surface, zinc will experience oxidation or corrosion as illustrated in Figure 16.1, and according to the reaction

$$Zn \longrightarrow Zn^{2+} + 2e^- \tag{16.8}$$

Since zinc is a metal, and therefore a good electrical conductor, these electrons may be transferred to an adjacent region at which the H^+ ions are reduced according to

$$2H^+ + 2e^- \longrightarrow H_2\,(\text{gas}) \tag{16.9}$$

If no other oxidation or reduction reactions occur, the total electrochemical reaction is just the sum of reactions 16.8 and 16.9, or

$$\begin{array}{r} Zn \longrightarrow Zn^{2+} + 2e^- \\ 2H^+ + 2e^- \longrightarrow H_2\,(\text{gas}) \\ \hline Zn + 2H^+ \longrightarrow Zn^{2+} + H_2\,(\text{gas}) \end{array} \tag{16.10}$$

Another example is the oxidation or rusting of iron in water, which contains dissolved oxygen. This process occurs in two steps; in the first, Fe is oxidized to Fe^{2+} [as $Fe(OH)_2$],

$$Fe + \tfrac{1}{2}O_2 + H_2O \longrightarrow Fe^{2+} + 2OH^- \longrightarrow Fe(OH)_2 \tag{16.11}$$

and, in the second stage, to Fe^{3+} [as $Fe(OH)_3$] according to

$$2Fe(OH)_2 + \tfrac{1}{2}O_2 + H_2O \longrightarrow 2Fe(OH)_3 \tag{16.12}$$

The compound $Fe(OH)_3$ is the all too familiar rust.

As a consequence of oxidation, the metal ions may either go into the corroding solution as ions (reaction 16.8), or they may form an insoluble compound with nonmetallic elements as in reaction 16.12.

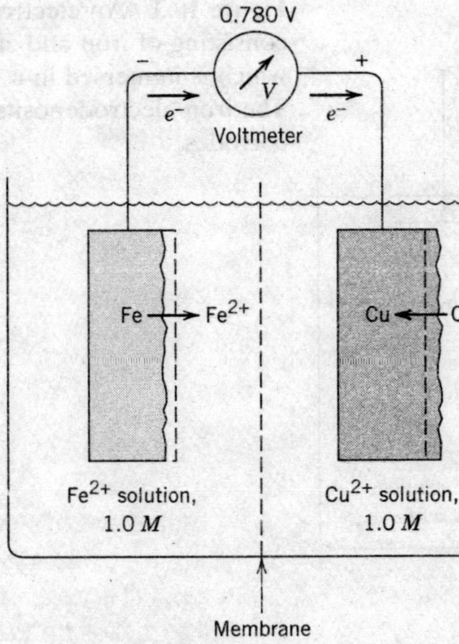

Figure 16.2 An electrochemical cell consisting of iron and copper electrodes, each of which is immersed in a $1M$ solution of its ion. Iron corrodes while copper electrodeposits.

Concept Check 16.1

Would you expect iron to corrode in water of high purity? Why or why not?

[The answer may be found in enclosed CD.]

Electrode Potentials

Not all metallic materials oxidize to form ions with the same degree of ease. Consider the electrochemical cell shown in Figure 16.2. On the left-hand side is a piece of pure iron immersed in a solution containing Fe^{2+} ions of $1M$ concentration.[1] The other side of the cell consists of a pure copper electrode in a $1M$ solution of Cu^{2+} ions. The cell halves are separated by a membrane, which limits the mixing of the two solutions. If the iron and copper electrodes are connected electrically, reduction will occur for copper at the expense of the oxidation of iron, as follows:

$$Cu^{2+} + Fe \longrightarrow Cu + Fe^{2+} \tag{16.13}$$

or Cu^{2+} ions will deposit (electrodeposit) as metallic copper on the copper electrode, while iron dissolves (corrodes) on the other side of the cell and goes into solution as Fe^{2+} ions. Thus, the two half-cell reactions are represented by the relations

$$Fe \longrightarrow Fe^{2+} + 2e^- \tag{16.14a}$$

$$Cu^{2+} + 2e^- \longrightarrow Cu \tag{16.14b}$$

When a current passes through the external circuit, electrons generated from the oxidation of iron flow to the copper cell in order that Cu^{2+} be reduced. In addition, there

[1] Concentration of liquid solutions is often expressed in terms of **molarity,** M, the number of moles of solute per million cubic millimeters (10^6 mm^3, or 1000 cm^3) of solution.

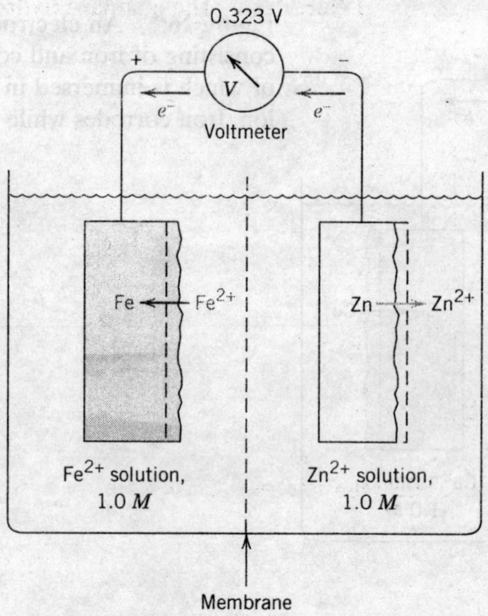

Figure 16.3 An electrochemical cell consisting of iron and zinc electrodes, each of which is immersed in a 1*M* solution of its ion. The iron electrodeposits while the zinc corrodes.

will be some net ion motion from each cell to the other across the membrane. This is called a *galvanic couple*—two metals electrically connected in a liquid **electrolyte** wherein one metal becomes an anode and corrodes, while the other acts as a cathode.

An electric potential or voltage will exist between the two cell halves, and its magnitude can be determined if a voltmeter is connected in the external circuit. A potential of 0.780 V results for a copper–iron galvanic cell when the temperature is 25°C.

Now consider another galvanic couple consisting of the same iron half-cell connected to a metal zinc electrode that is immersed in a 1*M* solution of Zn^{2+} ions (Figure 16.3). In this case the zinc is the anode and corrodes, whereas the Fe now becomes the cathode. The electrochemical reaction is thus

$$Fe^{2+} + Zn \longrightarrow Fe + Zn^{2+} \tag{16.15}$$

The potential associated with this cell reaction is 0.323 V.

Thus, various electrode pairs have different voltages; the magnitude of such a voltage may be thought of as representing the driving force for the electrochemical oxidation–reduction reaction. Consequently, metallic materials may be rated as to their tendency to experience oxidation when coupled to other metals in solutions of their respective ions. A half-cell similar to those described above [i.e., a pure metal electrode immersed in a 1*M* solution of its ions and at 25°C] is termed a **standard half-cell.**

The Standard emf Series

These measured cell voltages represent only differences in electrical potential, and thus it is convenient to establish a reference point, or reference cell, to which other cell halves may be compared. This reference cell, arbitrarily chosen, is the standard hydrogen electrode (Figure 16.4). It consists of an inert platinum electrode in a 1*M* solution of H^+ ions, saturated with hydrogen gas that is bubbled through the solution at a pressure of 1 atm and a temperature of 25°C. The platinum itself does not take part in the electrochemical reaction; it acts only as a surface on which hydrogen atoms may be oxidized or hydrogen ions may be reduced. The **electromotive force (emf) series** (Table 16.1) is generated by coupling to the standard hydrogen electrode.

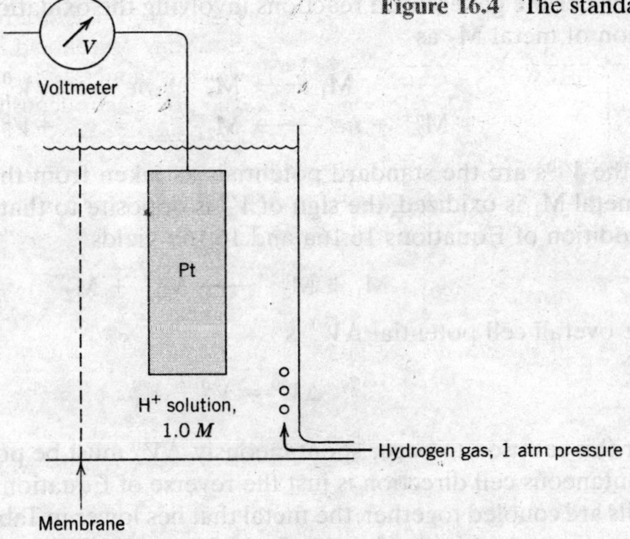

Figure 16.4 The standard hydrogen reference half-cell.

standard half-cells for various metals and ranking them according to measured voltage. Table 16.1 represents the corrosion tendencies for the several metals; those at the top (i.e., gold and platinum) are noble, or chemically inert. Moving down the table, the metals become increasingly more active, that is, more susceptible to oxidation. Sodium and potassium have the highest reactivities.

The voltages in Table 16.1 are for the half-reactions as *reduction reactions,* with the electrons on the left-hand side of the chemical equation; for oxidation, the direction of the reaction is reversed and the sign of the voltage changed.

Table 16.1 The Standard emf Series

	Electrode Reaction	*Standard Electrode Potential, V^0(V)*
↑	$Au^{3+} + 3e^- \longrightarrow Au$	+1.420
	$O_2 + 4H^+ + 4e^- \longrightarrow 2H_2O$	+1.229
	$Pt^{2+} + 2e^- \longrightarrow Pt$	~+1.2
	$Ag^+ + e^- \longrightarrow Ag$	+0.800
Increasingly inert	$Fe^{3+} + e^- \longrightarrow Fe^{2+}$	+0.771
(cathodic)	$O_2 + 2H_2O + 4e^- \longrightarrow 4(OH^-)$	+0.401
	$Cu^{2+} + 2e^- \longrightarrow Cu$	+0.340
	$2H^+ + 2e^- \longrightarrow H_2$	0.000
	$Pb^{2+} + 2e^- \longrightarrow Pb$	−0.126
	$Sn^{2+} + 2e^- \longrightarrow Sn$	−0.136
	$Ni^{2+} + 2e^- \longrightarrow Ni$	−0.250
	$Co^{2+} + 2e^- \longrightarrow Co$	−0.277
	$Cd^{2+} + 2e^- \longrightarrow Cd$	−0.403
	$Fe^{2+} + 2e^- \longrightarrow Fe$	−0.440
Increasingly active	$Cr^{3+} + 3e^- \longrightarrow Cr$	−0.744
(anodic)	$Zn^{2+} + 2e^- \longrightarrow Zn$	−0.763
	$Al^{3+} + 3e^- \longrightarrow Al$	−1.662
	$Mg^{2+} + 2e^- \longrightarrow Mg$	−2.363
	$Na^+ + e^- \longrightarrow Na$	−2.714
↓	$K^+ + e^- \longrightarrow K$	−2.924

Consider the generalized reactions involving the oxidation of metal M_1 and the reduction of metal M_2 as

$$M_1 \longrightarrow M_1^{n+} + ne^- \qquad -V_1^0 \tag{16.16a}$$

$$M_2^{n+} + ne^- \longrightarrow M_2 \qquad +V_2^0 \tag{16.16b}$$

where the V^0's are the standard potentials as taken from the standard emf series. Since metal M_1 is oxidized, the sign of V_1^0 is opposite to that as it appears in Table 16.1. Addition of Equations 16.16a and 16.16b yields

$$M_1 + M_2^{n+} \longrightarrow M_1^{n+} + M_2 \tag{16.17}$$

and the overall cell potential ΔV^0 is

$$\Delta V^0 = V_2^0 - V_1^0 \tag{16.18}$$

For this reaction to occur spontaneously, ΔV^0 must be positive; if it is negative, the spontaneous cell direction is just the reverse of Equation 16.17. When standard half-cells are coupled together, the metal that lies lower in Table 16.1 will experience oxidation (i.e., corrosion), whereas the higher one will be reduced.

Influence of Concentration and Temperature on Cell Potential

The emf series applies to highly idealized electrochemical cells (i.e., pure metals in $1M$ solutions of their ions, at 25°C). Altering temperature or solution concentration or using alloy electrodes instead of pure metals will change the cell potential, and, in some cases, the spontaneous reaction direction may be reversed.

Consider again the electrochemical reaction described by Equation 16.17. If M_1 and M_2 electrodes are pure metals, the cell potential depends on the absolute temperature T and the molar ion concentrations $[M_1^{n+}]$ and $[M_2^{n+}]$ according to the Nernst equation:

$$\Delta V = (V_2^0 - V_1^0) - \frac{RT}{n\mathcal{F}} \ln \frac{[M_1^{n+}]}{[M_2^{n+}]} \tag{16.19}$$

where R is the gas constant, n is the number of electrons participating in either of the half-cell reactions, and $\mathcal{F}$ is the Faraday constant, 96,500 C/mol—the magnitude of charge per mole (6.023×10^{23}) of electrons. At 25°C (about room temperature), equation 16.19 simplifies to

$$\Delta V = (V_2^0 - V_1^0) - \frac{0.0592}{n} \log \frac{[M_1^{n+}]}{[M_2^{n+}]} \tag{16.20}$$

to give ΔV in volts. Again, for reaction spontaneity, ΔV must be positive. As expected, for $1M$ concentrations of both ion types (that is, $[M_1^{n+}] = [M_2^{n+}] = 1$), Equation 16.19 simplifies to Equation 16.18.

Concept Check 16.2

Modify Equation 16.19 for the case in which metals M_1 and M_2 are alloys.

[The answer may be found in enclosed CD.]

EXAMPLE PROBLEM 16.1

Determination of Electrochemical Cell Characteristics

One-half of an electrochemical cell consists of a pure nickel electrode in a solution of Ni^{2+} ions; the other half is a cadmium electrode immersed in a Cd^{2+} solution.

(a) If the cell is a standard one, write the spontaneous overall reaction and calculate the voltage that is generated.

(b) Compute the cell potential at 25°C if the Cd^{2+} and Ni^{2+} concentrations are 0.5 and 10^{-3} *M*, respectively. Is the spontaneous reaction direction still the same as for the standard cell?

Solution

(a) The cadmium electrode will be oxidized and nickel reduced because cadmium is lower in the emf series; thus, the spontaneous reactions will be

$$Cd \longrightarrow Cd^{2+} + 2e^-$$

$$\frac{Ni^{2+} + 2e^- \longrightarrow Ni}{Ni^{2+} + Cd \longrightarrow Ni + Cd^{2+}} \qquad (16.21)$$

From Table 16.1, the half-cell potentials for cadmium and nickel are, respectively, −0.403 and −0.250 V. Therefore, from Equation 16.18,

$$\Delta V = V_{Ni}^0 - V_{Cd}^0 = -0.250 \text{ V} - (-0.403 \text{ V}) = +0.153 \text{ V}$$

(b) For this portion of the problem, Equation 16.20 must be utilized, since the half-cell solution concentrations are no longer 1*M*. At this point it is necessary to make a calculated guess as to which metal species is oxidized (or reduced). This choice will either be affirmed or refuted on the basis of the sign of ΔV at the conclusion of the computation. For the sake of argument, let us assume that in contrast to part (a), nickel is oxidized and cadmium reduced according to

$$Cd^{2+} + Ni \longrightarrow Cd + Ni^{2+} \qquad (16.22)$$

Thus,

$$\Delta V = (V_{Cd}^0 - V_{Ni}^0) - \frac{RT}{n\mathscr{F}} \ln \frac{[Ni^{2+}]}{[Cd^{2+}]}$$

$$= -0.403 \text{ V} - (-0.250 \text{ V}) - \frac{0.0592}{2} \log\left(\frac{10^{-3}}{0.50}\right)$$

$$= -0.073 \text{ V}$$

Since ΔV is negative, the spontaneous reaction direction is the opposite to that of Equation 16.22, or

$$Ni^{2+} + Cd \longrightarrow Ni + Cd^{2+}$$

That is, cadmium is oxidized and nickel is reduced.

The Galvanic Series

Even though Table 16.1 was generated under highly idealized conditions and has limited utility, it nevertheless indicates the relative reactivities of the metals. A more realistic and practical ranking, however, is provided by the **galvanic series,** Table 16.2. This represents the relative reactivities of a number of metals and commercial alloys in seawater. The alloys near the top are cathodic and unreactive,

Table 16.2 The Galvanic Series

	Platinum
	Gold
	Graphite
	Titanium
	Silver
	316 Stainless steel (passive)
	304 Stainless steel (passive)
↑	Inconel (80Ni–13Cr–7Fe) (passive)
	Nickel (passive)
	Monel (70Ni–30Cu)
Increasingly inert (cathodic)	Copper–nickel alloys
	Bronzes (Cu–Sn alloys)
	Copper
	Brasses (Cu–Zn alloys)
	Inconel (active)
	Nickel (active)
	Tin
	Lead
Increasingly active (anodic)	316 Stainless steel (active)
	304 Stainless steel (active)
	Cast iron
↓	Iron and steel
	Aluminum alloys
	Cadmium
	Commercially pure aluminum
	Zinc
	Magnesium and magnesium alloys

Source: M. G. Fontana, *Corrosion Engineering,* 3rd edition. Copyright 1986 by McGraw-Hill Book Company. Reprinted with permission.

whereas those at the bottom are most anodic; no voltages are provided. Comparison of the standard emf and the galvanic series reveals a high degree of correspondence between the relative positions of the pure base metals.

Most metals and alloys are subject to oxidation or corrosion to one degree or another in a wide variety of environments; that is, they are more stable in an ionic state than as metals. In thermodynamic terms, there is a net decrease in free energy in going from metallic to oxidized states. Consequently, essentially all metals occur in nature as compounds—for example, oxides, hydroxides, carbonates, silicates, sulfides, and sulfates. Two notable exceptions are the noble metals gold and platinum. For them, oxidation in most environments is not favorable, and, therefore, they may exist in nature in the metallic state.

16.3 CORROSION RATES

The half-cell potentials listed in Table 16.1 are thermodynamic parameters that relate to systems at equilibrium. For example, for the discussions pertaining to Figures 16.2 and 16.3, it was tacitly assumed that there was no current flow through the external circuit. Real corroding systems are not at equilibrium; there will be a flow of electrons from anode to cathode (corresponding to the short-circuiting of the electrochemical cells in Figures 16.2 and 16.3), which means that the half-cell potential parameters (Table 16.1) cannot be applied.

Furthermore, these half-cell potentials represent the magnitude of a driving force, or the tendency for the occurrence of the particular half-cell reaction. However, it should be noted that although these potentials may be used to determine spontaneous reaction directions, they provide no information as to corrosion rates. That is, even though a ΔV potential computed for a specific corrosion situation using Equation 16.20 is a relatively large positive number, the reaction may occur at only an insignificantly slow rate. From an engineering perspective, we are interested in predicting the rates at which systems corrode; this requires the utilization of other parameters, as discussed below.

The corrosion rate, or the rate of material removal as a consequence of the chemical action, is an important corrosion parameter. This may be expressed as the **corrosion penetration rate (CPR),** or the thickness loss of material per unit of time. The formula for this calculation is

$$\text{CPR} = \frac{KW}{\rho A t} \tag{16.23}$$

where W is the weight loss after exposure time t; ρ and A represent the density and exposed specimen area, respectively, and K is a constant, its magnitude depending on the system of units used. The CPR is conveniently expressed in terms of either mils per year (mpy) or millimeters per year (mm/yr). In the first case, $K = 534$ to give CPR in mpy (where 1 mil = 0.001 in.), and W, ρ, A, and t are specified in units of milligrams, grams per cubic centimeter, square inches, and hours, respectively. In the second case, $K = 87.6$ for mm/yr, and units for the other parameters are the same as for mils per year, except that A is given in square centimeters. For most applications a corrosion penetration rate less than about 20 mpy (0.50 mm/yr) is acceptable.

Inasmuch as there is an electric current associated with electrochemical corrosion reactions, we can also express corrosion rate in terms of this current, or, more specifically, current density—that is, the current per unit surface area of material corroding—which is designated i. The rate r, in units of mol/m^2-s, is determined using the expression

$$r = \frac{i}{n\mathcal{F}} \tag{16.24}$$

where, again, n is the number of electrons associated with the ionization of each metal atom, and $\mathcal{F}$ is 96,500 C/mol.

16.4 PREDICTION OF CORROSION RATES

Polarization

Consider the standard Zn/H_2 electrochemical cell shown in Figure 16.5, which has been short-circuited such that oxidation of zinc and reduction of hydrogen will occur at their respective electrode surfaces. The potentials of the two electrodes will not be at the values determined from Table 16.1 because the system is now a nonequilibrium one. The displacement of each electrode potential from its equilibrium value is termed **polarization,** and the magnitude of this displacement is the *overvoltage,* normally represented by the symbol η. Overvoltage is expressed in terms of plus or minus volts (or millivolts) relative to the equilibrium potential. For example, suppose that the zinc electrode in Figure 16.5 has a potential of -0.621 V after it has been connected to the platinum electrode. The equilibrium potential is -0.763 V (Table 16.1), and, therefore,

$$\eta = -0.621\text{ V} - (-0.763\text{ V}) = +0.142\text{ V}$$

There are two types of polarization—activation and concentration. We will now discuss their mechanisms since they control the rate of electrochemical reactions.

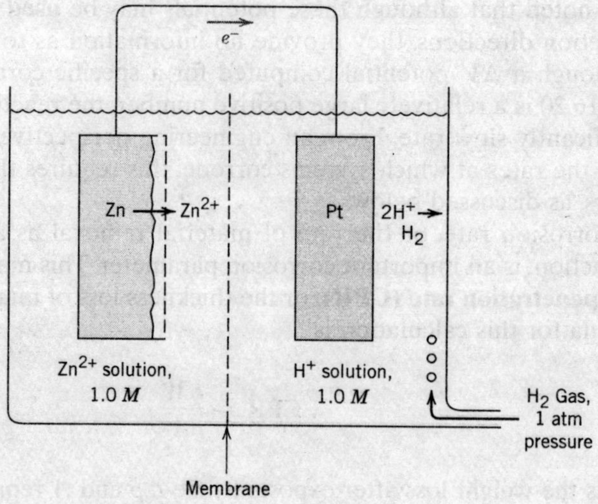

Figure 16.5 Electrochemical cell consisting of standard zinc and hydrogen electrodes that has been short-circuited.

Activation Polarization

All electrochemical reactions consist of a sequence of steps that occur in series at the interface between the metal electrode and the electrolyte solution. **Activation polarization** refers to the condition wherein the reaction rate is controlled by the one step in the series that occurs at the slowest rate. The term "activation" is applied to this type of polarization because an activation energy barrier is associated with this slowest, rate-limiting step.

To illustrate, let us consider the reduction of hydrogen ions to form bubbles of hydrogen gas on the surface of a zinc electrode (Figure 16.6). It is conceivable that this reaction could proceed by the following step sequence:

1. Adsorption of H^+ ions from the solution onto the zinc surface
2. Electron transfer from the zinc to form a hydrogen atom,

$$H^+ + e^- \longrightarrow H$$

3. Combining of two hydrogen atoms to form a molecule of hydrogen,

$$2H \longrightarrow H_2$$

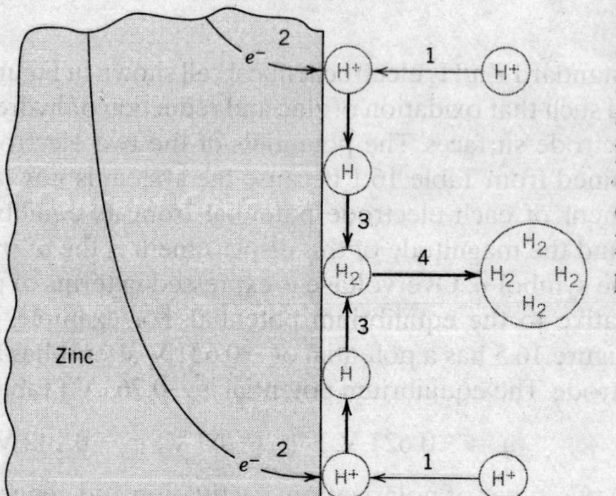

Figure 16.6 Schematic representation of possible steps in the hydrogen reduction reaction, the rate of which is controlled by activation polarization. (From M. G. Fontana, *Corrosion Engineering,* 3rd edition. Copyright © 1986 by McGraw-Hill Book Company. Reproduced with permission.)

4. The coalescence of many hydrogen molecules to form a bubble

The slowest of these steps determines the rate of the overall reaction.

For activation polarization, the relationship between overvoltage η_a and current density i is

$$\eta_a = \pm\beta \log \frac{i}{i_0} \tag{16.25}$$

where β and i_0 are constants for the particular half-cell. The parameter i_0 is termed the *exchange current density,* which deserves a brief explanation. Equilibrium for some particular half-cell reaction is really a dynamic state on the atomic level. That is, oxidation and reduction processes are occurring, but both at the same rate, so that there is no net reaction. For example, for the standard hydrogen cell (Figure 16.4) reduction of hydrogen ions in solution will take place at the surface of the platinum electrode according to

$$2H^+ + 2e^- \longrightarrow H_2$$

with a corresponding rate r_{red}. Similarly, hydrogen gas in the solution will experience oxidation as

$$H_2 \longrightarrow 2H^+ + 2e^-$$

at rate r_{oxid}. Equilibrium exists when

$$r_{red} = r_{oxid}$$

This exchange current density is just the current density from Equation 16.24 at equilibrium, or

$$r_{red} = r_{oxid} = \frac{i_0}{n\mathcal{F}} \tag{16.26}$$

Use of the term "current density" for i_0 is a little misleading inasmuch as there is no net current. Furthermore, the value for i_0 is determined experimentally and will vary from system to system.

According to Equation 16.25, when overvoltage is plotted as a function of the logarithm of current density, straight-line segments result; these are shown in Figure 16.7

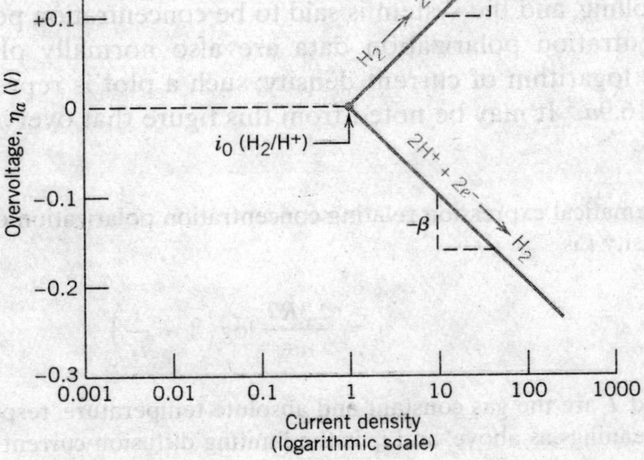

Figure 16.7 For a hydrogen electrode, plot of activation polarization overvoltage versus logarithm of current density for both oxidation and reduction reactions. (Adapted from M. G. Fontana, *Corrosion Engineering,* 3rd edition. Copyright © 1986 by McGraw-Hill Book Company. Reproduced with permission.)

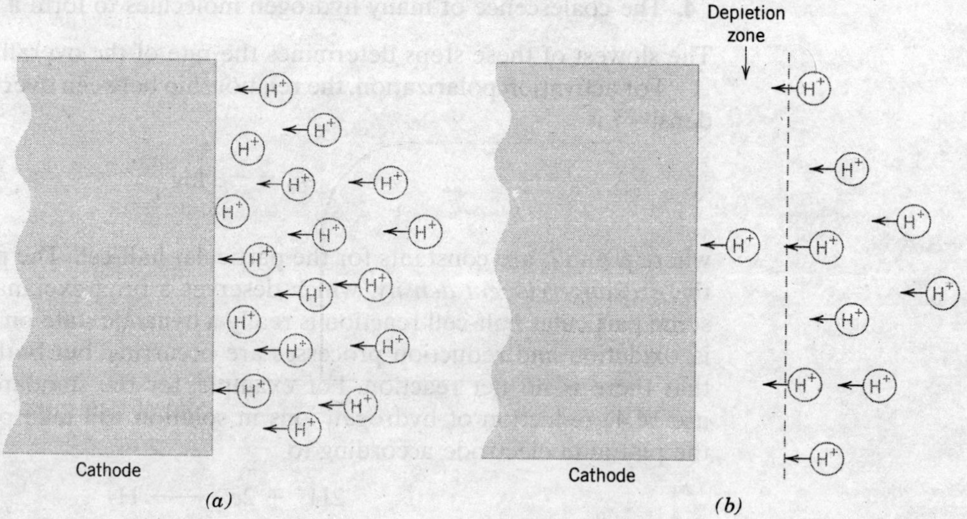

Figure 16.8 For hydrogen reduction, schematic representations of the H^+ distribution in the vicinity of the cathode for (*a*) low reaction rates and/or high concentrations, and (*b*) high reaction rates and/or low concentrations wherein a depletion zone is formed that gives rise to concentration polarization. (Adapted from M. G. Fontana, *Corrosion Engineering*, 3rd edition. Copyright © 1986 by McGraw-Hill Book Company. Reproduced with permission.)

for the hydrogen electrode. The line segment with a slope of $+\beta$ corresponds to the oxidation half-reaction, whereas the line with a $-\beta$ slope is for reduction. Also worth noting is that both line segments originate at i_0 (H_2/H^+), the exchange current density, and at zero overvoltage, since at this point the system is at equilibrium and there is no net reaction.

Concentration Polarization

Concentration polarization exists when the reaction rate is limited by diffusion in the solution. For example, consider again the hydrogen evolution reduction reaction. When the reaction rate is low and/or the concentration of H^+ is high, there is always an adequate supply of hydrogen ions available in the solution at the region near the electrode interface (Figure 16.8*a*). On the other hand, at high rates and/or low H^+ concentrations, a depletion zone may be formed in the vicinity of the interface, inasmuch as the H^+ ions are not replenished at a rate sufficient to keep up with the reaction (Figure 16.8*b*). Thus, diffusion of H^+ to the interface is rate controlling, and the system is said to be concentration polarized.

Concentration polarization data are also normally plotted as overvoltage versus the logarithm of current density; such a plot is represented schematically in Figure 16.9*a*.[2] It may be noted from this figure that overvoltage is independent

[2] The mathematical expression relating concentration polarization overvoltage η_c and current density i is

$$\eta_c = \frac{2.3RT}{n\mathcal{F}} \log\left(1 - \frac{i}{i_L}\right) \qquad (16.27)$$

where R and T are the gas constant and absolute temperature, respectively, n and $\mathcal{F}$ have the same meanings as above, and i_L is the limiting diffusion current density.

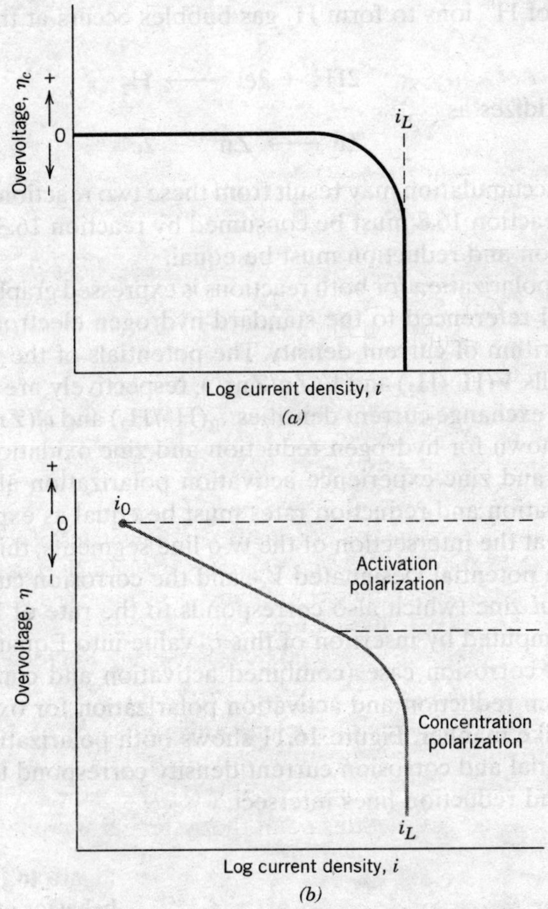

Figure 16.9 For reduction reactions, schematic plots of overvoltage versus logarithm of current density for (*a*) concentration polarization, and (*b*) combined activation–concentration polarization.

of current density until i approaches i_L; at this point, η_c decreases abruptly in magnitude.

Both concentration and activation polarization are possible for reduction reactions. Under these circumstances, the total overvoltage is just the sum of both overvoltage contributions. Figure 16.9*b* shows such a schematic η-versus-log i plot.

Concept Check 16.3

Briefly explain why concentration polarization is not normally rate controlling for oxidation reactions.

[*The answer may be found in enclosed CD.*]

Corrosion Rates from Polarization Data

Let us now apply the concepts developed above to the determination of corrosion rates. Two types of systems will be discussed. In the first case, both oxidation and reduction reactions are rate limited by activation polarization. In the second case, both concentration and activation polarization control the reduction reaction, whereas only activation polarization is important for oxidation. Case one will be illustrated by considering the corrosion of zinc immersed in an acid solution (see Figure 16.1).

The reduction of H^+ ions to form H_2 gas bubbles occurs at the surface of the zinc according to

$$2H^+ + 2e^- \longrightarrow H_2 \tag{16.3}$$

and the zinc oxidizes as

$$Zn \longrightarrow Zn^{2+} + 2e^- \tag{16.8}$$

No net charge accumulation may result from these two reactions; that is, all electrons generated by reaction 16.8 must be consumed by reaction 16.3, which is to say that rates of oxidation and reduction must be equal.

Activation polarization for both reactions is expressed graphically in Figure 16.10 as cell potential referenced to the standard hydrogen electrode (not overvoltage) versus the logarithm of current density. The potentials of the uncoupled hydrogen and zinc half-cells, $V(H^+/H_2)$ and $V(Zn/Zn^{2+})$, respectively, are indicated, along with their respective exchange current densities, $i_0(H^+/H_2)$ and $i_0(Zn/Zn^{2+})$. Straight line segments are shown for hydrogen reduction and zinc oxidation. Upon immersion, both hydrogen and zinc experience activation polarization along their respective lines. Also, oxidation and reduction rates must be equal as explained above, which is only possible at the intersection of the two line segments; this intersection occurs at the corrosion potential, designated V_C, and the corrosion current density i_C. The corrosion rate of zinc (which also corresponds to the rate of hydrogen evolution) may thus be computed by insertion of this i_C value into Equation 16.24.

The second corrosion case (combined activation and concentration polarization for hydrogen reduction and activation polarization for oxidation of metal M) is treated in a like manner. Figure 16.11 shows both polarization curves; as above, corrosion potential and corrosion current density correspond to the point at which the oxidation and reduction lines intersect.

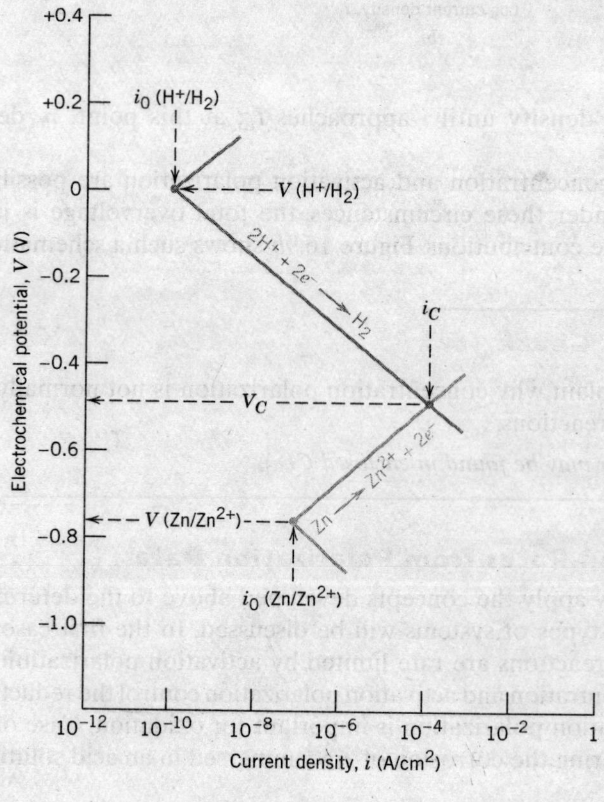

Figure 16.10 Electrode kinetic behavior of zinc in an acid solution; both oxidation and reduction reactions are rate limited by activation polarization. (Adapted from M. G. Fontana, *Corrosion Engineering,* 3rd edition. Copyright © 1986 by McGraw-Hill Book Company. Reproduced with permission.)

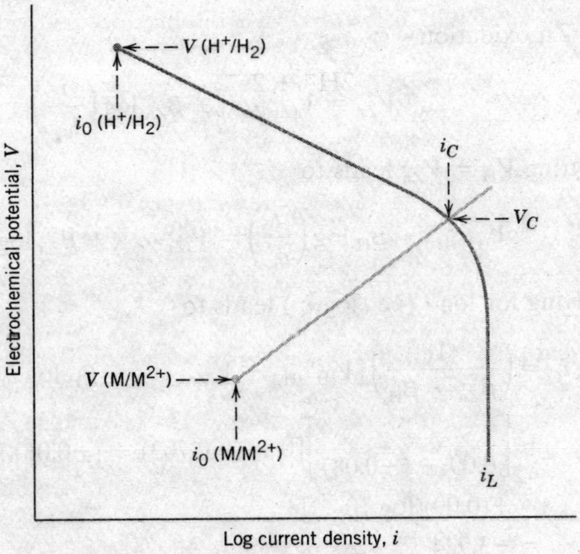

Figure 16.11 Schematic electrode kinetic behavior for metal M; the reduction reaction is under combined activation–concentration polarization control.

EXAMPLE PROBLEM 16.2

Rate of Oxidation Computation

Zinc experiences corrosion in an acid solution according to the reaction

$$\text{Zn} + 2\text{H}^+ \longrightarrow \text{Zn}^{2+} + \text{H}_2$$

The rates of both oxidation and reduction half-reactions are controlled by activation polarization.

(a) Compute the rate of oxidation of Zn (in mol/cm^2-s) given the following activation polarization data:

For Zn	*For Hydrogen*
$V_{(\text{Zn/Zn}^{2+})} = -0.763$ V	$V_{(\text{H}^+/\text{H}_2)} = 0$ V
$i_0 = 10^{-7}$ A/cm^2	$i_0 = 10^{-10}$ A/cm^2
$\beta = +0.09$	$\beta = -0.08$

(b) Compute the value of the corrosion potential.

Solution

(a) To compute the rate of oxidation for Zn, it is first necessary to establish relationships in the form of Equation 16.25 for the potential of both oxidation and reduction reactions. Next, these two expressions are set equal to one another, and then we solve for the value of i that is the corrosion current density, i_C. Finally, the corrosion rate may be calculated using Equation 16.24. The two potential expressions are as follows: For hydrogen reduction,

$$V_{\text{H}} = V_{(\text{H}^+/\text{H}_2)} + \beta_{\text{H}} \log\left(\frac{i}{i_{0_{\text{H}}}}\right)$$

and for Zn oxidation,

$$V_{Zn} = V_{(Zn/Zn^{2+})} + \beta_{Zn} \log\left(\frac{i}{i_{0_{Zn}}}\right)$$

Now, setting $V_H = V_{Zn}$ leads to

$$V_{(H^+/H_2)} + \beta_H \log\left(\frac{i}{i_{0_H}}\right) = V_{(Zn/Zn^{2+})} + \beta_{Zn} \log\left(\frac{i}{i_{0_{Zn}}}\right)$$

And solving for log i (i.e., log i_C) leads to

$$\begin{aligned}\log i_C &= \left(\frac{1}{\beta_{Zn} - \beta_H}\right)[V_{(H^+/H_2)} - V_{(Zn/Zn^{2+})} - \beta_H \log i_{0_H} + \beta_{Zn} \log i_{0_{Zn}}]\\ &= \left[\frac{1}{0.09 - (-0.08)}\right][0 - (-0.763) - (-0.08)(\log 10^{-10})\\ &\quad +(0.09)(\log 10^{-7})]\\ &= -3.924\end{aligned}$$

or

$$i_C = 10^{-3.924} = 1.19 \times 10^{-4}\ \text{A/cm}^2$$

And, from Equation 16.24,

$$\begin{aligned}r &= \frac{i_C}{n\mathcal{F}}\\ &= \frac{1.19 \times 10^{-4}\ \text{C/s-cm}^2}{(2)(96{,}500\ \text{C/mol})} = 6.17 \times 10^{-10}\ \text{mol/cm}^2\text{-s}\end{aligned}$$

(b) Now it becomes necessary to compute the value of the corrosion potential V_C. This is possible by using either of the above equations for V_H or V_{Zn} and substituting for i the value determined above for i_C. Thus, using the V_H expression yields

$$\begin{aligned}V_C &= V_{(H^+/H_2)} + \beta_H \log\left(\frac{i_C}{i_{0_H}}\right)\\ &= 0 + (-0.08\ \text{V}) \log\left(\frac{1.19 \times 10^{-4}\ \text{A/cm}^2}{10^{-10}\ \text{A/cm}^2}\right) = -0.486\ \text{V}\end{aligned}$$

This is the same problem that is represented and solved graphically in the voltage-versus-logarithm current density plot of Figure 16.10. It is worth noting that the i_C and V_C we have obtained by this analytical treatment are in agreement with those values occurring at the intersection of the two line segments on the plot.

16.5 PASSIVITY

Some normally active metals and alloys, under particular environmental conditions, lose their chemical reactivity and become extremely inert. This phenomenon, termed **passivity,** is displayed by chromium, iron, nickel, titanium, and many of their alloys. It is felt that this passive behavior results from the formation of a highly adherent and very thin oxide film on the metal surface, which serves as a protective barrier to further corrosion. Stainless steels are highly resistant to corrosion in a rather wide variety of atmospheres as a result of passivation. They contain at least 11% chromium that, as a solid-solution alloying element in iron, minimizes the formation of rust; instead, a protective surface film forms in oxidizing atmospheres. (Stainless steels are susceptible to corrosion in some environments, and therefore are not always "stainless.") Aluminum is highly corrosion resistant in many environments because it also passivates. If damaged, the protective film normally reforms very rapidly. However, a change in the character of the environment (e.g., alteration in the concentration of the active corrosive species) may cause a passivated material to revert to an active state. Subsequent damage to a preexisting passive film could result in a substantial increase in corrosion rate, by as much as 100,000 times.

This passivation phenomenon may be explained in terms of polarization potential–log current density curves discussed in the preceding section. The polarization curve for a metal that passivates will have the general shape shown in Figure 16.12. At relatively low potential values, within the "active" region the behavior is linear as it is for normal metals. With increasing potential, the current density suddenly decreases to a very low value that remains independent of potential; this is termed the "passive" region. Finally, at even higher potential values, the current density again increases with potential in the "transpassive" region.

Figure 16.13 illustrates how a metal can experience both active and passive behavior depending on the corrosion environment. Included in this figure is the S-shaped oxidation polarization curve for an active–passive metal M and, in addition, reduction polarization curves for two different solutions, which are labeled 1 and 2. Curve 1 intersects the oxidation polarization curve in the active region at point A, yielding a corrosion current density $i_C(\text{A})$. The intersection of curve 2 at point B is in the passive region and at current density $i_C(\text{B})$. The corrosion rate of metal M in solution 1 is greater than in solution 2 since $i_C(\text{A})$ is greater than $i_C(\text{B})$ and rate is proportional to current density according to Equation 16.24. This difference in corrosion rate between the two solutions may be significant—several orders of magnitude—when one considers that the current density scale in Figure 16.13 is scaled logarithmically.

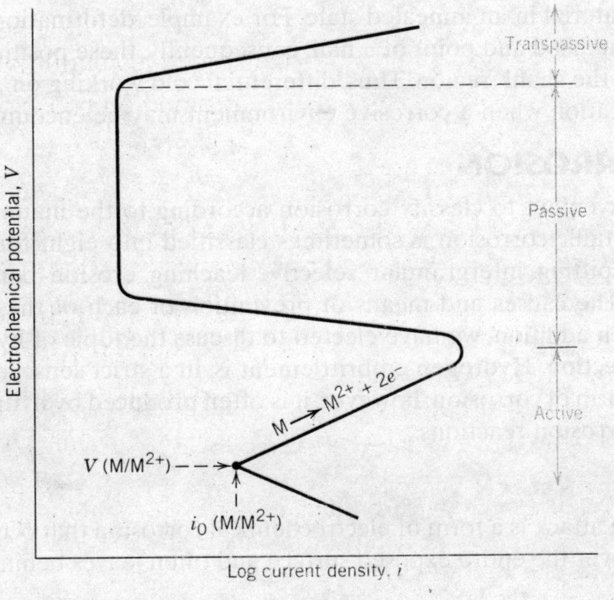

Figure 16.12 Schematic polarization curve for a metal that displays an active–passive transition.

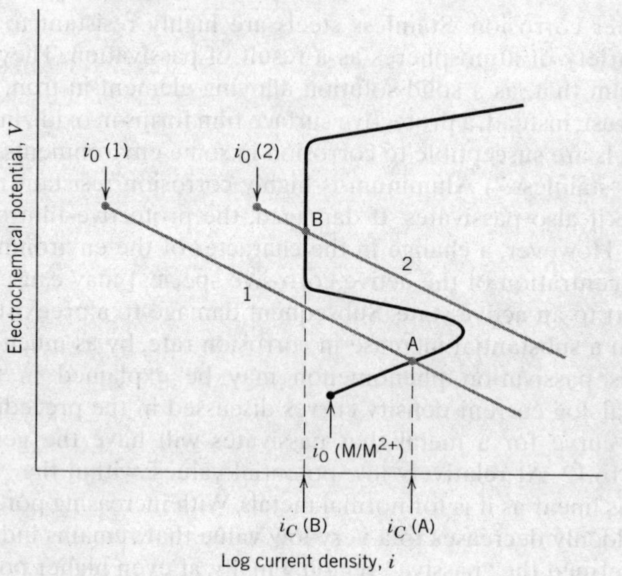

Figure 16.13 Demonstration of how an active–passive metal can exhibit both active and passive corrosion behaviors.

16.6 ENVIRONMENTAL EFFECTS

The variables in the corrosion environment, which include fluid velocity, temperature, and composition, can have a decided influence on the corrosion properties of the materials that are in contact with it. In most instances, increasing fluid velocity enhances the rate of corrosion due to erosive effects, as discussed later in the chapter. The rates of most chemical reactions rise with increasing temperature; this also holds for the great majority of corrosion situations. Increasing the concentration of the corrosive species (e.g., H^+ ions in acids) in many situations produces a more rapid rate of corrosion. However, for materials capable of passivation, raising the corrosive content may result in an active-to-passive transition, with a considerable reduction in corrosion.

Cold working or plastically deforming ductile metals is used to increase their strength; however, a cold-worked metal is more susceptible to corrosion than the same material in an annealed state. For example, deformation processes are used to shape the head and point of a nail; consequently, these positions are anodic with respect to the shank region. Thus, differential cold working on a structure should be a consideration when a corrosive environment may be encountered during service.

16.7 FORMS OF CORROSION

It is convenient to classify corrosion according to the manner in which it is manifest. Metallic corrosion is sometimes classified into eight forms: uniform, galvanic, crevice, pitting, intergranular, selective leaching, erosion–corrosion, and stress corrosion. The causes and means of prevention of each of these forms are discussed briefly. In addition, we have elected to discuss the topic of hydrogen embrittlement in this section. Hydrogen embrittlement is, in a strict sense, a type of failure rather than a form of corrosion; however, it is often produced by hydrogen that is generated from corrosion reactions.

Uniform Attack

Uniform attack is a form of electrochemical corrosion that occurs with equivalent intensity over the entire exposed surface and often leaves behind a scale or deposit. In a microscopic sense, the oxidation and reduction reactions occur randomly over the surface. Some familiar examples include general rusting of steel and iron and the tarnishing of silverware. This is probably the most common form of corrosion. It is also the least objectionable because it can be predicted and designed for with relative ease.

Galvanic Corrosion

Galvanic corrosion occurs when two metals or alloys having different compositions are electrically coupled while exposed to an electrolyte. This is the type of corrosion or dissolution that was described in Section 16.2. The less noble or more reactive metal in the particular environment will experience corrosion; the more inert metal, the cathode, will be protected from corrosion. For example, steel screws corrode when in contact with brass in a marine environment; or if copper and steel tubing are joined in a domestic water heater, the steel will corrode in the vicinity of the junction. Depending on the nature of the solution, one or more of the reduction reactions, Equations 16.3 through 16.7, will occur at the surface of the cathode material. Figure 16.14 shows galvanic corrosion.

Again, the galvanic series (Table 16.2) indicates the relative reactivities, in seawater, of a number of metals and alloys. When two alloys are coupled in seawater, the one lower in the series will experience corrosion. Some of the alloys in the table are grouped in brackets. Generally the base metal is the same for these bracketed alloys, and there is little danger of corrosion if alloys within a single bracket are

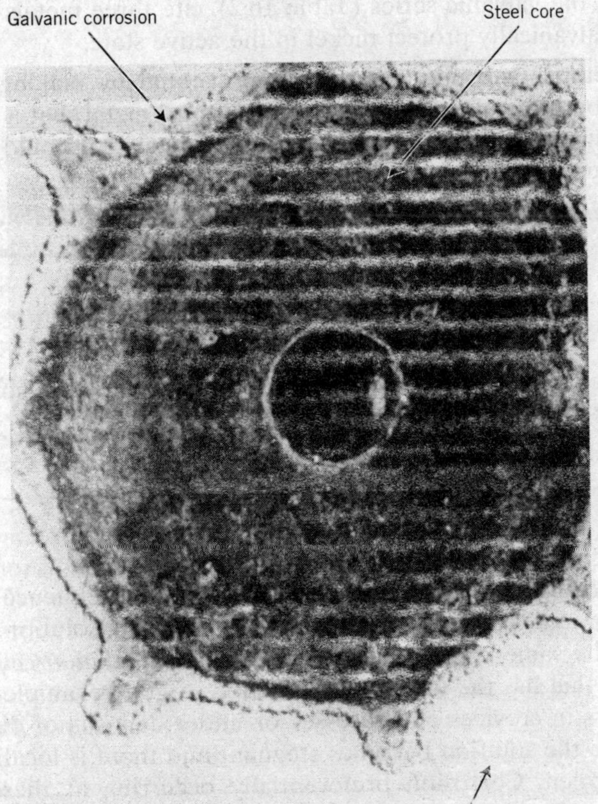

Figure 16.14 Photograph showing galvanic corrosion around the inlet of a single-cycle bilge pump that is found on fishing vessels. Corrosion occurred between a magnesium shell that was cast around a steel core. (Photograph courtesy of LaQue Center for Corrosion Technology, Inc.)

coupled. It is also worth noting from this series that some alloys are listed twice (e.g., nickel and the stainless steels), in both active and passive states.

The rate of galvanic attack depends on the relative anode-to-cathode surface areas that are exposed to the electrolyte, and the rate is related directly to the cathode–anode area ratio; that is, for a given cathode area, a smaller anode will corrode more rapidly than a larger one. The reason for this is that corrosion rate depends on current density (Equation 16.24), the current per unit area of corroding surface, and not simply the current. Thus, a high current density results for the anode when its area is small relative to that of the cathode.

A number of measures may be taken to significantly reduce the effects of galvanic corrosion. These include the following:

1. If coupling of dissimilar metals is necessary, choose two that are close together in the galvanic series.
2. Avoid an unfavorable anode-to-cathode surface area ratio; use an anode area as large as possible.
3. Electrically insulate dissimilar metals from each other.
4. Electrically connect a third, anodic metal to the other two; this is a form of **cathodic protection,** discussed presently.

Concept Check 16.4

(a) From the galvanic series (Table 16.2), cite three metals or alloys that may be used to galvanically protect nickel in the active state.

(b) Sometimes galvanic corrosion is prevented by making an electrical contact between both metals in the couple and a third metal that is anodic to these other two. Using the galvanic series, name one metal that could be used to protect a copper-aluminum galvanic couple.

[*The answer may be found in enclosed CD.*]

Concept Check 16.5

Cite two examples of the beneficial use of galvanic corrosion. *Hint:* One example is cited later in this chapter.

[*The answer may be found in enclosed CD.*]

Crevice Corrosion

Electrochemical corrosion may also occur as a consequence of concentration differences of ions or dissolved gases in the electrolyte solution, and between two regions of the same metal piece. For such a *concentration cell,* corrosion occurs in the locale that has the lower concentration. A good example of this type of corrosion occurs in crevices and recesses or under deposits of dirt or corrosion products where the solution becomes stagnant and there is localized depletion of dissolved oxygen. Corrosion preferentially occurring at these positions is called **crevice corrosion** (Figure 16.15). The crevice must be wide enough for the solution to penetrate, yet narrow enough for stagnancy; usually the width is several thousandths of an inch.

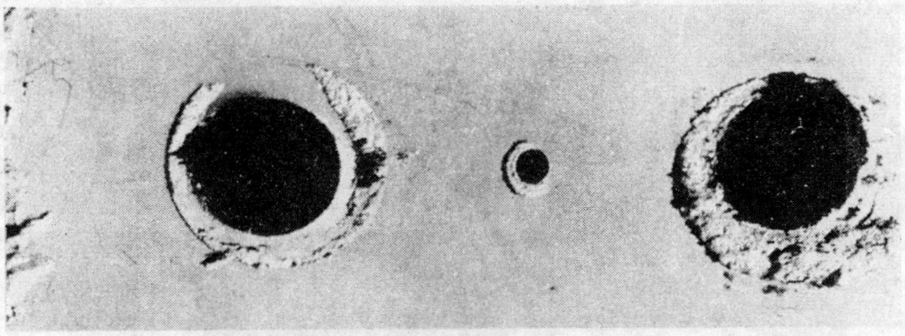

Figure 16.15 On this plate, which was immersed in seawater, crevice corrosion has occurred at the regions that were covered by washers. (Photograph courtesy of LaQue Center for Corrosion Technology, Inc.)

The proposed mechanism for crevice corrosion is illustrated in Figure 16.16. After oxygen has been depleted within the crevice, oxidation of the metal occurs at this position according to Equation 16.1. Electrons from this electrochemical reaction are conducted through the metal to adjacent external regions, where they are consumed by reduction—most probably reaction 16.5. In many aqueous environments, the solution within the crevice has been found to develop high concentrations of H^+ and Cl^- ions, which are especially corrosive. Many alloys that passivate are susceptible to crevice corrosion because protective films are often destroyed by the H^+ and Cl^- ions.

Crevice corrosion may be prevented by using welded instead of riveted or bolted joints, using nonabsorbing gaskets when possible, removing accumulated deposits frequently, and designing containment vessels to avoid stagnant areas and ensure complete drainage.

Pitting

Pitting is another form of very localized corrosion attack in which small pits or holes form. They ordinarily penetrate from the top of a horizontal surface downward in a nearly vertical direction. It is an extremely insidious type of corrosion, often going

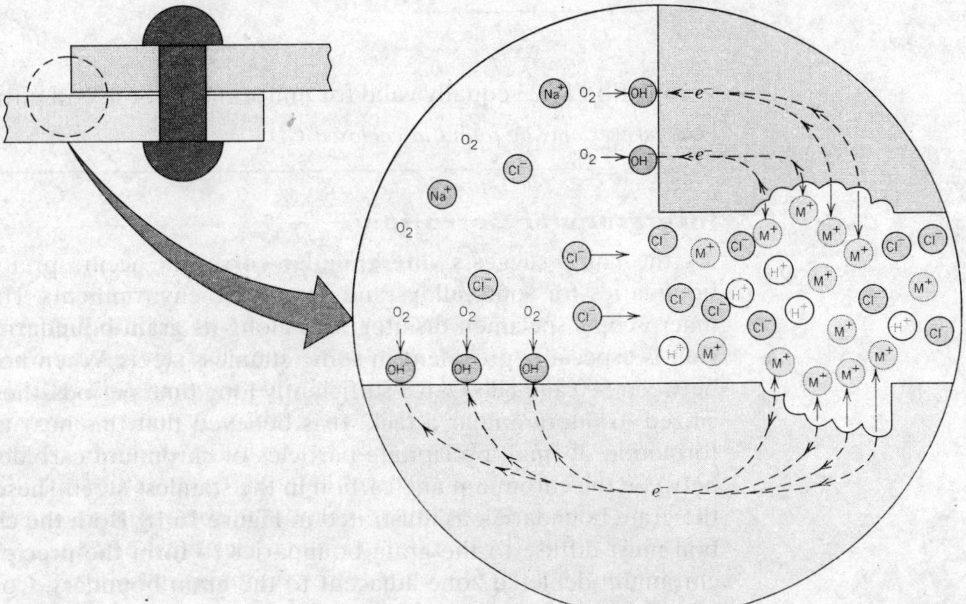

Figure 16.16 Schematic illustration of the mechanism of crevice corrosion between two riveted sheets. (From M. G. Fontana, *Corrosion Engineering*, 3rd edition. Copyright © 1986 by McGraw-Hill Book Company. Reproduced with permission.)

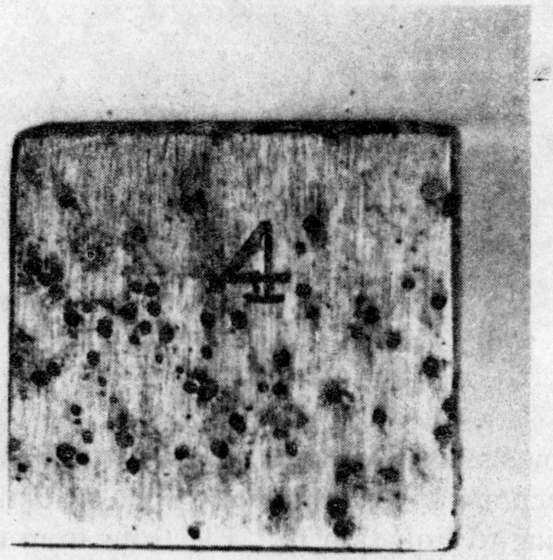

Figure 16.17 The pitting of a 304 stainless steel plate by an acid-chloride solution. (Photograph courtesy of Mars G. Fontana. From M. G. Fontana, *Corrosion Engineering*, 3rd edition. Copyright © 1986 by McGraw-Hill Book Company. Reproduced with permission.)

undetected and with very little material loss until failure occurs. An example of pitting corrosion is shown in Figure 16.17.

The mechanism for pitting is probably the same as for crevice corrosion in that oxidation occurs within the pit itself, with complementary reduction at the surface. It is supposed that gravity causes the pits to grow downward, the solution at the pit tip becoming more concentrated and dense as pit growth progresses. A pit may be initiated by a localized surface defect such as a scratch or a slight variation in composition. In fact, it has been observed that specimens having polished surfaces display a greater resistance to pitting corrosion. Stainless steels are somewhat susceptible to this form of corrosion; however, alloying with about 2% molybdenum enhances their resistance significantly.

Concept Check 16.6

Is Equation 16.23 equally valid for uniform corrosion and pitting? Why or why not?

[The answer may be found in enclosed CD.]

Intergranular Corrosion

As the name suggests, **intergranular corrosion** occurs preferentially along grain boundaries for some alloys and in specific environments. The net result is that a macroscopic specimen disintegrates along its grain boundaries. This type of corrosion is especially prevalent in some stainless steels. When heated to temperatures between 500 and 800°C for sufficiently long time periods, these alloys become sensitized to intergranular attack. It is believed that this heat treatment permits the formation of small precipitate particles of chromium carbide ($Cr_{23}C_6$) by reaction between the chromium and carbon in the stainless steel. These particles form along the grain boundaries, as illustrated in Figure 16.18. Both the chromium and the carbon must diffuse to the grain boundaries to form the precipitates, which leaves a chromium-depleted zone adjacent to the grain boundary. Consequently, this grain boundary region is now highly susceptible to corrosion.

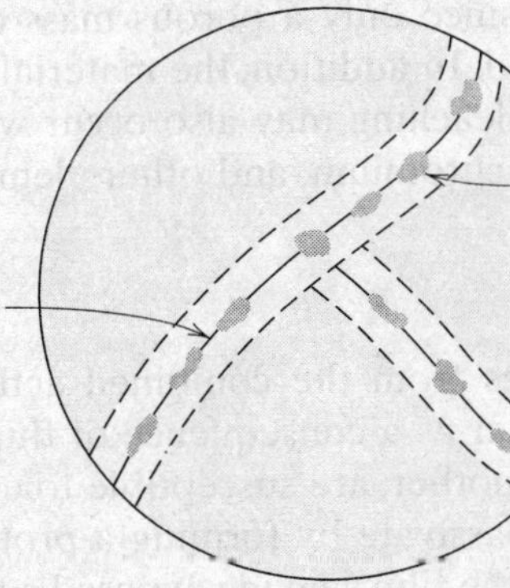

Figure 16.18 Schematic illustration of chromium carbide particles that have precipitated along grain boundaries in stainless steel, and the attendant zones of chromium depletion.

Intergranular corrosion is an especially severe problem in the welding of stainless steels, when it is often termed **weld decay.** Figure 16.19 shows this type of intergranular corrosion.

Stainless steels may be protected from intergranular corrosion by the following measures: (1) subjecting the sensitized material to a high-temperature heat treatment in which all the chromium carbide particles are redissolved, (2) lowering the carbon content below 0.03 wt% C so that carbide formation is minimal, and (3) alloying the stainless steel with another metal such as niobium or titanium, which has a greater tendency to form carbides than does chromium so that the Cr remains in solid solution.

Selective Leaching

Selective leaching is found in solid solution alloys and occurs when one element or constituent is preferentially removed as a consequence of corrosion processes. The most common example is the dezincification of brass, in which zinc is selectively leached from a copper–zinc brass alloy. The mechanical properties of the alloy are

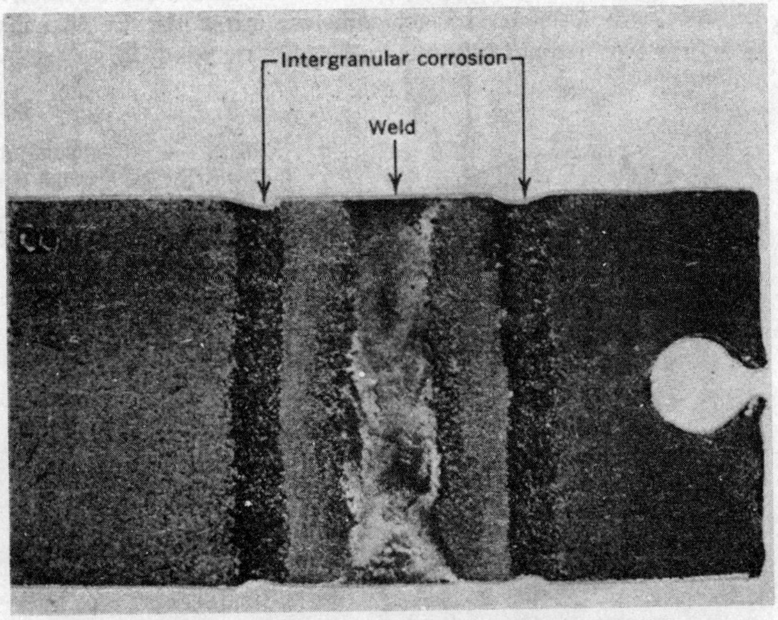

Figure 16.19 Weld decay in a stainless steel. The regions along which the grooves have formed were sensitized as the weld cooled. (From H. H. Uhlig and R. W. Revie, *Corrosion and Corrosion Control,* 3rd edition, Fig. 2, p. 307. Copyright © 1985 by John Wiley & Sons, Inc. Reprinted by permission of John Wiley & Sons, Inc.)

significantly impaired, since only a porous mass of copper remains in the region that has been dezincified. In addition, the material changes from yellow to a red or copper color. Selective leaching may also occur with other alloy systems in which aluminum, iron, cobalt, chromium, and other elements are vulnerable to preferential removal.

Erosion–Corrosion

Erosion–corrosion arises from the combined action of chemical attack and mechanical abrasion or wear as a consequence of fluid motion. Virtually all metal alloys, to one degree or another, are susceptible to erosion–corrosion. It is especially harmful to alloys that passivate by forming a protective surface film; the abrasive action may erode away the film, leaving exposed a bare metal surface. If the coating is not capable of continuously and rapidly reforming as a protective barrier, corrosion may be severe. Relatively soft metals such as copper and lead are also sensitive to this form of attack. Usually it can be identified by surface grooves and waves having contours that are characteristic of the flow of the fluid.

The nature of the fluid can have a dramatic influence on the corrosion behavior. Increasing fluid velocity normally enhances the rate of corrosion. Also, a solution is more erosive when bubbles and suspended particulate solids are present.

Erosion–corrosion is commonly found in piping, especially at bends, elbows, and abrupt changes in pipe diameter—positions where the fluid changes direction or flow suddenly becomes turbulent. Propellers, turbine blades, valves, and pumps are also susceptible to this form of corrosion. Figure 16.20 illustrates the impingement failure of an elbow fitting.

One of the best ways to reduce erosion–corrosion is to change the design to eliminate fluid turbulence and impingement effects. Other materials may also be utilized that inherently resist erosion. Furthermore, removal of particulates and bubbles from the solution will lessen its ability to erode.

Stress Corrosion

Stress corrosion, sometimes termed stress corrosion cracking, results from the combined action of an applied tensile stress and a corrosive environment; both influences are necessary. In fact, some materials that are virtually inert in a particular corrosive medium become susceptible to this form of corrosion when a stress is

Figure 16.20 Impingement failure of an elbow that was part of a steam condensate line. (Photograph courtesy of Mars G. Fontana. From M. G. Fontana, *Corrosion Engineering*, 3rd edition. Copyright © 1986 by McGraw-Hill Book Company. Reproduced with permission.)

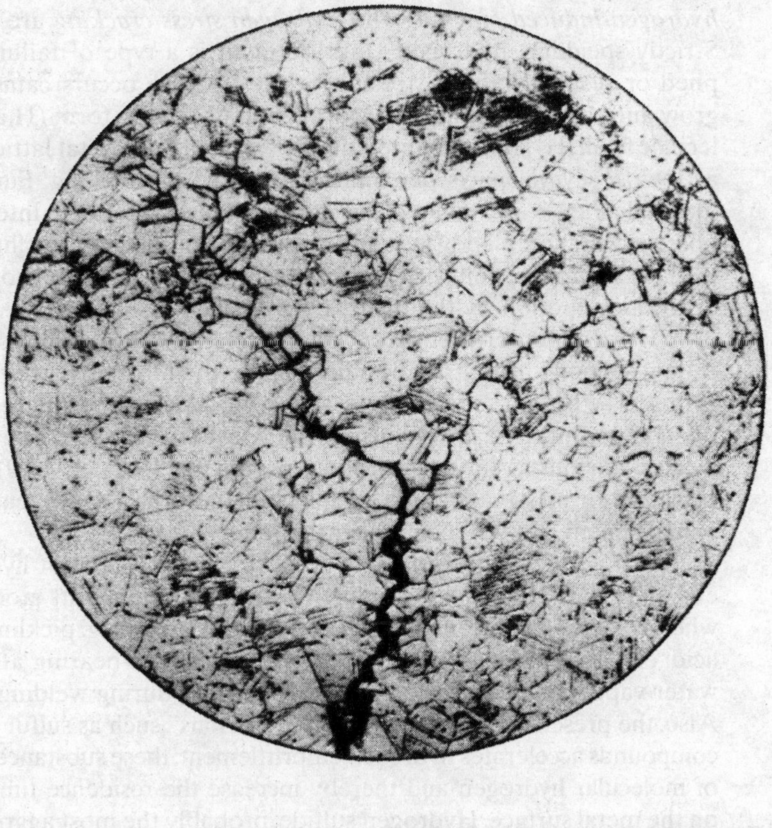

Figure 16.21 Photomicrograph showing intergranular stress corrosion cracking in brass. (From H. H. Uhlig and R. W. Revie, *Corrosion and Corrosion Control,* 3rd edition, Fig. 5, p. 335. Copyright 1985 by John Wiley & Sons, Inc. Reprinted by permission of John Wiley & Sons, Inc.)

applied. Small cracks form and then propagate in a direction perpendicular to the stress (see the chapter-opening photograph for this chapter), with the result that failure may eventually occur. Failure behavior is characteristic of that for a brittle material, even though the metal alloy is intrinsically ductile. Furthermore, cracks may form at relatively low stress levels, significantly below the tensile strength. Most alloys are susceptible to stress corrosion in specific environments, especially at moderate stress levels. For example, most stainless steels stress corrode in solutions containing chloride ions, whereas brasses are especially vulnerable when exposed to ammonia. Figure 16.21 is a photomicrograph in which an example of intergranular stress corrosion cracking in brass is shown.

The stress that produces stress corrosion cracking need not be externally applied; it may be a residual one that results from rapid temperature changes and uneven contraction, or for two-phase alloys in which each phase has a different coefficient of expansion. Also, gaseous and solid corrosion products that are entrapped internally can give rise to internal stresses.

Probably the best measure to take in reducing or totally eliminating stress corrosion is to lower the magnitude of the stress. This may be accomplished by reducing the external load or increasing the cross-sectional area perpendicular to the applied stress. Furthermore, an appropriate heat treatment may be used to anneal out any residual thermal stresses.

Hydrogen Embrittlement

Various metal alloys, specifically some steels, experience a significant reduction in ductility and tensile strength when atomic hydrogen (H) penetrates into the material. This phenomenon is aptly referred to as **hydrogen embrittlement;** the terms *hydrogen-induced cracking* and *hydrogen stress cracking* are sometimes also used. Strictly speaking, hydrogen embrittlement is a type of failure; in response to applied or residual tensile stresses, brittle fracture occurs catastrophically as cracks grow and rapidly propagate. Hydrogen in its atomic form (H as opposed to the molecular form, H_2) diffuses interstitially through the crystal lattice, and concentrations as low as several parts per million can lead to cracking. Furthermore, hydrogen-induced cracks are most often transgranular, although intergranular fracture is observed for some alloy systems. A number of mechanisms have been proposed to explain hydrogen embrittlement; most of them are based on the interference of dislocation motion by the dissolved hydrogen.

Hydrogen embrittlement is similar to stress corrosion (as discussed in the preceding section) in that a normally ductile metal experiences brittle fracture when exposed to both a tensile stress and a corrosive atmosphere. However, these two phenomena may be distinguished on the basis of their interactions with applied electric currents. Whereas cathodic protection (Section 16.9) reduces or causes a cessation of stress corrosion, it may, on the other hand, lead to the initiation or enhancement of hydrogen embrittlement.

For hydrogen embrittlement to occur, some source of hydrogen must be present, and, in addition, the possibility for the formation of its atomic species. Situations wherein these conditions are met include the following: pickling[3] of steels in sulfuric acid; electroplating; and the presence of hydrogen-bearing atmospheres (including water vapor) at elevated temperatures such as during welding and heat treatments. Also, the presence of what are termed "poisons" such as sulfur (i.e., H_2S) and arsenic compounds accelerates hydrogen embrittlement; these substances retard the formation of molecular hydrogen and thereby increase the residence time of atomic hydrogen on the metal surface. Hydrogen sulfide, probably the most aggressive poison, is found in petroleum fluids, natural gas, oil-well brines, and geothermal fluids.

High-strength steels are susceptible to hydrogen embrittlement, and increasing strength tends to enhance the material's susceptibility. Martensitic steels are especially vulnerable to this type of failure; bainitic, ferritic, and spheroiditic steels are more resilient. Furthermore, FCC alloys (austenitic stainless steels, and alloys of copper, aluminum, and nickel) are relatively resistant to hydrogen embrittlement, mainly because of their inherently high ductilities. However, strain hardening these alloys will enhance their susceptibility to embrittlement.

Some of the techniques commonly used to reduce the likelihood of hydrogen embrittlement include reducing the tensile strength of the alloy via a heat treatment, removal of the source of hydrogen, "baking" the alloy at an elevated temperature to drive out any dissolved hydrogen, and substitution of a more embrittlement-resistant alloy.

16.8 CORROSION ENVIRONMENTS

Corrosive environments include the atmosphere, aqueous solutions, soils, acids, bases, inorganic solvents, molten salts, liquid metals, and, last but not least, the human body. On a tonnage basis, atmospheric corrosion accounts for the greatest losses. Moisture containing dissolved oxygen is the primary corrosive agent, but other substances, including sulfur compounds and sodium chloride, may also contribute. This is especially true of marine atmospheres, which are highly corrosive because of the presence of

[3] *Pickling* is a procedure used to remove surface oxide scale from steel pieces by dipping them in a vat of hot, dilute sulfuric or hydrochloric acid.

sodium chloride. Dilute sulfuric acid solutions (acid rain) in industrial environments can also cause corrosion problems. Metals commonly used for atmospheric applications include alloys of aluminum and copper, and galvanized steel.

Water environments can also have a variety of compositions and corrosion characteristics. Freshwater normally contains dissolved oxygen, as well as other minerals several of which account for hardness. Seawater contains approximately 3.5% salt (predominantly sodium chloride), as well as some minerals and organic matter. Seawater is generally more corrosive than freshwater, frequently producing pitting and crevice corrosion. Cast iron, steel, aluminum, copper, brass, and some stainless steels are generally suitable for freshwater use, whereas titanium, brass, some bronzes, copper–nickel alloys, and nickel–chromium–molybdenum alloys are highly corrosion resistant in seawater.

Soils have a wide range of compositions and susceptibilities to corrosion. Compositional variables include moisture, oxygen, salt content, alkalinity, and acidity, as well as the presence of various forms of bacteria. Cast iron and plain carbon steels, both with and without protective surface coatings, are found most economical for underground structures.

Because there are so many acids, bases, and organic solvents, no attempt is made to discuss these solutions in this text. Good references are available that treat these topics in detail.

16.9 CORROSION PREVENTION

Some corrosion prevention methods were treated relative to the eight forms of corrosion; however, only the measures specific to each of the various corrosion types were discussed. Now, some more general techniques are presented; these include material selection, environmental alteration, design, coatings, and cathodic protection.

Perhaps the most common and easiest way of preventing corrosion is through the judicious selection of materials once the corrosion environment has been characterized. Standard corrosion references are helpful in this respect. Here, cost may be a significant factor. It is not always economically feasible to employ the material that provides the optimum corrosion resistance; sometimes, either another alloy and/or some other measure must be used.

Changing the character of the environment, if possible, may also significantly influence corrosion. Lowering the fluid temperature and/or velocity usually produces a reduction in the rate at which corrosion occurs. Many times increasing or decreasing the concentration of some species in the solution will have a positive effect; for example, the metal may experience passivation.

Inhibitors are substances that, when added in relatively low concentrations to the environment, decrease its corrosiveness. Of course, the specific inhibitor depends both on the alloy and on the corrosive environment. There are several mechanisms that may account for the effectiveness of inhibitors. Some react with and virtually eliminate a chemically active species in the solution (such as dissolved oxygen). Other inhibitor molecules attach themselves to the corroding surface and interfere with either the oxidation or the reduction reaction, or form a very thin protective coating. Inhibitors are normally used in closed systems such as automobile radiators and steam boilers.

Several aspects of design consideration have already been discussed, especially with regard to galvanic and crevice corrosion and erosion–corrosion. In addition, the design should allow for complete drainage in the case of a shutdown, and easy washing. Since dissolved oxygen may enhance the corrosivity of many solutions, the design should, if possible, include provision for the exclusion of air.

Physical barriers to corrosion are applied on surfaces in the form of films and coatings. A large diversity of metallic and nonmetallic coating materials are available. It is essential that the coating maintain a high degree of surface adhesion, which undoubtedly requires some preapplication surface treatment. In most cases, the coating must be virtually nonreactive in the corrosive environment and resistant to mechanical damage that exposes the bare metal to the corrosive environment. All three material types—metals, ceramics, and polymers—are used as coatings for metals.

Cathodic Protection

One of the most effective means of corrosion prevention is **cathodic protection;** it can be used for all eight different forms of corrosion as discussed above, and may, in some situations, completely stop corrosion. Again, oxidation or corrosion of a metal M occurs by the generalized reaction

$$M \longrightarrow M^{n+} + ne^- \tag{16.1}$$

Cathodic protection simply involves supplying, from an external source, electrons to the metal to be protected, making it a cathode; the reaction above is thus forced in the reverse (or reduction) direction.

One cathodic protection technique employs a galvanic couple: the metal to be protected is electrically connected to another metal that is more reactive in the particular environment. The latter experiences oxidation, and, upon giving up electrons, protects the first metal from corrosion. The oxidized metal is often called a **sacrificial anode,** and magnesium and zinc are commonly used as such because they lie at the anodic end of the galvanic series. This form of galvanic protection, for structures buried in the ground, is illustrated in Figure 16.22*a*.

The process of *galvanizing* is simply one in which a layer of zinc is applied to the surface of steel by hot dipping. In the atmosphere and most aqueous environments, zinc is anodic to and will thus cathodically protect the steel if there is any surface damage (Figure 16.23). Any corrosion of the zinc coating will proceed at an extremely slow rate because the ratio of the anode-to-cathode surface area is quite large.

For another method of cathodic protection, the source of electrons is an impressed current from an external dc power source, as represented in Figure 16.22*b* for an underground tank. The negative terminal of the power source is connected to the structure to be protected. The other terminal is joined to an inert anode (often graphite), which is, in this case, buried in the soil; high-conductivity backfill material provides good electrical contact between the anode and surrounding soil. A current

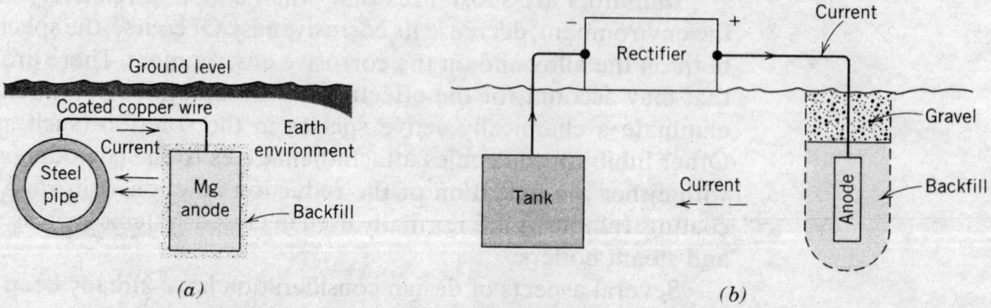

Figure 16.22 Cathodic protection of (*a*) an underground pipeline using a magnesium sacrificial anode, and (*b*) an underground tank using an impressed current. (From M. G. Fontana, *Corrosion Engineering,* 3rd edition. Copyright © 1986 by McGraw-Hill Book Company. Reproduced with permission.)

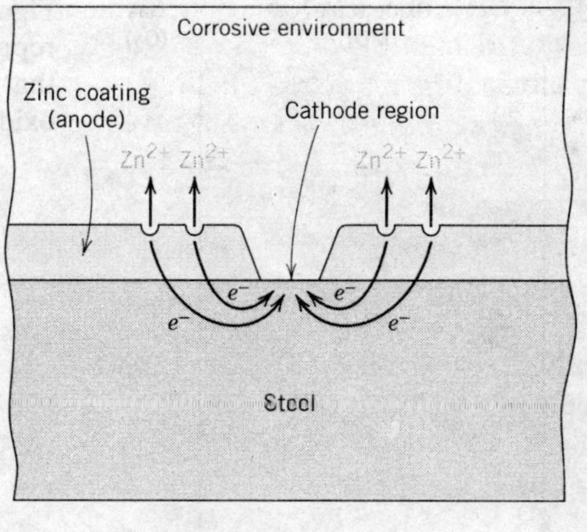

Figure 16.23 Galvanic protection of steel as provided by a coating of zinc.

path exists between the cathode and anode through the intervening soil, completing the electrical circuit. Cathodic protection is especially useful in preventing corrosion of water heaters, underground tanks and pipes, and marine equipment.

Concept Check 16.7

Tin cans are made of a steel the inside of which is coated with a thin layer of tin. The tin protects the steel from corrosion by food products in the same manner as zinc protects steel from atmospheric corrosion. Briefly explain how this cathodic protection of tin cans is possible, given that tin is electrochemically less active than steel in the galvanic series (Table 16.2).

[*The answer may be found in enclosed CD.*]

16.10 OXIDATION

The discussion of Section 16.2 treated the corrosion of metallic materials in terms of electrochemical reactions that take place in aqueous solutions. In addition, oxidation of metal alloys is also possible in gaseous atmospheres, normally air, wherein an oxide layer or scale forms on the surface of the metal. This phenomenon is frequently termed *scaling, tarnishing,* or *dry corrosion.* In this section we will discuss possible mechanisms for this type of corrosion, the types of oxide layers that can form, and the kinetics of oxide formation.

Mechanisms

As with aqueous corrosion, the process of oxide layer formation is an electrochemical one, which may be expressed, for divalent metal M, by the following reaction:[4]

$$\mathrm{M} + \tfrac{1}{2}\mathrm{O_2} \longrightarrow \mathrm{MO} \tag{16.28}$$

Furthermore, the above reaction consists of oxidation and reduction half-reactions. The former, with the formation of metal ions,

$$\mathrm{M} \longrightarrow \mathrm{M^{2+}} + 2e^- \tag{16.29}$$

[4] For other than divalent metals, this reaction may be expressed as

$$a\mathrm{M} + \frac{b}{2}\mathrm{O_2} \longrightarrow \mathrm{M}_a\mathrm{O}_b \tag{16.30}$$

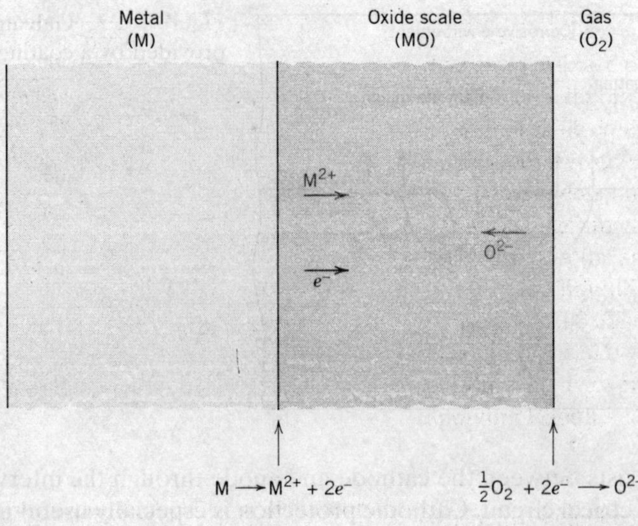

Figure 16.24 Schematic representation of processes that are involved in gaseous oxidation at a metal surface.

occurs at the metal–scale interface. The reduction half-reaction produces oxygen ions as follows:

$$\tfrac{1}{2}O_2 + 2e^- \longrightarrow O^{2-} \tag{16.31}$$

and takes place at the scale–gas interface. A schematic representation of this metal–scale–gas system is shown in Figure 16.24.

For the oxide layer to increase in thickness via Equation 16.28, it is necessary that electrons be conducted to the scale–gas interface, at which point the reduction reaction occurs; in addition, M^{2+} ions must diffuse away from the metal–scale interface, and/or O^{2-} ions must diffuse toward this same interface (Figure 16.24).[5] Thus, the oxide scale serves both as an electrolyte through which ions diffuse and as an electrical circuit for the passage of electrons. Furthermore, the scale may protect the metal from rapid oxidation when it acts as a barrier to ionic diffusion and/or electrical conduction; most metal oxides are highly electrically insulative.

Scale Types

Rate of oxidation (i.e., the rate of film thickness increase) and the tendency of the film to protect the metal from further oxidation are related to the relative volumes of the oxide and metal. The ratio of these volumes, termed the **Pilling–Bedworth ratio,** may be determined from the following expression:[6]

$$\text{P–B ratio} = \frac{A_O \rho_M}{A_M \rho_O} \tag{16.32}$$

---

[5] Alternatively, electron holes (Section 17.10) and vacancies may diffuse instead of electrons and ions.

[6] For other than divalent metals, Equation 16.32 becomes

Pilling–Bedworth ratio for a metal that is not divalent

$$\text{P–B ratio} = \frac{A_O \rho_M}{a A_M \rho_O} \tag{16.33}$$

where a is the coefficient of the metal species for the overall oxidation reaction described by Equation 16.30.

Table 16.3 Pilling–Bedworth Ratios for a Number of Metals

Protective		*Nonprotective*	
Ce	1.16	K	0.45
Al	1.28	Li	0.57
Pb	1.40	Na	0.57
Ni	1.52	Cd	1.21
Be	1.59	Ag	1.59
Pd	1.60	Ti	1.95
Cu	1.68	Ta	2.33
Fe	1.77	Sb	2.35
Mn	1.79	Nb	2.61
Co	1.99	U	3.05
Cr	1.99	Mo	3.40
Si	2.27	W	3.40

Source: B. Chalmers, *Physical Metallurgy*. Copyright © 1959 by John Wiley & Sons, New York. Reprinted by permission of John Wiley & Sons, Inc.

where A_O is the molecular (or formula) weight of the oxide, A_M is the atomic weight of the metal, and ρ_O and ρ_M are the oxide and metal densities, respectively. For metals having P–B ratios less than unity, the oxide film tends to be porous and unprotective because it is insufficient to fully cover the metal surface. If the ratio is greater than unity, compressive stresses result in the film as it forms. For a ratio greater than 2–3, the oxide coating may crack and flake off, continually exposing a fresh and unprotected metal surface. The ideal P–B ratio for the formation of a protective oxide film is unity. Table 16.3 presents P–B ratios for metals that form protective coatings and for those that do not. Note from these data that protective coatings normally form for metals having P–B ratios between 1 and 2, whereas nonprotective ones usually result when this ratio is less than 1 or greater than about 2. In addition to the P–B ratio, other factors also influence the oxidation resistance imparted by the film; these include a high degree of adherence between film and metal, comparable coefficients of thermal expansion for metal and oxide, and, for the oxide, a relatively high melting point and good high-temperature plasticity.

Several techniques are available for improving the oxidation resistance of a metal. One involves application of a protective surface coating of another material that adheres well to the metal and also is itself resistant to oxidation. In some instances, the addition of alloying elements will form a more adherent and protective oxide scale by virtue of producing a more favorable Pilling–Bedworth ratio and/or improving other scale characteristics.

Kinetics

One of the primary concerns relative to metal oxidation is the rate at which the reaction progresses. Inasmuch as the oxide scale reaction product normally remains on the surface, the rate of reaction may be determined by measuring the weight gain per unit area as a function of time.

When the oxide that forms is nonporous and adheres to the metal surface, the rate of layer growth is controlled by ionic diffusion. A *parabolic* relationship exists

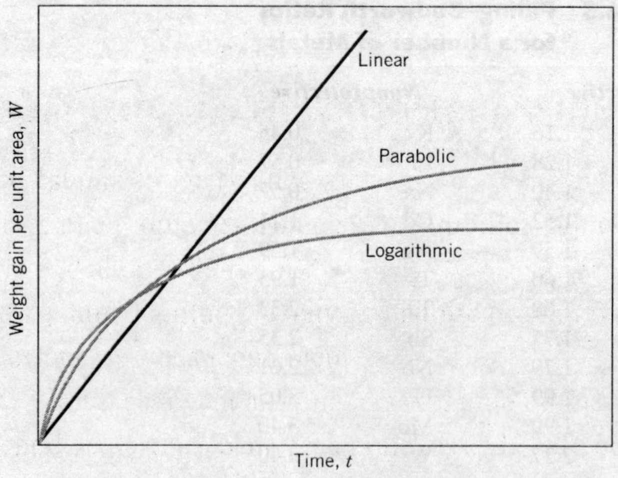

Figure 16.25 Oxidation film growth curves for linear, parabolic, and logarithmic rate laws.

between the weight gain per unit area W and the time t as follows:

$$W^2 = K_1 t + K_2 \tag{16.34}$$

where K_1 and K_2 are time-independent constants at a given temperature. This weight gain–time behavior is plotted schematically in Figure 16.25. The oxidation of iron, copper, and cobalt follows this rate expression.

In the oxidation of metals for which the scale is porous or flakes off (i.e., for P–B ratios less than about 1 or greater than about 2), the oxidation rate expression is *linear;* that is,

$$W = K_3 t \tag{16.35}$$

where K_3 is a constant. Under these circumstances oxygen is always available for reaction with an unprotected metal surface because the oxide does not act as a reaction barrier. Sodium, potassium, and tantalum oxidize according to this rate expression and, incidentally, have P–B ratios significantly different from unity (Table 16.3). Linear growth rate kinetics is also represented in Figure 16.25.

Still a third reaction rate law has been observed for very thin oxide layers (generally less than 100 nm) that form at relatively low temperatures. The dependence of weight gain on time is *logarithmic* and takes the form

$$W = K_4 \log(K_5 t + K_6) \tag{16.36}$$

Again, the K's are constants. This oxidation behavior, also shown in Figure 16.25, has been observed for aluminum, iron, and copper at near-ambient temperatures.

Corrosion of Ceramic Materials

Ceramic materials, being compounds between metallic and nonmetallic elements, may be thought of as having already been corroded. Thus, they are exceedingly immune to corrosion by almost all environments, especially at room temperature. Corrosion of ceramic materials generally involves simple chemical dissolution, in contrast to the electrochemical processes found in metals, as described above.

Ceramic materials are frequently utilized because of their resistance to corrosion. Glass is often used to contain liquids for this reason. Refractory ceramics must not only withstand high temperatures and provide thermal insulation but, in many instances, must also resist high-temperature attack by molten metals, salts, slags, and glasses. Some of the new technology schemes for converting energy from one form to another that is more useful require relatively high temperatures, corrosive atmospheres, and pressures above the ambient. Ceramic materials are much better suited to withstand most of these environments for reasonable time periods than are metals.

Degradation of Polymers

Polymeric materials also experience deterioration by means of environmental interactions. However, an undesirable interaction is specified as degradation rather than corrosion because the processes are basically dissimilar. Whereas most metallic corrosion reactions are electrochemical, by contrast, polymeric degradation is physiochemical; that is, it involves physical as well as chemical phenomena. Furthermore, a wide variety of reactions and adverse consequences are possible for polymer degradation. Polymers may deteriorate by swelling and dissolution. Covalent bond rupture, as a result of heat energy, chemical reactions, and radiation is also possible, ordinarily with an attendant reduction in mechanical integrity. It should also be mentioned that because of the chemical complexity of polymers, their degradation mechanisms are not well understood.

To briefly cite a couple of examples of polymer degradation, polyethylene, if exposed to high temperatures in an oxygen atmosphere, suffers an impairment of its mechanical properties by becoming brittle. Also, the utility of poly(vinyl chloride) may be limited because this material may become colored when exposed to high temperatures, although such environments do not affect its mechanical characteristics.

16.11 SWELLING AND DISSOLUTION

When polymers are exposed to liquids, the main forms of degradation are swelling and dissolution. With swelling, the liquid or solute diffuses into and is absorbed within the polymer; the small solute molecules fit into and occupy positions among the polymer molecules. Thus the macromolecules are forced apart such that the specimen expands or swells. Furthermore, this increase in chain separation results in a reduction of the secondary intermolecular bonding forces; as a consequence, the material becomes softer and more ductile. The liquid solute also lowers the glass transition temperature and, if depressed below the ambient temperature, will cause a once strong material to become rubbery and weak.

Swelling may be considered to be a partial dissolution process in which there is only limited solubility of the polymer in the solvent. Dissolution, which occurs when the polymer is completely soluble, may be thought of as just a continuation of swelling. As a rule of thumb, the greater the similarity of chemical structure between the solvent and polymer, the greater is the likelihood of swelling and/or dissolution. For example, many hydrocarbon rubbers readily absorb hydrocarbon liquids such as gasoline. The responses of selected polymeric materials to organic solvents are contained in Tables 16.4 and 16.5.

Swelling and dissolution traits also are affected by temperature as well as characteristics of the molecular structure. In general, increasing molecular weight, increasing degree of crosslinking and crystallinity, and decreasing temperature result in a reduction of these deteriorative processes.

Table 16.4 Resistance to Degradation by Various Environments for Selected Plastic Materials[a]

Material	*Nonoxidizing Acids (20% H_2SO_4)*	*Oxidizing Acids (10% HNO_3)*	*Aqueous Salt Solutions (NaCl)*	*Aqueous Alkalis (NaOH)*	*Polar Solvents (C_2H_5OH)*	*Nonpolar Solvents (C_6H_6)*	*Water*
Polytetrafluoroethylene	S	S	S	S	S	S	S
Nylon 6,6	U	U	S	S	Q	S	S
Polycarbonate	Q	U	S	U	S	U	S
Polyester	Q	Q	S	Q	Q	U	S
Polyetheretherketone	S	S	S	S	S	S	S
Low-density polyethylene	S	Q	S	—	S	Q	S
High-density polyethylene	S	Q	S	—	S	Q	S
Poly(ethylene terephthalate)	S	Q	S	S	S	S	S
Poly(phenylene oxide)	S	Q	S	S	S	U	S
Polypropylene	S	Q	S	S	S	Q	S
Polystyrene	S	Q	S	S	S	U	S
Polyurethane	Q	U	S	Q	U	Q	S
Epoxy	S	U	S	S	S	S	S
Silicone	Q	U	S	S	S	Q	S

[a] S = satisfactory; Q = questionable; U = unsatisfactory.

Source: Adapted from R. B. Seymour, *Polymers for Engineering Applications,* ASM International, Materials Park, OH, 1987.

In general, polymers are much more resistant to attack by acidic and alkaline solutions than are metals. For example, hydrofluoric acid (HF) will corrode many metals as well as etch and dissolve glass, so it is stored in plastic bottles. A qualitative comparison of the behavior of various polymers in these solutions is also presented in Tables 16.4 and 16.5. Materials that exhibit outstanding resistance to attack by both solution types include polytetrafluoroethylene (and other fluorocarbons) and polyetheretherketone.

Table 16.5 Resistance to Degradation by Various Environments for Selected Elastomeric Materials[a]

Material	*Weather Sunlight Aging*	*Oxidation*	*Ozone Cracking*	*Alkali Dilute/ Concentrated*	*Acid Dilute/ Concentrated*	*Chlorinated Hydrocarbons, Degreasers*	*Aliphatic Hydrocarbons, Kerosene, Etc.*	*Animal, Vegetable Oils*
Polyisoprene (natural)	D	B	NR	A/C-B	A/C-B	NR	NR	D-B
Polyisoprene (synthetic)	NR	B	NR	C-B/C-B	C-B/C-B	NR	NR	D-B
Butadiene	D	B	NR	C-B/C-B	C-B/C-B	NR	NR	D-B
Styrene-butadiene	D	C	NR	C-B/C-B	C-B/C-B	NR	NR	D-B
Neoprene	B	A	A	A/A	A/A	D	C	B
Nitrile (high)	D	B	C	B/B	B/B	C-B	A	B
Silicone (polysiloxane)	A	A	A	A/A	B/C	NR	D-C	A

[a] A = excellent, B = good, C = fair, D = use with caution, NR = not recommended.

Source: *Compound Selection and Service Guide,* Seals Eastern, Inc., Red Bank, NJ, 1977.

Concept Check 16.8

From a molecular perspective, explain why increasing crosslinking and crystallinity of a polymeric material will enhance its resistance to swelling and dissolution. Would you expect crosslinking or crystallinity to have the greater influence? Justify your choice. *Hint:* you may want to consult Sections 13.7 and 4.18.

[*The answer may be found in enclosed CD.*]

16.12 BOND RUPTURE

Polymers may also experience degradation by a process termed **scission**—the severence or rupture of molecular chain bonds. This causes a separation of chain segments at the point of scission and a reduction in the molecular weight. As previously discussed (Chapter 14), several properties of polymeric materials, including mechanical strength and resistance to chemical attack, depend on molecular weight. Consequently, some of the physical and chemical properties of polymers may be adversely affected by this form of degradation. Bond rupture may result from exposure to radiation or to heat, and from chemical reaction.

Radiation Effects

Certain types of radiation [electron beams, x-rays, β- and γ-rays, and ultraviolet (UV) radiation] possess sufficient energy to penetrate a polymer specimen and interact with the constituent atoms or their electrons. One such reaction is *ionization,* in which the radiation removes an orbital electron from a specific atom, converting that atom into a positively charged ion. As a consequence, one of the covalent bonds associated with the specific atom is broken, and there is a rearrangement of atoms or groups of atoms at that point. This bond breaking leads to either scission or crosslinking at the ionization site, depending on the chemical structure of the polymer and also on the dose of radiation. Stabilizers (Section 14.21) may be added to protect polymers from radiation damage. In day-to-day use, the greatest radiation damage to polymers is caused by UV irradiation. After prolonged exposure, most polymer films become brittle, discolor, crack, and fail. For example, camping tents begin to tear, dashboards develop cracks, and plastic windows become cloudy. Radiation problems are more severe for some applications. Polymers on space vehicles must resist degradation after prolonged exposures to cosmic radiation. Similarly, polymers used in nuclear reactors must withstand high levels of nuclear radiation. Developing polymeric materials that can withstand these extreme environments is a continuing challenge.

Not all consequences of radiation exposure are deleterious. Crosslinking may be induced by irradiation to improve the mechanical behavior and degradation characteristics. For example, γ-radiation is used commercially to crosslink polyethylene to enhance its resistance to softening and flow at elevated temperatures; indeed, this process may be carried out on products that have already been fabricated.

Chemical Reaction Effects

Oxygen, ozone, and other substances can cause or accelerate chain scission as a result of chemical reaction. This effect is especially prevalent in vulcanized rubbers that have doubly bonded carbon atoms along the backbone molecular chains, and that are exposed to ozone (O_3), an atmospheric pollutant. One such scission reaction may be represented by

$$-\mathrm{R}-\underset{\substack{|\\ \mathrm{H}}}{\mathrm{C}}=\underset{\substack{|\\ \mathrm{H}}}{\mathrm{C}}-\mathrm{R'}- + \mathrm{O_3} \longrightarrow -\mathrm{R}-\underset{\substack{|\\ \mathrm{H}}}{\mathrm{C}}=\mathrm{O} + \mathrm{O}=\underset{\substack{|\\ \mathrm{H}}}{\mathrm{C}}-\mathrm{R'}- + \mathrm{O}\cdot \qquad (16.37)$$

where the chain is severed at the point of the double bond; R and R′ represent groups of atoms that are unaffected during the reaction. Ordinarily, if the rubber is in an unstressed state, a film will form on the surface, protecting the bulk material from any further reaction. However, when these materials are subjected to tensile stresses, cracks and crevices form and grow in a direction perpendicular to the stress; eventually, rupture of the material may occur. This is why the sidewalls on rubber bicycle tires develop cracks as they age. Apparently these cracks result from large numbers of ozone-induced scissions. Chemical degradation is a particular problem for polymers used in areas with high levels of air pollutants such as smog and ozone. The elastomers in Table 16.5 are rated as to their resistance to degradation by exposure to ozone. Many of these chain scission reactions involve reactive groups termed *free radicals*. Stabilizers (Section 14.21) may be added to protect polymers from oxidation. The stabilizers either sacrificially react with the ozone to consume it, or they react with and eliminate the free radicals before they (the free radicals) can inflict more damage.

Thermal Effects

Thermal degradation corresponds to the scission of molecular chains at elevated temperatures; as a consequence, some polymers undergo chemical reactions in which gaseous species are produced. These reactions are evidenced by a weight loss of material; a polymer's thermal stability is a measure of its resilience to this decomposition. Thermal stability is related primarily to the magnitude of the bonding energies between the various atomic constituents of the polymer: higher bonding energies result in more thermally stable materials. For example, the magnitude of the C—F bond is greater than that of the C—H bond, which in turn is greater than that of the C—Cl bond. The fluorocarbons, having C—F bonds, are among the most thermally resistant polymeric materials and may be utilized at relatively high temperatures. However, due to the weak C—Cl bond, when poly(vinyl chloride) is heated to 200°C for even a few minutes it will discolor and give off large amounts of HCl that accelerates continued decomposition. Stabilizers (Section 14.21) such as ZnO can react with the HCl, providing increased thermal stability for poly(vinyl chloride).

Some of the most thermally stable polymers are the ladder polymers.[7] For example, the ladder polymer having the following structure

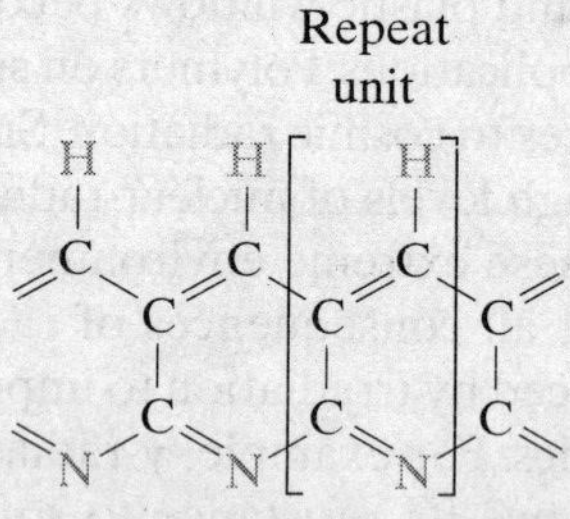

is so thermally stable that a woven cloth of this material can be heated directly in an open flame with no degradation. Polymers of this type are used in place of asbestos for high-temperature gloves.

16.13 WEATHERING

Many polymeric materials serve in applications that require exposure to outdoor conditions. Any resultant degradation is termed *weathering,* which may, in fact, be a combination of several different processes. Under these conditions deterioration

[7] The chain structure of a "ladder polymer" consists of two sets of covalent bonds throughout its length that are crosslinked.

is primarily a result of oxidation, which is initiated by ultraviolet radiation from the sun. Some polymers such as nylon and cellulose are also susceptible to water absorption, which produces a reduction in their hardness and stiffness. Resistance to weathering among the various polymers is quite diverse. The fluorocarbons are virtually inert under these conditions; but some materials, including poly(vinyl chloride) and polystyrene, are susceptible to weathering.

Concept Check 16.9

List three differences between the corrosion of metals and

(a) the corrosion of ceramics, and

(b) the degradation of polymers.

[*The answer may be found in enclosed CD.*]

SUMMARY

Electrochemical Considerations

Metallic corrosion is ordinarily electrochemical, involving both oxidation and reduction reactions. Oxidation is the loss of the metal atom's valence electrons; the resulting metal ions may either go into the corroding solution or form an insoluble compound. During reduction, these electrons are transferred to at least one other chemical species. The character of the corrosion environment dictates which of several possible reduction reactions will occur.

Not all metals oxidize with the same degree of ease, which is demonstrated with a galvanic couple; when in an electrolyte, one metal (the anode) will corrode, whereas a reduction reaction will occur at the other metal (the cathode). The magnitude of the electric potential that is established between anode and cathode is indicative of the driving force for the corrosion reaction.

The standard emf and galvanic series are simply rankings of metallic materials on the basis of their tendency to corrode when coupled to other metals. For the standard emf series, ranking is based on the magnitude of the voltage generated when the standard cell of a metal is coupled to the standard hydrogen electrode at 25°C (77°F). The galvanic series consists of the relative reactivities of metals and alloys in seawater.

The half-cell potentials in the standard emf series are thermodynamic parameters that are valid only at equilibrium; corroding systems are not in equilibrium. Furthermore, the magnitudes of these potentials provide no indication as to the rates at which corrosion reactions occur.

Corrosion Rates

The rate of corrosion may be expressed as corrosion penetration rate, that is, the thickness loss of material per unit of time. Mils per year and millimeters per year are the common units for this parameter. Alternatively, rate is proportional to the current density associated with the electrochemical reaction.

Prediction of Corrosion Rates

Corroding systems will experience polarization, which is the displacement of each electrode potential from its equilibrium value; the magnitude of the displacement is termed the overvoltage. The corrosion rate of a reaction is limited by polarization, of which there are two types—activation and concentration. Polarization data are plotted as potential versus the logarithm of current density. The corrosion rate for a particular reaction may be computed using the current density associated with the intersection point of oxidation and reduction polarization curves.

Passivity

A number of metals and alloys passivate, or lose their chemical reactivity, under some environmental circumstances. This phenomenon is thought to involve the formation of a thin protective oxide film. Stainless steels and aluminum alloys exhibit this type of behavior. The active-to-passive behavior may be explained by the alloy's S-shaped electrochemical potential-versus-log current density curve. Intersections with reduction polarization curves in active and passive regions correspond, respectively, to high and low corrosion rates.

Forms of Corrosion

Metallic corrosion is sometimes classified into eight different forms: uniform attack, galvanic corrosion, crevice corrosion, pitting, intergranular corrosion, selective leaching, erosion–corrosion, and stress corrosion. Hydrogen embrittlement, a type of failure sometimes observed in corrosion environments, was also discussed.

Corrosion Prevention

The measures that may be taken to prevent, or at least reduce, corrosion include material selection, environmental alteration, the use of inhibitors, design changes, application of coatings, and cathodic protection.

Oxidation

Oxidation of metallic materials by electrochemical action is also possible in dry, gaseous atmospheres. An oxide film forms on the surface which may act as a barrier to further oxidation if the volumes of metal and oxide film are similar, that is, if the Pilling–Bedworth ratio is near unity. The kinetics of film formation may follow parabolic, linear, or logarithmic rate laws.

Corrosion of Ceramic Materials

Ceramic materials, being inherently corrosion resistant, are frequently utilized at elevated temperatures and/or in extremely corrosive environments.

Swelling and Dissolution
Bond Rupture
Weathering

Polymeric materials deteriorate by noncorrosive processes. Upon exposure to liquids, they may experience degradation by swelling or dissolution. With swelling, solute molecules actually fit into the molecular structure. Scission, or the severance of molecular chain bonds, may be induced by radiation, chemical reactions, or heat. This results in a reduction of molecular weight and a deterioration of the physical and chemical properties of the polymer.

REFERENCES

ASM Handbook, Vol. 13, *Corrosion,* ASM International, Materials Park, OH, 1987.

ASM Handbook, Vol. 13A, *Corrosion: Fundamentals, Testing, and Protection,* ASM International, Materials Park, OH, 2003.

Craig, B. D. and D. Anderson, (Editors), *Handbook of Corrosion Data,* 2nd edition, ASM International, Materials Park, OH, 1995.

Fontana, M. G., *Corrosion Engineering,* 3rd edition, McGraw-Hill, New York, 1986.

Gibala, R. and R. F. Hehemann, *Hydrogen Embrittlement and Stress Corrosion Cracking,* ASM International, Materials Park, OH, 1984.

Jones, D. A., *Principles and Prevention of Corrosion,* 2nd edition, Pearson Education, Upper Saddle River, NJ, 1996.

Marcus, P. and J. Oudar (Editors), *Corrosion Mechanisms in Theory and Practice,* Marcel Dekker, New York, 1995.

Revie, R. W. (Editor), *Uhlig's Corrosion Handbook,* 2nd edition, John Wiley & Sons, New York, 2000.

Schweitzer, P. A., *Atmospheric Degradation and Corrosion Control,* Marcel Dekker, New York, 1999.

Schweitzer, P. A. (Editor), *Corrosion and Corrosion Protection Handbook,* 2nd edition, Marcel Dekker, New York, 1989.

Talbot, D. and J. Talbot, *Corrosion Science and Technology,* CRC Press, Boca Raton, FL, 1998.

Uhlig, H. H. and R. W. Revie, *Corrosion and Corrosion Control,* 3rd edition, John Wiley & Sons, New York, 1985.

QUESTIONS AND PROBLEMS

Electrochemical Considerations

16.1 **(a)** Briefly explain the difference between oxidation and reduction electrochemical reactions.

(b) Which reaction occurs at the anode and which at the cathode?

16.2 **(a)** Write the possible oxidation and reduction half-reactions that occur when magnesium is immersed in each of the following solutions: (i) HCl, (ii) an HCl solution containing dissolved oxygen, (iii) an HCl solution containing dissolved oxygen and, in addition, Fe^{2+} ions.

(b) In which of these solutions would you expect the magnesium to oxidize most rapidly? Why?

16.3 Demonstrate that **(a)** the value of $\mathcal{F}$ in Equation 16.19 is 96,500 C/mol, and **(b)** at 25°C (298 K),

$$\frac{RT}{n\mathcal{F}} \ln x = \frac{0.0592}{n} \log x$$

16.4 **(a)** Compute the voltage at 25°C of an electrochemical cell consisting of pure lead immersed in a 5×10^{-2} *M* solution of Pb^{2+} ions, and pure tin in a 0.25 *M* solution of Sn^{2+} ions.

(b) Write the spontaneous electrochemical reaction.

16.5 An Fe/Fe^{2+} concentration cell is constructed in which both electrodes are pure iron. The Fe^{2+} concentration for one cell half is 0.5 *M*, for the other, 2×10^{-2} *M*. Is a voltage generated between the two cell halves? If so, what is its magnitude and which electrode will be oxidized? If no voltage is produced, explain this result.

16.6 An electrochemical cell is composed of pure copper and pure cadmium electrodes immersed in solutions of their respective divalent ions. For a 6.5×10^{-2} *M* concentration of Cd^{2+}, the cadmium electrode is oxidized yielding a cell potential of 0.775 V. Calculate the concentration of Cu^{2+} ions if the temperature is 25°C.

16.7 An electrochemical cell is constructed such that on one side a pure Zn electrode is in contact with a solution containing Zn^{2+} ions at a concentration of 10^{-2} *M*. The other cell half consists of a pure Pb electrode immersed in a solution of Pb^{2+} ions that has a concentration of 10^{-4} *M*. At what temperature will the potential between the two electrodes be +0.568 V?

16.8 For the following pairs of alloys that are coupled in seawater, predict the possibility of corrosion; if corrosion is probable, note which metal/alloy will corrode.

(a) Aluminum and cast iron

(b) Inconel and nickel

(c) Cadmium and zinc

(d) Brass and titanium

(e) Low-carbon steel and copper

16.9 **(a)** From the galvanic series (Table 16.2), cite three metals/alloys that may be used to galvanically protect cast iron.

(b) As Concept Check 16.4(b) notes, galvanic corrosion is prevented by making an electrical contact between the two metals in the couple and a third metal that is anodic to the other two. Using the galvanic series, name one metal that could be used to protect a nickel-steel galvanic couple.

Corrosion Rates

16.10 Demonstrate that the constant K in Equation 16.23 will have values of 534 and 87.6 for the CPR in units of mpy and mm/yr, respectively.

16.11 A piece of corroded metal alloy plate was found in a submerged ocean vessel. It was estimated that the original area of the plate was 800 cm^2 and that approximately 7.6 kg had corroded away during the submersion. Assuming a corrosion penetration rate of 4 mm/yr for this alloy in seawater, estimate the time of submersion in years. The density of the alloy is 4.5 g/cm^3.

16.12 A thick steel sheet of area 100 $in.^2$ is exposed to air near the ocean. After a one-year period it was found to experience a weight loss of 485 g due to corrosion. To what rate of corrosion, in both mpy and mm/yr, does this correspond?

16.13 **(a)** Demonstrate that the CPR is related to the corrosion current density i (A/cm^2) through the expression

$$\text{CPR} = \frac{KAi}{n\rho} \quad (16.38)$$

where K is a constant, A is the atomic weight of the metal experiencing corrosion, n is the number of electrons associated with the ionization of each metal atom, and ρ is the density of the metal.

(b) Calculate the value of the constant K for the CPR in mpy and i in $\mu A/cm^2$ (10^{-6} A/cm^2).

16.14 Using the results of Problem 16.13, compute the corrosion penetration rate, in mpy, for the corrosion of iron in HCl (to form Fe^{2+} ions) if the corrosion current density is 8×10^{-5} A/cm^2.

Prediction of Corrosion Rates

16.15 **(a)** Cite the major differences between activation and concentration polarizations.

(b) Under what conditions is activation polarization rate controlling?

(c) Under what conditions is concentration polarization rate controlling?

16.16 **(a)** Describe the phenomenon of dynamic equilibrium as it applies to oxidation and reduction electrochemical reactions.

(b) What is the exchange current density?

16.17 Nickel experiences corrosion in an acid solution according to the reaction

$$Ni + 2H^+ \longrightarrow Ni^{2+} + H_2$$

The rates of both oxidation and reduction half-reactions are controlled by activation polarization.

(a) Compute the rate of oxidation of Ni (in mol/cm^2-s) given the following activation polarization data:

For Nickel	*For Hydrogen*
$V_{(Ni/Ni^{2+})} = -0.25$ V	$V_{(H^+/H_2)} = 0$ V
$i_0 = 10^{-8}$ A/cm^2	$i_0 = 6 \times 10^{-7}$ A/cm^2
$\beta = +0.12$	$\beta = -0.10$

(b) Compute the value of the corrosion potential.

16.18 The corrosion rate is to be determined for some divalent metal M in a solution containing hydrogen ions. The following corrosion data are known about the metal and solution:

For Metal M	*For Hydrogen*
$V_{(M/M^{2+})} = -0.90$ V	$V_{(H^+/H_2)} = 0$ V
$i_0 = 10^{-12}$ A/cm^2	$i_0 = 10^{-10}$ A/cm^2
$\beta = +0.10$	$\beta = -0.15$

(a) Assuming that activation polarization controls both oxidation and reduction reactions, determine the rate of corrosion of metal M (in mol/cm^2-s).

(b) Compute the corrosion potential for this reaction.

16.19 The influence of increasing solution velocity on the overvoltage-versus-log current density behavior for a solution that experiences combined activation–concentration polarization is

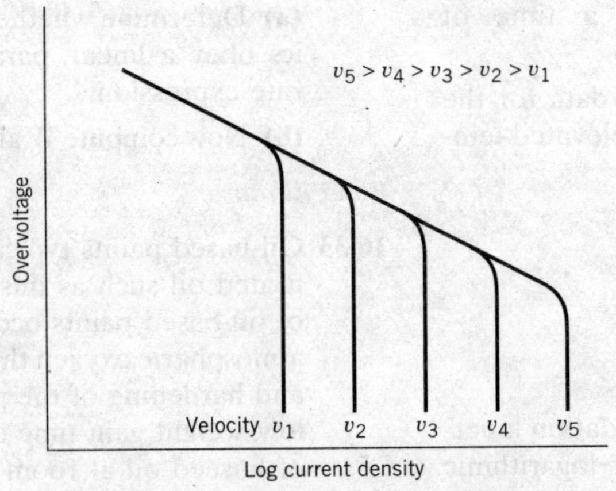

Figure 16.26 Plot of overvoltage versus logarithm of current density for a solution that experiences combined activation–concentration polarization at various solution velocities.

indicated in Figure 16.26. On the basis of this behavior, make a schematic plot of corrosion rate versus solution velocity for the oxidation of a metal; assume that the oxidation reaction is controlled by activation polarization.

Passivity

16.20 Briefly describe the phenomenon of passivity. Name two common types of alloy that passivate.

16.21 Why does chromium in stainless steels make them more corrosion resistant in many environments than plain carbon steels?

Forms of Corrosion

16.22 For each form of corrosion, other than uniform, do the following:

(a) Describe why, where, and the conditions under which the corrosion occurs.

(b) Cite three measures that may be taken to prevent or control it.

16.23 Briefly explain why cold-worked metals are more susceptible to corrosion than noncold-worked metals.

16.24 Briefly explain why, for a small anode-to-cathode area ratio, the corrosion rate will be higher than for a large ratio.

16.25 For a concentration cell, briefly explain why corrosion occurs at that region having the lower concentration.

Corrosion Prevention

16.26 **(a)** What are inhibitors?

(b) What possible mechanisms account for their effectiveness?

16.27 Briefly describe the two techniques that are used for galvanic protection.

Oxidation

16.28 For each of the metals listed in the table, compute the Pilling–Bedworth ratio. Also, on the basis of this value, specify whether or not you would expect the oxide scale that forms on the surface to be protective, and then justify your decision. Density data for both the metal and its oxide are also tabulated.

Metal	*Metal Density (g/cm^3)*	*Metal Oxide*	*Oxide Density (g/cm^3)*
Mg	1.74	MgO	3.58
V	6.11	V_2O_5	3.36
Zn	7.13	ZnO	5.61

16.29 According to Table 16.3, the oxide coating that forms on silver should be nonprotective, and yet Ag does not oxidize appreciably at room temperature and in air. How do you explain this apparent discrepancy?

16.30 In the table, weight gain–time data for the oxidation of nickel at an elevated temperature are tabulated.

W (mg/cm^2)	*Time (min)*
0.527	10
0.857	30
1.526	100

(a) Determine whether the oxidation kinetics obey a linear, parabolic, or logarithmic rate expression.

(b) Now compute W after a time of 600 min.

16.31 In the table, weight gain–time data for the oxidation of some metal at an elevated temperature are tabulated.

W (mg/cm^2)	*Time (min)*
6.16	100
8.59	250
12.72	1000

(a) Determine whether the oxidation kinetics obey a linear, parabolic, or logarithmic rate expression.

(b) Now compute W after a time of 5000 min.

16.32 In the table, weight gain–time data for the oxidation of some metal at an elevated temperature are tabulated.

W (mg/cm^2)	*Time (min)*
1.54	10
23.24	150
95.37	620

(a) Determine whether the oxidation kinetics obey a linear, parabolic, or logarithmic rate expression.

(b) Now compute W after a time of 1200 min.

Bond Rupture

16.33 Oil-based paints typically contain an unsaturated oil such as linseed oil. The "drying" of oil-based paints occurs by reactions with atmospheric oxygen that lead to crosslinking and hardening of the paint. In the table below, weight gain-time data for the oxidation of linseed oil at room temperature (298 K) are tabulated.

W (mg/cm^2)	*Time (min)*
0.053	18.6
0.100	39.0
0.158	57.1

(a) Determine whether the oxidation kinetics obey a linear, parabolic, or logarithmic rate expression.

(b) Compute the amount of time required for a weight gain of 0.120 mg/cm^2.

DESIGN PROBLEMS

16.D1 A brine solution is used as a cooling medium in a steel heat exchanger. The brine is circulated within the heat exchanger and contains some dissolved oxygen. Suggest three methods, other than cathodic protection, for reducing corrosion of the steel by the brine. Explain the rationale for each suggestion.

16.D2 Suggest an appropriate material for each of the following applications, and, if necessary, recommend corrosion prevention measures that should be taken. Justify your suggestions.

(a) Laboratory bottles to contain relatively dilute solutions of nitric acid

(b) Barrels to contain benzene

(c) Pipe to transport hot alkaline (basic) solutions

(d) Underground tanks to store large quantities of high-purity water

(e) Architectural trim for high-rise buildings

16.D3 Each student (or group of students) is to find a real-life corrosion problem that has not been solved, conduct a thorough investigation as to the cause(s) and type(s) of corrosion, and, finally, propose possible solutions for the problem, indicating which of the solutions is best and why. Submit a report that addresses the above issues.

Chapter 17 Electrical Properties of Materials

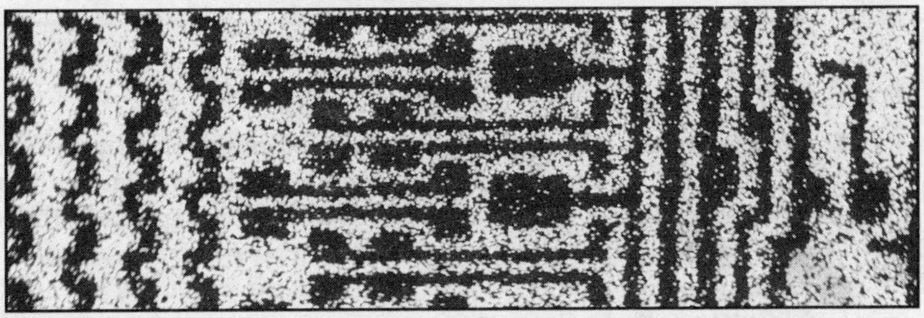

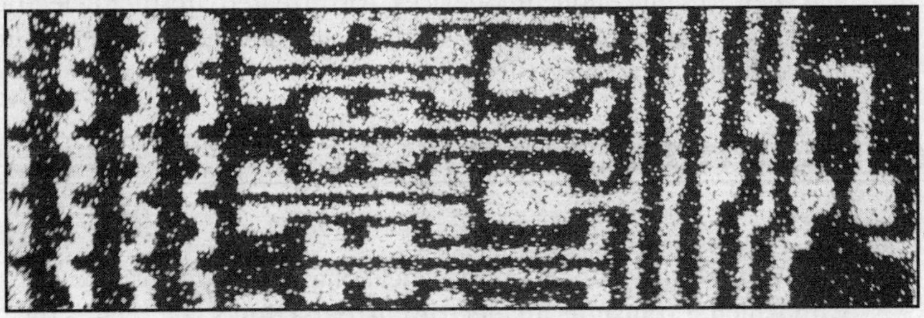

It was noted in Section 5.12 that an image is generated on a scanning electron micrograph as a beam of electrons scans the surface of the specimen being examined. The electrons in this beam cause some of the specimen surface atoms to emit x-rays; the energy of an x-ray photon depends on the particular atom from which it radiates. It is possible to selectively filter out all but the x-rays emitted from one kind of atom. When projected on a cathode ray tube, small white dots are produced that indicate the locations of the particular atom type; thus, a "dot map" of the image is generated.

Top: Scanning electron micrograph of an integrated circuit.

Center: A silicon dot map for the integrated circuit above, showing regions where silicon atoms are concentrated. Doped silicon is the semiconducting material from which integrated circuit elements are made.

Bottom: An aluminum dot map. Metallic aluminum is an electrical conductor and, as such, wires the circuit elements together. Approximately 200×.

Learning Objectives

After careful study of this chapter you should be able to do the following:

1. Describe the four possible electron band structures for solid materials.
2. Briefly describe electron excitation events that produce free electrons/holes in (a) metals, (b) semiconductors (intrinsic and extrinsic), and (c) insulators.
3. Calculate the electrical conductivities of metals, semiconductors (intrinsic and extrinsic), and insulators given their charge carrier density(s) and mobility(s).
4. Distinguish between *intrinsic* and *extrinsic* semiconducting materials.
5. (a) On a plot of logarithm of carrier (electron, hole) concentration versus absolute temperature, draw schematic curves for both intrinsic and extrinsic semiconducting materials.
   (b) On the extrinsic curve note freeze-out, extrinsic, and intrinsic regions.
6. For a *p–n* junction, explain the rectification process in terms of electron and hole motions.
7. Calculate the capacitance of a parallel-plate capacitor.
8. Define dielectric constant in terms of permittivities.
9. Briefly explain how the charge storing capacity of a capacitor may be increased by the insertion and polarization of a dielectric material between its plates.
10. Name and describe the three types of polarization.
11. Briefly describe the phenomena of *ferroelectricity* and *piezoelectricity.*

17.1 INTRODUCTION

The prime objective of this chapter is to explore the electrical properties of materials, that is, their responses to an applied electric field. We begin with the phenomenon of electrical conduction: the parameters by which it is expressed, the mechanism of conduction by electrons, and how the electron energy band structure of a material influences its ability to conduct. These principles are extended to metals, semiconductors, and insulators. Particular attention is given to the characteristics of semiconductors and then to semiconducting devices. Also treated are the dielectric characteristics of insulating materials. The final sections are devoted to the peculiar phenomena of ferroelectricity and piezoelectricity.

Electrical Conduction

17.2 OHM'S LAW

One of the most important electrical characteristics of a solid material is the ease with which it transmits an electric current. **Ohm's law** relates the current I—or time rate of charge passage—to the applied voltage V as follows:

$$V = IR \tag{17.1}$$

where R is the resistance of the material through which the current is passing. The units for V, I, and R are, respectively, volts (J/C), amperes (C/s), and ohms (V/A). The value of R is influenced by specimen configuration, and for many materials is independent of current. The **resistivity** ρ is independent of specimen geometry but related to R through the expression

$$\rho = \frac{RA}{l} \tag{17.2}$$

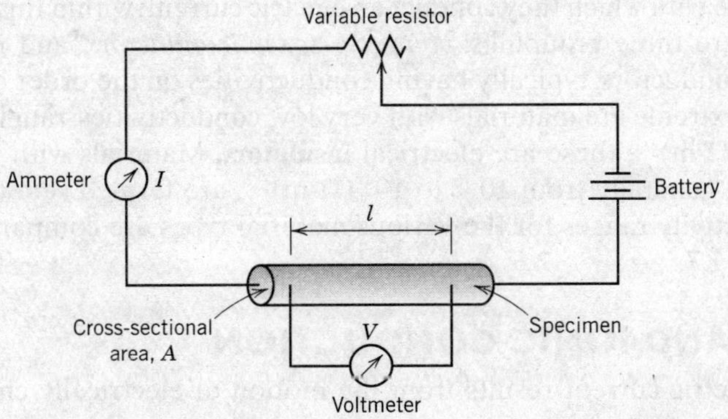

Figure 17.1 Schematic representation of the apparatus used to measure electrical resistivity.

where l is the distance between the two points at which the voltage is measured, and A is the cross-sectional area perpendicular to the direction of the current. The units for ρ are ohm-meters (Ω-m). From the expression for Ohm's law and Equation 17.2,

$$\rho = \frac{VA}{Il} \tag{17.3}$$

Figure 17.1 is a schematic diagram of an experimental arrangement for measuring electrical resistivity.

17.3 ELECTRICAL CONDUCTIVITY

Sometimes, **electrical conductivity** σ is used to specify the electrical character of a material. It is simply the reciprocal of the resistivity, or

$$\sigma = \frac{1}{\rho} \tag{17.4}$$

and is indicative of the ease with which a material is capable of conducting an electric current. The units for σ are reciprocal ohm-meters [$(\Omega\text{-m})^{-1}$, or mho/m]. The following discussions on electrical properties use both resistivity and conductivity.

In addition to Equation 17.1, Ohm's law may be expressed as

$$J = \sigma \mathscr{E} \tag{17.5}$$

in which J is the current density, the current per unit of specimen area I/A, and $\mathscr{E}$ is the electric field intensity, or the voltage difference between two points divided by the distance separating them; that is,

$$\mathscr{E} = \frac{V}{l} \tag{17.6}$$

The demonstration of the equivalence of the two Ohm's law expressions (Equations 17.1 and 17.5) is left as a homework exercise.

Solid materials exhibit an amazing range of electrical conductivities, extending over 27 orders of magnitude; probably no other physical property experiences this breadth of variation. In fact, one way of classifying solid materials is according to the ease with which they conduct an electric current; within this classification scheme there are three groupings: *conductors, semiconductors,* and *insulators.* **Metals** are good conductors, typically having conductivities on the order of 10^7 (Ω-m)$^{-1}$. At the other extreme are materials with very low conductivities, ranging between 10^{-10} and 10^{-20} (Ω-m)$^{-1}$; these are electrical **insulators.** Materials with intermediate conductivities, generally from 10^{-6} to 10^4 (Ω-m)$^{-1}$, are termed **semiconductors.** Electrical conductivity ranges for the various material types are compared in the bar-chart of Figure 1.7.

17.4 ELECTRONIC AND IONIC CONDUCTION

An electric current results from the motion of electrically charged particles in response to forces that act on them from an externally applied electric field. Positively charged particles are accelerated in the field direction, negatively charged particles in the direction opposite. Within most solid materials a current arises from the flow of electrons, which is termed *electronic conduction.* In addition, for ionic materials a net motion of charged ions is possible that produces a current; such is termed **ionic conduction.** The present discussion deals with electronic conduction; ionic conduction is treated briefly in Section 17.16.

17.5 ENERGY BAND STRUCTURES IN SOLIDS

In all conductors, semiconductors, and many insulating materials, only electronic conduction exists, and the magnitude of the electrical conductivity is strongly dependent on the number of electrons available to participate in the conduction process. However, not all electrons in every atom will accelerate in the presence of an electric field. The number of electrons available for electrical conduction in a particular material is related to the arrangement of electron states or levels with respect to energy, and then the manner in which these states are occupied by electrons. A thorough exploration of these topics is complicated and involves principles of quantum mechanics that are beyond the scope of this book; the ensuing development omits some concepts and simplifies others.

Concepts relating to electron energy states, their occupancy, and the resulting electron configuration for isolated atoms were discussed in Section 2.3. By way of review, for each individual atom there exist discrete energy levels that may be occupied by electrons, arranged into shells and subshells. Shells are designated by integers (1, 2, 3, etc.), and subshells by letters (s, p, d, and f). For each of s, p, d, and f subshells, there exist, respectively, one, three, five, and seven states. The electrons in most atoms fill only the states having the lowest energies, two electrons of opposite spin per state, in accordance with the Pauli exclusion principle. The electron configuration of an isolated atom represents the arrangement of the electrons within the allowed states.

Let us now make an extrapolation of some of these concepts to solid materials. A solid may be thought of as consisting of a large number, say, N, of atoms initially separated from one another, which are subsequently brought together and bonded to form the ordered atomic arrangement found in the crystalline material. At relatively large separation distances, each atom is independent of all the others and will have the atomic energy levels and electron configuration as if isolated. However, as the atoms come within close proximity of one another, electrons are acted upon, or perturbed, by the electrons and nuclei of adjacent atoms. This influence is such that each distinct atomic state may split into a series of closely spaced electron states in the solid, to form what is termed an **electron energy band.** The

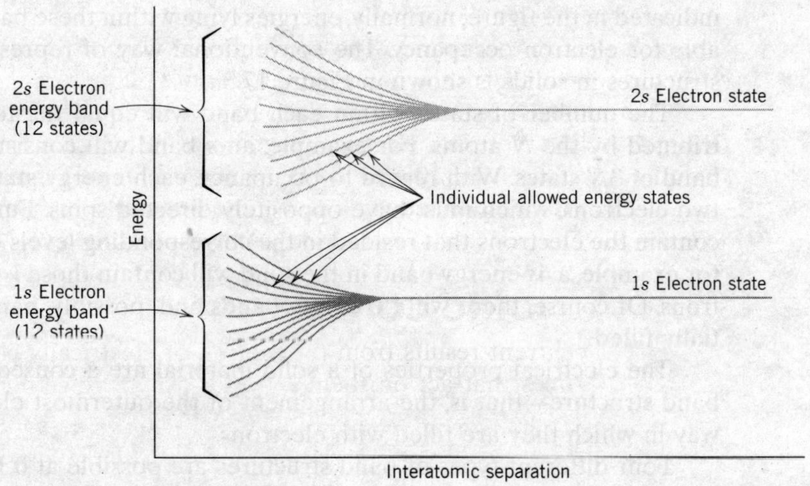

Figure 17.2 Schematic plot of electron energy versus interatomic separation for an aggregate of 12 atoms ($N = 12$). Upon close approach, each of the 1*s* and 2*s* atomic states splits to form an electron energy band consisting of 12 states.

extent of splitting depends on interatomic separation (Figure 17.2) and begins with the outermost electron shells, since they are the first to be perturbed as the atoms coalesce. Within each band, the energy states are discrete, yet the difference between adjacent states is exceedingly small. At the equilibrium spacing, band formation may not occur for the electron subshells nearest the nucleus, as illustrated in Figure 17.3*b*. Furthermore, gaps may exist between adjacent bands, as also

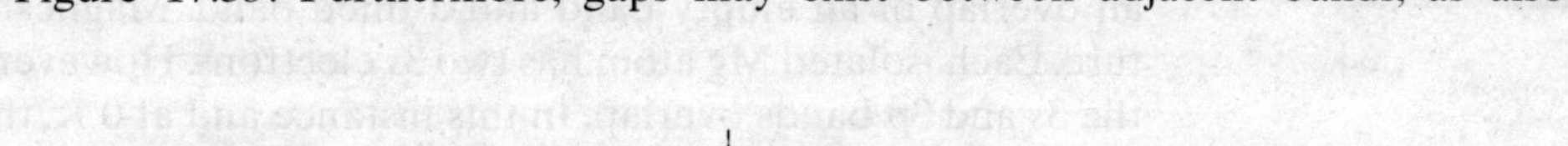

Figure 17.3 (*a*) The conventional representation of the electron energy band structure for a solid material at the equilibrium interatomic separation. (*b*) Electron energy versus interatomic separation for an aggregate of atoms, illustrating how the energy band structure at the equilibrium separation in (*a*) is generated. (From Z. D. Jastrzebski, *The Nature and Properties of Engineering Materials,* 3rd edition. Copyright © 1987 by John Wiley & Sons, Inc. Reprinted by permission of John Wiley & Sons, Inc.)

indicated in the figure; normally, energies lying within these band gaps are not available for electron occupancy. The conventional way of representing electron band structures in solids is shown in Figure 17.3*a*.

The number of states within each band will equal the total of all states contributed by the N atoms. For example, an s band will consist of N states, and a p band of $3N$ states. With regard to occupancy, each energy state may accommodate two electrons, which must have oppositely directed spins. Furthermore, bands will contain the electrons that resided in the corresponding levels of the isolated atoms; for example, a 4*s* energy band in the solid will contain those isolated atom's 4*s* electrons. Of course, there will be empty bands and, possibly, bands that are only partially filled.

The electrical properties of a solid material are a consequence of its electron band structure—that is, the arrangement of the outermost electron bands and the way in which they are filled with electrons.

Four different types of band structures are possible at 0 K. In the first (Figure 17.4*a*), one outermost band is only partially filled with electrons. The energy corresponding to the highest filled state at 0 K is called the **Fermi energy** E_f, as indicated. This energy band structure is typified by some metals, in particular those that have a single *s* valence electron (e.g., copper). Each copper atom has one 4*s* electron; however, for a solid comprised of N atoms, the 4*s* band is capable of accommodating $2N$ electrons. Thus only half the available electron positions within this 4*s* band are filled.

For the second band structure, also found in metals (Figure 17.4*b*), there is an overlap of an empty band and a filled band. Magnesium has this band structure. Each isolated Mg atom has two 3*s* electrons. However, when a solid is formed, the 3*s* and 3*p* bands overlap. In this instance and at 0 K, the Fermi energy is taken as that energy below which, for N atoms, N states are filled, two electrons per state.

The final two band structures are similar; one band (the **valence band**) that is completely filled with electrons is separated from an empty **conduction band,** and an **energy band gap** lies between them. For very pure materials, electrons may not

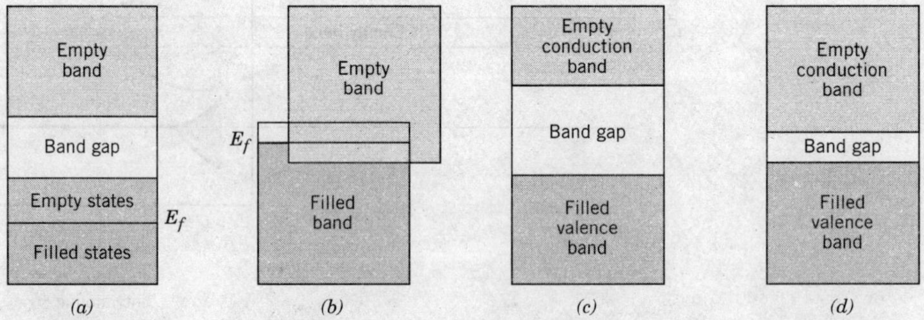

Figure 17.4 The various possible electron band structures in solids at 0 K. (*a*) The electron band structure found in metals such as copper, in which there are available electron states above and adjacent to filled states, in the same band. (*b*) The electron band structure of metals such as magnesium, wherein there is an overlap of filled and empty outer bands. (*c*) The electron band structure characteristic of insulators; the filled valence band is separated from the empty conduction band by a relatively large band gap (>2 eV). (*d*) The electron band structure found in the semiconductors, which is the same as for insulators except that the band gap is relatively narrow (<2 eV).

have energies within this gap. The difference between the two band structures lies in the magnitude of the energy gap; for materials that are insulators, the band gap is relatively wide (Figure 17.4*c*), whereas for semiconductors it is narrow (Figure 17.4*d*). The Fermi energy for these two band structures lies within the band gap—near its center.

17.6 CONDUCTION IN TERMS OF BAND AND ATOMIC BONDING MODELS

At this point in the discussion, it is vital that another concept be understood—namely, that only electrons with energies greater than the Fermi energy may be acted on and accelerated in the presence of an electric field. These are the electrons that participate in the conduction process, which are termed **free electrons.** Another charged electronic entity called a **hole** is found in semiconductors and insulators. Holes have energies less than E_f and also participate in electronic conduction. As the ensuing discussion reveals, the electrical conductivity is a direct function of the numbers of free electrons and holes. In addition, the distinction between conductors and nonconductors (insulators and semiconductors) lies in the numbers of these free electron and hole charge carriers.

Metals

For an electron to become free, it must be excited or promoted into one of the empty and available energy states above E_f. For metals having either of the band structures shown in Figures 17.4*a* and 17.4*b*, there are vacant energy states adjacent to the highest filled state at E_f. Thus, very little energy is required to promote electrons into the low-lying empty states, as shown in Figure 17.5. Generally, the energy provided by an electric field is sufficient to excite large numbers of electrons into these conducting states.

For the metallic bonding model discussed in Section 2.6, it was assumed that all the valence electrons have freedom of motion and form an "electron gas," which is uniformly distributed throughout the lattice of ion cores. Although these electrons are not locally bound to any particular atom, nevertheless, they must experience some excitation to become conducting electrons that are truly free. Thus, although only a fraction are excited, this still gives rise to a relatively large number of free electrons and, consequently, a high conductivity.

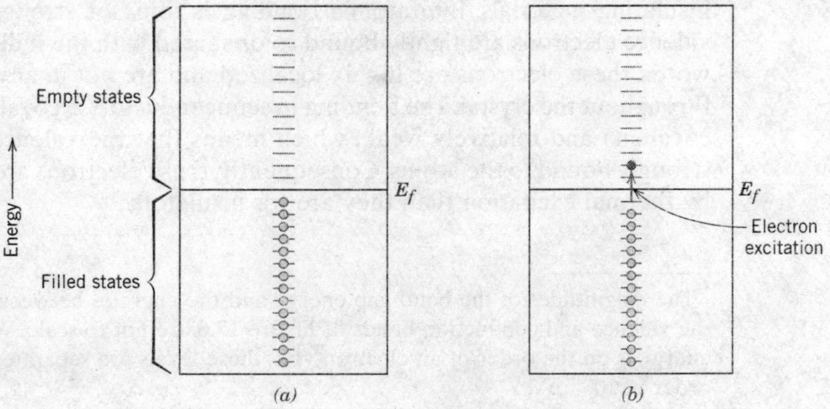

Figure 17.5 For a metal, occupancy of electron states (*a*) before and (*b*) after an electron excitation.

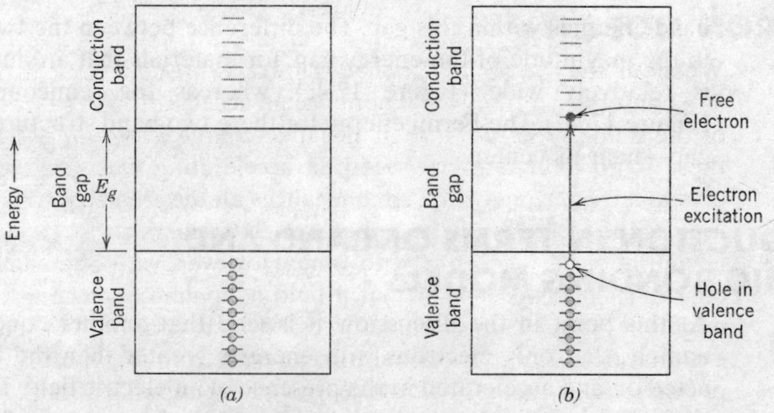

Figure 17.6 For an insulator or semiconductor, occupancy of electron states (*a*) before and (*b*) after an electron excitation from the valence band into the conduction band, in which both a free electron and a hole are generated.

Insulators and Semiconductors

For insulators and semiconductors, empty states adjacent to the top of the filled valence band are not available. To become free, therefore, electrons must be promoted across the energy band gap and into empty states at the bottom of the conduction band. This is possible only by supplying to an electron the difference in energy between these two states, which is approximately equal to the band gap energy E_g. This excitation process is demonstrated in Figure 17.6.[1] For many materials this band gap is several electron volts wide. Most often the excitation energy is from a nonelectrical source such as heat or light, usually the former.

The number of electrons excited thermally (by heat energy) into the conduction band depends on the energy band gap width as well as temperature. At a given temperature, the larger the E_g, the lower is the probability that a valence electron will be promoted into an energy state within the conduction band; this results in fewer conduction electrons. In other words, the larger the band gap, the lower is the electrical conductivity at a given temperature. Thus, the distinction between semiconductors and insulators lies in the width of the band gap; for semiconductors it is narrow, whereas for insulating materials it is relatively wide.

Increasing the temperature of either a semiconductor or an insulator results in an increase in the thermal energy that is available for electron excitation. Thus, more electrons are promoted into the conduction band, which gives rise to an enhanced conductivity.

The conductivity of insulators and semiconductors may also be viewed from the perspective of atomic bonding models discussed in Section 2.6. For electrically insulating materials, interatomic bonding is ionic or strongly covalent. Thus, the valence electrons are tightly bound to or shared with the individual atoms. In other words, these electrons are highly localized and are not in any sense free to wander throughout the crystal. The bonding in semiconductors is covalent (or predominantly covalent) and relatively weak, which means that the valence electrons are not as strongly bound to the atoms. Consequently, these electrons are more easily removed by thermal excitation than they are for insulators.

---

[1] The magnitudes of the band gap energy and the energies between adjacent levels in both the valence and conduction bands of Figure 17.6 are not to scale. Whereas the band gap energy is on the order of an electron volt, these levels are separated by energies on the order of 10^{-10} eV.

17.7 ELECTRON MOBILITY

When an electric field is applied, a force is brought to bear on the free electrons; as a consequence, they all experience an acceleration in a direction opposite to that of the field, by virtue of their negative charge. According to quantum mechanics, there is no interaction between an accelerating electron and atoms in a perfect crystal lattice. Under such circumstances all the free electrons should accelerate as long as the electric field is applied, which would give rise to an electric current that is continuously increasing with time. However, we know that a current reaches a constant value the instant that a field is applied, indicating that there exist what might be termed "frictional forces," which counter this acceleration from the external field. These frictional forces result from the scattering of electrons by imperfections in the crystal lattice, including impurity atoms, vacancies, interstitial atoms, dislocations, and even the thermal vibrations of the atoms themselves. Each scattering event causes an electron to lose kinetic energy and to change its direction of motion, as represented schematically in Figure 17.7. There is, however, some net electron motion in the direction opposite to the field, and this flow of charge is the electric current.

The scattering phenomenon is manifested as a resistance to the passage of an electric current. Several parameters are used to describe the extent of this scattering; these include the *drift velocity* and the **mobility** of an electron. The drift velocity v_d represents the average electron velocity in the direction of the force imposed by the applied field. It is directly proportional to the electric field as follows:

$$v_d = \mu_e \mathscr{E} \tag{17.7}$$

The constant of proportionality μ_e is called the electron mobility, which is an indication of the frequency of scattering events; its units are square meters per volt-second (m^2/V-s).

The conductivity σ of most materials may be expressed as

$$\sigma = n|e|\mu_e \tag{17.8}$$

where n is the number of free or conducting electrons per unit volume (e.g., per cubic meter), and $|e|$ is the absolute magnitude of the electrical charge on an electron (1.6×10^{-19} C). Thus, the electrical conductivity is proportional to both the number of free electrons and the electron mobility.

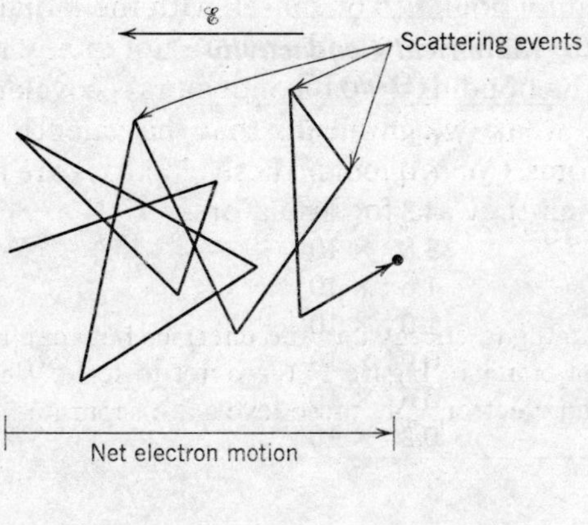

Figure 17.7 Schematic diagram showing the path of an electron that is deflected by scattering events.

Concept Check 17.1

If a metallic material is cooled through its melting temperature at an extremely rapid rate, it will form a noncrystalline solid (i.e., a metallic glass). Will the electrical conductivity of the noncrystalline metal be greater or less than its crystalline counterpart? Why?

[*The answer may be found in enclosed CD.*]

17.8 ELECTRICAL RESISTIVITY OF METALS

As mentioned previously, most metals are extremely good conductors of electricity; room-temperature conductivities for several of the more common metals are contained in Table 17.1. (Table B.9 in Appendix B lists the electrical resistivities of a large number of metals and alloys.) Again metals have high conductivities because of the large numbers of free electrons that have been excited into empty states above the Fermi energy. Thus n has a large value in the conductivity expression, Equation 17.8.

At this point it is convenient to discuss conduction in metals in terms of the resistivity, the reciprocal of conductivity; the reason for this switch in topic should become apparent in the ensuing discussion.

Since crystalline defects serve as scattering centers for conduction electrons in metals, increasing their number raises the resistivity (or lowers the conductivity). The concentration of these imperfections depends on temperature, composition, and the degree of cold work of a metal specimen. In fact, it has been observed experimentally that the total resistivity of a metal is the sum of the contributions from thermal vibrations, impurities, and plastic deformation; that is, the scattering mechanisms act independently of one another. This may be represented in mathematical form as follows:

$$\rho_{\text{total}} = \rho_t + \rho_i + \rho_d \tag{17.9}$$

in which ρ_t, ρ_i, and ρ_d represent the individual thermal, impurity, and deformation resistivity contributions, respectively. Equation 17.9 is sometimes known as

Table 17.1 Room-Temperature Electrical Conductivities for Nine Common Metals and Alloys

Metal	*Electrical Conductivity* $[(\Omega\text{-}m)^{-1}]$
Silver	6.8×10^7
Copper	6.0×10^7
Gold	4.3×10^7
Aluminum	3.8×10^7
Brass (70Cu–30Zn)	1.6×10^7
Iron	1.0×10^7
Platinum	0.94×10^7
Plain carbon steel	0.6×10^7
Stainless steel	0.2×10^7

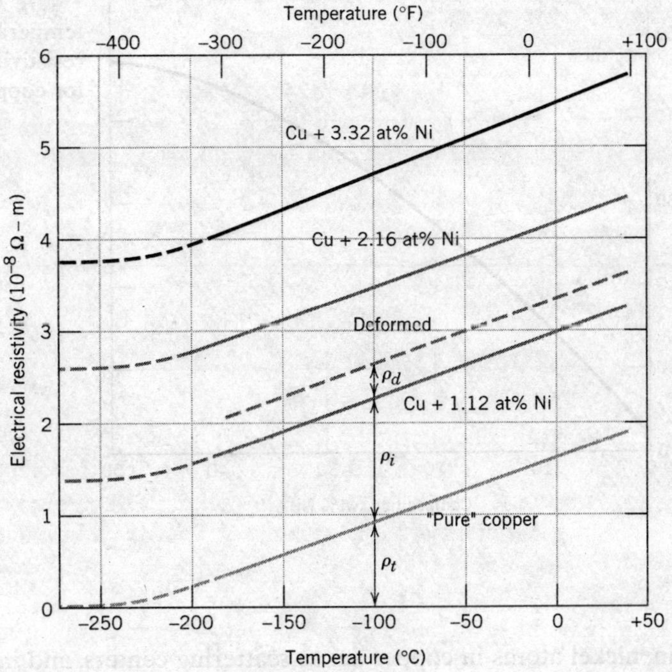

Figure 17.8 The electrical resistivity versus temperature for copper and three copper–nickel alloys, one of which has been deformed. Thermal, impurity, and deformation contributions to the resistivity are indicated at −100°C. [Adapted from J. O. Linde, *Ann. Physik*, **5**, 219 (1932); and C. A. Wert and R. M. Thomson, *Physics of Solids*, 2nd edition, McGraw-Hill Book Company, New York, 1970.]

Matthiessen's rule. The influence of each ρ variable on the total resistivity is demonstrated in Figure 17.8, a plot of resistivity versus temperature for copper and several copper–nickel alloys in annealed and deformed states. The additive nature of the individual resistivity contributions is demonstrated at −100°C.

Influence of Temperature

For the pure metal and all the copper–nickel alloys shown in Figure 17.8, the resistivity rises linearly with temperature above about −200°C. Thus,

$$\rho_t = \rho_0 + aT \tag{17.10}$$

where ρ_0 and a are constants for each particular metal. This dependence of the thermal resistivity component on temperature is due to the increase with temperature in thermal vibrations and other lattice irregularities (e.g., vacancies), which serve as electron-scattering centers.

Influence of Impurities

For additions of a single impurity that forms a solid solution, the impurity resistivity ρ_i is related to the impurity concentration c_i in terms of the atom fraction (at%/100) as follows:

$$\rho_i = Ac_i(1 - c_i) \tag{17.11}$$

where A is a composition-independent constant that is a function of both the impurity and host metals. The influence of nickel impurity additions on the room-temperature resistivity of copper is demonstrated in Figure 17.9, up to 50 wt% Ni; over this composition range nickel is completely soluble in copper (Figure 7.3*a*).

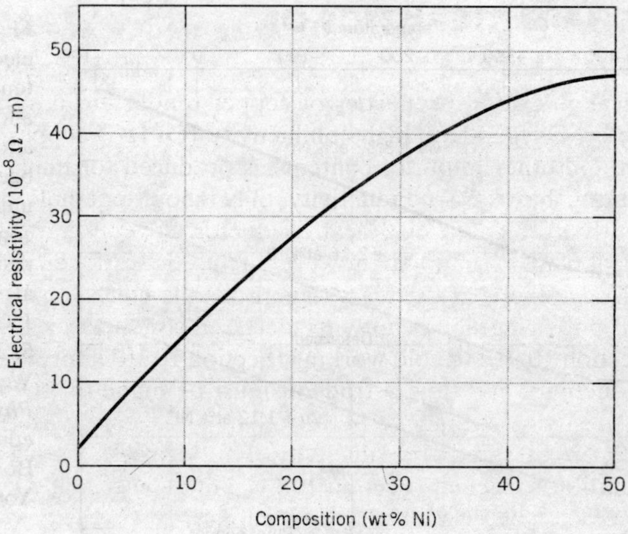

Figure 17.9 Room-temperature electrical resistivity versus composition for copper–nickel alloys.

Again, nickel atoms in copper act as scattering centers, and increasing the concentration of nickel in copper results in an enhancement of resistivity.

For a two-phase alloy consisting of α and β phases, a rule-of-mixtures expression may be utilized to approximate the resistivity as follows:

$$\rho_i = \rho_\alpha V_\alpha + \rho_\beta V_\beta \tag{17.12}$$

where the V's and ρ's represent volume fractions and individual resistivities for the respective phases.

Influence of Plastic Deformation

Plastic deformation also raises the electrical resistivity as a result of increased numbers of electron-scattering dislocations. The effect of deformation on resistivity is also represented in Figure 17.8. Furthermore, its influence is much weaker than that of increasing temperature or the presence of impurities.

Concept Check 17.2

The room-temperature electrical resistivities of pure lead and pure tin are 2.06×10^{-7} and 1.11×10^{-7} Ω-m, respectively.

(a) Make a schematic graph of the room-temperature electrical resistivity versus composition for all compositions between pure lead and pure tin.

(b) On this same graph schematically plot electrical resistivity versus composition at 150°C.

(c) Explain the shapes of these two curves, as well as any differences between them.

Hint: You may want to consult the lead-tin phase diagram, Figure 7.8.

[*The answer may be found in enclosed CD.*]

17.9 ELECTRICAL CHARACTERISTICS OF COMMERCIAL ALLOYS

Electrical and other properties of copper render it the most widely used metallic conductor. Oxygen-free high-conductivity (OFHC) copper, having extremely low oxygen and other impurity contents, is produced for many electrical applications. Aluminum, having a conductivity only about one-half that of copper, is also frequently used as an electrical conductor. Silver has a higher conductivity than either copper or aluminum; however, its use is restricted on the basis of cost.

On occasion, it is necessary to improve the mechanical strength of a metal alloy without impairing significantly its electrical conductivity. Both solid-solution alloying (Section 10.9) and cold working (Section 10.10) improve strength at the expense of conductivity, and thus, a tradeoff must be made for these two properties. Most often, strength is enhanced by introducing a second phase that does not have so adverse an effect on conductivity. For example, copper–beryllium alloys are precipitation hardened (Section 10.14); but even so, the conductivity is reduced by about a factor of 5 over high-purity copper.

For some applications, such as furnace heating elements, a high electrical resistivity is desirable. The energy loss by electrons that are scattered is dissipated as heat energy. Such materials must have not only a high resistivity, but also a resistance to oxidation at elevated temperatures and, of course, a high melting temperature. Nichrome, a nickel–chromium alloy, is commonly employed in heating elements.

MATERIALS OF IMPORTANCE

Aluminum Electrical Wires

Copper is normally used for electrical wiring in residential and commercial buildings. However, between 1965 and 1973 the price of copper increased significantly, and, consequently aluminum wiring was installed in many buildings constructed or remodeled during this period because aluminum was a less expensive electrical conductor. An inordinately high number of fires occurred in these buildings, and investigations revealed that the use of aluminum posed an increased fire hazard risk over copper wiring.

When properly installed, aluminum wiring can be just as safe as copper. These safety problems arose at connection points between the aluminum and copper; copper wiring was used for connection terminals on electrical equipment (circuit breakers, receptacles, switches, etc.) to which the aluminum wiring was attached.

As electrical circuits are turned on and off, the electrical wiring heats up and then cools down. This thermal cycling causes the wires to alternately expand and contract. The amounts of expansion and contraction for the aluminum are greater than for copper—i.e., aluminum has a higher coefficient of thermal expansion than copper (Section 19.3).[2] Consequently, these differences in expansion and contraction between the aluminum and copper wires can cause the connections to loosen. Another factor that contributes to the loosening of copper-aluminum wire connections is creep (Section 11.12); mechanical stresses exist at these wire connections, and aluminum is more susceptible to creep deformation at or near room temperature than copper. This loosening of the connections compromises the electrical wire-to-wire contact, which increases the electrical resistance at the connection and leads to increased heating. Aluminum oxidizes more readily than copper, and this oxide coating further increases the electrical resistance at the connection. Ultimately, a connection may deteriorate to the point that electrical arcing and/or heat build up can ignite any combustible materials in the vicinity of the junction. Inasmuch as most receptacles, switches, and other connec-

[2] Coefficient of thermal expansion values, as well as compositions and other properties of the aluminum and copper alloys used for electrical wiring are presented in Table 17.2.

Table 17.2 Tabulation of Compositions, Electrical Conductivities, and Coefficients of Thermal Expansion for Aluminum and Copper Alloys Used for Electrical Wiring

Alloy Name	*Alloy Designation*	*Composition (wt%)*	*Electrical Conductivity* $[(\Omega\text{-}m)^{-1}]$	*Coefficient of Thermal Expansion (°C)*$^{-1}$
Aluminum (electrical conductor grade)	1350	99.50 Al, 0.10 Si, 0.05 Cu, 0.01 Mn, 0.01 Cr, 0.05 Zn, 0.03 Ga, 0.05 B	3.57×10^7	23.8×10^{-6}
Copper (electrolytic touch pitch)	C11000	99.90 Cu, 0.04 O	5.88×10^7	17.0×10^{-6}

tions are concealed, these materials may smolder or a fire may spread undetected for an extended period of time.

Warning signs that suggest possible connection problems include: warm faceplates on switches or receptacles, the smell of burning plastic in the vicinity of outlets or switches, lights that flicker or burn out quickly, unusual static on radio/television, and circuit breakers that trip for no apparent reason.

There are several options available for making buildings wired with aluminum safe.[3] The most obvious (and also most expensive) is to replace all of the aluminum wires with copper. The next best option is the installation of a crimp connector repair unit at each aluminum-copper connection. With this technique, a piece of copper wire is attached to the existing aluminum wire branch using a specially designed metal sleeve and powered crimping tool; the metal sleeve is called a "COPALUM parallel splice connector." The crimping tool essentially makes a cold weld between the two wires. Finally, the connection is encased in an insulating sleeve. A schematic representation of a COPALUM device is shown in Figure 17.10. Only qualified and specially trained electricians are allowed to install these COPALUM connectors.

Two other less-desirable options are CO/ALR devices and pigtailing. A CO/ALR device is simply a switch or wall receptacle that is designed to be used with aluminum wiring. For pigtailing, a twist-on connecting wire nut is used, which employs a grease that inhibits corrosion while maintaining a high electrical conductivity at the junction.

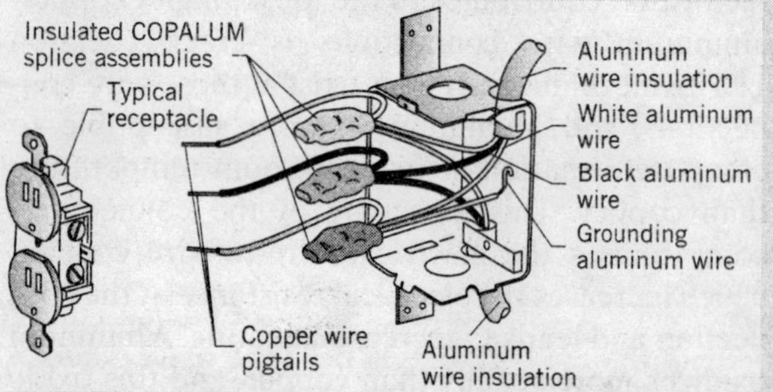

Figure 17.10 Schematic diagram of a COPALUM connector device that is used in aluminum wire electrical circuits. (Reprinted by permission of the US Consumer Product Safety Commission.)

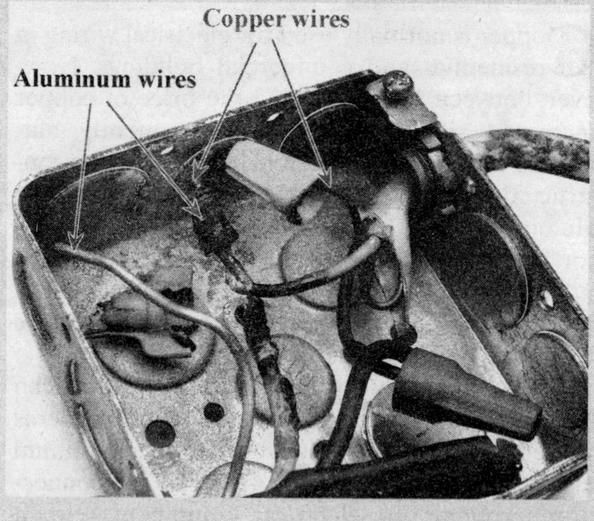

Photograph of two copper wire-aluminum wire junctions (located in a junction box) that experienced excessive heating. The one on the right (within the yellow wire nut) failed completely. (Photograph courtesy of John Fernez.)

[3] A discussion of the various repair options may be downloaded from the following Web site: http://www.cpsc.gov/cpscpub/pubs/516.pdf.

Semiconductivity

The electrical conductivity of the semiconducting materials is not as high as that of the metals; nevertheless, they have some unique electrical characteristics that render them especially useful. The electrical properties of these materials are extremely sensitive to the presence of even minute concentrations of impurities. **Intrinsic semiconductors** are those in which the electrical behavior is based on the electronic structure inherent in the pure material. When the electrical characteristics are dictated by impurity atoms, the semiconductor is said to be **extrinsic.**

17.10 INTRINSIC SEMICONDUCTION

Intrinsic semiconductors are characterized by the electron band structure shown in Figure 17.4*d*: at 0 K, a completely filled valence band, separated from an empty conduction band by a relatively narrow forbidden band gap, generally less than 2 eV. The two elemental semiconductors are silicon (Si) and germanium (Ge), having band gap energies of approximately 1.1 and 0.7 eV, respectively. Both are found in Group IVA of the periodic table (Figure 2.6) and are covalently bonded.[4] In addition, a host of compound semiconducting materials also display intrinsic behavior. One such group is formed between elements of Groups IIIA and VA, for example, gallium arsenide (GaAs) and indium antimonide (InSb); these are frequently called III–V compounds. The compounds composed of elements of Groups IIB and VIA also display semiconducting behavior; these include cadmium sulfide (CdS) and zinc telluride (ZnTe). As the two elements forming these compounds become more widely separated with respect to their relative positions in the periodic table (i.e., the electronegativities become more dissimilar, Figure 2.7), the atomic bonding becomes more ionic and the magnitude of the band gap energy increases—the materials tend to become more insulative. Table 17.3 gives the band gaps for some compound semiconductors.

Concept Check 17.3

Which of ZnS and CdSe will have the larger band gap energy E_g. Cite reason(s) for your choice.

[*The answer may be found in enclosed CD.*]

Concept of a Hole

In intrinsic semiconductors, for every electron excited into the conduction band there is left behind a missing electron in one of the covalent bonds, or in the band scheme, a vacant electron state in the valence band, as shown in Figure 17.6*b*.[5] Under the

[4] The valence bands in silicon and germanium correspond to sp^3 hybrid energy levels for the isolated atom; these hybridized valence bands are completely filled at 0 K.

[5] Holes (in addition to free electrons) are created in semiconductors and insulators when electron transitions occur from filled states in the valence band to empty states in the conduction band (Figure 17.6). In metals, electron transitions normally occur from empty to filled states *within the same band* (Figure 17.5), without the creation of holes.

Table 17.3 Band Gap Energies, Electron and Hole Mobilities, and Intrinsic Electrical Conductivities at Room Temperature for Semiconducting Materials

Material	*Band Gap (eV)*	*Electrical Conductivity* $[(\Omega\text{-}m)^{-1}]$	*Electron Mobility* $(m^2/V\text{-}s)$	*Hole Mobility* $(m^2/V\text{-}s)$
		Elemental		
Si	1.11	4×10^{-4}	0.14	0.05
Ge	0.67	2.2	0.38	0.18
		III–V Compounds		
GaP	2.25	—	0.03	0.015
GaAs	1.42	10^{-6}	0.85	0.04
InSb	0.17	2×10^4	7.7	0.07
		II–VI Compounds		
CdS	2.40	—	0.03	—
ZnTe	2.26	—	0.03	0.01

influence of an electric field, the position of this missing electron within the crystalline lattice may be thought of as moving by the motion of other valence electrons that repeatedly fill in the incomplete bond (Figure 17.11). This process is expedited by treating a missing electron from the valence band as a positively charged particle called a *hole*. A hole is considered to have a charge that is of the same magnitude as that for an electron, but of opposite sign ($+1.6 \times 10^{-19}$ C). Thus, in the presence of an electric field, excited electrons and holes move in opposite directions. Furthermore, in semiconductors both electrons and holes are scattered by lattice imperfections.

Intrinsic Conductivity

Since there are two types of charge carrier (free electrons and holes) in an intrinsic semiconductor, the expression for electrical conduction, Equation 17.8, must be modified to include a term to account for the contribution of the hole current. Therefore, we write

$$\sigma = n|e|\mu_e + p|e|\mu_h \tag{17.13}$$

where p is the number of holes per cubic meter and μ_h is the hole mobility. The magnitude of μ_h is always less than μ_e for semiconductors. For intrinsic semiconductors, every electron promoted across the band gap leaves behind a hole in the valence band; thus,

$$n = p = n_i \tag{17.14}$$

where n_i is known as the *intrinsic carrier concentration*. Furthermore,

$$\begin{aligned} \sigma &= n|e|(\mu_e + \mu_h) = p|e|(\mu_e + \mu_h) \\ &= n_i|e|(\mu_e + \mu_h) \end{aligned} \tag{17.15}$$

The room-temperature intrinsic conductivities and electron and hole mobilities for several semiconducting materials are also presented in Table 17.3.

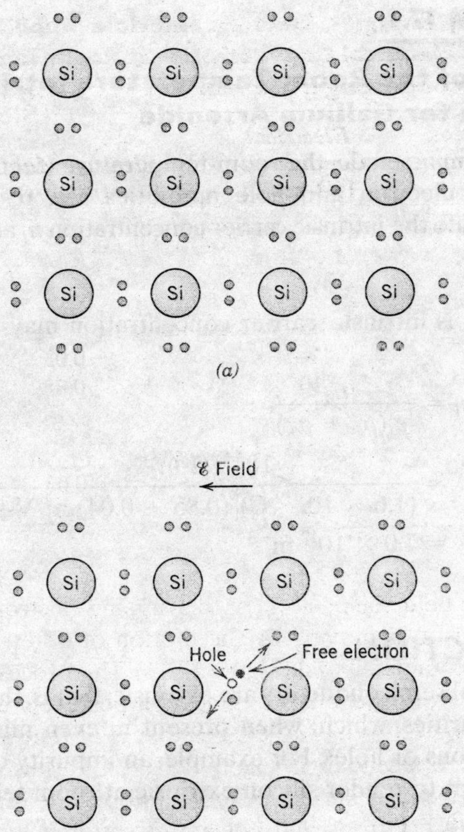

Figure 17.11 Electron bonding model of electrical conduction in intrinsic silicon: (*a*) before excitation, (*b*) and (*c*) after excitation (the subsequent free-electron and hole motions in response to an external electric field).

EXAMPLE PROBLEM 17.1

Computation of the Room-Temperature Intrinsic Carrier Concentration for Gallium Arsenide

For intrinsic gallium arsenide, the room-temperature electrical conductivity is $10^{-6}\,(\Omega\text{-m})^{-1}$; the electron and hole mobilities are, respectively, 0.85 and 0.04 m^2/V-s. Compute the intrinsic carrier concentration n_i at room temperature.

Solution

Since the material is intrinsic, carrier concentration may be computed using Equation 17.15 as

$$n_i = \frac{\sigma}{|e|(\mu_e + \mu_h)}$$

$$= \frac{10^{-6}(\Omega\text{-m})^{-1}}{(1.6 \times 10^{-19}\ \text{C})[(0.85 + 0.04)\text{m}^2/\text{V-s}]}$$

$$= 7.0 \times 10^{12}\ \text{m}^{-3}$$

17.11 EXTRINSIC SEMICONDUCTION

Virtually all commercial semiconductors are extrinsic; that is, the electrical behavior is determined by impurities, which, when present in even minute concentrations, introduce excess electrons or holes. For example, an impurity concentration of one atom in 10^{12} is sufficient to render silicon extrinsic at room temperature.

n-Type Extrinsic Semiconduction

To illustrate how extrinsic semiconduction is accomplished, consider again the elemental semiconductor silicon. An Si atom has four electrons, each of which is covalently bonded with one of four adjacent Si atoms. Now, suppose that an impurity atom with a valence of 5 is added as a substitutional impurity; possibilities would include atoms from the Group VA column of the periodic table (e.g., P, As, and Sb). Only four of five valence electrons of these impurity atoms can participate in the bonding because there are only four possible bonds with neighboring atoms. The extra nonbonding electron is loosely bound to the region around the impurity atom by a weak electrostatic attraction, as illustrated in Figure 17.12*a*. The binding energy of this electron is relatively small (on the order of 0.01 eV); thus, it is easily removed from the impurity atom, in which case it becomes a free or conducting electron (Figures 17.12*b* and 17.12*c*).

The energy state of such an electron may be viewed from the perspective of the electron band model scheme. For each of the loosely bound electrons, there exists a single energy level, or energy state, which is located within the forbidden band gap just below the bottom of the conduction band (Figure 17.13*a*). The electron binding energy corresponds to the energy required to excite the electron from one of these impurity states to a state within the conduction band. Each excitation event (Figure 17.13*b*) supplies or donates a single electron to the conduction band; an impurity of this type is aptly termed a *donor*. Since each donor electron is excited from an impurity level, no corresponding hole is created within the valence band.

At room temperature, the thermal energy available is sufficient to excite large numbers of electrons from **donor states;** in addition, some intrinsic valence–conduction band transitions occur, as in Figure 17.6*b*, but to a negligible degree. Thus, the number

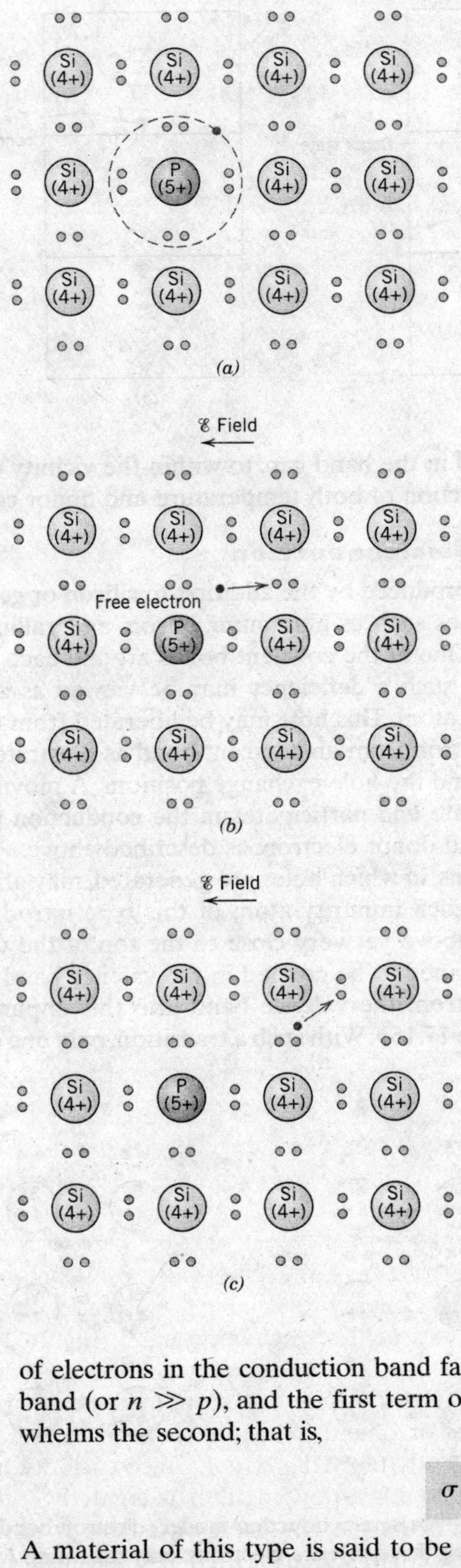

Figure 17.12 Extrinsic *n*-type semiconduction model (electron bonding). (*a*) An impurity atom such as phosphorus, having five valence electrons, may substitute for a silicon atom. This results in an extra bonding electron, which is bound to the impurity atom and orbits it. (*b*) Excitation to form a free electron. (*c*) The motion of this free electron in response to an electric field.

of electrons in the conduction band far exceeds the number of holes in the valence band (or $n \gg p$), and the first term on the right-hand side of Equation 17.13 overwhelms the second; that is,

$$\sigma \cong n|e|\mu_e \tag{17.16}$$

A material of this type is said to be an *n-type* extrinsic semiconductor. The electrons are *majority carriers* by virtue of their density or concentration; holes, on the other hand, are the *minority charge carriers*. For *n*-type semiconductors, the Fermi

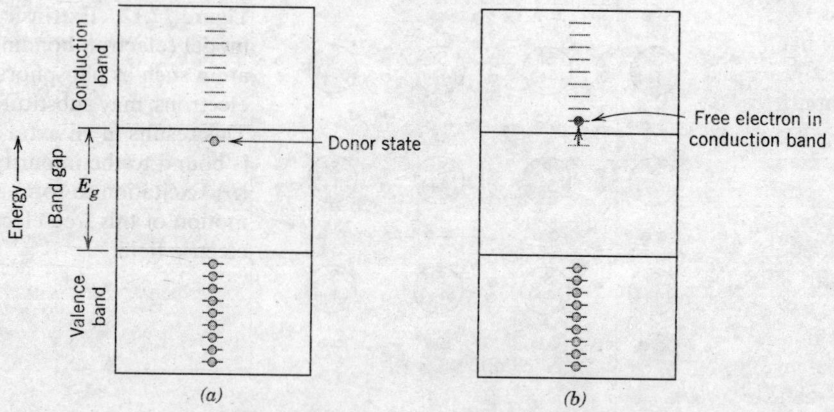

Figure 17.13 (*a*) Electron energy band scheme for a donor impurity level located within the band gap and just below the bottom of the conduction band. (*b*) Excitation from a donor state in which a free electron is generated in the conduction band.

level is shifted upward in the band gap, to within the vicinity of the donor state; its exact position is a function of both temperature and donor concentration.

p-Type Extrinsic Semiconduction

An opposite effect is produced by the addition to silicon or germanium of trivalent substitutional impurities such as aluminum, boron, and gallium from Group IIIA of the periodic table. One of the covalent bonds around each of these atoms is deficient in an electron; such a deficiency may be viewed as a hole that is weakly bound to the impurity atom. This hole may be liberated from the impurity atom by the transfer of an electron from an adjacent bond as illustrated in Figure 17.14. In essence, the electron and the hole exchange positions. A moving hole is considered to be in an excited state and participates in the conduction process, in a manner analogous to an excited donor electron, as described above.

Extrinsic excitations, in which holes are generated, may also be represented using the band model. Each impurity atom of this type introduces an energy level within the band gap, above yet very close to the top of the valence band (Figure 17.15*a*). A hole is imagined to be created in the valence band by the thermal excitation of an electron from the valence band into this impurity electron state, as demonstrated in Figure 17.15*b*. With such a transition, only one carrier is produced—

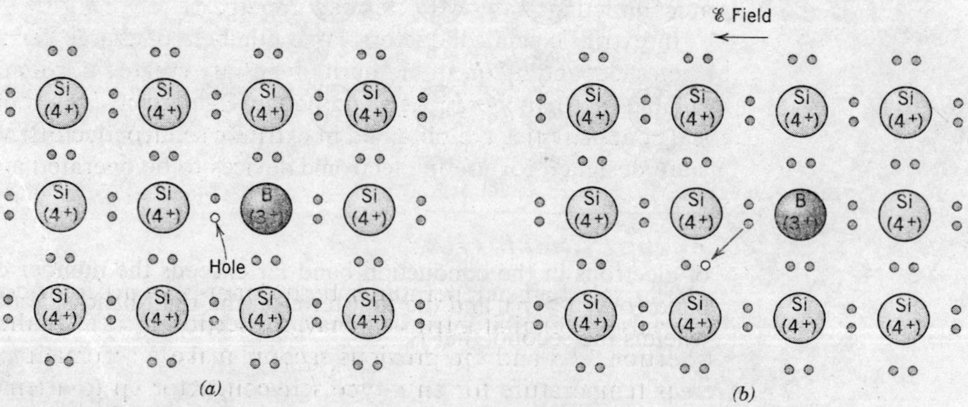

Figure 17.14 Extrinsic *p*-type semiconduction model (electron bonding). (*a*) An impurity atom such as boron, having three valence electrons, may substitute for a silicon atom. This results in a deficiency of one valence electron, or a hole associated with the impurity atom. (*b*) The motion of this hole in response to an electric field.

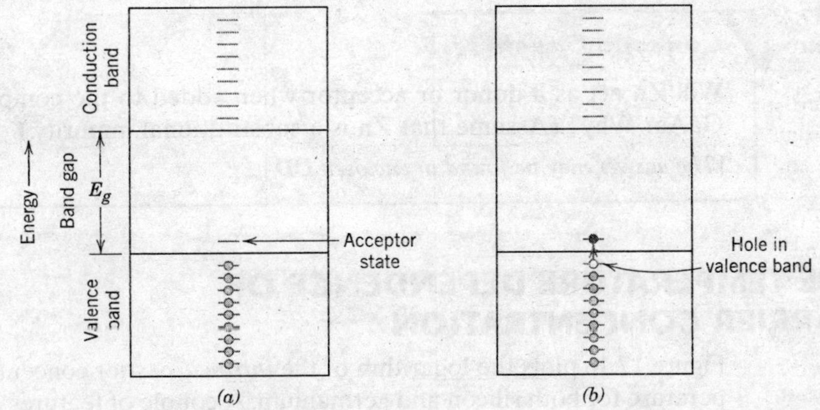

Figure 17.15 (*a*) Energy band scheme for an acceptor impurity level located within the band gap and just above the top of the valence band. (*b*) Excitation of an electron into the acceptor level, leaving behind a hole in the valence band.

a hole in the valence band; a free electron is *not* created in either the impurity level or the conduction band. An impurity of this type is called an *acceptor*, because it is capable of accepting an electron from the valence band, leaving behind a hole. It follows that the energy level within the band gap introduced by this type of impurity is called an **acceptor state.**

For this type of extrinsic conduction, holes are present in much higher concentrations than electrons (i.e., $p \gg n$), and under these circumstances a material is termed *p-type* because positively charged particles are primarily responsible for electrical conduction. Of course, holes are the majority carriers, and electrons are present in minority concentrations. This gives rise to a predominance of the second term on the right-hand side of Equation 17.13, or

$$\sigma \cong p|e|\mu_h \tag{17.17}$$

For *p*-type semiconductors, the Fermi level is positioned within the band gap and near to the acceptor level.

Extrinsic semiconductors (both *n*- and *p*-type) are produced from materials that are initially of extremely high purity, commonly having total impurity contents on the order of 10^{-7} at%. Controlled concentrations of specific donors or acceptors are then intentionally added, using various techniques. Such an alloying process in semiconducting materials is termed **doping.**

In extrinsic semiconductors, large numbers of charge carriers (either electrons or holes, depending on the impurity type) are created at room temperature, by the available thermal energy. As a consequence, relatively high room-temperature electrical conductivities are obtained in extrinsic semiconductors. Most of these materials are designed for use in electronic devices to be operated at ambient conditions.

Concept Check 17.4

At relatively high temperatures, both donor- and acceptor-doped semiconducting materials will exhibit intrinsic behavior (Section 17.12). On the basis of discussions of Section 17.5 and the previous section, make a schematic plot of Fermi energy versus temperature for an *n*-type semiconductor up to a temperature at which it becomes intrinsic. Also note on this plot energy positions corresponding to the top of the valence band and the bottom of the conduction band.

[*The answer may be found in enclosed CD.*]

Concept Check 17.5

Will Zn act as a donor or acceptor when added to the compound semiconductor GaAs? Why? (Assume that Zn is a substitutional impurity.)

[*The answer may be found in enclosed CD.*]

17.12 THE TEMPERATURE DEPENDENCE OF CARRIER CONCENTRATION

Figure 17.16 plots the logarithm of the *intrinsic* carrier concentration n_i versus temperature for both silicon and germanium. A couple of features of this plot are worth noting. First, the concentrations of electrons and holes increase with temperature because, with rising temperature, more thermal energy is available to excite electrons from the valence to the conduction band (per Figure 17.6*b*). In addition, at all temperatures, carrier concentration in Ge is greater than for Si. This effect is due to germanium's smaller band gap (0.67 versus 1.11 eV, Table 17.3); thus, for Ge, at any given temperature more electrons will be excited across its band gap.

On the other hand, the carrier concentration–temperature behavior for an *extrinsic* semiconductor is much different. For example, electron concentration versus temperature for silicon that has been doped with 10^{21} m^{-3} phosphorus atoms is plotted in Figure 17.17. [For comparison, the dashed curve shown is for intrinsic Si (taken from Figure 17.16)].[6] Noted on the extrinsic curve are three regions. At

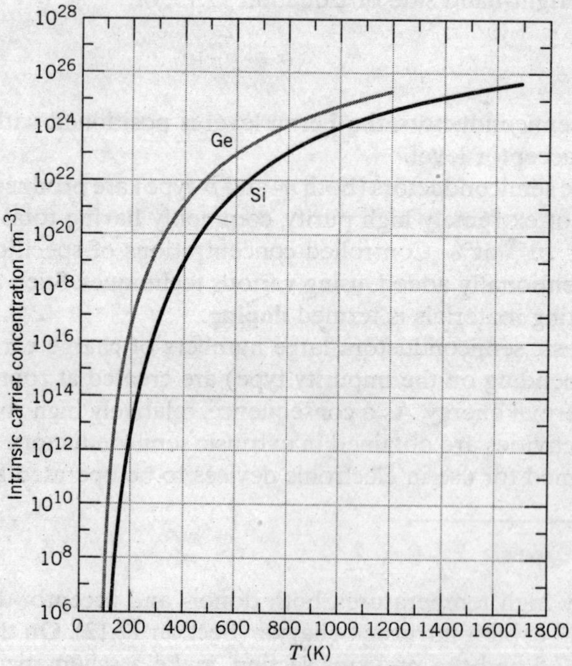

Figure 17.16 Intrinsic carrier concentration (logarithmic scale) as a function of temperature for germanium and silicon. (From C. D. Thurmond, "The Standard Thermodynamic Functions for the Formation of Electrons and Holes in Ge, Si, GaAs, and GaP," *Journal of The Electrochemical Society,* **122,** [8], 1139 (1975). Reprinted by permission of The Electrochemical Society, Inc.)

[6] Note that the shapes of the "Si" curve of Figure 17.16 and the "n_i" curve of Figure 17.17 are not the same even though identical parameters are plotted in both cases. This disparity is due to the scaling of the plot axes: temperature (i.e., horizontal) axes for both plots are scaled linearly; however, the carrier concentration axis of Figure 17.16 is logarithmic, whereas this same axis of Figure 17.17 is linear.

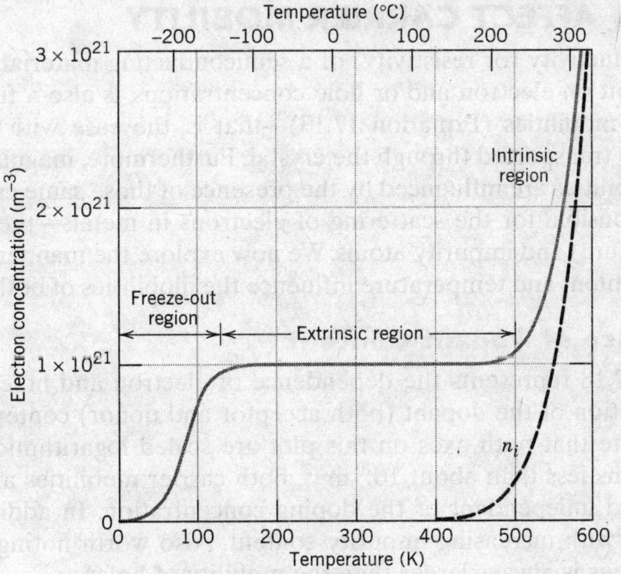

Figure 17.17 Electron concentration versus temperature for silicon (*n*-type) that has been doped with 10^{21} m^{-3} of a donor impurity, and for intrinsic silicon (dashed line). Freeze-out, extrinsic, and intrinsic temperature regimes are noted on this plot. (From S. M. Sze, *Semiconductor Devices, Physics and Technology*. Copyright © 1985 by Bell Telephone Laboratories, Inc. Reprinted by permission of John Wiley & Sons, Inc.)

intermediate temperatures (between approximately 150 K and 450 K) the material is *n*-type (inasmuch as P is a donor impurity), and electron concentration is constant; this is termed the "extrinsic-temperature region".[7] Electrons in the conduction band are excited from the phosphorus donor state (per Figure 17.13*b*), and since the electron concentration is approximately equal to the P content (10^{21} m^{-3}), virtually all of the phosphorus atoms have been ionized (i.e., have donated electrons). Also, intrinsic excitations across the band gap are insignificant in relation to these extrinsic donor excitations. The range of temperatures over which this extrinsic region exists will depend on impurity concentration; furthermore, most solid-state devices are designed to operate within this temperature range.

At low temperatures, below about 100 K (Figure 17.17), electron concentration drops dramatically with decreasing temperature, and approaches zero at 0 K. Over these temperatures, the thermal energy is insufficient to excite electrons from the P donor level into the conduction band. This is termed the "freeze-out temperature region" inasmuch as charged carriers (i.e., electrons) are "frozen" to the dopant atoms.

Finally, at the high end of the temperature scale of Figure 17.17, electron concentration increases above the P content, and asymptotically approaches the intrinsic curve as temperature increases. This is termed the "intrinsic temperature region" since at these high temperatures the semiconductor becomes intrinsic; that is, charge carrier concentrations resulting from electron excitations across the band gap first become equal to and then completely overwhelm the donor carrier contribution with rising temperature.

Concept Check 17.6

On the basis of Figure 17.17, as dopant level is increased would you expect the temperature at which a semiconductor becomes intrinsic to increase, to remain essentially the same, or to decrease? Why?

[*The answer may be found in enclosed CD.*]

[7] For donor-doped semiconductors, this region is sometimes called the *saturation* region; for acceptor-doped materials, it is often termed the *exhaustion* region.

17.13 FACTORS THAT AFFECT CARRIER MOBILITY

The conductivity (or resistivity) of a semiconducting material, in addition to being dependent on electron and/or hole concentrations, is also a function of the charge carriers' mobilities (Equation 17.13)—that is, the ease with which electrons and holes are transported through the crystal. Furthermore, magnitudes of electron and hole mobilities are influenced by the presence of those same crystalline defects that are responsible for the scattering of electrons in metals—thermal vibrations (i.e., temperature) and impurity atoms. We now explore the manner in which dopant impurity content and temperature influence the mobilities of both electrons and holes.

Influence of Dopant Content

Figure 17.18 represents the dependence of electron and hole mobilities in silicon as a function of the dopant (both acceptor and donor) content, at room temperature—note that both axes on this plot are scaled logarithmically. At dopant concentrations less than about 10^{20} m^{-3}, both carrier mobilities are at their maximum levels and independent of the doping concentration. In addition, both mobilities decrease with increasing impurity content. Also worth noting is that the mobility of electrons is always larger than the mobility of holes.

Influence of Temperature

The temperature dependences of electron and hole mobilities for silicon are presented in Figures 17.19*a* and 17.19*b*, respectively. Curves for several impurity dopant contents are shown for both carrier types; furthermore, both sets of axes are scaled logarithmically. From these plots, note that, for dopant concentrations of 10^{24} m^{-3} and below, both electron and hole mobilities decrease in magnitude with rising temperature; again, this effect is due to enhanced thermal scattering of the carriers. For both electrons and holes, and dopant levels less than 10^{20} m^{-3}, the dependence of mobility on temperature is independent of acceptor/donor concentration (i.e., is represented by a single curve). Also, for concentrations greater than 10^{20} m^{-3}, curves in both plots are shifted to progressively lower mobility values with increasing dopant level. These latter two effects are consistent with the data presented in Figure 17.18.

These previous treatments have discussed the influence of temperature and dopant content on both carrier concentration and carrier mobility. Once values of n, p, μ_e,

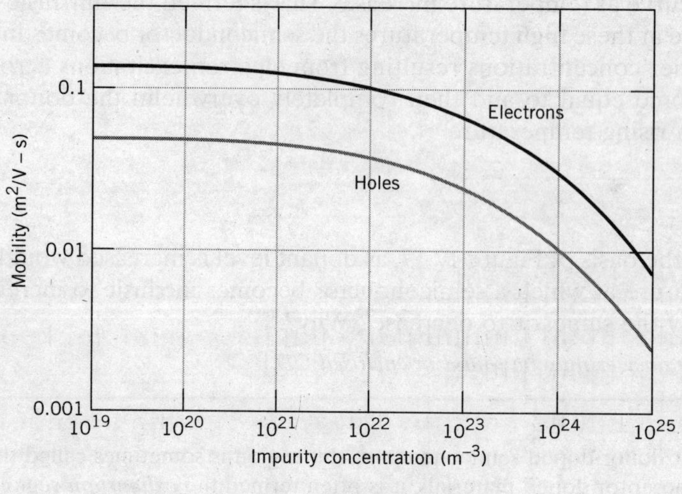

Figure 17.18 For silicon, dependence of room-temperature electron and hole mobilities (logarithmic scale) on dopant concentration (logarithmic scale). (Adapted from W. W. Gärtner, "Temperature Dependence of Junction Transistor Parameters," *Proc. of the IRE,* **45,** 667, 1957. Copyright © 1957 IRE now IEEE.)

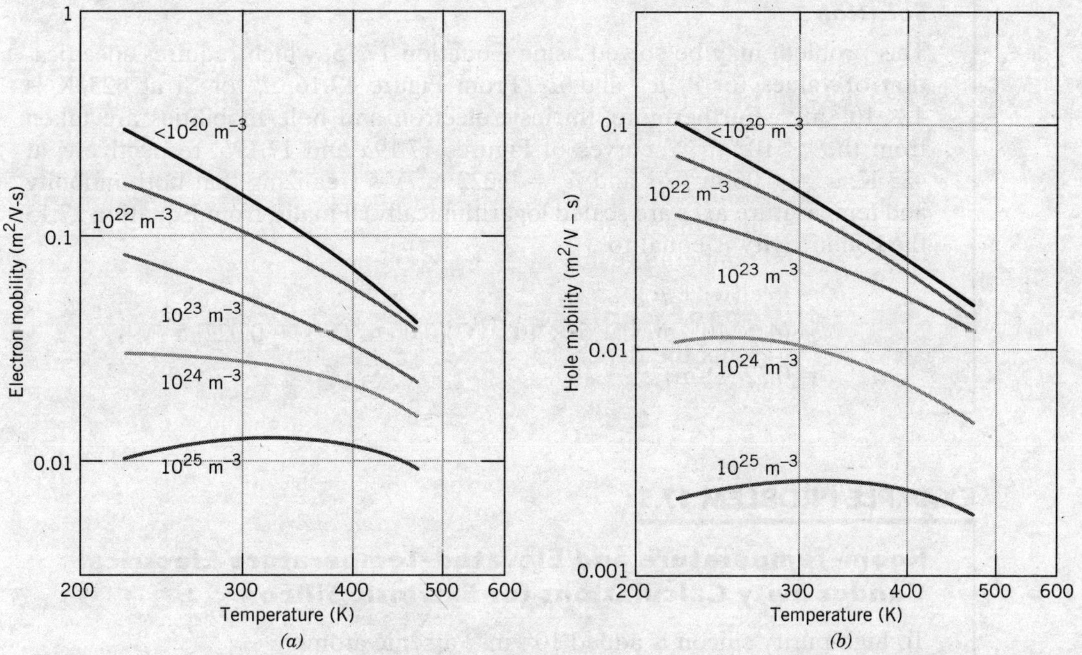

Figure 17.19 Temperature dependence of (*a*) electron and (*b*) hole mobilities for silicon that has been doped with various donor and acceptor concentrations. Both sets of axes are scaled logarithmically. (From W. W. Gärtner, "Temperature Dependence of Junction Transistor Parameters," *Proc. of the IRE,* **45,** 667, 1957. Copyright © 1957 IRE now IEEE.)

and μ_h have been determined for a specific donor/acceptor concentration and at a specified temperature (using Figures 17.16, 17.17, 17.18, and 17.19), computation of σ is possible using Equation 17.15, 17.16, or 17.17.

Concept Check 17.7

On the basis of the electron concentration-versus-temperature curve for *n*-type silicon shown in Figure 17.17 and the dependence of the logarithm of electron mobility on temperature (Figure 17.19*a*), make a schematic plot of logarithm electrical conductivity versus temperature for silicon that has been doped with 10^{21} m^{-3} of a donor impurity. Now briefly explain the shape of this curve. Recall that Equation 17.16 expresses the dependence of conductivity on electron concentration and electron mobility.

[*The answer may be found in enclosed CD.*]

EXAMPLE PROBLEM 17.2

Electrical Conductivity Determination for Intrinsic Silicon at 150°C

Calculate the electrical conductivity of intrinsic silicon at 150°C (423 K).

Solution

This problem may be solved using Equation 17.15, which requires specification of values for n_i, μ_e, and μ_h. From Figure 17.16, n_i for Si at 423 K is $4 \times 10^{19}\ \text{m}^{-3}$. Furthermore, intrinsic electron and hole mobilities are taken from the "$<10^{20}\ \text{m}^{-3}$" curves of Figures 17.19*a* and 17.19*b*, respectively; at 423 K, $\mu_e = 0.06\ \text{m}^2/\text{V-s}$ and $\mu_h = 0.022\ \text{m}^2/\text{V-s}$ (realizing that both mobility and temperature axes are scaled logarithmically). Finally, from Equation 17.15 the conductivity is equal to

$$\begin{aligned}\sigma &= n_i|e|(\mu_e + \mu_h)\\ &= (4 \times 10^{19}\ \text{m}^{-3})(1.6 \times 10^{-19}\ \text{C})(0.06\ \text{m}^2/\text{V-s} + 0.022\ \text{m}^2/\text{V-s})\\ &= 0.52\ (\Omega\text{-m})^{-1}\end{aligned}$$

EXAMPLE PROBLEM 17.3

Room-Temperature and Elevated-Temperature Electrical Conductivity Calculations for Extrinsic Silicon

To high-purity silicon is added $10^{23}\ \text{m}^{-3}$ arsenic atoms.

(a) Is this material *n*-type or *p*-type?

(b) Calculate the room-temperature electrical conductivity of this material.

(c) Compute the conductivity at 100°C (373 K).

Solution

(a) Arsenic is a Group VA element (Figure 2.6) and, therefore, will act as a donor in silicon, which means that this material is *n*-type.

(b) At room temperature (298 K) we are within the extrinsic temperature region of Figure 17.17, which means that virtually all of the arsenic atoms have donated electrons (i.e., $n = 10^{23}\ \text{m}^{-3}$). Furthermore, inasmuch as this material is extrinsic *n*-type, conductivity may be computed using Equation 17.16. Consequently, it is necessary for us to determine the electron mobility for a donor concentration of $10^{23}\ \text{m}^{-3}$. We can do this using Figure 17.18: at $10^{23}\ \text{m}^{-3}$, $\mu_e = 0.07\ \text{m}^2/\text{V-s}$ (remember that both axes of Figure 17.18 are scaled logarithmically). Thus, the conductivity is just

$$\begin{aligned}\sigma &= n|e|\mu_e\\ &= (10^{23}\ \text{m}^{-3})(1.6 \times 10^{-19}\ \text{C})(0.07\ \text{m}^2/\text{V-s})\\ &= 1120\ (\Omega\text{-m})^{-1}\end{aligned}$$

(c) To solve for the conductivity of this material at 373 K, we again use Equation 17.16 with the electron mobility at this temperature. From the $10^{23}\ \text{m}^{-3}$ curve of Figure 17.19*a*, at 373 K, $\mu_e = 0.04\ \text{m}^2/\text{V-s}$, which leads to

$$\begin{aligned}\sigma &= n|e|\mu_e\\ &= (10^{23}\ \text{m}^{-3})(1.6 \times 10^{-19}\ \text{C})(0.04\ \text{m}^2/\text{V-s})\\ &= 640(\Omega\text{-m})^{-1}\end{aligned}$$

DESIGN EXAMPLE 17.1

Acceptor Impurity Doping in Silicon

An extrinsic *p*-type silicon material is desired having a room-temperature conductivity of 50 $(\Omega\text{-m})^{-1}$. Specify an acceptor impurity type that may be used as well as its concentration in atom percent to yield these electrical characteristics.

Solution

First, the elements that, when added to silicon, render it *p*-type, lie one group to the left of silicon in the periodic table. These include the group IIIA elements (Figure 2.6): boron, aluminum, gallium, and indium.

Since this material is extrinsic and *p*-type (i.e., $p \gg n$), the electrical conductivity is a function of both hole concentration and hole mobility according to Equation 17.17. In addition, it will be assumed that at room temperature all of the acceptor dopant atoms have accepted electrons to form holes (i.e., that we are in the "extrinsic region" of Figure 17.17), which is to say that the number of holes is approximately equal to the number of acceptor impurities N_a.

This problem is complicated by the fact that μ_h is dependent on impurity content per Figure 17.18. Consequently, one approach to solving this problem is trial and error: assume an impurity concentration, and then compute the conductivity using this value and the corresponding hole mobility from its curve of Figure 17.18. Then on the basis of this result, repeat the process assuming another impurity concentration.

For example, let us select an N_a value (i.e., a p value) of 10^{22} m^{-3}. At this concentration the hole mobility is approximately 0.04 m^2/V-s (Figure 17.18); these values yield a conductivity of

$$\begin{aligned}\sigma &= p|e|\mu_h = (10^{22}\ \text{m}^{-3})(1.6 \times 10^{-19}\ \text{C})(0.04\ \text{m}^2/\text{V-s}) \\ &= 64\ (\Omega\text{-m})^{-1}\end{aligned}$$

which is a little on the high side. Decreasing the impurity content an order of magnitude to 10^{21} m^{-3} results in only a slight increase of μ_h to about 0.045 m^2/V-s (Figure 17.18); thus, the resulting conductivity is

$$\begin{aligned}\sigma &= (10^{21}\ \text{m}^{-3})(1.6 \times 10^{-19}\ \text{C})(0.045\ \text{m}^2/\text{V-s}) \\ &= 7.2\ (\Omega\text{-m})^{-1}\end{aligned}$$

With some fine-tuning of these numbers, a conductivity of 50 $(\Omega\text{-m})^{-1}$ is achieved when $N_a = p \cong 8 \times 10^{21}$ m^{-3}; at this N_a value, μ_h remains approximately 0.04 m^2/V-s.

It next becomes necessary to calculate the concentration of acceptor impurity in atom percent. This computation first requires the determination of the number of silicon atoms per cubic meter, N_{Si}, using Equation 5.2, which is as follows:

$$\begin{aligned}N_{\text{Si}} &= \frac{N_{\text{A}}\rho_{\text{Si}}}{A_{\text{Si}}} \\ &= \frac{(6.023 \times 10^{23}\ \text{atoms/mol})(2.33\ \text{g/cm}^3)(10^6\ \text{cm}^3/\text{m}^3)}{28.09\ \text{g/mol}} \\ &= 5 \times 10^{28}\ \text{m}^{-3}\end{aligned}$$

The concentration of acceptor impurities in atom percent (C'_a) is just the ratio of N_a and $N_a + N_{Si}$ multiplied by 100 as

$$C'_a = \frac{N_a}{N_a + N_{Si}} \times 100$$

$$= \frac{8 \times 10^{21}\ \text{m}^{-3}}{(8 \times 10^{21}\ \text{m}^{-3}) + (5 \times 10^{28}\ \text{m}^{-3})} \times 100 = 1.60 \times 10^{-5}$$

Thus, a silicon material having a room-temperature p-type electrical conductivity of 50 $(\Omega\text{-m})^{-1}$ must contain 1.60×10^{-5} at% boron, aluminum, gallium, or indium.

17.14 THE HALL EFFECT

For some material, it is on occasion desired to determine its majority charge carrier type, concentration, and mobility. Such determinations are not possible from a simple electrical conductivity measurement; a **Hall effect** experiment must also be conducted. This Hall effect is a result of the phenomenon whereby a magnetic field applied perpendicular to the direction of motion of a charged particle exerts a force on the particle perpendicular to both the magnetic field and the particle motion directions.

In demonstrating the Hall effect, consider the specimen geometry shown in Figure 17.20, a parallelepiped specimen having one corner situated at the origin of a Cartesian coordinate system. In response to an externally applied electric field, the electrons and/or holes move in the x direction and give rise to a current I_x. When a magnetic field is imposed in the positive z direction (denoted as B_z), the resulting force brought to bear on the charge carriers will cause them to be deflected in the y direction—holes (positively charged carriers) to the right specimen face and electrons (negatively charged carriers) to the left face, as indicated in the figure. Thus, a voltage, termed the *Hall voltage* V_H, will be established in the

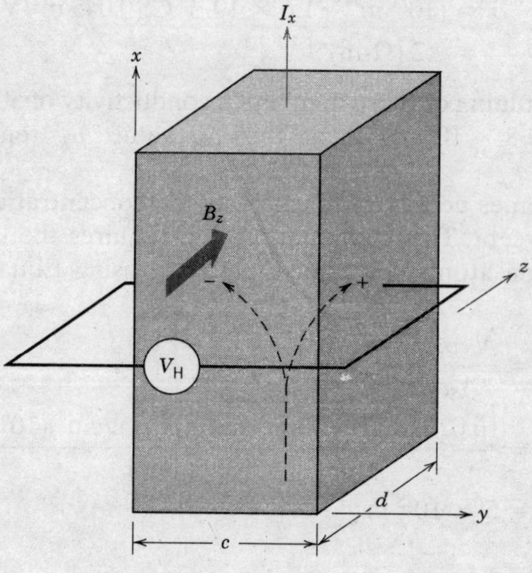

Figure 17.20 Schematic demonstration of the Hall effect. Positive and/or negative charge carriers that are part of the I_x current are deflected by the magnetic field B_z and give rise to the Hall voltage, V_H.

y direction. The magnitude of V_H will depend on I_x, B_z, and the specimen thickness d as follows:

$$V_H = \frac{R_H I_x B_z}{d} \tag{17.18}$$

In this expression R_H is termed the *Hall coefficient,* which is a constant for a given material. For metals, wherein conduction is by electrons, R_H is negative and equal to

$$R_H = \frac{1}{n|e|} \tag{17.19}$$

Thus, n may be determined, inasmuch as R_H may be measured using Equation 17.18 and the magnitude of e, the charge on an electron, is known.

Furthermore, from Equation 17.8, the electron mobility μ_e is just

$$\mu_e = \frac{\sigma}{n|e|} \tag{17.20a}$$

or, using Equation 17.19,

$$\mu_e = |R_H|\sigma \tag{17.20b}$$

Thus, the magnitude of μ_e may also be determined if the conductivity σ has also been measured.

For semiconducting materials, the determination of majority carrier type and computation of carrier concentration and mobility are more complicated and will not be discussed here.

EXAMPLE PROBLEM 17.4

Hall Voltage Computation

The electrical conductivity and electron mobility for aluminum are 3.8×10^7 $(\Omega\text{-m})^{-1}$ and 0.0012 $\text{m}^2/\text{V-s}$, respectively. Calculate the Hall voltage for an aluminum specimen that is 15 mm thick for a current of 25 A and a magnetic field of 0.6 tesla (imposed in a direction perpendicular to the current).

Solution

The Hall voltage V_H may be determined using Equation 17.18. However, it first becomes necessary to compute the Hall coefficient (R_H) from Equation 17.20b as

$$R_H = -\frac{\mu_e}{\sigma}$$

$$= -\frac{0.0012 \text{ m}^2/\text{V-s}}{3.8 \times 10^7 \,(\Omega\text{-m})^{-1}} = -3.16 \times 10^{-11} \text{ V-m/A-tesla}$$

Now, employment of Equation 17.18 leads to

$$V_H = \frac{R_H I_x B_z}{d}$$

$$= \frac{(-3.16 \times 10^{-11}\ \text{V-m/A-tesla})(25\ \text{A})(0.6\ \text{tesla})}{15 \times 10^{-3}\ \text{m}}$$

$$= -3.16 \times 10^{-8}\ \text{V}$$

17.15 SEMICONDUCTOR DEVICES

The unique electrical properties of semiconductors permit their use in devices to perform specific electronic functions. Diodes and transistors, which have replaced old-fashioned vacuum tubes, are two familiar examples. Advantages of semiconductor devices (sometimes termed solid-state devices) include small size, low power consumption, and no warmup time. Vast numbers of extremely small circuits, each consisting of numerous electronic devices, may be incorporated onto a small silicon chip. The invention of semiconductor devices, which has given rise to miniaturized circuitry, is responsible for the advent and extremely rapid growth of a host of new industries in the past few years.

The *p–n* Rectifying Junction

A rectifier, or **diode,** is an electronic device that allows the current to flow in one direction only; for example, a rectifier transforms an alternating current into direct current. Before the advent of the *p–n* junction semiconductor rectifier, this operation was carried out using the vacuum tube diode. The *p–n* **rectifying junction** is constructed from a single piece of semiconductor that is doped so as to be *n*-type on one side and *p*-type on the other (Figure 17.21*a*). If pieces of *n*- and *p*-type materials are joined together, a poor rectifier results, since the presence of a surface between the two sections renders the device very inefficient. Also, single crystals of semiconducting materials must be used in all devices because electronic phenomena that are deleterious to operation occur at grain boundaries.

Before the application of any potential across the *p–n* specimen, holes will be the dominant carriers on the *p*-side, and electrons will predominate in the *n*-region, as illustrated in Figure 17.21*a*. An external electric potential may be established across a *p–n* junction with two different polarities. When a battery is used, the positive terminal may be connected to the *p*-side and the negative terminal to the *n*-side; this is referred to as a **forward bias.** The opposite polarity (minus to *p* and plus to *n*) is termed **reverse bias.**

The response of the charge carriers to the application of a forward-biased potential is demonstrated in Figure 17.21*b*. The holes on the *p*-side and the electrons on the *n*-side are attracted to the junction. As electrons and holes encounter one another near the junction, they continuously recombine and annihilate one another, according to

$$\text{electron} + \text{hole} \longrightarrow \text{energy} \tag{17.21}$$

Thus for this bias, large numbers of charge carriers flow across the semiconductor and to the junction, as evidenced by an appreciable current and a low resistivity. The current–voltage characteristics for forward bias are shown on the right-hand half of Figure 17.22.

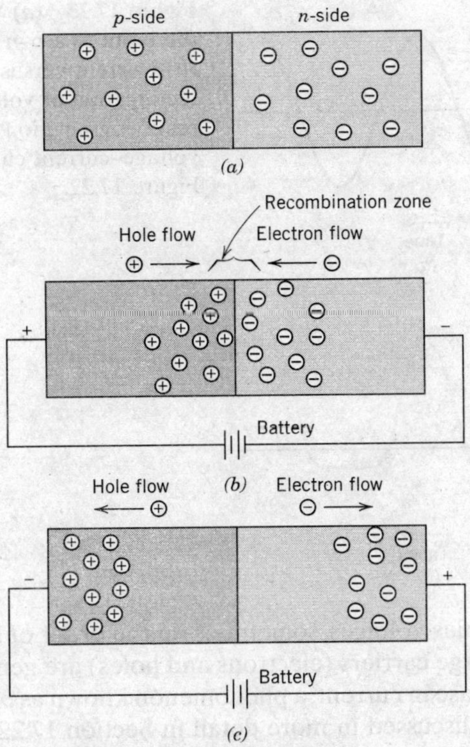

Figure 17.21 For a p–n rectifying junction, representations of electron and hole distributions for (a) no electrical potential, (b) forward bias, and (c) reverse bias.

For reverse bias (Figure 17.21c), both holes and electrons, as majority carriers, are rapidly drawn away from the junction; this separation of positive and negative charges (or polarization) leaves the junction region relatively free of mobile charge carriers. Recombination will not occur to any appreciable extent, so that the junction is now highly insulative. Figure 17.22 also illustrates the current–voltage behavior for reverse bias.

The rectification process in terms of input voltage and output current is demonstrated in Figure 17.23. Whereas voltage varies sinusoidally with time (Figure 17.23a), maximum current flow for reverse bias voltage I_R is extremely small in comparison to that for forward bias I_F (Figure 17.23b). Furthermore, correspondence between I_F and I_R and the imposed maximum voltage ($\pm V_0$) is noted in Figure 17.22.

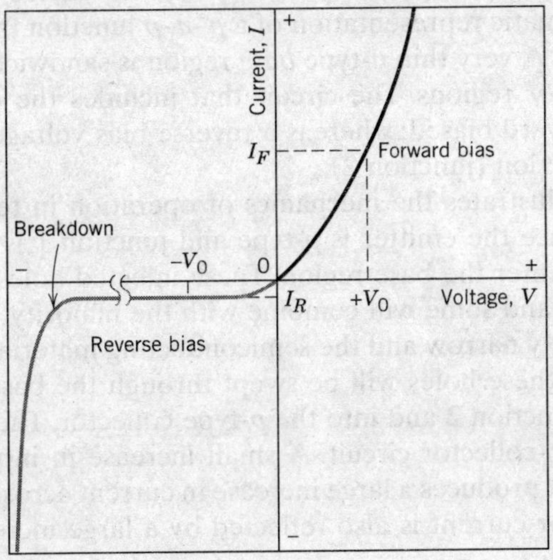

Figure 17.22 The current–voltage characteristics of a p–n junction for forward and reverse biases. The phenomenon of breakdown is also shown.

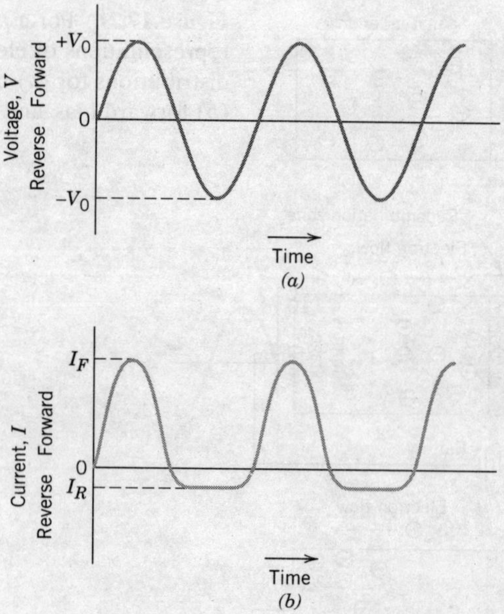

Figure 17.23 (*a*) Voltage versus time for the input to a *p–n* rectifying junction. (*b*) Current versus time, showing rectification of voltage in (*a*) by a *p–n* rectifying junction having the voltage–current characteristics shown in Figure 17.22.

At high reverse bias voltages, sometimes on the order of several hundred volts, large numbers of charge carriers (electrons and holes) are generated. This gives rise to a very abrupt increase in current, a phenomenon known as *breakdown,* also shown in Figure 17.22, and discussed in more detail in Section 17.22.

The Transistor

Transistors, which are extremely important semiconducting devices in today's microelectronic circuitry, are capable of two primary types of function. First, they can perform the same operation as their vacuum tube precursor, the triode; that is, they can amplify an electrical signal. In addition, they serve as switching devices in computers for the processing and storage of information. The two major types are the **junction** (or bimodal) **transistor** and the *metal-oxide-semiconductor field-effect transistor* (abbreviated as **MOSFET**).

Junction Transistors

The junction transistor is composed of two *p–n* junctions arranged back to back in either the *n–p–n* or the *p–n–p* configuration; the latter variety is discussed here. Figure 17.24 is a schematic representation of a *p–n–p* junction transistor along with its attendant circuitry. A very thin *n*-type *base* region is sandwiched in between *p*-type *emitter* and *collector* regions. The circuit that includes the emitter–base junction (junction 1) is forward biased, whereas a reverse bias voltage is applied across the base–collector junction (junction 2).

Figure 17.25 illustrates the mechanics of operation in terms of the motion of charge carriers. Since the emitter is *p*-type and junction 1 is forward biased, large numbers of holes enter the base region. These injected holes are minority carriers in the *n*-type base, and some will combine with the majority electrons. However, if the base is extremely narrow and the semiconducting materials have been properly prepared, most of these holes will be swept through the base without recombination, then across junction 2 and into the *p*-type collector. The holes now become a part of the emitter–collector circuit. A small increase in input voltage within the emitter–base circuit produces a large increase in current across junction 2. This large increase in collector current is also reflected by a large increase in voltage across

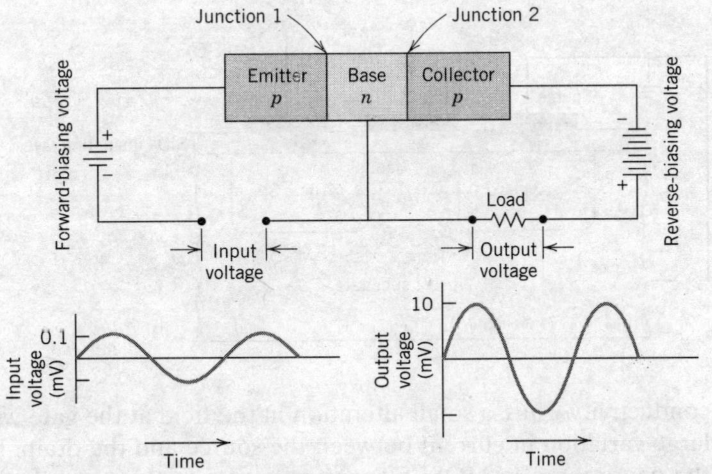

Figure 17.24 Schematic diagram of a *p–n–p* junction transistor and its associated circuitry, including input and output voltage–time characteristics showing voltage amplification. (Adapted from A. G. Guy, *Essentials of Materials Science,* McGraw-Hill Book Company, New York, 1976.)

the load resistor, which is also shown in the circuit (Figure 17.24). Thus, a voltage signal that passes through a junction transistor experiences amplification; this effect is also illustrated in Figure 17.24 by the two voltage–time plots.

Similar reasoning applies to the operation of an *n–p–n* transistor, except that electrons instead of holes are injected across the base and into the collector.

The MOSFET

One variety of MOSFET[8] consists of two small islands of *p*-type semiconductor that are created within a substrate of *n*-type silicon, as shown in cross section in Figure 17.26; the islands are joined by a narrow *p*-type channel. Appropriate metal connections (source and drain) are made to these islands; an insulating layer of silicon dioxide is formed by the surface oxidation of the silicon. A final connector (gate) is then fashioned onto the surface of this insulating layer.

The conductivity of the channel is varied by the presence of an electric field imposed on the gate. For example, imposition of a positive field on the gate will drive charge carriers (in this case holes) out of the channel, thereby reducing the electrical

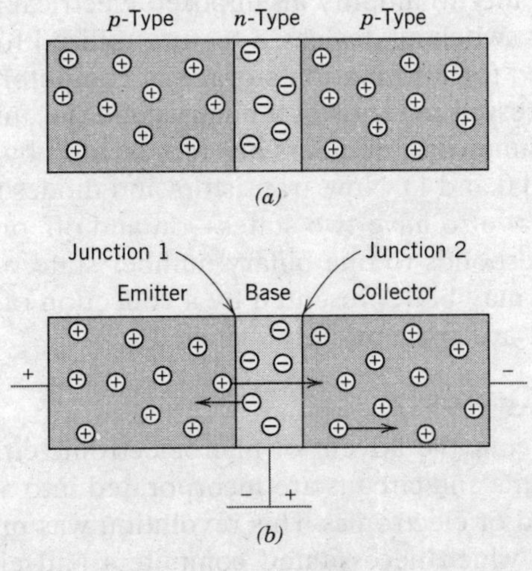

Figure 17.25 For a junction transistor (*p–n–p* type), the distributions and directions of electron and hole motion (*a*) when no potential is applied and (*b*) with appropriate bias for voltage amplification.

[8] The MOSFET described here is a *depletion-mode* p-*type*. A *depletion-mode* n-*type* is also possible, wherein the *n*- and *p*-regions of Figure 17.26 are reversed.

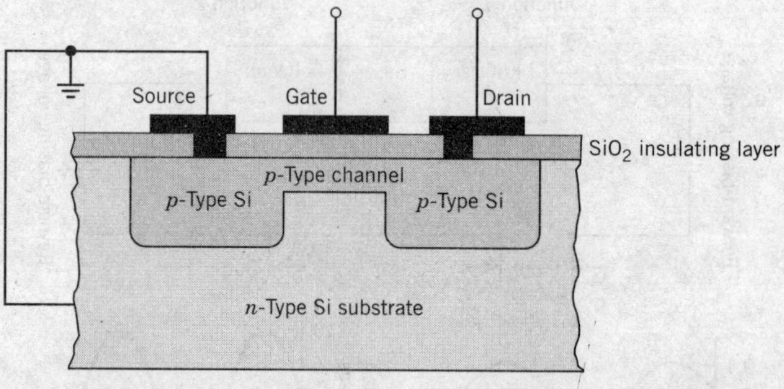

Figure 17.26 Schematic cross-sectional view of a MOSFET transistor.

conductivity. Thus, a small alteration in the field at the gate will produce a relatively large variation in current between the source and the drain. In some respects, then, the operation of a MOSFET is very similar to that described for the junction transistor. The primary difference is that the gate current is exceedingly small in comparison to the base current of a junction transistor. MOSFETs are, therefore, used where the signal sources to be amplified cannot sustain an appreciable current.

Another important difference between MOSFETs and junction transistors is that, although majority carriers dominate in the functioning of MOSFETs (i.e., holes for the depletion-mode *p*-type MOSFET of Figure 17.26), minority carriers do play a role with junction transistors (i.e., injected holes in the *n*-type base region, Figure 17.25).

Concept Check 17.8

Would you expect increasing temperature to influence the operation of *p–n* junction rectifiers and transistors? Explain.

[*The answer may be found in enclosed CD.*]

Semiconductors in Computers

In addition to their ability to amplify an imposed electrical signal, transistors and diodes may also act as switching devices, a feature utilized for arithmetic and logical operations, and also for information storage in computers. Computer numbers and functions are expressed in terms of a binary code (i.e., numbers written to the base 2). Within this framework, numbers are represented by a series of two states (sometimes designated 0 and 1). Now, transistors and diodes within a digital circuit operate as switches that also have two states—on and off, or conducting and nonconducting; "off" corresponds to one binary number state, and "on" to the other. Thus, a single number may be represented by a collection of circuit elements containing transistors that are appropriately switched.

Microelectronic Circuitry

During the past few years, the advent of microelectronic circuitry, where millions of electronic components and circuits are incorporated into a very small space, has revolutionized the field of electronics. This revolution was precipitated, in part, by aerospace technology, which necessitated computers and electronic devices that were small and had low power requirements. As a result of refinement in processing and fabrication techniques, there has been an astonishing depreciation in the cost of integrated circuitry. Consequently, at the time of this writing, personal computers are affordable to large segments of the population in many countries. Also, the use of **integrated circuits** has become infused into many other facets of our lives—calculators, communications, watches, industrial production and control, and all phases of the electronics industry.

Inexpensive microelectronic circuits are mass produced by using some very ingenious fabrication techniques. The process begins with the growth of relatively large cylindrical single crystals of high-purity silicon from which thin circular wafers are cut. Many microelectronic or integrated circuits, sometimes called "chips," are prepared on a single wafer; a photograph of one such wafer containing numerous chips is shown in Figure 21.27. A chip is rectangular, typically on the order of 6 mm ($\frac{1}{4}$ in.) on a side and contains millions of circuit elements: diodes, transistors, resistors, and capacitors. One such microprocessor chip is shown in its entirety in Figure 21.29*b*; also shown are the numerous electrical leads that are used to connect this chip to its

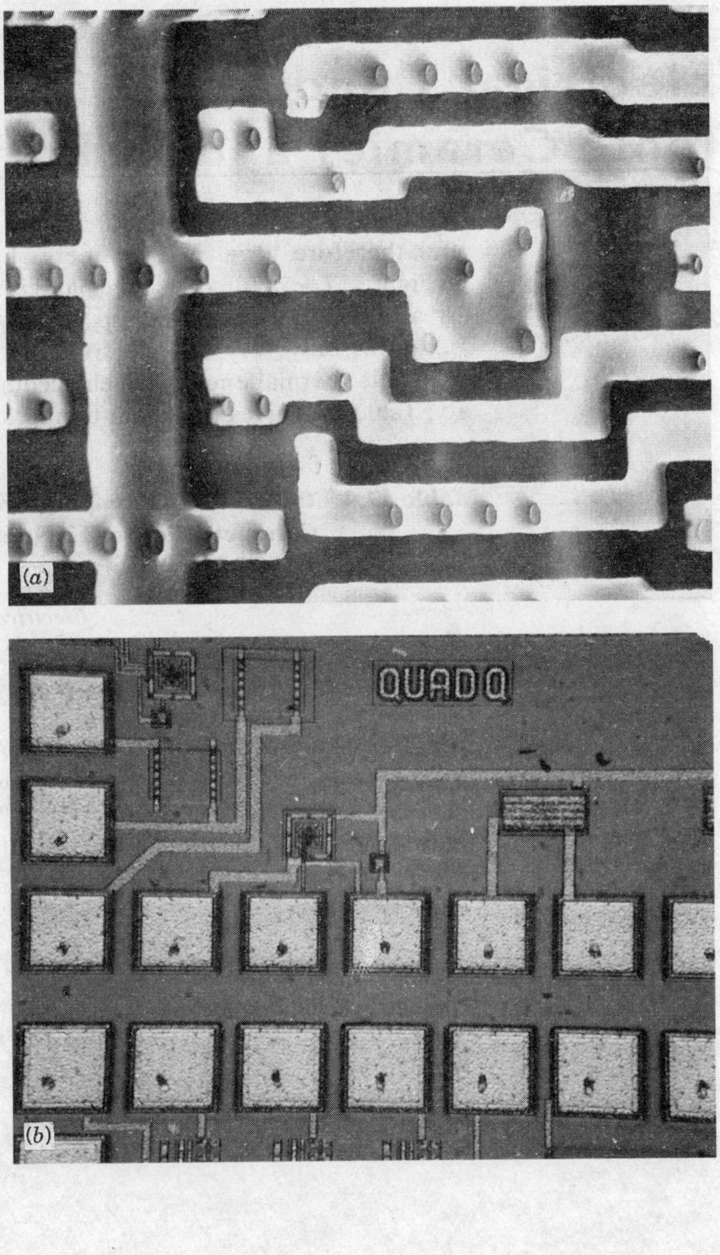

Figure 17.27 (*a*) Scanning electron micrograph showing a small region of a microprocessing chip (a 0.5-MB selected address device). The narrow, white regions are an aluminum top layer that serves as the wiring for this device. The gray regions are diffusion-layer doped silicon that have been coated with an interlayer dielectric. Approximately 2000×. (*b*) An optical photomicrograph showing a portion of a circuit that is used to test microprocessing chips. The narrow, light regions are aluminum connectors, and the white, square areas are test pads (semiconductor devices); test circuits (also composed of semiconductor devices) appear in the upper left-hand corner of the photograph. Approximately 50×. (Both photographs courtesy of National Semiconductor Corporation.)

leadframe, which in turn is bonded to a printed circuit board. Enlarged photographs of microprocessor chips at different magnifications are presented in Figures 17.27*a* and 17.27*b*; these micrographs reveal the intricacy of integrated circuits. At this time, microprocessor chips approaching one billion transistors are being produced, and this number doubles about every 18 months.

Microelectronic circuits consist of many layers that lie within or are stacked on top of the silicon wafer in a precisely detailed pattern. Using photolithographic techniques, for each layer, very small elements are masked in accordance with a microscopic pattern. Circuit elements are constructed by the selective introduction of specific materials (by diffusion or ion implantation) into unmasked regions to create localized n-type, p-type, high-resistivity, or conductive areas. This procedure is repeated layer by layer until the total integrated circuit has been fabricated, as illustrated in the MOSFET schematic (Figure 17.26). Elements of integrated circuits are shown in Figure 17.27 and in the chapter-opening photographs for this chapter.

Electrical Conduction in Ionic Ceramics and in Polymers

Most polymers and ionic ceramics are insulating materials at room temperature and, therefore, have electron energy band structures similar to that represented in Figure 17.4*c*; a filled valence band is separated from an empty conduction band by a relatively large band gap, usually greater than 2 eV. Thus, at normal temperatures only very few electrons may be excited across the band gap by the available thermal energy, which accounts for the very small values of conductivity; Table 17.4 gives the room-temperature electrical conductivities of several of

Table 17.4 Typical Room-Temperature Electrical Conductivities for 13 Nonmetallic Materials

Material	*Electrical Conductivity* $[(\Omega\text{-}m)^{-1}]$
Graphite	3×10^4–2×10^5
Ceramics	
Concrete (dry)	10^{-9}
Soda–lime glass	10^{-10}–10^{-11}
Porcelain	10^{-10}–10^{-12}
Borosilicate glass	$\sim 10^{-13}$
Aluminum oxide	$<10^{-13}$
Fused silica	$<10^{-18}$
Polymers	
Phenol-formaldehyde	10^{-9}–10^{-10}
Poly(methyl methacrylate)	$<10^{-12}$
Nylon 6,6	10^{-12}–10^{-13}
Polystyrene	$<10^{-14}$
Polyethylene	10^{-15}–10^{-17}
Polytetrafluoroethylene	$<10^{-17}$

these materials. (The electrical resistivities of a large number of ceramic and polymeric materials are provided in Table B.9, Appendix B.) Of course, many materials are utilized on the basis of their ability to insulate, and thus a high electrical resistivity is desirable. With rising temperature, insulating materials experience an increase in electrical conductivity, which may ultimately be greater than that for semiconductors.

17.16 CONDUCTION IN IONIC MATERIALS

Both cations and anions in ionic materials possess an electric charge and, as a consequence, are capable of migration or diffusion when an electric field is present. Thus an electric current will result from the net movement of these charged ions, which will be present in addition to current due to any electron motion. Of course, anion and cation migrations will be in opposite directions. The total conductivity of an ionic material σ_{total} is thus equal to the sum of both electronic and ionic contributions, as follows:

$$\sigma_{\text{total}} = \sigma_{\text{electronic}} + \sigma_{\text{ionic}} \tag{17.22}$$

Either contribution may predominate depending on the material, its purity, and, of course, temperature.

A mobility μ_I may be associated with each of the ionic species as follows:

$$\mu_I = \frac{n_I e D_I}{kT} \tag{17.23}$$

where n_I and D_I represent, respectively, the valence and diffusion coefficient of a particular ion; e, k, and T denote the same parameters as explained earlier in the chapter. Thus, the ionic contribution to the total conductivity increases with increasing temperature, as does the electronic component. However, in spite of the two conductivity contributions, most ionic materials remain insulative, even at elevated temperatures.

17.17 ELECTRICAL PROPERTIES OF POLYMERS

Most polymeric materials are poor conductors of electricity (Table 17.4) because of the unavailability of large numbers of free electrons to participate in the conduction process. The mechanism of electrical conduction in these materials is not well understood, but it is felt that conduction in polymers of high purity is electronic.

Conducting Polymers

Within the past several years, polymeric materials have been synthesized that have electrical conductivities on par with metallic conductors; they are appropriately termed *conducting polymers*. Conductivities as high as 1.5×10^7 $(\Omega\text{-m})^{-1}$ have been achieved in these materials; on a volume basis, this value corresponds to one-fourth of the conductivity of copper, or twice its conductivity on the basis of weight.

This phenomenon is observed in a dozen or so polymers, including polyacetylene, polyparaphenylene, polypyrrole, and polyaniline. Each of these polymers contains a system of alternating single and double bonds and/or aromatic units in the polymer chain. For example, the chain structure of polyacetylene is as follows:

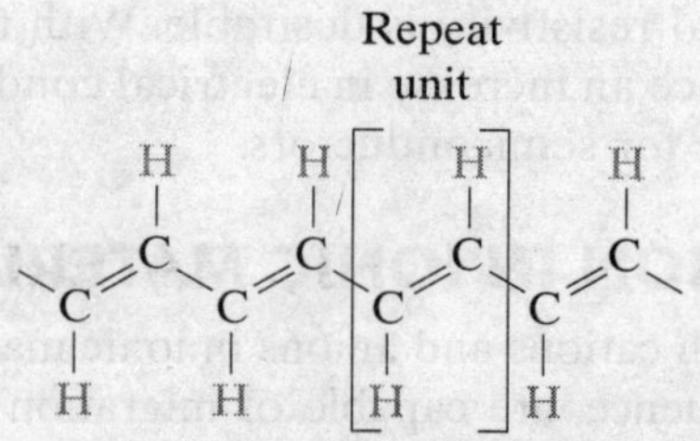

The valence electrons associated with the alternating single and double chain-bonds are delocalized, which means they are shared amongst the backbone atoms in the polymer chain—similar to the way that electrons in a partially filled band for a metal are shared by the ion cores. In addition, the band structure of a conductive polymer is characteristic of that for an electrical insulator (Figure 17.4*c*)—viz. at 0 K, a filled valence band separated from an empty conduction band by a forbidden energy band gap. These polymers become conductive when doped with appropriate impurities such as AsF_5, SbF_5, or iodine. As with semiconductors, conducting polymers may be made either *n*-type (i.e., free-electron dominant) or *p*-type (i.e., hole dominant) depending on the dopant. However, unlike semiconductors, the dopant atoms or molecules do not substitute for or replace any of the polymer atoms.

The mechanism by which large numbers of free electrons and holes are generated in these conducting polymers is complex and not well understood. In very simple terms, it appears that the dopant atoms lead to the formation of new energy bands that overlap the valence and conduction bands of the intrinsic polymer, giving rise to a partially filled band, and the production at room temperature of a high concentration of free electrons or holes. Orienting the polymer chains, either mechanically (Section 14.7) or magnetically, during synthesis results in a highly anisotropic material having a maximum conductivity along the direction of orientation.

These conducting polymers have the potential to be used in a host of applications inasmuch as they have low densities, are highly flexible, and are easy to produce. Rechargeable batteries and fuel cells are currently being manufactured that employ polymer electrodes. In many respects these batteries are superior to their metallic counterparts. Other possible applications include wiring in aircraft and aerospace components, antistatic coatings for clothing, electromagnetic screening materials, and electronic devices (e.g., transistors and diodes).

Dielectric Behavior

A **dielectric** material is one that is electrically insulating (nonmetallic) and exhibits or may be made to exhibit an **electric dipole** structure; that is, there is a separation of positive and negative electrically charged entities on a molecular or atomic level. This concept of an electric dipole was introduced in Section 2.7. As a result of dipole interactions with electric fields, dielectric materials are utilized in capacitors.

17.18 CAPACITANCE

When a voltage is applied across a capacitor, one plate becomes positively charged, the other negatively charged, with the corresponding electric field directed from the positive to the negative. The **capacitance** C is related to the quantity of charge stored on either plate Q by[9]

$$C = \frac{Q}{V} \tag{17.24}$$

where V is the voltage applied across the capacitor. The units of capacitance are coulombs per volt, or farads (F).

Now, consider a parallel-plate capacitor with a vacuum in the region between the plates (Figure 17.28*a*). The capacitance may be computed from the relationship

$$C = \epsilon_0 \frac{A}{l} \tag{17.25}$$

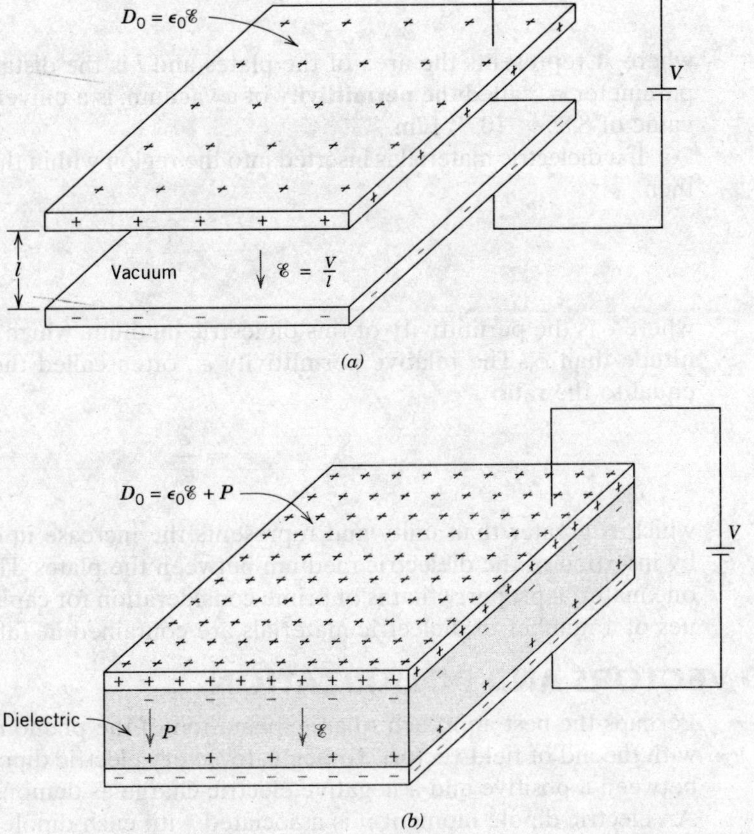

Figure 17.28 A parallel-plate capacitor (*a*) when a vacuum is present and (*b*) when a dielectric material is present. (From K. M. Ralls, T. H. Courtney, and J. Wulff, *Introduction to Materials Science and Engineering*. Copyright © 1976 by John Wiley & Sons, Inc. Reprinted by permission of John Wiley & Sons, Inc.)

[9] By convention, the uppercase "C" is used to represent both capacitance and the unit of charge, coulomb. To minimize confusion in this discussion, the capacitance designation will be italicized, as C.

Table 17.5 Dielectric Constants and Strengths for Some Dielectric Materials

Material	Dielectric Constant 60 Hz	Dielectric Constant 1 MHz	Dielectric Strength (V/mil)[a]
Ceramics			
Titanate ceramics	—	15–10,000	50–300
Mica	—	5.4–8.7	1000–2000
Steatite ($MgO–SiO_2$)	—	5.5–7.5	200–350
Soda–lime glass	6.9	6.9	250
Porcelain	6.0	6.0	40–400
Fused silica	4.0	3.8	250
Polymers			
Phenol-formaldehyde	5.3	4.8	300–400
Nylon 6,6	4.0	3.6	400
Polystyrene	2.6	2.6	500–700
Polyethylene	2.3	2.3	450–500
Polytetrafluoroethylene	2.1	2.1	400–500

[a] One mil = 0.001 in. These values of dielectric strength are average ones, the magnitude being dependent on specimen thickness and geometry, as well as the rate of application and duration of the applied electric field.

where A represents the area of the plates and l is the distance between them. The parameter ϵ_0, called the **permittivity** of a vacuum, is a universal constant having the value of 8.85×10^{-12} F/m.

If a dielectric material is inserted into the region within the plates (Figure 17.28*b*), then

$$C = \epsilon \frac{A}{l} \tag{17.26}$$

where ϵ is the permittivity of this dielectric medium, which will be greater in magnitude than ϵ_0. The relative permittivity ϵ_r, often called the **dielectric constant,** is equal to the ratio

$$\epsilon_r = \frac{\epsilon}{\epsilon_0} \tag{17.27}$$

which is greater than unity and represents the increase in charge storing capacity by insertion of the dielectric medium between the plates. The dielectric constant is one material property that is of prime consideration for capacitor design. The ϵ_r values of a number of dielectric materials are contained in Table 17.5.

17.19 FIELD VECTORS AND POLARIZATION

Perhaps the best approach to an explanation of the phenomenon of capacitance is with the aid of field vectors. To begin, for every electric dipole there is a separation between a positive and a negative electric charge as demonstrated in Figure 17.29. An electric dipole moment p is associated with each dipole as follows:

$$p = qd \tag{17.28}$$

where q is the magnitude of each dipole charge and d is the distance of separation between them. In reality, a dipole moment is a vector that is directed from

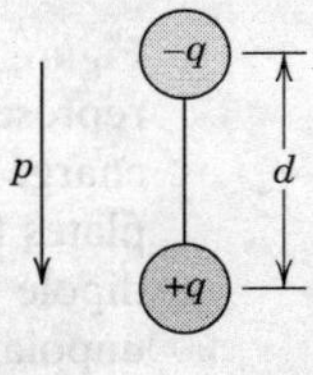

Figure 17.29 Schematic representation of an electric dipole generated by two electric charges (of magnitude q) separated by the distance d; the associated polarization vector p is also shown.

the negative to the positive charge, as indicated in Figure 17.29. In the presence of an electric field $\mathscr{E}$, which is also a vector quantity, a force (or torque) will come to bear on an electric dipole to orient it with the applied field; this phenomenon is illustrated in Figure 17.30. The process of dipole alignment is termed **polarization.**

Again, returning to the capacitor, the surface charge density D, or quantity of charge per unit area of capacitor plate (C/m^2), is proportional to the electric field. When a vacuum is present, then

$$D_0 = \epsilon_0 \mathscr{E} \tag{17.29}$$

the constant of proportionality being ϵ_0. Furthermore, an analogous expression exists for the dielectric case; that is,

$$D = \epsilon \mathscr{E} \tag{17.30}$$

Sometimes, D is also called the **dielectric displacement.**

The increase in capacitance, or dielectric constant, can be explained using a simplified model of polarization within a dielectric material. Consider the capacitor in Figure 17.31*a*, the vacuum situation, wherein a charge of $+Q_0$ is stored on the top plate and $-Q_0$ on the bottom one. When a dielectric is introduced and an electric field is applied, the entire solid within the plates becomes polarized (Figure 17.31*c*). As a result of this polarization, there is a net accumulation of negative charge of magnitude $-Q'$ at the dielectric surface near the positively charged plate and, in a similar manner, a surplus of $+Q'$ charge at the surface adjacent to the negative plate. For the region of dielectric removed from these surfaces, polarization effects are not important. Thus, if each plate and its adjacent dielectric surface are considered to be a single entity, the induced charge from the dielectric ($+Q'$ or $-Q'$) may be thought of as nullifying some of the charge that originally existed on the plate for a vacuum ($-Q_0$ or $+Q_0$). The voltage imposed across the plates is maintained at the vacuum value by increasing the charge at the negative (or bottom) plate by an amount $-Q'$, and the top plate by $+Q'$. Electrons are caused to flow from the positive to the negative plate by the external voltage source such that the proper voltage is reestablished. And so the charge on each plate is now $Q_0 + Q'$, having been increased by an amount Q'.

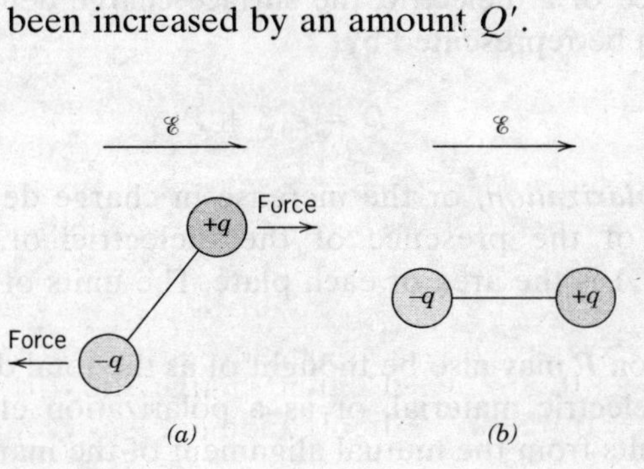

Figure 17.30 (*a*) Imposed forces (and torque) acting on a dipole by an electric field. (*b*) Final dipole alignment with the field.

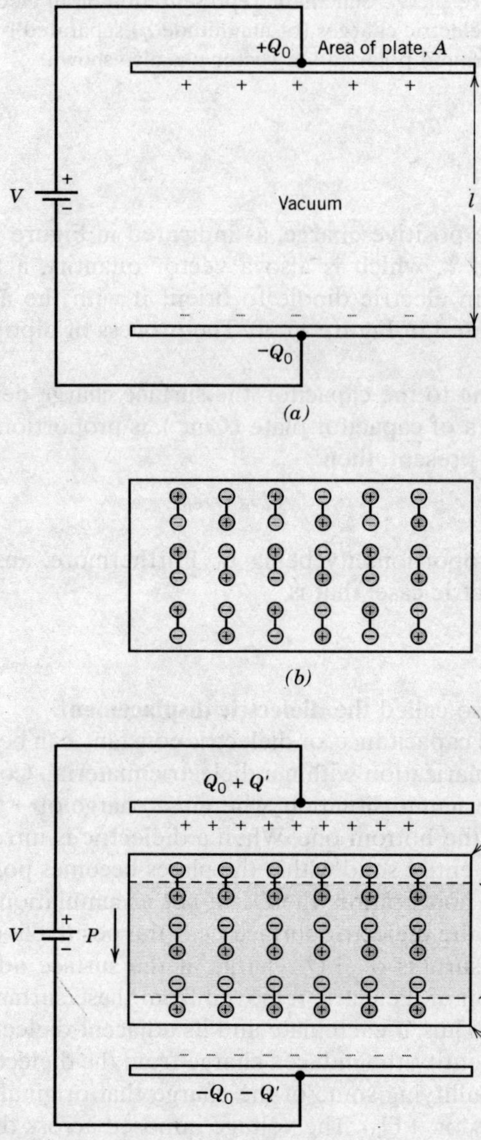

Figure 17.31 Schematic representations of (*a*) the charge stored on capacitor plates for a vacuum, (*b*) the dipole arrangement in an unpolarized dielectric, and (*c*) the increased charge storing capacity resulting from the polarization of a dielectric material. (Adapted from A. G. Guy, *Essentials of Materials Science,* McGraw-Hill Book Company, New York, 1976.)

In the presence of a dielectric, the surface charge density on the plates of a capacitor may also be represented by

$$D = \epsilon_0 \mathscr{E} + P \tag{17.31}$$

where P is the *polarization,* or the increase in charge density above that for a vacuum because of the presence of the dielectric; or, from Figure 17.31*c*, $P = Q'/A$, where A is the area of each plate. The units of P are the same as for D (C/m^2).

The polarization P may also be thought of as the total dipole moment per unit volume of the dielectric material, or as a polarization electric field within the dielectric that results from the mutual alignment of the many atomic or molecular

Table 17.6 Primary and Derived Units for Various Electrical Parameters and Field Vectors

Quantity	*Symbol*	*SI Units* *Derived*	*Primary*
Electric potential	V	volt	kg-m^2/s^2-C
Electric current	I	ampere	C/s
Electric field strength	$\mathscr{E}$	volt/meter	kg-m/s^2-C
Resistance	R	ohm	kg-m^2/s-C^2
Resistivity	ρ	ohm-meter	kg-m^3/s-C^2
Conductivity	σ	(ohm-meter)$^{-1}$	s-C^2/kg-m^3
Electric charge	Q	coulomb	C
Capacitance	C	farad	s^2-C^2/kg-m^2
Permittivity	ϵ	farad/meter	s^{2}C^2/kg-m^3
Dielectric constant	ϵ_r	ratio	ratio
Dielectric displacement	D	farad-volt/m^2	C/m^2
Electric polarization	P	farad-volt/m^2	C/m^2

dipoles with the externally applied field $\mathscr{E}$. For many dielectric materials, P is proportional to $\mathscr{E}$ through the relationship

$$P = \epsilon_0(\epsilon_r - 1)\mathscr{E} \tag{17.32}$$

in which case ϵ_r is independent of the magnitude of the electric field.

Table 17.6 lists the several dielectric parameters along with their units.

EXAMPLE PROBLEM 17.5

Computations of Capacitor Properties

Consider a parallel-plate capacitor having an area of 6.45×10^{-4} m^2 and a plate separation of 2×10^{-3} m across which a potential of 10 V is applied. If a material having a dielectric constant of 6.0 is positioned within the region between the plates, compute

(a) The capacitance.

(b) The magnitude of the charge stored on each plate.

(c) The dielectric displacement D.

(d) The polarization.

Solution

(a) Capacitance is calculated using Equation 17.26; however, the permittivity ϵ of the dielectric medium must first be determined from Equation 17.27 as follows:

$$\epsilon = \epsilon_r\epsilon_0 = (6.0)(8.85 \times 10^{-12}\ \text{F/m})$$
$$= 5.31 \times 10^{-11}\ \text{F/m}$$

Thus, the capacitance is

$$C = \epsilon\frac{A}{l} = (5.31 \times 10^{-11}\ \text{F/m})\left(\frac{6.45 \times 10^{-4}\ \text{m}^2}{2 \times 10^{-3}\ \text{m}}\right)$$
$$= 1.71 \times 10^{-11}\ \text{F}$$

(b) Since the capacitance has been determined, the charge stored may be computed using Equation 17.24, according to

$$Q = CV = (1.71 \times 10^{-11}\,\text{F})(10\,\text{V}) = 1.71 \times 10^{-10}\,\text{C}$$

(c) The dielectric displacement is calculated from Equation 17.30, which yields

$$D = \epsilon\mathscr{E} = \epsilon\frac{V}{l} = \frac{(5.31 \times 10^{-11}\,\text{F/m})(10\,\text{V})}{2 \times 10^{-3}\,\text{m}}$$
$$= 2.66 \times 10^{-7}\,\text{C/m}^2$$

(d) Using Equation 17.31, the polarization may be determined as follows:

$$P = D - \epsilon_0\mathscr{E} = D - \epsilon_0\frac{V}{l}$$
$$= 2.66 \times 10^{-7}\,\text{C/m}^2 - \frac{(8.85 \times 10^{-12}\,\text{F/m})(10\,\text{V})}{2 \times 10^{-3}\,\text{m}}$$
$$= 2.22 \times 10^{-7}\,\text{C/m}^2$$

17.20 TYPES OF POLARIZATION

Again, polarization is the alignment of permanent or induced atomic or molecular dipole moments with an externally applied electric field. There are three types or sources of polarization: electronic, ionic, and orientation. Dielectric materials ordinarily exhibit at least one of these polarization types depending on the material and also the manner of the external field application.

Electronic Polarization

Electronic polarization may be induced to one degree or another in all atoms. It results from a displacement of the center of the negatively charged electron cloud relative to the positive nucleus of an atom by the electric field (Figure 17.32*a*). This polarization type is found in all dielectric materials and, of course, exists only while an electric field is present.

Ionic Polarization

Ionic polarization occurs only in materials that are ionic. An applied field acts to displace cations in one direction and anions in the opposite direction, which gives rise to a net dipole moment. This phenomenon is illustrated in Figure 17.32*b*. The magnitude of the dipole moment for each ion pair p_i is equal to the product of the relative displacement d_i and the charge on each ion, or

$$p_i = qd_i \tag{17.33}$$

Orientation Polarization

The third type, **orientation polarization,** is found only in substances that possess permanent dipole moments. Polarization results from a rotation of the permanent moments into the direction of the applied field, as represented in Figure 17.32*c*. This alignment tendency is counteracted by the thermal vibrations of the atoms, such that polarization decreases with increasing temperature.

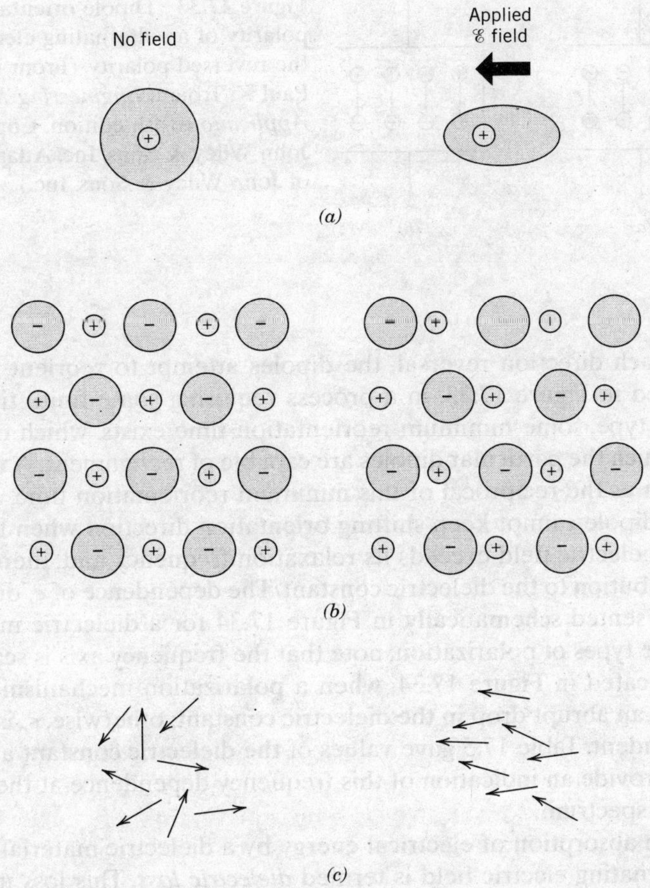

Figure 17.32 (*a*) Electronic polarization that results from the distortion of an atomic electron cloud by an electric field. (*b*) Ionic polarization that results from the relative displacements of electrically charged ions in response to an electric field. (*c*) Response of permanent electric dipoles (arrows) to an applied electric field, producing orientation polarization. (From O. H. Wyatt and D. Dew-Hughes, *Metals, Ceramics and Polymers,* Cambridge University Press, 1974.)

The total polarization P of a substance is equal to the sum of the electronic, ionic, and orientation polarizations (P_e, P_i, and P_o, respectively), or

$$P = P_e + P_i + P_o \tag{17.34}$$

It is possible for one or more of these contributions to the total polarization to be either absent or negligible in magnitude relative to the others. For example, ionic polarization will not exist in covalently bonded materials in which no ions are present.

Concept Check 17.9

For solid lead titanate ($PbTiO_3$) what kind(s) of polarization is (are) possible? Why? *Note:* lead titanate has the same crystal structure as barium titanate (Figure 17.35).

[*The answer may be found in enclosed CD.*]

17.21 FREQUENCY DEPENDENCE OF THE DIELECTRIC CONSTANT

In many practical situations the current is alternating (ac); that is, an applied voltage or electric field changes direction with time, as indicated in Figure 17.23*a*. Now consider a dielectric material that is subject to polarization by an ac electric field.

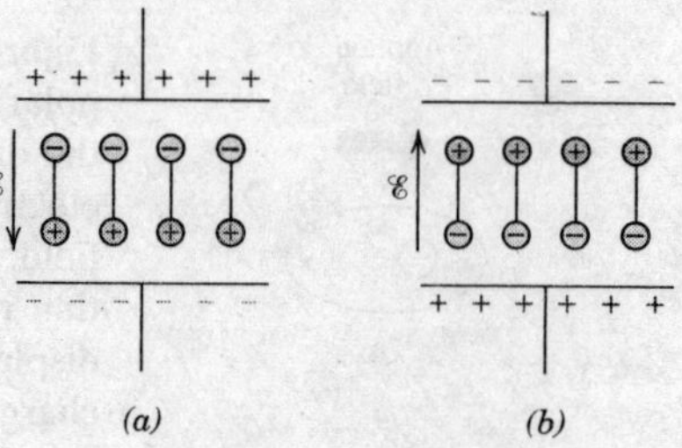

Figure 17.33 Dipole orientations for (*a*) one polarity of an alternating electric field and (*b*) for the reversed polarity. (From Richard A. Flinn and Paul K. Trojan, *Engineering Materials and Their Applications,* 4th edition. Copyright © 1990 by John Wiley & Sons, Inc. Adapted by permission of John Wiley & Sons, Inc.)

With each direction reversal, the dipoles attempt to reorient with the field, as illustrated in Figure 17.33, in a process requiring some finite time. For each polarization type, some minimum reorientation time exists, which depends on the ease with which the particular dipoles are capable of realignment. A **relaxation frequency** is taken as the reciprocal of this minimum reorientation time.

A dipole cannot keep shifting orientation direction when the frequency of the applied electric field exceeds its relaxation frequency and, therefore, will not make a contribution to the dielectric constant. The dependence of ϵ_r on the field frequency is represented schematically in Figure 17.34 for a dielectric medium that exhibits all three types of polarization; note that the frequency axis is scaled logarithmically. As indicated in Figure 17.34, when a polarization mechanism ceases to function, there is an abrupt drop in the dielectric constant; otherwise, ϵ_r is virtually frequency independent. Table 17.5 gave values of the dielectric constant at 60 Hz and 1 MHz; these provide an indication of this frequency dependence at the low end of the frequency spectrum.

The absorption of electrical energy by a dielectric material that is subjected to an alternating electric field is termed *dielectric loss*. This loss may be important at electric field frequencies in the vicinity of the relaxation frequency for each of the operative dipole types for a specific material. A low dielectric loss is desired at the frequency of utilization.

Figure 17.34 Variation of dielectric constant with frequency of an alternating electric field. Electronic, ionic, and orientation polarization contributions to the dielectric constant are indicated.

17.22 DIELECTRIC STRENGTH

When very high electric fields are applied across dielectric materials, large numbers of electrons may suddenly be excited to energies within the conduction band. As a result, the current through the dielectric by the motion of these electrons increases dramatically; sometimes localized melting, burning, or vaporization produces irreversible degradation and perhaps even failure of the material. This phenomenon is known as dielectric breakdown. The **dielectric strength**, sometimes called the breakdown strength, represents the magnitude of an electric field necessary to produce breakdown. Table 17.5 presented dielectric strengths for several materials.

17.23 DIELECTRIC MATERIALS

A number of ceramics and polymers are utilized as insulators and/or in capacitors. Many of the ceramics, including glass, porcelain, steatite, and mica, have dielectric constants within the range of 6 to 10 (Table 17.5). These materials also exhibit a high degree of dimensional stability and mechanical strength. Typical applications include powerline and electrical insulation, switch bases, and light receptacles. The titania (TiO_2) and titanate ceramics, such as barium titanate ($BaTiO_3$), can be made to have extremely high dielectric constants, which render them especially useful for some capacitor applications.

The magnitude of the dielectric constant for most polymers is less than for ceramics, since the latter may exhibit greater dipole moments: ϵ_r values for polymers generally lie between 2 and 5. These materials are commonly utilized for insulation of wires, cables, motors, generators, and so on, and, in addition, for some capacitors.

Other Electrical Characteristics of Materials

Two other relatively important and novel electrical characteristics that are found in some materials deserve brief mention—namely, ferroelectricity and piezoelectricity.

17.24 FERROELECTRICITY

The group of dielectric materials called **ferroelectrics** exhibit spontaneous polarization—that is, polarization in the absence of an electric field. They are the dielectric analogue of ferromagnetic materials, which may display permanent magnetic behavior. There must exist in ferroelectric materials permanent electric dipoles, the origin of which is explained for barium titanate, one of the most common ferroelectrics. The spontaneous polarization is a consequence of the positioning of the Ba^{2+}, Ti^{4+}, and O^{2-} ions within the unit cell, as represented in Figure 17.35. The Ba^{2+} ions are located at the corners of the unit cell, which is of tetragonal symmetry (a cube that has been elongated slightly in one direction). The dipole moment results from the relative displacements of the O^{2-} and Ti^{4+} ions from their symmetrical positions as shown in the side view of the unit cell. The O^{2-} ions are located near, but slightly below, the centers of each of the six faces, whereas the Ti^{4+} ion is displaced upward from the unit cell center. Thus, a permanent ionic dipole moment is associated with each unit cell (Figure 17.35*b*). However, when barium titanate is heated above its *ferroelectric Curie temperature* (120°C), the unit cell becomes cubic, and all ions assume symmetric positions within the cubic unit cell; the material now has a perovskite crystal structure (Section 4.13), and the ferroelectric behavior ceases.

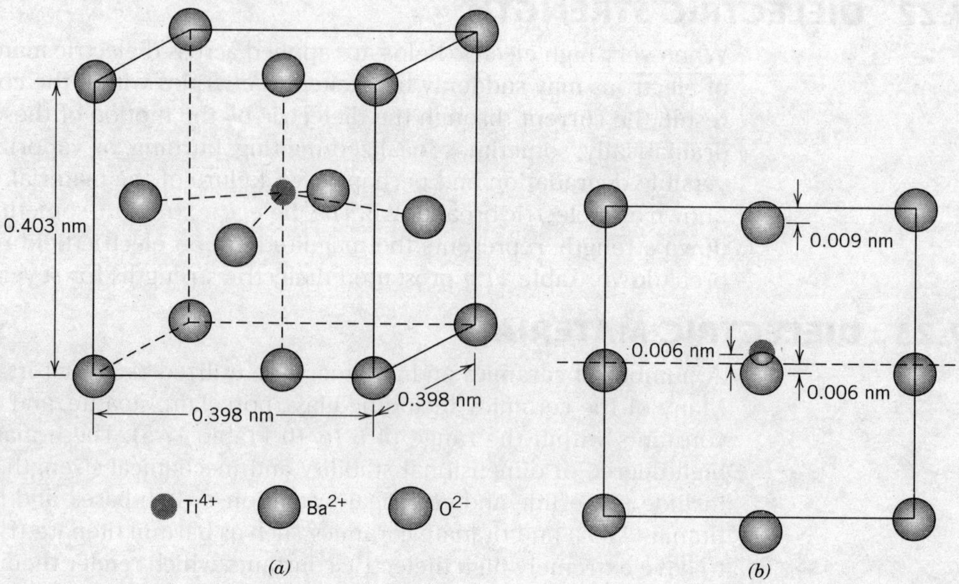

Figure 17.35 A barium titanate ($BaTiO_3$) unit cell (*a*) in an isometric projection, and (*b*) looking at one face, which shows the displacements of Ti^{4+} and O^{2-} ions from the center of the face.

Spontaneous polarization of this group of materials results as a consequence of interactions between adjacent permanent dipoles wherein they mutually align, all in the same direction. For example, with barium titanate, the relative displacements of O^{2-} and Ti^{4+} ions are in the same direction for all the unit cells within some volume region of the specimen. Other materials display ferroelectricity; these include Rochelle salt ($NaKC_4H_4O_6 \cdot 4H_2O$), potassium dihydrogen phosphate (KH_2PO_4), potassium niobate ($KNbO_3$), and lead zirconate–titanate ($Pb[ZrO_3, TiO_3]$). Ferroelectrics have extremely high dielectric constants at relatively low applied field frequencies; for example, at room temperature, ϵ_r for barium titanate may be as high as 5000. Consequently, capacitors made from these materials can be significantly smaller than capacitors made from other dielectric materials.

17.25 PIEZOELECTRICITY

An unusual property exhibited by a few ceramic materials is piezoelectricity, or, literally, pressure electricity: polarization is induced and an electric field is established across a specimen by the application of external forces. Reversing the sign of an external force (i.e., from tension to compression) reverses the direction of the field. The piezoelectric effect is demonstrated in Figure 17.36. This phenomenon and examples of its application were discussed in the Materials of Importance piece that follows Section 12.8.

Piezoelectric materials are utilized in transducers, which are devices that convert electrical energy into mechanical strains, or vice versa. Some other familiar applications that employ piezoelectrics include phonograph cartridges, microphones, speakers, audible alarms, and ultrasonic imaging. In a phonograph cartridge, as the stylus traverses the grooves on a record, a pressure variation is imposed on a piezoelectric material located in the cartridge, which is then transformed into an electric signal and is amplified before going to the speaker.

Piezoelectric materials include titanates of barium and lead, lead zirconate ($PbZrO_3$), ammonium dihydrogen phosphate ($NH_4H_2PO_4$), and quartz. This property is characteristic of materials having complicated crystal structures with a low degree of symmetry. The piezoelectric behavior of a polycrystalline specimen may

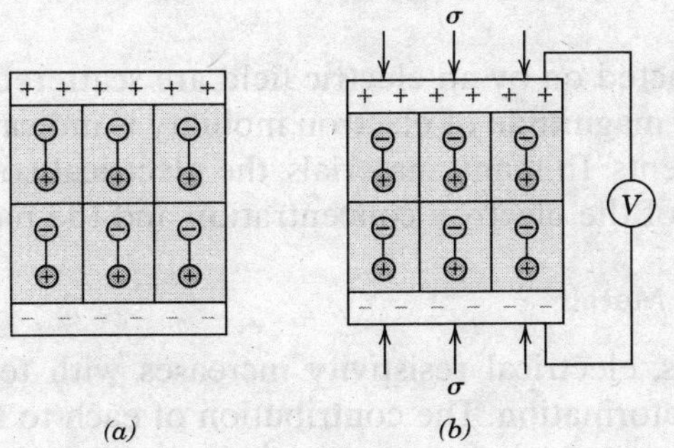

Figure 17.36 (*a*) Dipoles within a piezoelectric material. (*b*) A voltage is generated when the material is subjected to a compressive stress. (From Van Vlack, Lawrence H., *Elements of Materials Science and Engineering,* © 1989, p. 482. Adapted by permission of Pearson Education, Inc., Upper Saddle River, New Jersey.)

be improved by heating above its Curie temperature and then cooling to room temperature in a strong electric field.

Concept Check 17.10

Would you expect the physical dimensions of a piezoelectric material such as $BaTiO_3$ to change when it is subjected to an electric field? Why or why not?

[*The answer may be found in enclosed CD.*]

SUMMARY

Ohm's Law
Electrical Conductivity

The ease with which a material is capable of transmitting an electric current is expressed in terms of electrical conductivity or its reciprocal, resistivity. On the basis of its conductivity, a solid material may be classified as a metal, a semiconductor, or an insulator.

Electronic and Ionic Conduction
Energy Band Structures in Solids
Conduction in Terms of Band and Atomic Bonding Models

For most materials, an electric current results from the motion of free electrons, which are accelerated in response to an applied electric field. The number of these free electrons depends on the electron energy band structure of the material. An electron band is just a series of electron states that are closely spaced with respect to energy, and one such band may exist for each electron subshell found in the isolated atom. By "electron energy band structure" is meant the manner in which the outermost bands are arranged relative to one another and then filled with electrons. A distinctive band structure type exists for metals, for semiconductors, and for insulators. An electron becomes free by being excited from a filled state in one band, to an available empty state above the Fermi energy. Relatively small energies are required for electron excitations in metals, giving rise to large numbers of free electrons. Larger energies are required for electron excitations in semiconductors and insulators, which accounts for their lower free electron concentrations and smaller conductivity values.

Electron Mobility

Free electrons being acted on by an electric field are scattered by imperfections in the crystal lattice. The magnitude of electron mobility is indicative of the frequency of these scattering events. In many materials, the electrical conductivity is proportional to the product of the electron concentration and the mobility.

Electrical Resistivity of Metals

For metallic materials, electrical resistivity increases with temperature, impurity content, and plastic deformation. The contribution of each to the total resistivity is additive.

Intrinsic Semiconduction
Extrinsic Semiconduction
The Temperature Dependence of Carrier Concentration
Factors That Affect Carrier Mobility

Semiconductors may be either elements (Si and Ge) or covalently bonded compounds. With these materials, in addition to free electrons, holes (missing electrons in the valence band) may also participate in the conduction process. On the basis of electrical behavior, semiconductors are classified as either intrinsic or extrinsic. For intrinsic behavior, the electrical properties are inherent in the pure material, and electron and hole concentrations are equal; electrical behavior is dictated by impurities for extrinsic semiconductors. Extrinsic semiconductors may be either *n*- or *p*-type depending on whether electrons or holes, respectively, are the predominant charge carriers. Donor impurities introduce excess electrons; acceptor impurities introduce excess holes.

The electrical conductivity of semiconducting materials is particularly sensitive to impurity type and content, as well as to temperature. The addition of even minute concentrations of some impurities enhances the conductivity drastically. Furthermore, with rising temperature the intrinsic carrier concentration increases dramatically. For extrinsic semiconductors, with increasing impurity dopant content, the room-temperature carrier concentration increases whereas carrier mobility diminishes.

Semiconductor Devices

A number of semiconducting devices employ the unique electrical characteristics of these materials to perform specific electronic functions. Included are the *p–n* rectifying junction, and junction and MOSFET transistors. Transistors are used for amplification of electrical signals, as well as for switching devices in computer circuitries.

Capacitance
Field Vectors and Polarization
Types of Polarization
Frequency Dependence of the Dielectric Constant

Dielectric materials are electrically insulative, yet susceptible to polarization in the presence of an electric field. This polarization phenomenon accounts for the ability of the dielectrics to increase the charge storing capability of capacitors, the efficiency of which is expressed in terms of a dielectric constant. Polarization results from the inducement by or orientation with the electric field of atomic or molecular dipoles; a dipole is said to exist when there is a net spatial separation of positively and negatively charged entities. Possible polarization types include electronic, ionic, and orientation; not all types need be present in a particular dielectric. For alternating electric fields, whether a specific polarization type contributes to the total polarization and dielectric constant depends on frequency; each polarization mechanism ceases to function when the applied field frequency exceeds its relaxation frequency.

Ferroelectricity
Piezoelectricity

Also included in this chapter were brief discussions of two other electrical phenomena. Ferroelectric materials are those that may exhibit polarization spontaneously, that is, in the absence of any external electric field. Finally, piezoelectricity is the phenomenon whereby polarization is induced in a material by the imposition of external forces.

REFERENCES

Azaroff, L. V. and J. J. Brophy, *Electronic Processes in Materials*, McGraw-Hill, New York, 1963. Reprinted by TechBooks, Marietta, OH, 1990. Chapters 6–12.

Bube, R. H., *Electrons in Solids*, 3rd edition, Academic Press, San Diego, 1992.

Chaudhari, P., "Electronic and Magnetic Materials," *Scientific American*, Vol. 255, No. 4, October 1986, pp. 136–144.

Hummel, R. E., *Electronic Properties of Materials*, 3rd edition, Springer-Verlag, New York, 2000.

Kingery, W. D., H. K. Bowen, and D. R. Uhlmann, *Introduction to Ceramics*, 2nd edition, Wiley, New York, 1976. Chapters 17 and 18.

Kittel, C., *Introduction to Solid State Physics*, 8th edition, Wiley, New York, 2005. An advanced treatment.

Kwok, H. L., *Electronic Materials*, PWS Publishers, Boston, 1997.

Livingston, J., *Electronic Properties of Engineering Materials*, Wiley, New York, 1999.

Pierret, R. F. and K. Harutunian, *Semiconductor Device Fundamentals*, Addison-Wesley Longman, Boston, 1996.

Solymar, L. and D. Walsh, *Electrical Properties of Materials*, 7th edition, Oxford University Press, New York, 2004.

QUESTIONS AND PROBLEMS

Ohm's Law
Electrical Conductivity

17.1 (a) Compute the electrical conductivity of a 7.0-mm diameter cylindrical silicon specimen 57 mm long in which a current of 0.25 A passes in an axial direction. A voltage of 24 V is measured across two probes that are separated by 45 mm.

(b) Compute the resistance over the entire 57 mm of the specimen.

17.2 An aluminum wire 10 m long must experience a voltage drop of less than 1.0 V when a current of 5 A passes through it. Using the data in Table 17.1, compute the minimum diameter of the wire.

17.3 A plain carbon steel wire 3 mm in diameter is to offer a resistance of no more than 20 Ω. Using the data in Table 17.1, compute the maximum wire length.

17.4 Demonstrate that the two Ohm's law expressions, Equations 17.1 and 17.5, are equivalent.

17.5 (a) Using the data in Table 17.1, compute the resistance of an aluminum wire 5 mm in diameter and 5 m long. **(b)** What would be the current flow if the potential drop across the ends of the wire is 0.04 V? **(c)** What is the current density? **(d)** What is the magnitude of the electric field across the ends of the wire?

Electronic and Ionic Conduction

17.6 What is the distinction between electronic and ionic conduction?

Energy Band Structures in Solids

17.7 How does the electron structure of an isolated atom differ from that of a solid material?

Conduction in Terms of Band and Atomic Bonding Models

17.8 In terms of electron energy band structure, discuss reasons for the difference in electrical conductivity between metals, semiconductors, and insulators.

Electron Mobility

17.9 Briefly tell what is meant by the drift velocity and mobility of a free electron.

17.10 **(a)** Calculate the drift velocity of electrons in silicon at room temperature and when the magnitude of the electric field is 500 V/m. **(b)** Under these circumstances, how long does it take an electron to traverse a 25-mm length of crystal?

17.11 At room temperature the electrical conductivity and the electron mobility for aluminum are 3.8×10^7 $(\Omega\text{-m})^{-1}$ and 0.0012 m^2/V-s, respectively. **(a)** Compute the number of free electrons per cubic meter for aluminum at room temperature. **(b)** What is the number of free electrons per aluminum atom? Assume a density of 2.7 g/cm^3.

17.12 **(a)** Calculate the number of free electrons per cubic meter for silver, assuming that there are 1.3 free electrons per silver atom. The electrical conductivity and density for Ag are 6.8×10^7 $(\Omega\text{-m})^{-1}$ and 10.5 g/cm^3, respectively. **(b)** Now compute the electron mobility for Ag.

Electrical Resistivity of Metals

17.13 From Figure 17.37, estimate the value of A in Equation 17.11 for zinc as an impurity in copper–zinc alloys.

17.14 **(a)** Using the data in Figure 17.8, determine the values of ρ_0 and a from Equation 17.10 for pure copper. Take the temperature T to be in degrees Celsius. **(b)** Determine the value of A in Equation 17.11 for nickel as an impurity in copper, using the data in Figure 17.8. **(c)** Using the results of parts

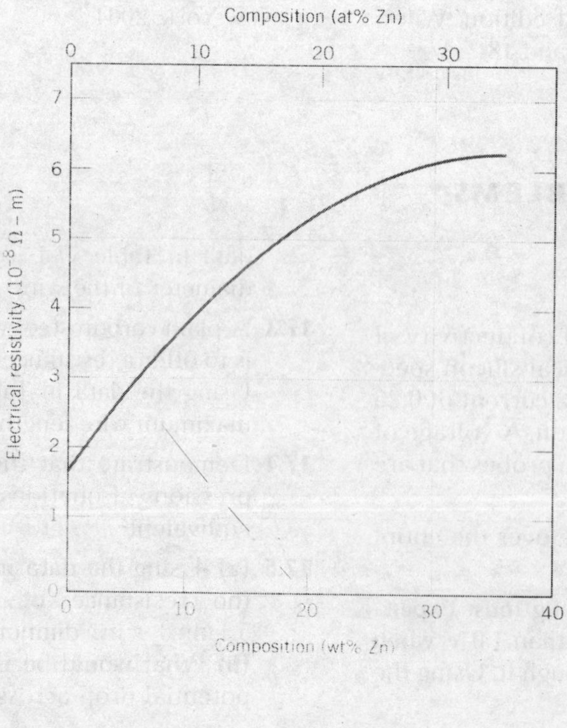

Figure 17.37 Room-temperature electrical resistivity versus composition for copper–zinc alloys. [Adapted from *Metals Handbook: Properties and Selection: Nonferrous Alloys and Pure Metals,* Vol. 2, 9th edition, H. Baker (Managing Editor), American Society for Metals, 1979, p. 315.]

(a) and (b), estimate the electrical resistivity of copper containing 2.50 at% Ni at 120°C.

17.15 Determine the electrical conductivity of a Cu-Ni alloy that has a tensile strength of 275 MPa. You will find Figure 10.16 helpful.

17.16 Tin bronze has a composition of 89 wt% Cu and 11 wt% Sn, and consists of two phases at room temperature: an α phase, which is copper containing a very small amount of tin in solid solution, and an ϵ phase, which consists of approximately 37 wt% Sn. Compute the room temperature conductivity of this alloy given the following data:

Phase	*Electrical Resistivity* $(\Omega\text{-}m)$	*Density* (g/cm^3)
α	1.88×10^{-8}	8.94
ϵ	5.32×10^{-7}	8.25

17.17 A cylindrical metal wire 3 mm in diameter is required to carry a current of 12 A with a minimum of 0.01 V drop per foot (300 mm) of wire. Which of the metals and alloys listed in Table 17.1 are possible candidates?

Intrinsic Semiconduction

17.18 **(a)** Using the data presented in Figure 17.16, determine the number of free electrons per atom for intrinsic germanium and silicon at room temperature (298 K). The densities for Ge and Si are 5.32 and 2.33 g/cm^3, respectively.

(b) Now explain the difference in these free-electron-per-atom values.

17.19 For intrinsic semiconductors, the intrinsic carrier concentration n_i depends on temperature as follows:

$$n_i \propto \exp\left(-\frac{E_g}{2kT}\right) \qquad (17.35a)$$

or taking natural logarithms,

$$\ln n_i \propto -\frac{E_g}{2kT} \qquad (17.35b)$$

Thus, a plot of $\ln n_i$ versus $1/T$ (K)$^{-1}$ should be linear and yield a slope of $-E_g/2k$. Using this information and the data presented in Figure 17.16, determine the band gap energies for silicon and germanium, and compare these values with those given in Table 17.3.

17.20 Briefly explain the presence of the factor 2 in the denominator of Equation 17.35a.

17.21 At room temperature the electrical conductivity of PbS is 25 $(\Omega\text{-m})^{-1}$, whereas the electron and hole mobilities are 0.06 and 0.02 m^2/V-s, respectively. Compute the intrinsic carrier concentration for PbS at room temperature.

17.22 Is it possible for compound semiconductors to exhibit intrinsic behavior? Explain your answer.

17.23 For each of the following pairs of semiconductors, decide which will have the smaller band gap energy, E_g, and then cite the reason for your choice. **(a)** C (diamond) and Ge, **(b)** AlP and InSb, **(c)** GaAs and ZnSe, **(d)** ZnSe and CdTe, and **(e)** CdS and NaCl.

Extrinsic Semiconduction

17.24 Define the following terms as they pertain to semiconducting materials: intrinsic, extrinsic, compound, elemental. Now provide an example of each.

17.25 An n-type semiconductor is known to have an electron concentration of 5×10^{17} m^{-3}. If the electron drift velocity is 350 m/s in an electric field of 1000 V/m, calculate the conductivity of this material.

17.26 **(a)** In your own words, explain how donor impurities in semiconductors give rise to free electrons in numbers in excess of those generated by valence band–conduction band excitations. **(b)** Also explain how acceptor impurities give rise to holes in numbers in excess of those generated by valence band–conduction band excitations.

17.27 **(a)** Explain why no hole is generated by the electron excitation involving a donor impurity atom. **(b)** Explain why no free electron is generated by the electron excitation involving an acceptor impurity atom.

17.28 Will each of the following elements act as a donor or an acceptor when added to the indicated semiconducting material? Assume that the impurity elementsare substitutional.

Impurity	*Semiconductor*
N	Si
B	Ge
S	InSb
In	CdS
As	ZnTe

17.29 **(a)** The room-temperature electrical conductivity of a silicon specimen is 500 $(\Omega\text{-m})^{-1}$. The hole concentration is known to be 2.0×10^{22} m^{-3}. Using the electron and hole mobilities for silicon in Table 17.3, compute the electron concentration. **(b)** On the basis of the result in part (a), is the specimen intrinsic, *n*-type extrinsic, or *p*-type extrinsic? Why?

17.30 Germanium to which 10^{24} m^{-3} As atoms have been added is an extrinsic semiconductor at room temperature, and virtually all the As atoms may be thought of as being ionized (i.e., one charge carrier exists for each As atom). **(a)** Is this material *n*-type or *p*-type? **(b)** Calculate the electrical conductivity of this material, assuming electron and hole mobilities of 0.1 and 0.05 m^2/V-s, respectively.

17.31 The following electrical characteristics have been determined for both intrinsic and *p*-type extrinsic gallium antimonide (GaSb) at room temperature:

	σ $(\Omega\text{-m})^{-1}$	n (m^{-3})	p (m^{-3})
Intrinsic	8.9×10^4	8.7×10^{23}	8.7×10^{23}
Extrinsic (*p*-type)	2.3×10^5	7.6×10^{22}	1.0×10^{25}

Calculate electron and hole mobilities.

The Temperature Dependence of Carrier Concentration

17.32 Calculate the conductivity of intrinsic silicon at 80°C.

17.33 At temperatures near room temperature, the temperature dependence of the conductivity for intrinsic germanium is found to equal

$$\sigma = CT^{-3/2}\exp\left(-\frac{E_g}{2kT}\right) \qquad (17.36)$$

where C is a temperature-independent constant and T is in Kelvins. Using Equation 17.36, calculate the intrinsic electrical conductivity of germanium at 175°C.

17.34 Using Equation 17.36 and the results of Problem 17.33, determine the temperature at which the electrical conductivity of intrinsic germanium is 40 $(\Omega\text{-m})^{-1}$.

17.35 Estimate the temperature at which GaAs has an electrical conductivity of 1.6×10^{-3} $(\Omega\text{-m})^{-1}$ assuming the temperature dependence for σ of Equation 17.36. The data shown in Table 17.3 might prove helpful.

17.36 Compare the temperature dependence of the conductivity for metals and intrinsic semiconductors. Briefly explain the difference in behavior.

Factors That Affect Carrier Mobility

17.37 Calculate the room-temperature electrical conductivity of silicon that has been doped with 10^{23} m^{-3} of arsenic atoms.

17.38 Calculate the room-temperature electrical conductivity of silicon that has been doped with 2×10^{24} m^{-3} of boron atoms.

17.39 Estimate the electrical conductivity, at 75°C, of silicon that has been doped with 10^{22} m^{-3} of phosphorus atoms.

17.40 Estimate the electrical conductivity, at 135°C, of silicon that has been doped with 10^{24} m^{-3} of aluminum atoms.

The Hall Effect

17.41 Some hypothetical metal is known to have an electrical resistivity of 3.3×10^{-8} $(\Omega\text{-m})$. Through a specimen of this metal 15 mm thick is passed a current of 25 A; when a magnetic field of 0.95 tesla is simultaneously imposed in a direction perpendicular to that of the current, a Hall voltage of -2.4×10^{-7} V is measured. Compute **(a)** the electron mobility for this metal, and **(b)** the number of free electrons per cubic meter.

17.42 Some metal alloy is known to have electrical conductivity and electron mobility values of 1.2×10^7 $(\Omega\text{-m})^{-1}$ and 0.0050 m^2/V-s, respectively. Through a specimen of this alloy that is 35 mm thick is passed a current of 40 A. What magnetic field would need to be imposed to yield a Hall voltage of -3.5×10^{-7} V?

Semiconducting Devices

17.43 Briefly describe electron and hole motions in a p–n junction for forward and reverse biases; then explain how these lead to rectification.

17.44 How is the energy in the reaction described by Equation 17.21 dissipated?

17.45 What are the two functions that a transistor may perform in an electronic circuit?

17.46 Cite the differences in operation and application for junction transistors and MOSFETs.

Conduction in Ionic Materials

17.47 We noted in Section 5.5 (Figure 5.3) that in FeO (wüstite), the iron ions can exist in both Fe^{2+} and Fe^{3+} states. The number of each of these ion types depends on temperature and the ambient oxygen pressure. Furthermore, we also noted that in order to retain electroneutrality, one Fe^{2+} vacancy will be created for every two Fe^{3+} ions that are formed; consequently, in order to reflect the existence of these vacancies the formula for wüstite is often represented as $Fe_{(1-x)}O$ where x is some small fraction less than unity.

In this nonstoichiometric $Fe_{(1-x)}O$ material, conduction is electronic, and, in fact, it behaves as a p-type semiconductor. That is, the Fe^{3+} ions act as electron acceptors, and it is relatively easy to excite an electron from the valence band into an Fe^{3+} acceptor state, with the formation of a hole. Determine the electrical conductivity of a specimen of wüstite that has a hole mobility of 1.0×10^{-5} m^2/V-s and for which the value of x is 0.040. Assume that the acceptor states are saturated (i.e., one hole exists for every Fe^{3+} ion). Wüstite has the sodium chloride crystal structure with a unit cell edge length of 0.437 nm.

17.48 At temperatures between 540°C (813 K) and 727°C (1000 K), the activation energy and preexponential for the diffusion coefficient of Na^+ in NaCl are 173,000 J/mol and 4.0×10^{-4} m^2/s, respectively. Compute the mobility for an Na^+ ion at 600°C (873 K).

Capacitance

17.49 A parallel-plate capacitor using a dielectric material having an ϵ_r of 2.2 has a plate spacing of 2 mm (0.08 in.). If another material having a dielectric constant of 3.7 is used and the capacitance is to be unchanged, what must be the new spacing between the plates?

17.50 A parallel-plate capacitor with dimensions of 38 mm by 65 mm and a plate separation of 1.3 mm must have a minimum capacitance of 70 pF (7×10^{-11} F) when an ac potential of 1000 V is applied at a frequency of 1 MHz. Which of the materials listed in Table 17.5 are possible candidates? Why?

17.51 Consider a parallel-plate capacitor having an area of 3225 mm^2, a plate separation of 1 mm, and with a material having a dielectric constant of 3.5 positioned between the plates. **(a)** What is the capacitance of this capacitor? **(b)** Compute the electric field that must be applied for 2×10^{-8} C to be stored on each plate.

17.52 In your own words, explain the mechanism by which charge storing capacity is increased by the insertion of a dielectric material within the plates of a capacitor.

Field Vectors and Polarization

Types of Polarization

17.53 For CaO, the ionic radii for Ca^{2+} and O^{2-} ions are 0.100 and 0.140 nm, respectively. If an externally applied electric field produces a 5% expansion of the lattice, compute the dipole moment for each Ca^{2+}–O^{2-} pair. Assume that this material is completely unpolarized in the absence of an electric field.

17.54 The polarization P of a dielectric material positioned within a parallel-plate capacitor is to be 4.0×10^{-6} C/m^2.

(a) What must be the dielectric constant if an electric field of 10^5 V/m is applied?

(b) What will be the dielectric displacement D?

17.55 A charge of 2.0×10^{-10} C is to be stored on each plate of a parallel-plate capacitor having an area of 650 mm^2 and a plate separation of 4.0 mm.

(a) What voltage is required if a material having a dielectric constant of 3.5 is positioned within the plates?

(b) What voltage would be required if a vacuum were used?

(c) What are the capacitances for parts (a) and (b)?

(d) Compute the dielectric displacement for part (a).

(e) Compute the polarization for part (a).

17.56 **(a)** For each of the three types of polarization, briefly describe the mechanism by which dipoles are induced and/or oriented by the action of an applied electric field.
(b) For gaseous argon, solid LiF, liquid H_2O, and solid Si, what kind(s) of polarization is (are) possible? Why?

17.57 **(a)** Compute the magnitude of the dipole moment associated with each unit cell of $BaTiO_3$, as illustrated in Figure 17.35.

(b) Compute the maximum polarization that is possible for this material.

Frequency Dependence of the Dielectric Constant

17.58 The dielectric constant for a soda–lime glass measured at very high frequencies (on the order of 10^{15} Hz) is approximately 2.3. What fraction of the dielectric constant at relatively low frequencies (1 MHz) is attributed to ionic polarization? Neglect any orientation polarization contributions.

Ferroelectricity

17.59 Briefly explain why the ferroelectric behavior of $BaTiO_3$ ceases above its ferroelectric Curie temperature.

DESIGN PROBLEMS

Electrical Resistivity of Metals

17.D1 A 90 wt% Cu–10 wt% Ni alloy is known to have an electrical resistivity of 1.90×10^{-7} Ω-m at room temperature (25°C). Calculate the composition of a copper–nickel alloy that gives a room-temperature resistivity of 2.5×10^{-7} Ω-m. The room-temperature resistivity of pure copper may be determined from the data in Table 17.1; assume that copper and nickel form a solid solution.

17.D2 Using information contained in Figures 17.8 and 17.37, determine the electrical conductivity of an 85 wt% Cu–15 wt% Zn alloy at −100°C (−150°F).

17.D3 Is it possible to alloy copper with nickel to achieve a minimum yield strength of 130 MPa (19,000 psi) and yet maintain an electrical conductivity of 4.0×10^6 (Ω-m)$^{-1}$? If not, why? If so, what concentration of nickel is required? You may want to consult Figure 10.16*b*.

Extrinsic Semiconduction
Factors That Affect Carrier Mobility

17.D4 Specify a donor impurity type and concentration (in weight percent) that will produce an *n*-type silicon material having a room temperature electrical conductivity of 200 (Ω-m)$^{-1}$.

17.D5 One integrated circuit design calls for diffusing boron into very high purity silicon at an elevated temperature. It is necessary that at a distance 0.2 μm from the surface of the silicon wafer, the room-temperature electrical conductivity be 1000 (Ω-m)$^{-1}$. The concentration of B at the surface of the Si is maintained at a constant level of 1.0×10^{25} m^{-3}; furthermore, it is assumed that the concentration of B in the original Si material is negligible, and that at room temperature the boron atoms are saturated. Specify the temperature at which this diffusion heat treatment is to take place if the treatment time is to be one hour. The diffusion coefficient for the diffusion of B in Si is a function of temperature as

$$D(\mathrm{m^2/s}) = 2.4 \times 10^{-4} \exp\left(-\frac{347\ \mathrm{kJ/mol}}{RT}\right)$$

Conduction in Ionic Materials

17.D6 Problem 17.47 noted that FeO (wüstite) may behave as a semiconductor by virtue of the transformation of Fe^{2+} to Fe^{3+} and the creation of Fe^{2+} vacancies; the maintenance of electroneutrality requires that for every two Fe^{3+} ions, one vacancy is formed. The existence of these vacancies is reflected in the chemical formula of this nonstoichiometric wüstite as $Fe_{(1-x)}O$, where x is a small number having a value less than unity. The degree of nonstoichiometry (i.e., the value of x) may be varied by changing temperature and oxygen partial pressure. Compute the value of x that is required to produce an $Fe_{(1-x)}O$ material having a p-type electrical conductivity of 1200 $(\Omega\text{-m})^{-1}$; assume that the hole mobility is 1.0×10^{-5} m^2/V-s, the crystal structure for FeO is sodium chloride (with a unit cell edge length of 0.437 nm), and that the acceptor states are saturated.

Semiconductor Devices

17.D7 One of the procedures in the production of integrated circuits is the formation of a thin insulating layer of SiO_2 on the surface of chips (see Figure 17.26). This is accomplished by oxidizing the surface of the silicon by subjecting it to an oxidizing atmosphere (i.e., gaseous oxygen or water vapor) at an elevated temperature. The rate of growth of the oxide film is parabolic—that is, the thickness of the oxide layer (x) is a function of time (t) according to the following equation:

$$x^2 = Bt \qquad (17.37)$$

Here the parameter B is dependent on both temperature and the oxidizing atmosphere.

(a) For an atmosphere of O_2 at a pressure of 1 atm, the temperature dependence of B (in units of μm^2/h) is as follows:

$$B = 800 \exp\left(-\frac{1.24 \text{ eV}}{kT}\right) \qquad (17.38a)$$

where k is Boltmann's constant (8.62×10^{-5} eV/atom) and T is in K. Calculate the time required to grow an oxide layer (in an atmosphere of O_2) that is 100 nm thick at both 700°C and 1000°C.

(b) In an atmosphere of H_2O (1 atm pressure), the expression for B (again in units of μm^2/h) is

$$B = 215 \exp\left(-\frac{0.70 \text{ eV}}{kT}\right) \qquad (17.38b)$$

Now calculate the time required to grow an oxide layer that is 100 nm thick (in an atmosphere of H_2O) at both 700°C and 1000°C, and compare these times with those computed in part (a).

17.D8 The base semiconducting material used in virtually all of our modern integrated circuits is silicon. However, silicon has some limitations and restrictions. Write an essay comparing the properties and applications (and/or potential applications) of silicon and gallium arsenide.

Chapter 18 Magnetic Properties

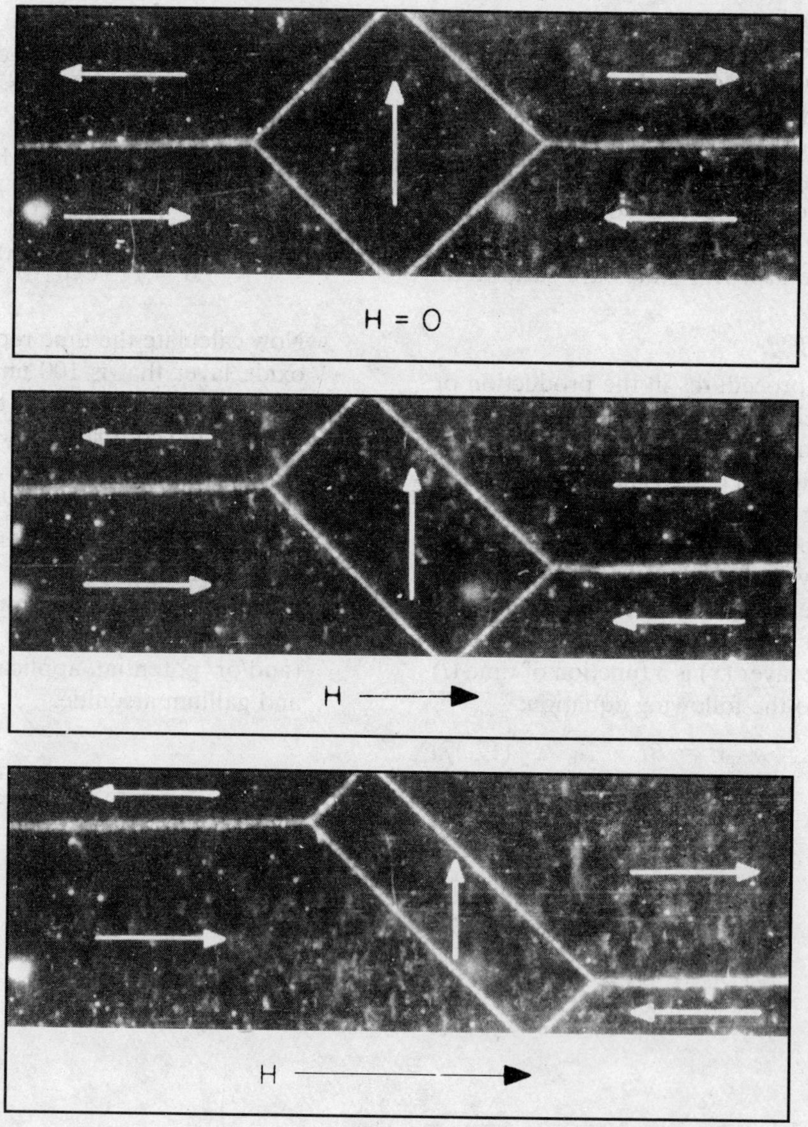

Photomicrographs of an iron single crystal, showing magnetic domains and their change in shape as a magnetic field (*H*) is applied. The magnetization direction of each domain is indicated by an arrow. Those domains that are favorably oriented with the applied field grow at the expense of the unfavorably oriented domains. (Photomicrographs courtesy of General Electric Research Laboratory.)

Learning Objectives

After careful study of this chapter you should be able to do the following:

1. **Determine the magnetization of some material given its magnetic susceptibility and the ap plied magnetic field strength.**
2. **From an electronic perspective note and briefly explain the two sources of magnetic moments in materials.**
3. **Briefly explain the nature and source of (a) diamagnctism, (b) paramagnetism, and (c) ferromagnetism.**
4. **In terms of crystal structure, explain the source of ferrimagnetism for cubic ferrites.**
5. **(a) Describe magnetic hysteresis; (b) explain why ferromagnetic and ferrimagnetic materials experience magnetic hysteresis; and (c) explain why these materials may become permanent magnets.**
6. **Note the distinctive magnetic characteristics for both soft and hard magnetic materials.**
7. **Describe the phenomenon of *superconductivity*.**

18.1 INTRODUCTION

Magnetism, the phenomenon by which materials assert an attractive or repulsive force or influence on other materials, has been known for thousands of years. However, the underlying principles and mechanisms that explain the magnetic phenomenon are complex and subtle, and their understanding has eluded scientists until relatively recent times. Many of our modern technological devices rely on magnetism and magnetic materials; these include electrical power generators and transformers, electric motors, radio, television, telephones, computers, and components of sound and video reproduction systems.

Iron, some steels, and the naturally occurring mineral lodestone are well-known examples of materials that exhibit magnetic properties. Not so familiar, however, is the fact that all substances are influenced to one degree or another by the presence of a magnetic field. This chapter provides a brief description of the origin of magnetic fields and discusses the various magnetic field vectors and magnetic parameters; the phenomena of diamagnetism, paramagnetism, ferromagnetism, and ferrimagnetism; some of the different magnetic materials; and the phenomenon of superconductivity.

18.2 BASIC CONCEPTS

Magnetic Dipoles

Magnetic forces are generated by moving electrically charged particles; these magnetic forces are in addition to any electrostatic forces that may prevail. Many times it is convenient to think of magnetic forces in terms of fields. Imaginary lines of force may be drawn to indicate the direction of the force at positions in the vicinity of the field source. The magnetic field distributions as indicated by lines of force are shown for a current loop and also a bar magnet in Figure 18.1.

Magnetic dipoles are found to exist in magnetic materials, which, in some respects, are analogous to electric dipoles (Section 17.19). Magnetic dipoles may be thought of as small bar magnets composed of north and south poles instead of positive and negative electric charges. In the present discussion, magnetic dipole moments are represented by arrows, as shown in Figure 18.2. Magnetic dipoles are influenced by magnetic fields in a manner similar to the way in which electric dipoles are affected by electric fields (Figure 17.30). Within a magnetic field, the force of the field itself exerts a torque that tends to orient the dipoles with the field. A familiar example is the way in which a magnetic compass needle lines up with the earth's magnetic field.

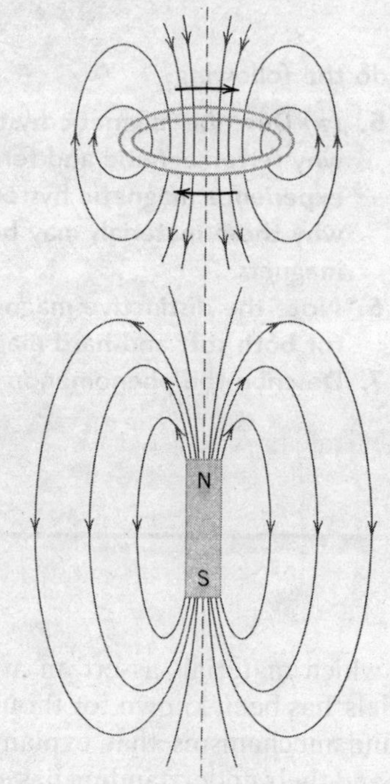

Figure 18.1 Magnetic field lines of force around a current loop and a bar magnet.

Magnetic Field Vectors

Before discussing the origin of magnetic moments in solid materials, we describe magnetic behavior in terms of several field vectors. The externally applied magnetic field, sometimes called the **magnetic field strength,** is designated by H. If the magnetic field is generated by means of a cylindrical coil (or solenoid) consisting of N closely spaced turns, having a length l, and carrying a current of magnitude I, then

$$H = \frac{NI}{l} \tag{18.1}$$

A schematic diagram of such an arrangement is shown in Figure 18.3*a*. The magnetic field that is generated by the current loop and the bar magnet in Figure 18.1 is an H field. The units of H are ampere-turns per meter, or just amperes per meter.

The **magnetic induction,** or **magnetic flux density,** denoted by B, represents the magnitude of the internal field strength within a substance that is subjected to an H field. The units for B are teslas [or webers per square meter (Wb/m^2)]. Both B and H are field vectors, being characterized not only by magnitude, but also by direction in space.

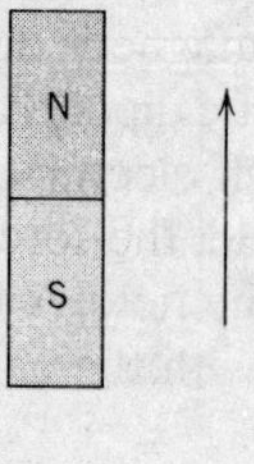

Figure 18.2 The magnetic moment as designated by an arrow.

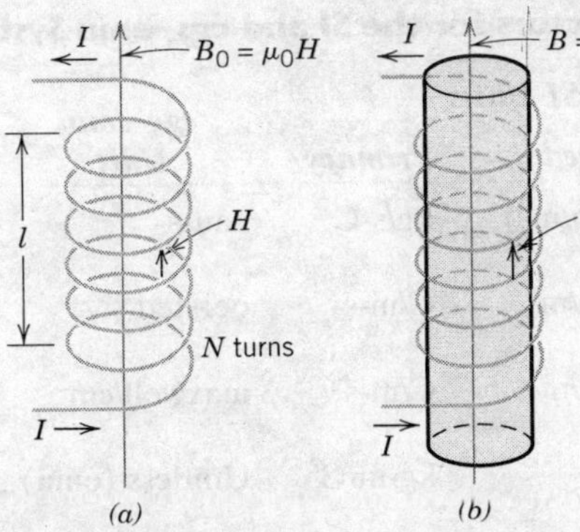

Figure 18.3 (*a*) The magnetic field H as generated by a cylindrical coil is dependent on the current I, the number of turns N, and the coil length l, according to Equation 18.1. The magnetic flux density B_0 in the presence of a vacuum is equal to $\mu_0 H$, where μ_0 is the permeability of a vacuum, $4\pi \times 10^{-7}$ H/m. (*b*) The magnetic flux density B within a solid material is equal to μH, where μ is the permeability of the solid material. (Adapted from A. G. Guy, *Essentials of Materials Science,* McGraw-Hill Book Company, New York, 1976.)

The magnetic field strength and flux density are related according to

$$B = \mu H \tag{18.2}$$

The parameter μ is called the **permeability,** which is a property of the specific medium through which the H field passes and in which B is measured, as illustrated in Figure 18.3*b*. The permeability has dimensions of webers per ampere-meter (Wb/A-m) or henries per meter (H/m).

In a vacuum,

$$B_0 = \mu_0 H \tag{18.3}$$

where μ_0 is the *permeability of a vacuum,* a universal constant, which has a value of $4\pi \times 10^{-7}$ (1.257×10^{-6}) H/m. The parameter B_0 represents the flux density within a vacuum as demonstrated in Figure 18.3*a*.

Several parameters may be used to describe the magnetic properties of solids. One of these is the ratio of the permeability in a material to the permeability in a vacuum, or

$$\mu_r = \frac{\mu}{\mu_0} \tag{18.4}$$

where μ_r is called the *relative permeability,* which is unitless. The permeability or relative permeability of a material is a measure of the degree to which the material can be magnetized, or the ease with which a B field can be induced in the presence of an external H field.

Another field quantity, M, called the **magnetization** of the solid, is defined by the expression

$$B = \mu_0 H + \mu_0 M \tag{18.5}$$

In the presence of an H field, the magnetic moments within a material tend to become aligned with the field and to reinforce it by virtue of their magnetic fields; the term $\mu_0 M$ in Equation 18.5 is a measure of this contribution.

Table 18.1 Magnetic Units and Conversion Factors for the SI and cgs–emu Systems

Quantity	*Symbol*	*SI Units* Derived	*SI Units* Primary	*cgs–emu Unit*	*Conversion*
Magnetic induction (flux density)	B	tesla (Wb/m^2)^a	kg/s-C	gauss	1 Wb/m^2 = 10^4 gauss
Magnetic field strength	H	amp-turn/m	C/m-s	oersted	1 amp-turn/m = $4\pi \times 10^{-3}$ oersted
Magnetization	M (SI) I (cgs–emu)	amp-turn/m	C/m-s	maxwell/cm^2	1 amp-turn/m = 10^{-3} maxwell/cm^2
Permeability of a vaccum	μ_0	henry/m^b	kg-m/C^2	Unitless (emu)	$4\pi \times 10^{-7}$ henry/m = 1 emu
Relative permeability	μ_r (SI) μ' (cgs–emu)	Unitless	Unitless	Unitless	$\mu_r = \mu'$
Susceptibility	χ_m (SI) χ'_m (cgs–emu)	Unitless	Unitless	Unitless	$\chi_m = 4\pi\chi'_m$

[a] Units of the weber (Wb) are volt-seconds.
[b] Units of the henry are webers per ampere.

The magnitude of M is proportional to the applied field as follows:

$$M = \chi_m H \tag{18.6}$$

and χ_m is called the **magnetic susceptibility,** which is unitless.[1] The magnetic susceptibility and the relative permeability are related as follows:

$$\chi_m = \mu_r - 1 \tag{18.7}$$

There is a dielectric analogue for each of the foregoing magnetic field parameters. The B and H fields are, respectively, analogous to the dielectric displacement D and the electric field $\mathscr{E}$, whereas the permeability μ parallels the permittivity ϵ (cf. Equations 18.2 and 17.30). Furthermore, the magnetization M and polarization P are correlates (Equations 18.5 and 17.31).

Magnetic units may be a source of confusion because there are really two systems in common use. The ones used thus far are SI [rationalized *MKS* (meter-kilogram-second)]; the others come from the *cgs–emu* (centimeter-gram-second-electromagnetic unit) system. The units for both systems as well as the appropriate conversion factors are contained in Table 18.1.

Origins of Magnetic Moments

The macroscopic magnetic properties of materials are a consequence of *magnetic moments* associated with individual electrons. Some of these concepts are relatively complex and involve some quantum-mechanical principles beyond the scope of this discussion; consequently, simplifications have been made and some of the details omitted. Each electron in an atom has magnetic moments that originate from two sources. One is related to its orbital motion around the nucleus; being a moving

[1] This χ_m is taken to be the volume susceptibility in SI units, which, when multiplied by H, yields the magnetization per unit volume (cubic meter) of material. Other susceptibilities are also possible; see Problem 18.3.

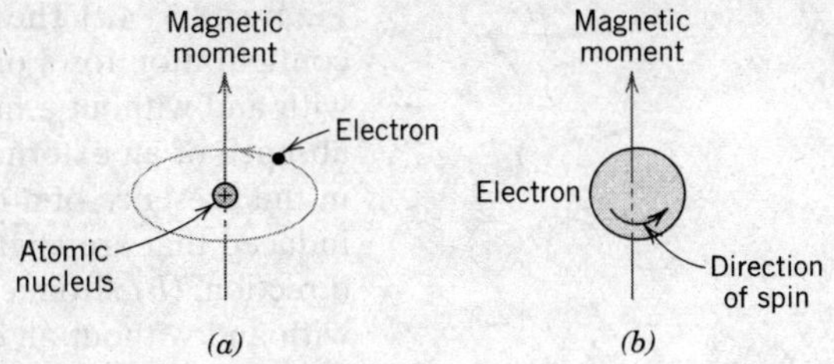

Figure 18.4 Demonstration of the magnetic moment associated with (*a*) an orbiting electron and (*b*) a spinning electron.

chargc, an clcctron may be considered to be a small current loop, generating a very small magnetic field, and having a magnetic moment along its axis of rotation, as schematically illustrated in Figure 18.4*a*.

Each electron may also be thought of as spinning around an axis; the other magnetic moment originates from this electron spin, which is directed along the spin axis as shown in Figure 18.4*b*. Spin magnetic moments may be only in an "up" direction or in an antiparallel "down" direction. Thus each electron in an atom may be thought of as being a small magnet having permanent orbital and spin magnetic moments.

The most fundamental magnetic moment is the **Bohr magneton** μ_B, which is of magnitude 9.27×10^{-24} A-m^2. For each electron in an atom the spin magnetic moment is $\pm\mu_B$ (plus for spin up, minus for spin down). Furthermore, the orbital magnetic moment contribution is equal to $m_l\mu_B$, m_l being the magnetic quantum number of the electron, as mentioned in Section 2.3.

In each individual atom, orbital moments of some electron pairs cancel each other; this also holds for the spin moments. For example, the spin moment of an electron with spin up will cancel that of one with spin down. The net magnetic moment, then, for an atom is just the sum of the magnetic moments of each of the constituent electrons, including both orbital and spin contributions, and taking into account moment cancellation. For an atom having completely filled electron shells or subshells, when all electrons are considered, there is total cancellation of both orbital and spin moments. Thus materials composed of atoms having completely filled electron shells are not capable of being permanently magnetized. This category includes the inert gases (He, Ne, Ar, etc.) as well as some ionic materials. The types of magnetism include diamagnetism, paramagnetism, and ferromagnetism; in addition, antiferromagnetism and ferrimagnetism are considered to be subclasses of ferromagnetism. All materials exhibit at least one of these types, and the behavior depends on the response of electron and atomic magnetic dipoles to the application of an externally applied magnetic field.

18.3 DIAMAGNETISM AND PARAMAGNETISM

Diamagnetism is a very weak form of magnetism that is nonpermanent and persists only while an external field is being applied. It is induced by a change in the orbital motion of electrons due to an applied magnetic field. The magnitude of the induced magnetic moment is extremely small, and in a direction opposite to that of the applied field. Thus, the relative permeability μ_r is less than unity (however, only very slightly), and the magnetic susceptibility is negative; that is, the magnitude of the B field within a diamagnetic solid is less than that in a vacuum. The volume susceptibility χ_m for diamagnetic solid materials is on the order of -10^{-5}. When placed between the poles of a strong electromagnet, diamagnetic materials are attracted toward regions where the field is weak.

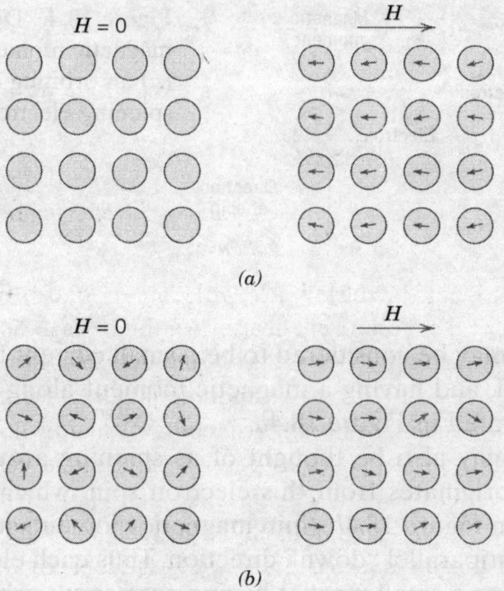

Figure 18.5 (*a*) The atomic dipole configuration for a diamagnetic material with and without a magnetic field. In the absence of an external field, no dipoles exist; in the presence of a field, dipoles are induced that are aligned opposite to the field direction. (*b*) Atomic dipole configuration with and without an external magnetic field for a paramagnetic material.

Figure 18.5*a* illustrates schematically the atomic magnetic dipole configurations for a diamagnetic material with and without an external field; here, the arrows represent atomic dipole moments, whereas for the preceding discussion, arrows denoted only electron moments. The dependence of B on the external field H for a material that exhibits diamagnetic behavior is presented in Figure 18.6. Table 18.2 gives the susceptibilities of several diamagnetic materials. Diamagnetism is found in all materials; but because it is so weak, it can be observed only when other types of magnetism are totally absent. This form of magnetism is of no practical importance.

For some solid materials, each atom possesses a permanent dipole moment by virtue of incomplete cancellation of electron spin and/or orbital magnetic moments. In the absence of an external magnetic field, the orientations of these atomic magnetic moments are random, such that a piece of material possesses no net macroscopic magnetization. These atomic dipoles are free to rotate, and **paramagnetism** results when they preferentially align, by rotation, with an external field as shown in Figure 18.5*b*. These magnetic dipoles are acted on individually with no mutual

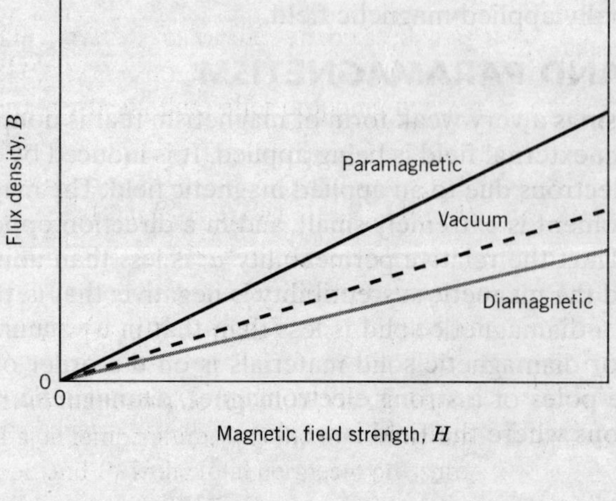

Figure 18.6 Schematic representation of the flux density B versus the magnetic field strength H for diamagnetic and paramagnetic materials.

Table 18.2 Room-Temperature Magnetic Susceptibilities for Diamagnetic and Paramagnetic Materials

Diamagnetics		*Paramagnetics*	
Material	*Susceptibility χ_m (volume) (SI units)*	*Material*	*Susceptibility χ_m (volume) (SI units)*
Aluminum oxide	-1.81×10^{-5}	Aluminum	2.07×10^{-5}
Copper	+°>96 $\times 10^{-5}$	Chromium	3.13×10^{-4}
Gold	-3.44×10^{-5}	Chromium chloride	1.51×10^{-3}
Mercury	-2.85×10^{-5}	Manganese sulfate	3.70×10^{-3}
Silicon	+°>41 $\times$ 10 ^{5}	Molybdenum	1.19×10^{-4}
Silver	-2.38×10^{-5}	Sodium	8.48×10^{-6}
Sodium chloride	-1.41×10^{-5}	Titanium	1.81×10^{-4}
Zinc	-1.56×10^{-5}	Zirconium	1.09×10^{-4}

interaction between adjacent dipoles. Inasmuch as the dipoles align with the external field, they enhance it, giving rise to a relative permeability μ_r that is greater than unity, and to a relatively small but positive magnetic susceptibility. Susceptibilities for paramagnetic materials range from about 10^{-5} to 10^{-2} (Table 18.2). A schematic B-versus-H curve for a paramagnetic material is also shown in Figure 18.6.

Both diamagnetic and paramagnetic materials are considered to be nonmagnetic because they exhibit magnetization only when in the presence of an external field. Also, for both, the flux density B within them is almost the same as it would be in a vacuum.

18.4 FERROMAGNETISM

Certain metallic materials possess a permanent magnetic moment in the absence of an external field, and manifest very large and permanent magnetizations. These are the characteristics of **ferromagnetism,** and they are displayed by the transition metals iron (as BCC α ferrite), cobalt, nickel, and some of the rare earth metals such as gadolinium (Gd). Magnetic susceptibilities as high as 10^6 are possible for ferromagnetic materials. Consequently, $H \ll M$, and from Equation 18.5 we write

$$B \cong \mu_0 M \tag{18.8}$$

Permanent magnetic moments in ferromagnetic materials result from atomic magnetic moments due to electron spin—uncancelled electron spins as a consequence of the electron structure. There is also an orbital magnetic moment contribution that is small in comparison to the spin moment. Furthermore, in a ferromagnetic material, coupling interactions cause net spin magnetic moments of adjacent atoms to align with one another, even in the absence of an external field. This is schematically illustrated in Figure 18.7. The origin of these coupling forces is not completely understood, but it is thought to arise from the electronic structure of the metal. This mutual spin alignment exists over relatively large volume regions of the crystal called **domains** (see Section 18.7).

The maximum possible magnetization, or **saturation magnetization** M_s, of a ferromagnetic material represents the magnetization that results when all the magnetic dipoles in a solid piece are mutually aligned with the external field; there

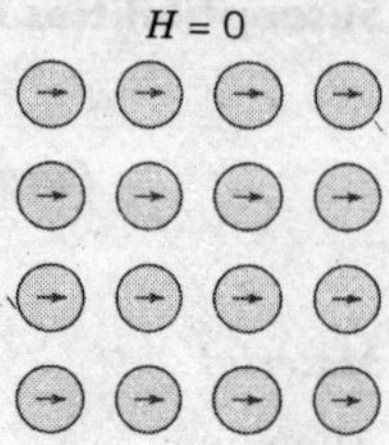

Figure 18.7 Schematic illustration of the mutual alignment of atomic dipoles for a ferromagnetic material, which will exist even in the absence of an external magnetic field.

is also a corresponding saturation flux density B_s. The saturation magnetization is equal to the product of the net magnetic moment for each atom and the number of atoms present. For each of iron, cobalt, and nickel, the net magnetic moments per atom are 2.22, 1.72, and 0.60 Bohr magnetons, respectively.

EXAMPLE PROBLEM 18.1

Saturation Magnetization and Flux Density Computations for Nickel

Calculate **(a)** the saturation magnetization and **(b)** the saturation flux density for nickel, which has a density of 8.90 g/cm^3.

Solution

(a) The saturation magnetization is just the product of the number of Bohr magnetons per atom (0.60 as given above), the magnitude of the Bohr magneton μ_B, and the number N of atoms per cubic meter, or

$$M_s = 0.60\mu_B N \tag{18.9}$$

Now, the number of atoms per cubic meter is related to the density ρ, the atomic weight A_{Ni}, and Avogadro's number N_A, as follows:

$$N = \frac{\rho N_A}{A_{Ni}} \tag{18.10}$$

$$= \frac{(8.90 \times 10^6 \text{ g/m}^3)(6.023 \times 10^{23} \text{ atoms/mol})}{58.71 \text{ g/mol}}$$

$$= 9.13 \times 10^{28} \text{ atoms/m}^3$$

Finally,

$$M_s = \left(\frac{0.60 \text{ Bohr magneton}}{\text{atom}}\right)\left(\frac{9.27 \times 10^{-24} \text{ A-m}^2}{\text{Bohr magneton}}\right)\left(\frac{9.13 \times 10^{28} \text{ atoms}}{\text{m}^3}\right)$$

$$= 5.1 \times 10^5 \text{ A/m}$$

(b) From Equation 18.8, the saturation flux density is just

$$B_s = \mu_0 M_s$$

$$= \left(\frac{4\pi \times 10^{-7} \text{ H}}{\text{m}}\right)\left(\frac{5.1 \times 10^5 \text{ A}}{\text{m}}\right)$$

$$= 0.64 \text{ tesla}$$

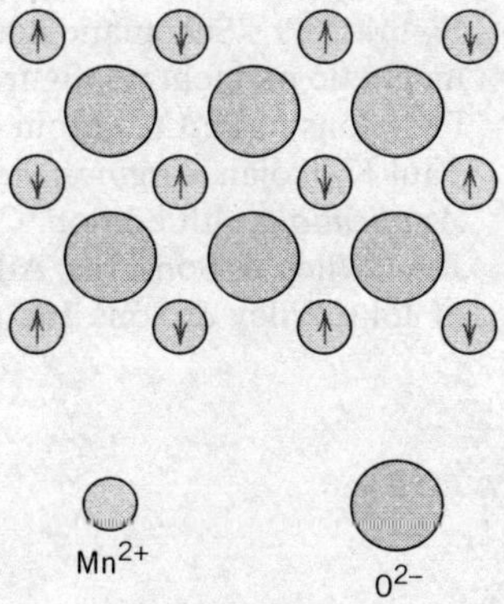

Figure 18.8 Schematic representation of antiparallel alignment of spin magnetic moments for antiferromagnetic manganese oxide.

18.5 ANTIFERROMAGNETISM AND FERRIMAGNETISM

Antiferromagnetism

This phenomenon of magnetic moment coupling between adjacent atoms or ions occurs in materials other than those that are ferromagnetic. In one such group, this coupling results in an antiparallel alignment; the alignment of the spin moments of neighboring atoms or ions in exactly opposite directions is termed **antiferromagnetism.** Manganese oxide (MnO) is one material that displays this behavior. Manganese oxide is a ceramic material that is ionic in character, having both Mn^{2+} and O^{2-} ions. No net magnetic moment is associated with the O^{2-} ions, since there is a total cancellation of both spin and orbital moments. However, the Mn^{2+} ions possess a net magnetic moment that is predominantly of spin origin. These Mn^{2+} ions are arrayed in the crystal structure such that the moments of adjacent ions are antiparallel. This arrangement is represented schematically in Figure 18.8. Obviously, the opposing magnetic moments cancel one another, and, as a consequence, the solid as a whole possesses no net magnetic moment.

Ferrimagnetism

Some ceramics also exhibit a permanent magnetization, termed **ferrimagnetism.** The macroscopic magnetic characteristics of ferromagnets and ferrimagnets are similar; the distinction lies in the source of the net magnetic moments. The principles of ferrimagnetism are illustrated with the cubic ferrites.[2] These ionic materials may be represented by the chemical formula MFe_2O_4, in which M represents any one of several metallic elements. The prototype ferrite is Fe_3O_4, the mineral magnetite, sometimes called lodestone.

The formula for Fe_3O_4 may be written as $Fe^{2+}O^{2-}–(Fe^{3+})_2(O^{2-})_3$ in which the Fe ions exist in both +2 and +3 valence states in the ratio of 1:2. A net spin magnetic moment exists for each Fe^{2+} and Fe^{3+} ion, which corresponds to 4 and 5 Bohr magnetons, respectively, for the two ion types. Furthermore, the O^{2-} ions are magnetically neutral. There are antiparallel spin-coupling interactions between the Fe ions, similar in character to antiferromagnetism. However, the net ferrimagnetic moment arises from the incomplete cancellation of spin moments.

Cubic ferrites have the inverse spinel crystal structure, which is cubic in symmetry, and similar to the spinel structure (Section 4.14). The inverse spinel crystal

---

[2] Ferrite in the magnetic sense should not be confused with the ferrite α-iron discussed in Section 7.18; in the remainder of this chapter, the term **ferrite** implies the magnetic ceramic.

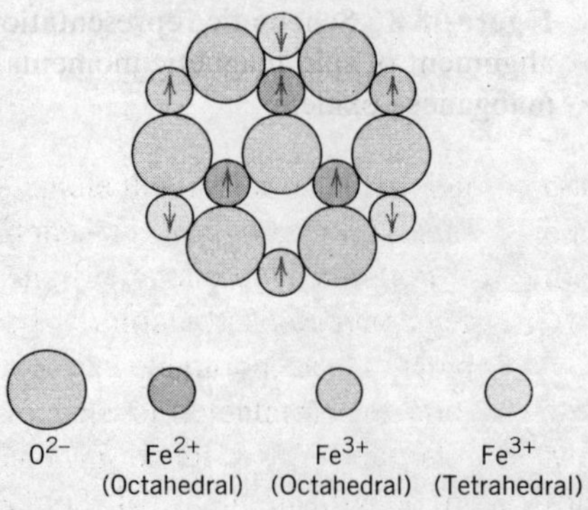

Figure 18.9 Schematic diagram showing the spin magnetic moment configuration for Fe^{2+} and Fe^{3+} ions in Fe_3O_4. (From Richard A. Flinn and Paul K. Trojan, *Engineering Materials and Their Applications,* 4th edition. Copyright © 1990 by John Wiley & Sons, Inc. Adapted by permission of John Wiley & Sons, Inc.)

structure might be thought of as having been generated by the stacking of close-packed planes of O^{2-} ions. Again, there are two types of positions that may be occupied by the iron cations, as illustrated in Figure 4.16. For one, the coordination number is 4 (tetrahedral coordination); that is, each Fe ion is surrounded by four oxygen nearest neighbors. For the other, the coordination number is 6 (octahedral coordination). With this inverse spinel structure, half the trivalent (Fe^{3+}) ions are situated in octahedral positions, the other half, in tetrahedral positions. The divalent Fe^{2+} ions are all located in octahedral positions. The critical factor is the arrangement of the spin moments of the Fe ions, as represented in Figure 18.9 and Table 18.3. The spin moments of all the Fe^{3+} ions in the octahedral positions are aligned parallel to one another; however, they are directed oppositely to the Fe^{3+} ions disposed in the tetrahedral positions, which are also aligned. This results from the antiparallel coupling of adjacent iron ions. Thus, the spin moments of all Fe^{3+} ions cancel one another and make no net contribution to the magnetization of the solid. All the Fe^{2+} ions have their moments aligned in the same direction; this total moment is responsible for the net magnetization (see Table 18.4). Thus, the saturation magnetization of a ferrimagnetic solid may be computed from the product of the net spin magnetic moment for each Fe^{2+} ion and the number of Fe^{2+} ions; this would correspond to the mutual alignment of all the Fe^{2+} ion magnetic moments in the Fe_3O_4 specimen.

Cubic ferrites having other compositions may be produced by adding metallic ions that substitute for some of the iron in the crystal structure. Again, from the

Table 18.3 The Distribution of Spin Magnetic Moments for Fe^{2+} and Fe^{3+} Ions in a Unit Cell Fe_3O_4[a]

Cation	*Octahedral Lattice Site*	*Tetrahedral Lattice Site*	*Net Magnetic Moment*
Fe^{3+}	↑↑↑↑ ↑↑↑↑	↓↓↓↓ ↓↓↓↓	Complete cancellation
Fe^{2+}	↑↑↑↑ ↑↑↑↑	—	↑↑↑↑

[a] Each arrow represents the magnetic moment orientation for one of the cations.

Table 18.4 Net Magnetic Moments for Six Cations

Cation	*Net Spin Magnetic Moment (Bohr magnetons)*
Fe^{3+}	5
Fe^{2+}	4
Mn^{2+}	5
Co^{2+}	3
Ni^{2+}	2
Cu^{2+}	1

ferrite chemical formula, $M^{2+}O^{2-}–(Fe^{3+})_2(O^{2-})_3$, in addition to Fe^{2+}, M^{2+} may represent divalent ions such as Ni^{2+}, Mn^{2+}, Co^{2+}, and Cu^{2+}, each of which possesses a net spin magnetic moment different from 4; several are listed in Table 18.4. Thus, by adjustment of composition, ferrite compounds having a range of magnetic properties may be produced. For example, nickel ferrite has the formula $NiFe_2O_4$. Other compounds may also be produced containing mixtures of two divalent metal ions such as $(Mn,Mg)Fe_2O_4$, in which the $Mn^{2+}:Mg^{2+}$ ratio may be varied; these are called mixed ferrites.

Ceramic materials other than the cubic ferrites are also ferrimagnetic; these include the hexagonal ferrites and garnets. Hexagonal ferrites have a crystal structure similar to the inverse spinel, with hexagonal symmetry rather than cubic. The chemical formula for these materials may be represented by $AB_{12}O_{19}$, in which A is a divalent metal such as barium, lead, or strontium, and B is a trivalent metal such as aluminum, gallium, chromium, or iron. The two most common examples of the hexagonal ferrites are $PbFe_{12}O_{19}$ and $BaFe_{12}O_{19}$.

The garnets have a very complicated crystal structure, which may be represented by the general formula $M_3Fe_5O_{12}$; here, M represents a rare earth ion such as samarium, europium, gadolinium, or yttrium. Yttrium iron garnet ($Y_3Fe_5O_{12}$), sometimes denoted YIG, is the most common material of this type.

The saturation magnetizations for ferrimagnetic materials are not as high as for ferromagnets. On the other hand, ferrites, being ceramic materials, are good electrical insulators. For some magnetic applications, such as high-frequency transformers, a low electrical conductivity is most desirable.

Concept Check 18.1

Cite the major similarities and differences between ferromagnetic and ferrimagnetic materials.

[*The answer may be found in enclosed CD.*]

Concept Check 18.2

What is the difference between the spinel and inverse spinel crystal structures? *Hint:* You may want to consult Section 4.14.

[*The answer may be found in enclosed CD.*]

EXAMPLE PROBLEM 18.2

Saturation Magnetization Determination for Fe_3O_4

Calculate the saturation magnetization for Fe_3O_4 given that each cubic unit cell contains 8 Fe^{2+} and 16 Fe^{3+} ions, and that the unit cell edge length is 0.839 nm.

Solution

This problem is solved in a manner similar to Example Problem 18.1, except that the computational basis is per unit cell as opposed to per atom or ion.

The saturation magnetization will be equal to the product of the number N' of Bohr magnetons per cubic meter of Fe_3O_4, and the magnetic moment per Bohr magneton μ_B,

$$M_s = N'\mu_B \tag{18.11}$$

Now, N' is just the number of Bohr magnetons per unit cell n_B divided by the unit cell volume V_C, or

$$N' = \frac{n_B}{V_C} \tag{18.12}$$

Again, the net magnetization results from the Fe^{2+} ions only. Since there are 8 Fe^{2+} ions per unit cell and 4 Bohr magnetons per Fe^{2+} ion, n_B is 32. Furthermore, the unit cell is a cube, and $V_C = a^3$, a being the unit cell edge length. Therefore.

$$M_s = \frac{n_B \mu_B}{a^3} \tag{18.13}$$

$$= \frac{(32 \text{ Bohr magnetons/unit cell})(9.27 \times 10^{-24} \text{ A-m}^2\text{/Bohr magneton})}{(0.839 \times 10^{-9} \text{ m})^3\text{/unit cell}}$$

$$= 5.0 \times 10^5 \text{ A/m}$$

DESIGN EXAMPLE 18.1

Design of a Mixed Ferrite Magnetic Material

Design a cubic mixed-ferrite magnetic material that has a saturation magnetization of 5.25×10^5 A/m.

Solution

According to Example Problem 18.2 the saturation magnetization for Fe_3O_4 is 5.0×10^5 A/m. In order to increase the magnitude of M_s it is necessary to replace some fraction of the Fe^{2+} with a divalent metal ion that has a greater magnetic moment—for example Mn^{2+}; from Table 18.4, note that there are 5 Bohr magnetons/Mn^{2+} ion as compared to 4 Bohr magnetons/Fe^{2+}. Let us first employ Equation 18.13 to compute the number of Bohr magnetons per unit cell

(n_B), assuming that the Mn^{2+} addition does not change the unit cell edge length (0.839 nm). Thus,

$$n_B = \frac{M_s a^3}{\mu_B}$$

$$= \frac{(5.25 \times 10^5 \text{ A/m})(0.839 \times 10^{-9} \text{ m})^3\text{/unit cell}}{9.27 \times 10^{-24} \text{ A-m}^2\text{/Bohr magneton}}$$

$$= 33.45 \text{ Bohr magnetons/unit cell}$$

If we let x represent the fraction of Mn^{2+} that have substituted for Fe^{2+}, then the remaining unsubstituted Fe^{2+} fraction is equal to $(1 - x)$. Furthermore, inasmuch as there are 8 divalent ions per unit cell, we may write the following expression:

$$8[5x + 4(1 - x)] = 33.45$$

which leads to $x = 0.181$. Thus, if 18.1 at% of the Fe^{2+} in Fe_3O_4 are replaced with Mn^{2+}, the saturation magnetization will be increased to 5.25×10^5 A/m.

18.6 THE INFLUENCE OF TEMPERATURE ON MAGNETIC BEHAVIOR

Temperature can also influence the magnetic characteristics of materials. Recall that raising the temperature of a solid results in an increase in the magnitude of the thermal vibrations of atoms. The atomic magnetic moments are free to rotate; hence, with rising temperature, the increased thermal motion of the atoms tends to randomize the directions of any moments that may be aligned.

For ferromagnetic, antiferromagnetic, and ferrimagnetic materials, the atomic thermal motions counteract the coupling forces between the adjacent atomic dipole moments, causing some dipole misalignment, regardless of whether an external field is present. This results in a decrease in the saturation magnetization for both ferro- and ferrimagnets. The saturation magnetization is a maximum at 0 K, at which temperature the thermal vibrations are a minimum. With increasing temperature, the saturation magnetization diminishes gradually and then abruptly drops to zero at what is called the **Curie temperature** T_c. The magnetization-temperature behavior for iron and Fe_3O_4 is represented in Figure 18.10. At T_c the mutual spin coupling forces are completely destroyed, such that for temperatures above T_c both ferromagnetic and ferrimagnetic materials are paramagnetic. The magnitude of the Curie temperature varies from material to material; for example, for iron, cobalt, nickel, and Fe_3O_4, the respective values are 768, 1120, 335, and 585°C.

Antiferromagnetism is also affected by temperature; this behavior vanishes at what is called the *Néel temperature.* At temperatures above this point, antiferromagnetic materials also become paramagnetic.

Concept Check 18.3

Explain why repeatedly dropping a permanent magnet on the floor will cause it to become demagnetized.

[*The answer may be found in enclosed CD.*]

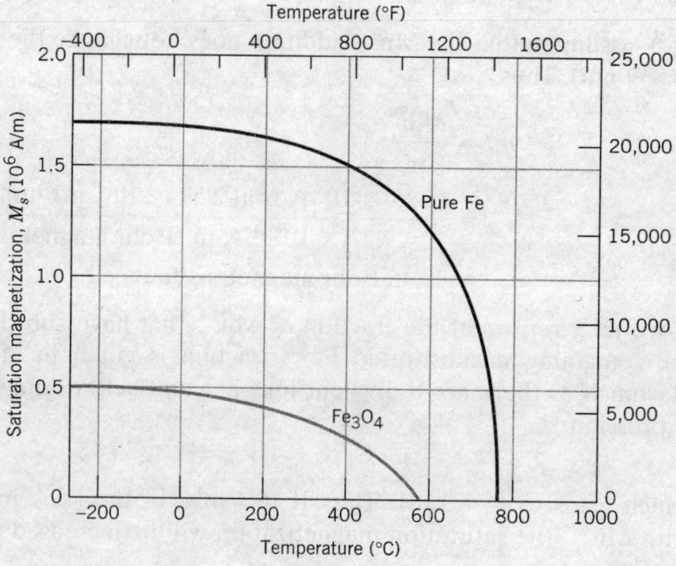

Figure 18.10 Plot of saturation magnetization as a function of temperature for iron and Fe_3O_4. [Adapted from J. Smit and H. P. J. Wijn, *Ferrites.* Copyright © 1959 by N. V. Philips Gloeilampenfabrieken, Eindhoven (Holland). Reprinted by permission.]

18.7 DOMAINS AND HYSTERESIS

Any ferromagnetic or ferrimagnetic material that is at a temperature below T_c is composed of small-volume regions in which there is a mutual alignment in the same direction of all magnetic dipole moments, as illustrated in Figure 18.11. Such a region is called a domain, and each one is magnetized to its saturation magnetization. Adjacent domains are separated by domain boundaries or walls, across which the direction of magnetization gradually changes (Figure 18.12). Normally, domains are microscopic in size, and for a polycrystalline specimen, each grain may consist of more than a single domain. Thus, in a macroscopic piece of material, there will be a large number of domains, and all may have different magnetization orientations. The magnitude of the M field for the entire solid is the vector sum of the magnetizations of all the domains, each domain contribution being weighted by its volume fraction. For an unmagnetized specimen, the appropriately weighted vector sum of the magnetizations of all the domains is zero.

Figure 18.11 Schematic depiction of domains in a ferromagnetic or ferrimagnetic material; arrows represent atomic magnetic dipoles. Within each domain, all dipoles are aligned, whereas the direction of alignment varies from one domain to another.

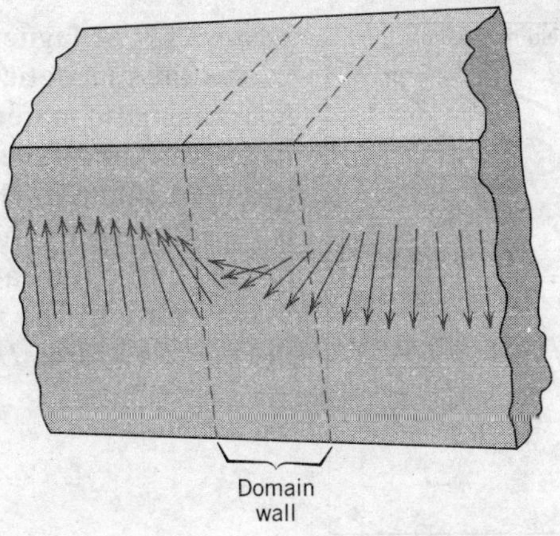

Figure 18.12 The gradual change in magnetic dipole orientation across a domain wall. (From W. D. Kingery, H. K. Bowen, and D. R. Uhlmann, *Introduction to Ceramics,* 2nd edition. Copyright © 1976 by John Wiley & Sons, New York. Reprinted by permission of John Wiley & Sons, Inc.)

Flux density B and field intensity H are not proportional for ferromagnets and ferrimagnets. If the material is initially unmagnetized, then B varies as a function of H as shown in Figure 18.13. The curve begins at the origin, and as H is increased, the B field begins to increase slowly, then more rapidly, finally leveling off and becoming independent of H. This maximum value of B is the saturation flux density B_s, and the corresponding magnetization is the saturation magnetization M_s, mentioned previously. Since the permeability μ from Equation 18.2 is the slope of the B-versus-H curve, note from Figure 18.13 that the permeability changes with and is dependent on H. On occasion, the slope of the B-versus-H curve at $H = 0$ is specified as a material property, which is termed the *initial permeability* μ_i, as indicated in Figure 18.13.

As an H field is applied, the domains change shape and size by the movement of domain boundaries. Schematic domain structures are represented in the insets (labeled U through Z) at several points along the B-versus-H curve in Figure 18.13. Initially, the moments of the constituent domains are randomly oriented such that there is no net B (or M) field (inset U). As the external field is applied, the domains that are oriented in directions favorable to (or nearly aligned with) the applied field

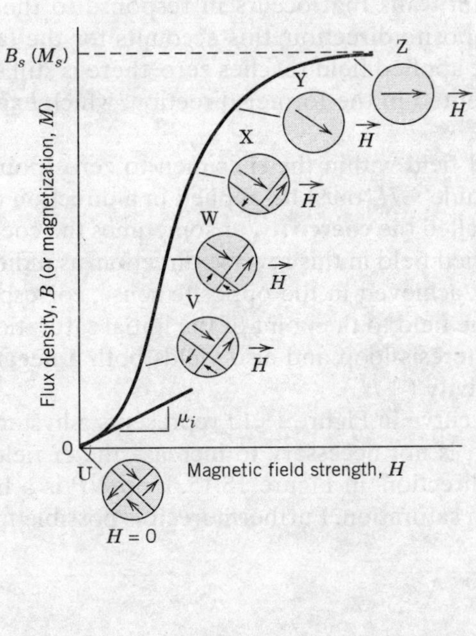

Figure 18.13 The B-versus-H behavior for a ferromagnetic or ferrimagnetic material that was initially unmagnetized. Domain configurations during several stages of magnetization are represented. Saturation flux density B_s, magnetization M_s, and initial permeability μ_i are also indicated. (Adapted from O. H. Wyatt and D. Dew-Hughes, *Metals, Ceramics and Polymers,* Cambridge University Press, 1974.)

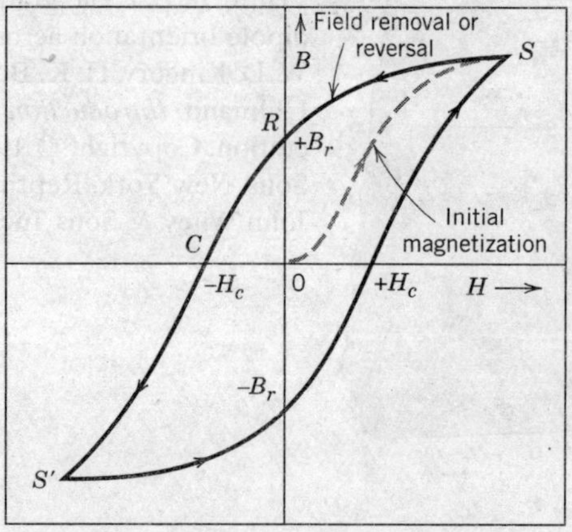

Figure 18.14 Magnetic flux density versus the magnetic field strength for a ferromagnetic material that is subjected to forward and reverse saturations (points S and S'). The hysteresis loop is represented by the solid curve; the dashed curve indicates the initial magnetization. The remanence B_r and the coercive force H_c are also shown.

grow at the expense of those that are unfavorably oriented (insets V through X). This process continues with increasing field strength until the macroscopic specimen becomes a single domain, which is nearly aligned with the field (inset Y). Saturation is achieved when this domain, by means of rotation, becomes oriented with the H field (inset Z). Alteration of the domain structure with magnetic field for an iron single crystal is shown in the chapter-opening photographs for this chapter.

From saturation, point S in Figure 18.14, as the H field is reduced by reversal of field direction, the curve does not retrace its original path. A **hysteresis** effect is produced in which the B field lags behind the applied H field, or decreases at a lower rate. At zero H field (point R on the curve), there exists a residual B field that is called the **remanence,** or remanent flux density, B_r; the material remains magnetized in the absence of an external H field.

Hysteresis behavior and permanent magnetization may be explained by the motion of domain walls. Upon reversal of the field direction from saturation (point S in Figure 18.14), the process by which the domain structure changes is reversed. First, there is a rotation of the single domain with the reversed field. Next, domains having magnetic moments aligned with the new field form and grow at the expense of the former domains. Critical to this explanation is the resistance to movement of domain walls that occurs in response to the increase of the magnetic field in the opposite direction; this accounts for the lag of B with H, or the hysteresis. When the applied field reaches zero, there is still some net volume fraction of domains oriented in the former direction, which explains the existence of the remanence B_r.

To reduce the B field within the specimen to zero (point C on Figure 18.14), an H field of magnitude $-H_c$ must be applied in a direction opposite to that of the original field; H_c is called the **coercivity,** or sometimes the coercive force. Upon continuation of the applied field in this reverse direction, as indicated in the figure, saturation is ultimately achieved in the opposite sense, corresponding to point S'. A second reversal of the field to the point of the initial saturation (point S) completes the symmetrical hysteresis loop and also yields both a negative remanence ($-B_r$) and a positive coercivity ($+H_c$).

The B-versus-H curve in Figure 18.14 represents a hysteresis loop taken to saturation. Of course, it is not necessary to increase the H field to saturation before reversing the field direction; in Figure 18.15, loop NP is a hysteresis curve corresponding to less than saturation. Furthermore, it is possible to reverse the direction

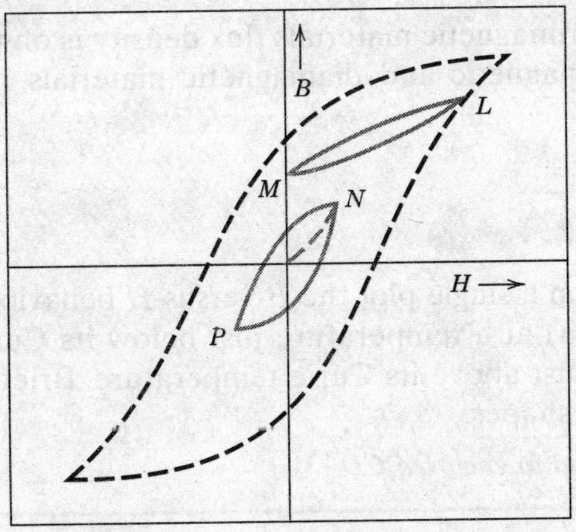

Figure 18.15 A hysteresis curve at less than saturation (curve *NP*) within the saturation loop for a ferromagnetic material. The *B–H* behavior for field reversal at other than saturation is indicated by curve *LM*.

of the field at any point along the curve and generate other hysteresis loops. One such loop is indicated on the saturation curve in Figure 18.15: for loop *LM*, the *H* field is reversed to zero. One method of demagnetizing a ferromagnet or ferrimagnet is to repeatedly cycle it in an *H* field that alternates direction and decreases in magnitude.

At this point it is instructive to compare the *B*-versus-*H* behaviors of paramagnetic, diamagnetic, and ferromagnetic/ferrimagnetic materials; such a comparison is shown in Figure 18.16. The linearity of paramagnetic and diamagnetic materials may be noted in the small inset plot, whereas the behavior of a typical ferromagnetic/ferrimagnetic is nonlinear. Furthermore, the rationale for labeling paramagnetics and diamagnetics as nonmagnetic materials is verified by comparing the *B* scales on the vertical axes of the two plots—at an *H* field strength of 50 A/m,

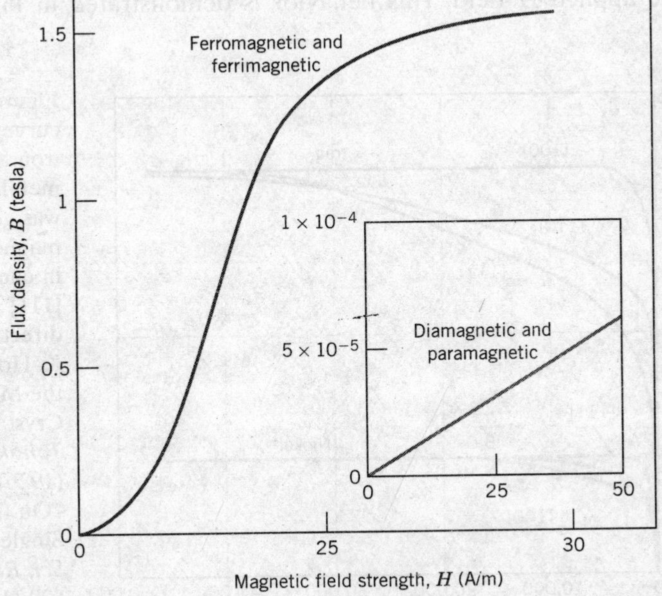

Figure 18.16 Comparison of *B*-versus-*H* behaviors for ferromagnetic/ferrimagnetic and diamagnetic/paramagnetic materials (inset plot). Here it may be noted that extremely small *B* fields are generated in materials that experience only diamagnetic/paramagnetic behavior, which is why they are considered to be nonmagnetics.

the ferromagnetic/ferrimagnetic materials flux density is on the order of 1.5 tesla, whereas for the parmagnetic and diamagnetic materials it is on the order of 5×10^{-5} tesla.

Concept Check 18.4

Schematically sketch on a single plot the *B*-versus-*H* behavior for a ferromagnetic material (a) at 0 K, (b) at a temperature just below its Curie temperature, and (c) at a temperature just above its Curie temperature. Briefly explain why these curves have different shapes.

[*The answer may be found in enclosed CD.*]

Concept Check 18.5

Schematically sketch the hysteresis behavior for a ferromagnet which is gradually demagnetized by cycling in an *H* field that alternates direction and decreases in magnitude.

[*The answer may be found in enclosed CD.*]

18.8 MAGNETIC ANISOTROPY

The magnetic hysteresis curves discussed in the previous section will have different shapes depending on various factors: (1) whether the specimen is a single crystal or polycrystalline; (2) if polycrystalline, any preferred orientation of the grains; (3) the presence of pores or second-phase particles; and (4) other factors such as temperature and, if a mechanical stress is applied, the stress state.

For example, the *B* (or *M*) versus *H* curve for a single crystal of a ferromagnetic material depends on its crystallographic orientation relative to the direction of the applied *H* field. This behavior is demonstrated in Figure 18.17 for single

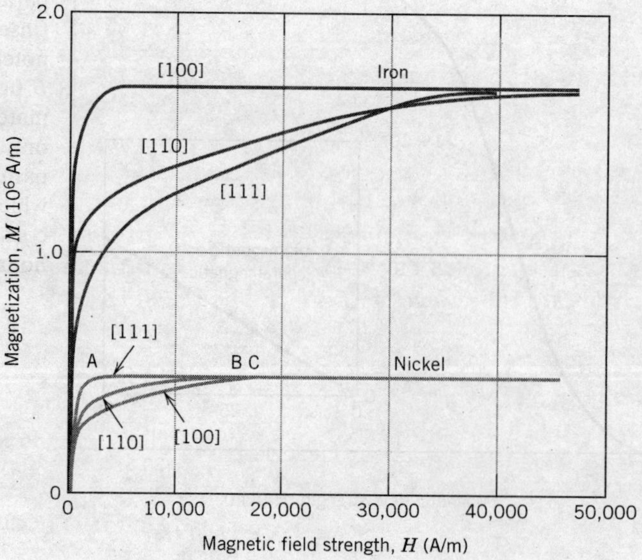

Figure 18.17 Magnetization curves for single crystals of iron and nickel. For both metals, a different curve was generated when the magnetic field was applied in each of [100], [110], and [111] crystallographic directions. [Adapted from K. Honda and S. Kaya, "On the Magnetisation of Single Crystals of Iron," *Sci. Rep. Tohoku Univ.,* **15,** 721 (1926); and from S. Kaya, "On the Magnetisation of Single Crystals of Nickel," *Sci. Rep. Tohoku Univ.,* **17,** 639 (1928).]

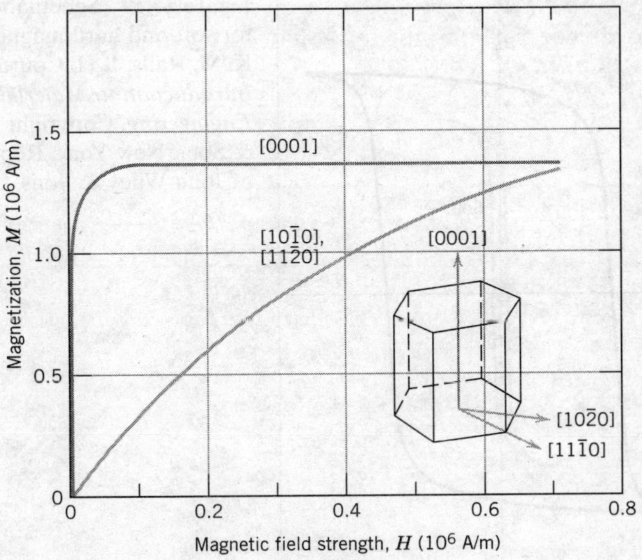

Figure 18.18 Magnetization curves for single crystals of cobalt. The curves were generated when the magnetic field was applied in [0001] and [10$\bar{1}$0]/[11$\bar{2}$0] crystallographic directions. [Adapted from S. Kaya, "On the Magnetisation of Single Crystals of Cobalt," *Sci. Rep. Tohoku Univ.*, **17**, 1157 (1928).]

crystals of nickel (FCC) and iron (BCC), where the magnetizing field is applied in [100], [110], and [111] crystallographic directions; and in Figure 18.18 for cobalt (HCP) in [0001] and [10$\bar{1}$0]/[11$\bar{2}$0] directions. This dependence of magnetic behavior on crystallographic orientation is termed *magnetic* (or sometimes *magnetocrystalline*) *anisotropy.*

For each of these materials there is one crystallographic direction in which magnetization is easiest—that is, saturation (of M) is achieved at the lowest H field; this is termed a direction of *easy magnetization.* For example, for Ni (Figure 18.17) this direction is [111] inasmuch as saturation occurs at point A; whereas, for [110] and [100] orientations, saturation points correspond, respectively, to points B and C. Correspondingly, easy magnetization directions for Fe and Co are [100] and [0001], respectively (Figures 18.17 and 18.18). Conversely, a *hard* crystallographic direction is that direction for which saturation magnetization is most difficult; hard directions for Ni, Fe, and Co are [100], [111], and [10$\bar{1}$0]/[11$\bar{2}$0].

As noted in the previous section, the insets of Figure 18.13 represent domain configurations at various stages along the B (or M) versus H curve during the magnetization of a ferromagnetic/ferrimagnetic material. Here, each of the arrows represents a domain's direction of easy magnetization; and domains whose directions of easy magnetization are most closely aligned with the H field grow, at the expense of the other domains that shrink (insets V through X). Furthermore, the magnetization of the single domain in inset Y also corresponds to an easy direction. And saturation is achieved as the direction of this domain rotates away from the easy direction into the direction of the applied field (inset Z).

18.9 SOFT MAGNETIC MATERIALS

The size and shape of the hysteresis curve for ferromagnetic and ferrimagnetic materials is of considerable practical importance. The area within a loop represents a magnetic energy loss per unit volume of material per magnetization–demagnetization cycle; this energy loss is manifested as heat that is generated within the magnetic specimen and is capable of raising its temperature.

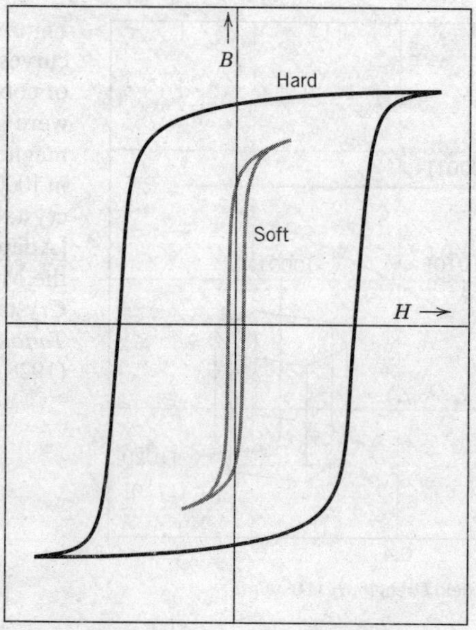

Figure 18.19 Schematic magnetization curves for soft and hard magnetic materials. (From K. M. Ralls, T. H. Courtney, and J. Wulff, *Introduction to Materials Science and Engineering*. Copyright © 1976 by John Wiley & Sons, New York. Reprinted by permission of John Wiley & Sons, Inc.)

Both ferromagnetic and ferrimagnetic materials are classified as either *soft* or *hard* on the basis of their hysteresis characteristics. **Soft magnetic materials** are used in devices that are subjected to alternating magnetic fields and in which energy losses must be low; one familiar example consists of transformer cores. For this reason the relative area within the hysteresis loop must be small; it is characteristically thin and narrow, as represented in Figure 18.19. Consequently, a soft magnetic material must have a high initial permeability and a low coercivity. A material possessing these properties may reach its saturation magnetization with a relatively low applied field (i.e., is easily magnetized and demagnetized) and still has low hysteresis energy losses.

The saturation field or magnetization is determined only by the composition of the material. For example, in cubic ferrites, substitution of a divalent metal ion such as Ni^{2+} for Fe^{2+} in $FeO–Fe_2O_3$ will change the saturation magnetization. However, susceptibility and coercivity (H_c), which also influence the shape of the hysteresis curve, are sensitive to structural variables rather than to composition. For example, a low value of coercivity corresponds to the easy movement of domain walls as the magnetic field changes magnitude and/or direction. Structural defects such as particles of a nonmagnetic phase or voids in the magnetic material tend to restrict the motion of domain walls, and thus increase the coercivity. Consequently, a soft magnetic material must be free of such structural defects.

Another property consideration for soft magnetic materials is electrical resistivity. In addition to the hysteresis energy losses described above, energy losses may result from electrical currents that are induced in a magnetic material by a magnetic field that varies in magnitude and direction with time; these are called *eddy currents.* It is most desirable to minimize these energy losses in soft magnetic materials by increasing the electrical resistivity. This is accomplished in ferromagnetic materials by forming solid solution alloys; iron–silicon and iron–nickel alloys are examples. The ceramic ferrites are commonly used for applications requiring soft magnetic materials because they are intrinsically electrical insulators. Their applicability is somewhat limited, however, inasmuch as they have relatively small

MATERIAL OF IMPORTANCE

An Iron-Silicon Alloy That is Used in Transformer Cores

As mentioned earlier in this section, transformer cores require the use of soft magnetic materials, which are easily magnetized and demagnetized (and also have relatively high electrical resistivities). One alloy commonly used for this application is the iron–silicon alloy listed in Table 18.5 (97 wt% Fe-3 wt% Si). Single crystals of this alloy are magnetically anisotropic, as are also single crystals of iron (as explained above). Consequently, energy losses of transformers could be minimized if their cores were fabricated from single crystals such that a [100]-type direction [the direction of easy magnetization (Figure 18.17)] is oriented parallel to the direction of an applied magnetic field; this configuration for a transformer core is represented schematically in Figure 18.20. Unfortunately, single crystals are expensive to prepare, and, thus, this is an economically unpractical situation. A better alternative—one that is used commercially, being more economically attractive—is to fabricate cores from polycrystalline sheets of this alloy that are anisotropic.

It is often the case that the grains in polycrystalline materials are randomly oriented, with the result that their properties are isotropic (Section 3.10). However, one way of developing anisotropy in polycrystalline metals is via plastic deformation, for example by rolling (Section 23.2, Figure 23.1*b*); rolling is the technique by which sheet transformer cores are fabricated. A flat sheet that has been rolled is said to have a *rolling* (or *sheet*) *texture*, or there is a preferred crystallographic orientation of the grains. For this type of texture, during the rolling operation, for most of the grains in the sheet, a specific crystallographic plane (*hkl*) becomes is aligned parallel (or nearly parallel) to the surface of the sheet, and, in addition a direction [*uvw*] in that plane lies parallel (or nearly parallel) to the rolling direction. Thus, a rolling texture is indicated by the plane–direction combination, (*hkl*)[*uvw*]. For body-centered cubic alloys (to include the iron–silicon alloy mentioned above), the rolling texture is (110) [001], which is represented schematically in Figure 18.21. Thus, transformer cores of this iron–silicon alloy are fabricated such the direction in which the sheet was rolled (corresponding to a [001]-type direction for most of the grains) is aligned parallel to the direction of the magnetic field application.[3]

The magnetic characteristics of this alloy may be further improved through a series of deformation and heat-treating procedures that produce a (100)[001] texture.

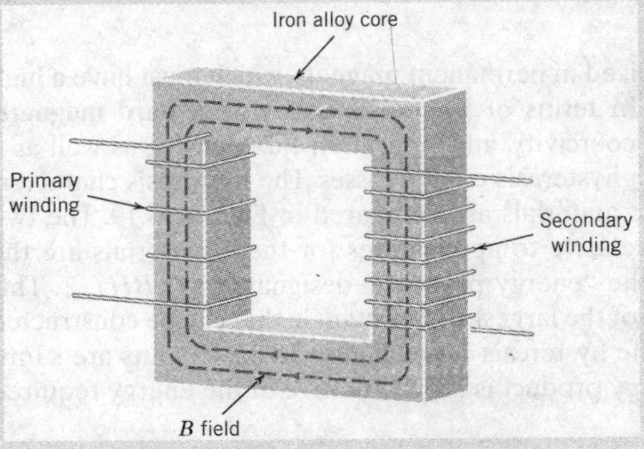

Figure 18.20 Schematic diagram of a transformer core, including the direction of *B* field that is generated.

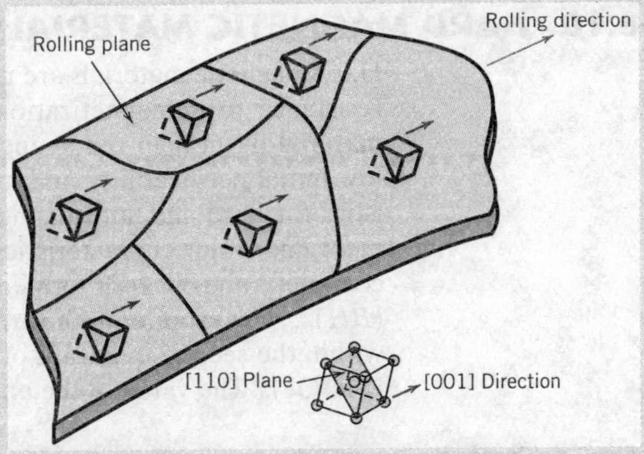

Figure 18.21 Schematic representation of the (110)[001] rolling texture for body-centered cubic iron.

[3] For body-centered cubic metals and alloys, [100] and [001] directions are equivalent (Section 3.7)—that is, both are directions of easy magnetization.

Table 18.5 Typical Properties for Several Soft Magnetic Materials

Material	*Composition (wt %)*	*Initial Relative Permeability* μ_i	*Saturation Flux Density* B_s *[tesla (gauss)]*	*Hysteresis Loss/Cycle* *[J/m³ (erg/cm³)]*	*Resistivity* ρ *(Ω-m)*
Commercial iron ingot	99.95Fe	150	2.14 (21,400)	270 (2700)	1.0×10^{-7}
Silicon–iron (oriented)	97Fe, 3Si	1400	2.01 (20,100)	40 (400)	4.7×10^{-7}
45 Permalloy	55Fe, 45Ni	2500	1.60 (16,000)	120 (1200)	4.5×10^{-7}
Supermalloy	79Ni, 15Fe, 5Mo, 0.5Mn	75,000	0.80 (8000)	—	6.0×10^{-7}
Ferroxcube A	$48MnFe_2O_4$, $52ZnFe_2O_4$	1400	0.33 (3300)	~40 (~400)	2000
Ferroxcube B	$36NiFe_2O_4$, $64ZnFe_2O_4$	650	0.36 (3600)	~35 (~350)	10^7

Source: Adapted from *Metals Handbook: Properties and Selection: Stainless Steels, Tool Materials and Special-Purpose Metals,* Vol. 3, 9th edition, D. Benjamin (Senior Editor), American Society for Metals, 1980.

susceptibilities. The properties of a half-dozen soft magnetic materials are shown in Table 18.5.

The hysteresis characteristics of soft magnetic materials may be enhanced for some applications by an appropriate heat treatment in the presence of a magnetic field. Using such a technique, a square hysteresis loop may be produced, which is desirable in some magnetic amplifier and pulse transformer applications. In addition, soft magnetic materials are used in generators, motors, dynamos, and switching circuits.

18.10 HARD MAGNETIC MATERIALS

Hard magnetic materials are utilized in permanent magnets, which must have a high resistance to demagnetization. In terms of hysteresis behavior, a **hard magnetic material** has a high remanence, coercivity, and saturation flux density, as well as a low initial permeability, and high hysteresis energy losses. The hysteresis characteristics for hard and soft magnetic materials are compared in Figure 18.19. The two most important characteristics relative to applications for these materials are the coercivity and what is termed the "energy product," designated as $(BH)_{max}$. This $(BH)_{max}$ corresponds to the area of the largest B-H rectangle that can be constructed within the second quadrant of the hysteresis curve, Figure 18.22; its units are kJ/m³ (MGOe).[4] The value of the energy product is representative of the energy required

[4] MGOe is defined as

$$1 \text{ MGOe} = 10^6 \text{ gauss-oersted}$$

Furthermore, conversion from cgs–emu to SI units is accomplished by the relationship

$$1 \text{ MGOe} = 7.96 \text{ kJ/m}^3$$

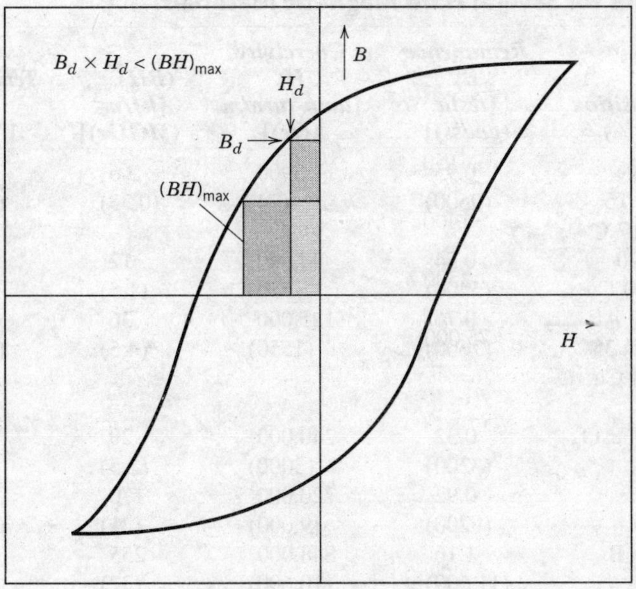

Figure 18.22 Schematic magnetization curve that displays hysteresis. Within the second quadrant are drawn two B–H energy product rectangles; the area of that rectangle labeled $(BH)_{max}$ is the largest possible, which is greater than the area defined by B_d–H_d.

to demagnetize a permanent magnet; that is, the larger $(BH)_{max}$ the harder is the material in terms of its magnetic characteristics.

Again, hysteresis behavior is related to the ease with which the magnetic domain boundaries move; by impeding domain wall motion, the coercivity and susceptibility are enhanced, such that a large external field is required for demagnetization. Furthermore, these characteristics are interrelated to the microstructure of the material.

Concept Check 18.6

It is possible, by various means (i.e., alteration of microstructure and impurity additions), to control the ease with which domain walls move as the magnetic field is changed for ferromagnetic and ferrimagnetic materials. Sketch a schematic B-versus-H hysteresis loop for a ferromagnetic material, and superimpose on this plot the loop alterations that would occur if domain boundary movement were hindered.

[*The answer may be found in enclosed CD.*]

Conventional Hard Magnetic Materials

Hard magnetic materials fall within two main categories—conventional and high energy. The conventional materials have $(BH)_{max}$ values that range between about 2 and 80 kJ/m^3 (0.25 and 10 MGOe). These include ferromagnetic materials—magnet steels, cunife (Cu–Ni–Fe) alloys, alnico (Al–Ni–Co) alloys—as well as the hexagonal ferrites (BaO–$6Fe_2O_3$). Table 18.6 presents some of the critical properties of several of these hard magnetic materials.

The hard magnet steels are normally alloyed with tungsten and/or chromium. Under the proper heat-treating conditions these two elements readily combine with carbon in the steel to form tungsten and chromium carbide precipitate particles, which are especially effective in obstructing domain wall motion. For the other metal

Table 18.6 Typical Properties for Several Hard Magnetic Materials.

Material	*Composition (wt %)*	*Remanence B_r [tesla (gauss)]*	*Coercivity H_c [amp-turn/m (Oe)]*	*$(BH)_{max}$ [kJ/m³ (MGOe)]*	*Curie Temperature T_c [°C(°F)]*	*Resistivity ρ (Ω-m)*
Tungsten steel	92.8 Fe, 6 W, 0.5 Cr, 0.7 C	0.95 (9500)	5900 (74)	2.6 (0.33)	760 (1400)	3.0×10^{-7}
Cunife	20 Fe, 20 Ni, 60 Cu	0.54 (5400)	44,000 (550)	12 (1.5)	410 (770)	1.8×10^{-7}
Sintered alnico 8	34 Fe, 7 Al, 15 Ni, 35 Co, 4 Cu, 5 Ti	0.76 (7600)	125,000 (1550)	36 (4.5)	860 (1580)	—
Sintered ferrite 3	$BaO–6Fe_2O_3$	0.32 (3200)	240,000 (3000)	20 (2.5)	450 (840)	$\sim10^4$
Cobalt rare earth 1	$SmCo_5$	0.92 (9200)	720,000 (9,000)	170 (21)	725 (1340)	5.0×10^{-7}
Sintered neodymium-iron-boron	$Nd_2Fe_{14}B$	1.16 (11,600)	848,000 (10,600)	255 (32)	310 (590)	1.6×10^{-6}

Source: Adapted from *ASM Handbook,* Vol. 2, *Properties and Selection: Nonferrous Alloys and Special-Purpose Materials.* Copyright © 1990 by ASM International. Reprinted by permission of ASM International, Materials Park, OH.

alloys, an appropriate heat treatment forms extremely small single-domain and strongly magnetic iron-cobalt particles within a nonmagnetic matrix phase.

High-Energy Hard Magnetic Materials

Permanent magnetic materials having energy products in excess of about 80 kJ/m³ (10 MGOe) are considered to be of the high-energy type. These are recently developed intermetallic compounds that have a variety of compositions; the two that have found commercial exploitation are $SmCo_5$ and $Nd_2Fe_{14}B$. Their magnetic properties are also listed in Table 18.6.

Samarium–Cobalt Magnets

$SmCo_5$ is a member of a group of alloys that are combinations of cobalt or iron and a light rare earth element; a number of these alloys exhibit high-energy, hard magnetic behavior,but $SmCo_5$ is the only one of commercial significance. The energy products of these $SmCo_5$ materials [between 120 and 240 kJ/m³ (15 and 30 MGOe)] are considerably higher than the conventional hard magnetic materials (Table 18.6); in addition, they have relatively large coercivities. Powder metallurgical techniques are used to fabricate $SmCo_5$ magnets. The appropriately alloyed material is first ground into a fine powder; the powder particles are aligned using an external magnetic field and then pressed into the desired shape. The piece is then sintered at an elevated temperature, followed by another heat treatment that improves the magnetic properties.

Neodymium–Iron–Boron Magnets

Samarium is a rare and relatively expensive material; furthermore, the price of cobalt is variable and its sources are unreliable. Consequently, the $Nd_2Fe_{14}B$ alloys have become the materials of choice for a large number and wide diversity of applications requiring hard magnetic materials. Coercivities and energy products of these materials rival those of the samarium–cobalt alloys (Table 18.6).

The magnetization–demagnetization behavior of these materials is a function of domain wall mobility, which, in turn, is controlled by the final microstructure—that is, the size, shape, and orientation of the crystallites or grains, as well as the nature and distribution of any second-phase particles that are present. Of course, microstructure will depend on how the material is processed. Two different processing techniques are available for the fabrication of $Nd_2Fe_{14}B$ magnets: powder metallurgy (sintering) and rapid solidification (melt spinning). The powder metallurgical approach is similar to that used for the $SmCo_5$ materials. For rapid solidification, the alloy, in molten form, is quenched very rapidly such that either an amorphous or very fine grained and thin solid ribbon is produced. This ribbon material is then pulverized, compacted into the desired shape, and subsequently heat treated. Rapid solidification is the more involved of the two fabrication processes; nevertheless, it is continuous, whereas powder metallurgy is a batch process, which has its inherent disadvantages.

These high-energy hard magnetic materials are employed in a host of different devices in a variety of technological fields. One common application is in motors. Permanent magnets are far superior to electromagnets in that their magnetic fields are continuously maintained and without the necessity of expending electrical power; furthermore, no heat is generated during operation. Motors using permanent magnets are much smaller than their electromagnet counterparts and are utilized extensively in fractional horsepower units. Familiar motor applications include the following: in cordless drills and screw drivers; in automobiles (starting, window winder, wiper, washer, and fan motors); in audio and video recorders; and in clocks. Other common devices that employ these magnetic materials are speakers in audio systems, lightweight earphones, hearing aids, and computer peripherals.

18.11 MAGNETIC STORAGE

Within the past few years, magnetic materials have become increasingly important in the area of information storage; in fact, magnetic recording has become virtually the universal technology for the storage of electronic information. This is evidenced by the preponderance of audio tapes, VCRs, disk storage media, credit cards, and so on. Whereas in computers, semiconductor elements serve as primary memory, magnetic disks are used for secondary memory because they are capable of storing larger quantities of information and at a lower cost. Furthermore, the recording and television industries rely heavily on magnetic tapes for the storage and reproduction of audio and video sequences.

In essence, computer bytes, sound, or visual images in the form of electrical signals are recorded on very small segments of the magnetic storage medium—a tape or disk. Transference to and retrieval from the tape or disk is accomplished by means of an inductive read–write head, which consists basically of a wire coil wound around a magnetic material core into which a gap is cut. Data are introduced (or "written") by the electrical signal within the coil, which generates a magnetic field across the gap. This field in turn magnetizes a very small area of the disk or tape within the proximity of the head. Upon removal of the field, the magnetization remains; that is, the signal has been stored. The essential features of this recording process are shown in Figure 18.23.

Furthermore, the same head may be utilized to retrieve (or "read") the stored information. A voltage is induced when there is a change in the magnetic field as

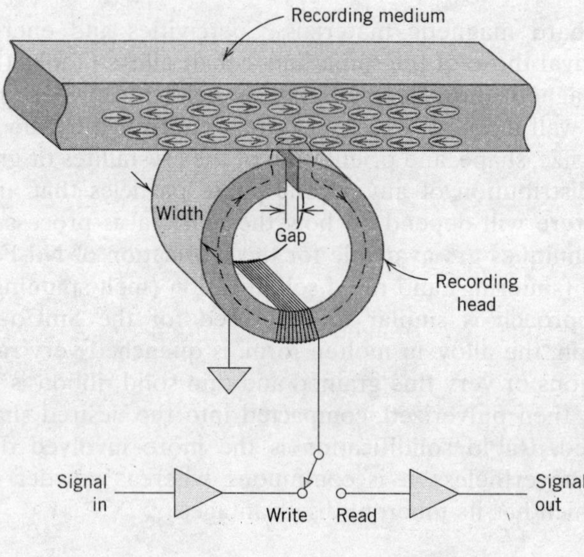

Figure 18.23 Schematic representation showing how information is stored and retrieved using a magnetic storage medium. (From J. U. Lemke, *MRS Bulletin,* Vol. XV, No. 3, p. 31, 1990. Reprinted with permission.)

the tape or disk passes by the head coil gap; this may be amplified and then converted back into its original form or character. This process is also represented in Figure 18.23.

Recently, hybrid heads that consist of an inductive-write and a magnetoresistive read head in a single unit have been introduced. In the magnetoresistive head, the electrical resistance of the magnetoresistive thin film element is changed as a result of magnetic field changes when the tape or disk passes by the read head. Higher sensitivies and higher data transfer rates make magnetoresistive heads very attractive.

There are two principal types of magnetic media—*particulate* and *thin film.* Particulate media consist of very small needle-like or acicular particles, normally of γ-Fe_2O_3 ferrite or CrO_2; these are applied and bonded to a polymeric film (for magnetic tapes) or to a metal or polymer disk. During manufacture, these particles are aligned with their long axes in a direction that parallels the direction of motion past the head (see Figures 18.23 and 18.24). Each particle is a

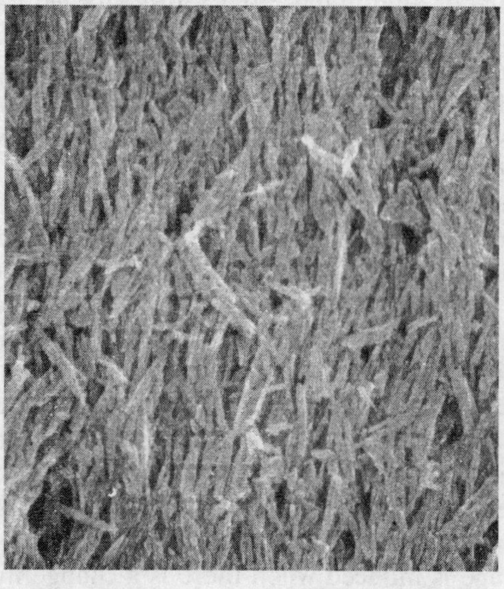

Figure 18.24 A scanning electron micrograph showing the microstructure of a magnetic storage disk. Needle-shaped particles of γ-Fe_2O_3 are oriented and embedded within an epoxy phenolic resin. 8000×. (Photograph courtesy of P. Rayner and N. L. Head, IBM Corporation.)

single domain that may be magnetized only with its magnetic moment lying along this axis. Two magnetic states are possible, corresponding to the saturation magnetization in one axial direction, and its opposite. These two states make possible the storage of information in digital form, as 1's and 0's. In one system, a 1 is represented by a reversal in the magnetic field direction from one small area of the storage medium to another as the numerous acicular particles of each such region pass by the head. A lack of reversal between adjacent regions is indicated by a 0.

The thin-film storage technology is relatively new and provides higher storage capacities at lower costs. It is employed mainly on rigid disk drives and consists of a multilayered structure. A magnetic thin-film layer is the actual storage component (see Figure 18.25). This film is normally either a CoPtCr or CoCrTa alloy, with a thickness of between 10 and 50 nm. A substrate layer below and upon which the thin film resides is pure chromium or a chromium alloy. The thin film itself is

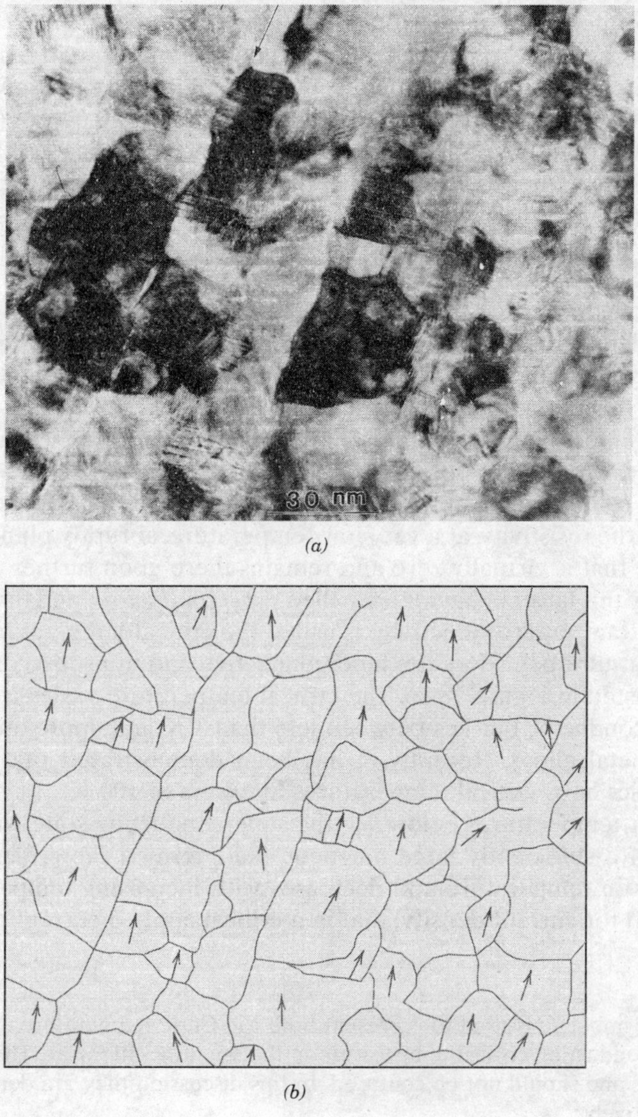

(a)

(b)

Figure 18.25 (*a*) A high-resolution transmission electron micrograph showing the microstructure of a cobalt–chromium–platinum thin film that is used as a high-density magnetic storage medium. The arrow at the top indicates the motion direction of the medium. 500,000×. (*b*) A representation of the grain structure for the electron micrograph in (*a*); the arrows in some of the grains indicate the texture, or the direction of easy magnetization. (From M. R. Kim, S. Guruswamy, and K. E. Johnson, *J. Appl. Phys.,* Vol. 74, No. 7, p. 4646, 1993. Reprinted with permission.)

polycrystalline, having an average grain size that is typically between 10 and 30 nm. Each grain within the thin film is a single magnetic domain, and it is highly desirable that grain shape and size be relatively uniform. For magnetic storage disks that employ these thin films, the crystallographic direction of easy magnetization for each grain is aligned in the direction of disk motion (or the direction opposite) (see Figure 18.25). The mechanism of magnetic storage within each of these single-domain grains is the same as for the needle-shaped particles, as described above—that is, the two magnetic states correspond to domain magnetization in one direction or its antiparallel equivalent.

The storage density of thin films is greater than for particulate media because the packing efficiency of thin-film domains is greater than for the acicular particles; particles will always be separated with void space in between. At the time of this writing, storage densities for particulate media are on the order of 1×10^8 bit/in.^{2} (1.5×10^5 bit/mm^2). For thin films, storage densities are approximately an order of magnitude greater [i.e., ~5×10^{10} bit/in.^{2} (8×10^7 bit/mm^2)].

Regarding specific magnetic properties, the hysteresis loops for these magnetic storage media should be relatively large and square. These characteristics ensure that storage will be permanent, and, in addition, magnetization reversal will result over a narrow range of applied field strengths. For particulate recording media, saturation flux density normally ranges from 0.4 to 0.6 tesla (4000 and 6000 gauss). For thin films, B_s will lie between 0.6 and 1.2 tesla (6000 and 12,000 gauss). Coercivity values are typically in the range of 1.5×10^5 to 2.5×10^5 A/m (2000 to 3000 Oe).

18.12 SUPERCONDUCTIVITY

Superconductivity is basically an electrical phenomenon; however, its discussion has been deferred to this point because there are magnetic implications relative to the superconducting state, and, in addition, superconducting materials are used primarily in magnets capable of generating high fields.

As most high-purity metals are cooled down to temperatures nearing 0 K, the electrical resistivity decreases gradually, approaching some small yet finite value that is characteristic of the particular metal. There are a few materials, however, for which the resistivity, at a very low temperature, abruptly plunges from a finite value to one that is virtually zero and remains there upon further cooling. Materials that display this latter behavior are called *superconductors,* and the temperature at which they attain **superconductivity** is called the critical temperature T_C.[5] The resistivity–temperature behaviors for superconductive and nonsuperconductive materials are contrasted in Figure 18.26. The critical temperature varies from superconductor to superconductor but lies between less than 1 K and approximately 20 K for metals and metal alloys. Recently, it has been demonstrated that some complex oxide ceramics have critical temperatures in excess of 100 K.

At temperatures below T_C, the superconducting state will cease upon application of a sufficiently large magnetic field, termed the critical field H_C, which depends on temperature and decreases with increasing temperature. The same may be said for current density; that is, a critical applied current density J_C exists below

[5] The symbol T_c is used to represent both the Curie temperature (Section 18.6) and the superconducting critical temperature in the scientific literature. They are totally different entities and should not be confused. In this discussion they are denoted by T_c and T_C, respectively.

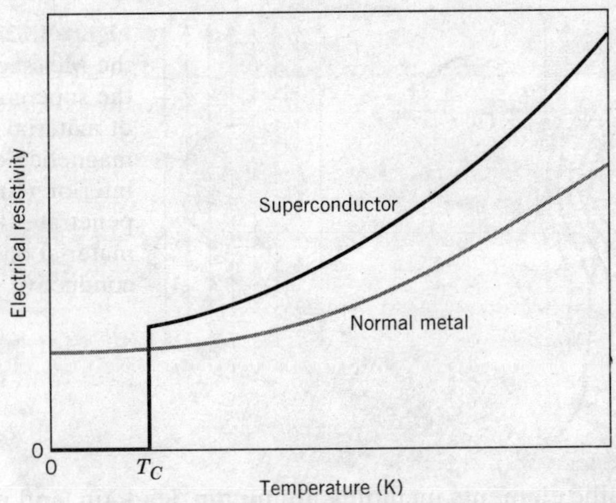

Figure 18.26 Temperature dependence of the electrical resistivity for normally conducting and superconducting materials in the vicinity of 0 K.

which a material is superconductive. Figure 18.27 shows schematically the boundary in temperature-magnetic field-current density space separating normal and superconducting states. The position of this boundary will, of course, depend on the material. For temperature, magnetic field, and current density values lying between the origin and this boundary, the material will be superconductive; outside the boundary, conduction is normal.

The superconductivity phenomenon has been satisfactorily explained by means of a rather involved theory. In essence, the superconductive state results from attractive interactions between pairs of conducting electrons; the motions of these paired electrons become coordinated such that scattering by thermal vibrations and impurity atoms is highly inefficient. Thus, the resistivity, being proportional to the incidence of electron scattering, is zero.

On the basis of magnetic response, superconducting materials may be divided into two classifications designated as type I and type II. Type I materials, while in the superconducting state, are completely diamagnetic; that is, all of an applied magnetic field will be excluded from the body of material, a phenomenon known as the *Meissner effect,* which is illustrated in Figure 18.28. As H is increased, the material remains diamagnetic until the critical magnetic field H_C is reached. At this point, conduction becomes normal, and complete magnetic flux penetration takes place.

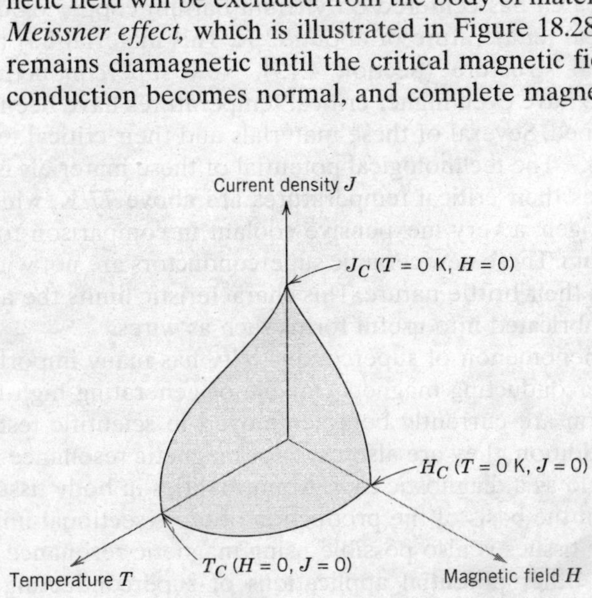

Figure 18.27 Critical temperature, current density, and magnetic field boundary separating superconducting and normal conducting states (schematic).

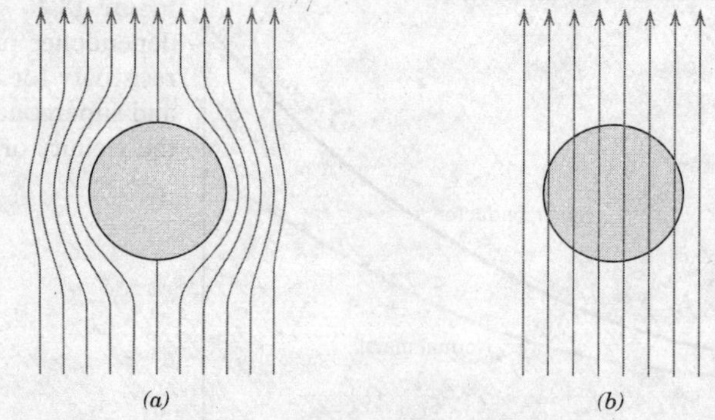

Figure 18.28 Representation of the Meissner effect. (*a*) While in the superconducting state, a body of material (circle) excludes a magnetic field (arrows) from its interior. (*b*) The magnetic field penetrates the same body of material once it becomes normally conductive.

Several metallic elements including aluminum, lead, tin, and mercury belong to the type I group.

Type II superconductors are completely diamagnetic at low applied fields, and field exclusion is total. However, the transition from the superconducting state to the normal state is gradual and occurs between lower critical and upper critical fields, designated H_{C1} and H_{C2}, respectively. The magnetic flux lines begin to penetrate into the body of material at H_{C1}, and with increasing applied magnetic field, this penetration continues; at H_{C2}, field penetration is complete. For fields between H_{C1} and H_{C2}, the material exists in what is termed a mixed state—both normal and superconducting regions are present.

Type II superconductors are preferred over type I for most practical applications by virtue of their higher critical temperatures and critical magnetic fields. At present, the three most commonly utilized superconductors are niobium–zirconium (Nb–Zr) and niobium–titanium (Nb–Ti) alloys and the niobium–tin intermetallic compound Nb_3Sn. Table 18.7 lists several type I and II superconductors, their critical temperatures, and their critical magnetic flux densities.

Recently, a family of ceramic materials that are normally electrically insulative have been found to be superconductors with inordinately high critical temperatures. Initial research has centered on yttrium barium copper oxide, $YBa_2Cu_3O_7$, which has a critical temperature of about 92 K. This material has a complex perovskite-type crystal structure (Section 4.13). New superconducting ceramic materials reported to have even higher critical temperatures have been and are currently being developed. Several of these materials and their critical temperatures are listed in Table 18.7. The technological potential of these materials is extremely promising inasmuch as their critical temperatures are above 77 K, which permits the use of liquid nitrogen, a very inexpensive coolant in comparison to liquid hydrogen and liquid helium. These new ceramic superconductors are not without drawbacks, chief of which is their brittle nature. This characteristic limits the ability of these materials to be fabricated into useful forms such as wires.

The phenomenon of superconductivity has many important practical implications. Superconducting magnets capable of generating high fields with low power consumption are currently being employed in scientific test and research equipment. In addition, they are also used for magnetic resonance imaging (MRI) in the medical field as a diagnostic tool. Abnormalities in body tissues and organs can be detected on the basis of the production of cross-sectional images. Chemical analysis of body tissues is also possible using magnetic resonance spectroscopy (MRS). Numerous other potential applications of superconducting materials also exist.

Table 18.7 Critical Temperatures and Magnetic Fluxes for Selected Superconducting Materials

Material	*Critical Temperature* T_C *(K)*	*Critical Magnetic Flux Density* B_C *(tesla)*[a]
	Elements[b]	
Tungsten	0.02	0.0001
Titanium	0.40	0.0056
Aluminum	1.18	0.0105
Tin	3.72	0.0305
Mercury (α)	4.15	0.0411
Lead	7.19	0.0803
	Compounds and Alloys[b]	
Nb–Ti alloy	10.2	12
Nb–Zr alloy	10.8	11
$PbMo_6S_8$	14.0	45
V_3Ga	16.5	22
Nb_3Sn	18.3	22
Nb_3Al	18.9	32
Nb_3Ge	23.0	30
	Ceramic Compounds	
$YBa_2Cu_3O_7$	92	—
$Bi_2Sr_2Ca_2Cu_3O_{10}$	110	—
$Tl_2Ba_2Ca_2Cu_3O_{10}$	125	—
$HgBa_2Ca_2Cu_2O_8$	153	—

[a] The critical magnetic flux density ($\mu_0 H_C$) for the elements was measured at 0 K. For alloys and compounds, the flux is taken as $\mu_0 H_{C2}$ (in teslas), measured at 0 K.
[b] **Source:** Adapted with permission from *Materials at Low Temperature,* R. P. Reed and A. F. Clark (Editors), American Society for Metals, Metals Park, OH, 1983.

Some of the areas being explored include (1) electrical power transmission through superconducting materials—power losses would be extremely low, and the equipment would operate at low voltage levels; (2) magnets for high-energy particle accelerators; (3) higher-speed switching and signal transmission for computers; and (4) high-speed magnetically levitated trains, wherein the levitation results from magnetic field repulsion. The chief deterrent to the widespread application of these superconducting materials is, of course, the difficulty in attaining and maintaining extremely low temperatures. Hopefully, this problem will be overcome with the development of the new generation of superconductors with reasonably high critical temperatures.

SUMMARY

Basic Concepts

The macroscopic magnetic properties of a material are a consequence of interactions between an external magnetic field and the magnetic dipole moments of the constituent atoms. Associated with each individual electron are both orbital and spin magnetic moments. The net magnetic moment for an atom is just the sum of the contributions of each of its electrons, wherein there will be spin and orbital moment cancellation of electron pairs.

Diamagnetism and Paramagnetism

Diamagnetism results from changes in electron orbital motion that are induced by an external field. The effect is extremely small and in opposition to the applied field. All materials are diamagnetic. Paramagnetic materials are those having permanent atomic dipoles, which are acted on individually and are aligned in the direction of an external field. Since the magnetizations are relatively small and persist only while an applied field is present, diamagnetic and paramagnetic materials are considered to be nonmagnetic.

Ferromagnetism

Large and permanent magnetizations may be established within the ferromagnetic metals (Fe, Co, Ni). Atomic magnetic dipole moments are of spin origin, which are coupled and mutually aligned with moments of adjacent atoms.

Antiferromagnetism and Ferrimagnetism

Antiparallel coupling of adjacent cation spin moments is found for some ionic materials. Those in which there is total cancellation of spin moments are termed antiferromagnetic. With ferrimagnetism, permanent magnetization is possible because spin moment cancellation is incomplete. For cubic ferrites, the net magnetization results from the divalent ions (e.g., Fe^{2+}) that reside on octahedral lattice sites, the spin moments of which are all mutually aligned.

The Influence of Temperature on Magnetic Behavior

With rising temperature, increased thermal vibrations tend to counteract the dipole coupling forces in ferromagnetic and ferrimagnetic materials. Consequently, the saturation magnetization gradually diminishes with temperature, up to the Curie temperature, at which point it drops to near zero; above T_c, these materials are paramagnetic.

Domains and Hysteresis

Below its Curie temperature, a ferromagnetic or ferrimagnetic material is composed of domains—small-volume regions wherein all net dipole moments are mutually aligned and the magnetization is saturated. The total magnetization of the solid is just the appropriately weighted vector sum of the magnetizations of all these domains. As an external magnetic field is applied, domains having magnetization vectors oriented in the direction of the field grow at the expense of domains that have unfavorable magnetization orientations. At total saturation, the entire solid is a single domain and the magnetization is aligned with the field direction. The change in domain structure with increase or reversal of a magnetic field is accomplished by the motion of domain walls. Both hysteresis (the lag of the B field behind the applied H field) as well as permanent magnetization (or remanence) result from the resistance to movement of these domain walls.

Magnetic Anisotropy

The M (or B) versus H behavior for a ferromagnetic single crystal is anisotropic—that is, dependent on the crystallographic direction along which the magnetic field is applied. The crystallographic direction for which M_s is achieved at the lowest H field is an easy magnetization direction; for Fe, Ni, and Co easy directions are, respectively, [100], [111], and [0001].

(d) At about what H field does this maximum permeability occur?

(e) To what magnetic susceptibility does this maximum permeability correspond?

18.20 An iron bar magnet having a coercivity of 7000 A/m is to be demagnetized. If the bar is inserted within a cylindrical wire coil 0.25 m long and having 150 turns, what electric current is required to generate the necessary magnetic field?

18.21 A bar of an iron–silicon alloy having the B–H behavior shown in Figure 18.29 is inserted within a coil of wire 0.40 m long and having 50 turns, through which passes a current of 0.1 A.

(a) What is the B field within this bar?

(b) At this magnetic field,

(i) What is the permeability?

(ii) What is the relative permeability?

(iii) What is the susceptibility?

(iv) What is the magnetization?

Magnetic Anisotropy

18.22 Estimate saturation values of H for single-crystal nickel in [100], [110], and [111] directions.

18.23 The energy (per unit volume) required to magnetize a ferromagnetic material to saturation (E_s) is defined by the following equation:

$$E_s = \int_0^{M_s} \mu_0 H \, dM$$

That is, E_s is equal to the product of μ_0 and the area under an M versus H curve, to the point of saturation referenced to the ordinate (or M) axis—for example, in Figure 18.17 the area between the vertical axis and the magnetization curve to M_s. Estimate E_s values (in J/m^3) for single-crystal iron in [100], [110], and [111] directions.

Soft Magnetic Materials
Hard Magnetic Materials

18.24 Cite the differences between hard and soft magnetic materials in terms of both hysteresis behavior and typical applications.

18.25 Assume the silicon–iron (97Fe, 3Si) in Table 18.5 just reaches the point of saturation when inserted within the coil in Problem 18.1. Compute the saturation magnetization.

18.26 Figure 18.30 shows the B-versus-H curve for a nickel–iron alloy.

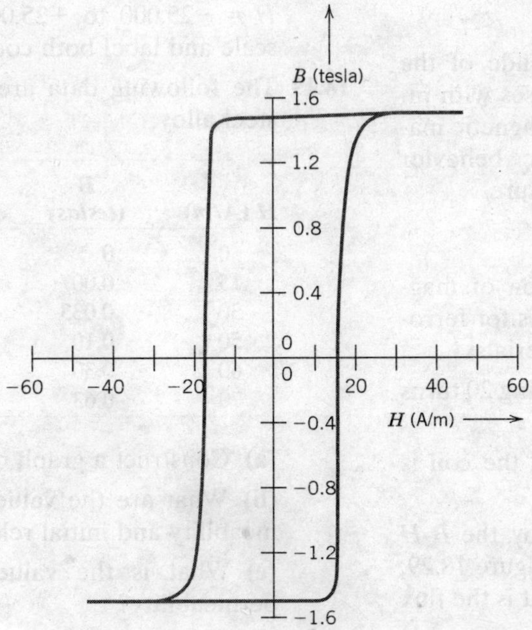

Figure 18.30 Complete magnetic hysteresis loop for a nickel–iron alloy.

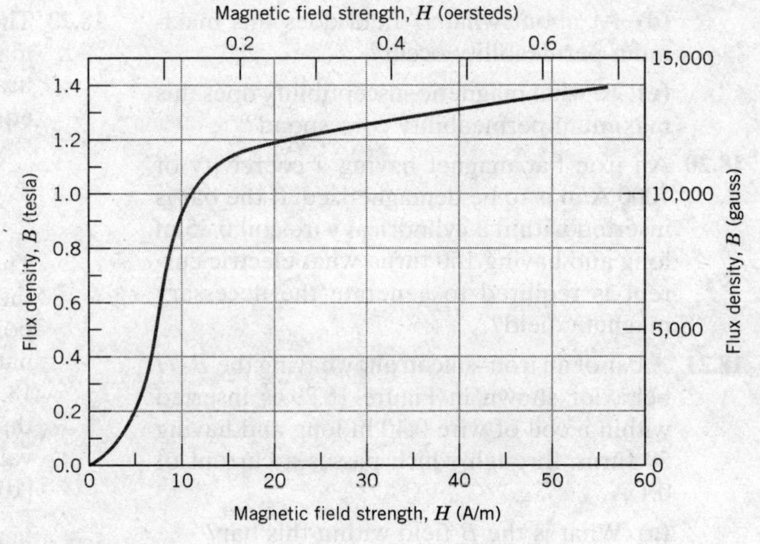

Figure 18.29 Initial magnetization B-versus-H curve for an iron-silicon alloy.

oriented parallel to one another and antiparallel to the Fe^{3+} ions in d sites. Compute the number of Bohr magnetons associated with each Sm^{3+} ion, given the following information: (1) each unit cell consists of eight formula ($Sm_3Fe_5O_{12}$) units; (2) the unit cell is cubic with an edge length of 1.2529 nm; (3) the saturation magnetization for this material is 1.35×10^5 A/m; and (4) assume that there are 5 Bohr magnetons associated with each Fe^{3+} ion.

The Influence of Temperature on Magnetic Behavior

18.15 Briefly explain why the magnitude of the saturation magnetization decreases with increasing temperature for ferromagnetic materials, and why ferromagnetic behavior ceases above the Curie temperature.

Domains and Hysteresis

18.16 Briefly describe the phenomenon of magnetic hysteresis, and why it occurs for ferromagnetic and ferrimagnetic materials.

18.17 A coil of wire 0.5 m long and having 20 turns carries a current of 1.0 A.

(a) Compute the flux density if the coil is within a vacuum.

(b) A bar of an iron–silicon alloy, the B-H behavior for which is shown in Figure 18.29, is positioned within the coil. What is the flux density within this bar?

(c) Suppose that a bar of molybdenum is now situated within the coil. What current must be used to produce the same B field in the Mo as was produced in the iron–silicon alloy (part b) using 1.0 A?

18.18 A ferromagnetic material has a remanence of 1.0 tesla and a coercivity of 15,000 A/m. Saturation is achieved at a magnetic field strength of 25,000 A/m, at which the flux density is 1.25 teslas. Using these data, sketch the entire hysteresis curve in the range $H = -25{,}000$ to $+25{,}000$ A/m. Be sure to scale and label both coordinate axes.

18.19 The following data are for a plain carbon steel alloy:

H (A/m)	***B (teslas)***	***H (A/m)***	***B (teslas)***
0	0	80	0.90
15	0.007	100	1.14
30	0.033	150	1.34
50	0.10	200	1.41
60	0.30	300	1.48
70	0.63		

(a) Construct a graph of B versus H.

(b) What are the values of the initial permeability and initial relative permeability?

(c) What is the value of the maximum permeability?

(a) What is the saturation flux density?

(b) What is the saturation magnetization?

(c) What is the remanence?

(d) What is the coercivity?

(e) On the basis of data in Tables 18.5 and 18.6, would you classify this material as a soft or hard magnetic material? Why?

Magnetic Storage

18.27 Briefly explain the manner in which information is stored magnetically.

Superconductivity

18.28 For a superconducting material at a temperature T below the critical temperature T_C, the critical field $H_C(T)$, depends on temperature according to the relationship

$$H_C(T) = H_C(0)\left(1 - \frac{T^2}{T_C^2}\right) \quad (18.14)$$

where $H_C(0)$ is the critical field at 0 K.

(a) Using the data in Table 18.7, calculate the critical magnetic fields for lead at 2.5 and 5.0 K.

(b) To what temperature must lead be cooled in a magnetic field of 15,000 A/m for it to be superconductive?

18.29 Using Equation 18.14, determine which of the superconducting elements in Table 18.7 are superconducting at 2 K and a magnetic field of 40,000 A/m.

18.30 Cite the differences between type I and type II superconductors.

18.31 Briefly describe the Meissner effect.

18.32 Cite the primary limitation of the new superconducting materials that have relatively high critical temperatures.

DESIGN PROBLEMS

Ferromagnetism

18.D1 A cobalt–iron alloy is desired that has a saturation magnetization of 1.47×10^6 A/m. Specify its composition in weight percent iron. Cobalt has an HCP crystal structure with c/a ratio of 1.623. Assume that the unit cell volume for this alloy is the same as for pure Co.

Ferrimagnetism

18.D2 Design a cubic mixed-ferrite magnetic material that has a saturation magnetization of 4.25×10^5 A/m.

Appendix A The International System of Units (SI)

Units in the *International System of Units* fall into two classifications: base and derived. Base units are fundamental and not reducible. Table A.1 lists the base units of interest in the discipline of materials science and engineering.

Derived units are expressed in terms of the base units, using mathematical signs for multiplication and division. For example, the SI units for density are kilogram per cubic meter (kg/m^3). For some derived units, special names and symbols exist; for example, N is used to denote the newton, the unit of force, which is equivalent to 1 $kg\text{-}m/s^2$. Table A.2 contains a number of the important derived units.

It is sometimes necessary, or convenient, to form names and symbols that are decimal multiples or submultiples of SI units. Only one prefix is used when a multiple of an SI unit is formed, which should be in the numerator. These prefixes and their approved symbols are given in Table A.3. Symbols for all units used in this book, SI or otherwise, are contained inside the front cover.

Table A.1 The SI Base Units

Quantity	*Name*	*Symbol*
Length	meter, metre	m
Mass	kilogram	kg
Time	second	s
Electric current	ampere	A
Thermodynamic temperature	kelvin	K
Amount of substance	mole	mol

Table A.2 Some of the SI Derived Units

Quantity	*Name*	*Formula*	*Special Symbol*[a]
Area	square meter	m^2	—
Volume	cubic meter	m^3	—
Velocity	meter per second	m/s	—
Density	kilogram per cubic meter	kg/m^3	—
Concentration	moles per cubic meter	mol/m^3	—
Force	newton	$kg\text{-}m/s^2$	N
Energy	joule	$kg\text{-}m^2/s^2$, N-m	J
Stress	pascal	$kg/m\text{-}s^2$, N/m^2	Pa
Strain	—	m/m	—
Power, radiant flux	watt	$kg\text{-}m^2/s^3$, J/s	W
Viscosity	pascal-second	kg/m-s	Pa-s
Frequency (of a periodic phenomenon)	hertz	s^{-1}	Hz
Electric charge	coulomb	A-s	C
Electric potential	volt	$kg\text{-}m^2/s^2\text{-}C$	V
Capacitance	farad	$s^2\text{-}C/kg\text{-}m^2$	F
Electric resistance	ohm	$kg\text{-}m^2/s\text{-}C^2$	Ω
Magnetic flux	weber	$kg\text{-}m^2/s\text{-}C$	Wb
Magnetic flux density	tesla	kg/s-C, Wb/m^2	(T)

[a] Special symbols in parentheses are approved in the SI but not used in this text; here, the name is used.

Table A.3 SI Multiple and Submultiple Prefixes

Factor by Which Multiplied	*Prefix*	*Symbol*
10^9	giga	G
10^6	mega	M
10^3	kilo	k
10^{-2}	centi[a]	c
10^{-3}	milli	m
10^{-6}	micro	μ
10^{-9}	nano	n
10^{-12}	pico	p

[a] Avoided when possible.

Appendix B Properties of Selected Engineering Materials

This appendix represents a compilation of important properties for approximately 100 common engineering materials. Each table contains data values of one particular property for this chosen set of materials; also included is a tabulation of the compositions of the various metal alloys that are considered (Table B.10). Data are tabulated by material type (viz., metals and metal alloys; graphite, ceramics, and semiconducting materials; polymers; fiber materials; and composites). Within each classification, the materials are listed alphabetically.

A couple of comments are appropriate relative to the content of these tables. First, data entries are expressed either as ranges of values or as single values that are typically measured. Also, on occasion, "(min)" is associated with an entry; this means that the value cited is a minimum one.

Table B.1 Room-Temperature Density Values for Various Engineering Materials

Material	*Density* (g/cm^3)
METALS AND METAL ALLOYS	
Plain Carbon and Low Alloy Steels	
Steel alloy A36	7.85
Steel alloy 1020	7.85
Steel alloy 1040	7.85
Steel alloy 4140	7.85
Steel alloy 4340	7.85
Stainless Steels	
Stainless alloy 304	8.00
Stainless alloy 316	8.00

Table B.1 (*Continued*)

Material	*Density* *(g/cm^3)*
Stainless alloy 405	7.80
Stainless alloy 440A	7.80
Stainless alloy 17-7PH	7.65
Cast Irons	
Gray irons	
• Grade G1800	7.30
• Grade G3000	7.30
• Grade G4000	7.30
Ductile irons	
• Grade 60-40-18	7.10
• Grade 80-55-06	7.10
• Grade 120-90-02	7.10
Aluminum Alloys	
Alloy 1100	2.71
Alloy 2024	2.77
Alloy 6061	2.70
Alloy 7075	2.80
Alloy 356.0	2.69
Copper Alloys	
C11000 (electrolytic tough pitch)	8.89
C17200 (beryllium–copper)	8.25
C26000 (cartridge brass)	8.53
C36000 (free-cutting brass)	8.50
C71500 (copper–nickel, 30%)	8.94
C93200 (bearing bronze)	8.93
Magnesium Alloys	
Alloy AZ31B	1.77
Alloy AZ91D	1.81
Titanium Alloys	
Commercially pure (ASTM grade 1)	4.51
Alloy Ti-5Al-2.5Sn	4.48
Alloy Ti-6Al-4V	4.43
Precious Metals	
Gold (commercially pure)	19.32
Platinum (commercially pure)	21.45
Silver (commercially pure)	10.49
Refractory Metals	
Molybdenum (commercially pure)	10.22
Tantalum (commercially pure)	16.6
Tungsten (commercially pure)	19.3
Miscellaneous Nonferrous Alloys	
Nickel 200	8.89
Inconel 625	8.44
Monel 400	8.80
Haynes alloy 25	9.13
Invar	8.05

Table B.1 (*Continued*)

Material	*Density* (g/cm^3)
Super invar	8.10
Kovar	8.36
Chemical lead	11.34
Antimonial lead (6%)	10.88
Tin (commercially pure)	7.17
Lead–tin solder (60Sn-40Pb)	8.52
Zinc (commercially pure)	7.14
Zirconium, reactor grade 702	6.51
GRAPHITE, CERAMICS, AND SEMICONDUCTING MATERIALS	
Aluminum oxide	
• 99.9% pure	3.98
• 96%	3.72
• 90%	3.60
Concrete	2.4
Diamond	
• Natural	3.51
• Synthetic	3.20–3.52
Gallium arsenide	5.32
Glass, borosilicate (Pyrex)	2.23
Glass, soda–lime	2.5
Glass ceramic (Pyroceram)	2.60
Graphite	
• Extruded	1.71
• Isostatically molded	1.78
Silica, fused	2.2
Silicon	2.33
Silicon carbide	
• Hot pressed	3.3
• Sintered	3.2
Silicon nitride	
• Hot pressed	3.3
• Reaction bonded	2.7
• Sintered	3.3
Zirconia, 3 mol% Y_2O_3, sintered	6.0
POLYMERS	
Elastomers	
• Butadiene-acrylonitrile (nitrile)	0.98
• Styrene-butadiene (SBR)	0.941
• Silicone	1.1–1.6
Epoxy	1.11–1.40
Nylon 6,6	1.14
Phenolic	1.28
Poly(butylene terephthalate) (PBT)	1.34
Polycarbonate (PC)	1.20
Polyester (thermoset)	1.04–1.46
Polyetheretherketone (PEEK)	1.31
Polyethylene	
• Low density (LDPE)	0.925
• High density (HDPE)	0.959

Table B.1 (*Continued*)

Material	*Density (g/cm^3)*
• Ultrahigh molecular weight (UHMWPE)	0.94
Poly(ethylene terephthalate) (PET)	1.35
Poly(methyl methacrylate) (PMMA)	1.19
Polypropylene (PP)	0.905
Polystyrene (PS)	1.05
Polytetrafluoroethylene (PTFE)	2.17
Poly(vinyl chloride) (PVC)	1.30–1.58
FIBER MATERIALS	
Aramid (Kevlar 49)	1.44
Carbon (PAN precursor)	
• Standard modulus	1.78
• Intermediate modulus	1.78
• High modulus	1.81
E-glass	2.58
COMPOSITE MATERIALS	
Aramid fibers-epoxy matrix ($V_f = 0.60$)	1.4
High modulus carbon fibers-epoxy matrix ($V_f = 0.60$)	1.7
E-glass fibers-epoxy matrix ($V_f = 0.60$)	2.1
Wood	
• Douglas fir (12% moisture)	0.46–0.50
• Red oak (12% moisture)	0.61–0.67

Sources: *ASM Handbooks, Volumes 1 and 2, Engineered Materials Handbook, Volume 4, Metals Handbook: Properties and Selection: Nonferrous Alloys and Pure Metals,* Vol. 2, 9th edition, and *Advanced Materials & Processes,* Vol. 146, No. 4, ASM International, Materials Park, OH; *Modern Plastics Encyclopedia '96,* The McGraw-Hill Companies, New York, NY; R. F. Floral and S. T. Peters, "Composite Structures and Technologies," tutorial notes, 1989; and manufacturers' technical data sheets.

Table B.2 Room-Temperature Modulus of Elasticity Values for Various Engineering Materials

Material	*Modulus of Elasticity (GPa)*
METALS AND METAL ALLOYS	
Plain Carbon and Low Alloy Steels	
Steel alloy A36	207
Steel alloy 1020	207
Steel alloy 1040	207
Steel alloy 4140	207
Steel alloy 4340	207
Stainless Steels	
Stainless alloy 304	193
Stainless alloy 316	193

Table B.2 (*Continued*)

Material	*Modulus of Elasticity (GPa)*
Stainless alloy 405	200
Stainless alloy 440A	200
Stainless alloy 17–7PH	204
Cast Irons	
Gray irons	
• Grade G1800	66–97[a]
• Grade G3000	90–113[a]
• Grade G4000	110–138[a]
Ductile irons	
• Grade 60-40-18	169
• Grade 80-55-06	168
• Grade 120-90-02	164
Aluminum Alloys	
Alloy 1100	69
Alloy 2024	72.4
Alloy 6061	69
Alloy 7075	71
Alloy 356.0	72.4
Copper Alloys	
C11000 (electrolytic tough pitch)	115
C17200 (beryllium–copper)	128
C26000 (cartridge brass)	110
C36000 (free-cutting brass)	97
C71500 (copper–nickel, 30%)	150
C93200 (bearing bronze)	100
Magnesium Alloys	
Alloy AZ31B	45
Alloy AZ91D	45
Titanium Alloys	
Commercially pure (ASTM grade 1)	103
Alloy Ti-5Al-2.5Sn	110
Alloy Ti-6Al-4V	114
Precious Metals	
Gold (commercially pure)	77
Platinum (commercially pure)	171
Silver (commercially pure)	74
Refractory Metals	
Molybdenum (commercially pure)	320
Tantalum (commercially pure)	185
Tungsten (commercially pure)	400
Miscellaneous Nonferrous Alloys	
Nickel 200	204
Inconel 625	207
Monel 400	180
Haynes alloy 25	236
Invar	141
Super invar	144

Table B.2 (Continued)

Material	*Modulus of Elasticity (GPa)*
Kovar	207
Chemical lead	13.5
Tin (commercially pure)	44.3
Lead–tin solder (60Sn-40Pb)	30
Zinc (commercially pure)	104.5
Zirconium, reactor grade 702	99.3
GRAPHITE, CERAMICS, AND SEMICONDUCTING MATERIALS	
Aluminum oxide	
• 99.9% pure	380
• 96%	303
• 90%	275
Concrete	25.4–36.6[a]
Diamond	
• Natural	700–1200
• Synthetic	800–925
Gallium arsenide, single crystal	
• In the ⟨100⟩ direction	85
• In the ⟨110⟩ direction	122
• In the ⟨111⟩ direction	142
Glass, borosilicate (Pyrex)	70
Glass, soda–lime	69
Glass ceramic (Pyroceram)	120
Graphite	
• Extruded	11
• Isostatically molded	11.7
Silica, fused	73
Silicon, single crystal	
• In the ⟨100⟩ direction	129
• In the ⟨110⟩ direction	168
• In the ⟨111⟩ direction	187
Silicon carbide	
• Hot pressed	207–483
• Sintered	207–483
Silicon nitride	
• Hot pressed	304
• Reaction bonded	304
• Sintered	304
Zirconia, 3 mol% Y_2O_3	205
POLYMERS	
Elastomers	
• Butadiene-acrylonitrile (nitrile)	0.0034[a]
• Styrene-butadiene (SBR)	0.002–0.010[a]
Epoxy	2.41
Nylon 6,6	1.59–3.79
Phenolic	2.76–4.83
Poly(butylene terephthalate) (PBT)	1.93–3.00
Polycarbonate (PC)	2.38
Polyester (thermoset)	2.06–4.41
Polyetheretherketone (PEEK)	1.10

Table B.2 (*Continued*)

Material	*Modulus of Elasticity (GPa)*
Polyethylene	
• Low density (LDPE)	0.172–0.282
• High density (HDPE)	1.08
• Ultrahigh molecular weight (UHMWPE)	0.69
Poly(ethylene terephthalate) (PET)	2.76–4.14
Poly(methyl methacrylate) (PMMA)	2.24–3.24
Polypropylene (PP)	1.14–1.55
Polystyrene (PS)	2.28–3.28
Poly(tetrafluoroethylene) (PTFE)	0.40–0.55
Poly(vinyl chloride) (PVC)	2.41–4.14
FIBER MATERIALS	
Aramid (Kevlar 49)	131
Carbon (PAN precursor)	
• Standard modulus	230
• Intermediate modulus	285
• High modulus	400
E-glass	72.5
COMPOSITE MATERIALS	
Aramid fibers-epoxy matrix ($V_f = 0.60$)	
Longitudinal	76
Transverse	5.5
High modulus carbon fibers-epoxy matrix ($V_f = 0.60$)	
Longitudinal	220
Transverse	6.9
E-glass fibers-epoxy matrix ($V_f = 0.60$)	
Longitudinal	45
Transverse	12
Wood	
• Douglas fir (12% moisture)	
Parallel to grain	10.8–13.6[c]
Perpendicular to grain	0.54–0.68[c]
• Red oak (12% moisture)	
Parallel to grain	11.0–14.1[c]
Perpendicular to grain	0.55–0.71[c]

[a] Secant modulus taken at 25% of ultimate strength.

[b] Modulus taken at 100% elongation.

[c] Measured in bending.

Sources: *ASM Handbooks, Volumes 1 and 2, Engineered Materials Handbooks, Volumes 1 and 4, Metals Handbook: Properties and Selection: Nonferrous Alloys and Pure Metals,* Vol. 2, 9th edition, and *Advanced Materials & Processes,* Vol. 146, No. 4, ASM International, Materials Park, OH; *Modern Plastics Encyclopedia '96,* The McGraw-Hill Companies, New York, NY; R. F. Floral and S. T. Peters, "Composite Structures and Technologies," tutorial notes, 1989; and manufacturers' technical data sheets.

Table B.3 Room-Temperature Poisson's Ratio Values for Various Engineering Materials

Material	Poisson's Ratio
METALS AND METAL ALLOYS	
Plain Carbon and Low Alloy Steels	
Steel alloy A36	0.30
Steel alloy 1020	0.30
Steel alloy 1040	0.30
Steel alloy 4140	0.30
Steel alloy 4340	0.30
Stainless Steels	
Stainless alloy 304	0.30
Stainless alloy 316	0.30
Stainless alloy 405	0.30
Stainless alloy 440A	0.30
Stainless alloy 17-7PH	0.30
Cast Irons	
Gray irons	
• Grade G1800	0.26
• Grade G3000	0.26
• Grade G4000	0.26
Ductile irons	
• Grade 60-40-18	0.29
• Grade 80-55-06	0.31
• Grade 120-90-02	0.28
Aluminum Alloys	
Alloy 1100	0.33
Alloy 2024	0.33
Alloy 6061	0.33
Alloy 7075	0.33
Alloy 356.0	0.33
Copper Alloys	
C11000 (electrolytic tough pitch)	0.33
C17200 (beryllium–copper)	0.30
C26000 (cartridge brass)	0.35
C36000 (free-cutting brass)	0.34
C71500 (copper–nickel, 30%)	0.34
C93200 (bearing bronze)	0.34
Magnesium Alloys	
Alloy AZ31B	0.35
Alloy AZ91D	0.35
Titanium Alloys	
Commercially pure (ASTM grade 1)	0.34
Alloy Ti-5Al-2.5Sn	0.34
Alloy Ti-6Al-4V	0.34
Precious Metals	
Gold (commercially pure)	0.42
Platinum (commercially pure)	0.39
Silver (commercially pure)	0.37
Refractory Metals	
Molybdenum (commercially pure)	0.32
Tantalum (commercially pure)	0.35
Tungsten (commercially pure)	0.28
Miscellaneous Nonferrous Alloys	
Nickel 200	0.31
Inconel 625	0.31
Monel 400	0.32
Chemical lead	0.44
Tin (commercially pure)	0.33
Zinc (commercially pure)	0.25
Zirconium, reactor grade 702	0.35
GRAPHITE, CERAMICS, AND SEMICONDUCTING MATERIALS	
Aluminum oxide	
• 99.9% pure	0.22
• 96%	0.21
• 90%	0.22
Concrete	0.20
Diamond	
• Natural	0.10–0.30
• Synthetic	0.20
Gallium arsenide	
• ⟨100⟩ orientation	0.30
Glass, borosilicate (Pyrex)	0.20
Glass, soda–lime	0.23
Glass ceramic (Pyroceram)	0.25
Silica, fused	0.17
Silicon	
• ⟨100⟩ orientation	0.28
• ⟨111⟩ orientation	0.36
Silicon carbide	
• Hot pressed	0.17
• Sintered	0.16
Silicon nitride	
• Hot pressed	0.30
• Reaction bonded	0.22
• Sintered	0.28
Zirconia, 3 mol% Y_2O_3	0.31
POLYMERS	
Nylon 6,6	0.39
Polycarbonate (PC)	0.36
Polystyrene (PS)	0.33
Polytetrafluoroethylene (PTFE)	0.46
Poly(vinyl chloride) (PVC)	0.38
FIBER MATERIALS	
E-glass	0.22

Table B.3 (*Continued*)

Material	*Poisson's Ratio*	*Material*	*Poisson's Ratio*
COMPOSITE MATERIALS			
Aramid fibers-epoxy matrix ($V_f = 0.6$)	0.34	E-glass fibers-epoxy matrix ($V_f = 0.6$)	0.19
High modulus carbon fibers-epoxy matrix ($V_f = 0.6$)	0.25		

Sources: *ASM Handbooks, Volumes 1 and 2,* and *Engineered Materials Handbooks, Volumes 1 and 4,* ASM International, Materials Park, OH; R. F. Floral and S. T. Peters, "Composite Structures and Technologies," tutorial notes, 1989; and manufacturers' technical data sheets.

Table B.4 Typical Room-Temperature Yield Strength, Tensile Strength, and Ductility (Percent Elongation) Values for Various Engineering Materials

Material/Condition	*Yield Strength (MPa)*	*Tensile Strength (MPa)*	*Percent Elongation*
METALS AND METAL ALLOYS			
Plain Carbon and Low Alloy Steels			
Steel alloy A36			
• Hot rolled	220–250	400–500	23
Steel alloy 1020			
• Hot rolled	210 (min)	380 (min)	25 (min)
• Cold drawn	350 (min)	420 (min)	15 (min)
• Annealed (@ 870°C)	295	395	36.5
• Normalized (@ 925°C)	345	440	38.5
Steel alloy 1040			
• Hot rolled	290 (min)	520 (min)	18 (min)
• Cold drawn	490 (min)	590 (min)	12 (min)
• Annealed (@ 785°C)	355	520	30.2
• Normalized (@ 900°C)	375	590	28.0
Steel alloy 4140			
• Annealed (@ 815°C)	417	655	25.7
• Normalized (@ 870°C)	655	1020	17.7
• Oil-quenched and tempered (@ 315°C)	1570	1720	11.5
Steel alloy 4340			
• Annealed (@ 810°C)	472	745	22
• Normalized (@ 870°C)	862	1280	12.2
• Oil-quenched and tempered (@ 315°C)	1620	1760	12
Stainless Steels			
Stainless alloy 304			
• Hot finished and annealed	205 (min)	515 (min)	40 (min)
• Cold worked ($\frac{1}{4}$ hard)	515 (min)	860 (min)	10 (min)
Stainless alloy 316			
• Hot finished and annealed	205 (min)	515 (min)	40 (min)
• Cold drawn and annealed	310 (min)	620 (min)	30 (min)
Stainless alloy 405			
• Annealed	170	415	20

Table B.4 (Continued)

Material/Condition	*Yield Strength (MPa)*	*Tensile Strength (MPa)*	*Percent Elongation*
Stainless alloy 440A			
• Annealed	415	725	20
• Tempered @ 315°C	1650	1790	5
Stainless alloy 17-7PH			
• Cold rolled	1210 (min)	1380 (min)	1 (min)
• Precipitation hardened @ 510°C	1310 (min)	1450 (min)	3.5 (min)
Cast Irons			
Gray irons			
• Grade G1800 (as cast)	—	124 (min)	—
• Grade G3000 (as cast)	—	207 (min)	—
• Grade G4000 (as cast)	—	276 (min)	—
Ductile irons			
• Grade 60-40-18 (annealed)	276 (min)	414 (min)	18 (min)
• Grade 80-55-06 (as cast)	379 (min)	552 (min)	6 (min)
• Grade 120-90-02 (oil quenched and tempered)	621 (min)	827 (min)	2 (min)
Aluminum Alloys			
Alloy 1100			
• Annealed (O temper)	34	90	40
• Strain hardened (H14 temper)	117	124	15
Alloy 2024			
• Annealed (O temper)	75	185	20
• Heat treated and aged (T3 temper)	345	485	18
• Heat treated and aged (T351 temper)	325	470	20
Alloy 6061			
• Annealed (O temper)	55	124	30
• Heat treated and aged (T6 and T651 tempers)	276	310	17
Alloy 7075			
• Annealed (O temper)	103	228	17
• Heat treated and aged (T6 temper)	505	572	11
Alloy 356.0			
• As cast	124	164	6
• Heat treated and aged (T6 temper)	164	228	3.5
Copper Alloys			
C11000 (electrolytic tough pitch)			
• Hot rolled	69	220	50
• Cold worked (H04 temper)	310	345	12
C17200 (beryllium–copper)			
• Solution heat treated	195–380	415–540	35–60
• Solution heat treated, aged @ 330°C	965–1205	1140–1310	4–10
C26000 (cartridge brass)			
• Annealed	75–150	300–365	54–68
• Cold worked (H04 temper)	435	525	8
C36000 (free-cutting brass)			
• Annealed	125	340	53
• Cold worked (H02 temper)	310	400	25
C71500 (copper–nickel, 30%)			
• Hot rolled	140	380	45
• Cold worked (H80 temper)	545	580	3

Table B.4 (*Continued*)

Material/Condition	*Yield Strength (MPa)*	*Tensile Strength (MPa)*	*Percent Elongation*
C93200 (bearing bronze)			
• Sand cast	125	240	20
Magnesium Alloys			
Alloy AZ31B			
• Rolled	220	290	15
• Extruded	200	262	15
Alloy AZ91D			
• As cast	97–150	165–230	3
Titanium Alloys			
Commercially pure (ASTM grade 1)			
• Annealed	170 (min)	240 (min)	30
Alloy Ti-5Al-2.5Sn			
• Annealed	760 (min)	790 (min)	16
Alloy Ti-6Al-4V			
• Annealed	830 (min)	900 (min)	14
• Solution heat treated and aged	1103	1172	10
Precious Metals			
Gold (commercially pure)			
• Annealed	nil	130	45
• Cold worked (60% reduction)	205	220	4
Platinum (commercially pure)			
• Annealed	<13.8	125–165	30–40
• Cold worked (50%)	—	205–240	1–3
Silver (commercially pure)			
• Annealed	—	170	44
• Cold worked (50%)	—	296	3.5
Refractory Metals			
Molybdenum (commercially pure)	500	630	25
Tantalum (commercially pure)	165	205	40
Tungsten (commercially pure)	760	960	2
Miscellaneous Nonferrous Alloys			
Nickel 200 (annealed)	148	462	47
Inconel 625 (annealed)	517	930	42.5
Monel 400 (annealed)	240	550	40
Haynes alloy 25	445	970	62
Invar (annealed)	276	517	30
Super invar (annealed)	276	483	30
Kovar (annealed)	276	517	30
Chemical lead	6–8	16–19	30–60
Antimonial lead (6%) (chill cast)	—	47.2	24
Tin (commercially pure)	11	—	57
Lead–tin solder (60Sn–40Pb)	—	52.5	30–60
Zinc (commercially pure)			
• Hot rolled (anisotropic)	—	134–159	50–65
• Cold rolled (anisotropic)	—	145–186	40–50
Zirconium, reactor grade 702			
• Cold worked and annealed	207 (min)	379 (min)	16 (min)

Table B.4 (*Continued*)

Material/Condition	*Yield Strength (MPa)*	*Tensile Strength (MPa)*	*Percent Elongation*
GRAPHITE, CERAMICS, AND SEMICONDUCTING MATERIALS[a]			
Aluminum oxide			
• 99.9% pure	—	282–551	—
• 96%	—	358	—
• 90%	—	337	—
Concrete[b]	—	37.3–41.3	—
Diamond			
• Natural	—	1050	—
• Synthetic	—	800–1400	—
Gallium arsenide			
• {100} orientation, polished surface	—	66[c]	—
• {100} orientation, as-cut surface	—	57[c]	—
Glass, borosilicate (Pyrex)	—	69	—
Glass, soda–lime	—	69	—
Glass ceramic (Pyroceram)	—	123–370	—
Graphite			
• Extruded (with the grain direction)	—	13.8–34.5	—
• Isostatically molded	—	31–69	—
Silica, fused	—	104	—
Silicon			
• {100} orientation, as-cut surface	—	130	—
• {100} orientation, laser scribed	—	81.8	—
Silicon carbide			
• Hot pressed	—	230–825	—
• Sintered	—	96–520	—
Silicon nitride			
• Hot pressed	—	700–1000	—
• Reaction bonded	—	250–345	—
• Sintered	—	414–650	—
Zirconia, 3 mol% Y_2O_3 (sintered)	—	800–1500	—
POLYMERS			
Elastomers			
• Butadiene-acrylonitrile (nitrile)	—	6.9–24.1	400–600
• Styrene-butadiene (SBR)	—	12.4–20.7	450–500
• Silicone	—	10.3	100–800
Epoxy	—	27.6–90.0	3–6
Nylon 6,6			
• Dry, as molded	55.1–82.8	94.5	15–80
• 50% relative humidity	44.8–58.6	75.9	150–300
Phenolic	—	34.5–62.1	1.5–2.0
Poly(butylene terephthalate) (PBT)	56.6–60.0	56.6–60.0	50–300
Polycarbonate (PC)	62.1	62.8–72.4	110–150
Polyester (thermoset)	—	41.4–89.7	<2.6
Polyetheretherketone (PEEK)	91	70.3–103	30–150
Polyethylene			
• Low density (LDPE)	9.0–14.5	8.3–31.4	100–650
• High density (HDPE)	26.2–33.1	22.1–31.0	10–1200
• Ultrahigh molecular weight (UHMWPE)	21.4–27.6	38.6–48.3	350–525
Poly(ethylene terephthalate) (PET)	59.3	48.3–72.4	30–300

Table B.4 ***(Continued)***

Material/Condition	*Yield Strength (MPa)*	*Tensile Strength (MPa)*	*Percent Elongation*
Poly(methyl methacrylate) (PMMA)	53.8–73.1	48.3–72.4	2.0–5.5
Polypropylene (PP)	31.0–37.2	31.0–41.4	100–600
Polystyrene (PS)	—	35.9–51.7	1.2–2.5
Polytetrafluoroethylene (PTFE)	—	20.7–34.5	200–400
Poly(vinyl chloride) (PVC)	40.7–44.8	40.7–51.7	40–80
FIBER MATERIALS			
Aramid (Kevlar 49)	—	3600–4100	2.8
Carbon (PAN precursor)			
• Standard modulus (longitudinal)	—	3800–4200	2
• Intermediate modulus (longitudinal)	—	4650–6350	1.8
• High modulus (longitudinal)	—	2500–4500	0.6
E-glass	—	3450	4.3
COMPOSITE MATERIALS			
Aramid fibers-epoxy matrix (aligned, $V_f = 0.6$)			
• Longitudinal direction	—	1380	1.8
• Transverse direction	—	30	0.5
High modulus carbon fibers-epoxy matrix (aligned, $V_f = 0.6$)			
• Longitudinal direction	—	760	0.3
• Transverse direction	—	28	0.4
E-glass fibers-epoxy matrix (aligned, $V_f = 0.6$)			
• Longitudinal direction	—	1020	2.3
• Transverse direction	—	40	0.4
Wood			
• Douglas fir (12% moisture)			
Parallel to grain	—	108	—
Perpendicular to grain	—	2.4	—
• Red oak (12% moisture)			
Parallel to grain	—	112	—
Perpendicular to grain	—	7.2	—

[a] The strength of graphite, ceramics, and semiconducting materials is taken as flexural strength.

[b] The strength of concrete is measured in compression.

[c] Flexural strength value at 50% fracture probability.

Sources: *ASM Handbooks, Volumes 1 and 2, Engineered Materials Handbooks, Volumes 1 and 4, Metals Handbook: Properties and Selection: Nonferrous Alloys and Pure Metals,* Vol. 2, 9th edition, *Advanced Materials & Processes,* Vol. 146, No. 4, and *Materials & Processing Databook (1985),* ASM International, Materials Park, OH: *Modern Plastics Encyclopedia '96,* The McGraw-Hill Companies, New York, NY; R. F. Floral and S. T. Peters, "Composite Structures and Technologies," tutorial notes, 1989; and manufacturers' technical data sheets.

Table B.5 Room-Temperature Plane Strain Fracture Toughness and Strength Values for Various Engineering Materials

Material	*Fracture Toughness* $(MPa\sqrt{m})$	*Strength*[a] *(MPa)*
METALS AND METAL ALLOYS		
Plain Carbon and Low Alloy Steels		
Steel alloy 1040	54.0	260
Steel alloy 4140		
• Tempered @ 370°C	55–65	1375–1585
• Tempered @ 482°C	75–93	1100–1200
Steel alloy 4340		
• Tempered @ 260°C	50.0	1640
• Tempered @ 425°C	87.4	1420
Stainless Steels		
Stainless alloy 17-7PH		
• Precipitation hardened @ 510°C	76	1310
Aluminum Alloys		
Alloy 2024-T3	44	345
Alloy 7075-T651	24	495
Magnesium Alloys		
Alloy AZ31B		
• Extruded	28.0	200
Titanium Alloys		
Alloy Ti-5Al-2.5Sn		
• Air cooled	71.4	876
Alloy Ti-6Al-4V		
• Equiaxed grains	44–66	910
GRAPHITE, CERAMICS, AND SEMICONDUCTING MATERIALS		
Aluminum oxide		
• 99.9% pure	4.2–5.9	282–551
• 96%	3.85–3.95	358
Concrete	0.2–1.4	—
Diamond		
• Natural	3.4	1050
• Synthetic	6.0–10.7	800–1400
Gallium arsenide		
• In the {100} orientation	0.43	66
• In the {110} orientation	0.31	
• In the {111} orientation	0.45	
Glass, borosilicate (Pyrex)	0.77	69
Glass, soda–lime	0.75	69
Glass ceramic (Pyroceram)	1.6–2.1	123–370
Silica, fused	0.79	104
Silicon		
• In the {100} orientation	0.95	—
• In the {110} orientation	0.90	—
• In the {111} orientation	0.82	—
Silicon carbide		
• Hot pressed	4.8–6.1	230–825
• Sintered	4.8	96–520

Table B.5 (*Continued*)

Material	*Fracture Toughness* ($MPa\sqrt{m}$)	*Strength*[a] (*MPa*)
Silicon nitride		
• Hot pressed	4.1–6.0	700–1000
• Reaction bonded	3.6	250–345
• Sintered	5.3	414–650
Zirconia, 3 mol% Y_2O_3	7.0–12.0	800–1500
POLYMERS		
Epoxy	0.6	—
Nylon 6,6	2.5–3.0	44.8–58.6
Polycarbonate (PC)	2.2	62.1
Polyester (thermoset)	0.6	—
Poly(ethylene terephthalate) (PET)	5.0	59.3
Poly(methyl methacrylate) (PMMA)	0.7–1.6	53.8–73.1
Polypropylene (PP)	3.0–4.5	31.0–37.2
Polystyrene (PS)	0.7–1.1	—
Poly(vinyl chloride) (PVC)	2.0–4.0	40.7–44.8

[a] For metal alloys and polymers, strength is taken as yield strength; for ceramic materials, flexural strength is used.

Sources: *ASM Handbooks, Volumes 1 and 19, Engineered Materials Handbooks, Volumes 2 and 4,* and *Advanced Materials & Processes,* Vol. 137, No. 6, ASM International, Materials Park, OH.

Table B.6 Room-Temperature Linear Coefficient of Thermal Expansion Values for Various Engineering Materials

Material	*Coefficient of Thermal Expansion* [$10^{-6}(°C)^{-1}$]
METALS AND METAL ALLOYS	
Plain Carbon and Low Alloy Steels	
Steel alloy A36	11.7
Steel alloy 1020	11.7
Steel alloy 1040	11.3
Steel alloy 4140	12.3
Steel alloy 4340	12.3
Stainless Steels	
Stainless alloy 304	17.2
Stainless alloy 316	15.9
Stainless alloy 405	10.8
Stainless alloy 440A	10.2
Stainless alloy 17-7PH	11.0
Cast Irons	
Gray irons	
• Grade G1800	11.4
• Grade G3000	11.4
• Grade G4000	11.4

Table B.6 (*Continued*)

Material	*Coefficient of Thermal Expansion* $[10^{-6}(°C)^{-1}]$
Ductile irons	
• Grade 60-40-18	11.2
• Grade 80-55-06	10.6
Aluminum Alloys	
Alloy 1100	23.6
Alloy 2024	22.9
Alloy 6061	23.6
Alloy 7075	23.4
Alloy 356.0	21.5
Copper Alloys	
C11000 (electrolytic tough pitch)	17.0
C17200 (beryllium–copper)	16.7
C26000 (cartridge brass)	19.9
C36000 (free-cutting brass)	20.5
C71500 (copper–nickel, 30%)	16.2
C93200 (bearing bronze)	18.0
Magnesium Alloys	
Alloy AZ31B	26.0
Alloy AZ91D	26.0
Titanium Alloys	
Commercially pure (ASTM grade 1)	8.6
Alloy Ti-5Al-2.5Sn	9.4
Alloy Ti-6Al-4V	8.6
Precious Metals	
Gold (commercially pure)	14.2
Platinum (commercially pure)	9.1
Silver (commercially pure)	19.7
Refractory Metals	
Molybdenum (commercially pure)	4.9
Tantalum (commercially pure)	6.5
Tungsten (commercially pure)	4.5
Miscellaneous Nonferrous Alloys	
Nickel 200	13.3
Inconel 625	12.8
Monel 400	13.9
Haynes alloy 25	12.3
Invar	1.6
Super invar	0.72
Kovar	5.1
Chemical lead	29.3
Antimonial lead (6%)	27.2
Tin (commercially pure)	23.8
Lead–tin solder (60Sn-40Pb)	24.0
Zinc (commercially pure)	23.0–32.5
Zirconium, reactor grade 702	5.9

Table B.6 (*Continued*)

Material	*Coefficient of Thermal Expansion* $[10^{-6}(°C)^{-1}]$
GRAPHITE, CERAMICS, AND SEMICONDUCTING MATERIALS	
Aluminum oxide	
• 99.9% pure	7.4
• 96%	7.4
• 90%	7.0
Concrete	10.0–13.6
Diamond (natural)	0.11–1.23
Gallium arsenide	5.9
Glass, borosilicate (Pyrex)	3.3
Glass, soda–lime	9.0
Glass ceramic (Pyroceram)	6.5
Graphite	
• Extruded	2.0–2.7
• Isostatically molded	2.2–6.0
Silica, fused	0.4
Silicon	2.5
Silicon carbide	
• Hot pressed	4.6
• Sintered	4.1
Silicon nitride	
• Hot pressed	2.7
• Reaction bonded	3.1
• Sintered	3.1
Zirconia, 3 mol% Y_2O_3	9.6
POLYMERS	
Elastomers	
• Butadiene-acrylonitrile (nitrile)	235
• Styrene-butadiene (SBR)	220
• Silicone	270
Epoxy	81–117
Nylon 6,6	144
Phenolic	122
Poly(butylene terephthalate) (PBT)	108–171
Polycarbonate (PC)	122
Polyester (thermoset)	100–180
Polyetheretherketone (PEEK)	72–85
Polyethylene	
• Low density (LDPE)	180–400
• High density (HDPE)	106–198
• Ultrahigh molecular weight (UHMWPE)	234–360
Poly(ethylene terephthalate) (PET)	117
Poly(methyl methacrylate) (PMMA)	90–162
Polypropylene (PP)	146–180
Polystyrene (PS)	90–150
Polytetrafluoroethylene (PTFE)	126–216
Poly(vinyl chloride) (PVC)	90–180

Table B.6 (*Continued*)

Material	*Coefficient of Thermal Expansion* $[10^{-6}(°C)^{-1}]$
FIBER MATERIALS	
Aramid (Kevlar 49)	
• Longitudinal direction	−2.0
• Transverse direction	60
Carbon (PAN precursor)	
• Standard modulus	
Longitudinal direction	−0.6
Transverse direction	10.0
• Intermediate modulus	
Longitudinal direction	−0.6
• High modulus	
Longitudinal direction	−0.5
Transverse direction	7.0
E-glass	5.0
COMPOSITE MATERIALS	
Aramid fibers-epoxy matrix ($V_f = 0.6$)	
• Longitudinal direction	−4.0
• Transverse direction	70
High modulus carbon fibers-epoxy matrix ($V_f = 0.6$)	
• Longitudinal direction	−0.5
• Transverse direction	32
E-glass fibers-epoxy matrix ($V_f = 0.6$)	
• Longitudinal direction	6.6
• Transverse direction	30
Wood	
• Douglas fir (12% moisture)	
Parallel to grain	3.8–5.1
Perpendicular to grain	25.4–33.8
• Red oak (12% moisture)	
Parallel to grain	4.6–5.9
Perpendicular to grain	30.6–39.1

Sources: *ASM Handbooks, Volumes 1 and 2, Engineered Materials Handbooks, Volumes 1 and 4, Metals Handbook: Properties and Selection: Nonferrous Alloys and Pure Metals,* Vol. 2, 9th edition, and *Advanced Materials & Processes,* Vol. 146, No. 4, ASM International, Materials Park, OH; *Modern Plastics Encyclopedia '96,* The McGraw-Hill Companies, New York, NY; R. F. Floral and S. T. Peters, "Composite Structures and Technologies," tutorial notes, 1989; and manufacturers' technical data sheets.

Table B.7 Room-Temperature Thermal Conductivity Values for Various Engineering Materials

Material	*Thermal Conductivity (W/m-K)*
METALS AND METAL ALLOYS	
Plain Carbon and Low Alloy Steels	
Steel alloy A36	51.9
Steel alloy 1020	51.9
Steel alloy 1040	51.9
Stainless Steels	
Stainless alloy 304 (annealed)	16.2
Stainless alloy 316 (annealed)	16.2
Stainless alloy 405 (annealed)	27.0
Stainless alloy 440A (annealed)	24.2
Stainless alloy 17-7PH (annealed)	16.4
Cast Irons	
Gray irons	
• Grade G1800	46.0
• Grade G3000	46.0
• Grade G4000	46.0
Ductile irons	
• Grade 60-40-18	36.0
• Grade 80-55-06	36.0
• Grade 120-90-02	36.0
Aluminum Alloys	
Alloy 1100 (annealed)	222
Alloy 2024 (annealed)	190
Alloy 6061 (annealed)	180
Alloy 7075-T6	130
Alloy 356.0-T6	151
Copper Alloys	
C11000 (electrolytic tough pitch)	388
C17200 (beryllium–copper)	105–130
C26000 (cartridge brass)	120
C36000 (free-cutting brass)	115
C71500 (copper–nickel, 30%)	29
C93200 (bearing bronze)	59
Magnesium Alloys	
Alloy AZ31B	96[a]
Alloy AZ91D	72[a]
Titanium Alloys	
Commercially pure (ASTM grade 1)	16
Alloy Ti-5Al-2.5Sn	7.6
Alloy Ti-6Al-4V	6.7
Precious Metals	
Gold (commercially pure)	315
Platinum (commercially pure)	71[b]
Silver (commercially pure)	428

Table B.7 (*Continued*)

Material	*Thermal Conductivity (W/m-K)*
Refractory Metals	
Molybdenum (commercially pure)	142
Tantalum (commercially pure)	54.4
Tungsten (commercially pure)	155
Miscellaneous Nonferrous Alloys	
Nickel 200	70
Inconel 625	9.8
Monel 400	21.8
Haynes alloy 25	9.8
Invar	10
Super invar	10
Kovar	17
Chemical lead	35
Antimonial lead (6%)	29
Tin (commercially pure)	60.7
Lead–tin solder (60Sn-40Pb)	50
Zinc (commercially pure)	108
Zirconium, reactor grade 702	22
GRAPHITE, CERAMICS, AND SEMICONDUCTING MATERIALS	
Aluminum oxide	
• 99.9% pure	39
• 96%	35
• 90%	16
Concrete	1.25–1.75
Diamond	
• Natural	1450–4650
• Synthetic	3150
Gallium arsenide	45.5
Glass, borosilicate (Pyrex)	1.4
Glass, soda–lime	1.7
Glass ceramic (Pyroceram)	3.3
Graphite	
• Extruded	130–190
• Isostatically molded	104–130
Silica, fused	1.4
Silicon	141
Silicon carbide	
• Hot pressed	80
• Sintered	71
Silicon nitride	
• Hot pressed	29
• Reaction bonded	10
• Sintered	33
Zirconia, 3 mol% Y_2O_3	2.0–3.3
POLYMERS	
Elastomers	
• Butadiene-acrylonitrile (nitrile)	0.25
• Styrene-butadiene (SBR)	0.25
• Silicone	0.23

Table B.7 *(Continued)*

Material	*Thermal Conductivity (W/m-K)*
Epoxy	0.19
Nylon 6,6	0.24
Phenolic	0.15
Poly(butylene terephthalate) (PBT)	0.18–0.29
Polycarbonate (PC)	0.20
Polyester (thermoset)	0.17
Polyethylene	
• Low density (LDPE)	0.33
• High density (HDPE)	0.48
• Ultrahigh molecular weight (UHMWPE)	0.33
Poly(ethylene terephthalate) (PET)	0.15
Poly(methyl methacrylate) (PMMA)	0.17–0.25
Polypropylene (PP)	0.12
Polystyrene (PS)	0.13
Polytetrafluoroethylene (PTFE)	0.25
Poly(vinyl chloride) (PVC)	0.15–0.21
FIBER MATERIALS	
Carbon (PAN precursor), longitudinal	
• Standard modulus	11
• Intermediate modulus	15
• High modulus	70
E-glass	1.3
COMPOSITE MATERIALS	
Wood	
• Douglas fir (12% moisture)	
Perpendicular to grain	0.14
• Red oak (12% moisture)	
Perpendicular to grain	0.18

[a] At 100°C.
[b] At 0°C.

Sources: *ASM Handbooks, Volumes 1 and 2, Engineered Materials Handbooks, Volumes 1 and 4, Metals Handbook: Properties and Selection: Nonferrous Alloys and Pure Metals,* Vol. 2, 9th edition, and *Advanced Materials & Processes,* Vol. 146, No. 4, ASM International, Materials Park, OH; *Modern Plastics Encyclopedia '96* and *Modern Plastics Encyclopedia 1977–1978,* The McGraw-Hill Companies, New York, NY; and manufacturers' technical data sheets.

Table B.8 Room-Temperature Specific Heat Values for Various Engineering Materials

Material	*Specific Heat (J/kg-K)*
METALS AND METAL ALLOYS	
Plain Carbon and Low Alloy Steels	
Steel alloy A36	486[a]
Steel alloy 1020	486[a]
Steel alloy 1040	486[a]
Stainless Steels	
Stainless alloy 304	500
Stainless alloy 316	500
Stainless alloy 405	460
Stainless alloy 440A	460
Stainless alloy 17-7PH	460
Cast Irons	
Gray irons	
• Grade G1800	544
• Grade G3000	544
• Grade G4000	544
Ductile irons	
• Grade 60-40-18	544
• Grade 80-55-06	544
• Grade 120-90-02	544
Aluminum Alloys	
Alloy 1100	904
Alloy 2024	875
Alloy 6061	896
Alloy 7075	960[b]
Alloy 356.0	963[b]
Copper Alloys	
C11000 (electrolytic tough pitch)	385
C17200 (beryllium–copper)	420
C26000 (cartridge brass)	375
C36000 (free-cutting brass)	380
C71500 (copper–nickel, 30%)	380
C93200 (bearing bronze)	376
Magnesium Alloys	
Alloy AZ31B	1024
Alloy AZ91D	1050
Titanium Alloys	
Commercially pure (ASTM grade 1)	528[c]
Alloy Ti-5Al-2.5Sn	470[c]
Alloy Ti-6Al-4V	610[c]
Precious Metals	
Gold (commercially pure)	130
Platinum (commercially pure)	132[d]
Silver (commercially pure)	235

Table B.8 (*Continued*)

Material	*Specific Heat (J/kg-K)*
Refractory Metals	
Molybdenum (commercially pure)	276
Tantalum (commercially pure)	139
Tungsten (commercially pure)	138
Miscellaneous Nonferrous Alloys	
Nickel 200	456
Inconel 625	410
Monel 400	427
Haynes alloy 25	377
Invar	500
Super invar	500
Kovar	460
Chemical lead	129
Antimonial lead (6%)	135
Tin (commercially pure)	222
Lead–tin solder (60Sn-40Pb)	150
Zinc (commercially pure)	395
Zirconium, reactor grade 702	285
GRAPHITE, CERAMICS, AND SEMICONDUCTING MATERIALS	
Aluminum oxide	
• 99.9% pure	775
• 96%	775
• 90%	775
Concrete	850–1150
Diamond (natural)	520
Gallium arsenide	350
Glass, borosilicate (Pyrex)	850
Glass, soda–lime	840
Glass ceramic (Pyroceram)	975
Graphite	
• Extruded	830
• Isostatically molded	830
Silica, fused	740
Silicon	700
Silicon carbide	
• Hot pressed	670
• Sintered	590
Silicon nitride	
• Hot pressed	750
• Reaction bonded	870
• Sintered	1100
Zirconia, 3 mol% Y_2O_3	481
POLYMERS	
Epoxy	1050
Nylon 6,6	1670
Phenolic	1590–1760
Poly(butylene terephthalate) (PBT)	1170–2300
Polycarbonate (PC)	840

Table B.8 (*Continued*)

Material	*Specific Heat (J/kg-K)*
Polyester (thermoset)	710–920
Polyethylene	
• Low density (LDPE)	2300
• High density (HDPE)	1850
Poly(ethylene terephthalate) (PET)	1170
Poly(methyl methacrylate) (PMMA)	1460
Polypropylene (PP)	1925
Polystyrene (PS)	1170
Polytetrafluoroethylene (PTFE)	1050
Poly(vinyl chloride) (PVC)	1050–1460
FIBER MATERIALS	
Aramid (Kevlar 49)	1300
E-glass	810
COMPOSITE MATERIALS	
Wood	
• Douglas fir (12% moisture)	2900
• Red oak (12% moisture)	2900

[a]At temperatures between 50°C and 100°C.

[b]At 100°C.

[c]At 50°C.

[d]At 0°C.

Sources: *ASM Handbooks, Volumes 1 and 2, Engineered Materials Handbooks, Volumes 1, 2, and 4, Metals Handbook: Properties and Selection: Nonferrous Alloys and Pure Metals,* Vol. 2, 9th edition, and *Advanced Materials & Processes,* Vol. 146, No. 4, ASM International, Materials Park, OH; *Modern Plastics Encyclopedia 1977–1978,* The McGraw-Hill Companies, New York, NY; and manufacturers' technical data sheets.

Table B.9 Room-Temperature Electrical Resistivity Values for Various Engineering Materials

Material	*Electrical Resistivity (Ω-m)*
METALS AND METAL ALLOYS	
Plain Carbon and Low Alloy Steels	
Steel alloy A36[a]	1.60×10^{-7}
Steel alloy 1020 (annealed)[a]	1.60×10^{-7}
Steel alloy 1040 (annealed)[a]	1.60×10^{-7}
Steel alloy 4140 (quenched and tempered)	2.20×10^{-7}
Steel alloy 4340 (quenched and tempered)	2.48×10^{-7}
Stainless Steels	
Stainless alloy 304 (annealed)	7.2×10^{-7}
Stainless alloy 316 (annealed)	7.4×10^{-7}
Stainless alloy 405 (annealed)	6.0×10^{-7}
Stainless alloy 440A (annealed)	6.0×10^{-7}
Stainless alloy 17-7PH (annealed)	8.3×10^{-7}

Table B.9 (*Continued*)

Material	*Electrical Resistivity* (Ω-*m*)
Cast Irons	
Gray irons	
• Grade G1800	15.0×10^{-7}
• Grade G3000	9.5×10^{-7}
• Grade G4000	8.5×10^{-7}
Ductile irons	
• Grade 60-40-18	5.5×10^{-7}
• Grade 80-55-06	6.2×10^{-7}
• Grade 120-90-02	6.2×10^{-7}
Aluminum Alloys	
Alloy 1100 (annealed)	2.9×10^{-8}
Alloy 2024 (annealed)	3.4×10^{-8}
Alloy 6061 (annealed)	3.7×10^{-8}
Alloy 7075 (T6 treatment)	5.22×10^{-8}
Alloy 356.0 (T6 treatment)	4.42×10^{-8}
Copper Alloys	
C11000 (electrolytic tough pitch, annealed)	1.72×10^{-8}
C17200 (beryllium–copper)	5.7×10^{-8}–1.15×10^{-7}
C26000 (cartridge brass)	6.2×10^{-8}
C36000 (free-cutting brass)	6.6×10^{-8}
C71500 (copper–nickel, 30%)	37.5×10^{-8}
C93200 (bearing bronze)	14.4×10^{-8}
Magnesium Alloys	
Alloy AZ31B	9.2×10^{-8}
Alloy AZ91D	17.0×10^{-8}
Titanium Alloys	
Commercially pure (ASTM grade 1)	4.2×10^{-7}–5.2×10^{-7}
Alloy Ti-5Al-2.5Sn	15.7×10^{-7}
Alloy Ti-6Al-4V	17.1×10^{-7}
Precious Metals	
Gold (commercially pure)	2.35×10^{-8}
Platinum (commercially pure)	10.60×10^{-8}
Silver (commercially pure)	1.47×10^{-8}
Refractory Metals	
Molybdenum (commercially pure)	5.2×10^{-8}
Tantalum (commercially pure)	13.5×10^{-8}
Tungsten (commercially pure)	5.3×10^{-8}
Miscellaneous Nonferrous Alloys	
Nickel 200	0.95×10^{-7}
Inconel 625	12.90×10^{-7}
Monel 400	5.47×10^{-7}
Haynes alloy 25	8.9×10^{-7}
Invar	8.2×10^{-7}
Super invar	8.0×10^{-7}
Kovar	4.9×10^{-7}
Chemical lead	2.06×10^{-7}
Antimonial lead (6%)	2.53×10^{-7}
Tin (commercially pure)	1.11×10^{-7}
Lead–tin solder (60Sn-40Pb)	1.50×10^{-7}

Table B.9 (*Continued*)

Material	*Electrical Resistivity* (Ω-m)
Zinc (commercially pure)	62.0×10^{-7}
Zirconium, reactor grade 702	3.97×10^{-7}
GRAPHITE, CERAMICS, AND SEMICONDUCTING MATERIALS	
Aluminum oxide	
• 99.9% pure	$>10^{13}$
• 96%	$>10^{12}$
• 90%	$>10^{12}$
Concrete (dry)	10^{9}
Diamond	
• Natural	$10–10^{14}$
• Synthetic	1.5×10^{-2}
Gallium arsenide (intrinsic)	10^{6}
Glass, borosilicate (Pyrex)	$\sim 10^{13}$
Glass, soda–lime	$10^{10}–10^{11}$
Glass ceramic (Pyroceram)	2×10^{14}
Graphite	
• Extruded (with grain direction)	$7 \times 10^{-6}–20 \times 10^{-6}$
• Isostatically molded	$10 \times 10^{-6}–18 \times 10^{-6}$
Silica, fused	$>10^{18}$
Silicon (intrinsic)	2500
Silicon carbide	
• Hot pressed	$1.0–10^{9}$
• Sintered	$1.0–10^{9}$
Silicon nitride	
• Hot isostatic pressed	$>10^{12}$
• Reaction bonded	$>10^{12}$
• Sintered	$>10^{12}$
Zirconia, 3 mol% Y_2O_3	10^{10}
POLYMERS	
Elastomers	
• Butadiene-acrylonitrile (nitrile)	3.5×10^{8}
• Styrene-butadiene (SBR)	6×10^{11}
• Silicone	10^{13}
Epoxy	$10^{10}–10^{13}$
Nylon 6,6	$10^{12}–10^{13}$
Phenolic	$10^{9}–10^{10}$
Poly(butylene terephthalate) (PBT)	4×10^{14}
Polycarbonate (PC)	2×10^{14}
Polyester (thermoset)	10^{13}
Polyetheretherketone (PEEK)	6×10^{14}
Polyethylene	
• Low density (LDPE)	$10^{15}–5 \times 10^{16}$
• High density (HDPE)	$10^{15}–5 \times 10^{16}$
• Ultrahigh molecular weight (UHMWPE)	$>5 \times 10^{14}$
Poly(ethylene terephthalate) (PET)	10^{12}
Poly(methyl methacrylate) (PMMA)	$>10^{12}$
Polypropylene (PP)	$>10^{14}$
Polystyrene (PS)	$>10^{14}$
Polytetrafluoroethylene (PTFE)	10^{17}
Poly(vinyl chloride) (PVC)	$>10^{14}$

Table B.9 *(Continued)*

Material	*Electrical Resistivity* (Ω-*m*)
FIBER MATERIALS	
Carbon (PAN precursor)	
• Standard modulus	17×10^{-6}
• Intermediate modulus	15×10^{-6}
• High modulus	9.5×10^{-6}
E-glass	4×10^{14}
COMPOSITE MATERIALS	
Wood	
• Douglas fir (oven dry)	
Parallel to grain	10^{14}–10^{16}
Perpendicular to grain	10^{14}–10^{16}
• Red oak (oven dry)	
Parallel to grain	10^{14}–10^{16}
Perpendicular to grain	10^{14}–10^{16}

[a]At 0°C.

Sources: *ASM Handbooks, Volumes 1 and 2, Engineered Materials Handbooks, Volumes 1, 2, and 4, Metals Handbook: Properties and Selection: Nonferrous Alloys and Pure Metals,* Vol. 2, 9th edition, and *Advanced Materials & Processes,* Vol. 146, No. 4, ASM International, Materials Park, OH; *Modern Plastics Encyclopedia 1977–1978,* The McGraw-Hill Companies, New York, NY; and manufacturers' technical data sheets.

Table B.10 Compositions of Metal Alloys for Which Data Are Included in Tables B.1 through B.9

Alloy (UNS Designation)	*Composition (wt%)*
PLAIN-CARBON AND LOW-ALLOY STEELS	
A36 (ASTM A36)	98.0 Fe (min), 0.29 C, 1.0 Mn, 0.28 Si
1020 (G10200)	99.1 Fe (min), 0.20 C, 0.45 Mn
1040 (G10400)	98.6 Fe (min), 0.40 C, 0.75 Mn
4140 (G41400)	96.8 Fe (min), 0.40 C, 0.90 Cr, 0.20 Mo, 0.9 Mn
4340 (G43400)	95.2 Fe (min), 0.40 C, 1.8 Ni, 0.80 Cr, 0.25 Mo, 0.7 Mn
STAINLESS STEELS	
304 (S30400)	66.4 Fe (min), 0.08 C, 19.0 Cr, 9.25 Ni, 2.0 Mn
316 (S31600)	61.9 Fe (min), 0.08 C, 17.0 Cr, 12.0 Ni, 2.5 Mo, 2.0 Mn
405 (S40500)	83.1 Fe (min), 0.08 C, 13.0 Cr, 0.20 Al, 1.0 Mn
440A (S44002)	78.4 Fe (min), 0.70 C, 17.0 Cr, 0.75 Mo. 1.0 Mn
17-7PH (S17700)	70.6 Fe (min), 0.09 C, 17.0 Cr, 7.1 Ni, 1.1 Al, 1.0 Mn
CAST IRONS	
Grade G1800 (F10004)	Fe (bal), 3.4–3.7 C, 2.8–2.3 Si, 0.65 Mn, 0.15 P, 0.15 S
Grade G3000 (F10006)	Fe (bal), 3.1–3.4 C, 2.3–1.9 Si, 0.75 Mn, 0.10 P, 0.15 S
Grade G4000 (F10008)	Fe (bal), 3.0–3.3 C, 2.1–1.8 Si, 0.85 Mn, 0.07 P, 0.15 S
Grade 60-40-18 (F32800)	Fe (bal), 3.4–4.0 C, 2.0–2.8 Si, 0–1.0 Ni, 0.05 Mg
Grade 80-55-06 (F33800)	Fe (bal), 3.3–3.8 C, 2.0–3.0 Si, 0–1.0 Ni, 0.05 Mg
Grade 120-90-02 (F36200)	Fe (bal), 3.4–3.8 C, 2.0–2.8 Si, 0–2.5 Ni, 0–1.0 Mo, 0.05 Mg

Table B.10 (*Continued*)

Alloy (UNS Designation)	*Composition (wt%)*
	ALUMINUM ALLOYS
1100 (A91100)	99.00 Al (min), 0.20 Cu (max)
2024 (A92024)	90.75 Al (min), 4.4 Cu, 0.6 Mn, 1.5 Mg
6061 (A96061)	95.85 Al (min), 1.0 Mg, 0.6 Si, 0.30 Cu, 0.20 Cr
7075 (A97075)	87.2 Al (min), 5.6 Zn, 2.5 Mg, 1.6 Cu, 0.23 Cr
356.0 (A03560)	90.1 Al (min), 7.0 Si, 0.3 Mg
	COPPER ALLOYS
(C11000)	99.90 Cu (min), 0.04 O (max)
(C17200)	96.7 Cu (min), 1.9 Be, 0.20 Co
(C26000)	Zn (bal), 70 Cu, 0.07 Pb, 0.05 Fe (max)
(C36000)	60.0 Cu (min), 35.5 Zn, 3.0 Pb
(C71500)	63.75 Cu (min), 30.0 Ni
(C93200)	81.0 Cu (min), 7.0 Sn, 7.0 Pb, 3.0 Zn
	MAGNESIUM ALLOYS
AZ31B (M11311)	94.4 Mg (min), 3.0 Al, 0.20 Mn (min), 1.0 Zn, 0.1 Si (max)
AZ91D (M11916)	89.0 Mg (min), 9.0 Al, 0.13 Mn (min), 0.7 Zn, 0.1 Si (max)
	TITANIUM ALLOYS
Commercial, grade 1 (R50250)	99.5 Ti (min)
Ti-5Al-2.5Sn (R54520)	90.2 Ti (min), 5.0 Al, 2.5 Sn
Ti-6Al-4V (R56400)	87.7 Ti (min), 6.0 Al, 4.0 V
	MISCELLANEOUS ALLOYS
Nickel 200	99.0 Ni (min)
Inconel 625	58.0 Ni (min), 21.5 Cr, 9.0 Mo, 5.0 Fe, 3.65 Nb + Ta, 1.0 Co
Monel 400	63.0 Ni (min), 31.0 Cu, 2.5 Fe, 0.2 Mn, 0.3 C, 0.5 Si
Haynes alloy 25	49.4 Co (min), 20 Cr, 15 W, 10 Ni, 3 Fe (max), 0.10 C, 1.5 Mn
Invar (K93601)	64 Fe, 36 Ni
Super invar	63 Fe, 32 Ni, 5 Co
Kovar	54 Fe, 29 Ni, 17 Co
Chemical lead (L51120)	99.90 Pb (min)
Antimonial lead, 6% (L53105)	94 Pb, 6 Sb
Tin (commercially pure) (ASTM B339A)	98.85 Pb (min)
Lead–tin solder (60Sn-40Pb) (ASTM B32 grade 60)	60 Sn, 40 Pb
Zinc (commercially pure) (Z21210)	99.9 Zn (min), 0.10 Pb (max)
Zirconium, reactor grade 702 (R60702)	99.2 Zr + Hf (min), 4.5 Hf (max), 0.2 Fe + Cr

Sources: *ASM Handbooks, Volumes 1 and 2,* ASM International, Materials Park, OH.

Appendix C Relative Costs for Selected Engineering Materials

This appendix contains price information for the same set of materials for which the properties are included in Appendix B. The collection of valid cost data for materials is an extremely difficult task, which explains the dearth of materials pricing information in the literature. One reason for this is that there are three pricing tiers: manufacturer, distributor, and retail. Under most circumstances, we have used distributor prices. For some materials (e.g., specialized ceramics such as silicon carbide and silicon nitride), it was necessary to use manufacturer's prices. In addition, there may be significant variation in the cost for a specific material. There are several reasons for this. First, each vendor has its own pricing scheme. Furthermore, cost will depend on quantity of material purchased and, in addition, how it was processed or treated. We have endeavored to collect data for relatively large orders—-that is, quantities on the order of 900 kg (2000 lb_m) for materials that are ordinarily sold in bulk lots—and, also, for common shapes/treatments. When possible, we obtained price quotes from at least three distributors/manufacturers.

This pricing information was collected between May and August 1998. As material prices change over time, it was decided to use a relative cost index; this index represents the per-unit mass cost (or average per-unit mass cost) of a material divided by the average per-unit mass cost of a common engineering material—A36 plain carbon steel. Although the price of a specific material will vary over time, the price ratio between that material and another will, most likely, change more slowly.

Material/Condition	*Relative Cost*
PLAIN CARBON AND LOW ALLOY STEELS	
Steel alloy A36	
• Plate, hot rolled	1.00
• Angle bar, hot rolled	1.6
Steel alloy 1020	
• Plate, hot rolled	0.8
• Plate, cold rolled	1.6
Steel alloy 1040	
• Plate, hot rolled	1.1
• Plate, cold rolled	1.9
Steel alloy 4140	
• Bar, normalized	2.6
• H grade (round), normalized	4.2

Material/Condition	*Relative Cost*
Steel alloy 4340	
• Bar, annealed	3.5
• Bar, normalized	4.7
STAINLESS STEELS	
Stainless alloy 304	
• Plate, hot finished and annealed	4.0
Stainless alloy 316	
• Plate, hot finished and annealed	5.3
• Round, cold drawn and annealed	8.9
Stainless alloy 440A	
• Plate, annealed	6.7
Stainless alloy 17-7PH	
• Plate, cold rolled	12.0
CAST IRONS	
Gray irons (all grades)	
• High production	1.9
• Low production	4.7
Ductile irons (all grades)	
• High production	2.4
• Low production	5.9
ALUMINUM ALLOYS	
Alloy 1100	
• Sheet, annealed	12.3
Alloy 2024	
• Sheet, T3 temper	14.1
• Bar, T351 temper	16.2
Alloy 6061	
• Sheet, T6 temper	7.6
• Bar, T651 temper	8.7
Alloy 7075	
• Sheet, T6 temper	13.4
Alloy 356	
• As cast, high production	7.9
• As cast, custom pieces	15.7
• T6 temper, custom pieces	16.6
COPPER ALLOYS	
Alloy C11000 (electrolytic tough pitch), sheet	7.9
Alloy C17200 (beryllium–copper), sheet	51.4
Alloy C26000 (cartridge brass), sheet	6.0
Alloy C36000 (free-cutting brass), sheet, rod	5.1
Alloy C71500 (copper–nickel, 30%), sheet	12.9
Alloy C93200 (bearing bronze)	
• Bar	7.9
• As cast, custom piece	17.4
MAGNESIUM ALLOYS	
Alloy AZ31B	
• Sheet (rolled)	15.7

Material/Condition	*Relative Cost*
• Extruded	12.6
Alloy AZ91D (as cast)	5.4
TITANIUM ALLOYS	
Commercially pure	
• ASTM grade 1, annealed	66.4
Alloy Ti-5Al-2.5V	157
Alloy Ti-6Al-4V	132
PRECIOUS METALS	
Gold, bullion	14,100
Platinum, bullion	18,400
Silver, bullion	271
REFRACTORY METALS	
Molybdenum	
• Commercially pure, sheet and rod	143
Tantalum	
• Commercially pure, sheet and rod	593
Tungsten	
• Commercially pure, sheet	111
• Commercially pure, rod (1/2–3/8 in. dia.)	166
MISCELLANEOUS NONFERROUS ALLOYS	
Nickel 200	31.4
Inconel 625	35.0
Monel 400	22.9
Haynes alloy 25	135
Invar	26.4
Super invar	39.3
Kovar	50.4
Chemical lead	
• Ingot	1.7
• Plate	2.5
Antimonial lead (6%)	
• Ingot	2.1
• Plate	3.4
Tin, commercial purity (99.9+%), ingot	11.2
Solder (60Sn-40Pb), bar	9.3
Zinc, commercial purity	
• Ingot	1.7
• Anode	2.9
Zirconium, reactor grade 702 (plate)	66.1
GRAPHITE, CERAMICS, AND SEMICONDUCTING MATERIALS	
Aluminum oxide	
• Calcined powder, 99.8% pure, particle size between 0.4 and 5 μm	2.1
• Ball grinding media, 99% pure, 1/4 in. dia.	41
• Ball grinding media, 96% pure, 1/4 in. dia.	42.5
• Ball grinding media, 90% pure, 1/4 in. dia.	21.7
Concrete, mixed	0.06
Diamond	
• Natural, 1/3 carat, industrial grade	90,000

Material/Condition	*Relative Cost*
• Synthetic, 30–40 mesh, industrial grade	27,000
• Natural, powder, 45 μm, polishing abrasive	7100
Gallium arsenide	
• Mechanical grade, 75 mm dia. wafers, ~625 μm thick	3100
• Prime grade, 75 mm dia. wafers, ~625 μm thick	13,200
Glass, borosilicate (Pyrex), plate	18.2
Glass, soda–lime, plate	2.9
Glass ceramic (Pyroceram), plate	22.5
Graphite	
• Powder, synthetic, 99% pure, particle size ~10 μm	7.1
• Powder, synthetic, 99.7% pure, particle size ~10 μm	10.7
• Extruded, high purity, fine (<0.75 mm) particle size	9.3
• Isostatically pressed parts, high purity, ~20 μm particle size	29
Silica, fused, plate	500
Silicon	
• Test grade, undoped, 100 mm dia. wafers, ~425 μm thick	2070
• Prime grade, undoped, 100 mm dia. wafers, ~425 μm thick	3300
Silicon carbide	
• α-phase sinterable powder, particle size between 1 and 10 μm	57.1
• α-phase, polishing abrasive	18.6
• β-phase sinterable powder, particle size between 1 and 10 μm	100
• β-phase, polishing abrasive, 1200 to 400 mesh	21.4
• α-phase ball grinding media, 1/4 in. dia., sintered	360
Silicon nitride	
• Sinterable powder, submicron particle size	143
• Balls, unfinished, 0.25 in. to 0.50 in. in diameter, hot isostatic pressed	1400
• Balls, finished ground, 0.25 in. to 0.50 in. diameter, hot isostatic pressed	4300
Zirconia, partially stabilized (3 mol% Y_2O_3)	
• Sinterable powder, submicron particle size	68
• Sinterable powder, particle size greater than a micron	39.3
• Ball grinding media, 15 mm dia., sintered	215
POLYMERS	
Butadiene-acrylonitrile (nitrile) rubber	
• Raw and unprocessed	4.1

Material/Condition	*Relative Cost*
• Extruded sheet ($^1/_4$–$^1/_8$ in. thick)	14.6
• Calendered sheet ($^1/_4$–$^1/_8$ in. thick)	12.0
Styrene-butadiene (SBR) rubber	
• Raw and unprocessed	1.7
• Extruded sheet ($^1/_4$–$^1/_8$ in. thick)	14.1
• Calendered sheet ($^1/_4$–$^1/_8$ in. thick)	9.7
Silicone rubber	
• Raw and unprocessed	7.9
• Extruded sheet ($^1/_4$–$^1/_8$ in. thick)	27.7
• Calendered sheet ($^1/_4$–$^1/_8$ in. thick)	50.0
Epoxy resin, raw form	5.0
Nylon 6,6	
• Raw form	7.4
• Extruded	13.4
Phenolic resin, raw form	13.2
Polybutylene terephthalate (PBT)	
• Raw form	5.7
• Sheet	13.9
Polycarbonate (PC)	
• Raw form	7.3
• Sheet	12.1
Polyester (thermoset), raw form	4.2
Polyetheretherketone (PEEK), raw form	143
Polyethylene	
• Low density (LDPE), raw form	1.8
• High density (HDPE), raw form	1.9
• Ultrahigh molecular weight (UHMWPE), raw form	8.2
Polyethylene terephthalate (PET)	
• Raw form	2.9
• Sheet	7.9
Polymethyl methacrylate (PMMA)	
• Raw form	3.4
• Calendered sheet	6.0
• Cell cast	8.4
Polypropylene (PP), raw form	1.8
Polystyrene (PS), raw form	1.5
Polytetrafluoroethylene (PTFE)	
• Raw form	33.2
• Sheet	54
Polyvinyl chloride (PVC), raw form	3.0
FIBER MATERIALS	
Aramid (Kevlar 49), continuous	44.3
Carbon (PAN precursor), continuous	
• Standard modulus	52.1
• Intermediate modulus	125
• High modulus	285
E glass, continuous	3.7
COMPOSITE MATERIALS	
Aramid (Kevlar 49) continuous-fiber, epoxy prepreg	84

Material/Condition	*Relative Cost*
Carbon continuous-fiber,	
epoxy prepreg	
• Standard modulus	71
• Intermediate modulus	164
• High modulus	340
E-glass continuous-fiber, epoxy prepreg	31.4
Woods	
Douglas fir	0.8
Red oak	4.2

Appendix D Repeat Unit Structures for Common Polymers

Chemical Name	*Repeat Unit Structure*
Epoxy (diglycidyl ether of bisphenol A, DGEPA)[1]	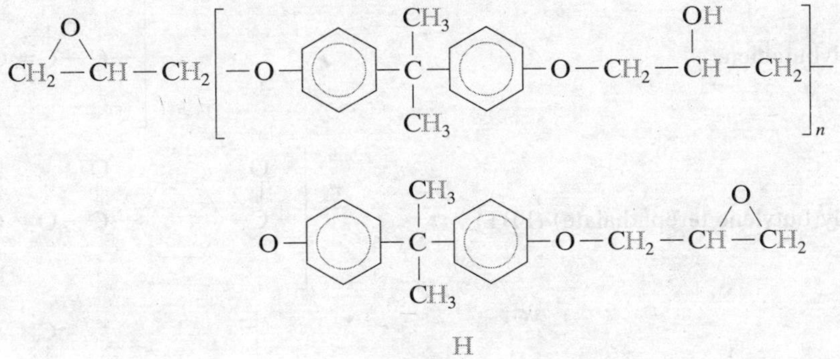
Melamine-formaldehyde (melamine)	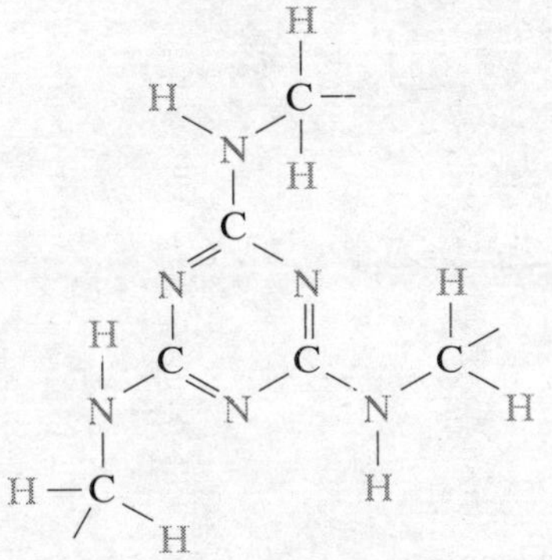
Phenol-formaldehyde (phenolic)	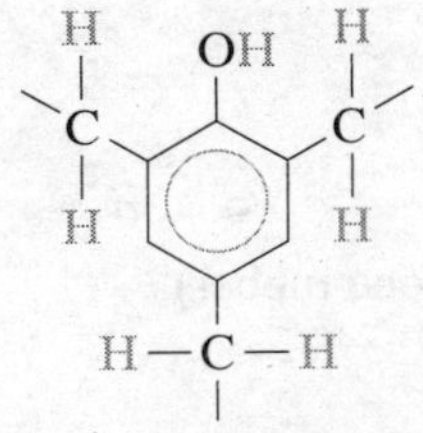

[1] The structure shown here is the monomer structure for this epoxy. Curing is accomplished by reaction of the epoxy with a "hardener" such as diamine. One example of a diamine is:

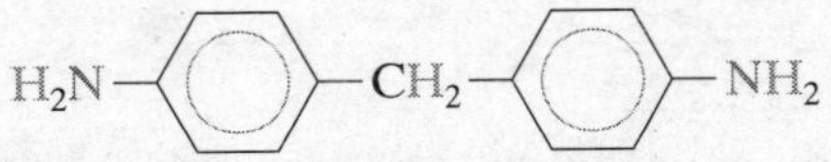

The hardener molecules react with and open up the epoxide rings (situated at both ends of the epoxy monomer), allowing the formation of a three-dimensional network polymer.

Chemical Name	*Repeat Unit Structure*
Polyacrylonitrile (PAN)	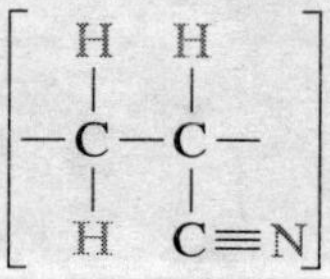
Poly(amide-imide) (PAI)	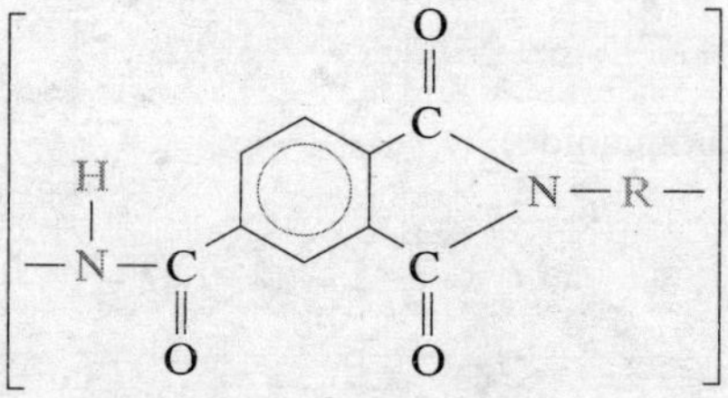
Polybutadiene	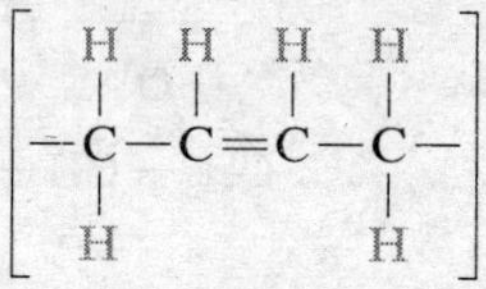
Poly(butylene terephthalate) (PBT)	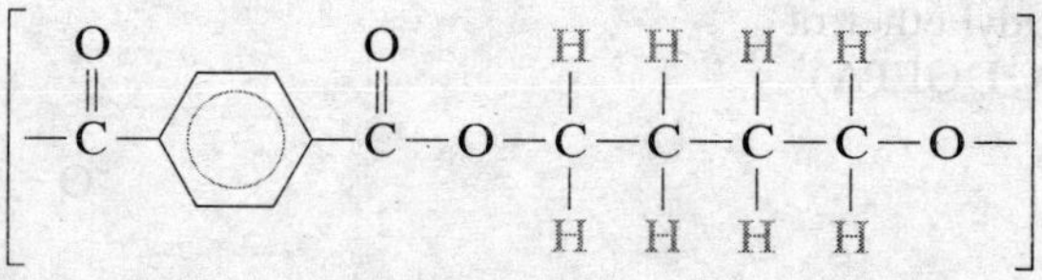
Polycarbonate (PC)	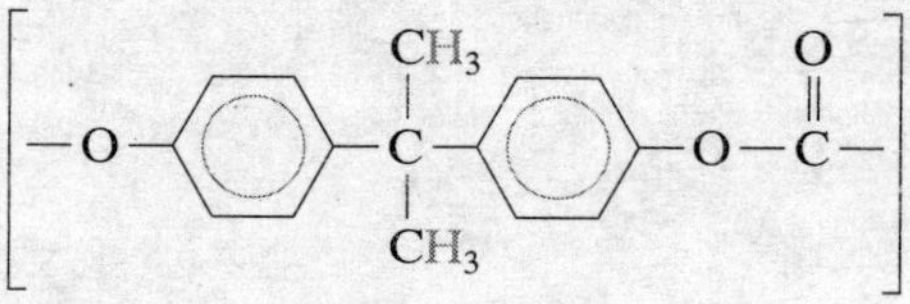
Polychloroprene	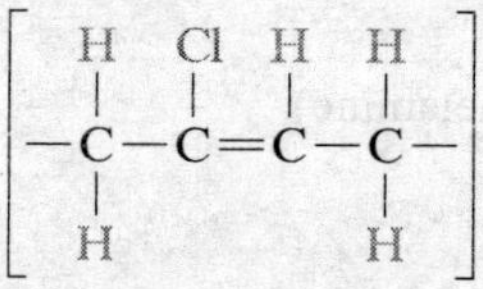
Polychlorotrifluoroethylene	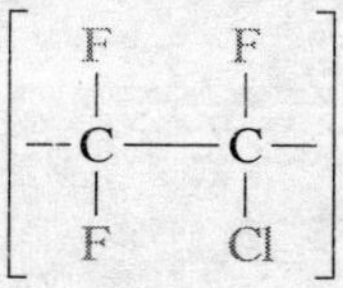
Poly(dimethyl siloxane) (silicone rubber)	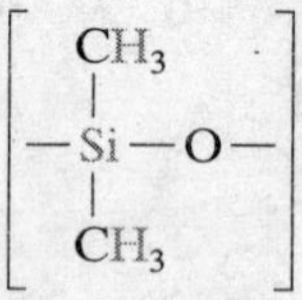
Polyetheretherketone (PEEK)	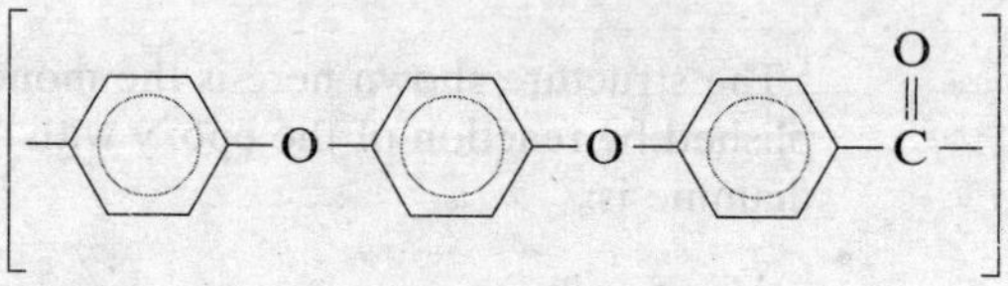
Polyethylene (PE)	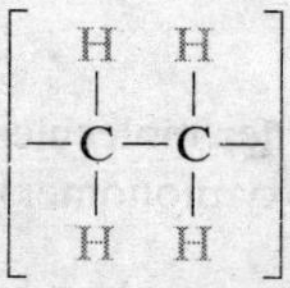

Chemical Name	*Repeat Unit Structure*
Poly(ethylene terephthalate) (PET)	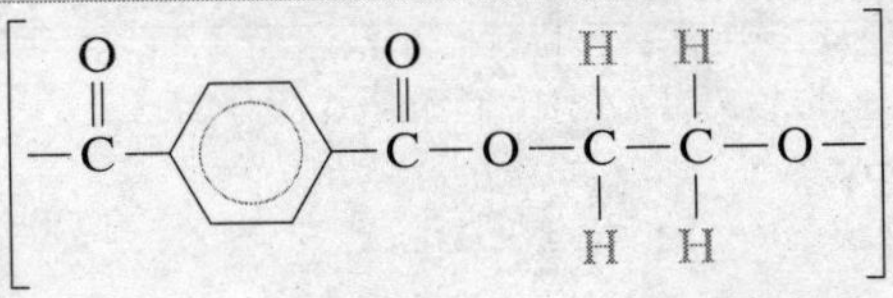
Poly(hexamethylene adipamide) (nylon 6,6)	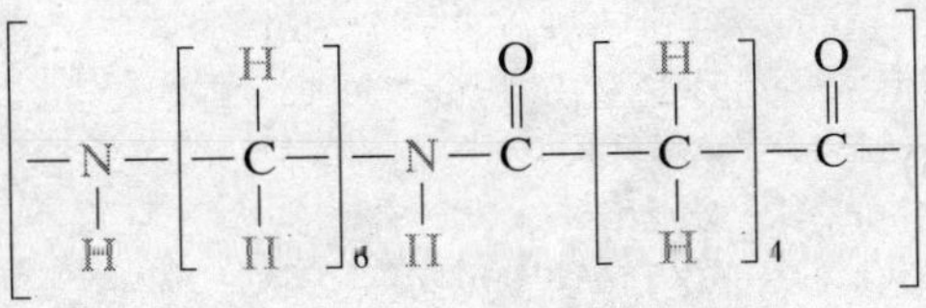
Polyimide	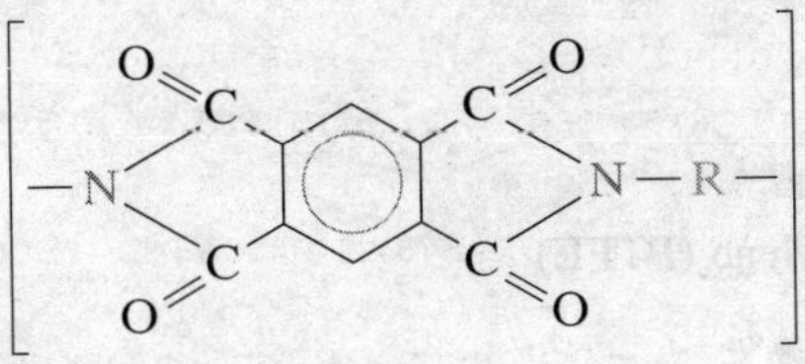
Polyisobutylene	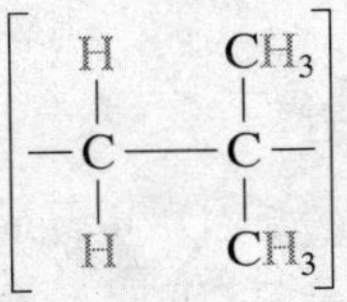
cis-Polyisoprene (natural rubber)	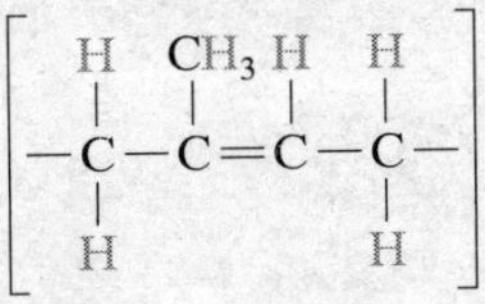
Poly(methyl methacrylate) (PMMA)	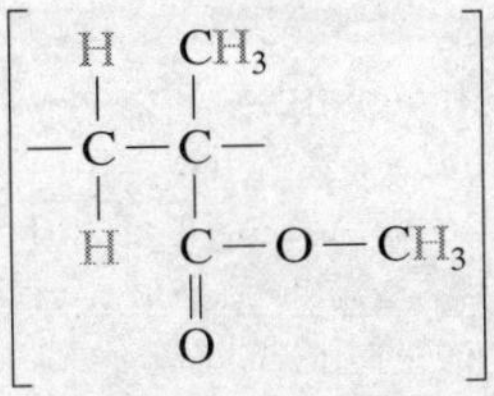
Poly(phenylene oxide) (PPO)	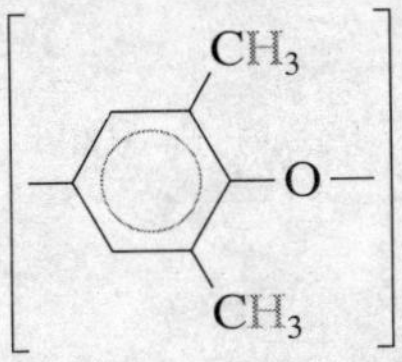
Poly(phenylene sulfide) (PPS)	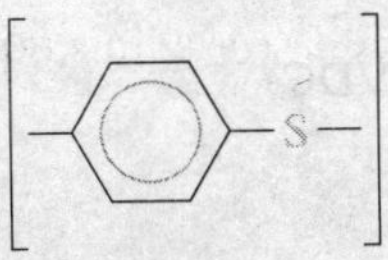
Poly(paraphenylene terephthalamide) (aramid)	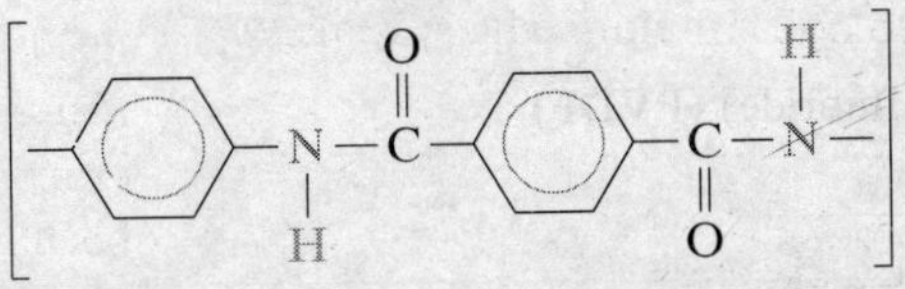

Chemical Name	*Repeat Unit Structure*
Polypropylene (PP)	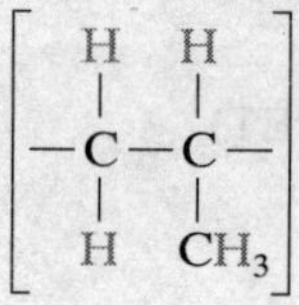
Polystyrene (PS)	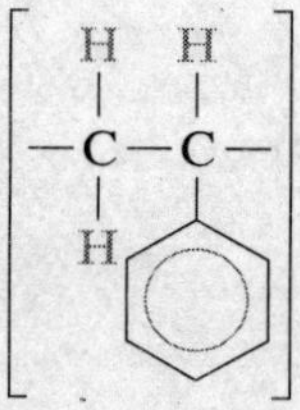
Polytetrafluoroethylene (PTFE)	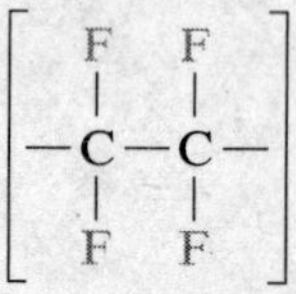
Poly(vinyl acetate) (PVAc)	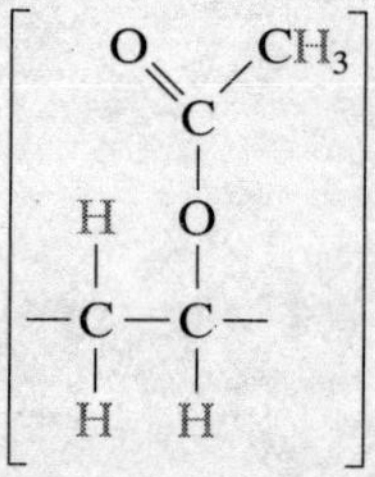
Poly(vinyl alcohol) (PVA)	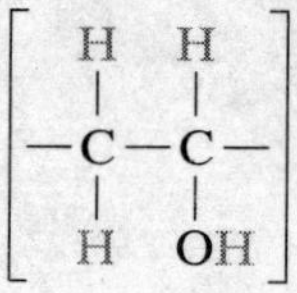
Poly(vinyl chloride) (PVC)	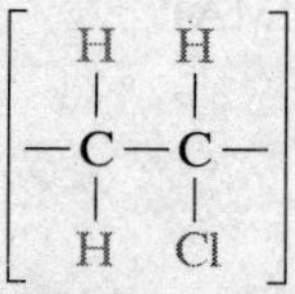
Poly(vinyl fluoride) (PVF)	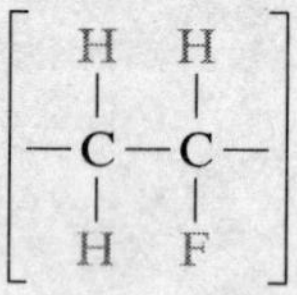
Poly(vinylidene chloride) (PVDC)	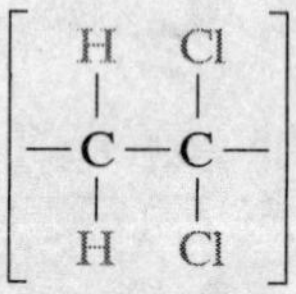
Poly(vinylidene fluoride) (PVDF)	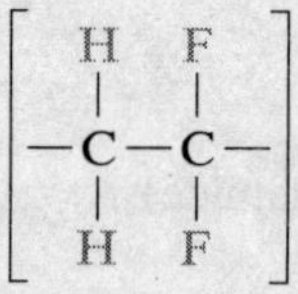

Appendix E Glass Transition and Melting Temperatures for Common Polymeric Materials

Polymer	*Glass Transition Temperature (°C)*	*Melting Temperature (°C)*
Aramid	375	~640
Polyimide (thermoplastic)	280–330	*a*
Polyamide-imide	277–289	*a*
Polycarbonate	150	265
Polyetheretherketone	143	334
Polyacrylonitrile	104	317
Polystyrene		
• Atactic	100	*a*
• Isotactic	100	240
Poly(butylene terephthalate)	—	220–267
Poly(vinyl chloride)	87	212
Poly(phenylene sulfide)	85	285
Poly(ethylene terephthalate)	69	265
Nylon 6,6	57	265
Poly(methyl methacrylate)		
• Syndiotactic	3	105
• Isotactic	3	45
Polypropylene		
• Isotactic	−10	175
• Atactic	−18	175
Poly(vinylidene chloride)	−17	198
• Atactic	−18	175
Poly(vinyl fluoride)	−20	200
Poly(vinylidene fluoride)	−35	—
Polychloroprene (chloroprene rubber or neoprene)	−50	80
Polyisobutylene	−70	128
cis-Polyisoprene	−73	28
Polybutadiene		
• Syndiotactic	−90	154
• Isotactic	−90	120
High density polyethylene	−90	137
Polytetrafluoroethylene	−97	327
Low density polyethylene	−110	115
Polydimethylsiloxane (silicone rubber)	−123	−54

[a] These polymers normally exist at least 95% noncrystalline.

Glossary

A

Abrasive. A hard and wear-resistant material (commonly a ceramic) that is used to wear, grind, or cut away other material.

Absorption. The optical phenomenon whereby the energy of a photon of light is assimilated within a substance, normally by electronic polarization or by an electron excitation event.

Acceptor level. For a semiconductor or insulator, an energy level lying within yet near the bottom of the energy band gap, which may accept electrons from the valence band, leaving behind holes. The level is normally introduced by an impurity atom.

Activation energy (*Q*). The energy required to initiate a reaction, such as diffusion.

Activation polarization. The condition wherein the rate of an electrochemical reaction is controlled by the one slowest step in a sequence of steps that occur in series.

Addition (or chain reaction) polymerization. The process by which monomer units are attached one at a time, in chain-like fashion, to form a linear polymer macromolecule.

Adhesive. A substance that bonds together the surfaces of two other materials (termed adherends).

Age hardening. See **Precipitation hardening.**

Allotropy. The possibility of the existence of two or more different crystal structures for a substance (generally an elemental solid).

Alloy. A metallic substance that is composed of two or more elements.

Alloy steel. A ferrous (or iron-based) alloy that contains appreciable concentrations of alloying elements (other than C and residual amounts of Mn, Si, S, and P). These alloying elements are usually added to improve mechanical and corrosion resistance properties.

Alternating copolymer. A copolymer in which two different repeat units alternate positions along the molecular chain.

Amorphous. Having a noncrystalline structure.

Anelastic deformation. Time-dependent elastic (nonpermanent) deformation.

Anion. A negatively charged, nonmetallic ion.

Anisotropic. Exhibiting different values of a property in different crystallographic directions.

Annealing. A generic term used to denote a heat treatment wherein the microstructure and, consequently, the properties of a material are altered. "Annealing" frequently refers to a heat treatment whereby a previously cold-worked metal is softened by allowing it to recrystallize.

Annealing point (glass). The temperature at which residual stresses in a glass are eliminated within about 15 min; this corresponds to a glass viscosity of about 10^{12} Pa-s (10^{13} P).

Anode. The electrode in an electrochemical cell or galvanic couple that experiences oxidation, or gives up electrons.

Antiferromagnetism. A phenomenon observed in some materials (e.g., MnO); complete magnetic moment cancellation occurs as a result of antiparallel coupling of adjacent atoms or ions. The macroscopic solid possesses no net magnetic moment.

Artificial aging. For precipitation hardening, aging above room temperature.

Atactic. A type of polymer chain configuration (stereoisomer) wherein side groups are randomly positioned on one side of the chain or the other.

Athermal transformation. A reaction that is not thermally activated, and usually diffusionless, as with the martensitic transformation. Normally, the transformation takes place with great speed (i.e., is independent of time), and the extent of reaction depends on temperature.

Atomic mass unit (amu). A measure of atomic mass; one-twelfth of the mass of an atom of C^{12}.

Atomic number (*Z*). For a chemical element, the number of protons within the atomic nucleus.

Atomic packing factor (APF). The fraction of the volume of a unit cell that is occupied by "hard sphere" atoms or ions.

Atomic vibration. The vibration of an atom about its normal position in a substance.

Atomic weight (*A*). The weighted average of the atomic masses of an atom's naturally occurring isotopes. It may be expressed in terms of atomic mass units (on an atomic basis), or the mass per mole of atoms.

Atom percent (at%). Concentration specification on the basis of the number of moles (or atoms) of a particular element relative to the total number of moles (or atoms) of all elements within an alloy.

Austenite. Face-centered cubic iron; also iron and steel alloys that have the FCC crystal structure.

Austenitizing. Forming austenite by heating a ferrous alloy above its upper critical temperature—to within the austenite phase region from the phase diagram.

B

Bainite. An austenitic transformation product found in some steels and cast irons. It forms at temperatures between those at which pearlite and martensite transformations occur. The microstructure consists of α-ferrite and a fine dispersion of cementite.

Band gap energy (E_g). For semiconductors and insulators, the energies that lie between the valence and conduction bands; for intrinsic materials, electrons are forbidden to have energies within this range.

Bifunctional. Designating monomers that may react to form two covalent bonds with other monomers to create a two-dimensional chain-like molecular structure.

Block copolymer. A linear copolymer in which identical repeat units are clustered in blocks along the molecular chain.

Body-centered cubic (BCC). A common crystal structure found in some elemental metals. Within the cubic unit cell, atoms are located at corner and cell center positions.

Bohr atomic model. An early atomic model, in which electrons are assumed to revolve around the nucleus in discrete orbitals.

Bohr magneton (μ_B). The most fundamental magnetic moment, of magnitude 9.27×10^{-24} A-m^2.

Boltzmann's constant (k). A thermal energy constant having the value of 1.38×10^{-23} J/atom-K (8.62×10^{-5} eV/atom-K). See also **Gas constant.**

Bonding energy. The energy required to separate two atoms that are chemically bonded to each other. It may be expressed on a per-atom basis, or per mole of atoms.

Bragg's law. A relationship (Equation 3.13) that stipulates the condition for diffraction by a set of crystallographic planes.

Branched polymer. A polymer having a molecular structure of secondary chains that extend from the primary main chains.

Brass. A copper-rich copper–zinc alloy.

Brazing. A metal joining technique that uses a molten filler metal alloy having a melting temperature greater than about 425°C (800°F).

Brittle fracture. Fracture that occurs by rapid crack propagation and without appreciable macroscopic deformation.

Bronze. A copper-rich copper–tin alloy; aluminum, silicon, and nickel bronzes are also possible.

Burgers vector (b). A vector that denotes the magnitude and direction of lattice distortion associated with a dislocation.

C

Calcination. A high-temperature reaction whereby one solid material dissociates to form a gas and another solid. It is one step in the production of cement.

Capacitance (C). The charge-storing ability of a capacitor, defined as the magnitude of charge stored on either plate divided by the applied voltage.

Carbon–carbon composite. A composite composed of continuous fibers of carbon that are imbedded in a carbon matrix. The matrix was originally a polymer resin that was subsequently pyrolyzed to form carbon.

Carburizing. The process by which the surface carbon concentration of a ferrous alloy is increased by diffusion from the surrounding environment.

Case hardening. Hardening of the outer surface (or "case") of a steel component by a carburizing or nitriding process; used to improve wear and fatigue resistance.

Cast iron. Generically, a ferrous alloy, the carbon content of which is greater than the maximum solubility in austenite at the eutectic temperature. Most commercial cast irons contain between 3.0 and 4.5 wt% C, and between 1 and 3 wt% Si.

Cathode. The electrode in an electrochemical cell or galvanic couple at which a reduction reaction occurs; thus the electrode that receives electrons from an external circuit.

Cathodic protection. A means of corrosion prevention whereby electrons are supplied to the structure to be protected from an external source such as another more reactive metal or a dc power supply.

Cation. A positively charged metallic ion.

Cement. A substance (often a ceramic) that by chemical reaction binds particulate aggregates into a cohesive structure. With hydraulic cements the chemical reaction is one of hydration, involving water.

Cementite. Iron carbide (Fe_3C).

Ceramic. A compound of metallic and nonmetallic elements, for which the interatomic bonding is predominantly ionic.

Ceramic-matrix composite (CMC). A composite for which both matrix and dispersed phases are ceramic materials. The dispersed phase is normally added to improve fracture toughness.

Cermet. A composite material consisting of a combination of ceramic and metallic materials. The most common cermets are the cemented carbides, composed of an extremely hard ceramic (e.g., WC, TiC), bonded together by a ductile metal such as cobalt or nickel.

Chain-folded model. For crystalline polymers, a model that describes the structure of platelet crystallites. Molecular alignment is accomplished by chain folding that occurs at the crystallite faces.

Charpy test. One of two tests (see also **Izod test**) that may be used to measure the impact energy or notch toughness of a standard notched specimen. An impact blow is imparted to the specimen by means of a weighted pendulum.

Cis. For polymers, a prefix denoting a type of molecular structure. For some unsaturated carbon chain atoms within a repeat unit, a side atom or group may be situated on one side of the double bond or directly opposite at a 180° rotation position. In a cis structure, two such side groups within the same repeat unit reside on the same side (e.g., *cis*-isoprene).

Coarse pearlite. Pearlite for which the alternating ferrite and cementite layers are relatively thick.

Coercivity (or coercive field, H_c). The applied magnetic field necessary to reduce to zero the magnetic flux density of a magnetized ferromagnetic or ferrimagnetic material.

Cold working. The plastic deformation of a metal at a temperature below that at which it recrystallizes.

Color. Visual perception stimulated by the combination of wavelengths of light that are transmitted to the eye.

Colorant. An additive that imparts a specific color to a polymer.

Compacted graphite iron. A cast iron that is alloyed with silicon and a small amount of magnesium, cerium, or other additives, in which the graphite exists as worm-like particles.

Component. A chemical constituent (element or compound) of an alloy, which may be used to specify its composition.

Composition (C_i). The relative content of a particular element or constituent (i) within an alloy, usually expressed in weight percent or atom percent.

Concentration. See **Composition.**

Concentration gradient (dC/dx). The slope of the concentration profile at a specific position.

Concentration polarization. The condition wherein the rate of an electrochemical reaction is limited by the rate of diffusion in the solution.

Concentration profile. The curve that results when the concentration of a chemical species is plotted versus position in a material.

Concrete. A composite material consisting of aggregate particles bound together in a solid body by a cement.

Condensation (or step reaction) polymerization. The formation of polymer macromolecules by an intermolecular reaction, usually with the production of a by-product of low molecular weight, such as water.

Conduction band. For electrical insulators and semiconductors, the lowest lying electron energy band that is empty of electrons at 0 K. Conduction electrons are those that have been excited to states within this band.

Conductivity, electrical (σ). The proportionality constant between current density and applied electric field; also a measure of the ease with which a material is capable of conducting an electric current.

Congruent transformation. A transformation of one phase to another of the same composition.

Continuous cooling transformation (*CCT*) diagram. A plot of temperature versus the logarithm of time for a steel alloy of definite composition. Used to indicate when transformations occur as the initially austenitized material is continuously cooled at a specified rate; in addition, the final microstructure and mechanical characteristics may be predicted.

Coordination number. The number of atomic or ionic nearest neighbors.

Copolymer. A polymer that consists of two or more dissimilar repeat units in combination along its molecular chains.

Corrosion. Deteriorative loss of a metal as a result of dissolution environmental reactions.

Corrosion fatigue. A type of failure that results from the simultaneous action of a cyclic stress and chemical attack.

Corrosion penetration rate (CPR). Thickness loss of material per unit of time as a result of corrosion; usually expressed in terms of mils per year or millimeters per year.

Coulombic force. A force between charged particles such as ions; the force is attractive when the particles are of opposite charge.

Covalent bond. A primary interatomic bond that is formed by the sharing of electrons between neighboring atoms.

Creep. The time-dependent permanent deformation that occurs under stress; for most materials it is important only at elevated temperatures.

Crevice corrosion. A form of corrosion that occurs within narrow crevices and under deposits of dirt or corrosion products (i.e., in regions of localized depletion of oxygen in the solution).

Critical resolved shear stress (τ_{crss}). The shear stress, resolved within a slip plane and direction, that is required to initiate slip.

Crosslinked polymer. A polymer in which adjacent linear molecular chains are joined at various positions by covalent bonds.

Crystalline. The state of a solid material characterized by a periodic and repeating three-dimensional array of atoms, ions, or molecules.

Crystallinity. For polymers, the state wherein a periodic and repeating atomic arrangement is achieved by molecular chain alignment.

Crystallite. A region within a crystalline polymer in which all the molecular chains are ordered and aligned.

Crystallization (glass-ceramics). The process in which a glass (noncrystalline or vitreous solid) transforms to a crystalline solid.

Crystal structure. For crystalline materials, the manner in which atoms or ions are arrayed in space. It is defined in terms of the unit cell geometry and the atom positions within the unit cell.

Crystal system. A scheme by which crystal structures are classified according to unit cell geometry. This geometry is specified in terms of the relationships between edge lengths and interaxial angles. There are seven different crystal systems.

Curie temperature (T_c). The temperature above which a ferromagnetic or ferrimagnetic material becomes paramagnetic.

D

Defect structure. Relating to the kinds and concentrations of vacancies and interstitials in a ceramic compound.

Degradation. A term used to denote the deteriorative processes that occur with polymeric materials. These processes include swelling, dissolution, and chain scission.

Degree of polymerization (*DP*). The average number of repeat units per polymer chain molecule.

Design stress (σ_d). Product of the calculated stress level (on the basis of estimated maximum load) and a design factor (which has a value greater than unity). Used to protect against unanticipated failure.

Diamagnetism. A weak form of induced or nonpermanent magnetism for which the magnetic susceptibility is negative.

Die. An individual integrated circuit chip with a thickness on the order of 0.4 mm and with a square or rectangular geometry, each side measuring on the order of 6 mm.

Dielectric. Any material that is electrically insulating.

Dielectric constant (ϵ_r). The ratio of the permittivity of a medium to that of a vacuum. Often called the relative dielectric constant or relative permittivity.

Dielectric displacement (*D*). The magnitude of charge per unit area of capacitor plate.

Dielectric (breakdown) strength. The magnitude of an electric field necessary to cause significant current passage through a dielectric material.

Diffraction (x-ray). Constructive interference of x-ray beams that are scattered by atoms of a crystal.

Diffusion. Mass transport by atomic motion.

Diffusion coefficient (*D*). The constant of proportionality between the diffusion flux and the concentration gradient in Fick's first law. Its magnitude is indicative of the rate of atomic diffusion.

Diffusion flux (*J*). The quantity of mass diffusing through and perpendicular to a unit cross-sectional area of material per unit time.

Diode. An electronic device that rectifies an electrical current—that is, allows current flow in one direction only.

Dipole (electric). A pair of equal yet opposite electrical charges that are separated by a small distance.

Dislocation. A linear crystalline defect around which there is atomic misalignment. Plastic deformation corresponds to the motion of dislocations in response to an applied shear stress. Edge, screw, and mixed dislocations are possible.

Dislocation density. The total dislocation length per unit volume of material; alternately, the number of dislocations that intersect a unit area of a random surface section.

Dislocation line. The line that extends along the end of the extra half-plane of atoms for an edge dislocation, and along the center of the spiral of a screw dislocation.

Dispersed phase. For composites and some two-phase alloys, the discontinuous phase that is surrounded by the matrix phase.

Dispersion strengthening. A means of strengthening materials wherein very small particles (usually less than 0.1 μm) of a hard yet inert phase are uniformly dispersed within a load-bearing matrix phase.

Domain. A volume region of a ferromagnetic or ferrimagnetic material in which all atomic or ionic magnetic moments are aligned in the same direction.

Donor level. For a semiconductor or insulator, an energy level lying within yet near the top of the energy band gap, and from which electrons may be excited into the conduction band. It is normally introduced by an impurity atom.

Doping. The intentional alloying of semiconducting materials with controlled concentrations of donor or acceptor impurities.

Drawing (metals). A forming technique used to fabricate metal wire and tubing. Deformation is accomplished by pulling the material through a die by means of a tensile force applied on the exit side.

Drawing (polymers). A deformation technique wherein polymer fibers are strengthened by elongation.

Driving force. The impetus behind a reaction, such as diffusion, grain growth, or a phase transformation. Usually attendant to the reaction is a reduction in some type of energy (e.g., free energy).

Ductile fracture. A mode of fracture that is attended by extensive gross plastic deformation.

Ductile iron. A cast iron that is alloyed with silicon and a small concentration of magnesium and/or cerium and in which the free graphite exists in nodular form. Sometimes called nodular iron.

Ductile-to-brittle transition. The transition from ductile to brittle behavior with a decrease in temperature exhibited by BCC alloys; the temperature range over which the transition occurs is determined by Charpy and Izod impact tests.

Ductility. A measure of a material's ability to undergo appreciable plastic deformation before fracture; it may be expressed as percent elongation (%EL) or percent reduction in area (%RA) from a tensile test.

E

Edge dislocation. A linear crystalline defect associated with the lattice distortion produced in the vicinity of the end of an extra half-plane of atoms within a crystal. The Burgers vector is perpendicular to the dislocation line.

Elastic deformation. Deformation that is nonpermanent—that is, totally recovered upon release of an applied stress.

Elastic recovery. Nonpermanent deformation that is recovered or regained upon the release of a mechanical stress.

Elastomer. A polymeric material that may experience large and reversible elastic deformations.

Electrical conductivity. See **Conductivity, electrical.**

Electric dipole. See **Dipole (electric).**

Electric field ($\mathscr{E}$). The gradient of voltage.

Electroluminescence. The emission of visible light by a *p–n* junction across which a forward-biased voltage is applied.

Electrolyte. A solution through which an electric current may be carried by the motion of ions.

Electromotive force (emf) series. A ranking of metallic elements according to their standard electrochemical cell potentials.

Electron configuration. For an atom, the manner in which possible electron states are filled with electrons.

Electronegative. For an atom, having a tendency to accept valence electrons. Also, a term used to describe nonmetallic elements.

Electron energy band. A series of electron energy states that are very closely spaced with respect to energy.

Electroneutrality. The state of having exactly the same numbers of positive and negative electrical charges (ionic and electronic)—that is, of being electrically neutral.

Electron state (level). One of a set of discrete, quantized energies that are allowed for electrons. In the atomic case each state is specified by four quantum numbers.

Electron volt (eV). A convenient unit of energy for atomic and subatomic systems. It is equivalent to the energy acquired by an electron when it falls through an electric potential of 1 volt.

Electropositive. For an atom, having a tendency to release valence electrons. Also, a term used to describe metallic elements.

Endurance limit. See **Fatigue limit.**

Energy band gap. See **Band gap energy.**

Engineering strain. See **Strain, engineering.**

Engineering stress. See **Stress, engineering.**

Equilibrium (phase). The state of a system where the phase characteristics remain constant over indefinite time periods. At equilibrium the free energy is a minimum.

Erosion–corrosion. A form of corrosion that arises from the combined action of chemical attack and mechanical wear.

Eutectic phase. One of the two phases found in the eutectic structure.

Eutectic reaction. A reaction wherein, upon cooling, a liquid phase transforms isothermally and reversibly into two intimately mixed solid phases.

Eutectic structure. A two-phase microstructure resulting from the solidification of a liquid having the eutectic composition; the phases exist as lamellae that alternate with one another.

Eutectoid reaction. A reaction wherein, upon cooling, one solid phase transforms isothermally and reversibly into two new solid phases that are intimately mixed.

Excited state. An electron energy state, not normally occupied, to which an electron may be promoted (from a lower energy state) by the absorption of some type of energy (e.g., heat, radiative).

Extrinsic semiconductor. A semiconducting material for which the electrical behavior is determined by impurities.

Extrusion. A forming technique whereby a material is forced, by compression, through a die orifice.

F

Face-centered cubic (FCC). A crystal structure found in some of the common elemental metals. Within the cubic unit cell, atoms are located at all corner and face-centered positions.

Fatigue. Failure, at relatively low stress levels, of structures that are subjected to fluctuating and cyclic stresses.

Fatigue life (N_f). The total number of stress cycles that will cause a fatigue failure at some specified stress amplitude.

Fatigue limit. For fatigue, the maximum stress amplitude level below which a material can endure an essentially infinite number of stress cycles and not fail.

Fatigue strength. The maximum stress level that a material can sustain, without failing, for some specified number of cycles.

Fermi energy (E_f). For a metal, the energy corresponding to the highest filled electron state at 0 K.

Ferrimagnetism. Permanent and large magnetizations found in some ceramic materials. It results from antiparallel spin coupling and incomplete magnetic moment cancellation.

Ferrite (ceramic). Ceramic oxide materials composed of both divalent and trivalent cations (e.g., Fe^{2+} and Fe^{3+}), some of which are ferrimagnetic.

Ferrite (iron). Body-centered cubic iron; also iron and steel alloys that have the BCC crystal structure.

Ferroelectric. A dielectric material that may exhibit polarization in the absence of an electric field.

Ferromagnetism. Permanent and large magnetizations found in some metals (e.g., Fe, Ni, and Co), which result from the parallel alignment of neighboring magnetic moments.

Ferrous alloy. A metal alloy for which iron is the prime constituent.

Fiber. Any polymer, metal, or ceramic that has been drawn into a long and thin filament.

Fiber-reinforced composite. A composite in which the dispersed phase is in the form of a fiber (i.e., a filament that has a large length-to-diameter ratio).

Fiber reinforcement. Strengthening or reinforcement of a relatively weak material by embedding a strong fiber phase within the weak matrix material.

Fick's first law. The diffusion flux is proportional to the concentration gradient. This relationship is employed for steady-state diffusion situations.

Fick's second law. The time rate of change of concentration is proportional to the second derivative of concentration. This relationship is employed in nonsteady-state diffusion situations.

Filler. An inert foreign substance added to a polymer to improve or modify its properties.

Fine pearlite. Pearlite for which the alternating ferrite and cementite layers are relatively thin.

Firing. A high temperature heat treatment that increases the density and strength of a ceramic piece.

Flame retardant. A polymer additive that increases flammability resistance.

Flexural strength (σ_{fs}). Stress at fracture from a bend (or flexure) test.

Fluorescence. Luminescence that occurs for times much less than a second after an electron excitation event.

Foam. A polymer that has been made porous (or sponge-like) by the incorporation of gas bubbles.

Forging. Mechanical forming of a metal by heating and hammering.

Forward bias. The conducting bias for a *p–n* junction rectifier such that electron flow is to the *n* side of the junction.

Fracture mechanics. A technique of fracture analysis used to determine the stress level at which preexisting cracks of known size will propagate, leading to fracture.

Fracture toughness (K_c). The measure of a material's resistance to fracture when a crack is present.

Free electron. An electron that has been excited into an energy state above the Fermi energy (or into the conduction band for semiconductors and insulators) and may participate in the electrical conduction process.

Free energy. A thermodynamic quantity that is a function of both the internal energy and entropy (or randomness) of a system. At equilibrium, the free energy is at a minimum.

Frenkel defect. In an ionic solid, a cation–vacancy and cation–interstitial pair.

Full annealing. For ferrous alloys, austenitizing, followed by cooling slowly to room temperature.

Functionality. The number of covalent bonds that a monomer can form when reacting with other monomers.

G

Galvanic corrosion. The preferential corrosion of the more chemically active of two metals that are electrically coupled and exposed to an electrolyte.

Galvanic series. A ranking of metals and alloys as to their relative electrochemical reactivity in seawater.

Gas constant (R). Boltzmann's constant per mole of atoms. $R = 8.31$ J/mol-K (1.987 cal/mol-K).

Gibbs phase rule. For a system at equilibrium, an equation (Equation 9.16) that expresses the relationship between the number of phases present and the number of externally controllable variables.

Glass–ceramic. A fine-grained crystalline ceramic material that was formed as a glass and subsequently crystallized.

Glass transition temperature (T_g). The temperature at which, upon cooling, a noncrystalline ceramic or polymer transforms from a supercooled liquid to a rigid glass.

Graft copolymer. A copolymer wherein homopolymer side branches of one monomer type are grafted to homopolymer main chains of a different monomer type.

Grain. An individual crystal in a polycrystalline metal or ceramic.

Grain boundary. The interface separating two adjoining grains having different crystallographic orientations.

Grain growth. The increase in average grain size of a polycrystalline material; for most materials, an elevated-temperature heat treatment is necessary.

Grain size. The average grain diameter as determined from a random cross section.

Gray cast iron. A cast iron alloyed with silicon in which the graphite exists in the form of flakes. A fractured surface appears gray.

Green ceramic body. A ceramic piece, formed as a particulate aggregate, that has been dried but not fired.

Ground state. A normally filled electron energy state from which an electron excitation may occur.

Growth (particle). During a phase transformation and subsequent to nucleation, the increase in size of a particle of a new phase.

H

Hall effect. The phenomenon whereby a force is brought to bear on a moving electron or hole by a magnetic field that is applied perpendicular to the direction of motion. The force direction is perpendicular to both the magnetic field and the particle motion directions.

Hardenability. A measure of the depth to which a specific ferrous alloy may be hardened by the formation of martensite upon quenching from a temperature above the upper critical temperature.

Hard magnetic material. A ferrimagnetic or ferromagnetic material that has large coercive field and remanence values, normally used in permanent magnet applications.

Hardness. The measure of a material's resistance to deformation by surface indentation or by abrasion.

Heat capacity (C_p, C_v). The quantity of heat required to produce a unit temperature rise per mole of material.

Hexagonal close-packed (HCP). A crystal structure found for some metals. The HCP unit cell is of hexagonal geometry and is generated by the stacking of close-packed planes of atoms.

High polymer. A solid polymeric material having a molecular weight greater than about 10,000 g/mol.

High-strength, low-alloy (HSLA) steels. Relatively strong, low-carbon steels, with less than about 10 wt% total of alloying elements.
Hole (electron). For semiconductors and insulators, a vacant electron state in the valence band that behaves as a positive charge carrier in an electric field.
Homopolymer. A polymer having a chain structure in which all repeat units are of the same type.
Hot working. Any metal-forming operation that is performed above a metal's recrystallization temperature.
Hybrid composite. A composite that is fiber reinforced by two or more types of fibers (e.g., glass and carbon).
Hydrogen bond. A strong secondary interatomic bond that exists between a bound hydrogen atom (its unscreened proton) and the electrons of adjacent atoms.
Hydrogen embrittlement. The loss or reduction of ductility of a metal alloy (often steel) as a result of the diffusion of atomic hydrogen into the material.
Hydroplastic forming. The molding or shaping of clay-based ceramics that have been made plastic and pliable by adding water.
Hypereutectoid alloy. For an alloy system displaying a eutectoid, an alloy for which the concentration of solute is greater than the eutectoid composition.
Hypoeutectoid alloy. For an alloy system displaying a eutectoid, an alloy for which the concentration of solute is less than the eutectoid composition.
Hysteresis (magnetic). The irreversible magnetic flux density-versus-magnetic field strength (B-versus-H) behavior found for ferromagnetic and ferrimagnetic materials; a closed B–H loop is formed upon field reversal.

I

Impact energy (notch toughness). A measure of the energy absorbed during the fracture of a specimen of standard dimensions and geometry when subjected to very rapid (impact) loading. Charpy and Izod impact tests are used to measure this parameter, which is important in assessing the ductile-to-brittle transition behavior of a material.
Imperfection. A deviation from perfection; normally applied to crystalline materials wherein there is a deviation from atomic/molecular order and/or continuity.
Index of refraction (*n*). The ratio of the velocity of light in a vacuum to the velocity in some medium.
Inhibitor. A chemical substance that, when added in relatively low concentrations, retards a chemical reaction.
Insulator (electrical). A nonmetallic material that has a filled valence band at 0 K and a relatively wide energy band gap. Consequently, the room-temperature electrical conductivity is very low, less than about 10^{-10} $(\Omega\text{-m})^{-1}$.
Integrated circuit. Millions of electronic circuit elements (transistors, diodes, resistors, capacitors, etc.) incorporated on a very small silicon chip.
Interdiffusion. Diffusion of atoms of one metal into another metal.
Intergranular corrosion. Preferential corrosion along grain boundary regions of polycrystalline materials.
Intergranular fracture. Fracture of polycrystalline materials by crack propagation along grain boundaries.
Intermediate solid solution. A solid solution or phase having a composition range that does not extend to either of the pure components of the system.
Intermetallic compound. A compound of two metals that has a distinct chemical formula. On a phase diagram it appears as an intermediate phase that exists over a very narrow range of compositions.
Interstitial diffusion. A diffusion mechanism whereby atomic motion is from interstitial site to interstitial site.
Interstitial solid solution. A solid solution wherein relatively small solute atoms occupy interstitial positions between the solvent or host atoms.
Intrinsic semiconductor. A semiconductor material for which the electrical behavior is characteristic of the pure material; that is, electrical conductivity depends only on temperature and the band gap energy.
Invariant point. A point on a binary phase diagram at which three phases are in equilibrium.
Ionic bond. A coulombic interatomic bond that exists between two adjacent and oppositely charged ions.
Isomerism. The phenomenon whereby two or more polymer molecules or repeat units have the same composition but different structural arrangements and properties.
Isomorphous. Having the same structure. In the phase diagram sense, isomorphicity means having the same crystal structure or complete solid solubility for all compositions (see Figure 9.3*a*).
Isotactic. A type of polymer chain configuration (stereoisomer) wherein all side groups are positioned on the same side of the chain molecule.
Isothermal. At a constant temperature.
Isothermal transformation (*T–T–T*) diagram. A plot of temperature versus the logarithm of time for a steel alloy of definite composition. Used to determine when transformations begin and end for an isothermal (constant-temperature) heat treatment of a previously austenitized alloy.
Isotopes. Atoms of the same element that have different atomic masses.
Isotropic. Having identical values of a property in all crystallographic directions.
Izod test. One of two tests (see also **Charpy test**) that may be used to measure the impact energy of a standard notched specimen. An impact blow is imparted to the specimen by a weighted pendulum.

J

Jominy end-quench test. A standardized laboratory test that is used to assess the hardenability of ferrous alloys.

Junction transistor. A semiconducting device composed of appropriately biased *n–p–n* or *p–n–p* junctions, used to amplify an electrical signal.

K

Kinetics. The study of reaction rates and the factors that affect them.

L

Laminar composite. A series of two-dimensional sheets, each having a preferred high-strength direction, fastened one on top of the other at different orientations; strength in the plane of the laminate is highly isotropic.

Large-particle composite. A type of particle-reinforced composite wherein particle-matrix interactions cannot be treated on an atomic level; the particles reinforce the matrix phase.

Laser. Acronym for *l*ight *a*mplification by *s*timulated *e*mission of *r*adiation—a source of light that is coherent.

Lattice. The regular geometrical arrangement of points in crystal space.

Lattice parameters. The combination of unit cell edge lengths and interaxial angles that defines the unit cell geometry.

Lattice strains. Slight displacements of atoms relative to their normal lattice positions, normally imposed by crystalline defects such as dislocations, and interstitial and impurity atoms.

Leadframe. Part of an integrated circuit package. A frame to which may be connected an array of electrical wire leads that are attached to an integrated circuit chip.

Lever rule. Mathematical expression, such as Equation 9.1b or Equation 9.2b, whereby the relative phase amounts in a two-phase alloy at equilibrium may be computed.

Light-emitting diode (*LED*). A diode composed of a semiconducting material that is *p*-type on one side and *n*-type on the other side. When a forward biased potential is applied across the junction between the two sides, recombination of electrons and holes occurs, with the emission of light radiation.

Linear coefficient of thermal expansion. See **Thermal expansion coefficient, linear.**

Linear polymer. A polymer produced from bifunctional monomers in which each polymer molecule consists of repeat units joined end to end in a single chain.

Liquid crystal polymer (*LCP*). A group of polymeric materials having extended and rod-shaped molecules, which, structurally, do not fall within traditional liquid, amorphous, crystalline, or semicrystalline classifications. In the molten (or liquid) state they can become aligned in highly ordered (crystal-like) conformations. They are used in digital displays and a variety of applications in electronics and medical equipment industries.

Liquidus line. On a binary phase diagram, the line or boundary separating liquid and liquid + solid phase regions. For an alloy, the liquidus temperature is the temperature at which a solid phase first forms under conditions of equilibrium cooling.

Longitudinal direction. The lengthwise dimension. For a rod or fiber, in the direction of the long axis.

Lower critical temperature. For a steel alloy, the temperature below which, under equilibrium conditions, all austenite has transformed to ferrite and cementite phases.

Luminescence. The emission of visible light as a result of electron decay from an excited state.

M

Macromolecule. A huge molecule made up of thousands of atoms.

Magnetic field strength (*H*). The intensity of an externally applied magnetic field.

Magnetic flux density (*B*). The magnetic field produced in a substance by an external magnetic field.

Magnetic induction (*B*). See **Magnetic flux density.**

Magnetic susceptibility (χ_m). The proportionality constant between the magnetization *M* and the magnetic field strength *H*.

Magnetization (*M*). The total magnetic moment per unit volume of material. Also, a measure of the contribution to the magnetic flux by some material within an *H* field.

Malleable cast iron. White cast iron that has been heat treated to convert the cementite into graphite clusters; a relatively ductile cast iron.

Martensite. A metastable iron phase supersaturated in carbon that is the product of a diffusionless (athermal) transformation from austenite.

Matrix phase. The phase in a composite or two-phase alloy microstructure that is continuous or completely surrounds the other (or dispersed) phase.

Matthiessen's rule. The total electrical resistivity of a metal is equal to the sum of temperature-, impurity-, and cold work-dependent contributions.

Melting point (glass). The temperature at which the viscosity of a glass material is 10 Pa-s (100 P).

Metal. The electropositive elements and alloys based on these elements. The electron band structure of metals is characterized by a partially filled electron band.

Metallic bond. A primary interatomic bond involving the nondirectional sharing of nonlocalized valence electrons ("sea of electrons") that are mutually shared by all the atoms in the metallic solid.

Metal-matrix composite (*MMC*). A composite material that has a metal or metal alloy as the matrix phase. The dispersed phase may be particulates, fibers, or whiskers that normally are stiffer, stronger, and/or harder than the matrix.

Metastable. Nonequilibrium state that may persist for a very long time.
Microconstituent. An element of the microstructure that has an identifiable and characteristic structure. It may consist of more than one phase such as with pearlite.
Microelectromechanical system (MEMS). A large number of miniature mechanical devices that are integrated with electrical elements on a silicon substrate. Mechanical components act as microsensors and microactuators and are in the form of beams, gears, motors, and membranes. In response to microsensor stimuli, the electrical elements render decisions that direct responses to the microactuator devices.
Microscopy. The investigation of microstructural elements using some type of microscope.
Microstructure. The structural features of an alloy (e.g., grain and phase structure) that are subject to observation under a microscope.
Miller indices. A set of three integers (four for hexagonal) that designate crystallographic planes, as determined from reciprocals of fractional axial intercepts.
Mixed dislocation. A dislocation that has both edge and screw components.
Mobility (electron, μ_e, and hole, μ_h). The proportionality constant between the carrier drift velocity and applied electric field; also, a measure of the ease of charge carrier motion.
Modulus of elasticity (E). The ratio of stress to strain when deformation is totally elastic; also a measure of the stiffness of a material.
Molarity (M). Concentration in a liquid solution, in terms of the number of moles of a solute dissolved in 10^6 mm^3 (10^3 cm^3) of solution.
Molding (plastics). Shaping a plastic material by forcing it, under pressure and at an elevated temperature, into a mold cavity.
Mole. The quantity of a substance corresponding to 6.023×10^{23} atoms or molecules.
Molecular chemistry (polymer). With regard only to composition, not the structure of a repeat unit.
Molecular structure (polymer). With regard to atomic arrangements within and interconnections between polymer molecules.
Molecular weight. The sum of the atomic weights of all the atoms in a molecule.
Monomer. A stable molecule from which a polymer is synthesized.
MOSFET. Metal-oxide-silicon field effect transistor, an integrated circuit element.

N

***n*-Type semiconductor.** A semiconductor for which the predominant charge carriers responsible for electrical conduction are electrons. Normally, donor impurity atoms give rise to the excess electrons.
Natural aging. For precipitation hardening, aging at room temperature.
Network polymer. A polymer produced from multifunctional monomers having three or more active covalent bonds, resulting in the formation of three-dimensional molecules.
Nodular iron. See **Ductile iron.**
Noncrystalline. The solid state wherein there is no long-range atomic order. Sometimes the terms *amorphous, glassy,* and *vitreous* are used synonymously.
Nonferrous alloy. A metal alloy for which iron is *not* the prime constituent.
Nonsteady-state diffusion. The diffusion condition for which there is some net accumulation or depletion of diffusing species. The diffusion flux is dependent on time.
Normalizing. For ferrous alloys, austenitizing above the upper critical temperature, then cooling in air. The objective of this heat treatment is to enhance toughness by refining the grain size.
Nucleation. The initial stage in a phase transformation. It is evidenced by the formation of small particles (nuclei) of the new phase, which are capable of growing.

O

Octahedral position. The void space among close-packed, hard sphere atoms or ions for which there are six nearest neighbors. An octahedron (double pyramid) is circumscribed by lines constructed from centers of adjacent spheres.
Ohm's law. The applied voltage is equal to the product of the current and resistance; equivalently, the current density is equal to the product of the conductivity and electric field intensity.
Opaque. Being impervious to the transmission of light as a result of absorption, reflection, and/or scattering of incident light.
Optical fiber. A thin (5–100 μm diameter) ultra high purity silica fiber through which may be transmitted information via photonic (light radiation) signals.
Overaging. During precipitation hardening, aging beyond the point at which strength and hardness are at their maxima.
Oxidation. The removal of one or more electrons from an atom, ion, or molecule.

P

Paramagnetism. A relatively weak form of magnetism that results from the independent alignment of atomic dipoles (magnetic) with an applied magnetic field.
Particle-reinforced composite. A composite for which the dispersed phase is equiaxed.
Passivity. The loss of chemical reactivity, under particular environmental conditions, by some active metals and alloys often due to the formation of a protective film.
Pauli exclusion principle. The postulate that for an individual atom, at most two electrons, which necessarily have opposite spins, can occupy the same state.
Pearlite. A two-phase microstructure found in some steels and cast irons; it results from the

transformation of austenite of eutectoid composition and consists of alternating layers (or lamellae) of α-ferrite and cementite.

Periodic table. The arrangement of the chemical elements with increasing atomic number according to the periodic variation in electron structure. Nonmetallic elements are positioned at the far right-hand side of the table.

Peritectic reaction. A reaction wherein, upon cooling, a solid and a liquid phase transform isothermally and reversibly to a solid phase having a different composition.

Permeability (magnetic, μ). The proportionality constant between B and H fields. The value of the permeability of a vacuum (μ_0) is 1.257×10^{-6} H/m.

Permittivity (ϵ). The proportionality constant between the dielectric displacement D and the electric field $\mathscr{E}$. The value of the permittivity ϵ_0 for a vacuum is 8.85×10^{-12} F/m.

Phase. A homogeneous portion of a system that has uniform physical and chemical characteristics.

Phase diagram. A graphical representation of the relationships between environmental constraints (e.g., temperature and sometimes pressure), composition, and regions of phase stability, ordinarily under conditions of equilibrium.

Phase equilibrium. See **Equilibrium (phase).**

Phase transformation. A change in the number and/or character of the phases that constitute the microstructure of an alloy.

Phonon. A single quantum of vibrational or elastic energy.

Phosphorescence. Luminescence that occurs at times greater than on the order of a second after an electron excitation event.

Photoconductivity. Electrical conductivity that results from photon-induced electron excitations in which light is absorbed.

Photomicrograph. The photograph made with a microscope, which records a microstructural image.

Photon. A quantum unit of electromagnetic energy.

Piezoelectric. A dielectric material in which polarization is induced by the application of external forces.

Pilling–Bedworth ratio (P–B ratio). The ratio of metal oxide volume to metal volume; used to predict whether or not a scale that forms will protect a metal from further oxidation.

Pitting. A form of very localized corrosion wherein small pits or holes form, usually in a vertical direction.

Plain carbon steel. A ferrous alloy in which carbon is the prime alloying element.

Planck's constant (h). A universal constant that has a value of 6.63×10^{-34} J-s. The energy of a photon of electromagnetic radiation is the product of h and the radiation frequency.

Plane strain. The condition, important in fracture mechanical analyses, wherein, for tensile loading, there is zero strain in a direction perpendicular to both the stress axis and the direction of crack propagation; this condition is found in thick plates, and the zero-strain direction is perpendicular to the plate surface.

Plane strain fracture toughness (K_{Ic}). For the condition of plane strain, the measure of a material's resistance to fracture when a crack is present.

Plastic. A solid organic polymer of high molecular weight that has some structural rigidity under load, and is used in general-purpose applications. It may also contain additives such as fillers, plasticizers, flame retardants, and the like.

Plastic deformation. Deformation that is permanent or nonrecoverable after release of the applied load. It is accompanied by permanent atomic displacements.

Plasticizer. A low molecular weight polymer additive that enhances flexibility and workability and reduces stiffness and brittleness resulting in a decrease in the glass transition temperature T_g.

Point defect. A crystalline defect associated with one or, at most, several atomic sites.

Poisson's ratio (ν). For elastic deformation, the negative ratio of lateral and axial strains that result from an applied axial stress.

Polar molecule. A molecule in which there exists a permanent electric dipole moment by virtue of the asymmetrical distribution of positively and negatively charged regions.

Polarization (P). The total electric dipole moment per unit volume of dielectric material. Also, a measure of the contribution to the total dielectric displacement by a dielectric material.

Polarization (corrosion). The displacement of an electrode potential from its equilibrium value as a result of current flow.

Polarization (electronic). For an atom, the displacement of the center of the negatively charged electron cloud relative to the positive nucleus, which is induced by an electric field.

Polarization (ionic). Polarization as a result of the displacement of anions and cations in opposite directions.

Polarization (orientation). Polarization resulting from the alignment (by rotation) of permanent electric dipole moments with an applied electric field.

Polycrystalline. Refers to crystalline materials that are composed of more than one crystal or grain.

Polymer. A compound of high molecular weight (normally organic) the structure of which is composed of chains of small repeat units.

Polymer-matrix composite (*PMC*). A composite material for which the matrix is a polymer resin, and having fibers (normally glass, carbon, or aramid) as the dispersed phase.

Polymorphism. The ability of a solid material to exist in more than one form or crystal structure.

Powder metallurgy (P/M). The fabrication of metal pieces having intricate and precise shapes by the compaction of metal powders, followed by a densification heat treatment.

Precipitation hardening. Hardening and strengthening of a metal alloy by extremely small and uniformly dispersed particles that precipitate from a supersaturated solid solution; sometimes also called *age hardening*.

Precipitation heat treatment. A heat treatment used to precipitate a new phase from a supersaturated solid solution. For precipitation hardening, it is termed *artificial aging*.

Prepreg. Continuous fiber reinforcement preimpregnated with a polymer resin that is then partially cured.

Prestressed concrete. Concrete into which compressive stresses have been introduced using steel wires or rods.

Primary bonds. Interatomic bonds that are relatively strong and for which bonding energies are relatively large. Primary bonding types are ionic, covalent, and metallic.

Primary phase. A phase that exists in addition to the eutectic structure.

Principle of combined action. The supposition, often valid, that new properties, better properties, better property combinations, and/or a higher level of properties can be fashioned by the judicious combination of two or more distinct materials.

Process annealing. Annealing of previously cold-worked products (commonly steel alloys in sheet or wire form) below the lower critical (eutectoid) temperature.

Proeutectoid cementite. Primary cementite that exists in addition to pearlite for hypereutectoid steels.

Proeutectoid ferrite. Primary ferrite that exists in addition to pearlite for hypoeutectoid steels.

Property. A material trait expressed in terms of the measured response to a specific imposed stimulus.

Proportional limit. The point on a stress–strain curve at which the straight line proportionality between stress and strain ceases.

***p*-Type semiconductor.** A semiconductor for which the predominant charge carriers responsible for electrical conduction are holes. Normally, acceptor impurity atoms give rise to the excess holes.

Q

Quantum mechanics. A branch of physics that deals with atomic and subatomic systems; it allows only discrete values of energy that are separated from one another. By contrast, for classical mechanics, continuous energy values are permissible.

Quantum numbers. A set of four numbers, the values of which are used to label possible electron states. Three of the quantum numbers are integers, which also specify the size, shape, and spatial orientation of an electron's probability density; the fourth number designates spin orientation.

R

Random copolymer. A polymer in which two different repeat units are randomly distributed along the molecular chain.

Recovery. The relief of some of the internal strain energy of a previously cold-worked metal, usually by heat treatment.

Recrystallization. The formation of a new set of strain-free grains within a previously cold-worked material; normally an annealing heat treatment is necessary.

Recrystallization temperature. For a particular alloy, the minimum temperature at which complete recrystallization will occur within approximately one hour.

Rectifying junction. A semiconductor *p–n* junction that is conductive for a current flow in one direction and highly resistive for the opposite direction.

Reduction. The addition of one or more electrons to an atom, ion, or molecule.

Reflection. Deflection of a light beam at the interface between two media.

Refraction. Bending of a light beam upon passing from one medium into another; the velocity of light differs in the two media.

Refractory. A metal or ceramic that may be exposed to extremely high temperatures without deteriorating rapidly or without melting.

Reinforced concrete. Concrete that is reinforced (or strengthened in tension) by the incorporation of steel rods, wires, or mesh.

Relative magnetic permeability (μ_r). The ratio of the magnetic permeability of some medium to that of a vacuum.

Relaxation frequency. The reciprocal of the minimum reorientation time for an electric dipole within an alternating electric field.

Relaxation modulus [$E_r(t)$]. For viscoelastic polymers, the time-dependent modulus of elasticity. It is determined from stress relaxation measurements as the ratio of stress (taken at some time after the load application—normally 10 s) to strain.

Remanence (remanent induction, B_r). For a ferromagnetic or ferrimagnetic material, the magnitude of residual flux density that remains when a magnetic field is removed.

Residual stress. A stress that persists in a material that is free of external forces or temperature gradients.

Resilience. The capacity of a material to absorb energy when it is elastically deformed.

Resistivity (ρ). The reciprocal of electrical conductivity, and a measure of a material's resistance to the passage of electric current.

Resolved shear stress. An applied tensile or compressive stress resolved into a shear component along a specific plane and direction within that plane.

Reverse bias. The insulating bias for a *p–n* junction rectifier; electrons flow into the *p* side of the junction.

Rolling. A metal-forming operation that reduces the thickness of sheet stock; also elongated shapes may be fashioned using grooved circular rolls.

Rule of mixtures. The properties of a multiphase alloy or composite material are a weighted average (usually on the basis of volume) of the properties of the individual constituents.

Rupture. Failure that is accompanied by significant plastic deformation; often associated with creep failure.

S

Sacrificial anode. An active metal or alloy that preferentially corrodes and protects another metal or alloy to which it is electrically coupled.

Safe stress (σ_w). A stress used for design purposes; for ductile metals, it is the yield strength divided by a factor of safety.

Sandwich panel. A type of structural composite consisting of two stiff and strong outer faces that are separated by a lightweight core material.

Saturated. A term describing a carbon atom that participates in only single covalent bonds with four other atoms.

Saturation magnetization, flux density (M_s, B_s). The maximum magnetization (or flux density) for a ferromagnetic or ferrimagnetic material.

Scanning electron microscope (SEM). A microscope that produces an image by using an electron beam that scans the surface of a specimen; an image is produced by reflected electron beams. Examination of surface and/or microstructural features at high magnifications is possible.

Scanning probe microscope (SPM). A microscope that does not produce an image using light radiation. Rather, a very small and sharp probe raster scans across the specimen surface; out-of-surface plane deflections in response to electronic or other interactions with the probe are monitored, from which a topographical map of the specimen surface (on a nanometer scale) is produced.

Schottky defect. In an ionic solid, a defect consisting of a cation–vacancy and anion–vacancy pair.

Scission. A polymer degradation process whereby molecular chain bonds are ruptured by chemical reactions or by exposure to radiation or heat.

Screw dislocation. A linear crystalline defect associated with the lattice distortion created when normally parallel planes are joined together to form a helical ramp. The Burgers vector is parallel to the dislocation line.

Secondary bonds. Interatomic and intermolecular bonds that are relatively weak and for which bonding energies are relatively small. Normally atomic or molecular dipoles are involved. Examples of secondary bonding types are van der Waals forces and hydrogen bonding.

Selective leaching. A form of corrosion wherein one element or constituent of an alloy is preferentially dissolved.

Self-diffusion. Atomic migration in pure metals.

Self-interstitial. A host atom or ion that is positioned on an interstitial lattice site.

Semiconductor. A nonmetallic material that has a filled valence band at 0 K and a relatively narrow energy band gap. The room temperature electrical conductivity ranges between about 10^{-6} and 10^4 $(\Omega\text{-m})^{-1}$.

Shear. A force applied so as to cause or tend to cause two adjacent parts of the same body to slide relative to each other, in a direction parallel to their plane of contact.

Shear strain (γ). The tangent of the shear angle that results from an applied shear load.

Shear stress (τ). The instantaneous applied shear load divided by the original cross-sectional area across which it is applied.

Single crystal. A crystalline solid for which the periodic and repeated atomic pattern extends throughout its entirety without interruption.

Sintering. Particle coalescence of a powdered aggregate by diffusion that is accomplished by firing at an elevated temperature.

Slip. Plastic deformation as the result of dislocation motion; also, the shear displacement of two adjacent planes of atoms.

Slip casting. A forming technique used for some ceramic materials. A slip, or suspension of solid particles in water, is poured into a porous mold. A solid layer forms on the inside wall as water is absorbed by the mold, leaving a shell (or ultimately a solid piece) having the shape of the mold.

Slip system. The combination of a crystallographic plane and, within that plane, a crystallographic direction along which slip (i.e., dislocation motion) occurs.

Softening point (glass). The maximum temperature at which a glass piece may be handled without permanent deformation; this corresponds to a viscosity of approximately 4×10^6 Pa-s (4×10^7 P).

Soft magnetic material. A ferromagnetic or ferrimagnetic material having a small B versus H hysteresis loop, which may be magnetized and demagnetized with relative ease.

Soldering. A technique for joining metals using a filler metal alloy that has a melting temperature less than about 425°C.

Solid solution. A homogeneous crystalline phase that contains two or more chemical species. Both substitutional and interstitial solid solutions are possible.

Solid-solution strengthening. Hardening and strengthening of metals that result from alloying in which a solid solution is formed. The presence of impurity atoms restricts dislocation mobility.

Solidus line. On a phase diagram, the locus of points at which solidification is complete upon equilibrium cooling, or at which melting begins upon equilibrium heating.

Solubility limit. The maximum concentration of solute that may be added without forming a new phase.

Solute. One component or element of a solution present in a minor concentration. It is dissolved in the solvent.

Solution heat treatment. The process used to form a solid solution by dissolving precipitate particles. Often, the solid solution is supersaturated and metastable at ambient conditions as a result of rapid cooling from an elevated temperature.

Solvent. The component of a solution present in the greatest amount. It is the component that dissolves a solute.

Solvus line. The locus of points on a phase diagram representing the limit of solid solubility as a function of temperature.

Specific heat (c_p, c_v). The heat capacity per unit mass of material.

Specific modulus (specific stiffness). The ratio of elastic modulus to specific gravity for a material.

Specific strength. The ratio of tensile strength to specific gravity for a material.

Spheroidite. Microstructure found in steel alloys consisting of sphere-like cementite particles within an α-ferrite matrix. It is produced by an appropriate elevated-temperature heat treatment of pearlite, bainite, or martensite, and is relatively soft.

Spheroidizing. For steels, a heat treatment normally carried out at a temperature just below the eutectoid in which the spheroidite microstructure is produced.

Spherulite. An aggregate of ribbon-like polymer crystallites (lamellae) radiating from a common central nucleation site; the crystallites are separated by amorphous regions.

Spinning. The process by which fibers are formed. A multitude of fibers are spun as molten or dissolved material is forced through many small orifices.

Stabilizer. A polymer additive that counteracts deteriorative processes.

Stainless steel. A steel alloy that is highly resistant to corrosion in a variety of environments. The predominant alloying element is chromium, which must be present in a concentration of at least 11 wt%; other alloy additions, to include nickel and molybdenum, are also possible.

Standard half-cell. An electrochemical cell consisting of a pure metal immersed in a 1*M* aqueous solution of its ions, which is electrically coupled to the standard hydrogen electrode.

Steady-state diffusion. The diffusion condition for which there is no net accumulation or depletion of diffusing species. The diffusion flux is independent of time.

Stereoisomerism. Polymer isomerism in which side groups within repeat units are bonded along the molecular chain in the same order but in different spatial arrangements.

Stoichiometry. For ionic compounds, the state of having exactly the ratio of cations to anions specified by the chemical formula.

Strain, engineering (ϵ). The change in gauge length of a specimen (in the direction of an applied stress) divided by its original gauge length.

Strain hardening. The increase in hardness and strength of a ductile metal as it is plastically deformed below its recrystallization temperature.

Strain point (glass). The maximum temperature at which glass fractures without plastic deformation; this corresponds to a viscosity of about 3×10^{13} Pa-s (3×10^{14} P).

Strain, true. See **True strain.**

Stress concentration. The concentration or amplification of an applied stress at the tip of a notch or small crack.

Stress corrosion (cracking). A form of failure that results from the combined action of a tensile stress and a corrosion environment; it occurs at lower stress levels than are required when the corrosion environment is absent.

Stress, engineering (σ). The instantaneous load applied to a specimen divided by its cross-sectional area before any deformation.

Stress raiser. A small flaw (internal or surface) or a structural discontinuity at which an applied tensile stress will be amplified and from which cracks may propagate.

Stress relief. A heat treatment for the removal of residual stresses.

Stress, true. See **True stress.**

Structural clay products. Ceramic products made principally of clay and used in applications where structural integrity is important (e.g., bricks, tiles, pipes).

Structural composite. A composite, the properties of which depend on the geometrical design of the structural elements. Laminar composites and sandwich panels are two subclasses.

Structure. The arrangement of the internal components of matter: electron structure (on a subatomic level), crystal structure (on an atomic level), and microstructure (on a microscopic level).

Substitutional solid solution. A solid solution wherein the solute atoms replace or substitute for the host atoms.

Superconductivity. A phenomenon observed in some materials: the disappearance of the electrical resistivity at temperatures approaching 0 K.

Supercooling. Cooling to below a phase transition temperature without the occurrence of the transformation.

Superheating. Heating to above a phase transition temperature without the occurrence of the transformation.

Syndiotactic. A type of polymer chain configuration (stereoisomer) in which side groups regularly alternate positions on opposite sides of the chain.

System. Two meanings are possible: (1) a specific body of material that is being considered, and (2) a series of possible alloys consisting of the same components.

T

Tape automated bonding (TAB). One type of integrated circuit leadframe design in which the substrate is a thin and flexible polymer film. Electrical contact between the IC chip and leadframe is via very thin and narrow copper fingers.

Temper designation. A letter–digit code used to designate the mechanical and/or thermal treatment to which a metal alloy has been subjected.

Tempered martensite. The microstructural product resulting from a tempering heat treatment of a martensitic steel. The microstructure consists of extremely small and uniformly dispersed cementite particles embedded within a continuous α-ferrite matrix. Toughness and ductility are enhanced significantly by tempering.

Tempering (glass). See **Thermal tempering.**

Tensile strength (*TS*). The maximum engineering stress, in tension, that may be sustained without fracture. Often termed *ultimate* (*tensile*) *strength*.

Terminal solid solution. A solid solution that exists over a composition range extending to either composition extremity of a binary phase diagram.

Tetrahedral position. The void space among close-packed, hard sphere atoms or ions for which there are four nearest neighbors.

Thermal conductivity (k). For steady-state heat flow, the proportionality constant between the heat flux and the temperature gradient. Also, a parameter characterizing the ability of a material to conduct heat.

Thermal expansion coefficient, linear (α_l). The fractional change in length divided by the change in temperature.

Thermal fatigue. A type of fatigue failure wherein the cyclic stresses are introduced by fluctuating thermal stresses.

Thermal shock. The fracture of a brittle material as a result of stresses that are introduced by a rapid temperature change.

Thermal stress. A residual stress introduced within a body resulting from a change in temperature.

Thermal tempering. Increasing the strength of a glass piece by the introduction of residual compressive stresses within the outer surface using an appropriate heat treatment.

Thermally activated transformation. A reaction that depends on atomic thermal fluctuations; the atoms having energies greater than an activation energy will spontaneously react or transform.

Thermoplastic (polymer). A semicrystalline polymeric material that softens when heated and hardens upon cooling. While in the softened state, articles may be formed by molding or extrusion.

Thermoplastic elastomer (*TPE*). A copolymeric material that exhibits elastomeric behavior yet is thermoplastic in nature. At the ambient temperature, domains of one repeat unit type form at molecular chain ends that crystallize to act as physical crosslinks.

Thermosetting (polymer). A polymeric material that, once having cured (or hardened) by a chemical reaction, will not soften or melt when subsequently heated.

Tie line. A horizontal line constructed across a two-phase region of a binary phase diagram; its intersections with the phase boundaries on either end represent the equilibrium compositions of the respective phases at the temperature in question.

Time–temperature–transformation (*T–T–T*) diagram. See **Isothermal transformation diagram.**

Toughness. A measure of the amount of energy absorbed by a material as it fractures. Toughness is indicated by the total area under the material's tensile stress–strain curve.

Trans. For polymers, a prefix denoting a type of molecular structure. To some unsaturated carbon chain atoms within a repeat unit, a single side atom or group may be situated on one side of the double bond, or directly opposite at a 180° rotation position. In a trans structure, two such side groups within the same repeat unit reside on opposite sides (e.g., *trans*-isoprene).

Transformation rate. The reciprocal of the time necessary for a reaction to proceed halfway to its completion.

Transgranular fracture. Fracture of polycrystalline materials by crack propagation through the grains.

Translucent. Having the property of transmitting light only diffusely; objects viewed through a translucent medium are not clearly distinguishable.

Transmission electron microscope (TEM). A microscope that produces an image by using electron beams that are transmitted (pass through) the specimen. Examination of internal features at high magnifications is possible.

Transparent. Having the property of transmitting light with relatively little absorption, reflection, and scattering, such that objects viewed through a transparent medium can be distinguished readily.

Transverse direction. A direction that crosses (usually perpendicularly) the longitudinal or lengthwise direction.

Trifunctional. Designating monomers that may react to form three covalent bonds with other monomers.

True strain (ϵ_T). The natural logarithm of the ratio of instantaneous gauge length to original gauge length of a specimen being deformed by a uniaxial force.

True stress (σ_T). The instantaneous applied load divided by the instantaneous cross-sectional area of a specimen.

U

Ultimate (tensile) strength. See **Tensile strength.**

Ultrahigh molecular weight polyethylene (*UHMWPE*). A polyethylene polymer that has an extremely high molecular weight (approximately 4×10^6 g/mol). Distinctive characteristics of this material include high impact and abrasion resistance, and a low coefficient of friction.

Unit cell. The basic structural unit of a crystal structure. It is generally defined in terms of atom (or ion) positions within a parallelepiped volume.

Unsaturated. A term describing carbon atoms that participate in double or triple covalent bonds and, therefore, do not bond to a maximum of four other atoms.

Upper critical temperature. For a steel alloy, the minimum temperature above which, under equilibrium conditions, only austenite is present.

V

Vacancy. A normally occupied lattice site from which an atom or ion is missing.

Vacancy diffusion. The diffusion mechanism wherein net atomic migration is from lattice site to an adjacent vacancy.

Valence band. For solid materials, the electron energy band that contains the valence electrons.

Valence electrons. The electrons in the outermost occupied electron shell, which participate in interatomic bonding.

van der Waals bond. A secondary interatomic bond between adjacent molecular dipoles, which may be permanent or induced.

Viscoelasticity. A type of deformation exhibiting the mechanical characteristics of viscous flow and elastic deformation.

Viscosity (η). The ratio of the magnitude of an applied shear stress to the velocity gradient that it produces; that is, a measure of a noncrystalline material's resistance to permanent deformation.

Vitrification. During firing of a ceramic body, the formation of a liquid phase that upon cooling becomes a glass-bonding matrix.

Vulcanization. Nonreversible chemical reaction involving sulfur or other suitable agent wherein crosslinks are formed between molecular chains in rubber materials. The rubber's modulus of elasticity and strength are enhanced.

W

Wave-mechanical model. Atomic model in which electrons are treated as being wave-like.

Weight percent (wt%). Concentration specification on the basis of weight (or mass) of a particular element relative to the total alloy weight (or mass).

Weld decay. Intergranular corrosion that occurs in some welded stainless steels at regions adjacent to the weld.

Welding. A technique for joining metals in which actual melting of the pieces to be joined occurs in the vicinity of the bond. A filler metal may be used to facilitate the process.

Whisker. A very thin, single crystal of high perfection that has an extremely large length-to-diameter ratio. Whiskers are used as the reinforcing phase in some composites.

White cast iron. A low-silicon and very brittle cast iron, in which the carbon is in combined form as cementite; a fractured surface appears white.

Whiteware. A clay-based ceramic product that becomes white after high-temperature firing; whitewares include porcelain, china, and plumbing sanitary ware.

Working point (glass). The temperature at which a glass is easily deformed, which corresponds to a viscosity of 10^3 Pa-s (10^4 P).

Wrought alloy. A metal alloy that is relatively ductile and amenable to hot working or cold working during fabrication.

Y

Yielding. The onset of plastic deformation.

Yield strength (σ_y). The stress required to produce a very slight yet specified amount of plastic strain; a strain offset of 0.002 is commonly used.

Young's modulus. See **Modulus of elasticity.**

Answers to Selected Problems

Chapter 2

2.3 **(a)** 1.66×10^{-24} g/amu;
(b) 2.73×10^{26} atoms/lb-mol

2.14

$$r_0 = \left(\frac{A}{nB}\right)^{1/(1-n)}$$

$$E_0 = -\frac{A}{\left(\frac{A}{nB}\right)^{1/(1-n)}} + \frac{B}{\left(\frac{A}{nB}\right)^{n/(1-n)}}$$

2.15 **(c)** $r_0 = 0.236$ nm, $E_0 = -5.32$ eV

2.19 73.4% for MgO; 14.8% for CdS

Chapter 3

3.4 000, 100, 110, 010, 001, 101, 111, 011, $\frac{1}{2}\frac{1}{2}0$, $\frac{1}{2}\frac{1}{2}1$, $1\frac{1}{2}\frac{1}{2}$, $0\frac{1}{2}\frac{1}{2}$, $\frac{1}{2}0\frac{1}{2}$, and $\frac{1}{2}1\frac{1}{2}$

3.11 Direction 1: $[2\bar{1}\bar{2}]$

3.13 Direction A: $[\bar{1}10]$;
Direction C: $[0\bar{1}\bar{2}]$

3.14 Direction B: $[\bar{4}0\bar{3}]$;
Direction D: $[\bar{1}1\bar{1}]$

3.15 **(b)** $[\bar{1}00]$, $[010]$, and $[0\bar{1}0]$

3.17 Direction A: $[\bar{1}\bar{1}23]$

3.22 Plane A: $(11\bar{1})$ or $(\bar{1}\bar{1}1)$

3.23 Plane B: (122)

3.24 Plane B: $(02\bar{1})$

3.25 **(c)** $[\bar{1}10]$ or $[1\bar{1}0]$

3.26 **(a)** (100) and $(0\bar{1}0)$

3.29 **(a)** $(0\bar{1}10)$

Chapter 4

4.1 $V_C = 1.213 \times 10^{-28}$ m^3

4.7 $R = 0.138$ nm

4.10 **(a)** $V_C = 1.06 \times 10^{-28}$ m^3;
(b) $a = 0.296$ nm, $c = 0.468$ nm

4.13 Metal B: simple cubic

4.15 **(a)** $n = 4$ atoms/unit cell;
(b) $\rho = 7.31$ g/cm^3

4.18 $V_C = 6.64 \times 10^{-2}$ nm^3

4.21 **(a)** $\mathrm{LD}_{100} = \dfrac{1}{2R\sqrt{2}}$

4.22 **(b)** $\mathrm{LD}_{111}(\mathrm{Fe}) = 4.03 \times 10^9$ m^{-1}

4.23 **(a)** $\mathrm{PD}_{111} = \dfrac{1}{2R^2\sqrt{3}}$

4.24 **(b)** $\mathrm{PD}_{110}(\mathrm{Mo}) = 1.014 \times 10^{19}$ m^{-2}

4.30 **(a)** Sodium chloride; **(d)** cesium chloride

4.32 APF = 0.79

4.33 **(a)** FCC; **(b)** tetrahedral; **(c)** one-half

4.35 **(a)** tetrahedral; **(b)** one-half

4.39 **(a)** $a = 0.437$ nm; **(b)** $a = 0.434$ nm

4.41 **(a)** ρ(calculated) = 4.11 g/cm^3;
(b) ρ(measured) = 4.10 g/cm^3

4.43 **(a)** $\rho = 4.20$ g/cm^3

4.45 Sodium chloride and zinc blende

4.47 APF = 0.84

4.49 APF = 0.68

4.54 **(a)** $\rho_a = 1.300$ g/cm^3, $\rho_c = 1.450$ g/cm^3;
(b) % crystallinity = 57.4%

4.57 $2\theta = 45.88°$

4.58 $d_{111} = 0.1655$ nm

4.60 **(a)** $d_{211} = 0.1348$ nm;
(b) $R = 0.1429$ nm

4.64 $d_{200} = 0.2455$ nm, $d_{311} = 0.1486$ nm, $a = 0.493$ nm

Chapter 5

5.1 $N_v/N = 4.56 \times 10^{-4}$

5.3 $Q_v = 1.10$ eV/atom

5.5 For FCC, $r = 0.41R$

5.7 $C'_{\mathrm{Ag}} = 87.9$ at%, $C'_{\mathrm{Cu}} = 12.1$ at%

5.8 $C_{\mathrm{Cu}} = 1.68$ wt%, $C_{\mathrm{Pt}} = 98.32$ wt%

5.10 $C'_{\mathrm{Cu}} = 41.9$ at%, $C'_{\mathrm{Zn}} = 58.1$ at%

5.14 $N_{\mathrm{Pb}} = 3.30 \times 10^{28}$ atoms/m^3

5.17 $a = 0.405$ nm

5.20 $N_{Mo} = 1.73 \times 10^{22}$ atoms/cm^3
5.24 $C_{Ge} = 11.7$ wt%
5.32 **(a)** Li^+ vacancy; one Li^+ vacancy for every Ca^{2+} added
5.39 **(a)** $d \cong 0.07$ mm
5.41 **(b)** $N_M = 320{,}000$ grains/in.^{2}
5.D1 $C_{Li} = 2.38$ wt%

Chapter 6

6.6 $M = 4.1 \times 10^{-3}$ kg/h
6.8 $D = 2.3 \times 10^{-11}$ m^2/s
6.11 $t = 31.3$ h
6.15 $t = 135$ h
6.18 $T = 901$ K (628°C)
6.21 **(a)** $Q_d = 315.7$ kJ/mol, $D_0 = 3.5 \times 10^{-4}$ m^2/s; **(b)** $D = 1.1 \times 10^{-14}$ m^2/s
6.24 $T = 900$ K (627°C)
6.29 $x = 15.1$ mm
6.D1 Not possible

Chapter 7

7.1 **(a)** $m_s = 2846$ g; **(b)** $C_L = 64$ wt% sugar; **(c)** $m_s = 1068$ g
7.5 **(b)** The pressure must be lowered to approximately 0.0014 atm.
7.8 **(a)** $\alpha + \beta$; $C_\alpha = 5$ wt% Sn-95 wt% Pb, $C_\beta \cong 98$ wt% Sn-2 wt% Pb; **(c)** $\beta + L$; $C_\beta = 92$ wt% Ag-8 wt% Cu, $C_L = 77$ wt% Ag-23 wt% Cu; **(e)** α; $C_\alpha = 8.2$ wt% Sn-91.8 wt% Pb **(g)** $L + Mg_2Pb$; $C_L = 94$ wt% Pb-6 wt% Mg, $C_{Mg_2Pb} = 81$ wt% Pb-19 wt% Mg
7.9 Is possible
7.12 **(a)** $T = 1320$°C; **(b)** $C_\alpha = 62$ wt% Ni-38 wt% Cu; **(c)** $T = 1270$°C; **(d)** $C_L = 37$ wt% Ni-63 wt% Cu
7.14 **(a)** $W_\alpha = 0.89$, $W_\beta = 0.11$; **(c)** $W_\beta = 0.53$, $W_L = 0.47$; **(e)** $W_\alpha = 1.0$; **(g)** $W_L = 0.92$, $W_{Mg_2Pb} = 0.08$
7.15 **(a)** $T = 280$°C;
7.18 **(a)** $T \cong 540$°C; **(b)** $C_\alpha = 26$ wt% Pb; $C_L = 54$ wt% Pb
7.19 $C_\alpha = 88.3$ wt% A-11.7 wt% B; $C_\beta = 5.0$ wt% A-95.0 wt% B
7.21 Possible at $T \cong 800$°C
7.24 **(a)** $V_\alpha = 0.84$, $V_\beta = 0.16$
7.30 Not possible because different C_0 required for each situation
7.33 $C_0 = 25.2$ wt% Ag-74.8 wt% Cu
7.35 Schematic sketches of the microstructures called for are shown below.

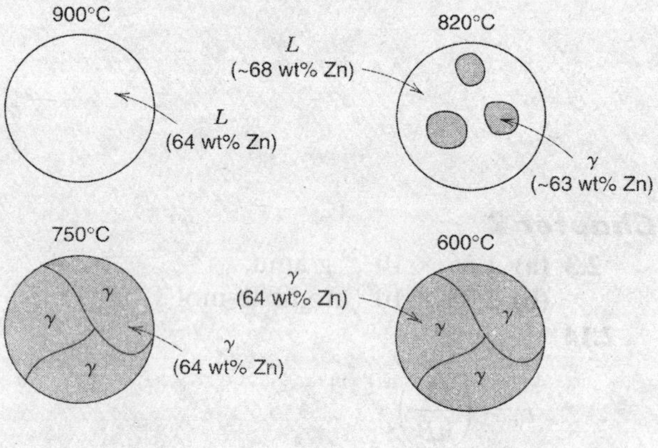

7.42 Eutectics: (1) 10 wt% Au, 217°C, $L \rightarrow \alpha + \beta$; (2) 80 wt% Au, 280°C, $L \rightarrow \delta + \zeta$;
Congruent melting point: 62.5 wt% Au, 418°C, $L \rightarrow \delta$
Peritectics: (1) 30 wt% Au, 252°C, $L + \gamma \rightarrow \beta$; (2) 45 wt% Au, 309°C, $L + \delta \rightarrow \gamma$; (3) 92 wt% Au, 490°C, $L + \eta \rightarrow \zeta$.
No eutectoids are present.
7.45 For point A, $F = 2$
7.48 $C_0' = 0.69$ wt% C
7.51 **(a)** α-ferrite; **(b)** 5.64 kg of ferrite, 0.36 kg of Fe_3C; **(c)** 2.52 kg of proeutectoid ferrite, 3.48 kg of pearlite
7.53 $C_0' = 0.63$ wt% C
7.55 $C_1' = 1.41$ wt% C
7.58 Not possible
7.61 Two answers are possible: $C_0 = 0.84$ wt% C and 0.75 wt% C
7.64 HB (alloy) = 141
7.66 **(a)** T(eutectoid) = 700°C; **(b)** ferrite; **(c)** $W_{\alpha'} = 0.20$, $W_p = 0.80$

Chapter 8

8.3 $r^* = 1.10$ nm
8.6 $t = 500$ s
8.8 $r = 8.76 \times 10^{-3}$ min^{-1}
8.10 $y = 0.65$
8.11 **(c)** $t \cong 250$ days

8.15 (b) 205 HB (93 HRB)
8.18 (a) 100% bainite;
(d) 100% spheroidite;
(e) 100% tempered martensite;
(g) 100% fine pearlite
8.20 (a) martensite; **(c)** bainite;
(e) cementite, medium pearlite, bainite, and martensite;
(g) proeutectoid cementite, pearlite, and martensite
8.23 (a) coarse pearlite
8.27 (a) proeutectoid ferrite and pearlite;
(c) martensite and bainite
8.36 (d) 87 HRB; **(g)** 27 HRC
8.38 (b) $TS = 930$ MPa
8.39 (b) Rapidly cool to about 630°C, hold for about 25 s, then cool to room temperature.
8.D1 Yes; coarse pearlite
8.D5 Temperature at between 320 and 400°C for 1 h

Chapter 9

9.4 $V_{Gr} = 8.1$ vol%
9.15 (a) At least 915°C
9.16 (b) 800°C
9.21 $l_0 = 475$ mm
9.24 (a) $F = 44{,}850$ N;
(b) $l = 76.25$ mm
9.26 $\Delta l = 0.43$ mm
9.29

$$\left(\frac{dF}{dr}\right)_{r_0} = -\frac{2A}{\left(\dfrac{A}{nB}\right)^{3/(1-n)}} + \frac{(n)(n+1)B}{\left(\dfrac{A}{nB}\right)^{(n+2)/(1-n)}}$$

9.31 (a) $\Delta l = 0.325$ mm;
(b) $\Delta d = -5.9 \times 10^{-3}$ mm, decrease
9.32 $F = 7{,}800$ N
9.33 $\nu = 0.367$
9.35 $E = 100$ GPa
9.38 (a) $\Delta l = 0.15$ mm;
(b) $\Delta d = -5.25 \times 10^{-3}$ mm
9.40 Steel and brass
9.43 (a) Both elastic and plastic;
(b) $\Delta l = 8.5$ mm
9.45 (b) $E = 200$ GPa;
(c) $\sigma_y = 750$ MPa;
(d) $TS = 1250$ MPa;
(e) %EL = 11.2%;
(f) $U_r = 1.40 \times 10^6$ J/m^3
9.48 Figure 6.12: $U_r = 3.32 \times 10^5$ J/m^3
9.50 $\sigma_y = 925$ MPa
9.54 $\epsilon_T = 0.311$
9.56 $\sigma_T = 460$ MPa
9.58 Toughness = 7.33×10^8 J/m^3
9.60 $n = 0.246$
9.62 (a) ϵ (elastic) $\cong 0.009$, ϵ (plastic) $\cong 0.011$;
(b) $l_i = 616.7$ mm
9.64 (a) 125 HB (70 HRB)
9.69 Figure 6.12: $\sigma_w = 125$ MPa
9.D7 (a) $\Delta x = 3.66$ mm;
(b) $\sigma = 5.50$ MPa

Chapter 10

10.9 Cu: $|\mathbf{b}| = 0.2556$ nm
10.11 $\cos\lambda \cos\phi = 0.490$
10.13 (b) $\tau_{crss} = 0.90$ MPa
10.14 $\tau_{crss} = 5.68$ MPa
10.15 For (111) – $[1\bar{1}0]$: $\sigma_y = 1.22$ MPa
10.24 $d = 4.34 \times 10^{-3}$ mm
10.25 $d = 6.9 \times 10^{-3}$ mm
10.28 $r_d = 8.80$ mm
10.30 $r_0 = 7.2$ mm
10.32 $\tau_{crss} = 6.28$ MPa
10.37 (a) $t \cong 3000$ min
10.38 (b) $d = 0.109$ mm
10.D1 Possible
10.D6 Cold work to between 26 and 27.5%CW [to $d_0' \cong 9.4$ mm], anneal, then cold work to give a final diameter of 7.6 mm.
10.D9 Heat for about 0.4 h at 204°C, or between 10 and 20 h at 149°C

Chapter 11

11.1 $\sigma_m = 2800$ MPa
11.3 $\sigma_c = 33.6$ MPa
11.6 Fracture will occur
11.8 $a_c = 18.2$ mm
11.10 Is subject to detection since $a \geq 3.0$ mm
11.12 (b) −100°C;
(c) −110°C
11.14 (a) $\sigma_{max} = 280$ MPa, $\sigma_{min} = -140$ MPa;
(b) $R = -0.50$;
(c) $\sigma_r = 420$ MPa
11.16 $N_f \cong 1 \times 10^7$ cycles
11.18 (b) $S = 100$ MPa;
(c) $N_f \cong 6 \times 10^5$ cycles
11.19 (a) $\tau = 74$ MPa; **(c)** $\tau = 103$ MPa
11.21 (a) $t = 30$ min; **(c)** $t = 27.8$ h

11.27 $\Delta\epsilon/\Delta t = 3.25 \times 10^{-2}\ \text{min}^{-1}$
11.28 $\Delta l = 4.9$ mm
11.30 $t_r = 10{,}000$ h
11.32 427°C: $n = 5.3$
11.33 **(a)** $Q_c = 186{,}200$ J/mol
11.35 $\dot{\epsilon}_s = 4.31 \times 10^{-2}\ (\text{h})^{-1}$
11.D4 $T = 1197$ K (924°C)
11.D6 For 1 year: $\sigma = 110$ MPa

Chapter 12

12.4 **(a)** $T = 2240$°C
12.6 **(a)** $W_L = 0.73$
12.7 **(b)** $T \cong 2800$°C; pure MgO
12.10 **(a)** 8.1% of Mg^{2+} vacancies
12.11 **(a)** $C = 45.9$ wt% Al_2O_3-54.1 wt% SiO_2
12.12 $\rho_t = 4.1$ nm
12.16 $R = 9.1$ mm
12.17 $F_f = 17{,}200$ N
12.20 **(a)** $E_0 = 265$ GPa;
(b) $E = 195$ GPa
12.22 **(b)** $P = 0.144$
12.28 **(b)** $Q_{vis} = 208$ kJ/mol

Chapter 13

13.3 $DP = 4800$
13.5 **(a)** $\overline{M}_n = 49{,}800$ g/mol; **(c)** $DP = 498$
13.8 **(a)** $C_{Cl} = 29.0$ wt%
13.9 $L = 2682$ nm; $r = 22.5$ nm
13.16 9333 of both acrylonitrile and butadiene repeat units
13.18 Vinyl chloride
13.21 f(styrene) = 0.32, f(butadiene) = 0.68

Chapter 14

14.3 $E_r(10) = 3.66$ MPa
14.14 $TS = 112.5$ MPa
14.22 Fraction sites vulcanized = 0.174
14.24 Fraction of repeat unit sites crosslinked = 0.356
14.37 **(a)** m(ethylene glycol) = 7.473 kg;
(b) m[poly(ethylene terephthalate)] = 25.304 kg

Chapter 15

15.2 $k_{max} = 31.0$ W/m-K; $k_{min} = 28.7$ W/m-K
15.6 $\tau_c = 43.1$ MPa
15.9 Not possible
15.10 $E_f = 104$ GPa;
$E_m = 2.6$ GPa
15.13 **(a)** $F_f/F_m = 44.7$;
(b) $F_f = 52{,}232$ N, $F_m = 1168$ N;
(c) $\sigma_f = 242$ MPa, $\sigma_m = 4.4$ MPa;
(d) $\epsilon = 1.84 \times 10^{-3}$
15.15 $\sigma^*_{cl} = 905$ MPa
15.17 $\sigma^*_{cd} = 822$ MPa
15.26 **(b)** $E_{cl} = 59.7$ GPa
15.D2 Carbon (PAN standard-modulus)
15.D3 Is possible

Chapter 16

16.4 **(a)** $\Delta V = 0.011$ V;
(b) $Sn^{2+} + Pb \rightarrow Sn + Pb^{2+}$
16.6 $[Cu^{2+}] = 0.784\ M$
16.11 $t = 5.27$ yr
16.14 CPR = 36.5 mpy
16.17 **(a)** $r = 4.56 \times 10^{-12}$ mol/cm²-s;
(b) $V_C = -0.0167$ V
16.28 Mg: P-B ratio = 0.81; nonprotective
16.30 **(a)** Parabolic kinetics;
(b) $W = 3.70$ mg/cm²

Chapter 17

17.2 $d = 1.3$ mm
17.5 **(a)** $R = 6.7 \times 10^{-3}\ \Omega$; **(b)** $I = 6.0$ A;
(c) $J = 3.06 \times 10^5$ A/m²;
(d) $\mathscr{E} = 8.0 \times 10^{-3}$ V/m
17.11 **(a)** $n = 1.98 \times 10^{29}\ \text{m}^{-3}$;
(b) 3.28 free electrons/atom
17.14 **(a)** $\rho_0 = 1.58 \times 10^{-8}\ \Omega$-m,
$a = 6.5 \times 10^{-11}$ (Ω-m)/°C;
(b) $A = 1.18 \times 10^{-6}\ \Omega$-m;
(c) $\rho = 5.24 \times 10^{-8}\ \Omega$-m
17.16 $\sigma = 5.56 \times 10^6\ (\Omega\text{-m})^{-1}$
17.18 **(a)** for Si, 6×10^{-13}; for Ge, 1.1×10^{-9}
17.25 $\sigma = 0.028\ (\Omega\text{-m})^{-1}$
17.29 **(a)** $p = 6.42 \times 10^{21}\ \text{m}^{-3}$;
(b) n-type extrinsic
17.31 $\mu_e = 0.50$ m²/V-s; $\mu_h = 0.14$ m²/V-s
17.33 $\sigma = 94.4\ (\Omega\text{-m})^{-1}$
17.37 $\sigma = 1040\ (\Omega\text{-m})^{-1}$
17.39 $\sigma = 128\ (\Omega\text{-m})^{-1}$
17.42 $B_z = 0.74$ tesla
17.49 $l = 3.36$ mm (0.135 in.)
17.53 $p_i = 1.92 \times 10^{-30}$ C-m
17.55 **(a)** $V = 40$ V; **(b)** $V = 139$ V;
(e) $P = 2.21 \times 10^{-7}$ C/m²
17.58 Fraction of ϵ_r due to $P_i = 0.67$
17.D2 $\sigma = 2.60 \times 10^7\ (\Omega\text{-m})^{-1}$
17.D3 Not possible

Chapter 18

18.1 **(a)** $H = 24{,}000$ A-turns/m;
(b) $B_0 = 3.017 \times 10^{-2}$ tesla;
(c) $B \cong 3.018 \times 10^{-2}$ tesla;
(d) $M = 7.51$ A/m
18.5 **(a)** $\mu = 1.26 \times 10^{-6}$ H/m;
(b) $\chi_m = 2.39 \times 10^{-3}$
18.7 **(a)** $M_s = 1.73 \times 10^6$ A/m
18.13 1.07 Bohr magnetons/Cu^{2+} ion
18.19 **(b)** $\mu_i \cong 2.5 \times 10^{-4}$ H/m, $\mu_{ri} = 200$;
(c) $\mu(\text{max}) \cong 3.0 \times 10^{-2}$ H/m
18.21 **(b)** (i) $\mu = 3.2 \times 10^{-2}$ H/m,
(iii) $\chi_m = 25{,}456$
18.25 $M_s = 1.58 \times 10^6$ A/m
18.28 **(a)** 2.5 K: 5.62×10^4 A/m; **(b)** 6.29 K

Chapter 19

19.2 $T_f = 65°\text{C}$ (149°F)
19.4 **(a)** $c_v = 47.8$ J/kg-K; **(b)** $c_v = 392$ J/kg-K
19.8 $\Delta l = -12.5$ mm
19.14 $T_f = 222.4°\text{C}$
19.15 **(b)** $dQ/dt = 2.88 \times 10^9$ J/h
(2.73×10^6 Btu/h)
19.22 k(upper) = 29.3 W/m-K
19.26 **(a)** $\sigma = -136$ MPa; compression
19.27 $T_f = 41.3°\text{C}$
19.28 $\Delta d = 0.0375$ mm
19.D1 $T_f = 41.8°\text{C}$
19.D4 Soda-lime glass: $\Delta T_f = 111°\text{C}$

Chapter 20

20.7 $v = 1.28 \times 10^8$ m/s
20.8 Fused silica: 0.53; polystyrene: 0.98
20.9 Fused silica: $\epsilon_r = 2.13$; polyethylene:
$\epsilon_r = 2.28$
20.16 $I'_T/I'_0 = 0.884$
20.18 $l = 29.2$ mm
20.27 $\Delta E = 1.78$ eV

Chapter 21

21.D3 **(a)** Stiffness: $P = \dfrac{\sqrt{E}}{\rho}$; strength: $P = \dfrac{\sigma_y^{2/3}}{\rho}$
21.D7 **(a)** $F = 36.8$ N
(b) F = 47.7 N

Chapter 23

23.D5 Maximum diameter = 50 mm
23.D6 Maximum diameter = 95 mm

Index

Page numbers preceded by an "A" or a "G" refer to the appendices and the glossary, respectively.

D

E

Q

R

U

Unit Conversion Factors

Length

$1\ \text{m} = 10^{10}\ \text{Å}$	$1\ \text{Å} = 10^{-10}\ \text{m}$
$1\ \text{m} = 10^{9}\ \text{nm}$	$1\ \text{nm} = 10^{-9}\ \text{m}$
$1\ \text{m} = 10^{6}\ \mu\text{m}$	$1\ \mu\text{m} = 10^{-6}\ \text{m}$
$1\ \text{m} = 10^{3}\ \text{mm}$	$1\ \text{mm} = 10^{-3}\ \text{m}$
$1\ \text{m} = 10^{2}\ \text{cm}$	$1\ \text{cm} = 10^{-2}\ \text{m}$
$1\ \text{mm} = 0.0394\ \text{in.}$	$1\ \text{in.} = 25.4\ \text{mm}$
$1\ \text{cm} = 0.394\ \text{in.}$	$1\ \text{in.} = 2.54\ \text{cm}$
$1\ \text{m} = 3.28\ \text{ft}$	$1\ \text{ft} = 0.3048\ \text{m}$

Area

$1\ \text{m}^2 = 10^4\ \text{cm}^2$	$1\ \text{cm}^2 = 10^{-4}\ \text{m}^2$
$1\ \text{mm}^2 = 10^{-2}\ \text{cm}^2$	$1\ \text{cm}^2 = 10^{2}\ \text{mm}^2$
$1\ \text{m}^2 = 10.76\ \text{ft}^2$	$1\ \text{ft}^2 = 0.093\ \text{m}^2$
$1\ \text{cm}^2 = 0.1550\ \text{in.}^2$	$1\ \text{in.}^2 = 6.452\ \text{cm}^2$

Volume

$1\ \text{m}^3 = 10^6\ \text{cm}^3$	$1\ \text{cm}^3 = 10^{-6}\ \text{m}^3$
$1\ \text{m}^3 = 35.32\ \text{ft}^3$	$1\ \text{ft}^3 = 0.0283\ \text{m}^3$
$1\ \text{cm}^3 = 0.0610\ \text{in.}^3$	$1\ \text{in.}^3 = 16.39\ \text{cm}^3$

Mass

$1\ \text{Mg} = 10^3\ \text{kg}$	$1\ \text{kg} = 10^{-3}\ \text{Mg}$
$1\ \text{kg} = 10^3\ \text{g}$	$1\ \text{g} = 10^{-3}\ \text{kg}$
$1\ \text{kg} = 2.205\ \text{lb}_\text{m}$	$1\ \text{lb}_\text{m} = 0.4536\ \text{kg}$
$1\ \text{g} = 2.205 \times 10^{-3}\ \text{lb}_\text{m}$	$1\ \text{lb}_\text{m} = 453.6\ \text{g}$

Density

$1\ \text{kg/m}^3 = 10^{-3}\ \text{g/cm}^3$	$1\ \text{g/cm}^3 = 10^3\ \text{kg/m}^3$
$1\ \text{Mg/m}^3 = 1\ \text{g/cm}^3$	$1\ \text{g/cm}^3 = 1\ \text{Mg/m}^3$
$1\ \text{kg/m}^3 = 0.0624\ \text{lb}_\text{m}/\text{ft}^3$	$1\ \text{lb}_\text{m}/\text{ft}^3 = 16.02\ \text{kg/m}^3$
$1\ \text{g/cm}^3 = 62.4\ \text{lb}_\text{m}/\text{ft}^3$	$1\ \text{lb}_\text{m}/\text{ft}^3 = 1.602 \times 10^{-2}\ \text{g/cm}^3$
$1\ \text{g/cm}^3 = 0.0361\ \text{lb}_\text{m}/\text{in.}^3$	$1\ \text{lb}_\text{m}/\text{in.}^3 = 27.7\ \text{g/cm}^3$

Force

$1\ \text{N} = 10^5\ \text{dynes}$	$1\ \text{dyne} = 10^{-5}\ \text{N}$
$1\ \text{N} = 0.2248\ \text{lb}_\text{f}$	$1\ \text{lb}_\text{f} = 4.448\ \text{N}$

Stress

$1\ \text{MPa} = 145\ \text{psi}$	$1\ \text{psi} = 6.90 \times 10^{-3}\ \text{MPa}$
$1\ \text{MPa} = 0.102\ \text{kg/mm}^2$	$1\ \text{kg/mm}^2 = 9.806\ \text{MPa}$
$1\ \text{Pa} = 10\ \text{dynes/cm}^2$	$1\ \text{dyne/cm}^2 = 0.10\ \text{Pa}$
$1\ \text{kg/mm}^2 = 1422\ \text{psi}$	$1\ \text{psi} = 7.03 \times 10^{-4}\ \text{kg/mm}^2$

Fracture Toughness

$1\ \text{psi}\sqrt{\text{in.}} = 1.099 \times 10^{-3}\ \text{MPa}\sqrt{\text{m}}$	$1\ \text{MPa}\sqrt{\text{m}} = 910\ \text{psi}\sqrt{\text{in.}}$

Energy

$1\ \text{J} = 10^7\ \text{ergs}$	$1\ \text{erg} = 10^{-7}\ \text{J}$
$1\ \text{J} = 6.24 \times 10^{18}\ \text{eV}$	$1\ \text{eV} = 1.602 \times 10^{-19}\ \text{J}$
$1\ \text{J} = 0.239\ \text{cal}$	$1\ \text{cal} = 4.184\ \text{J}$
$1\ \text{J} = 9.48 \times 10^{-4}\ \text{Btu}$	$1\ \text{Btu} = 1054\ \text{J}$
$1\ \text{J} = 0.738\ \text{ft-lb}_\text{f}$	$1\ \text{ft-lb}_\text{f} = 1.356\ \text{J}$
$1\ \text{eV} = 3.83 \times 10^{-20}\ \text{cal}$	$1\ \text{cal} = 2.61 \times 10^{19}\ \text{eV}$
$1\ \text{cal} = 3.97 \times 10^{-3}\ \text{Btu}$	$1\ \text{Btu} = 252.0\ \text{cal}$

Power

1 W = 0.239 cal/s	1 cal/s = 4.184 W
1 W = 3.414 Btu/h	1 Btu/h = 0.293 W
1 cal/s = 14.29 Btu/h	1 Btu/h = 0.070 cal/s

Viscosity

1 Pa-s = 10 P	1 P = 0.1 Pa-s

Temperature, T

$T(\text{K}) = 273 + T(°\text{C})$	$T(°\text{C}) = T(\text{K}) - 273$
$T(\text{K}) = \frac{5}{9}[T(°\text{F}) - 32] + 273$	$T(°\text{F}) = \frac{9}{5}[T(\text{K}) - 273] + 32$
$T(°\text{C}) = \frac{5}{9}[T(°\text{F}) - 32]$	$T(°\text{F}) = \frac{9}{5}[T(°\text{C})] + 32$

Specific Heat

1 J/kg-K = 2.39×10^{-4} cal/g-K	1 cal/g-°C = 4184 J/kg-K
1 J/kg-K = 2.39×10^{-4} Btu/lb_m-°F	1 Btu/lb_m-°F = 4184 J/kg-K
1 cal/g-°C = 1.0 Btu/lb_m-°F	1 Btu/lb_m-°F = 1.0 cal/g-K

Thermal Conductivity

1 W/m-K = 0.578 Btu/ft-h-°F	1 Btu/ft-h-°F = 1.730 W/m-K
1 cal/cm-s-K = 241.8 Btu/ft-h-°F	1 Btu/ft-h-°F = 4.136×10^{-3} cal/cm-s-K

Periodic Table of the Elements

Key: 29 ← Atomic number; Cu ← Symbol; 63.54 ← Atomic weight

- Metal
- Nonmetal
- Intermediate

IA	IIA	IIIB	IVB	VB	VIB	VIIB	VIII	VIII	VIII	IB	IIB	IIIA	IVA	VA	VIA	VIIA	0
1 H 1.0080																	2 He 4.0026
3 Li 6.941	4 Be 9.0122											5 B 10.811	6 C 12.011	7 N 14.007	8 O 15.999	9 F 18.998	10 Ne 20.180
11 Na 22.990	12 Mg 24.305											13 Al 26.982	14 Si 28.086	15 P 30.974	16 S 32.064	17 Cl 35.453	18 Ar 39.948
19 K 39.098	20 Ca 40.08	21 Sc 44.956	22 Ti 47.87	23 V 50.942	24 Cr 51.996	25 Mn 54.938	26 Fe 55.845	27 Co 58.933	28 Ni 58.69	29 Cu 63.54	30 Zn 65.41	31 Ga 69.72	32 Ge 72.64	33 As 74.922	34 Se 78.96	35 Br 79.904	36 Kr 83.80
37 Rb 85.47	38 Sr 87.62	39 Y 88.91	40 Zr 91.22	41 Nb 92.91	42 Mo 95.94	43 Tc (98)	44 Ru 101.07	45 Rh 102.91	46 Pd 106.4	47 Ag 107.87	48 Cd 112.41	49 In 114.82	50 Sn 118.71	51 Sb 121.76	52 Te 127.60	53 I 126.90	54 Xe 131.30
55 Cs 132.91	56 Ba 137.34	Rare earth series	72 Hf 178.49	73 Ta 180.95	74 W 183.84	75 Re 186.2	76 Os 190.23	77 Ir 192.2	78 Pt 195.08	79 Au 196.97	80 Hg 200.59	81 Tl 204.38	82 Pb 207.19	83 Bi 208.98	84 Po (209)	85 At (210)	86 Rn (222)
87 Fr (223)	88 Ra (226)	Acti- nide series	104 Rf (261)	105 Db (262)	106 Sg (266)	107 Bh (264)	108 Hs (277)	109 Mt (268)	110 Ds (281)								

Rare earth series	57 La 138.91	58 Ce 140.12	59 Pr 140.91	60 Nd 144.24	61 Pm (145)	62 Sm 150.35	63 Eu 151.96	64 Gd 157.25	65 Tb 158.92	66 Dy 162.50	67 Ho 164.93	68 Er 167.26	69 Tm 168.93	70 Yb 173.04	71 Lu 174.97
Actinide series	89 Ac (227)	90 Th 232.04	91 Pa 231.04	92 U 238.03	93 Np (237)	94 Pu (244)	95 Am (243)	96 Cm (247)	97 Bk (247)	98 Cf (251)	99 Es (252)	100 Fm (257)	101 Md (258)	102 No (259)	103 Lr (262)